Tradition Renewed

A HISTORY OF THE JEWISH THEOLOGICAL SEMINARY

"Evidence of our Seminary's
vitality is the fact that a century
of activity has not diminished our
eagerness to respond to our age in
terms of our tradition renewed,
and, if appropriate, reshaped."

—*Chancellor Gerson D. Cohen
on the eve of the JTS centennial
celebration, 26 August 1985.*

Tradition Renewed

A HISTORY OF THE
JEWISH THEOLOGICAL SEMINARY

VOLUME II

Beyond the Academy

AND THE BUSH והסנה
WAS NOT איננו
CONSUMED אכל

Edited by Jack Wertheimer

PUBLISHED BY THE JEWISH THEOLOGICAL SEMINARY OF AMERICA

First published in 1997 by
The Jewish Theological Seminary of America, Inc.
3080 Broadway
New York, New York 10027

Designed and produced by Scott-Martin Kosofsky at The Philidor Company, Boston.
Illustrations Editor, Julie Miller

FRONTISPIECE PHOTO: The outward view through the seminary gate.
Photo by Leo Choplin, Ratner Center, JTS.

Library of Congress Cataloging-in-Publication Data

Tradition renewed: a history of the Jewish Theological Seminary/
edited by Jack Wertheimer.—1st ed.
     p.   cm.
Includes bibliographical references and index.
Contents: v. 1. The making of an institution of Jewish higher learning.
ISBN: 0-87334-075-2
1. Jewish Theological Seminary of America—History.
2. Conservative Judaism—United States—History. I. Wertheimer, Jack.
BM90.J56T83   1997
296'.071'1747—dc21

First edition
Printed in the United States of America

TRADITION RENEWED: A HISTORY OF JTS

Edited by Jack Wertheimer

Contents

VOLUME II
Beyond the Academy

III. IN THE MAELSTROM OF JEWISH LIFE

IV. JTS and the World of Higher Education

DAVID WEINBERG

The Jewish Theological Seminary and the "Downtown" Jews of New York at the Turn of the Century

"The Jewish Theological Seminary, established to provide the East Side with Orthodox *rabbonim*, manufacturing rabbis for the West and South." In this cartoon, financier and Seminary supporter Jacob Schiff is shown lubricating the Seminary, in the form of a meat grinder with "gold oil" while Seminary president Solomon Schechter turns the crank. One of the Reform rabbis emerging at left is carrying a ham sandwich. Cartoon by Saul Raskin, *Der Groyser Kibetzer*, 22 January 1909.

DAVID WEINBERG

The Jewish Theological Seminary and the "Downtown" Jews of New York at the Turn of the Century

IT HAS BEEN commonly accepted wisdom among historians of Conservative Judaism that there is a direct relationship between the influx of East European immigrants to the United States at the end of the 19th century and the founding of the modern Jewish Theological Seminary in 1902. A critical reading of the standard works, however, suggests that the role and influence of immigrant Jews are far from clear. In simultaneously romanticizing and demonizing East European Jewry, studies of the early history of Conservative Judaism in America have only served to point up the many contradictions in the response of the movement and its leading institution to immigrants at the turn of the century.

On the one hand, scholars have portrayed Russian and Polish Jewish immigrants in the 1900s as pious believers who helped bolster American Jewry's commitment to religious observance. In particular, the arrival of thousands of Orthodox Jews is said to have provided the Conservative movement with spiritual direction and a mass base in an era when it was allegedly in danger of losing its way. Typical of this approach is that of Mordecai Waxman in his introductory essay to *Tradition and Change*, an anthology of essays on Conservative Judaism. For Waxman, Jewish immigration from Russia and Poland "offered an opportunity for the *tradition of life* which had prevailed in Eastern Europe to transfer itself to these shores."[1] According to the author, the influx of observant Russian and Polish Jews also provided the emergent Conservative movement with important spiritual leaven and with what he cryptically calls "a field for operation."[2] Similarly, in his classic work, *The Emergence*

3

of Conservative Judaism, Moshe Davis argues that, lacking mass support and a lay organization and desiring to counter the influence of Reform Judaism, the Seminary in the period of its restructuring sought to create "a lay synagogal body" through its outreach to East European Orthodoxy on the Lower East Side.[3]

While lauding East European Jews for their piety, historians of Conservative Judaism have also reflected in their writings the deep-seated fears that fueled the movement's desire to win over immigrants at the turn of the century. In this view, the influx of hundreds of thousands of Russian and Polish Jews created a financial burden and a social embarrassment for American Jewry and at times even posed a political danger. In particular, American Jewish religious leaders are said to have worried over the fate of immigrants who, in their desperate desire to assimilate, were said to be deserting Judaism en masse. Even traditional East European Jews were a source of concern. According to Norman Bentwich in his biography of Solomon Schechter, for example, leaders of the Old Seminary voiced concerns that the insistence of Orthodox immigrants upon maintaining their East European rituals and practices would balkanize American Jewish religious life at a crucial point in its development.[4] Still other immigrants were seen as feeding anti-Semitic sentiments among the general population through their participation in radical political activity. As the symbol of a religious movement that rested upon tradition yet remained open to the influences of modern American life, the restructured Seminary is described by its historians as having served a crucial role in "Americanizing" the new arrivals by drawing them and their children into the general orbit of Jewish communal life. Thus, for example, Richard Libowitz argues that the leaders of the Seminary were convinced that a "cadre of Yiddish-speaking Seminary graduates could . . . [lead] the latest arrivees to life styles more closely approaching the American norm."[5] Similarly, Abraham Karp cites a personal letter from Mordecai Kaplan to the author in which he claimed that the chief motivation of the new Seminary was "to establish a training school for American trained rabbis who might stem the proliferation of gangsterism on the Jewish East Side."[6] In his work, Moshe Davis summarizes, without awareness of their contradictory nature, the goals of Conservative Judaism vis-à-vis the immigrant population: to help them adjust to America, to save them for Judaism, and to help bolster support for traditional Jewish life in the United States.[7]

In all of the discussion, little attention has been paid to the attitudes of the immigrant Jewish population itself. In contrast to their discussions of later periods in the movement's history, historians of Conservative Judaism generally present a picture of a faceless and largely passive population on the Lower East Side at the turn of the century that in spite (or maybe because) of its spiritual fervor, remained largely without clear direction and leadership and that was wholly dependent upon "uptown" Jews for financial and institutional support. Thus, for example, Waxman defines the East European immigration simply as "a mass which settled in closely packed communities" while M. David Hoffman notes that the "Conservative group" was fortunate to find "men of affairs" who would "get a movement of the masses under away [*sic*]."[8] Most historians of Conservative Judaism seem to accept the paternalistic view of one Seminary supporter who commented at the turn of the century that "the uptown mansion never forgets the downtown tenement in distress."[9] At best, scholars frame the internal religious dynamics of the immigrant community in the 1890s and early 1900s in stereotypical and hyperbolic terms, in which radical anticlericalists and fanatical Orthodox vie with each other for political control of a naive and impotent population.[10]

The present essay represents a modest effort to fill the gap in our historical understanding of the first major encounter between the Jewish Theological Seminary and the immigrant Jewish population of the Lower East Side. I have deliberately chosen to limit my discussion to the crucial years directly before and after the reorganization of the Seminary because they best illustrate the inadequacy of previous analyses of the relationship between the emerging Conservative movement and newly arrived immigrants from Russia and Poland. For a brief moment, both American-born and immigrant traditionalists came together to press for the establishment of a distinctive school of rabbinic training. Far from the simple story of a self-confident institution seeking to partake of the immigrants' religious piety while at the same time steering them in the proper paths of Americanism, the history of the interaction between the Seminary and immigrants in the period surrounding the former's reorganization in 1902 reveals the complex interaction of three elements: an embryonic Conservative movement that was still in search of its own distinctive identity yet was strategically placed to assume leadership of the traditional community of both "uptown" and "downtown" Jews, an entrenched East European religious leadership that remained bitterly opposed to any accommodation with American life and regarded the Seminary as one of the preeminent symbols of religious assimilationism, and a small but influential group of immigrant businessmen and intellectuals troubled by what they saw as a serious crisis of religious leadership on the Lower East Side and searching for an institution that would further their goal of adapting traditional Judaism to the demands of American life.

The combination of these distinctive elements would not long survive, however. By the end of the first decade of the 20th century, the relationship between the Seminary and "downtown" Jews had changed dramatically. Under the guidance of Solomon Schechter, Conservative Judaism began to gain self-confidence. Gradually shifting its direction from the largely negative struggle against Reform, which necessitated searching out allies among traditionalist segments of Jewish society to support its fledgling rabbinical school, it began to mark out for itself a distinct and secure position within an American Jewish community that was no longer defined by the five boroughs of New York City. Even as the new movement continued to labor to win over the hearts and minds of immigrants, it followed their less observant sons and daughters out of the Lower East Side into the suburbs of New York and eventually beyond the Hudson River itself. By the 1920s, Conservative Judaism would no longer need to struggle to create a constituency for its spiritual message and its rabbinical graduates. Instead, it could now view its firmly established and highly visible rabbinical seminary as an important administrative, ideological, and financial base for a rapidly expanding movement.[11]

Changes within the immigrant community in the first two decades of the 20th century also affected relations between East European Jews and the Jewish Theological Seminary. More comfortable and self-confident in American society, the sons and daughters of East European immigrants no longer looked to "uptown" Jews for support and guidance. Those first-generation American Jews who continued to observe religious tradition tended to view their religious affiliation in the pragmatic and utilitarian terms of their fellow citizens. For many, membership in the Conservative movement and fidelity to its central institution became a convenient compromise between the competing loyalties of ethnic and national identity, rather than a matter of theology or denominationalism. At the same time, young Jews who maintained an attachment to Orthodox Judaism no longer found themselves divided, as their fathers had been, between those who saw the Seminary as the salvation of traditional Judaism and those who viewed it as its most bitter enemy. Instead, they borrowed the Seminary's basic approach of combining higher education in religious and secular study to create their own distinctive Orthodox institution—Yeshiva College.

More generally, the shifting relations between the Seminary and East European immigrants and between "uptown" and "downtown" Jews took place against the backdrop of the increasing self-confidence of immigrant Jews, as reflected in the founding of labor unions, the growth of economic self-sufficiency, and the rise of a new political consciousness. By 1914, the American Jewish community had begun to undergo a significant institutional restructuring and change in perspective. In place of the established Jew's struggle to find an appropriate balance between religious identity and participation in the larger society, a struggle that had led to the founding not only of the Jewish Theological Seminary but also of Hebrew Union College, the newly emboldened community, under the growing influence of immigrants, began increasingly to stress internal and decidedly "secular" issues such as social welfare, philanthropy, and political power. The dramatic changes in the relationship between East European Jewish immigrants and the Seminary in the prewar period may thus be said to reflect the growing integration of Russian and Polish Jewry into the Jewish community of New York in particular and into the American Jewish communal life in general.

The dimensions of the change were already evident to both "downtown" and "uptown" Jews concerned with the future of the Seminary in the early 1900s. As we shall see, those elements on the Lower East Side who championed the new rabbinical school recognized that graduates would have to serve not merely as interpreters of religious texts but as authentic representatives of a united Jewish community. At the same time, much of the established Seminary leadership of the period, including Solomon Schechter and Cyrus Adler, vehemently opposed efforts to solidify the communal structure of the Jewish community in New York. It was not only the growing influence of East European Jewry that so troubled them; it was also the decline of religion and religious values that the new forms of communal life seemed to presage.[12]

The genesis and early development of both the Seminary and the East European Jewish community in America took place primarily in New York City. The New York Jewish community of the early 1900s provided the founders of the Seminary with a distinctive constellation of supporters—wealthy German-born benefactors, modernizing Orthodox rabbis and intellectuals, and, increasingly, East European immigrants. At the same time, it seemed only logical and right that the central institution of higher Jewish learning in America at the turn of the century should be based in the city with the most dynamic growth in Jewish population. In 1890, there were approximately 225,000 Jews living in New York. Within a decade, the population had more than doubled to almost 600,000, and now represented well over half of American Jewry. The rapid increase in the city's population could be traced almost entirely to the arrival of East European immigrants. It is estimated that of the nearly one million Jews who landed at the port of New York between 1886 and 1906, almost 700,000 settled in the city.[13] Of the more than 600,000 East European Jewish immigrants in America in 1900, two-thirds lived in New York City, and almost all of them on the Lower East Side.[14]

For the majority of immigrant Jews attempting to eke out a living in the strange new environment of the Lower East Side at the turn of the century, the fate of the Seminary was of little concern. Two segments of the East European population, however, viewed the foundation of a religious institution that claimed to combine faithfulness to tradition with an openness to modern life with intense interest. First and foremost was the ultra-Orthodox community and its East European rabbis who, despite their migration to the New World, remained adamantly opposed to any accommodation to American life. Represented by the *Agudath ha-Rabbanim*, these "rejectionists" saw the Seminary as a mortal danger to the maintenance of traditional Jewish life in the New World. In this sense, they were more keenly aware than most other Jewish leaders at the time of the radical transformation in religious and communal life that was occurring in the United States. Though eventually to give way after World War I to a more moderate Orthodox leadership, members of the ultra-Orthodox community played a crucial role in defining the relationship between the Jewish Theological Seminary and East European immigrants in the early part of the 20th century.

The second group was comprised of a small but influential number of Orthodox writers, journalists, and businessmen who were struggling to find a way of balancing their commitments to Judaism with the attractions of the larger society in which they found themselves. Their quest for spiritual renewal—which the Yiddish newspaper editor Peter Wiernik, reflecting the state of mind of traditional-minded "modernizers" on the Lower East Side, awkwardly described as "a reformed Orthodoxy, or an Orthodox Reform"[15]—was fueled by the painful awareness of the decline in religious leadership and of the slow but inexorable erosion of religious values in the young immigrant community. At the same time, the "modernizers" were convinced that the American Jewish community was a unique phenomenon in Jewish history and could not become merely an extension of Russia and Poland.[16] The challenge was how to create a distinctive American Judaism which, unlike the *Nusach America* of the Reform movement, would be grounded in religious tradition.[17]

In pressing for the creation of a distinctive religious Jewish community in the United States, immigrant "modernizers" recognized the need to reach a modus vivendi with established Jewry. In contrast to other "downtown" Jewish leaders, however, they sought to transcend the contradictory attitudes of pride and self-assertiveness and deep insecurity, which Arthur Goren has incisively suggested had led in the past to both aggressive demands for recognition and hypersensitivity toward criticism.[18] Their vision was that of a united community in which German and Russian Jews would be equal partners. The Jewish Theological Seminary, with its support from both "uptown" assimilated and "downtown" observant Jews, seemed a logical vehicle for the forging of a new community. More important, as an institution that stressed the training of well-rounded religious leaders, the Seminary could help to create a new communal institutional framework resting on the multipurpose synagogue that would replace the factionalized and diffuse organizational structure of immigrant Jewish life. Admittedly, religious "modernizers" on the Lower East Side were not always comfortable with the pedagogical approach of the new rabbinical institution. Like many of the original founders of the Seminary itself, they often clung to the archetype of the East European yeshiva and found it difficult to agree on an appropriate balance between religious and secular education. As traditionalists, they also tended to place an overwhelming emphasis on the role of the rabbi while ignoring or minimizing the role of lay leadership and secular authority within the Jewish community. Nevertheless, for a brief moment in history, the reorganized rabbinical school pledged to train rabbis steeped in both tradition and modern life provided Lower East Side intellectuals with a symbol and an agency for the realization of their dreams of religious renewal.

The central vehicle that "modernizers" used to disseminate their ideas concerning the Seminary and its role in the revival of Judaism in America was the Yiddish press. Yiddish newspapers at the turn of the century not only served as the major source of information for the majority of immigrants, they also enabled Russian and Polish Jews to express their concerns in an era in which residents of the Lower East Side generally lacked political and economic power. For most immigrants, reading the Yiddish newspaper was both a daily obligation and an unremitting joy, as powerful a duty and as uplifting an experience as any religious ritual.[19] Reflecting its diverse readership, the Yiddish press espoused a wide variety of opinions and perspectives on contemporary Jewish issues. At the turn of the century, there were five dominant publications on the Lower East Side. The *Yidishe Velt* (Jewish World), which was published between 1902 and 1904, was heavily funded by wealthy German Jews and preached a moderate Orthodoxy to a small but devoted readership that numbered between five and ten thousand. The *Yidishes Tageblatt* (Jewish Daily), founded in 1885, claimed to sell between fifty and one hundred thousand copies a day. The *Tageblatt* had actually branched off from the *Yidishe Gazeten* (Jewish Gazette), whose masthead at the turn of the century proclaimed that it had the largest circulation of any Jewish newspaper in the world. Both papers represented the views of modernizing Orthodoxy and remained the most stalwart proponents of the Jewish Theological Seminary within the immigrant community. The *Morgen-Zhurnal* (Morning Journal), established in 1901 and claiming a readership of over fifty thousand, was the first morning Yiddish paper in America, a rarity in a community made up largely of laborers who arose early to go to work. It trumpeted the virtues of Orthodoxy and remained fairly conservative on both religious and secular matters. Finally, the *Forvertz* (Jewish Daily Forward), founded in 1897, claimed a circulation that matched that of the *Tageblatt*. It espoused the principles of socialism, albeit in the distinctively Americanized style of its fiery editor Abraham Cahan.[20]

In a period in which start-up money for publication was hard to find and reader loyalty was quixotic, financial exigency often overrode ideological principle in defining newspaper content.[21] The result was that a few enterprising owners and editors shaped the character and content of the Yiddish press in New York at the turn of the century. Given their entrepreneurial spirit and influence, it is not surprising that they also took a leading role in the effort to revitalize the immigrant community. As powerful voices in that community, they helped to publicize the program of the Jewish Theological Seminary on the Lower East Side.

Kasriel Sarasohn has been aptly described as the first newspaper magnate of the American Jewish press.[22] Born in the Suwalki province of northeastern Poland in 1835, Sarasohn was trained in his youth by his father to prepare for the rabbinate. Instead, he chose to become a merchant. In 1871, Sarasohn arrived in New York with a strong determination to put his religious training and his business skills to good use. Within a year, he had established a Yiddish newspaper, the *New Yorker Yidisher Tsaytung*, but it failed after only five months. After short stints first as a rabbi in an Orthodox synagogue in Syracuse, New York, and then as a manufacturer in Chicago, in 1874 "Reverend" Sarasohn, as he now called himself, returned to New York City to begin publishing the first American Yiddish weekly, the *Yidishe Gazeten*. This time he succeeded, in part because of his keen awareness of the interests and concerns of the growing immigrant Jewish population in New York, in part because of his remarkable ability to secure advertising and to find distributors for the paper. Within a few years, Sarasohn had all but established a monopoly in the field of Yiddish newspaper publishing by slowly acquiring his competitors, one by one.[23]

The influx to America in the 1880s of tens of thousands of Jews fleeing from pogroms in Russia convinced the aspiring editor that the time was ripe to establish a Yiddish daily. Not only were the new arrivals hungry for news about their homeland, they were also used to reading a Yiddish paper every day in Russia and Poland. In January 1885, Sarasohn began publishing the first continuing Yiddish daily in America (and in the world), the *Yidishes Tageblatt*. Its lively English page, edited by A. H. Fromenson, was a crucial factor in the success of the newspaper. Playing upon the immigrant and second-generation reader's desperate desire to master the new language, Sarasohn used the English editorial in the *Tageblatt* to publicize his ideas about religious renewal. In the meantime, the *Yidishe Gazeten* continued to appear as a weekly, serving as a condensed version of the *Tageblatt* for readers who lacked the time and/or the money to buy a daily newspaper.

Given Sarasohn's religious and conservative bent, it was not surprising that the editorials in the *Gazeten* and *Tageblatt* maintained a respectful attitude toward "uptown" Jews and continually reminded their immigrant readers of the debt they owed to their wealthier German coreligionists. At the same time, the two newspapers railed against the radical "nihilists" on the Lower East Side who were seen as threatening both Orthodox observance and the successful integration of East European Jews into American society. Such attitudes were reinforced by the strong support, including financial aid, that Sarasohn received from the New York Republican party, which at the turn of the century was engaged in a bitter struggle against Tammany Hall.[24] True to his own perspective as a successful businessman, Sarasohn's papers generally took the side of employers when immigrant employees went out on strike.[25] It was attitudes like these that undoubtedly endeared Sarasohn to wealthy "uptown" Jews affiliated with the Seminary.

In attacking the freethinking elements, Sarasohn also hoped to gain the support of traditionalists in the immigrant community. At first convinced that the movement for religious renewal would be led by members of the established East European Orthodox community, Sarasohn lobbied in the 1870s for the establishment of a chief rabbinate in New York. The subsequent failure of Rabbi Jacob Joseph to secure communal support angered Sarasohn. He was also sorely disappointed when ultra-Orthodox rabbis prohibited their followers from reading the *Gazeten*'s weekly edition on the Sabbath. Such experiences led Sarasohn to look beyond the religious leaders of the Lower East Side to traditional rabbis at the Seminary as sources for the religious revival in the immigrant community.

As one of the most powerful and influential figures on the Lower East Side, Sarasohn was an active force in the creation of a number of immigrant institutions. Like leaders of the Seminary, he wished to break down the ethnic and religious divisions that he was convinced prevented immigrants from becoming a major force in American Jewish life. By the time that Sarasohn died in 1905 at the age of sixty-nine, he was considered one of the powerful and articulate representatives of the immigrant community on the Lower East Side. It was estimated that between fifty and a hundred thousand people attended his funeral in New York.[26]

Zvi Hirsch Masliansky was undoubtedly the most popular and most polished *maggid* (religious orator) on the Lower East Side at the turn of the century. Born in a traditional family in the city of Slutzk in Byelorussia in 1856, he spent much of his youth as an itinerant preacher. Masliansky's oratorical ability brought him to the attention of the proto-Zionist movement, *Hibbat Zion*, which recruited him to preach the gospel of Jewish settlement in Palestine in houses of study throughout the Russian Pale of Settlement.

In 1895, Masliansky migrated to the United States after brief stops in a number of major cities of western Europe. The orator's fame preceded his arrival in New York, and he had little difficulty finding employment as a preacher. Beginning in 1898, Masliansky began to preach on Friday nights at the Educational Alliance. His sermons were a fascinating amalgam of religious traditionalism, Zionism, and Americanism in which diatribes against the persecution and misery facing the Diaspora Jew mingled with nostalgic evocations of the *heder* (traditional religious school) and paeans to America's commitment to science and religion.[27] Masliansky's program was quite simple—"Americanize" the older generation of immigrants and "Judaize" their children. His distinctive blending of religious tradition with what one writer has described as "the trends of the day" found a ready audience among immigrant Jews searching for a means of synthesizing their loyalties to the Old World with their commitments to the New.[28] Masliansky's ideas also brought him into contact with similarly minded "uptown" Orthodox Jews such as Bernard Drachman and Joseph Joffe who were affiliated with the Jewish Theological Seminary in the years before its reorganization. The result was that Masliansky soon became an ardent supporter of the Seminary, albeit in its pre-Schechter form.

Masliansky's views of the United States quickly drew the attention of "uptown"

Jews who saw him as an ideal interpreter of Americanism to immigrants and as a bulwark against the spread of radicalism on the Lower East Side. In 1902, with the help of a number of prominent Jews including Louis Marshall, Jacob Schiff, Frederick Stein, and Cyrus Sulzberger, Masliansky founded the Yiddish daily, *Yidishe Velt*. Attracting the most talented writers and journalists in the immigrant community with the lure of large salaries and bolstered by a loyal readership who idolized Masliansky, the *Velt* quickly assumed the status of the most prestigious newspaper on the Lower East Side. The editor of the English page was the renowned Joseph Jacobs, who himself had served as an editor of the *Jewish Encyclopedia*, the *American Jewish Year Book*, and the *American Hebrew*, as well as a lecturer at the Seminary. Faithfully reflecting the views of Masliansky and his backers, the *Velt* preached the virtues of Orthodoxy and Jewish nationalism but generally shunned political issues.

Despite its early success, however, the *Yidishe Velt* was far too tame to survive amid the more sensationalistic and more politicized Yiddish newspapers that emerged in the early 1900s. Ultimately, Masliansky was unable to translate his powerful oratory into the written word. Immigrants who flocked to his sermons were soon bored by his turgid essays and articles. After a bitter strike in 1905 that resulted in the decision by the *Velt*'s owners to cease publication,[29] Masliansky returned to his first love, preaching. During the remainder of his life, he delivered sermons in almost all of the major synagogues on the Lower East Side. At the same time, he continued his activity on behalf of Zionism, serving as vice-president of the Federation of American Zionists between 1902 and 1910. Throughout the 1920s and 1930s, Masliansky published extensively in the fields of Hebrew language and homiletics. He died in 1941 at the age of eighty-five.[30]

What primarily motivated immigrant "modernizers" like Sarasohn, Fromenson, and Masliansky to press for change in American Jewish life was the profound religious crisis in the downtown community. With more than two hundred established synagogues and another three hundred prayer halls serving East European Jews in Manhattan alone, religious life in the immigrant community in the 1890s and early 1900s was characterized by bitter factionalism, corruption, a lack of leadership, and the absence of a sound educational system. The majority of synagogues on the Lower East Side were little more than storefront operations with only a skeletal organizational structure. Most were affiliated with *landsmanshaftn*, or mutual aid societies, founded by immigrants to serve the needs of fellow Jews who had arrived from the same city or town in Eastern Europe. Those immigrants who were not members of *landsmanshaftn* or who were not especially observant attended *minyanim* (prayer quorums) that met on Rosh Hashanah and Yom Kippur in rented storefronts, dance halls, and even sweatshops. The establishment of temporary congregations led to wide-scale abuse. Immigrants would pay for High Holy Day tickets, only to arrive at the service to discover that the "rabbi" had absconded with the funds.[31] The result was that there was little coordination or direction in religious activity on the Lower East Side.[32]

To compound matters, there were no more than a handful of fully trained Orthodox rabbinical scholars in the United States at the end of the 19th century. Poorly paid, most were *poskim* (religious adjudicators) who spent their time in esoteric study. As the bitter and ineffective tenure of Jacob Joseph as chief rabbi of New York from 1888 to his death in 1902 demonstrated, immigrant religious leaders were ill-prepared to meet the challenges posed by life in the New World.[33] Trained in Eastern Europe, they were deeply pessimistic about the future of Jewish Orthodoxy in the New World. Old World rabbis also had great difficulty accepting the role of the state in regulating "secular" activities such as marriage and divorce.[34] Indifferent toward communal interests, they generally deferred all non-halakhic issues to wealthy lay leaders on the Lower East Side who cared little about the concerns of the majority of "downtown" residents. The spiritual vacuum led to the proliferation of *darshanim,* itinerant preachers who mingled religious thought with popular superstition and folklore. Ritual functions such as circumcisions and weddings, which East European rabbis regarded as unworthy of their time, were often handled by unprincipled and unschooled individuals. To make matters worse, in 1887 the New York legislature enacted a law that restricted the eligibility to perform marriages to judges, justices of the peace, government officials, and "ministers of legally incorporated religious congregations."[35] The result was that it became increasingly difficult for immigrant Jews to participate in a religious marriage ceremony that was recognized by the state.

The crisis in religious institutional life and leadership led to a marked decline in Jewish observance in the immigrant community, especially among youth. In 1904, it was estimated that no more than 25 percent of young Jewish men on the Lower East Side attended synagogue on a regular basis, and then only out of respect for their parents.[36] Missionaries were especially active in immigrant areas of settlement. Playing upon the young East European Jew's sense of deracination, Christian proselytizing groups offered material and spiritual comfort to the unemployed and the homeless. Many parents who worked on Sundays dropped their children off at schools conducted by Christian missionaries.[37] Local rabbis generally ignored the problem and did little to reach out to young Jewish men and women. An immigrant correspondent for the *American Hebrew,* commenting on the powerful influence of evangelical Christian missions established on the Lower East Side, bitterly noted in 1903 that "what we need down here is a liberal sprinkling of Judaism." Summing up the danger of proselytism among immigrants, he concluded: "We need [Jewish] missions to the Jews."[38]

Jewish education on the Lower East Side in the early 1900s was in an equally deplorable state. Most immigrant children attended public school. Only about one-quarter of them received religious instruction in the form of weekday or weekend schools sponsored by "uptown" synagogues or secular institutions such as the Educational Alliance. Many of the students were girls, since boys were expected either to study at yeshivas or to work full time.[39] Understaffed and underfunded, these schools spent most of their time competing with each other rather than creating a systematic curriculum. In classes, part-time students and teachers struggled to communicate with one another in two languages—English and Hebrew—and in innumerable local and regional East European Yiddish dialects. To add to their problems, most Jewish supplementary schools were overcrowded and unsanitary.[40] Parents who wanted a more traditional education sent their children to *heder* or employed tutors to come to their homes. In both cases, teachers were largely untrained, and learning involved little more than rote memorization. The few yeshivas that existed on the Lower East Side were poorly maintained and were dependent almost totally upon the beneficence of wealthy benefactors for survival.[41]

The result was a growing ossification of religious life in the East European Jewish community that disheartened would-be immigrant reformers and that raised serious doubts in the minds of outside observers as to the future of Judaism on the Lower East Side. Few would disagree with the Jewish philanthropist Louis Lipsky who summed up the state of Judaism on the Lower East Side at the turn of the century in the following terms:

> One third of the organized religious community was dead; another third was composed of 'sluggish minds,' or those whom habit conquers who cannot conceive of anything new. The other one-third is composed of the hangers-on, who are neither here nor there—too weak to organize on their own platform and too timid to tear away entirely from the old.[42]

Immigrant "modernizers" reacted bitterly to the lack of leadership and direction on the Lower East Side. Though as we have seen, some like Sarasohn applauded the appointment of a chief rabbi, it soon became painfully clear that the traditional East European religious leader was ill-adapted to the demands of the new community in America. For religious "modernizers," the idea of recreating an East European yeshiva in America, however romantic it may have seemed, was completely impractical. As one writer concluded in a series of articles published in the *Yidishe Velt* in 1903, the type of rabbi trained at a traditional yeshiva would be unable to minister to immigrants. Even the smallest synagogues in New York wanted a rabbi who could at least speak English.[43] Without proper guidance, the community would prove easy prey to dangerous internal and external forces that would not only threaten the traditional beliefs of immigrants but would also hinder the integration of their sons and daughters into the larger society. The continual diatribes against the evils of socialism, anarchism, and alcoholism that daily filled the pages of the *Gazeten* and the *Tagesblatt* point to the concerns of the "modernizers" with the dangers posed by the absence of a committed and concerned communal leadership. As one immigrant remarked bitterly in the pages of the English Jewish paper, the *American Hebrew*, in October 1903:

> What have they [rabbis] done to prevent or improve the conditions that are forcing themselves upon us? Besides marrying and burying people, and expounding the profundity of their thoughts on irrelevant topics, have the rabbis, our spiritual guardians so-called, done anything singly or collectively to maintain and foster the Jewish spirit in the growing men and women of our faith in the "ghetto," or its uptown offspring?[44]

Despite their criticism of the East European rabbinate on the Lower East Side, however, religious "modernizers" refused to embrace the views of Reform Judaism. Though it was important for the new rabbis to maintain "the manners and honorable character of gentlemen," an editorial in the *Yidishes Tagesblatt* commented in 1906, first and foremost they had to be well trained in traditional texts. In their acceptance of modernity, the American rabbi would not simply follow the dictates of his lay membership or the "anti-Semitic analyses" of Christian biblical scholars. Ultimately, the editorial maintained in a statement that reflected the newspaper's support of the ideals of the Seminary, Judaism meant stringently observing all laws and customs, while at the same time remaining sensitive to the needs of a changing environment and constituency.[45]

The growing concerns of immigrant Jewish "modernizers" dovetailed with a change in the attitudes of the Jewish Theological Seminary toward the Lower East Side. Though the rabbinical institution had existed since 1886, its relationship with the young immigrant community in the period before its reorganization was characterized by uncertainty and at times outright suspicion. Nevertheless, a number of prominent leaders of the early Seminary took an active interest in the plight of East European Jews. In 1890, for example, the orientalist Morris Jastrow and the future president of the Seminary Sabato Morais arbitrated a strike settlement between immigrant shirtmakers and their Jewish employers in Philadelphia. Similarly, the future founder of Hadassah and philanthropist Henrietta Szold helped immigrants find jobs in Baltimore and urged friends in other cities to do the same. It was Henry Pereira Mendes, the *hazzan* (cantor) and spiritual leader of Shearith Israel in New York, who seems to have been the first to suggest that American-born English-speaking rabbis move into immigrant areas of the major cities of America to serve them.[46]

Not all the efforts by the early Seminary leadership to cater to newly arrived immigrant Jews were characterized by such selfless idealism. As the *American Hebrew*, an ardent supporter of the Seminary, remarked in a hard-hitting editorial published on 8 March 1902, the Seminary afforded "the surest and safest means of handling the downtown problems of Americanizing the foreign element by sending among them trained and well-equipped rabbinical teachers."[47] Leaders of the early Conservative Judaism were active supporters of the work of the Jewish Alliance of America, which attempted to counter the possibility of a nativist backlash against immigrant Jews by settling them outside concentrated urban areas on the eastern seaboard. Such sentiments clearly motivated individuals like Cyrus Adler, the president of the Seminary's Board of Trustees from 1902 to 1905 and its future president, who generally expressed little interest in the plight of Russian and Polish Jews in America. In 1901, he had opposed granting scholarships to students simply because they were poor.[48] At best, Adler recognized the need to actively support the rapid assimilation of immigrant Jews into American life for the preservation of the community as a whole. As he stated in 1905 in a comment ostensibly made about anti-Semitism in Russia but equally applicable to the United States: "Where the Jews are segregated they are an easy mark and these thugs and criminals know that they can count upon the sympathy of the official classes and a portion of the populace."[49]

The 1890s saw the first active efforts by the Seminary to recruit students from the Lower East Side. At the Convention of the Seminary Association held in 1898, the new head of the faculty, Henry Pereira Mendes, stressed the role that immigrant graduates could play in the religious life of the "downtown" Jewish community. Though his speech paid tribute to the religious fervor of East European Orthodoxy, it was seeped in the paternalism that marked the attitude of the Old Seminary leadership toward immigrants. The Seminary, Pereira Mendes argued, had to respond to the crisis among newly arrived Jews from Russia and Poland. Though scholarship was treasured among the learning centers in the immigrant community, he maintained, it was obscurantist and rigid. In addition, services in Orthodox synagogues on the Lower East Side showed little love for culture and repelled children of the second generation. Alone among the religious institutions in the American Jewish life, Pereira Mendes concluded, the Seminary had a unique role to play in ministering to immigrant Jewry. Unlike other schools of rabbinical training, it was able to supply spiritual leaders who would be acceptable to the majority of the newly arrived Jews from Russia, "loving the religion which they love, practicing the law which they revere—yes setting the example of obedience to Israel's religion, respect for Israel's prophets and sages, and, above all, of reverence for Israel's God, and His word, the Torah."[50]

Given the attitudes of the Seminary leadership as well as the newness of the enterprise, it was not surprising that the problems facing immigrant students at the rabbinical school were often daunting. According to one teacher, almost all of the students from the Lower East Side at the turn of the century were desperately poor

Letter from Joshua Joffe to Percival Menken, a member of the Seminary's board of directors, 2 June 1902. The letter reads: My dear Doctor Menken: Our junior boys are scheduled for several hours work daily after 7 am from now until July 4th. They are very poor; they can not afford to spend $3. on carfare, nor spend some cents for luncheon unless someone gives it to them. And if not you—who? Please see to it that the following excellent boys receive some $5 each for the season. 1/Adlerblum; 2/Levy; 3/Rackowitz; 4/Rabbinowitz; 5/Rabbinowitz; 6/Melamet; 7/Schwartz. Yours very sincerely, Joshua Joffe. *Ratner Center, JTS.*

and would not have been able to pay carfare and buy lunch without financial aid.[51] Teachers at the Seminary were so concerned about the "uncultured" nature of the speech of immigrant students that in 1892, they created a special course in elocution taught by Professor Robert Houston of Columbia College.[52] Similarly, a report issued at the Third Biennial meeting of the Jewish Seminary Association in the same year talked of the need to introduce such students to "higher branches of English literature and give them a taste for reading such books as would give elegance to their style and refinement to their thoughts."[53] Despite the many obstacles, immigrant student enrollment increased throughout the last decade of the 19th century. By the time of the Seminary's reorganization in 1902, well over half of its students were of East European origin.[54]

By far the most direct reflections of the Seminary's outreach to the Lower East Side at the turn of the century were the Jewish Sabbath Observance Association and the Jewish Endeavor Society. The two organizations were established by a group of idealistic Seminary students and teachers with the approval of the administration and teaching staff. Their intention was both to ensure the maintenance of traditional practice on the Lower East Side and to demonstrate that ritual observance did not preclude participation in the larger society. Supporters of both organizations were convinced of the need to fill a vacuum left by the refusal of East European-trained rabbis to respond to the unprecedented challenges that American society posed for religiously observant immigrants.

The Jewish Sabbath Observance Association was created in 1894 at the Seminary to promote observance and to aid Sabbath observers in finding employment. Shortly after its founding, it opened an employment bureau on the Lower East Side and in the period before World War I, worked diligently though unsuccessfully to convince Jewish employers of the need to hire observant workers.[55] The organization was given new life and a new name in 1905. *Tomche Shabbat* (Supporters of the Sabbath), as it was now called, took a more aggressive role in stemming the growing influence of radical political movements. In particular, it sought to counter popular assumptions among socialist and anarchist elements that religious movements were solely concerned with defending the economic interests of their wealthy benefactors. In taking a proactive position, it not only promoted Sabbath observance but pressed to secure a five-day workweek.

Much more influential was the Jewish Endeavor Society, which was founded in 1901. Led by Seminary students and teachers, many of whom were of Russian and Polish origin, its major purpose was to hold regular religious services on the Lower East Side that would meld traditional and "modern" religious practices. In addition, the Society taught Bible classes and helped to establish religious schools. Ultimately, its members hoped to be able to establish a synagogue on the Lower East Side that would reflect the ritual practices of the Seminary. In doing so, as one historian states, the Society was helping to create a "prototype of the twentieth-century American Orthodox and Conservative synagogue."[56]

The supporters of such outreach programs were motivated by a number of concerns. On the most basic level, there was the fear that the alienation of immigrant youth from traditional religious leadership and observance would open the door to political radicalism, Reform and, even worse, Christian missionary activity.[57] Many also fervently believed in the need for "uptown" Jews to "Americanize" immigrants. Yet others had more grandiose designs for the two organizations. In concert with immigrant "modernizers," many of the Seminary students and teachers involved in these outreach programs were convinced that the influx of immigrants into the Conservative movement would act as a counterweight to the assimilationist tendencies of some of its "uptown" supporters and would ensure that the movement would remain wedded to the basic principles of Orthodoxy, albeit in modern garb. It was a view that would eventually lead to open conflict with the administration of the reorganized Seminary under the leadership of Solomon Schechter.

Such attitudes could be seen in the response of one of the most ardent supporters of the Jewish Endeavor Society, Rabbi Bernard Drachman. Drachman was born in New York City in 1861 but attended the Breslau Seminary in Germany. He thus found himself in the unique position of being an American-born English-speaking rabbi who had been trained in a traditional Central European seminary.[58] Much of his life was spent trying to find an appropriate religious venue to practice what he defined as a "refined" Orthodoxy. Disturbed by what he believed was the laxness of observance among more established Orthodox elements in the New York Jewish community and unable to find a position in a traditional immigrant synagogue on the Lower East Side, in 1889 he founded his own uptown Orthodox congregation, Zichron Ephraim. The cornerstones of the new congregation were laid by a number of the founders of the Jewish Theological Seminary Association, including Joseph Blumenthal and Henry Pereira Mendes. Shortly thereafter, Drachman was invited to become the first faculty member of the Seminary.

Drachman's view of religious modernization closely paralleled that of the German Neo-Orthodox thinker, Samson Raphael Hirsch. Though vehemently opposed to Reform, he was insistent upon the need to present Judaism "in an esthetic and impressive manner, worthy of the culture and refinement of the modern age."[59] It was for that reason that he opposed the appointment of Jacob Joseph as chief rabbi in the 1880s.[60] Indeed, he was convinced that a new religious perspective that rested upon a synthesis of traditional observance and modern propriety would easily break down the barriers between Reform and Orthodoxy. As the editor of Drachman's autobiography wrote in his introduction, the young rabbi was convinced that "complete loyalty to religious law, combined with beauty of ceremonial and propriety of manner, would prove an ideal combination that should . . . be acceptable to both parties."[61] Drachman also found himself closely allied with immigrant "modernizers." Always sensitive to the needs of the Lower East Side, he was convinced that it would be necessary to modify some religious practice to appeal to both immigrants and their children. Like Sarasohn and others, he placed great faith in the Seminary both as a meeting place for all observant Jews and as an agent of "modernization" for newly arrived East European Jews.[62]

The often conflicting views expressed by proponents of outreach to the immigrant community point up the fact that in the period before its reorganization, the Seminary had yet to successfully define its place in the American Jewish community. In general, supporters of the new institution seemed more confident explaining what it opposed than what it actually stood for. An important motivating factor for the establishment of the rabbinical school had been the perceived need to counter the influence of the Hebrew Union College in Cincinnati. Yet elements at the founding conference of the Seminary in 1886 successfully lobbied against calling it a "Conservative" institution, for fear that the institution would become too closely associated with Orthodoxy. At the same time, leading figures in the Seminary, most notably Pereira Mendes, played a central role in the formation of the Union of Orthodox Jewish Congregations of America in 1898. Not surprisingly, therefore, Seminary leaders in its early years found it difficult to explain the purpose of the school to the immigrant community. In 1888, for example, when asked by a Yiddish newspaper to define the religious orientation of the Seminary, the president of the Jewish Theological Seminary Association, Joseph Blumenthal, could only state that the rabbinical school would be neither Orthodox nor Reform.[63]

At the turn of the century, the Seminary could claim a constituency of twelve synagogues in New York City, Philadelphia, and Baltimore, each having its own distinctive attitude toward prayer books, seating arrangements, and the use of organs in religious services. The fact that the school and movement were led by a motley group that included assimilated Jews, old-line German Orthodox, and more established East European elements only complicated matters. The only perspective that its diverse membership could agree upon, the noted biblical scholar Max Margolis would later recall, was that "the Seminary is noncommittal and will remain noncommittal."[64] For opponents of the Seminary in the Reform movement, such attitudes smacked of outright hypocrisy. Rabbi Steven J. Wise, for example, dismissed the new institution as an Orthodox creation while at the same time attacking the traditionalist credentials of its leadership.[65] For others like Drachman and Sarasohn, the uncertain position of the Old Seminary in the American Jewish community provided them with an opportunity to steer the institution in a direction that they were convinced would ensure the survival of Orthodoxy in America.

Not surprisingly, therefore, "modernizers" on the Lower East Side generally responded with cautious optimism to the Seminary in its early years. In an editorial written in the *Yidishe Gazeten* in 1888, for example, Sarasohn warmly applauded the founding of a new "orthodox" institution in New York which he assured his readers would counter the obscurantism of East European rabbis.[66] In the 1880s and 1890s, the Yiddish newspaper magnate opened the pages of his newspapers to appeals by the Seminary for funds.[67] Yet the rabbinical school's efforts to incorporate secular knowledge into its curriculum continued to trouble individuals whose model of rabbinical training was Eastern Europe. Though impressed by the commitment of assimilationist German Jews to support a "traditional" institution and to involve leaders of the Lower East Side in the effort, immigrant "modernizers" were not always sure that the early Seminary could adequately prepare learned rabbis and spiritual leaders.[68] Thus, for example, an article in Sarasohn's *Ha-ivri*, which was noted for its cautious attitude toward the Seminary, bemoaned the fact that most of the teachers were not suitable to produce faithful students. Seminary-trained rabbis possessed secular knowledge but had little faith. Later articles in the Hebrew weekly commented on the inability of Seminary students to read halakhic sources. Despite the failure of Jacob Joseph's tenure, some immigrant religious reformers continued to hold to the belief that the future of American Orthodox Jewry lay not in an institution of higher learning but in a learned religious leader trained in Eastern Europe.[69]

There was no such hesitation in the response of the traditional religious leadership on the Lower East Side. In 1887, Moses Weinberger, an Orthodox rabbi from Hungary who settled in New York City, summed up the attitudes of many of his fellow rabbis in his book, *Jews and Judaism in New York*. Deriding the Seminary's alleged commitment to religious tradition, Weinberger dismissed the institution's supporters as "undecideds" whose only common reference point was the pursuit of money.[70] Conservatives were thus indistinguishable from Reform. Both of them were beyond the boundaries of normative Judaism; both would bring Judaism to ruin.[71] Many ultra-Orthodox Jews on the Lower East Side shared the attitude of Weinberger that "even if it [the Seminary] should somehow rise and establish itself on one foot, it will never be of any value to the Jewish people."[72] In public statements, East European rabbis cynically referred to the institution as the Jewish Theological "cemetery" and denounced it as the graveyard of Judaism. Local religious figures on the Lower East Side were especially hostile toward the activity of the Jewish Endeavor Society, which they saw, not unjustifiably, as a direct challenge to traditional religious leadership and as a devious attempt to foist the Seminary's brand of Judaism upon immigrants.

Despite continued appeals by the Seminary for teachers to teach Torah and *halakha* in English, Russian- and Polish-trained rabbis and scholars were reluctant to become affiliated with the new institution. For many, the Seminary's refusal to teach in Yiddish was indicative of a dangerous turning away from East European religious learning. More generally, the Seminary's emphasis upon an integrated curriculum that combined religious and secular study and that sought to place Judaic studies on equal footing with other scholarly disciplines was a direct challenge to the pedagogical approach of the traditional yeshiva. It was not coincidental that the ultra-Orthodox attacked Seminary teachers for their alleged reliance upon Higher Criticism. For East European rabbis on the Lower East Side, it was heresy for Jewish scholars to rely upon anything else but traditional Jewish sources to interpret the sacred texts of Judaism.[73]

In a larger sense, the establishment of the Seminary represented a threat to traditionalists because it signaled the growing self-confidence of American Jewry as an autonomous religious community. For most traditionalists, migration in America, whatever it may have meant for their economic and physical well-being, represented a distancing from the true source of Judaism. When the search committee for the chief rabbi decided to advertise the position, for example, it insisted that candidates be trained in an East European yeshiva. At the same time, its members all agreed that a Russian or Polish rabbi who came to the United States would be making an immense sacrifice.[74] The very idea that a rabbinical seminary claiming to be wedded to Jewish tradition could be established in the "*trefa* [unclean or unkosher] land" of America struck ultra-Orthodox Jewish leaders as nothing short of scandalous.[75]

For East European rabbis, the greatest challenge to religious life in the immigrant community was the lack of unified spiritual leadership.[76] In professing to be the institutional representative of Orthodoxy in the United States, the Seminary seemed to be laying claim as the sole religious authority for both established Jews and immigrants. The idea that American Jewry would no longer need to rely upon East European rabbis for its leadership was anathema to ultra-Orthodox elements. Thus, for example, immigrant rabbis were especially disturbed that they were not invited to visit or to examine students at the Seminary. In its desire to become the central focus of Jewish religious life, the Seminary also threatened the organizational structure of the immigrant community on the Lower East Side with its intermingling of houses of prayer and study, mutual aid societies, and burial societies and its clear differentiations according to geographical origin.

The ultra-Orthodox's hostility to the Seminary in its early years also stemmed from their contrasting visions of the role of the rabbi. For traditionalists, the rabbi's primary responsibility toward the community was to serve as the ultimate authority on all ritual and halakhic matters. From its inception, the Seminary sought to expand the role of the rabbi by insisting that its students be schooled in pastoral counseling, homiletics, and religious education. Equally important was the fact that Seminary graduates, though rooted in traditional Judaism, were trained to work in a pluralistic environment that included not only non-Jews but also leaders of other denominations in the Jewish community. It was for that reason that Henry Pereira

Mendes opposed the creation of the post of chief rabbi in the 1880s. "Judaism in America is without a head," he commented in an article written in the New York Herald on 21 July 1888; "Each congregation has its own rabbi."[77]

One of the most trenchant Orthodox critics of the early Seminary in the immigrant community was the Hebrew scholar and anthologist Yehuda David Eisenstein. In an essay written in 1887 entitled "*Yesod ha-Seminar he-hadash*" (The Foundation of the New Seminary), Eisenstein carefully outlined his objections to the new institution and to the movement it claimed to represent.[78] Like Weinberger, Eisenstein wondered where the Seminary stood in the spectrum of American Jewish religious life. The often confused efforts by the school's leadership to define its purpose and principles suggested to Eisenstein that the "Conservative" institution was neither fish nor fowl (*hayah o behemah*). As a logical outgrowth of the anarchic nature of American Jewish life, Conservatism allowed each individual to observe as much or as little as he wished. Ultimately, Eisenstein maintained, there was not much difference between the goals of the Reformers and of the Conservatives; it was only a matter of timing. While the former flaunted his hypocrisy, the latter disguised it. For all its much vaunted sophistication, Eisenstein concluded, "*Torat Conservatizm*" could be reduced to a simple rule: one observed Judaism in the synagogue and ignored it everywhere else. Ultimately, he maintained, the Conservatives "are weak of heart, like children hiding under the apron of their mothers, who are afraid to express their ideas in public; and from their mouths [one hears] pearls [of wisdom]: 'Do as I say, not as I do.'" In Eisenstein's view, the Seminary could only be accepted within the immigrant community if it adhered to the following stipulations: no Reform congregations could be admitted; administrators and teachers must be observant Jews; and students and teachers must study with covered heads and say nothing that contradicts the *Shulhan Arukh* (literally, a set table, a book of ritual laws). Eisenstein's last demand—that students should be between six and eight years old and should learn English only to prevent them from going to public school—pointed up the yawning gap between the aims of the Seminary and the interests of the traditional community.

The tendencies already noticeable in the 1890s were intensified as a result of the reorganization of the Seminary in 1902 and the appointment of Solomon Schechter as its new president. The reorganization, which led in 1903 to the construction of a new building on 122nd Street and Broadway, seemed to signal a firm commitment to develop Conservative Judaism as a distinctive and visible movement within American Jewry. The appointment of a renowned scholar as president was clearly meant to highlight the emphasis that the Seminary placed upon serious Jewish scholarship. The two events had a powerful effect upon immigrant "modernizers" on the Lower East Side. The fact that Schechter was born in Rumania and was familiar with East European Jewish life suggested that the Conservative movement had finally recog-

An article featured on the front page of the *Yidishe Gazeten* describes Solomon Schechter's arrival in the United States and his plans for the Seminary. Even his physical appearance is detailed for the readers: "His head is massive and covered with a mass of brown hair . . . ." "Rosh Yeshiva," *Yiddishe Gazeten*, 25 April 1902.

nized the centrality of immigrants in its future development as a powerful spiritual force in the American Jewish community. In turn, the construction of a new building seemed to signal the intention of the Seminary to establish itself as a permanent presence in the Jewish community and highlighted the need for the institution to clearly define its direction and goals.

Schechter himself made every effort to play upon his Central European Jewish heritage. Even before his arrival in America, he had expressed concern with what he regarded as the constant "bullying" of immigrants by rich British Jews.[79] Schechter's inaugural speech as president of the Seminary in November 1902 was highlighted by an attack upon Reform Judaism and a ringing commitment to prevent what the new president called the "occidentalization" of American Jewish religious life. Schechter also made sure to emphasize the importance of East European Jewry as the upholders of the traditions of the Torah. Throughout his tenure at the Seminary, he explicitly rejected the goal of Americanizing immigrants. He had not come to America for the purpose of converting the "downtown" Jews "to a more refined species of religion," Schechter would write to Louis Marshall, chairman of the Board of Trustees of the Seminary, in December 1913.[80] Instead he hoped to combine the "method" of western scholarship as practiced at Cambridge with the "madness" of East European spirituality that he had experienced during his schooling at Rumanian and Galician yeshivas.[81] It was the immigrant's almost visceral need to maintain Hebrew and traditional ritual as a means of retaining his spiritual ties to the Jewish people that would help rescue American Judaism from the evils of assimilationism and radicalism.[82] In 1913, Schechter would look back on his career and proudly note that it was the immigrant's strict adherence to tradition and his rejection of Reform that had brought Conservative Judaism to prominence.[83]

Schechter also pressed for the establishment of a cantorial school, a development that at least in part was intended to play on the Lower East Side's fascination with *hazzanim*.[84] Keenly aware of the desire of many immigrant women to engage in Jewish studies, he hoped to interest young girls in a career in Jewish education.[85] In 1904, Schechter helped found teacher training courses that were open to both men and women. Two years later, he unsuccessfully pressed for the establishment of a downtown branch of the Teachers Institute of the Seminary.

Recognizing the role that immigrant Jews could play in furthering the activity of the Seminary, Schechter also made a strong effort to popularize the activity of the institution on the Lower East Side. The new president was a warm supporter of the Jewish Endeavor Society which, shortly after his arrival, publicly announced plans to establish a "Conservative" synagogue to serve the "downtown" immigrant community.[86] At a meeting held in May 1904 at the Educational Alliance, Schechter outlined the role of the Seminary on the Lower East Side. A major goal of the institution, he proclaimed, was to "teach conservative or orthodox Rabbis who can speak

English and can relate to the younger generation."[87] In reaching out to immigrants, the Seminary wished to incorporate all of the best from the variety of national traditions that Jews had absorbed over the ages and had brought with them to America: the German scientific spirit of research, French love for ideals, Asiatic tendency to search out the mysteries of the world—and Russian-Polish enthusiasm. Only the Seminary, Schechter concluded, could embrace such a large, rich, and self-sacrificing community of Jews. Pereira Mendes, well known for his sympathetic views toward immigrants, concluded the meeting with a call for Jews of the Lower East Side to become members of the Jewish Theological Seminary Association.[88]

Schechter's outreach to the immigrant community had a profound effect on the religious moderates on the Lower East Side. One could see the growing confidence and enthusiasm in the response of the "modernizing" Yiddish press to the foundation of the new Seminary. "A Yeshiva for Everyone," the headline of the lead article in the *Yidishes Tagesblatt* boldly proclaimed on 18 April 1902. The article went on to explain in breathless terms that unlike previous Jewish schools of learning, the Seminary would be open even to Christians who wanted to attend.[89] Indeed, the rabbinical school would soon become a carbon copy of Cambridge where Schechter had first taught, thereby raising the image of the Jews in the world. At the same time, most Yiddish writers pointed approvingly to Schechter's denunciation of the idea of creating a distinctive American Judaism, as espoused by the Reform movement. Commenting on Schechter's invitation to serve on a doctoral committee in philosophy at Catholic University, one Yiddish journalist noted that the respect that Christian scholars showed the president of the Seminary demonstrated that Jews did not have to forsake their traditions in order to be accepted in the larger society.[90] The headline in the *Yidishe Velt* on the day after commencement of the reorganized Seminary's first graduating class pointed up the great hope that immigrant religious reformers placed in the reorganization institution after years of inner doubt and suspicion. It read simply: "The Old Seminary Has Been Left Behind."[91]

But it was Schechter's persona that had the most powerful effect upon immigrant "modernizers." To many, the new president's piercing eyes, long beard, and serious demeanor suggested an Old World rabbi who could well become the leader of the newly emerging American Jewish community. Yet unlike Rabbi Jacob Joseph, Schechter was no passive and hermited talmudist. As an individual of remarkable erudition, "one of the greatest Jewish scholars in the Diaspora" one writer commented, he was as familiar with secular literature as he was with sacred texts.[92] Alternatively tender and stern, Schechter seemed the ideal Moses to lead the Jews out of their spiritual slavery. From their first encounter with the new president of the Seminary, immigrant writers in the Yiddish press were convinced that he held the future of Judaism in America in his hands.[93]

On a more personal level, Schechter's ascension to the presidency of the Jewish

27

*The JTS
and the
"Downtown"
Jews of New
York at the
Turn of the
Century*

"Rosh Yeshiva. / Schechter's First Day. / The learned professor spends his first day in the New World with interviews and receiving visitors. / A Yeshiva for Everyone. / Christians will be able to visit.'" *Yidishes Tagesblatt*, 18 April 1902.

Solomon Schechter surrounded by Seminary students from his era.
Photo by Mandelkern. Ratner Center, JTS.

Theological Seminary seemed to symbolize the successful transformation from East to West that awaited all immigrants who persevered. Despite his erudition and his Cambridge airs, he had never denied his affinity to East European immigrants. As an important figure in American Jewish communal life, Schechter was also seen as being able to express the Russian and Polish Jew's secret resentments of the pretensions of "uptowners."[94] At the same time, Schechter gave immigrant intellectuals and businessmen entrée into established Jewish circles that they had never had before. At a reception in May 1902 for the new president at the home of Jacob Schiff, for example, Sarasohn was invited to serve as one of two representatives of the Lower East Side. At the door, he would tell his readers with pride, Schiff (undoubtedly mistaking the newspaperman for one of the newly hired faculty members of the Seminary) greeted him as "professor" and announced in English "I am very glad to meet with you"![95]

What most impressed "downtown" religious reformers was Schechter's seeming concern with the Lower East Side's lack of spiritual leadership and direction. As a Yiddish speaker, Schechter read the immigrant press closely. In his inaugural address, the new president echoed the central themes that had been sounded in the Yiddish press since the 1880s. Like the immigrant "modernizers," Schechter expressed concern that successive waves of arriving immigrants threatened to fragment the American Jewish community into "a multitude of petty Old Worlds."[96] Similarly, he saw religious traditionalists and political radicals locked in a bitter struggle for control of the Lower East Side that fragmented and weakened the community. As Schechter quipped in an interview with the editors of the *Yidishes Tageblatt* that was bound to appeal both to the paper's moderate readership and to its conservative editor, the Russian Jew was a creature of extremes: "He is either a 'zaddik' [righteous man] or a 'rosche' [evil man], a 'frum' [religious man] or a radical. And when he is a radical, he is such a 'rosche.'"[97] Like the immigrant "modernizers" as well, Schechter denounced East European Jews for letting their rabbis go hungry and called upon residents of the Lower East Side to have greater respect for the synagogue and for the rabbinate.[98] Schechter also echoed Sarasohn's and Masliansky's concerns over the alienation of immigrant youth. In order to win back young men and women to Judaism, he proclaimed, the immigrant community would have to adapt to the realities of American life. The Orthodox community would have to make sacrifices, the president of the Seminary commented to a Yiddish interviewer soon after his appointment, just as other Jews do. It was the least they could do for their children.[99]

The moderate Yiddish press covered Schechter's installation at the Seminary in November 1902 as if it were a coronation. Kasriel Sarasohn's ebullient editorial in the 5 December 1902 issue of the *Yidishe Gazeten* was typical. Schechter's appointment was "a new dawn," a breath of fresh air that had arisen from the East. His con-

"The Voice of the
Ghetto. Day
[Dawns]."
*Yidishes
Tagesblatt*,
English Depart-
ment, 24 Novem-
ber 1902.

THE VOICE OF THE GHETTO.
By A. M. F.

DAY DOWNS.

The sun of Judaism has risen; shadow and darkness are dispelled and there is light throughout the land. The East has triumphed over the West. Schechter has spoken, and Judaism has triumphed over the shadow of the borderland, over Occidentalism. The Judaism of the Torah, the plain, simple catholic Judaism of our fathers is in the ascendant, and under the leadership of the great, simple, courageous man who has come to us from the East it will become the dominating, impelling force in the lives of all Jews. Fad, fancies, modern mysticism, and reckless radicalism have failed. Ignorance will cease to be the fashion, flirtation with the whim and fancy of the hour will cease. Learning, spirituality and honesty will again be the standard for our Rabbis.

Schechter has spoken and all Jewry is refreshed. It rejoices that he takes his stand on the broad platform of the Torah, opposing with all the vigor of his master mind the shams, hypocrisies and expediencies of Reform. To him, and to the great movement of which he is the leader, religion is not a separate thing, but the essential factor in man's life.

Strongest of all is the stand he takes regarding the Jewish ministry. He insists, as the most uncompromising Orthodox insists, that our Rabbis must be men of learning. And, says this great man, there is no snap-shot method for requiring learning. As the office of the Jewish minister is to teach Judaism, he must be able to say: "Nothing Jewish is foreign to me." Ignorance is not such a bliss as to require special effort for its acquirement. Know-nothingism has been a miserable failure. And more than this: The spirit must accompany the letter. They cannot be separated, and Judaism cannot ignore the traditions of the past. The Torah is a part of ourselves, and there must be an end of all talk about Occidentalizing religion—as if the Occident had any genius for religion. The use of platitudes and stock-phrases must be abandoned.

Most interesting were his views on charity which he denied was synonymous with "that barbaric term altruism." It was born with the synagogue, and was not limited to any class. Gemilath Chasodim had no fixed measure. Charity should not be altogether scientific.

Prof. Schechter realizes that Judaism has suddenly grown old in this country, but we recognize that this optimism, his bravery, his broad, earnest spirit will give it new life, will regenerate it, will make it young again, and give it the strength and vigor that will lead it to mastery of the world.

The coming of Schechter is indeed a blessing to Judaism in America, whatever it may mean to "American Judaism," which he does not recognize. Those who invited him here, builded even better than they knew. He is great enough and strong enough and brave enough to put an end to all shams, fads and policies. He is the man to hold the banner of Judaism high, and bid all to follow whither he leads. For he will lead in the right path.

Orthodoxy certainly should welcome this man who is of themselves, to whom the Torah is sacred, and who has veneration for our history and traditions. Nor need Reform, honest Reform, look at him askance. The difference between Orthodoxy and Reform, are, after all, in details, and in matters of zeal, merely. The honest "Reformer"—men of the type of the late Isaac M. Wise, or Kaufman Kohler, or Gustav Gottheil, love the Torah as ardently as the most uncompromising Orthodox, and they surely can find nothing in Schechter's stand that is unacceptable to them. The task of reconciliation, the holy purpose of reuniting all factions in Judaism is certainly no impossible one, and in Schechter's optimistic notes we all find encouragement. For the "Radicals"—for those who have been dejudaizing Judaism, who have been tearing down the edifice reared through the centuries, Schechter will be the restraining hand. His, the voice to cry them "halt"—his, the finger to point out their error, and his the call to summon them back from their mad chase after fads and fancies, he the guide to lead them back to the right path. And, if they will not respond to his call, Judaism will do without them. They will be without sanction and support and their utterances will be vain.

To accomplish all that is within his power, Schechter must be more than the Dean of the Seminary. He must be the leader of the people. He must speak, not merely to the students, but to the entire community. His voice and his pen must be ever active in the service of the holy cause of the Torah, in which he has enlisted himself. He must captain the army of Judaism and lead it forward.

The day has dawned in the East. The dark clouds of the West, the mists of the border-land are dispersing. And the day has dawned gloriously.

demnation of "occidentalism" was nothing short of a reaffirmation of the basic principles of East European Jewish religious life. Despite his general unfamiliarity with American society, the editorial continued, Schechter had recognized almost immediately that American Judaism was in crisis. In publicly stating that neither religious radicalism nor obscurantism could save Orthodoxy, he had demonstrated his understanding of the need for a serious rethinking of the spiritual condition of American Jewry. With Schechter at the helm of Orthodox Judaism, an editorial written in the *Yidishes Tageblatt* the previous November had proclaimed, "Ignorance will cease to be the fashion, flirtation with the whim of and fancy of the hour will cease."[100] Sarasohn concluded his editorial written in December with an idyllic image of the new president that seemed to hark back to the editor's original hopes for a chief rabbi of the United States a decade and a half earlier. Schechter's optimism, bravery, and spirit would revivify Judaism in the New World. To accomplish his task, Schechter had to become more than the dean of the Seminary. He had to assume the leadership of the Jewish people and not merely to his students. In short, Schechter had to "captain the army of Judaism and lead it forward."[101]

Immigrant "modernizers" had yet another occasion to rejoice after the dedication of the new building of the Seminary on 123rd Street in April 1903. Beginning in January, articles began to appear on a daily basis chronicling its financing and construction. It was not only the new building that suggested the Seminary's permanency; it was also the fact that the rabbinical college had secured an endowment of a half million dollars.[102] And when the edifice was finally completed, the Yiddish press could not conceal its joy. Structurally, the new building was unrivaled. Articles in the Yiddish press marveled at the use of the most modern methods in its construction. Who would believe that you could erect a building that was completely fireproof with electric lighting throughout? Flanked by Columbia University to its south and a prospective new structure for the College of the City of New York to its north, an article in the *Velt* proclaimed, the new Seminary was truly deserving of an honored place among institutions of higher learning.[103]

Most important, of course, was the role of the new Seminary building in the revitalization of American Jewry. "A magnificent structure in the cause of Jewish learning," Masliansky's paper proclaimed. One Yiddish journalist described it as a *mishkan* (sanctuary) for the Torah. Yet another trumpeted it as a "fountain" of Torah.[104] At a time when the Kishinev massacre and dramatic developments in the Dreyfus Case aroused profound concern on the Lower East Side, the arrival of what one writer in the *Yidishes Gazeten* described as a new "epoch in the history of Judaism in America" was good news.[105] Indeed, the image of the Seminary as a unifying religious institution whose source was sacred learning meshed well with the emphasis upon unity in the immigrant community in a period of worldwide Jewish catastrophe.[106]

Moderate Yiddish newspapers were all in agreement that Schechter's accession to the presidency would lead to the expansion of outreach programs to the Lower East Side. Sarasohn and his supporters, in particular, believed that thanks to the renewed strength and visibility of the Seminary, the Jewish Endeavor Society would finally succeed in its effort to bridge the gap between the generations by synthesizing traditional observance with a modern aesthetic sensibility.[107] The most fervent hope of the "modernizers" was that immigrant youth would follow in the footsteps of the young students who ran the society. In an editorial entitled "*Idn fur idntum*" (Jews for Jewry) published in the *Yidishe Velt*, for example, Masliansky praised the organization in the following terms:

> It is a rare society comprised of rare individuals. Young men and young women who have graduated college, who have from their birth breathed the pure American air, young people who people can point with pride to as representatives of American Jews, young people who are more than students of secular studies but who count among them some who are well-versed in Talmud and *pesukim* [biblical verses].

Such individuals, Masliansky noted, should serve as the vanguard of a new rabbinate, comprised of "men who can speak English, and who are not afraid that they will overwork themselves." The new Seminary-trained rabbi would be available to the community seven days a week rather than only on the Sabbath. Constantly in the public eye, he would earn the respect of the community not only through his scholarship but by the exemplary life he led.[108]

In emphasizing the new type of religious leader that would emerge from the Seminary, some "modernizers" on the Lower East Side envisioned dramatic changes in the role of the synagogue in the American Jewish community. In contrast to the *shul* (traditional house of worship) of Eastern Europe, the American house of worship would combine both religious and secular concerns. In contrast to previous institutions in the Jewish community, it would not create artificial divisions between a scholarly elite and the masses. Instead, the new synagogue would incorporate all interested Jews, both old and young, into its activities. As Masliansky wrote in the previously cited editorial: "The synagogue must stand as the representative Jewish institution. It should be the unit of organization, and it should be more than a mere name. It should encourage kindergartens, young men's societies, young women's societies, and everything else that might attract young people." The Yiddish preacher's comments about the rabbinate and the synagogue could well have been written by Solomon Schechter himself.

In the heady first years of the Seminary's reorganization, the moderate Yiddish press served as a vehicle for the dissemination of its programs and ideals on the Lower East Side. Sarasohn's and Masliansky's newspapers were insistent that the

Seminary needed to be strongly supported by immigrants, if only to prevent it from being dominated by "uptowners." East European immigrants may not be the "'American Jews' of to-day," an article in the *Yidishes Tagesblatt* commented, "but they are likely to be the only American Jews of to-morrow."[109] In most cases, "modernizers" were quick to use immigrant complaints about the sad state of Jewish life on the Lower East Side to press their case for the need to support the Seminary and its effort to train new religious leaders.[110] For their part, Seminary officials continued to hold public meetings on the Lower East Side to publicize the school's activity, raise money, and gain new student recruits.[111] So successful was the Seminary's fund-raising campaign among East European Jews that it was rumored on the Lower East Side that the Hebrew Union College worried constantly over the loss of financial support from Russian Jews.[112]

Numerous letters in the Yiddish press attest to the fact that, despite the many obstacles, young immigrants were spurred by the rabbinical school's revitalized image on the Lower East Side to apply for admission. A typical letter was that from a yeshiva-trained immigrant in the *Yidishe Velt* published in February 1904, which voiced the writer's frustration over the Seminary's refusal to accept him without a bachelor's degree and pleaded for help in securing his admission. Masliansky responded in an editorial by noting that he had received a number of similar letters. Though recognizing that the Seminary might be too rigid at times in its standards for acceptance into its rabbinical school, he stressed the fact that a rabbi with "old *smicha* [rabbinical ordination]" had no future in America. Immigrants would simply have to adapt to the demands of the Seminary if they wished to succeed as American rabbis.[113] Enterprising teachers, some of whom were associated with the Seminary, were quick to take advantage of a new pool of prospective students. Throughout 1904, the Yiddish press ran an ad in its pages announcing preparatory classes offered by a teacher at the Seminary for anyone interested in entering a "rabbinical college or seminary the world over."[114]

Admittedly, there were some doubters among the immigrant moderates. For all his seeming enthusiasm, Masliansky had gnawing concerns about the direction of the new Seminary. The preacher and editor expressed only mild approval after witnessing the graduation of the first class of rabbis. There was no great spirit in the hall during the ceremony, an article published in the *Yidishe Velt* on 2 July 1902 remarked. The fact that people on the dais appeared to be asleep or at least lacked any enthusiasm created the impression that "neither the students nor the teachers are looking ahead with any shining hopes." Both the *Velt* and the *Tagesblatt* commented that many of the students and professors sat bareheaded during a presentation on the Talmud.[115] In an article written the next day, Masliansky wondered whether the spirit of Sabato Morais would live on in the new Seminary and stressed the need to carry on the great work of the more traditional teachers like Drachman and Joshua Joffe who "were almost the only ones who studied with their students and who put their whole heart and soul into it."[116]

Yet in the absence of any alternative for Orthodox Jews, even Masliansky could not deny the import of the new Seminary for the immigrant community. Despite its rocky beginnings, the *Yidishe Velt* commented, the Seminary remained "our great hope . . . an important moment in the Jewish history of the United States, a change in Jewish history of great significance."[117] No longer would the rabbinate be looked upon as a lowly profession. As for the Seminary's departure from religious tradition, Masliansky's paper wistfully commented, "This is America and one must take pride in what there is."[118] The rabbis who graduated from the Seminary may not be the geniuses turned out by the Volozhin Yeshiva, a writer remarked in an article published in the *Velt* in 1904, "but they are imbued with the Jewish spirit and viewing the world with a more general knowledge, know how to gain the love and respect of the younger generation for our Torah and our traditions."[119]

Not surprisingly, the changes in the Seminary created renewed opposition from ultra-Orthodox elements on the Lower East Side. Rejecting the moderates' call for a change in the curriculum of rabbinical schools, East European rabbis denounced the Seminary for its alleged willingness to introduce Higher Criticism in its biblical studies classes. Schechter's denigration of the Yiddish language and his refusal to allow its use in Seminary classrooms also raised the ire of many traditionalists in the immigrant community.[120] Local downtown rabbis were instrumental in blocking the attempt by the Jewish Endeavor Society to hold Sabbath prayers in one of the existing synagogues on the Lower East Side.[121] In some cases, student rabbis from the Seminary were evicted from synagogues; in others, local rabbis publicly disrupted classes and prayers.[122]

By far the most extreme opposition to the Seminary could be found in the *Agudath ha-Rabbanim* or Union of Orthodox Rabbis of America. Founded in July 1902, only a day after the death of Rabbi Jacob Joseph and coinciding with the graduation of the first group of rabbis from the reorganized Seminary, the *Agudah* quickly became the spokesman of the "rejectionist" elements of the East European rabbinate on the Lower East Side. Immigrant rabbis were led to create the *Agudah* in response to what they saw as the growing institutional strength of the "enemies" of Orthodoxy, including the Reform movement, the Jewish labor movement, and most important, the Jewish Theological Seminary. Organizers were also motivated by fears that rich Jews were systematically destroying traditional immigrant Jewish life by insisting upon assimilation in return for charitable aid.[123] The death of Rabbi Jacob Joseph only exacerbated fears of subversion by outside elements by highlighting the inner weaknesses of the Orthodox community on the Lower East Side. For the first time, Orthodox religious leaders felt the need to establish a unified stand against their common foes. Indeed, the fact that almost four-fifths of the founding members of the *Agudah* were actually from outside New York City suggested that immigrant rabbis faced with the challenge of maintaining Orthodoxy among Jews who had fled ghetto settlements were losing faith in the East European rabbinate of the Lower East Side and were seeking to create a new cadre of concerned and dynamic leaders.[124]

From its inception, the *Agudah* vehemently opposed any deviation from strict religious tradition. At its founding meeting, the organization passed a resolution proclaiming that no rabbinical institute could be established in the United States without its express consent. Similarly, it denounced efforts by some Orthodox synagogues to hold late after-dinner activities on Friday nights because they appeared to mimic the practices of Conservative (and Reform) temples.[125] Unlike members of the Jewish Sabbath Observance Society who were convinced that traditional observance was fully compatible with participation in civil society, members of the *Agudah* were mainly interested in ensuring that recent arrivals did not succumb to the attractions of the New World. As the historian Jeffrey Gurock suggests: "Ultimately the Agudat ha-Rabbanim was less concerned that American law respect the immigrant Jew and more interested that new Americans continue to respect Jewish law."[126]

For immigrant religious reformers, the creation of the *Agudah* seemed to signal the willingness of East European rabbis to assume their communal responsibilities. Here at last was an effort by immigrants to administer and coordinate their religious activity. Sarasohn had actually been one of the original proponents of the idea of creating an organization of Orthodox rabbis in the immigrant community. In 1901, he unsuccessfully lobbied for its establishment and hosted a number of its preliminary meetings in his home. Masliansky was equally enthusiastic. An article in the *Yidishe Velt* published at the time of the *Agudah*'s founding, for example, praised the group as a faithful copy of the great rabbinical assemblies of the past and claimed that its activity would ultimately demonstrate the need for the American rabbinate to free itself from fanaticism. A companion article compared the assembled rabbis to Moses and Joshua rising up to save the Jewish people in their time of trouble.[127] Indeed, Sarasohn and Masliansky's newspapers thought nothing of praising the *Agudah* and the Seminary in the same article as reflections of a revitalized Orthodoxy in America.[128] Blithely ignoring or badly misreading the potentially divisive nature of the *Agudah*'s agenda, an article in the *Yidishe Gazeten* described the meeting of rabbis as "a picture of Jewish unity, a picture of peace among all elements of Jewry."[129]

In actuality, the creation of the *Agudath ha-Rabbanim* served only to intensify a bitter battle within the Orthodox community for the right to carry the banner of traditional Judaism in America. It was a struggle in which East European rabbis found themselves pitted against many of the early founders of the Seminary. Four years before the creation of the Union of Orthodox Rabbis, leaders of the Seminary had helped to establish the Union of Orthodox Congregations in America. Their goal was to establish a constituency for the Seminary among traditional Jews by creating a vibrant movement responsive to both the spiritual and material needs of American Orthodox Jews. As late as June 1903, Henry Pereira Mendes, the president of the Union, could still praise the Seminary for strengthening a revitalized Orthodox Judaism.[130] Such statements were bound to anger ultra-Orthodox elements within the *Agudah* and to rouse them into taking action against the new rabbinical institution.

The *Agudah*'s attack upon the Seminary did not take long to develop. The first major salvo was launched against Mordecai Kaplan, a recent graduate of the rabbinical school, who had been hired in November 1903 to assume the pulpit as minister of Kehillat Jeshurun, a prominent Orthodox congregation in the Yorkville section of Manhattan. As news of Kaplan's appointment spread throughout the city, it soon proved to be a lightning rod for ultra-Orthodox elements on the Lower East Side. In the spring of 1904, the *Agudah* issued a circular denouncing the use of English in the pulpit of Kehillat Jeshurun and demanding that, as a general policy, all Orthodox congregations should refuse to hire graduates of the Seminary.[131] A few months later, the president and one of the trustees of the congregation, under pressure from supporters of the *Agudah* in the congregation, invited Jacob Willowsky, who was known as the "*Slutzker Rav*" and alternatively as the "*Ridbaz*," to preach for the High Holy Days. In his sermon, the "*Ridbaz*" denounced the use of English in sermons and refused to allow Kaplan to appear on the pulpit on Rosh Hashanah and Yom Kippur.[132] Though Kaplan survived the ordeal largely as a result of an intensive newspaper campaign by his loyal supporters within the congregation,[133] he was clearly unhappy with his situation. In 1909, Kaplan eagerly accepted Schechter's offer to teach at the Teachers Institute of the Seminary.

The controversy over Kaplan's appointment served to further widen the growing gap between moderate and ultra-Orthodox rabbis. In June 1904, Pereira Mendes had written to the *Agudah* on behalf of the Union of Orthodox Congregations in America inquiring about its attitude toward the Seminary. In response, the *Agudah* appointed a committee that included Moshe S. Margolies (later to be appointed rabbi at Kehillat Jeshurun alongside Kaplan), Joseph Peikes (whom Kaplan had replaced), and the "*Slutzker Rav*." For these individuals, the ordination of Seminary graduates represented a direct threat to the *Agudah*'s control over the Orthodox rabbinate in the United States. In its founding constitution, the *Agudah* had proclaimed that only those ordained by a religious scholar from Europe or the head of an established Orthodox congregation would be allowed to join.[134] It was not surprising, therefore, that the committee responded to Pereira Mendes by issuing a bitter condemnation of the Seminary that reiterated the *Agudah*'s opposition to the employment of its graduates as rabbis in Orthodox congregations. (The *American Hebrew* mistakenly claimed in its article on the decision that the *Agudah* had issued a *herem* [an edict of excommunication] against the Seminary.[135]) The decision of the ad hoc committee was reaffirmed at the Third Annual Convention of the *Agudath ha-Rabbanim* held in early July. In one of its public resolutions, the rabbinic body restated its intention not to recognize the Seminary as an Orthodox institution.[136] Though praising the commitment of the early founders of the Seminary to religious tradition, the organization stated in an allusion to Schechter that within a short time, "new spirits began to settle in this Seminary" who were intent upon bringing about changes that were antithetical to the beliefs and practices of all god-fearing Jews.[137] The *Agudah*'s president, Bernard Levinthal, was more direct in his public condemnation of the new president. In a play upon Schechter's name, he described the new head of the Seminary as a "butcher" who had come to America to slaughter Judaism.[138]

At the same time, members of the *Agudah* sought to drum up popular support for its stand among traditionalists on the Lower East Side. At a mass rally at the Bet Hamedrash Hagadol on Norfolk Street held in June 1904, speakers denounced the Seminary as a mortal danger to Judaism. Seminary graduates studied "seven languages and seven forms of wisdom," *Agudah* leaders declaimed, but they lacked knowledge of the essentials of Judaism. Instead of studying Talmud, they devised "evil plans" to weaken and even destroy Orthodoxy and its most ardent defender, the *Agudah*.[139] In the same month, Jehuda Eisenstein responded to a bitter editorial in the *American Hebrew* that had attacked the *Agudah*'s denunciation of the Seminary. The Seminary's reliance upon biblical Higher Criticism was anathema to any believing Jew, he argued. If anyone can claim such views as Orthodox, he wrote, then "Isaac M. Wise, the founder of Reform in America, who to his credit be it said, strenuously opposed High Criticism, may truly be called a pious Jew, a Hasid." Any individual who publicly denied the divine revelation of the Torah should be proclaimed "an apostate and a deserter of Judaism." If Schechter continued to teach Higher Criticism as part of his commitment to "Catholic Israel," Eisenstein concluded, then perhaps "it is high time to organize a 'Protestant Israel' to protest against such rot and decay in Judaism."[140]

The attack by the *Agudah* on the Seminary continued unabated throughout the summer of 1904. It was a testament to the growing influence of the Seminary, however, that the vehement reaction by both "uptown" and "downtown" Jews as well as opposition from members of the *Agudah* who lived outside New York City forced the organization to backtrack from some of its more extreme views. Already in July in his response to the *American Hebrew*, Eisenstein had argued that the organization was not opposed to the use of English in classrooms when that was the familiar language of the pupil. He was also willing to recognize that for some audiences, it might be preferable if sermons were given in English. In early August, leaders of the *Agudah* met again to reevaluate their position. They had never intended to proclaim a *herem* on the Seminary, the leaders announced in their concluding statement. Nevertheless, they demanded that the Seminary desist from calling itself an Orthodox institution, since none of its graduates could pass an examination before a competent Jewish authority for even the most minimal Orthodox ordination. At the same time, the statement ridiculed leaders of the Old Seminary such as Pereira Mendes who wished to unite Orthodox synagogues. In the near future, the *Agudah* would take it upon itself to establish a union of "real" Orthodox congregations.[141]

Ironically, many of the same criticisms leveled against the Seminary and its institutions by ultra-Orthodox elements could also be found among immigrant socialists and secularists. Like East European rabbis, socialists were convinced that the rabbinical institution and its "uptown" supporters were merely using religion to serve their own selfish ends and to prevent the development and growth of authentic immigrant organizations and movements. As for the belief of the "modernizers" in the need for a new type of rabbi attuned to both the material and spiritual concerns of the community, it was hardly worth discussing. Immigrant Jewish socialists saw little difference between graduates of the Seminary and of Hebrew Union College. Rabbis of whatever stripe who voiced concern for the social and economic conditions of the Lower East Side, an editorial in the *Forvertz* proclaimed in 1904, were little more than hypocrites. Their calls for ethical behavior were a mask for the class war that their bourgeois congregation members waged daily against immigrant workers.[142] For radicals, groups such as the Jewish Sabbath Observance Society and the Jewish Endeavor Society were nothing but desperate efforts by Jewish capitalists to obfuscate class consciousness and to block the inroads of socialists in the immigrant community. In any event, for most socialists, there were far more pressing problems to deal with on the Lower East Side than the fate of a dying and growingly irrelevant religious belief.[143]

Though only occasionally discussing the Seminary per se, the socialist press was unremitting in its attacks on the institution's defenders in the immigrant community. One of its favorite targets was Sarasohn, with whom the *Forvertz* competed for the Yiddish readership of the Lower East Side. Throughout the early 1900s, editorials in the socialist newspaper denounced the newspaper magnate as a plagiarizer, a slanderer, and a thief who masked his corruption with sweet words of social concern and religious piety.[144] In a veiled attack upon the Seminary and its outreach efforts among East European Jews, the socialists hammered home the theme that "uptown" religious reformers and their immigrant supporters like Sarasohn were only interested in exploiting immigrants for their own selfish ends. Traditional immigrants "would be a thousand times better off" if they sought unity with non-religious socialists, an article in the *Forvertz* commented in 1904, than with "the pseudo-religious capitalists and their toadies."[145]

Though diametrically opposed to one another, the ultra-Orthodox and the socialists on the Lower East Side clearly recognized at a very early stage the significance of the creation of an American rabbinical school pledged to meld tradition and modernity. Both groups understood that a movement and a rabbinate attuned to the challenges of daily life in the United States threatened proponents of both an unchanging Jewish past and a radical Jewish future. Most immigrants, however, dismissed their diatribes as the last gasp of a dying generation of transplanted East European rabbis on the one hand and the musings of anticlericalists on the other.

More significant was the growing frustration with Schechter's programs and policies on the part of many of the surviving founders and supporters of the Old Seminary such as Hirsch Masliansky, Bernard Drachman, and Henry Pereira Mendes. Part of the reason for their alienation was their personal animosity toward Schechter. Though he would never publicly admit it, Masliansky was undoubtedly jealous of the charismatic appeal and oratorical talent that the new president of the Seminary displayed in his public appearances on the Lower East Side. In an era when the great *maggid* was gradually losing favor among the immigrant masses, Schechter's self-fashioning as a defender of East European Jewish values seemed especially hurtful. Drachman's view of Schechter was even more antagonistic. As a successful teacher and respected scholar at the Old Seminary for fifteen years, he had naively assumed that he would succeed Sabato Morais as president in 1902.[146] To make matters worse, after Schechter's arrival, the new president demoted him from professor to instructor and refused to acknowledge his recently published book. In 1909, Drachman received a letter from Schechter announcing that his teaching appointment was being terminated.[147] As for Pereira Mendes, he was increasingly alarmed by the new president's dismissive attitudes toward the Old Seminary and its founders. Schechter himself generally ignored the Sephardic *hazzan*, regarding him as an insignificant rabbi and an inconsequential scholar.[148]

Ultimately, however, the hostility that many supporters of the Old Seminary in both the immigrant community and "uptown" Orthodoxy felt toward Schechter rested on serious religious differences. "Uptown" and "downtown" critics were unanimous in their conviction that the new president was fundamentally opposed to traditional Judaism. For Drachman, for example, Schechter's commitment to Orthodoxy was merely a strategic ploy to mask his real intention to carve out a distinctive path for a new form of "Conservative" Judaism that would depart significantly from religious traditions.[149] Others were convinced that the reorganized rabbinical school was a conspiracy by elements seeking to bolster the interests of Reform.[150]

By far the most concerned individual among the immigrant moderates was Hirsch Masliansky. As we have seen, throughout the first years after the reorganization of the Seminary, Masliansky positioned himself as a traditionalist gadfly who was intent on ensuring that the rabbinical school would retain its fundamental commitment to Orthodoxy. He was not afraid to criticize the new institution's activity when he thought that it departed from its original goal of training "orthodox rabbinical professors, rabbinical teachers, and rabbis who can hold high the banners of knowledge and Torah." There was little question that Schechter was an eminent scholar worthy of respect, Masliansky admitted. Yet the new president's ideas were potentially damaging to the original mission of the Seminary. In wishing Schechter well nevertheless, Masliansky would remain "a friend"— and a "pessimist."[151]

Masliansky was especially wary of Schechter's interest in the activities of the Jewish Endeavor Society, fearing that it represented an attempt to impose his own brand of Judaism on unsuspecting immigrants. In an editorial published in *Yidishe Velt* in January 1903, for example, the English page editor Joseph Jacobs questioned the decision to establish a special synagogue on the Lower East Side under the auspices of the society. Though insisting that the older generation needed to give the society a chance to succeed, he suggested that a separate institution would only result in "the formation of a ritual of the Endeavor [Society], which would only add to the 'minhagim,' which is not desirable, and be of no ultimate benefit to Judaism."[152] Masliansky's and Jacobs's fears of the loss of immigrant control over their religious activity were shared by other Orthodox Jews on the Lower East Side. In February 1903, one immigrant letter writer to the *American Hebrew* suggested that the Jewish Endeavor Society was grossly exaggerating its influence on the Lower East Side. The local synagogues established by the Seminary "do serve as a gathering place, week-days and on the Sabbath, of a comparatively small portion of the immigrant population of the 'Ghetto'," he commented, but their influence on the rising generation was "nil."[153] Similarly, in September 1903, the regular immigrant correspondent for the *American Hebrew,* who went under the pseudonym "A Voice from the Ghetto," commended the society for its efforts to counter missionaries but warned that the major responsibility had to rest with the residents of the Lower East Side.[154]

Despite Schechter's constant emphasis upon the Seminary's commitment to traditional Judaism, his efforts to steer a path between Orthodoxy and Reform after reorganization often created suspicion and confusion in the minds of immigrants. Some could not understand the excitement over what was, after all, merely another "orthodox" rabbinical school—and not a very observant one at that.[155] Others were distinctly uncomfortable with what they regarded as the Seminary's kowtowing to Reform leaders and to wealthy and assimilated members of the German Jewish community.[156] Still others feared that the Seminary's efforts to "Americanize" the rabbinate would lead only to the diminution of observance and materialist corruption.[157] "Downtown" Jews often had difficulty differentiating between the Seminary and the Reform Hebrew Union College. As late as 1903, for example, an English editorial in the Yiddish press could confuse the goals of the restructured Hebrew Union College under the new leadership of Kaufmann Kohler with those of the new Seminary. "The Cincinnati platform" was "wedged between orthodoxy and radical reform," the editorial commented, and "there is every promise of the present pupil becoming a fair scholar as well as a rabbi of the conservative type."[158] Even supporters like Sarasohn had to grudgingly admit that graduates of the Seminary would never have been deemed worthy of ordination in a Russian yeshiva.[159]

Whatever one may say about the criticisms of Schechter's plans for the Seminary by its early supporters, there seems little doubt that their assessment of the new president was more realistic than that of the more enthusiastic immigrant religious "modernizers." For all his sympathetic statements about immigrant culture and his denunciation of Reform, Schechter was no supporter of the "orientalization" of Jewish life. Schechter's attitude toward Yiddish was typical of his ambivalence toward East European Jews. The language was "a mere accident of our history," he had remarked in one of his early addresses at the Seminary, that was "doomed to die." To perpetuate Yiddish would endanger the Jewish future by making a virtue of what may once have been an "unfortunate necessity, but at present, thank God, is becoming an impossibility." Schechter's most fervent wish was that the children of immigrants would attend public schools and soon "compel their parents to speak English."[160]

Similarly, Jewish nationalists like Sarasohn chose to ignore Schechter's negative statements about Zionism. From the moment of his arrival in America, Schechter had voiced concern with what he regarded as the domination of the Zionist movement in the immigrant community by secularists and left-wing elements.[161] In April 1904, when a rumor circulated on the Lower East Side that Schechter would soon issue a statement openly supporting Herzl and his program, he was quick to quash it.[162] It was only at the end of 1906, and after much hesitation, that Schechter was willing to publicly state his support of the Jewish nationalist movement. In doing so, he reaffirmed his support of the ideals of Ahad Ha'am. Zionism's greatest accomplishments, Schechter remarked, were not political and socio-economic but cultural—a Hebrew press, a Hebrew literature, and Hebrew songs. Their major significance was that they had brought back many Jews to Judaism. Going beyond even Ahad Ha'am, Schechter insisted upon the centrality of religion in any effort to settle the Land of Israel.[163]

As Schechter's influence in the New York Jewish community grew, he began to openly voice the negative attitudes of "uptown" Jews toward immigrants. Paternalistic in his demeanor, he rejected all efforts by the Lower East Side to establish its own autonomous institutions.[164] Many of Schechter's supporters in the immigrant community took his comments about the extremist nature of immigrant behavior as a gentle jibe that masked a fervent love for East European Jewry. In actuality, he remained convinced throughout his life that immigrant Jews were volatile and irresponsible in their public actions and needed proper guidance from more established and cultured elements in the Jewish community. Schechter would undoubtedly have agreed with the assessment of the historian Gilbert Klaperman that East European Jews were often more responsive to immigrant socialists and Ethical Culture teachers than to German Jews, no matter how traditional the latter were.[165] Even Schechter's opposition to the "Americanization" of East European Jews, which had originally endeared him to religious "modernizers" on the Lower East Side, could be seen as less a reflection of his respect for religious tradition than of his deep distrust of American popular culture.[166] Though often lauded by the Yiddish press in his early years as president, Schechter would later remark that he had been ignored by journalists on the Lower East Side.[167] By the time of his death in 1915, Schechter was not nearly as optimistic about the prospects of winning over any new wave of immigrants from Eastern Europe to the cause of Conservative Judaism.[168]

In truth, Schechter's alienation from the East European Jewish community was based on more than suspicion and distrust. A determined individual, he soon realized that the Seminary could only thrive if it developed its own distinctive path, one which set it apart from any association with Orthodoxy. In helping to define a "third way" in American Jewish life, Schechter recognized instinctively that he could not rest the future of the Seminary on either supporters of the Old Seminary or moderates on the Lower East Side. The issue of exactly when the Seminary fashioned itself as the school of Conservative Judaism is far too complex to be dealt with in the context of this essay. Nevertheless, it is clear that the origins of that development can be seen almost immediately after the Seminary's reorganization and the accession of Schechter to power.

By the time that the Seminary had decided on its new direction as the representative of a distinctive religious movement, the ephemeral group of immigrant "modernizers" had all but disappeared. The death of Sarasohn in 1905 removed an important and influential supporter of the Seminary on the Lower East Side. His absence was clearly noticeable in the growing number of articles criticizing the "Conservative" movement that began to appear in the pages of the *Yidishes Tagesblatt*. Whatever Sarasohn's own concerns may have been about Schechter and the direction of the Seminary, it is doubtful that he would have ever allowed his newspaper to print the article on Conservatism that appeared on its English page in February 1906. In the article, the Reform rabbi Emil Hirsch described Schechter's movement in the following terms: "The Conservative—whatever this term may connote—segregate this country into conservative congregations, taking advantage of the elasticity and vagueness of their party label to constitute a great variety of more or less noticeable differentiations under the convenient and conventional shibboleth."[169]

Similarly, Masliansky's withdrawal from the newspaper business in 1904 also signaled the end of his efforts to serve as spiritual leader of the community. As we have seen, he had never been a strong supporter of Schechter's Seminary. Increasingly, his main concerns lay outside the American Jewish community in the development of the *yishuv* (Jewish settlement) in Palestine. Nevertheless, Masliansky would live to see not only the development of the Conservative movement but also the revitalization of American Orthodoxy.

Conclusion

For a brief period directly before and after the reorganization of the Jewish Theological Seminary in 1902, the goals and interests of moderate Orthodox immigrants and the Seminary leadership seemed to coincide. In actuality, each group was laboring under false assumptions about the other. Immigrant "modernizers" were searching for an institution that would train a dynamic new type of rabbi who would serve the interests of the emerging community on the Lower East Side. At the same time, they were looking for a way to gain acceptance for immigrants among established New York Jewry without having to demean themselves before their wealthier coreligionists. What the immigrant reformers could offer was the insight of Eastern Europe without the baggage of religious obscurantism. They thus envisioned the role of immigrants in the Seminary as a dynamic one, serving both to revivify and to expand the spiritual leadership and rank and file of a modern Orthodox movement in America.

As long as the Seminary struggled to gain a foothold in the American Jewish community, it was more than happy to reach out to the Lower East Side for support and for recruitment of rabbinical students. More generally, leaders of the reorganized Seminary were firmly convinced that, as Pereira Mendes claimed, "the future of traditional Judaism lies in this institution" and that religiously observant Jews on the Lower East Side would flock to it.[170] With the exception of the Jewish Endeavor Society, however, they made few efforts to develop an institutional support mechanism among immigrants themselves. Nor did they make any significant effort to respond to the concerns of immigrants as to the direction of the Seminary. In large part, the Seminary's hesitancy reflected the general confusion of the emerging Conservative movement in its first halting attempts to define its purpose and direction. As we have seen, Seminary leadership seemed both attracted to and repelled by immigrants, at times regarding them as the salvation of the rabbinical institution, at times viewing them as dangerous to its underlying goals. By the 1920s, Conservative Judaism would no longer need to rely upon what in any event was a rapidly disappearing immigrant constituency on the Lower East Side. Instead, it would concentrate its attention and effort on developing spiritual and lay leaders from within what was already an established and dynamic movement. By that time, few paid serious attention to the perspectives of Schechter and his contemporaries concerning "downtown" Jews that had helped shape the activity of the Seminary in the period immediately after its reorganization.

Despite the misunderstanding, there seems little question that for a short time, at least, immigrant "modernizers" (and indirectly East European rabbis) on the Lower East Side gave impetus and even direction to the development of the reorganized Seminary. In turn, the Seminary served as a model of rabbinic education and leadership for immigrant moderates seeking to create a distinctive American religious tradition that would temper the embracing of modernity with the rich religious heritage of the Lower East Side. In the end, however, the impact of Lower East Side immigrant "modernizers" at the turn of the century on the future of Conservative Judaism and the Jewish Theological Seminary proved to be an ambivalent one. While many of their sons and daughters would find their way into the Conservative movement and provide important financial support for the Seminary well into the 1950s and 1960s, other descendants would lay claim to their parents' dream of synthesizing contemporary life with tradition by creating their own movement of American Orthodoxy and by establishing their own Seminary in the form of Yeshiva College.

1. Mordecai Waxman, *Tradition and Change: The Development of Conservative Judaism* (New York: The Burning Book Press, 1958), p. 11. Italics in the original.
2. Ibid.
3. Moshe Davis, *The Emergence of Conservative Judaism* (Philadelphia: Jewish Publication Society, 1963), pp. 312–13.
4. Norman Bentwich, *Solomon Schechter, A Biography* (Philadelphia: Jewish Publication Society, 1940), pp. 173–74.
5. Richard Libowitz, "Kaplan and Cyrus Adler," in *The American Judaism of Mordecai M. Kaplan,* ed. Emanuel S. Goldsmith, Mel Scult, and Robert M. Seltzer (New York: New York University Press, 1990), p. 123. See also the comments by M. David Hoffman in his introduction to *Roads to Jewish Survival: Essays, Biographies, and Articles Selected from The Torch on its 25th Anniversary,* ed. Milton Berger, Joel S. Geffen, and M. David Hoffman (New York: Bloch Publishing Company/National Federation of Jewish Men's Clubs, 1967), p. 3.
6. Abraham Karp, "Solomon Schechter Comes to America," *American Jewish Historical Quarterly* 48, no. 1 (September 1963): pp. 60–61.
7. Davis, *Emergence of Conservative Judaism,* p. 188.
8. Waxman, *Tradition and Change,* p. 11; Hoffman, *Roads to Survival,* p. 4.
9. Cited in Karp, "Solomon Schechter Comes to America,"p. 61.
10. A notable exception is the American Jewish historian Arthur Goren in his work *New York Jews and the Quest for Community: The Kehillah Experiment, 1908–1922* (New York: Columbia University Press, 1970). See especially pp. 1–24.
11. See, for example, the comments of Elliot B. Gertel in his essay "The Jewish Theological Seminary of America," in *Jewish American Voluntary Organizations,* ed. Michael N. Dobkowski (New York/Westport, Conn.: Greenwood Press, 1986), p. 283.
12. See, for example, Adler's letter to Cyrus Sulzberger dated 5 December 1907, in *Cyrus Adler, Selected Letters,* ed. Ira Robinson (Philadelphia/New York: The Jewish Publication Society, 1985), vol. 1, p. 139 ; and Schechter's letter to Adler on 1 August 1914, cited in Bentwich, *Solomon Schechter,* p. 191.
13. Samuel Joseph, *Jewish Immigration to the United States from 1881 to 1910* (New York: Arno Press and the *New York Times,* 1969), p. 151.
14. See the statistics on the destination of Jewish immigration, 1899 to 1910, by principal states in Joseph, *Jewish Immigration,* p. 195. See also Richard Wheatley, "The Jews in New York," *Century Magazine* 43, 3 (January 1892): p. 328. In 1901, Cyrus Adler claimed that there were 650,000 Russian Jews in the United States. (Letter from Adler to Solomon Schechter, 2 October 1901, *Letters,* vol. 1, p. 95.)
15. Cited in Joseph Hirsch, "Peter Wiernik and his Views" (Ph.D. diss., Yeshiva University, 1974), p. 148.
16. See, for example, the article "Amerikanisher idishe geshikhte" in the *Idisher Zhurnal,* 17 June 1901, p. 1.
17. See, for example, the article "Unzere rabonim" in the *Yidishe Velt,* 27 January 1904, p. 4.
18. Goren, *New York Jews,* p. 30.
19. As the newspaper owner and editor Kasriel Sarasohn stated in his memoirs, for most readers on the Lower East Side, the Yiddish newspaper became in time "like a family member." (Kasriel Sarasohn, "Di biografie fun di 'Yidishe Gazeten' un fun dem 'Tageblatt,' geshribn fun Kasriel Zvi Sarasohn," in YIVO, *Yorbukh fun amopteyl* [New York: Yidishn visenshaftlikhn institut, amerikan opteyl, 1938], vol. 1, p. 283.)
20. Copies of all of the newspapers for the period under study, with the exception of the *Morgen Zhurnal,* are available at the New York Public Library or in the National Jewish Periodicals collection at the Joseph Klar Library of the Hebrew Union College in Cincinnati.

Though the *Morgen Zhurnal* began printing in 1901, I could find no extant copies before 1906. Circulation figures are taken from Mordecai Soltes, *The Yiddish Press: An Americanizing Agency* (New York: Teachers College of Columbia University, 1924), p. 38.

21. In his work on American Jewry, Judd Teller argues that one must be wary of the self-proclaimed ideological affiliations of the Yiddish press in New York City at the turn of the century. The "Orthodox" *Morgen Zhurnal*, for example, he notes,

> did not appear on Saturdays and holidays, but its staff worked on the sacred days to prepare the next morning's edition. On those days, its personnel entered the Journal's offices as if it were a speakeasy, looked around furtively, rattled the doorknob, and waited to be identified by the janitor who would peer out by lifting a corner of the rawn shutters. The Bowery's elevated trains were helpful, drowning out the roar of the presses. (Judd Teller, *Strangers and Natives: The Evolution of the American Jew from 1921 to the Present* [New York: Delacorte Press, 1968], pp. 28–29.)

22. Yosef Chaikin, *Yidishe bleter in amerike* (New York: J. Chaikin, 1946), p. 53.

23. Rischin, *The Promised City*, p. 118.

24. It was not uncommon for immigrant newspapers to accept financial support from political parties in return for favorable treatment in their editorial pages. See Chaikin, *Yidishe bleter*, p. 131.

25. See especially the comments of Y. Lipschitz in his article, "Di Yudishe Gazeten," in *Zukunft* 80, 5–6 (May–June 1974): p. 195. See also Chaikin, *Yidishe bleter*, p. 95. Sarasohn's hostility toward unions and strikes may also have resulted from his early struggles together with his two children to ensure the financial stability of the *Gazeten*. See especially Sarasohn's comments in "Di biografie fun di 'Yidishe Gazeten' un fun dem 'Tageblatt,'" pp. 280–81.

26. "Sarasohn, Kasriel," *Leksikon fun der nayer yidisher literatur* (New York: Alveltlikhe yidishn kongress, 1981), vol. 8, cols. 799–800; Moshe Shtarkman, "Di Sarasohn-zikhroynes vegn der yidisher presse in amerike," *Yorbukh fun amoptayl*, vol. 1, pp. 273–76; "Sarasohn, Kasriel H.," *The Jewish Encyclopedia* (New York: Funk & Wagnalls, 1905), vol. 11, col. 50.

27. For typical examples of Masliansky's sermons, see Reverend Zevi Hirsch Masliansky, *Sermons*, trans. Edward Herbert; rev. and ed. Rabbi Abraham J. Feldman (New York: Hebrew Publishing Company, 1926), pp. 86, 142, 249.

28. "Masliansky, Zvi Hirsch," *Leksikon fun der nayer yidisher literatur* (New York: Alveltlikhe yidishn kongress, 1965), col. 468; "Masliansky," *Universal Jewish Encyclopedia*, col. 396.

29. Chaikin, *Yidishe bleter*, pp. 142–43.

30. For further information on Masliansky, see Louis Lipsky, *Memoirs in Profile* (Philadelphia: Jewish Publication Society, 1975), pp. 237–42; and the article "Masliansky, Zvi Hirsch," in Zalmen Reisen, *Leksikon fun der yidisher literatur, presse un filologie* (Vilna: B. Kletzkin, 1927), vol. 5, cols. 321–24.

31. Jeffrey Gurock, "Jewish Endeavor Society," *Jewish American Voluntary Organizations*, p. 230. For a discussion of unscrupulous immigrants who posed as rabbis for the High Holy Days, see the article in the *Evening Post* from 26 June 1897, as reproduced in *Portal to America: The Lower East Side, 1870–1925*, ed. Allon Schoener (New York: Holt, Rinehart and Winston, 1967), p. 113.

32. For more information on religious life in New York at the end of the 19th century, see Wheatley, "Jews in New York," pp. 330–33, and *The Synagogues of the Lower East Side*, pp. 27–34.

33. For information on Jacob Joseph, see Abraham Karp, "New York Chooses a Chief Rabbi," in *Publications of the American Jewish Historical Society* 44, no. 3 (March 1955): pp. 129–98.

34. See, for example, the comments in the *New York Tribune*, 12 November 1899, as repro-

duced in *Portal to America*, p. 105.

35. Goren, *New York Jews*, p. 17.

36. *Yidishe Velt*, 2 February 1904, 1.

37. *Yidishe Velt*, 1 November 1903, English page. See also Klaperman, *Story of Yeshiva University*, p. 9.

38. *American Hebrew*, 72, 16 (6 March 1903): p. 535. Italics in the original.

39. In 1899, for example, of the 3200 students at the Educational Alliance school, only 15 percent were boys. (Figures cited in *New York Tribune*, 12 November 1899, as reproduced in *Portal to America*, p. 106.) In 1905, there were said to be 335 religious schools on the Lower East Side. (*The Synagogues of the Lower East Side*, p.31.)

40. See, for example, the comments by Richard Wheatley in "The Jews in New York—II," *Century Magazine* 43, 4 (February 1892): pp. 518–19.

41. See, for example, the discussion of the Makhzike Talmud Torah in Wheatley, "The Jews in New York—II," p. 519. For a general discussion of Jewish education on the Lower East Side at the turn of the century, see Klaperman, *Story of Yeshiva University*, pp. 6–16.

42. Cited in *The Russian Jews in the United States*, ed. Charles S. Bernheimer (Philadelphia: Winston, 1905), p. 152.

43. *Yidishe Velt*, 25 November 1903, p. 4; 3 December 1903, p. 4.

44. *American Hebrew*, 73, 23 (23 October 1903), p. 728.

45. *Yidishes Tageblatt*, 28 January 1906, p. 1. See also the comments about the appointment of Louis Ginzberg as professor of Talmud at the Seminary in the *Yidishe Velt*, 24 August 1902, English page; and 27 April 1903, p. 1.

46. Davis, *Emergence of Conservative Judaism*, pp. 263–64. See also Maxwell Whiteman, "Western Impact on East European Jews: A Philadelphia Fragment," in *Immigrants and Religion in Urban America*, ed. Randall M. Miller and Thomas D. Marzik (Philadelphia: Temple University Press, 1977), p. 133.

47. *American Hebrew*, 8 March 1902, p. 4.

48. Adler to Solomon Schechter, dated 26 August 1901, in *Adler, Selected Letters*, vol. I, pp. 91–92.

49. Adler to Oscar Straus, dated 12 November 1905, in *Adler, Selected Letters*, vol. I, p. 120. As late as 1925, Adler could still publicly state that Jewish life in Eastern Europe was characterized by "an abnormal attitude which, as it were, closed the Jewish mind in and limited it to its own literature, and ever to a small section of that." (Cited in Waxman, *Tradition and Change*, p. 181.)

50. Cited in Herbert Parzen, *Architects of Conservative Judaism* (New York: Jonathan David, 1964), p. 24.

51. Letter dated 2 June 1902, contained in Joshua Joffe Papers, Ratner Center, Jewish Theological Seminary.

52. A report issued on the Seminary's activities published in 1892 commented on the course in the following terms: "Even in the comparatively short time in which this course has been in progress, the desirable results attainable can already be appreciated in the improvement as regards pronunciation made by these pupils not native to the soil." (Jewish Theological Seminary, *Third Biennial Report*, 1892, p. 13.)

53. Jewish Theological Seminary, *Third Biennial Report*, pp. 26, 28.

54. The names of the students can be found in the Jewish Theological Seminary of America *Biennial Report, 1902–1904*, pp. 131–32.

55. For more information on the association, see Robert E. Fierstien, *A Different Spirit: The Jewish Theological Seminary of America, 1886–1902* (New York: The Jewish Theological Seminary of America, 1990), p. 105.

56. Jeffrey S. Gurock, *The Men and Women of Yeshiva: Higher Education, Orthodoxy, and Amer-*

ican Judaism (New York: Columbia University Press, 1988), pp. 27–28. See also Gurock's articles, "Resisters and Accommodators," in *American Jewish Archives* 35, no. 2 (November 1983): pp. 114–15; and "Jewish Endeavor Society," pp. 228–31. For an insight into the programs of the Jewish Endeavor Society, see the announcement of its activities in the *Yidishe Velt*, 22 January 1903, English page.

57. In 1903, the Temple Emanuel brotherhood began sponsoring services downtown in an attempt to compete with the Jewish Endeavor Society. See the comment by "An East Sider" in the *American Hebrew*, 74 (19 February 1904): p. 443. For an example of the Society's activities against missionaries, see the *Yidishes Tagesblatt*, 2 November 1903, English page; and 24 March 1904, English page.

58. See Drachman's own comments in his biography, *The Unfailing Light: Memories of an American Rabbi* (New York: Rabbinical Council of America, 1948), p. 167.

59. Drachman, *The Unfailing Light*, p. 168.

60. Karp, "New York Chooses a Chief Rabbi," pp. 153–54.

61. Drachman, *The Unfailiing Light*, p. xxii.

62. See, for example, Drachman's comments on the effect of "the miracle of America" on a young immigrant family, in Drachman, *The Unfailing Light*, p. 20.

63. *Yidishes Tagesblatt*, 18 March 1888, p. 1.

64. Cited in Mel Scult, *Judaism Faces the Twentieth Century: A Biography of Mordecai M. Kaplan* (Detroit: Wayne State University Press, 1993), p. 187.

65. As Wise remarked in an essay on the Seminary published in the *American Israelite* in March 1886, "The only orthodox man in that scheme is an Italian Hazan [Sabato Morais] who, God bless his soul, is unable to perpetrate a fraud otherwise, and appears in this connection as a deceived deceiver." Cited in Fierstien, *A Different Spirit*, p. 50.

66. *Yidishe Gazeten*, 6 March 1888, p. 1. See also the *Yidishe Gazeten*, 2 December 1896, pp. 2 a and b.

67. See, for example, the *Yidishes Tagesblatt*, 24 December 1897, English page. See also the article in the *American Hebrew*, 23 April 1886, p. 9.

68. Klaperman, *Story of Yeshiva University*, pp. 39–40, 42; *Yidishes Tagesblatt*, 12 May 1902, p. 1.

69. As an editorial in the *Yidishe Velt* entitled "A Chief Rabbi" published shortly after Jacob Joseph's death commented:

> To us of the East Side there is but one Judaism, and all others are but imitations which do not concern us. Then, again, he [a rabbi] must have been trained in Russia, and be an authority of the older type on Talmudic lore. Rabbis of the East Side are not interested in the historical development of the Halakha; they want to know what it is. They do not care about the relative age of the Talmud; they want to know how far such passages bear upon their present life. In other words, the Rav must be able to 'pasken' [make religious judgments] with undisputed authority. . . . It would be well if to all this were added a competent knowledge of English and some acquaintance with the conditions of modern culture. (*Yidishe Velt*, 3 August 1902, English page.)

70. Jonathan Sarna, *People Walk on their Heads: Moses Weinberger's Jews and Judaism in New York* (New York: Holmes and Meier Publishers, 1982), p. 64.

71. As Weinberger remarked: "Whatever their alleged opposition to Liberal Judaism, supporters of the Seminary are people who lie almost totally 'over the line' outside Judaism, and who distance themselves with all their might from the life of torah, the highest form of religious life." (Sarna, *People Walk on Their Heads*, p. 65.)

72. Ibid., p. 104.

73. *Ha-ivri*, 18 December 1896, 1. See also Klaperman, *Story of Yeshiva University*, pp. 40–41.

74. Karp, "New York Chooses a Chief Rabbi," p. 135.

75. See the comments by the Slutzker Rav, Rabbi Jacob David Willowsky, during his visit to the United States in 1900, as cited in Aaron Rothkoff, *Bernard Revel: Builder of American Jewish Orthodoxy* (Philadelphia: Jewish Publication Society, 1972), p. 4.

76. See, for example, the statement in *Sefer ha-yovel shel Agudat ha-Rabbanim ha-Ortodoksim, 1920–1927* (New York: Agudat Harabanim, 1928), p. 16.

77. Cited in Karp, "New York Chooses a Chief Rabbi," p. 151.

78. The essay is reproduced in Jehuda Eisenstein, *Otsar Zikhronotai* (New York: Eisenstein, 1929), pp. 206–11.

79. Letter to Mayer Sulzberger, 9 December 1900, cited in Karp, "Solomon Schechter Comes to America," p. 59.

80. Cited in Bentwich, *Solomon Schechter*, p. 191.

81. Solomon Schechter, *Studies in Judaism*, vol. 1 (Philadelphia: Jewish Publication Society, 1908), pp. 185–86.

82. Bentwich, *Solomon Schechter*, p. 217. See also the comments by Henrietta Szold cited in Waxman, *Tradition and Change*, p. 115.

83. Waxman, *Tradition and Change*, p. 165.

84. See the comments by Jonathan Sarna in *People Walk on their Heads*, p. 13.

85. For a contemporaneous discussion of the interest of immigrant women in Jewish education, see the article in the *New York Tribune*, 12 November 1899, reproduced in *Portal to America*, p. 108.

86. *Yidishes Tagesblatt*, 18 November 1902, English page; 7 February 1904, English page; and *American Hebrew*, 72 (30 January 1903): p. 368.

87. Cited in *Idishe Zeit*, 13 May 1904, p. 4. See also the article in *Yidishes Tagesblatt*, 5 May 1904, English page.

88. *Yidishes Tagesblatt*, 5 May 1904, English page; *Yidishe Velt*, 9 May 1904, p. 1.

89. *Yidishes Tagesblatt*, 18 April 1902, p. 1. See also the comments about Columbia University in *Yidishe Velt*, 3 July 1902, p. 4.

90. *Yidishe Velt*, 7 March 1904, p. 1. See also the *Yidishe Gazeten*, 26 April 1903, p. 15.

91. *Yidishe Velt*, 2 July 1902, p. 1.

92. *Yidishe Gazeten*, 25 April 1902, p. 1.

93. See, for example, the comments by A. H. Fromenson in *Yidishes Tagesblatt*, 31 August 1902, English page. The interview is reproduced in a slightly different form in the *Yidishe Gazeten*, 5 September 1902, English page. See also the article "A idishe universitet" in *Yidishe Velt*, 13 December 1903, p. 4.

94. In an interview with the *Yidishes Tagesblatt* in August 1902, Schechter recounted the story of a Jewish reverend in England who went to a photographer to have his portrait taken. In order to make the best impression, he dressed up in ostentatious attire that Schechter noted had recently been adopted by American rabbis. "Is that you, Goldstein?" the photographer asks. "I hardly recognized you; I thought you were a gentleman." (*Yidishes Tagesblatt*, 31 August 1902, English page.)

95. *Yidishes Tagesblatt*, 12 May 1902, p. 1.

96. Jewish Theological Seminary, *Biennial Report, 1902–1904*, p. 85.

97. Ibid. An editorial in the *Yidishe Gazeten* commented on Schechter's remarks by noting: "Let us hope that the professor can transform devils to angels." (*Yidishe Gazeten*, 5 September 1902, p. 5.)

98. Ibid.

99. Ibid., English Supplement, p. 3.

100. *Yidishes Tagesblatt*, 24 November 1902, English page. See also the editorial in the *Yidishes Tagesblatt*, 1 April 1903, English page.

101. See also the comments by Masliansky in the *Yidishe Velt*, 23 November 1902, English

page. The editorial shared Sarasohn's fascination with Schechter's denunciation of "occidentalism." "The religious pendulum is swinging, not violently, but definitely to the East," the paper commented. "Those who are in earnest in the revival must help increase the momentum."

102. *Yidishe Velt*, 27 January 1903, p. 3.

103. "The Jewish Theological Seminary," *Yidishe Velt*, 23 April 1903, English page. See also the response to Jacob Schiff's gift ensuring the construction of the Seminary in the *Yidishes Tagesblatt*, 9 January 1902, p. 1.

104. *Yidishe Gazeten*, 1 May 1903, p. 15. See also 26 April 1903, p. 1; 27 April 1903, p. 1; and the *Yidishes Tagesblatt*, 27 April 1903, p. 1.

105. *Yidishe Gazeten*, 27 April 1903, p. 1. See also the *Yidishe Gazeten*, 26 April 1903.

106. See, for example, the editorials "One for All, All for One" and "The Banner of Jewish Solidarity" in the *Yidishe Gazeten*, 8 May 1903, English supplement.

107. *Yidishes Tagesblatt*, 3 July 1902, English page.

108. *Yidishe Velt*, 2 February 1904, p. 1.

109. *Yidishes Tagesblatt*, 31 May 1904, English page. See also the article entitled "Yisroels universitet" in the *Yidishe Velt*, 21 March 1904, p. 1.

110. See, for example, the article "Ungliklikhe rabonim" by "Ish doyg" in the *Yidishe Velt*, 5 September 1904, p. 4.

111. See, for example, the discussion of plans for the public meeting held by the Seminary at the Educational Alliance Building on 8 May 1904, in the *Yidishe Velt*, 27 April 1904, English page. The writer commented that the meeting was "designed to secure sympathy and support for the Seminary from all classes of Hebrews, by impressing upon them the importance of its influence on the moral and religious life of the Jews in this country, so that it may become a real force for the uplifting of our brethren, and the general improvement of their condition."

112. *Yidishe Velt*, 22 July 1902, p. 3.

113. "Rabonim in amerike," *Yidishe Velt*, 25 February 1904, p. 4. See also the editorial "English–Speaking Rabbis" in the *Yidishe Velt*, 16 March 1904, English page.

114. See, for example, *Yidishe Gazeten*, 9 September 1904, English supplement, p. 8.

115. Ibid.; *Yidishes Tagesblatt*, 3 July 1902, p. 4.

116. *Yidishe Velt*, 2 July 1902, p. 1.

117. Ibid.

118. Ibid. See also the *Yidishes Tagesblatt*, 3 July 1902, p. 4.

119. *Yidishe Velt*, 6 June 1904, p. 4.

120. For Schechter's view of Yiddish, see p. 36 of the essay.

121. *American Hebrew*, 63, 6 (26 June 1903): p. 174.

122. See, for example, *Yidishe Velt*, 26 January 1903, English page.

123. *Sefer ha-yovel shel Agudat ha-Rabbanim*, p. 18.

124. For a listing of the cities represented at the founding conference, see Rothkoff, *Bernard Revel*, p. 14.

125. Gurock, *Men and Women of Yeshiva*, p. 124.

126. Gurock, "Resisters and Accommodators," p. 117.

127. *Yidishe Velt*, 1 August 1902, pp. 1, 3.

128. See, for example, the *Yidishes Tagesblatt*, 1 August 1902, p. 1.

129. *Yidishe Gazeten*, 5 August 1902, p. 1.

130. *Yidishe Gazeten*, 23 June 1903, English page; 25 June 1903, English page. For a discussion of Pereira Mendes's agenda in founding the Union, see Markovitz, "Henry Pereira Mendes," pp. 378–79.

131. For more details on the Orthodox response to Kaplan's appointment, see Scult, *Judaism*

51

*The JTS
and the
"Downtown"
Jews of New
York at the
Turn of the
Century*

Faces the Twentieth Century, pp. 65–76. In 1945, the *Agudath ha-Rabbanim* issued a *herem* against Kaplan who by then had formed the Reconstructionist movement. For details, see the tract by Shmuel Niger entitled *Unzer rekht tzu habn sfeykes* (Chicago: n.p., 1945).

132. In his book of religious responsa, Willowsky commented on English sermons in the following terms: "These sermons contain no true guidance for the Jewish people. They simply make the Jewish people like the rest of the nations. If these practices will not cease, there is no hope for the continuance of the Jewish religion. . . . If one does not have the power to stop this practice, he must leave the synagogue when such a preacher rises to ascend the pulpit." (Cited in Aaron Rothkoff, "The American Sojourn of Ridbaz: Religious Problems within the Immigrant Community," *American Jewish Historical Quarterly* 57, no. 4 [June 1968]: pp. 561–62.)

133. For examples of support for Kaplan, see the letter from Esther Ruskay, a member of the congregation, in *American Hebrew* 75, 14 (7 October 1904): pp. 549–50, and from "a woman of the synagogue" (Ruskay?) in 76, 5 (30 December 1904): pp. 192–93.

134. *Sefer ha-yovel shel Agudat ha-Rabbanim*, p. 22.

135. *American Hebrew*, 1 July 1904, pp. 178–79. The article concluded that the *Agudah* was free to criticize the Seminary but that in talking about an edict of excommunication they would "bring down upon them the ill-will of the people" and would "injure them[selves] in the eyes of their brethren of the world."

136. *Yidishes Tagesblatt*, 11 July 1904, English page.

137. *Sefer ha-yovel shel Agudat ha-Rabbanim*, p. 18.

138. Bernard Levinthal, *Message of Israel*, pp. 198–99. Ironically, Levinthal's son attended the Seminary and became a leading figure in the Conservative movement. For his part, Schechter denounced the *Agudah*'s members as "*hayot ha-kodesh*," as evil and destructive as "the Oyster Saints of the West" at the Hebrew Union College. (Letter from Schechter to Magnes, cited in Scult, *Judaism Faces the Twentieth Century*, p. 131. See also the interview with Schechter in the *Yidishes Tagesblatt*, 4 April 1905, p. 1.) As for its president, Bernard Levinthal, he was nothing but "an ambitious Jesuit." (Letter from Schechter to Judge Mayer Sulzberger, cited in Scult, *Judaism Faces the Twentieth Century*, p. 30.)

139. *Sefer ha-yovel shel Agudat ha-Rabbanim*, p. 31.

140. The article critical of the *Agudath ha-Rabbanim* can be found in the *American Hebrew*, 17 June 17, 1904, p. 130; Eisenstein's rebuttal is in the *American Hebrew*, 1 July 1904, p. 180. Eisenstein's response was reprinted in the *Yidishes Tagesblatt*, 11 July 1904, English page.

141. *Yidishe Velt*, 3 August 1904, English page; *American Hebrew*, 30 July 1904, p. 282. See also the discussion in Markovitz, "Henry Pereira Mendes," pp. 380–81. Despite its qualification, the *Agudah* continued to denounce the Seminary throughout the prewar period. In 1906, for example, Levinthal ridiculed the Seminary's insistence that rabbinical students needed a college education. (Rothkoff, *Bernard Revel*, p. 16.) A year later, the *Agudah* called upon Yiddish papers to refrain from referring to graduates of the Seminary as "rabbanim." (*Yidishe Gazeten*, 19 July 1907, p. 14; 6 September 1907, p. 4E.)

142. *Forvertz*, 9 March 1904, p. 4E.

143. See, for example, the editorial "An emes simpatisher klub" in the *Forvertz*, 8 July 1904, p. 4.

144. See, for example, *Forvertz*, 5 January 1904, p. 1; 9 January 1904, p. 1; and 29 April 1904, p. 1.

145. "A roshe fun a sotsialistisher magid," *Forvertz*, 30 July 1904, p. 5.

146. In an article published in the *Yidishe Velt* shortly before Schechter's appointment, Drachman was actually referred to as the "Head of the Seminary." (*Yidishe Velt*, 2 July 1902, p. 1a.)

147. Drachman, *Unfailing Light*, pp. 254, 260. In a personal footnote, the editor of Drachman's biography addressed the issue of Drachman's break with the Seminary. "In getting rid of him," he notes, "they were, then 'dropping the pilot,' shaking off the voice of their own Orthodox conscience." (Ibid., p. 261.)

148. Scult, *Judaism Faces the Twentieth Century,* p. 101. Pereira Mendes and Schechter would clash openly in 1912–13 during the unsuccessful effort to combine the Union of Orthodox Congregations in America and the United Synagogue of America. See especially Bentwich, *Solomon Schechter,* pp. 209–12.

149. Drachman, *Unfailing Light,* p. 259.

150. See, for example, the letter from "A Founder of the Old Seminary" in the *Yidishes Tagesblatt,* 23 May 1904, English page. See also the *Yidishes Tagesblatt,* 3 August 1904, English page.

151. *Yidishe Velt,* 22 August 1902, p. 4.

152. *Yidishe Velt,* 26 January 1903, English page.

153. *American Hebrew,* 62, 15 (27 February 1903): p. 501.

154. *American Hebrew,* 73, 17 (11 September 1903): p. 536.

155. See, for example, the letter to editor from Yehezkel Levitt in the *Yidishes Tagesblatt,* 5 February 1903, p. 4.

156. See, for example, the biting comments on the dedication of the Seminary building by an anonymous writer in the *Idishe Zeit,* 1 May 1903, p. 9. Among other things, the writer responded to Mayer Sulzberger's presentation with the "hope that the books that he donated are not as boring as his speech" and remarked that the Reform rabbi Kaufman Kohler spoke "English with a German accent and Hebrew with a Litisen [Lithuanian accent]." See also the comment by "an Orthodox Jew from the Lower East Side" cited in the *Yidishes Tagesblatt,* 23 November 1902, English page.

157. See, for example, the damning unsigned article on the Seminary rabbinate in the *Yidishes Tagesblatt,* 20 July 1905, English page.

158. "The Hebrew Union College," *Yidishe Velt,* 2 March 1903, English page.

159. See, for example, the article in the *Yidishe Gazeten,* 11 July 1902, p. 4.

160. Solomon Schechter, *Seminary Addresses and Other Essays,* pp. 88–89.

161. For a later reflection of his views, see Schechter's response to Magnes's decision to represent American Zionists at a memorial meeting honoring the Russian revolutionary hero Gregory Gershuni in 1908, as noted in Goren, *New York Jews,* p. 37. See also Bentwich, *Solomon Schechter,* p. 205.

162. *Yidishes Tagesblatt,* 21 April 1904, English page; *Yidishe Gazeten,* 29 April 1904, English page.

163. "Zionism: A Statement," *Seminary Addresses and Other Essays,* pp. 91–104. Interestingly, Bernard Drachman responded to Schechter's early support of Ahad Ha'am in the pages of the Yiddish press with a ringing endorsement of Herzl's agenda. In a veiled criticism of the president of the Seminary, Drachman called upon western Jews as "a patriotic duty . . . to assist in establishing a recognized home for the persecuted Jews and thus relieve the countries of their allegiance from the undue pressure of forced immigration." (*Yidishes Tagesblatt,* 11 May 1904, English page)

164. See, for example, Schechter's attitudes toward the establishment of the *kehillah* (central Jewish communal organization) in 1909, as noted in Goren, *New York Jews,* p. 52.

165. Klaperman, *Story of Yeshiva University,* p. 43.

166. See, for example, Schechter's comments concerning the influence of the press upon immigrants, as cited in Bentwich, *Solomon Schechter,* p. 216.

167. Schechter letter to Cyrus Adler, 1913, cited in Bentwich, *Solomon Schechter,* p. 190.

168. See, for example, Schechter's comments at the founding convention of the United Synagogue in 1913 concerning the danger of further immigration of Jews from Eastern Europe, as cited in Waxman, *Tradition and Change,* p. 166.

169. *Yidishes Tagesblatt,* 14 February 1906, English page.

170. *Yidishes Tagesblatt,* 4 April 1905, English page.

JONATHAN D. SARNA

Two Traditions of Seminary Scholarship

From left: Alexander Marx, Louis Finkelstein, and Saul Lieberman, ca. 1950.
Photo by Virginia F. Stern. Library, JTS.

JONATHAN D. SARNA

Two Traditions of Seminary Scholarship

THE 1902 CHARTER that incorporated the reorganized Jewish Theological Seminary listed "the advancement of Jewish scholarship" as the fourth of the institution's six aims.[1] This marked a significant change from the original charter of 1886 which had made no mention of Jewish scholarship at all.[2] But it also hinted at some disagreement with Solomon Schechter, who believed that the advancement of scholarship should be the Seminary's foremost priority. His goal, expressed in a letter to Mayer Sulzberger back in 1900, was to see the Seminary transformed into "a centre of Jewish *Wissenschaft* pure and simple."[3]

Schechter's audacious vision reflected the growing appreciation for Jewish scholarship that developed in the United States late in the 19th century. What Cyrus Adler described as a "Jewish Renaissance" seemed to be underway, and writing in 1894, Adler ticked off some of its achievements, including "the establishment of Oriental and Hebrew professorships in all of our large universities"; the growth of Hebrew Union College's library in Cincinnati, the establishment of the Jewish Theological Seminary (1886), the Jewish Publication Society (1888), and the American Jewish Historical Society (1892); the scholarly achievements of such men as Alexander Kohut, Marcus Jastrow, Moses Mielziner, Richard Gottheil, Morris Jastrow, Charles Gross, and Charles Waldstein [Walston]; and "the turning toward literary and scientific pursuits of a considerable number of Russian immigrants." "Is it possible," Adler wondered, "that the intellectual activity of the Jew in relation to Jewish learning is shifting to the English speaking world?" "I think," he answered tentatively, "it is."[4]

To strengthen the spirit of Jewish learning in the United States, Adler, in a follow-up article, proposed the establishment of a "Jewish Academy of America," akin to many a learned society founded in his day, charged with responsibility to "collect a library," "publish scientific researches," "provide facilities for students," convene scholars together, and "have connected with it a staff of men who would themselves be constantly engaged in advancing Jewish science."[5] The idea was wildly premature in 1894 and nothing came of it, but the fact that it received a hearing at all offers some indication of the elevated status that Jewish scholarship was beginning to enjoy in some circles of the American Jewish community. Just half a dozen years later, Henrietta Szold (who mixed in these same circles), writing in the *American Jewish Year Book* of 1900, found "striking evidence that the desire for Jewish scholarship is real and widespread." Impressed by the ongoing effort to produce the *Jewish Encylopedia*, by far the most ambitious scholarly project undertaken by American Jews to that time, she predicted "that in the not too distant future the United States will become a centre of Jewish scholarship."[6]

Actually, those eager to transform America into a center of Jewish scholarship faced substantial obstacles. Many other pressing problems (including the material needs of Jewish immigrants) competed for community attention. Besides, Jewish scholarship seemed to some lay leaders to be far too highbrow for American Jews. They sought to encourage elementary works and writings that appealed to "the popular taste." Recognizing that scholarship is expensive and often restricted to a "few choice spirits," even some of the trustees of the Jewish Theological Seminary thought to move cautiously. Rather than creating a great Jewish library, for example, they advocated a more modest one, kept within the bounds of an ordinary college library.[7]

Solomon Schechter, however, would have none of this. "The crown and climax of all learning is research," he announced in his 1902 inaugural address as Seminary president. "It is," he continued, "these fresh contributions and the opening of new sources, with the new currents they create, that keep the intellectual and the spiritual atmosphere in motion and impart to it life and vigor."[8] Judge Mayer Sulzberger heartily agreed, and early in 1904 he completed the gift of his own library to the Seminary with the "hope . . . that the Seminary may become the center for original work in the science of Judaism, to which end the acquisition of a great library is indispensable."[9]

Sulzberger had long cherished the goal of seeing his adopted land become a center of Jewish cultural life. This in large part accounts for his decision to collect rare Jewish books and manuscripts in the first place: "It was his idea. . .that the time was approaching when the need of such a library would be felt."[10] Now, with Solomon Schechter at the Seminary's helm and a promising group of young European-trained research scholars recruited to the faculty, he thought that time had arrived.

New York in the early years of the 20th century was home to the largest Jewish community in the world. In the United States as a whole, the Jewish population exceeded that of Germany, France, and the British Empire combined; only the Jewish communities in Russia and Austria-Hungary were larger. Europeans concerned

with the fate of world Jewry increasingly looked to America as the wave of the
future. It was the major bright spot (along with Zion) in a world where anti-
Semitism was growing and Russian Jewry lay imperiled.[11] So now it was up to
Schechter to mold a seminary worthy of this great new American Jewish population
center. The future of Jewish scholarship in the United States seemed to rest on his
shoulders.

In committing the Seminary to *Wissenschaft*, Schechter drew on German canons
of scholarship that had already made a substantial impact on American higher education. Columbia, Harvard, Michigan, and Wisconsin, as well as new universities
such as Johns Hopkins (where Cyrus Adler had received his Ph.D.), Clark, and
Chicago—all had come to emulate the German universities with their focus on
rigorous scholarship as the ultimate gauge of academic excellence. *Wissenschaft*, the
German word that characterized this rigorous scholarly methodology, literally
means "science"; in this case it implied a commitment to accuracy, neutrality, and
truth. As Peter Novick explains, the term also "signified a dedicated, sanctified
pursuit . . . not just knowledge, but self-fulfillment; not practical knowledge, but
knowledge of ultimate meanings."[12]

The pioneering German-Jewish scholar Leopold Zunz first applied these ideas
to Judaism, and he is credited with coining the term *Wissenschaft des Judentums* in
1822. This set off a revolution in Jewish studies that transformed both its methodology and its scope. Traditionally, much of Jewish learning had been Judeocentric,
"divorced from the rest of the world," "tied dogmatically to belief in an inviolable
tradition and the authority of its representatives," and dialectical in method. *Wissenschaft*, by contrast, "recognized the interrelationship of all intellectual forces,"
"attempted to explore and explain the connections between Jewish and non-Jewish
phenomena," considered itself independent, subject to free and unbiased critical
analysis, and "demanded concreteness and a sense of actuality." Where traditional
Jewish learning was a pious vocation, "a part of Jewish religiosity," *Wissenschaft* was
a scholarly vocation, a field of knowledge.[13]

Ismar Schorsch has recently argued that "Wissenschaft furnished the tools to
restore or remake a Judaism cut loose from its moorings by unimagined new knowledge, enemies and alternatives." *Wissenschaft*, he contends, was "a collective act of
translation, a sustained effort to cast the history, literature and institutions of
Judaism in Western categories." There was widespread hope, he observes, that Jewish scholarship would have profound social consequences: "Research would lead to
respect and finally acceptance, setting Jews free."[14]

These goals were shared by the great rabbinical seminaries of Europe, including
the Seminary's namesake, the Jewish Theological Seminary of Breslau, Berlin's
Hochschule für die Wissenschaft des Judentums, where Schechter himself had
studied, and the (Hildesheimer) Rabbiner Seminar für das Orthodoxe Judentum

where both Israel Friedlaender and Alexander Marx had been pupils. As distinct from traditional *yeshivot*, these seminaries promised to train *modern* rabbis, equipping them with traditional Jewish learning, a thorough mastery of the vernacular, and facility in both secular and extra-talmudic Jewish subjects. Faculty members at these institutions boasted rabbinic learning, secular training, and earned doctorates from major secular universities. Their research was academically oriented: it employed scholarly methodologies, paid strict attention to history and philology, and was always staunchly committed to the pursuit of "truth."[15]

Such was the legacy to which Schechter and the newly reorganized Jewish Theological Seminary of America fell heir in 1902. In the decades that followed, the Seminary would itself become a major conduit for the transmission of *Wissenschaft des Judentums* to the United States and one of the world's foremost centers of Jewish studies. In the process, however, it developed two distinct traditions of Jewish scholarship. The first, an elite tradition that commanded the highest institutional esteem and won the primary allegiance of the majority of the Seminary faculty, focused on timeless *texts*—rabbinic texts, midrashic texts, *Genizah* texts, historical texts, and literary texts. Textual projects, including critical editions, translations, commentaries, and reference aids, chiefly occupied these scholars and resulted in the distinguished corpus of publications on which the Seminary's scholarly reputation primarily rests. The second, a more popularly oriented engaged tradition that commanded less institutional esteem and won the primary allegiance of only a minority among the faculty, focused on timely *issues*. It produced highly influential work aimed at the larger community, Jewish and non-Jewish, and sought to combat ignorance and to apply Jewish teachings to problems of general concern. As we shall see, the Seminary's two greatest leaders, Solomon Schechter and Louis Finkelstein, appreciated, embraced, and personally exemplified both traditions, recognizing the value (although certainly not the equality) of each. The rest of the faculty, however, tended to embrace one tradition only, viewing the other with distaste if not disdain.[16]

The great tradition of textual scholarship dominated the Seminary's research agenda in each era of its history. Within each generation, an exemplar, a widely respected and highly productive senior scholar—first, Solomon Schechter, then Levi Ginzberg, and then Saul Lieberman—set the scholarly tone which those seeking status within the institution tried to follow. Through publications and influence, these exemplars defined the character of the faculty's work and established models of elite scholarship that the majority of colleagues strove to emulate. Since each exemplar saw textual research as the ne plus ultra of scholarship, that became the institutional test of merit, the standard which those seeking recognition among the elite had to maintain.

At other rabbinical seminaries, textual scholarship played a less substantial role.

The most significant work of the senior scholars at the Jewish Theological Seminary of Breslau, for example, was synthetic in character. Zacharias Frankel worked on the methodology of the *Mishna* and the Talmud, and Heinrich Graetz researched his magisterial history of the Jews. At Hebrew Union College in Cincinnati, the American Reform counterpart to the JTS, the most influential scholars focused on history, theology, and Bible. As for textual scholarship, there appeared, during the Cincinnati school's entire first century, exactly one "scientific publication of an entire major volume of rabbinic literature by an HUC faculty member"—Jacob Z. Lauterbach's *Mekilta de-Rabbi Ishmael*.[17]

The Seminary, from Schechter's day onward, was different. Schechter established the primacy of textual research at the Seminary, influenced in this by his beloved teacher, Meir Friedmann (Ish Shalom), whom he revered as "the pioneer in the art of critical editions of Rabbinic texts."[18] Schechter's own first book, back in England, had been a text, the *Aboth de Rabbi Nathan*, "edited from two Recensions and with the collation of all the manuscripts," and he continued to publish significant texts, particularly *Genizah* texts, throughout his life. He told his biographer that the proper study of Jews "necessitates the collation and accurate edition of the original sources and documents."[19] He also believed, according to his longtime friend and later colleague at the Seminary, Joseph Jacobs, "that the real training of a scholar was never complete and could not be completely tested until he had done something in the way of editing a MS., for this involved utilizing one's own resources as a scholar and not depending upon the scholarship of others."[20] This became a cardinal principle of Seminary pedagogy in later years. As a final test of scholarly worthiness, many a Seminary graduate was expected to demonstrate his prowess at editing a manuscript text.

For all of his allegiance to textual scholarship, however, Schechter also devoted a great deal of his talent to popular studies aimed at elucidating Judaism in terms that Jews and non-Jews alike could understand. Claude Montefiore, who brought Schechter to England as his tutor, was the major inspiration here. "I can't bear the idea of your devoting. . .your time to the publication of texts," he lectured his "Lieber Freund" Schechter. "You must train yourself to write & you must write not merely for the learned world."[21] Montefiore personally solicited many of Schechter's popular essays, later collected in his hugely popular *Studies in Judaism*, and was also the driving force behind Schechter's *Aspects of Rabbinic Theology*, a work consciously written with non-Jewish readers in mind. To be sure, Schechter never devoted as much time to such efforts as Montefiore wanted; in the final analysis he respected his teacher Friedmann more than the man who called him "Lieber Freund." Still, he learned from Montefiore to respect the art of writing for a general audience and ultimately did more than any other Jewish scholar of his generation to interpret Judaism to the English-speaking world.[22] This ability to reach beyond the academy served him well as the Seminary's president. Later, it also legitimated the tradition of engaged scholarship that lived on at the Seminary, albeit with greatly diminished status, during the terms of his successors.

When it came to making faculty appointments at the Seminary, however, Schechter looked primarily to scholars in the Friedmann tradition, men who shared his passion for textual research. Alexander Marx, whom Schechter had first met in Europe while Marx was researching his innovative doctorate on the text of the *Seder Olam* (based on manuscripts and early printed editions), for example, believed even as a young man that the production of "correct texts" was the central task of Jewish studies. "Facts, facts, facts, are paramount with him," his student Solomon Goldman later recalled, and for this reason in his position as the Seminary's librarian and professor of history he both sought to acquire rare books and manuscripts for the Seminary library and insisted that "texts be made the startingpoint for Jewish historiography."[23] Louis Ginzberg and Israel Davidson followed this lead, each producing significant textual studies after they joined the Seminary's faculty. Beginning in Ginzberg's case with his *Geonica* and in Davidson's with his edition of Joseph ibn Zabara's *Sefer Sha'ashu'im*, both men, for the remainder of their lives, pursued textual research with enthusiasm and ardor.[24] Israel Friedlaender, when he came to the Seminary, was already working on a textual project: a translation and commentary based on a manuscript by the Muslim historian Ali b. Ahmad ibn Hazm. Much to his colleagues' distress, however, his textual work went no further. Instead, he far exceeded Schechter in his involvement in community affairs, applying the fruits of his considerable learning to issues of the day and setting a model of popular engaged scholarship that Mordecai Kaplan later followed. After Schechter's death, he did undertake to produce a volume of Judeo-Arabic documents from the *Genizah*, but before that project got off the ground, he was murdered in the Ukraine.[25] Mordecai Kaplan, who personified the tradition of engaged popular scholarship within the Seminary for more than half a century, also sought initially to prove his mettle through textual scholarship. At Schechter's encouragement, he began work on a critical edition of *Shir Ha-Shirim Rabbah*, hoping in this way to gain the Seminary president's attention and approbation. The work was never completed, but Kaplan did eventually publish the other textual assignment he received from Schechter: an edition of Moses Hayim Luzzatto's 18th-century ethical text, *Mesillat Yesharim: The Path of the Upright*, commissioned by the Jewish Publication Society as part of what would become its Schiff Library of Jewish Classics.[26]

In preparing editions of texts, Seminary scholars felt that they were helping to build the field of Jewish Studies as a whole. Texts, they believed, were the "tools" and "building blocks" that scholars required, "the basis of every historical and literary investigation."[27] Marx spoke for many of them when he complained that "very little in comparison with other literatures has been done for producing correct texts of our standard works."[28] The great task that he and his like-minded colleagues set for themselves was to produce and elucidate these "correct texts" for the benefit of future generations of scholars.

Placed in a larger context, this quest for "correct texts" formed part of the legacy of both German historicism and the European Jewish enlightenment. A whole series of ambitious projects to produce scholarly editions of texts, Jewish and non-Jewish alike, developed on both sides of the Atlantic. As early as 1862, a modest program to publish "correct texts" had been established by European Jewish Hebraists. The society they founded bore the evocative name *Mekizei Nirdamim* ("Rousers of the Slumbering"), and significantly, it attracted support from traditional rabbis as well as from modern scholars. Its aim—to publish scholarly editions of medieval Hebrew manuscripts and rare books—was simultaneously both pious and academic.[29] In America, the most successful textual project undertaken by scholars (perhaps the one that Marx himself had in mind) was the Loeb Classical Library, established in 1910 to publish standard scholarly editions of the great works of Greek and Latin authors. The Loeb Classics also formed the model, if not the inspiration, for the Schiff Classics—Schiff was Loeb's brother-in-law.[30]

The Schiff Classics, although not itself a Seminary project, demonstrates the sharp imprint that the Seminary's textual focus made upon American Jewish scholarship as a whole. Previously, the Jewish Publication Society, the publisher of the series, had largely concentrated on history and Scripture and had excluded "works of a distinctively scientific character" from its publishing ambit. The bold project announced in 1915 to produce twenty-five volumes of carefully edited post-biblical Jewish classics with texts, translations, and scholarly notes represented an abrupt departure from this policy. Schechter, as chair of the JPS "Classics Committee," clearly played a central role in bringing this policy shift about. One of his last official acts was to address letters inviting Seminary colleagues and other scholars to contribute to the series. After his death, the Seminary continued for some time to dominate the project: eight of the scholars proposed as editors of different works came from the ranks of its faculty and alumni, twice as many as came from Hebrew Union College or from Dropsie College. Although on paper the steering committee overseeing the project was always carefully balanced, representing the full spectrum of Jewish religious life and the presidents of three different scholarly institutions, the plan itself bore the Seminary's unmistakable imprint. In effect, it represented a widening of the Seminary's research agenda to embrace the Anglo-American Jewish scholarly community as a whole.[31]

Apart from the Schiff Classics, the kind of textual scholarship that the Seminary considered the acme of learning won little public support and proved difficult to sustain. As early as 1909, for example, Louis Ginzberg wrote a formal letter to Solomon Schechter (intended, probably, for the eyes of the trustees) setting forth the heavy financial burdens that he had incurred "in the interests of Jewish scholar-ship," including hundreds of dollars to cover travel, research, and the publication of his *Genizah* studies. "I scarcely think it is creditable to the position of Jewish schol-arship in America that I should be placed in this position," he wrote, pointing out that European Jewish seminaries defrayed these kinds of costs.[32] The money in this case was found, and later (sometimes happily, sometimes not) Seminary trustees and friends would finance the publication of other textual studies undertaken by the faculty. The Stroock brothers, for example, subvented a variety of scholarly publi-cations as a memorial to their uncle, the Orthodox scholar Abraham Berliner, who had himself been a distinguished student of Jewish texts.[33] Later, the American Academy for Jewish Research (founded in 1919 under Ginzberg's leadership) and nonprofit foundations devoted to Jewish scholarship also assisted Seminary authors in publishing their books. Still, the nagging question persisted: for whom did the textually minded faculty toil?

First, as we have seen, the faculty toiled for the nascent field of Jewish Studies. By the early 20th century, an international community of *Wissenschaft* Jewish schol-ars existed, linked by a web of scholarly publications and personal communications. Jewish scholars on both sides of the Atlantic considered themselves part of a single Jewish scholarly fraternity. They pledged allegiance to the field as a whole.[34]

Second, as Ginzberg implied with his reference to the "position of Jewish schol-arship in America," the faculty felt that it was helping to raise the cultural level and prestige of the American Jewish community. Scholarship and learning had long served as determinants of status in Jewish history: they brought a community to the notice of the Jewish world and did much to establish its long-term reputation. Schechter and his cohort of young promising scholars, along with their enthusias-tic supporters (like Mayer Sulzberger), hoped that the Seminary's labors would have a similar effect. Scholarship produced within its portals, they believed, would lead American Jewry from the wilderness of insignificance into the promised land of Jewish cultural renown.

Even before he arrived in America, Schechter had begun to lay the groundwork for this effort. "I am now keeping back the best things for America as I think that such publication will give the Seminary a certain prestige," he wrote Mayer Sulzberger in 1901.[35] Having given up on Jewish cultural life in England, he now withheld his best scholarship with the intention of publishing it from his new perch in New York. For similar reasons, Schechter and the rest of the Seminary faculty took pains, in their first years, to issue the choicest fruits of their scholarship in English, rather than German. "Jewish learning in this country . . . will be American in language, in scope, in method, and yet be distinctively Jewish in essence," Israel Friedlaender predicted in 1914.[36] Refusing to pay obeisance to German centrality in the field of Jewish studies, the scholars of the new Seminary sought to place the distinctive stamp of their new American homeland on the Jewish scholarly map.

Third, the faculty saw its work as a contribution to the American Jewish quest for acceptance and respectability. This is most easily shown in the case of the Schiff Classics, for Schechter, in a private letter, frankly admitted that the undertaking "should, above all, result in raising the respect of Jew and Gentile for Jewish literature and the thoughts treasured up therein. . .[and] have besides all other results, also that of contributing to *kiddush hashem* [sanctification of the Divine name] and to the glory of Israel." Jewish classics that did not fulfill these criteria were, as a result, left out of the series.[37] The same desire to win non-Jewish respect for "Jewish contributions to Civilization" was reflected earlier in the *Jewish Encyclopedia*, and it underlay such popular volumes written by Seminary faculty members as Schechter's *Studies in Judaism* and *Some Aspects of Rabbinic Theology*, Louis Ginzberg's *Legends of the Jews*, and Joseph Jacobs's *Jewish Contributions to Civilization: An Estimate*. Jacobs, like Friedlaender a Seminary faculty member who wrote for a broad public and spoke out on contemporary issues, baldly stated what many a Jewish scholar of his day apparently assumed: "If it can be shown that Jews throughout the ages have contributed their share to the world's higher life and have, by their experiences, acquired specific capacities to continue to do so, they have a right to say to the world: 'Stand aside; let us to our appointed work.'" The honorary degrees that Schechter and Ginzberg both eventually won from Harvard University proved all the more meaningful in that they indicated that "the world"—at least the scholarly world—had paid some attention.[38]

Finally, the faculty aimed to broaden the canvas of Jewish studies, to demonstrate that post-biblical Judaism was culturally richer and religiously more variegated than generally recognized. This challenged at one and the same time the cherished assumptions of traditional Jews, who looked upon "the sea of the Talmud" as the major source of Jewish creativity, and the cherished assumptions of learned Christians, who questioned whether post-biblical Jews displayed any creativity at all. The treasure trove of documents that Schechter recovered from the Cairo *Genizah* gave great impetus to these scholarly efforts. Schechter himself delighted in the fragments that he characterized as "my Heretic's Gallery," the writings of Jews who rebelled against the rabbinic mainstream. The publication of these documents, he predicted (not inaccurately, as it turned out) "will surprise the world."[39] Ginzberg prefaced his *Legends*—"the first attempt to gather from the original sources all Jewish legends, in so far as they refer to Biblical personages and events"—with an attack on [non-Jewish] scholars and their "poetic phantasmagoria, frequently the vaporings of morbid visionaries." His work, a conscious refutation of Christian understandings of Judaism, demonstrated beyond the shadow of a doubt that "the fancy of the [Jewish] people did not die out in the post-Biblical time."[40] His very methodology served to buttress his case: where Christian scholars had so often rummaged Jewish sources to shed light on the origins of Christianity, he now did the same with Christian sources, prowling for lost Jewish legends. Israel Davidson's *Thesaurus of Mediaeval Hebrew Poetry*, a work no less massive in its dimensions, demonstrated that the poetic muse (religious and secular) did not die out from Israel either, notwithstanding the fact that, as Davidson lamented, neither Jews nor Christians properly appreciated this literature.[41] Saul Lieberman later followed in the footsteps of these early Seminary scholars with his studies of Greek and Hellenism in Jewish Palestine and his incomparable erudition that demonstrated how a thorough knowledge of antiquity could illuminate obscurities in rabbinic literature.[42]

Where faculty members divided, and the elite and popular traditions of Jewish scholarship at the Seminary parted company, was in their approach to modernity. The textual scholars, even as they extended the canvas of Jewish Studies and sought to rescue Judaism from those who misinterpreted its past, looked upon modernity as the strict chronological limit beyond which they refused to pass. With few exceptions, they restricted their scholarship to the premodern period. Davidson, for example, limited his listing of secular (but not religious) poetry to "those composed prior to the Haskalah [Jewish enlightenment]." He even excluded the religious poetry of Maskilic writers on the grounds that their prayers had not won popular acceptance and were imitative. As for the poems of Moses Hayyim Luzzatto, he explained that they "were deliberately excluded, because he is generally regarded, justly or unjustly, as the Father of the Haskalah Movement."[43] Earlier, in his doctoral dissertation, Davidson *had* paid attention to modern literature and the subject continued to interest him personally. At the Seminary, however, his scholarship was confined to the premodern era, in conformity with the elite institutional tradition to which he now subscribed. When once, as a diversion, he wrote a charming review of Sadie Rose Weilerstein's children's book, *The Adventures of K'tonton*, he carefully did so under a pseudonym.[44]

The Schiff Classics, overseen by Schechter and then Cyrus Adler, similarly eschewed modernity. Though Luzzatto was not in this instance excluded, other "modern" writers were. Classics, as defined by the series, had to be "sufficiently remote to be removed from present day controversies." The same disinclination to study modernity characterized the work of Alexander Marx (reputedly, he considered anything after 1789 to be "journalism") and later generations of textual scholars, through the Finkelstein years, as well.

By contrast, those scholars who wrote for more popular audiences, including Schechter, Friedlaender, and especially Mordecai Kaplan, focused sharply on modernity. Schechter used his wide-ranging learning to counter contemporary trends that he found antithetical to Judaism and to plead for a return to traditional observance. Friedlaender sought in his volume of essays entitled, significantly, *Past* and *Present*, "to interpret the events of the past in the light of the present and the problems of the present in the light of the past." Kaplan began his *Judaism as a Civilization* with a chapter entitled "The Present Crisis in Judaism." As engaged scholars writing for a concerned public, these men believed that their knowledge of the past contributed to their understanding of the present; they employed their learning to offer critical perspectives on contemporary developments. Friedlaender thus announced (perhaps with a hint of criticism for his colleagues) that he wrote "neither as an archeologist, with his eye riveted on the past, nor as a journalist, with his horizon limited to the present, but rather as an historian." He defended this approach as "imperative," since for Jews, "the past and the present are inextricably bound up with one another."[45]

Friedlaender's declaration serves as a reminder that Seminary faculty members, whatever their disagreements and sometimes in spite of themselves, reenacted and validated basic premises of the Conservative movement as a whole. They were traditional at their core and modern in their forms. They drew sustenance from texts and were expansive in defining and interpreting those texts. They sought legitimacy from the past and felt ambivalent toward changes demanded by the present. And, in very different ways, they optimistically believed (as Schechter, Friedlaender, Ginzberg, Marx, and Davidson all did) that tradition and modernity could safely be reconciled.

Of course, this nexus between the Seminary's scholarly agenda and the Conservative movement's religious agenda was never publicly articulated, least of all by those who felt that they were dispassionately establishing "correct texts." To have done otherwise would have undermined the very assumptions upon which *Wissenschaft* ideology was based. As a result, neither the students nor the supporters of the Seminary generally understood the relationship between the textual scholarship that the faculty pursued and the "vital issues" that the Conservative movement and the American Jewish community as a whole engaged. As Mel Scult and Baila Shargel demonstrate in their essays elsewhere in these volumes, student dissatisfaction at the Seminary was particularly acute. Alumnus Meyer Waxman spoke for many when in a thinly veiled critique published in 1941 he lamented both "the isolation of scholarship from life" among Jewish scholars in the United States and "the predominance of a general spirit of dryness."[46]

Mordecai Kaplan, by then, represented the antithesis of this critique. The exemplar, in his day, of scholarly engagement, he was neither isolated nor arid. Like Schechter and especially Friedlaender, both of whom he revered, he sought to mediate between the scholarly and popular worlds. His books and articles, written for the general public, ably demonstrated how old wisdom could shed light on contemporary issues, and they articulated an understanding of Judaism that proved powerfully influential.[47]

Textual scholarship at the Seminary, however, *had* become isolated and dry, and for understandable reasons. After an initial burst of enthusiasm, American Jewry lost interest in the Seminary and its work. Communal problems that some hoped it would resolve continued to fester, and the rarified scholarship that most of the faculty produced could not be appreciated. Worst of all, Schechter's death, in 1915, robbed the Seminary of its most colorful personality as well as its most effective advocate. Cyrus Adler, appointed to succeed Schechter, was not himself a significant scholar and failed to win the faculty's respect. It viewed his appointment as evidence of the Seminary board's "limited understanding of, and sympathy for, Jewish scholarship."[48] Since Adler simultaneously presided over Dropsie College in Philadelphia, he was not even full time at the Seminary and never moved to New York. Meanwhile, the board focused on the Seminary's burgeoning financial crisis, one that it faced in common with many another American Jewish cultural and religious institution in the 1920s and 1930s.[49] Economy soon became the watchword, funds to support scholarship grew scarce, and faculty morale plummeted. The dramatic opening in 1925 of the Hebrew University in Jerusalem, which now bid to make that city the center of Jewish studies, only underscored how much had changed from the heady days when Schechter had commanded the Seminary's ship and the faculty held themselves out as the American Jewish community's scholarly redeemers.

In response to these changes, much of the faculty turned inward. The elite textual scholars, taking their cue from Louis Ginzberg, focused on their own research and sought solace in the company of other scholars. Indeed, the very language of their discourse changed. Where earlier, as we have seen, their scholarship was patriotically "American in language," now, as if to symbolize their disaffection, they turned more and more to Hebrew. Davidson, for example, reissued his edition of *Sefer Sha'ashu'im* with a Hebrew introduction in 1925 and pointedly published the notes to his volume of *Genizah Studies in Memory of Dr. Solomon Schechter* (*Ginzei Schechter*) in Hebrew as well, although, he reports in the introduction, he had initially planned to write them in English.[50] Most of what he subsequently published was likewise in Hebrew, including the scholarly notes to his *Thesaurus*. Ginzberg too published his *Genizah Studies* in Hebrew—this despite the fact that Schechter, in whose memory the books appeared, was committed to publishing Jewish scholarship in English. He also published his commentary on the *Yerushalmi* in Hebrew and even found it necessary to explain why the long English introduction appeared in addition to the introduction in Hebrew—as if vernacular writing was now something for which a Seminary professor needed to apologize.[51] Later, of course, Saul Lieberman—once he succeeded Ginzberg as the exemplar of scholarship at the Seminary—also published the bulk of his scholarly writings in Hebrew. In his *Tosefta*, he did not even supply an English language preface and introduction, as

Davidson and Ginzberg generally had done. Instead, the work was explicitly geared to *b'nai Torah* (those well familiar with rabbinic literature) who could read the text in the original.[52]

Zionism and the ideology of Hebraism partly explain this transition to Hebrew. By writing in the "holy tongue," Seminary faculty members were consciously aligning themselves with the movements to create a Jewish homeland in Palestine and to revive Hebrew as a living language. Davidson and Ginzberg were also very much influenced by their experiences teaching at the Hebrew University, Davidson in 1926 and Ginzberg in 1928–29.[53] Other foreign-born faculty members wrote in Hebrew as a matter of expedience: they found it easier than English. Whatever the reasons, the fact that more and more Seminary scholarship appeared in Hebrew represented a dramatic shift. Where once Schechter and his colleagues had sought to shape a distinctively American center of Jewish scholarship that would translate classical Judaism into the English language, now the leading textual scholars at the Seminary turned away from America and wrote, in Hebrew, for like-minded Jewish scholars in Eretz Israel and around the world. This made the fruits of the Seminary's most highly prized elite scholarship even less accessible than before to the trustees and to most Conservative Jews.

The turn to Hebrew also markedly distinguished the Seminary's faculty from their contemporaries who produced Jewish scholarship at American colleges and universities and at the seminaries of the American Reform movement. Harry Wolfson at Harvard, Salo Baron at Columbia, Jacob Mann and Jacob Lauterbach at Hebrew Union College, Henry Malter and Solomon Zeitlin at Dropsie College, and most (but not all) of the faculty of the Jewish Institute of Religion—though conversant in Hebrew—published their most important scholarship in English.[54]

Within the Seminary itself, language now became yet another line of demarcation between the elite textual scholars who stood at the center of the institution and the engaged popular ones who found themselves more and more on the periphery. Mordecai Kaplan, unsurprisingly, wrote almost entirely in English. Later, Abraham Joshua Heschel, who like Kaplan reached out to the broader public, was deeply engaged with the events of his day, and never enjoyed the influence inside the Seminary that he won outside of it, likewise wrote most of his books in English. For other reasons, connected with the nature of their field, the Bible faculty (H. L. Ginsberg, Robert Gordis, Alexander Sperber, and later Nahum Sarna) also generally published in English, although the Canadian-born Ginsberg published two of his most significant books in Hebrew.[55] Most of the rest of the faculty wrote in Hebrew as a matter of choice. An analysis of the contributors to the dual-language *Festschriften* prepared for Louis Ginzberg (1946) and Alexander Marx (1950), for example, reveals that about two-thirds of the Seminary faculty who contributed wrote in the Hebrew section. By contrast, almost 80 percent of the other American-based contributors to these works composed their articles in English.[56] Well into the Finkelstein years, the choicest fruits of Seminary scholarship were reserved for other Hebrew-speaking Jewish scholars who could fully appreciate the momentous contributions that these textual studies represented. The publications brought the Seminary faculty surpassing stature with their colleagues in Israel and Europe. But they did so at a price, for by writing in Hebrew the faculty smartly turned its back on the English-speaking scholarly world, as well as on the vast majority of American Jews—among them, the lay leaders who supported the Seminary and most of the Conservative rabbis whom it trained.

Louis Finkelstein, who succeeded Adler as the Seminary's president in 1940 (renamed chancellor in 1951), sought to broaden the Seminary's sphere of influence. Having spent the bulk of his adult life at the Seminary, he appreciated each of the scholarly traditions that the institution perpetuated, and he understood that they appealed to different audiences. Like Schechter (with whom he had studied), and unlike most of the senior faculty of his own day, he himself sought to appeal to both audiences. His scholarly and educational efforts, as a result, moved in two directions. On the one hand, he devoted much of his own creative scholarship to textual studies of the *Sifre* and the *Sifra* that he published in Hebrew. On the other hand, he focused on "wider problems of Jewish life" and sought, invoking Schechter as his model, to reach "Christians, and Jews who know as little about Judaism as Christians."[57] He thus cast his lot with both traditions of Seminary scholarship and was able to draw upon both for his own purposes. Without directly challenging the Seminary's institutional culture, he worked to narrow the chasm that divided the faculty from the surrounding Jewish and non-Jewish communities and moved to place the fruits of faculty research at the service of American Jewry and the world.

Finkelstein accomplished this in three ways. First, he employed the tools of public relations to explain (and exalt) the faculty's highly specialized work in terms that ordinary lay people could appreciate. Second, he fostered scholarship that crossed the boundary into the modern period to confront, with others, the great ethical and spiritual dilemmas affecting the nation and the world. Third and most important, he promoted textbook syntheses that made the fruits of Jewish scholarship accessible, in English, to Jews and non-Jews alike.

Finkelstein's deft use of public relations, his first innovation, did much to break down the "ivory tower" image of elite Seminary scholarship that had developed under Adler. In 1944, for example, the Seminary published under his editorship a modest volume of essays entitled *Rab Saadia Gaon* drawn from lectures delivered at the Seminary and the University of Chicago in 1942 commemorating the thousandth anniversary of that great Jewish scholar and communal leader's death. Jewish and Christian scholars contributed to the volume—itself something of a new

Saul Lieberman
with *The Tosefta*,
1955. *Ratner Center,
JTS.*

departure for a Seminary publication. Beyond the focus on scholarship, however, the volume was also promoted by the Seminary as a timely contribution to wartime discourse. Finkelstein's introductory essay set the stage by describing Saadia as an "architect of peace." A canned review, distributed to newspapers, began with a reference to Adolf Hitler and pointed out that "despite periodic threats of extermination, Judaism survives as a living and vital force, as an immutable reminder to mankind of the fatherhood of God and the brotherhood of Man." It went on to assure readers that "much of permanent value" could be found in Saadia's writings and quoted approvingly Robert Gordis's call that "new Saadias" be produced by the Seminary in order to meet contemporary challenges.[58]

The appearance of the first three volumes of Saul Lieberman's *Tosefta* in 1955 set off something of a public relations frenzy. Finkelstein, in a letter to the American ambassador in Israel, Edward Lawson, described the publication of this halakhic compendium as "a most important event in the history of American Judaism and indeed, in the history of World Judaism." He asked the ambassador to present the work in a public ceremony to the president of the State of Israel as part of what he described as a "Spiritual Point Four program, by which America may contribute to older civilizations new insights into their own cultural products." Under the headline "U.S. Gives Israel New Study of Jewish Code," the subsequent ceremony

Louis Finkelstein
(left) and Chief
Justice Earl Warren
look over a page of
Talmud during
Warren's visit to the
Seminary in 1957.
*Photo by Guy
Gillette. Ratner
Center, JTS.*

received prominent coverage in the *New York Times*, where it was portrayed as a symbol of the close ties between the people of the United States and Israel. The Seminary's public relations office followed this up with an illustrated brochure (reprinted from *Seminary Progress*) entitled "The Tosefta: Its Meaning In Your Life." Most Seminary supporters, of course, could not read let alone appreciate what Lieberman had accomplished and had never heard of the *Tosefta*—but that made no difference. Thanks to Finkelstein, they could at least bask in the reflected glory of this incomparable work of scholarship knowing that in supporting the Seminary they were contributing to Israel, Judaism, American patriotism, and human betterment. Through the magic of public relations, Finkelstein had managed to make the esoteric popular and the aloof scholar seem engaged.[59]

Beyond public relations, Finkelstein also innovated in encouraging, as none of his predecessors ever had, serious scholarship devoted to modern and contemporary issues of Jewish concern. "More is known about the Jews of ancient Sura and Pumbedita than about those of modern New York," he publicly complained in an open letter to Judge Joseph M. Proskauer of the American Jewish Committee.[60] To rectify this problem, he, among many other projects, commissioned a wide range of scholarly essays on modern and contemporary Jewish life for his *The Jews* (see below); published under the Seminary's imprint Moshe Davis's important Hebrew volume on "The Shaping of American Judaism"[61]; initiated, at Davis's instance, an American Jewish History Center ("to find a way to interpret the impact of America on Jewish life and to indicate the significance of the American Jewish experience for the world Jewish community")[62]; and established under his own direction the Institute for Religious and Social Studies that sponsored regular lectures, conferences, and publications, and ultimately issued some fifty volumes devoted to contemporary social, ethical, and religious questions.[63]

Faculty members devoted to the elite textual tradition of Seminary scholarship and influential rabbis who sympathized with them challenged several of these initiatives, particularly the Institute which they considered ephemeral and a diversion from a rabbinical seminary's central mission. Yet, whatever their limitations, these forays into modern and contemporary studies did respond to the demands of the other Seminary tradition, which advocated such programs of outreach, and underscored the Seminary's deepening scholarly engagement with the central issues affecting Americans of the day. As a public relations letter put it on the occasion of a 1957 visit to the campus by Chief Justice Earl Warren and former President Harry Truman, "What better way to dramatize for the American public the values inherent in Judaism?" Regular interactions with non-Jewish scholars and notables offered the Seminary's supporters "increased pride in our ancient tradition, and increased respect for the Seminary's role in demonstrating the contemporary relevance of that tradition to the total American community."[64]

Similar objectives underlay Finkelstein's third initiative in the area of scholarship: his pioneering effort to produce readable syntheses that could bring the fruits of Jewish scholarship to a larger public. The most successful of these by far—billed as "an authoritative work on Judaism in its various phases" and "the most comprehensive discussion of the subject yet undertaken"[65]—was *The Jews*, first published under Finkelstein's editorship in 1949 and then revised through four different editions.

Finkelstein traced the genesis of this project to the dark days of World War II. As news of the Holocaust became known, he held discussions with such notables as Joseph M. Proskauer, Lewis L. Strauss, Irving Lehman, and Sol M. Stroock, leading figures at both the American Jewish Committee and the Seminary, concerning a book that would "serve as a living monument to the massacred."[66] Finkelstein had actually spoken out even earlier, in 1938, concerning the need for the Seminary to fight Hitler through "the preservation of the spiritual treasures of our people and of the human race." With remarkable prescience, he compared the Seminary's task then to that of the prophet Jeremiah when the Temple faced destruction: "the task of saving the Ark of the Covenant."[67]

As time passed and the project developed, however, its focus broadened in keeping both with the universalism that had become Finkelstein's trademark and with the postwar aims of the sponsor, the American Jewish Committee, which was simultaneously engaged in various efforts to promote interreligious harmony.[68] Finkelstein now promised to produce the first comprehensive scholarly treatment in English of "Judaism and the Jews," one that would promote "understanding in the world" both about Judaism as a religion and "about the nature of Jews as a group." His overall model was the prestigious Cambridge History series, where each part of a work was assigned to a different specialist in the field. But one significant difference distinguished the two projects. His, he felt, "should be important as a spiritual influence no less than for its learning." Multiple aims—scholarly, didactic, hortatory, and spiritual—thus underlay the whole enterprise from the beginning.[69]

As finally published, in 1949, *The Jews* filled two large volumes (four volumes in the Jewish Publication Society edition) and more than 1450 pages. Its thirty-five chapters, nine by members of the Seminary's faculty, divided unequally (and most revealingly) into four sections: "The History of Judaism and the Jews" (eight chapters); "The Role of Judaism in Civilization" (twenty-one chapters); "The Sociology and Demography of the Jews" (five chapters); and "The Jewish Religion" (one chapter, by Finkelstein himself). The disproportionate focus on Judaism's role in civilization evidenced a return to apologetic themes stressed back in Schechter's day and carried the same tacit assumptions. As Mordecai Kaplan explained, without specifically referring to *The Jews*:

> It was expected that such knowledge would open the eyes of non-Jews to the fact that the Jews, throughout their historical career, had been creators of significant cultural values. . . . It was assumed that non-Jews would change their attitude toward Jews as a result of this new knowledge concerning them. Thus not only would Jews gain the goodwill of their Gentile neighbors, but they themselves would also arrive at a better understanding of their own People and its past.[70]

Toward the same ends, and following the suggestion of Harry Wolfson, Finkelstein also wrote to several hundred educators and scholars "asking them to suggest the questions about Judaism and the Jews which they believed their acquaintances would most like to see answered." The answers ranged from the helpful to the bizarre (the most bizarre being a question concerning the reputed claim "that all Jews are born with tails and that Jewish doctors immediately remove them and . . . that circumcision is a cover-up for tail-removing") and probably formed the first piece of social research ever undertaken under the Seminary's auspices. In an appendix to *The Jews*, Finkelstein listed the most frequently asked of these questions and told where in the book to find appropriate answers—further evidence of the volume's apologetic intent. His conclusion was sobering: "Judaism [is] the unknown religion of our time."[71]

What nevertheless distinguished *The Jews* from the many other attempts to combat anti-Semitism through education was the solid scholarship that underlay the volume. Many of the book's articles were authored by the world's leading experts on their subject (including Seminary faculty members) and represented significant syntheses of their lives' work, in several cases the only such available in English. Finkelstein, to his "delight," found that certain chapters even included "original research of enduring value, some destined to change the whole course of study in their fields." Once again, as had earlier been the case with the *Jewish Encyclopedia* and much of *Wissenschaft* scholarship, apologetic motivations did not preclude the achievement of solid scholarly results. Thanks to Judah Goldin's careful stylistic editing, the chapters were even quite readable. Inevitably, some disappointed the editor, others (including the chapter on Jewish cultural life in Eastern Europe) never materialized, and still others (including the chapter on the Jews of Palestine/Israel) were too weak to publish.[72] Subsequent editions attempted to correct these and other shortcomings, and in the process expanded *The Jews* by more than four hundred additional pages. Even the first edition, however, was in terms of its ambitiousness, its synthetic quality, its attention to modern and contemporary developments, and its intended audiences unlike anything published by a Seminary faculty member before. Drawing upon both traditions of Seminary scholarship, it managed to be popular and scholarly at once. It reached beyond the normal confines of the Seminary, beyond the confines of the Conservative movement, and beyond even the boundaries of the Jewish people in an attempt to dispel ignorance, promote Judaism, and (in a reprise of Schechter's aim in the Schiff Classics) bring about *kiddush ha-shem*.[73]

Finkelstein attempted to follow up on the success of *The Jews* by editing a multivolume "cooperative" Jewish history on a similar basis. "Dr. [William F.] Albright is going to write a Biblical history; Professor [Elias] Bickerman is half through the Hellenistic history; [and] Moshe Davis is going to get up, at last, a history of the Jews in America," he informed Cecil Roth, hoping that he too would contribute to the effort. Salo Baron, however, refused to participate, both because he wanted to devote maximum attention to his own history and because he found Finkelstein's plan, with its aim of reaching both a scholarly and a popular audience, fatally flawed. The project died on the drawing board.[74]

In yet another fruitless effort to "achieve . . . two goals, rarely combined in the same literary work," Finkelstein in the late 1960s proposed the creation of a quarterly devoted to ethics. "It should be so written that it can be read with pleasure by the comparatively uneducated; and so profound that it can be studied with profit by scholars and in study groups," he wrote in his magniloquent statement of purpose. As so often before, he sought scholarship that would both bridge Seminary traditions and be all things to all people: at once timely and timeless, educational and inspirational, representing "the approach to life of Conservative Judaism" and beneficial to all humanity—in short, an extension of his vision for the Seminary as a whole.[75]

Many Seminary faculty members never fully subscribed to this vision. Saul Lieberman served as their scholarly role model, and as we have seen, he firmly perpetuated the more exclusive traditions of the Seminary's past. Textual scholarship, much of it in Hebrew, thus continued to dominate the institution through the 1960s, winning its practitioners singular esteem in the world of Jewish academics. The broader agenda represented by Finkelstein, Heschel, Kaplan, and younger scholars found a following as well.

Gerson Cohen, who succeeded Finkelstein as chancellor in 1972, identified for a time with both camps. He had trained at the Seminary, had written a textually-based doctoral dissertation in Jewish history inspired by Alexander Marx (though completed at Columbia University), had published his first major scholarly article in Hebrew in the *Mordecai M. Kaplan Jubilee Volume*, and was also vitally interested in contemporary issues. The study of Jewish history, his writings suggested, could help to span the abyss between textual scholarship and issues of concern to the contemporary Jew.[76] But as subsequent events demonstrated, the two traditions were not so easily reconciled. The polarizing debate over women's ordination revealed, among many other things, that the two types of scholarship—one rarified and exclusive, the other popular and inclusive—reflected profoundly different conceptions of the Seminary, its objectives, its obligations to the Conservative movement, and its mission to the world at large.

1. The charter is reprinted in Cyrus Adler, ed., *The Jewish Theological Seminary of America Semi-Centennial Volume* (New York: Jewish Theological Seminary of America, 1939), pp. 178–80. The first objective listed is "the perpetuation of the tenets of the Jewish religion." The last is "the education and training of Jewish rabbis and teachers."

2. *American Jewish Year Book* 1 (1899): pp. 58–59; Robert E. Fierstien, *A Different Spirit: The Jewish Theological Seminary of America, 1886–1902* (New York: Jewish Theological Seminary of America, 1990), p. 54.

3. Solomon Schechter to Mayer Sulzberger, 5 March 1900, in Meir Ben Horin, "Solomon Schechter to Judge Mayer Sulzberger: Part 1. Letters from the Pre-Seminary Period (1895–1901)," *Jewish Social Studies* 25 (October 1963): p. 276. In his 1902 inaugural address, Schechter restated the Seminary's mission in terms more to his liking: "The ideals at which the Directors of this institution aim are the promotion of Jewish learning and the training for the Jewish ministry." Solomon Schechter, *Seminary Addresses and Other Papers* (New York: Burning Bush Press, 1959), pp. 13–14.

4. Cyrus Adler, "A Jewish Renaissance," *American Hebrew* 56 (1894): p. 25. Some of these ideas had earlier been expressed when the Jewish Publication Society was established; see its "Announcement" reprinted in Jonathan D. Sarna, *JPS: The Americanization of Jewish Culture, 1888–1988* (Philadelphia: Jewish Publication Society, 1989) pp. 355–59. For further background, see Jonathan D. Sarna, "Cyrus Adler and the Development of American Jewish Culture: The 'Scholar-Doer' as a Jewish Communal Leader," *American Jewish History* 78 (March 1989): pp. 382–94; Jonathan D. Sarna, "The Making of an American Jewish Culture," in *When Philadelphia Was the Capital of Jewish America*, ed. Murray Friedman (Philadelphia: Balch Institute, 1993), pp. 145–55; and Jonathan D. Sarna, "A Great Awakening: The Transformation that Shaped Twentieth Century American Judaism & Its Implications for Today," *Council for Intiatives in Jewish Education Essay Series* (New York: Council for Initiatives in Jewish Education, 1995).

5. *American Hebrew* 56 (1894), p. 181. The letter is reprinted in *Cyrus Adler, Selected Letters*, ed. Ira Robinson (Philadelphia: Jewish Publication Society, 1985), vol.I, p. 70, where "not witnessing a revival" should be corrected to "now witnessing a revival." For parallel development in other American circles of learning, see Joseph C. Kiger, *American Learned Societies* (Washington D.C.: Public Affairs Press, 1963); and Alexandra Oleson and John Voss, eds., *The Organization of Knowledge in Modern America, 1860–1920* (Baltimore: Johns Hopkins University Press, 1979).

6. Henrietta Szold, "The Year 5660," *American Jewish Year Book* 2 (1900–1901), pp. 35–36. On the *Jewish Encyclopedia* and its significance, see Shuly Rubin Schwartz, *The Emergence of Jewish Scholarship in America: The Publication of the Jewish Encyclopedia* (Cincinnati: Hebrew Union College Press, 1991), esp. pp. 1–16.

7. Sarna, *JPS*, p. 36; Alexander Marx, "The Library," *Jewish Theological Seminary Semi-Centennial Volume*, p. 92.

8. Schechter, *Seminary Addresses and Other Papers*, pp. 16, 18.

9. Quoted in Marx, "The Library," p. 90. In his 10 December 1901 letter to Sulzberger finalizing his arrangements with the Seminary, Schechter also acknowledges the Judge's "generous intentions" concerning his library; see Ben-Horin, "Solomon Schechter to Judge Mayer Sulzberger," p. 286, and Herman Dicker, *Of Learning and Libraries: The Seminary Library at One Hundred* (New York: Jewish Theological Seminary of America, 1988), p. 17.

10. Alexander Marx, "Some Jewish Book Collectors," in Marx, *Studies in Jewish History and Booklore* (New York: Jewish Theological Seminary of America, 1944), p. 234.

11. Sarna, *JPS*, pp. 37, 67; Guido Kisch, "The Founders of 'Wissenschaft des Judentums' and America," *Essays in American Jewish History* (Cincinnati: American Jewish Archives, 1958), p. 160.

12. Peter Novick, *That Noble Dream* (New York: Cambridge University Press, 1988), p. 24; see also Paul Mendes-Flohr and Jehuda Reinharz, *The Jew in the Modern World: A Documentary History*, 2d ed. (New York: Oxford University Press, 1995), pp. 209–10.

13. Adapted from Ismar Elbogen, "A Century of Wissenschaft des Judentums," in *Studies in Jewish Thought: An Anthology of German Jewish Scholarship*, ed. Alfred Jospe, (Detroit: Wayne State University Press, 1981), pp. 26–27.

14. Ismar Schorsch, *From Text to Context: The Turn to History in Modern Judaism* (Hanover, N.H.: Brandeis University Press, 1994), pp. 4, 154, 164.

15. "Rabbinical Seminaries," *Encyclopaedia Judaica* 13 (1972): col. 1463–65.

16. For summaries and evaluations of the scholarship undertaken by the Seminary's leading scholars into the Finkelstein years, see especially Meyer Waxman, *A History of Jewish Literature*, 2d ed. (Cranbury, N.J.: Thomas Yoseloff, 1960), vols. 4, 5; Joshua Trachtenberg, "American Jewish Scholarship," *The Jewish People Past and Present* (New York: Jewish Encyclopedic Handbook, 1955), vol. 4, pp. 411–55; Ismar Elbogen, "American Jewish Scholarship: A Survey," *American Jewish Year Book* 45 (1943–44): pp. 47–65; and Samuel Rosenblatt, "American Jewish Scholarship and the Jewish Theological Seminary," *Proceedings of the Rabbinical Assembly* 5 (1933): pp. 372–87. Here my aim is neither to chronicle nor to evaluate the scholarship produced by Seminary faculty members, but rather to explore two traditions of Seminary faculty research and their implications.

17. Guido Kisch, ed., *Das Breslauer Seminar* (Tübingen: J. C. B. Mohr, 1963), esp. pp. 167–77, 187–203, 270–93; Samuel E. Karff, ed., *Hebrew Union College-Jewish Institute of Religion at One Hundred Years* (Cincinnati: Hebrew Union College Press, 1976), pp. 287–476, esp. p. 320.

18. Solomon Schechter, "Lector Meir Friedmann," *Seminary Addresses and Other Papers*, p. 137.

19. Norman Bentwich, *Solomon Schechter: A Biography* (Philadelphia: Jewish Publication Society, 1948), p. 259.

20. Joseph Jacobs, "Some Aspects of Schechter," *Jewish Theological Seminary Students Annual* 3 (1916): pp. 104–05.

21. Claude G. Montefiore to Solomon Schechter, 31 December 1885, in *Lieber Freund: The Letters of Claude Goldsmid Montefiore to Solomon Schechter 1885-1902*, ed. Joshua B. Stein (Lanham, Md.: University Press of America, 1988), p. 3. The version of this letter found in Bentwich, *Solomon Schechter*, p. 266, illustrates the kind of liberties that Schechter's biographer took with primary sources.

22. Bentwich surveys Schechter's popular writings in *Solomon Schechter*, pp. 266–80.

23. Alexander Marx, "What Our Library Offers to Our Students," *Jewish Theological Seminary Students Annual* 1 (1914): p. 218; Solomon Goldman, "The Man of the Book," *Alexander Marx Jubilee Volume* (New York: Jewish Theological Seminary, 1950), pp. 13, 30; see also Menahem H. Schmelzer, "Alexander Marx (On the Occasion of the 100th Anniversary of His Birth)," *Jewish Book Annual* 35 (1977-78): pp. 123–27.

24. Most, but not all, of Ginzberg's more popular writings, including his *Legends of the Jews*, were commissioned prior to his appointment to the Seminary. He did, however, publish a number of popular articles in the 1920s in the *United Synagogue Recorder*, and in 1928 he published a volume of popular essays with the Jewish Publication Society entitled *Students, Scholars and Saints*. See Boaz Cohen, "Bibliography of the Writings of Prof. Louis Ginzberg," English section of *Louis Ginzberg Jubilee Volume* (New York: American Academy for Jewish Research, 1945), pp. 19–47.

25. Baila Round Shargel, *Practical Dreamer: Israel Friedlaender and the Shaping of American Judaism* (New York: Jewish Theological Seminary, 1985), pp. 14, 68–70; *The Jewish Theological Seminary Register 1917–1918* (New York: Seminary Register, 1917), p. 26; Ginzberg

similarly lamented "that Friedlaender had largely squandered his very substantial talent." See Eli Ginzberg, *Keeper of the Law* (Philadelphia: Jewish Publication Society, 1966), p. 150; Eli Ginzberg, "The Seminary Family," in *Perspectives on Jews and Judaism: Essays in Honor of Wolfe Kelman*, ed. Arthur A. Chiel (New York: Rabbinical Assembly, 1978), p. 120.

26. Mel Scult, *Judaism Faces the Twentieth Century: A Biography of Mordecai M. Kaplan* (Detroit: Wayne State University Press, 1993), pp. 108, 388, n. 25; Sarna, *JPS*, pp. 157–58.

27. See, for example, Marx, "What Our Library Offers to Our Students, p. 218; Israel Davidson, preface to *Thesaurus of Mediaeval Hebrew Poetry* (1924; reprint, New York: Ktav, 1970), vol. 1, pp. xxxviii, xlvi.

28. Marx, "What Our Library Offers to Our Students," p. 218.

29. Mendes-Flohr and Reinharz, *Jew in the Modern World*, pp. 237–40.

30. Sarna, *JPS*, pp. 120, 125–26.

31. For the history and significance of the Schiff Library of Jewish Classics, see Sarna, *JPS*, pp. 120–30. JTS faculty and alumni recruited to produce volumes for the series include Israel Davidson, Louis Ginzberg, Moses Hyamson, Mordecai Kaplan, Alexander Marx, Louis M. Epstein, Jacob Minkin, and Meyer Waxman. Only the volumes by Davidson and Kaplan ultimately appeared in the series.

32. Louis Ginzberg to Solomon Schechter, 22 January 1909, JTS Archives, R.G. 1CC-1-1, and reprinted in Ginzberg, *Keeper of the Law*, pp. 93–94. In 1909, Ginzberg published two volumes of his *Geonica* and one volume entitled *Yerushalmi Fragments from the Genizah* as the first three volumes in a new series entitled *Texts and Studies of the Jewish Theological Seminary of America*.

33. See, for example, Louis Finkelstein, *Jewish Self-Government in the Middle Ages* (New York: Jewish Theological Seminary, 1924), pp. ix, xi. Louis Marshall and Felix Warburg funded the publication of *Ginze Schechter*, studies of *Genizah* texts published in Schechter's memory, while Nathan and Linda Miller subsidized Davidson's *Thesaurus of Medieval Hebrew Poetry* (see Wechsler and Ritterband, *Jewish Learning in American Universities*, p. 152).

34. Surviving correspondence and published *festschriften* demonstrate the existence of such a community of scholars. See also the international scope of the Alexander Kohut Memorial Foundation as portrayed in Rebekah Kohut, *His Father's House: The Story of George Alexander Kohut* (New Haven: Yale University Press, 1938), pp. 137–47.

35. Schechter to Sulzberger, 5 November 1901, in Ben-Horin, "Solomon Schechter to Judge Mayer Sulzberger," p. 285; see Joseph Jacobs, "Solomon Schechter as Scholar and as Man," *Jewish Theological Seminary Students Annual* 3 (1916): p. 99 ("Almost all he published after his coming to America had already been prepared in Cambridge").

36. Friedlaender, "Jewish Learning in America," *Past and Present*, p. 317.

37. Solomon Schechter to Cyrus Adler, 19 March 1914, as quoted in Sarna, *JPS*, p. 122.

38. Schwartz, *Emergence of Jewish Scholarship in America*, pp. 24–26 and passim; Solomon Schechter, *Studies in Judaism: First Series* (1896; reprint, Philadelphia: Jewish Publication Society, 1915), pp .xi–xxv; Louis Ginzberg, *The Legends of the Jews* (Philadelphia: Jewish Publication Society, 1909), vol. 1, p. vii; Joseph Jacobs, *Jewish Contributions to Civilization: An Estimate* (Philadelphia: Jewish Publication Society, 1919), pp. 9, 44–46 (quoted); Bentwich, *Solomon Schechter*, p. 272; Solomon Goldman, "The Portrait of a Teacher," *Louis Ginzberg Jubilee Volume* (New York: American Academy for Jewish Research, 1946), p. 6.

39. Schechter to Sulzberger, 5 November 1901, in Ben Horin, "Solomon Schechter to Judge Mayer Sulzberger," part 1, p. 285; the reference is to the material Schechter published in his *Documents of Jewish Sectaries*, 2 vols., (Cambridge: Cambridge University Press, 1910).

40. Louis Ginzberg, *The Legends of the Jews* (Philadelphia: Jewish Publication Society, 1909), pp. vii, x, xi.

41. Davidson, *Thesaurus of Mediaeval Hebrew Poetry*, pp. xxxvii–li.

42. Saul Lieberman, *Greek in Jewish Palestine* (New York: Jewish Theological Seminary, 1942); *Hellenism in Jewish Palestine* (New York: Jewish Theological Seminary, 1950); for his contributions to Jewish scholarship, see the Hebrew volume published in his memory by the Israel Academy of Arts and Sciences, *LeZikhro Shel Shaul Lieberman* (Jerusalem: World Union of Jewish Studies, 1983).

43. Davidson, *Thesaurus of Mediaeval Hebrew Poetry*, vol.1, p. xlvii (translation mine); vol. 4, pp. xiv-xv. Davidson notes that several modern poems, including "Ha-Tikwah," did for various reasons find their way into the thesaurus.

44. Israel Davidson, *Parody in Jewish Literature* (New York; Columbia University Press, 1907); Carrie Davidson, *Out of Endless Yearnings: A Memoir of Israel Davidson* (New York; Bloch, 1946), pp. 183–87.

45. Friedlaender, *Past and Present*, p. ix; see also Schechter's prefaces to his *Studies in Judaism* and *Seminary Addresses*; and Mordecai Kaplan, *Judaism as a Civilization* (New York: Schocken, 1967), pp. xi–xiv, 3–15.

46. Waxman, *A History of Jewish Literature*, vol. 4, pp. 1085–86; Marshall Sklare, *Conservative Judaism: An American Religious Movement* (New York: Schocken, 1972), pp. 180–84; cf. Mel Scult, *Judaism Faces the Twentieth Century: A Biography of Mordecai M. Kaplan* (Detroit: Wayne State University Press, 1993), p. 223 (citing Neil Gilman): "The faculty was clearly devoted to teaching classical texts, and the religious message, if any, 'was left to the student to ferret out on his own.' Questions of a fundamentally religious nature were simply not dealt with directly. The text was the focus, not the religious experiences that lay behind it."

47. Scult, *Judaism Faces the Twentieth Century*, esp. pp. 222–25.

48. Ginzberg, "The Seminary Family," p. 118. The fact that Ginzberg, Friedlaender, and Kaplan had all hoped to succeed Schechter only heightened their bitterness, which differences over Zionism then compounded. See Ginzberg, *Keeper of the Law*, pp. 132–33; Shargel, *Practical Dreamer*, pp. 15–16; Scult, *Judaism Faces the Twentieth Century*, pp. 108, 205–8; and more broadly, Ira Robinson, "Cyrus Adler and the Jewish Theological Seminary of America: Image and Reality," *American Jewish History* 78, no. 3 (March 1989): pp. 363–81.

49. Sarna, *JPS*, pp. 137–74, esp.142; Michael A. Meyer, *Response to Modernity: A History of the Reform Movement in Judaism* (New York: Oxford University Press, 1988), pp. 296–309.

50. Israel Davidson, *Sefer Sha'ashuim* (Berlin: Eshkol, 1925); Israel Davidson, *Genizah Studies in Memory of Doctor Solomon Schechter*, vol. 3, *Liturgical and Secular Poetry* (New York: Jewish Theological Seminary, 1928), Hebrew section, p. v. See also Isadore Twersky's discussion in *Jewish Studies in American Universities, Study Circle on Diaspora Jewry in the Home of the President of Israel*, 4th series, (Jerusalem: Institute of Contemporary Jewry, 1970), p. 31.

51. "My friend, Professor Frederick Fassett, Jr. . . . insisted that many students of history, literature, and archaeology would be much interested in my Commentary, but . . . lack of knowledge of Hebrew would bar their acquaintance with it." Louis Ginzberg, *A Commentary on the Palestinian Talmud* (New York: Jewish Theological Seminary, 1941), vol. 1, p. viii. Ginzberg also published one of his books in German, *Eine Unbekannte Jüdische Sekte* (1922; reprint, New York: G Olms, 1972).

52. Saul Lieberman, *The Tosefta: The Order of Zera'im*, 2d ed. (Jerusalem: Jewish Theological Seminary of America, 1992), p. xiii.

53. Davidson, *Out of Endless Yearnings*, pp. 121–38; Ginzberg, *Keeper of the Law*, pp. 140–41, 202–6.

54. For a comprehensive survey of Jewish Studies on the university level, see Paul Ritterband and Harold S. Wechsler, *Jewish Learning in American Universities: The First Century* (Bloomington: Indiana University Press, 1994).

55. H. L. Ginsberg, *Kitve Ugarit* (Jerusalem: Mehkarim Leshoniyim, 1936); *Kohelet* (Tel Aviv: Nyuman, 1961).

56. *Louis Ginzberg Jubilee Volume,* 2 vols. (New York: American Academy for Jewish Research, 1945); Saul Lieberman, ed., *Alexander Marx Jubilee Volume,* 2 vols., (New York: Jewish Theological Seminary of America, 1950). The somewhat different list of Seminary faculty contributors to the *Mordecai M. Kaplan Jubilee Volume* (New York: Jewish Theological Seminary, 1953) preferred English by a margin of nine (65 percent) to five (35 percent). Still, of the Diaspora scholars who published in the Hebrew volume, five were Seminary faculty and only two taught elsewhere.

57. Louis Finkelstein to Solomon Goldman, 20 September 1944, in Jacob J. Weinstein, *Solomon Goldman: A Rabbi's Rabbi* (New York: KTAV, 1973), pp. 259–64. For a related discussion of Finkelstein's aims, see Michael B. Greenbaum, "Mission Conflict in Religiously Affiliated Institutions of Higher Education: The Jewish Theological Seminary of America During the Presidency of Louis Finkelstein 1940–1955" (Ph.D. diss., Teachers College, Columbia University, 1994).

58. Louis Finkelstein, ed., *Rab Saadia Gaon: Studies in His Honor* (New York: Jewish Theological Seminary, 1944). The canned review by Sydney H. Zebel is preserved in the JTS Papers, R.G. 11C-12-1.

59. Louis Finkelstein to Edward Lawson, 13 July 1955; *New York Times,* 16 September 1955; "The Tosefta: Its Meaning In Your Life" [1955], all in JTS Papers, R.G. 11C-63-10. The Point Four Program, the last of four proposals to promote democracy outlined by Harry Truman in his 1949 inaugural address, aimed to make the benefits of American science and technology available to "under-developed" countries.

60. "Prefatory Letter (July 4, 1949)," in *The Jews,* 2 vols., ed. Louis Finkelstein (New York, Harper & Brothers, 1949), p. xv. Finkelstein attributed this observation to "a prominent Jewish scholar," but he subsequently made similar statements himself ("We understand Judaism in the first century better than we understand Judaism in the twentieth"). See Marshall Sklare, *The Jews* (New York: Free Press, 1958), p.v.

61. Moshe Davis, *Yahadut Amerika Be-Hitpathutah* (New York: Jewish Theological Seminary, 1951); Davis later produced a related volume in English, *The Emergence of Conservative Judaism* (Philadelphia: Jewish Publication Society, 1965).

62. Moshe Davis, preface to Louis J. Swichkow and Lloyd P. Gartner, *The History of the Jews of Milwaukee* (Philadelphia: Jewish Publication Society, 1963), p. xii.

63. See the list in *The Jewish Theological Seminary of America Register* (New York: Jewish Theological Seminary, 1970), pp. 155–58; this total includes the publications of the Conference on Science, Philosophy and Religion, which the Institute administered.

64. Undated [1957] letter to Seminary friends, JTS Papers, R.G. 11C-63-10.

65. Memorandum, 7 January 1947, JTS Papers, R.G. 36-1-22.

66. Finkelstein, *The Jews,* p. xiii; *Newsweek,* 6 March 1950, p. 70.

67. "Address delivered at the first Women's Conference on Jewish Affairs. . .November 15, 1938," Ratner Center, Marjorie Wyler Papers, 4/38.

68. Naomi W. Cohen, *Not Free to Desist: The American Jewish Committee 1906–1966* (Philadelphia: Jewish Publication Society, 1972), pp. 453-62.

69. "The Need for an Authoritative Comprehensive Book on Judaism" (n.d.), JTS Papers, R.G. 36-1-30.

70. Mordecai Kaplan, *The Greater Judaism in the Making* (New York: Reconstructionist Press, 1960), p. 357.

71. Finkelstein, *The Jews,* p. xvii, xxvi, 1391–97. Many of the original questionnaires, as well as those sent out in preparation for the second edition, are preserved in the JTS Papers, R.G. 36-6. For the bizarre question forwarded by Carleton S. Coon on the basis of a tale

that he had actually heard, see Coon to Finkelstein (n.d., c. March-April 1946), Ratner Center Archive, R.G.36-6-15.

72. Finkelstein, *The Jews*, pp. xvi, xviii.

73. Ibid., p. xxxiii.

74. Louis Finkelstein to Cecil Roth, 4 August 1950; Finkelstein to Salo Baron, 11 January 1951; Baron to Finkelstein, 1 February 1951—all in JTS Papers, Ratner Center, R.G.36-1-14. Hadassah initiated a similar project in 1952 that resulted in the publication of *Great Ages and Ideas of the Jewish People,* ed. Leo W. Schwartz (New York: Random House, 1956).

75. Louis Finkelstein, "Statement of Purpose Regarding the Proposed Quarterly," March 1965, JTS Papers, in R.G.35-2-7.

76. Gerson D. Cohen, ed., *Sefer Ha-Qabbalah: The Book of Tradition*, by Abraham Ibn Daud (Philadelphia: Jewish Publication Society, 1967), pp. vii, 347; idem, "Translating Jewish History into Curriculum: From Scholarship to Paideia—A Case Study," in ed. *From the Scholar to the Classroom* , ed. Seymour Fox and Geraldine Rosenfield (New York: Jewish Theological Seminary, 1977), pp. 31–58; idem, "The Shattered Tablets," *Moment* (October 1985): pp. 17–21; idem, *Studies in the Variety of Rabbinic Cultures* (Philadelphia: Jewish Publication Society, 1991), esp. pp. 320–23.

ALAN MINTZ

The Divided Fate of Hebrew and Hebrew Culture at the Seminary

Teachers Institute social room, ca. 1940s. This room, in the Unterberg Building,
was furnished on a Hebraic theme by the Institute's alumni.
Photo by Peyser and Patzig. Ratner Center, JTS.

ALAN MINTZ

The Divided Fate
of Hebrew and Hebrew
Culture at the Seminary

THE PREAMBLE to the establishment
of the United Synagogue of America went through many changes between 1911 and
1914, as Solomon Schechter sought to secure the degree of consensus necessary to
launch a movement. Two planks in the preamble, however, remained unchanged
throughout the revisions, and both had to do with the Hebrew language. These
formulations are significant both for what they say aloud about the relationship of
the Seminary and the Conservative movement to Hebrew as well as what they leave
unspoken.

The issuers of the preamble proposed to "establish the United Synagogue of
America, with the following ends in view":

> To maintain the traditional character of the liturgy, with Hebrew as the lan-
> guage of prayers.
>   To encourage the establishment of Jewish religious schools, in the curricula
> of which the study of the Hebrew language and literature shall be given a
> prominent place, both as the key to the true understanding of Judaism, and as
> a bond holding together the scattered communities of Israel throughout the
> world.[1]

Since there are only six issues mentioned in the preamble altogether, the attention
given to Hebrew is substantial, especially the lengthy remarks about the role of
Hebrew in Jewish education. (The four other planks are "loyalty to the Torah and
its historical exposition," "observance of the Sabbath and the Dietary laws," preserving "in the service the reference to Israel's past and the hopes for Israel's
restoration," and fostering "Jewish religious life in the home.")

The insistence on Hebrew should be taken, in keeping with the defensive posture
of the preamble as a whole, as a protest against the practices of Reform Judaism at

83

the turn of the century and its embrace of English as the principal language of both worship and religious instruction. But the emphasis on Hebrew should not be understood as being solely reactive. Of the six points of the preamble it is only the statement on education that departs from the laconic and apodictic formulation of the rest; and it is only here that Schechter provides a rationale, a kind of *ta'amei hamitsvot*, for the preamble's declarations. Of the two reasons he gives, the first is an epistemological-theological claim and the second is a sociological one. Schechter unequivocally asserts that a "true understanding of Judaism" cannot be attained without using Hebrew as a key. Schechter is not talking about the linguistic tools scholars need employ for the historical study of Judaism and its documents. Rather, given the educational frame of reference, he appears to be addressing the preparation necessary for a layperson to understand his religion and practice it. (This goes beyond the recitation of prayers in Hebrew, which is covered in the separate statement quoted above.) Hebrew is the key, and without it one is not simply disadvantaged but barred from entry into the edifice of Judaism.

The second reason pertains to the dispersed state of world Jewry. The emphasis on Hebrew's role as a unifying bond implies a state of affairs in which other forces, especially religion, can no longer perform that function. If Hebrew is seen as a bulwark against the disintegration of the Jewish people, how much more so must it be imperative for American Jews, whose characteristic resistance of foreign languages makes them doubly removed from their brethren in foreign lands.

The claims made by Schechter on behalf of Hebrew, as large as they were, must be understood in relation to the far more ambitious advocacy of Hebrew taking place in other quarters. By 1914, the year of the preamble, the Zionist movement was in high gear. Modern Hebrew had been recognized as the language of national rebirth, and at least in ideological thinking, Hebrew was considered the linguistic coefficient of territory. For the cultural Zionists led by Ahad Ha'am, Jewish nationalism was as much a matter of language as of land. A modern literature in Hebrew had already emerged in Eastern Europe in the 19th century, and it was hoped at the beginning of the new century that a vanguard would return to Palestine and revive the ancient tongue as a spoken language. The revival of Hebrew in the Land of Israel was expected to quicken the spiritual life of diaspora Jewry as a whole. This was the expectation and commitment of a small number of fervent Hebraists who arrived in America in the great waves of immigration as young people or as children brought by their parents. By the eve of World War I, there was a gathering Hebraist activity—mainly in New York but in other cities as well—which was the establishment of Hebrew clubs, Hebrew journals, at least one Hebrew college (none other than the Teachers Institute of the Seminary), and the beginnings of an indigenous creative literature in Hebrew, as well as the dissemination of the revived Hebrew literature that had earlier been written in Europe.

Now, Schechter himself had a positive attitude toward Zionism, and it was the impress of his views that made Conservative Judaism, alone of all three major synagogue movements in American life, affirm Zionism long before the general Zionization of American Jewry that followed the founding of the state. In his important 1906 essay, "Zionism: A Statement," Schechter espouses a version of Ahad Ha'amism—turned on its head, some would argue—that affirms Zionism more for its strengthening of Jewish identification in the Diaspora than for its building a spiritual center in Zion. As for Hebrew, Schechter mentions it only to decry the inability of American Jews to read the sources of their religion and to pray in the language of their ancestors. As in the 1914 preamble, there is no notice or encouragement given to a revived Hebrew as either a modern literary culture or as a contemporary spoken idiom.

I have adduced Solomon Schechter's partial and ambivalent endorsement of Hebrew as a way of introducing a sharply defined cleavage within the Seminary on the issue of Hebrew. On one side of this internal tension, in a way most continuous with Schechter's views, stood the Rabbinical School, which affirmed Hebrew as the fundamental language of Jewish learning and tradition but held no special brief for modern Hebrew and its cultural agenda. On the other side stood the Teachers Institute, which, through its faculty and curriculum, unreservedly advocated Hebrew as the banner of the nationalist cause. The Teachers Institute, to be sure, was a unit of the Seminary and dependent upon it, but in many crucial ways it proceeded along its own path. It is fair to say that as much as the Teachers Institute was a part of the Seminary it was also an outpost of an ideological movement called Hebraism that reached beyond the Seminary and on many points was at odds with the institution that housed it.

If by "Hebrew" we mean the passionate advocacy of the Hebrew language as a vehicle for a resurgent national Jewish life in the modern age, then by all accounts the story of Hebrew at the Seminary is surely the story of the Teachers Institute, its faculty, and its students. In the Rabbinical School the centrality of Hebrew obtained only to the degree to which it was considered a medium for classical Jewish civilization and the main language of texts to be scientifically studied; it was also designated as an irreducible marker of the literate worshiping Jew in the present. Yet rarely was Hebrew more than that for Solomon Schechter, Cyrus Adler, or Louis Finkelstein and many of the scholars they appointed to train rabbis for the American rabbinate. The development of Hebrew as a practical spoken language and as a modern literary culture was not their passion. While they might have viewed the flowering of Hebrew in Palestine approvingly as a development appropriate to the new Jewish settlement there, the claims for Hebrew being a necessary and creative force on the American scene did not persuade them. Given the real differences between the Rabbinical School and the Teachers Institute on this matter, it is a wonder that the two schools, however unequal their relationship, remained part of the same enterprise, and we shall be called upon to think about the bonds of common interest that offset the tensions around the Hebrew issue.

To say the Teachers Institute was "housed" by the Seminary is an ambiguous statement that calls attention to an important fact of geography. Although the Teachers Institute was a fully integrated and subsidized unit of the Seminary, it was physically separated from the main institution for most of the first twenty-five years of its existence. Although the Teachers Institute held its first classes at the Uptown Talmud Torah on East 111th Street, it soon relocated to the Lower East Side, eventually finding permanent quarters in the Hebrew Technical Institute on 1917. It remained there until 1930, when it occupied its present home as part of the colonial brick quadrangle on Morningside Heights together with the Rabbinical School. So while the Rabbinical School existed in the rarified orbit of Columbia University, Teachers College, and Union Theological Seminary, the Teachers Institute remained for a prolonged time at the hub of Hebraist and nationalist sentiment in the immigrant Jewish neighborhoods downtown.

The Rabbinical School-Teachers Institute split did have its crucial mediations, and certainly the chief among them was the figure of Mordecai Kaplan, who headed the Teachers Institute from its reorganization in 1909 to his retirement in 1945. Kaplan's relation to modern Hebrew was complex, as we shall see from an examination of his private journals. Although the instructors he appointed to the Teachers Institute faculty were largely unambivalent partisans of Hebrew nationalism, Kaplan himself stood apart from their enthusiasm and assigned to Hebrew a central but not dominating role in his vision of American Judaism. The institutional and temperamental tensions between Solomon Schechter and Mordecai Kaplan and Schechter's jealousy of Kaplan's alliance with Samson Benderly, the head of the Kehillah's Bureau of Jewish Education, is an important part of this story that has been told elsewhere.[2] What is relevant to this inquiry is the position relative to Hebrew that Kaplan worked out—in part out of his collaboration with Benderly— and how this position served as a counter-norm to the Hebraic maximalism of the rest of the Teachers Institute faculty. For reasons that will become apparent, I wish to put the cart before the horse, so to speak, by first delineating Kaplan's position, which, despite his headship of the school, was not the majority view, and then examining the Hebraist worldview of the faculty.

Kaplan began with an open but skeptical mind toward the Hebrew revival. In an entry from his earliest journal (the first night of Hannukah, 11 December 1906), he writes:

> I have just been reading two opposing views on a matter of great national importance viz: the question of Hebrew as a literature. One is the view of Achad-Haam as expressed in the "Hashiloach" (Heshvan, 5663), the other an

בית מדרש למורים
תרצ"ב - 1932

article in the Jewish Daily News by a man named Zeitlin. The former makes the revival of Hebrew a part of the national program, the latter proves the impossibility of a Hebrew literature. There are four requisites, Zeitlin says, for the creation of a national literature: (1) the nation must speak with one tongue, (2) must have one country, (3) must possess a national university and (4) a centre where her talent naturally finds a home. There is no doubt that Zeitlin takes the more correct view of the problem in being convinced that a literature cannot be artificially created as Achad-Haam proposes to do, least of all by the medium of a magazine.

And yet we all feel that it could hurt greatly the national cause were we to neglect the Hebrew tongue. On what logical basis, then, is it possible to maintain it? Certainly not on plea that by such interest you will get a literature. Never in history were a people requested to cultivate a certain language for the sake of what *will* be written in that language; which language has invariably been cultivated for what *has* been written of spoken or sung in it. Thus the only logical reason for making the interest of Hebrew part of the national program is that it contains, embodies in itself that Jewish consciousness which is the basis of Jewish nationality.[3]

Written several years before he undertook the headship of the Teachers Institute, this entry suggests something of the distance from which Kaplan, beginning a rabbinic career in America, viewed the emergence of a modern Hebrew literature in

Eastern Europe. The distance is palpable in the way Kaplan approaches the problem. He takes up the issue as if it were a proposition susceptible of logical proof, and he concludes that because there is no precedent for a people cultivating "a certain language for the sake of what *will* be written" in it then the only value of Hebrew can reside in the values of the past it embodies. Lost on him is the irony that one of the arguments he has read was written in English and the other in Hebrew. What is striking here is Kaplan's apparent lack of familiarity with—or his failure to bring to mind—the impressive achievements of contemporary Hebrew literature that could be readily adduced to give empirical validation to one side of the argument. By the end of 1906, after all, there were the oeuvres of Y. L. Gordon and Abramowitch (Mendele), the best work of Bialik, Berdichevsky, and Tchernichovsky, and the accomplished writings of many younger writers. The future fortunes of modern Hebrew literature were of course not decided at this point, but there is no question that the creature at issue was very much alive no matter how much Kaplan debated the theoretical possibility of its existence.

Some eight years later and after five years of grappling with the issues of Jewish education and teacher training as the head of the Teachers Institute, Kaplan appears to have revised his position on modern Hebrew. The transformation is in fact so thoroughgoing that it is hard to match the diarist who wrote the entry above with the diarist who recorded the following for 20 February 1915.

> After I heard Berkson give that model lesson of last Sunday which was conducted by him in stilted and incorrect Hebrew I was at first inclined to draw the inference that it was futile to attempt to make Hebrew a means of instruction and that it was more advisable to reintroduce instruction in English. But upon further reflection it occurred to me that no more fatal error could be committed than to surrender the last chance there exists of developing the use of Hebrew, the importance of which I have never realized as I do now. What brought home to me the value of Hebrew has been the realization of how little hope there seems to be of ever restoring the sense of Israel's unity in any other way than by means of that language. Nothing can be more visionary than to expect that the unity of Israel will in the future be based upon uniformity in matters of religious doctrine and practice. Hardly less visionary is the hope which we might repose in a Jewish centre, the realization of which is a thing of the very remote future; and in case such a centre would be established something else besides its mere existence would have to exercise the function of uniting Israel in the lands of the diaspora. The only means capable of exercising such a function is the Hebrew language. At present we cannot expect it to develop all the vigor and wealth of a spoken language, but there is every reason to believe that it can attain a high degree of development as a literary medium sufficient at least to maintain a cultural unity among all the Jews of the world. Out of this cultural unity would arise the spiritual unity which would be independent of uniform beliefs and observances.

When I spoke of the need of cultivating the Hebrew language before the Special Class of the Institute in my remarks yesterday (present were Dushkin, Berkson, Chipkin, Miss Aaronson, Brickner, Rosen, Isaacs & Honor) they acted at once on my suggestion and henceforth carried on all their discussions in Hebrew. On the other hand, when I tried to persuade some of the Seminary men to do the same thing, their reply was that they had never had the opportunity of learning to speak Hebrew. No one is more to blame for the lackadaisical spirit among Seminary students, for the general lack of initiative and enthusiasm, and particularly for the step-brotherly attitude towards everything that makes for a real revival of Jewish life than Dr. Schechter. One could hardly credit so well informed a man with such smallness of soul. Out of a personal dislike for some of the Hebraists, he ordered that the Seminary subscription of the Hashiloach be discontinued. The students in whom all courage has been stamped out by the scholarships which they receive from the Seminary have not ventured to utter a word.[4]

The occasion for Kaplan's new affirmation of Hebrew arises paradoxically from the experience of observing a student teacher performing rather pitiably in the national language. The student in question is Isaac Berkson, one of the elite group of young people chosen by Samson Benderly to pursue a special program in Jewish and general education (the "Special Class" mentioned below); Berkson would later become an important theorist of Jewish education and a professor of education at City College. At the awkward moment in his training in which Kaplan captures him, Berkson is trying to put into practice one of Benderly's innovations: *Ivrit bi-Ivrit*. This is a pedagogical principle (literally, "Hebrew In Hebrew") that called for using spoken Hebrew in the classroom to teach Hebrew language and culture, on the assumption that the medium reinforces and facilitates the message. (*Ivrit bi-Ivrit* was a concept that was revolutionary in its time and marked off the Hebraist regime of the Talmud Torah movement from both Sunday school and yeshiva education; it is one of those practices whose long and equivocal history makes it difficult to disentangle the components that were educationally efficacious from those that were driven by ideology and often acted to undermine its ostensible goals.) That the Teachers Institute was committed to the *Ivrit bi-Ivrit* method in the conduct of its own classes goes without saying; it was also the method it trained students to put into practice when they entered the field as teachers. In Kaplan's journal entry, Berkson's awkwardness gives him cause to reconsider the probity of this policy. But the moment passes; Kaplan is saved from revisionism, and renewed in his conviction, he goes on to pronounce a ringing affirmation of the importance of Hebrew.

The reasoning that causes Kaplan to pull up before the brink of "fatal error" is worth attending to. What brings home to him the "value of Hebrew" is profound disappointment with alternative sources of support for the unity of the Jewish people. It is fanciful to believe, he argues, that "religious doctrine and practice" can any longer guarantee that unity. Ahad Ha'am's idea of a spiritual center in Eretz Yisrael is held to be "hardly less visionary." Even if this dream were realized sometime in the distant future, Kaplan astutely observes, the mere existence of such a center would not be enough to overcome the dispersion of the Jewish people and the cleavages within it. Despairing of these paths, Kaplan is led to Hebrew. It is important to note that, consistent with his temperament, he makes his argument on pragmatic grounds rather than on the basis of any romantic linguistic nationalism. Hebrew is simply the "only means capable of exercising such a function." Kaplan's is a calculus of risk, and he wants to bet on the right horse. If Hebrew remains underdeveloped as a spoken language, "there is every reason to believe" that as a literary medium it can achieve what religion and territory cannot. From unity of language unity of the spirit must necessarily emerge.

Kaplan's scorn for Solomon Schechter's "smallness of soul" has a tinge of irony about it given certain similarities between the two men's rationales for Hebrew. In Schechter's final recension of the preamble to the founding of the United Synagogue of America a year earlier (1914), quoted above, he based his defense of Hebrew not just on Hebrew as the language of the liturgy or as the "only key to the true understanding of Judaism" but also on Hebrew's capacity to provide a "bond holding together the scattered community of Israel throughout the world." The difference, of course, lay in the conception of Hebrew. For Schechter, it meant a shared literacy based on the classics of Jewish culture; for Kaplan, it meant that plus the creative potential of the spoken language and the new literature. Kaplan had helped to create an institution that furthered this larger mission of Hebrew; he hired instructors who were greater enthusiasts than he who in turn attracted students quickened by the nationalist impulse. This success in addition to Kaplan's alliance with Benderly—on top of evident ideological reservations—explains Schechter's petty vindictiveness in canceling the institution's subscription to *Hashiloah* and thereby inflicting a wound that was at once symbolic and real.[5]

Kaplan's evident delight in the responsiveness of the members of the Special Class (the "Benderly Boys," thus despite the presence of Ms. Aaronson[6]) is indicative of his relation to Hebrew. Persuaded by an ideological necessity, Kaplan proposes the switch to Hebrew (out of the norm of English), and his proposal is gamely taken up—for more than that class session? one wonders—by his young disciples. This pattern of throwing himself into Hebrew and then withdrawing is one that repeated throughout Kaplan's long productive life. His journals record a personal struggle with Hebrew that is unparalleled for its honesty and insight in any other document of American Jewish life.[7] Kaplan's report of his sympathetic interaction with the students of the Special Class can aid us at this point in further refining the contours of Kaplan's public role in relation to Hebrew. The place of Hebrew in the educational program put into practice by the Benderly and Kaplan trained educators reflects back, I would argue, on the message of their teachers.

The influence of the Benderly Boys cannot be exaggerated. Trained as a kind of cadre, they spread out over the nation and put their stamp on Jewish education between the two world wars. In lieu of a comprehensive account of their work and their individual differences, I would venture a broad characterization of their program as an adaptation of Hebrew-oriented Jewish nationalism to the American scene. *Halakha* and *mitzvot* were translated into customs and ceremonies; the folk songs and myths being developed in the culture of the Yishuv were given precedence over synagogue practices; and modern spoken Hebrew was privileged over classical literacy. This was a program whose subversive revisionism has been generally underestimated; yet in a crucial way it undercut its own large ambitions. As Walter Ackerman has pointed out, the centralized Talmud Torah movement initiated by Benderly believed too fervently in the promise of American pluralism to make room for and protect minority cultures.[8] By investing all of its resources in afternoon schools that were supplemental to the main business of public school education, the movement underestimated the force of acculturation and had to settle for an outcome that rarely became more than supplemental. Kaplan criticized the Talmud Torah program for its deafness to religious issues and for its discounting of the educational potential of the synagogue, or in his terms, the synagogue center. When it came to Hebrew, however, I believe he had much in common with his former students. He may have stressed classical literacy more pointedly, but he joined them in advancing what might be called an integrationist model of Hebrew.

By integrationist I refer to the relationship to American culture and the English language. So, although Kaplan was convinced that Hebrew was a central pillar of Jewish education, that it was the major carrier of Jewish values and culture, and that the survival and unity of the Jewish people depended on the spread and growth of a revived Hebrew, he nevertheless believed that Hebrew culture could flourish and be enriched by its existence alongside American civilization. His sense of his own position is well conveyed in an account he gave in his journal (11 September 1925) of an informal get-together he hosted at his house for the faculty of the Teachers Institute to discuss issues of common concern about the school. Present were Hillel Bavli, Zevi Scharfstein, Leo Honor, Morris Levine, Paul Chertoff, Joseph Bragin, and Osher Ovsay.

> Most of the men, despite the fact that they have adequate knowledge of their respective subjects, have little mastery of the art of education, and still regard the purpose of any kind of education as being able to remember and quote text. In addition, being modern Hebraists, they are zealots for the employment of Hebrew as a medium of conversation. They almost refuse to recognize that we are living in an American environment, and view the encroachment of Americanism into the lives of our students with a good deal of jealous hostility. I must

confess that while on the positive side I am probably no less in favor of making as much use of Hebrew as possible, I part company with them when it comes to excluding the use of English. Being a compromiser and a syncretist by nature I try to abide by the principle enunciated in Kohelet: *ehoz bazeh vegam bazeh* [grasp both this *and* that]. The only one of the faculty who agrees with me in that respect is Honor. I should also mention Kedushin and Silk, but they wield little influence.

Does the fact that Kaplan was nearly a minority of one among his colleagues at the Teachers Institute make his position correspondingly unimportant? It is true that the faculty with their zealousness for Hebrew were in fact recruited by him and that he seemed to yield to their moral (though not intellectual) superiority, making his differences from them known only discreetly and diffidently. Nevertheless, if we widen the frame of reference beyond the cultural politics of the Teachers Institute faculty to encompass the larger world of Jewish education made by the students trained at the institution, it would have to be said that Kaplan's integrationist approach to Hebrew became the dominant model.[9]

Yet however dominant it might have been in the world of applied Jewish education, the integrationist model was most certainly not the one that set the tone of the Teachers Institute and its academic atmosphere. On a personal level, the faculty seems to have regarded Kaplan as a friend to Hebraism and a defender of the school's cause before a doubting Adler and the trustees, yet they undoubtedly did not count him as one of their own. On the level of institutional culture, it was they who ran the school on a day-to-day basis while Kaplan juggled his many roles in Jewish life, and it was they who suffused the classroom with their passionate Hebraism. In interviews with alumni of the Teachers Institute it is invariably the devotion of the faculty to modern Hebrew and the genuine employment of the language in the classrooms and the hallways that is recalled to mind, in addition to the encounter with the texts of the Bible, Ahad Ha'am, and Bialik. Implicit in the educational and cultural worldview of most of the faculty was what might be called (without prejudice) a separatist model of Hebrew; in this model, Hebrew language and culture determine an autonomous sphere of Jewish national culture whose connection to American culture is not hostile but wary and aloof. We shall first look at how this model was embodied in the curriculum of the Teachers Institute and where the school was located on the national and international map of the Hebraist movement. We will then turn our attention to a dimension less tangible but arguably more influential: the ethos of Hebraism.

The values of the institution are reflected in the distribution of the 132 credit hours required for the undergraduate degree (Bachelor of Jewish Pedagogy):

Bible	36 credit [hours]
Hebrew	36

History	20
Talmud	16
Education	12
Religion	12[10]

The large number of hours required in Bible warrants some explanation. In Hebraist-nationalist circles in America and abroad the Bible was esteemed not so much as a revealed religious text or as an object of scientific scholarly study but as the great saga of the beginnings of the Jewish people, whose greatest glory lay in the incomparable beauty of its Hebrew idiom. To study the Bible, then, beyond its inherent edification, was to immerse oneself in the primal font of the Hebrew language in its moment of greatest purity and vigor. In the nationalist outlook, the canon of Jewish knowledge was anchored by two great poles: the Bible in ancient times and modern Hebrew literature in our own. The study of history made its claims; Talmud less so. For certain intents and purposes, the study of Bible at the Teachers Institute can be considered a kind of extension or retrojection of the study of Hebrew; and indeed some of the most passionate Hebraists on the faculty—Morris Levine (Moshe Halevy), Joseph Bragin, Hillel Bavli, Benjamin Silk (Silkiner)—taught Bible as well as Hebrew, although they were not trained as Bible scholars and did not aspire to contribute to the critical comparative study of the Bible. Between Bible and Hebrew courses, 72 of the students' 132 credit hours were spoken for.

Even more indicative of the faculty's conception of the priorities of Jewish knowledge were the "minimum requirements for admissions" to the Teachers Institute. To enter the program in 1927 the applicant was expected to possess the following:

Bible: (a) Thorough knowledge of the contents of the Former Prophets.
(b) Ability to translate any text from the Former Prophets and easy portions from the Later Prophets.
Hebrew: (a) Ability to read at sight correctly and understand easy narrative Hebrew prose.
(b) Ability to express oneself correctly in Hebrew on simple topics.
(c) Knowledge of grammatical forms and ability to spell correctly.
History: Knowledge of the important events of Jewish history, as described in an outline of the type of Dubnow's *Koroth Ha'Ibrim*.

It is unclear whether these entry requirements were in fact a minimum or more often a maximum; it was a lot to expect of high school graduates at a time when there were very few day schools. But even as expectations, these norms serve to suggest the profile of competence that the Teachers Institute faculty sought to build upon. Again, we have the pairing of Bible and Hebrew. In Bible the emphasis is on knowing "the contents" of a body of material and facility in decoding the Hebrew text. In Hebrew the emphasis is not only on decoding but on grammatically correct communication.[11]

This curricular configuration identifies the Teachers Institute as belonging to a larger international phenomenon in modern Jewish life: the Hebraist-nationalist movement. Intertwined with the rise of political Zionism at the end of the 19th century was a culturalist movement inspired by the writings of Ahad Ha'am and Bialik that sought to base the renewal of the Jewish people upon the revival of the Hebrew language. This movement argued that language was as important as land and that the successful settlement of Eretz Yisrael was dependent upon—and would follow in time—the successful creation of a Hebrew culture. In contrast to its chief competitor Yiddish and obviously to European languages, it was felt by Ahad Ha'am and others that Hebrew alone possessed the capacity to negotiate the transition between the traditional religious culture of Judaism and the conditions of national existence in the modern world. Language, in the view of romantic nationalism, was conceived of as both conservative and creative. It preserved within the folds of its ancient garments the values and usages of the past at the same time as it enabled a newly revived national entity to give expression to its unique genius. Foreseeing the accelerated abandonment of religious faith and practice by the Jewish masses, Ahad Ha'am viewed Hebrew as the only vehicle for a modern Jewish culture that did not burn the bridges to the past.

The idea of a new Hebrew culture inflamed the minds of many in the Pale of Settlement at the end of the last century. It appealed to the older householders who had supported the Hibbat Zion movement as well as to young men who had left the culture of the *beit midrash* (study hall) in which they were raised yet sought to connect themselves with the renewed life of their people. As conditions worsened in Russia, these Hebrew nationalists began a series of displacements that took them to Berlin, Paris, or Vienna before setting off for Palestine, South Africa, or America. Among the millions of Jews who came to America during the great emigrations there were enough partisans of Hebrew by 1913 to create Hebrew journals, schools, and organizations. By the early 1920s Hebrew colleges were established in major Jewish population centers. These were post-secondary educational institutions in which modern Jewish studies were taught in Hebrew not only to train teachers but also to advance the Jewish knowledge of students at general colleges. Herzeliya in New York and the Hebrew Teachers College in Boston are paradigmatic examples of Hebraist institutions founded in the early 1920s. Gratz College in Philadelphia and the Teachers Institute itself were founded earlier but were reborn as Hebraist bulwarks during World War I.[12]

Viewed internationally, the American Hebrew colleges were but one of three centers created after the Revolution and the Civil War made Hebraist activity impossible in Russia. The two others were the Yishuv in Palestine and, taken together, Poland, Lithuania, Latvia, and Estonia. Although unique conditions produced widely divergent courses of development, each center represented an adaptation of a shared cultural and ideological agenda. The case of Palestine was the most radical and multi-layered. The mythic icon of Eliezer Ben-Yehudah's inventing modern Hebrew has less to do with the reality than does the transfer of Hebraist cultural institutions (journals, publishing houses, gymnasia) to the large cities and the fanatic devotion of veteran Hebrew teachers in the isolated settlements of the countryside.[13] The later success of Hebrew as an everyday spoken language and as a cultural medium in Israel, an achievement that exceeded the fantasies of the wildest Zionist visionaries, however, should not make us lose sight of the fact that in an earlier period, in the years after the Great War, Hebrew culture tried valiantly to root itself in other climes.

In interwar Poland and the Baltic states, the chief embodiment of Hebraism was the Tarbut schools. These were autonomous academic Jewish high schools in which most subjects were taught in Hebrew as well as the co-territorial language. The Jewish curriculum was heavily based on Hebrew language, modern Hebrew literature, Bible, and history. What set these schools apart from the Hebrew colleges in America was the relationship to the surrounding culture. The Tarbut schools took as their mission the training of an elite group of young people who would realize their Jewish lives by settling in Eretz Yisrael and contributing to its development. Like the Zionist youth movements that were profoundly influential in the formation of their students' loyalties, the Tarbut schools functioned as a kind of *hakhsharah*, a practical and spiritual preparation for a life that would unfold elsewhere. This purpose could be forcefully projected because of the relatively weak competition posed by the surrounding culture. Estonian and Lithuanian national cultures exerted little attraction, Polish somewhat more. But in no case was the ideal formulated as the establishment for the long term of a high Hebrew culture in these lands.[14]

The thrust of the Hebrew colleges in America was different, and this difference arose from the possibilities implicit in the promise of America. During World War I, it was believed by many that establishment of a center for Hebrew culture in America could come about. The Soviet Union was a dead end, and the war had shut down cultural organs both in Middle Europe and in Palestine. It was only in America that conditions of freedom prevailed. With its great universities and the populousness and increasing wealth of its Jewry, the American Jewish scene contrasted sharply with the cultural and material impoverishment of the tiny Yishuv. Later in the interwar period, even diehard Hebraists came to admit that the wished for creative center in America had not materialized; yet during the war and right afterward it was far from delusional to believe that it was possible. The focus on America did not mean that the Hebraists who staffed the Hebrew colleges were uninvolved with life in Eretz Yisrael. They followed political and cultural developments there closely and passionately identified with the fortunes of the Yishuv. Some even moved there.[15] And they may have been pleased if individual students realized their Zionist ideals and made *aliya* to Eratz Yisrael. Yet the main burden of their work was to train teachers of Hebrew in American Jewish schools and to create a literate laity conversant with Hebrew culture. If in time it became evident that the American milieu was not hospitable to their endeavor, America nevertheless remained the locus of their institutional and cultural activity.

How the American Hebrew colleges differed from their counterpart institutions in Palestine and Europe is clear enough; how they differed among themselves is more subtle. Two of the colleges, the Teachers Institute of the Seminary and the Teachers Institute of Yeshiva University (before that of Rabbi Isaac Elchanan Theological Seminary), were affiliated with religious movements, and this connection affected—in ways less consequential than one might imagine—the nature of the curriculum. Because most of the colleges came into being in the early 1920s, the two schools that were started earlier, Gratz College in Philadelphia and the Seminary's Teachers Institute, played host to a greater ideological and religious mix of students in this early period before more options became available. The Hebrew colleges that were established in major Jewish cities (Herzeliya in New York, the College of Jewish Studies [later Spertus] in Chicago, the Boston Hebrew Teachers College, the Baltimore Hebrew College, among others) tended to reflect something of the traits of the local Jewish community as well as the personality of the college's leader.

Unsurprisingly, New York City had the greatest number of options. After the war there were Herzeliya, the Seminary's Teachers Institute, and Yeshiva's Teachers Institute. In all three institutions, the unambivalent core of the curriculum was Bible and Hebrew language and literature. Yeshiva required more credits in Talmud and codes than the other two. Herzeliyah put somewhat more stress on history than did the Seminary; and the Seminary in turn required classes in religion (taught by Mordecai Kaplan), which Herzeliyah did not. Although there were observant students and faculty at Herzeliyah, its head, Moshe Feinstein, set more of an unapologetically secular tone. One imagines that Hebraists who joined the faculties of the Seminary's and Yeshiva's teachers institutes were not antagonistic to the particular religious climates of those institutions or were at least prepared to accommodate themselves at some level of public behavior.[16]

All of these differences considered, the sense of communality among the Hebrew colleges, especially at the level of the faculty, is overwhelming. So that if institutionally the Teachers Institute "belonged" to the Jewish Theological Seminary, culturally and ideologically it was a branch—though not of the sort for which franchises and charters are issued—of a larger international and national movement that intersected with the interests and outlooks of the Seminary and

Conservative Judaism but did not merge with them. The more radical dimension of difference, we have seen, is represented not as much by Kaplan's integrationist model as by the faculty he recruited and not as much by the formal curriculum they taught as by their ideological passions. This is the dimension of the Hebraist ethos; and although it was this quality that gave the Teachers Institute its personality, it is not easy to pin down.

A good place to capture something of this aura is an appreciation of the Teachers Institute written by Hillel Bavli on the occasion of the school's fiftieth anniversary in 1959.[17] The article is nostalgic and elegiac and begins by describing his arrival from Buffalo in 1917 as a very young man, his interview with Kaplan for appointment to the Teachers Institute, and his early years of teaching there. From his own attachment to the institution he proceeds to evoke the spirits of devoted teachers who, though now departed, set the tone in the period between the wars. (Abraham Halkin, Zevi Sharfstein, Moshe Davis, Reuven Wallenrod, Judah Goldin, and others, being among the living, were not dealt with.) A poet and an appreciative critic, Bavli is not the figure to look to for probing intellectual discriminations; but in striving to render some collective characterization of the outlook of the faculty, he gives us an evocative description of their common core of values.

> Despite all the individual differences among them, the members of the faculty were of one mind in their concern for Hebrew education in America and in their conviction that Hebrew education worthy of its name must be based both upon the foundations of Torah and Jewish tradition and upon the so-called secular cultural achievement of recent times. All of them carried with them a deep-rooted Hebraic consciousness that drew from ancient sources, and they were all devoted body and soul to the idea of national revival and the proud return of Israel to its land. It was in accordance with this inner awareness and conviction that they directed their teaching and shaped the program of study.

As impressionistic as this description is it nonetheless bares some of the assumptions that underlay the Hebraism of the faculty. To begin with, the enterprise of Hebrew education is presented as encompassing two bodies of knowledge: the "foundations of Torah and Jewish tradition" of the past and the "secular cultural achievements" of the present. But Bavli's formulation is not simply symmetrical; there is the implication that at the Teachers Institute as opposed to other institutions (and perhaps as opposed to the natural inclination of the students and their attraction to the current and the actual), when it comes to the study of modern Hebrew culture, largely secular by nature, there is a shared insistence (*tsarikh uvedin*) that the study of modern literature be firmly grounded upon and informed by the classical tradition. But it works the other way around as well. It is the great present cause of national revival that retroactively suffuses the ancient cultural achievements of the people with newly urgent relevance. It is this capacity not only to affirm simultaneously classical religious culture *and* contemporary secular Hebrew culture but also to see them as validating each other that formed the essential Hebraism of the Teachers Institute. Yet whereas the essence of classical culture may have been religious, the relationship of the Hebraists to the worldly culture of the national revival was anything but secular. In other words, however much they revered the classical religious literature of Israel, they did not approach it in a traditionally religious way. Rather, the rhetoric of religious belief, devotion, and ultimate concern is displaced onto the national cause. When it came to the revival of the Jewish people through the Hebrew language, they were transfixed by an ideological fervor that was religious in the sense that the great ideologies of the 19th and 20th centuries were capable of eliciting vision and commanding allegiance.

It is these qualities of faithfulness to the Hebrew cause and energetic participation in its culture rather than brilliant scholarly achievement that impress one in the shades of departed Hebraists that Bavli parades before the reader.[18] It is worth identifying some of these figures because it is they, more than any other factor, that contribute to the Hebrew mystique of the Teachers Institute. One of the most revered of the faculty was Morris D. Levine (Moshe Halevi in his Hebrew articles), whose coming to the Teachers Institute by all accounts signaled a substantial intensification of the Hebraist atmosphere of the institution. His articles in *Hatoren,* the Hebrew journal that began in 1913 and appeared with varying frequency for about ten years, contained the most thoughtful articulation of the ideals of a Hebraist culture in America and the most trenchant critique of the existing arrangements of the Jewish community considered from the Hebraist perspective. The source of his moral authority at the Teachers Institute was his enormous investment in preparing his classes, the high demands he placed on his students, and the uncompromising moral seriousness of his commitment to Hebrew.[19] Benjamin Silk, who wrote under the name of B. N. Silkiner, was a quiet and uncontentious presence at the Teachers Institute, where he taught Bible. In the larger world of American Hebraism, however, he had a large reputation as the first Hebrew poet to engage the mythic American past. His epic poem about native Americans during the Spanish conquest (*Mul ohel Timora; shivrei poema*)[20] inaugurated a genre of Indian epics contributed to by E. E. Lissitzky and Israel Efros. Silkiner was also well known internationally for his translation into Hebrew of *Macbeth*. Together with Bavli's own poetry, Silkiner's verse, which became more approachably lyrical after his epic, made the Teachers Institute into one of the centers for Hebrew poetry in America. Also mentioned with affection by Bavli were Joseph Bragin, a teacher of Bible and *Mishna* and a veteran educator who had directed the Bureau of Jewish Education's Hebrew high school with its many branches throughout the boroughs, and Osher Ovsay, who wrote with impressive facility in the Hebrew press about both Talmud and secular Hebrew literature, the subjects he taught at the Teachers Institute. The youngest and the only American-born member of the faculty was the school's registrar, Leo Honor, who taught education and history and was respected for his Hebraist passions by his older, European-born colleagues. A graduate of Benderly's program and Columbia Teachers College, he left the Teachers Institute in 1929 to become head of Jewish education in Chicago.

Still alive and very productive at the time of Bavli's semi-centenary memoir were Zevi Scharfstein, Abraham Halkin, and Reuven Wallenrod. Perhaps more than any other figure in his time, Scharfstein was responsible for disseminating the *Ivrit bi-Ivrit* method and developing materials for its implementation. At the Teachers Institute he was in charge of teacher training, and it was before his watchful eyes that all candidates for the pedagogy degree had to conduct their model classes in Hebrew. He was an astute businessman as well, who founded the Shilo publishing house (whose symbol was a deer after his first name Zevi) that flooded the extensive world of Hebrew education with its publications—as anyone who has ever held a Shilo prayer book in his hands will know. Abraham Halkin (brother to the Hebrew writer and critic Shimon Halkin and father to the writer and translator Hillel Halkin) was a genuine critical scholar of Jewish history in the Islamic period who, like Bavli, taught in both the Teachers Institute and the Rabbinical School. He taught in the former in Hebrew and in the latter in English, and he enjoyed telling his Teachers Institute students how much better informed they were than the rabbinic students he taught. He was known among the students and faculty for his uncompromising Zionism and for describing his living in the Diaspora—he retired to Israel—as living in sin. Finally, Reuven Wallenrod was, after Shimon Halkin, the most important writer of Hebrew fiction in America. An accomplished psychological realist, Wallenrod sensitively probed the vagaries of acculturation between the world wars. His novel of 1946, *Ki fanah yom* (At Day's End), is an extremely accomplished study of social shifts reflected in the changing seasons of a Catskill resort and the family that runs it.

And then there was Bavli himself. He had come to the Teachers Institute right after college, and by the time of his memoir in 1959 he had taught there for forty years, even longer than Kaplan. Although Bavli was one of the few faculty members invited to teach in the Rabbinical School, his loyalties were always to the Teachers Institute and its Hebraist atmosphere. He was central to the maintenance of this atmosphere not only because of his longevity and his conciliatory personality but also because he was a poet. He embodied the figure of the poet at a time when poets generally occupied a very exalted place in the cultural system of the Hebrew national revival.[21] To be a scholar was all very admirable, but to continue in the footsteps of Bialik and to serve the Hebrew muse in its purest form—this was a very high calling indeed. Bavli was a widely published poet who was especially admired for some of his long poems with settings in the American landscape, like his "Mrs. Woods." He was also very active as a critic who wrote appreciatively about the work of fellow poets. Bavli, like other members of the faculty who wrote for Hebrew journals, created a sense for the students of the Teachers Institute that they were moving among men who were in the midst of making the national culture.

One poem written by Bavli, which was well known in Hebraist circles, can serve as a bridge to a discussion of the place of Hebrew in the Rabbinical School. The following poem—with a prose translation I have provided—appeared in *Hadoar* in 1948 amidst the tumultuous celebrations of Israel's independence in the Hebraist world.[22]

גאים ועֲרירים

גאים ועֲרירים אתם פוסעים
על מרבדי דממה באולמי־חכמה אטומי קול,
משרברבים בעטרה של שלות־רוח עליונה
ובאדרת־היראה בה תתעטפו.
לא באה עדיכם שועת־היקוד של המכורה
המגעשה בסערות־אימים, מסות חרות;
לא להטו לבכם כפירי־עמכם האבירים
הממלטים תקות עתיד מלע אבדון —
להרעישכם ולאגדכם בברית חזון ועלילה
עם כואבי מולדת.

קהים, חרשים, נעולי לב, אביוני אמונה ומעש
אתם נושאים משאכם תפל, שמחים בצדקתכם,
על נצח וקדשה וישועת אל רחוק מכם,
וקהל פסוקים תלויים על שפתיכם כקמעות
בהם שדי כפירה ושעמום תבריחו,
שכחתם את שפת־מחצבתכם המטהרה,
בלשון־עועים את מיטב כל סגלה בכם תקפחו
ותתרפסו מרוששים לפני אלים זרים.

הה, אי יד־המרפא תנופף מול עיניכם תמיד,
כאבוקה של אש־פלדות מתרה ומצרף,
את מנלת הפלצות והגבורה של זה הדור ?
או מי יטיף לתוך כוס־דבשכם המסאבה
נטפי ענות, איל ומרי מרתיחי דם
עד אם תקומו, תחגנו משבי־שפלות, ממשאות־שוא
ותתפשטו כסות־הקלון, מסכת מקיונים,
ותשאגו, תתפללו כאבותיכם המומי לב,
ונשאתם את נפשכם הנהלאה
לקראת הפדות.

101

*Divided Fate
of Hebrew
and Hebrew
Culture at the
Seminary*

[Vain and barren you tread on hushed carpets in the sealed off halls of learning, sporting your crown of complacency and cloaked in your mantle of self-importance. The roar of freedom's bonfires has not gotten through to you, nor have you been stirred by the sight of brave young people snatching hope from the jaws of calamity, nor can you be moved to become part of the covenant of vision and deed with those who suffer with the homeland.

Deaf, dull, unfeeling, impoverished of faith and deed, contentedly self-righteous, you limply declaim your message of eternity, holiness and the salvation of a distant God; a gathering of verses hang from your lips like amulets through which the demons of apostasy and ennui will rush in. You have forgotten the purifying language of your source; in a muddled language you have deprived yourself of the best of your inheritance, and impoverished you grovel before alien gods.

Oh, which healing hand, like the purifying torch of tempering fire, will signal the scroll of daring and bravery of this generation? Or who will dispense into your putrefying honeyed cup a tincture of oppression, power and rebellion sufficient to boil your blood and make you arise from your abasement and false loyalties and cast off your rags of shame and clown's mask? Then roaring prayers like your astonished ancestors, your soul will be borne upward toward redemption.]

Given the mildness of Bavli's institutional persona, the searing invective of this poem must have been stunning. The rhetoric of the poem is unmistakably modeled on the public poems of Bialik in which the poet assumes the stance of the biblical prophet and attempts, through insult and hyperbole, to goad a vain and apathetic people into an active return to God's path. The volume of the invective is in proportion to the spiritual deafness of the addressees. They are so cut off by layers of prideful self-regard that they are insensible of the least echo of the extraordinary events that are noisily unfolding beyond their carpeted halls. The tragedy in this situation, of course, is not the

Hillel Bavli
(1893–1961).
*Ratner Center,
JTS.*

failure of those inside to come to the aid of those who are courageously striving on the outside but the spiritual consequences of remaining untouched by the spectacle. Not seeing and not hearing and continuing to make empty pronouncements about holiness and eternity lead to a dangerous alienation from real sources of divine truth and inspiration; and despite all the rhetoric of godliness and high purpose, this is a vacuum that invites invasion by the forces of disbelief and demoralization.

The reference to Hebrew at the end of the second stanza is hardly subtle, and it makes the connection between language and apostasy. You cannot grasp the redemptive drama of national liberation if you have abandoned the language of the nation. To abandon Hebrew is to divest yourself of your best resources and, denuded, to be forced to seek shelter among alien gods. The metaphor of clothing and nakedness is continued in the apocalyptic frenzy of the final verses. Only by voluntarily stripping off the garments of shame and the clown's mask (*kesut-haqalon, masekhet muqeyonim*) can the soul be exposed to possibility of redemption.

A poem is not an institutional manifesto nor a policy document, but it can suggest something of the unspoken tensions that prevailed in the relationship between the Rabbinical School and the Teachers Institute. This was a relationship that was inherently unequal. The price paid for relative autonomy in matters of culture and curriculum cast the Teachers Institute into the role of poor relation to the Rabbinical School, where faculty members received considerably higher salaries and students higher stipends. Moshe Davis recalls that when he took over the deanship from Kaplan in 1945 faculty salaries were so neglected that Zevi Scharfstein complained to him that his granddaughter, who had just begun work as a kindergarten teacher, was making more money than he. (Given the income from Scharfstein's publishing work, the insult to his dignity must have been the real rub.)[23] In discussing the Rabbinical School, a distinction should be made between Hebrew and Hebraism. The administration and much of the faculty of the Rabbinical School may not have been persuaded by Hebraism as an ideology with its demands for Hebrew speech and its privileging of modern Hebrew writing over almost all texts of Jewish civilization except the Bible. But this did not mean that they did not believe in the essential value of Hebrew as the main vehicle of classical Jewish knowledge and the necessity of Hebrew literacy for rabbis trained at the Seminary. From the late 1920s onward (after the founding of the Hebrew University) there was an increasing tendency among the Rabbinical School faculty to produce their scholarly work in Hebrew, despite the earlier example of Solomon Schechter and his call for the writing of American Jewish scholarship in English.[24]

The fact that the Rabbinical School was above all a professional training institution for American rabbis meant that if there was one language the students had to speak well it was not Hebrew. Especially before World War II, the Rabbinical School fulfilled a socializing function. Most of the young men who studied there were the children of immigrants, if not immigrants themselves, and during their years at the Seminary their accented speech had to be Americanized and their manner of speaking trained in the homiletical arts that could empower rabbis in the great age of public preaching.[25]

Nevertheless, from time to time the issue of Hebrew as a language of instruction was debated in the Rabbinical School, often at the urging of students. The most serious discussion of the issue took place in 1943. In the early 1940s some of the brightest rabbinical students were either avowed Hebraists or had considerable sympathies for the cause; they included Mordecai Waxman, Abraham Goldberg, Arthur Hertzberg, Herman Kieval, Moshe Davis, Sidney Greenberg, Jack Cohen, Jacob Kabakoff, Stanley Rabinowitz, Milton Arfa, Max Raskin, Abraham Kazis, Sidney Morgenbesser, and Gerson Cohen. Student pressure was apparently strong enough to force Louis Finkelstein to form a faculty committee to consider the merits and practicability of the demands. We are fortunate to have not only the minutes of that meeting, which was chaired by Mordecai Kaplan, but also Kaplan's journal entry for that day discussing the meeting. (See Appendix.[26]) The chain of events that brought about the meeting is filled in by Kaplan's account in his journal. The committee meeting was the result of an earlier discussion that took place at a meeting of the full faculty which was in turn prompted by a petition presented two months earlier by students who requested that Rabbinical School courses be taught in Hebrew.

The formal unanimity of the committee minutes masks the apparent contentiousness of the faculty meeting. Bavli's passionate support for the students was to be expected; Robert Gordis gave qualified support. The objections reported by Kaplan in his account were serious issues of policy and principle. Simon Greenberg's opposition was based on the grounds that the students will be "expected to preach and teach in English"; their effectiveness in the pulpit will depend on their communicative and performative skills in English. The general level of those skills among the students—to judge from item six in the committee minutes concerning the need for training in the "accurate and cultured use of English"—was already considered to be wanting. Saul Lieberman's objection stemmed less from the Seminary's role in professional training than from its tradition of Jewish scholarship. He argued that teaching in Hebrew—which was certainly no obstacle for Lieberman himself, who had come to the Seminary from Palestine—"would prevent the students from cultivating exactitude in grasping the subject matter." It is not clear whether Lieberman had in mind the students' awkward difficulties with spoken Hebrew or some inherent "inexactitude" in the language itself.[27] Whatever the case, it is likely that others among the faculty joined him in feeling that it was difficult enough to convey the complexities of difficult texts like the Talmud to rabbinical students without interposing an extra layer of difficulty.

Undecided, Kaplan remained silent at the faculty meeting, and he supposes that this was the reason why Finkelstein asked him to chair a committee (composed of Bavli, Greenberg, Gordis, and himself) that was charged with taking up the issue. As is true with most such documents, the minutes of the 5 May meeting reported the practical recommendations of the committee and recorded little of the substance of the discussion that preceded them. In his journal, however, Kaplan takes credit for framing the argument with such persuasive force that it carried the day, although in fact it was probably only Greenberg who needed convincing. The forcefulness seems to have derived from a very dramatic analogy: "Introducing Hebrew into the Seminary as the language of instruction might turn out to be as significant for the diaspora as introducing Hebrew into the Haifa Technicum a generation ago for the development of Jewish cultural and political life in Palestine." Nothing less. Yet despite the unanimous report in favor of introducing courses taught in Hebrew on a trial basis, there is little evidence that the recommendations were ever taken up.

The appointment of Moshe Davis to the deanship of the Teachers Institute in 1946 represented not only a changing of the guard generationally but a shift in the quality of Hebraism that informed the spirit of the school. The American-born Davis, who was an alumnus of both the Teachers Institute and the Rabbinical School, had served as president in the late 1930s of the *Histadrut Hanoar Ha'ivri*, a youth organization made up of students at the various Hebrew colleges and had edited its journal *Niv*. Davis was also the central figure in the Hebrew Arts Committee (*Va'ad Ha'omanut Ha'ivrit*), which sought to stimulate Jewish creativity in music, theater, and dance.[28] Sylvia Cutler and the man she later married, Moshe Ettenberg, were among the Teachers Institute students who were active along with Davis in these endeavors. Taken together, the *Histadrut Hanoar Ha'ivri, Niv,* and the Hebrew Arts Committee formed a kind of second act in the drama of American Hebraism, and if this new development did not immediately transform the culture of the Teachers Institute, whose teachers were older and central players in the earlier phases of the Hebrew movement, it was destined to do so somewhat later; for it was from these circles, directly though once removed, that Camp Ramah was to emerge. Ramah is one of most important developments in the life of the Seminary and the Conservative movement generally in the postwar years, and it is deservingly the subject of separate studies in these volumes. There is a dimension of the provenance of Ramah, however, which can be understood only through the connection with Hebrew and Hebraist movement.

The complex of *Hanoar Ha'ivri, Niv,* and the Hebrew Arts Committee represents the second generation of the Hebraist movement in America and one which was largely native born. Although the members of this generation did not neglect the duties of filial piety, they differentiated themselves from their predecessors by seeking to widen the horizons of the Hebraist enterprise and connect it to new sources of vitality. If you asked a member of the founding generation (like Bavli, Silkiner, or Ovsay on the Teachers Institute faculty) what it means to be a Hebraist and to participate in Hebrew culture, he would likely list the following: speaking Hebrew, being familiar with modern Hebrew literature as well as with classical Jewish texts, furthering Hebrew education, and contributing either creative or critical

Divided Fate of Hebrew and Hebrew Culture at the Seminary

Faculty of the Teachers Institute meeting under a map of Palestine, 1947. Clockwise from bottom left: H. L. Ginsberg, Reuben Wallenrod, Abraham S. Halkin, Judith Kaplan Eisenstein, Leo Rosenzweig, Sylvia Ettenberg, Moshe Davis, Zevi Scharfstein, Temima Gezari, Joshua Ovsay, Hillel Bavli, Paul Chertoff, Abraham Joshua Heschel. *Photo by Virginia F. Stern. Ratner Center, JTS.*

writing to Hebrew journals. Implicit in this description is a particular model of culture that turns almost entirely on the activities of speaking, reading, writing, and schoolroom pedagogy. For the younger Hebraists this essentially literary model was unacceptably constricting on two counts. The first was the constriction of literature in contrast to an embrace of the arts in all their dimensions. The Hebrew Arts Committee coordinated and publicized the activities of the Pargod Theater, the Galil Singers, the Kinor Sinfonietta, the Rikkud Ami dance group, and other artistic enterprises that stressed Hebrew and national material. Among the younger Hebraists there were some who wrote stories and verse, but this was not a general strength—T. Carmi and Gavriel Preil are exceptions—and one imagines that being born in America and living in a non-Hebrew-speaking environment must have made creative writing in Hebrew difficult.

This in fact was the grounds of the second constriction: the absence of a *havai 'ivri,* a Hebrew ambience or environment. The younger Hebraists chafed at the limitation of Hebrew speech to the schoolroom with its sense of artificiality and institutional propriety. They wished to see Hebrew plugged into the sources of vitality located in life as a whole. This was an aspiration, needless to say, that was very difficult to realize in America. For some the only solution lay in a life lived in Eretz Yisrael. Others were constrained to imagine new kinds of Jewish institutions in which this enlarged role for Hebrew could be experimented with. This was the radical innovation behind the founding of Camp Massad: to create within a sealed-off environment a total Hebrew reality. The fact that Massad had no formal classes was a sign of its desire to liberate Hebrew from the ghettoized demoralization of the classroom. Hebrew was to be lived in the day-to-day activities, events, and interactions, and this seems to be close to what in fact happened. Shlomo Shulzinger, the founder and dominant personality behind Massad, was among the leaders of *Hanoar Ha'ivri*, and his ideas were developed in the debates among members of the movement.

Seminary students were among the first campers and counselors at Massad, and it was they who seceded to form Camp Ramah in the late 1940s. Hebrew and an identification with the culture of the Yishuv in Eretz Yisrael were the supreme values at Massad; conformance to the practices of modern Orthodoxy was more an act of political good sense than a sign of the integration of religious issues into the educational agenda of the camp. The Ramah secession signaled the desire to make the issues of religious faith and observance of the commandments a central focus rather than a by-product of accommodation. The founders of Ramah did not intend to sell out, abandon, or marginalize Hebrew. Yet by taking seriously American Jewish religious experience they did undermine the paramount status of Hebrew.[29] Ideology was affected by sociology. The campers came from afternoon Hebrew schools rather than from institutions like the Yeshivah of Flatbush, and the Hebrew fluency of the counselors could not be counted on either. If the goal was to sensitize campers to the values of *Shabbat*, *kashrut*, prayer, and Jewish learning, then in order to accomplish this some sacrifice of Hebrew as a communicative medium would have to be made.[30]

The hold of Hebrew on the institutional culture of the Teachers Institute from the 1950s onward was affected in a similar way. As Jews moved out from city centers to the suburbs, their children left the central Talmud Torahs with their strong Hebraic emphasis for synagogue religious schools. Not only was their Hebrew preparation weaker when they arrived at the Teachers Institute but, perhaps more important, they were not exposed to the inspired zealotry of veteran educators for whom Hebrew was a life passion. Like the famous *midrash* of the Shekhinah departing the Temple precincts station by station after the Destruction, the presence of Hebrew shrunk progressively within the life of the Teachers Institute, beginning with informal exchanges between faculty and students and among the faculty themselves and proceeding to the language of instruction in the classroom. Exceptions to the rule of teaching in Hebrew multiplied until the province of Hebrew became limited to Hebrew classes themselves.

The weakening of Hebrew at the Teachers Institute is in no way remarkable and reflects the broad decline of Hebrew that resulted in the closing or severe diminishment of other Hebraist institutions. The reasons for this decline are many, but there is one that particularly relates to the Teachers Institute as a unit of the Seminary. The Seminary was a major participant in the explosion of Jewish Studies in America not only by training many of its major figures but also by refashioning itself as a university with graduate programs. In this reorganization, the divergent identities and functions of the Teachers Institute and the Rabbinical School were considerably blunted. The faculty from both units were regrouped within academic departments according to discipline that cut across the institution as a whole. While the undergraduate Joint Program (later the List College) and the Rabbinical School provided different professional training for students, they were both served by the same departments of history, Talmud, Jewish thought, and so forth.

Hebrew was similarly "reengineered" in this academic professionalization of Jewish Studies. Hebrew as a unified matrix of both language and literature—which was certainly the case in the mind of the Hebraists—was dismantled. Hebrew language became a separate department which, in addition to undertaking research in language acquisition and pedagogy, performed the service function of teaching Hebrew for the institution as a whole. This development reflected the growing professionalization of Hebrew teaching on college campuses generally. Hebrew literature was taught in its own department, which later incorporated Yiddish literature and was called the Department of Jewish Literatures. The teaching of Hebrew literature had similarly become professionalized, looking to modern literary criticism for its tools, in a way very much unlike the culture of the dedicated enthusiasts who had taught in the field for so long. Hebrew thus became caught between, on the one hand, the professionalization of academic disciplines and university culture, and, on the other, a loyalty to a cultural program that increasingly adopted a defensive posture. While the study and teaching of Hebrew were taken to new heights of insight and analysis, the era had ended in which Hebrew served as an inspiriting vision.

Appendix 1

Minutes of Meeting of Faculty Committee on Hebrew held on Wednesday, May 5th; present: Professors Bavli, Greenberg, Gordis, Kaplan in chair

Prof. Kaplan presented the character of the problem to which the Committee was to address itself and indicated its theoretic and practical aspects. After a thorough discussion in which every member of the Committee participated, the following conclusions were unanimously adopted as the recommendations of the Committee.

1. The introduction of Hebrew as a language of instruction in the Seminary curriculum possesses important consequences of the most beneficial kind, both for the scholarship of the students, their service to their congregations in later life and the quality of Jewish life in America.

2. The introduction of Hebrew presupposes the abolition of the cycle system, which on completely independent grounds is outworn and inefficient.

3. The principle of bi-lingualism in the judgment of the Committee is completely free from weaknesses. It will not impair the use of the English language by the student body and will, of course, stimulate enormously their interest, love and use of Hebrew.

4. In each instance, the Professor giving the course should decide the language in which he preferred to give it. With the abolition of the cycle system, certain years of a given subject might be given in English and others in Hebrew.

5. Obviously, certain courses would necessarily be given exclusively in English. Such are homiletics and Public Speaking.

6. The Committee feels the need of improving the use of English by the student body. It would suggest the introduction of special courses in literature and composition. This method will prove far more efficacious in bringing about an accurate and cultured use of English than the mere retention of English as the language of instruction.

7. The Committee was particularly impressed by the fact that the request for the introduction of Hebrew came from the student body. It therefore means that the experiment would have the enthusiastic cooperation of the students and therefore would be most likely to succeed.

8. The project would be entirely experimental in character. If after a year or two, the Faculty would feel that it had not justified itself, it could be abandoned without prejudice.

Respectfully submitted,
Robert Gordis

Appendix 2
(From the journal of Mordecai Kaplan, 5 May 1943)

This afternoon the committee to consider the question of Hebrew as the medium of instruction at the Seminary met in my office. The committee consisted of Bavli, Gordis, Greenberg, and myself as chairman. This meeting grew out of a petition that the Seminary students sent to the faculty about two months ago. Among other things they asked that we use Hebrew as its language of instruction. When the matter came up at the Faculty meeting, Bavli argued passionately in favor of granting the students' request. Greenberg was opposed, on the ground that the students are expected to preach and teach in English. Lieberman argued against granting the request on the ground that the use of Hebrew would prevent the students from cultivating exactitude in grasping the subject matter. Gordis rather favored the introduction of Hebrew in subjects which lent themselves most easily. I kept silent, because I could not make up my mind on the merits of either side. For that very reason, I suppose, Finklestein asked me to be chairman of the committee to study the problem. Since then I had been resolving it in my mind. After considerable thought I came to the conclusion that this was too important an opportunity to translate into practice the principle of striving for maximum Jewishness compatible with the conditions that exist in this country. Introducing Hebrew into the Seminary as the language of instruction might turn out as significant for diaspora Judaism as introducing Hebrew into the Haifa Technicum was a generation ago for the development of Jewish cultural and political life in Palestine. That was the basis upon which I put the question when I presented it to the committee this afternoon. Having won complete agreement on that score, I found no difficulty in arriving at a solution of the practical aspect of the question. I had decided to conduct the meeting in Hebrew, because I felt it would be paradoxical for us to prejudice our very decision if we conducted the meeting in English. It would show that even for us who are supposed to have a command of Hebrew, it was not easy or natural to use the language in discussing the feasibility of permanent use as a language of instruction.

1. Herbert Rosenblum, "The Founding of the United Synagogue of America, 1913," (Ph.D. diss., Brandeis University, 1970), pp. 196–209, 289–95.

2. Mel Scult, "Mordecai Kaplan, the Teachers Institute, and the Foundation of Jewish Education in America," *American Jewish Archives* 38, no. 1 (April 1986): pp. 57–84.

3. From the archives of the Reconstructionist Rabbinical College, with kind permission. The passage was provided to me by Rabbi Jacob J. Schacter, who rendered me a great service throughout by bringing to my attention material from Kaplan's diaries bearing on Hebrew.

4. This and all further quotations from Kaplan's diaries are taken from the manuscript of his journals in the Rare Book Room of the Library of the Jewish Theological Seminary; I thank Dr. Ismar Schorsch for permission to consult and quote from the journals.

5. Kaplan's efforts to raise funds for *Hashiloah* were continual; see entry for 24 July 1923.

6. Ms. Aaronson later married Barnett Brickner, a prominent Reform rabbi.

7. The issue of Hebrew in Kaplan's journals is a subject unto itself. There are large portions of the journals that are written in fluid modern Hebrew, and not only on the occasion of Kaplan's trips to Palestine. Although he loved Hebrew, Kaplan was not entirely at home in speaking the language, and he felt intimidated by the fluency of his Hebraist faculty. Taken together, the many entries in the journal concerning his approach-and-avoidance relationship to Hebrew form an important document.

8. Walter Ackerman, "The Americanization of Jewish Education," *Judaism* 24 (1975): pp. 416–35.

9. Kaplan had an astute awareness of the larger political forces among which he navigated as head of the Teachers Institute. In a journal entry for 1 May 1922, Kaplan reflects on a meeting of a committee of the Seminary trustees in the offices of the Strook brothers in which educational matters were taken up and much abuse heaped upon modern Hebrew and Yiddish literature:

   > Here is my situation. I am in the center of a four-cornered fight. At one corner the orthodox abuse me and the Teachers Institute as turning out heretics and nonobservant teachers. At the second corner are the Hebraists who claim that we send out men and women who are totally ignorant of Hebrew and Hebrew literature and only good for what they term "religious schools of the Yahudeim." At the third corner the members of the faculty of the Institute who resent any kind of religious emphasis as being ecclesiastical and would have the Institute turned into a school for Jewish nationalism. And finally Adler and the Trustees who want the Institute to give public school teachers a few lessons in Jewish religion and ethics and lessons in translating its order of prayers. This is their idea of the type of teachers we ought to train.

10. The source of these figures and the general information about requirements of admission are taken from the Seminary Register for 1927. In addition to the full program for the degree, which was aimed at young people training as professionals in Jewish education, there were diploma programs that required eighty-six credits; of these credits, the same proportions were devoted to Hebrew and Bible.

11. Kaplan's remark (see note 7 above) about the Hebraists' preoccupation with quoting text and speaking Hebrew is not far off the mark.

12. Although most Hebraists were Zionists—the exception of Shimon Rawidowicz is an illuminating case—this is not to say that the Zionist movement, as reflected in the array of Zionist parties, and the Hebrew movement were the same thing or always viewed their interests as convergent. It was typical for Hebraists to feel a sense of moral superiority both because of and despite the fact that they exercised little political leverage within the various Zionist movements. Hebraism and Zionism are best conceived of as intertwined rather

III

*Divided Fate
of Hebrew
and Hebrew
Culture at the
Seminary*

than identical. A modern history of the Hebrew movement has not been written and remains a great desideratum. See A. Levenson, *The Hebrew Movement in the Diaspora* (Hebrew) (London, 1935).

13. For a recent account that stresses the latter, see Benjamin Harshav, *Language in Time of Revolution* (Berkeley: University of California Press, 1993).

14. On the Tarbut schools, see Walter Ackerman, "'Nach Palastina Durch Wirballen'—A Hebrew Gymnasium in Lithuania," in *Origins: The Beginnings of Jewish Educational Institutions*, vol. 7, Studies in Jewish Education, pp. 38-53. See Ackerman, note 8, p. 42 for bibliography on the Tarbut schools.

15. Most of the well-known Hebraists who settled in Palestine were not, however, on the faculty of the Hebrew colleges. These included Avraham Regelson, Shimon Ginsberg, Shimon Halkin, and Avinoam Grossman. An exception, Israel Efros, did teach at the Baltimore Hebrew College.

16. For a systematic survey of the colleges, see Isidor Margolis, *Jewish Teacher Training Schools in the United States* (New York: National Council for Torah Education of Mizrachi–Hopoel Hamizrachi, 1964). It is interesting to note that the Baltimore Hebrew College apparently rejected participation in Margolis's survey. See also Walter Ackerman, "A World Apart: Hebrew Teachers Colleges and Hebrew-Speaking Camps," in *Hebrew in America: Perspectives and Prospects*, ed. Alan Mintz (Detroit: Wayne State University Press, 1993), pp. 105-28.

17. "Image of an Institution" (Hebrew), *Hadoar* 14 Iyyar 1959, pp. 486-88; this is a version of a talk given before the Educators Assembly of the United Synagogue on 20 Adar II of that year.

18. Bavli also includes Israel Friedlaender, who was well known for his writings and played a role in the Rabbinical School and at the level of national Jewish affairs. Along with Kaplan, he taught the special classes provided for the Benderly Boys. His murder in the Ukraine in 1920 put an untimely end to an advocate for Hebrew and the national idea.

19. On the journal and Levine's participation in it, see the author's "Sanctuary in the Wilderness: *Hatoren* and the Beginnings of the Hebraist Movement in America" in Mintz, *Hebrew in America*, pp. 29-67. See also the posthumous volume of his writings: *Kitve Moshe Halevi* (New York: Hotsa'at Keren Yisra'el Mats, 5693).

20. Jerusalem, 1910. On Silkiner, see Menahem Ribalow, ed., *Sefer zikaron leB. N. Silkiner* (New York, 5694).

21. See Moshe Davis's admiration for Bavli in the oral history interview with Davis conducted by Mychal Springer, 18 June 1990, p. 19, Ratner Center.

22. Hillel Bavli, *Aderet hashanim* (Jerusalem, 1955), pp. 72-73.

23. It should be noted that between 1938 and 1940, the Seminary was in a severe financial crisis. Funding from the great German-Jewish families had waned, and the strategy of raising money from conservative synagogues had not yet been put into place. The idea of closing the Teachers Institute altogether was discussed. Characteristic of their devotion to the school, the faculty volunteered to take cuts in salary in order to keep the Teachers Institute open (Simon Greenberg, interview by author, 29 June 1992).

24. Jonathan Sarna in his contribution to this work suggests several reasons for this phenomenon; among them were the faculty's feeling of distance from Cyrus Adler and the constituency he represented and the ascendancy of Hebrew as the international language of advanced Jewish scholarship after the founding of the Hebrew University of Jerusalem.

25. Simon Greenberg, interview.

26. The minutes of the faculty meeting are found in R. G. 3B, faculty files, box 1, folder 18 (Robert Gordis file).

27. This second reason would seem strange in light of the fact that Lieberman wrote his mon-

umental work on the Tosefta, with its minute analyses of realia, in Hebrew.

28. The Seminary's Communications Department handled publicity for the Hebrew Arts Committee, and there is correspondence about its activities in R. G. 11, Communications Dept., box 33, folders 30–31. Davis explained the rationale for the undertaking in an article in *The New Palestine* 35, no. 5, (15 December 1944): pp. 2–63.

29. For an account of this period, see Shuly Rubin Schwartz, "Camp Ramah: The Early Years, 1947–1952," *Conservative Judaism* 40, no. 1, (fall 1987): pp. 12–42.

30. For a thoughtful overview of the fate of Hebrew at Ramah, see Robert Abramson, "The Indispensibility of the Hebrew Language" in *The Ramah Experience: Community and Commitment,* ed. Sylvia C. Ettenberg and Geraldine Rosenfeld (New York: Jewish Theological Seminary of America, 1989), pp. 71–84.

NAOMI W. COHEN

"Diaspora plus Palestine, Religion plus Nationalism"

The Seminary and Zionism 1902–1948

Solomon Schechter with Zionist colleagues at Tannersville, New York, around 1909. Front row, from left: Louis Ginzberg, Judah Magnes, Schechter, Samson Benderly, Henry Malter. Back row: Z. H. Bernstein, Alexander Marx, Newman Cowen, M. Schloessinger, A. E. Lubarsky. *Photo by Bickelmann. Ratner Center, JTS.*

NAOMI W. COHEN

"Diaspora plus Palestine, Religion plus Nationalism"

The Seminary and Zionism, 1902–1948

I
T HAS LONG BEEN commonplace in scholarly accounts to note the special bond between Conservative Judaism and Zionism. In *The Political World of American Zionism*, for example, Samuel Halperin wrote more than thirty years ago: "The American Zionist movement derived its most unanimously enthusiastic and dedicated supporters from the ranks of Conservative Judaism."[1] Yet the role played by the Jewish Theological Seminary, the acknowledged head of the movement, in forging the Conservative-Zionist nexus is less obvious. A study of the Seminary and Zionism from 1902 until the establishment of the State of Israel reveals neither unanimity nor ongoing consensus. Among the components that made up the school—administration, faculty and students, Board of Directors—different views of Zionism, reflecting a variety of backgrounds, religious beliefs, and political values, prevailed. At times the subject of Zionism exposed serious differences between the Seminary's administration and the affiliated arms of the Conservative movement—the Rabbinical Assembly and the United Synagogue—who usually outpaced the school in support of Jewish nationalist activities. The overall picture differed markedly from that at the Seminary's older counterpart, Reform's Hebrew Union College (HUC). There, despite sporadic manifestations of Zionist sympathies from students and faculty, a tighter institutional structure (HUC was directly controlled by Reform's Union of American Hebrew Congregations) allowed the first presidents to steer the college along an official anti-Zionist course in tandem with Reform's rabbinical and congregational organizations.[2]

Before 1948 the Seminary never sought or mandated conformity on Zionism. Sabato Morais, who headed the school from its inception in 1886 until his death in 1897, broke with his rabbinical colleagues by speaking out against a man-made restoration of Jews to Eretz Yisrael. In his case, an upbringing in a home of fervent Italian nationalists dedicated to Italian unification failed to elicit his support for modern Jewish nationalism.[3] Unconstrained by those views, Morais's successor, Solomon Schechter, allied himself in 1905 with the Zionist movement. Nevertheless, Schechter insisted that his action in no way bound the Seminary: "I should like it to be distinctly understood that this allegiance cannot be predicated of the Institution over which I have the honor to preside, and which has never committed itself to the [Zionist] Movement, leaving this to the individual inclination of the students and Faculty, composed of Zionists, anti-Zionists, and indifferentists." Since Louis Marshall, chairman of Schechter's Board of Directors, agreed that each director as well as student and faculty member was free to take his own stand, Zionism early on became an extra-institutional matter and, within the walls of the Seminary, a subject that on occasion aroused heated debate.[4]

In large measure differences over Zionism stemmed from variant readings of the Seminary's mission. The religious founding fathers, the pre-Herzl generation of Morais as well as the generation of Schechter and his faculty, envisioned a school for the propagation of historical Judaism in accommodation with modernity. With an emphasis on scholarship, the Seminary would train rabbis committed to *halakha* (traditional Jewish law) but conversant and comfortable with modern intellectual trends and scholarly methods. Aiming for "conservative progress" (Alexander Kohut's term) that would safeguard the future of Judaism against the inroads of Reform and assimilation, the Seminary was pledged to defend the cardinal principles of normative Judaism—the synagogue, *kashrut*, the Sabbath, and Eretz Yisrael. Jewish peoplehood was axiomatic, and a divinely sanctioned return to Palestine was nonnegotiable. All of the Seminary's academic heads before 1948—Morais, Schechter, Cyrus Adler, Louis Finkelstein—subscribed to that mission despite differences in interpretation and differences over political Zionism.

Unlike the religionists, the laymen, who reorganized the Seminary at the turn of the century and set the pattern for the first and for succeeding boards of directors, stressed an American agenda. The patrician circle led in 1902 by Jacob H. Schiff and Louis Marshall were not averse to Jewish tradition in modern dress, but most refused to countenance the idea of a discrete Jewish nationality. They saw the Seminary primarily as an Americanizing agency, one that would produce modern rabbis and teachers to ease the acculturation of the East European immigrant masses and, equally important, to guard them against the nefarious and "un-American" doctrines of secularism and radicalism. More than another philanthropic organization created by the German Jewish establishment, the Seminary took on a practical urgency. It would teach the East Europeans how to retain their religion in a form both respectable and acceptable to Americans. To be sure, Zionists sat alongside non-Zionists and anti-Zionists on the board, but all agreed that Zionism as well as Palestine, a land significant chiefly as a possible haven for persecuted European Jews, was extraneous to the Seminary's program.

Although one vision emphasized the preservation of *Judaism* and the other focused on shoring up the security of *Jews*, the two converged on a critical point. Neither one negated the American Diaspora. Until 1948 the lay leaders for the most part summarily rejected the notion that America was *galut* (exile). They believed that America alone held out the promise of permanent Jewish survival and that it alone demanded undivided Jewish allegiance. The religionists followed a two-centered approach. Nationalists at least in the traditional religious sense, they prayed for a return to Zion, but they deemed the ongoing exilic experience essential to the unfolding of modern Zionism.[5] At the same time, they dedicated themselves to service the religious needs of an American Jewry and to perpetuate the Jewish heritage in the United States. A genuine love of the country also underlay their insistence that Judaism and Americanism were eminently compatible. Thus, however justified, acceptance of Diaspora survivalism united both groups and allowed each to invest in the future of the Seminary.

The outlook of the students reinforced the two-centered vision. The students took pride in their Americanism and were grateful for the country's bounties. Moreover, their education and professional ambitions were predicated on an American future. Like the lay founders of the institution and like American Jews in general, including Zionists, they emended Herzl's laws with respect to the United States. The virulent anti-Semitism that menaced European Jewish well-being and physical security, the base on which Herzl rested his case, did not obtain in America. But although the students also agreed that America was different, their highly developed sense of Jewish ethnicity was virtually ineradicable. Overwhelmingly of East European origin, they bore a cultural baggage steeped in both religious and secular concepts of Jewish peoplehood and nationality. A few of the early ones recalled the Zionist influences that touched them as youngsters in the Old World or in American immigrant homes.[6] Since Zionism was neither taught nor officially sanctioned in the Rabbinical School, it became a popular extracurricular activity. To be sure, not every rabbi ordained by the Seminary was an ardent Zionist; Gerson B. Levi, class of 1904, preached rabid anti-Zionist views when he edited the Chicago-based *Reform Advocate*. But overwhelmingly, in a pattern set by the first graduate, England's Chief Rabbi Joseph Hertz (class of 1894),[7] Seminary men went on to develop their Zionist leanings more fully during their pulpit careers.

Actual clashes within the Seminary between defenders of the one-centered and two-centered approaches were avoided so long as Zionism was little more than a pious dream or an exercise in philanthropy. Tensions mounted, however, whenever Zionism as a secular political movement raised its head or appeared to threaten the image of American Jews that the Jewish establishment so assiduously cultivated. What in each instance determined the administration's position, or its response to conflicting Zionist and anti-Zionist pressures from within the Seminary and from the Jewish and American communities, depended on diverse factors, ranging from the nature of the presidential leadership to the school's financial needs.

Controversy ended with the establishment of Israel in 1948. Then the various components of the Seminary, together with the organizational affiliates of the Conservative movement, united in forging ever closer ties with the Jewish state.

Schechter's Legacy

A CONFIDENT AND OPTIMISTIC Solomon Schechter arrived in New York in 1902. A native of Romania who had received a training in scientific scholarship in Western Europe, Schechter left his post at Cambridge University to undertake a singular mission, the establishment of a rabbinical school and a center of Jewish scholarship dedicated to the teaching of modern traditional Judaism. Convinced that the future of Israel was in America, he believed that the new institution, a "Conservative School removed alike from both extremes, Radical-Reform and Hyper-Orthodoxy," would capture the allegiance of American Jews.[8] Schechter, who had developed a passion for American history and literature and who was a fervent admirer of Abraham Lincoln, delighted in American democratic institutions, which, he was fond of saying, had been inspired by the Hebrew Bible. He judged the practice of Judaism to be fully compatible with Americanism. Indeed, in the free American environment Judaism would flourish, and he, as one admirer put it, would be the new Ezra propagating the Torah in exile.[9]

Almost from the outset, the Seminary's President encountered obstacles that cooled his optimism. Attacks from both Orthodox and Reformers, budgetary needs, the rise of new communal organizations that deflected support from the Seminary, and his own shortcomings as an administrator seriously threatened the viability of the school and its potential for attracting American Jews. Nor did the New World look as rosy as it had from across the Atlantic. Schechter was most troubled by the rapid inroads of assimilation among immigrant Jews. The major problem confronting the community, he wrote, was "not so much the Americanizing of the Russian Jew as his Judaizing." The antireligious stand of the immigrants was partially to blame, but Reform posed an even graver threat to Jewish identity and to the very survival of American Judaism.[10]

Schechter had lashed out in articles against Reform "radicals" while he was still in England. He intensified the attack in the United States, where his new office exposed him to the workings of a Reform movement stronger than in Europe. Time and again he disputed Reform's teachings that divorced mission from nationhood and spirituality from *halakha*, and he repeatedly sniped at the catch phrases of the Reform movement—"prophetic Judaism," "universalism," and "progress." Bent on recapturing the Prophets from skewed interpretations, he charged that Reform's definition of prophetic Judaism amounted to "the giving up of the Torah and uniting with the left wing of the Christians." According to Schechter, the Reformers' cry of "de-Orientalization" was no more than "a piece of theological anti-Semitism . . . copied from Christian theologians," and the Reformers' creed as formulated in the Pittsburgh Platform of 1885 "was bound in the end to land us into what I may call 'No Man's Country,' or 'No Jew's Religion.'" In his inaugural address Schechter warned against such self-destructive tendencies that presaged an inevitable drift to "Paulinism."[11]

His outward friendship with prominent American Reform leaders notwithstanding, the Seminary's President kept up his harsh criticism, even cautioning his graduates against Reform practices ostensibly made in the name of religion. Finding Reform guilty of disloyalty, betrayal, and destruction and sneering at its "Christianizing" and "skyscraping" rabbis, he became, in the words of his biographer, "the leader of a Counter-Reformation."[12]

At the heart of Schechter's counterreformation lay his unshakable belief in Jewish nationhood and nationalism. His East European origins and rich Jewish education had made him a "natural Zionist." His twin brother, a *hovev Zion* (member of the *hibbat Zion* or Love of Zion movement), was among the first settlers of Zikhron Ya'akov; Solomon himself had told Mathilde Roth that if she turned down his proposal of marriage he would become a farmer in Palestine. A Zionist before there was a Zionist movement, Schechter always longed for a Jewish Palestine—"Zionism was, and still is, the most cherished dream I was worthy of having," he wrote at the end of his life.[13] His ongoing battle with Reform revealed his almost instinctive aversion to that movement's repudiation of Jewish nationhood. He by contrast always posited that a Jewish national consciousness was inseparable from the Jewish religious faith. Committed to the survival of the Jews as a distinct people, Schechter judged Reform's antinationalist posture to be untenable, un-Jewish, and, in terms of the community, downright destructive.

When he assumed the presidency of the Seminary, Schechter made use of Zionism as a weapon against Reform. Defining the Jewish problem as Reform-abetted assimilation that was gnawing away at the vitals of Judaism, he saw an antidote in Zionism, a force for the reinvigoration of Jewish life throughout the world. Like Ahad Ha'am (pen name for Asher Ginzburg, a Russian Jewish intellectual), but essentially concerned with religious fundamentals, he dreamed of Palestine as a spiritual and cultural center whose influence would radiate throughout the Jewish Diaspora. The ideal Palestine did not negate the legitimacy of Jewish centers elsewhere; in fact, it depended for its realization on a Diaspora that was religiously and culturally vibrant. In Schechter's words, "There will be no redemption without the proper preceding preparation of the captivity." Thus, from the beginning, he reconciled his hopes for a restored Jewish homeland with American Jewish survivalism.[14]

Schechter's counterreformation served an institutional as well as ideological purpose. The Seminary promised the new immigrants a viable option between the antithetical poles of European Orthodoxy and classical Reform, but in order to attract the religious element who might be influenced by Orthodox taunts at Schechter's *shmadhoys* (house of apostasy), it had to prove that its commitment to tradition radically distanced it from Reform. Furthermore, to gain the confidence of the ethnic-minded East Europeans generally, it had to repudiate Reform's anti-Zionism and show a sympathy for Jewish national aspirations. At the same time, it needed to demonstrate to those most concerned with Americanization that it, no less than Reform, stood for modernity and Americanism. In a letter to Mayer Sulzberger, a trusted friend and a founder of the reorganized Seminary, Schechter explained: "We cannot allow the ignoramuses of the West [i.e., HUC in Cincinnati], who are unfortunately too strongly represented in the East, to monopolize all the patriotism."[15] For all those reasons it behooved Schechter to become the anti-Reformer—to carve out a distinctive traditional yet modern American image for the Seminary and to cast his lot with the Zionist cause.

While in Europe Schechter had refused to join the movement launched in 1897 by Theodor Herzl. To be sure, he recognized the pressures of fin de siècle anti-Semitism, but to his way of thinking, the irreligious, if not antireligious, attitudes of the Zionist leaders distorted the national ideal. "Zionism diverted from the religious idea is a very monster," he said. Schechter had promised Israel Zangwill, an active English Zionist, that he would join the movement when he arrived in the United States, but religionless Zionists looked no more palatable from an American vantage point.[16] The weak and fragmented Federation of American Zionists (FAZ) was, in 1902, a strange alliance of opposites. Its leaders came from the German Jewish establishment—Gustav Gottheil, his son Richard, and Stephen Wise were Reform Jews—but the rank and file were principally of East European stock. Neither group championed Zionism on religious grounds. Nevertheless, if secular nationalism was un-Jewish to Schechter, unchecked assimilation appeared even worse.

From 1902 to 1905 the Seminary's President inched ever closer to announcing his support of the Zionist movement. In a very short statement in the spring of 1904 he publicly endorsed "moral Zionism, which is so wonderfully described by Achad Haam" as the necessary safeguard against assimilation. Although some Zionists resented the implied criticism of their political approach, the arch-Reformer and president of HUC, Kaufmann Kohler, was most outraged. His shrill rebuttal insisted that American Jews were not in exile, that Ahad Ha'amism in America was an anachronism, and that Zionism, however labeled, turned the Jew away from his true mission. Kohler, who was then embarking on a purge of Zionists from his faculty, interpreted Schechter's words as a public challenge to Reform ideology which he, Kohler, could not ignore.[17] While the gap between the two seminaries widened, Schechter recognized the need to mend his institutional fences. Leaning toward formal Zionist affiliation but always aware that several of his most prominent board members were Reform Jews, he deemed it prudent to explain his position privately. As he confided to a close friend in the summer of 1904, "I was lately spending a good deal of time making [Zionist] propaganda . . . among the Jewish aristocracy here." To them too he preached a moral and spiritual Zionism.[18]

Not only did Reformers refuse to yield, but other immediate factors apparently hardened Schechter's resolve to commit himself to Zionism publicly. For one thing, the rupture in the Zionist organization over the issue of territorialism underscored the need to press from within the ranks for a Jewish restoration to the true Zion. Second, Herzl's death in 1904, which Schechter called a "great calamity," exposed a serious void in Zionist leadership. He may well have been intrigued by the prospect of sharing in the choice of Herzl's successor, someone, he said, who could simultaneously "manage" the East Europeans and command the respect of Western Jews. Finally, Schechter was doubtless influenced by his close friendship with Israel Friedlaender. The latter, who joined the Seminary faculty in 1903, shared Schechter's views on Reform and assimilation and on Ahad Ha'am and a creative Jewish Diaspora. A diligent Zionist worker and propagandist, Friedlaender, along with Conservative Jews like Judah Magnes and Harry Friedenwald, was shifting the focus of the FAZ to spiritual and cultural Zionism.[19] In that more comfortable setting, Schechter may have reasoned, his official presence could help bring about the necessary correctives to Herzlian secular Zionism.

Schechter publicly cast his lot with the Zionist movement in a speech delivered in December 1905 at a Zionist meeting and, exactly a year later, in a famous written endorsement entitled "Zionism: A Statement."[20] In both versions he bemoaned Jewish assimilation, particularly spiritual assimilation, or *galut ha-nefesh*. Zionism, he maintained, negated that slow but tortuous process of dying—"Zionism declares boldly to the world that Judaism means to preserve its life by *not* losing its life." He added that the Zionist movement had already begun, and would continue, to strengthen the synagogue, the Hebrew language, and Jewish cultural creativity. Again he scoffed at the Reformers—the "prophetic" Jews who misinterpreted the Bible, called Zionism retrogressive, and marked *tisha b'Av*, signifying the liberation of spiritual Judaism from its nationalist shackles, as a day for rejoicing. Schechter countered that the nationalistic and universalistic elements in Judaism worked in harmony, that "Israel must first effect its own redemption and live again its own life, and be Israel again, to accomplish its universal mission." Zionism, he wrote impassionedly, was the "Declaration of Jewish Independence," the reassertion of the Jewish soul "as natural and instinctive as life itself."

Nothing in Schechter's words contradicted his vision of the Seminary's mission.

To be sure, he stated that "it is not only desirable, but absolutely necessary, that Palestine . . . should be recovered with the purpose of forming a home for at least a portion of the Jews, who would lead there an independent national life." Nevertheless, his approach remained two-centered; his focus was on the Diaspora as much as on Palestine. He neither accepted Herzl's gloomy predictions of exilic conditions nor called for a mass *aliya*. On another level, his Zionist affiliation added strength to the distinctive image that Schechter sought to cultivate for the Seminary. It publicly distanced him, and perforce his institution, further from Reform, and helped by a widely circulated Yiddish translation of the 1906 statement,[21] it doubtless enhanced the attractiveness of the Seminary for the new immigrants.

Coming at a time when, as the quip went, "no gentleman was a Zionist and no Zionist was a gentleman," Schechter's move was a coup for the FAZ and a setback for the anti-Zionists. The abuse heaped by Reform spokesmen on Schechter—he betrayed his own principles as well as the Jewish cause, Kohler charged; he joined the Zionist "Salon de Refuses," the *American Israelite* taunted—supports the contention that Schechter's adversaries also saw Zionism as a significant weapon of a counterreformation.[22]

The Seminary's President was primarily concerned, however, with a controversy that erupted with his board. The fifteen-member board was dominated by banker Jacob H. Schiff, a Reform Jew by affiliation and an opponent of political Zionism. Unassuaged by Schechter's private explanations and prodded by Kohler and other Reformers, Schiff made public a letter to Schechter in criticism of Zionism. More than Reform sympathies prompted the action. Schiff's priorities at that time were first, to alleviate the sufferings of the Jews in Russia, and second, to combat the mounting tide of American immigration restrictionism that threatened to curb the entry of East European Jews. Zionism, which might conceivably cast the Jew in an unfavorable light, could prove highly detrimental to both. Schiff offered religious and practical arguments against Zionism, but the crux of his opposition concerned Jewish loyalties. "Speaking as an American," he wrote, "I cannot for a moment concede that one can be at the same time a true American and an honest adherent of the Zionist movement." Zionists who labored for the establishment of a Jewish nation placed "a prior lien upon their citizenship"; the realization of their hopes would compromise their loyalty to the United States.[23]

The issue of dual allegiance had first been raised in 1904 in Kohler's response to Schechter's "moral Zionism." Schechter answered in his 1905 speech but ignored the subject in his written statement. Nevertheless, the charge of un-Americanism from a man of Schiff's power and influence, and which was pounced on by the press, demanded a forceful rejoinder. An emotional Schechter refused to be drawn into a public fight, but he revealed his deep feelings to Harry Friedenwald, another board member and president of the FAZ:

Both Wall Street and the Pulpit have arrayed against us—by us I mean not only the Zionists, but . . . the Jews who still act and live and believe Judaism. I was and am still contemplating to present a memorandum [to] the Board . . . that though I do not make propaganda for Zionism in the institution I recognize and teach no other theology than that given to us by the Prayer Book and Rabbinic Judaism which is that *u-mipnei hataenu galinu meartzenu* [because of our sins we were exiled from our land] that America is not the final destiny of Judaism, that we believe in the advent of the Messiah who will redeem Israel and bring us back to the Holy Land etc. If they think that these doctrines are incompatible with Americanization as they understand it and which they believe to be the salvation of the Jews they can have my resignation at once. I would prefer to starve than to keep them under any illusion or to abandon my principles.[24]

Friedenwald, scion of a prominent Baltimore family known for general community service as well as Zionist activities, was sensitive to the slight against his father's honor implicit in Schiff's letter. He rose to Schechter's defense and, with the help of Israel Friedlaender and other Zionists, formulated a public response. At a Zionist mass meeting he attacked the Jewish banker, although not by name, for branding his fellow Jews with the charge of treason. On the shoulders of such Jews, Friedenwald intoned, lay the guilt of fomenting anti-Semitism. By formal resolution the Zionists repudiated Schiff's charges, affirmed their loyalty to the country, and called upon Jewish anti-Zionists to desist from harmful accusations.[25]

Schiff was forced to retreat. In a second published letter he denied having ever said that Zionism was incompatible with patriotism, but he still insisted that it placed a "lien" on citizenship. Schechter neither answered nor resigned, and harmonious relations with Schiff were restored. In the long run, the incident did not diminish Schechter's influence over the board. When the directors questioned whether it was proper for him to permit a student Zionist society to meet in the building, the President's view prevailed. In that instance he reportedly thundered to Louis Marshall: "The money bags are not going to rule the Seminary."[26]

An important note to the Schiff/Schechter controversy was added in a public letter by Marshall. The latter abhorred publicity surrounding Jewish differences, but he felt impelled to answer a charge by the *American Israelite* that Schechter had violated a board-imposed taboo on Zionism. Marshall defended Schechter's right to support Zionism publicly; the board, he said, never sought to control the judgment of individual directors, faculty members, or students. He emphatically denied the incompatibility of Zionism with American patriotism, a notion that the *American Israelite* shared with Schiff and which, the chairman of the board insisted, supplied ammunition for anti-Semites. A self-styled non-Zionist who was critical of political Zionism, Marshall nonetheless praised Zionist accomplishments in words strikingly similar to Schechter's:

[Zionism] has been productive of immense benefits to Judaism. It has stimulated a living interest in its history and development among thousands who have hitherto been indifferent to things Jewish, and among many who otherwise would have been lost to Israel. It has rescued Hebrew from the category of dead languages. It has given birth to a manly Jewish consciousness, in refreshing contrast with the apologetic attitude which precedes it. It . . . has made Jewish culture signify something that is positive instead of the shadow of a name.[27]

Ten years later Marshall openly acknowledged the influence of the Seminary's President: "In common with the late Dr. Schechter, I have the greatest sympathy with the cultural Zionism of Ahad Ha'am . . . , and have been interested in the establishment of a Jewish spiritual center in Palestine." Ironically, by then Schiff too had modified his position. Considering affiliation with the Zionists in 1917, he endorsed the establishment of a homeland in Palestine which, he said in Schechter-like terms, would infuse Jews throughout the world with religious inspiration and cultural creativity. Neither Marshall nor Schiff, however, ever joined the FAZ.[28]

Most of the Seminary's directors opposed *political* Zionism; even Friedenwald cast Zionism primarily into a religious mold. But that opposition made them non-Zionists sooner than anti-Zionists. As non-Zionists they sympathized with and contributed to the economic rebuilding of Palestine and its development as a religio-cultural center. Marshall and also Schiff were active sponsors of Aaron Aaronsohn's agricultural experiment station and the Haifa Technion.[29] Indeed, much as they deplored schemes that categorized Jews as a race, nationality, or nation-in-the-making, they shared a deeply ingrained attachment to Palestine. At the same time, they preferred to express their sentiments in arenas other than the Seminary. Friedenwald operated through the FAZ; Schiff, Marshall, and Cyrus Adler fashioned non-Zionist policies through the American Jewish Committee (AJC). Just as Schechter refused to impose his Zionist views on the school, the directors never committed the institution to their opinions. The controversy of 1907 caused no changes in the makeup of the board, and Schiff and Friedenwald continued to serve side by side.

The Seminary's President actively participated in Zionist affairs after 1906, and in 1913 he spoke at the Zionist Congress in Vienna. That same year he, along with Friedlaender and Judah Magnes, influenced the American directors of the Haifa Technion to cast the decisive vote for the use of Hebrew rather than German as the primary language at that school. Schechter also aired his opinions more informally. Since he vacationed some years in Tannersville, New York, where the Zionists held their conventions, he enjoyed opportunities to debate Jewish issues privately as well as publicly.[30]

His Zionist activities never muted Schechter's criticism of secular Zionism, which he deemed as alien to normative Judaism as the teachings of Reform. In *Some*

Aspects of Rabbinic Theology he wrote: "The brutal Torah-less nationalism promulgated in certain quarters would have been to the Rabbis just as hateful as the suicidal Torah-less universalism preached in other quarters." In light of the "radical" (read: irreligious) tendencies among Zionists, he saw a positive value in the Orthodox Zionist organization, Mizrachi. Schechter also found fault with the secularist policies of the leaders of the *yishuv* (Jewish settlement in Palestine before 1948), "a de-Judaized clique . . . who have not a spark of religion in them." Distinguishing now between the "real [read: spiritual] Zionists" and the "Nationalists," he said of the latter: "Theirs is the worst kind of assimilation from which we would shrink back even in America." To Ahad Ha'am he confided grave doubts about religionless schools in Palestine built by secularists—"unripe men, imbued with the most wild theories about religion and social problems, and . . . as fanatical and dogmatic in their statements as their antagonists of the Orthodox party." Shortly before his death, when the religious focus of the FAZ had faded, Schechter warned again of the "spiritual disaster" that irreligious Zionists courted:

> There is such a thing as the assimilation of Judaism even as there is such a thing as the assimilation of the Jew, and the former is bound to happen when religion is looked upon as a negligible quantity. When Judaism is once assimilated the Jew will surely follow in its wake, and Jew and Judaism will perish together.[31]

Schechter's religious Zionism found a ready response among Seminary students, many of whom were already Zionist sympathizers. The young men flocked to sermons and lectures by prominent Zionists and took an active part in Zionist youth and Hebrew-speaking organizations. Jacob Kohn, class of 1907, recalled how he and his schoolmates would travel to the Lower East Side for group meetings and for talks by Magnes, Shmaryahu Levine, and Zvi Hirsch Masliansky. Zionism, Kohn said, made them feel the unity of Israel and the Jewish heritage. The students venerated their President, and the rapport between them was strengthened by Schechter's Zionist stand. At an alumni meeting in 1908 Kohn, then a new rabbi, argued in Schechterian fashion on the legitimacy of preaching Zionism from the pulpit. "The return to Palestine," he stated in part, "was necessary for a proper development of Judaism and Jewish culture and for 'the spark of religious devotion to serve the flame of national enthusiasm.'" Thanks to their own leanings and to the input of Schechter and his faculty, more than 60 percent of the Seminary-trained rabbis in 1914 were, according to one estimate, active Zionists.[32]

True to Marshall's word, the board's views did not intimidate the faculty, and the latter fully supported Schechter's Zionist position. Like the President, all were traditionalist Jews who subscribed to the two-centered vision and the cultural theories of Ahad Ha'am. Their Zionism, however, was a private and low-keyed affair. As Alexander Marx, professor of history, explained, "We were all Zionists—but not active." Except for Friedlaender and the young Mordecai Kaplan, the luminaries of the faculty—Marx, Louis Ginzberg, Israel Davidson—confined their organized Zionist activities primarily to participation in the short-lived Achavah Club. A small group of Jewish intellectuals from a variety of backgrounds who discussed aspects of contemporary Jewish problems from a learned perspective, Achavah limited its membership to "adherents of National Judaism."[33] Rabbi Meyer Berlin, head of the Mizrachi, once expressed his surprise that neither Friedlaender nor Kaplan, the only Zionist activists on the faculty, could induce his colleagues to engage actively in propagandizing for the cause. But the research-oriented scholars structured their priorities differently from the activists. A bitter Kaplan believed that at bottom the faculty was unconcerned with both the training of American rabbis (at whom they sneered) and with the future of Judaism in America.[34]

Friedlaender and Kaplan, who regularly attended Zionist meetings and delivered Zionist lectures, helped to offset the passive Zionism of their colleagues. Their wives followed suit; Lilian Friedlaender, Lena Kaplan, and Mathilde Schechter were among the first directors of Hadassah. Within the Schechter circle, however, it was Israel Friedlaender who chalked up the most impressive Zionist record before the war. An exponent of the two-centered vision, the professor of Bible demonstrated his faith in the future of American Jewry through articles and through his work for communal projects like the New York *kehilla* and Jewish education. At the same time he played a multifaceted Zionist role: organizer, committeeman, polemicist, and, above all, theoretician. Friedlaender credited both Theodor Herzl and Ahad Ha'am with awakening the Jewish national consciousness, but his theory of Zionism was fundamentally Ahad Ha'amism with religious emendations. He saw in Zionism a movement that transcended statehood. Not only was it a powerful tool for Jewish unity but its objective, a normal Jewish life in a new Palestine, promised to revitalize Judaism. By working for a religiously vibrant Palestine where the prophetic ideals could be realized, Zionism would establish a center of religious significance for the Jewish Diaspora and for all humanity. The explicator of "Diaspora plus Palestine, Religion plus Nationalism," Friedlaender aired his beliefs to Jewish and non-Jewish audiences and, privately, even to non-Zionists on the Seminary's board. His views, like Schechter's but developed in far greater detail, made him a major influence on Seminary students, who knew him as the Zionist "par excellence."[35]

Schechter and Friedlaender cast Zionism in spiritual terms and bound it securely to the Jewish Diaspora experience. The resultant product was well suited to take root in American soil. A comfortable Zionism, it satisfied the Jewish ethnic urge, and since it posited the legitimacy of a Jewish center in the United States, it required no personal sacrifice like *aliya*. A religious interpretation and an aversion to secular Jewish nationalism also fit Zionism into the American scheme of things, where Jews were defined as a religious community. Thus, an American Jew could in all good conscience easily hold on to both worlds. At the same time, as the cases of Schiff and Marshall suggest, the religious emphasis slowly succeeded in bridging the gap between Zionists and non-Zionists. By adapting Zionist theory to the preferences of Jews and the host country, Schechter's circle nurtured the prospect of an American Jewish consensus on Zionism.[36]

Adler and "Palestinianism"

Schechter served as President until his death in 1915, long enough to set his style upon the Seminary and its faculty. Although his successor, Cyrus Adler, had been associated with the Seminary for many years—he had taught Bible for Morais, played a critical role in the reorganization of the post-Morais institution, and sat on Schechter's Board of Directors—he seemed a breed apart. His very appearance was different; the native-born President was clean-shaven, his mannerisms and accent were American rather than European. Unlike Schechter, Adler lived in Philadelphia and not Morningside Heights; he neither met the students in the classroom nor entertained them regularly at home; his closest associates were the Schiff-Marshall circle and not the faculty; and his scholarly expertise was in Semitics rather than rabbinic studies. Nor was Adler's daily routine confined to the Seminary, for he devoted at least as much time to Dropsie College, where he served as president, and to the American Jewish Committee. And, in contrast to Schechter and his faculty, Adler was a non-Zionist.

Adler's non-Zionism, Rabbi Israel Goldstein recalled, created an emotional barrier between the President and the Seminary family. But even if he had so desired, Adler was hardly in a position to sway the school to his stand on Zionism. Since the board appointed him temporary President (the temporary was dropped only in 1924), his freedom to shape policy was significantly limited. Moreover, the faculty resented the appointment. Although the Schechter/Adler correspondence reveals Schechter's genuine respect for Adler's scholarly knowledge, those of the inner Schechter circle, notably Ginzberg, Marx, Friedlaender, and Davidson, could not understand how Adler's "un-Jewish" academic credentials allowed him to fill Schechter's shoes. A few had privately harbored hopes of succeeding Schechter. Mordecai Kaplan, whose pronounced dislike of the man lasted throughout Adler's tenure, dismissed the President as a mere flunky of the board.[37] Seemingly cold and stiffly aloof, Adler worked neither at cultivating support among the faculty and students nor at generating the rapport that his predecessor had enjoyed. On the matter of Zionism, he never thought of tailoring his views for the sake of institutional unity. Nor did he labor, the way Schechter had, to integrate his views on Zionism with a philosophy of Conservative Judaism. While he formulated non-Zionist responses to new developments through the AJC, Schechter's Zionist legacy lived on. Borne by the early rabbinical graduates, it stamped the character of the Rabbinical Assembly and the United Synagogue, thereby sowing seeds for tension between Adler and the branches of the Conservative movement.

For a short while Adler seemed a likely recruit for the Zionist movement. When in 1891 he visited Palestine as American commissioner of the World's Colombian Exposition, his emotions were stirred by the beauty of the land, its antiquities, and the exotic customs of native Jews. Simultaneously, his practical sense, alert to the need of a haven for oppressed Russian Jews, led to conversations with the American minister to Constantinople and the Turkish Grand Vizier on the prospects for expanded Jewish settlement in the Ottoman empire. Palestine was the "great hope" of every East European community, Adler said, and he even toyed with the idea that "the Jews of the world can now buy Palestine back." The twenty-eight-year-old American sounded very much a proto-Zionist when he deplored the fact that the destiny of world Jewry depended on the policies and vagaries of the European powers. That situation would persist, he stated, "until we have our own strip of land and our own gunboats." Seven years later Adler heard Herzl speak in London, and although somewhat skeptical of the message, he was charmed by the charismatic Zionist leader.[38]

After 1900, however, Adler turned his back on the Zionist movement, and over the years gained the dubious distinction of being the only prominent Conservative leader unaffiliated with the nationalist cause. Why he became a non-Zionist, or one who outspokenly opposed Jewish statehood but loyally supported cultural and scientific projects in the *yishuv*, has called forth various explanations, some noting in particular his staunch American loyalties and the influence of the leaders of the German Jewish establishment with whom he associated.[39] Those answers are partially illuminating, but only a greater emphasis on Adler's strict religious principles resolves some of the seeming ambiguities of his behavior.

A traditionalist Jew, Adler prayed daily for a return to Zion. Since he believed that "Every good Jew longs . . . for the restoration of Palestine and the coming of the Messiah," he repudiated Reform's contradictory tenets. Adler never disputed the concept of Jewish peoplehood, but loyal to the teachings of his mentor, Sabato Morais, he refused to translate it into a movement for a modern Jewish state. The reader of his letters and speeches senses a pervasive distrust of man-made schemes, be they Reform or Zionist, that tampered with the traditional and divinely ordained roles for Judaism and Eretz Yisrael. Palestine was promised to Abraham for "a holy purpose," Adler once wrote, so that "there might arise upon it a kingdom of priests and a holy nation." He saw a "mystical" element in the hope for a restored Zion, a hope that bound Jews around the world and one generation to the next.[40]

To Adler, Jews were essentially a religious community, one whose distinctive badge and sole justification for existence was its faith. In a dichotomy between

Judaism and Jews, he ranked the former above the latter: "I know that we can have no Judaism without Jews," he told Israel Zangwill, "but I am very little interested in Jews, as Jews, without Judaism." For the sake of Judaism Adler immersed himself in numerous projects that aimed at promoting a Jewish cultural renascence in the United States. Institutions of learning like the Seminary bore special responsibilities since they were the prime defenders of traditional religion. "The 'Paramount' duty of the Jews in America," Adler insisted, "is the maintenance of Judaism in America."[41]

But while his immediate focus was on American Judaism, he never lost sight of Zion. Different from other non-Zionists who contributed to Jewish settlement in Palestine out of sentiment or humanitarianism, Adler emphasized religious objectives: "The Jewish hope is for a restoration to Palestine where upon the historical soil of the Holy Land with the Holy City as its center Judaism may be cultivated with renewed vigor and from there as a center radiate out to the Jews of the entire world and revive the religion where it is growing cold or colorless." A defender of multiple centers for the growth of Judaism, he disputed the negation of the *galut* that deflected Jews from their religious obligations in the Diaspora. Besides, dispersion had enriched Judaism, and a Diaspora was necessary for the upbuilding of a Jewish Palestine. A contributor to a variety of cultural, religious, and even economic institutions in the *yishuv*, Adler preferred the label of "pro-Palestinian" rather than non-Zionist. At times he distinguished between Zionists and nationalists (as Schechter had), implying that his kind and not the "radical" and religionless nationalists were the true Zionists.[42] He long cherished the hope of making non-Zionism an organized cohesive force within the community, but his sporadic efforts along those lines proved futile.

In accordance with his deep religious convictions, Adler was repelled by Herzl's policies, and any youthful fantasies about gunboats or strips of land quickly evaporated. The Basle program was critically flawed precisely because it did not mention religion, and political Zionism, or a secularist movement for Jewish statehood, betrayed the essence of Judaism. Ignoring the existence of God, Zionism "has . . . promoted a pagan idea which deified the soil and the people." Nor had Zionists "discovered" Palestine for Jews. Rather, they were the upstart usurpers who laid fraudulent claims to a land that throughout history had belonged to all Jews. Since Zionism divided the community, shortchanged both Judaism and Jews, and threatened to derail them from their proper course, it boded only ill. "I would consider a settlement in Palestine on an anti- or non-religious basis the greatest misfortune that has happened to the Jews in modern times," Adler once stated. There was only one way for Zionism to establish its legitimacy—i.e., if Zionists acknowledged the importance of religion and indicated that their objective was the cultivation of Judaism on Palestinian soil. In that case, Adler later said, he would have favored the movement "even with the view at some future time of the creation of a Jewish commonwealth."[43]

To be sure, Schechter too opposed secular Zionism, but he compromised in order to counteract Reform and assimilation. While he also emphasized the preservation of Judaism, he never subscribed to Adler's arbitrary distinctions between Jews and Judaism. Whereas Schechter linked nationhood with the enrichment of Jewish cultural creativity, Adler concentrated on the renewal of a religious tradition, be it in the Diaspora or Palestine, that was seemingly independent of territorial moorings. Schechter, an East European by birth, empathized with the victims of anti-Semitism; the American Adler understood their plight only intellectually. Since Schechter shared Jewish aspirations for political autonomy, which Adler did not, he was prepared to work from within the Zionist fold to correct perceived abuses. Adler, more rigid and uncompromising, and more bitter about Zionist heresies, stayed aloof. "The hope for a restoration of Israel to Palestine is a part of my Judaism and I do not have to join a party which has not recognized Judaism as a part of its platform in order to realize my own Judaism."[44]

Practical considerations hardened Adler's opposition to Zionism. He long thought that Mesopotamia was a wiser choice for beleaguered European Jews looking for a haven, and it is quite possible that he helped in the formulation of the early Mesopotamia plan, usually accredited to one of Adler's teachers at Johns Hopkins, Paul Haupt. Adler reasoned that Mesopotamia offered distinct advantages over Palestine—fertile land, far less chance of Christian, and hence Turkish, opposition, and a possibility of outright purchase from the sultan.[45] Solely a pragmatic choice, Mesopotamia neither raised the dreaded specter of Jewish statehood nor interfered with the traditionalist hope for Eretz Yisrael. Moreover, colonization there instead of in Palestine might easily win the support of anti-Zionist Jewish philanthropists.

Shortly before the Basle Congress of 1897, perhaps in a purposeful effort to defuse the popular enthusiasm generated by the nascent Zionist movement, Adler raised the matter of Mesopotamia with Herzl. But the latter failed to respond. The American was not a man who took such rebuffs lightly or readily forgave them, and although Herzl contacted Adler some two years later, he had little use for the Zionist leader from then on. Alluding to Jewish hopes raised and then dashed by false messiahs, he once referred to Herzl as "the *mashiach* from Vienna." Adler's interest in Mesopotamia persisted, and in 1909, encouraged by the appointment of a close friend, Oscar Straus, as ambassador to Turkey, Adler and his circle seriously considered it again.[46]

On a different level but equally unpalatable was the democratic format of the Zionist organization. (Herzl had initially hoped that Baron de Rothschild would underwrite his plans, but in light of the baron's disinterest he fashioned a democratic movement that was pitched to the masses.) Although the American Adler gloried in the blessings of democracy for the United States, he was an elitist with respect to the Jewish community. One prominent Zionist complained that Adler "does not concede to the discussion of Jewish problems the same degree of freedom and frankness which he would concede to discussions of American policies." Adler's devotion to the AJC, a hand-picked group that arrogated to itself the right to speak for American Jewry, was accompanied by an aversion to democratic organizations and democratic political tactics on the part of the Jewish minority. Publicity and noise invariably accompanied mass meetings, popular elections, petitions, and demonstrations, and unlike quiet diplomacy they succeeded only in awakening anti-Jewish sentiments in the larger society. Personal resentment on Adler's part crept in too. To him and his associates, the untutored immigrant masses who used Zionist fronts for challenging the wisdom and practical experience of the AJC were foolhardy as well as ungrateful.[47] Too thin-skinned for the give-and-take of a democratic forum, Adler would turn increasingly bitter in the open fight with the Zionists over a Jewish congress.

Unlike Reform anti-Zionists in the prewar era, Adler gave little credence to the charge of dual allegiance. His own "Palestinianism" neither contradicted America's definition of Jews as a religious community nor suggested any incompatibility with Americanism. When the Schiff/Schechter controversy erupted, Adler maintained that he as an American citizen was not obliged to account for the religious convictions that underlay his views of a restored Zion. Privately he defended the Zionists too. The ever cautious Adler feared a public uproar that could impact adversely on the Seminary, and although he admitted that Schechter may have erred in arousing Schiff, the latter's statement that Zionists could not be good Americans was "indefensible."[48] His criticism of Schiff proves that Adler's religious principles rather than the influence of his associates, or for that matter his patriotism, constituted the bedrock of his opposition to Zionism.

Adler assumed his Seminary post at a time when the crusade for Americanization, generated by the outbreak of the war, was reaching new heights. Jews and other minorities could not escape popular insistence on conformity and 100 percent Americanism. Some Jews, as Mordecai Kaplan recounted in his commencement address of 1916, expressed their ardent patriotism by ranking America above Judaism on their scale of loyalties.[49] But others, like American Poles, Czechs, and Irish, were fired by the Wilsonian principle of national self-determination to press for the creation of an independent homeland. When, in the Balfour Declaration of November 1917, England vindicated Herzl by approving "the establishment in Palestine of a national home for the Jewish people," Zionists were elated. They, as did many Christian Americans, regarded it as a promise of statehood.

At the Seminary, Israel Goldstein recalled, reaction to the Declaration was surprisingly low-keyed. The students, all Zionists, appreciated its significance, but

Goldstein thought it curious that not one felt impelled to enlist in the Jewish Legion. Since the faculty for their part did not interrupt their scholarly pursuits, the normal routine prevailed.[50] Outside the school's walls the Balfour Declaration elicited more animated responses. Israel Friedlaender, for example, publicly applauded the British statement, and along lines drawn earlier, underscored the need of a physical homeland for the recharging of Jewish unity and religious creativity.[51] At the same time, through the AJC, Cyrus Adler and his influential board members responded differently, demonstrating that the Declaration had not closed the gap within the Seminary family over Jewish nationalism.

In 1915, acting as chairman of the AJC's executive committee, Adler had informed a senator from Arkansas that "although I am not a Zionist I think that it could easily be recognized that upon religious grounds, even without considering political grounds, the Jews have a claim to some sort of specially favored treatment in Palestine." He did not elaborate on what he desired, but in 1917 he didn't find the answer in the British statement. Practical obstacles stood in the way of its implementation, and even its very words were ridiculous—a national home, he once said, reminded him of "a big orphan asylum." At bottom, Adler was objecting to the politicization of Zion implicit in the Declaration and its recognition of the Jews as a political entity rather than a religious people. He reiterated his hope for a restoration to Zion, but again he insisted that Palestine belonged to all Jews and was not the exclusive province of the Zionists and again he emphasized the religious purpose of a Jewish home in Palestine. "Whether it be as an independent state or under English or Turkish sovereignty, Palestine is sacred and should be for those Jews who want to go to Palestine to practice Judaism."

The capture of Jerusalem by the British in December 1917, another boost to the Zionists, prompted Adler to push for an immediate response from the non-Zionists. He reasoned that if they failed to seize the opportunity, leadership on the Palestine question would go by default to the Zionist movement. Ever eager to legitimate non-Zionism as a viable option for American Jews, he drafted a statement again indicting the religionless Zionists and suggesting a Zionist-called conference representative of the major Jewish organizations to formulate common objectives. In deference to the AJC, which had yet to be heard from, Adler was persuaded, however, not to publicize his statement.[52]

The formal response of the AJC to the Balfour Declaration, written by Adler and two others, gave the British pronouncement a bland non-Zionist endorsement. Expressing sympathy with the traditional Jewish hope for a home in Palestine, the committee promised to cooperate "with those who, attracted by religious or historic association, shall seek to establish in Palestine a center for Judaism, for the stimulation of our faith, for the pursuit and development of literature, science and art in a Jewish environment, and for the rehabilitation of the land." The AJC narrowly construed the Declaration: it talked of "a" center and not "the" center, it limited its support to a religious and cultural center, and it ignored the controversial word "national." The committee's response signaled no retreat on Adler's part but merely reconciled his long-held convictions with the dramatic turn of events. His non-Zionism, or the pursuit of a restoration for the sake of Judaism, remained very much alive. The coincidence of British imperialist interests with the Zionist hope dispelled some of his doubts about the practicality of the Zionist movement, and the ambiguous wording of the Declaration allowed him to interpret England's approval of Jewish settlement in Palestine to be as much a victory for his side as for the Zionists. To be sure, his aversion to Jewish nationalism increased during the war years, but like Schiff and Marshall he refused to endorse the plan of Reform Rabbi David Philipson in 1918 for a conference to combat Zionism.[53]

The idea of a democratically chosen congress to represent American Jews and speak on behalf of Jewish rights at the postwar peace conference challenged the elitist AJC and its self-assumed prerogative over Jewish diplomacy. Enthusiastically endorsed by the Zionists under the magnetic leadership of attorney Louis Brandeis, a congress readily appealed to the East European masses. Communal pressure and a fear for its very survival compelled the AJC to search for a compromise with the Zionists, causing Adler, who headed the negotiations for the committee, to grow increasingly bitter. He had no respect for Brandeis, an "agitator" who had turned his back on the Jewish people until his mid-fifties and was unmoved by the plight of Russian Jewry "before we poor Jews attracted his august and interested attention." Adler strongly believed that the propaganda for a congress in the name of democracy, but which actually bore the stamp of radical socialist influence, was in fact a Zionist plot to capture control of the Jewish community. Machine-like political tactics of the congress partisans disgusted him, and attacks on the committee's leaders led him, along with Schiff and Marshall, to consider resigning from Jewish communal affairs. In the end, the AJC was forced to yield, and Marshall joined the delegation of the American Jewish Congress to the peace conference. Although Adler categorically refused to be involved with the new organization, he was persuaded to go to Versailles in 1919 as special representative of the AJC.[54]

The congress issue exposed a major point of contention between Adler and the Zionists—Diaspora nationalism. Since Adler construed the words "national" and "nationality" narrowly, in the sense of discrete political identity and citizenship, he deemed them utterly repugnant to modern Diaspora life. Moreover, a congress that attempted to organize Jews along national lines appeared downright dangerous, particularly at a time when hyperpatriotism gripped the country.[55] Objecting also to the Zionist demand for national rights in postwar Eastern Europe, he thought that proportional representation for Jews as a separate nationality was doubly impossible—it was impossible to achieve, and were it achieved, it would place the Jews in an impossible situation. After the war Adler blamed the idea of a separate Jewish nationality, a product of political Zionism, for contributing to the ugly wave of anti-Semitism in America.[56]

The historic events of the war years mellowed the views of his friends, Schiff and Marshall, on Zionism, but Adler was unmoved. Indeed, the congress experience hardened his resolve to distance himself from the Zionists. Harboring a permanent grudge against Brandeis and his circle, he explained that he preferred not to associate with those who were indifferent or hostile to Judaism. Nor did he change his mind about Jewish nationality or any Zionist view that defined Jews as a nation. The Torah and not race or nationality was the true bond of Israel, he told the Seminary graduating class of 1920, but Zionism shifted the center of gravity from the Torah to the land and the people. The Seminary's President pledged his continued help in the upbuilding of Palestine, but he turned down an invitation to join the newly established Zionist Organization of America (ZOA) in 1918. Religion was still uppermost in his brief against the movement, and he charged Zionist unwillingness to interpret their program Jewishly with failure to secure the allegiance of American Jews. It was strange, he mused, that while Americans saw fit to recognize God in the Declaration of Independence, Jews, "whose specialty is religion," ignored God.[57]

The Seminary still refrained from taking an official stand on Zionism, but as wartime events transformed Zionism from a largely theoretical to a real and immediate issue, Schechter's policy of institutional noninvolvement appeared increasingly illogical. Prominent members of the Seminary family in addition to Adler were very much involved in the congress episode. Zionist board member Harry Friedenwald, in opposition to the non-Zionism of the AJC and of fellow board members Schiff and Marshall, resigned in protest from the committee. Professor Israel Friedlaender, whose attempted reconciliation of the AJC and the congress supporters failed, washed his hands of both groups. Schechter himself had objected to the idea of a congress. He did not live long enough to fight alongside Adler, but nationalist agitation may have fed into the warning he gave of the potential "nightmares" in political Zionism shortly before he died.[58]

Adler's activities through the AJC were bound to affect his influence within the Seminary community. True, he wore two separate hats, but assessments of the man who qualified the promise of the Balfour Declaration and who fought Brandeis, the American Jewish Congress, and national rights hardly distinguished between the non-Zionist chairman of the AJC's executive committee and the Conservative leader. Nor was it natural for Adler himself to put aside his views upon entering the Seminary's doors. The gap between the non-Zionist President and board on the one hand, and the Zionist faculty and students on the other, widened. As Seminary graduates went on to bring the Zionist message to the rapidly multiplying Conser-

vative synagogues after the war, the differences with their President strained both
Conservative unity and the Seminary's leadership of the movement.

A major crisis over Zionism within Conservative ranks erupted at the United
Synagogue convention of 1917. Hitherto the organization, controlled at that time
by rabbis and faculty members, had glossed over Zionism. Now, in line with a community effort to show support of England's anticipated Declaration, it considered a
resolution that would have formally joined it with the Zionists in endorsing the
claim to a legally recognized homeland in Palestine. Adler, president of the United
Synagogue, immediately protested, insisting that the matter lay beyond the constitutional purview of the organization. Furthermore, he in all good conscience could
not vote for the Basle program. A stormy debate followed. Although the vast majority of delegates were affiliated Zionists, many found serious fault with Zionist leaders and tactics. (Samuel Cohen, class of 1912, who subsequently served as executive
director of the United Synagogue, called the Zionist organization in America "cor-
rupt, atheistic, and anti-Jewish.") Some countered, however, that the issue was
more important than the Zionists. How could they, men who prayed daily for Zion,
not do a thing to help realize the restoration? Moreover, as Friedlaender insisted,
many of them shared the conviction that there was no hope for Judaism without
Zionism. Finally, the delegates agreed to a resolution couched in religious terms:
"The United Synagogue of America reaffirms its faith in the fulfillment of our
ancient Zionist hope in the early restoration of Palestine as the Jewish homeland as
the means for the consummation of the religious ideals of Judaism."

Adler's defeat had been cushioned, but since the United Synagogue had in effect
allied itself with the irreligious Zionists, it was nonetheless a defeat. The convention dealt him a second blow by proceeding to elect a delegate to the American Jewish Congress. Adler had threatened to resign over the matter as early as 1915, and
interpreting the convention's act in 1917 as a vote of no confidence, he carried out
the threat. His words at the session betrayed a stubbornness and inability to compromise: "It seems that the Jewish people consider their interests at the present time
differently from the way I consider their interests. But I still believe I am right. I can
never believe in the majority. If I had believed in the majority, I should never have
been a Jew." Convinced that the convention scenario had been written and executed
by the "inner council" of Zionists, he bitterly contemplated the misguided delegates who had fallen into the Zionist trap. As in the AJC/congress controversy, he
preferred to withdraw entirely if the game was not played on his terms.[59]

Adler's wartime behavior, and his near paranoia about Zionist plots, accentuated
the rift between him and the Zionist graduates of the Seminary. Sermons and articles by a few of the prominent Zionist rabbis—Solomon Goldman, Israel Goldstein, Israel Levinthal, Simon Greenberg—as well as *Proceedings* of the Rabbinical
Assembly conventions, reveal some of the salient differences.[60] The rabbis too

aimed for a spiritual-cultural center in Palestine, but they did not limit their Zionism to that end alone. Enthusiastic about what a restored Zion could do for *Jews* and not only Judaism, they optimistically viewed the Balfour Declaration as a license for a Jewish homeland. (Adler on the other hand insisted that the Declaration meant only "home" and not homeland.[61]) It was incumbent upon American Jews, the rabbis said, not to let that license lapse but to turn their religious sentiments into concrete actions for the rebirth of Palestine. Buttressed by the philosophy of cultural pluralism, they did not fear the word "national," as in Jewish "national" homeland or Jewish "national" interest, nor did the bogey of secular nationalism deter them from positions of leadership within the Zionist movement. Solomon Goldman served as president of the ZOA (1938–40), and so too did Israel Goldstein (1943–45). Ironically, the Conservative rabbis, who ministered to an upwardly mobile middle class in the United States, supported a labor-oriented economy in the *yishuv*. In 1935 the Rabbinical Assembly, along with 241 Reform rabbis, publicly endorsed the programs of the Histadrut and the League for Labor Palestine.[62]

During the interwar period the rabbis infused their congregations through the pulpit and Hebrew schools with strong Zionist sentiments. Opposition from congregants was minimal, usually limited as in the case of Goldstein's B'nai Jeshurun or Milton Steinberg's Park Avenue Synagogue to the older Germanic element in the community. The overwhelming consensus that the rabbis forged testifies to their own Zionist commitment and to the ethnic needs of their members. It also lends credence to the idea that Zionism in the synagogue filled an ideological void in Conservative Judaism. Indeed, so attractive was Zionism to the congregations that even Solomon Goldman worried lest it secularize the synagogue. At the same time, the rabbis, the bearers of the two-centered vision, sought ways of making Zionism applicable and relevant for American Jews. At convention after convention the Rabbinical Assembly discussed not only the need to inculcate a *spiritual* Zionism among the laity but also ways of integrating cultural developments in the *yishuv*—Hebrew pronunciation, art, music—into American Jewish life.[63]

To be sure, on certain key matters the rabbis and the Seminary President thought alike. Both stood for loyalty to America—the rabbis no less than Adler—and for the upbuilding of the *yishuv*—Adler no less than the rabbis. Both affirmed a Jewish future in the Diaspora; neither asked for *aliya* from America, which was "home"; and both preached an American Judaism that was synagogue-centered. The rabbis too opposed secular Zionism, and even those actively engaged in Zionist affairs insisted at almost every convention on a restored Palestine grounded in Jewish religious values. (Robert Gordis recalled how he and several colleagues belonged for a short time to Hapoel Hamizrachi just because it combined a loyalty to traditional Judaism with a progressive social orientation.)[64] In 1937 the Rabbinical Assembly formulated its "Pronouncement on Zionism," a statement that stressed the spiritual and ethical essence of the Zionist movement. Since it skirted the issue of statehood, and since, like Adler, it criticized Zionist bans on the use of Arab labor, the statement was hardly a challenge to the President's views.[65]

Differences, however, outweighed similarities. Kaplan's characterization of Adler as a "fanatical anti-Zionist" who always found reason to complain about Zionism was exaggerated, but others agreed. When Adler delivered a glowing report to the Rabbinical Assembly in 1929 on the accomplishments of the *yishuv*, one rabbi wryly commented that the President's show of enthusiasm warranted the *she-hehiyyanu* blessing.[66] At bottom, Zionism was a "gut" issue, and deep emotions overlay reasoned arguments. Adler never shared the ethnic yearnings of the rabbis, and his religious and "mystical" bond with Palestine did not satisfy them.

On the surface, tensions between Adler and the Zionist rabbis eased in the 1920s. England's acceptance of a mandate over Palestine put the issue of statehood on hold, and the resignations of Brandeis and his lieutenants weakened the popular attractiveness of the ZOA. On both the world and American scenes political Zionism gave way to Palestinianism, permitting Zionists and non-Zionists to unite in the common goal of building up the land. Chaim Weizmann successfully wooed American non-Zionists like Marshall and Adler, in part by minimizing the importance of political agitation, and differences over matters like Jewish nationalism and the religious component in Zionism were suspended. Marshall, who more than anyone labored to establish a pro-Palestine consensus, argued that it behooved non-Zionists no less than Zionists to provide a haven for Jewish immigrants, now barred by restrictive legislation from entering the United States. Moreover, since the Balfour Declaration was written into the mandate and hence sanctioned by international law, American Jews, the most powerful Jewish community in the world, courted disgrace if they remained aloof or indifferent to the opportunity of establishing a home in Palestine.

Adler fully agreed, noting too that America's association with the Allies insured the compatibility of Palestinianism and American interests. He joined Marshall in support of economic ventures on behalf of the *yishuv*, including the Weizmann-sponsored Keren Hayesod, and ultimately in the formation of an enlarged Jewish Agency comprised of both non-Zionists and Zionists. To be sure, the non-Zionists were forced to accept the phrase "Jewish National Home" in the preamble to the constitution of the enlarged agency, but Marshall reassured them that the likelihood of a Jewish majority in Palestine, with the attendant possibility of calls for statehood, was unreal. While their goodwill was genuine, the non-Zionists doubtless also hoped that cooperation in the agency and a course of active Palestinianism would help them regain the ground they had lost to the Zionists in the wartime struggle for communal leadership.[67]

Palestinianism suited the rabbis too. Sermons that stressed the similarities between spiritual Zionism and American values, and hence the legitimacy of two centers for the American Jew, were now very much in place. At the same time, the Conservative message of spiritual Zionism injected a needed and meaningful ideological note into a cause that had lost the vigor and glamour of the Brandeis era and had become little more than a philanthropy. Palestinianism also spared the rabbis, who like American liberals generally recoiled in the aftermath of the war from extreme nationalism and from the need to square their universalist ideals with the aim of Jewish statehood. Perhaps most important, a Zionism linked primarily to religion and the synagogue well served the wishes of the congregations. In a decade whose hallmark was national conformity, the Jewish masses, shedding their immigrant status and intent upon acculturation and mobility, were afraid to affirm more than a religious identity. Not to accommodate to societal pressures, or to magnify separate ethnic or Jewish national interests, fed into the ugly anti-Semitism that echoed at the time from the circulation of the *Protocols of the Elders of Zion*, the Ku Klux Klan, and Henry Ford's *Dearborn Independent*.

In the cooling-off period that Palestinianism provided, Adler found common cause with the arms of the Conservative movement in support of religious and cultural undertakings for the *yishuv*. One shared venture was a plan for the construction of Jeshurun, an American-like synagogue-center in the Rehavia section of Jerusalem. Before the war Adler had spoken of the need for synagogues in Palestine to represent religious Jews with "dignity," and in the 1920s, concentrating anew on the spiritual development of a Jewish Palestine, he interested board member and philanthropist Felix Warburg in the Jeshurun idea.[68] The United Synagogue enthusiastically sponsored the project, which secured endorsements from the Rabbinical Assembly, the Women's League, and from Jews in the *yishuv*. To the Conservative rabbis and the congregations Jeshurun presented a concrete answer to a much-discussed question: What can we contribute, other than money, to a Jewish homeland? Conservative leaders believed that it was their right no less than their duty to nurture religious life in the *yishuv*. Rabbi Max Drob, president of the Rabbinical Assembly in 1927, stated bluntly: Since our men bear the brunt of the United Palestine Appeal, "we are therefore justified in demanding that the upbuilding of Palestine should be spiritual as well as economic." In a sentence that Adler himself could have written, Drob added: "We should make it clear that a God-less Palestine is a contradiction in terms."[69] The Jeshurun project dragged on, still unfinished at the end of World War II. Meantime, in 1935, the synagogue was donated to the *yishuv*.[70]

Support of the Hebrew University in Jerusalem also united Adler and the rabbis. The idea of a modern university was first raised in the 1880s with the *hibbat Zion* movement, and it slowly captured the interest of leading Jews. Adler too endorsed the idea shortly after it was discussed at the World Zionist Congress of 1913. The barriers against Jewish students in European universities, which, he predicted, would spread to the United States, called for the consideration of a university in Palestine. By the early 1920s the Seminary's President was fully immersed in overall planning for the institution—governance, budget and fund-raising, curriculum and faculty. Just as he believed that Palestine belonged to all Jews, so did he view the Hebrew University as an institution to serve Jews throughout the world.[71]

Adler served on the university's board of governors and academic council, but his particular interest was the Institute of Jewish Studies. True to his principles, he hoped that rabbinic Judaism would be the regnant philosophy at the institute and that Jewish studies would be "Jewish" as well as Hebrew. "The Institute," he wrote, "should not be a merely cold-blooded theoretical establishment, but one which in some way may tend to a religious and spiritual revival." As he explained in a statement prepared for the formal opening of the university: "The two thousand and more years of the development of the Jewish people as a religious people has created a point of view which has a right to find a place in all subjects where opinions play a part."[72] At the inauguration ceremonies in 1925 Mordecai Kaplan spoke in Hebrew for the Seminary. He too expressed hope that the university would become a "spiritual center" where *Torat Yisrael* would be joined with secular knowledge.[73]

With Adler's blessing other members of the Seminary family became involved in the operations of the university. Louis Ginzberg chaired a committee of the American Academy for Jewish Research (which included Adler) that helped shape the character of the institute, and in 1928–29, beginning a tradition of service by Seminary faculty members as visiting professors in Jerusalem, he taught Talmud at the university. The Hebrew University also gained the generous financial support of Felix Warburg, Jacob Schiff's son-in-law and friend of the university's chancellor, Judah Magnes. Warburg and his wife were captivated by Palestine and Chaim Weizmann during a visit in 1923, and the board member shared some glowing memories of the land in his address at the next Seminary commencement. (Nevertheless, he took care to add that his support of the university allied him not with the statists but with those who believed in Palestine as a center for Jewish learning.) Although his Jewish consciousness never approximated that of

Felix Warburg (1871–1937). *Photo by Underwood and Underwood. Ratner Center, JTS.*

Adler or Schiff, it was Warburg ironically who suggested that rabbinical students spend a year in Jerusalem for religious inspiration. Opposition to political Zionism remained, but Adler and the board felt sufficiently comfortable with Palestinianism to relax their suspicions and display a warmer interest in the *yishuv*. In 1926 the Seminary voted an honorary degree to Hebrew poet, Hayyim Nahman Bialik.[74]

Not all the branches of the Seminary during Adler's tenure were content merely with Palestinianism. The Teachers Institute (established in 1909) and its affiliated department, the Seminary College of Jewish Studies (1931), which catered to men and women who sought professional training as Jewish teachers as well as those intent on pursuing a Jewish education for its own sake, were far more nationalistic than the administration and the Rabbinical School. Unlike the Rabbinical School, the Teachers Institute chose modern Hebrew as its language of instruction, and the students took courses dealing with Zionism and the "Neo-Hebraic Renaissance" as well as with the geography and history of Palestine. The popular extension classes of the Teachers Institute, the Israel Friedlaender Classes, which trained communal workers and leaders of Zionist youth organizations, also contained a strong Zionist component. The bent of the Institute's curriculum reflected the powerful Zionist commitment of the faculty. Indeed, Mordecai Kaplan, principal and later dean of the Teachers Institute, complained about those faculty members "who resent any kind of religious emphasis as being ecclesiastical and would have the Institute turned into a school for Jewish nationalism." He also charged that most of the staff dismissed his attempts to adjust Jewish life to American conditions, preferring, he said, "self-withdrawal" into a Hebrew ghetto and eventual *aliya*. Kaplan was himself an active Zionist, but he opposed both a secularist bias and the negation of the Diaspora. Simultaneously, he resisted the pressures of Adler and the board who questioned the curriculum's emphasis on modern Hebrew belles-lettres and who, according to Kaplan, would have preferred to see the Teachers Institute limit its instruction to prayer and religion. He, like Schechter before him, believed that Hebrew was an indispensable tool for cultivating Jewish consciousness and survival. The Hebraic and nationalistic core of the Teachers Institute and Seminary College held fast, and it deeply influenced hundreds of students.[75]

Moshe Davis, a distinguished alumnus of both the Teachers Institute and Rabbinical School, fondly recalled Kaplan's faculty of the 1930s—learned teachers who loved their students, were American *maskilim* (followers of the Jewish Enlightenment), and were all deeply "Zionist motivated." He singled out the foremost Zionists—Kaplan, Morris Levine (Moshe Halevi), Hillel Bavli, and Abraham Halkin. Halkin, for one, unabashedly used the classroom to preach *sh'lilat ha-golah* (negation of the Diaspora). Davis cogently contrasted the "two Seminaries" of his time: (1) a non-Hebraic Talmud-centered rabbinical department whose focus was on scholarship and where Zionism was passive, and (2) the Teachers Institute which emphasized Hebrew and Jewish nationalism and which propagated active Zionism among its students.[76] (Indeed, as this writer recalls, Teachers Institute students boasted of such distinctions between them and the rabbinical students.) Davis himself was one of approximately 250 graduates of the Teachers Institute who, as of 1993, had gone on *aliya*.[77]

Zionism at the Teachers Institute called down neither the wrath nor the censorship of the administration. Adler disliked Kaplan primarily for two reasons—his religious philosophy and, in the eyes of the President and the board, his attempt to carve out an independent empire on Seminary turf. Kaplan's Zionism did not enhance his palatability, but since Adler was squarely opposed to "heresy-hunting," he did not ban Reconstructionism much less nationalism from the classroom.[78] The Zionist stance of the Teachers Institute left its mark on two generations of graduates who went on to teach at Jewish day and afternoon schools, and like Schechter's legacy to the rabbis, it strengthened the ties between the Zionist and Conservative movements.

The deeper question of how Zionism was relevant to an American Jew of the 20th century was tackled by Mordecai Kaplan and his Reconstructionist philosophy. In early articles and in his magnum opus, *Judaism as a Civilization* (1934), Kaplan laid out a program that was eminently suited to the contemporary American environment. Influenced by American pragmatic thinkers, he consistently affirmed Diaspora survivalism as well as strong American loyalties. At the same time, however, Jewish peoplehood and Palestine were central to his thought. In the Reconstructionist formula Palestine was the hub of the Jewish wheel, the source and inspiration for a vibrant civilization in the Diaspora. Kaplan once referred to himself as a "Judaist" rather than Zionist, for he ranked cultural Zionism, a means of preventing Jewish life from being "submerged" in a non-Jewish environment, above *aliya* or political statehood. He also posited that a successful *yishuv* depended on a flourishing Diaspora. A center in Palestine that both nurtured and was nurtured by the Diaspora community constituted an elemental, and indeed unquestionable, component of Jewish survival: "Any healthy minded Jew," Kaplan wrote in 1929, "could not help but feel to the very marrow of his bones . . . that without Palestine reclaimed by the Jews there was nothing left for the Jews to do in the world."[79]

Kaplan's popularity in more than fifty years of teaching at the Rabbinical School and the Teachers Institute crested between 1920 and 1945, corresponding roughly to Adler's tenure. An important study by sociologist Charles Liebman explains that his attractiveness to students, usually the best and the brightest, lay in his understanding of their problems with Orthodoxy and his willingness to address issues, religious and social, that the rest of the faculty avoided. Students of that generation found Kaplan "politically correct": he was unafraid to challenge religious traditions; he drew from the same philosophical, anthropological, and sociological ideas that they imbibed at secular colleges; he was the social justice liberal of the New Deal era. In short, Kaplan put Zionism in a context most meaningful to children of immigrants grappling toward a reconciliation of their American and Jewish identities and priorities. Reconstructionism bridged their two worlds, and Kaplan's Zionism, stripped of theological imperative but buttressed by modern scholarship and encased in a larger philosophical framework, satisfied their ethnic consciousness.[80]

The relative tranquility of the Palestinian era was shaken by the Arab riots of 1929. American Jews united in a mammoth relief drive for the Jewish victims, but questions surfaced again within the community, as well as from the government and non-Jewish opinion makers, about the legitimacy of Zionist aims. Compounding the divisions of opinion on how to react both to the Arabs and the British, Chancellor Judah Magnes of the Hebrew University, a disciple of Schechter and close friend of the Adler circle, injected his own scheme for peace in Palestine. Independently of Weizmann and the Jewish Agency, Magnes called for direct negotiations with the Arabs for a democratic binational state. He defended his plan on the grounds of spiritual Zionism and Ahad Ha'amism; the choice, he said, was political, military Zionism—concretized in the imperialistically motivated Balfour Declaration and mandate that flew in the face of Jewish ethical and universalist principles—or "pacific, international, spiritual Zionism." The plan was well calculated to attract the American non-Zionists, providing them with a platform on which to support Palestinianism, decry the evils of political nationalism, and defend the liberal cause of Arab rights. Seminary board member Felix Warburg, for example, was one such supporter, since the plan jibed with his vision of Palestine as a vibrant interreligious center of Jews, Christians, and Arabs.[81]

Magnes's plan, which suited the anti-imperialist and pacifist mood of postwar liberal intellectuals, relates to the Seminary story precisely because it exposed a crucial juncture at which the Schechter legacy of spiritual Zionism diverged from political Zionism. Classical Zionists found the plan unpalatable and downright destructive. Was a Zionism predicated on the vision of a Jewish state that functioned ethically as the "light unto the nations" realistic in a modern world where the amoral base of statecraft was the norm? Should a Jewish state judge itself, and expect to be judged, by moral standards that did not apply to other nations? The binationalist solution, failing to satisfy the Jewish nationalist impulse or the practical urgency that gave rise to Zionism in the first place, automatically dashed all hope for a Jewish state in Palestine, at least so long as Jews constituted a minority within an Arab majority. The plan also fell short of the dream of cultural Zionists, for it was hardly likely that a Jewish minority in a binationalist state, without ironclad guarantees of physical security, political equality, and economic opportunity, could create a culture vibrant enough to invigorate Diaspora Judaism. Magnes, however, who

posed his solution in the either/or terms of normative political Zionism or religious
and ethical values, was not budged. Better to renounce a national home and to
return Jews to the ghetto, he said, than to compromise Jewish spiritual integrity.[82]
Other spiritual Zionists may have not gone that far, but the tension between spiritual Zionism and pragmatic statecraft has sustained an ongoing debate in American
Jewish circles ever since.

At the Seminary in 1929 opinions divided too. Mordecai Kaplan and Louis
Finkelstein, then a lecturer in theology, favored negotiations with the Arabs, but
broaching the idea at that time aroused student resentment and ran the danger of
being branded "traitor." Adler too desired a Jewish/Arab understanding, and he
agreed, albeit vaguely, that Magnes's thinking was "on the right track." But, he was
far less enthusiastic than Kaplan. The latter gave his "hearty approval" to the
Magnes plan, and he even sought out Joseph Levy, the *New York Times* correspondent in Palestine who had acted as an intermediary between Magnes and the Arab
side. Kaplan was also critical of the Balfour Declaration—"a foreign body in the
system of Jewish revival . . . liable to set up a dangerous poison"—and of Zionist
relationships with the Arabs. As in the case of Magnes, the principle of "ethical
nationhood" qualified his Zionist vision.[83]

In the immediate aftermath of the riots Adler's importance in the Jewish diplomatic arena grew. He succeeded to the presidency of the AJC upon Louis Marshall's
death, and in the enlarged Jewish Agency he and Warburg assumed Marshall's
unofficial role as the ranking non-Zionist. (Adler was a member of the agency's
council and administrative committee, and Warburg chaired the administrative
committee.) Both Adler and Warburg were committed to the upbuilding of Palestine, Adler from the vantage point of a religious Jew and Warburg from an interreligious interest. Neither one possessed Marshall's statesmanlike abilities or his
understanding of ethnic sensibilities. Of the two, Adler was more sympathetic to
the *yishuv* and to cooperation with the Zionists. He was still critical of certain
Zionist policies, particularly those that he thought contributed to the riots, but
unyielding on the principle of free Jewish immigration into Palestine, he pressured
Warburg to resist any such curtailment by the British. Nor did Adler encourage
Magnes, who was bitterly denounced by the Zionists, the way Warburg did. He
found fault with certain points of the Magnes plan, and above all he chided its
author on the need for "corporate responsibility." It was inappropriate and ill-
advised for anyone, particularly the head of the Hebrew University, to launch a
course of independent diplomacy that bypassed Weizmann and the agency executive.[84] Adler was a legalist and strict constructionist; a team player in the agency, he
called for the policy making through the proper channels.

Adler's role in the agency brought him closer to Zionists and Zionist goals than
ever before. Having voluntarily assumed responsibilities in the agency, he felt hon-

orbound to uphold its constitution, no longer to question the wisdom of the Balfour Declaration or even the term "Jewish National Home." To be sure, his support of the public campaign after the riots for the physical reconstruction of the *yishuv* did not weaken his personal religious sentiments regarding Palestine. Building up the land, he told a Jewish audience in 1930, transcended pragmatic concerns: "There are many more reasons in Jewish history, in Jewish sentiment, and in Jewish religious feeling, why it is a happiness for a person who really possesses these feelings to take part in the rebuilding of the Old Land." Nor did participation in the Jewish Agency alter Adler's priorities. The desire to nurture Judaism, and in Palestine too, remained primary. As he insisted when endorsing the need for religious schools in the *yishuv*, a Jew's religious duties were not fulfilled merely by settlement in Palestine. Nevertheless, responsibility to the enlarged agency, which he regarded as pivotal for Jewish unity, mellowed his earlier criticisms of the Zionist movement. Adler also came to recognize, sooner than most, that the non-Zionist approach of separating philanthropic from political involvement was logically untenable. Economic aid, he told Warburg, could not but affect public policies regarding taxation, industry, and military security. Although he implicitly acknowledged that aid to the *yishuv* in whatever form contributed to the growth of an independent state, he personally was not deterred.[85]

Adler's loyalty to the agency was strengthened by Weizmann's request that he prepare a position paper on the Jewish right of access to the Western Wall. Rival claims to the Wall by Arabs and Jews had triggered the riots, and the League of Nations appointed a special committee to decide the issue. The task appealed to Adler; it drew upon his scholarship as well as his religious interests, and he liked to think that he was chosen because he was a "moderate" who headed a modern religious institution like the Seminary. In a well-researched memorandum, he showed the sanctity of the Wall to Jews ever since the destruction of the Temple. His argument was that the unbroken Jewish customs of pilgrimage and prayer at the Wall, attested to in both Christian and Jewish sources, had never been forbidden by Ottoman authorities and therefore still obtained.[86]

A committee of the League ultimately upheld the Jewish right of free access, but the overall Palestinian situation ended on the gloomy note of the Passfield White Paper (1930). Recommending restrictions on Jewish immigration and land settlement, it outraged both Zionists and non-Zionists. Although Adler publicly counseled continued reliance on England's good faith, he shared the community's anger and despair. Very likely his feelings were echoed in a resolution drafted by his wife, Racie Adler, and adopted by the Women's League. Registering its "deep sorrow and bitter disappointment" with England's policy, the Women's League stated: "We had so completely trusted the oft-repeated assertion that the Mandate which embodies the Balfour Declaration would be fully carried out, that we had come to regard this as something fixed, the answer to our prayers for 2,000 years." Adler himself tore apart the major points of the White Paper. He reiterated at a council meeting of the agency that the Jewish national home was internationally guaranteed—"We belong in Palestine as of right and not on sufferance." Again he insisted that the honor of all Jews was at stake.[87]

The problems of Palestine increased in the new decade. As the partners in the enlarged Jewish Agency squabbled over power, the fallout of the Great Depression threatened fund-raising and the very solvency of the agency. At the same time, persecution unleashed by Adolf Hitler underscored the need of Palestine as a secure refuge.[88] In Palestine itself, Arab riots broke out again in the mid-1930s. Admitting the unworkability of the mandate and the futility of seeking an Arab/Jewish modus vivendi, England's Peel Commission in 1937 proposed the creation of separate Arab and Jewish states. Against the backdrop of Nazi terror, Chaim Weizmann convinced the badly divided Twentieth Zionist Congress to give its qualified acceptance to England's offer. The plan, however, aroused the resistance of American non-Zionists and many Zionists. When the Rabbinical Assembly, for example, alluded to partition in its "Pronouncement on Zionism" (1937), it affirmed that no political settlement could be construed as a renunciation of the Jewish claim to "the whole of Palestine."[89]

At the opening reception of the Seminary's academic year in 1937, Adler registered his opposition to partition, stating that it would not contribute to peace in Palestine. Like others, including Weizmann, he had never believed that a Jewish state was a forseeable possibility, and now he was less than sanguine about its viability. He couched his objections in terms of the practical fiscal and military difficulties that a Jewish state would face. Resistant to any radical change, he faulted England for failing to live up to the terms of the mandate and for failing to hammer out amicable relationships between the Arabs and Jews. As the alternative to partition he and his circle suggested that England fulfill its obligations as the mandatory power and that the Arabs and Jews continue to negotiate toward a peace within a united Palestine. Toward that end they mounted an aggressive campaign, cooperating with English non-Zionists and American Zionists to pressure Weizmann. Some held separate talks with Arab leaders in New York; others muttered about leaving the agency. Desperately seeking the maintenance of the mandate as it was created, their plan was at best a holding action.[90]

The very idea of Jewish statehood alarmed some non-Zionists, but Adler now appeared less rigid. "As a non-Zionist," he wrote, "I do not at all deplore, or indeed did not deplore the establishment of a Jewish commonwealth." He didn't explain what he meant by a "commonwealth," but neither did he reject out of hand the mention of political autonomy. Agonizing over the plight of German Jewry, and as a loyal member of the Zionist/non-Zionist partnership in the agency, he pledged continued financial support of the *yishuv* regardless of the outcome of partition. Nor did he fall back upon the binationalist solution that Warburg preferred. While the banker ranted about "that miserable Jewish State" that threatened all sorts of complications, Adler rejected permanent minority status for the Jews in Palestine or any stoppage of Jewish immigration, especially if similar bans were not imposed on the Arabs. According to Morris Waldman, executive secretary of the AJC, Adler resisted not statehood but Diaspora nationalism, or attempts to organize Diaspora Jews along political lines. True, the expectation that Diaspora Jews would continue to fund what would become a foreign state might raise problems of divided loyalties, but Adler denied that the status of Western Jews would be compromised. Under pressure of world events, and as a policy maker in the agency, he had shifted his views considerably since 1917. Indeed, had England interpreted the Balfour Declaration and mandate along the lines laid down by Adler in 1937, an autonomous Jewish commonwealth might well have emerged. But after a year and a half of wrangling, England abandoned the partition scheme.[91]

The partition episode not only testified to differences of opinion within the non-Zionist camp, it also revealed the sentiments of the Seminary's board. Adler and Warburg, the leading American non-Zionists in the Jewish Agency until their deaths, were both life directors of the Seminary, and so were non-Zionists Sol Stroock and Irving Lehman. The same men dominated the non-Zionist AJC, whose response to partition mirrored Adler's stand. In both the committee and the Seminary Adler was very much an influential policy maker and, Mordecai Kaplan's comment to the contrary notwithstanding, never a mere flunky of the board. Whereas Schechter officially had been only an employee of the board, Adler, a board member too, was a peer.[92]

The non-Zionist views that Adler shared with the board made themselves heard on occasion within the Seminary's walls. On the one hand, the significance of Palestine as a Jewish center was always acceptable. At a Conference on Jewish Affairs, which the Seminary sponsored in 1937 as part of its semicentennial celebration, one of the dozen roundtable discussions dealt with "The Place of Palestine in the Development of Jewish Ideals." The very title reflected Adler's approach, and a paper delivered by Rabbi Abraham Heller, himself an ardent Zionist, emphasized the positive results of Zionism—the regeneration of Jewish values and Jewishness, a sense of Jewish unity, a haven for the persecuted—results that could hardly have offended the non-Zionists.[93] On the other hand, the idea of a separate Jewish nationality, particularly at a time when Nazis were propagating racial theories and when even the liberal *Christian Century* doubted that Jewish peoplehood made for proper Americanism, was anathema. The drive for a World Jewish Congress, a body predicated on the assumption that Jews constituted a discrete national group, raised the hackles of Adler and the board, and both the President and director Sol Stroock used the podium at two Seminary graduations to counter the nationalists. Adler, who expounded on the dangers of claiming that Jews were more than a religious group, even faulted a student sermon for its discussion of Jewish nationalism. But the President never attempted more serious indoctrination within the Seminary, and the faculty and students of the 1930s—"We were *all* Zionists," Judah Nadich (class of 1936) recalled—continued to march to a different drummer.[94]

The MacDonald White Paper of 1939, which drastically reduced Jewish immigration to Palestine, was bitterly condemned by both non-Zionists and Zionists. Unity was still elusive, but the Nazi terror compelled some non-Zionists to think more positively about a state in Palestine. Less than a year before his death, Adler and five other leading non-Zionists drafted a letter to Chaim Weizmann listing their criticisms of Zionist policies and setting forth their terms for remaining in the agency. Since they disapproved of the White Paper and minority status for Jews in Palestine, they had little recourse but to accept the solution of statehood. They now called for a state in which all lived together as equal citizens free from the domination of any one group. When and, more important, how to achieve a state that guaranteed political democracy but where Jews were not a permanent minority were, perhaps intentionally, left unexplained.[95]

Adler headed the Seminary until his death in 1940, but his tenure of twenty-five years had no telling effect on either the faculty or the students, much less on the affiliated branches of the Conservative movement, with respect to issues of Jewish nationalism and Zionism. Although all agreed on the need to build up the *yishuv*, unity ended there. In a pattern fixed during World War I, when Adler was most resistant to political Zionism, the President and the board pulled one way and the faculty and students another. Meantime, the Rabbinical Assembly and United Synagogue charted their independent courses, looking sooner to the ideas of Schechter, the revered colleague and teacher, than of Adler, the aloof, part-time administrator.

During the interwar period, Adler dealt with Zionism through the AJC and the Jewish Agency, and his activities reflected upon the Seminary because he happened to be President of the institution and not because he was *the* Conservative spokesman. The challenge of making the Seminary *in fact* the recognized leader of a unified Conservative movement devolved upon his successor. Like Schechter, Adler died at the beginning of a world war that dramatically altered the course of political Zionism. In the onrush of events the non-Zionist position of Adler and the board became increasingly untenable, and the next administration would be pressed to take a stand either for or against a Jewish state.

A Time of Crisis

The succession of Louis Finkelstein to the presidency came as no surprise to the Seminary family. Finkelstein had risen through the ranks; ordained in 1919, he left his congregation in 1931 to teach full time at the Seminary and to serve as Adler's assistant and provost. Recognized unofficially as heir apparent, he enjoyed a warm and congenial relationship with his chief. The two men shared a commitment to scientific scholarship and to traditional observance both as a personal and institutional norm.[96] Even the sensitive issue of Zionism, which had aroused considerable anti-Adler sentiment among Finkelstein's rabbinical colleagues, did not strain the bonds of mutual trust and respect. To be sure, Finkelstein was a card-carrying member of the Zionist Organization, but since he was a staunch opponent of political as well as secular nationalism, his Zionism was purely of a spiritual nature. Indeed, an early statement of his—"We want to see Palestine rebuilt; we have for it . . . an intuitional, unreasoning, and mystic love"[97]—could very well have been made by Adler. Finkelstein's stand on a Jewish Palestine presaged no significant change in administration policy, and had critical events between 1940 and 1948 not intervened, it would hardly have aroused any debate.

The new President had a passion for study and for scholarship—by 1940 he had produced major works on the Pharisees and Rabbi Akiba—but, so different from his oldest friend, Solomon Goldman, he took little interest in the politics or strategy of modern Jewish state-building. Unlike Schechter and Adler, Finkelstein neither engaged in public polemics on Zionist policies or personalities nor campaigned actively, the way the non-Zionist Adler had, for building up the *yishuv*. He followed Adler into the executive councils of the AJC but not into the Jewish Agency. His popular writings that touched on Zionism reveal how he concentrated on fitting modern Zionism into the religious chain welded by his heroes, the Prophets and the spiritual leaders of the Second Commonwealth. Seeking to apply his scholarship to this-worldly activities, he viewed the establishment of a Jewish Palestine through an historical-religious lens.[98]

Finkelstein began with two premises. One affirmed the need of Palestine for the religious Jew: "I believe that every Jew has a religious duty to strive to live in Palestine as the Holy Land of Israel; that because of the association of prayer and ceremonial with the Holy Land, he can worship God in Palestine in a manner in which he cannot worship Him anywhere else in the world."[99] The second underscored the place of Palestine in a vibrant Judaism: in his words "Judaism without Palestine is spiritually retarded." The land, he maintained, was necessary for the development of the prophetic teachings of peace, equality, and social justice. His objective was a Jewish community in Palestine dedicated to the observance of the Torah, the living word of God, and one that would, as the spiritual center of Israel, spark Jewish creativity. He spoke vaguely at times of a predominantly Jewish Palestine[100] or of an autonomous community, but substance always took precedence over political form.

A religious community in Palestine had a larger purpose as well. Citing the views of Rabbi Akiba, Finkelstein insisted that nationhood had meaning only if Israel existed for an ideal outside itself. Upon a Jewish Palestine lay the responsibility of contributing to the survival of civilization by making God's reality manifest to the world and by transmitting the message of the fatherhood of God and brotherhood of man. He liked to think of a restored Palestine as the "third commonwealth," infused with the same spiritual vitality that inspired the deeds of Ezra, the Hasideans, and the Pharisees and that molded the spiritual life of both Israelites and non-Israelites. It followed that if the world cherished the prophetic ideals taught by the Jews, it would help in the rebuilding of Palestine.

Finkelstein's form of spiritual Zionism emphasized the universalist role of Judaism but did not delimit it, as classical Reform did, to religious contributions. Israel as the kingdom of priests had more to impart than a message of monotheism. Positing the ongoing creativity of Israel, Finkelstein affirmed in an early talk that the people's historical contributions to civilization in prophecy, religious law, philosophy, and poetry had not exhausted their potential: "What future creations lie latent in the still growing mind of Israel we do not know." All attempts at creativity deserved encouragement: "Jewish art, Jewish music, the renaissance of the Hebrew language as the medium of daily intercourse, and above all the rebuilding of the Jewish homeland, have all our enthusiastic support." The Hebrew University, for example, to which he promised Seminary cooperation early on, illustrated his point.[101] Zionism was therefore a good; itself a product of Jewish creativity, it held out the promise of renewed creativity for the benefit of mankind through a Jewish center.

Palestine as the spiritual hub of Judaism—and Finkelstein usually used the term "Judaism" in preference to "Jews"—never negated the viability or desirability of the American Diaspora. Jews had found spiritual as well as material well-being in America, for the ethical values of the Founding Fathers were identical to those of the Pharisees. Moreover, American Jews too were called upon to render service to God, Torah, and mankind. The Seminary in particular, which Finkelstein likened to the academy at Yavneh, had a universal mission. Just as the spiritual influence of Yavneh transcended the material glories of the Hellenistic world, so might the Seminary (with Finkelstein perhaps as the American Yohanan ben Zakkai?) similarly serve mankind. Privately Finkelstein may have agonized that he, an observant Jew, could not live a full religious life outside Eretz Yisrael,[102] but his beliefs reinforced the two-centered vision of the Seminary.

Finkelstein's emphasis on universalism and on spiritual rather than political Zionism bore distinct traces of the American liberal creed. Coming to maturity during the Great War, his generation repudiated the militarism and hypernationalism that in their opinion had precipitated the world conflict. Their faith in a new postwar world was rudely shaken by the failure of the League of Nations and the rise of totalitarianism, but they held fast to the twin beliefs of universalism and pacifism. In the case of Finkelstein, who found reinforcement for them in rabbinic teachings, the ideals assumed even greater significance.[103] They fed his aversion to power politics in general and to the politics of Jewish state-building in particular.

Finkelstein's refusal to make Jewish political sovereignty a Seminary objective never seriously undermined his control over the students and faculty. The more nationalistically minded grumbled, but since the Seminary did not mandate conformity, they were free to act out their Zionist sentiments independently. Besides, the President had a singular ability to keep his institution in line. A forceful and magnetic leader, charming and hospitable, worldly but unassuming, he could reason, cajole, conciliate, and, above all, inspire loyalty. Unlike his predecessor he was a "hands on" president, a respected teacher as well as astute administrator, whose single-minded dedication to the Seminary was exemplary and whose scholarship earned universal admiration. Students and faculty neither rebelled against his determination to keep the Seminary more traditionalist than Conservative nor forced his hand on Zionism.

The Rabbinical Assembly and United Synagogue, despite some disaffection with Finkelstein's Zionist approach and administrative policies, were similarly captivated by the personality and achievements of their classmate and colleague. When the Seminary launched a joint fund-raising campaign, which gave the school the power to allocate funds to the arms of the movement, their submission to the President and the Seminary was virtually total.[104] In fact as well as in theory the school under its fourth President spoke for a centralized movement. And, just as the Seminary was the fount of Conservative Judaism, Louis Finkelstein was the Seminary.

The Board of Directors of the Seminary also accepted Finkelstein's religious Zionism. No more representative of Conservative Judaism than their predecessors, the members lacked the deep Jewish attachments of a Schiff and a Marshall. But although they were predominantly anti-Zionists or non-Zionists, they could empathize with the principles of universalism and mission that suffused the President's ideology and rhetoric. They genuinely revered Finkelstein for his piety and his learning,[105] and they too responded to his charm and charisma. To this author's knowledge, he functioned for some as personal counselor and spiritual guide. The board also saw that Zionism did not impede Finkelstein's major plans to broaden the institution's outreach to Christians, principally intellectuals, as well as to Jews. In 1937 when Finkelstein, then provost, coordinated the Seminary's semicentennial celebration that featured prominent Christian academics, he was chided by Solomon Goldman for "constantly running after the goyim." Finkelstein solemnly answered that American Jews were obliged to educate others in Jewish values, for without a relationship with American Christians, Judaism would survive only as a reaction to anti-Semitism. Nor did he find it inappropriate, the way Goldman had, for board member Lewis L. Strauss, a Reform Jew and anti-Zionist, to serve as chairman of the celebration.[106]

The board cheered on Finkelstein's interreligious projects. Through ongoing conferences and institutes—the Institute for Religious and Social Studies (1938) brought together Christian and Jewish clergymen; the Conference on Science, Philosophy and Religion (1940) joined Jewish and Christian scholars—and by educational devices like *The Eternal Light* radio programs (1944), Finkelstein succeeded in stamping the importance of Judaism on the religious map of the United States. At a time when Americans invoked the religious roots of democracy to provide the antidote to totalitarianism, he taught that Judaism, at least as much as Christianity, deserved proper recognition. The man who did most to gain respectability among Christian leaders for the "Judeo" component of the "Judeo-Christian" tradition, Finkelstein strengthened the board's pride in the Seminary. Doubtless in their eyes he was transforming the institution from a parochial yeshiva geared to service East European immigrants into a creative intellectual center harnessed to the needs of the entire nation.[107]

Zionism became a potentially disruptive force to the smooth administration of the Seminary only when demands for an independent Palestine resurfaced in the 1940s against the backdrop of the Holocaust. At that time Finkelstein was forced to confront the issue of Jewish political nationalism and somehow reconcile three discrete factors: his personal convictions, the board's hostility, and the Zionist loyalties of the students, faculty, and Conservative movement at large.

Finkelstein's views of Zionism did not arouse public comment before he became President. His interest after the riots of 1929 in Jewish negotiations with the Palestinian Arabs was a topic of conversation only among Seminary students; his opposition to partition in 1937 was voiced privately and merely to show his support of the Adler-Warburg stand.[108] Less than a year after he assumed office, however, Zionists pounced upon the man who now headed the Conservative movement.

In March 1941 Lord Halifax, British ambassador to the United States, invited three rabbis—David de Sola Pool, Louis Finkelstein, and Israel Goldstein—to a private conference on the issues facing American Jews. Halifax raised the subject of Zionism, and the rabbis assured him that while they differed on minor points they were all Zionists. In the course of the conversation Finkelstein commented on the irreligiosity of modern Jews in Palestine which shocked Christian leaders but which, he had reason to hope, would change. Immediately after the meeting, when Pool and Goldstein rebuked him for those gratuitous remarks, he replied that he believed in being honest about such matters, and besides Halifax, a religious man, was probably well aware of the facts. Finkelstein may have felt that a defense of spiritual rather than political Zionism would appeal to the ambassador, but in Zionist eyes he had tarnished the image of a united Jewry in support of the *yishuv*. Although the conference was supposed to remain confidential, Goldstein leaked the substance to several leading Zionists, including Chaim Weizmann and Stephen Wise, and the Seminary's President became fair game for the nationalists.

A Zionist smear campaign ensued: Finkelstein had maligned the *yishuv*, and, at a time when the British White Paper had cut the sole remaining lifeline for Jews trapped by the Nazis, he was no better than a *moser* (informer against the Jews). Weizmann did not return Finkelstein's call; Wise refused to shake Finkelstein's hand at a social occasion. Furious with a now contrite Goldstein (who at once attempted to defend Finkelstein to Weizmann), the Seminary's President told his colleague that the "poison" was rapidly spreading. "If unchecked, the trouble will spread to Palestine; it is all over Brooklyn now, and will be told to Chief Rabbi Herzog." He claimed that he was concerned more for his institution than for himself.[109] Different from Adler, Finkelstein wanted to be, and was, judged as the leader of the Seminary and the Conservative movement. His office gave him public recognition and clout, but as this episode taught, it put constraints upon his speech and behavior.

World War II radically changed the course of American Zionism. British intransigence with respect to Jewish immigration into Palestine, compounding the horrors of Hitler's war against the Jews, testified to the inadequacy of a passive Palestinianism or gradualist Zionism. The crisis demanded an immediate refuge for European Jewish survivors, and since refugees had long been a drug on the international market, Zionists fixed upon Jewish political autonomy as the one solution for keeping open the gates to Palestine. Under the influence of a new generation of leaders, David Ben-Gurion in Palestine and Abba Hillel Silver in the United States, they assumed a more militant approach. At a Zionist conference at New York's Biltmore Hotel in May 1942, more than six hundred delegates, calling for unity within the movement, demanded free entry into Palestine, control over immigration and land development by the Jewish Agency, and the establishment of Palestine "as a Jewish commonwealth integrated in the structure of the new democratic world." In order to make support of a commonwealth coextensive with the Jewish community and to force the non-Zionists into line, the Zionists orchestrated the organization of an American Jewish Conference. At dramatic sessions in August 1943, representatives of more than a million and a half American Jews endorsed the Biltmore program and thus resurrected Herzl's call for a Jewish state. Their action, Mordecai Kaplan predicted, "will probably figure prominently in the annals of the modern Jewish renaissance."[110]

The new Zionist militancy revitalized the die-hard anti-Zionists. In the summer of 1942 a small group of Reform rabbis initiated what soon became the American Council for Judaism. Embittered by the Biltmore program and by the action of Reform's Central Conference of American Rabbis (CCAR) endorsing the creation of a Jewish army in Palestine to fight alongside the Allies, the dissidents published a statement in condemnation of political Zionism. It denied neither the plight of the refugees nor the admirable achievements of the *yishuv*, but it contended that a nationalistic and secularistic movement contradicted the cardinal tenets of Judaism.[111]

Rabbi Philip Bernstein, also a Reform rabbi but an active Zionist, immediately consulted with several prominent rabbis, including the presidents of the Rabbinical Assembly, CCAR, and Rabbinical Council of America (Orthodox), who proceeded to draft a counterstatement. Arguing that Zionism was fully compatible with Judaism and its universalistic teachings, that Jews like other peoples enjoyed the right to political self-determination, and that Zionism did not weaken the undivided loyalty of Jews to the United States, the statement lashed out at the anti-Zionists for their disservice to beleaguered Jews and for providing aid to the enemies of a Jewish homeland. Bernstein then called upon Finkelstein, along with twenty other leading rabbis, to sponsor a letter soliciting endorsement of the statement from fellow rabbis from all wings of American Judaism. Although several members of the Rabbinical Assembly signed that letter, Finkelstein refused. He said that the statement was open to misinterpretation and that it could trigger a full-blown controversy and thus actually harm the Zionist cause. Disturbed, however, that his refusal was construed by some as anti-Zionist, he wrote Bernstein a week later adding that he, as President of the Seminary, had been advised not to sign. Since the advice came from a Zionist, indeed a sponsor of the counterstatement, he labored to prove that his decision in no way reflected any personal opposition to Zionism.[112]

Caught between Zionist pressure on the one hand and an unwillingness to ally himself with the statehood movement on the other, Finkelstein wrote Bernstein yet again, stating that he was well aware of the "whispering campaign" against him, even though no American Jew had cause to presume "that I am not deeply concerned about the future of our homeland in Palestine." He reiterated his fear of communal disunity generated by the controversy and its adverse effect on Jewish restoration to Palestine. Perhaps the American Council for Judaism was not totally in error; he noted that some of his Christian friends had modified their views on Zionism under the influence of the organization's propaganda. Calling for Zionist patience and *heshbon ha-nefesh* (soul-searching), he urged above all the need to square Zionist thought with religious principles. Only a Zionism grounded fully in religion stood the chance of furthering Jewish aspirations in Palestine. It could possibly win over many anti-Zionists—and here he referred to private conversations with members of the council—and thereby achieve a basic unity among American Jews. In no way did Finkelstein condone the council's activities (despite a council newsletter that once "welcomed" him into their ranks), but clearly the principal culprit in his analysis was the the Zionist movement.[113]

The letters to Bernstein reveal how Finkelstein groped for a way out of the conflicting pressures that beset him. His validation of Zionism solely on religious grounds, now largely ignoring the factors of Jewish peoplehood and creativity, became the most expedient way for him to operate publicly. It involved no compromise of principle on his part, and neither Zionists nor anti-Zionists could very well dispute his vision of a Torah-true community in Palestine. Perhaps too, as he suggested, Jewish consensus on a religious homeland would more readily evoke a positive response in Christian circles, doubtless the same circles to which he turned in his outreach programs. As the spiritual guide who tried to stand above the contending factions and judge them according to religious norms, Finkelstein donned the mantle of arbiter, pleading for Jewish unity and chiding those whose communal in-fighting injured the cause of a legitimate (read: religious) Jewish homeland.

Zionists were persuaded neither by appeals for a transcendent Jewish unity, unattainable in the best of times, nor by what they regarded as pious platitudes. World Jewry in crisis could not afford the luxury of religious visions, and after Biltmore, a true Zionist did not equivocate about statehood. In the flareup over the council, Bernstein never even acknowledged the receipt of Finkelstein's letters. While the Seminary's President genuinely believed that Zionist attacks on him were totally unwarranted, his attempts to appear as the principled Zionist ended in failure. Moshe Davis once explained: "He tried to straddle, . . . to stick to both sides of the issue. And . . . that's why there is to this day the recollection on the part of many students at the time . . . of his non-Zionism and anti-Zionism."[114]

The counterstatement of the Bernstein group eventually garnered more than eight hundred signatures. Attacks on the council followed from the Rabbinical Assembly, which called upon rabbis to repudiate and frustrate the purposes of the organization. The Seminary's rabbinical students followed suit; allied with students from Orthodox and Reform seminaries, they unanimously endorsed a program advocating Jewish membership in the United Nations, a Jewish army, and the establishment of a Jewish state in Palestine.[115] Publicly, however, the Seminary's administration kept silent. Virtually the only rabbi who refused to sign the Rabbinical Assembly statement, Finkelstein attempted to placate both sides. He explained to a Zionist colleague: "I, of course, agreed with my colleagues in their basic strictures against the Council. . . . On the other hand, I simply could not sign a statement which equated Judaism with American, British and French nationalism."[116] At the same time, when board member Arthur Hays Sulzberger of the *New York Times*, a rabid anti-Zionist, wondered suspiciously what the connection of the Rabbinical Assembly was to the Seminary, Finkelstein assured him that although the Rabbinical Assembly "as a whole is very much under the influence of the Zionist Organization," it had no control over the policy of the school. He added that the statement of the students, who were caught up in a Zionist-fomented "wave of hysteria," was considerably stronger and "more foolish." He had convinced them, he claimed, that they had misunderstood the situation, and had they not already sent their statement to the Zionist organization, they would have withdrawn it. Sulzberger's sympathies with the council notwithstanding, Finkelstein mildly criticized the anti-Zionists for their "injudicious" behavior, but conforming to his role as spiritual arbiter, he preferred to stay above the controversy. He suggested that the situation called for an "educational effort," perhaps along the lines of a new religious journal.[117]

Where the Seminary stood on the fight between the Zionists and the council became a public issue when the Independent Jewish News Service reported that several board members were associated with the council. (A story from the news service in the Zionist *New Palestine*, purportedly exposing secret meetings of the council, included Sulzberger's name. A letter by Finkelstein, citing the same report, mentioned Henry Hendricks, Edgar Nathan, and Alan Stroock as well as Sulzberger.) Finkelstein called the report "unscrupulous propaganda," charging that it contained "misinterpretations" if not "actual falsities." He explained to the faculty that none of the board members under attack was, or intended to become, associated with the council. In no way, moreover, was the Seminary obligated to defend the statements of any individuals connected with it.[118]

That Finkelstein felt impelled to offer an explanation suggests first, a widespread awareness of the positive interest in the council on the part of several board members (notably Sulzberger, Strauss, and Stroock), and second, a fear on the part of the faculty that the council sympathizers would attempt to impose an anti-Zionist policy upon the Seminary. At this juncture the respected talmudist, Professor Louis Ginzberg, intervened. He called the incident "much ado about nothing," but he reminded Finkelstein that Schechter's answer to Schiff back in 1907 had shown American Jews where the Seminary stood on Zionism. Implying that Finkelstein could take similar action with respect to *his* board, he hoped at least that the Seminary's laissez-faire policy on Zionism would prevail and "that the members of the Board will . . . not object to any pro-Zionistic declarations by members of the Faculty expressed by them as individuals."[119]

A few months after the uproar over the Council for Judaism, another crisis erupted, this one concerning the withdrawal of the AJC from the American Jewish Conference. The non-Zionist committee, a reluctant participant from the beginning, suffered a major defeat when the conference dismissed its pleas to defer the issue of Jewish statehood and roundly endorsed the Biltmore program. The committee's executive voted in October 1943 to leave the conference, thereby breaking the impressive show of Jewish unity on the Palestine issue. The action called forth torrents of abuse, and 10 percent of the committee's membership resigned in protest.[120]

The arms of the Conservative movement stood in the forefront of the opposition; the Rabbinical Assembly, United Synagogue, and Women's League all dissociated themselves from the committee. From Conservative rabbis and congregations came cries for Louis Finkelstein, a member of the committee's executive, to follow suit. Milton Steinberg, rabbi of New York's Park Avenue Synagogue, called the committee's withdrawal "an expression of the most dejudaized and detraditionalized elements in American Jewish life" that fed into the hands of the anti-Zionists. The president of a congregation in Pottsville, Pennsylvania, similarly inveighed against the committee's "irresponsible" action "which flouts those very religious principles and democratic ideals to which we in our small way are dedicated." Both the prestigious rabbi and the obscure layman, allied in a movement that had from its inception linked Zionism with Judaism, asked Finkelstein to resign from the committee. As Steinberg diplomatically put it: "You do serve as spokesman for Conservative Judaism in this country. And, ideally, there ought not to be a sharp dichotomy between the leadership of a movement and the overwhelming sentiment of its following."[121]

Again Finkelstein was forced to balance institutional pressures and personal beliefs. He had stated his own views at the meeting of the committee's executive; he was against the White Paper and in favor of a refuge in Palestine but against Jewish statehood. He argued that if a commonwealth meant a less-than-equal political status for Christians and Muslims in Palestine, then he opposed it. Furthermore, he thought it bad statesmanship to ask for the unattainable: "There isn't one possibility in five hundred that there will be established in the course of the next twenty-five years what is called a Jewish state in Palestine." Jewish political impotence did not trouble him. In line with earlier remarks he now stated: "It is not a fact that Jews have been praying for two thousand years that there should be a Jewish president in Palestine. What the Jews have been praying for two thousand years is that the Kingdom of God shall be restored in Palestine." Finkelstein abstained on the vote to withdraw from the Conference. Emphasizing the need for communal unity he preferred to negotiate further with the Zionists. If they refused to change the statehood resolution, only then was withdrawal in order.[122] Except for that qualification, his spiritual Zionism along with his suspicions of nationalism led to a conclusion identical to the committee's.

Seminary tradition also worked to keep Finkelstein loyal to the committee. The school and the defense agency had been closely linked throughout their histories. In the days of Schechter and Adler the same prominent few who ran the committee sat on the Seminary's board; Adler was a lynchpin of the committee while he headed the Seminary. During Finkelstein's administration traces of the interlocking directorate persisted, most notably in the persons of Sol Stroock and his son Alan. Finkelstein himself served on various committees of the AJC, and the AJC in turn helped fund the Seminary's Conference on Science, Philosophy and Religion.[123]

Were Finkelstein to resign from the committee and thereby sever the long-standing relationship, he doubtless would have precipitated a major crisis with the board.

Nevertheless, the President could not ignore the pressures from his own rank and file. Milton Steinberg, for one, probed beyond the conference episode and asked for answers to a series of pointed questions: Did Finkelstein envision a Jewish Palestine solely as "a community of Saints such as that of Safed in the sixteenth century" or as a home for "many Jews even if not all of them are saints and scholars"? On what basis did Jews have the right to demand free entry into Palestine? Was the Western world still bound by the promises of the Balfour Declaration and mandate? Did Finkelstein deny Jewish nationhood? Would he favor Jewish political self-determination if Jews constituted a majority in Palestine?

Finkelstein answered forthrightly: Palestine was not only for saints and scholars; the Balfour Declaration and mandate were permanent covenants; the right to enter Palestine stemmed primarily from the right of any Jew to fulfill a religious obligation—"The question of whether the Jew who comes to Palestine is himself religious in other respects, is not a relevant issue. . . . His desire to come to Palestine is a desire to perform a religious act." Yes, he believed in Jewish peoplehood ("nation" was too loose a term), but he did not regard Jews as a political group. Nor did present circumstances warrant statehood:

> I believe the interest of Palestine and the world requires that for the time being, it should remain under international control. If, at sometime in the future, the Jews constitute a majority of the land, and as such a majority desire that the land be reconstituted as the Republic of Eretz Israel (with guarantees of full and equal rights to all individuals and groups), I would regard it as the duty of the world to grant that request, insofar as it will grant similar requests to other small countries.

Although Steinberg the Zionist concluded that at least for the moment Finkelstein's response "leaves little to be desired," the question of why the President opposed the conference resolution and sided with the AJC remained. Finkelstein explained at length to the rabbi that since the committee's attempts at unity had been rebuffed, the fault for the rupture lay with the Zionists. He personally was dismayed by Zionist tactics at the conference and the fact that sessions were held on the Sabbath. More important, he thought the Palestine resolution was intrinsically flawed. The word "commonwealth," which connoted an arrogation of political power on the part of Jews at the expense of non-Jews in Palestine, was morally and religiously indefensible as well as potentially harmful to Diaspora Jews. Long the universalist, he was also concerned lest the resolution, drawn along lines of narrow nationalism, cause Jews to forget their mission to the world at large. He had suggested, Finkelstein said, that the word "homeland" be substituted for "commonwealth," but the Zionists turned him down.[124]

Finkelstein's explanations jibed with his remarks at the AJC meeting and his most recent article for the *New Palestine*. But a private letter to Steinberg illuminated more clearly than before the essential distinction drawn by Finkelstein between his spiritual Zionism and political Zionism. "The primary question is not one of political control of the land," he said, "but whether the Jews are given the opportunity to perform their religious duty, and to develop their spiritual and cultural life in the Holy Land, and whether they are there in such numbers and preponderance as to make the development of their religious and spiritual life basic elements in the civilization of the country." It followed, therefore, that a Jewish majority in Palestine might be desirable, but the concept of a majority in a political sense carried no special merit.[125] Finkelstein held fast to his principles, but his position on "political control" hardly endeared him in 1943 to the American Zionist rank and file.

The Seminary's President discussed the AJC/conference rupture with a hand-picked committee that consisted of four board members, four alumni, and four faculty members. The group, of whom he said "virtually everyone . . . is an ardent Zionist," agreed that he should remain in the AJC with a view towards achieving collaboration between the committee and the Zionists. There the matter was dropped, and a letter of resignation from the AJC, which Finkelstein had drafted earlier, was never sent. Nevertheless, disaffection with his close ties to the committee lingered.[126]

By 1943, as thoughts turned to plans for a postwar world, Finkelstein's universalist and antinationalist leanings grew more pronounced. In articles that appeared in the *New Palestine* he ranked national sovereignty well below internationalism: "The creation of an enduring peace presupposes an active cooperative relationship among nations and peoples, which makes the question of statehood less and less relevant; while emphasis on national sovereignty anywhere must be fatal to civilization." He spoke on the need for a restored Jewish homeland—never did he use the words "state" or "commonwealth"—but again he depicted a center through which a revitalized Judaism (not Jews) would effectively disseminate the spiritual values required for the survival of civilization. The political contours of that center remained fuzzy. Emphasizing the need for a postwar association of nations committed to the prophetic ideals of peace and justice, he saw a Jewish homeland under the "aegis" of that association. A restored Palestine and a new world order were interlocked. Indeed, the former was "indispensable to a reformation of world culture as well as one of the major expressions of that reformation itself." Since he decried secular Jewish nationalism in particular, the editor of the *New Palestine* pressed him for a similar denunciation of anti-Zionism. All Finkelstein agreed to, however, was one mild sentence in strict keeping with his religious focus: "To oppose this effort to restore the Jewish settlement of the Holy Land," he said, "is to repudiate a cardinal tradition of Judaism."[127]

Spiritual Zionism grounded in a universal mission and laced with international-ism did not satisfy the Zionists who looked rather for a positive endorsement from the leader of Conservative Jewry. They had drawn the line between Zionist and anti-Zionist on the issue of Jewish political autonomy, and a "homeland" or "settle-ment" under international control fell short of that objective. Yet, out of principle as well as a healthy fear of antagonizing his board, Finkelstein would venture no fur-ther. Sulzberger's behavior, for example, proved that antinationalists were at least as uncompromising as the political Zionists. Moving from non-Zionism to anti-Zionism in response to nationalist militancy,[128] the publisher aired his bias publicly through the powerful *New York Times*. Privately he needled Finkelstein repeatedly whenever he suspected Seminary identification with Jewish nationalism. On one occasion Sulzberger mistakenly detected a Jewish flag in a *Times* photograph of a Seminary convocation, and he protested that the display of a flag "which is not my national emblem again raises the issue which has so much disturbed me."[129]

The President trod warily with the board. As early as 1941 he began to clear with members of his board matters that smacked of Seminary involvement with Pales-tine or Zionism: Should he sign a statement in support of the Hebrew University? Should he attend a luncheon tendered by Chaim Weizmann?[130] At one faculty meeting he described his difficulties with individual board members after the initial two-year honeymoon period and the countless hours he was forced to spend in pla-cating them. Since financial pressures fostered a dependence on the goodwill of Sulzberger and Lewis Strauss, the two most likely to expand the Seminary's circle of large contributors, it was also politic to keep any Zionist sentiments in check. Mordecai Kaplan reported that the President agreed to certain conditions that Sulzberger thought would help chances of reaching the "big money": the Seminary would not limit itself to servicing Conservative Judaism; the Seminary would con-tinue its interfaith work; and, the Seminary would not commit itself to political Zionism. The cynical Kaplan suspected that Finkelstein himself and not the two board members had formulated those conditions.[131]

Finkelstein loyally sprang to Sulzberger's defense in a dispute between the pub-lisher and Abba Hillel Silver. In the wake of the American Jewish Conference, the Reform rabbi, now the recognized voice of an aggressive Zionism, publicly denounced "the spirit of Arthur Hays Sulzberger" which had turned the *Times* into "the channel for anti-Zionist propaganda." Finkelstein, who claimed both men as his friends but deplored the injurious effect of such quarrels on the causes of both Jews and Judaism, blamed the Zionist leader. He told Sulzberger that Silver had chosen a path of "violence and vehemence." Perhaps recalling that Silver was most responsible for the passage of the Palestine resolution and hence for Finkelstein's

WESTERN UNION (45)

CLASS OF SERVICE
This is a full-rate Telegram or Cablegram unless its deferred character is indicated by a suitable symbol above or preceding the address.

A. N. WILLIAMS
PRESIDENT

1201

SYMBOLS
DL = Day Letter
NL = Night Letter
LC = Deferred Cable
NLT = Cable Night Letter
Ship Radiogram

The filing time shown in the date line on telegrams and day letters is STANDARD TIME at point of origin.   Time of receipt is STANDARD TIME at point of destination

JN173 47=WASHINGTON DC 12 1212P

DR LOUIS FINKELSTEIN, PRESIDENT JEWISH
    THEOLOGICAL SEMINARY=BROADWAY & 122 ST

=THE PICTURE OF PROCEEDINGS AT SEMINARY
PUBLISHED IN THE TIMES THIS MORNING SHOWS A
FLAG WHICH IS NOT MY NATIONAL EMBLEM AND
AGAIN RAISES THE ISSUE WHICH HAS SO MUCH
DISTURBED ME. I SHALL BE BACK IN MY OFFICE
WEDNESDAY & HOPE TO HEAR FROM YOU REGARDS=
    :ARTHUR HAYS SULZBERGER.

THE COMPANY WILL APPRECIATE SUGGESTIONS FROM ITS PATRONS CONCERNING ITS SERVICE

Telegram, Arthur
Hays Sulzberger
to Louis Finkel-
stein, 16 Septem-
ber 1946. Letter,
Arthur Hays
Sulzberger to
Louis Finkelstein,
17 September
1946. Finkelstein's
"reassuring note"
to Sulzberger
read: "I have just
received your
telegram. What
looks like a flag in
the "Times"
picture is the
Seminary banner
containing the
Seminary seal
which you have
very often seen. . .
No other flag or
emblem is used by
the Seminary."
*Ratner Center,
JTS.*

The New York Times
Times Square

ARTHUR HAYS SULZBERGER
PUBLISHER

September 17, 1946

Dear Dr. Finkelstein:

                Thanks for
your reassuring note of September 16th. I am glad I didn't
get more excited than I did at
what looked to me like a Zionist flag !

            Won't you suggest some dates
for the meeting?

                Faithfully yours,

Dr. Louis Finkelstein
3080 Broadway
New York, N.Y.

own difficulties after the AJC/conference rupture, the Seminary's President may have unconsciously identified with Sulzberger: "It is obviously the fate of the men who try to civilize the world to be misinterpreted and maligned by their contemporaries who resist being civilized." Nothing from "our hysterical friends," he assured his board member, could undermine "your place in American religious life and in Judaism, and your magnificent contributions to civilization in our time." Writing to Silver at the same time, Finkelstein also called Sulzberger "a loyal and devout Jew trying to serve his faith and his people" whose outlook on Jewish life was, indeed, not that different from the rabbi's. He did not neglect, however, to lavish equally high praise on the Zionist leader: "There are few men in public life for whose abilities I have greater admiration, and of whose wholehearted devotion to the service of God and the Jewish faith, I have greater certainty."[132]

Again, as in the episodes of the Bernstein letter and the AJC's withdrawal from the American Jewish Conference, the Seminary's President attempted to juggle conflicting pressures—his own principles, his dependence on the board, and the need to appease his Conservative constituency. Again, professing a simultaneous loyalty to both Zionists and anti-Zionists, he sought a way out of the maze by shifting the focus from political Zionism to Jewish unity. Finkelstein failed to defuse the Sulzberger/Silver controversy, and the publisher and the rabbi exchanged heated letters replete with accusations and ad hominen attacks. (A near-hysterical Sulzberger even charged that the Zionists, who perverted and distorted facts, were employing "Goebbels' tactics.")[133]

When in 1945 the board officially considered the President's views on Zionism, it showed how sensitive the entire body, and not just Sulzberger and Strauss, had become to the subject. Finkelstein drafted a frank statement:

> He described his attitude toward the reestablishment of a Jewish settlement in Palestine as being precisely that of Doctor Schechter, and wholly within the Jewish tradition. He stated that it was his conviction that in this sense, every member of the Faculty, every alumnus of the Seminary, and he believed also, every member of the Board, was a Zionist. On the other hand, while he did not wish to make a public statement on the subject, . . . he wished the Board to know what he had believed had been made obvious from all his writings over many years, . . . namely, that he does not regard the Jews of the world as a political unit. He considers that the effort to describe them that way is extremely dangerous, not only to the Jews, but to democracy, generally, and that, though he hopes that events will prove him wrong, the concentration of the Zionist effort on the conception of Palestine as a "Jewish Commonwealth," rather than on widespread immigration will have a harmful effect on the future of the Yishub.

The board accepted the President's statement. They may have thought that his spiritual Zionism posed no immediate challenge, or they may well have assumed, as did some faculty members, that he was not a Zionist.[134]

Meanwhile, Conservative Jews waited in vain for Finkelstein to endorse the Zionist demand for statehood. A cover story featuring Finkelstein that appeared in *Time* reported that at least one large contributor to the Seminary "tore up his usual check." Within the Rabbinical Assembly rumblings of discontent with Finkelstein's attempts to keep one foot in both the Zionist and anti-Zionist camps were also heard. As Milton Steinberg put it, "I want Dr. Finkelstein . . . to stop pussy-footing on Zionism."[135] The opposition came to a head in 1944–45 when several prominent rabbis, led by Steinberg and Solomon Goldman, prepared a list of grievances against the Seminary's President. Their lengthy indictment criticized Finkelstein for initiating new programs of an interfaith or public relations nature that had little relevance to the Seminary as a seat of learning, for ignoring the need to formulate a Conservative theology, and for wielding too much power over the Rabbinical Assembly and United Synagogue. Furthermore, and this was the heart of their complaint, they charged that Finkelstein's board was a body unrepresentative of, and unsympathetic toward, Conservative Judaism. Although Zionism was not specifically included as a grievance, it was implicit in the bill of particulars. One could well deduce from the rabbis' brief that if the Seminary stayed on a proper course—committed to the interests and spirit of Conservative Judaism and heedful of its rabbis and congregations—it would emerge as an active supporter of the Zionist program.

Steinberg and Goldman presented harsh criticisms to Finkelstein privately. Steinberg, who canceled the annual appeal for the Seminary at the Park Avenue Synagogue, also aired the charges publicly in three sermons entitled "Crises in Conservative Judaism." Not only did he pointedly question Finkelstein's power but he lashed out against the board, men "who are anti-traditionalist, anti-Zionist, even assimilationist" and "flagrantly out of harmony with everything the Seminary represents." Finkelstein handled the dissidents with consummate skill. He patiently answered them individually; he arranged meetings where he, flanked by senior members of the faculty, entertained their complaints; and he flattered them with friendly invitations. In the end, his strategy wore them down. That plus a genuine loyalty to their teacher and friend on the part of the rabbis broke the back of the "Steinberg-Goldman revolt." In the long run not all was lost. The administrative organization of the Seminary was modified to include a larger Board of Overseers, representative of Conservative Jewry, that would share some authority with the board of directors. Finkelstein also promised that so long as he was President no one would be appointed a director without the endorsement of the Rabbinical Assembly's executive.[136]

For the time being, the President and the board of directors reigned supreme with respect to political Zionism. Indeed, at the very moment that he was negotiating with the rabbis, Finkelstein again refused to sign a Zionist statement responding to charges from the American Council for Judaism. This time he explained that if the text of the statement were properly altered, he might be able to induce Lessing Rosenwald, president and strong financial backer of the council, to withdraw his support of that organization. He did meet with Rosenwald, but his attempt at peacemaking between Zionists and anti-Zionists failed.[137] Whether in the interest of Jewish unity, or merely "pussyfooting" as Steinberg had said, Finkelstein refused to burn his bridges to either group.

Within the walls of the Seminary, faculty and student anger also smoldered. Finkelstein's approach to Zionism was never debated publicly; in Moshe Davis's words, it generated only "corridor, cafeteria and house talk."[138] On several occasions, however, the opposition surfaced. In 1944 the Seminary awarded an honorary degree to Chaim Weizmann,[139] but to the consternation of the students the citation made no mention of Zionism. It referred to Weizmann's scientific contributions to the cause of democracy in World War I and his lifelong struggle to alleviate the sufferings of Israel and the world. A mirror of Finkelstein's own views, the citation compared the Zionist leader to Rabbi Yohanan ben Zakkai, commending his efforts through the founding of the Hebrew University to further the "development of the spiritual values of Israel." "His pursuit of the prophetic vision," the text concluded, "is motivated by an earnest conviction that a Jewish community, reestablished in the Holy Land, can once more be a source of inspiration and moral strength to all mankind." In the eyes of the students, "spiritual values," "prophetic vision," and "Jewish community" ignored Weizmann's herculean tasks on behalf of Jewish nationhood. More important, the citation could hardly be construed as a message of encouragement to a *yishuv* bent on political independence. Several students complained jointly to the administration, but Finkelstein offered no explanation. Student bitterness mounted when the class of 1945 requested and was denied permission to sing "Hatikva" at their commencement.[140]

Aside from his sensitivity to the board's outlook, Finkelstein's own opposition to political Zionism had not changed as the war wound down. He confided to board member Frieda Warburg in October 1944 that "I sympathize greatly" with Judah Magnes's binationalist scheme for Palestine. Moreover, he thought that the "temporary difficulties" in Palestine were overshadowed by larger issues—like "seeing that the Jews shall be the best kind of people possible"—to which the Seminary was committed.[141] The letter coincided in time with student reaction to the Weizmann degree and the onset of the confrontation with Goldman and Steinberg. In spite of, or perhaps in answer to, the challenges from colleagues and students, Finkelstein stiffened both his resistance to statehood and his determination to launch projects beyond the conventional parameters of a rabbinical school.

Nor did Finkelstein emend his position in the final months before the state of Israel came into being. The United Nations had voted for partition in November

1947, but diplomatic shifts until the very last days threatened to jettison international approval of a Jewish state. Meanwhile the *yishuv* was caught in a stranglehold between Arab guerilla warfare and British restrictions on Jewish self-defense. On all levels—political, material, and moral—it desperately needed American Jewish support. Finkelstein, the confirmed pacifist, recoiled at the thought of a Jewish-Arab war. Like others, he believed the warnings from high American officials that the establishment of a state might actually lead to the military destruction of a Jewish Palestine.[142] If a state was not viable at that time, there was no imperative for altering his course.

On the eve of Israel's independence, Zionist members of the faculty stood up to the President. A dispute over a seemingly trivial issue, an honorary degree to be awarded at commencement, captured the bitterness that had built up over the years between the Zionists and Finkelstein. At a meeting in January, the president's recommendation of the AJC's president, Joseph Proskauer, drew opposition because of the latter's anti-Zionism, and a compromise was reached whereby an award would also go to Moshe Shertok, head of the political department of the Jewish Agency and a leading force for statehood. Unhappy with Shertok, Finkelstein tried a month later to substitute Paul Baerwald of the Joint Distribution Committee, also an antinationalist. Although the president promised a special convocation to honor Zionist leaders if and when partition was favorably resolved, Professors Hillel Bavli and Shalom Spiegel argued that it was the Seminary's duty to take an immediate public stand on the side of the *yishuv*. Mordecai Kaplan's diary provides a detailed description of how tempers flared: "Both Bavli and Spiegel spoke sharply and bitterly of the ivory tower attitude of the Seminary, an attitude that is responsible for the tendency on the part of the Jewish masses to ignore the Seminary. At one point Finkelstein screamed at Bavli, and Bavli paled with anger." Not only had faculty members worked individually for Zionism, the president shouted, but no group in America had done more for Zionism than the Rabbinical Assembly. When Shertok's name was brought up once more in April, Finkelstein again lost his temper. Maintaining that it was a matter of conscience, he said that "he had no faith in the Zionist leaders who have made the issue of Jewish statehood paramount." In the end, honorary degrees went to both Zionists and anti-Zionists but not to Shertok.[143]

Barely a month after the birth of Israel, the Seminary held its graduation. On that day the students rebelled. As the popular story goes, they draped an Israeli flag on the Seminary tower only to have it whisked away by the administration before the ceremonies began. Since their request for "Hatikva," in which Professor Bavli joined, was also turned down (a foreign anthem, nonreligious to boot), they arranged with the carillonneur at Union Theological Seminary to play the melody during commencement. Elated and triumphant, the students heard the bells formally announce their identification with the new Jewish state.[144]

Louis Finkelstein presents a Seminary honorary degree to David Ben-Gurion, Jerusalem, 1952. *Photo by Braun. Ratner Center, JTS.*

The birth of Israel brought a dramatic shift in Seminary policy. Like its affiliated branches, the school now stood proudly behind the Jewish state. In 1952 the Seminary in conjunction with the Jewish Agency launched the Seminary Israel Institute, and that same year it awarded an honorary degree to David Ben-Gurion. Ten years later the Seminary opened a *pnimiyah* (dormitory) in Jerusalem, thereby establishing a permanent presence in the land.[145]

Finkelstein, still very much the spiritual Zionist, warmly endorsed the ties of active cooperation. The very existence of a state recharged his vision of a third commonwealth committed to the universal ideals and mission of Judaism, a vision in which American Jews also played a part. The latter, he said, like Babylonian Jewry of old "who brought the vision of Judaism to bear upon the practical affairs of the world," were fully prepared to help their Israeli brethren in the service of God. "If we can labor with them toward a solution of the vast human problem, that in itself will be a privilege."[146] At Finkelstein's suggestion Chaim Weizmann presented President Truman with a *sefer Torah* as a token of gratitude from the people of Israel.[147] No other object could have better conveyed Finkelstein's view, unchanged over many years, of the raison d'être of a Jewish state.

Finkelstein openly emended his position after 1948 in one significant respect. Now, for the first time, he articulated a belief in a special bonding between Conservative Judaism and Zionism. Reverting to the theme of Jewish creativity which he had raised before the Rabbinical Assembly in 1927, he explained that a common base of self-confidence generated by that creativity underlay both ideologies. The self-confidence born of Zionism, he said, allowed Conservative Judaism to take root and flourish in the United States: "That enormous faith in ourselves and in our tradition—which has enabled us, like our predecessors, to assert that . . . we can participate fully in the life of America and yet hold fast to the traditions of our fathers; the faith that convinced Solomon Schechter that the Seminary he was reorganizing was at once a Jewish Seminary and an American Seminary . . . this faith and self-confidence were, in my opinion, by-products of the vast effort which had already begun to lay the foundations of a resurrected Jewish commonwealth in *Eretz Yisrael*." According to that reasoning, he concluded, "In a certain sense, it may be said that Conservative Judaism is itself the first-born child of the marriage of Zionism and Americanism."[148] Thus, Finkelstein put himself and the Seminary squarely back on the track originally laid by Solomon Schechter.

THE THREE MEN who headed the Seminary from 1902 to 1948 were all imbued with a love of Zion. Against the backdrop of an evolving Zionist movement, each affirmed the centrality of Palestine in Jewish religious thought, and each envisioned a modern Palestine that would serve as a spiritual center for observant Jews throughout the world. Although they also shared a dislike of Jewish secular nationalism, they differed on basic issues of Jewish peoplehood and political Zionism. Schechter, concerned with the survival of his people, saw in Zionism a weapon for battling Reform and assimilation. Adler, whose chief priority was the survival of Judaism, found the concept of Jewish nationality distasteful if not dangerous to Diaspora Jewry. Finkelstein, preferring to skirt the subject of peoplehood, opposed Jewish nationalist activities that contradicted his universalist and pacifist principles.

Of the three, Schechter's Zionist stand commanded the strongest and most lasting support from the Seminary family and the Conservative ranks. Even his dispute with Schiff, at a time when the Seminary was at its weakest and most vulnerable, ended in a victory for the President. By contrast, Adler and Finkelstein often stood at odds with the Rabbinical Assembly and the United Synagogue as well as the faculty and students. Yet, even from a position of non-Zionism or Zionism with qualifications, each president contributed to the course of Zionism in the United States: Schechter pioneered in the Americanization of Jewish nationalism in accordance with the sentiments of an immigrant generation; Adler mobilized non-Zionists to contribute to the upbuilding of the *yishuv*; Finkelstein, notably after 1948, cemented a spiritual partnership between American Jews and Israel. In their separate ways they defended the compatibility of Jewish interest in Palestine with Americanism.

The legacy of religio-cultural Zionism bequeathed by Schechter and never supplanted by his successors irrevocably stamped the character of the Seminary and of Conservative Judaism. It lent substance both to the Seminary's two-centered vision and to the institution's role as propagator of historical Judaism. Outliving political Zionism and the attainment of Jewish statehood, it promised a permanent relationship between the Jews of Israel and America whereby each center would continue to enrich the other.

I am grateful to the late Professor Moshe Davis for his wise counsel on several aspects of this essay.

1. Samuel Halperin, *The Political World of American Zionism* (Detroit: Wayne State University Press, 1961), p. 101.

2. Michael A. Meyer, "A Centennial History," in *Hebrew Union College-Jewish Institute of Religion at One Hundred Years*, ed. Samuel E. Karff (Cincinnati: Hebrew Union College Press, 1976), pp. 44–46, 62–69.

3. Moshe Davis, *The Emergence of Conservative Judaism* (Philadelphia: Jewish Publication Society, 1963), p. 354; David G. Dalin, "Cyrus Adler, Non-Zionism, and the Zionist Movement," *AJS Review* 10 (Spring 1985): p. 68.

4. Solomon Schechter, *Seminary Addresses and Other Papers* (New York: Burning Bush Press, 1959), pp. xxiii–xxiv; *American Hebrew*, 30 September 1907.

5. For a recent analysis, see Allon Gal, "The Historical Continuity Motif in Conservative Judaism's Concept of Israel," *Journal of Jewish Thought and Philosophy* 2 (1993): pp. 157–83.

6. See, for example, Herman H. and Mignon L. Rubenovitz, *The Waking Heart* (Cambridge: Nathaniel Dame, 1967), pp. 1–7; Israel Goldstein, *My World As a Jew*, 2 vols. (New York: Herzl Press; London: Cornwall Books, 1984), vol. 1, p. 32; Jacob Kohn, Memoirs, Kohn Papers. (Unless otherwise noted, all manuscript material is in the JTS archives.)

7. Abraham J. Karp, "Reaction to Zionism and to the State of Israel in the American Jewish Religious Community," *Jewish Journal of Sociology* 8 (September 1966): p. 153.

8. Norman Bentwich, *Solomon Schechter* (Philadelphia: Jewish Publication Society, 1938), pp. 94, 97, 167, 192; draft of S. Schechter to L. Marshall, 23 December 1913, Schechter Papers.

9. Bentwich, *Solomon Schechter*, pp. 164, 273–74; Schechter, *Seminary Addresses*, pp. 2, 48–50, 145–68; report of Schechter's address in *American Hebrew*, 1 April 1904.

10. Herbert Rosenblum, "The Founding of the United Synagogue of America" (Ph.D. diss., Brandeis University, 1970), chaps. 1–2; p. 5. Schechter to S. Greenbaum, 28 February 1912, Schechter Papers; report of Schechter's address in *American Hebrew*, 1 April 1904.

11. Robert E. Fierstien, "Solomon Schechter and the Zionist Movement," *Conservative Judaism* 29 (spring 1975): p. 6; S. Schechter to H. Bentwich, 7 July 1904, 1 November. [1909], Schechter Papers; Schechter, *Seminary Addresses*, pp. 22–23; Solomon Schechter, "The Seminary and the Community," *American Hebrew*, 25 March 1904; Bentwich, *Solomon Schechter*, p. 329. On the competition between the Seminary and HUC sparked by Schechter's arrival and the almost simultaneous appointment of Kaufmann Kohler to head the Cincinnati school, see Meyer, "A Centennial History," pp. 53–54, 71–73.

12. Schechter, *Seminary Addresses*, pp. 23, 203; S. Schechter to H. Bentwich, 6 June, 30 November 1904, Schechter Papers; Bentwich, *Solomon Schechter*, pp. 97, 105–06, 180, 205–07, 296, 304–08, 314, 336; Meir Ben-Horin, "Solomon Schechter to Judge Mayer Sulzberger," *Jewish Social Studies* 27 (April 1965): pp. 79, 81, 83, 85–86; Naomi W. Cohen, "The Challenges of Darwinism and Biblical Criticism to American Judaism," *Modern Judaism* 4 (May 1984): p. 134.

13. Bentwich, *Solomon Schechter*, pp. 309–10; Schechter, *Seminary Addresses*, p. xxiv.

14. Bentwich, *Solomon Schechter*, pp. 311–15; Louis Finkelstein, "Solomon Schechter as a Zionist," *New Palestine*, 13 December 1940.

15. Ben-Horin, "Solomon Schechter to Judge Mayer Sulzberger," p. 95.

16. I. Zangwill to S. Schechter, 21 December 1903, 5. Schechter to I. Zangwill, 27 February 1904, to H. Bentwich, 30 November 1904, Schechter Papers; Bentwich, *Solomon Schechter*, pp. 311–15.

17. *American Hebrew* editorial, 15 April 1904; Kaufmann Kohler in *Menorah* 36 (June 1904): pp. 327–29; Herbert Parzen, "The Purge of the Dissidents, Hebrew Union College and Zionism," *Jewish Social Studies* 37 (summer-fall 1975): pp. 291–315.

18. S. Schechter to H. Bentwich, 7 July 1904, Schechter Papers; J. Schiff to S. Schechter, 12

July 1904, Schiff Papers (American Jewish Archives, Cinncinnati).

19. Bentwich, *Solomon Schechter*, p. 320; S. Schechter to H. Bentwich, 7 July, 30 November 1904, Schechter Papers; Evyatar Friesel, "Jacob H. Schiff Becomes a Zionist," *Studies in Zionism*, no. 5, April 1982, p. 60.

20. "Dr. Schechter on Zionism," *American Hebrew*, 29 December 1905; Schechter, *Seminary Addresses*, pp. 91–104.

21. Bentwich, *Solomon Schechter*, p. 316.

22. Robert Gordis, *Understanding Conservative Judaism* (New York: Rabbinical Assembly, 1978), p. 122; Kaufmann Kohler, "Zionism or Judaism—Which?" *Menorah* 42 (January 1907): pp. 40–43; *American Israelite*, 4 April 1907.

23. S. Schechter to H. Friedenwald, 29 [August] 1907, Friedenwald Papers; Cyrus Adler, *Jacob H. Schiff*, 2 vols. (Garden City: Doubleday Doran, 1929), vol. 2: pp. 164–66. Similar remarks that Schiff made before the Jewish Chautauqua Society were publicly distributed. *American Hebrew*, 2 August 1907; *New York Times*, 29 July 1907.

24. Kohler in *Menorah* 36 (June 1904): pp. 327–28; *American Hebrew*, 29 December 1905; *New York Times*, 23 August 1907; S. Schechter to H. Friedenwald, 29 [August] 1907, Friedenwald Papers.

25. Harry Friedenwald, *The Attitude of the American Zionist*, 1907, JTS library, Zionist pamphlets; I. Friedlaender to H. Friedenwald, 8 September, 1 October 1907, Friedenwald Papers; *American Hebrew*, 30 August, 20 September 1907; *New York Times*, 15 September 1907.

26. Adler, *Jacob Schiff*, vol. 2, p. 167; *New York Times*, 30 September 1907; Rubenovitz, *The Waking Heart*, pp. 17–18.

27. *American Hebrew*, 20 September 1907.

28. Friesel, "Jacob H. Schiff Becomes a Zionist," pp. 73, 91.

29. Friedenwald letter to *American Hebrew*, 30 August 1907; Stuart E. Knee, "Jewish Non-Zionism in America and Palestine Commitment 1917–1941, *Jewish Social Studies* 39 (summer 1977): pp. 209–22; Friesel, "Jacob H. Schiff Becomes a Zionist," p. 64.

30. Bentwich, *Solomon Schechter*, pp. 322–23; Herbert Parzen, "Conservative Judaism and Zionism," *Jewish Social Studies* 23 (October 1961): p. 244; Rubenovitz, *The Waking Heart*, p. 102; Louis Lipsky, *Memoirs in Profile* (Philadelphia: Jewish Publication Society, 1975), p . 234.

31. Solomon Schechter, *Some Aspects of Rabbinic Theology* (New York: Macmillan, 1910), p. 105; idem, *Seminary Addresses*, xxiv–xxv; Bentwich, *Solomon Schechter,* pp. 322–24, 327; S. Schechter to N. Bentwich, 26 February 1914, 23 February 1915; to A. Ginzberg, 3 December 1913; to N. Isaacs, 30 April 1914. Schechter Papers.

32. JTS *Students' Annual*, 1915, p. 52; Jacob Kohn, *Memoirs*, Kohn Papers; *Jewish Exponent*, 12 June 1908; Parzen, "Conservative Judaism and Zionism," p. 239. On participation of early Seminary students in an organization called Young American Zionists, see Herbert Parzen, "Conservative Judaism and Zionism, A Documentary Account," *Herzl Year Book* 6 (1964–65): pp. 312–13.

33. Moshe Davis, "Israel Friedlaender's Minute Book of the Achavah Club" in *Mordecai M. Kaplan Jubilee Volume*, English section (New York: Jewish Theological Seminary, 1953), pp. 157–213; Eli Ginzberg, *Keeper of the Law* (Philadelphia: Jewish Publication Society, 1966), pp. 324–26. Ginzberg, professor of Talmud, was a delegate to the Sixth Zionist Congress (1903) where he voted against the Uganda proposition. Simcha Kling, "Zionism in the Early Days of Conservative Judaism," in *Judaism*, ed. Arthur A. Chiel (New York, 1978), p. 264.

34. Mordecai M. Kaplan diary, 10, 13 October 1914, 15 August 1916.

35. Rose G. Jacobs, "Beginnings of Hadassah," in *Early History of Zionism in America*, ed. Isidore S. Meyer (New York: American Jewish Historical Society and Herzl Foundation, 1958), pp. 242–43; Israel Friedlaender, *Past and Present* (Cincinnati: Ark Publishing Com-

pany, 1919), pp. x–xi, chaps. 15, 18, 21; Baila R. Shargel, *Practical Dreamer* (New York: Jewish Theological Seminary, 1985), especially chaps. 8–9; I. Friedlaender to J. Schiff, 10 April 1911, to C. Adler, 7 June 1915, Friedlaender Papers; Goldstein, *My World as a Jew*, vol. 1, p. 39.

36. Ben Halpern, "The Americanization of Zionism," *American Jewish History* 69 (September 1979): pp. 22, 33; Friesel, "Jacob H. Schiff Becomes a Zionist," pp. 86–87.

37. Ira Robinson, "Cyrus Adler and the Jewish Theological Seminary of America," *American Jewish History* 78 (March 1989): pp. 366–75; Kaplan diary, 12 September 1922; Goldstein, *My World As a Jew*, vol. 1, p. 40.

38. Cyrus Adler, *Selected Letters*, ed. Ira Robinson, 2 vols. (Philadelphia: Jewish Publication Society, and New York: Jewish Theological Seminary, 1985), vol. 1, pp. 39–45, 50, 53–54, 117; idem, *I Have Considered the Days* (Philadelphia: Jewish Publication Society, 1945), chaps. 5-6.

39. Simcha Kling, "Cyrus Adler and Zionism," *Conservative Judaism* 33 (fall 1979): pp. 22–27; Dalin, "Cyrus Adler, Non-Zionism," pp. 56–61; Herbert Parzen, *Architects of Conservative Judaism* (New York: J. David, 1964), pp. 87–89.

40. Adler, *Selected Letters*, vol. 1, p. 174, vol. 2, p. 209; C. Adler to M. Warburg, 23 November 1934, Adler Papers; Abraham A. Neuman, *Cyrus Adler* (New York: American Jewish Committee, 1942), p. 198.

41. C. Adler to J. Mack, 21 March 1921, Adler Papers (AJC); C. Adler to F. Warburg, 2 December 1925, to H. P. Mendes, 9 March 1933, Adler Papers; Adler, *Selected Letters*, 1: pp. 118, 187; Naomi W. Cohen, *Encounter with Emancipation* (Philadelphia: Jewish Publication Society, 1984), pp. 203-10.

42. Adler, *Selected Letters*, vol. 1, pp. 189, 243, 248-49, 253, 262, 339; vol. 2, 154, 209; C. Adler to L. Marshall, 20 July 1914, Adler Papers; Neuman, *Cyrus Adler*, pp. 200–3; Kling, "Cyrus Adler and Zionism," pp. 22–23.

43. Adler, *Selected Letters*, vol. 1, pp. 330, 334, 339, 349; vol. 2, p. 49; Adler's letter to *Jewish Exponent*, 27 December 1918; minutes of AJC executive committee, 2 February 1918 (AJC). For similar reasons Adler refused to go along with Israel Zangwill's territorialist scheme despite the contrary views of close friends like Oscar Straus and Mayer Sulzberger. Adler, *Selected Letters*, vol. 1, pp. 117–19. In 1936 he opposed Russia's Birobidjan project, stating that "we do not give encouragement to a Jewish State which will not only be non-religious but anti-religious." C. Adler to L. Noss, 12 June 1936, Adler Papers.

44. C. Adler to S. Rosenbloom, 10 May 1922, Adler Papers.

45. Moshe Perlmann, "Paul Haupt and the Mesopotamian Project," *Publication of the American Jewish Historical Society* 47 (March 1958).

46. Ibid., pp. 168–73; Neuman, *Cyrus Adler*, pp. 190–97; Adler, *Selected Letters*, vol. 1, p. 82; C. Adler to R. Gottheil, 26 February 1909, to J. Magnes, 14, 20 May 1909, Adler Papers.

47. L. Lipsky to H. Friedenwald, 27 September 1915, Friedenwald Papers; Adler, *Selected Letters*, vol. 1, pp. 109, 212, 227, vol. 2, p. 13; Naomi W. Cohen, *Not Free to Desist* (Philadelphia: Jewish Publication Society, 1972), pp. 104–5.

48. Adler, *Selected Letters*, vol. 1, pp. 136–37.

49. Kaplan diary, 30 June 1916.

50. Goldstein, *My World As a Jew*, vol. 1, p. 48. On commencement day Goldstein's valedictory address hailed the Declaration and joined it with a Schechter-like message on the religious stimulus that Palestine would provide for the Diaspora. Ibid., p. 50.

51. Friedlaender, *Past and Present*, chaps. 24–26; Shargel, *Practical Dreamer*, pp. 171–73, 179–81.

52. C. Adler to C. Jacobson, 21 June 1915, Adler Papers (AJC); minutes of AJC executive committee, 2 February 1918 (AJC); Adler, *Selected Letters*, vol. 2, pp. 336, 338–41, 344–45. Religious objections to political Zionism also accounted for Adler's opposition to Congress's endorsement of the Declaration in the Lodge-Fish resolution of 1922. Ibid., vol. 2, p. 49.

53. Cohen, *Not Free to Desist*, pp. 109–10; Neuman, *Cyrus Adler*, p. 205; Parzen, "Conservative Judaism and Zionism," p. 242; Knee, "Jewish Non-Zionism in America," p. 211; Adler, S*elected Letters*, vol. 2, p. 203.

54. Cohen, *Not Free to Desist*, pp. 90–98, 114, 116; Adler, *Selected Letters*, vol. 1, pp. 273–74, 276–87, 290–93, 307–08, 312–14, 323–24, 392; C. Adler to L. Marshall, undated, Adler Papers.

55. Adler, *Selected Letters*, vol. 1, pp. 313, 349; Adler letter to *Jewish Comment*, 8 June 1917, to the *Jewish Exponent*, 27 December 1918.

56. C. Adler to J. Mack, 3 May 1920; to O. Janowsky, 6 October 1931; to S. Wolf, 4 August 1920, Adler Papers; Adler, *Selected Letters*, vol. 2, pp. 9–10, 20.

57. Adler, *Selected Letters*, vol. 1, p. 349, vol. 2, pp. 25, 34; C. Adler to J. Hack, 30 September 1918, Adler Papers; Cyrus Adler, *Address Delivered at the Commencement Exercises of the Jewish Theological Seminary of America*, 4 June 1920; Adler letter to *Jewish Exponent*, 27 December 1918.

58. Cohen, *Not Free to Desist*, p. 95; Friedlaender, *Past and Present*, chap. 18; Bentwich, *Solomon Schechter*, p. 328; Schechter, *Seminary Addresses*, p. xxiv.

59. Rosenblum, "Founding of the United Synagogue," p. 244; United Synagogue of America, *Fourth Annual Report*, 1916, pp. 43-44, *Fifth Annual Report*, 1917, pp. 66–79; minutes of the United Synagogue, Kohn Papers; Parzen, *Architects of Conservative Judaism*, pp. 112, 120–24; Kaplan diary, 6 June 1915; Adler, S*elected Letters*, vol. 1, p. 332.

60. For published writings of the individual rabbis (which pertain to this and the following two paragraphs), see bibliographical entries in Pamela S. Nadell, *Conservative Judaism in America* (New York: Greenwood Press, 1988). See also Milton Steinberg, "Current Philosophies of Jewish Life in America," in *The American Jew*, ed. Oscar I. Janowsky (New York: Harper and Brothers, 1942), pp. 215-16.

61. United Synagogue of America, *Sixth Annual Report*, 1918, p. 16.

62. *The Rabbis of America to Labor Palestine* (New York: The League for Labor Palestine, 1935), p. 12; Mark Raider, "Zion and America," *Jewish Frontier* 60 (March–April 1993): p. 18.

63. Halperin, *Political World of American Zionism*, pp. 105-7; Goldstein, *My World As a Jew*, vol. 1, pp. 55-60, 68–69; Simon Noveck, *Milton Steinberg* (New York: Ktav, 1978), p. 137; Simon Greenberg, interview by author, 18 August 1992; Marshall Sklare, *Conservative Judaism* (New York: Schocken Books, 1972), p. 220; *Proceedings of the Rabbinical Assembly*, 1928, pp. 53–59, 1929, p, 97, 1930, pp. 35, 41–42; 1933, pp. 44–46; 1939, pp. 30–31.

64. Quickly becoming the target of Orthodox suspicion, the Conservative rabbis were, however, forced to withdraw. Gordis, *Understanding Conservative Judaism*, p. 119.

65. *Proceedings of the Rabbinical Assembly*, 1937, pp. 388–400.

66. Kaplan diary, 1 May 1922, 12 March 1925, 11 July 1929.

67. L. Marshall to C. Adler, 3 May 1921, C. Adler to L. Marshall, 30 June 1925, to J. Billikopf, 16 January 1931, to W. Fineshriber, 16 March 1931, Adler Papers; C. Adler to S. Schimmel, 29 March 1921, Adler Papers (AJC); Adler, *Selected Letters*, vol. 2, pp. 34–35, 47, 49, 69; Charles Reznikoff, ed., *Louis Marshall*, 2 vols. (Philadelphia: Jewish Publication Society, 1957), vol. 2, pp. 731–92; Herbert Parzen, "The Enlargement of the Jewish Agency for Palestine," *Jewish Social Studies* 39 (winter-spring 1977): pp. 129–58; Morris D. Waldman, *Nor By Power* (New York: International Universities Press, 1953), p. 204; Naomi W. Cohen, "An Uneasy Alliance," in *A Bicentennial Festschrift for Jacob Rader Marcus* (Waltham and New York: Ktav, 1976), pp. 108–12.

68. Cyrus Adler, *Lectures, Selected Papers, Addresses* (Philadelphia: Privately printed, 1933), pp. 313–14; minutes of the Board of Directors, 2 March 1919, C. Adler to F. Warburg, 13 May 1924.

69. *Proceedings of the Rabbinical Assembly*, 1927, p. 22, 1930, p. 42. *United Synagogue Recorder*, April 1924, p. 11; April 1925, pp. 9–10; May 1925, pp. 4-5; October 1925; pp. 6–7, July 1927, p. 5; October 1928, p. 5; July 1929, p. 10. *Herald* of the *United Synagogue Recorder*, 1 May

1925, pp. 4-5. Israel H. Levinthal, *Steering or Drifting—Which?* (New York: Funk and Wagnalls, 1928), pp. 269-76.

70. *Proceedings of the Rabbinical Assembly*, 1948, pp. 257-58; Abraham J. Karp, *A History of the United Synagogue of America* (New York: United Synagogue of America, 1964), pp. 63, 73.

71. Adler, *Selected Letters*, 1: p. 234, 2: p. 298; *Proceedings of the Rabbinical Assembly*, 1934, p. 67. A voluminous correspondence relating to the Hebrew University exists in the Adler Papers, especially for the years 1922-26.

72. C. Adler to S. Rosenbloom, 20 March 1925, Record Group (hereinafter R.G.) 1A-Hebrew University file; C. Adler to F. Warburg, 13 July 1932, 27 January 1933, 1925 statement, Adler Papers; Adler, *Selected Letters*, 2: pp. 111-13.

73. Kaplan also spoke at another session as the representative of the ZOA. *The Hebrew University-Jerusalem Inauguration, April 1, 1925* (Jerusalem, 1925), pp. 67, 100.

74. Ginzberg, *Keeper of the Law*, p. 168, chap. 9; C. Adler to F. Warburg, 13 May 1924, Adler Papers; J. Magnes to L. Finkelstein, 13 May 1940, R.G. 1A, Hebrew University file; *United Synagogue Recorder*, June–July 1924, p. 11; Jerome M. Kutnick, "Non-Zionist Leadership: Felix M. Warburg" (Ph. D. diss., Brandeis University, 1983), pp. 147-51; Adler, *Selected Letters*, 2: p. 125.

75. Mordecai M. Kaplan, "The Teachers Institute and Affiliated Departments," in *Jewish Theological Seminary of America Semi-Centennial Volume*, ed. Cyrus Adler (New York: Jewish Theological Seminary, 1939); JTS *Register*, 1926–27, p. 67, 1927–28, pp. 71, 77, 114–15; Kaplan diary, 1 May 1922, 29 October 1934, 31 December 1944.

76. Moshe Davis oral history interview, 18 January, 1, 27 February, 7 March 1990; 18 April 1991, Davis Papers, Ratner Center archives.

77. The figures have been graciously compiled for me by Dr. Sylvia Cutler Ettenberg. They do not include other *olim* who studied at the Teachers Institute but did not receive a degree.

78. L. Marshall to C. Adler, 25 May 1922, 24 September 1923, Adler Papers; Adler, *Selected Letters*, 2: pp. 26, 80; Richard Libowitz, "Kaplan and Cyrus Adler," in *The American Judaism of Mordecai M. Kaplan*, eds. Emanuel S. Goldsmith, Mel Scult, and Robert M. Seltzer (New York: New York University Press, 1990), pp. 122–39.

79. Early articles by Kaplan appeared in *Menorah Journal* for 1915-16 and 1920. See also Kaplan diary, 16 June 1921, 16 June 1928, 11 July 1929, 22 September 1939; *The American Judaism of Mordecai M. Kaplan*, pp. 41-44, 75–76, chap. 20.

80. Charles S. Liebman, "Reconstructionism in American Jewish Life," *American Jewish Year Book* 71(1970): pp. 3–99.

81. Naomi W. Cohen, *The Year After the Riots* (Detroit: Wayne State University Press, 1988), especially chap. 2.

82. Ibid., p. 74.

83. Ibid., p. 75; Kaplan diary, 16 September, 20 November 1929, 7 January, 3 June 1930; Adler, *Selected Letters*, vol. 2, pp. 181, 186–87; *The American Judaism of Mordecai N. Kaplan*, pp. 41-42, 412.

84. Kutnick, "Non-Zionist Leadership," pp. 148–51, 416–17; Cohen, *Year After the Riots*, pp. 79, 97-98, 117, 164; Adler, *Selected Letters*, vol. 2, pp. 177, 181, 185–89, 198–99; C. Adler to J. Billikopf, 16 January 1931, Adler Papers.

85. C. Adler to J. Rosenberg, 15 May 1930, *Philadelphia Ledger*, 3 September 1929, Adler Papers; Adler's address to Washington Conference, 8 March 1930, Adler Papers-JTS microfilm, reel 46; Adler, *Selected Letters*, vol. 2, pp. 218, 298-300.

86. C. Adler to L. Namier, 30 June 1930, Adler Papers; Cyrus Adler, *Memorandum on the Western Wall Prepared for the Special Commission of the League of Nations on Behalf of the Jewish Agency for Palestine* (Philadelphia: Privately printed, 1930). (The title of the memorandum was slightly changed in a second emended version.)

87. Adler, *Selected Letters*, 2:200, 208; *Women's League Outlook*, December 1930, p. 3; Cyrus Adler, *Lectures, Selected Papers, Addresses*, pp. 318–31, 341.

88. In the early 1930s Adler neither admitted the possibility of a "catastrophe" in Germany nor agreed that Palestine was the only hope for German Jews. Cohen, *Not Free to Desist*, p. 188; Cyrus Adler, "An Essay in Self-Searching," *The Day*, 4 November 1934.

89. Maurice J. Karpf, *Partition of Palestine and Its Consequences*; *Jewish Social Sciences Quarterly* 14, no. 3, pp. 1–16 (reprint); *Proceedings of the Rabbinical Assembly*, 1937, p. 400.

90. *JTA News*, 10 October 1937; *American Jewish Year Book* 40(1938–39): pp. 108, 585–86, 619–20, 625–28; W. Fineshriber to C. Adler, 9 March 1931, C. Adler to W. Fineshriber, 16 March 1931, Adler Papers; O. d'Avigdor-Goldsmid to C. Adler, 6 December 1937, R.G. 1A-Jewish Agency file; Adler, *Selected Letters*, vol. 2, pp. 333–42; Cyrus Adler, *Observations on the Report of the Palestine Royal Commission* (New York, 1938); Halperin, *Political World of American Zionism*, p. 119.

91. Adler, *Selected Letters*, vol. 2, pp. 335–36, 344–45; C. Adler to F. Warburg, 24 August, 20 November, 24 December 1936, F. Warburg to O. d'Avigdor-Goldsmid, 20 July 1937, Warburg Papers (American Jewish Archives); W. Senator to C. Adler, 13 January 1938, Adler Papers; Halperin, *Political World of American Zionism*, p. 359; Waldman, *Nor By Power*, p. 207.

92. Knee, "Jewish Non-Zionism in America," pp. 217–19; *American Jewish Year Book* 40(1938–39): pp. 586–87, 618–19, 625–26; Kaplan diary, 12 September 1922.

93. *American Jewish Year Book* 39 (1937–38): p. 276; Abraham M. Heller, *Jewish Survival* (New York: Behrman's Jewish Book House, 1939), pp. 149–54. My thanks to Rabbi Zachary Heller for the reference to his father's sermons.

94. Adler, *Selected Letters*, vol. 2, pp. 274, 293, 316, 330; *American Jewish Year Book* 37 (1935–36): p. 145, 438; *New York Times*, 22 June 1932; Kaplan diary, 15 June 1933, 9 October 1934, 11 June 1935; Judah Nadich to author, 5 May 1993. For Adler's clash with the Rabbinical Assembly over the World Jewish Congress see Kaplan diary, 17 March, 8 May, 15 June 1933, 11 June 1935.

95. "The Jewish Agency and the Non-Zionists," AJC memo, 14 June 1944, pp. 16–18.

96. Parzen, *Architects of Conservative Judaism*, pp. 207–9.

97. Louis Finkelstein, "The Things that Unite Us," *Proceedings of the Rabbinical Assembly*, 1927, p. 51.

98. Unless otherwise noted, the material in the next five paragraphs has been culled from the following pre-1948 articles and speeches by Finkelstein: "The Things that Unite Us"; "Jewish Nationalism and the Hebrew Language," *Avukah Annual* (1925–1930); "Some Aspects of Rabbinic Nationalism," *Brandeis Avukah Annual*, ed. J.S. Shubow (New York: Avukah, American Student Zionist Federation, 1932); "Need for Land to Develop Teachings," *New Palestine*, 25 January 1935; "Address," *New Palestine*, 17 July 1936; "A Program for Positive Judaism," *American Hebrew*, 11 March 1938; "Tradition in the Making," in *Jewish Theological Seminary of American Semi-Centennial Volume*; "The Duty of the Jew," *Jewish Exponent*, 4 October 1940; "Reflections on Judaism, Zionism and Enduring Peace," *New Palestine*, 21 May 1943; "Zionism and World Culture," *New Palestine*, 15 September 1944; draft of radio address, 17 June 1938, R.G. 1A-Zionist Organization of America file. See also Menahem Schmelzer's sensitive analysis in "Rabbi Louis Finkelstein," (Hebrew) *Mada'ei ha-Yahadut* 32 (1992). See Moshe Davis, "To Our Teacher, Rabbi Louis Finkelstein, on the First Anniversary of His Death," (Hebrew) *Hadoar*, 1 January 1993.

99. L. Finkelstein to M. Steinberg, 9 November 1943, R.G. 1B-AJC file.

100. Ibid.

101. L. Finkelstein to J. Kahn, 28 December 1931, to J. Magnes, 17 June 1940, R.G. 1A-Hebrew University file.

102. M. Davis to author, 27 September 1992.

103. In 1937, for example, in reference to the heated disputes generated by the Arab riots and the Palestine partition proposal, Finkelstein recalled the words of Rabbi Joshua ben Hananiah urging his brethren always to resolve their problems peaceably. L. Finkelstein to F. Warburg, 3 September 1937, R.G. 1A-Warburg file.

104. Nadell, *Conservative Judaism in America*, pp. 86, 279–80.

105. Moshe Davis oral history interview, 15 April 1990, Davis Papers, Ratner Center archives.

106. Adler, *I Have Considered the Days*, pp. 422–24; S. Goldman to L. Finkelstein, 12 November 1936, L. Finkelstein to S. Goldman, 27 November 1936, R.G. 1A-Goldman file.

107. See for example *American Jewish Year Book* 43 (1941-42): pp. 29, 45(1943–44): pp. 138–39; Louis Finkelstein, "Hope as Well as Despair," *American Hebrew*, 27 September 1940, "The Duty of the Jew," *Jewish Exponent*, 4 October 1940, "For a Complete Democracy," *Atlantic Monthly* 168 (September 1941), "America and a World of Darkness," *Jewish Forum* 24 (September 1941). Finkelstein spoke of the Judeo-Christian tradition as early as the Semi-Centennial. Finkelstein, "Tradition in the Making," p. 27; Schmelzer, "Rabbi Louis Finkelstein," p. 41.

108. Kaplan diary, 14 September 1929; L. Finkelstein to Frieda Warburg, 1 September 1937, R.G. 1A-Warburg file.

109. Memorandum of conference with Lord Halifax, 27 March 1941, L. Finkelstein's memorandum of telephone conversation with Dr. Israel Goldstein, 9 April 1941, I. Goldstein to S. Wise, 11 April 1941, to C. Weizmann, 11 April 1941, R.G. 1A-Goldstein file; Finkelstein memorandum, 27 March 1941, R.G. 1A-minutes of a meeting file.

110. Melvin I. Urofsky, *We Are One!* (Garden City, N.Y.: Anchor Press, 1978), pp. 3-30; Kaplan diary, 2 September 1943.

111. Thomas A. Kolsky, *Jews Against Zionism* (Philadelphia: Temple University Press, 1990), chap. 2.

112. P. Bernstein to L. Finkelstein, 6, 8 October 1942, L. Finkelstein to P. Bernstein, 9, 16 October 1942, R.G. 1A-Bernstein file; L. Finkelstein to L. Levinthal, 22 October 1942, R.G. 1A-Levinthal file; *New Palestine*, 20 November 1942; Howard R. Greenstein, *Turning Point* (Ann Arbor: Brown Judaic Studies 12, 1981), p. 144.

113. L. Finkelstein to P. Bernstein, 30 December 1942, R.G. 1A-Bernstein file; L. Finkelstein to A. Lelyveld, 24 April 1946, R.G. 1A-responses to Finkelstein's Rabbinical Assembly address file.

114. Moshe Davis oral history interview, 15 April 1990, Davis Papers, Ratner Center archives.

115. Urofsky, *We Are One!* p. 67; *New York Times*, 23 January 1943; *Reconstructionist*, 5 February 1943; *New Palestine*, 19 February 1943.

116. L. Finkelstein to M. Steinberg, 9 November 1943, R.G. 1B-Steinberg file.

117. A. Sulzberger to L. Finkelstein, 25 January 1943, L. Finkelstein, 27 January 1943, R.G. 1B-Sulzberger file. On Sulzberger's anti-Zionism, see *New Palestine*, 20 November 1942, 7 January 1944; Kolsky, *Jews Against Zionism*, pp. 55, 58; Gay Talese, *The Kingdom and the Power* (New York: World Publishing Company, 1969), pp. 90–91.

118. *New Palestine*, 8 January 1943; L. Finkelstein to H. Bavli, 20 January 1943, R.G. 1A-Bavli file, to A. Sulzberger, 27 January 1943, R.G. 1B-Sulzberger file.

119. Kolsky, *Jews Against Zionism*, pp. 42, 46, 58, 79; L. Ginzberg to L. Finkelstein, 2 February 1943, R.G. 1A-Ginzberg file.

120. Cohen, *Not Free to Desist*, pp. 249–60; Waldman, *Nor by Power*, chap. 22.

121. *American Jewish Year Book* 46 (1944–45): p. 557; M. Steinberg to L. Finkelstein, 29 October 1943, R.G. 1B-Steinberg file; M. Hanin to L. Finkelstein, 5 November 1943, R.G. 1B-AJC file.

122. Waldman, *Nor by Power*, pp. 280-81; S. Schulman to L. Finkelstein, 28 October 1943, L. Finkelstein to S. Schulman, 1 November 1943, R.G. 1B, Schulman file; L. Finkelstein to

M. Steinberg, 9 November 1943, R.G. lB-AJC file.

123. S. Wallach to L. Finkelstein, 15 August 1941, R.G. lA-AJC file; for a view of Finkelstein's participation in the AJC see all AJC files in R.G. 1.

124. M. Steinberg to L. Finkelstein, 11, 18 November 1943, L. Finkelstein to M. Steinberg, 12, 24 November 1943, R.G. lB-Steinberg file, to M. Steinberg, 9 November 1943, R.G. lB-AJC file.

125. Louis Finkelstein, "Reflections on Judaism, Zionism and Enduring Peace," *New Palestine*, 21 May 1943; L. Finkelstein to M. Steinberg, 9 November 1943, R.G. lB-AJC file.

126. L. Finkelstein to "Dear Colleague," 28 December 1943, R.G. lB-AJC file; L. Finkelstein to J. Proskauer, 20 October 1943, R.G. lB-Proskauer file; Jacob J. Weinstein, *Solomon Goldman* (New York: Ktav, 1973), p . 44.

127. "Reflections on Judaism, Zionism and Enduring Peace," *New Palestine*, 21 May 1943; "Zionism and World Culture," *New Palestine*, 15 September 1944; C. Alpert to L. Finkelstein, 22 April 1943, L. Finkelstein to C. Alpert, 30 April 1943, R.G. lB-*New Palestine* file.

128. Talk by Sulzberger to a Baltimore temple group, 5 November 1942, R.G. lA-Sulzberger file; A. Sulzberger to L. Finkelstein, 21 May 1945, 12 August 1946, R.G. lC-Sulzberger file; Kaplan diary, 17 March 1948; Sulzberger's letter to Abba Hillel Silver, *New Palestine*, 7 January 1944. On Milton Steinberg's interchange with Sulzberger, see Simon Noveck, *Milton Steinberg*, pp. 134-36.

129. A. Sulzberger to L. Finkelstein, 16 Sept, 1946, R.G. lC-Sulzberger file.

130. L. Finkelstein to S. Stroock, 1 July 1941, R.G. lA-Stroock file; note on C. Weizmann to L. Finkelstein, 2 May 1941, R.G. lA-Weizmann file.

131. Kaplan diary, 26 March, 24 September 1945.

132. *New York Times*, 29 October 1943; L. Finkelstein to A. Silver, 3 November 1945, R.G. lB-Silver file; L. Finkelstein to A. Sulzberger, 5 November 1943, R.G. lB-Sulzberger file.

133. *New Palestine*, 7 January 1944.

134. Minutes, Board of Directors JTS, 17 April [1945]; Kaplan diary, 17 April 1945.

135. *Time*, 15 October 1951; Weinstein, *Solomon Goldman*, p. 44.

136. Steinberg's sermons, "Crises in Conservative Judaism," in R.G. lB-Steinberg file; Weinstein, *Solomon Goldman*, 42–49, 259–70; Noveck, *Milton Steinberg*, pp. 171–79; Kaplan diary, 20 November 1944, 23 January, 17 June 1945; unsorted Steinberg papers: Finkelstein-Steinberg correspondence for January–July 1945.

137. Kaplan diary, 29 June 1945.

138. Moshe Davis to author, 28 October 1992.

139. A degree was first considered in 1942. At that time the only one to question it, on the grounds that Weizmann was a secularist, was Zionist Simon Greenberg. Kaplan diary, 23 October 1942.

140. Copy of citation and JTS news release 8 December 1944, R.G. llC-Communications; Abraham Karp to author, 4 December 1992; Arthur Hertzberg, "The Changing Rabbinate," *Proceedings of the Rabbinical Assembly*, 1975, p. 67.

141. L. Finkelstein to Frieda Warburg, 27 October 1944, R.G. lB-Warburg file; L. Finkelstein to J. Magnes, 31 March 1947, R.G. lD-Magnes file; Arthur A. Goren, ed., *Dissenter in Zion* (Cambridge: Harvard University Press, 1982), p. 483.

142. Simon Greenberg to author, 18 August 1992.

143. Kaplan diary, 7 January, 22, 28 February, 17 March, 27 April 1948; *New York Times*, 7 June 1948. In protest against the Seminary's attitude, Bavli published a bitter poem, "Gayim v'Aririm," that appeared in his *Aderet Ha-shanim* (Jerusalem: Bialik Institute, 1955), pp. 72-73. (My thanks to Professor Alan Mintz for calling the poem to my attention.)

144. Morton Leifman to author, 30 August 1992; Yaakov Rosenberg to author, 7 November 1992. Moshe Davis disputes the story of "Hatikva" at the 1948 graduation, claiming that

the carilloneur played a melody that only sounded like the Jewish anthem. Moshe Davis oral history interview, 20 November 1990, Davis Papers, Ratner Center archives.

145. Moshe Davis, ed., *Israel: Its Role in Civilization* (New York: Israel Institute of the Jewish Theological Seminary, 1956), introduction; idem, "Our Share in Eretz Yisrael," symposium in *Conservative Judaism* 11 (spring 1957): pp 26–36; *New York Times*, 29 April 1952.

146. Finkelstein's address at a dinner in honor of Maxwell Abbell, 31 October 1948, R.G. lE-Abbell file; Louis Finkelstein, "The State of Israel as a Spiritual Force," in *Israel: Its Role in Civilization*, p. 16.

147. Board of Directors *Newsletter*, 17 June 1948, R.G. lE-JTS Board of Directors file.

148. Finkelstein, "State of Israel as a Spiritual Force," p. 6.

ELI LEDERHENDLER

The Ongoing Dialogue

*The Seminary and the
Challenge of Israel*

Louis Finkelstein at a Seminary convocation in Jerusalem, 1952.
Ratner Center, JTS.

ELI LEDERHENDLER

The Ongoing Dialogue
The Seminary and the Challenge of Israel

In memory of Moshe Davis

"We go to Zion to be ourselves. The function of those who go to Zion is to teach
the eternal (and necessarily eternal) masses in the Galut to be themselves. Self-
affirmation as a people and as individuals must be our aim."—Ludwig
Lewisohn, *Israel* (1925).

As the Seminary's history as a fountainhead of Judaic values is one that is fraught
with great complexity and inner contradiction, it should therefore come as no shock
to discover that in the Seminary's approach to the State of Israel, we can identify
similar complexities and conflicts. Our goal here will be to understand the Seminary's relationship with Israel in terms of the *distance* between the two as well as the
closeness between them. This essay endeavors to place Israel within the developing
ethos of the Seminary.

The Source Traditions

One might describe the Seminary as the product of three compelling streams in the
history of modern Judaism: first, the academic traditions of *Wissenschaft des Judentums* (modern Jewish scholarship); second, the forces of Americanization that have
re-formed the patterns of Jewish life in the United States; and third, the rabbinic
tradition itself. All three of these "heritage" sources of the Seminary's ethos were
historically marked by ambivalence, or some essential difference, vis-à-vis the ethos
that produced the Zionist movement and the State of Israel. The Seminary, as the
"child" of such godparents, is heir to these conflicts.

Originating in Europe in the early modern period, the development of modern
Jewish scholarship within the parameters of the European scholarly canon was
inextricably linked with the politics of religious toleration, the privatization of religion, and the public debate over Jewish civil enfranchisement. The *Wissenschaft* of
those devoted to the modern study of Judaism was programmed to fit Judaism into
Western social, intellectual, and religious patterns so that Jews, as individuals,

might also be enabled to fit into Western society. Simultaneously, "Jewish science" made available to modernizing Jews, already living beyond the separatist norms of their ancestors, a language of Jewish continuity that was acceptable and apprehensible, both because its discourse took place in Western languages and because it lent to Judaism a sophisticated, idealist, universalist-ethicist cast.

The Seminary likes to trace its lineage to the *Wissenschaft* tradition through one of its important branches: the "Positive-Historical School" identified with Zacharias Frankel. The name of the institution itself testifies to that claim of spiritual parenthood, harking back to Frankel's Jewish Theological Seminary in Breslau. Frankel's ideological emendation of the basic *Wissenschaft* tradition included three main elements: the preeminence of *rabbinic* scholars in the formulation of the learned culture of Judaism; the combination of scholarly concerns with the practice of a living Judaism (thus departing from a merely antiquarian model of research); and an ethnocentric "ism" of Jewish peoplehood that preferred a pan-Jewish cultural nationalism to the radical, universalistic-monotheistic ethic being propounded by other contemporaries.

Yet, even this Positive-Historical *Wissenschaft* remained focused on text-oriented scholarship, which was both in keeping with its philological and philosophical roots in Central European intellectual history and fully compatible with the rabbinic heritage as such. It remained dedicated to Judaism as a developing Idea or Law, with the Jews as the bearers and interpreters of that Idea. It was devoted to the creation of the intellectual apparatus required to enable the Jews to continue to bear and to interpret that Idea into the modern period, and thus to overcome the forces threatening the Jewish people with cultural distintegration.[1]

Zionism, on the other hand, did not perceive Jewish existence as something that could be assured through intellectual means. It saw Jewry as a political entity (a "nation") that was suffering under a political handicap: the lack of a homeland. That handicap, the Zionists taught, was responsible for the fact that the integration of Jews as individuals within European society was faltering. Indeed, it was doomed to fail. The problem could be rectified *only* through political means: through a politics of self-determination.

We can see certain points of contact between Frankel's ethnocentric *Wissenschaft* and political Zionism: the elevation of Hebrew to the status of a national language; the apotheosis of the Jewish people as a historical, creative, and unitary *Volk*; and the intention to preserve that unity by recreating new foci of activity and authority. But the intellectual-religious project of the Frankel school found its chief raison d'être in the elaboration of a viable modern Judaism suited to European Jewish life; while Zionism projected a new Jewish *polis* (in Herzl's terms, a *Judenstaat*) capable of sustaining a corporate Jewish community—something that was quite *unsuited* to the conditions of life in Europe.

Thus, even in its Frankelean variation, the *Wissenschaft* approach did not form a neat match with the Zionist enterprise. (The gap between the two positions could be negotiated by some Jewish scholar-intellectuals—Martin Buber, Gershom Scholem, Akiva Ernst Simon—who brought Central European Jewish *Wissenschaft* to Palestine in the 20th century, although they could not reconcile themselves to the militant nationalism that characterized much of the leadership of the *yishuv*—pre-state Jewish Palestine.)

In actuality, not only was Frankel's system essentially suited for Europe but it was drawn to the specific template of conditions in the German and Habsburg imperial lands in the mid- to late-19th century. Frankel's philosophy faced enormous structural barriers outside its native Central European habitat. It fared best where the professionalization of the modern rabbinate intersected with the intellectualization (read: academicization) of highbrow Jewish culture and where both of these trends triangulated with the national question, so endemic to Central Europe. Frankel's Seminary was a natural development in Breslau but probably could not have been located in London, Paris, or even Hamburg, let alone Warsaw or Vilna.

That the Jewish Theological Seminary of America, under Solomon Schechter, could successfully readapt some major planks of Frankel's program had a good deal to do with the replication in America of some of the conditions that had obtained in Central Europe; but it had even more to do with peculiarly American conditions that maximized the need for a Judaism that was Western in form but ethnocentric in content, while reducing to a minimum any obstacles that stood in the way of an untrammeled freedom of religion and freedom of scholarly enquiry.

In America at the turn of the 20th century the desperate need for a trained professional rabbinate to serve a community that was growing by quantum leaps each year, and a parallel demand for the cultural resources that might be provided by a sophisticated Jewish scholarship, coincided (as in Central Europe) with tremendous flux and tension regarding ethnic, racial, and national identity.[2] This was, after all, the height of the "new immigration" that changed Protestant America forever, the gestation period of an urban, industrial America that definitively transformed the old agrarian society and its social values, and the time of America's emergence as a major power with global responsibilities. The mass Jewish migration from Eastern Europe brought a vast Jewish population to live under conditions that were conducive to the Seminary's approach (the attraction made itself felt over time, rather than immediately)—a historic convergence of crucial importance. America made possible that which Germany never could, both in terms of the mass concentration of America's Jewish population—its cultural capabilities and its world-Jewish (*klal yisrael*) sensibilities—and in terms of America's denominationalism that fostered a legitimate, institutionalized, "established" religious diversity.

When Schechter and others in the Seminary orbit (Israel Friedlaender, for example) elaborated a pro-Zionist, Conservative position,[3] their intellectual cloth was cut to American patterns. Zionism's cultural agenda (revitalization of Hebrew language and letters without renouncing Western culture and science), as well as its social program (dignifying the Jewish masses through a democratization of Jewish community life), resonated with a newly emerging, post-migration American Judaism that championed ethnocultural and religious distinctiveness as a necessary concomitant and fulfillment of equality and democracy.

Yet, at the same time, a bald assertion of Jewish distinctiveness would have condemned the Conservatives to a position on the margins of American Jewry had it not been qualified by an equally powerful commitment to America. In an urban America that was developing its own cultural style, Jews stood athwart an ongoing public discussion of conformity and nonconformity that has lasted from the 1870s through the 1960s and continues even today. By lending its sponsorship to a cultural compromise between East European Orthodox traditionalism and English-speaking, liberal, middle-class Judaism, the Seminary and the rabbis that it trained affirmed the compatibility of this Judaism with life in the mainstream of American society and culture.[4] This essential qualification created ideological "space" between American-based Conservatism and Palestine-based Zionism, so that on this count, too (as with the *Wissenschaft* tradition), one had either to "bridge" the gap or to acknowledge and affirm it.

We come, finally, to the rabbinic tradition itself. The complexity of rabbinic literature is such that any generalization may appear reductionist. Certainly there is in the rabbinic tradition enough (in liturgy and ritual, in *halakha* and *aggadah*) that is rooted in a desire to perpetuate the tie between Judaism and the land of its birth. But without pretending to engage in a thorough analysis of rabbinic teachings relating to Exile and Redemption, it can be stated in shorthand form that the originality of rabbinism as a system lay in the textualization of cultic center and territory (the Yavneh solution), combined with an Eretz-Israelism that was wrapped in a messianic "envelope" (and thus removed from a this-worldly plane). "Thus," Eliezer Schweid has observed, "ritual patterns were created that perpetuated the memory of the Land of Israel and endowed it with supreme *symbolic* signficance. . . . The idealization of the land culminated in its absolute spiritualization." Even when rabbinic discourse revolved around the ultimate theological and political issues attendant upon "the Land," they became enmeshed in what another keen observer has called "ontological complexities—even ambiguities—rooted in the classical sources themselves"; thus, "The problem is not . . . '*Eretz Yisrael* or not . . .' [but] 'What is *Eretz Yisrael* supposed to be, to represent, to promise?'"[5]

The rabbinic reformation, taken as a whole, created the mechanism for a religious authority that was at once decentralized *and* normative. It thus made Judaism less dependent on any one central hierarchy and correspondingly more dependent on consensual arrangements, on local initiative, and on the transmission of knowledge throughout a widening periphery. It also made possible survival in dispersion across generations and centuries. Rabbi Samson Raphael Hirsch, in restating the rabbinic posture in 19th-century Germany, stated, "From where Torah emanates, there is my Zion"—an apt if ironic recasting of the classical "For out of Zion shall go forth the Law."[6] Or, to take a more recent example, from within the Seminary itself, Professor Neil Gillman recently noted that *halakha* "represents a quasi-realized eschatology which enables us to structure our lives in the here and now, deal with the chaos that is inevitable in our age of history, and await the ultimate *eschaton* to come. It is precisely the power of this quasi-realized eschatological structure that impelled Judaism's resistance to the more aggressive eschatological movements that arose in the course of its history."[7] And, it should be noted, it is also this structure that implies a dissonance between rabbinic Judaism as a system and Zionism.

The teleology of Exile and Redemption is firmly rooted in the entire rabbinic corpus, as it is in the Zionist philosophy. But in rabbinic Judaism, as Gillman noted, the Law and its interpretation perform the key function of maintaining the "here and now" of Judaism wherever Jews happen to live. Most Jews happen to live in the Diaspora and will continue to do so, if current demographic trends hold, until the community in Israel begins to outweigh those abroad (probably some time in the mid-21st century). The thrust of Zionism, like rabbinic Judaism, was to neutralize messianism; but unlike the rabbinic-halakhic approach, it did so by coopting the political utopia embedded in Jewish eschatology—and to this day the Zionist state is at loggerheads with Jewish messianism.[8]

The Seminary, which has prided itself on maintaining its link to a continued halakhic process (identifying itself with the interpretive enterprise begun by the Tanaim and Amoraim), is similarly implicated in the logic of rabbinic ex-territoriality: the condition of holiness is predicated on religious practice *(mitsvot)*, participation in and adherence to communal norms, and personal closeness to God, rather than on the maintenance of one national-religious community in the Land of Israel.

Secular Zionism, which emerged as an overthrow of traditional Jewish politics, could remain practically removed from matters of "religion," which were ceded to the Orthodox because these matters were ostensibly irrelevant to the *realpolitik* of diplomacy and state-building. But the Seminary could hardly relegate the rabbinic tradition to the Orthodox and still claim to be a flagship institution of modern Judaism. From the period of Frankel, on through the Schechter era and into the post-1948 years, what developed as Conservatism was a self-conscious reworking of the rabbinic tradition, including aspects of its ex-territorial bias. Some of the most respected intellectual formulations within (or close to) the Positive-Historical and Conservative tradition that deal with the issues of nationality, peoplehood, and territoriality come to a decidedly non-political, non-territorial conclusion. One may cite Graetz's 19th-century spiritual nationalism or Baron's 20th-century emphasis on "history" over "nature"; Heschel's similar location of the sacred in the realm of "time" (more than in "space") and his aggadic-mystical personal religiosity of "awe"; or Lieberman's normative *halakha* as a surer guide to religious authenticity than "catholic Israel" could ever be in a post-traditional community. Conversely, Kaplan, the "naturalist," was marginalized within the Seminary in part because he insisted that a reconstituted Jewish peoplehood-community, when closely associated with a viable and creative Israel, was necessary for Jewish existence: Jewish civilization required visible objectification. But his was not the dominant view at the Seminary.

The Jewish State and the Seminary

I have emphasized the problematic aspects of the Seminary's intellectual "baggage" with regard to Zionism and Israel in order to point up some of the deeper sources of the ambivalence that we will confront in the following discussion. Yet, just as Orthodox and Reform Judaism in their respective ways have wrestled with and discovered ways to reconcile the post-exilic rabbinic tradition with the imperatives of the Zionist struggle and the reality of Jewish statehood, so, too, did the Seminary find ways that led toward a reconciliation of its own. To the extent that its mode of reconciliation has borne the stamp of its own philosophy, we will find much in the Seminary's Israel component that speaks to the distinctiveness of the Seminary's position in American Jewry.

In affirming a nexus with Israel, the Seminary has assumed a role that is neither political nor philanthropic, nor even purely intellectual; rather, this role is *religious*. The articulation of Israel's meaning for Jewish life, conceived broadly, is part of the religious task of the Seminary: to shape and to disseminate Judaism in the contemporary world in the light of historical scholarship and modern existential concerns. Israel is the great unavoidable presence on the late 20th-century Jewish scene. It virtually demands to be recognized and dealt with by dint of its historic importance to the Jewish people at large. All contemporary Jewish issues, sooner or later, intersect with Israeli ones. No Jewish institution that claims to represent a significant segment of Jewry today, anywhere in the world, can fail to take Israel into account without running the risk of irrelevancy. To teach Judaism as if nothing had changed in 1948 would be akin to teaching nuclear physics as if there had been no Hiroshima: theoretically feasible but tunnel-visioned and intellectually dishonest.

We will see that a strong attachment to Israel, over the years, has clearly affected the Seminary's ethos and that of its graduates. It is the Seminary's ambition to return the favor. How and how well it has done so is a question that remains open, but one that will also concern us toward the end of this inquiry.

Though the Seminary's name indicates a "theological" purpose, Judaism is the theology of a particular ethno-national group. The Seminary's ethos has always taken that as fundamental. In its formative period, the Seminary developed characteristic approaches to the issue of Jewish nationalism: as Israel Friedlaender had put it, "Diaspora plus Palestine, religion plus nationalism."[9] Those approaches tell much about the intellectual pedigree of the Seminary faculty as well as about the preferences of the Seminary's wider constituency, for whom peoplehood issues were paramount.[10]

185

*The Ongoing
Dialogue:
The Seminary
and the
Challenge of
Israel*

In the year of Jewish statehood, 1948, the biennial convention of the United Synagogue took place in Chicago from May 13 to 17: that is, continuing through the crucial weekend on which Israel was established and the War of Independence officially began. According to reports of the convention, "numerous speakers" cited "the religious, cultural, and moral impact of the creation of the state of Israel upon the potentialities of Jewish life in America."[11] United Synagogue executive director Rabbi Albert I. Gordon told a press conference that "Palestine Jewry is endowing its American brethren with a heightened sense of dignity and self-respect by demonstrating that the social and religious principles of Judaism are as valid today as they were in Biblical times."[12] Dr. Moshe Davis, then the dean of the Seminary's Teachers Institute, predicted that "as the political situation stabilizes, the influence of Eretz Israel upon the spiritual and cultural life of American Israel will increase beyond our powers of anticipation."[13]

And yet, notwithstanding the celebratory rhetoric, the establishment of the State of Israel was not a clear-cut or assured triumph, marked as it was by prolonged political struggle, bloodshed, the unresolved problems of Holocaust survivors, and the challenge of the mass *aliya* (immigration) about to begin, as well as the ominously looming struggle for international supremacy between the two major world powers. Moreover, the precise impact of the *yishuv* on the numerically far stronger American Jewish community was to remain unclear for some time to come. On the eve of independence, the Jewish population in Israel numbered some six hundred thousand. Israel's basic assertion, that the Jewish people was itself a political entity that—albeit dispersed throughout the world—retained sufficient political coherence to warrant the establishment of a sovereign Jewish state, was still open to question and qualification in many American Jewish circles (including some at the Seminary) on both philosophical and practical grounds. The Jewish people, still staggering from the losses sustained in the Holocaust, was spread across the globe, both East and West, and internally divided by politics, theology, and culture. Jews throughout the world owed their primary political or civic loyalty to the countries under whose flags they had just fought for six years to defeat Nazi Germany. By declaring the independent State of Israel, the leaders of the *yishuv* gave an inspired ideal—Jewish peoplehood—its first fair chance in many centuries; but by the same token, they created a series of new dilemmas for existing Jewish communities: not least, those in the United States.

There was, for instance, the question of resource allocation. The War of Independence and the ensuing period of large-scale immigration imposed enormous financial obligations upon the new state, whose leaders naturally turned to the Jewish Diaspora communities for support. The outpouring of American Jewish support was being orchestrated even before May 1948. The first day of Pesach, Saturday, 24 April, was declared "UJA [United Jewish Appeal] Sabbath," and the New York Board of Rabbis urged all rabbis and congregations to participate in assuring the success of the nationwide campaign to raise $250 million: "With our help—and help can come *only* from us—the 700,000 [*sic*] Jews in Palestine now defending their lives and their homes can win ultimate peace and security—and the opportunity to build homes for the thousands of homeless Jews wishing to join them. . . . It has been given into our hands to give this help. . . . We, the Jews of America, are their one 'last, best hope on earth.'"[14]

Rabbi Louis Finkelstein, as President (Chancellor) of the Seminary, was faced with an unpromising situation in his own institution, which he described at the time in a letter to Judah L. Magnes, president of the Hebrew University:

> As you probably know, the United Jewish Appeal has made it virtually impossible for any of the educational institutions here to raise the sum they had hoped for. Our own Seminary is probably the chief sufferer because we ourselves are so deeply involved with the United Jewish Appeal and most of our laymen are among its leading workers. Without complaining in any way of the conditions, we have to face the fact that we are ending this year with a substantial deficit, and I have had to promise the Board of Directors that I would not request any expansion of our budget.[15]

At the time, the Seminary was poised upon the brink of a major new project: the opening of a Seminary branch or school in Los Angeles (which became the University of Judaism).[16] A new strategic position on the question of priorities for the Jewish public in resource allocation was a pressing necessity for an institution like the Seminary. By the spring of 1949, the outlines of such a position were discernible. Simon Greenberg, filling in for Louis Finkelstein (then on a year's leave of absence), argued (at the Seminary's National Planning and Campaign Committee in Philadelphia): "The persistent calls we hear for a moratorium on constructive Jewish effort in America come only from those who timidly underestimate our energies and our resources. We must prove to them that the lives of our brethren and the security of Israel need not be purchased at the expense of building a vibrant, meaningful Judaism on our own continent. . . . [N]o civilized people invokes sacrifices from its colleges and universities in a period of crisis."[17]

Finkelstein himself echoed this theme upon his return, in a letter sent to members of the Rabbinical Assembly:

> Ever since the first Jewish immigrants arrived in this land, almost three centuries ago, a continuous effort has been made to establish America as another center of Jewish spiritual life. This effort reached its culmination in the past ten years, which have witnessed the development of our synagogue and religious educational life in a manner which could not but hold enormous promise for the future. It seemed as if the American Jews had declared that their answer to the destruction of the great centers of Jewish learning and faith abroad would be the establishment of even greater ones on this continent. . . . It is hard to think of any duty more urgent than the continuation of this promising effort to make Judaism once more one of the great, vital, spiritual forces in the world. . . . The new responsibilities which are falling on us abroad are urgent and must be met. At the same time, we must not desist for a moment from the effort to establish ourselves as a center of the religious resurgence, which will ultimately make America a spiritual leader of the world. . . . Sharing with all other Jews in the development of the State of Israel, Conservative Jewry in America will continue . . . its effort to establish on this continent, through the Seminary, a University of Judaism worthy of the great academies of the past: of Yabnah, of Sura, of Pumbedita.[18]

Fighting on "two fronts" simultaneously (as Finkelstein put it), or insisting that the new rules of allocating Jewish public resources need not entail a zero-sum calculus, was a fitting public stance for the Seminary to take. This position affirmed *both* American Jewish and Israeli priorities without seeming to place one higher than the other. But in the allocation of some resources, particularly human resources, a choice was necessary, and such a case presented itself to the Seminary almost immediately after the State of Israel was established. The episode provides what I believe to be a key to Louis Finkelstein's entire approach, not just to the narrower matter of the division of resources in the post-1948 world, but even more, to the wider question of Jewish peoplehood and the relative significance of Israel in the Jewish world.

During 1947–48, Professor Ernst Simon, then on leave from the Hebrew University's School of Education, taught at the Seminary's Rabbinical School and Teachers Institute. As the academic year came to a close, Finkelstein strongly urged him to remain at the Seminary at least another year and, if possible, permanently. He summed up their conversations in a lengthy letter to Simon:

> It seems to me that, at least for the immediate future, you have a more significant contribution to make here even than in Jerusalem. This is because at the Hebrew University you offer instruction in philosophy of education and education, a field in which there are others. . . . At the Seminary and in American Judaism you have a unique contribution to make, namely that which can be

offered through the integration of philosophy with Jewish tradition and by a person who has had the rare experience among our people of deliberately choosing the path of Jewish life against assimilation. . . . *I have always felt that we must regard ourselves as soldiers and serve where we are called upon to serve and where we can render the most significant service we are able to give*[19] [my emphasis—EL].

The offer of a permanent post, he went on to say, would be held open for two years. Finkelstein took into account that Simon would undoubtedly have to consult the Hebrew University: "We would not wish to do anything which might in any way injure the Hebrew University, believing that its establishment and advancement are primary obligations for all Jews, and having faith that in the future it will serve as a great spiritual center for the whole Jewish community." Professor Simon, in his reply, noted his profound appreciation of Finkelstein's "insight into another man's heart who has to make a very grave decision and is thrown into a genuine moral conflict."[20] (Simon returned to Jerusalem in November 1948.)

By presenting the issue as one of conscience, Finkelstein portrayed the Jewish world as one, global, all-embracing framework. Within that framework, no one field of action was in principle to be preferred over any other, but to Finkelstein's mind, a rational division of resources was possible and, indeed, necessary. Such a division would place the unique talents of an Ernst Simon at the disposal of American Jewry, hungry for spiritual sustenance and able to elevate him to a position of influence in the community at large, rather than have him toil among the ranks of those who were intently (but with less immediate impact on the world at large) building "a spiritual center for the whole Jewish community" in Jerusalem. Moreover, although Israel could spare Simon, American Jewry could not.

There are three motifs that bear notice here: (1) Israel has a status worthy of support by all Jews; (2) Israel can serve as a reservoir of scholarship for the Diaspora and it should accept that role graciously; (3) one must serve where one is "called upon" to serve, like any good soldier, where one can do the most good. The fact that Finkelstein himself had lived in Palestine in 1924, had been offered a senior post there in the educational field, and, although tempted, had decided to return to the United States where he could "render the most significant service" adds authenticity, pathos, and depth to this episode with Simon.[21]

Finkelstein felt so strongly on the matter that when the Hebrew University turned down a request to extend Simon's leave for another year, he voiced his frustration in an irate letter to Judah Magnes:

It seems to be an almost hopeless task to get people in one country to have a clear notion of what is going on in the other. Instead of our begging them [the Hebrew University] to let us have Prof. Simon, I would have expected that if they knew anything about America, and what a personality like Prof. Simon might mean simply in dollars and cents [as a spokesman in America] for the University, not to speak of increasing [the University's] prestige [in American academic circles], they would beg us to hold him for another year.[22]

Simon Greenberg saw to it that a more positive public relations "spin" was attached to this episode. In a communique he composed in October 1948, Greenberg maintained that Ernst Simon's sojourn at the Seminary had provided "the best answer" to the pressing question of what relationship ought to exist between Israel and U.S. Jewry. "He brought to us in his own personality, in the clarity of his thought, and in the purity of his spirit the noblest spiritual and intellectual achievements of the Jewish community in Israel. He will bring back, we hope, to the citizens of Israel, all that is good and noble not only in American Jewish life but in the great democratic tradition of our country. It is on that high plane of cultural and spiritual partnership that the relationship of Israel and Jewry throughout the world will and should be developed."[23]

Finkelstein's attachment to the Land of the Sages was profound, an attachment that he would renew annually for many years, and when his daughter settled and established a family in Jerusalem, his visits took on even greater personal significance. ("When I was her age, I too thought I was going to spend my life in Jerusalem, but I did not.") A chronic sufferer from insomnia and a man whose daily schedule was rigidly disciplined, he found that his brief interludes in Israel offered precious respite and renewal. "I really think that I live more happily all year because of the two weeks I spend in Jerusalem each year," he would later write to his younger colleague and friend, Moshe Davis.[24] Yet, Finkelstein, as a disciplined "soldier"— or, more aptly, as the chief executive officer of a major Jewish institution of learning upon whose shoulders rested what he believed was a significant share of responsibility for the future of the Jewish people in America—was able to put the interests of his Seminary first and foremost when it came to critical choices.

That Finkelstein had no real doubt as to the validity of such a position, in terms of the inner history of rabbinic Judaism, is confirmed by something that he wrote some thirty-five years after the Simon episode. In a *Festschrift* honoring Moshe Davis, published by the Hebrew University's Institute of Contemporary Jewry (the institute founded by Davis in 1959), Finkelstein contributed a short "Note on Rab Pirqoi Ben Baboi," a Babylonian sage of the Geonic period. In a volume otherwise devoted to 20th-century Jewry, this one contribution stands out as exceptional. It can only be regarded (and, indeed, Moshe Davis always understood it) as a personal communication on the subject of Israeli-Diaspora relations and on their mutual agreement to disagree. The "Note" concerns the arguments used by Pirqoi Ben Baboi to delegitimize the practice by Jews living in Eretz Israel of distinctive customs that set them apart from the community in Babylonia. Although Ben Baboi's arguments lacked historical or halakhic merit, they were in a sense validated by history: Given the overriding need for Jewish unity in the face of the schismatic challenge of Karaism, it was historically justifiable that Babylonian rabbinic customs be imposed even on Eretz-Israel Jewry, who had their own traditions. Even if Ben Baboi bent the facts to suit his case (a remarkable procedure for a scholar!), Babylonian practice did override Palestinian ones, the Karaite challenge was eventually repulsed, and the commitment of Oral Law to writing (which Finkelstein described as a stage in the anti-Karaite reformation) created a new rabbinic literature that animated Judaism for centuries. Finkelstein chose, through this historic example, to explain his devotion to his own academy and his own community, while recognizing that Davis, in making his home at the Hebrew University, had chosen a different (though equally legitimate) route.[25]

Moreover, Finkelstein had a clearly developed sense of *why* the Seminary (more precisely, the values that the Seminary stood for) deserved such devotion. At stake was not mere institutional survival, nor even the "mere" survival of Conservative Jewry or the American Jewish community as a whole. What was at stake was the survival (quite literally) of the human race, which had in two world wars proved itself capable of wanton and brutal destruction, had shown how a "civilized" society could so lose its grip on essential moral values that murder and tyranny could be considered normal, and was about to launch itself on a path of nuclear armament that could spell the final catastrophe. In such a world, an effective humane message of universal ethics was the only antidote, and Judaism, with its accumulated wisdom, could fulfill such a role in the world only if it did not shirk its responsibilities. The call for a return to humane values could come from anywhere—indeed, it could (and would, Finkelstein believed) come from Jerusalem itself. But such a message, if it was to become a force for salvation in the world, had to find a ready reception within the leading nation of the free world, the United States of America. The Seminary was located *not* on a far periphery but at the eye of the contemporary human storm. Its mission, to bring Judaism out "from under wraps" and into the light of day where all humanity might benefit, was a mission of ultimate importance.

This basic argument was one that Finkelstein would reiterate and elaborate on over the years, and it was an argument that he used in reference to Israel, placing it within the context of a wider, human, moral struggle. Thus:

> Israel is the more likely to succeed in this enterprise (of achieving the glory of the new Israel . . .) if, even beyond its magnificent predecessors, it can achieve the formulation of a prophetic idea, as powerful and significant in the affairs of men as theirs were in their time. . . . That the world needs a prophetic insight in which the concept of human dignity and worth will be integrated with advancing science and scholarship can scarcely be questioned. Never in many generations have men been so utterly confused about their own purposes and aims as

they are today. Never have nations been given so completely to drift, and unable to find an intellectual rudder as today. . . . Is it a vain hope that the children of the Jewish tradition, living partly amidst their brethren of other faiths in the free countries of the world, and partly on the holy soil of Zion, will find some way of formulating that which is implicit in the life of monotheistic religion, of democracy, and human dignity at their best?[26]

Our military victory over the Nazis prevented the collapse of democratic civilization in the face of an imminent threat of one form of totalitarianism. That victory has not eliminated the peril arising from another and stronger form of totalitarianism. But it has given to the free peoples a breathing spell, which we can utilize to bring about a spiritual re-awakening of mankind, so as to lay the foundations for permanent, continuous growth of peace and freedom throughout the world. . . . The struggle to make the world safe for democracy is now transferred in fact from the battlefields to our own consciences. . . . This is the task which falls, with especial weight, on the religious leaders of America— Catholic, Protestant, and Jewish.[27]

Alas, it is too late to try to stop the galloping catastrophe once it has covered itself with the cloak of patriotism, glory, and idealism. Therefore I do not have to tell you, dear colleagues, that the place to change the course of human events is not in the chancelleries of the world, but in the homes, the schools, and the houses of worship. . . . Your task and mine, it seems to me, is to initiate the kind of thought, study, and religious development which would make such an approach to the problems of life not a dream, but a reality. Let us begin then with the consideration of our central institution—the Seminary—as a potential moral force in the world.[28]

Or, to take the starkest statement of this kind: "Unless the Jewish people leads mankind in the spiritual and moral sphere, we have no rational justification for existence at all. Whether we like it or not, we are the corporate Servant of the Lord."[29]

When we combine the various components of this worldview, the result is more or less as follows: Israel reborn is a sign of moral hope for the world, because the restoration of the Jews to their land signifies the possibility of change in history. Israel has the potential to contribute to the spiritual dialogue that will be necessary to restore moral balance in the world, and such potential rests on the religious and historical tradition that the Jews in their own land might revitalize in some unique way. But this spiritual enterprise must cross boundaries in order to succeed: There must be an effort to communicate across religious and geographic lines, and the process of moral persuasion entails grassroots education more than politics. The Jews, led by their rabbis and scholars, have a responsibility to take up that challenge, not only in Israel but also (or especially) in America, where democratic and humane values are validated by the system of government and where the balance of power in the world is currently vested.

To fully understand Israel's role in Louis Finkelstein's conception of Jewish peoplehood and of the job of the Seminary, we need to locate Israel along both a "vertical" or historical-Jewish axis, on which the Land was and would always be the Land of the Sages, to which one must turn, as a Jew, to discover the ultimate truths embodied in Judaism, and along a "horizontal" or contemporary world-ethical axis, where Israel's significance lay in the role that it might (ought to) play in the crucial human drama of our own day. The Jews, as a people, stood at the intersection of those two axes. Their presence as a moral force in the world transcended questions of place, but in fact it was their presence *in Israel and in the United States* that mattered most of all: in Israel, in close proximity to the wellsprings of their religious genius and, in America, situated within a pluralistic community of religions that alone could hope to mend the world.

It remained for the Seminary to determine just how it would set about promoting a spiritual link with Israel, as Finkelstein envisioned. In a letter to Rabbinical Assembly members in November 1951 (composed by Simon Greenberg to be sent out over Finkelstein's signature), Conservative rabbis were informed of a variety of steps that the Seminary was taking or planning in order to develop "common spiritual aims between the Jewries of Israel and America." Noting that most synagogues and rabbis were already actively engaged in Zionist and Israel-related affairs, the letter affirmed that "the Conservative movement has been the very heart of Zionist effort in this country." Finkelstein was able to report that, "at the suggestion of the Rabbinical Assembly," the Seminary was planning to establish a Seminary-Israel Institute that would "have as its purpose the clarification of the aims and purposes of the State of Israel and discussion of the common problems of the Jewries of that state and of the United States."[30]

In fact, the conception grew out of discussions held over the course of 1950–51 between the Seminary and the Jewish Agency: specifically, conversations that included Finkelstein himself, Moshe Davis (then provost of the Seminary), Hayim Greenberg (the American Zionist leader and member of the Zionist Executive), and Moshe Sharett (representing the State of Israel).[31] According to Davis, who actually ran the Israel Institute, it had not been easy to persuade the Chancellor to agree to establish a forum whose purpose lay outside the Seminary's formal academic function. The Israel Institute was a "compromise." Much of the credit for the initiative belongs to Hayim Greenberg. As head of the Education and Culture Department of the Jewish Agency, he was not only an active supporter of the Seminary's plan to develop an intellectual role vis-à-vis Israel, but he also encouraged the Seminary's neighbor, Columbia University, which was then developing its own Israel Institute within its School of International Affairs.[32]

It remained for the Seminary to choose its own approach if it was going to offer something of significance to the academic community. Describing the rationale behind the Israel Institute to Maurice Samuel, Finkelstein wrote the following:

193

*The Ongoing
Dialogue:
The Seminary
and the
Challenge of
Israel*

The Seminary Israel Institute
of
The Jewish Theological Seminary of America

cordially invites you to attend the lectures on

"A RE-ORIENTATION TO ZIONISM"

to be given by

DOCTOR MORDECAI M. KAPLAN
Professor of Philosophies of Religion
The Jewish Theological Seminary of America

on Tuesdays at 11:15 A.M.
at
THE SEMINARY
Northeast corner, Broadway and 122nd Street

I. WHY A REFORMULATION OF ZIONISM?

February 16, 1954
THE CRISIS IN ZIONISM AS CRISIS IN JUDAISM

February 23, 1954
THE BACKGROUND OF THE ZIONIST MOVEMENT

March 2, 1954
THE LIMITED PERSPECTIVE OF PRE-STATE ZIONISM

II. THE NEW ZIONISM (REDEMPTION OF THE
JEWISH PEOPLE AND REGENERATION OF THE JEWISH SPIRIT)

March 9, 1954
THROUGH REAFFIRMATION OF JEWISH PEOPLEHOOD

March 16, 1954
THROUGH RECLAMATION OF *ERETZ YISRAEL*

March 23, 1954
THROUGH REPLENISHMENT OF TORAH

There will be a registration fee of $1.00 for the series

The Seminary Israel Institute is conducted under the joint auspices of
THE JEWISH AGENCY FOR PALESTINE AND
THE JEWISH THEOLOGICAL SEMINARY OF AMERICA

For information regarding the course and luncheon lectures, please write

THE SEMINARY ISRAEL INSTITUTE
3080 Broadway • New York 27, New York

Two posters for
Seminary Israel
Institute lectures,
1954 and 1956.
*Ratner Center,
JTS.*

THE SEMINARY ISRAEL INSTITUTE
OF
THE JEWISH THEOLOGICAL SEMINARY OF AMERICA

*cordially invites you to attend a series of lectures
at the Seminary, Tuesdays, 12 o'clock noon, on*

ZION IN JEWISH THOUGHT

Doctor Abraham S. Halkin, Moderator

February 14, 1956 **BIBLICAL PERIOD** DOCTOR ABRAHAM S. HALKIN Associate Professor of Jewish History and Institutions at the Seminary	**March 6, 1956** **MEDIEVAL PROSE** DOCTOR NAHUM GLATZER Associate Professor of Jewish History, Brandeis University
February 21, 1956 **TALMUDIC PERIOD** RABBI GERSON D. COHEN Librarian and Instructor in Jewish History and Institutions at the Seminary	**March 13, 1956** **MODERN PROSE** DOCTOR BEN HALPERN Editor, The Jewish Frontier
February 28, 1956 **MEDIEVAL POETRY** DOCTOR CHAIM DIMITROVSKY Lecturer in Talmud at the Seminary	**March 20, 1956** **MODERN POETRY** DOCTOR HILLEL BAVLI Associate Professor of Hebrew Literature at the Seminary

THE SEMINARY ISRAEL INSTITUTE AWARD LUNCHEON

Tuesday, March 20, 1956   1:00 P.M., the Seminary

Presentation of the Seminary Israel Institute Award for 1955-1956 to

PROFESSOR MORDECAI M. KAPLAN

Address: Mordecai M. Kaplan — Ahad Ha'am of American Jewry
by
Doctor Samuel M. Blumenfield

There will be a registration fee of $1.00 for the
lecture series and a charge of $1.00 for the luncheon

The Seminary Israel Institute is conducted under the joint auspices of
THE JEWISH AGENCY FOR PALESTINE AND
THE JEWISH THEOLOGICAL SEMINARY OF AMERICA

The purpose of this Institute is to emphasize the role of the State of Israel and the Land of Israel as a spiritual influence on the lives of the Jews everywhere and also on world affairs. Obviously, in many respects that is a vision of the future, but I think that both of us agree that in a very real measure the Yishuv and now the State have fulfilled and are fulfilling this hope. Indeed, from my point of view, *it is the main function of the State of Israel.* . . . The audience . . . will consist of academicians on this hill [i.e., Morningside Heights], other academicians in New York, and people who influence public opinion [my emphasis—EL].[33]

The Institute, inaugurated (in cooperation with the Jewish Agency) in February 1952, was officially described as intended

to strengthen the spiritual and cultural bonds between the State of Israel and America; to offer Americans an interpretation of the spiritual and cultural values of the State of Israel; to foster an understanding of the potential role of the State of Israel as intermediary between the Orient and the Occident; and to help develop a recognition of the State of Israel as a spiritual center for Jewry everywhere.[34]

The wording of the statement of purpose was vintage Finkelstein. This was explicitly reemphasized in the Chancellor's own address to the inaugural session: "We are hoping that ultimately the Institute may help implement the dream we have long cherished: that through the combined efforts of American and Israeli Jewries, the State of Israel may become not only a spiritual and cultural center for all Jews, but a great center for mutual understanding of all peoples, particularly between the East and the West."[35]

For its first season (February–April 1952), the Israel Institute scheduled a series of lecture sessions and another series of shorter luncheon talks. The lectures, delivered by Professor Shalom Spiegel on "Zion in Jewish Tradition," traced "the place of Eretz Israel in the religious life of the Jews" from "Biblical Foundations" through the modern "Return to Zion." The first in the series of luncheon meetings was devoted to Finkelstein's address on "The State of Israel as a Spiritual Force in the Modern World." Succeeding Tuesday sessions featured such luminaries as Professor Saul Lieberman ("Jewish Life in Eretz Israel as Reflected in the Talmud *Yerushalmi*"), Hayim Greenberg ("Religion and State in Israel"), and Professor Martin Buber ("The Emerging Character Type in Contemporary Israel and the Future World Society").[36]

In succeeding years, the Seminary Israel Institute featured further lecture series and, beginning in 1954, sponsored an annual Chaim Weizmann Memorial Lecture.[37] Among the prominent speakers at the Institute were archaeologist and former Israeli army chief of staff, Yigael Yadin; archaeologist and Hebrew University rector, Dr. Benjamin Mazar; and such Seminary luminaries as H. L. Ginsburg,

Abraham S. Halkin, Hillel Bavli, and Mordecai M. Kaplan. By the end of the 1950s, the activity of the Institute ceased (coinciding with Moshe Davis's departure for Jerusalem). One lasting result of the Institute was the publication of a volume of essays called *Israel: Its Role in Civilization*[38] and a volume written by Mordecai Kaplan, *A New Zionism*[39] (to be discussed further on in this essay).

Israel: Its Role in Civilization is notable, inter alia, for Louis Finkelstein's essay, "The State of Israel as a Spiritual Force," which constitutes his definitive statement on the subject, drawing on the themes that we have already noted. Here he also elaborated on the relationship, as he saw it, between Zionism and Conservative Judaism:

> In a certain sense it may be said that Conservative Judaism is itself the firstborn child of the marriage of Zionism and Americanism. The enormous faith in ourselves and in our tradition—which has enabled us, like our predecessors, to assert that we can defy the standardization of modern industrial life; that, rejecting ghettoization, we can participate fully in the life of America and yet hold fast to the traditions of our fathers; . . . the daring that emboldened [Solomon Schechter] and his associates to undertake the establishment of [a] great center of Torah in what was then, from the Jewish point of view, an intellectual and spiritual wilderness—this faith and self-confidence were, in my opinion, by-products of the vast effort which had already begun to lay the foundations of a resurrected Jewish commonwealth in *Eretz Israel*.[40]

The essay restated Finkelstein's basic theses on the ethical implications of Israelite institutions and Pharisaic thought. He averred, again, that Israel might yet "beget" an idea "so powerful that it may itself redeem mankind" from its current troubled existence.

> Is it not possible, and even probable, that precisely at this turn in human events so many of us have been called to Zion because part of the clarification of Torah in our day must come out of Zion? . . . Freed at last from the burdens of ghetto life and the fear of persecution, the Jewry of the free lands on the one hand, and that of Israel on the other, can think normally and creatively. Searching into the depths of their own tradition, their own hearts . . . , they may yet find the Ariadne's thread that will lead mankind out of its present intellectual maze and chaos.[41]

Most intriguing, however, was a passage toward the end of the essay, in which Finkelstein enunciated what seemed to be a coherent picture of the place of the Seminary with regard to Israel in the Jewish world community:

> We at the Seminary regard ourselves and American Jewry neither as one of the foci of a great ellipse of Judaism nor the center of a circle, with only mystic connections with a similar circle surrounding Jerusalem. We recognize that we stand on the periphery of Jewish inspiration; and if we are content with our position, it is only because we believe that the service we can render God,

Torah, and mankind from this stance is one *to which we have been called and
which we cannot neglect.* Yet always we turn to Zion not only in prayer but also in
the hope of instruction. We gladly assume the role of amanuensis to our
brethren who have been given the superior privilege of serving God and studying Torah in the land in which both were uniquely revealed. If the experiences
we have garnered in our efforts . . . may prove of some use, they are at the disposal of our masters and teachers in Israel and Zion. If we can labor with them
toward a solution of the vast human problem, that in itself will be a privilege.
[my emphasis—EL][42]

Jakob Petuchowski (of Hebrew Union College) took Finkelstein to task over his
apparent consigning of American Jewry to second-class spiritual status vis-à-vis
Israel (an "unwelcome and completely unnecessary note of self-abasement") and
challenged the leadership of Conservatism to come up with a theology of greater
content than an ersatz Zionism.[43] The tone of humility and subordination does
require some explanation, in light of all that we have seen until now regarding
Finkelstein's understanding of the vital importance of the Seminary—indeed, its
centrality.

One possible explanation is that the phrase was mere rhetorical flourish. (I have
it on good authority that considerations of a rhetorical or public relations nature did
enter into this and other statements of this kind.)[44] On the other hand, the statement is consistent with Finkelstein's general and long held reverence for the high
level of scholarship in all areas of Jewish *Wissenschaft* that had been attained by certain scholars in Israel. In the 1950s, the academic and intellectual community in the
fields of Judaica in Israel outclassed in quality and quantity the Hebraic scholarly
resources of the native-born American Jewish community. Finkelstein's admiration
for those scholars is undoubtedly what he had in mind when he wrote to Maurice
Samuel that "in a very real measure the Yishuv and now the State have fulfilled and
are fulfilling this hope" (of spiritual leadership).[45] It is also what prompted him to
try to recruit Ernst Simon for the Seminary faculty. It is what made him crow, in a
newsletter to the Seminary Board of Directors in January 1948, that the publication
of Saul Lieberman's book on Maimonides "was chronicled [in Palestine] on the
front page of the newspapers and seems to have aroused tremendous interest. As
one example, the Chief Rabbi [Isaac Halevi Herzog] cabled Professor Lieberman,
asking that a copy of the book be shipped to him immediately airmail."[46] Lieberman
himself, of course, was a "catch" brought over from Israel, where he had been in the
Hebrew University's first graduating class (in 1925). The admiration of the Israeli
public was important for Finkelstein precisely because he believed that Israeli standards were not easily met.

In describing the steps being taken by the Seminary to bring it into line with the
post-1948 reality, Finkelstein dwelled on the intellectual resources that Israel was

providing the Seminary and on the ensuing scholarly interface between the two Jewish scholarly communities.

> The third step [in the development of relations between Israel and the Seminary] came with bringing to America a group of scholars from Israel who have helped stimulate the minds of our students and all of us to further thought of Israel as *the great center of Jewish learning.* Among these scholars are Professor Saul Lieberman and such younger men as Rabbis Shraga Abramson and Zalman Dimitrowsky. We now have in our midst the impressive personality of Professor Martin Buber. . . . Various delegations have been sent to Israel by the Seminary and the Rabbinical Assembly. The visit of Professor Saul Lieberman and Doctor Moshe Davis to Israel [to scout for new faculty talent] in 1950 had results which are only now becoming apparent. . . . Under the influence of Professor Lieberman, who is its President, the American Academy of Jewish Research is now publishing jointly with the Government of Israel a critical edition of *Vayyikra Rabba.* We are hoping that this will be the first of many common ventures between the Government and the educational institutions of Israel and those over which we have influence in America. . . . Partly as a result of the growing intimacy between Israeli institutions and the Seminary, the revolution in *hokhmat yisrael* [Jewish scholarship], so long desired by lovers of Hebrew everywhere, has at last come to pass. The vast majority of Seminary scholarly publications are now in Hebrew.[47]

It would take another decade and a half before the first major cadre of locally trained American Jewish scholars would take its place at institutions of higher learning: meanwhile, Jewish studies in America were still dependent largely upon immigrant scholars. With the destruction of the great spiritual and scholarly reservoir of European Jewry (especially East European Jewry), Israel, which had absorbed many of those who left Europe in the interwar period, emerged as the new "home" of—and a potential source of talent from—a vigorous intellectual community of Torah and its allied sciences. Finkelstein could honestly say, in the early 1950s, that he would be happy if the Seminary might work alongside (or co-opt) Judaica scholars in Israel.

Finally, there is the testimony of Rabbi Israel Goldstein, the longtime Conservative Zionist leader, who referred to the question of Louis Finkelstein's posture on Israel in a letter he wrote to Simon Greenberg at the end of 1968, in which the issue was apparently Finkelstein's omission of Israeli matters from a recent public letter: "I have had conversations with Dr. Finkelstein which did reveal a great feeling on his part about Israel's indispensability. He remarked once that *from the standpoint of Jewish scholarship, Israel is indispensable to the Diaspora.* It is because I was so warmed by his very sincere avowal that he had not done enough during the great political struggle to secure the Jewish State, that I was sensitive to what I thought was an omission in his latest letter" (my emphasis—EL).[48]

This question of scholarship as the linchpin of Israel's proper significance in the Seminary ethos can be addressed in another way, too, in which the *limitations* of scholarship as such come into play. It may be that the conflicts at the heart of the Israel question at the Seminary stem from a more general syndrome that has been ascribed to the Seminary experience: an inadequate integration of scholarly and academic concerns with "life issues" or experiential concerns. During the early 1950s, sociologist Marshall Sklare noted the primacy that Seminary faculty assigned to scholarship and their concomitant devaluation of the work done by the Seminary's own rabbinical graduates "out in the field," in congregations.[49] Another perspective on the same issue was expressed by Seminary professor Neil Gillman (former dean of the Rabbinical School). By separating scholarship from religion, he contended, the Seminary was able to avoid the pursuit of ideological issues to their undesired conclusions.[50]

Hence, it is revealing that Saul Lieberman, one of the Seminary faculty with very close ties to the scholarly community in Israel, reacted negatively one morning in 1975 when a rabbinical student, leading the morning service, began to recite the *Hallel* prayers to mark the special character of *Yom Yerushalayim* (the 28th of *Iyar*). Simon Greenberg, who was present, reflected on the incident in a letter to his grandson: "Professor Lieberman, like I, who did not recall that this was the anniversary of the capture of the Old City in 1967, at first objected. Even after he was told [why the Hallel was being injected in the service], he still thought that the *berakha* [blessing] should not be made. . . . And so the *hazan* did not recite the closing *berakha*." What was a matter of *klal yisrael* (ideological-ethnic) identification for the students was, for their teacher, a matter of "the law not yet [having] been fixed [so that] it is preferable to perform the act but not recite the *berakha* so that God's name may not be taken in vain."[51] Lieberman's own attachment to Israel was apparently not communicated in this episode: it was not relevant to the question of rabbinical practice that was at hand, namely, the question of normative ritual.

The fact that *Wissenschaft* (which could be attuned very closely to developments in Israel) was set off from matters of professional training (which was the Seminary's avowed mission and was strongly America-oriented) also accounts for Finkelstein's paradoxical ability simultaneously to hold Israel up as the recognized home of Jewish spiritual genius and to make sure that the rabbinical students at the Seminary (each new crop of "good soldiers") received clear marching orders to serve American Jewry first of all.

One alumnus, now living in Israel, who studied at the Seminary from 1950 to 1959, recalled that, "Each month there would be a breakfast meeting of the students with Finkelstein, at which he spoke about the mission of the American rabbi. Israel just did not enter Finkelstein's world [as far as the students were concerned]: not that he was 'anti', but he would simply not mention it. Our job, he would stress, and he believed it in the depths of his heart, was to save the Jewish people [in America]. Only we were capable of rescuing it through values, tradition. . . . He gave us a guilt trip that was extremely difficult to get rid of."[52]

Thus the problematic nature of Israel's place within the Seminary ethos can well be understood. The dilemmas posed by the establishment of the State of Israel did not so much *change* the Seminary: they were merely internalized along lines determined by preexisting rhythms of the Seminary's inner pendulum. "Diaspora plus Palestine, religion plus nationalism" was a formula that still applied. Assertions of Israel's spiritual value to "civilization" went hand in hand with the demand that Israel's chief benefit to humanity ought to be channeled through a revitalization of Jewish communities abroad, in particular in the United States. Territory and sovereignty were ultimately "good" only if they could be textualized. Jerusalem's path to its true historical destiny lay through Yavneh.

A New Zionism

The message sent out by Finkelstein to Rabbinical Assembly members in November 1951 contained one of the first public references to the Seminary's plan to build itself a center in Jerusalem. "Perhaps the most significant single step in cementing cultural relations between the American Jewish community and that of Israel," the message said, "will come about when the project, which we have so long envisaged, of an estate in Israel to be used as a center for study, research and instruction for our students, alumni, faculty and other scholars and creative spirits is realized."[53] He went on to say that he intended to visit Israel in the coming spring to begin to make arrangements for the acquisition of such property.

Prime Minister David Ben-Gurion seemed almost to echo the strains of the Seminary's *niggun* (melody) at a convocation held by the Seminary in Jerusalem on 25 May 1952. His speech, upon receiving an honorary degree from the Seminary, began as follows:

> The rise of the State of Israel has had revolutionary political and territorial results that are obvious to all, but it has at the same time brought about a far-reaching spiritual and cultural change which may not yet be easily discernible, but which is bound to make its impress felt increasingly in the course of time.[54]

Some years later, in 1958, when the Seminary invited Ben-Gurion once again to speak at a major Seminary event in Israel—the laying of the cornerstone of what was to become the Seminary's Student Center in Jerusalem—he seemed to press this point even more strongly: "It is not the purpose of the State of Israel merely to add one more state to the many that already exist or may yet be created in the world; Israel is the bearer of the historic and spiritual ideals with which the Jewish people has been imbued ever since its beginnings, ideals which have been given supreme

*The Jewish
Theological
Seminary
of America*

David Ben-Gurion
speaks at the cor-
nerstone laying
ceremony for the
Seminary's Ameri-
can Student Cen-
ter in Jerusalem,
Hebrew Univer-
sity amphitheater,
29 July 1958.
Ratner Center, JTS.

and eternal expression in the Book of Books and in the immortal messages of
Israel's prophets."[55]

But the apparent similarity between this approach and that articulated by Louis
Finkelstein and others at the Seminary is partial at best—even deceptive. Ben-
Gurion's model was not Yavneh at all, but the prophets, Joshua, and the revolution-
ary, militant Akiva.

Yavneh, a lifeboat salvaged from the wreck of a besieged and burning vessel, may
in fact have found its way to safer shores and reconstituted the Jewish people in new
form; but to a nation-builder like Ben-Gurion, it was unthinkable that Yavneh
should remain the model once the mother ship had been raised from the bottom,
restored, outfitted, and put out to sea once more with a new crew. It was up to the
lifeboat to find its way back to its point of origin or, at the very least, to help captain
and crew insure that the vessel would really be seaworthy. In the 1952 speech, this
trend of thought is easily discerned:

> Rabbi Yohanan Ben Zakai who asked the Roman conqueror for the boon of
> Yavneh and its wise men, may well have preserved Israel's existence and

fortified its spirit against the misfortunes and sorrows it was to encounter during its prolonged wanderings. But the greatest among the disciples of Rabbi Yohanan Ben Zakai's disciples—Rabbi Akiva, son of Joseph, the outstanding figure in Judaism after the second destruction—*was not satisfied merely with the existence of Yavneh and its wise men, but aided Bar-Kochba in the revolt intended to restore Israel's political sovereignty and freedom.* It was only after the failure of that desperate and heroic attempt that the Jews became "the people of the Book," endeavoring to make commentaries on the Bible and commentaries on those commentaries fill the great gap left by the destruction of their sovereignty. . . .

But all those commentaries, . . . grow pale when they are contrasted with the brilliant light shed on Joshua's struggle by the battles fought in our modern war of independence. . . .

The mighty task of Israel's cultural development in its own land, like the tasks of gathering together the exiled children of our people and building the country, cannot possibly be accomplished by the small, young state itself, depending entirely upon its own resources. . . . *We need scholars and scientists and men of vision . . . from among the Jews of America, if we are to build that new wisdom of Israel [hokhmat yisrael].* . . . Even in the special field of research into Jewish history and the history of the Land of Israel—the field which in the lands of the exile we called the wisdom of Israel, in its narrowest sense—there is room and need for cooperation between scholars in Israel and scholars in the dispersion, particularly America [my emphasis—EL].[56]

The textualization of territory was to be reversed: Text ("commentaries") would become once again a living source when read in the light of contemporary action. Yavneh would survive alongside and within a rebuilt Jerusalem—that was *its* true destiny—and would thrive only when its text was reunited with its *Ur*-text. "Anyone who intends to become a teacher or rabbi in any Jewish community in the world," Ben-Gurion argued, "will not be faithful to his mission unless he drinks of the twofold and indivisible well: the Book of Books in its Hebrew original and the free and independent Jewish homeland."[57]

Ben-Gurion, having only just launched his ship of state, wanted the Jews of the America, including the Seminary, *to help Israel.* He wanted (and would welcome) all the creative spirit manifested by Jews from any part of the world which could be transplanted in Israel or otherwise harnessed to the goals of nation-building.

Finkelstein, who thought of his society (American and Jewish-American) as caught in the throes of spiritual crisis, wanted *Israel* to help *him* in his struggle to articulate a humane spiritual vision for the world. The fact is that each one had his eye on a different priority altogether.

Simon Greenberg's authorship of the November 1951 letter to Conservative rabbis (cited above) is discernible in the fact that it spoke of the Seminary's potential contribution *to Israel.*[58] Greenberg's views ran along lines different from Finkelstein's. Over the years, it would be Greenberg, in partnership with Bernard Mandelbaum, who would campaign for and raise the necessary funds to build the Student Center in Jerusalem; help organize groups of intellectuals, students, educators, and academics in Israel; encourage the formation of a *gar'in aliya* (core group to settle in Israel) among Seminary students; direct the Schocken Institute (to be discussed later), support the creation of a Conservative seminary for Israeli rabbis, and generally act as the Seminary's Israel activities coordinator. His argument in the fall of 1951 encapsulated his point of view:

> The acquisition of this . . . estate will bring nearer the realization of our great hope and aspiration *to render the unique service which we associated with the Seminary have to offer Israel,* quite aside from what we are doing with the rest of American Jewry. We can bring its [Israel's] valiant and bold spiritual power to bear on the problems of our lives and the world. We can serve as the channels through which its [Israel's] people respond to the currents of world thought. If it be given the State of Israel to serve once more, as it did in antiquity, as a bridge between . . . rival cultures and civilizations, we can contribute greatly to its effectiveness and usefulness in that role [my emphasis—EL].[59]

This offering of "a unique contribution" would come to predominate in Seminary rhetoric much later, under the administration of Gerson D. Cohen as Seminary Chancellor (1972–86). At the outset, however, the other aspect—that of Israel's contribution to the strengthening of the Diaspora—was what prevailed. Finkelstein, who returned from five weeks in Israel and England in August 1952, spoke enthusiastically about the "remarkable results" achieved in Israeli intellectual life, despite the most trying material conditions, and stated, "Anyone aspiring to the Jewish ministry . . . ought to spend at least a year in Israel, studying the Scriptures and the Mishna, and later Talmudic works, in the land of their origin. . . . *Because of the lessons to be learned in Israel, both in relation to the Jewish community, and in its bearing on world affairs, I am urging our Faculty and Board of Directors . . . to establish a Dormitory for our Rabbinical students and alumni in Jerusalem, so that they can spend a year in study at the Hebrew University and other institutions of higher learning*" [my emphasis—EL].[60] (Nevertheless, the implementation of a period of study in Israel for aspiring Conservative rabbis was not completed, despite Finkelstein's stated enthusiasm for the idea, until 1964. Students at the Rabbinical School in the 1950s faced difficulties in persuading the Seminary to grant academic credit for courses taken at the Hebrew University.)[61]

The vision here is far more circumscribed than in the Greenberg memo: it speaks modestly in terms of a "dormitory," of studying at other institutions, not of a center or a "channel" through which Israel, enriched by the Conservative and American Jewish spirit, might encounter the rest of the world and develop in new directions. If Finkelstein thought there was a contribution that America and its Jews might make (speaking generally about postwar Europe as well as Israel), that contribution was in the form of the positive example set by American interfaith cooperation and tolerance.[62]

The fact that it was Greenberg who had developed a grander vision of what a Conservative center in Israel might become suggests that either he himself or someone who supported his viewpoint was the unnamed Conservative figure whose views were cited in a meeting of Israeli government and Jewish Agency officials held in Ben-Gurion's office in July 1950. The meeting, devoted entirely to the question of relations with the American Jewish community, ranged over ideological and practical as well as cultural issues. During the discussion, MK (member of Knesset) Eliezer Livneh (Libenstein) stated that a number of American Jewish organizations were hoping to establish a base for themselves for ongoing programs in Israel, including the major synagogue associations—Orthodox, Conservative, and Reform—and the Hillel Foundation, B'nai B'rith, and the Jewish Welfare Board. Livneh, who was at the time a "goodwill ambassador" on Israel's behalf in the United States, noted that he had been told unofficially that the Conservative movement intended to build a center in Israel that would bring about five hundred young American Jews annually to Israel for a six-month to twelve-month stay either during high school or after college. It was anticipated that most would return afterwards to the United States but that some might choose to remain in Israel. The Conservative movement hoped, Livneh reported, to create congregations in Israel (unlike the Reform movement, which at that stage was sceptical of its chances to establish a presence in the form of synagogues).[63]

The scale of the project as conceived was much larger than what was eventually realized. Certainly the intention to establish a wider presence, in the form of Conservative synagogues, went beyond Finkelstein's idea of a dormitory for students and a study center for visiting scholars. The question of scale and scope was to remain open through the 1950s and 1960s, until it was subjected to a thorough review in the mid-1970s.

Yet it was not entirely true that the Seminary ethos in the 1950s remained largely unchanged by the advent of Israel. It fell to Mordecai M. Kaplan, whose thinking was unconventional in Seminary terms, to argue the urgent necessity of an intellectual, philosophical, and political engagement with the essential challenges to the Jewish people and to Judaism posed by Israeli statehood. Not only did he demand that the Seminary and the Conservative movement come to grips with the new balance in the Jewish world, but he also challenged Israel to abandon pre-state Zionist concepts of Diaspora-negation and to fully accept its stake in the revitalization of Jewish peoplehood throughout the Diaspora. As he wrote in *A New Zionism*, he viewed such revisions as the only ultimate guarantors of Jewish collective survival in the new era. Moreover, there was the question of the *content* of Jewish culture and identity—a question that was equally relevant to the new state and to the Jewries of the Diaspora, since Israel could hardly do without what he called "Western civilization" any more than could the Diaspora communities.[64]

The core solution that Kaplan formulated was both radical and amorphous: the Jewish people was to be *reconstituted as an international People, with its nucleus in Israel.*

> The New Zionism should teach all Jews to regard their sense of unity and mutual responsibility both as a means and as a goal of their personal salvation. . . . It should aim to foster, on the basis of our common history and tradition, a sense of interdependence and a process of interaction between the Jews of Israel and the Jews of the rest of the world. The societal organism that will evolve out of this interaction will be differently structured from the Jewish People of the past, but it will be morally and spiritually continuous with that People.[65]

This was radical in that it called for a formal process, essentially political in nature (a declaration of Peoplehood, to be recognized by the international community). It was based on a social ("this-worldly") conception of the Jewish people that went far beyond traditional religious notions of *klal yisrael* (Schechter's "catholic Israel" or what Kaplan termed the "Ecclesia of Israel"). It went beyond even the early 20th-century formulas of "national cultural autonomy" advocated for some Diaspora communities and favored by Jewish nationalists, chiefly in Russia and Eastern Europe: formulas that had made no provision for an international dimension of the kind envisaged by Kaplan, nor, for that matter, had they posited an Israeli "nucleus."

But Kaplan's vision was amorphous, too, in that there was no established precedent for an "international People" in international law or historical practice. One knowledgeable observer noted that even Diaspora Zionists, to say nothing of Israeli Zionists, found the concept of a "new type of transterritorial people" incomprehensible.[66] Kaplan himself made the point that the new status of the Jews was an unresolved issue:

> What kind of society is present day Israel? It certainly is not an ancient kind of nation, such as the Jews constituted in the past, since non-Jews are to have equality in every respect with Jews. Nor does it constitute the "Ecclesia of Israel," or religious nomocracy, which is what Rabbinism has made of world Jewry. What kind of society is World Jewry to be henceforth? It certainly cannot become a modern nation, since there is no political relationship between it and the State of Israel.[67]

The need to pin down what precisely he meant by "reconstituting Jewish peoplehood" led Kaplan to speak of a formal act or "covenant" of Jewish reunification. With Israel as a central focus for this renewed covenant, the degenerative processes at work within world Jewry since the Emancipation could be reversed. Without Israel—or, conversely, with *only* Israel—the whole of the Jewish people could never be restored or reconstituted. As a "people," Jews could act in concert despite existing differences between secular and religious Jews, Jews of different nationalities, Jews with differing theologies:

> We must begin at once to agitate for a great demonstrative reaffirmation of Jewish unity throughout the world. . . . Such a reaffirmation should take the form of a solemn covenant to be enacted in Jerusalem. Every segment of Jewry should be represented there, and the day on which it would take place should be celebrated each year as Jewish unity day, the day when we shall have become an *'Am berit,* a Covenant People [emphasis in the original—EL].[68]

Kaplan held to his conviction that a public act of reconstitution was required, keeping up a running correspondence on the matter with Moshe Davis (among others) throughout the 1960s and well into the 1970s, in which he repeatedly castigated the Zionist movement and others for failing to see his point.[69]

The persistent urgency of Kaplan's concern over this matter ought to be understood in light of his failure over the period of 1957–75 to persuade the Conservative movement, as represented by the United Synagogue, to formally affiliate itself with the World Zionist Organization. He believed that the Zionist body could be transformed into the kind of pan-Jewish representative organ he envisioned, but only if all branches of Judaism would affiliate and thus infuse Zionism with new purpose. Otherwise, Zionism would retain a partisan, unrepresentative character that would perpetuate the cleavages within world Jewry. Eventually, the Diaspora would wither and Israel would lose its historic link to the Jewish past. The Diaspora desperately needed to be linked to Israel, but Israel and the Zionist movement desperately needed an injection of religion (in the Kaplanian sense). In short, as he put it, he saw "the need of having both the Diaspora problem and the Israeli problem fitted into a [common] frame of reference."[70]

The "great debate" over affiliation to the World Zionist Organization took place in several rounds. Kaplan originally brought the proposal to affiliate before the United Synagogue's biennial convention in 1957. The issue was next discussed at the 1958 convention of the Rabbinical Assembly under the heading "Yisrael: Am, Eretz, Medinah," which featured addresses by Abraham Joshua Heschel and Kaplan. Heschel began by stating for the record his view that the Land of Israel was always and would always be central to Judaism, that "a mysterious relationship obtains between the Jewish people and the Jewish land which remained throughout the ages a challenge to the Jews."[71] He confirmed that America is, indeed, Exile and referred to "the shame of being absent [from Israel]": he observed that "one feels abashed at the thought of being a distant spectator while the most dramatic act of building and defending the land is being enacted by others." But he preferred to raise the concept of Exile (*galut*) from the material and political plane to the spiritual plane, where even "the vital, unquestionable, and indisputable need of maintaining an Israeli army is *galut*, too." The rest of his address was devoted to the development of his main thesis: that, for those living in America, the best way to participate in the national rebirth of the Jews and, incidentally, to overcome the "embarrassment of being absent" was to "bring about an inner spiritual and cultural *aliya* on the soil of America."[72]

Kaplan, for his part, spoke of Israel and Zionism along the lines already outlined. He bemoaned the "superfluous" quality of a Zionism that was merely philanthropic; but he also linked the survival of the Jews as a people to a restoration of their dignity, status, security, and "self-fulfilment or salvation as human beings"— conditions that were dependent on Israel, which could become "a catalytic agent in reconstituting the Jewish People."[73]

Having laid the ideological groundwork, Kaplan, together with World Zionist Organization chairman Nahum Goldmann, then reintroduced his proposal at the 1959 convention of the United Synagogue, only to see his initiative postponed amid bitter controversy. According to Kaplan, the proposal was filibustered by Simon Greenberg and Abraham J. Heschel. Kaplan was finally allowed a few more minutes for rebuttal but to no avail.[74] He felt he had been personally attacked and railroaded, and angrily described the proceedings as "trickery"; the convention, a "spiritual desert."[75] Indeed, he felt personally betrayed by Greenberg, with whom he had spent three hours prior to the convention hammering out a formula for a consensus on affiliation to the World Zionist Organization, only to hear Greenberg back out at the last minute.[76]

Simon Greenberg himself recalled the incident years later in a letter to Moshe Davis, in which he contended:

> [I opposed] having the United Synagogue of America join, as a branch of the
> W.Z.O., even though I was very active in the W.Z.O. I could not see how an
> organization which is based on the belief in the centrality of . . . the synagogue
> in Jewish life, could become a branch of an organization that in essence denies
> that centrality to the synagogue.[77]

Greenberg's memory served him very well, for in his address at the United Synagogue convention of 1959 he laid great emphasis on the idea that any impulse to assign to the Jewish people a false "status" in the world would be harmful; that only the synagogue "adequately embodies that concept of Jewish status which I believe to be the only ultimately valid one. . . . Any organization that implicitly, let alone explicitly, rejects this conception of Jewish status will . . . undermine the foundations upon which the whole structure of Jewish life everywhere, including the State of Israel, ultimately depends."[78]

The affair seemed to poison the atmosphere in the Seminary faculty for weeks thereafter, possibly longer. Finkelstein wrote to Davis (then living in Jerusalem) about the acrimony of the debate. Davis responded cautiously, but directly:

> Our movement, and most particularly the Seminary, must evolve a clear-cut position and action based on that position vis-à-vis the Eretz Israel content of our lives in America. Statements and addresses are important but not sufficient. We came to this pass because the Eretz Israel area was permitted to lag behind in our program.... When we will have found the way in which to *live* in Eretz Israel even while our residence is in New York, I believe we will suggest a path to the entire American Jewish community."[79]

Finkelstein made an effort to smooth things over in his Seminary household: at a meeting of Seminary alumni held over the following weekend, Heschel spoke at a dinner in honor of Kaplan, which apparently did much to ease the tension between them.[80] In early February Finkelstein called on Kaplan to discuss the substantive issues still unresolved. Kaplan urged Finkelstein to think about a compromise, according to which the world Jewish religious, philanthropic, and defense organizations would band together, with the World Zionist Organization at their head, in a federal structure. Finkelstein agreed to submit the plan to an informal committee.[81] The idea of some trans-territorial, overarching framework was what Kaplan then continued to pursue, alone, for years. In the fall of 1976, the World Council of Synagogues, representing the Conservative movement, and whose chosen spiritual head was Seminary Chancellor Gerson D. Cohen, decided to affiliate with the World Zionist Organization. The affiliation took place a half year after the affiliation of three other world Jewish bodies: the Maccabi World Union, the World Federation of Sephardic Communities, and (most pertinently) the World Union of Progressive Judaism—the worldwide representative of the Reform movement.[82]

More important than the interpersonal rancor that the issue of political affiliation with the Zionist movement aroused are the deeper roots of the debate within the Seminary itself. Greenberg's original position can be understood in terms of a principled separation between questions properly related to citizenship and political sovereignty, on the one hand, and those, on the other, that are related to the moral and ethical (religious) sphere, at both the individual and the societal level. Greenberg could champion a major investment by the Seminary *in* Israel, to further the cause of Jewish religious development, while opposing anything that smacked of political subordination of the religious conscience. The state could not become an end in itself, and as long as the ultimate ends remained in the religious sphere, the latter must remain autonomous. Moreover, he felt that Zionism, as a movement in Jewish life, had never articulated a new direction or goal, once it had attained the object of its political program: the establishment of Jewish statehood. The Conservative movement, on the other hand, was already engaged in creating "close bonds" with Israel through its youth movement, through academic ties with the Hebrew University, through the planned Student Center, and through the newly formed World Council of Synagogues. "We should and shall fashion more such bonds and strengthen the existing ones. But in all these matters, I do not see how closer association with the Zionist Organization . . . as [it is] presently constituted could be of help to us."[83]

Ultimately, in the wake of the Yom Kippur War and amid growing concern over anti-Jewish and anti-Israel activities around the world, he came to the conclusion that the Conservative movement ought to reexamine the question. The Zionist movement could meet the conditions he had in mind for Conservative affiliation if it were to revise its program with a "preamble," the text of which, he suggested, should be as follows:

> Zionism aims to enhance the religio-cultural heritage of the Jewish people and to make it an increasingly vital factor in molding the character of the individual Jew, the Jewish community, and of human civilization and believes that the existence of a sovereign, politically democratic, physically secure, economically viable, and spiritually sensitive State of Israel on the soil with which that heritage is theologically, historically, and emotionally intertwined, to be indispensable to the achievement of that aim.[84]

His basic position is best conveyed, however, in a discussion on the religious significance of Jewish statehood in which he participated in August 1973 at the Hillel Foundation's center at the Hebrew University. Rejecting the idea that the state *as such* had any religious significance, he went on to reformulate the issue of religion, the individual, and the state in a way that not only explains Greenberg's own philosophy but also illuminates the problem (as he conceived it) of the Seminary's role with regard to Israel:

> I would ask, instead, how does the state afford to us the possibility of attaining religious significance in our lives as individuals? . . . Religious significance resides in the life of the individual [not the state], and as a Jew I therefore ask, how does the state enhance my chance to live a religiously significant life? . . . I observe the same mitsvot here as I would abroad, and indeed one can say that there are many Jews who come here and abandon or neglect the religious aspect of the lives they led when they lived outside of Israel, because here they no longer feel the need for it. . . . [But] as for me personally, I have no doubt that God works in history, and I have seen things happen [in Israel] in my lifetime that could not have happened naturally.[85]

It was this gift of *a religious sensibility* that endowed Israel with religious significance for Greenberg. By the same token, the Seminary's position in Israel would have to be an extension of its own religious principles—not an adjunct to Israel's national or political agenda.

Kaplan, on the other hand, could not permit himself to rely on the individual's capacity for religious sensitivity. All around him he saw spiritual failure—even in his own efforts. In February 1961 he wrote to Moshe Davis, complaining of the Seminary's curricular overemphasis on "Talmudism, at the expense of a knowledge of what is happening to Jewish life and Jewish religion and . . . what ought to be done to save them from disintegration. . . . The letters I get from a number of Seminary graduates who are outwardly successful in the rabbinate reveal an inner spiritual rottenness which cannot but ultimately lead to an utter collapse in the entire structure of synagogue Judaism."[86] Again in March 1962 he wrote in an embittered vein:

> It has been forty years since I founded the Society for the Advancement of Judaism. In those same years I ran a school for teachers [the Seminary's Teachers Institute], taught at the Seminary and at a school to train Jewish public servants. I devoted a great deal of time to the improvement of Jewish education and to the enhancement of Zionism. Along the way I published books and articles, all focused on the aim of restoring our people and our faith. Throughout, I endeavored to frame these tasks within a coherent ideology that cut to the core [of the problems]. But when I survey the fruit of my labors, I see precious little that augurs well for the future of Judaism. . . . In place of Torah and learning—ignorance; in place of a desire to unify the people—fragmentation into parties and a bitter rivalry; and instead of serious consideration of the crisis plaguing our faith—avoidance and recourse to empty phraseology. Compared with forty years ago, I think we have actually regressed.[87]

Kaplan's sense of urgency, of impatience with opponents, of the need to tackle all problems at once and to look for a *combined* solution in one simply grasped formula—as opposed to Greenberg's willingness to *separate* different spheres and pursue incremental growth—stemmed from his deeply felt pessimism.

In a basic way, Mordecai Kaplan and Louis Finkelstein shared a common premise. Kaplan (like Finkelstein) looked to Israel for help in bolstering the spiritual resources of the Diaspora, especially in America. American Jewry, on its own, had as yet little of authentically Jewish value to offer Israel. The difference between the two men lay in this: To Finkelstein, Judaism was eternal, an unbroken spiritual chain of tradition. Israel represented a great heartland of Jewish scholarship, a new link in the chain that led from the Sages through the European rabbinic tradition, and culminating in a fascinating combination of Western *Wissenschaft* and East European *lamdoness* (learnedness) in the original setting and in the original language of rabbinic Judaism. To be able to tap into a resource of that kind would open the Seminary—and, through it, American Jewry—to a wellspring of spiritual stimuli that it sorely needed.

To Kaplan, on the other hand, Israel's significance lay elsewhere. It was only in Israel that modern Jews had managed to reverse the disintegrative effects of the

Emancipation and to reconstitute themselves as a collective community. Only where Jews lived as a "people" could they effectively produce a Judaism creative enough and naturalistic enough (i.e., in keeping with the humanistic requirements demanded by modern people) to engage the commitment and the energies of Jews everywhere. Unless the Diaspora could "plug in" to the Israeli enterprise, and unless Israel made itself receptive to and responsible for the Jews of the Diaspora, there would no longer remain a significant *ethnos* (*klal yisrael*). With the disappearance of the *klal*, its creature—Judaism—would by definition also disappear. Therefore, the breakdown of the *klal* occasioned by Emancipation had to be rolled back *or there was no future for Judaism.* The study of texts ("talmudism") would not suffice, just as Israeli patriotism alone would not suffice.

The debate over Israel and Zionism was no formal or academic matter, nor was it incidental to the Seminary's raison d'être. The category of "peoplehood" (or *klal yisrael)* was one that was intrinsic to the Conservative position on Judaism, based as it has been on the proposition that Judaism *evolves* through the historical experience of the Jews. That is what allows intellectual "space" for an ongoing, progressive "revelation" of Torah that may be traced to Sinai but does not cease. Torah is revealed in the religious life of the community as interpreted by its scholar-elite, the rabbis. The logic of that position is undermined when the religious life of the community becomes impoverished. Yet that was precisely the situation facing the Seminary in the 1950s. In light of that predicament, Conservative ideologist Rabbi Robert Gordis was forced to reformulate Schechter's notion of "Catholic Israel":

> Catholic Israel must be conceived of differently from hitherto accepted views.
> . . . Catholic Israel embraces all those who observe Jewish law in general, although they may violate one or another segment of it, and who are sensitive to the problem of their non-observance because they wish to respect the authority of Jewish law.[88]

The existence of such a halakhic community was a sine qua non for the continued existence of Conservative Judaism (or, in Seminary terms, of Judaism itself). The community, once delimited by Gordis's strictures, was no longer a community of the whole: the "whole" being no longer available (in theological terms) as the living embodiment of Torah. Now it was to be *one part* of the community that would have to serve "as if" it were the whole. Ben Halpern, the American Zionist historian, responded with trenchant criticism to the new formulation devised by Gordis:

> Dr. Gordis wishes to include under the title "Catholic Israel" a vague group not confined to a particular denomination. But whom, in fact does this definition suit more perfectly than the adherents of Conservative Judaism in America—or, even more specifically, of the "group mind" emerging out of the collective cogitations of the Law Committee of the Conservative Rabbinical Assembly? It is to this that Catholic Israel has shrunk. . . . [But] Catholic Israel

can only create new religious insights through history if it is a body capable of having a history.[89]

Kaplan's position was essentially similar. He could see no alternative to rebuilding an "organic" community—that is, one in which no segment acted "as if" it were the whole; rather, only when the segments were joined could a whole exist. His reliance on Israel to provide the necessary linkages was therefore absolute.[90]

Not so for Louis Finkelstein: The community was itself dependent on the existence in its midst of a great academy of Jewish learning. As others have noted, his was an elitist position in principle, backed up by his reading of Jewish history.[91] It will therefore suffice to illustrate this with one explicit passage from his private correspondence. In December 1967 he wrote a confidential letter to Moshe Davis that, more than anything else, explains his policies:

> The strength of the Conservative Movement emanates in my opinion from the fact that its fulcrum is a house of learning. In this respect, as in others, *our movement has adopted for itself the structure of ancient Pharasaism*, the fulcrum of which too was a house of learning, where research could be pursued freely. Dr. Schechter probably consciously adopted this structure for our Movement. In a way, the Seminary plays the same role in the Conservative Movement that the individual rabbi has to play in his congregation. *His authority arises from the fact that he has devoted himself . . . to the study of Judaism.* The structure of our Movement, *unique in the modern world*, is well understood, I believe, by the overwhelming majority of the members of the Rabbinical Assembly. However, it is apparently difficult for some laymen to understand it. This became evident at the [last] convention of the United Synagogue. . . . There is an obvious peril to our whole Movement in widespread ignorance of this basic conception [my emphasis—EL].[92]

In this scheme of things, then, Israel's role was related to the enhancement of the authority and scholarly quality of Finkelstein's academy. Only thus could the Seminary fulfill its mission as a religious "fountainhead." Israel was, indeed, vital; but in essence it was subordinate to the priority assigned to the continuity of scholarship. The question of formal affiliation of the Conservative movement with the World Zionist Organization was, therefore, beside the point; moreover, it injected a lay body, the United Synagogue, into a representative position vis-à-vis Israel, and hence vis-à-vis *klal yisrael*, that would constitute a usurpation of the Seminary's primacy.

Rather than place the Seminary within a world Jewish body whose essential contribution to the future of Judaism would be symbolic, the policy of the Seminary, guided by Finkelstein and supported by Simon Greenberg, would be to place the Seminary—as a place of learning—in greater proximity to the world of learning in Israel. The chosen instrument was not the Zionist movement but the Seminary's own center to be built in Jerusalem.

The Seminary in Israel, Stage One

The decision was taken in principle during the first year of Israeli statehood to foster a Seminary presence in Israel, but its implementation was to take over a decade to achieve.[93] Architectural plans were drawn up for a complex of three buildings, which together would comprise what was then called a "Spiritual-Cultural Center in Jerusalem." The plan called for a residence hall with accommodations for about two hundred people; a library, study hall, and lecture hall; and a synagogue large enough for a congregation of 500 to 750.[94] Groundbreaking, as we know, took place 29 July 1958, but construction was delayed until the beginning of 1960, and the only structure that was built (completed in 1962) was the residence hall, referred to in the correspondence of the Seminary as "the *Pnimiyah*" (dormitory) or "American Students' Center." In the spring of 1961, with construction already well under way, Finkelstein and the Seminary board met to discuss a report by United Synagogue president Charles Rosengarten that the quality of construction fell woefully short of expectations. Finkelstein was embarrassed, especially in front of those board members who had opposed the plan all along—Alan Stroock and Herbert H. Lehman. "I am almost sorry that we ever started this project," Finkelstein complained.[95] Nevertheless, construction was completed the following spring. The American Student Center, as it was actually realized, comprised dormitory rooms for forty-two students (ten couples and twenty-two singles), two faculty apartments, a library and study hall (*beit midrash*), a seminar room, dining room and kitchen, and a lounge.[96]

In the meantime, the Seminary had also acquired an already existing structure in Jerusalem, the centrally located Schocken residence, which contained an impressive private library of Judaica ("the world's largest [private] collection of medieval Hebrew literature and Kabbalah . . . [in addition to] incunabula and rare manuscripts and books").[97] The Schocken Library, or Institute, was to serve as the Seminary's center for research and related scholarly activity (originally envisioned as part of the master plan for a Seminary campus at Neve Schechter) and was placed directly under the supervision of the Seminary Chancellor. An agreement with the Schocken family in February 1961 transferred the property to the Seminary (although ownership of most of the collection itself was retained by the family). Finkelstein asked Hebrew University president Mazar to serve on the Schocken Institute's board of directors—thereby indicating the Seminary's intention to refrain from "invading" the university's sphere. In actuality, little was done to alter the existing staff and program arrangements at the library until the 1970s.[98]

That the Seminary's foothold in Israel was founded on a library-research center and a dormitory for visiting rabbinical students is understandable in light of our prior discussion. It was not, however, a policy that was free from controversy or easy to implement from an administrative point of view. Both Moshe Davis and Saul

Design for the American Student Center in Jerusalem, ca. 1958. *Ratner Center, JTS.*

Lieberman, who supported the plan for an academic center, lobbied strongly for a first-rank scholar [a *talmid hakham*] to be placed in charge of the Seminary's Israel program, both to raise the Seminary's "profile" in the Israeli intellectual community and to lend scholarly rigor to the program. At the same time, some Rabbinical Assembly members (and supported, among others, by Professor Ephraim Urbach of the Hebrew University), lobbied for a heavy investment in the building of local Conservative congregations. Davis argued, along lines similar to Finkelstein's views, that local community ties were secondary, whereas an academic presence was primary.[99]

This controversy was to resurface over the years, but the Seminary's policy has remained generally consistent in assigning priority to its academic program. It is therefore perhaps surprising that Finkelstein did not assign responsibility for the Seminary's Jerusalem program to one of his top-ranking faculty members or administrators. As late as May 1962 he still had no idea who could run the *Pnimiyah*.[100] Davis would later recall that Finkelstein's attitude toward those who were sent off to work in Jerusalem was akin to "sending them into exile": 3080 Broadway would always come first in his thinking, and Jerusalem was an adjunct activity.[101]

By the academic year 1964–65, Seminary rabbinical students were formally given the option to spend a year of study (with full academic accreditation) while in residence at the Students' Center. As the program developed over the next few years, students were given classes in Bible, Talmud, philosophy, and history. The center was run by Rabbi Raphael Posner, and the faculty included (among others) Professors Davis, Ernst Simon, Dr. Avraham Goldberg, Posner himself, and guest lecturers (Dr. Nehamah Leibowitz, for example, taught at the *Pnimiyah* in 1967).[102] Students took a seminar with Professor Davis on the development of Conservative

Judaism in America. As one participant in the seminar in 1964–65 later recalled, the notion of spending precious time on such a course struck the students as surprising and irksome at first, for they had come to Israel ostensibly to enrich their learning in other ways—not by studying American Jewry. Yet, by the time the course ended, the "hidden agenda" became clear: Davis was endowing the students with the mental equipment and the ideological motivation *to return to America* and to serve congregations without "feeling badly" about leaving Israel (although he hoped that some might return—as at least one did).[103]

It was also at about that time, once the program was in place, that the Chancellor's thinking also began to undergo a shift. In an open letter written at the end of June 1964, Finkelstein reflected on his latest stay in Israel and on the impression he gained there that the Seminary was held in high regard in government and in progressive religious circles. On this occasion, too, he made the point that the Seminary had "much to give Israel in the spiritual and moral dimension." He continued as in the past to remind his colleagues that "Israel has much to give us, too; and further, when we make our contribution, it will be refined and improved in ways possible only to Jews living in the Holy Land." Yet, taking note of the absence of any school like the Seminary in Israel, he made clear his opinion that, insofar as religious development was concerned, American Jewry need not feel inferior. Most important, however, was a new and optimistic perception that the climate in Israel, insofar as the Seminary's role there was concerned, had turned a corner: "In light of conversations which I had, I am confident that our difficulties in Israel will be ended in the very near future—indeed, to all intents and purposes that chapter is already closed."[104]

The "difficulties" referred to by Finkelstein were the roadblocks placed by the Orthodox rabbinate in Israel in the way of a pluralistic and voluntaristic religious life, including opposition to the expansion of Conservative and Reform institutions in the country. These problems had been on the agenda for years. As far back as 1950, the Rabbinical Assembly had passed a resolution on "Religion in Israel," which stated:

> Because we see our relationship with Israel as resting primarily on the level of culture and religion, we are especially anxious about the status of Judaism in Israeli life. We are concerned over the present rift between the secular and religious groups in the country. We trust that the religious forces in Israel will find the necessary approach to the masses of Israeli Jews and the means of impressing them with the continuing validity of Jewish religious doctrine for the moral and spiritual needs of our time. . . . The American Jewish community, including all its religious groups, has some valuable experience in dealing with the challenge of secularism to the religious life. . . . We feel that especially in our own Conservative group, with its unique program of blending tradition with modernism, there are many precedents that can aid the synagogue in Israel. . . .

Students at the American Student Center in Jerusalem, 1987. *Communications Department, JTS.*

The future of Judaism in Israel rests primarily upon . . . revitalization and renewal rather than upon political victories in the councils of government.[105]

The resolution went on to "deplore" the practice of the Chief Rabbinate in barring non-Orthodox rabbis from performing any official functions in Israel. The lack of religious pluralism in Israel continued with seemingly little or no change, however, just as there was little change in the public status of religion in general (referred to as the "status quo" agreement between the Orthodox sector and the government with respect to the place of Judaism in Israel's public life). As of the summer of 1962, for example, Finkelstein was still convinced that it was only in the long run that any basic changes might be anticipated:

I have come to the conclusion that most of the people who oppose us in Israel really disagree with our whole approach to Judaism . . . , and one expects one's opponents not to be very fond of one. I am now sorry that I did not arrange for that lunch with [Zerach] Warhaftig [Minister of Religions]. I do not think it would have done much good in the short run, but it would do a great deal of good in the long run for all these men to understand that they are playing with fire when they denounce our people generally.[106]

Yet soon afterward, in 1964, it seemed that he was given certain assurances that changed his mind.

During his own visit to Israel in May 1965, Professor Lieberman also spoke about religious dialogue in Israel, but he was less sanguine than Finkelstein. He saw little to indicate that the yeshiva world was about to change its views on Conservatism. Lieberman felt that the Seminary, whose hallmark was its commitment to freedom of research as the best expression of Torah, could not help but constitute a threat to those with a narrower view of the Judaic tradition. Lieberman took pains to deny that there were plans to "import" artificially a Conservative movement or to establish a Conservative rabbinical school for Israel. Such developments, he stated (in an interview in *Haaretz*) would have to grow slowly from within Israeli society.[107]

The issue of religious pluralism in Israel did not go away, of course. The possibilities of opening certain doors for Conservative Judaism in Israel—but also the overall sense that a personal, cautious, and very gradual approach was necessary—were underscored by Moshe Davis's experience in the fall of 1967, when he officiated at his daughter's wedding in the presence (and under the jurisdiction) of Chief Rabbi Yitzhak Nissim. He wrote to Finkelstein: "It bore out many of my own theories of how we can establish a Conservative religious presence here, but that is 'future music.'" At the end of 1967, Finkelstein would still have to conclude: "While the vast majority of the leaders of the State of Israel would like the Seminary to expand its commitments there . . . , some are definitely opposed to us."[108]

Over the years, this would remain a constant source of tension. Responding in 1972 to Simon Greenberg's requests for funds for the Seminary's Israel projects, Rabbi Jacob Agus of Baltimore would write: "The failure of our movement to make headway in Israel aggravates the cause of Judaism throughout the world. Because of our inaction, the gangrene of polarization creeps relentlessly on the body and soul of the Israeli."[109] Greenberg himself would write to University of Judaism chairman Isadore Familian in 1974 in an optimistic but rather equivocal vein, "[Chancellor] Gerson Cohen has been here [in Israel] this past month and has met with everyone from the Prime Minister down. We have every reason to believe that the presence of the Seminary and the Conservative movement in Israel *will within the reasonably near future* be increasingly felt, particularly in the areas of the intellectual and spiritual bonds that should unite our two great communities."[110] A year later, Greenberg would confide to his grandson the impression (after a meeting with David Glass, bureau director of the Minister of Religions):

> The Ministry of Religion [*sic*] had very little power over the attitude and activities of the Rabbinate. They cannot order them to accept the divorces, marriages, or conversions performed by Conservative rabbis. The other thing that became clear is that he as well as the present head of the Ministry, Dr. Raphael, have a good deal of good will towards the Conservative movement and are ready to be of help in such areas as they have authority, as, for example, making a financial contribution towards a synagogue building fund, which he promised to do if we made a proper application. . . . My colleagues think that I am too easy on the Chief Rabbinate when I discuss these matters.[111]

The issues continued to be raised throughout the period under study, and we will have reason to return to the attitude of and actions undertaken by the Seminary leadership in this regard.

The Orthodox rabbinate's monopoly over the sphere of personal status law did not, however, block the Seminary's academic and educational activities in Israel. Indeed, on the academic front and in related activities the Seminary faced no resistance and enjoyed cordial relations with the Israeli scholarly community. Thus, it was the Seminary's academic ties within Israel that came to the fore when disaster struck in the form of the fire at the Seminary's library in the spring of 1966. Eliahu Elath, president of the Hebrew University, cabled at once with an offer to help replace destroyed books, wherever possible, from the National and University Library in Jerusalem. The Seminary's Dr. Menaham Schmelzer was in touch with his counterpart at the university, and Saul Lieberman was dispatched as well.[112] It was against this background that the Seminary built its program in Israel from the mid-1960s through the mid-1970s, a period that spanned the last years of Louis Finkelstein's tenure as Chancellor and the first years of Gerson Cohen's.

This was, in addition, one of the most turbulent periods in the history of American colleges, universities, and theological seminaries, as in America in general. The rapidly escalating war in Vietnam, the political and geostrategic implications of both the Arab-Israeli War in June 1967 and the Soviet invasion of Czechoslovakia in 1968, major domestic upheavals such as inner-city rioting, political assassinations, and widespread unease over changing social mores shook the American public. America's academic sector felt (and fueled) the reverberations in a magnified way. Colleges were going through a period of especially rapid, large-scale growth and, in particular, experienced a period of strife over power and priorities on campus amid open challenges to existing authority structures. Universities and seminaries were flashpoints of violent confrontation and political dissent. Perhaps not coincidentally (given the greater awareness of overseas events and the turbulence at home), a semester or year of study abroad, which had always before been a privilege reserved for the elite of America's youth, became more widely available as an option in American higher education. The Seminary's program was not unlike those in other specialized fields or advanced-study programs in the humanities and social sciences.

The winds of change did not stop at the Seminary gates, as is indicated in the following excerpts from letters written by Finkelstein to Davis:

> I think you will be astonished to hear, for the first time in the history of the Seminary, the Chief Executive [i.e., Finkelstein] was publicly attacked in a student periodical. It is not serious and I am not worried about it, but it is a sign of the times. . . .
>
> [T]here is a great deal to be achieved in Israel . . . for the fulfillment of our hopes and aspirations. I am thinking not only of what we can give to Israel, but *primarily of what Israel can do for us.* The problems of American adolescents . . . , Christian and Jewish, are staggering. The alienated may be a minority but they certainly are a very effective minority and they manage to poison everything. *I do not know of any cure for our disease except the possible influence of Jerusalem and Israel and its youth on us* [my emphasis—EL].[113]

In 1969 the Seminary administration was still talking about the possibility of raising $3.5 million to erect two additional buildings on the Neve Schechter site. Rabbi David Goldstein of Har Zion in Philadelphia was appointed to direct the effort as a separate campaign, under Simon Greenberg's leadership and in cooperation with the Seminary's development committee (but outside regular Seminary funding channels).[114] Nevertheless, such plans faced enormous difficulties and did not come to fruition. The Seminary was finalizing its plans to open a graduate studies division—the Institute for Advanced Studies in the Humanities (IASH)—and was raising funds to build an additional building for the Seminary's campus. Finkelstein and his Board of Directors worried that government funding for IASH might not come through as expected, and there was the additional anxiety that constructing the new building might necessitate budgetary cutbacks in other areas (and conversely, that any new expenditure might imperil the building program). It was Finkelstein's intention that IASH should bring the Bible, Talmud, and other Jewish texts into the forefront of humane discourse in America, and dovetailing with that conception, he believed that the Seminary ought to expand its activities in Israel to promote global prominence for Jewish studies at an advanced level. But he felt constrained by the scarcity of resources and was pessimistic about receiving support from within the Seminary: "There is no way I could persuade [Jerusalem mayor Teddy Kollek] that our Board of Directors and our Faculty just will not go along [with expanding the Seminary's work in Jerusalem]."[115]

A year of study in Israel for all rabbinical students was not made obligatory, at least partly due to such considerations. The Seminary could not afford to subsidize the cost of tuition and travel for its students (and their spouses). By 1970, only two junior-year students out of twenty were able to go. The Seminary had been receiving a modest subsidy from the Jewish Agency's Student Authority ($1,000 per student), but travel and living expenses for a married couple were then estimated at $5,000. The Seminary, which was spending about $200,000 a year in Israel, asked the Jewish Agency for an additional $25,000 subvention for student stipends, which it received.[116] This could not offer a fundamental solution, however, to the larger problem of putting the Seminary's Israel programs on a secure, long-term footing.

It was therefore apparent that a more focused effort was needed in order to advance projects in Israel that had been begun but then allowed to falter or slow down. In 1971 Finkelstein saw the wisdom of Moshe Davis's view that the Seminary needed "somebody in Jerusalem who will be our representative at the level on which Nelson Glueck intended to be for [the Reform movement]." At a meeting of the executive committee of the Seminary Board of Directors that September, he reported that progress in Israel had been stymied, but he also noted that a cadre of some sixty Seminary graduates were living in Israel (in 1970–71, ten thousand American Jews had made *aliya*), and that Simon Greenberg was prepared to settle in Israel himself to facilitate new expansion plans for the Seminary. Late the next year, Finkelstein wrote to Greenberg in Israel: "The more I think of Israel, the more I feel convinced that it offers us a great opportunity which ought not to be missed." (At the same time, he expressed the hope that Greenberg would continue to put in time at the Seminary in New York.)[117]

In 1972, Dr. Gerson D. Cohen became Chancellor of the Seminary. A man with a strong personal commitment to Zionism, Hebrew culture, and Israel, he went ahead with plans to have Greenberg direct a three-year "Special Seminary-Israel Pilot Project" inaugurated in September of that year "to reexamine the activities that have been conducted . . . since 1958 and to chart a course for the future." The project's agenda included: "a) an enlarged program of accredited undergraduate and graduate courses in the areas of [the Seminary's] competence; b) a . . . program of public lectures for adult Jewish studies, wherever possible in cooperation with our affiliated synagogues in Israel; c) Hebrew publications of works dealing with the history and philosophy of the Conservative Movement; d) the reorganized utilization of the voluntary services of the students resident in the Student Center and of the large number of Seminary graduates, Rabbinical Assembly members, United Synagogue laymen resident in Israel, and others, for cultural and religious activities among youth and adults in Israel."[118] Rabbi David Goldstein was appointed as consultant to the Chancellor on Seminary-Israel Affairs, with a mandate to raise funds independently of normal Seminary funding sources.[119] Extended in 1976 for an additional three years, the project run by Greenberg and Goldstein raised more than $200,000, which was used to fund the lectures and publishing activities outlined above, as well as to organize seminars of Israeli educators and courses on

Judaica for Israelis (notably at the Oranim Teachers' College of the United Kibbutz Movement) and to lend support to fledgling Conservative congregations in Israel.[120] At the same time, the dormant research program once envisioned for the Schocken Institute was reexamined. Saul Lieberman agreed to transfer his own collection of rabbinica to the library at Schocken, and the Seminary assured the Schocken family that, with an expanded Seminary program in Jerusalem, erstwhile plans to run a proper research facility would now be implemented.[121]

The new Chancellor enunciated a number of new policies. First, the year-in-Israel program would become mandatory for rabbinical students, despite misgivings by faculty that a full year was not justified, being both expensive for the Seminary and "not sufficiently profitable educationally to make it worthwhile."[122] Second, Cohen spoke about the Seminary's ties with Israel from a new sense of confidence in the importance of the Seminary and its activities for Israeli society. He emphasized the mutuality of Diaspora-Israel relations: the "common" or "dual" set of objectives joining Israel and American Jewry. "Israel has always occupied a place in the value system of the diaspora. Now diaspora Jewry must occupy a place in the value system of Israel."[123]

Underlying Cohen's "high profile" posture were a number of significant factors. In the new, post-1967 Jewish world, Israel itself had assumed a new position. By 1972, no serious claimant to the mantle of Jewish leadership in America could afford merely to bask passively in the sunshine of Israel as a center of scholarship. After the Yom Kippur War (October 1973), solidarity with an internationally isolated Israel became even more crucial: by 1975 the Conservative movement overcame its earlier reservations about affiliation with the World Zionist Organization. But, perhaps in response to the upsurge in pro-Israel support in American Jewry, the Seminary had to compete once again (as it had in 1948) for its fair share of communal resources.

A further factor was the maturation of American Jewish scholarship. In the twenty years since Finkelstein had framed an Israel policy for the Seminary, a new American-born and American-trained generation of Judaica scholars—of which Cohen himself was a part—was taking its place in a growing number of American universities. The Seminary faculty itself was going to be rejuvenated as part of that process, and as a result the Seminary would no longer need to recruit faculty from Israel.

A good indication of the new tone at the Chancellor's office is conveyed by a letter that Gerson Cohen wrote to Simon Greenberg in February 1975. He reported to Greenberg that the Israeli Consul General in New York had informed him that President Ephraim Katzir would be stopping at the Seminary in early March but would remain only briefly. There were to be no honorary degrees (as there had been for past presidents and prime ministers of Israel), as Katzir had already accepted a degree from Brandeis and from Brooklyn Polytechnic Institute. Cohen noted, "I

Israeli president Ephraim Katzir (center) at the Seminary library with Chancellor Gerson Cohen (left) and Menahem Schmelzer, Seminary librarian, 1975. *Photo by Arnold Katz. Ratner Center, JTS.*

was distressed that while we had invited Katzir for a degree some two years ago, he was now following a pattern that we do not particularly like in other Jews who accept degrees from *goyim* rather than from Jewish institutions." But he went on to say, in a tone far different from that of his predecessor, "I think Israel is going to be the loser if it does not understand that *the greatest Jewish scholarly institution* deserves more than a visit" [my emphasis—EL].[124]

The incident represents a "coming of age" that permitted a sense of independence. By the same token, however, the Seminary could now reasonably formulate a rationale for becoming more actively involved elsewhere in the Jewish world, and particularly so in Israel. This is precisely what Cohen (Chancellor until 1986) and his successor, Ismar Schorsch, would indeed do. The keynote of that rationale was mutuality rather than competition. The Seminary would not constitute an alternative to Israel but, rather, a bulwark of strength that was simultaneously the strength of the Diaspora and of Israel. Cohen, though disturbed by the slighting of the Seminary by Katzir, was even more disturbed by his fear that Israel, in underestimating the status and needs of the Diaspora, was figuratively cutting off the branch that it was sitting on. As he wrote to Greenberg:

> Last Saturday night, I was at a private party . . . and the thesis was advanced that while Israel is in great trouble, much more emphasis has to be placed on the identity of American Jewry because American Jewry is slowly finding its identification with Israel being attenuated. I think the Israelis simply do not understand the temper of the leadership of American Jewry. They make the great mistake of talking to [prominent lay leaders] Max Fisher, Jack Stein, and Arthur Levine, thinking they represent the power base of American Jewry. They do not, and it is important the Israelis get to know this [through the Seminary]. . . . *I will not change my posture of complete identification with the cause of Israel, which I believe is the cause of world Jewry.* I will continue to emphasize the Israeli component in Seminary activities, but I feel very strongly that Israel is simply acting in poor taste in terms of . . . American Jewry [my emphasis— EL].[125]

Israel on the Mind of the Seminary, 1967–1987

The new rationale for integrating the Seminary into a Jewish world where Israel was increasingly central evolved over time. To take the full measure of the overall place of Israel in the Seminary ethos, it is important to look at the qualitative significance of the Israel dimension *in New York*, "at home," and not simply in terms of the programs that the Seminary built in Israel from the 1970s through the 1980s. An appreciation of later developments requires first a backward glance at the later 1960s.

The war of June 1967 had caught the Seminary, like the rest of the Jewish community, off guard. The first Seminary representative to react publicly was Saul Lieberman, who issued a forceful and passionate statement on 5 June. Calling upon "all the Jews in the world" but addressing the Conservative movement specifically, through its rabbis and congregations, he let it be known that this was the critical hour in which loyal Jews had to stand by Israel, at the very least by sending financial support. "The Jewish people has never in its history passed through an hour of such danger," he said, warning: "Its entire existence is gravely threatened. . . . This is our great opportunity, one that may never repeat itself [if we fail to act], to help save Klal Yisrael." He exhorted the community to dig deeply into its pockets, he himself and his wife serving as personal examples (they had given $25,000 to the Israel Emergency Fund).[126]

Louis Finkelstein had planned to spend part of the summer (as he did each year) in England and in Israel, leaving New York by 21 June and arriving in Israel on 2 July. The fifth of June thus found Finkelstein still in New York and unable at that late stage to change his plans, despite Moshe Davis's urging him to leave for Israel at once.[127] In the meantime, Dr. Nelson Glueck, president of Hebrew Union College, arrived on 12 June "with the assistance of the U.S. government," and empowered by the American School of Oriental Research to take official possession of the school's premises in East Jerusalem, cut off in Jordanian territory since 1948. (Dr. Glueck had headed the school during the 1930s and from 1942 to 1947.)[128] Finkelstein agreed to try to move up his own arrival from England, but he resisted any suggestion that his presence, paralleling that of Dr. Glueck's, should be given a public relations character: "I do not think—and Professor Lieberman agrees with me in this— that we want in any way to seem to be exploiting this occasion for institutional purposes. This is a temptation that just has to be resisted."[129] One result was that the Reform movement was publicly present in Jerusalem, as were students from Yeshiva University, working as volunteers; but the contingent of Seminary students, as active as they were, formed only a minimal Conservative presence, easily overlooked.[130]

As for other members of the Seminary community, Mordecai Kaplan wrote to Davis, on the eve of *Shavuot* in 1967, a week after East Jerusalem surrendered to Israeli troops:

> I hope that our political and military leaders will realize fully the two main obstacles to a satisfactory peace settlement: 1) the underdeveloped fanatically emotional character of the Arabs combined with a holy megalomania which makes it impossible for them to accept defeat, and 2) the chicaneries of Russia that is prepared to go all out for the Arabs in order to have a monopoly on their oil reserves. Under those circumstances it is up to our political and military leaders to neutralize the force of these two obstacles by making a dramatic surprise move: They should accept the internationalization of the Old City of Jerusalem as a concession in advance as the price they are ready to pay for direct negotiations with the defeated nations.[131]

A month later he followed this up with a chagrined note, when the Israeli government showed no signs of moving in that direction:

> I am no prophet, but I have enough common sense to have realized at once the danger of Israel's insistence on reclaiming the old Jerusalem [*sic*]. The one sure outcome of Israel's stubbornness is the continuance of a state of belligerency. Such a state of belligerency is bound, God forbid, to bring an end to the Jewish people. . . . Please communicate my suggestion to someone in the Government who has a head on his shoulders, a head which has not become intoxicated by the success of the week's war. In the final analysis this is a war not alone against the Moslem world but also against the Communist world. Let us remember what the Zealots did to us during the Second Commonwealth. The Zealots of today are likely to do the same in shorter shrift to our Third Commonwealth.[132]

Kaplan was being fully consistent with his long held principles regarding the nature of Israel as a center to serve world Jewry—a center that did not necessitate any one specific political or territorial configuration, just as long as it was the keystone in a restructured world Jewish people. But in addition, Kaplan's fear that Israel was too small and too isolated to stand up indefinitely against the combined might of the Soviet Union and the Arab and Moslem world (and that to try to do so was unconscionable hubris) ought to be read within the context of contemporary American reactions, especially in the Christian community. The durability of Israel's newly won military and strategic security was placed in question not only by Israel's foes, but also by the seeming indifference of those who (in the eyes of those at the Seminary) should have been among Israel's most vocal supporters. The silence of the Christian churches in America in the weeks prior to the war and some of the criticism leveled at Israel in the wake of the ceasefire had been particularly disturbing to those at the Seminary who had for years championed the cause of interfaith understanding. The failure of the churches to perceive that the fate of Israel was inseparable from that of the Jews appeared to indicate that either the Jews themselves had failed to communicate this point adequately, or (even more disturbing) that Christian goodwill toward Judaism and the Jewish people had not progressed as far as had been thought (or both). Louis Finkelstein, for example, wrote to Moshe Davis on 2 October 1967:

> Together with the affirmative response, there has also been a very negative one in the circles of some of our Christian friends. Very few people here who are non-Jews realize quite what Jerusalem means to Jews and how central it has been in all Jewish thought. We always took for granted that men understood this and have never taken the trouble to explain it. Now we have to do the job when it is difficult and late.[133]

That job was undertaken by the member of the Seminary faculty who was, perhaps, the most well placed to speak openly about interfaith dialogue, Abraham J. Heschel. His book, *Israel: An Echo of Eternity*, was first published in late 1967. It is a pro-Israel religious and political polemic in the guise of a lyrical psalm, sprinkled with pointed remarks directed explicitly at the non-Jewish theological community. At the same time, it succeeds in communicating to Jewish readers, as well, that the time had come for a new reckoning with the reality of Israel. It contains little of an original nature: rather, it restates in Heschel's unique poetic style the case for Israel's existence, the historical ties of the Jewish people and Jewish faith with the land of the Bible, the character of Judaism as a historical religion, and the religious—indeed, biblical—significance for all humanity of an Israel reborn, precisely in a generation radically traumatized by genocide. It challenges the reader—Christian as well as Jew—to partake in a commitment to a redemptive history. Quoting the vision of universal peace in Isaiah 2:1–4 ("For out of Zion shall go forth the law and the word of the Lord from Jerusalem"), he turned to his reader with this plea:

> But that word will not go forth from Jerusalem unless all of us—Jews and non-Jews—have tasted profoundly the intensity of waiting for the word. The bur-

den is upon us Jews but we will not and must not do it alone. All of us must learn how to create in this dreadful emptiness of our lives, how to be illumined by a hope beyond disaster and dismay. The Bible is an unfinished drama. Our being in the land is a chapter of an encompassing, meaning-bestowing drama. . . . The State of Israel is not the fulfillment of the Messianic promise, but it makes the Messianic promise plausible.[134]

In the aftermath of the war, in an attempt to launch a new initiative under the influence of that summer's drama, Louis Finkelstein tried to interest his colleagues and board in a new Israel-related project. He had, while in Israel, discussed the possibility of establishing in Jerusalem, under Seminary auspices, a "world academy of ethics" to focus world and Diaspora Jewish attention on the positive (non-military) prospects of Israel, quite apart from the humanitarian and academic functions of such an academy. Such a magnet institution was, to his way of thinking, a far more effective means of propagandizing for *aliya* than were messages based on Israel's vulnerability. In this he was seconded by Simon Greenberg, who had in July 1967 addressed a gathering of American Zionists in Tel-Aviv on the subject of *aliya* from the West:

> We must change the image of Israel almost exclusively as a place for the perse-cuted. We must return to the original vision of Zionism, the vision of a State of Israel as the center of a flourishing creative Jewish culture, as the place where Judaism can renew itself . . . and where as a people we shall be able to build a social order that will represent a significant contribution to the welfare not only of the residents of Israel, but of mankind.[135]

The concept of such an academy as Finkelstein had in mind was drawn from his own long-standing conviction that Judaism had a vital role to play in the world as a universal ethical system and that Israel's role in history was bound up with the revival of Judaism's ethical genius. However, this plan, too, ran afoul of resistance both in Israel and at home in New York. In Israel, Yaakov Herzog, director-general of the prime minister's office (and son of the former Israeli chief rabbi, Isaac Halevi Herzog), strenuously objected to the idea of tying a nonsectarian and international academy to sectarian auspices. In addition, the Hebrew University's plans for its own peace institute (the Truman Institute) on Mount Scopus took precedence over Finkelstein's proposal. In New York, among the Seminary's Board of Directors and faculty, the reaction of most people was to call Finkelstein's notion a "pipe dream." He wrote to Davis: "I think the upshot of it all is really that everybody here has cooled off [since June]. . . . We are up against something very, very difficult which I had not anticipated . . . namely, the simple lack of enthusiasm of American Jews to themselves participate in the building of the State of Israel."[136]

The war of 1967 may not have left immediate or tangible changes in its wake. Indeed, it stands to reason that an institution like the Seminary, with a long internal tradition of dealing with both Israel and Jewish peoplehood in general, would not undergo any major revolution in this regard under the immediate influence of a particular series of events. Major shifts in expressions of Jewish identity and pro-Israelism were more discernible in those sectors of American Jewry where peoplehood and Israel consciousness had been more muted or peripheral but were now suddenly coming to the fore.

Nonetheless, the building of a more ambitious program for the Seminary in Israel in the 1970s was probably related to gravitational shifts in the Jewish world that became more apparent after 1967. Among these were a sustained, long-term increase in American Jewish funding for Israel, a small wave of *aliya* from America that lasted through the mid-1970s (continuing afterward in more modest dimensions), and a new preoccupation with Soviet Jewish emigration to Israel. All of this impinged on the Seminary in some way, whether directly or indirectly.

The Seminary, Israel, and Aliya *as Seen by Alumni*

The question of immigration to Israel takes on much greater historical significance, for example, than is indicated by Finkelstein's perception of a lack of enthusiasm for it at the Seminary. But rather than look at the faculty or administration, in this regard we need to examine the student body. Ten percent of the membership of the Rabbinical Assembly (the overwhelming majority of them graduates of the Seminary's Rabbinical School) have moved to Israel—a proportion that is *ten times* the corresponding proportion in American Jewry at large. This statistic raises the possibility that, despite the lukewarm attitude of Seminary faculty, Seminary-trained rabbis carried with them out of JTS a disproportionately high appreciation for Israel's centrality in modern Jewish life (or in their own Jewish lives, at any rate). Placing Israel on their personal agenda in this way may or may not have something to do with the education that they received at the Seminary. It was partly out of a desire to investigate this question that a survey of Rabbinical School alumni was carried out.

Those polled were 470 men and women who had graduated between 1972 and 1993, including 441 living in the United States and Canada and 29 living in Israel; 291 (62 percent) returned completed questionnaires. Seventy-six percent (208) of those who replied listed their occupation as "congregational rabbi." An additional 3 percent are chaplains, 8 percent work in Jewish education, 3 percent in informal education, 7 percent in higher education, and 2 percent in Jewish communal agencies. Twenty-five (or almost 9 percent) of the respondents are residents of Israel, most having made *aliya* between 1975 and 1992 (though one respondent settled in Israel in 1968.) Several other respondents reported having lived in Israel for periods of two to five years before returning to the United States. Thus, the group reflects rather closely the overall figures on *aliya* among Conservative rabbis.[137]

A great many factors, both personal and societal as well as historical, need to be taken into account in determining the sources of the *aliya* phenomenon in the Conservative movement. Clearly, no one factor will explain it, even in the case of a given individual. Parental influence, early education, summer camp and youth group experiences, historical events, in addition to intellectual influences inside and outside the Seminary, must be considered. Family considerations (spouse, children) enter the picture for some *olim* (immigrants). Finally, there is the influence of the year of study in Israel that most of the respondents (73 percent) spent while they were Seminary students. This figure goes up to 80 percent among the *olim*. Given the small sample of Israeli residents, we will not be able to draw definitive conclusions, but we may be able to identify suggestive trends, especially when the Israeli residents can be compared to their American counterparts.

It should first be noted that a large majority of all the respondents—79 percent— answered "yes" when asked whether they had "ever considered living in Israel."[138] Similarly, in choosing a "label" for themselves—Zionist, religious Zionist, pro-Israel, non-Zionist, or post-Zionist—68 percent chose a label that affirmed a Zionist or religious Zionist orientation; a further 27 percent chose a label that omitted the term "Zionist" but was still "pro-Israel"; 5 percent called themselves "post-Zionist"; no one chose the label "non-Zionist."[139] We may therefore begin our evaluation by noting a general readiness among the alumni to identify positively with Zionism or with Israel generally (95 percent Zionist or pro-Israel) and a level of personal awareness on the question of *aliya* that surely exceeds by far the general level in the American Jewish population.

Whether or not this wide consensus has something to do with their common Seminary background is the next question we should ask. Students may, of course, have brought certain attitudes with them when they came to the Seminary—in fact, those attitudes may have prompted them to apply to the Seminary's Rabbinical School in the first place. Still, their Seminary experience either reinforced such pre-existing attitudes or else it failed to reinforce them. Either way, the Seminary factor remains relevant.

We elicited various kinds of information on this score. First of all, although one respondent was born in 1933, all of the others came of age in a world that included the State of Israel and it was thus part of their general Jewish awareness: 52 percent of the respondents were born by 1953 and 48 percent were born between 1954 and 1968.

Only 36 percent confirmed that either one of their parents had belonged to a Zionist organization while the respondents were growing up (44 percent among the *olim*). An identical proportion (36 percent) had been campers at Camp Ramah (24 percent of the *olim* had been campers there); but fully 68 percent of the respondents had worked there as staff (80 percent of the *olim*). Fifty-nine percent had been members of USY (only 48 percent of the *olim*).

Finally, we asked the Israeli residents several specific questions: To what extent did they believe their learning experiences at the Seminary were a factor that contributed to their move to Israel? To what extent had their experiences prior to their student years at the Seminary been such a factor? To what extent had family considerations been a factor? And would they agree or disagree with the following statement: "My decision to move to Israel went against the grain of my experience as a Seminary student"? (See Appendix, Table 1.) The alumni themselves assigned a low priority to their learning experience as such in their later decision to make their homes in Israel—34 percent rating it "not at all" significant or just "a little," while only 17 percent thought that it had been significant "to a great extent." Prior experiences and family considerations were far more important. At the same time, the question of whether or not *aliya* had been consistent with the spirit of the Seminary elicited both strong agreement and strong disagreement. That suggests the possibility of "mixed messages" having been received on the part of students. While only 39 percent agreed that their *aliya* was a nonconformist act in Seminary terms, they expressed this conviction in a more vehement way than did the majority (52 percent) who claimed the reverse. Significantly, almost 10 percent were unsure one way or the other.

When we probe further among those who agreed that *aliya* went against the grain of their Seminary education, we find that almost half (45 percent) of them had graduated from the Seminary after 1982 (specifically, between 1984 and 1992), whereas those who thought their Seminary education was quite in keeping with their decision to live in Israel *had overwhelmingly studied at JTS in an earlier period:* 86 percent had graduated before 1982. Only two of the later graduates (one from the class of 1986 and one from the class of 1990) had come away with the feeling that the Seminary had supported their plans for *aliya*. If this is an accurate indication (and caution is required in view of the small size of the sample), then it might indicate that the Seminary of the 1980s and early 1990s was perceived by its students as being more of a diasporist institution than was the case previously. (Alternatively, there may be other factors involved that will have to be examined.) We shall return to this hypothesis later.

If we attempt to create a profile of the Seminary *oleh* (immigrant), we will find the following: The typical Seminary *oleh* is older than the average among alumni in our sample, graduated earlier than the average, is more likely to have had Zionism in his or her family background, less likely to have been in USY (oriented strongly toward congregational life), more likely to have spent a year of Rabbinical School in Israel, and more likely to have been a staffer at one of the Ramah camps. (See Appendix, Table 2.)

The issue of time of graduation is suggestive in and of itself. If we take into account that the general *aliya* of Jews from America peaked during the early to mid-

1970s, it is noteworthy that 62 percent of our Israeli respondents moved to Israel *after* 1980—that is, their individual experiences both inside and outside the Conservative movement and the Seminary were of greater importance in their decision than was the possible influence of their American Jewish counterparts and peers. This *aliya* has its own characteristics.

It would be helpful to know whether or not the Israeli respondents were influenced any differently by modern Jewish intellectual figures than were their classmates. Comparing the *olim* with the entire group polled (see Appendix, Table 3), the Israeli residents appear to have been influenced to a smaller degree by Heschel and Kaplan (the most important American Jewish theologians included in the question on intellectual influences). They were also slightly less inspired by either Buber or Rosenzweig (with their individualist-existentialist theologies); but they were significantly more influenced by Ahad Ha'am—whose cultural Zionist ethos was strongly oriented toward a collective, nationalist view of Jewish life and toward Palestine as the nation's focal point. Although Kaplan was, to that extent, similarly oriented, Kaplan was, unlike Ahad Ha'am, positively supportive of the Western Diaspora, particularly in the United States.

Pursuing the question of ideological and religious identity and commitment, the *olim* were asked to agree or disagree with the following statements: "Having served as a rabbi abroad, I felt I could not live my life as a Jew the way I wanted to, unless I moved to Israel"; "As a Conservative Jew, I felt that moving to Israel would fulfill my commitment to my principles."

While 59 percent of the *olim* agreed or agreed strongly with the first statement, a significant proportion (19 percent) did not agree. This smaller group thus affirmed that one could indeed live as a Jew and as a rabbi in the Diaspora in accordance with fundamental Jewish principles (a premise that the Seminary supports), but that they nevertheless chose Israel as a personal option. An additional 23 percent were not sure one way or the other. When the question focused specifically on the Conservative element in their identity, 65 percent agreed or agreed strongly with the statement that linked Conservatism with living in Israel, but 31 percent disagreed or disagreed strongly. (Only 4 percent were unwilling to take a position on this.) This is a clear-cut split. There is a clear link in the minds of most rabbinical *olim* between the kind of Judaism they identify with (presumably, the kind of Judaism they learned and practiced at JTS) and their decision to make their lives in Israel; but there clearly is also a fairly prominent difference of opinion in that regard— indicating, once again, a possible problem of "mixed messages."

A few respondents used the space in the margins to add further information. Some pointed out that the questionnaire was not sensitive enough an instrument to record nuances or to probe the deeper sources of a person's attitude and commitment to Israel. One Diaspora respondent, for example, wrote that he had lived in

Israel from 1988 to 1991, intending to settle permanently, and that this had had much to do with the fact that he had spent three separate periods in Israel while in college or at the Seminary. Another Diaspora respondent noted that, "The most important element in my relationship to Israel was my involvement in Hillel as a student." A third (also a Diaspora resident) complained that the entire area of childhood level of observance had been left out of the questionnaire, as had the Hebraic content of Jewish day school education. Having been to Israel six times, including his year of study while at the Seminary, this respondent concluded: "The Seminary experience as well as emotional ties to Israel are both life choices growing out of other factors in our backgrounds. The Seminary is not causal of feelings for Israel. Jewish feelings and loyalties and literate Hebrew skills are!"[140]

Although we have so far been entertaining the hypothesis that there is a direct relationship (positive or negative) between the Seminary experience, as seen by the students, and the question of *aliya*, the possibility exists that the relationship between the Seminary as a life and learning experience and the extremely high proportion of *olim* among alumni is, or is also, an *indirect* one. This was suggested to me in an interview I conducted with a Rabbinical School alumnus from an earlier period (a member of the class of 1959), who had served as a rabbi in two American congregations before moving to Israel in 1970. What he had to say is consistent with Marshall Sklare's analysis of Conservative rabbis in the 1950s. My interviewee recalled a study that was conducted on the relative levels of job satisfaction reported by Reform and Conservative rabbis, in which Reform rabbis were overwhelmingly satisfied with their work, while Conservative rabbis were just as overwhelmingly frustrated. The sources of his own frustration, the alumnus related, were similar to the kinds of frustration that faced his Conservative peers: Although he had wanted to go out and "serve" American Jewry and had a high degree of empathy for his congregants, he was isolated in the community by his high personal commitment to observance. Second, the supreme value of learning, instilled in him while at the Seminary, proved difficult if not impossible to maintain once he was out in the field. Finally, he (and others he knew) keenly felt the attraction to Israel and experienced their ties to America as a conflict.[141]

That is to say, that the Seminary itself (and its allied institutions, like Camp Ramah), by creating an intense, all-embracing Jewish environment and by instilling the values it did, set up an uncomfortable dissonance for rabbis who went out to work in the American Jewish community. That, in turn, led them to consider Israel as an option. Trained as a self-conscious elite, educated to believe in the charismatic force of learning and imbued with a sense of mission, they came up against a folk religion that left many of them feeling inadequate, as if they had somehow failed. The value of *klal yisrael* that was meant to motivate alumni to serve where they had been called to serve, also motivated them to consider settling in Israel. Israel, too, was the home of *klal yisrael,* and the history of the Jewish people was unfolding there as well as in America.[142]

The survey of alumni did not focus on *aliya* alone, however, even though that is the most striking feature of Seminary graduates' attitudes and behavior when compared with general American Jewish norms. Given the fact that they were trained, after all, to serve American Jewry primarily, and given that most American Jews (and most Conservative rabbis) express a sense of commitment to and identification with Israel in other ways than settling there, the survey asked questions relating to current personal and professional matters relating to Israel. Because the alumni living in North America far outnumber those living in Israel (by a factor of nine to one), it may be possible to test hypotheses raised with regard to the place of Israel in the consciousness of Seminary graduates and to see whether those hypotheses are confirmed or denied.

Respondents who currently serve with congregations were asked how many times within the most recent six months their sermons had dealt with Israel; how many times their messages to congregants in synagogue bulletins had, in the same period, dealt with Israel; and whether they could compare themselves to other Conservative rabbis in terms of the priority of Israel on their synagogue agendas (higher priority, lower, the same?). They were asked about their synagogues' calendar for the current year, and whether any of the following activities were planned: adult Hebrew classes, Israel Bonds function(s), Jewish National Fund fund-raising function(s), function(s) to promote America-Israel Public Affairs Committee activities, speaker(s) on Israeli public affairs, parlor meeting(s) and other fund-raising functions for Israel's Masorti (Conservative) movement, presentations related to Israeli tourism, congregational trip to Israel, and other Israel-related functions (*Yom Ha'atzmaut,* youth-related activities, United Jewish Appeal–related activity, Israel fair, discussion group or *hug*). Rabbis were asked whether they had served in the last two years on a local or national committee or organization devoted to Israel and how many times they had had telephone contact with someone (non-family-related) in Israel within the most recent two months. (See Appendix, Table 4.)

The assumption underlying this set of questions was that, although congregations' Israel activity is partly determined by lay leadership, there are some areas that come directly under the influence of the rabbi: sermons, bulletin messages, adult education, and other programs. Indeed, rabbis can and do seek to alter their congregations' programming priorities and are active in promoting some activities. One respondent, who believed that the questionnaire he was returning showed a congregation deficient in Israel programming, wrote the following, indicating just how much initiative is available to the rabbi in some congregations:

> I only came to this congregation [six months prior to the survey], so programming was pretty much out of my hands. I am amazed (shocked!) at how little

consciousness there is of Israel. I am trying to turn it around next year: adding an Israel component to the school curriculum; getting Israeli pen pals for the religious school students; bringing [the local Israeli *shaliah*—emissary/program coordinator] to speak to various synagogue groups . . . , trying to interest a few congregants in visiting Israel. It's a start, and it's a 100% improvement over what I found here.[143]

When the sum of all responses was computed, it was found that no respondent listed more than eight of the nine specified items (the tenth item was the write-in "other" or miscellaneous category), and very few listed none at all.[144] Local variations among the congregations would certainly account for some of the results obtained, but because our object is to trace latent or more direct influences deriving from the rabbis' Seminary experience, we need to put the rabbis themselves into sharper focus. Hence, the frequency of their own sermons dealing with Israel was compared with their own assessment of the "priority" assigned to Israel on their synagogues' agendas relative to other rabbis' congregations and then compared with their personal affinity for an ideological position on Zionism and Israel. (See Appendix, Tables 5 and 6.)

It would appear that the rabbis responding to the survey share the view that a moderate number of sermons devoted to Israel (on average, between one a month and one every other month) is consistent with current practice. A sermon count that falls below once in three months correlates with a self-perceived image of a lower-than-average Israel priority in synagogue life. That is to say, rabbis who rate their congregations on the weak side of a scale of Israel-orientation also appear to do less themselves (at least from the pulpit) to alter that orientation. The question we should then ask is, who are these rabbis? Is there any discernible pattern among them? Do they as individuals assert a position relative to Israel?

More than 60 percent of the rabbis who identify themselves as Zionist used the sermon at least four times in six months to convey a message dealing with Israel. There is a clear distinction in practice between those rabbis and the ones who chose a label of either "pro-Israel" (a lowest common denominator label among Jews) or "post-Zionist": among the former, more than 60 percent were in the zero-to-three sermon category, while the latter were evenly divided between the more frequent (four or more sermons) and the less frequent (three or less).[145] Again, there appears to be a relationship between the personal position chosen by the rabbi and the various measurements of what goes on in the synagogue with regard to Israel. The Israel profile is not necessarily lay leader driven. We should therefore probe what the rabbis themselves have in common. Do congregations differ in terms of their Israel-activities calendar according to the period in which their rabbis studied for the rabbinate? (See Appendix, Table 7.) In fact, we see that a progression exists from later to earlier Seminary graduates that correlates with the progression of intensity (from lower to higher) of Israel-related activities on synagogue calendars—which is in turn correlated with rabbis' own chosen ideological position and with the use of the pulpit for bringing Israel into the synagogue. That is to say, later graduates (after 1982) are associated with congregations where Israel takes a lower profile both in the calendar of events and in the sermons. This finding is consistent with the impression, gained previously from the much smaller sample of Seminary *olim*, that the 1980s were associated in the minds of some alumni with a more diasporist Seminary. (It should be borne in mind, too, that 1982–83 represents the mean year for *aliya* for respondents who moved to Israel, and that 75 percent of those in our survey who eventually settled in Israel had been ordained by 1983.) At the very least, the results corroborate a "mixed message" syndrome. We need, then, to return to the Seminary itself and the explicit positions taken by its leadership during the 1970s and 1980s.

The Seminary's Israel Program

At the end of October 1974, Simon Greenberg submitted a twenty-two-page memorandum to Chancellor Cohen—the most substantive such document in Greenberg's files—which Cohen was to use in his effort to raise the funds necessary to make the year-in-Israel program compulsory for rabbinical students and (no doubt) to sway the Board of Directors away from the positions that had hampered Finkelstein. In a handwritten note attached to the draft memorandum, Cohen commended the text as "brilliant" and observed that it represented a "historic

Seminary officials meet with Shimon Peres in Israel, 1970s. From left: Reuven Hammer, Morton Leifman, Gerson Cohen, Peres. *Ratner Center, JTS.*

document." The contents of the memo were determined during consultations held between the two men in Jerusalem over the month of July 1974. Cohen was thus in full sympathy with the policies outlined, and he believed that it represented a major turning point for the Seminary. I will therefore quote its relevant portion at length.[146]

Apart from its review of events and projects going back to the days of Solomon Schechter, the memorandum contained a summary of discussions at the Seminary's top administrative level since 1973. In a section called, "The Ideological Basis," the memo outlined a rationale for a new Seminary policy:

> 1. The Seminary's fundamental and overriding purpose . . . is to train professional Rabbinic, scholarly, educational and Jewishly committed lay leadership, primarily *but not exclusively* for the American Jewish community. Seminary graduates are today serving in a variety of capacities in many countries outside the U.S.A. A very substantial number of them are now serving religious, educational and social welfare institutions in Israel. *The Seminary today is not merely a Jewish-American institution. It is the recognized outstanding Jewish world center for the development of a historically grounded, halachically traditionally oriented approach to Judaism, set within an overall theological framework and striving to achieve a viable theoretical and practical synthesis between the national and the universal, the ethical and the ritual, within Judaism, and between Judaism and the modern intellectual climate. As such it has a responsibility towards the Jewish people as a whole.*
>
> 2. Since environmental conditions affecting the American Jewish community are in many significant instances *sui generis*, many aspects of the training of leaders for American Jewry must be *sui generis*. . . . However, the ideational, the ceremonial and the literary factors which stamp the life of a given community as Jewish, cannot be Jewishly totally *sui generis*. If they were, there would be no sense of identity between one Jewish community and another. Hence, in the training of leaders for the American Jewish community, wisdom requires that *emphasis should be placed upon the factors that make for identity between it and other Jewish communities.*
>
> 3. The spiritual and cultural vigor of the Jewish component in the life of American Jewry will in the foreseeable future be, in extraordinarily large measure, dependent upon the continued existence of the State of Israel. . . . American Jewry must therefore be deeply concerned with the quality of the religio-cultural component of the life of the Jews in Israel. . . . [A]n increasing number of [Jews in Israel] are experiencing the need and *asking for aid in developing their religio-cultural life along the lines developed by the Seminary*.
>
> 4. The Seminary's program for the training of American Jewish religio-cultural leaders must therefore include . . . all that will be deemed indispensable to a thorough knowledge and significant experiencing of the land, the people, the culture and the social and political structure of the State of Israel, and . . . do all that it can to help Israelis acquire a knowledge of the Seminary's method of

studying the Jewish heritage and of implementing its ideals and practices. *It may hopefully be able to contribute towards the training of Israelis for religio-cultural leadership in Israel.*[147]

Greenberg went on to anchor this policy as a natural continuation of Louis Finkelstein's legacy of "reaching out beyond the confines of the Jewish community and of narrowly conceived theological concerns [t]hrough the Institute for Religious and Social Studies and through the Conference of Science, Philosophy and Religion.... In his 1952 report, Dr. Finkelstein proposed that a permanent academy be established in Jerusalem, where scholars and men of affairs of all faiths, and from all free countries, might meet to discuss common problems."[148]

The memorandum recommended making a year's study in Israel compulsory for every Rabbinical School student, "and eventually . . . for everyone who is working for a professional degree from the Seminary." It advocated that courses be given at the doctoral level at Neve Schechter, open to Seminary graduates living or visiting in Israel, and that "an effort should be made to have the Hebrew University and other schools in Israel accept those credits towards their own higher degrees in related areas of study." It proposed creating in Jerusalem a "center for the ongoing study of problems confronting Judaism" so that the Seminary's involvement in Israel would be "identified with a center of distinctive study and research in an area reflecting one of the Seminary's primary interests." That center (the memo continued) "would be to the United Synagogue of Israel and to traditionally-oriented non-fundamentalists of Israel what the Seminary is to the United Synagogue of America—their spiritual and cultural fountainhead." Such a center would also eventually come to serve as a base "for an ongoing dialogue between Israeli fashioners of public opinion and American Conservative leaders." Finally, the memorandum pointed to the need for a complete overhaul of the existing arrangements for the Schocken Institute.[149]

Several months later, Cohen was in Jerusalem once again and asked Greenberg to prepare for his signature a new communique outlining progress on the Israel projects. Cohen praised the successful efforts to open a class in rabbinic sources at the Oranim teachers' college, activities of religious outreach organized by Neve Schechter director Rabbi Reuven Hammer in the immediate neighborhood of the school, the opening of thirteen to fifteen Conservative congregations in Israel, and the year-abroad program at Neve Schechter itself, which was then running at full capacity. He concluded that he was now "quite certain that there is a small but highly articulate group of young and older people [in Israel] who are beginning to view us as the channel whereby they might acquire a more objective, balanced and sympathetic view of our religious tradition by studying the text of that tradition as we have, over the decades, studied them."[150] By October 1976, Cohen issued a memorandum (again drafted by Greenberg) that stated, "The Seminary has no intention of withdrawing from its activities in Israel or curtailing them. On the contrary, it is and should be the policy of the Seminary, not only to maintain the activities . . . but to seek opportunities for extending them."[151]

This activity was clearly indicative of a new demarche on the part of the Seminary, as an institution, toward inscribing its imprint on Israeli society and, likewise, toward intensifying the Israeli component of the Seminary's overall program. Putting Israel closer to the top of the school's agenda than ever before required laying the organizational and ideological groundwork both in Israel and in New York. The intention is explicitly stated, but the policies outlined rested on ambiguities: constructive ambiguities, perhaps, but nonetheless potentially perplexing.

The vision outlined by Greenberg, with Cohen's support, contained more than a small measure of Conservative triumphalism, as reflected in the global centrality claimed for the Seminary and its unique ability to transmit the Judaic heritage. That claim was backed up by the further assertion that recognition of the Seminary as "the" channel for exploration and crystallization of a modern Jewish worldview was spreading to small but growing segments of Israeli society. Yet, at the same time, the deepening of the Seminary's linkage with Israel—in terms of the Seminary's own needs as an American Jewish institution—was justified by *Israel's* contribution to "the spiritual and cultural vigor" of American Jewish life. The Seminary, by involving itself in the "religio-cultural life" of Israel and by emphasizing for Seminary students the "factors that make for identity between" the two communities, was positioning itself as the keystone in an overarching, late-20th-century world Judaism, upon which would rest the quality of Jewish life in Israel and in America. Indeed, Judaism's role in world civilization as a whole was at stake.

The vision was supported by an underlying passion for Israel and a historical understanding of the significance of its presence for American Jewry. But it was informed as well by an acute sense of Israel's incompletion. In honor of Israel's twenty-fifth anniversary in 1973, *Conservative Judaism* published a series of essays called "Israel: Anticipation and Reality." Chancellor Cohen's own essay on "The Meaning of Israel in the Perspective of History" opened the issue. In 1977 he published a further assessment of Israel's role within world Jewry, "From *Altneuland* to *Altneuvolk*: Toward an Agenda for Interaction between Israel and American Jewry." The following year, he contributed a short essay on "The Meaning of Liberty in Jewish Tradition" to a volume on *Jewish Life in America*.[152] In all three, Cohen articulated a coherent ideology to support the "keystone" theory of the Seminary in relation to Israel and American Jewry. The essays are worth a close examination: an understanding of Cohen's position will enable us to better assess the question of "mixed messages" that we noted in our survey of alumni of the 1970s and 1980s.

Gerson Cohen's carefully argued essays bristle with both insight and passion, and his points are stated with a characteristic vehemence. As significant as their content, however, is their rhetorical structure. His essays are models of dialectical presentation, carefully balancing an initial thesis with its antithesis, leading to a coherent conclusion that seems to resolve the tension between the two. As a historian, fully aware of the complexities of the Jewish past, he could not accept clear and simplistic formulas. If Israel reborn is unmatched as a significant event in the course of many centuries of Jewish history, it is also flawed by Israel's self-dissociation from the history of those accumulated centuries. If its existence and survival are the heartbeat of world Jewish survival, the heart is never the *only* vital organ and thus cannot be said to be "more important" than brain, lungs, nervous system, etc. If American Jewry, as a community of faith, has accomplished less than it should have in terms of its resources and talent, it has still accomplished much more than other Diaspora communities in the West and has replenished its own professional and scholarly elite from within. The conditions of freedom in America have perhaps contributed to a loosening of Jewish bonds, but also to the articulation of a positive ideology of Judaism: a Judaism of free will, not merely of rejection by the "other." If the Jews are once again, because of Israel, an *'am*, a "corporate kinship group," the very existence of that concept is still fundamentally grounded upon the people's covenant with God, which alone—over and above secular, national loyalty or territorial independence—constitutes a mandate to perpetuate the Jewish people. If Israel has demonstrated an extraordinary ability to defend itself, it has also demonstrated that the laws of Jewish history still apply: that a small people is dependent in the long run on powerful patrons. Qualitatively, Israel is still part of the patterns of Jewish history (and thus shares equally in the diasporic experience); it has not negated or transcended the basic paradigms. Israel's existence has restored Jewish collective pride and rendered it possible for Jews as well as non-Jews to recognize in the Jewish heritage a living culture of the present, not merely a relic of the past. But it was in America that Jewish professors succeeded in winning a place for Judaism in the Western academy, "and consequently as part of the spiritual fabric of society as a whole."[153]

The heart of Cohen's argument is an indivisibility of Jewish history and Jewish peoplehood that renders the dualistic tensions (differences in space or in time between Jewish communities) not merely secondary but actually irrelevant. The different parts must reinforce one another, on a mutual basis, or forfeit their own raison d'être. The only authentically Jewish goals are goals held in common between Diaspora and Israel, though their implementation may vary in style or substance from place to place. The special qualities that characterize one community must be used to replenish and stimulate the Jewishness of the other community. Hebrew, Israel's national language, must be reinforced in American Jewry, for example, but Israel, for its part, needs to recognize the intrinsic *spiritual* merit of Diaspora Judaism, or else lose its ties to the only heritage that is legitimately and authentically

Israel's own. Cohen writes:

> As a consequence of my Jewishness I not only can, but do and must, feel a deep kinship with other Jews that transcends citizenship and time and place. As a Jew, I find the demands of secular nationalist totalism as a yardstick of legitimate loyalties an idolatry. I feel a special relationship with the Land of Israel, for my being a Jew makes it my Land. And I feel a special sense of solidarity with the State of Israel, for it is the institutional embodiment of my people's relationship to its Land. But that Land derives its special place in my life from my religious heritage. . . .
>
> The State is only one aspect of Jewish rebirth. But the State is not the sum and substance of either Jewish identity or of Jewish eschatology. And these two categories embrace the whole of the Jewish People not only of our day but of every age. . . .
>
> Indeed, only from the Diaspora can there come an over-arching commitment to Judaism based not on political statehood or upon geography but solely on the idea of covenant and commitment to ethos. . . . While I do not believe we can prescribe a religious vision to the Israeli in search, I do know that the impact of some of our young people on intellectuals in Israel has been enormous. . . .
>
> [T]he State of Israel and our own American Jewish community are the living links of continuity with [the modern Jewish] great mass drive for liberation.[154]

The tensions inherent in the binary dialectic could only be released if the "two" became "one." American Jewry was incomplete without Israel, but the reverse was also true.

Cohen had "reconstituted" the Jewish people—as per Kaplan's dictum—as an *'am*. The existence of the State of Israel constituted proof positive of that peoplehood. But unlike Kaplan, Cohen saw no need for a new constitutional or covenantal act, since the original covenant of the people with its God was still operative, and it was the only historically valid basis for the existence of the whole collective.

For Kaplan there was a ruptured covenant (as reflected in the fragmentation of the Jewish people): the establishment of a Jewish state was a necessary but not a sufficient condition for the restoration of a fully covenantal relationship between the Jews, their Torah, and their land. For Finkelstein, as long as Yavneh (Jewish learning) flourished, the covenant was by definition maintained and a channel kept open for its perennial renewal. Cohen had added a further argument: as long as Jews adhered to a primordial identity between their peoplehood and their religion, the original covenant was maintained. It was threatened only when the one was separated from the other. Insofar as Israel supports both Jewish peoplehood and the Jews' attachment to their own tradition, it is a positive force that has to be reinforced. By the same token, any Israeli act or policy that places in question the basic equation of peoplehood and religion has to be resisted.

In this sweeping argument, Cohen rendered obsolete such classical Zionist ideas as rejection of the Exile (in his system, such rejection amounted to *self*-rejection), and he neutralized the Copernican revolution in Jewish culture that Zionist secularism once had wrought.

Zionism, as a political movement, was based on a radical reassessment of the Jews' place in the world, a reassessment that had necessarily and thoroughly broken with long held theological principles. In traditional Judaism, as reformulated in the wake of the destruction of the Second Temple, the people Israel continued to occupy a central place in the history of the world (*ata bachartanu*), indeed of the cosmos. While the lives and welfare of individual Jews or Jewish communities were not axiomatically guaranteed, the divine covenant with a saving remnant was unalterable and eternal. God's power to cause redemption at the "end of days" would ultimately prove the truth of that proposition. Yet, the 19th and 20th centuries had shaken to the foundations the confidence of many Jews in God's providential involvement in the world and in the metahistorical significance of their lives. Zionists were, by and large, Jews who declared baldly that they possessed no special dispensation from heaven. They owed their existence to their own efforts, just like other nations; Jewish survival was contingent, not axiomatic, and therefore required positive action to restore the Jews' political independence; and the proper status for the Jews in the world was not central, but equal ("normal"). It was this set of convictions that equipped them with the will to act, despite the opposition and indifference of major segments of world Jewry.

Cohen did not reject secular Zionism or the Zionist state out of objection to the antitraditional thrust of its founding principles. But he called upon Israel and Israelis to transcend their initial act of revolution, now that statehood was accomplished, and to rediscover the positive content of Jewish history, culture, and religion. That content, produced in the Diaspora and never really supplanted, was in the final analysis all the positive content that Israel could ever identify itself with, if it was to be an authentic expression of Jewish peoplehood.[155]

The careful balancing of *yin* and *yang*, of thesis and antithesis, enabled Cohen personally to live in the Diaspora while acknowledging the definitive change in the Jewish world since the rise of Israel. He rejected as empty phraseology, however, any claims to the "centrality" of Israel in Jewish life, if by that was meant that the state had any greater importance than the Jewish people itself, in all its parts and in all its historical manifestations.

In July 1981 Cohen and the Conservative movement reacted sharply, out of their strong sense of kinship with Israel, when government coalition negotiations in Israel came around (as they had done at various times in the past) to the question of the religious status quo, and it was proposed to amend the country's Law of Return—a "Basic Law," that is, one with constitutional status, that confers on every

Jew or anyone married to or immediately descended from a Jew, the right to automatic sanctuary and citizenship. The proposed amendment would have defined the term "Jew" according to Orthodox standards (i.e., barring anyone converted to Judaism under non-Orthodox auspices from inclusion under the law), thus further entrenching the institutionalization of Orthodox Judaism in Israeli law and delegitimizing the non-Orthodox movements in Judaism. Cohen called an emergency meeting to express "our dismay and alarm" and to "condemn the claim of a small minority who have set themselves up as an exclusive legitimate religious spokesman and as sole representatives of the Torah."[156] The challenge to the Seminary inherent in the proposed amendment could only have been taken as "alarming" within the context of a deep-rooted identification with Israel and concern for its ties with Jews worldwide.

Thus, Israel was a powerful presence at the Seminary of the 1970s and early 1980s, as reflected in the actions and words of the Seminary's leading figures. Simon Greenberg wrote to one of the financial backers of the "Israel Pilot Project," early in 1975, that "Dr. Cohen, who was [in Israel] for some ten days, was impressed by what had been achieved and I think that we now have a much clearer idea of what the Seminary ought to be doing in Israel. . . . [These plans] will . . . be an integral part of the Seminary's total program, and not merely an experimental activity. . . ."[157] It was this quality of making Israel a more integral aspect of the Seminary's work that characterized this period. By 1979, Cohen had given his approval for the Conservative beachhead in Israel to constitute itself as an Israeli movement in its own right—the movement for *Masorti* (Traditional) Judaism. By 1982 he had set up within the Seminary a foundation to raise funds for the *Masorti* movement, had recruited its personnel, and had secured its original funding.[158]

But at the same time, the Seminary's mission was said to be also an American Jewish mission and indeed a worldwide one. "The future of Judaism, here [in America] as well as in Israel and elsewhere, will be largely determined by the present state of things within the central institutions of Conservative Judaism," Cohen wrote in 1977.[159] Cohen's position is a perfect illustration of the juxtaposition of ambivalences, outlined in the introduction of this essay. The theology of rabbinic Judaism, with its subordination of national cultic center to a personal and collective redemptive holiness (through *halakha*) was reaffirmed. Scholarship had finally, in America, proven its ability to win for the Jews a recognized and respected place in the comity of international cultures. And American freedom had permitted the creation of authentic Jewish institutions and creative Jewish survival, which had the potential to enrich the culture and the Jewishness of Israel itself.

To those closest to him, Cohen spoke in later years of his hope to be remembered primarily for what he had built for the Seminary in Israel—not (as he suspected might be the case) for the decision to admit women to the Rabbinical School.[160] Yet, others—students in particular—could scarcely be held accountable if the message they heard was a confusing one (not everyone could achieve Cohen's synthesis) or if their hearing was selective.

There was a good deal more involved than the Chancellor's speeches and essays, however, in the process that ensued, particularly in the early 1980s. Recall that our survey of alumni seemed to point to 1982–83 as a watershed time, after which the students believed that the Seminary was (for better or worse) more focused on American Jewish matters, a time when the salience of Israel within the Seminary ethos began to be blurred and perhaps even overlooked. There were powerful structural factors that combined to make that so.

The last years of the 1970s had engendered a faltering confidence in and around the Seminary, given the relatively underdefined and "soft" commitment of the Conservative laity to the Seminary and to its ideology. In 1975, partly in response to the sense of internal confusion, a formal course on Conservative Jewish ideology was introduced at the Rabbinical School for the first time since the 1940s and 1950s, when such a course was taught by Moshe Davis. The question of whether or not to admit women to the ordination program prompted the Seminary to commission a survey of the religious views of the Conservative laity, and the results were felt to be profoundly disturbing. The movement seemed to be losing ground, especially among younger Jews.[161] Plans were made to revamp the entire rabbinical curriculum to better equip graduates for their pastoral work in congregational life. In the meantime, the issue of women's ordination was tabled pending further discussion.

The ambiguous status of the Israel question at the Seminary in the early 1980s, when seen in terms of a wider process of reevaluation of American Jewish realities, takes on greater contextual comprehensibility. The question of women's ordination was itself indicative of the compelling significance of the American social context for the Seminary and for its self-image as the preeminent fountainhead of religious values for the contemporary Jew. Taking this into account, we may indeed see 1983, the year in which the women's ordination question was finally resolved, as a year that marked a turning inward to American Jewry and to other issues most relevant close to home, as is suggested by our survey data.

What is more, the results of an in-house survey of Rabbinical School students conducted in 1985 tend to support the argument being presented here. The survey was conducted by Drs. Aryeh Davidson and Jack Wertheimer.[162] Among the pertinent data that emerged at the time were the following:

Three-quarters of all rabbinical students enrolled at that time were third-generation American Jews: that is, native-born children of native-born American parents (whereas in 1967, only 55 percent of the students were third-generation). This is a social and cultural factor of some importance and, independent of any other factors, may have played a role in fostering an "inward-turning" trend.

When asked what they regarded as the most important skills and functions associated with the rabbinic profession (out of a list of seventeen items), skills related to teaching and counseling were selected as the most essential (respectively, by 86 percent and 77 percent of the students). "The importance of serving as a model of spirituality," living as "an halakhic Jew" and as "a religious person" were all ranked as extremely important by 50 to 67 percent of the students. Promoting the study of Hebrew and promoting Zionism were rated as only "moderately important," and only by 46 percent and 44 percent of the students, respectively.

The study concluded that the students had developed an image of the rabbinical role that placed the greatest emphasis on the rabbi's leadership and educational or counseling functions. Fully 87 percent said that they hoped to serve in a congregation.[163] Bearing this in mind, it is not surprising that Israel, a Jewish arena that presented to the students few if any opportunities to exercise these functions, would be overshadowed by American communal priorities. Conversely, it is quite possible that rabbinical students in the mid-1980s revealed in their choices, their intellectual preoccupations, and their professional aspirations a culturally determined pattern that is primarily the *result* of an American orientation.

Clearly, such characteristics were not new in the 1980s. Perhaps the supreme emphasis placed on values of spirituality, pastoral work, and religious leadership simply emerged with greater salience, relative to "peoplehood" and Zionist (ethnic) values. A poignant reminder of the importance of religious leadership to Seminary graduates, even from earlier years, is conveyed in a letter that Simon Greenberg wrote in 1973 to the head of the student organization of the Rabbinical School:

> A number of [our colleagues in Jerusalem] who had in the past expressed all kinds of doubts and misgivings about the significance of the congregational set-up . . . , about the blessings that adhere in the relationship between the Rabbi and his congregants, all realize afresh that they had not sufficiently appreciated what we have in our movement in the United States. It is only when you don't have a synagogue and don't have a congregation of which you could feel a part, that you begin to feel and understand the blessings in having one.[164]

Among the likely reasons for a growing emphasis in the 1980s on the personal, on the spiritual, and on rabbinical-pastoral roles were probably:(a) the perception that the American rediscovery of ethnicity of the 1970s had waned, leaving ethnic (secular) Jewishness in a cultural cul-de-sac; (b) a reassertion of the importance of "content" issues in Jewish life, in reaction to an overbalanced emphasis on "survivalism" that came in the wake of the 1967 and 1973 Israeli wars (which had brought to the fore in Jewish affairs the lay leadership of the fund-raising apparatus, at the expense of the synagogal sector); and (c) an internalization of the general

American trend toward self-actualization of the individual (aptly reflected in the women's ordination issue).

Epilogue: New Directions and Prospects

The argument that emerges from our discussion so far is as follows: The Seminary had striven historically to graft its own religious, cultural, and intellectual vision onto American Jewish life. That vision always included an Israel dimension, which the Seminary tried to ground in the twin realities of Jewish life in America, on the one hand, and in Israel, on the other. The Seminary found its efforts in Israel to be rewarding—though also frustrating—but it was never the central or guiding policy of the institution to focus its main energies on Israel. By the 1980s, American Jewish realities were even more dominant in the ethos of the Seminary than before.

It is certainly consistent with the foregoing assessment that the Seminary's Holocaust memorial reflects an absence of any Israeli motif or reference point. The memorial is mounted in the Seminary's new library (built during Gerson Cohen's tenure), situated on the north wall of the main floor. It consists of a work in marble and brass by Nathan Rapoport that embodies six memorial candles. It is entitled "The Last March, 1939–1945."

There is a Hebrew inscription, with its English translation, "This has befallen us. Of it we tell constantly as we pour out our hearts, subdued and grieving." Below this there appear three inscriptions in English. The first, situated centrally, alludes to the symbolism of the six candles and speaks of the horrible deaths suffered by one-third of the Jewish people. It concludes, "Let the treasures of this library enshrine their sacred memory."

The second, situated to the left, states: "We are grateful to all the allied nations who liberated our people and other peoples from Nazi torture and threat of death. The humanitarian and heroic acts of the people of Denmark and Sweden shall never be forgotten by us."

The last inscription, on the right panel, states: "These also shall we remember. As we mourn our people's tragic fate, we should also recall the massacre of millions of innocent non-Jewish people who suffered similar deaths. May their memory never be forgotten."

Having been sensitized in recent years to the underlying structures of memory, to the mechanisms by which memory is created for us by such memorials (the Seminary's own Jewish Museum mounted an impressive exhibit on the subject of Holocaust memorials and Holocaust memory during 1994), one cannot help but be struck by the distinction between this Holocaust memorial and any memorial that has ever been erected or designed in Israel. No Holocaust memorial in Israel is complete without a reference either to the heroism of the Jewish resistance during the war, or to the State of Israel as an embodiment of the spirit of the victims and an affirmation of the people's collective will to live—usually both. The Seminary's memorial studiously avoids any reference at all to the commonplace Israeli themes of memory. In its patriotic gratitude to the Allies, in the universalism of its last panel, it is an American Jewish memorial.

Whether the Israeli approach or the American approach is "more fitting" is beside the point. There is no intrinsic reason why the Seminary's Holocaust memorial should be identical with Israeli memorials, given the different public agendas that find their expression through such shrines. The library memorial accurately reflects the cultural distance between the two communities, and therefore, it offers graphic illustration of the inward-looking or self-sufficient tendencies at the Seminary of the latter 1980s.

In the meantime, in a manner that demonstrates the complexity of the issue, a different dynamic was also at work. At the institutional level, flesh was being put on the notion of a Seminary "contribution" to Israeli religious life. Once established, institutions acquire momentum of their own.

It was Gerson Cohen himself who had, in March 1979, explicitly noted the fact that "despite the consistently positive attitude toward Jewish nationalism within the Conservative movement, we are the last of the major American Jewish groups to establish an institutional presence in Israel."[165] Perhaps because of the need to reassert the Seminary's claim to a central role in world Jewish life (a role that was being questioned in the late 1970s), the Seminary's stake in Israel began to grow considerably.[166] It was during the late 1970s and on through the mid-1980s that the population of Seminary alumni in Israel grew, the compulsory one-year program for rabbinical students at Neve Schechter was fully implemented, and a separate and innovative program of text-study (*Midreshet Yerushalayim*) was established for visiting students and others, under the leadership of Rabbi Baruch Feldstern. A Lieberman Institute for Talmudic Research was established in 1985 under Rabbi Shamma Friedman to honor the memory of the late Professor Lieberman (who died in 1983). Based at the Schocken building, the institute thus brought to fruition the Seminary's long-standing undertaking to use the facility of the Schocken Library to develop an active program of research.

An increasing number of Conservative congregations became active in Israel, and a *gar'in aliya* settled a new kibbutz in the Galilee, Kibbutz Hanaton. Not the least of the impressive "firsts" was the material and conceptual support given to a new type of school within the Israeli public school system. Known by the acronym TALI (for *Tigbur Limudei Yahadut*: "enhanced Judaic studies"), the idea spread from a pilot school in Jerusalem to other areas around the country, bringing to Israeli families a third option never before available to them, between the rigorously Orthodox school and the rigorously secular school. TALI schools retained the dominant secular curriculum of the Education Ministry's system but used the discretionary hours of instruction provided for in the public education law to supplement the regular program with greater Judaic content. The schools' approach resembles that of the American Solomon Schechter schools in that Judaic studies are fully integrated into the curriculum, with an emphasis on Jewish religious values, expanded study of traditional texts, prayer and prayer skills, and a positive approach to the Jewish heritage as a whole.

In 1984, Simon Greenberg's proposal of a decade earlier, to establish a Seminary program for Israelis, came to fruition with the founding of the Beit Midrash L'limudei Yahadut (Seminary of Judaic Studies) in Jerusalem. Gerson Cohen, Simon Greenberg, and Reuven Hammer, at the urgent request of the Israeli Masorti movement, had organized a feasibility discussion with leading Seminary alumni in the country and sympathetic Israeli intellectual figures in 1982, and within two years the Beit Midrash opened its doors to its first class of students.[167] The school was headed by Reuven Hammer, who was later succeeded by Professor Lee Levine of the Hebrew University (a Seminary alumnus who had lived in Israel since 1971). Temporarily housed at the Schocken premises, the school, though small, soon required its own building. (Although the Seminary offered the new program space at Neve Schechter, the offer was declined at the time, given the desire of the Beit Midrash administration to avoid the situation of a small Israeli student body "lost" among the more numerous American contingent from the one-year program.)[168] Subsequent developments, however, produced a very different situation.

First, the number of American rabbinical students who participated in the one-year program began to decline as the Rabbinical School administration waived the requirement in a growing number of individual cases (generally for reasons related to spouses unable to leave their jobs for an entire year). Second, the fiscal crisis that wreaked havoc in many sectors of the American economy in the 1980s made itself felt at the Seminary by the last years of the decade, forcing budgetary cutbacks. By 1990, Professor Ismar Schorsch, the Chancellor as of September 1987, shut down the *Midreshet Yerushalayim* program and decided to close Neve Schechter altogether. Simultaneously, the Israeli rabbinical school, having ordained its first locally trained class in 1988, was searching for new quarters at the end of 1989. Professor Levine proposed that the Beit Midrash move into the Seminary's building and take over responsibility for the few American students that were now involved in the year-in-Israel program. (Earlier fears that the fledgling Israeli program might lose its identity within a larger American program had dissolved. If anything, American students in the first year after the new arrangement reported that they were the ones to feel isolated.)[fl.] By 1994, the Beit Midrash grew beyond its rabbinical program to include up to three hundred students in various graduate-level and professional certification programs. The successful expansion of course offerings and the growth of the student body at the Beit Midrash were due partly to the tremendous growth in Israel of the demand for alternative higher education programs outside the major universities. During the 1980s, as the population reached five million, community colleges and certification schools mushroomed (in fields ranging from public and business administration through law school), and the Beit Midrash was thus able to tap into a newly awakened academic sector. Meanwhile, the annual American contingent also began to grow again, coming to include virtually the entire third-year class of some twenty-five students by 1994.

The fiscal problems of the eighties had led the Seminary to alter its previous arrangement with the Foundation for Masorti Judaism in Israel. Joint fund-raising on a movement-wide basis in the United States gave way to a decision to fund the Beit Midrash alone, leaving the Israeli Conservative congregations, youth movement, adult education programs, and other activities to raise funds independently through the foundation.[170] The resultant revision of the relationship between the Seminary and the movement in Israel tended to underscore an inherent tension that fully reflected the Seminary's own past experience. The policy that was adopted in Israel was based upon a long held conception—shared by Finkelstein, Cohen, and now Schorsch—that the truly significant contribution the Seminary could make to Jewish life lay in the excellence of its academic program. Everything else would flow naturally from that source. It was as if the Seminary's "genetic" imprint was being replicated in Israel, even though the disposition of the Seminary in America itself was now to pay closer attention to the needs of the laity.[171]

The commitment to fostering an Israeli rabbinical school imbued with the Seminary's ethos and, indeed, formally attached to the Seminary (although it had its own Israeli board of directors), was a natural position for the new Chancellor to take. His background as a scholar of European Jewish intellectual history predisposed him to view Jewish *Wissenschaft* as the main axis for modern Jewish religious renewal. In a talk given in Jerusalem in 1986, on the occasion of the Seminary's centenary year, Schorsch had forcefully stated his belief that Zionism, and then the State of Israel, had condemned Judaism to wither by failing to take positive steps toward the establishment of a modern rabbinate in the country, thus allowing traditionalist Orthodoxy to assert its own antimodernist program.[172]

Like his predecessor, Schorsch called upon Israel to transcend its own origins by engaging the Judaic tradition as part of the *modern* reality of Jewish life—not merely as a historic relic that had preserved Judaism in Exile but had outlived its purpose. The path to take, therefore, was the introduction of a modern (academically trained) rabbinate that, through combining the "old" and the "new," could help revive a positive religious dialogue within Israel and between Israel and the Diaspora.

In terms of his own values, then, Schorsch was able to justify his focus on the rabbinical training program (as compared with congregational work). A corollary policy of support for the TALI schools, under the umbrella of the Beit Midrash, was also favored, insofar as it had the potential to affect much wider sections of Israeli society.[173]

Schorsch reiterated his reasons for supporting the Seminary's role in Israel in an address delivered in New York in 1988, at a special conference of Conservative leaders on "Zionism and the Conservative/Masorti Movement." "Israel," he told the group, "embodies a unique historical achievement. . . . For Conservative Jews, as heirs of the Historical School, it would be a travesty to observe from the sidelines this adventure in overcoming historical inertia and political difficulties." He went on to argue that the State of Israel "represents the most potent unifying force in a secular age in which the Jewish people have become deeply fragmented religiously. . . . Nothing endangers its centrality in Jewish life more gravely than the continued growth of Orthodox power in public life. . . . Genuine religious pluralism is vital not only to improve Israel-Diaspora relations but also to reconnect Israeli Jews to Judaism."[174] At that time, as well, Schorsch protested vigorously against the attempt (once again, a result of post-election coalition building in Israeli politics) to alter the Law of Return. As it had to Cohen before him, the distancing of Israel from Diaspora communities seemed to Schorsch to augur only disaster.

Ironically, Schorsch's support for the growth of the Beit Midrash has raised the issue of the Seminary's central status within the Conservative movement. As the Beit Midrash expands its sphere of academic activity, involving not only rabbinical students in Israel but also visiting students from Latin America and new educational programs in Eastern Europe and the former Soviet Union, Jerusalem's Seminary may develop, in time, as an ideological and institutional center in its own right. It is Schorsch's stated position that such a development would be welcome, despite the American orientation of so many JTS faculty, students, and graduates. This point of view, that argues against a "middleman" role for the Seminary in America, envisions world Jewish communities drawing closer to modern Jewish religion through Israel's Hebrew-speaking Conservative base, rather than through the mediating English culture of American Judaism.[175]

The ever present need to anchor the Seminary's own position more strongly within American Jewry, however, has simultaneously led Schorsch to reassert the vital purposes served by the Seminary in its own milieu. The National Jewish Population Study of 1990 conducted in the United States left the impression in many Jewish circles that a crisis of morale of major significance was plaguing American Jewry, placing in doubt its long-term vitality as a creative minority in American society. This sparked new efforts to channel resources to programs aimed at enhancing anything related to "Jewish continuity." At the same time, Israel gained an unprecedented margin of strategic security and a more favorable position in international trade when years of frustrating and painful efforts resulted in peace agree-

Israeli Prime
Minister David
Ben-Gurion
(third from left) at
the Seminary dur-
ing a visit to New
York, 1960. Louis
Finkelstein is to
his left. *Photo by
Maurey Garber.
Ratner Center,
JTS.*

ments and economic relations with some of its most stubborn enemies in the Arab
world (and new ties with nations further afield), during the years 1992–94. Relieved
of the need to regard Israel's security and economic safety as chronically endangered, it was possible for Schorsch, in announcing a major new grant received by the
Seminary for graduate studies in Jewish education, to tell the *New York Times* that
American Jews needed "to focus on their own future." The welcome changes in the
status of Israel opened the door to reordered priorities at home: "This is where the
battlefield for Judaism is."[176]

AN INSTITUTION WHOSE OWN FINANCIAL BASE is still vulnerable faces enormous
dilemmas when it commits itself to a two-front "battlefield." That is especially true
when it embarks on a course that may someday see its own offspring abroad take the
lead within its own sphere. There is cogent justification for such a course, within the
terms defined by Cohen and Schorsch, presupposing that Israel and American
Jewry form one indivisible whole: what reinforces the one does not weaken the
other. It is worth pondering, nonetheless, some other factors that would explain the
Seminary's stake in maintaining its foothold in Jerusalem. We should also ask to
what extent are its efforts likely to bear fruit? And what, in the final analysis, makes
the Seminary's active engagement with Israel of historical interest and significance,
beyond issues of theology?

In the mid-1950s, Ben Halpern observed the following:

The more one insists on the religious character of American Jewry, the less can one regard its essential beliefs as specifically American. There is certainly a minimum degree of universality which anything worthy of the name religion must not only claim but exhibit. In the case of the Jewish religion, a claimant to that title must certainly show that it makes sense to (or at least has validity for) the Jews everywhere. Above all, any form of belief and practice that wishes to call itself Jewish is called upon to show that in Israel, the only community where Jews live on their own terms, there are some Jews who can identify themselves with it.[177]

It is not necessarily the case that every form of Judaism, to be authentic, must be universally applicable—sects and cults within Judaism (or adjacent to it) can and do function without universal applicability: witness Satmar Hasidism, Beta Israel Ethiopian Judaism, and the Samaritans. But Halpern's argument touches upon some of the core issues for Conservative Judaism, given its ambitions to continue to represent *mainstream* Judaism.

It was Marshall Sklare whose sociological analysis of the movement concluded that it was indeed a local American phenomenon, largely the product of a demographic and socioeconomic wave that occurred because of the mass migration of Jews from Eastern Europe to the United States between 1881 and 1924. Riding the crest of that wave, he argued, the Conservative synagogue emerged as an expression of immigrant and second-generation acculturation and upward social mobility. It was a path to a middle-class American Judaism that, in contrast to Reform (at that time), retained enough of the immigrant culture to be appealingly familiar: Hebrew, as a significant element in synagogue ritual; requisite physical "accessories" (*talit* [prayershawl] and head-covering); and an unabashed ethnocentrism that included support for Zionism. This argument implied very strongly that once the demographic wave had passed, the rationale for a Conservative synagogue would also pass.

Hence, in its search for an ongoing Conservative philosophy and way of life, the Seminary must show that it does in fact represent more than a one-time, sociodemographic "blip" in Jewish history: it must demonstrate that it is a historically valid and religiously potent process within Judaism. Halpern's argument becomes, then, extremely relevant to the core issues of Conservative continuity. Unless the Seminary can project its vision onto the Israeli religious scene, it will remain America-bound and, implicitly, limited to the social basis that originally served as its developmental context.

Second, the reasons that militate towards a deeply engaged relationship with Israel, even at a time when concerns at home seem to be paramount, lie within the particular kind of religious philosophy espoused by the Seminary. Conservatism has posited a developmental model of law and theology. It argues for the validity, not of a permanently defined traditionalist code, but of a rabbinic *procedure* or *method* that will continually bring Jewish beliefs and practices into line with the conditions of life as most Jews live it. Insofar as the rabbinic code can be kept fluid, it retains authenticity and authority *even while it undergoes revision.*

Since it is not contested that the conditions of Jewish life in the modern world have been changed by virtue of Israel's existence, the question then becomes one of Judaism's capacity to absorb this change. Can Conservative Judaism, as a religious way of life, be made to accord with *this particular change* in the same way as it has been made to accord, for example, with the equalization of men's and women's roles in society? Unless Conservative Judaism can demonstrate its ability to bring its religious worldview into conformity with something as existentially compelling and as central to Judaism as Jewish statehood in Eretz Israel, its claim to have found the proper method for conserving Jewish values in a changing world must remain truncated. The key issue, then, is the assertion that rabbinic tradition and praxis are indeed as malleable as the Seminary says they are. As long as Conservative Judaism's neat "fit" with Zionism was based on the ethnocentrism of its laity, the deeper theological issues hardly arose. Once the Seminary looked beyond the social basis of its congregations' original growth to a more enduring religious system, however, it had to come to grips with Israel in a more profound way. All of the foregoing may be inferred from Schorsch's perception that "as heirs of the Historical School, it would be a travesty to observe from the sidelines" as Israel continues to reshape the history of the Jews. The Israel issue is not an adjunct to the core of Seminary Judaism: it goes right to the heart of that Judaism.

But the Seminary and the philosophy that it fosters face numerous obstacles in Israel, and the Orthodox establishment's hold on the rabbinate is the least of them—even if it *is* the cause of much frustration and does tend to alienate American Conservative Jews. More critical problems exist that may be summarized under three related subheadings: a weak demographic base, doubts about the depth of American Jewish religious life, and the rather alien ethic of voluntarism and pluralism in religion.

First, the Conservative demand for mutuality and parity in religious dialogue in Israel falls short of being convincing to many Israelis because the movement's presence in the country is so small. It does not even compare to the Orthodox sector (about 20 percent), let alone the much larger non-Orthodox or "secular" sector. The failure to create demographic facts—the high *aliya* rate among Conservative rabbis notwithstanding—has consequences. The goal of reaching out to a larger population is being addressed through the TALI schools, it is true; but this is a long-term investment in "souls" that still has not altered the current perception that Conservative Jews, like other American Jews, are largely content to keep Israel at a distance. Consequently, the role of Conservatism in Israel is perceived to be minor. Two hundred congregations—rather than the current forty—would constitute a strong argument in and of themselves. This may develop in time, with or without increased Conservative *aliya* from America. But it is at least relevant to ask about the connection between the place of Israel and of *aliya* on the American Jewish *religious* agenda and the place of Conservatism in Israeli life.

Second, the validity of the Conservative/*Masorti* paradigm for modern Jewish life is constantly undermined in the public eye by the widely published statistics on assimilation and intermarriage in American Jewry. Those at the Seminary who speak of the critical situation of American Judaism and of the consequent need to focus on America first, to reeducate and rebuild the communities at home, simply reinforce the belief of many in Israel that American forms of Judaism have not been a resounding success even where they have been given ample opportunity to develop. The inference is that these forms of Judaism have little to offer Israel, since they argue from weakness. There are those who go further, particularly in the Orthodox sector and among its sympathizers, and say that they see a *causal* relationship between liberal Judaism and assimilation. They are convinced that Israel has enough difficulties with secularism without compounding the problem by introducing religious "sectarianism" (as they would have it).

Third, for reasons having to do mainly with the social ethic of Israel itself, a Judaism that is predicated on a pluralist ethos of voluntarism and choice is not acceptable to anyone whose own socialization has been monist and collectivist. The appeal of liberal Judaism may be greater among Israel's own liberal pluralists—but most of these happen also to be secularists (whether by choice or through lack of alternatives).

Contrary to popular belief, however, the majority of Israelis are not philosophically secular. There is a folk religion that is developing in the country (just as Conservatism can arguably be described as an American Jewish folk religion). The elements of that folk religion include the overwhelmingly normative life-cycle rites; the sanctity of Yom Kippur (abstention from vehicular travel is virtually total on that day, except in non-Jewish areas); ethnic folk festivals (such as the *Maimouna*, popularized by Moroccan Jews); grave-pilgrimages (some of the traditional type, some of a more national nature, such as *Yad Vashem* and youth trips to sites in Poland associated with the Holocaust, that have taken on a sanctified character); but above all, an amorphous blend of beliefs surrounding Israel (the people and the land) as a central, abiding presence in the salvational history of the world. This last is shared by circles far beyond the Orthodox and far beyond the religious nationalists of *Gush Emunim:* rather, there is a widespread belief in the "providential" character of the state's existence and of its experience and struggle in war and peace. The Seminary, with its elitist approach, channeling its best efforts through a school for advanced Jewish studies, simply does not tap into this level of Israel's religious life.

The reader might recall at this point what was said at the outset about the Seminary's intellectual genealogy, specifically its self-avowed debt to the *Wissenschaft* heritage in the spirit of Zacharias Frankel. We took note that Frankel's intellectual and religious endeavor was suited to a very specific environment and to a particular moment in history. Outside that particular framework, the Positive-Historical school and Conservative Judaism fared well only where similarly auspicious conditions obtained—namely, in the United States. In asserting a worldwide mission, the leaders of the Seminary have chosen to disregard, or perhaps to transcend, the historical origins of their movement. (I believe that they have done this for cogent philosophical reasons, which I have outlined in the previous few pages.) But, while claiming a Conservative religious and intellectual advantage even for a society as dissimilar from the American one as Israel's is, they have (until now) made little progress in projecting their vision onto Israel's type of "self-evident" Jewishness. Israeli Jewishness, when compared to the American form, is less dependent on intellectual endeavor or deliberate, individual practice; it is far more dependent on the shared commonalities of language, nationality, social interaction, and public ritual. In other words, whereas in America Conservative Judaism might need to emphasize collective values of communal attachment, communal norms, and common historical awareness, it is relatively less important to do so in a country where *Hatikva* is the national anthem.

One of the ironies of history, however, is that as Israeli society becomes more heavily influenced by American culture, it is undergoing a slow process of change that may open parts of Israel to American forms of Judaism. The old collectivist-elitist models (the kibbutz, the Palmach, the Histadrut, Ben-Gurion's *mamlakhtiut* [statism]) are giving way—at least in the private professional and business-oriented sectors of society—to new, individual-centered and consumer-driven models that are much more in line with American norms. The status of the individual and of women (civil liberties issues have come to the fore, spurred by an activist Supreme Court); the search for new sources of meaning that so often accompanies a successful materialism; the legitimacy, above all, of choice, self-expression, and openness have become far more significant in Israel's public discourse since the 1980s.

The implications insofar as the Seminary and Conservative Judaism are concerned are rather astonishing: it may well be that the Conservative movement's *American values of individualism, choice, egalitarianism, and pluralism* are the most important ones that it can emphasize in Israel, at least as important as the Judaic religious values of halakhic authority, *masoret* (tradition), and talmudic textual virtuosity that have animated the best Seminary minds for decades. The movement's appeal is geared to a limited group in any case. It can to a degree broaden its scope—perhaps by looking more closely into the values of the secular sector and by addressing them more directly. In most other sectors, the Seminary and the Conservative

Saul Lieberman (standing) with Golda Meir (left), and Louis Finkelstein (right) in the Seminary Sukkah, 1961. *Ratner Center, JTS.*

movement face intimidating obstacles that can only be neutralized through the direct infusion of a Conservative constituency—American Conservative *olim*.

THE HISTORY THAT HAS BEEN DESCRIBED in the foregoing pages reflects an older division between Herzl's Zionism—a political mobilization of Jewish resources to solve the *Judennot* ("plight of the Jews")—and spiritual-cultural Zionism, which was a way of thinking and primarily of *educating*, with the focus on national values, culture, and morale.

After 1948, Israeli ideology combined Herzlean political Zionism with Ben-Gurion's statism. It tended, by and large, to relegate Ahad Ha'am's mandate to create a modern Jewish culture to a secondary status. This was perhaps inevitable, given the enormous tasks awaiting the new nation in immigrant absorption, in security, and in productivization.

Post-1948 Conservative Judaism combined Schechter's spiritual nationalism with Heschel's moralism and religious experientialism. It relegated to the sidelines Kaplan's naturalism and his intellectual quest for a new "peoplehood." The Seminary's basic intent and program is to create a scholarly-rabbinic elite whose power lies in its ability to articulate the hows and whys of Judaic practice. It believes that no one else on the religious scene combines the elements of virtuosity in the handling of classical texts, a commitment to traditional practice, and a commitment to modernism. Therefore, it must ultimately become a "natural," magnetic authority.

Zionism's claims for Jewish statehood may be understood in a somewhat analogous vein: Israel will become the natural center of gravity of the Jewish people because it is the best, most viable option available. It alone can perceive and embody the Jewish national will, provide a basis for collective Jewish survival, insure Jewish cultural development and continuity.

The juxtaposition of these two claims may be the source of competition or it may be the basis for a fruitful collaboration. From our vantage point at the end of the 20th century, we stand at an extremely interesting crossroads. The two most important modern models of Jewish community life are placed face to face—the American model of a Jewish community of choice within a tolerant non-Jewish majority culture, and the Israeli model of Jewish majority rule in a sovereign state. Both Israel and the Seminary are rooted in some of the same modern Jewish values: humanism (in its basic sense) and Jewish self-emancipation. The two encounter one another in an exchange that we can imagine as the one "telling" the other that "religion is not enough," while the second replies, "politics is not enough."

On another level, the dialogue is one between epochal events and long-term social processes: between the advent of Israel and the elaboration of a Jewish way of life in America over generations. The profound grappling of the Seminary's leaders, teachers, and students with the emergence of a Jewish state is ample testimony to the compelling nature of that event. The need to feel part of the process, to be directly and intimately engaged, is expressed in the form of a demand that Israel pay heed to the Seminary's reality and to its message.

The Israel factor at the Seminary cannot be adequately summed up in theoretical and academic formulas. Some of the children and grandchildren of Louis Finkelstein, Gerson D. Cohen, and Simon Greenberg live in Israel, as do hundreds of alumni, former faculty, and the sons and daughters of Seminary faculty and Conservative rabbis. Their impact on Israeli academic life, Israeli culture and religion, and Israel-Diaspora relations cannot yet be fully assessed, but it has already been significant. One of the Seminary's own, Professor Moshe Davis, trying to account for this phenomenon, told me that "history is stronger than ideology." By the same token, however, the strength of an ideology lies in its historical awareness. The Seminary's historical and ideological sides are both inseparable from modern Judaism itself. That, in the last analysis, is what ties it to Israel.

The data appearing in these tables were calculated on the basis of the survey of Rabbinical School alumni described in the essay section headed "Israel on the Mind of the Seminary, 1967–1987," pp. 222–233.

Table 1: *Olim* Evaluate Their Seminary and Other Experiences with Reference to their *Aliya*

FACTORS IN *ALIYA*	EXTENT OF THEIR INFLUENCE			
	not at all	*a little*	*to some extent*	*to a great extent*
Seminary learning	17%	17%	48%	17%
Prior experiences	4	9	17	70
Family factors	35	0	4	61

Table 1A: *Aliya* is "against the grain" of the Seminary

agree	*agree strongly*	*disagree*	*disagree strongly*	*not sure*
17%	22%	35%	17%	9%

Table 2: Profile of Seminary *Olim* Relative to Other Alumni

CHARACTERISTIC	ALL ALUMNI	*OLIM* ONLY [n=25]
Parent a Zionist	36%	44%
Camper at Ramah	36	24
Staffer at Ramah	68	80
Member of USY	59	48
Year at Neve Schechter	73	80
Born by 1954	55	72
Graduated JTS by 1983	55	75
[total number of respondents = 290]		

Table 3: Modern Jewish Thinkers and Their Influence on Rabbinical Students

Question: "To what extent do you think each of the following affected the crystallization of your religious worldview?" [number of respondents = 283]

	to a great extent	*somewhat/a little*	*not at all*
Abraham J. Heschel	57%	38%	5%
Mordecai M. Kaplan	27	62	10
Franz Rosenzweig	22	62	15
Martin Buber	17	60	22
Ahad Ha'am	11	62	27
Saul Lieberman	9	50	41
Gershom Scholem	7	50	43

Table 3A: Thinkers' Influence: All Alumni Compared to *Olim* ("to a great extent"):

	All alumni	*Olim only*
Abraham J. Heschel	57%	28%
Mordecai M. Kaplan	27	12
Franz Rosenzweig	22	20
Martin Buber	17	16
Ahad Ha'am	11	28
Saul Lieberman	9	8
Gershom Scholem	7	8

Table 4: Israel-Related Activities on Synagogue Calendars (American respondents)

Adult Hebrew classes	83%
Public affairs speakers on Israeli issues	74
Israel Bonds functions	61
JNF functions	37
Masorti movement fund-raising	36
Functions related to Israel tourism	35
Congregational trip to Israel	34
Parlor meetings with *Masorti* representatives	16
AIPAC-related activities	14
Other	20

Table 5: Sermons on Israel and Self-Rating on Relative Priority of Israel (American respondents)

NUMBER OF ISRAEL-RELATED SERMONS WITHIN 6 MONTHS	PERCEIVED PRIORITY OF ISRAEL IN CONGREGATION			
	Higher priority	*Lower priority*	*About the same*	*Not sure*
0	0%	75%	0%	25%
1	6	41	35	18
2	4	30	52	13
3	13	25	51	11
4	29	14	45	12
5 or more	31	3	48	19

[number of respondents = 211]

Table 6: Sermon Frequency and Zionist Label of Rabbi (American respondents)

SELF-APPLIED LABEL	FREQUENCY OF ISRAEL-RELATED SERMONS IN 6-MONTH PERIOD					
	0	*1*	*2*	*3*	*4*	*5 or more*
Zionist	1%	6%	8%	24%	28%	33%
Religious Z.	2	8	5	25	24	39
Pro-Israel	4	9	20	31	16	20
Post-Zionist	0	20	20	10	30	20

[number of respondents = 209]

Table 7: Scale of Congregational Israel Activities According to Rabbi's Year of Ordination

GROUP OF RESPONDENTS	MEAN YEAR OF ORDINATION
All respondents [number of respondents = 288]	1982
Respondents with 1–2 Israel activities on calendar	1984
Respondents with 3 Israel activities on calendar	1983
Respondents with 4–5 Israel activities on calendar	1982
Respondents with 6–8 Israel activities on calendar	1980

My thanks to Julie Miller, Tim Hanssen, and other staff of the Ratner Center for the Study of Conservative Judaism, who helped enormously in expediting my research at the archives of the Jewish Theological Seminary. Some of their work involved retrieving boxes and files from storage before they were fully processed (and as a result, the annotation of files cited does vary in form). I owe special thanks to the late Professor Moshe Davis of the Hebrew University who initiated me into the world of the Seminary of the 1940s and 1950s and shared with me his own files of correspondence. In the design and implementation of the alumni survey that figures in this study, I received vital and expert advice from Professor Steven M. Cohen of the Hebrew University, for which I am very grateful.

1. Ismar Schorsch, "Zacharias Frankel and the European Origins of Conservative Judaism," in Schorsch, *From Text to Context: The Turn to History in Modern Judaism* (Hanover and London: University Presses of New England/Brandeis: 1994), pp. 255–65; idem, "Emancipation and the Crisis of Religious Authority: The Emergence of the Modern Rabbinate," in *Revolution and Evolution: 1848 in German Jewish History*, ed. Werner E. Mosse, Arnold Paucker, and Reinhard Rürup (Tübingen: JCB Mohr, 1981), pp. 205–47.

2. Naomi W. Cohen, *Encounter With Emancipation, The German Jews in the United States, 1830–1914* (Philadelphia: Jewish Publication Society, 1984), pp. 203–10; Shuly Rubin Schwartz, *The Emergence of Jewish Scholarship in America: The Publication of the* Jewish Encyclopedia (Cincinnati: Hebrew Union College Press, 1991), pp. 5–15, 165–73. Cf. Jonathan Sarna, *JPS: The Americanization of Jewish Culture, 1888–1988* (Philadelphia: The Jewish Publication Society, 1989).

3. See the essay by Naomi W. Cohen in these volumes, "Diaspora Plus Palestine, Religion Plus Nationalism."

4. See Marshall Sklare's pioneering study, *Conservative Judaism, An American Religious Movement* (1955; reprint New York: Schocken, 1972), esp. chaps. 1 and 3.

5. Eliezer Schweid, in his entry on the "Land of Israel" in *Contemporary Jewish Religious Thought*, ed. Arthur A. Cohen and Paul R. Mendes-Flohr (New York and London: Macmillan, 1987), pp. 535–41; Avraham Feder, "The Sanctity of Eretz Yisrael: A Basic Ambivalence," *Forum* no. 54/55 (1984–85): pp. 89–90. For further extensive discussion of the issues, sources, and their treatment by modern Jewish philosophers, see Arnold Eisen, *Galut: Modern Jewish Reflections on Homelessness and Homecoming* (Bloomington: Indiana University Press, 1986); cf. Ephraim Urbach, "Center and Periphery in Jewish Historic Consciousness: Contemporary Implications," in *World Jewry and the State of Israel*, ed. Moshe Davis (New York: Arno Press, 1977), pp. 217–35.

6. Saemy Japhet, "The Secession from the Frankfurt Jewish Community Under Samson Raphael Hirsch," *Historia Judaica* 10 (1948): p. 106.

7. Neil Gillman, "When the Messiah Dies," *Sh'ma, A Journal of Jewish Responsibility* 25, no. 480 (28 October 1994): p. 3.

8. See Eli Lederhendler, "Interpreting Messianic Rhetoric in the Russian *Haskalah* and Early Zionism," *Studies in Contemporary Jewry: Vol. VII: Jews and Messianism in the Modern Era* (1991), pp. 14–33; and, in the same volume, Yaacov Shavit, "Realism and Messianism in Zionism and the Yishuv,"pp. 100–27; ibid., Hannan Hever, "Poetry and Messianism in Palestine Between the Two World Wars," pp. 128–58; ibid., Janet Aviad, "The Messianism of Gush Emunim," pp. 197–213. Cf. Gideon Aran, "From Religious Zionism to Zionist Religion: The Roots of Gush Emunim," *Studies in Contemporary Jewry* 2 (1986): pp. 116–43.

9. Naomi W. Cohen (see infra); cf. Lloyd P. Gartner, "Conservative Judaism," section on "Israel's Place in World Jewry" (separate pagination: pp. 20–29), *Forum* no. 57/58 (spring 1986), following p. 182; also idem, "*Hayahadut hakonservativit vehatsiyonut: melumadim,*

darshanim, ufilantropim" ["Conservative Judaism and Zionism: Scholars, Preachers, and Philanthropists"] in *Tsiyonut vedat* [*Zionism and Religion*], ed. Shmuel Almog, Jehuda Reinharz, and Anita Shapira (Jerusalem: Zalman Shazar Center for Jewish History, 1994), pp. 245–62.

10. Sklare, *Conservative Judaism*, pp. 219–21.

11. *Seminary Progress*, June 1948, p. 13; *New York Times*, 15 May 1948, p. 4.

12. *Seminary Progress*, June 1948, p. 13.

13. *New York Times*, 15 May 1948, p. 4.

14. Rabbi Theodore N. Lewis, president of the New York Board of Rabbis, to Rabbi Louis Finkelstein, letter dated 12 April 1948. Ratner Center, JTS General Files, 1E–75–32.

15. Louis Finkelstein to Judah L. Magnes, 31 March 1948. Ratner Center, JTS General Files, 1E–73–46. In a similar vein, Finkelstein wrote a confidential letter the following year, on 20 July 1949, to Rabbi Judah Nadich, in which he stated that at the end of the fiscal year 1948–49, the Seminary had "a staggering deficit. If we are not to eliminate whole departments and activities, we shall have to undertake curtailment throughout the Institution." Ratner Center 1-E–75–12 (1948–49), Judah Nadich file.

16. 21 November 1948 was fixed as the date for dedicating the West Coast building in Los Angeles: Ratner Center 1-E–70–7 (Simon Greenberg file); cf. Louis Finkelstein, newsletter to Board of Directors, 17 June 1948; Finkelstein to board, 13 April 1949; cf. Deborah Dash Moore, *To the Golden Cities* (New York: The Free Press, 1994), pp. 124, 127–33.

17. *Seminary Progress*, May 1949, p. 8.

18. Finkelstein to Rabbinical Assembly members with congregations, 13 September 1949. Accordingly, the Seminary set a record fund-raising goal for 1949–50: $1,972,000. See *Seminary Progress*, May 1949, p. 22.

19. Finkelstein to Ernst Simon, 1 July 1948. Ratner Center, 1-E–78–23.

20. Simon to Finkelstein, 15 July 1948.

21. Finkelstein had been offered a post as superintendent for schools in the Mizrachi stream (about 1924) and was highly tempted to accept the offer. In later years, he expressed regret that he had not settled in Eretz Israel when he had the chance. "He felt the conflict, he felt that perhaps he did not choose the right path for himself, but he repressed it." Moshe Davis, interview by author, 16 November 1993.

22. Finkelstein to Magnes, 25 August 1948. Ratner Center 1E–73–46.

23. Ratner Center 1E–78–23 (1948–49), Ernst Simon file.

24. Finkelstein to Moshe Davis, 15 July 1960 and 14 July 1964. Correspondence from private files of Moshe Davis in Jerusalem.

25. Louis Finkelstein, "Note on Pirqoi Ben Baboi," in *Contemporary Jewry: Studies in Honor of Moshe Davis,* ed. Geoffrey Wigoder (Jerusalem: Institute of Contemporary Jewry, 1984), pp. 267–69. According to Professor Davis, the "Note" was submitted very late, but Finkelstein was most insistent that the brief article appear in the *Festschrift*. The "Note" is accompanied by a two-paragraph preamble, in which Finkelstein wrote of his indebtedness over the years to Moshe Davis's counsel and contributions. "One of his main interests has been the relation of the Jewish community of Israel to the Diaspora. As Professor Mordecai M. Kaplan once called him, he is a *pontifex*, a bridge-builder . . . between Israel and the Diaspora. . . . In the present article I wish to discuss the work of a man who approached this problem quite differently from Professor Moshe Davis." The implication was that Finkelstein saw himself as a modern-day Pirqoi Ben Baboi (who could see long-term importance in the survival of his Diaspora community and its academy). "Pirqoi Ben Baboi was Finkelstein looking at himself in the mirror. He [like Ben Baboi] had had to make compromises, too as a practitioner [of Jewish leadership], for the sake of Judaism." Moshe Davis, interview, 16 November 1993.

26. "Excerpts from address by Dr. Louis Finkelstein, Chancellor, the Jewish Theological Seminary," for release, Tuesday, 26 February 1952 (address at the Seminary Israel Institute luncheon session). Ratner Center, JTS Seminary-Israel Institute, 24.

27. Statement by Dr. Louis Finkelstein, Chancellor, Jewish Theological Seminary of America, upon his return from Israel and England, 4 August 1952.

28. Open letter to rabbinical colleagues, 19 July 1961 (from Edinburgh). Moshe Davis files.

29. Finkelstein, draft of open letter to rabbinical colleagues, 4 July 1971 (written in Jerusalem). Ratner Center, General Files, 1AA.

30. Ratner Center, Seminary-Israel Institute files, 24.

31. Finkelstein to Maurice Samuel, 7 December 1951. Ratner Center: Seminary-Israel Institute, Letters 2/29.

32. Moshe Davis, interviews by author 16 November 1993 and 18 December 1994. In July 1950, Columbia University's School of International Affairs announced that in the fall it would inaugurate an "Israel Institute" to be headed by Columbia's eminent incumbent professor of Jewish history, Salo W. Baron. The purpose of the Institute at Columbia, which would offer courses in Jewish and Israeli history, Middle Eastern studies, and Judaism, would be "to produce those with the qualifications necessary to understand the specific processes reflected in Jewish life throughout the world and in the State of Israel in particular." (Clipping from an unidentified New York Yiddish newspaper, 30 July 1950, placed in Finkelstein's personal files. Ratner Center, General Files, 1F–84–20, 1950.)

33. Finkelstein to Maurice Samuel, 7 December 1951. Ratner Center: Seminary-Israel Institute, 24: Letters, 2/29.

34. Invitation to the inauguration of the Seminary Israel Institute, Ratner Center, Seminary Israel Institute, 24, 1952. The gala inauguration was the occasion for the first official visit to the Seminary by Ambassador Abba Eban.

35. "News from The Jewish Theological Seminary of America: Address by Doctor Louis Finkelstein . . . at the Inauguration of the Seminary Israel Institute," 21 February 1952. Ratner Center, Seminary Israel Institute, 24, press release dated 22 February 1952.

36. Ratner Center, Seminary Israel Institute, 24: 1952.

37. Harvard philosopher Harry Austryn Wolfson was invited to deliver the first annual Chaim Weizmann Memorial Lecture, but he declined. Finkelstein's letter of invitation, dated 22 November 1954, stated the following:

> I am sure you know about the Seminary-Israel Institute we conduct here in cooperation with the Jewish Agency. It is an effort to help the State of Israel get itself and its background better understood in academic circles, especially here on Morningside Heights. The Government of Israel is very much interested in this effort and in past years has sent eminent representatives like Abba Eban to participate in our lectures.
>
> [. . .] Both our Israeli brethren and we here believe that your agreeing to give this lecture would be an eminent service of the kind which you alone can give to the State of Israel. (Ratner Center, Seminary Israel Institute 24 box 7.).

38. Moshe Davis, ed., *Israel: Its Role in Civilization* (New York: Harper, 1956).

39. Mordecai M. Kaplan, *A New Zionism* (New York: Herzl Press and The Jewish Reconstructionist Press, 1959).

40. Louis Finkelstein, "The State of Israel as a Spiritual Force," in *Israel: Its Role in Civilization*, ed. Davis, p.6.

41. Ibid., pp. 14–15.

42. Ibid., p. 16.

43. Jakob Petuchowski, review of *Israel: Its Role in Civilization*, ed. Davis, in *American Jewish*

Archives 9, no. 2 (October 1957): pp. 144–48.

44. Moshe Davis, interview, 18 December 1994.

45. See above, n. 33.

46. Third monthly newsletter to the board, 16 January 1948. Ratner Center, General Files, 1–E.

47. Open letter to Rabbinical Assembly members, 5 November 1951, Ratner Center: Seminary-Israel Institute files, 24.

48. Israel Goldstein to Simon Greenberg, 18 December 1968. Ratner Center: Simon Greenberg Papers 2/12.

49. Sklare, *Conservative Judaism*, pp. 185–190, 221–222.

50. Neil Gillman, "The Changing Paradigm of the Conservative Rabbi," *Conservative Judaism* 43, no. 2 (winter 1990–91): p. 8.

51. Letter dated 9 May 1975. Ratner Center, Simon Greenberg Papers 1/5.

52. Dr. Aaron Singer, interview by author, 20 October 1994.

53. Memorandum from Simon Greenberg to Louis Finkelstein, 8 November 1951, with letter attached. Ratner Center, Seminary-Israel Institute, 24.

54. "Address by Prime Minister David Ben-Gurion at the Convocation of the Jewish Theological Seminary of America, Jerusalem, May 25, 1952." Ratner Center: Simon Greenberg Papers 12/23.

55. *United Synagogue Review* (autumn 1958): p. 8: Remarks by Ben-Gurion at the cornerstone-laying of the Seminary's Student Center in Jerusalem, 29 July 1958.

56. See n. 54, above.

57. See n. 55, above.

58. See n. 53, above.

59. Ibid. For a more detailed blueprint for the Seminary's Israel Student Center, see Greenberg's address to the 1958 convention of the Rabbinical Assembly: *Proceedings of the Rabbinical Assembly of America*, vol. 22, 1958 (New York: Rabbinical Assembly, 1959), pp. 161–66.

60. Statement by Doctor Louis Finkelstein, Chancellor, Jewish Theological Seminary of America, upon his return from Israel and England aboard SS United States, 4 August 1952. Ratner Center, Simon Greenberg Papers, 12/23, p. 1.

61. Neil Gillman, *Conservative Judaism, The New Century* (West Orange: Behrman House, 1993), p. 172: "Prior to the 1960s a Seminary rabbinical student who wanted to spend a year studying for academic credit in Israel had to petition the faculty for permission. To this day Seminary alumni recall the difficulty in obtaining this permission, and although it was usually granted, many simply decided to go on their own and forgo academic credit." This statement was confirmed in a personal communication by the late Rabbi Alexander Shapiro (one of the first Seminary students to apply for permission to study in Israel, in 1953) to Amy Levin, and through her to me.

62. Ibid., p. 2.

63. "'Al haperek: gishateinu leyahadut amerika,' protokol pegisha bemisrad rosh hamemshala David Ben-Gurion miyom 27.7.1950" ["On the Agenda: Our Approach to American Jewry, Protocol of a Meeting at the Office of Prime Minister David Ben-Gurion, 27 July 1950"], published by Zvi Ganin in *Kivunim* 4 (new series), 1993, p. 57. The minutes are located in the Israel Defense Forces Archives (IDF), 230/72, file 656. In December 1954, Greenberg wrote to an American Jewish supporter of the Seminary's fund-raising campaign for its Jerusalem compound that "ultimately [the center would] accommodate some 200 students. . . . We plan to make it obligatory for every one of our rabbinical students to spend one year of study in Israel." Simon Greenberg to Marvin Itts (of Youngstown, Ohio), 6 December 1954. Ratner Center: Simon Greenberg Papers, 12/52.

64. Kaplan, *A New Zionism*, pp. 95, 98.

65. Ibid., p. 99.

66. Jack J. Cohen, "Reflections on Kaplan's Zionism," in *The American Judaism of Mordecai M. Kaplan*, ed. Emanuel S. Goldsmith, Mel Scult, and Robert M. Seltzer (New York: New York University Press, 1990), p. 410.

67. Kaplan, *A New Zionism*, p. 95.

68. Mordecai M. Kaplan, "Toward the Formulation of Guiding Principles for the Conservative Movement," published as a supplement to *Conservative Judaism* 6, no. 4 (May 1950): p. 18; cf. chap. 4 in Kaplan, *A New Zionism*.

69. The point is stressed in various letters that Kaplan wrote to Moshe Davis over the years, which Professor Davis was kind enough to show me. In 1963 Kaplan wrote: "I received the draft of your article about the organization of the Jewish communities in the Western hemisphere. . . . My impression from reading it was that Diaspora Jewry lacks a spirit of creative initiative and that it is capable only of reacting to its environment. . . . I think that there is only one way in which it can extract itself from this predicament: if the Zionist movement . . . will take upon itself the mission of rebuilding the House of Israel from its ruins" [translated from the Hebrew, EL]. Kaplan to Davis, 4 June 1963. Moshe Davis's private files.

Once again, on 1 August 1967, Kaplan wrote to Davis: "You are probably aware that the Jewish Agency was created at the demand of the British Government to award the Balfour Declaration, not to the World Zionist Organization, but to the Jewish People. The conversion of the Jewish Agency into the Executive of the W.Z.O. was one of the stupid errors of the Zionist leaders who haven't the least notion of the significance of Jewish peoplehood for Jewish creative survival." Kaplan encouraged Davis to think "ultimately" in terms of supporting "a world conference for the *reconstitution* of the Jewish People" [emphasis in the original—EL].

In a further letter, dated 16 August 1970, Kaplan noted that Jewish members of the New Left in the United States were siding with the Palestinians against Israel. "As far as I am concerned, the attitude of those Jewish students is only one of the results of the polarization of Jews and Zionists, which the latter have permitted to come about, as a consequence of the fact that Zionism is regarded [as] a self-contained movement of a small minority of the Jewish people, instead of the creation of the Jewish people as a whole. Matters are bound to go from bad to worse as long as the Diaspora Jewry will continue to exist in its present hodge-podge condition. . . . In my opinion it would be best for the call for the reconstitution of the Jewish People to come from the State of Israel, in the interests of its own survival."

And on 26 July 1975, Kaplan urged that Davis (together with Gerson Cohen) take specific and immediate action, this time to have the "call" for a reconstitution come from Diaspora Jewry: "The way Zionism is functioning at the present time, it is endangering by its negation of American Judaism the survival of the Jewish People as a whole. In the series you got me to deliver on [A New] Zionism, I clearly foresaw such a possibility. It is therefore important that steps be taken as soon as possible to publicly reconstitute world Jewry by convening a Congress representative of world Jewry, and draw up a constitution. . . . I have been working on Mr. Philip Klutznik [*sic*] to call into being such a congress. He has promised to do so, but he is very dilatory. This is where you come in. Get yourself and Chancellor Gerson D. Cohen after him to take action which is extremely urgent" [emphasis in the original—EL].

70. Kaplan to Davis, 14 April 1958. Davis's private files.

71. *Proceedings of the Rabbinical Assembly of America* vol. 22 (1958), p. 118.

72. Ibid., pp. 119, 121.

263

*The Ongoing
Dialogue:
The Seminary
and the
Challenge of
Israel*

73. Ibid., pp. 137–139.

74. See Kaplan's speech and his reaction to the proceedings at the convention in *The Recon-structionist* 225, no. 16 (11 December 1959): pp. 8–15; cf. the prior note about the upcoming convention, *The Reconstructionist* 225, no. 12 (16 October 1959): p. 4.

75. Kaplan to Davis, 4 January 1960. Davis's private files.

76. "We both committed ourselves to support this platform, [and] even though each of us retained the right to interpret this or that detail according to his own lights, with regard to the question of affiliation as such, there was no doubt. But at the dinner session itself, at which the three of us spoke, Goldmann, Greenberg, and I, Greenberg backed out of his promise." Ibid. Moshe Davis states that Greenberg was fulfilling the role of spokesman, acting under Finkelstein's instructions on that occasion. Moshe Davis, interview, 16 November 1993.

77. Simon Greenberg to Moshe Davis, 15 February 1993. Davis's private files.

78. "On the Problem of Jewish Unity and Jewish Status, by Dr. Simon Greenberg, Vice Chancellor, Jewish Theological Seminary of America. Address Delivered at the Biennial Convention of the United Synagogue of America on Monday, 16 November 1959." Ratner Center, Greenberg Papers 14/22.

79. Davis to Finkelstein, 14 December 1959. Davis's private files.

80. Finkelstein to Davis, 22 December 1959. Davis's private files.

81. Kaplan to Davis, 25 February 1960. Davis's private files.

82. See "Affiliation of World Council of Synagogues with the World Zionist Organization, statement by Dr. Israel Goldstein," Jerusalem, 25 September 1976; with attached letter from Goldstein to Samuel Rothstein, chairman, World Council of Synagogues, 19 September 1976; and letter from Simon Greenberg to Israel Goldstein, 15 October 1976: Ratner Center, Simon Greenberg Papers 14/29; cf. "Memorandum" by Wolfe Kelman, 12 January 1976, Ratner Center, Simon Greenberg Papers 15/5. Kelman, who had attended the Jerusalem meetings of the World Zionist Action Committee, was in favor of the Conservative movement's affiliation with the W.Z.O., but only if more favorable terms could be worked out. He claimed that the Reform movement's affiliation was historically necessary "in order to finally lay to rest the subliminal association, in many Jewish minds, between Reform and anti-Zionism"; but this was not necessary for the Conservative movement, which had always been closely associated with Zionism. On the other hand, the W.Z.O. had incorporated the Reform movement into its governing bodies as a nonvoting affiliate. Kelman was in favor of having the Conservative movement join the W.Z.O. only as a voting party, fully on a par with large Zionist organizations like Hadassah. He suggested, therefore, the formation of a new, mass-membership Conservative Zionist organization. This proposal was eventually accepted, with the creation of MERCAZ, the Conservative Zionist movement.

83. "The Relationship of the Conservative Movement in Judaism to the Zionist Movement, the Zionist Organization of America, the State of Israel, the World Zionist Organization and to Klal Yisrael, by Simon Greenberg (for presentation to the National Convention of the Rabbinical Assembly—5724—April 1964)." Ratner Center, Simon Greenberg Papers, 14/23. Even after the affiliation of the World Council of Synagogues with the W.Z.O., Greenberg remained sceptical: "I am not sure about the benefits that may come either to the W.Z.O. or to the Conservative movement as a result of the present action, although I had something to do with getting the final approval of the Executive Council [of the World Council of Synagogues] in this matter." Greenberg to Israel Goldstein, 15 October 1976. Ratner Center: Simon Greenberg Papers 14/29.

84. "Draft for a Position Paper of the Rabbinical Assembly on Zionism, presented to the Rabbinical Assembly Convention April 1975, by Simon Greenberg." Ratner Center, Simon

Greenberg Papers, 14/23. Cf. "The Conservative Movement and the World Zionist Organization" (January 1975). Ratner Center: Simon Greenberg Papers, 15/13.

85. Transcript of remarks at Beit Hillel, Jerusalem, 26 August 1973. Ratner Center, Simon Greenberg Papers 2/70.

86. Kaplan to Davis, 8 February 1961. Davis's private files.

87. Kaplan to Davis, 18 March 1962.

88. Robert Gordis, *Judaism for the Modern Age* (New York, 1955), pp. 176–77.

89. Ben Halpern, *The American Jew, A Zionist Analysis* (1956; reprint New York: Schocken, 1983), p. 109.

90. Ibid., p. 109–10.

91. See, e.g., Abraham J. Karp, "Louis Finkelstein (1895–1991)," *American Jewish Year Book* 93 (1993):p. 533; cf. Louis Finkelstein, "The Ideals of the Founders," *Judaism* 26, no. 3 (1977): pp. 265–67; cf. Pamela S. Nadell, *Conservative Judaism in America: A Biographical Dictionary and Sourcebook* (Westport, Conn.: Greenwood Press, 1988), p. 280.

92. Finkelstein to Davis, 21 December 1967, marked "Confidential." Davis's private files.

93. Finkelstein to Selig Brodetsky, president of the Hebrew University, 1 February 1949. Ratner Center, JTS General Files: 1–E–66 (3). Nevertheless, Simon Greenberg later stated for the record that the plan to construct a Seminary Center in Jerusalem "was first conceived in the course of a conversation between Dr. Louis Finkelstein, Seminary Chancellor, and Prime Minister David Ben-Gurion" in 1952 (during Finkelstein's visit to Israel that summer). "Memorandum on Seminary Center in Jerusalem," 20 February 1957. Ratner Center: Simon Greenberg Papers 12/44.

94. "Memorandum on plans for A Spiritual-Cultural Center in Jerusalem," Simon Greenberg, fall 1952.Ratner Center, Simon Greenberg Papers 12/44. Cf. his further memorandum of 26 April 1956 (same file).

95. Finkelstein to Davis, 8 June 1961. The identification of the board members was supplied to me by Moshe Davis, interview, 16 November 1993. Davis reported: "If Finkelstein could be given a good legitimate reason to withdraw, he would have."

96. Memorandum re Seminary–Israel Program. Bernard Mandelbaum to members of the Rabbinical Assembly, September 1963. Ratner Center, Simon Greenberg Papers 12/44. Cf. "The Seminary and Israel, Memorandum B," by Simon Greenberg, November 1974 (Ratner Center: Simon Greenberg Papers, 12/44), in which Greenberg relates the following:

> The sum needed to construct all of the buildings envisioned for the Seminary Center was estimated at a million and a half to two million dollars. We had in sight by 1959–60 only some $400,000. It was decided then to construct but one building for the time being which would have dormitory facilities for some eight couples, 25 single students, two modest faculty apartments for visiting faculty, a dining room, student lounge, two classrooms and a large room to serve as both library and synagogue. That would require $500,000. Rabbi David Goldstein of Har Zion Temple, Philadelphia, volunteered to raise the necessary $100,000, which he did. . . . On May 30, 1962, the building was dedicated in ceremonies held at the Binyaney Haumah in Jerusalem as part of the convention program of the World Council of Synagogues and again with the participation of Premier David Ben Gurion and other Israeli notables. That fall the building housed its first group of Seminary and [8–10] Israeli students. . . . They had classes at the Center led by members of the Seminary or Hebrew University faculty. . . . During . . . twelve years [1962–1974] the lives of some 350 future religious [and] educational leaders of the American and Israeli Jewish community were thus beneficently affected.

265

*The Ongoing
Dialogue:
The Seminary
and the
Challenge of
Israel*

97. Ibid.

98. Finkelstein to Davis, 23 February 1961, and 16 March 1961. Davis's private files. Cf. Mandelbaum memorandum, September 1963 (above, n. 96).

99. Moshe Davis, interview, 16 November 1993. Cf. Davis to Finkelstein, 7 May 1962. Davis's private files.

100. Davis to Finkelstein, 7 May 1962. Davis's private files. Cf. Finkelstein to Davis, 16 March 1961; cf. Finkelstein to Davis, 28 March 1960.

101. Moshe Davis, interview by author, 23 November 1993.

102. "Memorandum on the Student Center in Jerusalem," from Raphael Posner to Marjorie Wyler, JTS, 29 May 1967. Ratner Center, Simon Greenberg Papers 12/44.

103. "A recollection of a seminar in Jerusalem with Moshe Davis, 1964–65," by Avraham Herbert Feder (unpublished), October 1992. Davis's private files.

104. "Dear Colleague," letter sent by Dr. Finkelstein from Jerusalem for distribution in his absence, 30 June 1964. Ratner Center: Boaz Cohen Papers 9/Finkelstein file). My thanks to Rabbi Dr. David Golinkin who drew my attention to this letter.

105. Rabbinical Assembly resolutions . . . 1950, "Religion in Israel."

106. Finkelstein to Davis, 29 July 1962. Davis's private files.

107. "*Hakanaut—mithara kasha vetahlif zol letorah, siha 'im prof' shaul lieberman*" ["Fanaticism—Difficult Opponent, and A Cheap Substitute for Torah: A Conversation with Prof. Saul Lieberman"], *Haaretz,* 7 May 1965.

108. Davis to Finkelstein, 22 November 1967; Finkelstein to Davis, 21 December 1967. Davis's private files. Davis was personally known to Rabbi Nissim and in local synagogue life in Jerusalem. Nissim's response, when Davis raised the matter of his officiating at his daughter's wedding, was to offer Davis rabbinical recognition on a permanent basis. Davis declined, asking only to be given a one-time-only dispensation, which Nissim readily granted. Nissim's position, as he explained it to Davis at the time, was that it mattered little from which institution a rabbi had received ordination—the crucial criterion was whether or not someone was recognized as a trustworthy rabbinical authority (*kerav mukar*). On that basis, Nissim was prepared to accept Seminary or even Hebrew Union College rabbis, and by the same token, would apply the same criterion to rabbis ordained at Yeshiva University's RIETS rabbinical school (i.e., even those ordained under Orthodox auspices had no automatic claim on the Israeli rabbinate, unless they were known locally). Davis's point to Finkelstein was that, to achieve recognition in Israel, Seminary rabbis would have to live there and function within the community long enough to become known quantities; de facto recognition would eventually follow. Moshe Davis, interview by author, 27 November 1994.

109. Agus to Greenberg, 20 June 1972. Ratner Center, Simon Greenberg Papers, 12/45.

110. Greenberg to Familian, 24 July 1974. Ratner Center, Simon Greenberg Papers, 2/75.

111. Letter, 30 May 1975. Ratner Center, Simon Greenberg Papers, 1/5.

112. Elath to Finkelstein, cable, 4 May 1966; also Davis to Finkelstein, 20 May 1966. Davis's private files.

113. Finkelstein to Davis, 7 March 1969 and 2 August 1971. Davis's private files.

114. Minutes of meeting, 12 February 1969, in Dr. Finkelstein's office, on "The Seminary Student Center and other Israel Activities," attended by Dr. Louis Finkelstein, Dr. Bernard Mandelbaum, Rabbi David Goldstein, and Rabbi Simon Greenberg. Ratner Center, Simon Greenberg Papers, 12/34.

115. Finkelstein to Davis, 6 February 1968; same to same, 7 March 1969. Davis's private files. The Seminary adopted an austerity budget for 1970–71. See: "Diary of events associated with the plans for the founding of a university of Judaism in Jerusalem under the auspices of the Seminary," 13 October 1971. Ratner Center, Simon Greenberg Papers, 12/34.

116. Louis Finkelstein to Louis Pincus, 5 January 1970. Ratner Center: Simon Greenberg Papers, 12/44. Same to same, 4 March 1971, and 28 September 1971. Ratner Center, Simon Greenberg Papers, 12/34.

117. Minutes of executive committee meeting held 9 September 1971: memorandum for Dr. Simon Greenberg (dated 18 October 1971). Ratner Center, Simon Greenberg Papers, 12/34. Finkelstein to Greenberg, 5 December 1972. Ratner Center, 1–BB–286/48 (Simon Greenberg file).

118. "The Seminary in Israel, Memorandum # 3," 15 October 1972; cf. "The Seminary in Israel, Memorandum #4," 15 May 1973; "The Special Seminary-Israel Project, Memorandum No. 7," 11 December 1975, Ratner Center, Simon Greenberg papers, 12/44. Cf. "The Seminary and Israel, Memorandum B," November 1974, Ratner Center: Simon Greenberg Papers, 12/9.

119. Cohen to Greenberg, with enclosure (to David Goldstein), 18 September 1973; cf. minutes, "Decisions at a meeting which was attended by Dr. Gerson Cohen, Mrs. Sylvia Ettenberg, Rabbis Shamma Friedman, Simon Greenberg, Avraham Holtz, Wolfe Kelman, David Kogen and Stanley Schachter, Thursday 12 April 1973," Ratner Center, Simon Greenberg Papers, 15/7.

120. Simon Greenberg interview, Ratner Center, 18 June 1990. Cf.: transcript of discussions held in 1972 at the Schocken Institute, with Rabbi Herbert Weinberg, Rabbi Joseph Wernick, Rabbi David Clayman, Rabbi Philip Spectre, Dr. Pesach Schindler, Rabbi David Hartman, Dr. Pinhas Peli, Dr. Uri Tal, Dr. Eliezer Schweid, Dr. Moshe Greenberg; cf. memorandum, 2 February 1976 (Sylvia Ettenberg to Gerson Cohen), re programs of cooperation between the Jewish Theological Seminary of America and the Ministry of Education and Culture of Israel, Ratner Center, Simon Greenberg papers, 15/1; memorandum, 20 October 1976, and minutes, 24 November 1976: re: Israel project. Ratner Center, Simon Greenberg papers, 12/35; draft for brochure on "The Special Seminary Program in Israel" (1976), Ratner Center, Simon Greenberg Papers, 12/7.

121. Micha J. Schocken to Gerson D. Cohen, 11 August 1974. Ratner Center, Simon Greenberg Papers, 2/72. In actual fact, Lieberman's collection was not transferred to Jerusalem until 1990, and rather than have it housed at the Lieberman Research Institute at the Schocken building, the collection was kept at the Neve Schechter building.

122. Greenberg to Cohen, 31 March 1974, Ratner Center, Simon Greenberg Papers, 12/34; same to same, 24 December 1974, with draft for "Memo C," Ratner Center, Simon Greenberg Papers, 2/72; Robert Hammer to Gerson Cohen, 15 September 1974, Ratner Center: Simon Greenberg Papers, 15/7.

123. Marjorie Wyler to Murray Kass, 24 October 1972, in preparation for publicity arrangements for Cohen's speech in Jerusalem in November. Ratner Center, Record Group 1.

124. Cohen to Greenberg, 18 February 1975. Ratner Center, Simon Greenberg Papers, 12/8.

125. Ibid.

126. Quoted in Lucy Dawidowicz, "American Public Opinion" [on the Arab-Israel War of 1967], *American Jewish Year Book* 69 (1968): p. 209. The degree to which Israel's crisis caught the Seminary off guard is reflected in a survey of Rabbinical School students conducted early in 1967 by Charles S. Liebman. The results, obtained prior to May 1967, indicated that 0 percent of the students enrolled at that time believed the "strength and survival of Israel" to be a problem of the highest priority, among various problems facing American Jewry. The problems that were felt to be critical were Jewish education (42 percent) and assimilation (12 percent), followed by Soviet Jewry and "social and ethical values of American Jews" (both chosen by 9 percent of the student body). "Greater Jewish unity," intermarriage, and anti-Semitism in the United States were also completely dismissed (i.e., chosen by 0 percent) as being high priority problems. See Charles S. Liebman, "The

Training of American Rabbis," *American Jewish Year Book* 69 (1968): p. 87.

Training of American Rabbis," *American Jewish Year Book* 69 (1968): p. 87.

127. Finkelstein to Davis, 28 December 1966 and 3 January 1967; cable from Davis to Finkelstein, 11 June 1967: "After Sabbath prayer and meditation respectfully urge you to advance visit Israel earliest possible date and come with Professor Lieberman and minyan representative personalities Seminary, Rabbinical Assembly, and United Synagogue STOP Undoubtedly all Seminary school graduates, families and friends will wish to join you at prayers Old City STOP This mitzvah for itself will create indispensable solidarity with yishuv." Finkelstein wrote back that he could not change his plans to that extent, but that he would leave England earlier than he had planned to. "I do not have to tell you," he wrote, "that I am more eager than ever to see the children and grandchildren, but even more to see the old Jerusalem and the Kotel Maaravi which I have not seen since 1925." Finkelstein to Davis, 16 June 1967. Davis's private files.

128. *The Jerusalem Post*, 13 June 1967, p. 4.

129. Finkelstein to Davis, 16 June 1967. Davis's private files.

130. Moshe Davis interview, 23 November 1993.

131. Kaplan to Davis, '*Erev Shavuot* 5727. Davis's private files.

132. Kaplan to Davis, 14 July 1967. Davis's private files.

133. Finkelstein to Davis, 2 October 1967. Davis's private files. A. Roy Eckardt in particular was outspoken in his criticism of his colleagues in the Christian world, publishing articles in both the *Christian Century* (26 July and 2 August 1967) and the *New York Times* ("Letters to the Editor," 8 July 1967). Both Simon Greenberg and Naomi W. Cohen, in interviews, have noted the depth of concern in Seminary circles over the failure of years of interfaith work to inspire a deeper understanding in the Christian churches of Israel's importance to the Jewish community. Greenberg, in a taped interview (Ratner Center archives, interview date, 6 March 1991) mentioned Abraham J. Heschel's chagrin, in particular; and Naomi Cohen, in an interview with the author (26 July 1994), recalled that her late husband, Gerson D. Cohen, had taken the churches' attitude to heart. He had replied to one particularly "nasty" article, which he felt represented a "betrayal" of the Jewish people, but was told that his article arrived too late to be published.

134. Abraham Joshua Heschel, *Israel: An Echo of Eternity* (1967; reprint New York: Farrar, Straus and Giroux, 1973), pp. 222–23; cf. 48–49, 51, 112–15, 120–22, 134–35, 213ff. Cf. David Hartman, *Conflicting Visions. Spiritual Possibilities of Modern Israel* (New York: Schocken, 1990), pp. 174–76.

135. Simon Greenberg, "On Aliyah from the West," remarks at Convention of ZOA held in the ZOA House, Tel-Aviv on 23 July 1967. Ratner Center, Simon Greenberg Papers, 14/23.

136. Finkelstein to Davis, 6 February 1968; cf. same to same, 6 September 1967 and 13 December 1967. Davis's private files.

   On 25 September 1967 Finkelstein wrote to Davis that he had arranged a meeting with Louis Pincus (of the Jewish Agency) together with Rabbi Wolfe Kelman. "Wolfe was quite adamant in saying that he thought this was no time to discuss aliyah. Mr. Pincus could not persuade him."

137. I would like to acknowledge the help of the staff of the Ratner Center for the Study of Conservative Judaism who, under the supervision of Professor Jack Wertheimer of JTS, organized the collection of addresses, printing and mailing of questionnaires, and general technical support. The Seminary History Project (also headed by Professor Wertheimer) provided the necessary funding for the survey. Data analysis was performed in Jerusalem by Zvi Richter and invaluable advice was received from Uzi Rebhun of the Institute of Contemporary Jewry of The Hebrew University (division of Jewish demography). I am very grateful to all of them for their assistance.

   The decision to limit the survey to alumni of the Rabbinical School alone was made for practical and financial reasons. A survey of all JTS alumni, even for the period of 1972–93, would have been beyond the resources available for the current study.

138. Although not all respondents answered the question, 216 did so; those who left the question unanswered included twenty of our Israeli residents. Thus, 171 alumni, of whom 166 live in the Diaspora, responded positively to the question, while forty-five answered "no."

139. The question read: "Which of the following terms most suitably characterizes your views: 1-Zionist, 2-religious Zionist, 3-pro-Israel, 4-non-Zionist, 5-post-Zionist." There was no provision made for "not applicable" or "not sure."

140. The respondent grew up in Philadelphia, was born in 1946, and graduated in 1972 from the Rabbinical School.

141. Dr. Aaron Singer, interview, 20 October 1994.

142. Ibid.

143. The respondent was born in 1947, serves with a congregation in the New England area, and did not participate in the Seminary's year program in Jerusalem while a student in Rabbinical School.

144. The proportional breakdown of congregations according to the *number* of different Israel-related activities on their calendar for the year 1993–94 is as follows:

COUNT OF ACTIVITIES	PERCENT OF CONGREGATIONS*
None of the listed activities	3
One	6
Two	12
Three	27
Four	15
Five	15
Six	10
Seven	7
Eight	8

*There are slight inconsistencies in the number of responses obtained for each type of activity: percentages are rounded off to the average whole percentage point and therefore the total slightly exceeds 100 percent.

145. The fact that the "post-Zionists" speak about Israel relatively more often than the "pro-Israel" group may be a distortion due to the small size of the "post-Zionist" group (only ten individuals), or it may reflect the fact that they have chosen a position that is more specifically related to Israel (*post-Zionist*) and not merely "pro" something in general.

146. "The Seminary and Israel, Memorandum B," November 1974, with letter attached from Cohen to Greenberg, dated 30 October 1974. Ratner Center, Simon Greenberg Papers, 12/44. Cf. "Memorandum A," 31 July 1974, summarizing discussions held by Greenberg and Cohen in Jerusalem on 12 July 1974, following Cohen's four-week stay in Israel. Ratner Center: Simon Greenberg Papers, 12/44.

147. Ibid., pp. 13–14.

148. Ibid., pp. 14–15.

149. Ibid., pp. 16–18, 20.

150. Draft memorandum, prepared by Simon Greenberg at the request of Dr. Gerson Cohen when in Jerusalem, 15 January 1975. Ratner Center, Simon Greenberg Papers, 12/44.

151. "A memorandum summarizing the consensus reached by Chancellor Gerson Cohen, Rabbi Stanley Schachter, and Rabbi Simon Greenberg at a meeting held in Chancellor Cohen's office on 1 October 1976, regarding: The Future of the Seminary-Israel Pilot Project." Ratner Center, Simon Greenberg Papers, 12/35.

152. Gerson D. Cohen, "The Meaning of Israel in the Perspective of History," *Conservative Judaism* 27, no. 3 (1973): pp. 3–14; idem, "From *Altneuland* to *Altneuvolk*: Toward an

269

*The Ongoing Dialogue:
The Seminary
and the
Challenge of
Israel*

Agenda for Interaction between Israel and American Jewry," in *World Jewry and the State of Israel*, ed. Moshe Davis (New York: Arno Press, 1977), pp. 237–57; idem, "The Meaning of Liberty in Jewish Tradition," in *Jewish Life in America: Historical Perspectives*, ed. Gladys Rosen, (New York: Ktav and American Jewish Committee—Institute of Human Relations Press, 1978), pp. 1–7.

153. Ibid., passim. Quoted phrase is from Cohen, "*Altneuvolk*," p. 253.

154. Cohen, "*Altneuvolk*," pp. 251, 256; "Meaning of Israel," p. 14; "Meaning of Liberty," p.5.

155. Naomi Cohen, interview by author, 26 July 1994. "He, too [like Solomon Schechter] thought that religion was the core of Judaism, but didn't go as far as Schechter in denouncing secular Zionism. He did see JTS as having a historic mission—to bring the religion factor more into focus for Israel. . . . Privately, [Gerson Cohen] was very much a Zionist. He had been raised in Hebrew and spoke it fluently. [The family] had considered *aliya*. His father lived there at the end of his life. [Israel] was part of him, part of his life. It was his country, his people, he identified fully. But he was also a historian, and that meant that he did not buy the Zionist interpretation that Jews were only 'in' history thanks to Israel. Nor did Israel solve antisemitism. This kept him more balanced."

156. Simon Greenberg to Gerson D. Cohen, cable, 8 July 1981, in reply to a previous cable summoning Greenberg to the meeting scheduled for 13 July. Greenberg's reply apparently quotes passages from Cohen's cable to him. Ratner Center, Simon Greenberg Papers, 2/72.

157. Simon Greenberg to Sydney M. Baer, 29 January 1975. Ratner Center, Simon Greenberg Papers, 2/70.

158. Professor Lee Levine, interview by author, 16 November 1994. Cf. Neil Gillman, *Conservative Judaism, The New Century* (West Orange, N.J.: Behrman House, 1993), pp. 177–80.

159. Gerson D. Cohen, "The Present State of Conservative Judaism," *Judaism* 26, no. 3 (1977): p. 268.

160. Naomi Cohen, interview, 26 July 1994 (see n. 155).

161. Gillman, *Conservative Judaism*, pp. 117, 134–35.

162. Aryeh Davidson and Jack Wertheimer, "The Next Generation of Conservative Rabbis: An Empirical Study of Today's Rabbinical Students," in *The Seminary at 100. Reflections on the Jewish Theological Seminary and the Conservative Movement*, ed. Nina Beth Cardin and David Wolf Silverman (New York: The Rabbinical Assembly and The Jewish Theological Seminary of America, 1987), pp. 33–46.

163. Ibid., pp. 38–40.

164. Greenberg to Richard Hammerman, copy to Rabbi David Kogan, 7 January 1973. Ratner Center: Simon Greenberg Papers, 2/77.

165. Memorandum, 20 March 1979, with attached minutes of a meeting, 11 March 1979, of representatives of the Jewish Theological Seminary of America and the Masorti movement, in Jerusalem. Ratner Center: Simon Greenberg Papers, 12/53.

166. Dorff wrote in 1984 that "For decades Orthodox synagogues and schools [in Israel] have been supported by direct allocations from the government, while Conservative institutions have received next to nothing. Moreover, the marriages and divorces performed by Conservative rabbis there have not been legally recognized. Until recently, Conservative leaders have been reluctant to press too hard for changes in these policies because of Israel's severe military and financial problems. In 1981, however, the Foundation for the Conservative Movement in Israel was established in order to raise funds to support directly Conservative Movement projects there, without going through the governmental agencies. . . . *In the years to come, the movement will press for local Jewish community federations to contribute directly to the Foundation in order to insure that a proper percentage of American funds raised for Israel are used for Conservative projects there*" [my emphasis—EL]. Dorff, "Ideology of Conservative Judaism," p. 114.

167. Professor Lee Levine, interview by author, 16 November 1994. Memorandum, Reuven Hammer to David Gordis, 22 December 1982, and Hammer's lecture notes (in longhand) from the rabbinical school conference, held at Neve Schechter, 5 December 1982. Ratner Center: Simon Greenberg Papers, 16/5.

168. Professor Lee Levine, interview by author, 16 November 1994.

169. Ibid.

170. Gillman, *Conservative Judaism*, pp. 184–85.

171. Dr. Ismar Schorsch, interview by author, 10 February 1994.

172. Ismar Schorsch, "Shaping the Image of the Modern Rabbi: Let the Old Be Made New and the New Be Made Holy," translated from the original Hebrew in Ismar Schorsch, *Thoughts from 3080, Selected Addresses and Writings* (New York: The Jewish Theological Seminary of America, 1987), pp. 17–24.

173. Dr. Ismar Schorsch, interview, 10 February 1994. Personal communication to the author, 14 December 1994.

174. John S. Ruskay and David M. Szonyi, eds., *Deepening the Commitment: Zionism and the Conservative/Masorti Movement* (New York: The Jewish Theological Seminary of America, 1990), pp. 2–3.

175. Schorsch and Levine, interviews, 10 February 1994 and 16 November 1994, respectively. Cf. Ruskay and Szonyi (eds.), *Deepening the Commitment*, pp. 12–13.

176. *New York Times*, 13 October 1994, pp. B1 and B10; personal communication to the author, 14 December 1994.

177. Halpern, *The American Jew*, p. 137.

MARSHA L. ROZENBLIT

The Seminary during the Holocaust Years

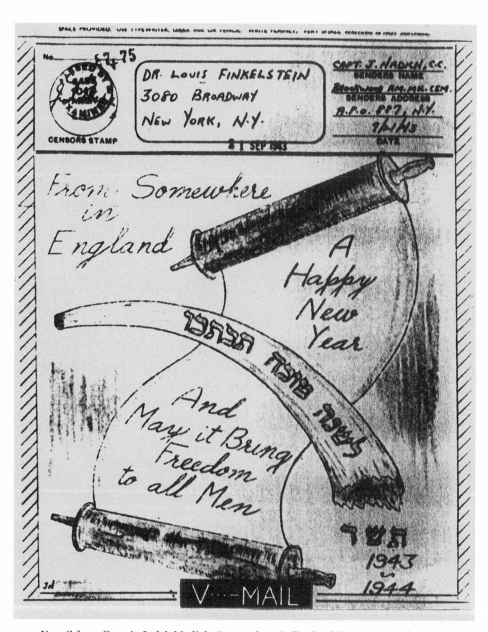

V-mail from Captain Judah Nadich, "somewhere in England," to Louis Finkelstein, Rosh Hashanah, 1943. *Ratner Center, JTS.*

MARSHA L. ROZENBLIT

The Seminary during the Holocaust Years

Iᴺ THE YEARS WHEN THE JEWS of Europe suffered persecution and extermination, the Jewish Theological Seminary responded to the crisis in ways that reflected the fundamental convictions of its leaders about the role of the institution in the Jewish world. In the 1930s, as the Nazis mounted a campaign to drive Jews from the cultural, political, and economic life of Germany, president Cyrus Adler and provost Louis Finkelstein, and the Seminary faculty, worked hard to save Jewish scholars and bring them to America where they could continue to devote themselves to Jewish scholarship. During World War II, when it became obvious that the Nazis had embarked on a campaign to annihilate European Jewry, Seminary President Louis Finkelstein labored tirelessly on projects that he believed would fight the forces of totalitarianism and safeguard both democracy and religion. Thus he, the faculty, and the board viewed his work on the Institute for Religious Studies, an effort at interfaith understanding, and on the Conference on Science, Philosophy and Religion, bringing prominent intellectuals together to answer the most pressing questions of the day, as the Seminary's contribution to the fight against Nazism.

Both during and after the war, Seminary leaders firmly believed that the destruction of European Jews gave the Seminary the responsibility of safeguarding Jewish learning and ensuring the continuity of Judaism. Throughout the Holocaust the Seminary saw its mission as protecting scholars and using scholarship to fight the enemies of Judaism. Such a position may not have satisfied those who sought political action to save Jews, but it reflected the deeply held convictions of Seminary leaders about the imperative to preserve Jewish culture.

The 1930s: Rescuing Scholars and Rabbis

When the Nazis came to power in Germany in 1933 they began a campaign of persecution against the Jews aimed at removing them from all positions in public life. Nazi edicts mandated the wholesale firing of Jews in civil service and university

273

positions, created a quota for Jewish students in high schools and universities, barred Jews from participating in German cultural life, and made it increasingly difficult for Jewish lawyers and doctors to work.[1] Seminary President Cyrus Adler expressed deep concern about the situation of the Jews in Germany, believing that the Nazi government was "endeavoring to destroy the Jews who have been there for 2000 years."[2] As early as April 1933, years before the Nazis systematically sought to make Germany *judenrein*, Adler felt that all the Jews of Germany should leave.[3] By 1937 Adler was convinced that Nazi persecution of the Jews meant "that the burden of keeping up Jewish learning not only in America but for other parts of the world, will be shifted to the United States."[4]

Beginning in 1933 Adler received numerous requests for assistance for unemployed German Jewish academics.[5] Throughout the 1930s he attempted to find them positions in America, and in particular, he tried to arrange positions at the Seminary or Dropsie College, the other institution he headed, for scholars in Jewish Studies. Naturally, the depression-related financial difficulties of both institutions constrained this effort. Nevertheless, Adler felt compelled to assist these men by raising money to fund positions.

Adler asked the JTS faculty, many of whom also received requests for assistance, to inform him of any German Jewish scholar appropriate for the Seminary faculty.[6] A request by Professor Louis Ginzberg to invite the Aramaic scholar Eugen Mittwoch to lecture at the Seminary did not work out, but Adler still tried to find a post for him.[7] In 1934 and 1935 Adler spent some time helping Dr. Leo Rosenzweig, whom he labeled "a combination of the Slobodka Yeshiva and Hermann Cohen" but did not want to hire him at the Seminary, not least because the man did not know English.[8]

Adler had far more success with Alexander Sperber and Julius Lewy. In August 1933 and January 1934 Professor William Foxwell Albright of Johns Hopkins University urged Adler to hire Alexander Sperber, a young former lecturer at Bonn now destitute in Palestine, "the best Jewish authority on Greek and Aramaic versions of the Bible," who "would make a great addition to American scholarship." He also recommended Julius Lewy, a professor of Assyriology from Giessen, who was to be a visiting professor at Johns Hopkins in the fall of 1934.[9] Adler at first lamented that "I have not one penny free,"[10] but then he obtained $3000 from the newly formed Emergency Committee in Aid of Displaced German Scholars and $1000 from the Rockefeller Foundation so he could invite Lewy for the spring of 1935 and Sperber for the full academic year 1934–35.[11] Lewy only taught at JTS one semester,[12] but Adler obtained continued funding for Sperber from the Emergency Committee through 1937–38, and in 1938 the Seminary placed Sperber on its permanent faculty at the munificent salary of $2500 a year.[13] Sperber lived in the Seminary dormitory for many years.[14]

While the Seminary felt obligated to help German Jewish scholars, it did not intend to alter its standards just to save them. Only those Judaica scholars would be hired who fit its model of dispassionate scholarship and commitment to Jewish tradition. Scholars also had to understand the needs of American students and speak English perfectly. The case of Guido Kisch, a specialist in medieval Jewry law from Halle, illustrates how these standards posed a dilemma for JTS leaders. When Kisch first requested Adler's assistance in November 1933, Adler merely forwarded his request to the Emergency Committee in Aid of Displaced German Scholars, informing Kisch that it was not likely that an American law school would hire him.[15] In the spring of 1934, however, Alexander Marx, the Seminary's historian and librarian, and Salo Baron of Columbia University, proposed to give Kisch a research fellowship at the American Academy for Jewish Research, the scholarly organization to which most Seminary faculty belonged. They had already collected $1250 from the members of the academy for the purpose and sought additional funding from the American Jewish Joint Distribution Committee and the Rockefeller Foundation.[16] Kisch did receive a fellowship at the academy, with the Emergency Committee providing two-thirds of the money through 1936.[17] In 1936, the Seminary faculty considered whether it should hire Kisch but decided that his field did not suit the curriculum, and that in any case he did not possess sufficient knowledge of rabbinics to teach in a rabbinical seminary. Nevertheless, faculty members desired to help him. Louis Finkelstein, then provost and a member of the academy's committee to raise funds for Kisch, wrote to Adler on 4 February 1936: "For Kisch it is: either some provision here or *H'V [chas v'chalilah*, 'God forbid'] the calamity of a forced return to the *Gai Hinom* [hell] of Hitlerland."[18] Adler responded by raising money for Kisch's fellowship from the Joint Distribution Committee, the American Jewish Committee, and B'nai B'rith.[19]

The Seminary extended a warm welcome to Professor Ismar Elbogen, the Jewish historian from the Lehranstalt für die Wissenschaft des Judentums in Berlin, to whom it had awarded an honorary degree in 1937. Because he was not a university professor, the Emergency Committee in Aid of Displaced German Scholars could not assist him. In late 1937–early 1938, after Elbogen indicated that he wanted to leave Germany, Cyrus Adler worked feverishly with (Reform) Rabbi William Rosenau of Baltimore; Max Currick of the Central Conference of American Rabbis; Julius Morgenstern, president of Hebrew Union College; Stephen Wise, head of the Jewish Institute of Religion; and Zionist Julian Mack to create a research fellowship for Elbogen under the auspices of JTS, HUC, JIR, and Dropsie. Elbogen, whom Adler considered "the foremost Jewish scholar in Germany," was to receive $4000 a year ($1000 from each institution) beginning with the academic year 1938–39, and he was completely free to pursue his own research without any obligation to teach at the participating institutions.[20]

The Seminary also provided some financial assistance to Professor Samuel Krauss from Vienna, who had fled to Cambridge in 1938.[21] On the other hand, in March 1938 Cecilia Rozovsky of the National Coordinating Committee for Aid to Refugees and Emigrants Coming from Germany asked JTS if it could offer a position to Dr. Elieser Ehrman of Berlin, but Finkelstein replied that "unfortunately, no department of this institution is in a position to add to its staff at the present time. I deeply regret this, but at the moment there does not seem to be anything that could be done to remedy the situation."[22] While no explanation is provided in the letter, Finkelstein probably wrote this because Ehrman would not have fit in at the Seminary.

The most frustrating case for the Seminary was its attempt to save Professor Moses Schorr, a Jewish historian from Lwow, Poland, to whom it had given an honorary degree in 1937. In the spring of 1940, the Seminary learned that Schorr, living in the Soviet zone of Poland, had been arrested by the Russians because of his anti-Communist sympathies. Hoping that an American visa would convince the Russians to release Schorr, the Seminary, now under Finkelstein's presidency, offered Schorr a professorship and obtained $1200 from the Emergency Committee in Aid of Displaced Foreign Scholars to provide partial subvention for the position. Throughout the summer and fall Finkelstein implored the Polish and Russian embassies and the State Department to intervene, nervous that the Emergency Committee's financial commitment would expire before Schorr was released. Nothing came of his efforts, and Schorr died in a Soviet prison in 1941.[23]

In 1938 the intensification of Nazi persecution of the Jews in Germany moved the Seminary to focus on a second group of Jews whom it perceived as deserving its assistance: German rabbis. At that point the Nazis had made it impossible for Jews to earn a living and had virtually outlawed organized Jewish life in Germany, now including Austria. All German Jews—not least its rabbis—sought to flee.[24] The Seminary was besieged with requests to help rabbis locate positions in America.[25] At first Adler and Finkelstein tried to find jobs for them—a difficult task if the rabbis knew no English.[26] In November 1938, for example, Erich Warburg wrote to Adler asking him to assist Theodor Herzl Weiss of Altona. Finkelstein handled the case, a task made easier because Warburg had agreed to pay the rabbi's salary. He arranged a position for Weiss with a congregation in Palisades Park, New Jersey, and did considerable paperwork to arrange a visa for this Yiddish-speaking German Orthodox rabbi.[27]

Adler quickly realized, however, that the job was too great for him alone, and thus he persuaded the Rabbinical Assembly to create a committee to help German rabbis. Writing to Simon Greenberg, head of the Rabbinical Assembly, on 29 July 1938, Adler lamented that the National Coordinating Committee that helped German Jewish refugees showed far more interest in assisting potential artisans and governesses than rabbis. He suggested that Greenberg appoint a committee to assist the coordinating committee in placing rabbis. Advising Greenberg to work with the other rabbinical associations, he acknowledged all the difficulties attendant on retraining and placing German refugee rabbis but reminded Greenberg of the importance of Jewish solidarity: "We all have to bear in mind the difficulties and distressing conditions which have come quite unmeritedly to our colleagues in Germany and what used to be Austria, and that we all have to share them in greater or lesser measure."[28] Greenberg appointed Rabbi Herbert Parzen to coordinate the Rabbinical Assembly efforts on behalf of refugee rabbis.[29]

Realizing the need for even greater coordination than the Rabbinical Assembly could provide, Adler helped create the Committee on Refugee Jewish Ministers, a subdivision of the National Coordinating Committee. Meeting at the Seminary on 13 October 1938, the newly formed committee, with members from all three major branches of American Judaism, discussed how they could retrain and place German refugee rabbis so they could most effectively serve American congregations.[30] Adler also arranged for JTS graduate Rabbi Alexander Burnstein of Newark to serve as secretary of this agency beginning 1 December 1938.[31] Adler helped Burnstein in his work, urgently reminding him in January 1939 that "we must do what we can and in every direction to save as many rabbis and students as possible."[32] Burnstein felt that Adler had "done more toward the consummation of this project than any other man."[33] He regularly consulted with Adler and reported his accomplishments.[34]

Once the Committee on Jewish Refugee Ministers had been formed, the Seminary simply forwarded all requests from German and Austrian rabbis and cantors to Burnstein.[35] Adler's replies to rabbis reflected his anguish at not being able to help all of these men. He wrote to Harry May in August 1938, "I wish from the bottom of my heart that I could send you a completely favorable reply but I cannot. Believe me." Similarly, in December 1938 he seemed genuinely upset when he told Edith Taglicht that it would probably be impossible to place her seventy-six-year-old father, Viennese chief rabbi Israel Taglicht.[36] On the other hand, Seminary secretary Joseph Abrahams, who increasingly responded to inquiring German rabbis, replied curtly to them, showing them no warmth or concern. On 12 April 1939, for example, he wrote a Golvard [*sic*, probably Eduard] Steinberg in Vienna: "Doctor Adler has already done so much for foreigners who wish to come to this country that it is impossible for him to be of assistance to you."[37] Finkelstein, who took on many of Adler's duties in 1939 as the latter became ill, also responded officially, without warmth. He replied, for example, to Rabbi Herbert Finkelscherer of Stettin on 17 May 1939: "Unfortunately, there is nothing that any of us at the Seminary can do in the matter."[38]

In some cases, the Seminary provided additional assistance to refugee rabbis. Burnstein sometimes called upon Finkelstein for assistance in placing rabbis, and

Finkelstein wrote to congregations urging them to hire the rabbis he recommended.[39] Finkelstein also regularly wrote letters on behalf of refugee rabbis so that they could officiate at marriages in America.[40] Sometimes, however, he was annoyed by requests regarding rabbis. He promised board member Frieda Schiff Warburg, for example, that he would help Julius Bach, an Austrian rabbi who was trying to create a congregation of Austrian Jews in New York, but his limited help was often only grudgingly provided.[41]

The most important assistance that the Seminary extended to refugee rabbis was the classes it hosted beginning in 1939 for German and Austrian rabbis eager to retrain for the American rabbinate. Funded by the National Refugee Service, these classes provided instruction in English, public speaking, and synagogue and school problems. In 1939 twenty-five students attended these classes in the old Seminary building on 123rd Street.[42] The Seminary coordinated this effort, helped raise funds, and provided space.[43] The classes continued at least through 1943.[44]

The Seminary also extended itself to Rabbi Max Gruenewald, generously permitting him to live in the dormitory, at first without charge and then for minimal rent, while he pursued his scholarly work and became acquainted with America. Gruenewald, later president of the Leo Baeck Institute, probably began his American career as a dorm resident on a scholarship from the American Academy for Jewish Research. Later, the Seminary tried to find him a position with a congregation. Finkelstein's letters to him were always gracious and generous. In 1946, after Gruenewald was firmly ensconced in a pulpit in Milburn, New Jersey, and reunited with his wife and son who had been in Palestine during the war, Finkelstein wrote to him, repeating what he had said to him many times before: "We regard it as a great privilege to have had you as a resident of the dormitory."[45]

The Seminary assisted famous Jewish scholars, and it tried to help German rabbis, but both the leadership and the faculty refused to use the Seminary simply to save German Jews. In the 1930s, but especially after 1938, many young German Jews applied to be students at the Seminary in order to get visas to America. The Seminary did reluctantly admit a few, but it refused to alter its admissions standards in order to fulfill the Jewish commandment of "redeeming captives." Committed to its mission to provide a first-rate, modern, scholarly education for rabbis, possibly insecure about its status as a truly American institution preparing American rabbis for American congregations, and constrained by financial considerations, the Seminary did not open its doors in any significant way to German Jewish students.

Throughout the 1930s, even after the escalation of Nazi persecution in 1938, the Seminary faculty remained steadfast in its insistence that all applicants for admission to the Rabbinical School meet its stringent requirements and know English perfectly. Seminary faculty regularly sent exams to Germany for students, but admitted only those students who passed the rigorous exams and came highly recommended. Thus, upon Ismar Elbogen's recommendation, they admitted Berthold Woythaler in 1936 but refused admission to many others, either because their Judaic background was weak or they had not attended a university, closed to them since 1933.[46] In January 1938, the faculty admissions committee had determined "that we already have under consideration so many foreign students that it is inadvisable to admit a new student unless he is of exceptional ability."[47]

In 1938 the number of foreign applicants escalated dramatically. By the middle of the year the Seminary faculty felt overwhelmed by requests for admission. At a 9 June meeting it voted to inform the present crop of applicants "that the Seminary cannot at present consider the admission of any more foreign students," although, in fact, the Seminary did admit one or two more.[48] Adler explained faculty concerns to the Seminary board at its 2 May 1938 meeting. "The suggestion has been made," he noted, "that in view of the great catastrophe which has befallen the German and Austrian Jews, we ought to modify our standards, but the members of the Faculty feel that to do this would be to negate what we have striven after for fifty years, and to undermine the Seminary as an educational force in this community."[49] This reluctance to admit foreign students was shared by other American rabbinical schools.[50]

Finkelstein, then provost, felt compelled to explain Seminary policy to Ismar Elbogen, who had recommended many of his students to the Seminary. Finkelstein presented two arguments: first, German students were linguistically and culturally unprepared for the American rabbinate, and second, the Seminary simply did not have the financial resources to admit many German students. In April 1938, he told Elbogen that it would take years for foreign students to understand how rabbis functioned in American congregations, and in any case they did not fit well in classes with American students. Moreover, he reminded Elbogen, the Seminary could not lower its standards for less well-prepared students. Such lowering of standards was not in the interests of Judaism in America or the world at large, he asserted.[51] One month later he emphasized financial considerations in explaining the Seminary's reluctance to admit German students.[52]

The financial problems were real enough. Seminary deficits had mounted steadily through the depression years. In 1938–39 the Seminary had a deficit of $44,900, and a cumulative deficit since 1934 of $142,900.[53] There is no evidence, however, that the Seminary tried to raise money in order to rescue German Jews by admitting them as students. Finkelstein may have assured Elbogen in January 1939 that "I have been making strenuous efforts to obtain the means for bringing some of the German students here,"[54] but he does not seem to have done so. He was more concerned with the needs of Judaism than with those of individual German Jews.

In some cases the Seminary actively helped students, but often this help was tinged with annoyance. While the Seminary seemed genuinely concerned about

Sally Skrcyzpce, the son of a Danzig cantor, who came to the Seminary briefly on a Hebrew Immigrant Aid Society (HIAS) scholarship,[55] it became increasingly annoyed with Helmut Galliner, the son of a Berlin rabbi, whom it accepted in 1937 as a special student in bibliography because he lacked the necessary credentials for the Rabbinical School. Galliner studied with Alexander Marx, worked in the library thirty hours a week, and received free room and board for several years. The Seminary helped him obtain his student visa and assisted him in obtaining a permanent visa in Cuba in 1938 and 1939, even lending him money to spend the necessary three months there. The faculty decided, however, that Galliner should not take courses at the Seminary, and he was not offered a permanent job in the library.[56] In 1941 Finkelstein expressed his annoyance with Galliner, who wanted a job or the continuation of his fellowship, to board member Frieda Schiff Warburg, to whom Galliner had appealed. Finkelstein made it clear to Mrs. Warburg that there were many people, scholars in particular, who deserved Seminary resources far more than Galliner, who had responded to the Seminary's assistance with "impossible demands." Moreover, Finkelstein asserted, he did not want to violate the immigration laws by keeping Galliner as a student more than four years.[57]

In some cases, Seminary efforts on behalf of students came to naught because the U.S. State Department refused them visas. The files offer heartbreaking testimony to the difficulties German Jews had in obtaining visas to America between 1938 and 1941. One case was Nahum Stechler, a Polish-born Berlin Jew who applied in elegant Hebrew for admission to the Teachers Institute in January 1938. Despite repeated entreaties by the Seminary to the State Department, Stechler, safe in England, never received his visa.[58]

Other cases expose not only the "paper walls" that the State Department erected to prevent German Jewish immigration but also the Seminary leaders' lack of sympathy for the plight of these poor young Jews. Two examples will suffice. In July 1938, Werner Lampel, the son of a cantor in Leipzig, applied for admission and was rejected. In December the Seminary reversed itself when Marx discovered that Lampel met Seminary requirements. Unfortunately, the American consul in Berlin rejected Lampel's application for a student visa because Lampel could not prove that he would return to Germany after he completed his studies. Throughout the early months of 1939 Lampel's father wrote several urgent appeals to Finkelstein, begging him to do what he could for his son. Finkelstein did nothing, explaining his inaction to Lampel, then in England, on 9 May 1939: "Once we have issued the statements which were sent to you we must abide by the decisions of the Consulate with regard to the whole matter. Naturally we wish to help you, but I feel that the Seminary has done everything it can."[59]

Finkelstein was less sympathetic to Curt Arndt, a student from Berlin, who had completed his rabbinical studies in Rome. In December 1938, the faculty admitted him to the Seminary College of Jewish Studies. In 1940, he was stuck in England

awaiting a regular quota number for a visa because he could not prove he would
return to Germany after he completed his studies in America. Finkelstein wrote
letters to the American consul there, attesting that Arndt had been accepted as a
student and would receive free room and board, but he told Marx, who was concerned about Arndt: "As you yourself realize, there is, unfortunately nothing that
the Seminary can do in the matter."[60] In late 1940 and 1941 Finkelstein refused to
help Arndt any further. He declined to write letters attesting that Arndt had indeed
been accepted as a student, informing Alexander Burnstein, "It would not be possible to send him a certificate stating he had been admitted to the College, or letter
such as you suggest." He also refused to appeal to the American consul to waive the
requirement that Arndt return to England (from an internment camp in Canada)
for his physical exam, informing Arndt, "Under present circumstances I cannot
undertake the action you suggest."[61]

Seminary leaders worried about those few German students who actually
arrived, reflecting the Seminary's anxieties about its role in training "American"
rabbis. A memorandum of 17 May 1939 expressed Finkelstein's deep concern that
the foreign students—Meir Engel, Sigmund Szobel, Leo Wind (from Poland), and
Berthold Woythaler—had not adjusted to America or learned English adequately.
He argued that, with the exception of Woythaler, the foreign students "cannot be
classified as our regular students are" and that their attendance in regular classes
should be "curtailed."[62] Over a year later the faculty wanted Szobel to withdraw
from the Rabbinical School because he could never graduate as a rabbi. This concern had nothing to do with his intellectual abilities or his character, which all
agreed were excellent. Rather, the faculty doubted whether he could overcome his
foreign accent and foreignisms, and whether he could ever find employment. Szobel
absolved the faculty of the obligation to help him find a job, which he expected to
secure through his own contacts. Given this promise, the faculty allowed him to
continue in the Rabbinical School, advising him to correct his accent and get an
American roommate.[63] The Seminary faculty was consistently pleased with
Berthold Woythaler, presumably because he had Americanized rapidly.[64]

It was not only German Jewish scholars, rabbis, and students who turned to the
Seminary for assistance after 1938; many ordinary people did so as well. In most
cases, Seminary officials simply forwarded these requests to the National Refugee
Service and officiously informed the applicants that Adler or Finkelstein had
"already undertaken as much as he can possibly do with regard to the refugee problem," or, as Finkelstein put it, "I deeply regret that there is nothing that I can do to
be of assistance to you and your family."[65] As individuals, Adler, Finkelstein, and
other members of the Seminary faculty issued affidavits to Jews seeking to immi-
grate to the United States and helped them once they had come to America. There

seems to be no pattern that would explain whom they chose to help. Adler, for example, arranged a job as a West Coast salesman for the Jewish Publication Society for a refugee he met in 1935, and he proposed contacting New York's leading furriers to arrange an affidavit for Otto Kernisch of Vienna in 1939.[66]

Finkelstein was at his most helpful in assisting Ferdinand Buchsbaum, the sexton (*shammes*) of a synagogue in Frankfurt, and his family to come to America in 1939, when he signed an affidavit on their behalf.[67] In the summer of 1941 he was willing to sign an affidavit for Helene Bloch, the sister of Henry Graetz for whom he had signed an affidavit four years earlier.[68] He also assisted relatives and friends of relatives, writing a letter of support for Emanuel Strauss, his nephew's brother-in-law, in June 1941, and providing character references for Max and Elsa Nathan so they could buy a chicken farm in New Jersey.[69] Sometimes Finkelstein seemed genuinely upset when he could not provide an affidavit, as in the case of Paul Bettlin, a Joint Distribution Committee worker in Marseilles, in 1941–42.[70] Similarly, he seemed quite distressed that he was unable to help Solomon Joelsons, a Latvian Jew who managed to get to Sweden.[71] On the other hand, Finkelstein often replied curtly to those he chose not to assist.[72]

Other members of the Seminary faculty also helped refugees. Zvi Scharfstein, a prominent member of the Teachers Institute faculty, and his wife signed many affidavits.[73] Alexander Sperber, who had been a refugee, frequently asked Finkelstein to intervene on behalf of friends from Rumania and Vienna, and he himself went to Washington to appeal the case of his cousin.[74] As an institution, the Seminary regularly provided refugees with twenty-five seats at High Holy Day services and a number of places at its Passover seder.[75]

The Seminary also concerned itself with the fate of Jewish books and ceremonial objects. It thus naturally agreed to accept the Judaica collection of the Danzig Jewish community in 1939. The shipment, which included fifty-one Torahs earmarked for American congregations to remind them of the plight of German Jewry, arrived in July 1939 and was placed on display in the Seminary museum.[76] Alexander Marx aptly summed up the mood of the Seminary in October 1939: "The tragic events occurring in Europe placed upon us the sad responsibility to take care of a number of treasures."[77] The Seminary also accepted the Benjamin Mintz collection from Poland[78] and worried about Jewish books in Europe.[79]

In the early years of World War II, the plight of ordinary Jews in Eastern Europe did not occupy Finkelstein's attention. Instead, he focused on the destruction of Jewish institutions of learning. Serving on the board of the Joint Distribution Committee, Finkelstein attended its August 1940 conference on Lithuanian yeshivas and drafted the JDC's statement appealing for assistance for rabbis and yeshiva students in the Soviet zone of Poland in early 1941.[80] He also advised Rabbi Gershon Hadas in early 1941 on how to send money to schools in Eastern Europe.[81] In 1941

DANZIG MUSEUM IN EXILE
SEMINARY IS HAVEN FOR COLLECTION
SAVED FROM NAZIS DESTRUCTION

Professor Max Arzt (left) of The Jewish Theological Seminary of America, and Rabbi Berthold Woythaler, Rabbi of Temple Beth Sholom, Manchester, Conn., inspect articles of the Danzig Collection at the Seminary prior to their removal to public exhibition in Scribner's Book Store window, New York, beginning September 1, the fifth anniversary of the Nazi occupation of Danzig. Rabbi Woythaler formerly lived in Danzig and worshipped in the synagogue in which the articles were displayed. The articles were sent to the Seminary for safekeeping a few weeks before the Nazi invasion of Danzig in 1939.

From The Jewish Theological Seminary of America
Broadway and 122nd Street, New York 27, N. Y.

Ratner Center, JTS.

Finkelstein inquired about photocopying the Günzberg manuscript collection in the Soviet Union.[82]

The 1940s: Fighting Totalitarianism through Scholarship

During the 1930s, indeed through the middle of 1941 when the State Department effectively barred refugees from coming to America, the Seminary had to cope with individual Jews desperately seeking its assistance. Once the Nazis began the systematic annihilation of European Jewry, however, such assistance—dealing at all with individual Jews—became impossible. Instead the Seminary concerned itself with preserving Judaism. Seminary leaders all believed that the study of Jewish tradition and the revitalization of Jewish learning were the most powerful vehicles for Jewish survival. Finkelstein, who became Seminary President in 1940, led the Seminary firmly according to his own vision, central to which was the belief that serious scholarly efforts toward interfaith understanding and measures to strengthen true religion and democracy were the best antidotes to Hitlerism and totalitarianism. Thus during the Holocaust itself the Seminary as an institution did not engage in direct activity on behalf of the suffering Jews in Europe but devoted itself to the more immediate yet abstract goal of furthering Judaism in America. Such preoccupation with life in America was typical of the American Jewish community in this period.[83]

Committed to democracy and convinced that democracy derived from and depended on religious faith, Finkelstein believed that democracy imbued with faith in God was the best weapon against Nazism. Thus in 1940 he wrote to Abraham Meyers in Chicago blaming the defeat of the Western democracies on their lack of religion and asserting that American democracy would not last long without belief in God.[84] Similarly, in a 1941 lecture at New York's Town Hall, Finkelstein declared that "only a democracy animated by profound religious conviction is capable of offering serious resistance to either ideational or military enemies." He feared for American democracy if people lost their faith in God.[85]

Finkelstein sought to employ the Seminary to augment Jewish religious faith and interfaith understanding. He outlined his priorities to board member Alan Stroock in December 1940: to strengthen the concept of Judaism as a religion among Jews, to cooperate with other religions in safeguarding democracy, and to work with intellectuals "to preserve civilized life in our generation."[86] Similarly, in a letter to Judge Joseph Proskauer of the American Jewish Committee in October 1943, Finkelstein argued that the best way for Jews "as a group" to help solve the present world crisis would be to preserve their religious faith and demonstrate to others how that faith could contribute to the advancement of civilization. He observed:

> The ineffectiveness of our efforts on behalf of our brothers in Nazi-occupied
> Europe, our failure to overcome the callousness of the world toward this

unprecedented catastrophe, are, in my opinion, to a great extent the results of our own misunderstanding of the real significance of the tragic events of our time, and our falling away from the religious traditions and the high ideals of Prophetic and Rabbinic Judaism.[87]

During the war years the Seminary hosted a series of conferences to spread this message to ordinary Conservative Jews.[88]

Finkelstein's reports to the Board of Directors in 1940, 1941, and 1942 offer excellent insights into his understanding of how the Seminary should respond to the crisis posed by Nazism to the Jews. He announced to the board on 29 October 1940 that the Seminary had to work on four fronts. It must remain committed to its basic mission to train rabbis and teachers and promote Jewish scholarship. It must also devote itself to adult Jewish education in order to increase both religious consciousness and the love of democracy among American Jews. Further, it must interpret Judaism to the Christian world through the Institute for Religious Studies. Finally, it must bring together scholars "to formulate a united spiritual front to totalitarian philosophy" through the ongoing Conference on Science, Philosophy and Religion.[89]

These goals derived from Finkelstein's fear that anti-Semitism would flourish in America after the war, as well as from his awareness, as early as 1941, that European Jewry could no longer sustain world Jewry. In his report to the Board of Directors on 6 April 1941, before America even entered World War II, Finkelstein graphically described how the absence of idealism and the prevalence of lower moral standards in postwar America would lead to the proliferation of anti-Semitism. He reiterated his commitment to the Institute for Religious Studies and the Conference on Science, Philosophy and Religion as a means not only of improving intergroup understanding but also of "strengthening the moral and spiritual fiber of the American people." At the same time, he argued that "our responsibility for the preservation of Jewish ideals and traditions becomes the more urgent and must be accepted the more solemnly because of the suppression of many older institutions, from which we have derived inspiration," that is, from the great institutions of rabbinic learning in Europe, which no longer existed and whose students and faculty would be lucky if they escaped concentration camps and forced labor. With extraordinary prescience for early 1941, before the Nazis began the systematic extermination of the Jews, Finkelstein asserted that American Jewry must look at this destruction and echo Elijah: "And I, even I only, am left and they seek my life and take it away." While he hoped this situation would be temporary, in the meantime American Jewry had a great responsibility "as trustees of the inherited spiritual treasures of our faith."[90]

The following year Finkelstein seemed even more worried about the rise of anti-Semitism in postwar America and therefore even more insistent on the need to sup-

A luncheon
meeting of the
Institute for Reli-
gious Studies,
1944. Louis
Finkelstein is at
left in the group
standing at the
dais. *Photo by
Virginia F. Stern.
Ratner Center,
JTS.*

port democracy through religion, especially through his Institute for Religious
Studies and Conference on Science, Philosophy and Religion. In his May 1942
report to the board, he declared anti-Semitism a "pagan anachronism" that must be
destroyed or it would destroy not only Judaism and the Jews but civilization itself.
He feared that in a war-weary postwar America totalitarianism and anti-Semitism
would triumph. Jews, he asserted, needed to fight this anti-Semitism not as Jews but
as Americans, defending the spiritual interests of all American people. In addition,
of course, Finkelstein continued to worry about Judaism and the disaffection of so
many American Jews from Judaism's religious values. He concluded by stating that
the activities of the Seminary made a major contribution "to the preservation of the
American belief in democratic tradition."[91]

Given these convictions, it is no wonder that Finkelstein and his assistant Jessica
Feingold devoted most of their prodigious energies to the Conference on Science,
Philosophy and Religion[92] and to the Institute for Religious Studies. Organized in
1938 as the Institute for Interdenominational Studies with a $5000 grant from
Lucius Littauer,[93] the Institute for Religious Studies brought together Protestant,
Catholic, and Jewish clergy and scholars for courses on the various religious traditions. From the beginning Finkelstein made it clear that this Institute would serve
as a weapon against anti-Semitism in America. Sincerely believing that knowledge
destroyed prejudice, he hoped "that many misunderstandings and misconstruc-

tions of Judaism can be dissipated by a careful study of the facts." By teaching Christian clergy about Judaism and by making all clergy aware of the common elements of the "Judeo-Christian tradition," the Institute would help dispel anti-Semitism, which was a threat to democracy itself.[94] In a 1944 letter that accompanied the distribution of *Group Relations and Group Antagonisms*, one of the publications of the Institute, Finkelstein asserted that "this work is of the essence in attacking the problems of post-war America and overcoming the tendency toward increasing group tensions which constitute so great a peril to us all."[95] During the war Finkelstein sought to expand the Institute, raising money from Littauer, the Warburgs, and other Seminary contributors, and obtaining a $20,000 grant from the New York Foundation.[96] He also opened branches of the Institute in Chicago (1944) and Boston (1945).[97]

Finkelstein believed that the Institute fulfilled its mission. In a letter to Frieda Schiff Warburg on 18 May 1944, he declared that "the Institute is gradually becoming a potent force for overcoming the hostilities due to differences of religion."[98] Seminary treasurer Arthur Oppenheimer similarly felt that the Institute was central to the mission of JTS. He told Seminary fund-raiser Rabbi Max Arzt that "the Institute for Religious Studies has evoked such high praise in many quarters, and has done such effective work, that I am sure all of us agree it must be kept open and expanded at all costs."[99] Not everyone at the Seminary agreed. Apparently some JTS alumni, led by Milton Steinberg and Solomon Goldman, opposed the Institute. Finkelstein viewed this opposition as "isolationist," concerned, that is, only with internal Jewish affairs. Moreover, he felt that Zionism colored the views of his opponents, making them hostile to "the concept of the Seminary as a religious and educational institution." He remained committed to the Seminary's religious mission and successfully neutralized the opposition, confident he had "the backing of the members of the faculty," as he told his ally, board member and *New York Times* publisher Arthur Hays Sulzberger.[100]

Finkelstein also enlisted scholarship in the service of his cause. He arranged a fellowship at the Institute for Religious Studies for Elias Bickerman, an historian of antiquity, so that he could study minority problems in pagan and Christian Rome;[101] and he himself edited a three-volume collection of essays on the Jews and Judaism. Funded by the American Jewish Committee, these volumes, which appeared in 1949, contained essays by leading scholars on Jewish religion, history, and culture. Finkelstein viewed these volumes as a way to combat anti-Semitism and ignorance.[102] At the same time, he promoted the Seminary as a center of dispassionate scholarship and resisted efforts of some members of the Rabbinical Assembly to make the Seminary serve just the needs of Conservative Judaism.[103]

The Seminary did, however, broadcast its conviction that the abiding moral and spiritual truths of Judaism were valuable for Jews and non-Jews alike. Thus in October 1944 it inaugurated a regular weekly radio program called *The Eternal Light*. The half-hour broadcast on the NBC network contained a dramatic presentation on some significant issue in Jewish tradition, along with choir music and a short talk, all designed to show how Judaism was a "moral force" in history, so that Jews and Christians would understand "the basic moral values which Judaism has contributed to the world."[104] In a press release in May 1946, the Seminary noted that *The Eternal Light* program "contributes in a worthy manner to the spread of the ideals of brotherhood and mutual understanding."[105]

Though terribly saddened by the ongoing Nazi annihilation of European Jewry, Seminary leaders thus spent the war years focusing on how to strengthen American Judaism as the best antidote to such evil. This was certainly the message of the commencement addresses delivered by prominent members of the board during World War II. These addresses all alluded to Nazi atrocities but never dwelled on them. Instead they enjoined the rabbis to make Judaism strong and thus ultimately victorious against all enemies. Edgar Nathan delivered the commencement address in November 1942 to the first class of rabbis to graduate from the accelerated ordination program for chaplains. He affirmed that Judaism would survive wherever people recognized God and reminded the young rabbis that the history of the Jews proved that might does not make right, concluding with the hope that those who came back from the war would "make this country and the world a fit place for noble living."[106] Louis Epstein, another board member, spoke even more dramatically in his commencement address in June 1943. He reminded his audience that the strength of Judaism lay in its commitment to study and in its idealism. He urged the graduates to become models of true Judaism, leading Israel to ever higher levels of perfection.[107] Alan Stroock echoed Finkelstein's views when he declared at the October 1944 commencement that "the Seminary would be unworthy of its heritage were it not today to lend its every energy to the struggle to attain the only kind of world in which Judaism and civilization can live and breathe." All religious groups, but especially the Jews, with their particular genius for democracy, must take the lead in creating a better world. The Seminary, he felt, was particularly well suited to craft the Jewish contribution to a peaceful and just world. He concluded with a call for brotherhood, enjoining Finkelstein to proclaim on behalf of the Seminary and all Jews that

> the Jew has come through the horror of the last decade with the eternal light still burning at his altar and in his heart—not poisoned by the beast of hate, but in spite of pillage and starvation, indignity and death—looking forward to the dawning of the day when he can say in the great words of Lincoln: 'We are not enemies, but friends.'[108]

One wonders how he could speak so optimistically in 1944.

There is no doubt that Seminary leaders, faculty, and students knew of Nazi atrocities against the Jews during World War II. As a member of the boards of the American Jewish Committee and the Joint Distribution Committee, Finkelstein regularly received reports about Nazi atrocities, and his references to the situation of the Jews in Europe, like the one to Elijah cited above, reflect his awareness of the magnitude of the Nazi assault. A few of his letters indicate that during the war he had not yet internalized the reality of this assault,[109] and in the middle of the war he probably did not have a clear sense that European Jewry would not be able to reconstitute itself.[110] He did misunderstand the reasons for the Nazi assault on the Jews, blaming it on Nazi animosity toward the monotheistic idea.[111] Although moved by the plight of European Jewry, he nevertheless neither responded to direct appeals to participate in protest actions on their behalf[112] nor involved the Seminary in any public activity about the Holocaust.

By contrast, some JTS students tried to protest Nazi atrocities. Like most concerned American Jews, students knew by late 1942 that the Nazis had embarked on a campaign to annihilate European Jewry,[113] even if not everyone understood the full extent or meaning of its horror.[114] As Rabbi J. Leonard Azneer remembers, "The ache of the holocaust was constant."[115] Nearly all the students joined in the mass demonstrations protesting the Holocaust at Madison Square Garden.[116] Three rabbinical students—Noah Golinkin, Jerome Lipnick, and Bertram Sachs—organized a European Committee in the fall of 1942 to draw attention to the catastrophe and to formulate plans to rescue the Jews of Europe.[117]

Disappointed that Stephen Wise did not encourage them in their actions, the committee tried to enlist the support of non-Jewish theological students in its enterprise.[118] In February 1943 students at the Seminary joined with students of ten other Jewish and Christian seminaries in New York to protest Nazi atrocities and discuss rescue strategies for European Jews "who have been marked for complete extermination." This Inter-Seminary Conference, held 22 February 1943 at JTS and at Union Theological Seminary and attended by about two hundred people, featured lectures on such topics as "Hitler's Policy of Extermination," workshops on what religious groups could do to help the Jews of Europe, and a session on Palestine as a place of refuge. Finkelstein himself delivered the final talk, calling for brotherhood and common action to solve world problems.[119] In a series of resolutions, the Inter-Seminary Conference called for an end to immigration restrictions for refugees, the opening of Palestine to Jewish immigrants and the creation of a Jewish homeland there, negotiations with Germany to release all Jews and political prisoners, special efforts on behalf of children, and food for the starving populations of Europe.[120]

The European Committee also appealed to the American Jewish community to work to save the Jews of Europe. In an article in *The Reconstructionist* in March 1943, Golinkin, Lipnick, and Sachs outlined a course of action, including prayers, meet-

The Inter-
Seminary Con-
ference meets
at the Jewish
Theological Sem-
inary, 11 February
1943. *Fellman
Photo Service.
Ratner Center,
JTS.*

ings, vigils, and protests for American Jewry.[121] On 25 April 1943, the committee issued a "program of action," a detailed plan for marshaling the resources of the American Jewish community to protest the annihilation of European Jewry. This program expressed the anguish and the impatience of its drafters. It declared that "Hitler is determined to blot out the Jew; [so] we must be determined to save him.... Thousands of Jewish lives are being destroyed daily, and American Jewry has not yet found its soul." The students urged that the effort to rescue the remaining Jews of Europe become the highest communal priority of American Jews.[122] The European Committee worked with the Synagogue Council of America in planning a period of mourning and special prayers for the Jews of Europe, and in the summer of 1943 it called on the American Jewish Conference to devote itself to rescuing European Jewry.[123] The Rabbinical Assembly also urged protest and action on behalf of European Jewry.[124]

Students at the Seminary held occasional memorial services for victims of the Holocaust. In particular, they memorialized in their prayers the Jewish victims of Nazi liquidations of various ghettos in Eastern Europe. On 19 April 1944, students in the Rabbinical School and Teachers Institute conducted a memorial service commemorating the Warsaw Ghetto uprising the year before, paying tribute to the leaders of the uprising, and praying for the same kind of courage "to aid in speeding the day of victory."[125] Some of these special services touched students deeply. Max

Ticktin, a student at JTS from 1942 to 1947, recalled that at one service when the leader began chanting psalms everyone present began to cry.[126] Herman Grossman remembered that on *Tisha B'Av* 1943, Professor Louis Ginzberg, who was leading the *mincha* (afternoon) service, burst into tears. For Grossman, "It was one of the most moving and memorable events of my life."[127]

Perhaps the most common response to the Holocaust among students was the intensification of their commitment to Zionism and to establishing a Jewish state. Rabbi Simon Glustrom, a student at JTS from 1944 to 1948, recalls that "in retrospect, . . . interest in Zionism . . . seemed to take on a greater sense of urgency during those years."[128] Rabbi Stanley Rabinowitz, a student from 1939 to 1943 and on the staff until 1945, noted that the students, all of them Zionists, felt that the only answer to the Holocaust was to open the gates of Palestine and create a Jewish homeland. Students pressed Seminary leaders, not all of whom were sympathetic to Zionism, to sing *Hatikvah* at graduation and other convocations and to fly the Zionist flag, now the flag of Israel. "These two elements," he observed, "the flag and the anthem, became symbols of student identification with the Holocaust."[129] Increased Zionist allegiance and insistence on a Jewish homeland were common American Jewish responses to the Holocaust.[130]

Members of the Seminary community stopped a few times during the war to reflect on, protest, and memorialize the persecuted Jews of Europe. Most of the time, however, they did not think, or they did not want to think, about the situation of European Jewry, nor did they stop studying Bible and Talmud in order to do so.[131] Abraham Karp, who graduated in 1945, feels that this behavior was a mechanism for avoiding utter despair but admits that such an evaluation derives from hindsight.[132] Like most American Jews—indeed, like most Americans—Seminary students and faculty focused on World War II itself and on how they could best contribute to the war effort. Even before America entered the war, Seminary graduate Ben Zion Bokser prepared, at Adler's request, an essay on the Jewish attitude to war. In May 1940 Seminary board member Henry Hendricks revised its final paragraph to emphasize that if aggression threatened America "Jews will stand, as always, shoulder to shoulder with all other Americans in unflinching, loyal and devoted defense of their country."[133] When America entered the war in December 1941, Finkelstein immediately wrote to President Roosevelt wishing him strength and assuring him "that, like all our fellow citizens, I am ready and eager to do anything in my power to assist you."[134] During the war Finkelstein made it clear that studying at the Seminary was not a way to avoid military service.[135]

As a religious institution, the Seminary devoted itself to the religious needs of Americans Jews during the war. Thus in the summer of 1942 Finkelstein, possibly worried about anti-Semitic consequences if Jews violated blackout regulations on Friday nights, protested that such regulations in New York unfairly discriminated

*The Jewish
Theological
Seminary
of America*

Captain Samuel
Cass, Jewish The-
ological Seminary
Rabbinical School
class of 1933,
Senior Jewish
Chaplain for the
Army and Navy in
Canada, presides
over Yom Kippur
services while
Morris Wilansky,
a local civilian,
blows the shofar,
1945. *Signal Corps
Photo. Ratner
Center, JTS.*

Rabbi Judah
Nadich (Seminary
class of 1936)
meets with com-
bat chaplains in
Namur, Belgium,
January 1945.
Other seminary
graduates present
include Ario
Hyams, Samuel
Cass, Marvin
Goldfine, and
Harry Essrig
(third, sixth,
eighth, and
eleventh from left
in the back row)
and Max Wall
(first row, right).
*Signal Corps
Photo. Courtesy
of Rabbi Judah
Nadich.*

against Sabbath-observing Jews and asked city officials not to hold air-raid practices on Friday nights.[136] Most of the Seminary's attention, naturally, went to the wartime needs of Jewish soldiers. The Seminary prepared several brochures for distribution to Jewish soldiers, which, in the words of administrator Max Arzt, were "designed to maintain and advance their moral faith as Jews and as Americans."[137] Although some people criticized these pamphlets for not meeting the religious needs of ordinary Jewish soldiers,[138] they reflected the Seminary's conviction that belief in God, justice, and civilization would lead to the destruction of the "domination of arrogance" and the liberation of Israel.[139] The Seminary also sent sermon texts to Jewish soldiers in areas where there were no chaplains.[140] With the help of the Jewish Welfare Board, the Seminary regularly arranged religious services and Passover seders for about 150 Jewish midshipmen training at Columbia University.[141] For its part the Rabbinical Assembly tried to solve the problems of potential *agunot* (women whose soldier husbands might die without witnesses and who therefore would not be able to remarry) by preparing a special *get* that granted a divorce to women whose husbands had not returned three years after demobilization.[142]

The Seminary concentrated most of its efforts during World War II on producing Jewish chaplains for the American and Canadian armed forces. Recognizing both the need of soldiers for religious guidance and the opportunity the war afforded to popularize Conservative Judaism among young American Jews, the Seminary developed an accelerated course of study so that rabbis could graduate in three years instead of the normal four. Finkelstein explained to the faculty in July 1942 his reasons for proposing this acceleration. He worried that many Conservative rabbis would be physically disqualified for the chaplaincy and hoped to avoid the problems that would be caused by drafting into the chaplaincy older rabbis who had children and congregations. The government, moreover, required that chaplains have a year of pastoral experience before they entered the service. Thus Finkelstein felt that the war required an accelerated program even if such acceleration was not academically wise.[143] Hence the faculty accepted a plan by which the June 1943 class would graduate in November 1942 and the June 1944 class would graduate in June of 1943.[144] In the winter of 1943 the faculty decided that alumni should teach the summer sessions so faculty would still be free for "creative work," and it refused to accelerate the program further.[145] By 1943, Finkelstein observed in a letter that the Rabbinical School had "virtually become a chaplaincy school."[146] The Seminary assisted those congregations whose rabbis had entered military service as chaplains, providing them with faculty guest rabbis or recent graduates.[147]

Seeing an opportunity to propagandize for Conservative Judaism, Finkelstein was eager to get as many of his graduates into the chaplaincy as possible. In 1942, for example, he urged the Jewish Welfare Board to press the army to relax its rules about pre-chaplaincy pastoral work.[148] In March 1943, Finkelstein wrote of his interest in placing more chaplains "from our group" in the armed forces.[149] Later in the war, when more than ninety JTS graduates served as chaplains in the American and Canadian armies,[150] both Seminary leaders and the chaplains themselves felt that their army experiences would prepare them well for the challenges of postwar American Jewish life. Max Arzt, for example, felt "that the work of the chaplains will result in a revitalization of Jewish life and interest in the post-war period."[151] Chaplains, he told Chaplain Herbert Ribner in October 1943, "will return to the civilian fold much better equipped to deal with the problem of evolving a rich and creative Jewish life in this country."[152] Israel Kazis, who served as a chaplain in North Africa and Italy, felt that the experience of Jewish soldiers with the Jewish chaplains would create a "hunger" in Jewish men for Conservative Judaism and increase lay respect for rabbis. Both Finkelstein and Arzt agreed with him.[153]

Hence the Seminary and the chaplains were far more concerned with American Jewish needs than with the terrible situation of the Jews in Europe. Many chaplains corresponded regularly with Finkelstein and Max Arzt. Virtually none of their letters mentioned Nazi atrocities, even in 1944 and 1945 when American troops were liberating Europe. Instead they focused on the religious needs of American Jewish soldiers or on larger issues confronting American Judaism.[154] Chaplains took pleasure in the defeat of the Nazis, of course, and they delighted in describing the Jewish religious services they conducted in former Nazi territory, regarding them as proof of the Jewish triumph over Nazism. Israel Kazis, for example, positively crowed when he described High Holy Day services in Italy in 1944. "To me," he wrote,

> there was something symbolic in the situation: We were proclaiming our faith in God in the face of the godless Germans; a symbol perhaps of the long history of Israel proclaiming his faith and remaining loyal to it in spite of opposition of his enemies.[155]

Most of his letters, however, deal with the future of American Jewry.

Indeed, Seminary leaders devoted much effort during the war to planning for the growth of Conservative Judaism. The Wartime Emergency Commission for Conservative Judaism headed by Norman Salit, for example, concerned itself with the specific needs of chaplains and how they would be reintegrated in congregations after the war.[156] Similarly, the Seminary hosted several conferences on the future of Judaism in America and the role of returning chaplains.[157] Convinced that Conservative Judaism best met the needs of 20th-century American Jewry, Seminary leaders felt an enormous responsibility to educate American Jews, to teach them the beauty of Jewish religious tradition, and to instill in them a sense of pride in their heritage.[158] In this regard as well, Seminary leaders focused on American Jewry and on Judaism, not on the suffering Jews of Europe.

Postwar Reaffirmation

295

*The Seminary
during the
Holocaust
Years*

In the immediate aftermath of World War II, when consciousness of the Nazi extermination of European Jewry finally set in fully, the Seminary continued to pursue the goals that Finkelstein had set for it in 1940. It devoted itself to training rabbis and teachers, promoting Jewish scholarship, working for interfaith understanding, and coping with the problems of the postwar world. Just as it had during the war years, the Seminary focused on the needs of American Jewry, a natural focus for an institution that saw itself as leading the American Jewish community. Seminary leaders viewed their agenda as the best response to the terrible crisis that beset world Jewry with the annihilation of six million Jews. At a 17 April 1945 meeting, members of the JTS board rededicated themselves to Finkelstein's vision, affirming that the Seminary itself was an academic institution devoted to Judaism as a spiritual force and pledging the Seminary to increased cooperation with other religious and intellectual leaders "with the aim of strengthening democracy as a spiritual and cultural force in the United States."[159]

The attitude of the Seminary was best summed up by a confidential statement prepared by the faculty, probably in 1945.[160] The faculty expressed its grief over the catastrophe that beset Jewry and urged generous help for the survivors, but the eight-page document does not dwell on European Jewry. Instead, the faculty emphasized the responsibility that American Jews now faced "to rededicate ourselves to the cause of a renaissance of our people," to the "preservation and advancement of Judaism, its ideas and spiritual values." To that end, the faculty advocated stronger Jewish education and more Jewish scholarship.[161] It also called for a Jewish homeland in Palestine, at the same time declaring a commitment to brotherhood, social justice, and cooperation with other religious groups.

Seminary leaders certainly worried about Jewish survivors in Europe and hoped to attend to their religious needs. As early as May 1945 Finkelstein urged the Joint Distribution Committee to send kosher food to Europe as quickly as possible.[162] In the summer the Seminary considered dispatching Robert Gordis, Max Arzt, and Simon Greenberg to Europe to study "the spiritual conditions of the Jews there, and to find out how we can be of assistance."[163] Jewish chaplains certainly aided survivors.[164] In 1946 the Seminary board consulted frequently with Judge Simon Rifkind, then advisor for Jewish affairs to the European Theater commander, on how the Seminary could help survivors, especially those with rabbinic training, although nothing concrete seems to have emerged from those discussions.[165] The Seminary sent books, pamphlets, and other literature to many surviving Czech Jewish communities.[166] As individuals many Seminary leaders also helped survivors.[167]

Finkelstein's concern for brotherhood and democracy prompted him to extend sympathy also to the Germans, and he urged the Allied occupation forces to treat them benignly. In particular, he wanted fair Allied treatment of German religious institutions, as he wrote in a letter to the *New York Times* on 11 August 1945. This letter caused a stir in American Jewish circles. Finkelstein had stated that most German Jews thought Germany "in the right" in the war. Although he had referred only to Germany's anger over the provisions of Versailles, the letter made it seem that German Jews more generally agreed with Germany during World War II, and many Jews naturally took offense. Finkelstein never apologized or rectified the misconception publicly.[168]

The Seminary, as usual, expressed great interest in the fate of scholarship. In particular, the Seminary took it upon itself to provide assistance to the rabbinical seminary in Budapest. Samuel Löwinger, director of the Budapest Seminary, had appealed to JTS for aid in April 1945, and Finkelstein worked closely with the Joint Distribution Committee in arranging a monthly stipend. JTS also sent many books to Budapest, mostly post-1938 publications of Seminary faculty.[169] Finkelstein was concerned with the fate of Jewish libraries that had survived the war, urging that they be sent to the Hebrew University.[170] He was delighted that the library of the *Alliance israélite universelle* had survived and inquired if the *Alliance* could microfilm its *Genizah* manuscripts for JTS.[171] He wondered if copies of his own publication, an edition of the *Sifra* of Deuteronomy published in Germany in 1938, still existed and could be retrieved.[172] The Seminary museum received many artifacts testifying to Nazi depredations against the Jews, which it displayed as "an unfailing reminder of our fellow men and women in Europe who have suffered so much for our sake."[173] The Seminary did not, however, devote its resources to assisting scholars among the survivors, declining, for example, to arrange a fellowship for Mark Wischnitzer similar to the one established earlier for Ismar Elbogen, because the conditions that had operated in Elbogen's case, "the necessity for saving one of the most eminent Jewish scholars of our time," no longer existed.[174]

The Seminary did see fit to honor several notable Jewish Holocaust survivors. In February 1945, the Seminary granted honorary degrees to Chief Rabbi Jacob Kaplan and Judge Leon Meiss of France. Explaining why he wished to honor them, Finkelstein praised their "heroic achievements on behalf of French Jewry during the difficult days of the occupation" and their "determination to maintain Judaism . . . in the days to come."[175] A year later, the Seminary awarded an honorary degree to German rabbi and Theresienstadt survivor Leo Baeck.[176]

The special convocation to award Baeck his degree on 6 January 1946, attended by three hundred people, may have served as the Seminary's major ceremony of mourning for the murdered Jews of Europe. It also provided the Seminary with an opportunity to dedicate itself publicly to the future of Judaism. Baeck provided the Seminary with the perfect foil for expressing its anguish about the destruction of European Jewry and its hope for a better world. Not only was Baeck a Holocaust victim who had survived the war while devoting himself to the spiritual needs of Jews

Leo Baeck (right) about to receive an honorary degree from Louis Finkelstein at the convocation in his honor, 6 January 1946. Abraham Joshua Heschel is behind Baeck. *Photo by Virginia F. Stern. Ratner Center, JTS.*

but he was the perfect role model of rabbi, scholar, and advocate for better Jewish-Christian relations. At the convocation, Finkelstein expressed eloquently the Seminary's grief for "the millions of our brethren who have had to make the supreme sacrifice for their faith" and for "the disaster which has come upon our faith and our people." At the same time, he expressed his joy that Baeck, a "colleague and co-worker in the preservation and advancement of Judaism in our time," had survived "to see the dawn of a brighter day." Finkelstein praised Baeck extravagantly for his dedicated leadership of German Jewry throughout the horrors of the Nazi period and lauded him for sanctifying God's name in the face of evil, thereby demonstrating "the abiding power of the Jewish tradition as a spiritual force." Baeck's devotion to God served, he declared, to prepare his followers "to be builders of a better world," "to rebuild civilization" in the aftermath of the defeat of Nazism.[177] Seminary graduate Jacob Milgrom remembers how exhilarated everyone felt when the Seminary honored Baeck, a symbol of the Holocaust and of the survival of Jewry.[178]

FROM 1933 TO 1946 THE LEADERS, faculty, and students of the Jewish Theological Seminary conducted themselves much as did most American Jews. They were concerned about the plight of European Jewry in the face of Nazism, but they chose to focus primarily on the needs of American Jewry and American Judaism. If they were active Zionists—as many students and faculty were—they advocated the establishment of a Jewish state. It would have been surprising if the Seminary community had behaved otherwise. Children of America and the American Jewish community, beset by the depression and American anti-Semitism and devoted to Americanization, members of the Seminary naturally adopted as their priority the fortification of American Jewish identity. Moreover, Seminary leaders sincerely believed that a stronger American Judaism provided the best antidote to Nazism and the best insurance for the continued survival of Judaism and the Jewish people in the face of the Nazi slaughter of European Jewry. Similarly, Zionist students and faculty felt that a Jewish homeland would best ensure Jewish continuity.

Devotion to these ideals may not have satisfied those who insisted then and later that American Jews should have cared more about European Jewry and should have exerted themselves more vigorously on its behalf. Many who were students in those years express dismay in retrospect that they did not do more, that they focused on study, personal concerns, and the needs of American Jewry. Saul Teplitz, for example, a student at the Seminary from 1941 to 1945, whose wedding ceremony took place at JTS in June 1944, has expressed "deep regret" that "we didn't give a second thought to the appropriateness of a celebration on the day when thousands of Jews were being murdered."[179] Similarly, Baruch Silverstein, a rabbinical student from 1936 to 1940, has wondered why Seminary students and faculty did not arrange hunger strikes, chain themselves to the White House, or at least stand sobbing at street corners and subway entrances.[180] Such guilt feelings aside, members of the Seminary community responded to the Holocaust in ways that reflected their fundamental convictions and commitments at that time. Their behavior reflected that of the American Jewry they so eagerly sought to lead.

1. Raul Hilberg, *The Destruction of the European Jews,* rev. and definitive ed. (New York and London: Holmes and Meier, 1985), vol. 1, pp. 65–94; Karl A. Schleunes, *The Twisted Road to Auschwitz: Nazi Policy toward German Jews, 1933–1939* (Urbana: University of Illinois Press, 1970), pp. 62–132.

2. Letter to Wilbur Thomas, Carl Schurz Memorial Foundation, 15 June 1933, in *Cyrus Adler, Selected Letters,* 2 vols., ed. Ira Robinson, (Philadelphia and New York: Jewish Publication Society and Jewish Theological Seminary, 1985), vol. 2, p. 269.

3. Adler to Horace Stern, 7 April 1933, ibid., vol. 2, p. 260.

4. Report of Adler to board meeting, 23 June 1937, JTS Archives, Board of Directors minutes, JTS, 1933–41.

5. See, for example, letters of Adler to Paul Baerwald of the Joint Distribution Committee, 3 May 1933; to Professor Seligman of Columbia, 3 May 1933; and to E.R. Murrow of the Emergency Committee, 13 March 1934, JTS, Ratner Center for the Study of Conservative Judaism, Records of the Jewish Theological Seminary (hereinafter: Ratner Center), 1A/7/37. See also Adler's report (p. 11) to 15 April 1934 meeting of the JTS Board of Directors, JTS Archives, Board of Directors minutes, 1933–41, and Adler's letter to Sol Stroock, board member, 27 October 1933, Ratner Center, 1A/25/47.

6. Minutes of faculty meeting, 10 May 1933, Ratner Center, 3A/1, faculty minutes 1932–33.

7. Correspondence on Mittwoch between Adler, Louis Ginzberg, Felix Warburg, and Stephen Duggan of the Emergency Committee in Ratner Center, 1A/18/28. On Adler's efforts in 1938, see Adler to Alexander Sperber, 7 December 1938, 1A/18/28; Sperber to Finkelstein, 21 July 1938, 3B/2/14. In 1941 the Institute for Advanced Study in Princeton tried to enlist Finkelstein's assistance for Mittwoch, 1A/18/28.

8. Caricature of Rosenzweig in Adler to Dr. Harry Dawidowitz, 19 December 1934. Ratner Center, 1A/23/1.

9. Albright to Adler, 17 August 1933 and 17 January 1934, Ratner Center, 3B/2/15.

10. Adler to Albright, 23 January 1934, Ratner Center, 3B/2/16.

11. Correspondence between Adler and Lewy, Sperber, and E.R. Murrow of the Emergency Committee, 1934, Ratner Center, 3B/2/15. The Rockefeller Foundation only provided money for Lewy, who received $2000 for his semester, while Sperber received $2000 for the year. See also Board of Directors minutes, JTS, 25 April 1934 and report of Adler to 21 November 1934 board meeting, p. 9. At first Sperber taught at JTS and Dropsie.

12. Adler continued to assist Lewy after he left the Seminary; see Adler to Julian Morgenstern, president of the Hebrew Union College, 31 January 1935, in *Cyrus Adler, Selected Letters,* vol. 2, pp. 289–90. Lewy ultimately became a professor at the Hebrew University.

13. See correspondence between Adler and the Emergency Committee and with Sperber, Ratner Center, 3B/2/14 and 3B/2/15. Apparently the Seminary was supposed to regularize Sperber first in 1936, then in 1937, but deficit problems forced it to request a third and fourth year of support from the Emergency Committee.

14. Sperber to Adler, 12 September 1934; to Joseph Abrahams, August 1937, Ratner Center, 3B/2/15; and Sperber to Abrahams, October 1940, indicating that he would move out of his room (216) by 15 October 1940, 3B/2/14. A letter of the summer of 1945, however, indicates that Sperber was still living in the Seminary dormitory, 1C/54/1.

15. Kisch to Adler, 14 December 1933; Adler to Kisch, 20 December 1933, Ratner Center, 1A/15/5.

16. Adler to Paul Baerwald, 25 April 1934, Ratner Center, 1A/15/5. Edward Baerwald, a Frankfurt attorney and brother of the Joint Distribution Committee head Paul Baerwald, had written to Adler, 3 April 1934, on Kisch's behalf.

17. Adler to Dr. Alfred Cohn, Rockefeller Institute, 27 February 1936, Ratner Center, 1A/15/5. Kisch arrived in America in January 1935. Kisch to Adler, 3 February 1935, 1A/15/5.

18. Finkelstein to Baron, 6 January 1935 (*sic*, 1936), Ratner Center, 1A/15/5; Finkelstein to Adler, 4 February 1936, 1A/14/21. There were a few people at the academy who did not want to continue the fellowship. Finkelstein was so angry with these people that he thought "it the duty of every right-thinking person to resign and to organize a new Academy" if the academy did not help Kisch. Letter of Finkelstein to Rabbi Leo Jung, 10 February 1936, 1A/14/21.

19. See correspondence of 1936 and 1937 in Ratner Center, 1A/15/5. Finkelstein to Marx, 20 February 1946, 1C/50/53, indicates that in 1946 Kisch was still on an academy fellowship.

20. Ratner Center, 1A/18/42 and 3B/1/9. Wise and Morgenstern did try to get Elbogen to teach, but Adler remained adamant that Elbogen should be free of all obligations. Adler's opinion of Elbogen in his proposal to the JTS board meeting, 20 December 1937, 3B/1/9. See also Adler to Felix Warburg, 24 June 1937, in *Cyrus Adler, Selected Letters*, vol. 2, pp. 331–32. After Elbogen died in 1943 the four institutions paid his widow a pension, 1B/42/15, 1C/49/13.

21. Adler to Herbert Loewe, 13 July 1938, Ratner Center, 1A/15/64, and Finkelstein to Loewe, 7 July 1938, 1A/16/94. See also Adler to Simon Greenberg, 29 July 1938, 1A/19/17. JTS provided Loewe, who was raising money for Krauss, with $50 a year. Apparently Adler also personally provided some assistance to Professor Kaminka of Vienna who had fled to Tel Aviv. Adler to Greenberg, cited above.

22. Finkelstein to Razovsky, 10 March 1938, Ratner Center, 1A/19/20.

23. Ratner Center, 1A/23/35. Both Stephen Wise, head of Jewish Institute of Religion and the American Jewish Congress, and Kurt Blumenfeld, of the Jewish National Fund in Jerusalem, had urged Finkelstein to act in this matter. See also Adler to Cordell Hull, 2 February 1940, in *Cyrus Adler, Selected Letters*, vol. 2, pp. 374–75.

24. Hilberg, vol. 1, pp. 81–144; Schleunes, pp. 133–254.

25. See, for example, letter of British Chief Rabbi Joseph Hertz (a JTS graduate) to Adler, 28 June 1938, Ratner Center, 1A/9/62 or letter of Max Warburg to Adler, 14 October 1938, 1A/28/6. See also correspondence on Dr. Max Köhler, 1A/15/30.

26. Adler to Rabbi Joseph Hertz, 29 July 1938, Ratner Center, 1A/9/62.

27. See correspondence in Ratner Center, 1A/28/6. It is not clear if Weiss ever came to America. The State Department gave him visa problems in England in April 1939, and there is no further record of Weiss in the Seminary archives.

28. Adler to Greenberg, 29 July 1938, Ratner Center, 1A/19/17.

29. Greenberg to Adler, 7 August 1938; Greenberg to Finkelstein, 25 August 1938, Ratner Center, 1A/9/62.

30. Adler to William Rosenwald of the National Coordinating Committee, 2 November 1938, and minutes of special committee meeting, Ratner Center, 1A/19/17. One copy of the minutes indicates that the meeting took place on 24 October, but another copy indicates 13 October.

31. Adler's recommendation for Burnstein, 10 November 1938, and Burnstein-Adler correspondence, November and December 1938, Ratner Center, 1A/19/17.

32. Adler to Burnstein, 12 January 1939, Ratner Center, 1A/19/17.

33. Burnstein to Adler, 25 November 1938, Ratner Center, 1A/19/17.

34. See Burnstein-Adler 1939 correspondence, Ratner Center, 1A/19/18. On 1 May 1939, Burnstein told Adler he had already placed thirty-three rabbis, including Rabbi Emil Schorsch of Hanover, the father of the present Chancellor of JTS.

35. See, for example, list of forwarded requests of 29 November 1938, Ratner Center, 1A/19/17. See also Finkelstein to Burnstein, 21 October 1940, 1A/4/17; Abrahams to Alfred Kober, 13 June 1939 and Finkelstein to Kober, 24 April 1939, 1A/15/27; Finkelstein to Walter Strauss, 31 March 1942, 1A/25/39; and correspondence with Dr. Max Köhler in 1A/15/30.

36. Adler to May, 15 August 1938; Adler to Edith Taglicht, 14 December 1938, Ratner Center, 1A/19/17. See other letters of Adler, 1A/19/18.

37. Ratner Center, 1A/19/17. Abrahams wrote more or less the same letter to several other rabbis, including Rabbi Samuel Glueck of Hungary, on 12 April 1939. Sometimes, he was less curt, replying to rabbis: "I deeply regret that there is nothing we can do for you at the Seminary." See his letters, 1A/19/18.

38. Finkelstein to Finkelscherer, 17 May 1939, Ratner Center, 1A/19/18. Finkelstein was equally curt to Max Warburg, who, in April 1940 had asked Finkelstein to help Rabbi Paul Holzer from Hamburg, then in England. Finkelstein wrote to Warburg: "Much to my regret, I know of no way in which I myself can be of use in this instance." See Max Warburg to Finkelstein, 16 April 1940, and Finkelstein to Warburg, 19 April 1940, 1A/27/46.

39. See correspondence, Ratner Center, 1A/19/18; Finkelstein to Rabbi David Goldstein, 31 March 1939, 1A/9/29; Finkelstein to Rabbi Herman Rubenovitz, 8 January 1940, 1A/23/6.

40. See, for example, Finkelstein's letters on behalf of Dr. Alfred Kober, 24 January 1940, Ratner Center, 1A/15/27; or on behalf of Rabbi Ira Sud, 13 and 14 December 1939, 1A/26/1.

41. See correspondence between Finkelstein and Bach, Ratner Center, 1A/2/41, and Finkelstein to Mrs. Warburg, 19 October 1939, 1A/27/43 and 22 April 1940, 1A/27/44.

42. *JTSA Register*, 1940-41, p. 18; Adler's report to Board of Director's meeting, 25 April 1939, in JTS Archives, Board of Directors minutes, JTS, 1933-41; Finkelstein's report to Board of Directors meeting, 25 October 1939, Ratner Center, 2/2/3; supplement to the President's report, 1940, 1/2/3. See also auditor's report, 30 January 1941, 1A/19/19.

43. Finkelstein to speech professor A. B. Williamson, 10 July 1939, Ratner Center, 1A/28/19; Finkelstein to Dr. Israel Goldstein, 1A/9/30; Finkelstein to Mrs. Warburg, 8 August 1939, 1A/27/43.

44. See correspondence in 1940, 1941, and 1943 between the Committee for Refugee Education and the Seminary, Ratner Center, 1A/5/39. Not all the people who took these English classes were rabbis. One thank you note to the Seminary (1A/22/15) signed by eleven students reveals that at least four of the members of one class were women!

45. Correspondence on Gruenewald in 1943 and 1944, Ratner Center, 1B/34/19; Finkelstein to Baron, 15 November 1943, 1B/30/20; Finkelstein to Frieda Schiff Warburg, 13 September 1943, 1B/41/37; and 1946 correspondence, 1C/48/17; quotation in Finkelstein to Gruenewald, 5 March 1946, 1C/48/17. At Ingrid Warburg's request, the Seminary also provided a dorm room for a few months to Rabbi Ernst Jacob from Augsburg. See Ingrid Warburg to Finkelstein, 3 October 1938; Finkelstein to Warburg, 14 October 1938, Ratner Center, 1A/27/46.

46. Ratner Center, 3A/1, faculty minutes 1935-36, pp. 60, 99; faculty minutes 1937-38, pp. 8, 23, 48-52, 54-55, 60-61, 77; faculty minutes 1938-39, pp. 21, 25, 28, 38.

47. Ratner Center, 3A/1, faculty minutes 1937-38, p. 52.

48. Ratner Center, 3A/1, faculty minutes 1937-38, p. 77; faculty minutes 1938-39, pp. 25, 38. One student it did not admit was Emil Fackenheim. See Finkelstein to Rabbi Jonah Wise, 7 September 1938, 1A/28/22.

49. Report of Adler to board, 2 May 1939, JTS Archives, Board of Directors minutes, JTS, 1933-41.

50. Finkelstein inquired about the policies of the other rabbinical schools, and they responded. See Finkelstein to Stephen Wise, Jewish Institute of Religion, 10 June 1938, and response of Gertrude Adelstein, secretary, 21 June 1938, Ratner Center, 1A/12/92; Finkelstein to Julius Morgenstern, Hebrew Union College, 10 June 1938, and Morgenstern to Finkelstein, 15 June 1938, 1A/18/42.

51. Finkelstein to Elbogen, 19 April 1938, Ratner Center, 3B/1/9.

52. Finkelstein to Elbogen, 12 May 1938, Ratner Center, 3B/1/9.

53. Treasurer's report for 2 May 1938 meeting, JTS Archives, Board of Directors minutes, JTS, 1933–41.

54. Finkelstein to Elbogen, 20 January 1939, Ratner Center, 3B/1/9.

55. Ratner Center, 1A/24/46.

56. See correspondence, Ratner Center, 1A/8/48; Finkelstein to Alexander Marx, 27 October 1938, 3B/2/6; correspondence between Finkelstein and Sperber, 3B/2/14; library report, 2 May 1938 board meeting, JTS Archives, Board of Directors minutes, JTS, 1933–41.

57. Finkelstein to Mrs. Warburg, 2 May 1941, Ratner Center, 1A/8/48; Finkelstein to Mrs. Warburg, 1 May 1941, 1A/27/44.

58. See Ratner Center, 1A/25/15.

59. Ratner Center, 1A/15/88.

60. Ratner Center, 1A/2/17.

61. Arndt to Finkelstein, 17 December 1940; Finkelstein to Arndt, 20 January 1941; Burnstein to Finkelstein, 7 February 1941; Finkelstein to Burnstein, 10 February 1941; Finkelstein to Arndt, 10 March 1941, Ratner Center, 1A/2/17. A year later (7 May 1942), Burnstein coldly informed Finkelstein that he had found Arndt a job with the Spanish-Portugese synagogue in Montreal, 1A/2/17.

62. Ratner Center, 3A/1, faculty minutes 1938–39, pp. 42–43.

63. Ratner Center, 3A/2, faculty minutes, 1940–41, pp. 2, 16–17.

64. Finkelstein later warmly recommended him for a rabbinical position. See letter to Rabbi Jacob Kohn, Ratner Center, 1B/36/5.

65. Abrahams to Hebrew Immigrant Aid Society, 7 April 1939, Ratner Center, 1A/10/94; Finkelstein to Hermann Vogelstein, 30 January 1940, 1A/27/26; Finkelstein to Alex Scharfstein, 5 December 1938 in 1A/19/20. See also correspondence, 1A/19/19 and 1A/19/20.

66. Adler to Cecilia Razofsky, National Refugee Service, 30 January 1939, Ratner Center, 1A/19/19; Adler to Razofsky, 29 October 1935, 1A/19/20.

67. Ratner Center, 1A/4/24.

68. Ratner Center, 1A/9/49. It is possible that Henry Graetz and his sister are descendants of the Jewish historian Heinrich Graetz since they came from Breslau.

69. On behalf of Strauss, see affidavit and correspondence in Ratner Center, 1A/8/38; on the Nathans, see 1A/18/72. Max Nathan was the nephew of a friend of Finkelstein's.

70. Ratner Center, 1A/3/24; see also Finkelstein to Norman Bentwich, 16 February 1943, 1B/30/26.

71. Finkelstein to Charles Beth, 3 November 1941, and other correspondence, October and November 1941, Ratner Center, 1A/13/26. For another example, see Finkelstein to J. Brettholz, 12 February 1940, 1A/15/30.

72. See, for example, Finkelstein to Leo Finkelstein (no relation), 13 April 1939, Ratner Center, 1A/8/4.

73. Ratner Center, 1A/23/21.

74. Sperber to Finkelstein, 3 February 1941, 23 February 1942, 8 May 1942, Ratner Center, 3B/2/17.

75. Ratner Center, 1A/19/19. In 1943 the Seminary was still providing High Holy Day seats to some refugees, 1B/41/2.

76. Ratner Center, 1A/6/37; statement of Alexander Marx on the library and museum (20 October 1939) to 25 October 1939 Board of Directors meeting in 2/2/3 and Board of Directors minutes, JTS, 1933–41. See also 11C/24/40. The collection was open to the public only on Monday afternoons, by appointment. In September 1944 the Seminary arranged a public display at Scribner's bookstore., 11C/25/2.

77. Marx statement to Board of Directors meeting, 25 October 1939, JTS Archives, Board of Directors minutes, JTS, 1933–41.

78. Ibid.

79. See correspondence between Finkelstein and Elbogen on the issue of books in 1939, Ratner Center, 1A/7/29.

80. Ratner Center, 1A/18/33. For statement, see 1A/12/7. See also Finkelstein's concern in his letter to Rabbi A. Kalmanowitz of the Mirer Yeshiva, Brooklyn, 26 September 1940, 1A/14/37.

81. Finkelstein to Hadas, Ratner Center, 1A/10/30.

82. See correspondence with Natalia Ashkenazi of the Polish Embassy, Ratner Center, 1A/2/23.

83. On American Jewry generally, see David Wyman, *The Abandonment of the Jews: America and the Holocaust, 1941–1945* (New York: Pantheon Books, 1984), and Henry Feingold, *The Politics of Rescue: The Roosevelt Administration and the Holocaust, 1933–1945* (New Brunswick, N.J.: Rutgers University Press, 1970).

84. Finkelstein to Meyers, 8 August 1940, Ratner Center, 1A/18/18. See also Finkelstein's report to the 5 June 1940 board meeting, JTS Archives, Board of Directors minutes, JTS, 1933–41.

85. This lecture was printed as the "Jewish Viewpoint" in a book, *Faith for Today,* published by Doubleday, Doran in 1941. 1A/26/30, Ratner Center.

86. Finkelstein to Stroock, 4 December 1940, Ratner Center, 1A/25/40.

87. Finkelstein to Proskauer, 20 October 1943, Ratner Center, 1B/38/60.

88. Ratner Center, 1B/31/58, 1B/32/5, 1B/32/7, 1B/35/19.

89. JTS Archives, Board of Directors minutes, JTS, 1933–41, Finkelstein's report to the board, 29 October 1940. See also his report on 5 June 1940.

90. JTS Archives, Board of Directors minutes, JTS, 1933–41, Finkelstein's report to board, 6 April 1941. See also preliminary draft in Ratner Center, 1A/21/37. Similar sentiments about the responsibility of American Jewry were voiced by Seminary administrator and Rabbinical Assembly president Max Arzt in his presidential address, June 1940. See *Proceedings of the Rabbinical Assembly* 7, (1940): pp. 71–80.

91. Ratner Center, 1A/21/37.

92. See essay by Fred Beuttler in these volumes.

93. See Finkelstein to board member Sol Stroock, 12 July 1939 Ratner Center, 1A/25/47.

94. Mimeographed report on the Institute, n.d., in Ratner Center, 1B/35/8; pamphlet describing JTS, 1940s, 11C/50/31. See also Finkelstein to Arthur Hays Sulzberger, 24 June 1942, 1A/26/2. The Institute was later renamed the Institute for Religious and Social Studies.

95. Draft of letter, 17 August 1944, to be sent by board member Alan Stroock but written by Finkelstein, Ratner Center, 1B/40/38.

96. Finkelstein correspondence with Littauer, 1943, Ratner Center, 1B/36/48; with Frieda Schiff Warburg and the Warburg Foundation, 1943 and 1944, 1B/41/35 and 1B/41/37, and 1946, 1C/55/16; with Paul Baerwald of the New York Foundation, 1946, 1C/51/36. Sulzberger was honorary chair of this foundation and helped arrange the grant. See Finkelstein to Sulzberger, 12 January 1945, 1C/54/21. The foundation gave the Institute $10,000 in 1943. Finkelstein to Littauer, 24 March 1943, 1B/36/48.

97. Ratner Center, 1B/35/8.

98. Ratner Center, 1B/41/35.

99. Oppenheimer to Arzt, n.d., but probably in 1943 or 1944, Ratner Center, 1B/38/23.

100. Finkelstein to Sulzberger, 12 February 1945, Ratner Center, 1C/54/20.

101. See Bickerman's report, June 1944, Ratner Center, 1C/44/2.

102. Finkelstein to Judge Proskauer, 19 March 1943, Ratner Center, 1B/38/60; Finkelstein to Alan Stroock, 8 October 1943, 1B/40/38; and correspondence, 1B/41/4. The volumes, *The Jews: Their History; The Jews: Their Religion and Culture*; and *The Jews: Their Role in Civilization*, were published in 1949 by Harper and Row.

103. See Finkelstein to Eli Ginzberg, son of faculty member Louis Ginzberg, 30 April 1945, Ratner Center, 1C/47/48.

104. Finkelstein to Niles Trammell, NBC, 11 February 1944, Ratner Center, 1A/26/33; Finkelstein to Rabbi Jessurun Cardoza, 12 September 1944, 1B/31/28; material in 1B/32/49; Finkelstein's remarks at *The Eternal Light* luncheon, 1 October 1945, in 1C/46/48.

105. Press release, 10 May 1946, Ratner Center, 1C/46/46.

106. Ratner Center, 1A/18/71.

107. Ratner Center, 1C/53/65.

108. Ratner Center, 1B/40/38. The Seminary probably printed this address (see Finkelstein to Stroock, asking for corrections, 4 December 1944). Robert Gordis's commencement address on 15 September 1946, 11C/52/18, also emphasized the need for a strong Judaism.

109. See, for example, Finkelstein to Max Gottschalk, 1 June 1943, Ratner Center, 1B/34/6, in which he tells Gottschalk, in a totally non-ironic tone, to talk to someone who has recently arrived from Poland about the folk religious customs of the Jews there. Gottschalk was equally guilty of disbelief, because he had inquired in the first place on behalf of the American Jewish Committee.

110. See, for example, JTS resolution, on the fifth anniversary of receiving the Danzig Collection (1944), Ratner Center, 1B/35/19.

111. See Finkelstein's speech to Inter-Seminary Conference, 22 February 1943, in newsletter, *The Challenge*, Ratner Center, 1A/12/34.

112. He did not respond, for example, to circular letters from Rabbi Jonah Wise, an activist for the Joint Distribution Committee, of 29 October 1943 and 12 January 1944, Ratner Center, 1B/42/14. He never responded to the American Federation of Polish Jews, on whose board he sat, about its publication, *The Black Book of Polish Jewry*, 1A/1/38 and 1B/29/20. His lack of response to appeals for help from various Jewish organizations can be seen in 1A/1/1, 1A/2/3, and elsewhere in the archives.

113. In order to ascertain student attitudes and behavior during these years, I wrote to all graduates of the Rabbinical School between 1935 and 1948 who are still alive, approximately one hundred people. I received responses from twenty-three of them. In addition, I interviewed eight graduates as well as Sylvia Ettenberg, a former administrator. On the issue of knowledge, letters to the author by Rabbi Stanley Rabinowitz, 9 November 1994; Rabbi Norman Shapiro, 6 November 1994; Rabbi Morris Fishman, 20 November 1994; and Rabbi Lewis Weintraub, interview by author, 15 November 1994. On information on the Holocaust available to the public see Deborah Lipstadt, *Beyond Belief: The American Press and the Coming of the Holocaust, 1933–1945* (New York: Free Press, 1986).

114. Some graduates, for example, Jacob Milgrom (letter to the author, 6 November 1994, and interview by author, 17 November 1994) and Max Ticktin (interview by author, 22 November 1994), insist that despite reports, most students did not really know about mass murder until after the war. See also Rabbi Allan Langner, 4 November 1994; Rabbi Jack Cohen, 15 November 1994; and Rabbi David Lieber, 6 January 1995, letters to the author.

115. Letter to author, 10 November 1994.

116. Rabbi Stanley Rabinowitz, 31 October 1994 and 9 November 1994, letters to the author, and interview by author, 15 November 1994; Rabbi Simon Glustrom, letter to the author, 6 November 1994; Rabbi Baruch Silverstein, letter to the author, 7 November 1994; Rabbi Lewis Weintraub, interview by author, 15 November 1994. On the Madison Square Gar-

den rallies, see David Wyman, *The Abandonment of the Jews*, pp. 24–25, 87–92.

117. Noah Golinkin, interview by author, 29 November 1994. Some material on the activities of this committee is also in the Ratner Center Archives (see below).

118. Noah Golinkin, interview.

119. Ratner Center, 1A/12/34. This file contains the program of the conference as well as several issues of a mimeographed newsletter, *The Challenge*, which reported on the conference.

120. Ratner Center, 1A/12/34. See also *Seminary Progress* 2, no. 3 (May 1943) in 1B/39/89.

121. "Retribution Is Not Enough," *The Reconstructionist* 9, no. 2 (5 March 1943), pp. 19–21. I would like to thank Rabbi Noah Golinkin for giving me a copy of this article.

122. "A Program of Action," 25 April 1943, Ratner Center, 1A/12/46.

123. Noah Golinkin, interview. Two of the prayers distributed by the Synagogue Council to all American synagogues were written by Golinkin himself. After one final letter of protest to Breckenridge Long, the European Committee became dormant.

124. See Rabbinical Assembly form letter to rabbis, 30 December 1942, Ratner Center, 1A/22/2.

125. See report in mimeographed newsletter, *Seminary Corner*, 1 May 1944, Ratner Center, 11C/52/15. On memorial services generally, Stanley Rabinowitz interview, 15 November 1994.

126. Interview by author, 22 November 1994.

127. Herman Grossman, letter to the author, n.d., [November 1994].

128. Letter to author, 6 November 1994. Such intensification was also noted by other graduates; for example, Rabbi Allan Langner, letter to author, 4 November 1994; Abraham Karp, Arthur Hertzberg, Jacob Milgrom, interviews by author, 17 November 1994; Max Ticktin, interview, 22 November 1994; Noah Golinkin, interview, 29 November 1994.

129. Letter to author, 31 October 1994; interview, 15 November 1994; Allan Langner, letter, 4 November 1994; Abraham Karp, interview, 17 November 1994.

130. Naomi W. Cohen, *American Jews and the Zionist Idea* (New York: Ktav, 1975), pp. 36–71; Wyman, *The Abandonment of the Jews*, pp. 157–177.

131. *Seminary Progress*, a glossy newsletter that reported on Seminary activities, almost never mentioned the Holocaust or actions on behalf of European Jewry in the 1940s. Most of the letters that I have received from former students attest to the fact that study continued uninterrupted. For example: Rabbi Saul Teplitz, letter to the author, 2 November 1994; Rabbi Simon Glustrom, letter to the author, 6 November 1994; Rabbi Jack Cohen, letter to the author, 15 November 1994; Max and Esther Ticktin, interview by author, 22 November 1994.

132. Abraham Karp, interview, 17 November 1994.

133. Finkelstein to Hendricks, 23 May 1940, and Hendricks to Finkelstein, 29 May 1940, Ratner Center, 1A/11/23.

134. Finkelstein to FDR, 10 December 1941, Ratner Center, 1A/22/38.

135. Finkelstein to Rabbi Herman Cohen, 22 February 1943, Ratner Center, 1B/31/50, and Finkelstein to Dr. Samuel Kohs, Jewish Welfare Board, 24 October 1943, 1B/35/21. Finkelstein was also cold to one person who inquired about conscientious objector status: Finkelstein to Herschel Zackheim, 28 January 1942, 1A/29/4.

136. Ratner Center, 1A/3/35, and Finkelstein to Rabbi de Sola Pool, 12 June 1942, 1A/21/25.

137. Arzt form letter to Seminary benefactors, 17 March 1944, Ratner Center, 1B/33/13. See also Finkelstein to Milton Steinberg, 15 July 1943, 1A/25/19; Finkelstein's correspondence with Jewish Welfare Board, summer and fall 1944, 1B/35/2.

138. See, for example, complaint of Meir Engel to Max Arzt, 20 December 1944, Ratner Center, 1B/32/45; Chaplain Edward Sandrow to Finkelstein, February 14, 1944, 1B/39/48;

Judah Nadich to Finkelstein, 28 March 1944, 1B/37/40. The Jewish Welfare Board, which distributed the pamphlets, complained that the one Finkelstein had written was inappropriate. Letter of Finkelstein to JWB, 29 September 1944, 1B/35/21.

139. See Morris Kertzer's pamphlet, *A Faith to Live By,* Ratner Center, 1B/35/50.

140. Finkelstein to Rabbi Elias Charry, 18 February 1943, 6 April 1943, Ratner Center, 1B/31/37; Finkelstein to Louis Kraft, Jewish Welfare Board, 6 April 1943, 1B/35/21.

141. See correspondence in Ratner Center, 1A/13/20, 1B/33/48, 1B/35/21, 1B/41/12; Finkelstein to Mrs. Warburg, 28 March 1945, 1C/55/15; Finkelstein to Alexander Marx, 2 September 1943, 3B/2/8; Finkelstein to Marx, 20 July 1942, 3B/2/9. The Seminary did not hold its usual public seder during the war because of rationing.

142. See copies of this special *get* in Ratner Center, 1A/22/2.

143. For examples of Finkelstein's individual letters to faculty members on 21 July 1942, see Finkelstein to Hillel Bavli, Ratner Center, 1A/2/60; to Mordecai Kaplan, 1A/14/62; to Max Arzt, 3B/1/1; to Alexander Marx, 3B/2/9.

144. Faculty meeting 22 September 1942, Ratner Center, 3A/2; faculty meetings 1942–43, pp. 8–9. The early graduates had to remain "under the practical guidance" of the Seminary for the rest of the year. The board approved the plan at its 29 September 1942 meeting, JTS Archives, Board of Directors minutes, JTS, 1942–44.

145. Faculty meeting 11 February 1943 and 17 March 1943, Ratner Center, 3A/2, faculty meetings 1942–43, pp. 59–60 and 88. See also Board of Directors minutes, meeting, 23 February 1943, 2/1/9.

146. Finkelstein to Dr. Samuel Feinstein, 6 April 1943, Ratner Center, 1B/32/52. Interestingly, the Seminary did not want members of its own staff to enter the chaplaincy and, deeming them indispensable, pleaded with the Chaplaincy Availability Committee to exempt them. See correspondence in 1B/31/34 and discussion at 19 May 1943 and 4 July 1943 faculty meetings, 3A/2, faculty meetings, 1942–43.

147. Finkelstein to Hillel Bavli, 15 September 1943, Ratner Center, 1B/30/21; Max Arzt to Judah Nadich, 26 August 1943, 1B/37/40; Nathan Nichols to Max Arzt, 14 February 1944, 1B/38/12.

148. Finkelstein to Rabbi David de Sola Pool, 14 October 1942, Ratner Center, 1A/21/24.

149. Finkelstein to Rabbi Philip Bernstein, 19 March 1943, Ratner Center, 1B/35/21. At that point, of 129 Jewish chaplains, seventy-two were Reform, twenty-seven Orthodox, and thirty Conservative. JWB report in same file.

150. Max Arzt reported to Nathan Levitsky, 28 March 1944, Ratner Center, 1B/36/35, that there were seventy-eight JTS graduates in the armed forces of whom three served in Canada. As of 26 June 1944, eighty-seven Rabbinical Assembly members served in the armed forces, 1B/38/71. By March 1945, ninety-five JTS alumni served as chaplains. See JTS Archives, Board meeting minutes, 1 March 1945, JTS, 1944–46. On Canadian chaplains see correspondence, Ratner Center, 1B/29/14, 1B/30/18, and 1B/31/26.

151. Arzt to Major Myron Ball, 7 January 1944, Ratner Center, 1B/30/17.

152. Arzt to Ribner, 24 October 1943, Ratner Center, 1B/39/7.

153. Kazis to Finkelstein, 15 November 1943, 31 January 1944; Finkelstein to Kazis, 17 November 1943, 16 February 1944; Kazis to Max Arzt, 27 April 1944, Ratner Center, 1B/35/46.

154. See, for example, correspondence between Rabbi Isaac Klein and Finkelstein, Ratner Center, 1B/36/1. After the war as well, Conservative rabbis focused on the needs of American Jews and not on the destruction. There was almost no mention of the destruction of European Jewry at the Rabbinical Assembly conventions in 1945 and 1946. See *Proceedings of the Rabbinical Assembly of America,* volume 9 (1945) and volume 10 (1946).

155. Kazis to Finkelstein, 10 October 1944, Ratner Center, 1B/35/46. See also correspondence between Judah Nadich and Finkelstein, 1B/37/40.

156. Reports and newsletters, Ratner Center, 1B/41/41 and 1C/55/18. Max Arzt and Simon Greenberg represented the Seminary on this commission. See also *Proceedings of the Rabbinical Assembly of America* 9 (1945): p. 13.

157. See reports and programs of these conferences, Ratner Center, 1B/32/1, 1B/35/8. See also Max Routtenberg to Finkelstein, 3 August 1944, in 1B/39/29.

158. "American Judaism Faces the Future," preliminary draft, 20 June 1944, Ratner Center, 1B/35/19. See also Robert Gordis, "The Tasks Before Us" *Conservative Judaism* 1, no. 1 (January 1945): pp. 1–8.

159. Resolutions, 17 April 1945, JTS Archives, Board of Directors minutes, JTS, 1944–46.

160. Copies of this statement can be found in Ratner Center, 1A/7/50, 1C/47/6, 1C/47/28, and 1C/49/22. The document is undated, but internal evidence necessitates a post-V-E Day date, probably in 1945. The copies read "Confidential, Not for Publication or Distribution," and so it is not clear if this statement was ever made public.

161. Finkelstein expressed his concern with exactly these issues in a letter he wrote on 23 August 1945 to Louis Ginzberg, Ratner Center, 1C/47/49. It may be that the faculty prepared the statement at Finkelstein's behest.

162. Finkelstein to Joseph Hyman, 8 May 1945, Ratner Center, 1C/48/65a.

163. Correspondence between Finkelstein and Congressman Sol Bloom, whose help was enlisted in getting the necessary permits, Ratner Center, 1A/44/9. Only Gordis ended up traveling to Europe.

164. Such assistance is well known, although not much direct evidence of it exists in the JTS Archives. Judge Simon Rifkind, advisor on Jewish Affairs to the European Theater Commander, wrote to Finkelstein 8 December 1945, 1C/53/2, thanking God for the work of the chaplains on behalf of the survivors.

165. Interim report, Finkelstein to Board of Directors, 19 April 1946, Ratner Center, 1C/44/12; circular letter of Finkelstein, 7 May 1946, 1C/45/17; Finkelstein to Emanuel Neumann, 27 May 1946, 1C/51/28.

166. See letters of 29 August 1946 from Finkelstein to Gertrude Lichtensternova in Marianska Lazne, Ratner Center, 1C/50/23; to Abraham Brandstein, Liberec, 1C/44/22; to Rudolf Schreiber, Ceska Lipa, 1C/53/36; to Karel Stein, Prague, 1C/54/4; and to Dr. Karol Zimmer, Karlovy Vary, 1C/55/47a. Finkelstein also sent the same material to Bernhardt Braver, Vienna 1C/44/22. Why the Seminary focused on Czechoslovakia is not at all clear.

167. Max Arzt, for example, devoted considerable energy to try to get a relative of his to come to America from Poland. See his letters on the subject in Ratner Center, 1B/37/50, 1C/44/9, 1C/49/58, 1C/54/11, 1C/55/47a. Finkelstein was involved in assisting a relative of Saul Lieberman's, 1C/43/14 and 1C/53/40a and his own cousin, 1C/43/14. Jessica Feingold also helped some people find relatives. See 1C/46/38, 1C/49/49.

168. Finkelstein, 11 August 1945, Ratner Center, 1C/51/67; Benno Liegner to Finkelstein, 13 August 1945, 1C/50/23; Rudolf Callmann to Finkelstein, 17 August 1945, and Finkelstein to Callman, 27 August 1945, 1C/44/37; M. Novella to the *New York Times*, 2 September 1945, 1C/51/45; Herbert Seeliger to Finkelstein, 14 September 1945, 1C/53/42; Finkelstein to Arthur Hays Sulzberger, 1 October 1945, 1C/54/20. On Finkelstein's general concern for the situation of Germans see Finkelstein to Samuel Rosenman, 1 May 1945, 1C/53/15, and his correspondence with Prince Huburtus zu Löwenstein, 1C/50/32. Naturally Prince Huburtus, an anti-Nazi who had spent the war years in America, liked Finkelstein's letter.

169. Appeal from Budapest, Ratner Center, 1C/44/32 and 1C/50/32; Finkelstein's efforts with the Joint Distribution Committee and his correspondence with Budapest in 1945 and 1946, 1C/43/14, 1C/49/37, and 1C/50/32.

170. See correspondence between Finkelstein and Major Sholom Pomrenze, spring and sum-

mer 1946, Ratner Center, 1C/52/4.

171. Finkelstein to Maurice Liber, 3 June 1946, Ratner Center, 1C/50/23.

172. Finkelstein to Eli Ginzberg, 14 August 1945, Ratner Center, 1C/47/48; Finkelstein to Chaplain Abraham Horvitz, 1 June 1945, 1C/48/57.

173. Finkelstein-Marx correspondence, May 1946, Ratner Center, 1C/50/53; Marx to Joel Geffen, 8 May 1945, ibid.; Finkelstein to Juliette Stern, 22 May 1946, 1C/54/4; Finkelstein to Abraham Horvitz, 1 June 1945, 1C/48/57.

174. Finkelstein to Julius Morgenstern, 3 October 1946, Ratner Center, 1C/48/39.

175. Finkelstein to Kaplan, 10 January 1945, Ratner Center, 1C/49/41; Finkelstein to Meiss, 10 January 1945, 1C/50/61. In October 1944, at Alexander Sperber's suggestion, the Seminary had honored Professor Paul Kahle, a non-Jewish Bible scholar from Bonn, in exile in England because he opposed the Nazi regime's anti-Jewish policy in the 1930s. See 1B/35/33 and Sperber to Finkelstein,16 June 1944, 1B/40/23.

176. Finkelstein to Baeck, 26 December 1945, Ratner Center, 1C/43/36.

177. Remarks at convocation for Leo Baeck, 6 January 1946, Ratner Center, 1C/47/28.

178. Jacob Milgrom, interview, 17 November 1994.

179. Letter to author, 2 November 1994.

180. Letter to author, 7 November 1994.

JULIE MILLER &
RICHARD I. COHEN

A Collision of Cultures:

The Jewish Museum and the Jewish Theological Seminary, 1904-1971

Opening of the Robert Rauschenberg retrospective at the Jewish Museum, 29 March 1963.
Photo by Hans Namuth. © Hans Namuth Estate.
Center For Creative Photography, University of Arizona.

JULIE MILLER & RICHARD I. COHEN

A Collision of Cultures:

The Jewish Museum and the Jewish Theological Seminary, 1904-1971[1]

DURING THE NINETEEN SIXTIES the Jewish Museum came to be known as the foremost showplace for contemporary art among New York's museums. For many in the city's art world, the sixties were the museum's "heyday."[2] Under the leadership of Alan Solomon, its dynamic young director, the museum mounted influential exhibits of the work of Robert Rauschenberg (1963) and Jasper Johns (1964). "Primary Structures" (1966) organized by curator Kynaston McShine during the tenure of Solomon's successor, Sam Hunter, was "the first comprehensive showing" of Minimalist art.[3]

Recognizing the Jewish Museum's primacy in the field of contemporary art, the U.S. Information Agency asked Alan Solomon, in his role as director of the Jewish Museum, to serve as the commissioner of the United States' exhibit at the 1964 Venice Biennale, the international exhibition of art.[4] Solomon brought the work of eight contemporary painters: Morris Louis, Kenneth Noland, Robert Rauschenberg, Jasper Johns, John Chamberlain, Claes Oldenberg, Jim Dine, and Frank Stella to Venice. Some of them had already exhibited at the Jewish Museum; others would later on. When Robert Rauschenberg won the Biennale's international prize for painting, the first American ever to do so, it seemed as if the Jewish Museum had reached the highest pinnacle of international regard a museum could reach.

Yet not everyone was pleased with the museum's new focus on contemporary art. One visitor to the 1963 Rauschenberg show complained to the director:

> Yesterday a dear friend of mine from Boston and I made a special effort to come to the museum. Naturally we look to the museum as a repository of the finest examples of art—Jewish art—and what did we find? An assortment of the most repulsive and nauseating modern (?) art ever collected in one place. And to learn that some of the creators of this exhibition of bad taste are not even Jewish was the crowning insult to our intelligence.[5]

Administrators at the Jewish Theological Seminary of America, the Jewish Museum's parent institution, were similarly discomfited by the art they saw at the museum. How, they wondered, did the Jewish Museum's contemporary art program express the values of the Jewish Theological Seminary? The Jewish Museum, officially described as being "under the auspices" of the Seminary, remained, after all, a Seminary department along with the Rabbinical School and training schools for cantors and Jewish teachers. And just how had the Jewish Museum, once a modest Museum of Jewish Ceremonial Objects housed in the Seminary's library, managed to stray so far from its parent?

Strain between the museum and the Seminary over these issues came to a head in the 1960s, resulting in the abolition of the contemporary art program at the museum in 1971. But confusion and discomfort about the museum on the part of the Seminary did not materialize for the first time in the sixties; it already had a history decades old by the time Alan Solomon took over as director in 1962.

The Earliest Years (1904-1931)

In 1904 Mayer Sulzberger, the Philadelphia judge and Jewish book collector, presented the Seminary with about 7,500 Hebrew and Jewish books and 750 manuscripts. These formed the foundation of the Seminary's library.[6] Librarian Alexander Marx (1878-1953), then a young historian freshly arrived from Germany and the tutelage of eminent Jewish bibliographer Moritz Steinschneider, made it his life's work to build on Sulzberger's gift. Marx devoted half a century of labor to the Seminary library. At his death, it had become one of the foremost Judaica libraries in the world.

Sulzberger's gift included more than books and manuscripts; it also contained a small addendum of Jewish ceremonial objects. In the letter formally presenting his gift Sulzberger wrote Marx: "I have added thereto a number of objects used in the various rites and ceremonies, to serve as a suggestion for the establishment of a Jewish museum in connection with the library."[7] But despite Sulzberger's wish, the museum remained little more than a suggestion for years afterward. A photograph of the library's reading room on the top floor of the Seminary's building on West 123rd Street shows a single exhibit case standing disregarded behind a table where Dr. Marx and a group of students are seated.[8]

The Jewish Museum's difficulty in establishing itself was not unique; European Jewish museums faced similar problems. Inspired by the late 19th-century movement to establish museums in major European cities, Jews, and even some who were not Jewish, recognized the need to collect and preserve the art and artifacts of Jewish life. Jewish museums were established in Vienna, Prague, Frankfurt, Danzig, and other cities during the late 19th and early 20th centuries, yet their beginnings were often tenuous. Sometimes their collections consisted of objects rescued from

313

*A Collision
of Cultures:
The Jewish
Museum and
the Jewish
Theological
Seminary*

Library reading
room in the Semi-
nary's former
building on West
123rd Street, early
1920s. One
exhibit case is
placed in front of
the fireplace.
*Photo by Peyser
and Patzig Indus-
trial Photogra-
phers. Library,
JTS.*

abandoned synagogues, once the main repositories for Jewish ritual art. The first
arrangements these new museums made to house and display their collections were
often makeshift, and even afterwards they encountered countless problems in
turning their fledgling collections into real museums. Once established, Jewish
museums needed the backing of philanthropists in order to survive. They also
needed to situate themselves in Jewish communities whose members were accultur-
ated enough to feel comfortable about putting their private ritual objects on public
display. Perhaps most important of all, Jews themselves had to be willing to accept
art as a legitimate mode of expression.[9]

New Jewish museums faced entrenched attitudes within Jewish society towards
art and its significance in Jewish life. "Jewish art" encountered skepticism, denial,
and outright debunking from members of rabbinic circles as well as educated
laypeople. Along with the prevalent belief that Jewish art was aesthetically well
below that produced by other nations were notions that Judaism and art were inim-
ical by nature, and that Jews themselves lacked artistic ability. Thus, conflicting
ideas about acculturation, art, and the nature of Judaism were at the heart of the
difficulties European Jewish museums faced as they struggled to establish themselves.

Solomon Schechter, President of the Seminary when Sulzberger made his donation, was among those who were unfriendly towards Jewish art. His attitude was
typical of many 19th-century exponents of *Wissenschaft des Judentums* in his tendency to hold the study of Jewish art and ritual objects in low esteem.[10] Even if he

had been enthusiastic about art, Schechter still had to devote most of his energy to running the recently reorganized Seminary.

Amid these concerns, and with a lack of interest in establishing a Jewish museum on Schechter's part, Jewish art and artifacts were not priorities at the early 20th-century Seminary as they rarely had been in Jewish life in other times and places.

At the inauguration of the West 123rd Street building in 1903, Sulzberger spoke eloquently, even passionately about his hopes for the library:

> The Bodleian Library at Oxford and the British Museum at London are, and perhaps will always remain, the most magnificent and complete Hebrew book museums in the world. But it is our business on this side of the Atlantic to hope and to work, undaunted by the magnitude of others' achievements; we should hold in view the purpose to make our collection as nearly complete as the resources of the world may render possible, and in so doing we should spare neither thought nor labor nor money.[11]

In dedicating himself as he did to the library, Marx took Sulzberger's words to heart. He also understood that his main responsibility was to build a collection of books, and only secondarily to gather a museum of objects. To the extent that the library carried out a museum function at all during these early years, it was truly as a "book museum." Exhibits staged by Marx in the West 123rd Street building reflected his own bibliographical and Jewish historical interests. His first, in 1905, was organized to celebrate the seven hundredth anniversary of the death of Moses Maimonides. Marx later recalled how: "The small number of rare books and Mss. by Maimonides then owned by the Library were arranged on a few small tables in the Lecture Hall of the old Seminary building."[12] Other exhibits organized by Marx similarly drew from the library's collections of books and manuscripts. "Biblical Manuscripts and Books" (1913); works of the Vilna Gaon displayed to celebrate his two hundredth birthday (1920); "Judaeo-Arabic and Judaeo-Persian Manuscripts" and "Hebrew Printing in Asia and Africa" (1924); "Illuminated and Beautifully Written Manuscripts" (1930), are some examples.[13]

The Museum of Jewish Ceremonial Objects (1931–1946)

In 1930, the Seminary moved around the corner to a new set of buildings at Broadway and West 122nd Street. The move was a significant step forward for the museum. It gained a room of its own on the first floor of the new Jacob H. Schiff Memorial Library building; a name, the Museum of Jewish Ceremonial Objects; a curator, Dr. Paul Romanoff; and a major collection of Judaica—the one formerly owned by Sephardic antiquities dealer Hadji Ephraim Benguiat.

Cyrus Adler, who became the Seminary's Acting President after Solomon Schechter's death in 1915, first saw Benguiat's collection in 1893 at the dealer's shop in Boston. Although Adler (1863–1940) later earned a reputation as an important

315

*A Collision
of Cultures:
The Jewish
Museum and
the Jewish
Theological
Seminary*

The Museum of
Jewish Ceremo-
nial Objects, first
floor of the Schiff
Library Building,
1940s. *Photo by
Virginia F. Stern.
Ratner Center,
JTS.*

figure in Jewish communal affairs, he began his career as a museum curator at the Smithsonian Institution. After receiving a doctorate in Semitics (the first to receive that degree at an American university) at Johns Hopkins University in 1887, Adler took a job as a curator at the United States National Museum's Section of Oriental Antiquities. By 1905 he had risen to become the Smithsonian's assistant secretary. In 1893 Adler was on a leave of absence from the Smithsonian to serve as a United States commissioner to the World's Columbian Exposition to be held in Chicago that year. He was scouting for material for his exhibit at the exposition when he found himself in Benguiat's shop.

According to Adler, the Benguiat family "spread over the larger cities in Europe and America" collecting and selling antiques but keeping all they gathered of Judaica. Adler convinced Benguiat to lend him the collection for his exhibit at the Chicago exposition. After the exposition ended, the loan was transferred to the United States National Museum where Adler by then held the formidable title of Custodian of the Section of Historic Religious Ceremonials.

The Benguiat Collection, as described by Adler and his colleague Immanuel Moses Casanowicz in their 1901 catalog, consisted of sixty-two items dating from the 16th through 19th centuries, from Europe, Asia, the Middle East, and North Africa. There were Torah wrappers, silver pointers, Hanukkah menorahs, candle-sticks, Passover dishes, mezuzzahs, and other objects for use in religious practice in home and synagogue. Even after the collection was at the United States National

Museum, Benguiat continued to add to it. (Adler had hoped to acquire the collection for the Smithsonian but received little support from its directors.[14]) By 1908 Benguiat's loan made up most of the United States National Museum's holdings in Judaica. The most prized of the additions was a 16th-century wooden ark from Urbino, Italy.[15]

By the time Benguiat died and his family decided to sell the collection, Cyrus Adler had left the Smithsonian and become the president of the Seminary. In 1925 Felix Warburg, "with the assistance of a few friends," bought the Benguiat Collection for the Seminary. Warburg (1871-1937) the banker, art collector, and tireless worker for Jewish causes was, like his father-in-law Jacob Schiff, a member of the Seminary's Board of Directors. He was also an experienced museum benefactor, having served as a trustee of New York's Museum of Natural History since 1910.[16]

When the Benguiat Collection was put on display at the Museum of Jewish Ceremonial Objects for the first time at the museum's dedication in November 1931, the new room was large enough to hold it but the museum's two exhibit cases—bought by Felix Warburg in 1923—were not. Six more had to be borrowed from the Museum of Natural History. Yet one object was still missing from the museum's opening exhibit. The Benguiat Collection's prize object, the Urbino ark, had been placed in the library's manuscript room instead of in the museum, a sign that despite its new status, the distinction between the museum and the much larger library of which it was still just a small part, was not yet completely clear.[17]

During the lifetime of the Museum of Jewish Ceremonial Objects, exhibits continued to be organized according to the themes favored by Alexander Marx. Some, as before, were devoted exclusively to books. Examples of illuminated marriage contracts from the library's collection were exhibited several times. Other exhibits commemorated the births and deaths of Jewish historical figures, ancient and modern.

A few exhibits during these years were about the Jewish contribution to American life. This was a meaningful theme for the Seminary, which strove to Americanize its overwhelmingly foreign-born rabbinical students and, through them, their immigrant congregations. For Columbus Day 1937, the museum displayed the almanac by the Jewish astronomer Abraham ben Samuel Zacuto used by Columbus on his voyage, thus demonstrating a Jewish presence at the very moment of European contact with the New World. To show the tenacity of Jews and their language in America, the museum exhibited the oldest Hebrew grammar books printed in the United States.

Holiday exhibits regularly featured such objects as seder plates and Hanukkah menorahs. In 1938, ceramic figurines of "Jewish types in the Ukraine" by Issachar Ryback, were exhibited. During the winter of 1938–39, ancient Jewish coins borrowed from the collection of novelist and collector Sholem Asch were displayed, and Jewish medals from the collection of Samuel Friedenberg were shown in 1940.

The most popular exhibit at the museum during these years was the one held in 1935 to celebrate the octocentennial of the birth of Moses Maimonides. Unlike the museum's first, modest Maimonides exhibit, this one was part of a monthlong, national celebration organized by a special committee which Cyrus Adler served as a cochairman. A brochure put out by the committee related the life of Maimonides to contemporary concerns:

> Amongst thoughtful minds, this more intimate contact with the thought and work of Maimonides will result in stimulating contrasts and comparisons between the philosophic and religious perplexities of his era and those of our own time. During these days when Jewry is especially conscious of the oppressive measures directed against it in many lands, the observance will serve to emphasize the spiritual and cultural achievements of the great Jewish minds, in spite of the persecution they have always been forced to face.[18]

This reasoning must have struck a chord, since crowds turned out to see the exhibit. The Seminary opened the museum extra evenings to accommodate them. The exhibit was responsible for a rise in attendance to 22,845 in 1935 from 14,026 the previous year.[19]

The museum brought its collection to an even wider audience by establishing a lending program during these years. Books, manuscripts, and objects were lent out for exhibits at such disparate organizations as the Trenton Section of the National Council of Jewish Women; the Reformed Church in the suburb of Bronxville, New York; branches of the New York Public Library; the Menorah Society at Brooklyn College; the Temple of Religion at the 1940 Golden Gate International Exposition in San Francisco; the army camp at Fort Dix, New Jersey; and Bamberger's department store.[20]

Along with the Sulzberger and Benguiat collections, smaller donations of objects—mostly Jewish ceremonial objects but also prints and drawings on Jewish themes, coins, and other items—trickled in steadily. This willingness on the part of collectors and the public to donate objects to the museum indicates that it had come to be viewed by Jews in the United States and abroad as a suitable repository for Jewish objects of value, both personal and communal. But it was Harry George Friedman (1881-1965), an investment banker originally from Poland, who launched patronage at the museum into a new era.[21]

H. G. Friedman (as he signed his letters) was a banker and a nonpracticing rabbi who began collecting Judaica during the 1920s. As his collection grew, Friedman started lending ceremonial objects from it to the Seminary museum for its holiday exhibits.[22] In 1941 he decided to convert his loans into a gift. In a letter to Marx written on this occasion, Friedman expressed his understanding of the meaning of his collection:

In making this Collection, my motive has been primarily to assemble objects which broadly served the Synagogue or the home. I have been, therefore, more nearly interested in objects that had popular vogue and which represented the craftsmanship that existed in the larger Jewish communities. For these reasons it is my wish that such objects, though of comparatively little financial value, be retained. I have regarded such objects as having possibly a higher historical importance than objects of greater artistic value which represent, in many instances, the work of non-Jewish craftsmen for more limited and wealthier individuals and communities. I do not under-rate the importance of such objects, particularly Synagogue objects, for these reflect the general cultural life which Jews shared.[23]

For the next two decades Friedman continued to donate Jewish objects to the Seminary. His gifts were made in the most unrestricted and self-effacing way. Uninterested in creating a personal memorial, Friedman wanted his collection to serve the needs of the museum and its public. All told, Friedman gave the museum more than six thousand objects.

Such patronage as Friedman's raised the museum's profile in the Jewish world both in the United States and abroad.[24] Thus, when Europe became dangerous for Jews in the thirties, some turned to the Seminary's museum as a place to safeguard their own or institutional collections. Ernest Wolf, the son of Albert Wolf, an important collector of Judaica from Berlin, proposed that the Seminary help to bring the collection of Berlin's Jewish museum to New York. Adler and Marx showed little inclination to intervene in this case and, consequently, nothing was done.[25] But soon after, when Danzig's Jewish museum was threatened, Adler took action.

Like the Seminary's museum, Danzig's Jewish museum, housed in the city's Great Synagogue, was founded in 1904. Its contents were the gift of Lesser Gieldzinski (1830-1910) a wealthy grain merchant, collector of art and Judaica, and a member of the synagogue's board of directors. In the spring of 1939, members of the Danzig Jewish community, the American Jewish Joint Distribution Committee, and Cyrus Adler began negotiating to have the contents of the museum shipped to the Seminary for safekeeping.[26] In July, ten crates containing hundreds of ceremonial objects, textiles, books, and Torah scrolls dating from the 17th through the 20th centuries arrived at the Seminary. Many of these objects had filled the Danzig museum, formerly Gieldzinski's collection. Others had been in use in the Great Synagogue itself or in other synagogues in the city. Some additional objects probably came from the homes of members of the Danzig Jewish community whose own departures had been financed by the sale of the community's synagogues and cemeteries.[27] Instead of putting the Danzig objects in storage, the Seminary took advantage of the summertime absence of students to display them in five dormitory rooms. Visitors were invited to view them there by appointment. Five years later the Seminary displayed the Danzig objects in the window of Scribner's book store on

Fifth Avenue.[28] Amid the bustle of Fifth Avenue, even greater numbers of people were able to see them. This very public anti-Nazi statement was, among other things, a demonstration of the security New York's Jews had come to feel in their own city and a sign of the museum's growing confidence.

The Seminary agreed to keep the objects for safekeeping during the war, and then return them to Danzig if the Jewish community managed to reestablish itself there within fifteen years. In August 1939, the Nazis invaded Danzig. The Great Synagogue was dismantled, the Danzig community did not reestablish itself, and the Danzig objects remain in the collection of the Jewish Museum today.[29]

The Mintz collection of Judaica also arrived at the museum by means of a near escape. Benjamin Mintz was an antiques dealer in Warsaw who, like Benguiat, held on to his purchases of Judaica. He and his wife Rose came to the United States in 1939 with their collection, intending to display it at the Polish Pavilion at the New York World's Fair. When Poland was invaded, the Mintzes and their collection remained in the United States. They lent it to the Museum of Jewish Ceremonial Objects where it was exhibited during the winter of 1939-40. In 1947, after Benjamin Mintz died, the Jewish Museum bought the collection from his widow.[30]

Just as Friedman's donations to the museum raised its stature to a higher level than Seminary officials had ever planned for, the arrival of refugee objects put additional pressure on the Seminary to invest both funds and effort. Thus a pattern developed in which forces from outside the Seminary worked to promote the museum even at cross-purposes to the intentions of the Seminary's leaders. Another example of this pattern can be seen in the problematic relationship that developed between Cyrus Adler and his appointee as curator of the museum, Paul Romanoff.

Romanoff was born in Russia, emigrated to the United States, and earned a doctorate in "Palestininan topography" at the Dropsie College for Hebrew and Cognate Studies in Philadelphia.[31] He was appointed to the post of curator soon after the museum's dedication in 1931. Adler, who was president of Dropsie College while Romanoff was studying there, recommended Romanoff for the job.[32] When Romanoff arrived at the Seminary, taking up residence in a dormitory room, Adler was the only person he knew.[33]

Adler's years at the Smithsonian and his personal involvement with the Benguiat Collection seem to suggest that he had a special interest in the museum. The purchase of the Benguiat Collection and the inclusion of a separate room for the museum in the Seminary's new complex of buildings during Adler's presidency are proof that he did remain interested. Yet Adler did not choose to invest further in the museum. The economic stresses resulting from the depression certainly played a role in this decision.[34] Adler's unusually heavy workload as president simultaneously of the Seminary in New York and Dropsie College in Philadelphia was presumably another factor in his unwillingness to take on the development of a new institution. Also, many years separated Adler from his Smithsonian career, and in the interim he had developed new interests. Thus, Adler's decision to hire Romanoff was probably motivated more by his desire to help a poor scholar by offering him a temporary job than by a deliberate decision to provide the museum with a permanent curator. When Romanoff appealed to the Seminary for a raise in pay, the Seminary's treasurer commented: "The salary which we are paying him was all that the position was worth to us; that the job had been given to him as a stopgap because he was out of employment at the time."[35]

Poverty made the job a necessity for Romanoff. He supported relatives in Europe and, after he married in 1937, a wife.[36] Romanoff also pursued his ambitions as a scholar; he lectured, wrote, and published during the years he was at the museum.[37] Romanoff consulted Adler about the publication of his thesis and told him that if he failed to publish it there would be no chance of his getting "any position of importance in the field of scholarship."[38] He must have seen the job as a way to remain close to Adler, whom he saw as his mentor, and to advance himself in the scholarly world.

Adler turned out to be a very reluctant mentor. The tone of his letters to Romanoff is usually chilly and brusque (although Adler rarely wrote warmly to anyone).[39] Alexander Marx was no more helpful. Louis Finkelstein, who succeeded Adler as the Seminary's President in 1940, was even less interested. Adler offered Romanoff no encouragement in his curatorial efforts and, at times, actively discouraged him.[40] One summer, during the imbroglio over Romanoff's request for a raise in pay, Adler wrote him from Woods Hole:

> I told you on several occasions, and rather emphatically I thought, this winter in a talk that was interrupted that there was no real place at the Seminary for you. I told you that I regarded the little museum as a more or less fixed thing. I have no desire to build up a great museum nor have we the means. The post there is that of caretaker and whatever your merits, does not justify, in the present condition of the Seminary, a salary for a man with a family. I urged you on several occasions to consider this and to try to find yourself another place. . . . At all events I think the kindest thing I can say to you is that you ought not look to the Seminary for any real position for your future.[41]

The kind of relationship that could produce such a letter was obviously painful for both. Romanoff responded: "Both the contents and your indifferent attitude surprised and shocked me." Adler wrote Louis Finkelstein: "I hate very much to send a letter like this to Doctor Romanoff and I hesitate not to."[42]

During Romanoff's years as curator, the museum's fate was captive to the inattention of Adler, Marx, and Finkelstein but also to the dynamics of this uncomfortable relationship. Some of Adler's failure to support the museum was certainly due to his other preoccupations and to the economic constraints of the time, yet some was also the result of Adler's inability either to work with or dislodge Romanoff.

Despite the lack of any encouragement from his superiors, Romanoff hung onto the job desperately, pouring unwanted energy, initiative, and long hours into the museum until his death in 1943 at the age of forty-five.[43] Anxious to prove his worth to his employers, Romanoff carved out a place for himself as the museum's publicist. As a result, he was the first to define what the museum's public mission should be. In letters, reports, and neatly drawn charts, Romanoff detailed his activities and the museum's growing public reputation.

One of Romanoff's responsibilities was to guide visitors through the museum. Most of these visitors were Jewish and came in groups from synagogues, yeshivas, Hebrew schools, labor unions, clubs, and Zionist, women's, and refugee organizations. A significant number of others came from organizations that were not Jewish, such as servicemen's associations, public and private schools, local colleges, and Christian churches.[44] During the years that Romanoff was curator, attendance at the museum more than doubled, rising from 10,768 in 1932 to 26,555 in 1940.[45] Romanoff told Adler that he was so busy guiding and lecturing to visitors that he had no time for his own scholarly work: "In March alone," he wrote, "I have devoted every Friday and seven entire evenings to the museum."[46]

To show Adler, Marx, and later Finkelstein, the appreciation he was receiving from these visitors (even while he failed to receive it from them), Romanoff typed out copies of letters he received from his admiring visitors. Anna Wright, a teacher at St. James Church School, Upper Montclair, New Jersey, wrote Romanoff to report on the reactions of her students after their visit. One girl described her experience in rapturous detail:

> Listening to Dr. Romanoff was not like a lecture. It was like looking at a pageant or as if he were unrolling a long beautiful tapestry of gorgeously colored pictures of the outstanding religious experiences. It wasn't so much that you saw Jewish ideas, but as if he unfolded in front of you the essentials of human religious feeling back, back, back to the very beginning of mankind's idea of God. It was *just gorgeous!*

Another remarked: "I never understood the Jewish ideas before. Why didn't they teach us the way Dr. Romanoff did?"[47]

As domestic anti-Semitism increased during this period, Romanoff saw the museum as an institution that could foster understanding and, thereby, tolerance of Jews by other groups. This goal was central to his conception of the museum's mission. He wrote: "We serve as a medium for better understanding and have become the place where one can learn of the beauty of our rituals and holidays, and of the common background of all faiths,"[48] and "Our museum has become a medium for inter-racial tolerance and understanding."[49]

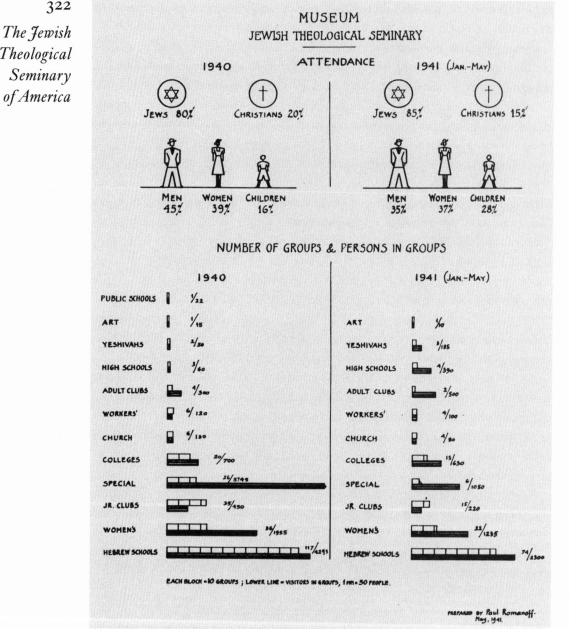

Museum attendance chart for 1940-41 by Paul Romanoff. *Ratner Center, JTS.*

That anti-Semitism was a local, even a neighborhood reality is demonstrated by the following situation described by Romanoff to Finkelstein in 1939. Romanoff told how local children were throwing rocks at the windows of the Seminary and breaking panes of glass. Some of these children attended the school run by Corpus Christi Church, one block from the Seminary. According to Romanoff, "Social conditions and their ignorance of our Institution are to blame. In view of the fact that Coughlin meetings are constantly being held on the street corners near the Seminary, all this feeling has been intensified." After Romanoff guided groups of nuns and children from the church through the museum and lectured to them about the Jewish roots of Christianity, "not only have the above mentioned incidents almost disappeared, but the children are cordial when they now visit the museum." Romanoff added, "I am sure you will agree, that these visits have accomplished a great deal in establishing good feeling and understanding in our immediate neighborhood."[50]

323

*A Collision
of Cultures:
The Jewish
Museum and
the Jewish
Theological
Seminary*

Even as the museum's reputation as an instrument of interfaith understanding grew, its relationship with the Seminary's own faculty and students failed to develop. By neglecting to establish a study collection for history or biblical archaeology at the museum, the Seminary failed to connect the museum's work with that of its own scholars.

By contrast, the library was meant to support the scientific, historical study of Judaism to which the Seminary was dedicated. In 1904 Mayer Sulzberger wrote to Marx: "My hope is that the Seminary may become the center for original work in the science of Judaism, to which end the acquisition of a great library is indispensable."[51] Most Seminary scholars did not recognize that the museum could serve a similar function. Cyrus Adler was one of only a few Jewish scholars who recognized objects as sources of information.[52]

One of the museum's rare purchases serves as evidence that a study collection was at least considered. When a group of visiting schoolchildren sent in a small collection of money to express appreciation for its visit, the museum used it to buy "two pieces of ancient Palestinian pottery . . . dating from the beginning of the Common Era. One of these, an oil lamp, is in the shape of an elephant."[53] Had the Seminary decided to use this elephant and its companion as the basis of a study collection, it might have succeeded in binding the loyalties of faculty, students, and alumni to the museum. Instead, the Museum of Jewish Ceremonial Objects remained disconnected from the central activities of its parent institution.

In 1941 Paul Romanoff made another in his long series of pleas for a raise in pay. Instead of giving Romanoff any hope that the new regime might bring a more positive attitude towards himself and the museum, Finkelstein responded by quoting almost the whole of Adler's Woods Hole letter. Then he added: "This is of course true today, as it was in 1938."[54]

The Move to Fifth Avenue (1947)

Just two and a half years later, it was no longer true. In January 1944, Frieda Schiff Warburg, widow of Felix Warburg and, by then, the only surviving child of Jacob Schiff, donated her house at 1109 Fifth Avenue at 92nd Street to the Seminary to use as a new home for the museum. (Paul Romanoff, who died on 13 December 1943, missed this event by less than one month.) It is not clear where the idea came from. Given Finkelstein's statement to Romanoff in 1941, his new duties as President, and his preoccupation with other Seminary programs, it is difficult to believe that the idea originated with him. Frieda Warburg credited Alan Stroock—her lawyer and a fellow member of the Seminary's Board of Directors—for the idea in the speech she gave when the Jewish Museum opened in her former home. The transformation of 17 East 80th Street, the home of Nina Loeb Warburg—who was at once Frieda War-burg's aunt, sister-in-law, and beloved friend—into New York University's Institute of Fine Arts in the thirties might also have inspired her.[55]

Regardless of where the idea came from, a gift from Frieda Warburg was simply impossible to turn down. Jacob Schiff had long been one of the Seminary's most important benefactors. He provided it with its first two buildings and contributed substantially to its endowment fund. His family funded the construction of the Schiff library building at 3080 Broadway. Schiff's son, Mortimer, was a benefactor of the library, and Felix Warburg was important to the museum. Both served on the Seminary's Board of Directors. Frieda Schiff Warburg (1876-1958) was well tutored by her father in her responsibilities as a philanthropist. She became the first woman to serve on the Seminary's Board of Directors when her husband's death left the seat open. As the heiress not only of her family's fortune, but also of its tradition of crucial acts of philanthropy in the Jewish world, Frieda Schiff Warburg had become a figure to reckon with.[56]

Other important changes accounted for the Seminary's new interest in the museum. One was World War II and the resulting destruction of Jewish culture in most of Europe. Alexander Marx recognized that the library must assume a new responsibility: "The main centers of Jewish learning of the last century are disintegrating, and it is evidently the task of American Jewry, together with the newly growing center in Palestine, to uphold the banner of Jewish learning."[57] This was equally true for the museum. As we have seen, objects from European Jewish museums, collectors, private individuals, and families managed to escape the destruction in Europe and find their way to the safety of Morningside Heights and, later, Fifth Avenue.

Frieda Schiff Warburg (1876–1958). *Photo by Foyer. Ratner Center, JTS.*

Human refugees also made their way from Europe to the Seminary's museum. The first was Guido Schoenberger, an art historian who had been a curator at the museum of the City of Frankfurt and taught at the local university. After he lost these positions with the rise of Hitler, he was associated with Frankfurt's Museum of Jewish Antiquities (the Rothschild Museum). In 1939 he emigrated to the United States, and soon after he was hired by the museum, first as a cataloger, then as research associate, the title he retained until his retirement in the early 1960s. After the war, Schoenberger played an important role in bringing fifty objects formerly belonging to the Frankfurt Jewish Museum to the Jewish Museum.[58]

Another change occurred within the Seminary itself. During the late thirties Louis Finkelstein, then still the Seminary's provost, became concerned about the rifts between peoples of different religions, nationalities, races, and even scholarly points of view—the results of which he believed were being horribly played out in Europe. He felt that the Seminary should broaden its mission to help in the effort to bridge these gaps. The Institute for Religious and Social Studies, a program for clergy of all faiths founded in 1938, and the Conference on Science, Philosophy and Religion, a series of conferences for scholars in sciences and the humanities that began in 1940, were the two central programs founded and run by Finkelstein to address what came to be called "intergroup relations."

Two other projects instigated by Finkelstein in the forties blended the aims of presenting Jews and Judaism to the broader American public—a kind of popular, domestic intergroup relations—with outreach to American Jews who, Finkelstein feared, were becoming increasingly estranged from Judaism. In 1943 Finkelstein proposed editing a comprehensive book about Jews and Judaism meant for the general reader. Funded by the American Jewish Committee and published by the Jewish Publication Society, the first edition of *The Jews: Their History, Culture, and Religion* appeared in four volumes in 1949.

As it turned out, Finkelstein had reason to be concerned about the level of public knowledge about Jews. While the book was in preparation he sent out a survey to the people he envisioned would make up its readership. These were highly educated people from around the country, largely not Jewish, some prominent in their fields. They included college administrators and professors, government officials, doctors, scientists, and authors. In response to the request to list "questions which should be answered in the book on Judaism and the Jews, including queries I have frequently heard" many of the 209 recipients included responses that revealed a willingness to believe and repeat common prejudices about Jews and Judaism combined with a lack of any substantive knowledge. Respondents wanted to know why Jews "controlled" various industries and "crowded" certain professions, why they engaged in "sharp business practices," and why they "insisted" on following Jewish religious and cultural practices rather than abandoning them for Christian ones. There were criticisms of Jewish "aggressiveness," "clannishness," and "hyper-sensitivity." One respondent asked: "Why do not the synagogues have steeples?"[59]

Commenting on the results of the survey Finkelstein wrote: "The replies I have received are indeed astonishing. It is clear that the world in general, and this includes many Jews, just do not know the ABC about Judaism. . . . I suppose education on the intellectual level is not the final answer to the difficulties of human life but it is certainly indispensable. The more I see of the troubles of the world, the more I turn in some hope to this little Institution which can do so much."[60]

The second of Finkelstein's popular outreach programs was the Seminary's weekly radio show, *The Eternal Light*, founded in 1944. Produced by the Seminary and broadcast over NBC, *The Eternal Light* consisted of dramatizations and interviews on Jewish themes. It also made use of Jewish music. Like the Conference, the Institute, and *The Jews*, *The Eternal Light*'s "great purpose" was "to increase understanding among people, knowing that tolerance, understanding and peace go hand in hand."[61] Of all of Finkelstein's outreach and intergroup programs *The Eternal Light*, with its use of culture—drama and music, in this case—and its appeal to a broad, general audience, was the one most similar to the museum. Finkelstein compared them, stating that the museum could be "from a visual point of view what the Eternal Light is to its listening audience, that is, a means for making Judaism understood by all groups."[62]

Given Louis Finkelstein's immersion in his intergroup and outreach programs at the time that Frieda Warburg donated her house to the Seminary, it is not surprising that he began to think of the museum as one of them. In his correspondence with Mrs. Warburg as the museum was being planned, Finkelstein described his own vision of how 1109 Fifth Avenue would be used. In addition to providing space for the museum, Finkelstein envisioned meeting rooms and classrooms for the Conference and Institute and an office for his principle assistant, Jessica Feingold, who played an important administrative role in both programs. "As you know," Finkelstein wrote, "my own conception is that it shall be an academic center, housing not only the museum, but the Conference on Science, Philosophy and Religion, the Institute for Religious Studies and other activities of the Seminary." There, the Institute would grow "as an effective instrument, making for national solidarity and for increased good will among men across differences of creed." The museum would share this mission: "The museum itself, it seems to me, is an instrument for . . . understanding across differences."[63]

To have brought the museum into the fold of the intergroup programs and made it a messenger of goodwill between peoples—ironically following the lead established by Paul Romanoff not so many years earlier—would have fulfilled the mission closest to Finkelstein's heart. Yet Finkelstein also understood that the site of the museum's new home, on upper Fifth Avenue in the heart of New York's museum district, meant that for the first time it would have to establish its legitimacy as a museum among museums. The Metropolitan Museum of Art, and other neighbors such as the Museum of Modern Art and the Whitney and Guggenheim museums, became models to live up to—as well as sources of some competitive anxiety. When Frieda Warburg suggested establishing a "women's house committee" Finkelstein vetoed the idea, arguing that the Metropolitan and "the other great museums" had no such committee and that "we should not do anything that would be less dignified than their practice."[64]

The location of the museum's new building, among institutions of like kind but far from New York's Jewish neighborhoods, mirrored the situation of its parent institution. When the Seminary moved to Morningside Heights in 1903, it was settling in New York's rising "acropolis on the Hudson," a neighborhood of academic and religious institutions with Columbia University as its "Parthenon."[65] The Seminary made this move at considerable inconvenience to its students, most of whom lived in the Jewish immigrant neighborhoods of Brooklyn or the Lower East Side. Yet this choice of neighborhood expressed the Seminary's vision of where Jews should situate themselves in American society.

The Seminary opposed ghettoization—and in particular the influences of the actual Jewish ghetto from which it drew most of its students. The fresh air of the Heights was meant to blow away the redolence of the East Side's religious backwardness, atavistic foreign practices, and socialist and Yiddishist secularism. By choosing Morningside Heights in 1903 and then confirming that choice in 1930 with the construction of a new campus in the same neighborhood, the Seminary was expressing in bricks and mortar an aim central to Conservative Judaism: that American Jews, even while maintaining the integrity of their religious traditions, should claim their rightful place in America's pluralistic society. Of course, Felix and Frieda Warburg chose the site of their house based on where they wanted to live in 1907.[66] But when the Seminary agreed to move its museum there, it found itself in a situation that it had deliberately chosen twice before, one not incongruent with its sense of itself.

The makeup of the Museum Advisory Committee Finkelstein assembled similarly expressed his understanding that the museum should take its place as a museum among museums, rather than as a Jewish institution among other Jewish institutions. The makeup of this committee was also a tacit admission of the lack of museum expertise—with the exception of Guido Schoenberger, whose proposal for the museum was one among several considered—available at the Seminary. In addition to Moshe Davis, Simon Greenberg, and Alexander Marx, all Seminary administrators, the advisory committee included scholars and curators from the Metropolitan Museum of Art, the Brooklyn Museum, the Museum of Modern Art, the United States National Museum, the Juilliard School of Music, Johns

The Warburg house at 1109 Fifth Avenue, ca. 1944. *Photo by Virginia F. Stern. Ratner Center, JTS.*

Hopkins University, Columbia University (Meyer Schapiro), Harvard University, and Yale Divinity School.[67] The absence of any representative from the Educational Alliance, which ran an influential art school on the Lower East Side, is notable.[68]

In his search for a director of the museum, Finkelstein looked for someone who was eminent in the field of art history. As he explained to Frieda Warburg:

> [The museum] must be regarded not simply as another museum, but that to be successful at all it would have to be, in its own way, *the* museum in the city of New York. Although it is small, my conception of it is similar to my conception of the Seminary generally, namely, that although it may be limited in scope it must compare in standing with the finest institutions of its type. That is why I impressed upon our Executive Committee and Board of Directors the necessity of having as head of the museum, even before it was opened, a man of unquestioned eminence in the whole field of art.[69]

Judging from the choices he made, Finkelstein clearly also hoped that the director would be Jewish. Finkelstein's first choice was the art historian Richard Krautheimer, to whom he offered the job in 1944. Like Schoenberger, the German-born Krautheimer lost his university job with the rise of Hitler. In 1933 he left for Rome, where he began a study of the churches of that city that would occupy him for the next half century.[70] Krautheimer came to the United States in 1935 where, at the time Finkelstein offered him the directorship, he was teaching at Vassar and occupied with wartime work for the Office of Strategic Services in Washington,

D.C. His scholarly work by that time had overwhelmingly been on early Christian church architecture, although he had also written an important book on medieval synagogues.[71] Finkelstein wrote of Krautheimer: "I am convinced that he is the best possible person for the position and earnestly hope that he will accept."[72] Krautheimer's knowledge of synagogues was not unrelated to the kind of research that could be done on the Jewish ceremonial objects in the museum's collection. Still, his specialty was Christian art and not the history, iconography, or religious and cultural meanings specific to Jewish objects. Finkelstein, seeking legitimacy for the museum in the broader world of art and museums, valued Krautheimer's eminence as an art historian over his familiarity with the museum's collections.

Krautheimer did not accept the directorship, telling Finkelstein that he was unwilling to give up his teaching and wartime work. Yet, perhaps feeling some desire to ally himself with a Jewish institution as a result of his own experiences in Nazi Germany, Krautheimer did not reject Finkelstein's offer altogether. When Finkelstein offered him the part-time position of director of research at the museum, Krautheimer, despite his other commitments, accepted.[73]

Finkelstein turned next to Meyer Schapiro, to whom he offered the directorship in December 1945. Schapiro, an art historian on the faculty of Columbia University, grew up, like Finkelstein, in Brownsville, Brooklyn, and, also like Finkelstein, spent his professional life in the rarefied academic atmosphere of Morningside Heights. There the similarity between the two men ended. Schapiro's involvement with art, artists, and left-wing causes and his distance from things religious made him an unlikely partner for Finkelstein. As Schapiro himself later remarked: "They sought my help even though they knew I was not a believer."[74]

Schapiro, who was then at the beginning of a long and eminent career as an interpreter, principally, of modern art and a supporter of contemporary American artists, also turned down the offer. But, like Krautheimer, Schapiro did not entirely disappoint Finkelstein. He agreed to serve on the Museum Advisory Committee, and later on, after the Jewish Museum was established, Finkelstein continued to seek his advice informally when problems arose.[75]

Finally, in September 1946, Finkelstein settled on Stephen Kayser, an art historian of lesser eminence than either Krautheimer or Schapiro, but one who was perhaps more suitable for the job. As if to express his disappointment at failing to get a luminary like either of his first two choices, Finkelstein divided the position in half, downgrading Kayser's title to curator and giving the title of director to the Seminary's provost, Simon Greenberg, a rabbi with no background in museum work or the visual arts.[76]

Stephen Kayser (1900-1988), another refugee, received his doctorate in 1922 from the University of Heidelberg, taught in German and Czechoslovakian universities, then left Europe for the United States in 1938.[77] Unlike Schapiro or

Krautheimer, Kayser specialized in Jewish art. At the time Finkelstein began negotiating with him, Kayser had succeeded in establishing himself as a professor of art
history at San Jose State College. Finkelstein's offer raised conflicting feelings in
Kayser. While he was not happy at the prospect of leaving the job which finally
made him feel secure in the United States—nor did he want to leave his "lovely
California house, with nine fruit trees in the backyard"—he was also strongly drawn
to work with a Jewish collection:[78]

> It is not easy for those who like me have come from the continent to get
> definitely located in an educational institution in this country. I have seen in
> many cases that men with fame were appointed only year by year. Although I
> have been working at the University of California for four years, I could not get
> rooted . . . Here in San Jose I feel firm ground for the first time ever since I came
> to this country. . . . I am highly satisfied with my position here which will
> increase in the course of time. But how can I make them [the president of San
> Jose State College and the head of his department] understand that the inner
> voice who calls me to New York is something else again!? Can anyone non-Jew-
> ish fully understand what we feel when besides all the good things which the
> outside offers us and which are of God's blessing too, there is something more
> inside?[79]

Kayser wrote Guido Schoenberger just before he left California: "Believe me it is
not easy to leave this part of the country, but I found the job in New York too challenging."[80]

Almost three and a half years passed between Frieda Warburg's donation of the
house and the opening of the Jewish Museum on 8 May 1947, the second anniversary of V-E Day. This left plenty of time for the Museum Advisory Committee,
Louis Finkelstein, and the largely internal Museum Committee and the "Inner"
Museum Committee to debate and plan the physical and theoretical design of the
reborn museum. The latter two committees' shifting and overlapping memberships
consisted of, among others, Simon Greenberg, Stephen Kayser, Guido Schoenberger, Alexander Marx and his assistant Anna Kleban, Jessica Feingold, and the
two advisors, Richard Krautheimer and Meyer Schapiro. Percival Goodman, the
architect chosen to modify the house, and Frieda Schiff Warburg also
contributed their opinions.[81]

The difficulty these advisors had in coming up with a new name for the museum
symbolizes the trouble they had in agreeing on the more important question of how
to formulate its mission. Some of the names proposed would have been suitable for
an art museum: Museum of Jewish Art; Museum of Arts, Jewish Theological Seminary of America; or Art Museum of the Jewish Theological Seminary. Others suggested an emphasis on religion, culture, and history: Museum of Jewish Culture,
Museum of Jewish Religion and Culture, and Museum of Jewish Cultural History.

331

*A Collision
of Cultures:
The Jewish
Museum and
the Jewish
Theological
Seminary*

Alexander Marx,
Stephen Kayser,
and Louis Finkel-
stein (left to right)
stand before the
Urbino ark at the
opening of the
Jewish Museum
in the Warburg
house, 8 May
1947. *Photo by
Virginia F. Stern.
Ratner Center,
JTS.*

A few, such as American Jewish Museum and Jewish Museum of America, stressed the museum's American orientation. Some, such as Judaic Museum or Jewish Museum, were more vague.[82] Richard Krautheimer favored "Jewish Museum" since "it is simple, unpretentious, and at the same time wider and more flexible than any other name I can think of."[83] It also expressed little about the mission of the museum and thus could accommodate all points of view. By January 1947, after several years of debate, the museum was only a few months away from opening but it still had no name. A sign posted outside the building blandly designated it the "Museum of the Jewish Theological Seminary."[84] Only later that month did the Seminary's executive committee finally approve "The Jewish Museum."[85]

When they were not struggling over what to call the museum, the advisors considered a series of plans prepared by Guido Schoenberger, Richard Krautheimer, and, interestingly, the author Paul Goodman, brother of architect Percival Goodman.[86] In the first section of his plan, titled "Classification of the Museum-type and Name of the Museum," Schoenberger states categorically—in the by now old-fashioned 19th-century classificatory spirit of Cyrus Adler—that "A Jewish Museum belongs to the group of History Museums." Richard Krautheimer and Paul Goodman, with his collaborator Benjamin Nelson, essentially agreed with that characterization. But when it came to the question of how to express Jewish history, all four also shared an unease about the visual appeal of the ceremonial objects that made up the bulk of the Jewish Museum's collection. As Goodman and Nelson phrased it: "The truth is that in these objects *considered by themselves* not enough is expressed. The paucity of plastic expression among the Jews of at least the last thousand years, is well known."[87] Richard Krautheimer concurred:

> It has been suggested from various sides to constitute the new institution as a *Museum of Jewish Art*. The difficulty of such a scheme lies in the limited amount of material available. It lies even more in the fact that the quality of Jewish art is rarely so outstanding in itself as to make it an object of purely aesthetic interest. Jewish life and thought has never been expressed as predominantly in the field of art as, for example, in the life and thought of the Italian Renaissance or of seventeenth century Holland; rarely has it created any great work in the field of art. Jewish art is to a large extent folk art and its position in the life of the Jewish community resembles very much the position of art in the life of colonial America: rarely outstanding and never on a pedestal, yet part of the community's religious and daily life.[88]

To make up for what they agreed to be the lack of inherent visual interest in Jewish objects, all emphasized the importance of careful selection and good interpretation. Schoenberger, conscious of what a jumble of spice boxes or Torah crowns could look like, warned that "A careful selection of the most important types and examples of cultural monuments and documents has to be maintained to avoid a tiresome accumulation by the display of similar objects."[89] Schoenberger's plan, "to illustrate Jewish cultural life by monuments and documents," emphasized the use of labels, photographs, maps, and charts to fill in the historical gaps in the collection—as well as to make up for the physical impossibility of displaying large monuments. Goodman and Nelson similarly proposed the use of "plenty of manuscripts and books" and "mighty mottoes and texts."

When Krautheimer read Schoenberger's and Goodman and Nelson's plans he concluded that their approaches relied too much on words and not enough on objects. In his critique of Schoenberger's plan he wrote: "The accent must be placed on the visual rather than the literary or documentary approach. Therefore I would seriously propose formulating as the aim of the museum, *the presentation of Jewish life in visual form*." Writing to Finkelstein about Goodman and Nelson's plan, Krautheimer stated: "I should like to emphasize that a museum must be more than an illustrated primer, be it of Jewish history or Jewish culture or of the Jewish faith. Such a concept is quite obsolete because it appeals to reason rather than to the visual impressions of the visitor."[90] Kayser, although not present for these discussions, concurred with this point of view, writing later: "To put up a museum which teaches Judaism, that is to say, which enters into the task of the Sunday Schools and of the Jewish parent, would be something very worthwhile I admit, but that would be a product of Jewish education in general and not of a museum which places its main emphasis upon the visual part of tradition."[91]

Still, Krautheimer and his fellow planners remained concerned about the objects' lack of visual appeal. To make up for this lack Goodman and Nelson, in particular, proposed that the museum present other arts and areas of learning, ones in which Jewish culture and religion had expressed themselves more prolifically. They felt that "the Jews have been a people great in poetry, in legend, in philosophy, and law; and a people whose music and dance is interesting and very influential." They proposed "regular performances of record-concerts, dance recitals, and other music and drama" and they thought that Seminary students could "recite poems" as they led visitors on guided tours.[92]

The planners agreed that the proposed audience for the museum should be scholars as well as the general public, Jews, and, pursuing the interfaith theme, everyone else. For scholars, all proposed a study collection; Krautheimer and Schoenberger thought there should be a research program. Krautheimer hoped there would be a catalog, guidebook, lecture program, a series of publications on Jewish art, and a periodical. He also hoped that the Jewish Museum would collaborate with the U. S. Monuments Commission in investigating what was left of Jewish art in Europe.[93] As for the general public, Goodman and Nelson echoed Finkelstein's sentiments: "If a Jew, he would be fired in the faith . . . if a gentile, he would be moved to tolerance, admiration, and gratitude."[94]

By early 1945 wartime shortages, financial problems, the physical difficulties involved in modifying the house, the continuing failure to find a director, and disagreements among the planners about the mission of the museum all combined to bring the project to a halt. Writing to Krautheimer in a tone that turned out to be prematurely elegiac, Finkelstein remarked: "The more I think of it the more I feel that the difficulties attendant upon the building at 1109 Fifth Avenue were comparatively unimportant and that the question of overall direction is our fundamental problem."[95]

This crisis served to bring out each planner's deepest concerns. While Finkelstein came to see the crisis as a way to jettison the museum plan entirely and replace it with an intergroup relations project, both Krautheimer and Schoenberger voiced concern in terms of the Seminary's responsibility in the face of wartime destruction in Europe.

Finkelstein at first proposed the intermediate step of abandoning the project and instead, "at some future time," constructing a building on the Seminary's campus to be used for an extension program in the arts. A museum would be included only as one part of a program that would offer classes in art, theater, dance, and music. When Richard Krautheimer learned of this plan, he resigned. Among his reasons, he emphasized the urgency of acting at "the present moment" to establish a museum:

Indeed the time places, in this writer's opinion, a duty on the shoulders of the Jewish Theological Seminary of America and on those of the Jews all over the country. The almost complete destruction of Jewish life in Central and Eastern Europe including its monuments, museums, libraries and research centers is the worst cultural loss Judaism has suffered in the last five hundred years. The last remnants of Jewish art and history in these countries must be collected now, if at all, and this can be done only in this country or else in Palestine. Judaism's cultural monuments must be preserved and should be made available to the world not only in writing but also visually. The Seminary, through the planned Museum and Research Center is in a position to fulfil this task. To let this opportunity pass would be difficult to explain to future generations.[96]

Guido Schoenberger voiced the same concern:

The Jewish Question is in the limelight of the entire world just now. To provide a refuge for the treasures of pillaged Synagogues, to rebuild at least in effigy a part of the spiritual and material achievements of the European communities which have been destroyed, is a task of the greatest importance; and it would have the greatest effect right now.[97]

Finkelstein next proposed dispensing with the whole project. When Frieda Warburg suggested selling the house, Finkelstein did not protest. Instead he suggested—in an unsent letter—that the proceeds from the sale could fund the construction of "another building on our campus dedicated to the very subject of better understanding among all peoples."[98] Weary, presumably, of the debates and difficulties that had engulfed the museum project, Finkelstein hoped to redirect Warburg's gift to finance the intergroup programs that interested him much more at that time.

The Seminary and the Arts

The crisis lasted for most of 1945, but by the spring of 1946 work on the museum had resumed. In June, Meyer Schapiro submitted a plan that, like the others, included exhibits of the permanent collection, tours, lectures, research, and publication. Schapiro also suggested adding the entirely new element of modern and contemporary art to the museum's exhibition program.

Meyer Schapiro was an advocate of contemporary American art, and he hoped he could convince Louis Finkelstein and the others to make the Jewish Museum a venue for it. In the plan he submitted in June 1946, Schapiro suggested an exhibit of contemporary art—loans—consisting of paintings, sculptures, and prints executed by Jewish artists, whether living or dead, who worked "within the modern tradition." The names he suggested included Marc Chagall, Jacques Lipchitz, Max Weber, Abraham Walkowitz, Jacob Epstein, Alfred Stieglitz, William Zorach, Moise Kisling, Chaim Gross, Jack Levine, Ben-Zion, the Soyers, Adolph Gottlieb, and Marc Rothko, among the living. Among the modern dead, he mentioned Pissarro, Soutine, and Modigliani. Schapiro noted: "Where possible, the artists should be approached personally and invited to send work with Jewish themes or with a marked Jewish sentiment; but this is not a dogmatic requirement; the aim of the exhibit is to show the accomplishment of Jewish artists, rather than a particular trend of art."[99] Although he did not propose it in this plan, Schapiro also hoped that the museum would "find its way to the exhibit of contemporary art" not necessarily of Jewish content, and not necessarily by Jewish artists.[100]

The museum accepted Schapiro's suggestion. The opening exhibit in May 1947 included a show of the work of contemporary Jewish artists on Jewish themes in one of the main galleries on the first floor. The artists shown included Ben-Zion, Marc Chagall, Jacques Lipchitz, Reubin Rubin, Jennings Tofel, Max Weber, William Zorach, and others. While this exhibit was in preparation, Schapiro suggested to Kayser, by then installed as the curator, that he "could also take any non-Jewish subjects for the opening exhibit."[101] Kayser chose not to take this suggestion although he did share Schapiro's interest in modern art, albeit Jewish art.

The opening exhibit was the museum's first manifestation of an interest in modern art. Its collection, after all, was made up not of paintings and sculptures, but of Jewish ceremonial objects. Even such collectors as H. G. Friedman valued these objects more as artifacts of Jewish life than as art objects. A desire to make the Jewish Museum dynamic and appealing to visitors combined with Finkelstein's regard for Schapiro's judgment were certainly factors in the decision to show modern art. But art was a problematic subject for the Seminary. It turned out to be the hinge on which relations between the Seminary and the museum turned for the worse.

The incorporation of contemporary art into the museum's program seemed possible at that time to such disparate personalities as Finkelstein and Schapiro in part because of a larger transformation that had taken place in the culture of New York's Jews. As they joined the middle class, these Jews adopted standards of refinement and aesthetics borrowed from the larger culture just as the Jews of Berlin, Vienna, and Paris had done before them. This aspect of acculturation not only affected middle-class mores but also made it possible for individual Jews to participate in the creative world of the visual arts. Starting around the turn of the century, New York produced an increasing number of Jewish artists, art critics, and art patrons, most of them divorced from religious life.[102] Yet these developments meant little to Jewish religious institutions in the city such as the Seminary. Whether as the result of religious proscription, culture, or habit, the practice or study of the visual arts was simply absent from the Seminary's curriculum. Louis Finkelstein himself personified the model of the rabbi indifferent to the arts. Whenever he was drawn into any artistic question he always hastened to protest his ignorance. Stephen Kayser's request, early on, for Finkelstein's participation on the museum's painting jury drew a refusal and this comment: "With regard to the choice of paintings, I am afraid I would be quite useless." Even many years later Finkelstein replied to a question about an Israeli sculptor: "As I am sure you know, I have no competence in the field of sculpture whatever."[103]

Simon Greenberg, the museum's director, was slightly more curious about art. He carried on an informal correspondence course on the subject with Stephen Kayser, who responded to Greenberg's questions with lengthy explanations. Greenberg appreciated Kayser's instruction: "I believe I have on more than one occasion told you how deeply indebted I feel to you for what I have learned from you about art in general and Jewish art in particular."[104] And yet Greenberg continued to feel unequal to the contemporary art he was seeing at the Jewish Museum. After his visit to the 1957 exhibit of contemporary art, "The New York School: Second Generation," he commented, self-effacingly, to Meyer Schapiro, "I spent a good bit of time looking at the paintings of these young artists. I find all of them interesting. They undoubtedly reflect a sincere effort to give honest expression to some inner mood or search or aspiration. But only about a half dozen of them seem to say something significant to me. I am not so sure that it is not my fault."[105]

Yet the arts, as an element of growing importance in American life, were increasingly filtering into the world of Conservative Judaism. At the Brooklyn Jewish Center, the model synagogue center founded on Eastern Parkway in 1919, "culture"—in the form of lectures, a library, and a drama club—played an important role by the twenties. In 1947 Stephen Kayser convinced sculptor Jacques Lipchitz to speak at the Rabbinical Assembly's convention when its members asked to be addressed by "a living artist."[106]

Conservative Jews found themselves face-to-face with aesthetic issues most frequently as a result of the postwar boom in synagogue construction. On synagogue building committees, congregants and their rabbis had to make decisions about design and decoration for which they were generally ill-prepared. Kayser wanted to address the aesthetic gap in the training of Conservative rabbis and their increasingly suburban congregants. In 1948 he wrote Simon Greenberg: "I do hope that in the course of time we can actually train our rabbis also in this field, [synagogue design] which is of such far-reaching importance for the future of American Judaism."[107] The only headway Kayser made with the rabbis was one course, "The Functions of Jewish Art in Jewish Life," which he taught in a special summer session for alumni. Kayser may have been more successful with the informal advisory services he provided to synagogue building committees under the museum's auspices during his years as curator. In a report delivered in early 1958 there is a reference to the "scores of hours" Kayser was spending with "building committees throughout the country."[108]

The Seminary's Rabbinical School offered no courses in the visual arts. Kayser's summer course for alumni was the only foray in this direction. But the arts did begin to find their way into other, less central, Seminary schools and programs. As early as 1943 a meeting of the Conference on Science, Philosophy and Religion, whose overall theme was "Approaches to World Peace," included sessions on "Art and Letters and Enduring Peace" and "Art as a Means to Unify Mankind." In 1947 Conference participants discussed "Contemporary Art and the Churches." Stephen Kayser spoke on "The Jewish View" of church and synagogue architecture (others delivered talks on the Catholic and Protestant views) at a 1947–48 Institute for Religious and Social Studies seminar.[109]

The Institute's Tuesday lecture series sometimes included speakers in the arts such as composer Henry Cowell, architect Frank Lloyd Wright, modern dancer Ted Shawn, painter Ben Shahn, poet Delmore Schwartz, critics Philip Rahv and Lionel Trilling, and Dr. Robert W. Spike, a representative of the Board of Home Missions of the Congregational and Christian Churches who spoke, incongruously, on beat author Jack Kerouac's novel *The Subterraneans*. By the sixties, at a series of lectures titled "Encounter With the Arts: The Clergyman and the Surrounding Culture," speakers addressed popular dances ("the Twist, the Hully Gully, the Bossa Nova"), popular music ("Rock'n Roll, Folk Music, Jazz"), and contemporary art ("the Abstract, the Pop, Assemblage").[110]

At the Seminary's Teachers Institute, students, mostly women, could study "Arts and Crafts in the Hebrew School," music, drama, and dance, but not visual arts. At the Women's Institute of Jewish Studies, a non-degree extension program, students could learn about "Jewish Customs and Ceremonies with special reference to Jewish art" or "How the Bible Inspires the Arts."[111]

The closest the Seminary came to a real arts program during the forties and fifties was the one established at the University of Judaism in Los Angeles. The School of the Creative Arts founded there offered training in drama, dance, music, and arts and crafts. Training in the visual arts was, again, absent, although a branch of the Jewish Museum was established at the University of Judaism.[112]

This continuing reluctance to acknowledge the importance of painting and sculpture was typical of the Seminary's point of view, although some softening here and there was evident. Finkelstein's inclusion of a chapter on "Judaism and Art" by Rachel Wischnitzer in his *The Jews* is one example.[113] In 1950, planning a "Rabbi Akiba Memorial Month," Finkelstein showed an understanding that an aesthetic element added to what was essentially an outreach and educational project would enhance its appeal. As he wrote Kayser: "We would like to place inside the tower a perpetual light. *This should be something of esthetic value.* I would very much like to know whether you have in the museum collection any suitable light that could be used."[114]

After the years of planning and the excitement of the opening of the Jewish Museum, the Seminary's attention receded. The museum's director, Simon Greenberg, more a representative of the Seminary than a hands-on administrator, was heavily overextended. He served on the Seminary's faculty and, additionally, at different times during this period as its provost, vice-chancellor, and Acting President. Greenberg helped found the University of Judaism and in 1948, just a year after the Jewish Museum's opening, became its president, a job that required shuttling back and forth between Los Angeles and New York. Greenberg's directorship of the museum was only one of his many administrative duties—and far from being his primary one.[115]

During the late forties and fifties, the staff at the Jewish Museum, led by Kayser, was minimal, the budget was small, and the director was largely absent. Kayser occasionally had to pay for museum expenses out of his own pocket. A committee of the Seminary's Board of Overseers advised the Jewish Museum during this period, but Stephen Kayser, with the assistance of his wife, artist Louise Kayser, and his small staff was left to guide the Jewish Museum mostly on his own.[116]

Kayser arrived at the Jewish Museum only at the tail end of the 1944–47 planning period, and while many of the plans discussed then were, in fact, adopted, Kayser's vision was also important in setting the tone of the reborn museum. Like Krautheimer's and Schoenberger's, Kayser's dedication to and vision of the Jewish Museum was colored to some extent by his experiences as a refugee. Compared to the leaders of today's Holocaust museums, this generation of refugee curators and scholars was less inclined to look directly into the eye of the storm they had so recently fled.[117] Instead of focusing on destruction, Kayser's plan was to support Jewish cultural regeneration in his adopted country. In his first report to the Board of Overseers, Kayser connected this aim with the overall work of the Seminary: "Our whole program can only be understood fully within the framework of a regeneration of Jewish forms and Jewish life, and we consider the museum therefore, as a part of the activities of the Jewish Theological Seminary in spiritual guidance of the greater Jewish public in this country and by that, throughout the world."[118]

Kayser's work with synagogue building committees was one element in his program of Jewish cultural regeneration. Another was his effort to make the Jewish Museum "a home for living Jewish artists."[119] At the Jewish Museum's opening exhibit a pattern was set that persisted throughout the fifties: while Judaica exhibits took place on the upper floors, the museum's important first floor gallery space—which Kayser once referred to emotionally as "the child of my sorrows"—was devoted to work by contemporary Jewish artists.[120] During the Jewish Museum's first decade there were shows featuring the work of Max Band, Ben-Zion, Ismar David (Hebrew letter design), Chaim Gross, A. Raymond Katz (synagogue art and

Judaica exhibit upstairs at the Jewish Museum, 1947. *Photo by Virginia F. Stern. Ratner Center, JTS.*

decoration), Yehoshua Kovarsky, Arthur Szyk, Abraham Walkowitz, Max Weber, and others—Jewish artists some or all of whose work featured Jewish or biblical themes. At the same time, the upstairs rooms held exhibits on Jewish holidays and the sabbath, Jewish music, children's art, and the new Jewish state.

During these years Stephen Kayser struggled to keep the aesthetic foremost in the exhibition program of the Jewish Museum. At the opening he sought, for instance, to define the archaeological artifacts on display as art: "The material will not be on display under the heading of archaeology, but as art objects only."[121] Writing to Finkelstein about the Judaica he planned to display at the opening exhibit, Kayser pointed out rather agitatedly: "I am taking the liberty of emphasizing that my main task is to put up an artistic exhibit."[122]

Kayser pursued his aim of supporting Jewish artists, making contacts with a few in New York. Jacques Lipchitz and Marc Chagall, each of whom had work in the opening exhibit, visited the museum as it prepared to open. Chagall offered to decorate the museum's auditorium with a series of murals depicting scenes of contemporary Jewish life. Pointing out that 350,000 people had attended a recent Chagall exhibit at the University of Chicago, Kayser wrote: "A room covered with wall paintings by him would be a sensation, aside from the artistic value and significance which they would represent." Despite Kayser's eager recommendation of this project, the Seminary failed to pursue it. The murals, which would have almost certainly been an important draw for visitors, were never painted.[123]

Sculptor Jacques
Lipchitz (right)
with curator
Stephen Kayser at
the opening of the
Jewish Museum, 8
May 1947. *Photo
by Virginia F.
Stern. Ratner
Center, JTS.*

Kayser struggled valiantly to keep his end up, but by 1950 interest in the Jewish Museum, as measured by visitor attendance and coverage in the press, was declining. In a memorandum to Simon Greenberg, Kayser reported on a disturbing trend: attendance between 1948 and 1950 had dropped by more than half. Kayser was reduced to suggesting that "refreshments be served [at special press previews] in an effort to bring more critics to the Museum."[124] In 1953 the Jewish Museum faced the embarrassing possibility that the national committee set up to celebrate the tercentenary of the Jews' arrival in North America was considering the Metropolitan Museum of Art as the site of its official exhibit. This crisis passed when the committee finally did choose the Jewish Museum. Yet even the overseers' museum committee, where one member bemoaned the "characteristic lack of visual appeal" of the Judaica, did not feel fully confident of the appeal of the museum's collection.[125]

Thus, as the Jewish Museum's tenth anniversary in the Warburg house approached, it was apparent that some kind of change was necessary to pull the museum out of its doldrums. With the reluctant acquiescence of Louis Finkelstein, the Jewish Museum finally decided to accept Meyer Schapiro's suggestion that it display contemporary art regardless of whether or not it had any Jewish content.

Thus, in 1957, the Jewish Museum moved one step toward the New York art world and one step away from the Seminary when it opened itself up to contemporary art.[126]

Contemporary Art at the Jewish Museum: Success and Controversy

"The New York School: Second Generation," one of the exhibits arranged to celebrate the Jewish Museum's tenth anniversary in 1957, was the first exhibit at the Jewish Museum to present art for its own sake rather than for the sake of its Jewish content. The twenty-three artists, chosen by Meyer Schapiro, included Elaine de Kooning, Helen Frankenthaler, Jasper Johns, Robert Rauschenberg, and George Segal, all of whom were represented by abstract works. In the introduction to the exhibit's catalog, the art historian Leo Steinberg found a link between abstract art and Judaism:

> Both Jewry and modern art are masters of renunciation, having at one time renounced all the props on which existence as nation, or art, once seemed to depend. Jewry survived as an abstract nation, proving, as did modern art, how much was dispensable. I would add also that, like modern painting, Jewish religious practices are remarkably free of representational content, the ritual being largely self-fulfilling, rather than the bearer of a detachable meaning. Lastly, both Judaism and contemporary art established themselves by uncompromising exclusiveness. And if I said before that it is hard to be a modern painter, there is an old Jewish proverb to match that sentiment. Which possibly explains why many young Jews find it easy to become modern painters.[127]

Stephen Kayser also strained to find some connection with Judaism, pointing out that some of the work was, in fact, by "prominent young Jewish artists."[128] The foreword to the show's catalog referred to the painters, a bit self-consciously, as "Christian as well as Jewish." But for Meyer Schapiro, who helped organize the exhibit and delivered an address at its opening, the religion of the artists was of no particular importance. In the address, Schapiro explained how the challenges of contemporary art could revive and train the vision of museum-goers, providing them with tools they could then bring to Judaica exhibits. Contemporary art and Judaica, which seemed to have nothing in common, could be complementary:

> This relation to contemporary art is of vital importance even for the maintenance of an art of older works, and it is that which gives the real lover of art the opportunity to see the older works in a fresh way and to make his own, his personal, discriminations among them.[129]

"The New York School: Second Generation" was a breakthrough, a cure for the doldrums of the fifties. In its 1957 report to the Board of Overseers, the Museum Committee declared: "Gradually, the function of a Jewish Museum is evolving in our minds: to so present the particular as to strip it of parochialism: so to illumine Jewish art that it reflects universal light."[130] This balance between the "particular" and the "universal" was reflected in the Jewish Museum's exhibit program for the next few years. While exhibits on Jewish themes continued (Contemporary Ceremonial and Synagogue Art, 1958; Ben-Zion's paintings on Jewish and biblical themes, 1959; The American Jew in the Civil War, 1960-61) the Jewish Museum also gave one-person shows to the abstract painters Adolph Gottlieb (1957) and Helen Frankenthaler (1960).

In his introductory essay for the Adolph Gottlieb exhibit catalog, the art critic Clement Greenberg congratulated the Jewish Museum for its daring and discernment in exhibiting an artist whose work was still evolving, one among only a "handful of artists on whom the immediate future of painting itself depends."[131] The museum's new willingness to plunge bravely into the world of contemporary art also attracted the attention of wealthy donors. In 1961 Albert and Vera List, collectors of contemporary art, donated $500,000 to the Seminary for the construction of a new wing to be built adjacent to the Warburg House. Generous as the Lists' gift was, it also demonstrated the museum's continuing vulnerability, in the absence of set policies of its own, to the influence of outside forces. While the Lists' offer of a new building proved that exhibits of contemporary art could attract significant funding, the expanded museum would require even more funds to operate. The Seminary had always provided the lion's share of the museum's budget, but it would clearly be unable to meet these new financial requirements. Faced with this reality, the Seminary solidified its commitment to contemporary art at the museum.

The rethinking of this period is expressed by a 1962 statement of the Jewish Museum's new goals. Along with specific Jewish objectives ("to represent the continuity of Jewish history and tradition," "to help relate Jews to the current society by representing the contribution of contemporary Judaica to the social scene"), it included a third purpose: "to contribute to the aesthetic life of the general community." To fulfill that purpose, the museum decided to offer "a program of contemporary art of a general nature" in order to contribute "to the contemporary art scene."[132] In 1962 the Seminary replaced both Stephen Kayser and Simon Greenberg with Alan Solomon, a forty-two-year-old art historian with a specialty in modern art, as the Jewish Museum's first resident, full-time director. At the same time it appointed a Board of Governors for the Jewish Museum with Vera List as its chair.[133]

Thus, by the time the List Building opened in early 1963, the Jewish Museum had adopted a policy that effectively divided its exhibition program into two parts: Judaica, and "contemporary art of a general nature." The first exhibits in the List Building expressed the Jewish Museum's new duality: immediately following "The Hebrew Bible in Christian, Jewish, and Muslim Art" and "The Silver and Judaica

343
*A Collision
of Cultures:
The Jewish
Museum and
the Jewish
Theological
Seminary*

Albert and Vera
List at the Jewish
Museum,
ca. 1963. *Ratner
Center, JTS.*

Entrance to the
List Building,
ca. 1963. The
sculpture group is
Elbert Weinberg's
"Procession."
*Ratner Center,
JTS.*

Collection of Mr. and Mrs. Michael M. Zagayski" came the Robert Rauschenberg retrospective that caused so much unhappiness.[134]

As the abstract paintings of the fifties evolved into the collages, combines, and happenings of the sixties, the Jewish Museum's contemporary art program, under the direction of Alan Solomon, Sam Hunter, and Karl Katz, successively, catapulted the museum to the head of New York's art world. Art critic Emily Genauer described the Jewish Museum as: "the city's 'in' museum. . . . Its shows, almost invariably the first 'official' presentation hereabouts of new art forms and isms still in the making and testing, have become a magnet for all the with-it kids." The press, which once had to be lured to the museum with refreshments, now followed developments there with interest.[135] Yet these same developments caused distress among visitors who were used to more traditional displays of Judaica. As a result, the Jewish Museum developed two separate audiences that had little in common with one another. At sixties openings the denizens of the art scene (the "with-it kids") and more traditional museum visitors collided. Art critic Calvin Tomkins described the scene at the opening of the 1963 Rauschenberg show:

> The opening, on the evening of March 29, 1963, was an astonishing event in itself, the first of the wide-open, see-and-be-seen, roaring art world galas that became such a part of the sixties scene. All the younger New York artists were there, and the still somewhat unfamiliar, sweetish scent of marijuana cut through the haze of cigarette smoke in the dignified, high-ceilinged rooms. Ascending the mansion's baronial staircase, men and women in evening clothes gazed with amazement and apprehension at the mass of disheveled art lovers above and below, some of whom looked almost as outlandish as the art on display.[136]

Meyer Schapiro's expectation that exhibits of contemporary art and Judaica could work naturally together seemed illusory when faced with this reality. The response of a rabbi's wife who had brought her Bible study group to the museum during the Rauschenberg show demonstrated just how illusory it was. "I was so embarrassed," she wrote. "As a matter of fact, I believe the women felt insulted. By the time we reached the third floor, psychologically they were completely unresponsive to the Judaica."[137]

The rift between the Jewish Museum's two audiences was paralleled by the one that developed between the museum and the Seminary. Members of the Seminary's executive committee objected to the museum's dual program, arguing that contributors to the Seminary would feel they were being asked to support "an art program completely unrelated to Judaism and inconsistent with their intentions in making gifts." It was even suggested that the Seminary withdraw its sponsorship from the contemporary art program and support only the Judaica.[138]

During the sixties, as the Jewish Museum moved increasingly in the orbit of New York's art world, it felt less and less obligated to align its aims with those of the Seminary. The dynamism of the art world at that time drew the Jewish Museum in directions unimaginable, incomprehensible, to its parent. Yet the parent remained concerned. Under pressure from the Seminary, the museum reformulated its policy three times and ran through three directors (Alan Solomon, 1962-64; Sam Hunter, 1965-67; and Karl Katz, 1968-71) during this period. Tensions were explicitly expressed in a list of governing principles drafted by the Seminary that included the order that "the Director will not arbitrarily curtail or compromise the Judaica offerings of the museum."[139]

When the Jewish Museum aligned itself with the contemporary art movement in the sixties, it was joining what appeared to be the most exciting force in art at that time. The perceived failure of the three New York museums devoted to modern art, the Museum of Modern Art, the Whitney, and the Guggenheim, to keep up with contemporary art made the challenge seem even more tempting, especially in light of the museum's long felt sense of competition with New York's more established museums.[140] Alan Solomon, Sam Hunter, and Karl Katz all had backgrounds in contemporary art and were led to understand that the Jewish Museum wanted to enter that field.[141] Louis Finkelstein and others at the Seminary were fully aware of the contemporary art orientation of the museum's directors—in fact the three directors were hired because they had such backgrounds—they just could not have predicted the direction in which sixties art would go, or their own difficulty in understanding or approving of it.[142]

As the sixties wore on, Finkelstein, personally, felt distressed by the art he saw at the Jewish Museum. In 1965 Vera List and Sam Hunter reported to Finkelstein that Elbert Weinberg's "Procession," a sculpture group abstractly depicting men bearing a Torah (which had stood in the museum's small sculpture garden since 1959) had been put in storage to make way for sculpture by artist Larry Rivers in conjunction with his 1965 show. Finkelstein reacted angrily to the sculpture's removal:

> As I told Mr. Hunter, it seems to me, despite my ignorance of art, that this particular piece of sculpture ought to be continuously on view before the museum because it symbolizes, as very few other works of art do, what the museum itself stands for and also what the Seminary stands for . . . I do not know why it should be removed simply for the sake of showing pieces of art which are unconnected with the meaning of the museum, or the meaning of the Seminary, or the meaning of Judaism.[143]

H. G. Friedman also expressed growing distress: "I can only say to you that in Paradise it must be a bit disturbing even to the equanimity of the souls of Mr. and Mrs. Warburg to find that the Jewish Museum to which they gave their home and important collections can only publicize what is not Jewish."[144]

Exasperation, bewilderment, and anger were present on the museum's side as well. Sam Hunter voiced some of this in a reminiscence of his era at the museum:

The Jewish Museum belongs to the Jewish Theological Seminary, which is completely parochial and subject to the most incredibly conservative pressures in the Jewish community. Modern art was like a thorn in the trustees' side. The more successful we were the more depressed they became. It's an absolute coincidence that we did so much with a tenth of the budget other museums had and under such parochial auspices. It was the right thing at the right time but the wrong place.[145]

Underlying this conflict were sharp differences of opinion about the role Jews should play in American life and culture, particularly when it came to art. In creating cultural programs with Jewish content—such as the radio programs broadcast by *The Eternal Light* or the essays in *The Jews*—and casting them out onto the mainstream of American cultural life, Louis Finkelstein had hoped to teach all Americans something about Jews and Judaism. But Jewish art, whether it was defined as ceremonial objects or as paintings by Jewish artists on Jewish themes, was, as the experience of the fifties proved, not consistently appealing enough to the general public to serve as an effective medium for conveying Judaism or Jewish culture.

And yet, when the Jewish Museum began showing contemporary art, its directors and supporters had to struggle to explain this art's relation to Judaism. The first attempt at this was Leo Steinberg's equation of Judaism with the Abstract Expressionist paintings on view at the "New York School" show. In his effort to find an affinity between abstraction and Judaism, Steinberg represented Judaism as something essentially formless—very different from the solid themes and values presented by Finkelstein in his outreach programs.

While Steinberg strained to make a connection between Judaism and contemporary art, neither Alan Solomon nor Sam Hunter was concerned with extracting specifically Jewish meanings from it. Instead, they understood Jewish contributions to contemporary art in terms of patronage, or else they noted Jews' contributions, broadly, to "contemporary life." Alan Solomon's definition of what was Jewish in contemporary art was as nebulous as Steinberg's. He noted that due to the turn towards the abstract in art, Jewish themes could literally no longer be discerned in painting. "Plainly then," he wrote,

> Jewish contributions to contemporary art, like Jewish contributions to contemporary life, have to do not with specific 'facts' or subjects or styles but with predispositions toward and affinities for certain ethical values, spiritual ideas, or cultural attitudes, for which, even acknowledging their specifically Jewish sources, it is extremely difficult to make exclusive claims.

To make such claims would be, according to Solomon, to court charges of "parochialism." Solomon felt that the Jewish Museum could model itself after such institutions as Brandeis University or the 92nd Street YM–YWHA, both of which were institutions under Jewish sponsorship that ran cultural programs directed at "the cultural life of the whole community."[146]

347

*A Collision
of Cultures:
The Jewish
Museum and
the Jewish
Theological
Seminary*

Sam Hunter, who took over as director in 1965, equated Judaism with the broad themes of modernity and humanism and, like Solomon, compared the Jewish Museum to other Jewish institutions that ran programs of general culture. He saw the museum "as a product and instrument of Jewish humanism which seeks full participation in American life without surrendering Jewish identity."[147] Hunter's first policy statement on assuming the directorship was in the form of an article in the *New York Times*, since by then the mission of the Jewish Museum had become a matter of heated public debate:

> That the Seminary could look with favor on an advanced art program is not astonishing in terms of the efforts of the official Jewish community and its spokesmen ever since the so-called "enlightenment" period of the early nineteenth century to seek full intellectual participation in Western culture. Without losing touch with its historic roots, Judaism has continued to reconstruct itself to meet the challenge of modern life.

Hunter referred to *Commentary* magazine (published by the American Jewish Committee) and the *Menorah Journal*, both "distinguished precedents for the two distinct involvements of the Jewish Museum, and for the consensus view that such a duality of interests could be creative rather than restricting."[148]

A commitment to modernity and humanity, vital involvement in contemporary American life—these were important to Conservative Judaism and to Louis Finkelstein. Yet the Seminary could not continue to accept such formless definitions of Judaism—especially when, to Finkelstein and others at the Seminary, the art being shown at the Jewish Museum was not only incomprehensible but disagreeable. Finally, its patience worn to the breaking point, the Seminary brought the museum's contemporary art program to a halt in January 1971.[149]

Conclusion

The Jewish Museum was similar to the outreach and intergroup programs established by Louis Finkelstein, but there was an important difference. That difference was art, the medium through which the museum hoped to express itself, especially from 1947 to 1970. The failure of specifically Jewish art to attract a wide audience by the fifties—a diminution of the appeal it seemed to hold for the public during the thirties and early forties—caused the Jewish Museum to turn to a general contemporary art program experimentally in 1957 and formally by 1963. The Seminary's lack of sympathy with this art program led to seismic rifts between the two institutions during the sixties and the ending of the contemporary art program in 1971.

Yet a sizable gap between the two institutions existed even before the Jewish Museum's move to the Warburg house in 1947. The Seminary was a bad parent to the museum, submitting it to long periods of neglect punctuated by periodic short bursts of attention. It was repaid for this neglect in the sixties when, in the spirit of the times, the museum rebelled to follow an independent path. But if the museum was a troublesome child, this may have been partly due to the fact that it was an unwanted one. The Seminary, even during the Adler years, never actively chose to establish a museum. The influence such important donors as H. G. Friedman, Frieda Schiff Warburg, and Albert and Vera List had over the programs and policies of the museum is an example of how vulnerable an institution can be when it has no fully enunciated policies of its own.

Given all that we know about dysfunctional families, the Jewish Museum should have turned out badly—but it did not. During the thirties, when Jews in Germany were feeling the first constraints of repression, the Museum of Jewish Ceremonial Objects was able to bolster the spirits and repair the pride of American Jews with the popular Maimonides exhibit. The museum was also able to provide a home for the expelled Danzig Museum and, after the war, to serve as a repository for some of the former collections of other destroyed European Jewish museums. Even before Louis Finkelstein conceived of his intergroup programs, the museum, under Paul Romanoff, took a stance against local anti-Semitism.

During the sixties the Jewish Museum played a crucial role in the advancement of contemporary art, gaining status in the eyes of New York's art world—even though it did so at the price of consternation and incomprehension among the city's traditional Jews. Yet even while controversy swirled around the exhibits of contemporary art, exhibits on Jewish themes continued and the dual program remained truly dual, even vital. Pursuing a theme that had long been of interest to Stephen Kayser, Alan Solomon presented "Recent American Synagogue Architecture" in 1963. "*Habdalah*," 1964, showed the spice boxes, kiddush cups, and candlesticks in the museum's collection. "The Lower East Side: Portal to American Life (1870-1924)," curated by the museum's assistant director, Allon Schoener, was pathbreaking in its use of audiovisual effects and photographic blow-ups. The exhibit attracted crowds when it opened in the fall of 1966, leading the museum to reopen it the following spring.[150] "Masada: A Struggle for Freedom," fall 1967, illustrating the archaeological discoveries made by Yigael Yadin, also attracted crowds of visitors. That this exhibit came only months after the Six-Day War doubtless contributed to its popularity.[151]

The popularity of the Jewish Museum's Lower East Side and Masada exhibits reflected a new interest in ethnicity that continues to the present day. Other "ethnic" museums, such as the *Museo del Barrio* and the Studio Museum in Harlem, were founded in the late sixties. The Museum of Chinese in the Americas, pursuing

349

*A Collision
of Cultures:
The Jewish
Museum and
the Jewish
Theological
Seminary*

Visitors at the
museum's Masada
exhibit, 1967-68.
*Ratner Center,
JTS.*

the same trend, was founded more recently.[152] In 1969 Allon Schoener brought both the ethnic theme and the technical effects he developed at the Lower East Side exhibit to the controversial but influential show he curated at the Metropolitan Museum of Art: "Harlem on My Mind."[153]

Between them, the Jewish Museum and the Jewish Theological Seminary created a forum—at times a battlefield—of debate about what a Jewish museum should be. The strain between the two institutions may even be said to have leavened the debate, producing a wealth of ideas in the effort to satisfy often conflicting concerns. The answers they arrived at were never absolute; different times and circumstances required different solutions.

These debates paralleled struggles taking place on the broader field of American and, more specifically, New York Jewish culture. From 1904 to 1971 New York's Jewish community was culturally recast several times. From a community that at the turn of the century had only begun to integrate the mass immigration of Jews from Eastern Europe, it was, by the early seventies, a vibrant, if still evolving, entity with prestige beyond its numbers in American society. Certainly by the sixties and seventies, Jewish involvement in many areas of the arts had become commonplace.

Yet despite the acculturation of New York's Jews, and despite the Seminary's commitment to Americanization, the visual arts marked a boundary on the American cultural scene beyond which the Seminary simply did not want to go. The Jewish Museum, staffed by people whose foremost interest was the visual arts, chafed at this limitation. Thus, despite their close family relationship, the institutional cultures of the Seminary and the museum were distinctly different. The contrasting spirits of the two institutions can be felt in their halls even today.

1. The authors would like to thank Jenna Weissman Joselit, Sharon Liberman Mintz, and Rebecca Jacobs, who read and commented on an earlier version of this essay. My work on this essay is dedicated to the memory of my grandmothers, Minnie Singer Miller and Mollie Meyerowitz Silver—JM.

2. See, for instance, Tom L. Freudenheim, "The Jewish (Jewish) Museum," *Moment 2* (1976): pp. 27-29; 51-52, 28, for this characterization of the sixties at the Jewish Museum.

3. Calvin Tomkins, *Off the Wall: Robert Rauschenberg and the Art of Our Time* (New York: Doubleday, 1980), p. 255.

4. Donald M. Wilson, acting director of the U.S. Information Agency, to Alan Solomon, 7 November 1963, Jewish Theological Seminary of America, Ratner Center for the Study of Conservative Judaism, Records of the Jewish Theological Seminary, Record Group 11, Communications Department, Series C, box 47, folder 4. Collections from the Ratner Center will hereinafter be abbreviated using the following format: R.G.11C-47-4.

5. S.M.F. to Alan Solomon, 26 April 1963, R.G.25-2-9.

6. Alexander Marx, "The Library," in *The Jewish Theological Seminary of America, Semi-Centennial Volume*, ed. Cyrus Adler (New York: Jewish Theological Seminary of America, 1939), pp. 89-90.

7. Marx, "The Library," p. 90. See also Emily D. Bilski, "Seeing the Future Through the Light of the Past: The Art of the Jewish Museum," in *The Seminary at 100. Reflections on the Jewish Theological Seminary and the Conservative Movement*, ed. Nina Beth Cardin and David Wolf Silverman (New York: The Rabbinical Assembly and the Jewish Theological Seminary of America, 1987), p. 143, and registrar's card files, S501-526, Jewish Museum.

8. Reproduced in *Register of the Jewish Theological Seminary of America* (New York: Jewish Theological Seminary, 1922), facing p. 12.

9. See Joseph Guttman, "Is There A Jewish Art?" in *The Visual Dimension: Aspects of Jewish Art*, ed. Clare Moore (Boulder, San Francisco, and Oxford: Westview Press, 1993), pp. 1-19. On some of the social processes involved, see Pierre Birnbaum and Ira Katznelson, "Emancipation and the Liberal Offer," in *Paths of Emancipation: Jews, States, and Citizenship*, ed. Pierre Birnbaum and Ira Katznelson (Princeton: Princeton University Press, 1995), pp. 3-36.

10. See Richard I. Cohen, "Self-Image Through Objects: Toward a Social History of Jewish Art Collecting and Jewish Museums," in *The Uses of Tradition: Jewish Continuity in the Modern Era*, ed. Jack Wertheimer (New York: Jewish Theological Seminary of America; Cambridge, Mass.: distributed by Harvard University Press, 1992), p. 215, for a discussion of Solomon Schechter's conflict with Joseph Jacob over the Anglo-Jewish Exhibition, London, 1887. See also Schechter's review of Israel Abrahams, "Jewish Life in the Middle Ages," *Critical Review of Theological and Philosophical Literature* 7 (1897): pp. 16-21, which criticizes Abrahams's interest in the daily life of Jews. Our thanks to Elliott Horowitz of Bar-Ilan University for this reference.

11. Marx, "The Library," p. 91.

12. Ibid., p. 117.

13. Ibid., p. 118.

14. Grace Cohen Grossman, "Judaica at the Smithsonian," unpublished essay, pp. 46-47. We thank Ms. Grossman, curator of the Skirball Museum in Los Angeles, for sharing her essay with us and allowing us to refer to it in various contexts in this essay.

15. At that time the ark was thought to have been given by the Duke of Urbino to the Jewish community there in 1451. See JTS *Register*, p. 154. A recent Jewish Museum catalog describes it as dating from 1533, with no mention of the Duke. See Norman L. Kleeblatt and Vivian B. Mann, *Treasures of the Jewish Museum* (New York: Universe Books, 1986), pp. 52-53.

16. Cyrus Adler, *I Have Considered the Days* (Philadelphia: Jewish Publication Society, 1941); Cyrus Adler, "Semi-Centennial Address," in *Semi-Centennial Volume*, p. 14; Cyrus Adler and I. M. Casanowicz, *Descriptive Catalogue of a Collection of Objects of Jewish Ceremonial Deposited in the U.S. National Museum by Hadji Ephraim Benguiat* (Washington D.C.: U.S. Government Printing Office, 1901); Cyrus Adler and I. N. Casanowicz, *The Collection of Jewish Ceremonial Objects in the United States National Museum* (Washington D.C.: U.S. Government Printing Office, 1908); JTS *Register*, 1931-1932, pp. 154-55; Abraham A. Neuman, "Cyrus Adler, A Biographical Sketch," in *American Jewish Year Book*, vol. 42, ed. Harry Schneiderman (Philadelphia: Jewish Publication Society, 1940), pp. 23-144; A. S. W. Rosenbach, "The Seminary Museum," in Adler, *Semi-Centennial Volume*, pp. 145-46; Frieda Schiff Warburg, *Reminiscences of a Long Life* (New York: Privately printed, 1956), pp. 102, 110.

17. JTS *Register*, 1931-1932, pp. 154-55. Alexander Marx used the ark to store rare books and manuscripts. Later on Stephen Kayser, the Jewish Museum's curator, 1947-1962, had to convince Marx to give the ark up to the museum. See Grace Cohen Grossman, "Stephen S. Kayser: A Personal Testimony," in *Threescore and Ten: Essays in Honor of Rabbi Seymour J. Cohen on the Occasion of His Seventieth Birthday*, ed. Abraham J. Karp, Louis Jacobs, and Chaim Zalman Dimitrovsky (Hoboken: KTAV, 1991), p. 415.

18. Maimonides Octocentennial Committee, "Celebration of the Eight Hundredth Birthday of Moses Maimonides," (pamphlet), Ratner Center Vertical File for Maimonides.

19. For the increase in hours, see news release, 22 January 1933, R.G.1A-17-20. Also see the correspondence in this file for the work of the Maimonides Octocentennial Committee and especially Adler's involvement in it. For these attendance statistics and others, see note 45.

20. JTS *Register*, 1934-1935—1942-1943.

21. Maurice Hexter, "Necrology, H. G. Friedman, 1881-1965," *American Jewish Historical Quarterly* 55 (1965): pp. 541-44.

22. Alexander Marx to Cyrus Adler, 17 March 1938, R.G.1A-16-65. See also JTS *Register* for these years.

23. H. G. Friedman to Alexander Marx, 24 December 1941, R.G.1A-8-39.

24. The reputation of Alexander Marx as a bibliographer and scholar may have also helped to make the museum known outside the United States. Marx maintained a worldwide correspondence with rabbis, Jewish scholars, dealers in Jewish books, and librarians throughout his life. See the Alexander Marx papers (Arch 80) in the library of the Jewish Theological Seminary.

25. See correspondence between Cyrus Adler and Alexander Marx, May 1938, R.G.1A-16-65.

26. In the course of these negotiations Adler asked Henrietta Buchman of the JDC about the welfare of other Judaica collections: "In this connection, I am wondering what is happening to the Jewish collections of the Berlin Gemeinde or the Seminaries, as well as the collections in Breslau." Cyrus Adler to Henrietta K. Buchman, JDC, 14 March 1939, R.G.1A-6-37. Earlier, Adler had shown little initiative in the effort to try to save Judaica collections from Jewish seminaries in Germany. See Israel Schapiro, Library of Congress, to Cyrus Adler, 15 February 1939, and Cyrus Adler to Alexander Marx, 20 February 1939, R.G.1A-16-65.

27. Joseph Gutman, "The Danzig Treasures," in *Danzig 1939: Treasures of a Destroyed Community*, The Jewish Museum (Detroit: Wayne State University Press for The Jewish Museum, 1980), p. 37, and "Museum Collection of the Danzig Jewish Community," R.G.11C-25-1.

28. JTS *Register*, 1940-1941, pp. 77-78. For Scribner's window display, see news reprint, no citation, "Danzig Museum in Exile. Seminary is Haven for Collection Saved from Nazis Destruction," [summer 1945], R.G.11C-25-2. It is reproduced as an illustration in the

essay by Marsha Rozenblit in these volumes.

29. For information about the Danzig Museum, see Jewish Museum, *Danzig, 1939*. Archival material documenting negotiations for the collection and its arrival in New York can be found in R.G.1A-6-37, R.G.11C-24-40 to 42, R.G.11C-25-1 and 2, and Jewish Museum Records, Arch. 60, Jewish Theological Seminary Library. See also JTS *Register*, 1940-1941, pp. 77-78.

30. Grace Cohen Grossman, "Stephen S. Kayser," pp. 410-11; Joan Rosenbaum, introduction to Kleeblatt and Mann, *Treasures*, p. 10; JTS *Register*, 1940-1941, p. 80; R.G.11C-46-17 and 18; Simon Greenberg to Rose Mintz, 12 May 1947, R.G.25-1-3. Grossman elaborates on this story, revealing that the Mintzes' plan was a "ruse" meant to enable him and his wife to leave Warsaw for the United States, display the collection, then sell it to raise funds for their eventual settlement in Palestine. Grossman, "Stephen S. Kayser," p. 424, note 21.

31. For Romanoff's thesis topic: Paul Romanoff to Cyrus Adler, 6 March 1934, R.G.1A-22-39.

32. Adler's years as president of Dropsie College for Hebrew and Cognate Studies in Philadelphia (1908-40) overlapped with his years as President of the Seminary (Acting President, 1916-24; President, 1924-40), requiring him to commute between New York and Philadelphia. For a reference to Adler's recommendation of Romanoff, see Paul Romanoff to Cyrus Adler, 22 December 1931, R.G.1A-22-39.

33. Louis Finkelstein to Cyrus Adler, 14 January 1932, R.G.1A-22-39.

34. See Adler's 6 July 1938 letter to Paul Romanoff, cited on p. 19, below.

35. A[rthur] O[ppenheimer] to Cyrus Adler, 24 August 1938, R.G.1A-22-39.

36. For Romanoff's pleas for raises in pay and descriptions of his poverty and family obligations, see his letters to Cyrus Adler and Louis Finkelstein in R.G.1A-22-39.

37. Romanoff wrote three books: *Onomasticon of Palestine: A New Method in Post Biblical Topography* (New York, 1937), reprinted from *The Proceedings of The American Academy for Jewish Research* 7 (1935–36), pp. 147–227; *The Fox in Jewish Tradition* (New York: Columbia University Press, 1942), and *Jewish Symbols on Ancient Jewish Coins* (Philadelphia: Dropsie College, 1944). He published reviews and articles, some based on the museum's collections, in *Horeb, Bitzaron, Review of Religion* and other journals, and lectured at the American Academy of Jewish Research, the Metropolitan Museum of Art (see Romanoff's letters to Adler, 10 June and 12 November 1936, R.G.1A-22-39), and the American Numismatic Society (see R.G.1A-22-39).

38. Paul Romanoff to Cyrus Adler, 19 October 1933, R.G.1A-22-39.

39. See Ira Robinson, ed. *Cyrus Adler, Selected Letters* (Philadelphia: Jewish Publication Society; New York: Jewish Theological Seminary, 1985).

40. When Romanoff attempted to take on projects on his own initiative, he received rebuffs from all three. For his efforts to catalog the collection and to give Sunday afternoon lectures and radio talks, see his correspondence with Adler, Marx, and Finkelstein in R.G.1A-22-39.

41. Cyrus Adler to Paul Romanoff, 6 July 1938, R.G.1A-22-39.

42. Cyrus Adler to Louis Finkelstein, 6 July 1938; Paul Romanoff to Cyrus Adler, 17 July 1938, R.G.1A-22-39.

43. Biographical information about Romanoff comes from an obituary in Jewish Theological Seminary Library, Arch. 60, Jewish Museum Files, box 2, and from letters there and in R.G.1A-22-39 and R.G.1B-39-14.

44. Romanoff's attendance chart for 1940 and 1941 breaks down visitors by religion, sex, age, and type of group, R.G.1A-22-39. It is interesting that the smallest (1941) and second smallest (1940) percentage of visitors recorded on the chart came from art groups.

45. According to Romanoff's attendance charts for December 1931—April 1939 and 1932-1941, visitor figures for these years are: 1932, 10,768; 1933, 12,875; 1934, 14,026; 1935,

22,845 (the popularity of the Maimonides exhibition accounts for this jump); 1936, 13,727; 1937, 14,243; 1938, 20,180; 1939, 20,853; 1940, 26,555, R.G.1A-22-39. JTS *Register* for 1939-1940 (p. 87), 1940-1941 (p. 76), and 1942-1943 (p. 82) provide the following figures which are calculated by academic year: 1938-1939, 19,672; 1939-1940, 26,686; 1940-41—1941-42, nearly 44,000 for the two academic years.

46. Paul Romanoff to Cyrus Adler, 30 March 1933, R.G.1A-22-39.

47. Anna Wright to Paul Romanoff (copy), 5 December 1939, R.G.1A-22-39.

48. Paul Romanoff, report, 18 May 1939, p. 2, R.G.1A-22-39.

49. Paul Romanoff to Cyrus Adler, 10 May 1939, R.G.1A-22-39.

50. Paul Romanoff to Louis Finkelstein, 24 November 1939, R.G.1A-22-39. Romanoff is referring to the anti-Semitic radio priest, Father Charles Coughlin.

51. Marx, "The Library," p. 90. Freudenheim, "The (Jewish) Jewish Museum," p. 28, and Avram Kampf, "The Jewish Museum: An Institution Adrift," *Judaism* 3 (summer 1968): p. 290, both mention the Seminary's failure to develop a study collection at the museum.

52. See, for instance, Adler's "Museum Collections to Illustrate Religious History and Ceremonials," (Washington D.C.: U. S. Government Printing Office, 1895).

53. JTS *Register*, 1940-1941, p. 79.

54. Louis Finkelstein to Paul Romanoff, 3 June 1941, R.G.1A-22-39.

55. "Speech by Mrs. Felix M. Warburg at the Dedication of The Jewish Museum, 7 May 1947," R.G.11-44-29. Frieda Warburg describes her relationship with Nina Warburg throughout her *Reminiscences*. The purchase of the house from the estate of Nina Warburg's husband, Felix Warburg's brother Paul Warburg, is mentioned in Harry Bober, "The Gothic Tower and the Stork Club," *Arts and Sciences* (a New York University publication) (spring 1962): p. 5. See also Julie Miller, "Planning the Jewish Museum, 1944-1947," *Conservative Judaism* 47 (fall 1994): pp. 72-73 for a (similarly inconclusive) discussion of where the idea for using the Warburg house for the Jewish Museum could have come from.

56. For more on Frieda Schiff Warburg, her family, and her role in the development of the Jewish Museum see: Ron Chernow, *The Warburgs: The 20th-Century Odyssey of a Remarkable Jewish Family* (New York: Random House, 1993); Miller, "Planning the Jewish Museum;" Warburg, *Reminiscences;* and the correspondence of Louis Finkelstein and Jessica Feingold with Frieda Schiff Warburg in R.G.1, Series B, C, and D.

57. Marx, "The Library," p. 87.

58. Schoenberger also lectured at New York University's Institute of Fine Arts. For Schoenberger's career see "Academic Record of Guido Schoenberger," and Walter W. S. Cook to Frieda Schiff Warburg, 17 January 1944, R.G.1B-39-66; Rachel Wischnitzer, "Guido Schoenberger (1891-1974)," *Journal of Jewish Art* 3-4 (1977), p. 132; Felicitas Heimann-Jelinek, *Was uebrig blieb. Das Museum Juedischer Altertuemer in Frankfurt, 1922-1938* (Frankfurt: Juedisches Museum Frankfurt, 1988), p. 37. For Schoenberger's role in recovering the Frankfurt objects see: Grace Grossman, "Stephen Kayser," p. 412; Helen Hirsch, "The Jewish Museum Observing the Tenth Anniversary," *The Jewish Standard*, Jersey City, New Jersey, 27 September 1957, and Stephen Kayser, "The Jewish Museum After Ten Years," *Adult Jewish Education* (spring 1957): pp. 6-9, 7.

59. Louis Finkelstein, ed. *The Jews: Their History, Culture, and Religion* (Philadelphia: Jewish Publication Society, 1949). Subsequent editions were published in 1955, 1960, and 1971. Records documenting the conception, preparation, publication, and reception of the first three editions of *The Jews* are in R.G. 36, *The Jews: Their History, Culture, and Religion*. For Finkelstein's reasons for undertaking the book, see his "The Need for an Authoritative, Comprehensive book on Judaism," R.G. 36-1-30. The questionnaires and related interpretative material are also in R.G. 36. It is possible that the distancing effect of the question

355

*A Collision
of Cultures:
The Jewish
Museum and
the Jewish
Theological
Seminary*

had something to do with the tone of the responses. In 1957 Finkelstein sent out a similar questionnaire and received essentially the same result. R.G. 36 also documents the later survey.

60. Louis Finkelstein to Sholome Gelber, American Joint Distribution Committee, Bergen-Belsen, Germany, 5 April 1946, R.G. 36-1-21.

61. "The Eternal Light, Tenth Anniversary," Ratner Center for the Study of Conservative Judaism Vertical Files, file for *The Eternal Light*.

62. Louis Finkelstein to Irving Bennett, 21 May 1947, R.G. 25-1-16.

63. Louis Finkelstein to Frieda Warburg, 6 January 1944, R.G.11C-48-25; Louis Finkelstein to Frieda Warburg, 6 April 1944, R.G.1B-41-38; Louis Finkelstein to Frieda Warburg, 28 September 1945 (marked "not sent, to be filed") R.G.1C-55-15. Jessica Feingold became the executive director of the Institute in 1951 and the executive vice-president of the Conference in 1956. From 1959 until her retirement in 1983 she was the Seminary's director of intergroup activities.

64. Kenneth T. Jackson, ed., *The Encyclopedia of New York City* (New Haven: Yale University Press, 1995), entry on museums. Quotation is as cited in Julie Miller, "Frieda Schiff Warburg, First Woman Member of the Jewish Theological Seminary's Board of Directors," unpublished essay, Ratner Center, Vertical File.

65. Robert A. M. Stern, *New York 1930: Architecture and Urbanism Between the Two World Wars* (New York: Rizzoli, 1987), p. 109. See also Jackson, *Encyclopedia of New York City*, entry on Morningside Heights, and Elliot Willensky and Norval White, *AIA Guide to New York City* 3d ed. (New York: Harcourt, Brace, Jovanovich, 1988), pp. 418-27.

66. Warburg, *Reminiscences*, p. 130. Two museums, the Metropolitan (1874) and the American Museum of Natural History directly across Central Park (1869), were already long established when the Warburgs moved into the house in 1908. More were founded during the years they lived there: the Museum of Modern Art (1929), Whitney Museum of American Art (1931), Guggenheim Museum (1937). The Warburg's youngest son, Edward M. M. Warburg, an important patron of modern art, was involved in the founding of the Museum of Modern Art. See Nicholas Fox Weber, *Patron Saints: Five Rebels Who Opened America to a New Art, 1928-1943* (New York: Alfred A. Knopf, 1992). Weber describes how Frieda and Felix Warburg did not really understand modern art, but they were willing to be the financial backers of their son's projects. Louis Finkelstein attempted to involve Edward Warburg in the Jewish Museum, but he only very occasionally succeeded. See, for instance, Edward Warburg's "A Report to the Committee of the Board of Trustees of the Jewish Theological Seminary on the Possible Reorientation of the Jewish Museum" [1950], R.G.21-1-58.

67. Museum Advisory Committee members are listed in the catalog, *Inaugural Exhibition: The Giving of the Law and the Ten Commandments, Jewish Art of Late Antiquity, Works of Contemporary Artists, The Torah in Synagogue Art* (New York: The Jewish Museum, [1947]), Ratner Center vertical file for the Jewish Museum.

68. For a description of Jewish art organizations in New York, see Norman L. Kleeblatt and Susan Chevlowe, "Painting a Place in America: Jewish Artists in New York, 1900-1945," in *Painting a Place in America: Jewish Artists in New York, 1900-1945, A Tribute to the Educational Alliance Art School*, ed. Norman L. Kleeblatt and Susan Chevlowe (New York: The Jewish Museum; Bloomington: Indiana University Press, 1991), pp. 89-149.

69. Louis Finkelstein to Frieda Warburg, 10 September 1944, R.G.1B-41-38.

70. Richard Krautheimer, *Corpus Basilicarum Christianarum Romae* [The early Christian basilicas of Rome], (Citta del Vaticano: Pontificio Instituto di Archeologia Cristiana, 1937-1977).

71. Richard Krautheimer, *Mittelalterliche Synagogen* (Berlin: Frankfurter Verlags-Anstalt, 1927).

72. Louis Finkelstein to Frieda Warburg, 19 June 1944, R.G.1B-41-38.

73. For Finkelstein's negotiations with Krautheimer, see Louis Finkelstein to Frieda Warburg, 1 June , 19 June, 22 June, 11 July, 13 July, 14 July 1944, R.G.1B-41-38. Slobodan Curcic et al., "Richard Krautheimer" [obituary] *Speculum* 70 (1995): pp. 731-32.

74. Helen Epstein, "Meyer Schapiro: A Passion to Know and Make Known," Part 2, *Art News* (summer 1983): pp. 91. For more on Schapiro see: John Russell, "Meyer Schapiro, 91, Is Dead; His Work Wove Art and Life," *New York Times*, 4 March 1996.

75. Louis Finkelstein to Meyer Schapiro, 13 December 1945, R.G.1C-53-33. This was the beginning of a long relationship between Meyer Schapiro and the Jewish Museum. Letters in the Jewish Museum records at the Seminary and at the museum document his role as a respected advisor over a period of many years.

76. Simon Greenberg is first listed as the Jewish Museum's director in the JTS *Register* for 1951-1952, but it is clear that he occupied a supervisory role over Kayser from the time the museum opened in 1947. On 3 December 1946 Greenberg wrote Stephen Kayser, "Now that I have assumed my duties as Provost at the Seminary, Doctor Finkelstein has asked me to take a closer interest in all matters referring to the Museum." R.G.25-1-3. On 9 October 1947, Finkelstein wrote Frieda Warburg that he was planning to appoint Greenberg as director, R.G.1D-63-17. Avram Kampf states that Greenberg was named director at the time Kayser was hired in "An Institution Adrift," p. 285. Marjorie Wyler, then head of the Seminary's office of public relations, remembers that Greenberg was put over Kayser in order to ensure that the Seminary's interests were represented (Marjorie Wyler, interview by Julie Miller, 14 November 1995). Finkelstein's 9 October 1947 letter to Warburg (see above) implies the same thing.

77. Biographical statement in Stephen Kayser Papers, box 1, Jewish Museum archives; Steven Fine, "Professor Stephen S. Kayser (1900-1988)," [obituary] *Jewish Art* 15 (1989): pp. 120-21; Grossman, "Stephen Kayser," pp. 403-26; Stephen Kayser, "After Displacements I Find Coherence Again," in R. M. MacIver, *The Hour of Insight* (New York: Institute for Religious and Social Studies, 1954), pp. 41-50. Kayser edited *Jewish Ceremonial Art*, a catalog of the Jewish Museum's collections (Philadelphia: Jewish Publication Society, 1955, 1959) and was the author of "Defining Jewish Art" in *Mordecai M. Kaplan Jubilee Volume* (New York: Jewish Theological Seminary, 1953) vol. 1, pp. 457-69.

78. Kayser, "After Displacements," p. 48.

79. Stephen Kayser to Louis Finkelstein, 28 March 1946, R.G.1C-49-45.

80. Stephen Kayser to Guido Schoenberger, 18 December 1946, R.G.25-1-3.

81. See minutes of the Museum Committee and Inner Museum Committee, R.G.25-1-21 and 28. For Percival Goodman's description of his work on the house and his relationship with Louis Finkelstein, see Bernard Rosenberg and Ernest Goldstein, *Creators and Disturbers: Reminiscences by Jewish Intellectuals of New York* (New York: Columbia University Press, 1982), p. 315.

82. Guido Schoenberger, "General Plan for a Museum of Jewish Culture in New York," 15 September 1944; Richard Krautheimer, "Comments on the Memorandum, 'General Plan for a Museum of Jewish Culture in New York'" [29 September 44]; minutes, Museum Advisory Committee, 31 October 1944, all R.G.25-1-27a, and minutes, Inner Museum Committee, 9 January 1947, R.G.25-1-21.

83. Krautheimer, "Comments on the Memorandum."

84. Minutes, Inner Museum Committee, 9 January 1947, R.G.25-1-21.

85. Ibid., 20 January 1947, R.G.25-1-21.

86. Schoenberger, "General Plan"; Krautheimer, "Comments on the Memorandum"; Paul Goodman and Benjamin Nelson, "Notes for a Museum of the Jewish Faith," n.d. [late 1944], R.G.25-1-29; Richard Krautheimer to Louis Finkelstein, 29 December 1944, com-

ments on the Goodman and Nelson plan, R.G. 25-1-29; memorandum by Guido Schoenberger to Louis Finkelstein, "Notes on a Memorandum for a Museum of the Jewish Faith by Dr. Paul Goodman and Dr. Benjamin N. Nelson," 29 December 1944, R.G. 25-1-29; Richard Krautheimer, "Memorandum Concerning Changes in Plan for the Jewish Museum," n.d. [1 May 1945], R.G.1C-49-64; Meyer Schapiro, "Memo for Conference," 26 June 1946, and "Memo for J.M." 25 June 1946, R.G. 25-1-3. Paul Goodman, author of *Growing Up Absurd: Problems of Youth in the Organized System* (New York: Random House, 1956) was later known as an inspiration for the youth movement of the sixties.

87. Goodman and Nelson, "Notes for a Museum," p. 2.

88. Krautheimer, "Comments on the Memorandum," p. 2.

89. Schoenberger, "General Plan for a Museum," p. 3.

90. Krautheimer, "Comments on the Memorandum," p. 3, the underlining is his; Krautheimer to Finkelstein, 29 December 1944, R.G.25-1-29.

91. Stephen Kayser to Harry G. Friedman, 7 September 1948, R.G.25-1-21.

92. Goodman and Nelson, "Notes for a Museum," pp. 2, 3.

93. Krautheimer, "Memorandum Concerning Changes," p. 3.

94. Goodman and Nelson, "Notes for a Museum," p. 11.

95. Louis Finkelstein to Richard Krautheimer, 2 May 1945, R.G.1C-49-64.

96. Krautheimer, "Memorandum Concerning Changes," p. 2.

97. Guido Schoenberger to Louis Finkelstein, 21 February 1945, R.G.1C-53-38.

98. Louis Finkelstein to Frieda Warburg, 28 September 1945, R.G.1C-55-15.

99. Schapiro, "Memo for J.M." The word "expression" is typed over "sentiment." Schapiro lists "Soyer" without indicating if he meant Moses or Raphael.

100. "Address of Dr. Meyer Schapiro, presented at the opening of the exhibit, 'The New York School, Second Generation,' at the Jewish Museum . . . 7 March 1957," verbatim transcript, R.G.1M-160-18.

101. Stephen Kayser to Louis Finkelstein, 31 March 1947, Stephen Kayser files, Jewish Museum.

102. See, for instance, William Innes Homer, *Alfred Stieglitz and the American Avant-Garde* (Boston: New York Graphic Society, 1977) for discussions of Stieglitz, Abraham Walkowitz, and Max Weber; Irving Howe, *World of Our Fathers* (New York: Harcourt Brace Jovanovich, 1976), especially the section on painters and sculptors, pp. 573-85; and Kleeblatt and Chevlowe, eds. *Painting a Place in America*.

103. Louis Finkelstein to Stephen Kayser, 1 April 1947, Stephen Kayser files, Jewish Museum; Louis Finkelstein to Israel Goldstein, 13 June 1955, Sam Hunter files, Jewish Museum. Finkelstein's daughter Hadassah Davis describes her father's indifference to the arts in a recent article: "LF was deaf to music, except for liturgical melodies; art meant nothing to him; he hardly ever attended theatrical performances of any kind." Hadassah Davis, "My Father, Louis Finkelstein," *Conservative Judaism* 47 (summer 1995): p. 87. Simon Greenberg and Moshe Davis both played significant roles in the Hebrew Arts Committee, but the committee's focus was on the performing arts, not the visual arts. See, for instance, Moshe Davis, *The Hebrew Arts Committee* (1944).

104. Simon Greenberg to Stephen Kayser, 14 February 1950, Stephen Kayser files, Jewish Museum. See other letters in these files for the "correspondence course" on art. In one exchange Kayser refutes the claim of a newspaper article Greenberg sent him that equated abstract art with Communism. In another, Kayser and Greenberg discuss the issue of whether one reads from left to right or right to left in a painting.

105. Simon Greenberg to Meyer Schapiro, 21 March 1957, R.G.1M-160-18. To understand, by way of contrast, what that exhibit meant to members of New York's art world, Calvin Tomkins describes how art dealer Leo Castelli had "his first great epiphany" on seeing

Jasper Johns's "Green Target" there. It was the first time a Johns painting had been publically exhibited. Tomkins, *Off the Wall*, p. 140.

106. See Deborah Dash Moore, "A Synagogue Center Grows in Brooklyn," in *The American Synagogue: A Sanctuary Transformed*, ed. Jack Wertheimer (Hanover, N.H.: University Press of New England, 1987), pp. 297-326; Stephen Kayser to Louis Finkelstein, 26 June 1947, Stephen Kayser files, Jewish Museum.

107. Stephen Kayser to Simon Greenberg, 15 April 1948, Stephen Kayser Files, Jewish Museum.

108. One of the aims of this course was to enable the rabbi "to deal practically with the questions which come up continually in connection with synagogue building and decoration," JTS *Register,* 1948-1949, p. 63. The report noting Kayser's "scores of hours" with synagogue building committees is: "Jewish Museum, January 1st to November 30, 1957, Report to the Board of Overseers, January 8, 1958," R.G.21-3-12. There are references to Kayser's advisory service in other reports to the Board of Overseers, his letters to Greenberg, clippings of articles about the Jewish Museum in scrapbooks in R.G.11, and in his "The Jewish Museum After Ten Years." The service was essentially informal, with no separate office or personnel.

109. Lyman Bryson, ed. *Approaches to World Peace* (New York: Conference on Science, Philosophy and Religion, 1944); Lyman Bryson, ed. *Learning and World Peace* (New York: Conference on Science, Philosophy and Religion, 1948); program for the Chicago Institute for Religious and Social Studies series on "Current Religious Thought," 1947-1948 in Stephen Kayser files, Jewish Museum.

110. Information about Institute lectures comes from the Institute's publicity posters, found in R.G. 16, Institute for Religious and Social Studies, box 97. The posters are undated, but the ones mentioned here probably come from the fifties and sixties.

111. JTS *Register,* 1930-1931 to 1951-1952; catalog, "The Women's Institute of Jewish Studies, Morning Classes, 1958-1959" Ratner Center Vertical Files, file for JTSA-Women's Institute of Jewish Studies.

112. University of Judaism, *Register,* 1958-1959; 1959-1960. For references to the museum branch at the University of Judaism, see Stephen Kayser's correspondence with Simon Greenberg, Stephen Kayser files, Jewish Museum, and scrapbooks, R.G.11.

113. Rachel Wischnitzer, "Judaism and Art," in Finkelstein, *The Jews*, vol. 3, pp. 984-1010.

114. Louis Finkelstein to Stephen Kayser, Stephen Kayser files, Jewish Museum. The emphasis is ours.

115. For Simon Greenberg's career, see Pamela S. Nadell, *Conservative Judaism in America: A Biographical Dictionary and Sourcebook* (New York: Greenwood Press, 1988), pp. 120-23.

116. For Kayser's expenses see Stephen Kayser to Simon Greenberg, 13 and 27 February 1948, Stephen Kayser files, Jewish Museum. The Museum's "shoe-string budget" of $1,750 per year for exhibitions is mentioned in Will Kramer's letter to the editor of *Judaism* 18 (winter 1969), p. 106. This letter was actually written by Kayser, as Grace Grossman reveals in her "Stephen Kayser," p. 426, note 47. Kampf ("An Institution Adrift," pp. 286-87) describes the lack of resources available to the Jewish Museum in this period. For a description of how the Jewish Museum was financed during these years see also Herbert Unterberger, "Survey—The Jewish Museum," draft, 10 April 1962, Marjorie Wyler Papers, box 2, folder 12, Ratner Center.

117. In 1948 two exhibitions did directly address destruction in Europe: photographs of ghetto life by George Kadish and drawings of destroyed synagogues by Georges Loukomski. The "Report to the Museum Committee of the Board of Overseers for Meeting, December 15, 1948," mentions these, R.G.21-1-31. Stephen Kayser also proposed an exhibit of destroyed European synagogues; see Miller, "Planning the Jewish Museum," p. 64.

118. "Jewish Museum Report to the Board of Overseers," 6 May 1947, R.G.21-1-20, p. 6.

119. For this phrase, and the account of the Jewish Museum's opening exhibition, see the catalog to the "Inaugural Exhibition," Ratner Center vertical file for the Jewish Museum.

120. Stephen Kayser to Simon Greenberg, 3 November 1947, Stephen Kayser files, Jewish Museum.

121. Stephen Kayser to Simon Greenberg, memorandum on "Plans and Activities of the Museum During Your Absence," 27 March 1947, Stephen Kayser files, Jewish Museum. For more on the archaeology exhibition at the opening, see Miller, "Planning the Jewish Museum."

122. Stephen Kayser to Louis Finkelstein, 31 March 1947, Stephen Kayser files, Jewish Museum.

123. "Jewish Museum Report to the Board of Overseers," 6 May 1947, R.G.21-1-18. For additional references to the proposed Chagall mural, see Stephen Kayser to Louis Finkelstein, 17 March 1947, Stephen Kayser files, Jewish Museum; minutes, Inner Museum Committee, 11 September 1947, R.G.25-1-21; Grossman, "Stephen Kayser," p. 414; Kampf, "An Institution Adrift," p. 284.

124. Stephen Kayser to Simon Greenberg, 3 November 1950, R.G.21-2-14. Kayser cites attendance figures for the month of October for the three years: 1948, 5480; 1949, 4606; 1950, 2438. Museum Administration Committee minutes, 12 December 1953, R.G.25-11-17.

125. For discussions about the Tercentenary exhibit see minutes of the Museum Committee for 28 April, 26 May, 16 June, 15 September, 29 September, 10 November, and 12 December 1953, and "Report On the Jewish Museum of the Jewish Theological Seminary," February-March 1954, all in R.G.25-11-17. The Tercentenary exhibit, "Under Freedom," was arranged under the sponsorship of the American Jewish Tercentenary Committee and the Jewish Museum and opened at the Jewish Museum on 1 December 1954. It traveled afterward to the Smithsonian Institution and the Metropolitan Museum of Art.

126. Lillian M. Schapiro, widow of Meyer Schapiro, remembers that Meyer Schapiro persuaded "the reluctant Louis Finkelstein" to allow "The New York School" to open at the museum. Lillian M. Schapiro, letter to Julie Miller, 1 April 1996.

127. Leo Steinberg, introduction in catalog, "The New York School: Second Generation," Jewish Museum, 10 March–28 April 1957, R.G.25, box 6. Another copy can be found in the exhibition archives at the Jewish Museum.

128. Stephen Kayser, "After Ten Years," in Jewish Museum tenth anniversary brochure, unpaged, Ratner Center vertical file for Jewish Museum.

129. "Address of Dr. Meyer Schapiro," p. 3.

130. Jewish Museum Report to the Board of Overseers, 8 January 1958, R.G. 21-3-12.

131. Clement Greenberg, "Adolph Gottlieb," in *An Exhibition of Oil Paintings by Adolph Gottlieb,* the Jewish Museum, 1957, catalog, R.G. 25, box 6.

132. "Objectives and Functions of the Jewish Museum, Revised Draft," 10 September 1962, Marjorie Wyler Papers, box 2, folder 12.

133. For the Jewish Museum's decision to let Stephen Kayser go, see Grossman, "Stephen Kayser," p. 417. For Kayser's displeasure with the turn the museum took after his departure, see Will Kramer's letter to the editor in *Judaism,* pp. 104-106. See note 116.

134. Jewish Museum Report for Board of Overseers, May 1963, in Jewish Theological Seminary Board of Directors minutes, 1963.

135. Emily Genauer, "Crowds See Jewish Museum's Exhibit on East Side Life," *World Journal Tribune,* 22 September 1966. Exhibits, controversies, and the rapid arrivals and departures of the Jewish Museum's three directors of the sixties were followed closely by the press. See, for instance, from the *New York Times:* "Jewish Museum Names Director of Operations" (Alan Solomon), 8 July 1962; "Director of Jewish Museum Named" (Sam Hunter),

19 March 1965; Sam Hunter, "The Jewish Museum: What Is It, Why Is It, and What Next?" 8 August 1965; Richard F. Shepard, "Jewish Museum Depicts a Ghetto. Lower East Side is Subject of a Magnificent Show," 21 September 1966 (this article asks: "Is it art? Is it Jewish? Who cares? Whatever it is, it is long overdue."); Milton Esterow, "Director of Jewish Museum Quits in Policy Rift" (Sam Hunter), 25 October 1967; Milton Esterow, "Jewish Museum Finds its New Director, Brooklyn-Born Karl Katz, in Israel," 3 April 1968; Grace Glueck, "Fingers, Jackstraws, and Lincoln Logs," 21 April 1968 ("the embattled outpost on upper Fifth that's perpetually torn between sacred [Jewish history and religion] and secular [Pop, Op, Primary Structures."]); Grace Glueck, "Museum Turns to All-Jewish Shows," 5 January 1971; Arthur A. Cohen, "Museum or Mausoleum?" 7 February 1971.

136. Tomkins, *Off the Wall,* p. 208.

137. S. K. to Mrs. Albert Fried, president, National Women's League of the United Synagogue of America, 16 May 1963, R.G.25-2-9.

138. JTS Board of Directors, executive committee minutes, 18 January 1963.

139. "Governing Principles: The Jewish Museum, 3 February 1966, suggested revisions and additions to Mr. [Arthur] Jacobs' memorandum from the director of the Museum." Sam Hunter files, Jewish Museum.

140. For this view of the Modern, Whitney, and Guggenheim, see Emily Genauer, "Crowds See Jewish Museum's Exhibit on East Side Life"; Kampf, "An Institution Adrift," p. 292; and Tomkins, *Off the Wall,* pp. 205-6.

141. The contemporary art program was adopted by the museum before Alan Solomon, the first director to work under the dual program, was hired. During negotiations for the job the Seminary's vice-president wrote Solomon: "A new major wing is currently under construction which will accommodate in addition to the present outstanding collection of Jewish ceremonial and traditional art a new focus on contemporary and modern art." Arthur Katz to Alan Solomon, 19 March 1962, R.G.1R-209-56. During the interval between Alan Solomon's resignation and the hiring of Sam Hunter, Hans van Weeren-Griek served as acting director.

142. For Avram Kampf's angry analysis of the financial reasoning behind Finkelstein's dismissal of Stephen Kayser in order to start a contemporary art program, see his letter in *Judaism* 18 (winter 1969): p. 108.

143. Vera List to Louis Finkelstein, 3 November 1965; Louis Finkelstein to Vera List, 8 November 1965, Sam Hunter files, Jewish Museum. "Procession," which had been the gift of Vera List, was reinstalled in the museum's sculpture garden in 1972. See "Report for the Board of Overseers," May 1972, R.G.21-7-22. Today it is in the courtyard of JTS.

144. Harry G. Friedman to Hans van Weeren-Griek, 4 August 1964.

145. Roberta Brandes Gratz, "Daily Close-Up. Wall-To-Wall Friends." *New York Post,* 12 January 1973.

146. "Some Observations on the Exhibition and Acquisition Policies of the Jewish Museum" transcript, n.d., unsigned, R.G.11C-47-35. This copy of Solomon's statement, found in the files of the Seminary's public relations department, has been almost completely crossed out, presumably by members of that department. The JTS *Register,* 1964-1966, contains a recognizable excerpt from the document and identifies it as Solomon's initial policy statement (p. 114). Another draft of the statement, also unsigned, but dated 1 August 1962, is in the Sam Hunter files at the Jewish Museum.

147. Sam Hunter to David Finn, 18 June 1965, Sam Hunter Files, Jewish Museum.

148. Sam Hunter, "The Jewish Museum: What Is It, Why Is It, and What Next?"

149. Grace Glueck, "Museum Turns to All-Jewish Shows," *New York Times,* 5 January 1971; press release, 11 January 1971, R.G.11C-47-16. See also: Daniel M. Friedenberg, "Can a

Jewish Museum Live by Art Alone?" *New York Times*, 29 August 1971.

150. See press releases and clippings of articles about the Lower East Side show in R.G. 11C-46-5.

151. For the Masada show, see publicity material in R.G. 11C-46-8 to 15.

152. The Museum of Chinese in the Americas was founded in 1980 as the Chinatown History Museum.

153. Michael Kimmelman, "Culture and Race: Still on America's Mind," *New York Times*, 19 November 1995.

.

JEFFREY SHANDLER & ELIHU KATZ

Broadcasting American Judaism

The Radio and Television Department of the Jewish Theological Seminary

David Sarnoff (left) and Louis Finkelstein in an NBC broadcasting studio, 1940s.
Ratner Center, JTS.

JEFFREY SHANDLER & ELIHU KATZ

Broadcasting American Judaism

The Radio and Television Department
of the Jewish Theological Seminary

Early in the tenure of
President Louis Finkelstein, the Jewish Theological Seminary took to the airwaves
in order to reach out to American Jews and their non-Jewish neighbors. By turning
to radio and, shortly thereafter, television, JTS embraced media with which it had
little experience, and to which, apparently, Finkelstein personally paid scant
attention.[1] This foray into broadcasting took place at a strategic moment both in the
Seminary's history and in the development of American broadcasting. During its
early years of production, JTS's Radio and Television Department[2] provided the
Seminary with its most extensive outreach to the world for several decades and
made a significant contribution towards the shaping of public affairs broadcasting.
From the mid-1940s through the late 1980s, JTS produced hundreds of hours of
broadcasting in conjunction with the three major national commercial networks
under various titles— *The Eternal Light* (on NBC radio and television), *Frontiers of
Faith* (NBC television), *Directions* (ABC television), *Lamp Unto My Feet* (CBS television)—reaching millions of Jews and non-Jews across the United States and
abroad.

In several ways, the agenda of the Radio and Television Department and its
output epitomize Finkelstein's vision for transforming the role of the Seminary and
of the Conservative movement during the middle decades of the 20th century. In
their content and configuration, the broadcasts produced by JTS also reflect larger
notions of Jews and Judaism, of religiosity and of ecumenism in post-World War II
America. An examination of these broadcasts (as well as correspondence and other
archival records pertaining to the Radio and Television Department and interviews
with some of its former employees) also raises a number of issues regarding the
particular opportunities and challenges that radio and television have offered Jews
for the presentation of self in the American context.

Revealing "the world's best kept secret":
The Seminary Begins Broadcasting

Although the emergence of the Radio and Television Department is closely identified with the Finkelstein administration, the Seminary made its first broadcasts under the tenure of Cyrus Adler. During the 1930s JTS produced a number of radio broadcasts on an ad hoc basis in conjunction with either local stations or one of the national networks. Among the earliest documented broadcasts was a speech by James Bryant Conant, president of Harvard University, on the occasion of the Seminary's fiftieth anniversary. The speech was broadcast on 15 March 1937 over New York station WEAF and the NBC Red network, and it was aired on W1XAL, an experimental international shortwave station devoted to nonprofit educational broadcasting.[3] During the late 1930s JTS essayed its first regular series of broadcasts with *The Women's Hour*, a weekly half-hour program aired on New York station WHN.[4] By 1939, JTS had engaged the services of Milton Krents, an attorney for the American Jewish Committee, to assist in arranging the Seminary's broadcasting efforts.[5]

The idea for a regular radio program presented by the Seminary in conjunction with a national network began to take shape during the late 1930s and early 1940s. According to Marjorie Wyler, who worked in the Seminary's Office of Public Information beginning in 1938 and became head of the Radio and Television Department in the 1980s, Finkelstein was interested in making appropriate and effective use of radio "to explain Judaism to the American public and to give Jews a better appreciation of their own heritage." These radio broadcasts, Finkelstein believed, would reveal Judaism, "the world's best kept secret," to both unaffiliated Jews and many non-Jews. Wyler reports that the facilitation of this agenda began with a meeting between Finkelstein and NBC president David Sarnoff, which was arranged by Seminary board member Arthur Sulzberger.[6] Sarnoff, who was interested in presenting a Jewish program on his network, agreed to underwrite a series produced in association with JTS.[7] According to Wyler, he stipulated that, as "Judaism was entitled to time as *one* of the major faiths in the United States," the Seminary's programming would have to represent Judaism as a whole and not just the Conservative movement.[8]

In 1944 the Seminary engaged Krents on a contingency basis to oversee the production of a then unnamed, regularly scheduled series of radio broadcasts.[9] (He continued to serve as producer of JTS's radio and television programming through the early 1980s.) Krents had proposed to Finkelstein that the JTS radio series could best fulfill its mission by broadcasting original dramas, as opposed to worship services, concerts of sacred music, or sermons, which had been the staples of most American religious broadcasting.[10] Radio drama had emerged as a "high" art form in the late 1930s; until then, dramatic broadcasts had largely been limited to soap operas and suspense serials. Landmark scripts by Norman Corwin (e.g., *They Fly Through the Air*, aired on CBS's *Words without Music* in 1939), Archibald MacLeish (*The Fall of the City*, aired by CBS's *Columbia Workshop* in 1937), and Orson Welles (CBS's *War of the Worlds*, aired on *Mercury Theater on the Air* in 1938) demonstrated that radio drama could effectively present topics of serious social concern to general audiences (all three of the aforementioned dramas were conceived as anti-Fascist allegories).[11]

At Krents's suggestion, the Seminary engaged playwright Morton Wishengrad to prepare a number of scripts for the series. Once an employee of the International Ladies Garment Workers Union's education department, Wishengrad had written plays for stage and radio. Among his broadcast credits were scripts for *Lands of the Free*, a Sunday afternoon drama series on the history of Latin America presented on NBC's *University of the Air*.[12] One of Wishengrad's first works for JTS, aired before the series proper had begun, was *The Battle of the Warsaw Ghetto*, a half-hour play that fuses elements of documentary and drama to recount the story of Jewish resistance against Nazi persecution. First aired on NBC in October 1943, only a few months after the uprising, the drama proved extremely effective, prompting extensive response from enthusiastic listeners.[13] During the remaining war years the network presented the play another two times, and it was broadcast internationally on Armed Forces Radio.[14] NBC reaired *The Battle of the Warsaw Ghetto* as late as 1977.[15]

After a close vote by its Board of Directors, JTS agreed to undertake the creation of a weekly series of dramatic broadcasts in conjunction with NBC. Wyler writes that the board "debated long and seriously, reluctant to commit scarce dollars to an avowedly experimental project."[16] In a recent interview, she also recalled that a considerable number of board members then feared that regular broadcasts on national radio would make Jews too "conspicuous" in the American public sphere.[17] Originally to be called "Synagogue of the Air," the series was eventually named *The Eternal Light*.[18] From its inception, *The Eternal Light* pursued an ambitious and complex agenda that distinguished it from other religious and cultural affairs broadcasting. A press release issued by the Seminary on the occasion of the series's premiere in the fall of 1944 explains that *The Eternal Light* "is designed to show Judaism as a moral force in important moments of history."[19] In other early publicity materials, the Seminary articulated the series's "basic precepts": "to extol all who sanctify God's name; to emphasize the sanctity of the human personality; to demonstrate the fundamental character of the democratic impulse in a good society; to define the place of Palestine in Jewish religious aspiration; to introduce, elucidate and interpret Jewish ritual, ceremonial and folk-lore."[20] A promotional poster from the early 1940s depicting the Seminary's various departments and activities describes *The Eternal Light* as "dramatizing the ideals of Judaism" and "attacking apathy and ignorance," reaching "a weekly national audience of millions." The poster features a schematic diagram, which positions *The Eternal Light* parallel to the Institute for Religious and Social Studies (IRSS), the Seminary's educational program for "clergymen of all faiths," inaugurated in 1938. By implication, what the IRSS sought to do for clerics—"cure group tensions and racial and religious bigotries"—*The Eternal Light* offered to its national lay audience, which was linked by a "coast to coast network" of NBC stations.[21]

A "move into America": JTS's Broadcasts and the Postwar Context

The Seminary's outreach via radio and television was consonant with developments in American Jewish life in the years immediately following World War II: the growth of the Conservative movement, itself part of a rapid rise in religious affiliation among American Jews; the internal migration of American Jews from the major cities of the Northeast and Midwest to points south and west and from urban enclaves to suburban communities; and the emergence of American Judeo-Christian ecumenism. Conservativism was, as Arthur Goren notes, the most rapidly expanding organized movement within American Judaism during the postwar years, as "a new religious emphasis" prevailed in American life.[22] Marshall Sklare links the advent of the Conservative movement to American Jewry's rapid upward socioeconomic mobility, internal migration to "third settlement areas," and integration into an American cultural mainstream.[23] This demographic shift, especially the mass movement to the suburbs, constituted, in Arthur Hertzberg's words, a symbolic "move into America."[24]

Albert Gordon also ties the move to the suburbs to significant changes in "the character of Jewish community life in America. . . . The new Jewish suburbanites believe . . . that since we are all Americans, it is not good for Jews—or any other ethnic or religious group—to live together, forming their own community. They *fear* segregation, in contrast to their parents, who in many cases sought it."[25] So powerful is the impact of suburban migration in the postwar years on American Jewish culture, according to Nathan Glazer, that he considers this "great movement" to be "more persuasive" an explanation for the transformation of American Jewry in the postwar period "than either Hitler or Zionism. . . . [A]side from the economic and social shift, though certainly allied to it, was the rise of new values in American life, values that may be included under the general heading of . . . middle-class respectability."[26] The broadcast media served both the geographic decentralization of American Jews and their entry into the American cultural mainstream by offering them direct and simultaneous access to the centers of culture (Jewish as well as general), regardless of where Jewish radio and television audiences resided.

369

*Broadcasting
American
Judaism:
The Radio
and Television
Department
of the JTS*

This geographic and cultural integration of America's Jews also coincided with the advent of postwar Judeo-Christian ecumenism. Geoffrey Wigoder notes that "new Christian perceptions [of Jews and Judaism] emerged only after World War II. The first step came with the realization that the traditional Christian teaching of contempt had created the atmosphere in which a Holocaust was possible."[27] The principles of ecumenism, stressing harmony and commonalities among religious faiths, were fundamental to the notion of network-sponsored religious broadcasting exemplified by *The Eternal Light* and the various television series in which JTS participated. According to the Television Code of the National Association of Radio and Television Broadcasters, the producers of these programs were committed to "apportion[ing] . . . time fairly among the representative faith groups," along the model of presenting "balanced" news coverage of political issues. Content of the programs was to "place emphasis on broad religious truths, excluding the presentation of controversial or partisan views."[28]

Sponsorship and scheduling also marked these ecumenical broadcasts as different in form, content, and agenda from the genres and protocols of prime-time and weekday daytime programming. These ecumenical series were among the variety of public affairs and cultural programs presented in accordance with the FCC's Communications Act of 1934, which mandated that licensed broadcasters demonstrate their commitment to the public interest by presenting a regular number of hours of noncommercial programming each week. Intended to edify rather than entertain, these programs were to demonstrate broadcasters' respect for the principle that the airwaves were a public trust licensed to them by the federal government. This was underscored by the fact that these programs were often aired in "sustaining time"—i.e., they were presented at the broadcasters' expense, without the benefit of a sponsor's underwriting.[29] Other religious programs involved the purchase of air time by an individual church or movement and often included proselytizing on behalf of its particular doctrine or the soliciting of contributions.

Innovative as they were, these programs were usually aired on Sunday mornings and afternoons, a time period in the weekly broadcasting schedule that had proved relatively unprofitable for commercial broadcasting. Wishengrad noted that "the sustaining, non-commercial, network-sponsored drama . . . is cursed by adjectives like 'educational,' 'religious,' 'historical,' 'public-service,' and other audience-deterrents. . . . To the public the sustainer is a test of stamina, doggedness, and the spirit of adventure. For it is hidden away or actually buried in time-slots accessible only to insomniacs, people who never eat lunch or dinner, reluctant students under compulsion of their teachers, and other marginal listeners."[30] Within the broadcasting industry the time period in which *The Eternal Light* and many other public service programs were aired was known as the "Sunday ghetto." (However, the thoughtful, relaxed mood of this time of the week—what media critic Goodman

Ace dubbed "a brainy Sunday afternoon"[31] —may not have been altogether inappropriate for cultivating the kind of audiences to which such programs aspired. Moreover, ecumenical broadcasting symbolically transformed Sundays from what had been, according to Richard Niebuhr, the day that American Christians retreated into a host of denominational factions, marked not only by doctrinal but also by ethnic, class, racial and regional divides,[32] into a day for exploring and celebrating common interests.)

A key organizing principle of ecumenical broadcasts presented in the "Sunday ghetto" was NBC president Sarnoff's vision, shared by the other networks, of Judaism as "one of the major faiths in the United States," alongside Catholicism and Protestantism.[33] This trinitarian conceptualization of American religion figures frequently in postwar American ecumenical writing as well as in studies of American religion, notably Will Herberg's 1955 book, *Protestant—Catholic—Jew: An Essay in American Religious Sociology*. In this study, the author identifies religiosity as essential to the American character: "American religion and American society would seem to be so closely interrelated as to make it virtually impossible to understand either without reference to the other." Whereas the progeny of immigrants could be expected to change their language, nationality, and ethnic traditions, he argues, they would not change their religion, because "from the beginning the structure of American society presupposed diversity and substantial equality of religious associations."[34] Herberg thus conceptualizes America as a "triple melting pot," in which citizens of diverse ethnic heritages are united in a national commitment to religiosity that includes respect for the freedom of worship (as a Protestant, Catholic, or Jew).[35] This model, which implicitly traces Herberg's own journey from Communist ideologue in the 1920s and 1930s to postwar conservative (in the mid-1950s he was religion editor of *The National Review*), had special implications for American Jews at the end of World War II. While they continue to figure as a minority in this configuration, their symbolic status as one-third of the "triple melting pot" far exceeds national demographic proportions (Jews then comprised no more than 3 percent of the American population) vis-à-vis the Christian majority.

Significantly, Herberg and others link this (re)turning to religiosity to the mores of middle-class respectability. Looking back on this period from the vantage point of the late 1980s, Arthur Hertzberg notes that American Christians were expected to "exercise neighborliness" toward the arrival of Jews into previously restricted suburban enclaves: "Whatever the theological differences, they were now expected to behave, in practice, as if they accepted each other as equals." No less a figure than President Eisenhower "had pronounced all religion to be good." Identifying oneself as a member of a religious community "was the way to be a respectable 'American' in those Eisenhower years."[36]

Using the media to enact this vision of American religiosity also had particular significance for Jews during the first years of the Cold War, when they were frequent, if often oblique, targets of American anti-Communist activists' scrutiny of the broadcasting industry. Moreover, the broadcasting media were themselves targeted as potential instruments of "un-American" propaganda. In 1950, for example, the right-wing magazine *Counterattack* warned readers that "at any given time, it would require only three . . . subversives . . . in a radio studio . . . to reach 90 million American people with a [propaganda] message."[37] But ecumenical programs allowed the broadcasting industry to situate itself at the center of American values. Thus NBC's president, David Sarnoff, proclaimed, on the occasion of the tenth anniversary of *The Eternal Light*, that "radio waves, which are a manifestation of an 'Infinite Reason,'. . . do not discriminate against race, religion or creed. Freedom is their essence—and they enter the homes of Protestants, Catholics and Jews alike."[38] Ecumenical programming on radio and television thereby also provided another venue for the new kind of contact between American Jews and non-Jews within the middle-class culture epitomized by the suburbs. Through these domestic media Jews would, in effect, be inviting themselves into the homes of their new neighbors for a Sunday social call.

"Dramatizing the ideals of Judaism": The Eternal Light *on Radio*

The realization of JTS's first network broadcasting series in 1944 involved a collaboration of Seminary scholars, lay personnel, and outside advisors, who were responsible for the content of the broadcasts, with writers, performers, and NBC's production and technical staff. While the network underwrote some of the production costs for *The Eternal Light*, the Seminary was responsible for developing scripts and supervising their realization. JTS's costs—some $22,000 for the initial pilot series of thirteen episodes—included the hiring of actors, scriptwriters, and musicians.[39] In addition to commissioning Krents to produce the series and Wishengrad to write the scripts, Finkelstein appointed Moshe Davis, then a dean of the Teachers Institute of the Seminary, to serve as program editor for *The Eternal Light* shortly after regular production commenced. (Davis held this position through 1952 and was succeeded by Ben Zion Bokser.[40]) Krents, Davis, and Wishengrad worked closely with NBC personnel—including Max Jordan, the network's director of religious programs; Frank Papp, who directed the series; and Milton Katims, who conducted the NBC orchestra, which accompanied the broadcasts.

The official, full-time participation of Seminary academicians in the realization of JTS's broadcasts was limited to the program editor, although individual faculty were occasionally consulted on an ad hoc basis, and Seminary students were hired as research assistants to help find material that would become the basis for scripts. The staff of *The Eternal Light* also consulted with an outside advisory committee, whose

From left: *Eternal
Light* scriptwriter
Morton Wish-
engrad, program
editor Moshe
Davis, producer
Milton Krents,
and director
Frank Papp,
1940s. *Photo by
Virginia F. Stern.
Ratner Center,
JTS.*

members included rabbis representing the various major religious movements of
American Jewry. In addition to Finkelstein, Louis Mann represented the Reform
movement, while Leo Jung and David da Sola Pool served as the spokespersons for
Ashkenazic and Sephardic Orthodoxy.[41]

Wishengrad wrote numerous scripts for *The Eternal Light* and other Seminary
broadcasts from 1944 until his death in 1963. Over the years he was joined by a number of other scriptwriters for the radio series—including such writers for television
and the theater as Erik Barnouw, Ernest Kinoy, Arnold Perl, and Shimon
Wincelberg.[42] Regular performers on *The Eternal Light* included Sam Jaffe, Alexander Scourby, and Roger DeKoven. Although as a rule the producers of *The Eternal
Light* eschewed the pursuit of celebrity performers, a number of prominent
actors—including Ralph Bellamy, Joseph Cotton, Melvyn Douglas, John Garfield,
Eva LeGallienne, Paul Muni, and Edward G. Robinson—appeared on occasional
episodes.[43] During four and a half decades the Seminary produced nearly nineteen
hundred radio broadcasts under the name *The Eternal Light*.

Initially, NBC broadcast *The Eternal Light* on Sunday mornings from 11:00 to
11:30 A.M.; in the autumn of 1946 the series was rescheduled to air between 12:30
and 1:00 P.M.[44] Within the limitations of the relatively unpopular "Sunday ghetto,"
The Eternal Light acquired a considerable following. In its inaugural season the
series was aired by thirty-three of NBC's affiliated stations and was carried in
Canada over the CBC. By the mid-1950s, *The Eternal Light* was presented by more
than a hundred stations across the United States. The earliest ratings information
on the series are "Hooper ratings" for the autumn of 1946; these figures suggest that

373

*Broadcasting
American
Judaism:
The Radio
and Television
Department
of the JTS*

From left: actor
John Garfield,
Morton Wishen-
grad, orchestra
conductor Milton
Katims, and
Milton Krents at
an NBC micro-
phone, 1940s.
*Photo by Virginia
F. Stern. Ratner
Center, JTS.*

The Eternal Light then reached an audience of more than five million in the United States alone, comparable in size to the number of listeners recorded for other religious, cultural, and public affairs programs of the time.[45] Early publicity materials for *The Eternal Light* frequently mentioned an audience of six million.[46] Five years after inaugurating the series, the Seminary reported receiving an average of five hundred letters a week from listeners; in addition, there were nine hundred regular subscribers to offprints of scripts for the dramas.[47]

The Eternal Light was almost as widely recognized as an important contribution to the development of radio drama as it was for its innovative approach to religious broadcasting. Among its earliest admirers was Eleanor Roosevelt, who mentioned the program in "My Day," her nationally syndicated column, two days after the series's debut.[48] *Variety* praised both the agenda of *The Eternal Light* and the series's production values:

> NBC rates a nod for this Sunday noontime public service show. Any attempt in these crucial times to further goodwill and tolerance, break down homefront prejudices and foster greater understanding of minority groups should of necessity be encouraged. . . . [NBC] has projected itself as a definite force for good. . . . The dramatizations are of a pattern that reflect painstaking effort to realize a fuller understanding of the problems and invest them with top entertainment values: the acting [is] . . . out of the top drawer, and the direction and all around production [is] a distinct credit.[49]

A 1948 manual on how to produce religious radio programming cited *The Eternal Light* as a pioneer of broadcast drama and praised it for being "not only one of the best religious programs on the air, but also one of the leading dramatic shows in all radio."[50] Reviewing the series for the *New York Times* in 1950, Val Adams wrote that *The Eternal Light* "bubbles with more real sense of good theatre than some of radio's star studded productions" and praised the series for its "fundamental new approach . . . to religious broadcasting," which "suggests spiritual uplift and moral integrity with never a trace of sanctimony."[51] In its first ten years on the air, *The Eternal Light* received awards from the National Conference of Christians and Jews; Ohio State University's Institute for Education by Radio; the Radio–TV Critics Circle of New York; and *Variety*, the entertainment weekly, among others.[52] In later years, the series twice received the George Foster Peabody Broadcasting Award.[53]

During the early postwar years, various efforts were made to bring *The Eternal Light* to audiences beyond North America. Transcripts of the series were printed regularly in *Jüdische Rundschau*, a periodical for Jewish Displaced Persons in Germany, and episodes were performed in German and Yiddish for live audiences in DP camps. The *Ewige Licht Programme* was also aired over German-language radio stations in Munich, Frankfurt, Bremen, and Cologne. Selected installments of *The Eternal Light* were presented in Hebrew by the Palestine (later Israel) Broadcasting Service during these years and into the 1950s. For many years *The Eternal Light* was also carried by the Voice of America and by Armed Forces Radio Service.[54]

At this time the Seminary also developed other means for extending the impact of *The Eternal Light* broadcasts. Listeners could write to JTS for copies of individual offprints of scripts (at a cost of ten cents each) or could receive them by subscription. To encourage Jewish educators to make use of the broadcasts or scripts in their classes, the Radio and Television Department prepared teachers' guides that would facilitate classroom discussion of individual broadcasts.[55] A volume of twenty-six of Wishengrad's radio plays for *The Eternal Light* was published in 1947,[56] and that same year recordings of ten episodes were made available for purchase.[57] In more recent years, the Seminary has distributed tape recordings of individual radio broadcasts as well as films and, later, videotapes of selected episodes of its television series.

"Alien modalities?": Creating Jewish Drama

During the formative period of the Radio and Television Department, the question of format for JTS's broadcasting series proved to be especially challenging. Wyler reports that the advisory committee for *The Eternal Light* regarded established forms of religious programming—worship services, sacred music, and sermons— as either violations of Jewish tradition or inappropriate for the largely non-Jewish audience.[58] The issue was resolved when Krents

> suggested drama as a way of conveying ideas and values painlessly to a radio audience. He introduced Dr. Finkelstein to Morton Wishengrad, a talented

375
*Broadcasting
American
Judaism:
The Radio
and Television
Department
of the JTS*

Poster for *Das Ewige Licht*, 1947. *Photo by Virginia F. Stern. Ratner Center, JTS.*

young playwright—and an avowed agnostic. After a luncheon which lasted several hours, Wishengrad found it hard to maintain his skepticism. There was a real challenge in working with Seminary scholars, translating traditional Jewish values into the vocabulary of radio drama. The dramatist left the Seminary with an armful of books, and by midsummer, he was ready to begin a task which would engage him for the rest of his life.[59]

Although Wyler relates this as a story of conversion for the spiritually dubious Wishengrad, the decision to enter the realm of drama also involved a considerable leap of faith on the part of the leadership of the Conservative movement. Indeed, the choice of a dramatic format, which so distinguished the early broadcasts on *The Eternal Light*, constitutes an especially interesting opportunity to consider Wigoder's observation that "for Jews, interreligious dialogue can pose the problem of entry into alien modalities."[60] The dramatic mode—unlike the narrative and lyric modes of the Bible, the dialogic mode of Talmudic writing and scholarship, or the ritual mode of communal worship—is largely alien to traditional Jewish religious culture. Moreover, the modern Jewish stage and the involvement of Jews in Western theater in general have been, on the whole, decidedly secular enterprises.

Though some scholars see the influence of ancient Greek drama on parts of the Bible (notably the Song of Songs and the Book of Job), they regard the absence of an ancient Hebrew dramatic literature as indicative of an incompatibility between the drama and Jewish ritual practice, law, or philosophy. The conflict applies both to subject matter or themes and to the distinctive performative context of drama, which—with the very circumscribed exception of *purim-shpiln* (skits)—is absent from traditional Jewish cultural practice. The notion of the theater as an alien and anti-traditional phenomenon has its origins in the Talmudic period and continues through the *Haskalah* into the modern era.[61]

By contrast, the playwrights, rabbis, and others involved in JTS's ecumenical broadcasts envisioned drama and religion as culturally compatible and their respective practitioners as capable of a collaboration both aesthetically and spiritually valid. In his foreword to the 1947 anthology of Wishengrad's radio scripts for *The Eternal Light*, Finkelstein writes of the need for "the team of scholar-artist . . . to interpret Judaism. . . . *The Eternal Light* suggests how an artist and a group of [religious] scholars can co-operate to translate ancient, abstract ideas into effective modern dramatics."[62] These are similar to the terms with which Pamela Ilott, vice-president for religious and cultural affairs broadcasts at CBS News, described the mission of the ecumenical television series *Lamp Unto My Feet* on the occasion of its thirtieth anniversary: "The creation of works of art represents man's striving to express his highest aspirations, to reflect his own world and, at the same time, to influence the condition of man. Religious television presentations . . . provide a common ground for artists and theologians to work toward these ends."[63]

Indeed, JTS's religious dramas for American radio and television figure as part of a larger interest in aestheticizing Judaism that flourished during the early postwar years. Tied to the embourgeoisement of the American Jewish community, this interest informed American Jewish practice in the synagogue, school, and community, as well as in home decor and cuisine. As Barbara Kirshenblatt-Gimblett notes in her work on Jewish cookbooks, these various activities strive to demonstrate that "civility and aesthetics" could be compatible with traditional practice.[64]

Central to these acts of aestheticizing Judaism—whether at the synagogue, in the kitchen, on the airwaves, or elsewhere—is a concern for respectability in the eyes of mainstream American middle-class culture. This can be seen, for example, in the debate surrounding the plans for an expansion of the Jewish Museum of New York, which was originally based at the Seminary, when Frieda Schiff Warburg donated her former home on Fifth Avenue to JTS for this purpose. In Julie Miller's study of this period of the museum's formation, which took place during the years that *The Eternal Light* was first heard regularly on NBC radio, she observes that Seminary leaders envisioned the future of its modest in-house display of Judaica as an "institution of the highest quality, one worthy of competing with a neighbor like the Metropolitan Museum of Art."[65]

Similarly, in his 1959 dissertation on American Jewish broadcasting, Zev Zahavy argues that aesthetic concerns for respectability are essential to realizing the "gracious opportunity" that broadcasting provides for "expanding the moral, ethical and divine principles of Jewish life." Apparently written, in part, to make the case for Orthodox religious broadcasts, Zahavy's dissertation disapproves of programming that "encourages sensuous behavior which motivates materialistic pursuits," such as the (unidentified) telecast of a Passover ballet with "improperly attired" dancers performing "acrobatic gyrations" that were "strongly suggestive." The "proper utilization" of Jewish religious broadcasting, Zahavy maintains, "may create tastes and motives for better Jewish living."[66] The Seminary developed its own protocols regarding the propriety of religious broadcasting. According to Davis, the creators of *The Eternal Light* discovered early on that Bible stories did not lend themselves to dramatic presentation in a series: "The Bible," he explained, "is such an epic, its passages so sacred that it cannot be transferred suitably to the medium of radio."[67]

Concern for the moral responsibility of broadcasting and the aesthetics of programming was itself the subject of discussion on occasional JTS broadcasts—for example, on an installment of the televised version of *The Eternal Light* aired on 9 December 1962. In a conversation with Newton Minow, then chairman of the FCC, on "the ethical responsibilites of communications in a space age," Finkelstein championed the possibilities of using "this new medium for the betterment of the human condition."[68] Reiterating his famous speech before the National Association of Broadcasters of the previous year, denouncing much of American television as being a "vast wasteland,"[69] Minow commented that "the potential of this most miraculous means of communication has not been fulfilled." Advocating use of the medium "not just to mirror the public taste . . . [but] to advance it," he cites the example of broadcasting classical music "when it was certainly not popular. . . . But by being on the air, millions and millions of people were exposed to good music who probably never would have had that chance before." As evidence of the edifying effect that this use of television had on the American public, Minow notes that "more money was spent on [classical music] concerts last year than on going to the baseball games."[70]

JTS realized these highbrow aspirations in broadcasts that maintained an elevated, dignified tone, whether striving for an earnest, histrionic, or comical affect. The aesthetics of JTS's broadcasts are epitomized by the voices of such performers as Alexander Scourby and Roger De Koven, who were regularly heard as narrators or protagonists on the radio version of *The Eternal Light*. The carefully inflected speech of these resonant baritones bore no trace of "ethnic" accent or rhythm; it performed the equivalent of the ideal sound that JTS sought for its rabbinical students, who had been required to study elocution during the Seminary's early years.[71] Thus, the aesthetic of the Department of Radio and Television conforms with JTS's long-standing agenda of "Americanizing" the "East European" sensibilities of the majority of American Jews.[72]

"Stories of a People": Programming Genres, Subjects, and Themes of The Eternal Light

Within a unifying aesthetic of respectability, the hundreds of radio broadcasts presented on *The Eternal Light* explored a wide range of subjects through a variety of genres. For many years each installment began with the cantorial chanting of the Hebrew folksong "Shomer Yisrael"[73] as arranged by Morris Mamorsky, who also composed original music for the series. This signature melody was followed by a reverberating male voice that intoned the following Biblical passage: "And the Lord spake unto Moses, saying, 'Command the children of Israel that they bring unto thee pure olive oil beaten for the light, to cause lamps to burn continually in the tabernacle of the congregation, and it shall be a statute forever in your generations.'"[74] During the first years of broadcasting, episodes of *The Eternal Light* consisted of an original drama or dramatic adaptation, followed by a brief commentary on the episode's subject. Initially, these commentaries were delivered by rabbis and lay leaders, selected "to give the different Jewish religious groups equal representation."[75] Later they also included such public figures as Ludwig Lewisohn, Edgar J. Nathan, Jr., and Fiorello H. LaGuardia.

At Finkelstein's suggestion, *The Eternal Light* was inaugurated with a series of thirteen dramas about synagogues throughout Jewish history.[76] The first episode, aired on 8 October 1944, was *A Rhode Island Refuge*, which presented the story of the Touro synagogue, founded in Newport in 1763. A second series of broadcasts presented the life stories of "builders of Judaism," including profiles of Louis Brandeis, Emma Lazarus, Sholem Aleichem, and Isaac M. Wise. Biographies of noteworthy figures, Jewish and non-Jewish, would be among the most enduring genres of *The Eternal Light* dramas. In addition to the lives of important historical figures of Jewish letters and thought (e.g., Rabbi Akiba, Solomon Ibn Gabirol, Moses Mendelssohn, the Vilna Gaon[77]), *The Eternal Light* called attention to the diverse contributions of Jews to general culture, with biographical dramas about Dr. Bela Schick, who helped fight diphtheria; Edward Rosewater, telegraphist for President Lincoln; and Ludwig Zamenhof, inventor of Esperanto, among others.[78]

As the inaugural broadcast of *The Eternal Light* demonstrates, JTS was committed to using radio to situate Jews within American life and demonstrate the compatibility of Jewish and American values. This notion was fundamental to the Seminary's rationale for religious broadcasting. Thus, in an address delivered at an ecumenical seminar on religious broadcasting convened at Ohio State University in 1946, Davis called upon fellow broadcasters to "rededicate ourselves with passion to the social contract . . . of America" and "to tap the sources of democracy, the religious traditions: for religion declares that spiritual and moral imperatives have an independent value in society."[79] This agenda was also realized in installments of *The Eternal Light* devoted to American holidays, especially Thanksgiving,[80] and to the American Revolution and Civil War,[81] as well as in profiles of important figures, both Jewish and non-Jewish, in American history and culture. Among these were educator Mary McLeod Bethune, labor leader David Dubinsky, poet Emma Lazarus, and inventor George Washington Carver.[82] The Seminary also produced special broadcasts in 1954 as part of the commemoration of the Tercentenary of American Jewry.[83] (Similarly, in 1976 the Radio and Television Department helped produce special programs for ABC and NBC television honoring the American bicentennial.[84])

While many of the dramas presented on *The Eternal Light* focused on the past, the series also addressed various contemporary issues. Occasional scripts articulated links between biblical teachings and present concerns. In October 1946, for example, as the United Nations General Assembly convened for the first time, *The Eternal Light* presented *Isaiah and the Nations*.[85] In this script by Stanley Silverman, "the Prophet Isaiah appears at the opening session of the General Assembly to bring the voice of the holy scripture to the delegates."[86]

During its first years of broadcasting, *The Eternal Light* also devoted a considerable number of episodes to the experiences of European Jewry during and after World War II. In addition to programs about the struggle to survive Nazi persecution—including one of the first American media adaptations of Anne Frank's wartime diary[87]—were dramas about Displaced Persons and refugees building new lives in the postwar era.[88] The series also addressed moral concerns beyond the Jewish community, through occasional episodes honoring the life of Mahatma Gandhi or documenting an effort to bring Japanese women, scarred as a result of the atomic bomb, to the United States for reconstructive plastic surgery.[89] *Hunger*, a 1946 drama by Wishengrad, employed the "living newspaper" technique of fusing elements of drama and documentary, which had been developed by the WPA Federal Theater in the 1930s, to present an overview of hunger around the world in the wake of World War II and to argue the need for an American response.[90] "In this form the narration extends like a clothesline between one pole marked 'Famine' and another marked 'American Relief,'" Wishengrad explained in a prefatory note to the published version of the script. "Pinned to the clothesline are statistics, medical data, actuarial reports, quotations, and dramatic vignettes. But it is the narrative clothesline upon which the data, quotations, and short scenes are suspended, and which gives the whole an emotional unity."[91]

Other programs explored various means of linking moral edification with entertainment, presenting adaptations of Jewish folklore and literature (including works by S. Y. Agnon, Isaac Babel, David Bergelson, Y. L. Peretz, Henry Roth, Isaac Bashevis Singer, and Sholem Aleichem).[92] During its first seasons, *The Eternal Light* also offered occasional adaptations of works of world literature that deal with Jewish characters (Steven Vincent Benet's *Joseph and the Indians*, Gotthold Ephraim Lessing's *Nathan the Wise*, Jean Baptiste Racine's *Athalie*).[93] Moral instruction was offered even within the occasional humorous episode, whether an adaptation of the tales of the wise men of Chelm or an original script, such as Marc Siegel's *How Manny Got into the Seventh Grade*, the story of a ten-year-old schoolboy's search for a sign from God that he would be promoted to the next grade.[94]

In the summer, when many radio series aired reruns during their regular time periods, *The Eternal Light* presented a separate series—entitled, at first, *Stories of a People* and later, *Words We Live By*—which replaced dramas with adaptations and discussions of the Bible and related literary works. In 1952 the replacement series offered programs based on the Psalms, with readings by Raymond Massey and musical selections performed by a choir under the direction of Hugo Weisgall. The following year, the summer series presented ten programs in which Mark Van Doren and Maurice Samuel discussed Thomas Mann's *Joseph and His Brothers*. The success of their appearance together led to repeated collaborations on both the radio and television versions of *The Eternal Light*. Each year the two men discussed some aspect of the Bible—such as minor characters in the Bible and the Bible in translation—until both died in 1972. These on-air discussions resulted in the pub-

Mark Van Doren (left) and Maurice Samuel on the set of *Mr. Lincoln and the Bible*, 1960, one in a series of discussions aired on *The Eternal Light. Photo by Maurey Garber. Ratner Center, JTS.*

lication of several books: Samuel's *Certain People of the Book*, and two posthumous volumes, *In the Beginning, Love: Dialogues on the Bible* and *The Book of Praise: Dialogues on the Psalms*, edited by Edith Samuel.[95]

Although JTS and its collaborators at NBC pursued an original course in radio programming with *The Eternal Light*, the format of the series responded to signal changes in American broadcasting policy. Beginning in 1960 a series of FCC rulings eliminated the requirement that broadcasters offer sustaining-time programs as part of their licensing. Stewart Hoover notes that during this decade "the time and money available to mainline [religious] groups through their sustaining-time relationships with the networks began to deteriorate."[96] As a result of ensuing budgetary constraints, the Radio and Television Department produced fewer original dramas on *The Eternal Light* in the 1960s. In their stead the program offered series of conversations with Jewish authors (e.g., Leslie Epstein, Bel Kaufman, Cynthia Ozick, Chaim Potok, Leo Rosten), scholars (Lucy Dawidowicz, Barbara Myerhoff, Irving Howe), performing artists (Giora Feidman, Jan Peerce, Molly Picon), and other personalities, many of whom were interviewed by Martin Bookspan. Beginning in the late 1960s, Elie Wiesel presented an annual series on *The Eternal Light*, aired on several consecutive Sundays, which explored biblical literature, hasidic lore, the Holocaust, and other topics. *The Eternal Light* also continued to present special holiday programs and to rebroadcast dramas first presented during the series's early years.

"Portraying Judaism visually to a mass audience": JTS on Television

At the same time that the Seminary maintained a long-standing commitment to its radio series on NBC, it entered into arrangements, at one time or another, with all three major commercial networks to produce religious television broadcasts. Whereas on radio *The Eternal Light* was the Seminary's own weekly series, its various television productions all involved sharing a series or a weekly timeslot with non-Jewish producers of ecumenical media. JTS's first venture into television broadcasting took place in 1948. During the fall of this year, CBS initiated production of *Lamp Unto My Feet*, an ecumenical series presented on Sunday afternoons at 4:30. The first installments of the series were devoted to "the instruction of children in the rituals and traditions of their respective religions." In addition to JTS, participants included New York's Riverside Church, the Fifth Avenue Presbyterian Church, and Corpus Christi Church. The first installment of *Lamp Unto My Feet* involving the Seminary was presented on 28 November 1948. The broadcast, a lesson on the Sabbath, featured explanations of ritual objects and traditional holiday foods as well as "a completely prepared Sabbath table." In addition to presenting a children's choir performing Sabbath songs, "the highlight of the program came with the introduction of the special Sabbath guests, two recently arrived D.P. children, among the first to come under the new quota, who spoke in Yiddish of the happiness of their first Thanksgiving in America."[97]

In 1951 JTS reported that its relationship with NBC had expanded beyond radio to "portray Judaism visually to a mass audience."[98] Alternating with the Protestants' National Council of Churches and the National Council of Catholic Men, the Seminary created episodes for *Frontiers of Faith*, NBC's first televised ecumenical religion series. In its initial season, *Frontiers of Faith* was carried on Sundays by forty-seven NBC television stations. While continuing to present *The Eternal Light* on radio, Davis, Krents, and Wishengrad also worked on the new television series.[99] The network's staff for *Frontiers of Faith* included producer Doris Ann and director Martin Hoad. The Jewish segments on the premiere season of *Frontiers of Faith* explored some of the different possibilities offered by the medium of television. Dramatic presentations included a semi-staged reading of Maurice Samuel's *The World of Sholom Aleichem*, featuring Aline MacMahon, Sam Levine, Joseph Wiseman, and Ezra Stone, and a fully staged dramatization of Anne Frank's diary,

383

*Broadcasting
American
Judaism:
The Radio
and Television
Department
of the JTSA*

Shooting
*Kasrilevka on the
Mississippi*, by
James Yasse and
William Wise, the
story of a fictional
encounter
between Sholem
Aleichem and
Mark Twain. It
was broadcast in
1955 as part of the
Frontiers of Faith
television series.
*Photo by Gedalia
Segal. Ratner
Center, JTS.*

adapted by Wishengrad.[100] Perhaps the most ambitious of these earliest install-ments of *Frontiers of Faith* was a documentary entitled *The Days of Our Years*. Also scripted by Wishengrad, the program examined the challenges of aging, while stressing the resilience of senior citizens. Broadcasting from the Kingsbridge House, a home for the aged in the Bronx, television cameras "eavesdrop[ped] on the occupational therapy rooms and upon a rehearsal of the residents' choir."[101]

Starting in 1958, those episodes of the series that were produced by JTS were aired under the title *The Eternal Light*;[102] Catholic installments were presented as *The Catholic Hour* (later known as *Guideline*), while *Frontiers of Faith* continued as the name for episodes produced by the National Council of Churches. These three series maintained the rotating format established when they had shared the title *Frontiers of Faith*—in effect, situating Jews as one-third of America's spirituality. In his 1969 survey of American religious television of the mid-1960s, William Bluem reported: "Carried on over 100 TV stations throughout the nation, the televised version of *The Eternal Light* has a weekly audience of four million and receives over 4,000 letters each week."[103] The series continued to present original dramas, some of them televised versions of scripts originally performed on the radio version of *The Eternal Light*. In the 1960s the television version of the series began presenting pro-grams recorded at various locations; these included a profile of Solomon Schechter taped at Christ College, Cambridge University; documentaries on Jewish themes in Rembrandt's art, filmed in Amsterdam, and on the Jewish contribution to the

Renaissance, shot in Italy; and a biography of Elie Wiesel that follows the author to his hometown of Sighet, Hungary, and to Jerusalem.[104] During this decade *The Eternal Light* also began to present interviews with prominent public figures, including Ambassador Sol M. Linowitz, author James Michener, violinist Itzhak Perlman, Jewish Museum director Karl Katz, and theologian Abraham Joshua Heschel.[105]

Beginning in 1961 JTS and ABC coproduced installments of *Directions*, that network's Sunday ecumenical television series. Like *Frontiers of Faith*, the ABC series alternated presentations of Protestant, Catholic, and Jewish segments. The format of the installments produced by JTS was originally conceptualized as a "living magazine," whose "editor" was actor and folksinger Theodore Bikel. In a press release, Bikel is quoted as saying that, "within the heritage of each of the three great faiths, there is guidance and direction which can serve all men in the sometimes difficult task of living. . . . [T]he interpretation of the impact of Judaism on our time, and the impact of our times on Judaism, is a challenge of the first order."[106] The concern of the series with addressing (if, perhaps, obliquely) serious, even controversial topical issues is suggested by the Seminary's first installment of *Directions*, aired on 1 January 1961. This broadcast featured performances by actor Morris Carnovsky, who read from the works of Albert Einstein, and the folksinging quartet, The Weavers, all of whom had been victims of anti-Communist blacklisting during the 1950s.[107]

The magazine format of *Directions* soon gave way to dramas, documentaries, interviews, panel discussions, and other forms of programming similar to those presented on the televised version of *The Eternal Light*. The ABC series paid particular attention to the arts and explored the links between various forms of artistic creativity and religious spirituality. In addition to airing original dramas, *Directions* presented a dance by Pearl Lang's company, a concert of Jewish folksongs by Martha Schlamme, and a performance of Handel's oratorio *Israel in Egypt*.[108] Visual artists profiled include photographer Roman Vishniac and painter Marc Chagall.[109] Perhaps the series's most ambitious artistic efforts were the production of original operas and concert works, such as *The Thief and The Hangman*, based on a Yemenite folktale with a score by Abraham Ellstein set to Morton Wishengrad's text; *The Fifth Cup: A Cantata for Passover*, a contemporary musical version of the seder narrated by Theodore Bikel, with text by Norman Simon and music by Gershon Kingsley; and *The Final Ingredient*, a Holocaust drama, composed by David Amram to a libretto by Arnold Weinstein.[110]

Documentaries presented on *Directions* include a five-part series on Israel's archeological past and cultural present. Other episodes took viewers to the Anne Frank House in Amsterdam, a communal *havurah* in Madison, Wisconsin, and the burial society of a Conservative congregation in Minneapolis. A special broadcast on 1 January 1967 dealt with the April 1966 fire that had heavily damaged the JTS library.[111] Panel discussions on *Directions* brought together clergy and lay leaders of different faiths to consider contemporary moral issues. For example, *Ethics in Five Acts*, a five-part discussion series written by Robert Lewis Shayon, explored ethical concerns connected to integration, youth culture, business, science, and international affairs. Other broadcasts dealt with theological responses to student uprisings, bioethics, and the aftermath of the Vietnam War, or explored connections between Jewish thought and various intellectual disciplines, such as psychology and physics.[112] Jewish religious leaders interviewed on *Directions* ranged from JTS Chancellor Louis Finkelstein (who made several appearances on the Seminary's various broadcast series) to Sally Priesand, the first woman rabbi ordained by the Reform movement.[113]

"Living in an era of the bottom line": The Recent History of the Radio and Television Department

By the 1980s, JTS's religious broadcasting ventures had diminished in scope, responding to changes both at the Seminary and in American broadcasting. At a time when the commercial networks' domination of American television was being challenged by the advent of the home videotape recorder, the spread of cable and satellite systems, and changes in the federal regulation of television broadcasting, the networks' long-standing commitment to public service programming declined. At the same time, increasing numbers of network affiliates and independent stations were dropping the ecumenical series produced by the networks or similar syndicated programs. Having discovered, as Hoover observes, that "religion could be a profit center," broadcasters turned instead to evangelical groups, who transformed the "Sunday ghetto" into profitable air time. Eventually, mainstream religious groups, which had formerly enjoyed the networks' economic support through sustaining-time programming, were obliged either to purchase air time for religious programs or to watch the size of their audience dwindle.[114] Thus, whereas the television version of *The Eternal Light* was carried by more than a hundred stations in the early 1970s, a Hanukkah special presented on the series in 1982 was aired by only twenty-two stations.[115]

At this time the Radio and Television Department began to distribute old episodes of the radio version of *The Eternal Light* for rebroadcast on dozens of public service stations, through the Communications Center of the University of Texas.[116] But stations that continued to air *The Eternal Light* and other similar series often presented them during the most marginal times in their schedules. Krents noted, in an article published in 1981, that "there are centers of Jewish population today where devoted listeners must tune in at 5:30 AM to hear Eternal Light."[117] With regard to the decline of the commercial networks' commitment to ecumenical programming, Helen Marmor, NBC executive director for religious programs during the early 1980s, commented, "We live in an era of the bottom line, I'm afraid."[118]

These negative developments also created new opportunities for Jewish religious broadcasting. In 1981, for example, the Jewish Television Network, "the first experiment in the United States featuring regularly scheduled programming aimed at a Jewish audience," debuted on Los Angeles's Theta Cable system.[119] But JTS did not aggressively pursue new ventures in radio and television during the 1980s. Rather, the steadily rising costs of media production, as well as institutional shifts in agenda away from general public outreach and toward concerns within the Conservative Jewish community, led to a reduction of resources committed to the Radio and Television Department. The Seminary produced only a few new television programs each year during this period; on radio, *The Eternal Light* continued to rebroadcast old episodes and offer new series of interviews. During the late 1980s and early 1990s, JTS joined forces with the National Council of Churches, the Southern Baptist Radio and Television Commission, and the United States Catholic Conference to form the Interfaith Broadcasting Commission (IBC), which presented a series of telecasts on ABC-TV entitled *Visions and Values*. The Seminary's productions for IBC have included *I Ask for Wonder* (1988–89 season), *Rituals* (1989–90), *Saying Kaddish* (1990–91), and *Oasis in Time* (1991–92).[120] Other programs produced by the Radio and Television Department in years past have been reaired on the religious cable television channel VISN.

"By Jews? Of Jews? For Jews?":
JTS's Broadcasts as a Case Study in Identifying "Jewish media"

The broadcasts produced by the Radio and Television Department constitute a distinctive corpus of Jewish self-portraiture in mass media. As artifacts of popular culture, they reflect signal changes experienced by American Jews during and immediately after World War II, and they are responsive to the dynamics of the community's concerns over the course of the ensuing decades. Their analysis also raises a number of larger issues, including the challenge of identifying broadcasts (or, by extension, other works of popular culture) as "Jewish." In addition, these series present an opportunity for examining how television and radio provide a venue for Jews in the virtual landscape of American public culture.

As examples of "Jewish broadcasting," the programs produced by JTS demonstrate the complex implications inherent in identifying a work of mass media with a particular cultural group. Such identification can variously refer to the creators ("by" Jews), the subjects ("of" Jews), or the audience ("for" Jews) of the works in question. With regard to all three of these aspects, the Seminary's radio and television series—seemingly forthright examples of "Jewish media"—evince a complex interrelationship of Jewish and non-Jewish elements.

387

*Broadcasting
American
Judaism:
The Radio
and Television
Department
of the JTS*

"By Jews?": The radio version of *The Eternal Light* and the various television series for which JTS produced programs were the work of employees of the Seminary and of the various commercial networks. While these parties nominally represent "Jewish" and "general" interests, the commitments of the various individuals involved in the realization of these broadcasts were much more nuanced. Those working for the Seminary included not only members of the rabbinate and lay leaders of the Conservative movement but also writers whose Jewish identity was often decidedly secular, as well as many non-Jewish performers. Network employees similarly included Jews and non-Jews with a range of spiritual convictions.

Indeed, the Seminary occasionally pointed with pride to the opportunities that its radio and television series provided for bringing together Jewish and non-Jewish talent, thereby enacting "behind the scenes" a dramatic lesson in tolerance and integration. In listing actors who performed on the radio version of *The Eternal Light* over the years, for example, a twenty-fifth anniversary press release mentions "Juano Hernandez, an extremely gifted Negro actor who found on the Eternal Light the opportunity to play a wider range of roles than he was able to secure in commercial radio. The program has never used the shield of 'type casting' to bar performers of any race or creed."[121]

"Of Jews?": The range of subjects addressed on the Seminary's radio and television series demonstrates an expansive approach to the subject of "Jewish" broadcasting that, like Jewish identity in the modern age, defies easy classification within a single paradigm—religious, ethnic, national, cultural, linguistic, etc. (In a 1949 essay on Jewish identity, written for an anthology edited by Finkelstein, anthropologist Melville Herskovits wrote that while "the Jews . . . represent a historic continuum, [and] have survived as an identifiable, yet constantly shifting series of groups, . . . no word . . . means more things to more people than does the word 'Jew.'"[122]) The decision to abandon the working title of the Seminary's radio series, "Synagogue of the Air," in favor of *The Eternal Light* evinces a desire on the part of its producers to present something other than conventional American religious programming rooted in some aspect of public worship. While the name *The Eternal Light* metonymizes the synagogue, it also invokes an image of Jews as a timeless moral "light unto the nations"—which may have had special appeal for Finkelstein.[123]

The producers of these broadcasts intended that the moral light imparted by Jews be valued as a universalist and humanist resource. This reflects what Wigoder characterizes as an "asymmetry" in the relation of Christians and Jews within the rubric of American ecumenism: "For the Jews, Christianity does not pose a theological problem, and Jewish participation in the dialogue does not have the same level of theological motivation as among the Christians. . . . The Jew is motivated more by historical and pragmatic considerations, based on the conviction that mutual understanding is the key to coexistence."[124] Thus, Parker, Barry, and

Smythe note in their pioneering study of American religious broadcasting and its audience that "the policy of *The Eternal Light* does not envisage men as puppets, either of God or of the Devil. The semantic framework of this program sees men as complex mixtures of motives and as being endowed with both personal autonomy and dignity. Indeed, the purpose of the program was stated to be: 'to affirm the dignity of all human beings.'"[125]

Despite their situation within the rubric of religious broadcasting, the scope of JTS's radio and television series often extended beyond theological matters, presenting Jewishness as a national, cultural, or ethnic identity. Davis termed this a *"klal-yisrael"* approach to programming, and it no doubt reflected the influence of JTS faculty member Mordecai Kaplan's notion of "Judaism as a civilization."[126] Moreover, the articulation of this range of Jewish interests was variously intertwined with ecumenical, patriotic, and humanist concerns. Consequently, the content of some of JTS's broadcasts provoked debate over the proper scope of "Jewish" programming: Thus, Davis recalls that

> as *[The Eternal Light]* became a *klal-yisrael* program, the question came up from time to time, why are you doing it under the guise of religious programming? . . . The other groups began to complain. . . . One day the man in charge of Public Affairs at NBC came to see Dr. Finkelstein to complain . . . about the Solomon Schechter program, . . . [which] was geared around the [Cairo] Geniza findings. He . . . says, "What's religious about this? A hole in the wall, and a little pussycat goes through, and the man follows the pussycat . . ., and why is this a religious program for NBC to put on?" . . . Dr. Finkelstein said to him, "You know, what I'd like to tell you is that for us study is prayer." And the man said, "Well, I never knew, I never understood it that way."[127]

If, in fact, an overarching goal united the far-ranging scope and mission of the Seminary's radio and television broadcasts, it was a commitment to demonstrating that Jewish particularism—whether realized in ancient ritual, traditional lore, or contemporary Zionist activism—is incidental to the fundamental universalism of Judaism and its compatibility with mainstream American values and principles. Just as the lore and rites of Judaism could be easily rendered accessible to both non-Jews and estranged coreligionists, Jews could be presented to the general American public as loyal and well-integrated fellow citizens.

Moreover, the dignified presentation of Jews heard on *The Eternal Light* and seen on JTS's television series provided a marked contrast to most other Jewish characters and performers who populated these media during the middle decades of this century. Like other ethnic and racial types featured in American popular culture of the time, characters identified as Jewish were largely comic figures. As Henry Sapoznik notes, identifying characters as Jews on English-language radio in America during the medium's heyday in the 1930s and 1940s was largely a matter of "'funny' names (both real and pseudo-ethnic) and 'funny' speech—mangled grammar, inverted syntax, malapropisms, and, above all, the conventions of dialect."[128] He cites a 1943 *Manual of Foreign Dialects for Radio, Stage and Screen*, which instructs performers that "the pitch of Yiddish is much higher than in American [English] and the falsetto is reached many times, especially under the stress of emotion. . . . The Yiddish dialect should have wide pitch range which reaches almost incredible, squeaking peaks."[129] Similarly, the Jews who appeared in the Seminary's Sunday television series contrasted with their presence elsewhere on the medium as "'outsider' figures,"[130] as David Marc notes in his study of American television situation comedies. The portraits of Jews broadcast by JTS also differed significantly with what Sig Altman observed, circa 1970, to be the prevailing comic image of Jews on American television "and by extension in the public eye," where, he argues, "even the very word 'Jewish' has become laden with humorous overtones."[131]

"For Jews?": While committed to an ecumenical focus on the commonalities among different faiths and their followers, the Seminary also envisioned a double agenda in its programming for an audience divided between Jews and non-Jews. For Jews, JTS's broadcasts would provide a point of entry for the unaffiliated, isolated, or culturally illiterate members of the community. For non-Jews, the series would serve to demystify Jewish history, beliefs, and practices, and, by eradicating ignorance about Jews, eliminate anti-Semitic prejudice.

Audience responses collected over the years by the Seminary reflect, albeit selectively, some of the extent to which listeners and viewers of its broadcasts conformed to these expectations. In files from JTS's Public Relations Department are dozens of excerpts from letters (selected by the staff for potential use in press and publicity materials) written by non-Jewish audience members, expressing their gratitude to the Seminary for its broadcasts, such as the following:

> I always make it a point to listen to your Sunday morning program, "Eternal Light." I am a Gentile who is finding it easier to admire and like the Jewish people thru your broadcast.
>
> I am 21 and a soldier's wife. Your program has helped me to understand the problems of the Jewish race. My husband recently brought home a Jewish soldier and his wife whom he liked and wanted me to also. They are grand people. We have carried on conversations with them about the Jewish religion and their historical background. Many times my only knowledge was what I absorbed from the "Eternal Light."
>
> I believe your program will do much to help other Americans understand the Jews, and thus foster a better relationship between them. Our post-war world needs just that. You are doing a fine work.
>
> —North Charleston, S[outh] C[arolina][132]

Responses on file from Jews in the audience speak of the value that the broadcasts had for those situated remote from major centers of Jewish life: "We Jewish people who are scattered in all the small towns throughout the land are very much in need of spiritual guidance, and any little bit we hear through means of radio is like a bit of Manna from heaven," writes a listener from Lyndonville, Vermont.[133] In addition, the radio version of *The Eternal Light* and, to a lesser extent, JTS's television broadcasts became fixtures of mainstream American Jewish life as an ongoing source of Jewish pride: "My little girl who is 8 is glued to the radio during the program and she beams that she was born a Jewess and has such a fine heritage," a listener to *The Eternal Light* from Passaic, New Jersey, writes.[134] In one of his semi-autobiographical novels, Philip Roth recalls the place of the series in a Sunday ritual duplicated in many American Jewish homes during the early post–World War II years:

> Fifty-two Sundays a year, for most of my lifetime, my father went out to the corner for the smoked fish and the warm rolls, my brother and I set the table and squeezed the juice. . . . Then, after my parents had read the Newark Sunday papers and listened on the radio to *The Eternal Light*—great moments from Jewish history in weekly half-hour dramatizations—we two boys were rounded up and the four of us set off in the car to visit relatives.[135]

In a recent interview, Davis described *The Eternal Light* in those years as having become "a kind of sacred hour for Jews all over America."[136] Indeed, the Sunday routine that Roth recounts constitutes a (virtual) public ritual that "defin[es] and symboliz[es] . . . a moral community,"[137] exemplifying what Jonathan Woocher has labeled American civil Judaism. Even the Seminary's oft-mentioned statistic of six million listeners for its radio series constitutes a symbolic, definitional act for the American Jewish community, invoking both the estimated Jewish population of postwar North America and the number of Jewish victims of the Holocaust.

Yet Wyler recollects that, while the Seminary's official agenda placed equal emphasis on its Jewish and non-Jewish audiences, the Radio and Television Department in fact considered its primary audience to be non-Jews. Wyler recently reported that, even after regular production of the series had ceased, the Seminary continued to receive requests for copies of old broadcasts, almost all of which came from Christian groups.[138] This non-Jewish audience was also of strategic symbolic value to Jewish producers and listeners, allowing them to perceive themselves through the image of Jews projected to non-Jews. Thus, Jews might value these presentations of Jewry before a general American audience in several respects: as instruments for combating anti-Semitism; as objects of Jewish achievement and pride; and as oblique means of inspiring Jews, by presenting them as a worthy subject not merely within the community but before a much larger non-Jewish audience.

Thus, beyond the seeming forthrightness of the Seminary's radio and television series's identity as "Jewish media" lies a complex of aspects, relations, and agendas. As Kirshenblatt-Gimblett observes, speaking more generally on Jewish culture, the question of ethnic identity is best understood as "a social construction," best discussed when situated in a particular context: "Perhaps the question should be rephrased: not, What is Jewishness? but rather, When does an individual foreground his identity as Jewish, by what means, and to what ends? What is the cultural content of this social differentiation? What is the display of Jewishness counterposed to? Who are the relevant others?"[139]

A Ghetto in the Democracy of the Airwaves?
Jews in the Landscape of American Broadcasting

These complex nuances of the "Jewishness" of JTS's broadcasts and their implications did not figure in the official discourse of Seminary administrators associated with the Radio and Television Department. Rather, they were fond of celebrating the compatibilities of broadcasting, democracy, and religion. For example, in 1946 Moshe Davis told an interfaith audience:

> If there is any validity to this faith in the indispensability of religion to democracy, then the religious traditions have but one choice: to draw out of their own traditions those elements which may help them raise to universal heights for the greater benefit of all mankind. . . . Of all the opportunities granted to the church and synagogue to transmit their message, radio transmission is of singular effectiveness. Radio is democracy's and, therefore, religion's most vital means of communication.[140]

Yet, while the networks and the Seminary hailed broadcasting as a virtual locus of spiritual democracy, American radio and television provided Jews with a marginal and highly circumscribed, albeit respectable, venue in which to present themselves to the American public. When broadcasting professionals referred to this time period as a "ghetto," they no doubt employed the word to describe, in the general meaning that it has acquired, a segregated and undesirable area, usually populated by a group regarded as deviant. The "Sunday ghetto" does not allude specifically to Jews, since it also includes Protestants and Catholics, as well as various artists and public figures. Indeed, it can also be seen—as actual ghettos have been—as offering a protected space for its inhabitants, in which they can flourish in ways impossible beyond the ghetto's parietal confines. Louis Wirth characterizes this phenomenon, in his landmark 1928 sociological study of the ghetto, as an "accommodation, to distinguish it from the assimilation that takes place when two people . . . come to share each other's inner life and thus become one."[141]

The ecumenical broadcasting series produced by JTS's Radio and Television Department thus situated Jews in a segregated and restricted "neighborhood" to inhabit, ostensibly "separate but equal," within the virtual "cultural forum" or public "gathering place" of American broadcasting.[142] By designating the "Sunday ghetto"—which had been "set aside for meditation, introspection, and a general inventory of life"[143]—as an appropriate time and place in which Jews might regularly appear forthrightly and with dignity as Jews on national radio and television, broadcasters implicitly established all other venues in the "democracy" of the airwaves as inappropriate for such appearances.

The programs produced by JTS during the heyday of the Radio and Television Department were pioneering efforts both as a form of Jewish outreach and as a use of drama in public service broadcasting. They are best appreciated as the results of a distinctive constellation of agendas and opportunities at the Seminary, within the American Jewish community, and among the commercial networks during the middle decades of this century. The many hours of radio and television produced by the collaboration of these forces evince distinctive strategies to accommodate Jewish particularism and multiple understandings of Jewish identity and creativity within a conceptual and aesthetic framework that the producing organizations considered palatable to the general American public, compatible with enduring American values.

Looking back at the history of the Seminary's Radio and Television Department from the vantage of the late 1980s, Wyler notes that this constellation has shifted considerably. In addition to changes in the finances and priorities of both the broadcasting industry and the Seminary, she observes that "our society is far more sophisticated about the media than it was a half-century ago."[144] One consequence of this increased sophistication has been the adoption of these media—especially television—as venues for American Jewish self-portraiture. Indeed, the Sunday ghetto began to disappear as Jews started to appear regularly as other than comic foils on national prime-time television broacasts.

In the past two decades, subjects of Jewish interest that once were addressed only on *The Eternal Light* or JTS's other series now appear frequently in multiple locations within the geography of American broadcasting. In episodes of prime-time entertainment series such as *LA Law*, *Northern Exposure*, and *thirtysomething*, Jewish protagonists grapple with questions of religious practice, faith, and identity. Prime-time television miniseries have presented dramas on the Nazi persecution of European Jewry (*Holocaust: The Story of the Family Weiss*, 1978), the life of Golda Meir (*A Woman Called Golda*, 1985), and the Jewish immigrant experience (*Evergreen*, 1985). Broadcast documentaries explore subjects ranging from Jewish popular culture to the broad sweep of Jewish history (*Heritage: Civilization and the Jews*, 1984) and profile figures such as Raoul Wallenberg and Elie Wiesel. Jews as a political force, both in Israel and in the Diaspora, are regularly discussed on local and national newscasts. A variety of Jewish broadcasting efforts continues to flourish on local radio stations and cable television channels, and the advent of home videotape recorder-players has extended the opportunities for disseminating and collecting media of Jewish interest.

Recent years have also witnessed the creation of Jewish media archives at institutes ranging from the Hebrew University in Jerusalem to the Jewish Museum of New York.[145] The broadcasts of JTS's Radio and Television Department, some of which now repose in archival collections, provide a strategic vantage point from which to contemplate the significance of these ecumenical series within the relation of Jews to America's broadcast media and American popular culture in general. Now, as artifacts, these programs continue to provide valuable insights into the values and sensibilities of American Jews and American broadcasting during the crucial middle decades of the 20th century.

The authors of this essay wish to thank Milton Krents, Marjorie Wyler, and the late Moshe Davis, former staff members of JTS's Department of Radio and Television, and Tim Hanssen and Julie Miller, of the Ratner Center for the Study of Conservative Judaism, for their assistance and insights.

1. With regard to Finkelstein's interest in radio at the time that the Seminary began plans for regular broadcasts, former JTS staff member Marjorie Wyler commented, "I don't think that he even turned on the radio. I doubt very much whether he had one in the house." Marjorie Wyler, interview by Jeffrey Shandler, New York, 7 December 1994.

2. The Radio and Television Department acquired this name in the early 1950s; before that, it was generally referred to as "The Eternal Light," the name of its first and most enduring broadcast series. Throughout this essay, "the Radio and Television Department" will refer to the division of JTS devoted to broadcasting and associated activities (e.g., the distribution of scripts and recordings of broadcasts) from the beginning of regular broadcasts of *The Eternal Light* in 1944.

3. Untitled typescript [speech? 1937?], JTS Archives, RG 11C, box 18, folder 22.

4. *Jewish Theological Seminary of America Register* 1938–1939 ([New York: Jewish Theological Seminary, 1939]), p. 25. Wyler recalls that the series presented "all kinds of esoteric subjects"—for example, a broadcast on gardening—and that, with *The Women's Hour*, the Seminary was "feeling our way into that medium." Interview, 7 December 1994.

5. The Seminary's earliest extant documentation of Krents's work on its behalf with regard to broadcasting is a telegram, dated 28 March 1939, in which Krents cabled Finkelstein regarding a "forthcoming Passover broadcast." JTS Archives, RG 1A, box 15, folder 67.

6. Marjorie G. Wyler, "*The Eternal Light*: Judaism on the Airwaves," *Conservative Judaism* 39, no. 2 (winter, 1986–87): pp. 18–19. According to Wyler, Finkelstein first met Sarnoff in 1939-1940. Interview, 7 December 1994.

7. According to Krents, NBC was motivated to approach JTS about creating a radio series as a consequence of the sale of NBC Blue, one of the company's two networks, in 1943. The newly formed ABC network acquired *Message of Israel*, a Jewish religion series produced in conjunction with the Reform movement, which had been on NBC Blue's roster, and NBC (formerly NBC Red) was left without a Jewish program. Milton Krents, telephone conversation with Elihu Katz, New York, 15 November, 1994.

8. Wyler, "*The Eternal Light*," p. 18. Emphasis in original.

9. According to a letter from Finkelstein to Krents dated 5 September 1944, Krents was to be paid a flat fee for his work that year "in regard to the seminary program" (JTS Archives, RG 1B, box 36, folder 13). Finkelstein proposed making similar contingency arrangements with others involved in the production of the first episodes of what would be *The Eternal Light*. In a letter to Krents dated 11 August 1944, Finkelstein wrote that "it will not be necessary at the present time to make an annual contract with the script writers in view of the the fact that there is, of course, the possibility that we may be taken off the air in the course of the year." See Marjorie Wyler Papers, Ratner Center for the Study of Conservative Judaism (unprocessed collection).

10. This was true not only for Christian radio programming but also for the earliest Jewish broadcasting efforts. For an overview of the early history of American Jewish broadcasting, see Zev Zahavy, *A History and Survey of Jewish Religious Broadcasting* (Ph.D. diss., Yeshiva University, 1959). According to Zahavy, the earliest known Jewish broadcast on American radio was a half-hour Selihot program by the Conservative movement's United Synagogues of America, aired by WEAF on 30 August 1923 (p. 147).

11. See Erik Barnouw, *The Golden Web: A History of Broadcasting in the United States; Volume II—1933–1953* (New York: Oxford University Press, 1968), pp. 66–70, 85–89, 116–21.

395

*Broadcasting
American
Judaism:
The Radio
and Television
Department
of the JTS*

12. Ibid., p. 231.

13. A press release marking the twenty-fifth anniversary of the radio series claims that listeners sent some ten thousand letters responding to Wishengrad's Warsaw Ghetto drama. "*The Eternal Light*" [press release], 26 September 1969; hectograph, p. 2. JTS Archives, RG 11C, box 30, folder 42.

14. Morton Wishengrad, *The Eternal Light* (New York: Crown, 1947), p. 32.

15. *The Eternal Light*, program no. 1294, aired 11 December 1977.

16. Wyler, "*The Eternal Light*," p. 19.

17. Wyler interview, 7 December 1994. During a televised conversation with Newton Minow aired on *The Eternal Light*, Finkelstein commented that when the radio series was first proposed to the Seminary's board of directors, "there was great opposition to it . . ., and it passed our board of directors by one vote." *The Ethical Responsibilities of Communications in a Space Age* (program no. T-102, aired 9 December 1962); transcript, p. 4.

18. See the minutes of the Board of Directors of the Jewish Theological Seminary of America, JTS Archives, RG 2, executive committee meeting, 17 August 1944. Other names under consideration for the series, according to a handwritten note by Finkelstein[?], included "The People of the Book," "The Voice of Judaism," "The Voice of the Synagogue," and "The Light of Judaism." Letter from Milton Krents to Finkelstein, 8 August 1944. Ratner Center for the Study of Conservative Judaism, JTS, Marjorie Wyler Papers (unprocessed collection). According to Wyler, the name "The Eternal Light" was proposed by JTS board member Alan M. Strook, and it "immediately won unanimous approval." (Wyler, "*The Eternal Light*," p. 19)

19. "'*The Eternal Light*,' Program Series Drawn from Jewish Culture, Begins on NBC Oct. 8" [press release], 29 August [1944]; hectograph. JTS Archives, RG 11C, box 26, folder 38.

20. "The 'Eternal Light' Celebrates Its First Birthday" [press release, October(?) 1945]; hectograph, 4-5. These "basic precepts" were repeated elsewhere, including in an expanded form in Everett C. Parker, Elinor Inman, and Ross Snyder, *Religious Radio: What to Do and How* (New York: Harper & Brothers, 1948), p. 7.

21. The poster is reproduced in Michael Greenbaum's article, "The Finkelstein Years," in volume one of this book.

22. Arthur A. Goren, *The American Jews* (Cambridge, Mass.: Belknap/Harvard University Press, 1982), p. 102.

23. Marshall Sklare, *Conservative Judaism: An American Religious Movement*, rev. ed. (New York: Schocken, 1972) pp. 25-32, 66-72.

24. Arthur Hertzberg, *The Jews in America: Four Centuries of an Uneasy Encounter* (New York: Simon & Schuster, 1989), p. 322.

25. Albert I. Gordon, *Jews in Suburbia* (Boston: Beacon, 1959), p. 16. Emphasis in original.

26. Nathan Glazer, *American Judaism*, 2d ed., rev. (1957; reprint, Chicago: University of Chicago Press, 1989), pp. 116-17.

27. Geoffrey Wigoder, "Ecumenism," in *Contemporary Jewish Religious Thought: Original Essays on Critical Concepts, Movements and Beliefs*, eds. Arthur A. Cohen and Paul Mendes Flohr (New York: Charles Scribner's Sons, 1987), p. 148.

28. "The Television Code of the National Association of Radio and Television Broadcasters," in William Y. Elliott, ed., *Television's Impact on American Culture* (East Lansing: Michigan State University Press, 1956), p. 334.

29. See Stewart M. Hoover, *Mass Media Religion: The Social Sources of the Electronic Church* (Newbury Park, Calif.: SAGE, 1988), pp. 49-55, and Peter G. Horsfield, *Religious Television: The American Experience* (New York: Longman, 1984), pp. 3-7.

30. Morton Wishengrad, *The Eternal Light* (New York: Crown, 1947), pp. xiv-xv.

31. Goodman Ace, "On a Brainy Sunday Afternoon," *The Book of Little Knowledge: More Than*

You Want to Know About Television (New York: Simon & Schuster, 1955), pp. 125–27.

32. See H. Richard Niebuhr, *The Social Sources of Denominationalism* (1929; reprint, New York: Henry Holt, 1954). Thanks to Eugene Lowe of Princeton University for contributing this insight.

33. Wyler, *"The Eternal Light,"* p. 18.

34. Will Herberg, *Protestant—Catholic—Jew: An Essay in American Religious Sociology* (Garden City, N. Y.: Doubleday, 1955), pp. 15, 40.

35. Herberg's configuration canonizes major corporate religious movements as the American mainstream, thereby excluding organized secular Jews (e.g., the Workmen's Circle or the Jewish People's Fraternal Order), Reconstructionists, black Jews, and hasidim. In addition, various Christian groups not affiliated with mainstream coalitions such as the National Council of Churches are implicitly omitted. Moreover, the complete absence of Islam, Native American religious traditions, and all Asian faiths locates them beyond the nation's spiritual pale—to say nothing of excluding from the American spectrum those who are atheist or who claim no religious identity. Herberg's model also fails to account for African Americans and others whose ancestry does not fit his model of voluntary emigration to America.

36. Hertzberg, *The Jews in America*, pp. 322-23.

37. As cited in John Cogley, *Report on Blacklisting, Volume II: Radio-Television* ([New York]: The Fund for the Republic, 1956), p. 15.

38. *The Eternal Light: Tenth Anniversary Year*, [New York?, 1954?]; brochure, p. 7. JTS Archives, RG 11C, box 30, folder 33.

39. Wyler, *"The Eternal Light,"* p. 19. According to a letter from Krents to Finkelstein (8 August 1944) about a projected production budget for the series, the Seminary was to be responsible for the cost of a choir (including a cantor, accompanist, and choirmaster), scriptwriters, and actors. In addition, JTS incurred "incidental expenses such as clerical work, publicity and promotion, administative, etc." See Ratner Center for the Study of Conservative Judaism, JTS, Marjorie Wyler Papers (unprocessed collection).

40. Other program editors for the Radio and Television Department's various radio and television programs included Arthur Chiel, Gerson Cohen, Edward Gershfield, Bernard Mandelbaum, Max Routtenberg—all rabbis ordained at JTS.

41. Wyler, *"The Eternal Light,"* p. 19. Other members of the initial committee included Mrs. Felix M. Warburg, Judge Irving Lehman, Judge Joseph M. Proskauer, Charles J. Rosenbloom, James Marshall, Albert D. Lasker, Mendel Silberberg, Jesse Steinhardt, and Rabbis Edgar F. Magnin, Jeshurun Cardozo, and Louis M. Levitsky. ("*The Eternal Light*," Program Series Drawn From Jewish Culture, Begins on NBC Oct. 8"), p. 2.

42. Others who wrote scripts for *The Eternal Light* include Arthur Arent, Peter Barry, Sylvia Berger, Ben Kagan, Joseph Liss, Alan Lomax, Alan Marcus, Peter Lyon, Eve Merriam, Sigmund Miller, Joseph Mindel, Seymour Reit, Hedda Rosten, Norman Rosten, Marc Siegel, Irve Tunick, and Marion Voigt.

43. "*The Eternal Light*" [press release], 26 September 1969; hectograph. JTS Archives, RG 11C, box 30, folder 42.

44. "*The Eternal Light*" [report, 1946?]; hectograph. JTS Archives, RG 11C, box 26, folder 40. Some local stations aired recordings of the broadcasts later in the day.

45. The first Hooper ratings were 3.3 (6 October 1946), 3.6 (20 October), and 4.4 (3 November). The document reporting this information notes that "Comparative Hooper ratings here may be of interest: The Catholic Hour, after more than 15 years on the network, at the excellent listening hour of 6 PM, had a Hooper, on October 6, of 3.9. On November 3, the University of Chicago Round Table had a 3.6 Hooper, while the Toscanini NBC Orchestra had a 3.3 Rating." ("*The Eternal Light*" [report, 1946?]; hectograph. JTS Archives, RG

397

*Broadcasting
American
Judaism:
The Radio
and Television
Department
of the JTS*

11C, box 26, file 40.)

46. E.g., "6,000,000 Listen . . . ," a twelve-page fund-raising brochure published by JTS, ca. 1947. JTS Archives, RG 11C, box 27, file 30. The brochure cites the "latest Hooper rating," noting that *The Eternal Light* is carried by "more than 75 [of NBC's] affiliated stations."

47. "Report to the Board of Overseers: *The Eternal Light*," December 1948; hectograph, p. 2. JTS Archives, RG 11C, box 26, folder 38.

48. See "*The Eternal Light* Celebrates Its First Birthday," p. 1. Mrs. Roosevelt's syndicated column appeared on 10 October 1944; see, e.g., "Hyde Park Visit; New Radio Series," *New York World-Telegram*, p. 17.

49. Rose., "*The Eternal Light*," *Variety*, 25 October 1944, p. 38.

50. Parker, Inman, and Snyder, *Religious Radio*, p. 7.

51. Val Adams, "'*The Eternal Light*': Religion Series Appeals to All Faiths and Stresses Dramatic Values," *New York Times*, 8 January 1950, sec. 2, p. 15.

52. *The Eternal Light: Tenth Anniversary Year*, p. 8; "*The Eternal Light*" [press release], 26 September 1969, p. 2. JTS Archives, RG 11C, box 30, folder 42.

53. *The Eternal Light* received the Peabody award for radio in 1962 and 1967. In addition, JTS received a Peabody award in 1978 "for '*The Eternal Light*,' a consistently noteworthy program broadcast for 35 years on the NBC Radio Network." See Gita Siegman, ed., *World of Winners: A Current and Historical Perspective on Awards and Their Winners*, 2d ed. (Detroit: Gale Research, 1992), pp. 688, 686.

54. "*The Eternal Light*: Fact Sheet," 22 October 1953; hectograph. JTS Archives, RG 11C, box 26, folder 38.

55. See, e.g., Jacob S. Golub, "Teacher's Guide for Scripts of '*The Eternal Light*' Broadcasts," 15 January 1945; hectograph. JTS Archives, RG 11C, box 26, folder 39.

56. Wishengrad, *The Eternal Light*. The volume includes an introductory essay on the art of radio playwrighting by Wishengrad.

57. [Untitled press release], 19 January 1947; hectograph. JTS Archives, RG 11C, box 26, folder 40. According to the release, "Each program is produced on three [78-rpm] twelve inch unbreakable Vinylite records."

58. Other Jewish groups did not consider the broadcast of worship services on the radio to be a problem. For example, beginning in the 1950s Friday evening services were aired on New York City station WQXR from Temple Emanu-El, a Reform synagogue (Zahavy, *A History and Survey of Jewish Religious Broadcasting*, p. 6).

59. Wyler, "*The Eternal Light*," p. 19.

60. Wigoder, "Ecumenism," p. 150.

61. See "The Jewish Stage," in Gustav Karpeles, *Jewish Literature and Other Essays* (Philadelphia: Jewish Publication Society, 1895), pp. 229-48.

62. Wishengrad, *The Eternal Light*, p. viii.

63. "Art and Religion in Atmosphere of Creative Freedom Characterize 30 Years of '*Lamp Unto My Feet*' Series," CBS News press release, 22 February 1978. National Jewish Archive of Broadcasting, The Jewish Museum of New York.

64. Barbara Kirshenblatt-Gimblett, "Kitchen Judaism," in *Getting Comfortable in New York: The American Jewish Home, 1880–1950*, eds. Susan L. Braunstein and Jenna Weissman Joselit (New York: The Jewish Museum, 1990), p. 78.

65. Julie Miller, "Planning the Jewish Museum, 1944–1947," *Conservative Judaism* 47, no. 1 (fall 1994): p. 61.

66. Zahavy, *A History and Survey of Jewish Religious Broadcasting*, pp. 5–22, passim.

67. Adams, "'*The Eternal Light*,'" sec. 2, p. 15. Despite Davis's comment, episodes from the Bible were dramatized on the series, often incorporating traditional or modern commentaries on the original texts.

68. *The Ethical Responsibilities of Communications in a Space Age*, p. 1.

69. See Newton Minow, *Equal Time* (New York: Atheneum, 1964), chap. 1, "The Vast Wasteland," pp. 45–69; the speech is reproduced on pp. 48–64.

70. *The Ethical Responsibilities of Communications in a Space Age*, pp. 2–4, passim.

71. See, e.g., the records of speech teacher Arleigh Williamson, JTS Archives, RG 3B, box 2, folders 21–27.

72. See Sklare, *Conservative Judaism*, pp. 191–95.

73. Text of the song: "*Shomer Yisrael sh'mor sh'erit Yisrael v'al yovad Yisrael ha-omrim sh'ma Yisrael.*"

74. Exodus 27:20.

75. Form letter (addressed to "Dear Colleague") from Louis Finkelstein, 7 September 1944; hectograph. JTS Archives, RG 11C, box 26, folder 39.

76. Moshe Davis, interview by Pamela Jay, Jerusalem, 25 December 1990 (transcript), p. 6. Ratner Center for the Study of Conservative Judaism, JTS.

77. *Akiba* (program no. 29, aired 29 April 1945); *The Days of a Poet* (Solomon Ibn Gabirol; program no. 692, aired 12 February 1961); *Moses Mendelssohn* (program no. 68, aired 24 February 1946); *A Lifetime Is Long Enough* (Vilna Gaon; program no. 570, aired 8 December 1957).

78. *A Heart of Wisdom* (Schick) by Joseph Mindel (program no. 576, aired 19 January 1958); *The Man Who Knew Lincoln* (Rosewater) by Virginia Mazer (program no. 489, aired 1 January 1956); *The Language of Hope* (Zamenhof) by Judah Stampfer (program no. 653, aired 7 February 1960).

79. Moshe Davis, "Voice in the Wilderness," in *Education on the Air: Sixteenth Yearbook of the Institute for Education by Radio*, eds. I. Keith Tyler and Nancy Mason Dasher (Columbus: Ohio State University, 1946), p. 248.

80. E.g., *An Unlikely Story* by Joseph Mindel, based on Ida Uchill's *Pioneers, Peddlers and Tzadikim* (program no. 642, aired 22 November 1959).

81. E.g., *The Man Who Rode Like Revere* by William Wise, the story of Francis Salvador, a Revolutionary War hero in South Carolina (program no. 513, aired 17 June 1956); *Mr. Flanagan, the Chaplain and Mr. Lincoln* by Marc Siegal, which tells of a rabbi's efforts during the Civil War to allow Jewish clergy to serve in the chaplaincy (program no. 723, aired 14 January 1962).

82. *Enter to Learn, Depart to Serve* (Bethune) by Joseph Bruck (program no. 616, aired 18 January 1959); *David Dubinsky* by Harry Gersh (program no. 597, aired 29 June 1958); *Emma Lazarus: A Modern Esther* by Morton Wishengrad (program no. 21, aired 25 February 1945); *The Big Road* (Carver) by Virginia Mayer (program no. 726, aired 4 February 1962).

83. E.g., *An American Sampler* by Marc Siegal, "a dramatic narrative sung in ballad style which recollects a few of the incidents in 300 years of American Jewish history" (program no. 444, aired 21 November 1954). CBS, NBC, and the Dumont networks all aired special television programs in conjunction with the Tercentenary. See David Bernstein, "The American Jewish Tercentenary," *American Jewish Year Book* 67 (1956): pp. 101–02. According to Bernstein, CBS's William S. Paley and NBC's David Sarnoff were among those who were on the Tercentenary's program policy committee. Sarnoff is credited with proposing the theme for the celebration, "Man's Opportunities and Responsibilities Under Freedom."

84. *Jewish Theological Seminary of America Register* 1977–1982 ([New York: JTS, 1982]), p. 101.

85. *Isaiah and the Nations* (program no. 102, aired 20 October 1946).

86. "*The Eternal Light* Celebrates its First Birthday," p. 6.

87. *Anne Frank: Diary of a Young Girl* by Meyer Levin (program no. 366, aired 14 December 1952). The drama starred Jeff Chandler as Otto Frank and Anne Whitfield as Anne. For an account of the subsequent controversy surrounding Levin's adaptation of the diary, see his

399

*Broadcasting
American
Judaism:
The Radio
and Television
Department
of the JTS*

Obsession (New York: Simon & Schuster, 1973), and Lawrence Graver, *An Obsession with Anne Frank: Meyer Levin and the Diary* (Berkeley: University of California Press, 1995).

88. E.g., *My Father's Tallis* (program no. 49, aired 14 October 1945); *A Sound of Music* (program no. 59, aired 23 December 1945); *The Voice of Rachel* (program no. 60, aired 30 December 1945).

89. *Gandhi* by Morton Wishengrad (program no. 252, aired 1 January 1950); *Light Against the Dark* by Marion Voigt (program no. 473, aired 12 June 1955).

90. *Hunger* (program no. 82, aired 2 June 1946). The speaker at the conclusion of the broadcast was Fiorello H. LaGuardia, Director General of United Nations Relief and Rehabilitation Administration.

91. Wishengrad, *The Eternal Light*, p. 188.

92. S. Y. Agnon's *The Betrothed*, adapted by Joseph Mindel (program no. 1260, aired 9 January 1977); Isaac Babel's *The Phonograph*, adapted by James Yaffe (program no. 1264, aired 6 Febuary 1977); a David Bergelson story adapted by Morton Wishengrad as *The Tender Grass* (program no. 75, aired 14 April 1946); Y. L. Peretz's *If Not Higher* (program no. 47, aired 16 September 1945); Henry Roth's *Call It Sleep*, adapted by Shimon Wincelberg (program no 1259, aired 2 January 1977); Isaac Bashevis Singer's *Zlateh the Goat* (program no. 1373, aired 9 December 1979); Sholem Aleichem's *The Pocketknife* (program no. 1103, aired 27 October 1946).

93. *Joseph and the Indians* (program no. 3, aired 22 October 1944); *Nathan the Wise* (program no. 92, aired 11 August 1946); *Athalie* (program no. 91, aired 4 August 1946).

94. *The Wise Men of Chelm* by Morton Wishengrad[?] (program no. 87, aired 7 July 1946); *How Manny Got into the Seventh Grade* by Marc Siegel (program no. 649, aired 10 January 1960).

95. Maurice Samuel, *Certain People of the Book* (New York: Knopf, 1967); Mark Van Doren and Maurice Samuel, *In the Beginning, Love: Dialogues on the Bible*, ed. Edith Samuel (New York: John Day, 1973); Mark Van Doren and Maurice Samuel, *The Book of Praise: Dialogues on the Psalms*, ed. Edith Samuel (New York: John Day, 1975).

96. Hoover, *Mass Media Religion*, pp. 54–55.

97. Report to the Board of Overseers: *The Eternal Light*, December 1948; hectograph, pp. 4–6. JTS Archives, RG 11C, box 26, folder 38.

98. *Jewish Theological Seminary of America Register*, 1951-1952/5712 (New York: JTS, 1952), p. 124.

99. For *Frontiers of Faith*, according to Moshe Davis, the network made an exception to its policy forbidding those employed in its radio division to work on television programs as well. Moshe Davis, interview by Pamela Jay, Jerusalem, 10 January 1991 (transcript), p. 9. Ratner Center for the Study of Conservative Judaism, JTS.

100. *The World of Sholom Aleichem* aired 9 November 1952; *Anne Frank: The Diary of a Young Girl* aired 16 November 1952.

101. [Untitled press release], 14 November 1952; hectograph. JTS Archives, RG 11C, box 32, folder 37. The program was aired 23 November 1952.

102. The first television program aired under the series title *The Eternal Light* was *The Broken Sabbath of Rabbi Asher* by Morton Wishengrad, on 4 November 1958. The cast of this dramatic reading included William Shatner, Reuben Singer, and Charlotte Rae.

103. A. William Bluem, *Religious Television Programs: A Study of Relevance* (New York: Hastings House, 1969), p. 31.

104. *Schechter Revisited at Cambridge University* (program no. 128, aired 15 November 1965); *The World of Rembrandt* (program no. 154, aired 10 December 1967); *A Talent for Life: Jews of the Italian Renaissance* (program no. 253, aired 2 December 1979); *The Itinerary of Elie Wiesel: From Sighet to Jerusalem* (program no. 200, aired 21 May 1972)

105. *A Conversation with Ambassador Sol M. Linowitz* (program no. 151, aired 19 November

1967); *A Conversation with James Michener* (program no. 160, aired 23 June 1968); *A Conversation with Itzhak Perlman* (program no. 231, aired 7 November 1976); *A Conversation with Karl Katz* (program no. 172, aired 8 June 1969); *A Conversation with the Late Dr. Abraham Joshua Heschel* (program no. 205, aired 4 February 1973). The last program, an hour-long interview conducted by Carl Stern of NBC News, was taped ten days prior to Heschel's death.

106. [Untitled press release], 22 December 1961; hectograph. JTS Archives, RG 11C, box 25, folder 8. According to this press release, the segments of the series produced in conjunction with the Seminary were titled *Directions '61: A Jewish Perspective*, with parallel titles for Protestant and Catholic segments. Milton Krents served as producer of the series for the Seminary, along with Wiley Hance, manager of public affairs for ABC. The program editor for JTS was Arthur Chiel.

107. The subject of anti-Communist blacklisting within the entertainment industry was directly discussed on television for the first time on the CBS public affairs program *Small World*, hosted by Edward Murrow, on 8 March 1959. (See J. Fred MacDonald, *Television and the Red Menace: The Video Road to Vietnam* [New York: Praeger, 1985], p. 25.)

108. *Shirah* (Pearl Lang; program no. 21, aired 8 April 1962); *A Life in Song* (Martha Schlamme; program no. 78; aired 28 May 1967); *Israel in Egypt* (program no. 31a[?], aired 7 April 1963).

109. *The Concerns of Roman Vishniac* (program no. 112, aired 12 December 1971); *A Glimpse of the Inner Life of Marc Chagall* by Marc Siegal (program no. 16, aired 7 January 1962).

110. *The Thief and the Hangman* (program no. 13, aired 15 October 1961) was based on a television drama of the same name written by Morton Wishengrad for *The Eternal Light* (program no. 7, aired 11 May 1952); *The Fifth Cup: A Cantata for Passover* (program no. 161, aired 23 March 1975); *The Final Ingredient* (program no. 54, aired 11 April 1965) was based on a television drama of the same name written by Reginald Rose for ABC (aired 19 April 1959).

111. *Directions in Israel* (programs nos. 34–38, aired 6, 13, 20, 27 October and 3 November 1963); *The Heritage of Anne Frank* (program no. 119, aired 3 December 1972); *Kibbutz Langdon: U.S.A.* (program no. 135, aired 21 April 1974); *A Plain Pine Box* (program no. 168, aired 16 October 1977); *. . . And the Bush Was Not Consumed* (program no. 68, aired 1 January 1967).

112. *Ethics in Five Acts* (programs nos. 27–31, aired 3, 10, 17, 24, 31 March 1963); *Campus Crisis '70* (program no. 104, aired 5 July 1970); *Tampering with Genes: Serving God or Playing God?* (program no. 163, aired 1 May 1977); *Vietnamese Refugees* (aired in 1975); *Man's Understanding of Himself* (program no. 11, aired 1 October 1961); *A Conversation with Isidor I. Rabi* (program no. 146, aired 6 October 1974).

113. *A Conversation with Dr. Louis Finkelstein* (program no. 110, aired 13 June 1971); *The Woman Rabbi and Judaism* (program no. 128, aired 25 November 1973).

114. Hoover, *Mass Media Religion*, p. 56.

115. Form letter from Stanley J. Schachter, vice-chancellor of JTS (addressed to "Dear Colleague"), 16 February 1983; hectograph. JTS Archives, RG 11C, box 27, folder 16.

116. *Jewish Theological Seminary of America Register* 1977–1982, p. 100.

117. Milton E. Krents, "The Realities of Religious/Electronics Economics," *Women's League Outlook* 52, no. 1 (fall 1981): p. 22.

118. As cited in Michael Gallagher, "Caution: Lower Clearance," [draft of essay, 1982(?)]; hectograph. JTS Archives, RG 11C, box 62, folder 21.

119. Carol Sorgen, "Jews Discovering Cable TV Potential," *Jewish Times* (Baltimore), 10 April 1981, p. 5.

120. Videocassettes of these and a selection of earlier telecasts from *The Eternal Light* are available from the Radio and Television Department.

121. "*The Eternal Light*" [press release], 26 September 1969; hectograph, p. 4.

401

*Broadcasting
American
Judaism:
The Radio
and Television
Department
of the JTSA*

122. Melville J. Herskovits, "Who Are the Jews?" in *The Jews: Their History, Culture and Religion*, ed. Louis Finkelstein (Philadelphia: Jewish Publication Society, 1949), p. 1168.

123. When Finkelstein's portrait appeared on the cover of *Time* magazine on 15 October, 1951 (vol. 58, no. 16), in conjunction with a cover story on trends in the American Jewish community's religious life, he was depicted standing under an eternal light.

124. Wigoder, "Ecumenism," p. 149.

125. Everett C. Parker, David W. Barry, and Dallas W. Smythe, *The Television-Radio Audience and Religion* (New York: Harper & Brothers, 1955), pp. 113–14.

126. Mordecai Kaplan, *Judaism as a Civilization: Toward a Reconstruction of American-Jewish Life*, rev. ed. (1934; reprint, New York: Thomas Yoseloff, 1957).

127. Davis interview, 25 December 1990, pp. 12–13.

128. Henry Sapoznik, "Broadcast Ghetto: The Image of Jews on Mainstream American Radio," *Jewish Folklore and Ethnology Review* 16, no. 1 (1994): p. 37.

129. Lewis Herman and Margueritte Shallet Herman, *Manual of Foreign Dialects for Radio, Stage and Screen* (New York: Ziff Davis, 1943), p. 393, as cited in Sapoznik, "Broadcast Ghetto," p. 38.

130. David Marc, "Comic Visions of the City: New York and the Television Sitcom," *Radical History Review* 42 (1988): p. 61.

131. Sig Altman, *The Comic Image of the Jew: Explorations of a Pop Culture Phenomenon* (Rutherford, N. J.: Fairleigh Dickinson University Press, 1971), p. 11.

132. Untitled and undated compilation of listener letters, JTS Archives, RG 11C, box 26, folder 40, p. 7. Spellings and punctuation in original typescript.

133. Ibid., p. 11.

134. Ibid., p. 15.

135. Philip Roth, *The Ghost Writer* (1979; reprint, New York: Ballantine Books/Fawcett Crest, 1983), pp. 106-107.

136. Davis interview, 25 December 1990, p. 7.

137. Jonathan S. Woocher, *Sacred Survival: The Civil Religion of American Jews* (Bloomington: Indiana University Press, 1986), p. 14.

138. Marjorie Wyler, interview by Jeffrey Shandler, New York, 1 July 1992.

139. Barbara Kirshenblatt-Gimblett, "The Folk Culture of Jewish Immigrant Communities: Research Paradigms and Directions," in *The Jews of North America*, ed. Moses Rischin (Detroit: Wayne State University Press, 1987), p. 87.

140. Davis, "Voice in the Wilderness," p. 248.

141. Louis Wirth: *The Ghetto* (1928; reprint, Chicago: University of Chicago Press, 1956), p. 283. See also Max Weinreich, "The Reality of Jewishness Versus the Ghetto Myth: The Sociolinguistic Roots of Yiddish," in *To Honor Roman Jakobson: Essays on the Occasion of His Seventieth Birthday* (The Hague: Mouton, 1967), pp. 2199–211.

142. See Horace M. Newcomb and Paul Hirsch, "Television as a Cultural Forum: Implications for Research," *Quarterly Review of Film Studies* 8, no. 3 (summer 1983): pp. 45–56; Paul C. Adams, "Television as Gathering Place," *Annals of the Association of American Geographers* 82, no. 1 (1992): pp. 117–35.

143. Ace, "On a Brainy Sunday Afternoon," p. 125.

144. Wyler, "*The Eternal Light*," p. 21.

145. Copies of episodes from the various television series that JTS helped produce (*Frontiers of Faith, The Eternal Light, Directions, Lamp Unto My Feet*) are housed in the National Jewish Archive of Broadcasting at The Jewish Museum of New York, 1109 Fifth Avenue; see *National Jewish Archive of Broadcasting: Catalog of Holdings*, 2d ed. (New York: The Jewish Museum, 1995).

JACK WERTHEIMER

JTS and the Conservative Movement

Attendees at the Rabbinical Assembly's golden jubilee convention assemble on the Seminary lawn, 1950. The front row contains several past presidents of the RA. From left: Max Routtenberg, Theodore Friedman, Charles Kauvar, Aaron Blumenthal, Louis Finkelstein, David Aronson, Max Davidson, Ira Eisenstein, Robert Gordis, Jacob S. Minkin. *Photo by Empire Photographers. Ratner Center, JTS.*

JACK WERTHEIMER

JTS and the
Conservative Movement

TOWARD THE BEGINNING
of 1979, the Chancellor of JTS and his board chairman exchanged a series of letters
about a matter of pressing concern: How shall the Seminary conceive of its relationship to the Conservative movement? Alan M. Stroock, the chairman of the
board, maintained that "the Movement is an arm of the Seminary, and the Seminary is not an arm of the Movement, and, in many ways, is independent of it."
Gerson D. Cohen responded as follows:

> Of course, the Seminary is independent in the sense that it has complete free-
> dom in academic matters, the *sine qua non* for maintaining its scholarly
> integrity. On the other hand, a truer picture of the relationship today would be
> to say that the Seminary and the Conservative Movement are interdependent.
> We provide leaders and spiritual guidance for the Movement, and in turn
> depend heavily upon the Movement for support. This means that we rely heav-
> ily on the rabbis who are the intermediaries between us and the laity. We can no
> longer stand aloof from the Conservative Movement as a whole, nor can we
> ignore the burning issues that confront these ambassadors and our Movement
> daily. The Seminary cannot afford to maintain a neutral position, which in the
> final analysis is a euphemism for the Orthodox position, while the Conservative
> movement as a whole goes its own way. If the Seminary is to be the fountain-
> head of Conservative Judaism, it must be in contact with the Movement and
> give it guidance. . . . While we at the Seminary have always seen ourselves as
> being "above the battle" as you say, others have seen the Seminary as evading
> the issues facing our Movement, because it was bankrupt and ill-equipped to
> confront them.[1]

This exchange, written during the heat of controversy over the admission of
women to the JTS Rabbinical School, is remarkable for a number of reasons, not the
least of which is its candor. Stroock apparently viewed the Conservative movement

with its eight hundred congregations and nearly two million adherents as an appendage of the Seminary, even as he urged JTS to maintain its independence. Cohen, in turn, while defending the academic freedom of his institution, frankly admitted that the Seminary needed the movement and had failed its constituency in the past by standing aloof on key issues. The role reversal here is quite striking, for we might have expected the head of an academic institution to fight for independence and his board chairman to argue for the pragmatic necessity of bending to the needs of potential donors. But Cohen and Stroock came at this issue from precisely the opposite perspectives: Stroock urged JTS to stand aloof from the Conservative movement and Cohen argued for greater involvement with denominational concerns.[2] Perhaps even more noteworthy was the fact that nearly a century after the founding of JTS in 1886, the two individuals most responsible for guiding that institution were still struggling to define the proper relationship between JTS and the Conservative movement. The primary issues addressed by this essay are why this relationship was so difficult to define and what the sources were for the underlying tension between JTS and the leading organizations of the Conservative movement in the United States.[3]

The Fountainhead

The Jewish Theological Seminary and its denominational partners were somewhat at odds virtually from the founding of the key institutions of the Conservative movement. Indeed, some of the subsequent difficulties can be traced directly to the manner in which Conservative institutions came into existence. The Jewish Theological Seminary was created before there was a Conservative movement. It functioned for a quarter century as a rabbinical seminary and academic center unconnected to a movement or denomination. In time, its leaders created the infrastructure of the Conservative movement—but they took such steps primarily to promote the needs of JTS. We may note, by way of contrast, that the Reform movement developed quite differently: first came the congregational organization (the Union of American Hebrew Congregations) established in 1873, which then founded a rabbinical school (the Hebrew Union College) in 1875.[4] While conflicts between seminaries and congregational bodies are not unusual, they are exacerbated when the seminary possesses greater financial and political clout than the denomination—and when it relates to the denomination with great ambivalence. Such ambivalence has marked the relationship between the Seminary and the organizations of the Conservative movement ever since JTS brought the latter into existence.

The first such organization, in fact, began as an association of Seminary graduates. Founded on 4 July 1901 as the Alumni Association of the Jewish Theological Seminary, this body renamed itself the Rabbinical Assembly of the Jewish Theo-

The JTS Rab-
binical School
class of 1909.
Morris D. Levine,
later on the fac-
ulty of the Teach-
ers Institute, is
second from left.
The other class
members (in
alphabetical
order) are Hirsch
Goldberg, Louis
I. Goldberg, and
Raphael H.
Melamed. *Ratner
Center, JTS*

logical Seminary (RA) in 1919 after it had grown to some 116 members.[5] For its first quarter century, the alumni association relied entirely on the President and faculty of JTS to manage a primary function of any rabbinical organization—the placement of rabbis. Cyrus Adler, in his capacity as chairman of the board and later President, involved himself directly in the process of matching JTS rabbinical students with particular congregations. And when some of these former students were ready to move on to other pulpits, they appealed directly to Adler and members of the faculty for help. Their often plaintive and sometimes boastful letters to their alma mater perpetuated a dependency that could only lead to resentment. Rabbis in the field wrote of their loneliness and frustration and also pleaded for help in finding a congregation that treated its rabbi better. The response from JTS was often sympathetic but not necessarily helpful.[6]

The responsibility for placement matters only gradually began to shift away from Seminary officials. In 1927 a placement committee was created that consisted of six Rabbinical Assembly representatives and two delegates each from the United Synagogue (the congregational body) and the Seminary. Almost another two decades elapsed before the Rabbinical Assembly hired a full-time executive. The RA thus remained a weak and poorly financed operation subject to the wishes of the Seminary for more than four decades.[7]

The next organization was founded far more deliberately by the Seminary. Although Solomon Schechter conceived of JTS as the leader of "Catholic Israel" and openly expressed early in his administration the sagacity of "avoiding sectarianism, for it is an especial American feature that no preference is given to any denomination or sect or theological '*Richtung*' [orientation],"[8] he gradually came to the realization that a "Conservative Union" was a necessary addition to the American Jewish community. By 1909 plans for such a union were taking serious shape and prominent individuals in the circle around Schechter lobbied to define its mission. Herbert Rosenblum, the historian who has studied this process most closely, astutely captures the conflicting positions in his detailed analysis of the events leading up to the founding of the United Synagogue. Rosenblum writes:

> The projected Conservative Union meant different things to different people. To Schechter it was intended to become a bulwark against the further erosion of his Seminary following and a pipeline for his "message" into previously inaccessible communities. To [Rabbi Judah] Magnes, it offered the possibility of structuring a positively tradition-oriented new alignment along moderate lines. To [Rabbi Herman] Rubenovitz, it meant the building of a Conservative Movement devoted to the teachings of Solomon Schechter. To [Rabbi Charles I.] Hoffman, it intimated the organization of a national (or international) apparatus for coordinating the religious observances of the Torah. [Cyrus] Adler saw in the proposed Union a possible source of future problems for the Seminary and traditional standards. [Israel] Friedlaender envisioned in it the possibility of strengthening the Jewish ethnic and national consciousness along cultural and religious lines. [Louis] Marshall, we may legitimately conjecture, saw in the developing Union a possible new source of energy and support for the Seminary.[9]

It is striking that none of these prominent individuals wished to create a Conservative Union as a service institution for congregations. They all regarded the union as a means to another end. And significantly, both Schechter and his board chairman, Louis Marshall, viewed the future Conservative Union as an instrument to help the Seminary spread its Jewish message and recruit funders.

At the founding convention of the United Synagogue on 23 February 1913, Schechter declared his intention "not to create a new party, but to consolidate an old one."[10] But the organization quickly became a rallying point and central address for congregations seeking a course between traditional practices and moderate innovations in congregational life—that is, its affiliates developed the synagogue program of Conservative Judaism. Under the leadership of Rabbi Samuel Cohen, its first executive, the United Synagogue aggressively courted newly formed congregations, as well as established synagogues that were changing their practices.[11]

In order to attract a broad membership to its congregations, the United Synagogue established a series of auxiliaries: In 1916, the Women's Religious Union of the United Synagogue was formed with Mathilde Schechter, the widow of

Solomon, assuming the position of president.[12] In 1921 synagogue clubs for young people were organized nationally as the United Synagogue's Young People's League (later renamed the United Synagogue Youth).[13] And a few years later, Samuel Cohen created a National Federation of Jewish Men's Clubs of the United Synagogue of America, which in time served not only as a men's auxiliary but also as a vehicle for leadership training and the nurturing of promising youth.[14] These efforts yielded impressive gains: some seventy societies affiliated with the renamed Women's League of the United Synagogue by 1920. And the United Synagogue itself grew dramatically from the twenty-two congregations represented at the founding meeting in 1913 to 229 affiliates by 1929.[15]

Brooklyn branch of the National Women's League, luncheon at Beth Shalom of King's Bay, 1963. From left: Isabel Josephberg, Torah Fund chair, and Sophie Adler, branch president. *Courtesy of Torah Fund Campaign, JTS.*

Despite its relatively rapid growth in membership, the United Synagogue long remained a weak organization, heavily dependent upon the Seminary for financing and programmatic guidance. Its first three presidents were JTS personnel: Schechter, who not only founded the United Synagogue but served as its first president, was succeeded by Cyrus Adler and then by the noted Seminary talmudist, Louis Ginzberg. Every executive director of the United Synagogue was ordained at JTS, a tie that may have impeded their independence. And for many decades, the organization was physically housed at the Seminary.

Sources of Friction

Tensions between these organizations and JTS flared almost immediately after their founding, undoubtedly fueled by the disparity between the prestige and financial security enjoyed by JTS and the relative weakness of denominational organizations. But there were deeper sources of dissatisfaction as well, rooted in alternative visions of the Seminary's mission.[16] From the start, organizations of the Conservative movement urged JTS to focus sharply on denominational concerns: they wanted the Seminary to function as the pedagogic arm of a denomination, training its rabbis and later other personnel, specifically for leadership within Conservative synagogues. JTS leaders viewed the institution's mission more broadly—as serving the American Jewish community and eventually addressing non-Jews as well. One resolution to such tensions would have been for the Conservative movement and JTS to part company, but that proved unfeasible because the various parties needed each other too much. Thus, the tensions persisted—and created a long-standing ambivalence in the relationship between the various arms of the Conservative movement.

Expressions of this ambivalence, which simultaneously included barbed criticism and pleas for greater cooperation and respect, recur along predictable lines throughout the century and can be traced back to the earliest contacts between these organizations. Thus, in a letter to Cyrus Adler written just a few years after the founding of the United Synagogue and his appointment as the executive of that organization, Samuel Cohen lamented the inadequate preparation of rabbis ordained at JTS for congregational leadership: "It is a deplorable fact but the average Seminary graduate does not know how to deal with practical communal problems.... It might be well to consider the advisability of establishing a regular course treating adequately the problems of communal endeavor, religious education and pastoral theology."[17] Long after the types of courses recommended by Cohen became part of the required curriculum of the Rabbinical School, the criticism of JTS products persisted.

Even as he criticized JTS, Cohen also urged the Seminary to appreciate the virtues of the United Synagogue—and the role it could play as the Seminary's partner. He touted the ability of the United Synagogue to improve relations between Seminary alumni and congregations, as well as to educate congregants "to understand the problem Judaism is facing and the way in which progress may be made towards a solution." According to Cohen, "This work can be done only by one agency, the United Synagogue."[18]

Fifteen years later, Cohen was still urging the arms of the Conservative movement to treat each other with greater respect and to increase their levels of cooperation. He portrayed his organization as the most important force for "building loyalty to our movement on the part of the lay leaders in the various congregations in the United States and Canada." And he contended that "a study of the actual procedure followed by the various congregations in calling their rabbis, indicates that the most important factor is their affiliation with one of our regional branches." The message here was quite explicit: the United Synagogue could help the Seminary place its graduates in pulpits, win adherents to Conservative Judaism, and find work for members of the Rabbinical Assembly.[19]

A similar ambivalence—carping criticism coupled with calls for greater cooperation—would come to characterize relations between the Rabbinical Assembly and JTS. Already during the Schechter period some recent graduates were urging the Seminary to take a more active role in shaping congregational life. Two years after his ordination, Herman Rubenovitz wrote to Schechter arguing that "a program of educational work carried on by the Seminary branches under the auspices of the Seminary, a species of Seminary-extension, would tend to make of them rallying

points for the conservatively inclined of all congregations, and would then spread
Seminary influence." Rubenovitz was among the first, but certainly not the last, to
urge JTS to engage the American Jewish community far more directly.[20]

Not long afterwards, JTS alumni petitioned the Seminary's leading talmudist to
clarify the nature of Judaism espoused by JTS, a theme that would recur for many
decades in exchanges between rabbis and their alma mater. Several alumni and
younger JTS faculty members addressed a letter to Louis Ginzberg urging the
Seminary to

> formulate in terms of beliefs and practice, the type of Judaism that we believe
> you profess in common with us. We have failed as a group to exert an influence
> on Jewish life in any way commensurate with the truth and strength of our
> position, and that, primarily, because we have never made our position clear to
> the rest of the world. . . . we maintain that the time has come for us to state
> frankly and emphatically what we believe in and what we regard as authorita-
> tive in Jewish practice. . . . We feel that no good can come to Judaism either from
> petrified traditionalism or from individualistic liberalism, and that it is our
> duty to point the way to a Judaism that shall be both historical and progres-
> sive.[21]

The failure of the Seminary to articulate a distinctive ideology, coupled with its
involvement in matters quite removed from the Conservative movement, would
serve as a persistent source of resentment on the part of the rabbis.

And yet, like the United Synagogue, the rabbis were beholden to the Seminary.
As noted, they depended on the goodwill of Seminary administrators and faculty
when it came to placement matters. The Rabbinical Assembly also drew most of its
membership from JTS alumni and in fact granted nearly automatic membership to
rabbis ordained at the Seminary. [22] When the Rabbinical Assembly eventually
opened a permanent office, it would be housed in the JTS complex. The RA and
JTS, in short, were institutionally intertwined, even as friction between them
continued to mount during the thirties and forties.

Leaders of JTS, in turn, were even more ambivalent toward the denominational
organizations. They continually criticized those agencies for being too weak and
ineffectual, even as they simultaneously felt ill at ease whenever those denominational arms acted decisively. As the fountainhead institution from which the
denominational organizations emerged, the Seminary insisted on serving as the
official voice of the Conservative movement. Indeed, even before the United Synagogue was founded, Cyrus Adler cautioned Schechter not to relinquish authority to
the yet to be founded "Conservative union":

> It is not that I shrink from a new organization, but I would have the Seminary
> not only a place for education and research and not only a center of personal
> influence but so organized as to speak with authority for all conservative

Congregations. It might even be possible to create a Commission on which there would be representatives of the Faculty, the Trustees, the Alumni and the Teachers' College that would be in a way authorized to speak unitedly with regard to public questions which arise from time to time, where public expression is necessary.[23]

Although presumably each of the four bodies mentioned by Adler would have an equal say, there was little doubt that from the perspective of JTS leaders, the Seminary had to serve as the authoritative voice. Adler continually fretted over the possibility that the "Conservative Union" would "overshadow the Alumni of the Seminary and may even detract somewhat from the Seminary as the authoritative center of Conservative Judaism in this country."[24]

Given this approach, it is not surprising that Seminary leaders expressed embarrassment and anger when prominent individuals within these organizations publicly espoused positions at variance with JTS policies—especially when such statements alienated wealthy donors. Already at the beginning of the century, Solomon Schechter confronted a situation that would become all too common in later decades. Responding to a letter of complaint from a well-to-do patron, Schechter sought to put some distance between JTS and its alumni:

> I can very well understand your annoyance at reading the communication [a press clipping about an address delivered by a JTS alumnus] and yet I wish to appeal to your sense of justice and upon reflection not to withdraw your friendship from an Institution which is promoting the ideals which I know you as well as I have at heart. There is no University or College or Theological Institution in this land some of whose graduates have not occasionally erratic views not entirely in accord with its teachings and its policy. But this is unavoidable. All an Institution of learning can do is to give its best to the young men under its charge with the hope that they will continue to walk in the paths which their feet have set.[25]

Sol M. Stroock, chairman of the Seminary's board of directors (1929-1941), speaks at commencement, 1940. *Photo by Fellman Photo Service. Ratner Center, JTS.*

This incident was one of many in which the Seminary was held accountable for the lapses—real or imagined—of its graduates.

In truth, JTS leaders expected alumni to serve as goodwill ambassadors for the institution, providing entree to potential donors. This expectation was explicitly articulated during the Schechter presidency by a future board chairman. Writing to Adler in 1911, Sol M. Stroock observed,

"Our main hope for the continued support of the Seminary must come through the Alumni. . . . If each of these young Rabbis could not succeed in getting a considerable number of the members of his Congregation to contribute something annually to the Seminary, I think he could succeed in getting the trustees and the principal members so to contribute. The personal influence of the Rabbi with these members I think would effectually quicken the interest of the members in the Seminary." Stroock also suggested the designation of a Seminary Day on one *shabbat* a year. "I think we ought also in this regard to enlist not only the services of the graduates, but also every Rabbi of every Orthodox Congregation."[26] Here again we see the dual relationship between JTS and its alumni: the latter were relied upon virtually from the outset to serve as liaisons with wealthy potential donors, but they were not to be outspoken—especially as advocates of positions that embarrassed the Seminary.

But the latter was unavoidable, especially as the disparity between congregational practices and Seminary religious norms increased. Cyrus Adler addressed this issue with much equivocation when a correspondent inquired about the stance of the Seminary regarding the playing of an organ in congregations on the Sabbath.[27] Adler took pains to emphasize that "the Seminary is a teaching institution, and does not undertake to pass upon the conduct of congregations. Its sister body, the United Synagogue of America, has a Committee on the Interpretation of Jewish Law, of which members of our Faculty and some of our graduates are members. This Committee makes formal reply to inquiries submitted to it by congregations."

Men's choir with organ at the Brooklyn Jewish Center, 1960s. *Ratner Center, JTS.*

Adler promptly proceeded to inform his correspondent that the "Seminary conducts a small synagogue of its own. In this Synagogue there is no instrumental music. It is the hope and desire of the Faculty of the Seminary that as our graduates go out they will establish services of the same general character as those they see in the Seminary Synagogue"—i.e., without organs. He then qualified this position and acknowledged, "Nevertheless it is fair to say that the Seminary does not prohibit its graduates from going to a synagogue in which the organ is used if these men themselves have no objection to it." Finally, he conceded that "we prefer the traditional Synagogue without change in method of worship or liturgy." However, "where a congregation has departed from this but is yet minded to be conservative, we do not withdraw our aid from them. . . . Were we to refuse this we would simply drive them into the reform or radical wing, where they themselves do not wish to go."

Here quite dramatically, the inner contradictions of the Seminary, which so affected its relationship with the Conservative movement, were exposed. To begin with, Adler espoused neutrality—the Seminary is merely an academic institution; he then shifted to advocacy—JTS favors traditional synagogue practices; then to a pragmatic engagement with the realities faced by rabbis—they need to take congregations with organs; and finally to the espousal of an ideological position—the Seminary must resist the tide of radical reform. Adler also openly acknowledged the division of labor that would long dominate the Conservative movement: the Seminary would serve as the bastion of traditionalism, while its rabbinic alumni would contend with less than traditional synagogue practices. Adler's letter underscores the impossible bind in which the Seminary and its rabbinical alumni found themselves. The latter repeatedly called for their Seminary to take a more active role in denominational life, but had the institution done so, it would have promoted positions at variance with—even quite critical of—congregational practices because of the high level of religious traditionalism that characterized the key administrators and faculty members at JTS. The Seminary, in turn, lamented the religious laxity tolerated by its alumni but relied upon the rabbis to serve as its ambassadors. Little wonder that Seminary officials often found it more satisfying to deal with academic and intergroup concerns than to face the insoluble dilemmas posed by denominational politics!

The relationship between the Seminary and the United Synagogue was fraught with the same irresolvable tensions and yet further complicated by the barely concealed contempt of JTS administrators for what they regarded as the incompetence of the synagogue body. Whatever the tensions with the rabbis, a special relationship existed between the mother institution and her alumni. Genuine bonds of friendship forged between Seminary professors and their students often lasted for a lifetime. They were reinforced at rabbinical conventions and through ongoing correspondence. Such human contacts mitigated tensions. The same cannot be said of relations between JTS and the United Synagogue.

The festering issues were laid bare in great detail in a memorandum written by Louis Finkelstein, then provost of the Seminary, to Cyrus Adler in late 1936. Responding to a declaration by Samuel Cohen of the United Synagogue, which touted the achievements of his organization, Finkelstein wrote with withering derision about the damage sustained by the Seminary through actions of the United Synagogue.[28] He begins by noting:

> Rabbi Cohen says nothing about the important congregations with regard to which the United Synagogue, far from being of help to the Seminary, is an actual detriment. Some of them have refused to elect graduates of the Seminary because they thought that would identify them with the United Synagogue, and others were persuaded to elect Seminary graduates only through the use of other agencies and by keeping the United Synagogue in the background.... At every one of the last three conventions of the Rabbinical Assembly, the Rabbis have complained that the United Synagogue, by admitting into full membership congregations with so-called "free-lance" rabbis, is actually helping to undermine the status of the rabbinate in this country, which the Seminary is trying to build up.... [Moreover] the bad state of the United Synagogue finances has alienated some of the prominent leaders of the Jewish community who were previously associated with the organization, and who thus have become hostile to our whole movement.[29]

Thus, Finkelstein contended that the United Synagogue was not a boon to the Seminary; in fact, it subverted Seminary fund-raising efforts.

He further expressed deep embarrassment over the religious laxity of the congregational body:

> In such questions as our relations with the Kashruth Organizations, the tactlessness and impetuosity of the United Synagogue representatives made any arrangement between us and the so-called orthodox group more difficult and practically impossible.... The Seminary is held to account for what the United Synagogue does in public, to individual congregations and members of the community; but neither the President, nor the Faculty, nor the Directors of the Seminary, are in any position to prevent the United Synagogue from carrying out the policies of which they disapprove.

Finkelstein went on to cite examples of laxity in the observance of Jewish law at United Synagogue functions: he described a Young People's League program held at the Seminary "to which all the delegates who were housed at the Commodore Hotel had to ride [because of the vast distances], publicly violating the Sabbath." And he referred to conventions scheduled by the United Synagogue where no kosher meat was available and delegates were incorrectly informed that a restaurant was kosher.[30]

All of this was terribly damaging to the Seminary, Finkelstein claimed, because "individuals and congregations outside of New York seem to regard the Seminary· and the United Synagogue as one institution."[31] The Rabbinical Assembly too, according to Finkelstein, had lost confidence in the congregational body. The executive committee of the RA had questioned the financial integrity of the United Synagogue and called for an independent auditor to review its records. The RA also took control of placement matters from the United Synagogue, charging that there had been serious breaches in confidence.[32]

Thus, fifty years after the establishment of JTS and over two decades after Solomon Schechter founded a "Conservative Union," relations between the Seminary and the major arms of the Conservative movement were tense and rife with contradictions. Both Adler and his lieutenant, Finkelstein, sought to place greater distance between the Seminary and its presumed partners. Adler had already written testily in 1930 that "one thing seems clear to me: these cooperative arrangements do not seem to work out very well." Regarding the placement of rabbis, he wrote:

> If the Seminary is to be in effect responsible . . . , then I would prefer to have it done definitely by the Seminary and have nothing to do with either the Rabbinical Assembly or the United Synagogue. If the United Synagogue feels that it is its function and wants to undertake it, then the Seminary would have nothing to do with it. . . . As for the Rabbinical Assembly, so far as I have been able to see, their contribution has been that of complaint.[33]

Only a set of dramatically new circumstances would prompt the major arms of the Conservative movement to intensify their coordination.

The Finkelstein Era

The intractable fiscal crises brought on by the Great Depression, coupled with the dramatic expansion of the Conservative movement in the postwar era, forced the various agencies of Conservative Judaism to rethink their relationship to one another and their proper place within American Judaism. The upshot was a paradoxical situation in which the various arms of the Conservative movement established new vehicles for cooperation during the Finkelstein years even as the rancor increased to unprecedented levels and each arm moved to distance itself from other agencies of the Conservative movement.

The first steps to achieving economic coordination were taken in 1938, during the waning years of the Adler administration. As a result of the combined effects of the depression, the failing health of Adler, and the deaths of several leading Seminary supporters, JTS found itself in dire economic straits. Even after the faculty and personnel took deep salary cuts and the budget was slashed, the institution ran annual deficits of $40,000 in the late thirties. Adler and his primary assistant, Louis Finkelstein, turned to the Rabbinical Assembly for help, and they found it in the persons of Simon Greenberg, then the RA president, and Solomon Goldman, a prominent pulpit rabbi in Chicago. The latter urged the RA convention of 1938 to adopt a resolution to initiate a $100,000 campaign by the rabbis for their alma mater. Greenberg, in turn, appealed to the RA membership to act because "a critical turning point has been reached in the Movement to which we have dedicated our lives and upon which we believe the future welfare of American Jewry directly, and world Jewry, depends."

Louis Finkelstein addresses the 1957 United Synagogue convention. *Ratner Center, JTS*

He recommended the creation of a systematic national program for rabbis to appeal to their congregants on the High Holy Days in behalf of JTS. For the first time, the Rabbinical Assembly became a full-fledged partner in assuring the fiscal needs of JTS.[34] Almost instantaneously, the Rabbinical Assembly's campaign raised substantial new funds, and it was continued indefinitely.

As the war years unfolded, even this campaign proved insufficient to meet new needs. The institutions of the Conservative movement were under great pressure to expand their scope of operations in these years: Finkelstein launched his interfaith and intergroup activities to enhance the visibility of Jews and Judaism on the American scene; the Rabbinical Assembly threw itself into wartime efforts and especially the task of providing support to chaplains in the armed forces; and during the post-depression boom, the United Synagogue found itself attracting new affiliates that required guidance.[35] Not surprisingly, as these institutions expanded their programs, their budgets ballooned: expenditures by JTS, alone, rose from slightly over a quarter of a million dollars in 1942 to over two million in 1947; the Rabbinical Assembly budget jumped from $2,000 in 1940 to $23,000 in 1946; and the United Synagogue's expenditures rose from $12,000 in 1940 to over $100,000 in 1946.[36] But even these vastly increased budgets could not cover all the programming required by the burgeoning Conservative movement.

In 1944, joint fund-raising was placed under a new banner, "The Campaign for the Jewish Theological Seminary of America, in cooperation with the Rabbinical Assembly and the United Synagogue." Under this arrangement, all fund-raising by the three organizations was merged into one campaign, which developed an apparatus to reach some ten thousand donors.[37] Most important for relations between JTS and the arms of the Conservative movement, the three partners created a Liaison

Committee primarily to negotiate the proper division of funds. As fund-raising reached new heights, the existing system of allocations required an overhaul so that the comparatively huge new sums of money raised would be divided more equitably.

The Liaison Committee, which functioned for more than twenty years, served as "managing partner" for the Conservative movement. Its primary function was to oversee the allocation of funds raised by the joint campaign, but in so doing, it often dealt with other matters of coordination. Among the items considered by the committee were the opening of a central office in midtown Manhattan, the creation of a national publication for the Conservative movement, and the most efficient means to utilize personnel for the benefit of all three partners.[38]

The spirit of cooperation embodied in the creation of the Liaison Committee proved short-lived. Despite the merging of the campaign and the very significant growth of sums raised by the joint campaign, budget deficits continued to climb. Already by 1945, the campaign no longer covered the expenses of the three organizations. Within three years, the accumulated deficit had risen to half a million dollars.[39] Under such circumstances, each partner in the joint campaign subjected the budgets of the other partners to increased scrutiny and asked, "Is this program necessary?" Such meddling in the affairs of autonomous organizations subverted goodwill.

In addition, the relationship of JTS and its campaign partners grew increasingly strained as those other institutions gained confidence. In the postwar era, the Conservative movement rode the crest of a wave that swept up ever greater numbers of adherents. Between 1955 and 1961, the time of most rapid expansion, some two hundred and fifty new affiliates joined the United Synagogue.[40] Not surprisingly, the new leaders who assumed positions of prominence as professionals and volunteers within the Rabbinical Assembly and the United Synagogue wanted to flex their muscles. The time had come to try new approaches and gain some independence from the Seminary.

In contrast to earlier decades, the two partners most at odds in the postwar period were the Seminary and the Rabbinical Assembly. The nadir in relations came in the late 1940s with the reorganization of the Law Committee and the decision to explicitly ban rabbis who were members of the Seminary faculty from "acting as voting members of the Committee on Jewish Law of the RA."[41] In his contemporaneous analysis of these events, Rabbi Simon Greenberg, then serving as vice-chancellor and provost of JTS, explained that this decision followed from "the Faculty's determined policy not to be considered as a body making authoritative pronouncements on dogma or law, [and therefore] the RA members who are also Faculty members accepted this limitation upon their rights as RA members without protest."[42] From the perspective of Rabbi David Aronson, the president of the RA, matters looked quite different. Aronson claimed that "The Seminary faculty—as a faculty— is not

ready to join our committee on Jewish law. It really comes down to the one man on the faculty whose presence would make any difference, and that is Prof. [Saul] Lieberman."[43]

Within a short time, Seminary faculty members did join the reorganized Law Committee, and JTS and the RA even formed a joint *Beit Din* (tribunal) to deal with a range of marital issues. But relations with the RA remained tense. In 1952, for example, Finkelstein, while traveling abroad, learned from Simon Greenberg, his most trusted advisor, that the RA was planning to convene a conference on Jewish law. Finkelstein was furious because he had previously agreed to participate in a joint Seminary-RA conference and, during his travels, had even enlisted the support of Prime Minister David Ben-Gurion to convene an international conference on Jewish law in Israel that would feature JTS faculty and Conservative rabbis. He immediately urged Greenberg to contact Max Davidson, the president of the RA: "Please request—beseech—Max in my name not to permit any precipitate action, which in view of our aspirations and the RA as well as, I hope, the United Synagogue, on the world scene, in Washington, etc., would just about finish us, and mean a break, either formal or informal, between us and the RA organization." In the event that this approach by Greenberg would fail, Finkelstein drafted his letter of resignation from the Law Committee, which explicitly accused the RA of reneging on its promise to convene with JTS a jointly sponsored conference on Jewish law. And leaving nothing to chance, Finkelstein ordered Greenberg to have every member of the JTS administration attend the RA convention to monitor developments and insure that the proposed conference would not be approved. They were also to make sure that "the next Vice President [of the RA], whoever he may be, is a man of high moral integrity. If one of the men of lesser integrity is elected, I fear the results for our movement will be catastrophic at once."[44]

Why had relations between JTS and the RA reached such a level of distrust? Michael Greenbaum has written trenchantly of the clash of views between Finkelstein and his rabbinic critics:

> While critics like Solomon Goldman and Milton Steinberg wanted the Seminary to embrace and favor the synagogue and its leadership, the Seminary under Finkelstein chose to embrace the broader (not necessarily synagogue affiliated) community and its leadership. Dr. Mordecai Kaplan described the tension between the critics and the Seminary as being between intensification and expansion. Was the Seminary to intensify its work internally? . . . Was it to concentrate on the Conservative movement or was it to concentrate on expansion outward toward the entire Jewish community? More broadly expressed, was the Seminary to emphasize merely the Conservative movement, or rather the perpetuation of Judaism and the survival of the Jewish people in America? . . . Finkelstein believed that "You can't have a little Seminary and do anything

to save American Judaism." His critics, however, were not interested so much in saving American Judaism as they were in developing the Conservative movement and defining Conservative Judaism in the process.[45]

Here, then, were fundamental differences in the way Finkelstein and his critics understood the proper mission of JTS.

Many rabbis also criticized JTS for its unbending traditionalism and were particularly bitter at the failure of leading Talmud professors to find warrants in Jewish law to address new challenges. After decades of frustration and complaints, the RA established an independent Law Committee in 1948, which moved swiftly to address the difficulties of Sabbath observance. In 1950, the committee issued a far-reaching *Takkanah* (rabbinic decree) permitting driving on the Sabbath in order to attend synagogue services. It coupled this act with a Sabbath Revitalization Program, aimed at increasing synagogue attendance and intensifying other forms of Sabbath observance.[46] To the dismay of rabbinic leaders involved in these programs, neither the United Synagogue nor the Seminary supported these efforts. Summing up the tepid response, Rabbi Jacob Agus, a leading proponent of the changes, wrote with great bitterness:

> In a logically organized movement, the ideological decisions of the rabbinate become the policy of the lay organization, and the various executives of the central agencies regard it as their duty to put into effect the proposals of the rabbinic authorities. No such situation obtained in the past decade within the Conservative organization. In the opinion of those who do control our central institutions, the Responsum on the Sabbath in particular and the Sabbath Revitalization effort in general were ill-advised and even harmful. The national publications did not publicize it. . . . The United Synagogue could find neither the time nor money for this project. When the extent of publicity accompanying other projects in our national organization is remembered, we realize that the indifference of our central agencies to this project was indeed monumental."[47]

From the perspective of the Seminary, of course, the Sabbath responsum was precisely as Agus intimated—"ill-advised and even harmful."[48]

In addition to these differences in ideology and vision, tensions flared because many pulpit rabbis resented the domineering posture assumed by the Seminary in general—and Finkelstein in particular—especially at a time when rabbis had become such important partners in financing Seminary programs through their fund-raising activities. At the annual convention of the Rabbinical Assembly in 1955, these resentments were aired publicly in an unusually candid address by Rabbi Aaron Blumenthal entitled, "The Status of the Rabbinical Assembly in the Conservative Movement." In Blumenthal's view, three major circumstances marred the relationship between the RA and JTS: "1. The fact that the Seminary is responsible for the raising of funds for our movement. 2. The public affairs activities of the Seminary. 3. The suspicion that the Seminary's officials strive to dominate the RA." Blumenthal acknowledged the need for a joint campaign and the reality that most funds would have to be raised within congregations. But he lamented the tendency for fund-raisers to think of rabbis mainly as campaign assistants. "'Rabbi X,' they tell us, 'has never done anything for the Seminary.' What they mean is he has not been very helpful in the campaign. In every other respect he may be doing very much for the movement."[49]

Then there was the matter of how the Seminary spent its money. Blumenthal examined the Seminary's "outside" activities, such as *The Eternal Light* radio programs and the Institute for Religious and Social Studies:

> Some of us endorse some of these projects and criticize others, but many of us, at one time or another, are afraid of the very fertile mind of this man called Louis Finkelstein. What will he think of next? Tomorrow's newspaper may bring us information about a new project which he has started—a project which commits the Conservative movement to a course of action or to a specific goal, and for which we are expected to find the funds! Even if the project is a perfect one, we wonder with varying degrees of indignation why we were not consulted about it.[50]

Finally, Blumenthal gave voice to claims that "the Seminary seeks to dominate the RA, to thwart us in our desire to deal effectively with the problems of the American Jewish community." He cited unending debates over questions of Jewish law that never found resolution, perhaps because the Seminary was stalling indefinitely. And he charged that the RA and the United Synagogue were manipulated by the Seminary "to make [their] program conform to that of the Seminary."[51] Why is the RA "drifting" and the Seminary "steering?" Blumenthal asked rhetorically. Because the RA has not yet "let go of the apron strings and map[ped] out its own future, independent of Seminary thinking." Blumenthal went on to declare: "We, the RA, simply have no program for Conservative Judaism."[52]

Blumenthal's severe strictures of his own organization notwithstanding, in the mid-1940s the RA had begun a process of defining a distinctive position. Through its enactments in the realm of Jewish law and its public pronouncements, the RA asserted its independence from JTS. Members of the Rabbinical Assembly—as individuals and as organized lobbies—challenged the policies of JTS and articulated their own conceptions of how the Conservative movement should develop. The RA also expanded its institutional structure by hiring a full-time executive and office staff, thereby creating the infrastructure to operate independently.

Within the Rabbinical Assembly, members differed as to the best way for the RA to deal with the Seminary. Some rabbis preferred a firm yet conciliatory approach, summed up as follows by Rabbi Judah Nadich at a meeting of RA members with Finkelstein:

> We all feel that not enough give and take exists between the Seminary and the rabbis. We need this for a united movement (and we are not) to help in the fight (and it's a joint battle). We are in rare contact with the Seminary, and usually only for fundraising, so it is good that we meet on other matters. These occasions are rare and always linked with finance, however. I hope that there will be not only more such meetings where we can discuss what is close to us, but that we may establish machinery for colleagues to be in continuous close touch with the Seminary and with each other. A convention once a year is not enough. We need close communication.[53]

Others, such as Rabbi Jacob Agus, despaired of cooperation and called for the RA to circumvent the Seminary and define its own course of action:

> Sadly, I have come to the conclusion that the Seminary group will not permit an ideological position to emerge, except if they control it. They do not regard us as partners, but as a constituency which they have to "handle," or to manipulate. Our best approach, therefore, is to prevent stagnation and to encourage a continuous exploration of the broad belt of religious ideology, extending from the line of Orthodoxy to that of Classical Reform. We must not strive for a unitary approach—only for standards of quality.[54]

Following this line of reasoning, Rabbi Wolfe Kelman, the longtime executive of the RA, hinted that the time had come to displace the Seminary as the authoritative

Abraham Joshua Heschel, left, with Wolfe Kelman at JTS, 1967. *Photo by John H. Popper. Ratner Center, JTS.*

voice of the Conservative movement: "Perhaps, the . . . leadership of the Seminary does not know what to make of the Conservative movement, and prefers not to come to grips with this fact. It is a pure accident that the Chancellor of the Seminary had been *de facto* head of the movement for the past number of years."[55] Thus, toward the close of the Finkelstein era, the accumulated frustration of decades impelled the top leadership of the Rabbinical Assembly to consider means of supplanting the Seminary and its Chancellor as the spokesman for the Conservative movement.

The United Synagogue also asserted its independence from JTS during the Finkelstein era. In 1966 it began a process of removing itself physically from the JTS campus and eventually relocated its entire operation to new headquarters near midtown Manhattan. Significantly, it took this action despite the strong objections of Finkelstein, who urged George Maislen, the president of the congregational body, to stay put:

> Anyone who has any experience in administration recognizes the importance of physical propinquity among leaders of various organizations so that they have opportunity for free exchange of opinions before issues become crystallized and action is taken in which one of them is opposed to the other. I am sure that one of the reasons that the Conservative movement stands out in American Judaism through the good relationships between its various branches is due to the fact that our various offices are located near one another. . . . All experience in administration shows that physical separation of offices tends to bring about ultimately also spiritual separation.[56]

In truth, JTS and the United Synagogue had undergone a "spiritual separation" long before. The Seminary under Finkelstein continued to harbor mistrust of the congregational body and impatience with its poor organization. Undoubtedly, the periodic need of JTS to bail out the United Synagogue when it had overspent did not improve relations. The congregational body, for its part, resented the Seminary's forays into programming that fell within its own domain. Finkelstein was eager to communicate directly with laypeople in order to strengthen the Seminary's fund-raising, and he often worked around the leadership of the United Synagogue. Writing of these efforts, Michael Greenbaum has aptly described how the Seminary's direct contacts with laypeople subtly undermined the United Synagogue: "While [Finkelstein's programs for lay leaders] could be described as educational ventures totally benefitting an academic center, they, nonetheless, represented an extensive outreach effort by the Seminary to Jewish laity which, given the weakness of the United Synagogue, could only be seen as a threat to its future success."[57]

Despite these turf issues, the Seminary's relationship with the United Synagogue was never as tense as with the Rabbinical Assembly, perhaps because the congregational body was too preoccupied with its own internal problems to challenge the

The Joint Prayer
Book Commission
of the Rabbinical
Assembly and the
United Syna-
gogue, ca. 1946.
From left: Max
Arzt, Elias
Solomon, Robert
Gordis, Morris
Silverman, Israel
Levinthal. *Photo
by Virginia F.
Stern. Courtesy of
the Rabbinical
Assembly.*

policies of JTS leaders directly. For one thing, the United Synagogue had to struggle to keep up with the vast expansion of Conservative congregations and the
services they required. For another, it had to contend with the departure of two
major constituents. During the 1940s both the Women's League and the Federation
of Jewish Men's Clubs moved toward independence from the congregational body
and worked directly with the Seminary's leaders.

The Women's League had traditionally focused its attention on strengthening
the Jewish home and supporting Seminary students. During the early 1940s, the
Women's League assumed increasing responsibility for raising scholarship funds
for students. Beginning with an initial goal of $10,000 in 1941, the Women's League
Torah Scholarship Fund was raising $150,000 by 1948. Within a few years, the
League set itself the goal of raising a half million dollars to fund a new dormitory
for Seminary students.[58] These activities won it the praise of Seminary leaders.
Finkelstein saluted the Women's League as "the strongest organization in our
Movement, with a record of great achievements, and with even greater aspirations,
coupled with almost unlimited opportunities for future service."[59] He also
rewarded the organization with its own seat on the Liaison Committee in 1956.[60]
The Women's League became the closest ally of JTS in this period, even as it simultaneously grew apart from the United Synagogue.

The National Federations of Jewish Men's Clubs (NFJMC) also broke away
from the congregational body in the 1940s. Rabbi Samuel Cohen, the longtime
executive of the United Synagogue, had also administered the Federation of Men's
Clubs, but in 1945 Finkelstein appointed Rabbi Joel Geffen, a JTS administrator
and fund-raiser, as the "spiritual advisor" of the organization. Within a few years,
the United Synagogue began to reduce its financial subvention; by 1967 it no longer
supported the Federation of Jewish Men's Clubs. Through publications such as *The*

National Enroll-
ment Plan display
at a United Syna-
gogue convention,
1957. *Ratner Center, JTS.*

TORCH and its programs to underwrite educational ventures spearheaded by the Seminary, such as the Leadership Training Fellowship and Ramah Camps, the NFJMC also became a partner of JTS, although it was long treated as a very junior partner.[61]

Despite the shifting relationships and frequent eruption of tensions between the various arms of the Conservative movement, several new initiatives were launched during the Finkelstein years to strengthen coordination and cooperation. The following is a brief listing of some of the more enduring programs: (1) A Liaison Committee served as a "clearinghouse for all matters which concern the three bodies"—JTS, the RA, and the United Synagogue. This committee also devised a formula for the allocations of funds to maintain the three organizations. (2) A Joint Retirement Board, consisting of representatives of all three groups, developed a pension plan. (Eventually members of the Cantors Assembly also joined.) (3) A Placement Commission funded by the RA, included lay representatives from the United Synagogue and also JTS personnel. (4) The Chaplaincy Availability Board was administered by the RA and was mainly concerned with JTS students. (5) The Prayer Book Committee of the RA committee included two lay representatives of the United Synagogue. (6) The Commission on Jewish Education was primarily a partnership of the RA and United Synagogue and was financed by royalties from the jointly issued *Sabbath and Festival Prayer Book*. (7) A Social Action Committee was funded by contributions from the RA, the United Synagogue, and the Women's League. (8) The Commission on Marriage and the Family was a joint project of the RA and United Synagogue. (9) The Joint Commission on Israel and Zionism also constituted a partnership of the United Synagogue and the Rabbinical Assembly. (10) A Youth Commission of the United Synagogue included two members appointed by the RA. (11) The Conference on Jewish Law was an experimental three-year partnership between the RA and JTS. It produced a revised *ketubah* (marriage document) and established a *Beit Din* (a rabbinic court). (12) The Rabbinic Cabinet functioned as a committee of rabbis who assisted in fund-raising for JTS.[62] (13) A National Enrollment Plan (NEP) sought to enlist congregations in fund-raising for the Conservative movement through a per capita contribution for each synagogue member.[63] Taken together, these joint ventures bound the organizations of the Conservative movement more tightly to one another and suggested a sense of cohesion and unity of purpose.

Nevertheless, a balance sheet of the Finkelstein era would be incomplete without an acknowledgment of the severe strains in relations between JTS and some of the other arms of the Conservative movement, and especially with the rabbinate. We have already explored some of the ideological and programmatic differences that divided JTS and its rabbinic critics. Structural problems also brought them into conflict— particularly over the question, "Who speaks for the Conservative movement?"

Finally, we ought not to minimize the impact of budgetary crises, which resulted in mutual recrimination. Beginning in 1938, Finkelstein needed to turn to the Rabbinical Assembly every few years with pleas for increased financial help. Such appeals were necessary until the end of his administration. In 1958, for example, Finkelstein warned the RA membership: "The entire Seminary program is imperiled by serious budgetary demands. Unless substantial financial help is forthcoming no later that June 20, our services must face drastic curtailment." He went on to urge every rabbi to raise at least an additional $500, convince his synagogue's sisterhood to make a treasury gift and then make a personal gift too.[64] By the mid-1960s, the Seminary had run up a debt of eight to nine million dollars through borrowing from its endowment fund; annual budget shortfalls ranged between one-half and three-quarters of a million.[65] And on the eve of Finkelstein's retirement in the early 1970s, the budgetary crisis loomed large yet again. Writing to a leading Conservative rabbi, Finkelstein noted in 1970:

> The tornado which struck the American economy last spring hit the Seminary with particular force. . . . At the end of June 1970 . . . we found ourselves $600,000 poorer than at the beginning of the year. . . . No such calamity has befallen the Seminary in my memory. . . . To survive as a great institution, the Seminary must find ways to convince at least 2,000 more people in the Conservative movement that their annual support must be given top priority. . . . In addition, and no less important, is our urgent need for some method of regular consultation with you and your colleagues on all developments at the Seminary.[66]

As a consequence of these shortfalls, the budgets of the Rabbinical Assembly and the United Synagogue were adversely affected—hardly a circumstance that made for amicable relations.

Seminary leaders vented their frustration by questioning the dedication of rabbis to their alma mater and belittling their contribution. "We just cannot build this institution in the way you, Arthur Sulzberger, and I conceived it, if it has to be an inverted pyramid, wobbling, as it were, on the support of the Rabbinical Assembly alone," wrote Louis Finkelstein to a prominent board member.[67] For its part, the Rabbinical Assembly doubted the fiscal responsibility and competence of the Seminary's administration. Shortly after the retirement of Finkelstein, Wolfe Kelman, the RA's executive, compared the condition of the State of Israel and the Conservative movement: "Amongst other parallels, to which you can add your own, both were led by people with entrepreneurial and mercurial personalities who cared very little about the nuts and bolts of organizational structure, prudent budgetary management, careful systems analysis, and all the other corporate criteria, which probably would have killed the growth of both, had they been applied during their periods of spectacular growth." But at a time of greater austerity for the Conservative movement, Kelman favored the centralization of all dues, membership, and fund-raising.

> In other words, we should work toward a structure whereby every member of our constituency would know, both by the ideology we espouse, and the contribution he makes, including membership fees, that he is part of one Conservative movement. That would mean eventually eliminating separate NEP and United Synagogue collections, R.A. membership dues, separate Torah Fund structures, etc. It would also mean the centralization of ideological articulation and the avoidance of competition, and often, mutually irreconcilable, ideological postures.[68]

Kelman, of course, was expressing his hope for institutional and ideological unity within the Conservative movement, a goal that proved elusive in the Finkelstein era, as well as in the subsequent administration of Gerson Cohen.

The Cohen Years: JTS as "the Nerve-Center of the Conservative Movement"

The election of Gerson D. Cohen as Finkelstein's successor raised expectations within the Conservative movement of dramatic changes in the offing. Conservative rabbis, in particular, viewed the changing of the guard as an opportunity to renew the Conservative movement and improve relations between the Seminary and its alumni. One rabbi wrote to the Seminary's board chairman in strong support of Cohen's candidacy and in the harshest of terms expressed his dismay at the prevailing state of affairs:

> The Conservative rabbinate is in a state of despair. Overwhelmed by forces in our general society which militate against religious commitment, and particu-

Gerson Cohen
with a United
Synagogue group
in the Seminary
sukkah, 1977.
From left: Oscar
Dane, Cohen, Joel
Geffen, Harry
Merrsman, Ben-
jamin Kreitman.
*Photo by Arnold
Katz. Ratner Cen-
ter, JTS.*

larly, the specific commitment required by the Jewish tradition, they have
looked to the leadership of our Movement for strength and guidance. It has not
been forthcoming. That the Seminary and the Conservative Movement has
steadily declined in the past twenty years no keen observer of the American
Jewish scene will deny. . . . The selection of a Chancellor for the Seminary could
be the turning point in American Judaism for a century to come. It could either
bring together the marvelous young forces that are still possible in our Movement and fulfill the dream of Schechter, or plunge the Seminary and our
Movement into their final doldrums.[69]

Another Midwestern rabbi echoed these views and attributed the decline of JTS to
its distance from congregational life: "The services of the Seminary Synagogue—
with its 'segregated seating' are not representative of our movement—in fact are a
living contradiction of what we stand for." He also itemized other weaknesses of
JTS, ranging from its failure to create a program of study in Israel for its rabbinical
students to the absence of a strong Conservative religious and ideological component at Ramah camps to the poor relations between JTS and its rabbis.[70] And still
another rabbi of a well-to-do Philadelphia synagogue wrote to warn Gerson Cohen
of the "total disenchantment of our [synagogue] leadership with the Seminary and
the Conservative movement." According to this rabbi, the source of the problem
was clear:

> There is no direction from the Seminary. In recent years it has been only a ser-
> vice institution which will ask us for money and will supply us with a rabbi or
> teacher if one is available. We have poured fortunes into the Seminary and have
> been completely abandoned when we need something in return. . . . What
> amaze[s] me . . . is that this [is] being said by men who are members of your
> Board of Directors and Board of Overseers.[71]

For many rabbis and lay leaders of the Conservative movement, Gerson Cohen offered the hope of a new beginning. By virtue of his profound scholarship and impeccable academic credentials, he followed in the footsteps of his illustrious predecessors. As a youthful man fully conversant with American culture and the needs of the hour, he would, it was believed, renew the movement. Cohen encouraged these hopes. He moved quickly to rebuild and expand the Seminary, hire a younger faculty and staff, restructure the academic programs of the institution—and reach out to the Conservative movement.

In line with Cohen's aspiration to rebuild the Seminary and transform its programs, a good deal of time was devoted early in his administration to questions of self-definition. In the mid-1970s, he initiated a self-study process to clarify how the Seminary wished to present itself to the larger American public. In contrast to the Finkelstein administration's efforts to serve all of American Jewry, and indeed, mankind in general, Cohen forthrightly linked JTS to the Conservative movement. When pressed by his public relations advisors to define the Seminary's mission, Cohen responded with the following manifesto:

> I want to articulate what I consider to be a statement of goals of the Seminary. I want the Seminary to become the central institution of the Conservative movement *de facto* as well as *de jure*. The Seminary should not only be the institution for ordaining Conservative rabbis, but the supreme academic center for quality Jewish education on the collegiate, graduate and post-graduate levels. It should also be the source or clearing-house of educational policy for the afternoon school, the Hebrew day school and adult education throughout the Conservative laity and Conservative professional groups. . . . The Seminary can no longer afford to remain neutral on major issues—not that it must take a positive stand on such issues as abortions, transplants, war and peace, the West Bank of the State of Israel and the like—but must provide the fora for the discussion of these issues in the light of Jewish values, Jewish theology, Jewish ethics and the historical situation of the Jews. I believe that the Conservative Movement can no longer afford to develop policy without the Seminary at the heart of the discussion. If this does not change, the Seminary will lose the impact it claims to have and which it pretends to have in the context of the Conservative movement.[72]

No previous Seminary head had ever linked JTS so closely to the Conservative movement.

The next year, Cohen circulated an internal memorandum to his top administrative colleagues designed to follow up on this mission statement with a concrete program of action to lead the Conservative movement.

> I am beginning to get rumblings from all corners of the country that the Seminary is losing contact with the men [of the RA]. For better or worse, we have to tackle this part of our public relations and of our continuing relationship with

the [former] students. We are not just a "school" we are the nerve-center of the Conservative Movement and I think we must begin to take action.[73]

It was, of course, precisely when Cohen began to "take action" that he experienced firsthand how frustrating it was to work closely with the other arms of the Conservative movement. Within a year of assuming office, Cohen embroiled himself in a debate that would eventually shadow him for most of his years at the helm of JTS: Should women be admitted to a program leading to rabbinic ordination? Writing in the Women's League *Outlook*, Cohen took a forthright stand against such a course of action. He contended that admitting a woman "to candidacy for ordination *at this time* [emphasis included] would hardly reflect the consensus of the Conservative movement, whether of its laity or its professional leadership."[74] The article elicited a large number of responses from Women's League members sharply critical of his position. Here is a sampling: "Our Jewish Women's Consciousness Raising Group was upset and distressed . . . [by the article]. None of us desire to be ordained as Rabbis. We do, however, demand that we—and all Jewish women—be given the opportunity to experience a full Jewish life. . . . We demand the right to choose a career based on our interests and qualifications."[75] Another correspondent concluded her letter, "I want to add that I have withdrawn my financial support from the Seminary, until such time as this problem is rectified. I will enlist the support of like-minded friends."[76] The thorny issue of women's ordination raised many questions about Jewish law, halakhic process in the Conservative movement, the principles of equality and fair play; but as Cohen quickly discovered, it also entangled him in a dispute with some of the Seminary's staunchest financial supporters and allies—a fact that was quickly brought home when in November 1973, the United Synagogue resolved at its convention "That it looks with favor on the admission of qualified women to the Rabbinical School of the Jewish Theological Seminary of America."[77]

The following summer, Cohen took a step in the other direction—toward the expansion of religious opportunities for females. In his capacity as the principle overseer of policies at the Ramah camps sponsored by JTS, Cohen approved the calling up of girls to the Torah (*aliyot*) as of the summer of 1974.[78] In short order, a member of the JTS Talmud faculty lambasted Cohen for not informing the entire Conservative movement that the faculty disassociated itself from this step—and indeed had never been consulted about it.[79] And Cohen began to receive angry letters from pulpit rabbis who interpreted this step as an infringement upon their authority. One of the most stinging rebukes argued as follows:

> The Ramah Camps are now being used as an instrument for coercion to force acceptance of a responsum of the RA Committee on Law and Standards. . . . By using the Ramah Camps for a political purpose, the Seminary puts unwar-

ranted and undue pressure upon the traditional elements within the Conservative Movement to accept a decision that conflicts with their principles and their practice. . . . It is, I submit, blatantly unfair to use the children of my congregation, whom I have personally persuaded to go to a Ramah Camp . . . as a lever to pressure me to grant Aliyot to women in my congregation because they have already done it at Ramah: "If the Seminary can do it, why can't you?" This is "brainwashing" of my children and I strongly object to this unconscionable tactic.[80]

Thus within two years of taking office, Gerson Cohen quickly learned that there was a steep price to be paid for taking "direct action" in denominational life. Throughout his years in office, he was violently buffeted by the diverse factions that were loosely allied within the Conservative movement.

The flash point during those years was the question of women's admission to the Rabbinical School, a debate that began in earnest in 1977 when Cohen created a national commission to examine the matter. Significantly, he acted at the urging of the Rabbinical Assembly, which had resolved that a commission was needed.[81] As the debate unfolded, it was clear that virtually all the major arms of the Conservative movement officially endorsed the ordination of women. Cohen was therefore under constant pressure to admit women to the Rabbinical School. No sooner had the JTS faculty voted to table the ordination issue in 1979 than the Rabbinical Assembly forced Cohen to reopen the question. At its 1983 convention, the RA narrowly failed to approve the admission of a woman to its ranks. Because she had not been ordained at JTS, Rabbi Beverly Magidson needed the support of three-quarters of the convention attendees to win membership in the RA. She failed to receive the necessary votes but did win the support of the majority (the vote was 206 in favor and 72 opposed). Cohen feared that the admission of a woman to RA membership who had not been ordained at JTS would undermine the prestige of the Seminary within the movement, and so he urged the convention to let him try one more time to deliver the JTS faculty.[82] In November 1983, the faculty voted to admit women to the Rabbinical School and even before the first woman was ordained, the RA resolved that "any rabbi ordained by the Jewish Theological Seminary of America will be automatically accepted for membership in the Rabbinical Assembly, [the] international association of Conservative rabbis."[83]

The ordination question proved a milestone in relations between the Seminary and the Conservative movement. Never before had the organizations of the denomination intruded so deeply into the internal policies of JTS. The matter at hand, after all, concerned the Seminary's admissions policies. But the leaders of the lay and rabbinic organizations of the denomination felt justified in pressing their perspective on the institution—a development without precedent in the history of JTS, but certainly not without analogues within other seminaries and denominations. Moreover, denominational interference was encouraged by some faculty members, even as others sought support from factions within the RA and United Synagogue that opposed the move. The controversy over women's ordination, in short, produced a dramatically new type of interaction—marked by much outside meddling—between the Seminary and the Conservative movement, one that rendered Cohen's call a decade earlier for the Seminary to become the "nerve-center of the Conservative movement" ironically prophetic.

Perhaps it also indicated a shift in the power relationships within the Conservative movement. This certainly was the way the president of the Rabbinical Assembly, Rabbi Alexander Shapiro, read the resolution of the question in his address to the RA convention of 1985. "Although . . . the Seminary had its own reasons for Ordination, clearly it felt itself pressed by an increasingly large majority of members of the Assembly who felt that for reasons theological and religious the time had come to complete the process begun so many years ago when first we began the education of women to finally close the circle and to bring women colleagues into our midst as equal in every way to each and every one of us."[84] The ordination battle thus cast into question who really spoke for the Conservative movement and who set its agenda. Thirty years after Aaron Blumenthal lamented the impotence of the rabbinate, it appeared that the RA was quite actively steering the Seminary, rather than vice versa.

The Cohen era was marked by several new initiatives in denominational cohesion. At the prompting of the Women's League, a series of meetings were organized to strengthen ties between the denominational arms. In late August 1977, a "Summit Conference" was convened (significantly, it was held on neutral turf at a midtown Manhattan hotel) and attended by representatives of the RA, JTS, University of Judaism, the United Synagogue, and the Women's League.[85] The group discussed a range of issues concerning impediments to the growth and staffing of the Conservative movement, as well as means to expand the international role of the movement. When it came to the question of "Intra-Movement Relationships," some tough questions were placed on the table. This is how the minutes of the meeting summarized the discussion:

> The Conservative movement is a coalition of various arms and it was considered advantageous by some of the fathers of the movement to keep it a loose coalition. It was noted with regret that institutionally, it has now become advantageous for every arm to prevent more cohesive work. The Rabbinical Assembly and the United Synagogue make it clear that the great scholars of the Seminary are not their authorities so, for example, the greatest authorities in liturgy are not involved in liturgical compilation. . . . We have never tried to work together and respect each other. . . . We are now a loose coalition of organizations that gets together at various times under various situations. . . . We have a unique system, where the center of gravity is an academic institution

which also allocates funds to the other groups, which causes tensions and rivalry, but it works; it is the only way.[86]

This forthright airing of basic truths, in fact, encouraged sustained conversations between the leaders of the denominational arms and the Seminary for decades to come.

A second critical initiative in movement cooperation, this one personally spearheaded by Cohen himself, was the development of coordinated programs in Israel. Beginning in 1981, JTS organized the Conservative movement to expand its presence in Israel. Collaborative fund-raising and other shared activities were established to aid the *Masorti* movement. Cohen invested a great deal of the Seminary's prestige and his administration's time in winning the support of the other arms of the movement for these Israeli ventures.[87]

Still another set of new initiatives were undertaken cooperatively to strengthen Conservative Judaism on university campuses. Perhaps the best known was called Ometz, the Center for Conservative Judaism on Campus. A joint project of the National Federation of Jewish Men's Clubs, JTS, and the United Synagogue, Ometz sought to coordinate programs at college campuses through a central office at JTS, a vast and perhaps overwhelming challenge.[88]

Finally, JTS and the Rabbinical Assembly created a Commission on the Ideology of Conservative Judaism in the last year of Cohen's administration. Although there had been calls for the convening of such a commission at least since the 1920s, nothing was ever done—perhaps out of fear that the Conservative movement would splinter if too much ideological clarity was sought. But in 1985 such a commission was founded and eventually included lay members of every arm of the movement in addition to RA and JTS representatives. Only after Cohen's retirement, early in the administration of Ismar Schorsch, did the commission conclude its work and issue its Statement of Conservative Principles, *Emet Ve-Emunah*.

The genesis of this project is somewhat shrouded in mystery. Some have linked it to the bruising debate over women's ordination and the desire to create movement consensus. Others have regarded it as a bid by the Rabbinical Assembly to press the Seminary to align itself even more closely to the Conservative movement. And there is some evidence, too, that the JTS administration saw such a project as a fitting way to mark the Seminary's centennial in 1986.[89] Regardless of the motives, upon its appearance, *Emet Ve-Emunah* was hailed by Chancellor Ismar Schorsch as a tangible expression of the unity within the Conservative movement and "the genuine consensus which prevails in its ranks."[90]

Despite these enormous strides toward cooperation within the Conservative movement, the Cohen era ended amid deep concern over the unity of the movement. The high hopes for reconciliation and unity attendant at the outset of the Cohen administration had not been realized. When the Seminary's board met to choose Cohen's successor, the issue of denominational disunity loomed large. The diagnosis: the Conservative movement was ailing. In his announcement to the board that a process to select a new Chancellor would commence, the chairman of the board, Stephen Peck, expressed his hope that the selection would "be a healing process and will result in all concerned with the Conservative Movement becoming as one."[91] Shortly after his appointment, Ismar Schorsch noted that "one of the things that came out in the search committee was a hunger for healing, for reconciliation. I'm going to strive to do that," he promised.[92] A century after the seminary's founding in 1886, JTS and the Conservative movement continued to stand in somewhat tense relation to one another; the need for unity and healing was as great as ever.

How are we to understand the persistence of friction and disunity, particularly during an administration as committed to strengthening ties between JTS and the Conservative movement as was that of Gerson Cohen? Undoubtedly, it could be argued that the closing years of the Cohen administration were especially contentious because of the extended battle over women's ordination, a conflict that rent the fabric of denominational unity. This conflict centered less on combat between the Seminary and other arms of the denomination than between factions within each arm. Pro-ordination forces within the Seminary administration and faculty were closely allied with the leadership of the Rabbinical Assembly and the United Synagogue. And opposing groups also formed a coalition that cut across institutional boundaries.

Still, with the resolution of the ordination question—and the departure of many combatants in the battle over women's ordination—unity remained elusive. This would suggest that deeper conflicts had been at work. Some of these conflicts resulted from the almost inevitable friction between seminaries and denominations, particularly in those seminaries that eschew a strong orthodoxy and aspire to academic excellence. In such institutions "theological education has been pulled in two directions," characterized by historian Conrad Cherry as "two 'yokes of obedience'—to the church and to the academy,"[93] or in the case of JTS, between the religious needs of Conservative Judaism and academic norms. The most overt expression of such disputes usually centers on the "products" of a seminary education. Denominations often question whether the clerics produced by the seminary are adequately prepared for congregational life. Seminaries, in turn, question whether "the chief purpose of theological education is training in the clerical functions."[94] Still another topic of perennial debate concerns the relationship between religious practice and theoretical discussion that often occurs in the academic setting of seminaries: should "the practice follow from theory?"[95] All of these issues arose with regularity in discussions between JTS and the arms of the Conservative movement.

In addition to these nearly universal sources of tension, the unique historical development of Conservative Judaism's institutions has furthered discord. The fact that JTS was the first institution founded and that, like other Jewish seminaries but unlike most Christian ones, it (rather than the congregation or the denomination) ordains clergy, has given JTS a great deal of independence. In addition, JTS from its inception has relied heavily on the largess of benefactors whose support did not necessarily come through the Conservative movement; especially during the early history of the Seminary, most board members and large donors did not even identify with Conservative Judaism. Moreover, the prestige of JTS has not derived from its relationship with the Conservative movement, but rather from the quality of its faculty (who have never been required to demonstrate personal allegiance to Conservative Judaism) and the contribution of the institution to Jewish culture at large. These have been the sources of institutional glory and acclaim. By contrast, it has always been a far more treacherous undertaking for Seminary leaders to involve themselves in denominational concerns, particularly because the Conservative movement has long consisted of a broad and deeply divided coalition of forces. One faction or another has often sought the Seminary's intercession in disputes, but such involvement has also alienated other segments of the Conservative coalition (a fundamental reality clearly attested by the ordination controversy). All of these factors have historically encouraged JTS to maintain a certain degree of independence from the Conservative movement.

And yet the Seminary and the arms of the Conservative movement have long needed each other. We have examined the financial needs that prompted the Seminary and the arms of the Conservative movement to work cooperatively in the raising of funds. JTS in time grew dependent on benefactors who were recruited from the pews of Conservative congregations. Also, the professionals trained at JTS—the rabbis, cantors, educators, communal workers, and other members of the Jewish civil service—served as vital intermediaries linking the Seminary and the denomination. Strong bonds forged through professional and personal interactions continually overcame some of the institutional rivalries and conflicts that divided the denominational organizations from the Seminary. Finally, JTS presidents and administrators have provided the Conservative movement with a constancy of leadership, which cannot be matched by volunteer heads of denominational organizations who come and go at two-year intervals. For all of these reasons leaders of the Jewish Theological Seminary and the denominational organizations of the Conservative movement have historically engaged one another and sought to work in concert, sometimes with great success but often with much ambivalence and tension.

I wish to thank Timothy Hanssen for his superb assistance in the researching of this essay and Dr. Michael Greenbaum for many fruitful conversations on this topic.

1. Undated letter from Gerson Cohen to Alan M. Stroock, which refers to the latter's letter of 5 February 1979. Ratner Center, JTS Records, R.G. 11C-14-26, Communications, Gerson Cohen correspondence, 1979.

2. In truth, Stroock was concerned about another constituency—the board itself. He apparently feared that by linking itself too closely with the Conservative movement, JTS would alienate board members who did not share that allegiance. Hence, Cohen reassured him: "I agree with you that members of the Seminary Board need not be affiliated with the Conservative Movement. On the other hand, there has been occasional restiveness on the part of some members of the Conservative Rabbinate and laity because the Board has not been more articulate in its Conservative posture." Ibid., p. 3.

3. The present essay cannot, of course, substitute for a history of the Conservative movement, a subject that has yet to find its historian. Rather the focus here is on the interaction of JTS with the primary arms of the Conservative movement, particularly the rabbinical and congregational organizations. (Relations between JTS and Conservative organizations abroad are also omitted here.) This essay primarily examines the sources of conflict, rather than chronicling each denominational program that was managed cooperatively.

4. Michael A. Meyer, *Response to Modernity: A History of the Reform Movement in Judaism.* (New York and Oxford: Oxford University Press, 1988), pp. 260–63, and idem, " A Centennial History," in *Hebrew Union College-Jewish Institute of Religion at One Hundred Years,* ed. Samuel E. Karff (Cincinnati: Hebrew Union College Press, 1976), pp. 3–283.

5. "The Rabbinical Assembly of America," Rabbinical Assembly presidential files, c. 1950, typescript, p. 1. I am grateful to Rabbi Joel Meyers, executive vice-president of the RA, for graciously granting me access to the files of the Rabbinical Assembly.

6. See Jack Wertheimer, " Pioneers of the Conservative Rabbinate: Reports from the Field by Graduates of 'Schechter's Seminary,'" *Conservative Judaism* 47, no. 3, (spring 1995): pp. 53–70. The correspondence published in this essay includes details about the ill-treatment suffered by rabbis at the hands of arrogant or foolish lay leaders and precise information about actual salaries and financial needs. One cannot imagine that rabbis who felt compelled to write in such humiliating detail to their former teachers could have maintained a positive relationship to their alma mater.

7. "75 Years of Changing Concerns—Emphasis and Philosophy." Rabbinical Assembly subject files, no date or author specified. Internal evidence suggests that this brief historical overview was probably written by Rabbi Wolfe Kelman, who served as the executive vice-president of the Rabbinical Assembly for nearly forty years. The essay's title suggests that the document was probably written around the year 1976. (See especially pages 2–3 on the early history.) It should be noted that the Rabbinical Assembly had become active in placement matters in the later 1920s—first through the efforts of appointed members such as Rabbis Louis Schwefel and Henry Fisher and later through executive directors such as Rabbis Bernard Segal, Max Routtenberg, and Wolfe Kelman. See the letter of Edward T. Sandrow to David C. Kogen in the RA presidential files, 1960, dated 1 July 1960.

   As late as 1936, the Rabbinical Assembly still sought the advice of Seminary leaders about internal matters. Thus when Rabbi Eugene Kohn wrote to Professor Louis Finkelstein about a proposal to alter the name of the rabbinical group from the Rabbinical Assembly of the JTS to the Rabbinical Assembly of America, Finkelstein argued against a name change: "The Rabbinical Assembly's relation to the Seminary is a very intimate one and not to be disturbed. The slight advantage which would come to the RA from having a shorter name would, in my opinion, be more than offset by the disadvantage of disassociating it from the mother institution." Finkelstein to Eugene Kohn, 15 June 1936. Rabbinical Assembly executive committee minutes, 1936.

8. Solomon Schechter, "The Seminary as a Witness," *Seminary Addresses and Other Papers* (New York: Burning Bush Press, 1959), p. 48.

9. Herbert Rosenblum, "The Founding of the United Synagogue of America, 1913" (Ph.D. diss., Brandeis University, 1970), p. 151.

10. Schechter's address is reprinted in *The United Synagogue Report*, 1913, pp. 14–23.

11. On these developments, see the author's essay on "The Conservative Synagogue," in *The American Synagogue: A Sanctuary Transformed*, ed. Jack Wertheimer (New York and Cambridge: Cambridge University Press, 1987), especially pp. 115–19.

12. See the minutes of the meeting of the executive council of the Women's Religious Union of the United Synagogue, 29 January 1916. Archives of the Women's League for Conservative Judaism. I thank the Women's League and its executive, Bernice Balter, for granting me access to the archival collection of the league. See also Abraham J. Karp, *A History of the United Synagogue of America, 1913–63* (New York: United Synagogue of America, 1964), pp. 30–37 on these developments.

    The independence of the Women's League from the United Synagogue was a matter of concern to its leaders virtually from its inception. In 1919, Mathilde Schechter pointedly questioned the United Synagogue leadership as to "whether our organization is to be swallowed into the United Synagogue entirely or in what way we are to work together." The Women's League from the outset had its own agenda—"the self-education of Conservative Jewish women"— and sought to maintain a degree of independence. On these matters, see Mel Scult, "The Baale Boste Reconsidered: The Life of Mathilde Roth Schechter (M.R.S.)," *Modern Judaism* (February 1987): pp. 17–19; and Hanna Marx, "Mathilde Schechter: An Appreciation," published by the National Women's League of the United Synagogue of America, n.d.

13. On the Young People's League, see *The United Synagogue Recorder* 1, no. 2 (1921): p. 3.

14. Charles E. Simon and Joel B. Sperber, "The Federation of Jewish Men's Clubs, 1929–1989," typescript dated 8 February 1990. In 1983 the word "National" was dropped from the organization's name to acknowledge its ties with Canadian congregations and international concerns. The link with the United Synagogue ended earlier. The Federation of Jewish Men's Clubs and its executive, Rabbi Charles Simon, generously provided me with access to organizational records.

15. See the *Annual Reports of the United Synagogue* for 1917, 1922, and 1929 to track the rapid growth of affiliated congregations.

16. This subject has been explored in depth and with great attention to nuance by Michael B. Greenbaum in several works. See his "Mission Conflict in Religiously Affiliated Institutions of Higher Education: The Jewish Theological Seminary of America during the Presidency of Louis Finkelstein, 1940–1955." (Ph.D. diss.,Columbia University, Teachers College, 1994). See also his essay on "The Finkelstein Era" in the present history and his essay, "Finkelstein and His Critics," *Conservative Judaism* 47 (summer 1995): p. 3–78. The present essay builds upon Greenbaum's work and carries the story through the era of Gerson Cohen. In addition, the present essay focuses more on structural tensions than on mission conflicts. Greenbaum's work in the latter area is indispensable, particularly for an understanding of the Finkelstein era..

17. Samuel M. Cohen to Cyrus Adler, 23 November 1917. Ratner Center, JTS Records, R.G. 15A-5-9. (The entirety of this letter appears in Wertheimer, "Pioneers of the Conservative Rabbinate," pp. 62–63.)

18. Ibid., p. 62.

19. Samuel M. Cohen to the leadership of the United Synagogue, 29 September 1932, in the

Rabbinical Assembly files, 1932.

20. Wertheimer, "Pioneers of the Conservative Rabbinate," pp. 58–59. The letter dates to 1 June 1910.

21. Quoted by M. Greenbaum, "Mission Conflict," p. 30. The letter was dated 9 June 1919.

22. It was a symptom of the dependent relationship of the RA that when the organization drafted a new constitution in 1928, its president sent a copy to Cyrus Adler (who was not an ordained rabbi) in order "to benefit from [his] counsel." Norman Salit to Cyrus Adler, 30 March 1928. JTS library, Cyrus Adler Papers, box 12, "Rabbinical Assembly." We may note in this context that JTS leaders regarded the women's auxiliaries primarily as service agencies for the Seminary and the spread of Conservative Judaism. At the founding of the United Synagogue, Schechter declared: "I would even suggest that the [Conservative] Union assign a certain portion of its work to women and give them a regular share in its activities. They can become more than an auxiliary to us; indeed helpful in many respects where, as conditions are in this country, their influence is more far-reaching than that of their husbands." Quoted by Gerson D. Cohen in a letter to Mrs. M. [Ruth] Perry, president of the Women's League, 9 December 1977. Ratner Center, JTS Records, R.G. 11C-14-24. Communications, Gerson Cohen Correspondence, 1967–83. See also Greenbaum, "Mission Conflict," p. 119.

23. Adler to Schechter, 3 August 1909. JTS library, Cyrus Adler Papers, box 18, "1906–1910."

24. Quoted by Ira Robinson in his essay on the Adler period in volume 1 of this history, note 120.

25. JTS library, Solomon Schechter Papers, 101–5, n.d. Schechter to an unspecified individual.

26. Sol M. Stroock to Cyrus Adler, 8 November 1911. JTS library, Cyrus Adler Papers, box 7, "Stroock, Sol. M."

27. Cyrus Adler to S. D. Tulin of Hartford, 31 October 1923. JTS Library, Cyrus Adler Papers, box 3, "Finkelstein, Louis (1919–1932)."

28. Louis Finkelstein to Cyrus Adler, 26 October 1936. JTS library, Cyrus Adler Papers, box 3, "Finkelstein, Louis, January–October 1936."

29. Ibid., pp. 1–2.

30. Ibid., pp. 2–3.

31. Ibid., p. 3.

32. Ibid., pp. 4–6. The RA, for its part, had virtually given up on the United Synagogue in this period. A "Committee on Cooperation with the United Synagogue and Seminary" offered the following scathing assessment in a report to the Rabbinical Assembly's 1938 convention: "This committee is of the opinion that [close] cooperation does not now exist. A careful canvas of the situation leads this committee to the conclusion that of the three branches, the United Synagogue is the weakest, due to the failure of the executive personnel of the United Synagogue to win the cooperation and the support of the members of the Rabbinical Assembly who, by their positions, carry the movement of American Jewry. This committee regretfully concludes that the situation cannot be remedied without a change in the personnel of the executive office of the United Synagogue . . . [and] that in making this change it should arrange for the satisfactory payment of the existing financial obligation and for additional financial adjustment in recognition of his many years of devoted service." "Committee on the Report of the Committee on Cooperation with the United Synagogue and Seminary" of the RA." RA files, "Convention Proceedings, 1938."

33. Adler to Finkelstein, 14 May 1930. JTS library. Cyrus Adler Papers, box 3, "Finkelstein, Louis (1919–1932)."

34. See the letter dated 20 September 1938 and marked "Personal and Confidential," written by Simon Greenberg in his capacity as president to the membership of the RA. Ratner Center, Simon Greenberg Papers, unprocessed collection, 1938. Greenberg explains why circumstances have become so dire: "We were fortunate and blessed with the fact that while

our Movement was young, the Seminary had a few good friends who were financially able to carry on its work without appealing to the community at large. Some of these friends are no longer with us among the living. Others can no longer be as generous as they were in the past. And while we have reason to hope that the Seminary may still benefit of the generosity of one or another wealthy man amongst us, we cannot depend upon miracles and upon the type of help which is uncertain and sporadic." It should be noted that individual rabbis had played a role in the past as fund-raisers for JTS within their communities, and some cooperative campaigns had occurred for specific projects at JTS. But the effort to initiate an RA campaign with a targeted monetary goal was unprecedented.

35. The United Synagogue, which had conducted its own fund-raising to meet its annual budget of $20–25,000, ran up a $50,000 debt that was eventually paid only when JTS lent it the money to wipe out its debt. "The Jewish Theological Seminary of America, the United Synagogue, the Rabbinical Assembly: The Nature of the Spiritual and Organizational Relationship That Exists and Should Exist Among Them." First draft signed by S[imon] G[reenberg], undated. (References in the draft to money expended in 1949 and budgets projected for 1950 suggest the document was drafted during the fiscal year that began on 1 July 1949.) Ratner Center, Simon Greenberg Papers, unprocessed collection, p. 13.

36. Greenbaum, "Mission Conflict," p. 182, note 654.

37. Ibid., pp. 172–74. Greenbaum claims that the donor base for the campaign grew from a thousand in 1936 to ten times that number in 1943.

38. This information on the Liaison Committee is based on Greenbaum, "Mission Conflict," pp. 162–68.

39. "The Jewish Theological Seminary of America, the United Synagogue, the Rabbinical Assembly: The Nature of the Spiritual and Organizational Relationship That Exists and Should Exist Among Them." First draft signed by S[imon] G[reenberg], undated, p. 16.

40. On this postwar expansion, see Wertheimer, "The Conservative Synagogue," pp. 123–32.

41. Greenberg, "The Nature of the Spiritual and Organizational Relationship That Exists and Should Exist," p. 9.

42. Greenberg, "The Nature of the Spiritual and Organizational Relationship," p. 9.

43. David Aronson to Rabbi Max Routtenberg, 1 August 1949, RA executive council minutes, 1949.

44. Ratner Center, Simon Greenberg Papers, box 10, Louis Finkelstein correspondence, 1952.

45. Greenbaum, "Mission Conflict," pp. 215–16.

46. Some of the key documents are printed in "Responsum on the Sabbath," *Proceedings of the Rabbinical Assembly* 14 (1950): pp. 112–188. In addition to the question of driving a car on the Sabbath, the Law Committee addressed the permissibility of using electricity on the Sabbath and introduced a "Program for the Revitalization of the Sabbath."

47. "Reevaluation of the Responsum on the Sabbath," by Jacob Agus. Ratner Center Collection, R.G. 1Q-199-9.

48. In the late 1960s, religious warfare erupted even more vehemently over another decision of the Law Committee that rendered it optional for congregations to observe *yom tov sheni shel galuyot* (a day added to the celebration of Jewish festivals for Jews living outside of Israel). The chairman of the Law Committee bitterly denounced "the vituperative attacks upon the authors of a responsum and on the Committee in general by some highly placed officials of the Seminary administration and Seminary faculty." Benjamin Z. Kreitman, "Committee on Jewish Law and Standards," *Proceedings of the Rabbinical Assembly* 34 (1970): pp. 194–95.

49. *Proceedings of the Rabbinical Assembly* 19 (1955): p. 133.

50. Ibid., pp. 133–34.

51. Ibid., p. 135.

52. Ibid., p. 135.

53. Meeting of Louis Finkelstein with RA rabbis on 6 February 1961. R.G. 1Q, 1961, p. 19. A few days after this meeting, Rabbi Edward T. Sandrow, then the president of the RA, called upon Finkelstein to form a joint committee with the rabbis to smooth relations between the RA and JTS and "to overcome many of the fears, tensions and suspicions which have arisen on both sides and which prevent the creation of sound and dynamic communication between us." RA presidential files, 1961. Sandrow to Finkelstein, 10 February 1961.

54. Letter from Rabbi Jacob B. Agus, dated 8 February 1966. RA files, Wolfe Kelman correspondence, miscellaneous.

55. "Committee on Conservative Judaism," meeting of 10 March 1966, p. 3. RA files, Wolfe Kelman correspondence, miscellaneous.

56. Louis Finkelstein to George Maislen, 26 December 1963. Ratner Center, General Files, R.G. 1S-216-30.

57. Greenbaum, "Mission Conflict," p. 116. An exchange between a lay leader of the United Synagogue and a JTS administrator is quite revealing about the doubts each organization harbored toward the other. In 1968 Dr. Arthur Jacobs asked for an explanation of the services provided to the United Synagogue by JTS. The response from JTS begins, revealingly, with the assertion that "obviously, without the Seminary there would be no United Synagogue, since it is a fact that we train rabbis for our Conservative congregations upon which rests the whole foundation of a synagogue group with certain interests and concerns." This is followed by a description of the role of the Seminary in providing staff members for a broad range of educational ventures. The letter concludes: "Part of this is, of course, the natural family relationship which causes the United Synagogue to 'boost' the Seminary wherever it is possible to do so, but a good deal of it is indicative simply of the intellectual and educational dependence which inevitably exists." Marjorie Wyler to Arthur Jacobs, Ratner Center, JTS Records, R.G. 11C 63-33, Communications, United Synagogue, 1960s–1980.

58. Greenbaum, "Mission Conflict," pp. 118–20.

59. Draft of speech delivered at the Women's League Convention. Ratner Center, Marjorie Wyler Papers, unprocessed collection, 1964.

60. Louis Finkelstein to Mrs. Louis Sussman, president of the Women's League, 31 May 1956. Ratner Center, JTS Records, R.G. 1L-150-67.

61. Milton Nevins, "A Brief History of the National Federation of Jewish Men's Clubs," in *Men's Club Manual*, ed. Jerome Labovitz (New York: National Federation of Jewish Men's Clubs, 1953), pp. 6–11. (In 1987, under the administration of Ismar Schorsch, the NFJMC was given a seat on the JTS board.) In the mid-1950s, the NFJMC formed a National Committee on Seminary Affairs and appointed a seminary affairs chairman in each club to develop support for JTS. See the letter from Bernard Rackmil to club presidents, 6 February 1956. Ratner Center, Joel Geffen Papers, 2a-15-35, NFJMC Seminary Committee, 1954–56. The essay of Michael Brown in volume 1 of this history traces the role of the Seminary in the founding and guidance of Ramah and the Leadership Training Fellowship, two programs through which JTS supervised the education of young Conservative Jews.

62. Most of these are itemized in Aaron Blumenthal, "The Status of the Rabbinical Assembly in the Conservative Movement," *Proceedings of the Rabbinical Assembly*, 1955, pp. 131–32.

63. The National Enrollment Plan was begun in the late 1950s. According to an independent advertising firm that studied the functioning of the NEP in 1972, only one hundred of the 850 United Synagogue congregations organized satisfactory NEP programs in which more than 75 percent of members contributed dues to the plan. In another three hundred synagogues, the congregation had officially voted to join the NEP, but participation was "not satisfactory." NEP was either rejected or never proposed at 450 United Synagogue

congregations. The Seminary maintained no effective control over NEP collections or the power to audit congregational accounts to ensure it received its proper NEP remittances. Harold Weinberger of Dobbs Advertising Company to Rabbi Henry Michelman, assistant to the Chancellor, 23 January 1973. R.G. 1 unprocessed addition, 1973.

64. Louis Finkelstein to the RA membership, 29 May 1958. Ratner Center, Joel Geffen Papers, 4b-25-36, Rabbinical Assembly, 1954–71.

65. Simon Greenberg, confidential memo to Louis Finkelstein, 17 February 1966, p. 5. Ratner Center, Simon Greenberg Papers, box 10.

66. Louis Finkelstein to all Seminary department heads, 4 December 1970. Ratner Center. Marjorie Wyler Papers, unprocessed collection, 1970. Finkelstein to Rabbi Mayer Abramowitz, 4 September 1970. Gerson Cohen, General Files, unorganized, 1970.

67. Quoted in Greenbaum, "Mission Conflict," p. 180, note 544. This letter was written in 1945, a period of cooperation between JTS and the RA.

68. RA Papers, Wolfe Kelman correspondence, 10 October 1974. Memorandum, addressee not named.

69. Letter from a Midwestern rabbi to Alan M. Stroock, 6 October 1971. RA Subject Files, 1971.

70. Letter dated 10 December 1971. Ratner Center, JTS Records, R.G. 1 BB-289-46, General Files, 1972.

71. Letter to Cohen from Philadelphia, 11 January 1972. R.G. 1, unprocessed addition, 1972.

72. Ratner Center, JTS Records, R.G. 11C-37-1, Communications, Gershon Kekst, 1975.

73. Memorandum dated 18 February 1976. Gerson Cohen, General Files, unprocessed, 1976.

74. Gerson D. Cohen, "Women in the Conservative Movement," Women's League *Outlook* (winter 1973).

75. Letter dated 15 March 1974 from Philadelphia. R.G. 1, unprocessed addition, 1974.

76. Letter from Philadelphia, 20 February 1974. R.G.1, unprocessed addition, 1974.

77. Letter from Willima Abrams, 3 March 1975. R.G. 1, unprocessed addition, 1975.

78. There is no evidence that Cohen altered his policies due to the hostile response to his article in the *Outlook*. To the contrary, shortly after taking office, he already indicated in a private letter that he personally favored granting girls *aliyot* in Ramah camps. Letter to Max Routtenberg, 23 February 1972. Ratner Center, JTS Records, R.G. 1BB-290-2, General Files, 1972.

79. Letter from a Talmud faculty member, 21 August 1974. R.G. 1, unprocessed addition, 1974.

80. Letter from a rabbi in Queens, New York, dated 1 July 1974. R.G. 1, unprocessed addition, 1974.

81. Press release, 30 January 1979. Ratner Center, JTS Records, R.G. 11B-8-18, Communications, press releases, July 1978-January 1979.

82. On the debate over Magidson's application to the RA, *Proceedings of the Rabbinical Assembly* 45 (1983): pp. 218–51.

83. Press release, 14 February 1985. Ratner Center, Marjorie Wyler Papers, unprocessed collection, 1985.

84. Report to the Convention, May 1985. Ratner Center, Alexander Shapiro Papers, unprocessed collection, 1986.

85. See the letters of Mrs. Ruth Perry to Gerson Cohen, 18 May 1977 and 2 August 1977. Gerson Cohen General Files, unorganized, 1977.

86. Minutes of the Conservative movement "Summit Conference" held on 30 August 1977. Women's League Archives, Subject Files, 1977, especially p. 5. The minutes do not indicate the name of the speaker of these words.

87. See, for example, Ratner Center, Simon Greenberg's draft memorandum of agreement for

such a cooperative venture with the United Synagogue, RA, Women's League, and the World Council of Synagogues. 2 November 1981. Simon Greenberg Papers, unprocessed. Greenberg formally headed these initiatives, but Cohen was personally active in seeing them through and often traveled to Israel.

88. See, for example, the Ometz brochure in Ratner Center, JTS Records, R.G. 11C-50-21, Communications, Ometz brochure, 1982–83.

89. In a draft proposal for "Conservative Movement-Wide Participation in the Seminary's Centennial," it is suggested that self-study "would constitute an act of unity which would be greeted with approval throughout the movement." It would address questions of ideology and also formulate an agenda for action. The document is in the Ratner Center, Alexander Shapiro Papers, box 6, folder 5. In his foreword to *Emet Ve-Emunah*, Kassel Abelson links the commission to the impending JTS centennial, p. 1.

90. *Emet Ve-Emunah: Statement of Principles of Conservative Judaism* (New York: Jewish Theological Seminary, 1988), foreword.

91. JTS library, board minutes, 19 June 1985, p. 98. In his effort to achieve such unity, Peck convinced the JTS board to amend its bylaws "to include the three largest constituent organizations by naming the chief elected officers of the Women's League for Conservative Judaism, the RA, and the United Synagogue to the Search Committee." Ibid., p. 99.

92. Sheldon Engelmayer, "Conservative 'Healer': Seminary Chancellor-elect to Strive for Reconciliation." *Jewish Week* (New York), 7 March 1986, p. 4.

93. Conrad Cherry, *Hurrying Toward Zion: Universities, Divinity Schools and American Protestantism* (Bloomington: Indiana University Press, 1995), p. 156.

94. Ibid., p. 299.

95. Ibid., p. 299.

DAVID GOLINKIN

The Influence of Seminary Professors on Halakha in the Conservative Movement: 1902-1968

Louis Ginzberg (1873–1953). *Photo by Virginia F. Stern. Ratner Center, JTS.*

DAVID GOLINKIN

The Influence of Seminary Professors on Halakha in the Conservative Movement: 1902-1968

IF ONE WERE TO ASK the average Conservative rabbi ordained by the Jewish Theological Seminary between 1950 and 1980 about the influence of Seminary professors on *halakha* (Jewish law) in the Conservative movement, he would no doubt reply that such influence was negligible or nonexistent. Indeed, in 1979 when the Seminary faculty was forced to deal with the issue of ordaining women rabbis, many rabbis and students remarked that this was the first time that Seminary professors had ever come down from their ivory tower to deal with the practical halakhic problems of the real world.[1]

Indeed, this popular perception was verbalized by Chancellor Ismar Schorsch in 1986:

> The . . . Seminary . . . inherited from Breslau a tradition that abdicated the responsibility to provide halakhic guidance for its own day. The twin model of the *Rosh Yeshiva* [head of a talmudic academy] and the German professor combined to raise the academic at Breslau or New York above the level of a mere *moreh hora'a* or halakhic decisor. No discrepancy was felt between devoting the bulk of the curriculum to the study of rabbinic literature and ignoring the halakhic needs of the contemporary community.[2]

More recently, Neil Gillman wrote as follows:

> From the middle of the twentieth century through 1972, Conservative Judaism presented two faces. One was the Seminary's—highly intellectual and academic, extraordinarily open to the most critical and scientific scholarly research, yet traditionalist in practice, barely tolerating changes in ritual observance, and

445

largely unaware of the issues faced by the masses of Jews in Conservative congregations throughout the country.[3]

In the following essay, we shall prove that this common perception is probably an accurate portrayal of Professor Saul Lieberman's approach to practical *halakha* and he, of course, was the leading talmudist at the Seminary from 1953, when Louis Ginzberg died, until his own death in 1983. It is not, however, an accurate portrayal of the attitude of *all* Seminary professors toward practical *halakha*. Rather, during the period we shall examine, three different and distinct approaches can be discerned: The first group—Solomon Schechter and Saul Lieberman—did not view themselves as *poskim* (decisors of Jewish law) and refrained, for the most part, from *pesak halakha* (legal decision making). The second group—Mordecai Kaplan and Louis Finkelstein—did not write many responsa but served on the Committee on Jewish Law of the Rabbinical Assembly and worked actively behind the scenes to mold Conservative *halakha*. The third group—Louis Ginzberg and Boaz Cohen— were halakhic activists, who dominated the various law committees of the Conservative movement for thirty-one years (1917–48) and wrote hundreds of responsa between 1917 and 1968.

Before we examine these approaches, a word is in order about the time frame of this study. We begin in 1902 because it was in that year that Solomon Schechter became President of the Jewish Theological Seminary.[4] We have concluded our study in 1968 because that is the year in which Boaz Cohen passed away.[5] His death symbolizes the end of an era, since he and Ginzberg dominated Conservative *halakha* for fifty years. Stopping in 1968 also gives us the historical perspective needed to analyze the events of the past.[6]

Those Who Refrained from Pesak Halakha: *Schechter and Lieberman*[7]

PROFESSOR SOLOMON SCHECHTER (1849–1915) was President of the reorganized Seminary, founder of the United Synagogue, and, for all intents and purposes, founder of what is today known as the Conservative movement.[8] He was a traditional Jew, fully committed to *halakha* and *mitzvot* (the commandments), a fact he stressed on numerous occasions.[9] In 1902, he stated in his oft-quoted inaugural address as President of the Jewish Theological Seminary:

> Judaism is not a religion which does not oppose itself to anything in particular. Judaism is opposed to any number of things and says distinctly "thou shalt not." It permeates the whole of your life. It demands control over all your actions, and interferes even with your menu. It sanctifies the seasons, and regulates your history, both in the past and in the future. Above all, it teaches that disobedience is the strength of sin. It insists upon the observance both of the spirit and of the letter; spirit without letter belongs to the species known to the mystics as "nude souls," *nishmatin artilain*, wandering about in the universe

without balance and without consistency, the play of all possible currents and changes in the atmosphere. In a word, Judaism is absolutely incompatible with the abandonment of the Torah.[10]

Furthermore, as many have noted, Schechter was a master of the catchy phrase or bon mot.[11] Some of his most memorable expressions were coined in the defense of *halakha* and *mitzvot*: "The frequent appeals to 'prophetic Judaism' are largely verbiage; you cannot live on oxygen alone."[12] "There is nothing in American citizenship which is incompatible with our observing the dietary laws, our sanctifying the Sabbath, our fixing a *Mezuzah* on our doorposts, our refraining from leavened bread on Passover, or our perpetuating any other law essential to the preservation of Judaism. . . . In this great, glorious and free country, we Jews need not sacrifice a single iota of our Torah."[13] "Ethics are good, but laws and commandments, bidden and commanded by God, are better."[14] "For me the *Tephillin* are my banner, the *Sepher Torah* our *Magna Charta*, the Synagogue our Parliament. The Dietary Laws are consequences of holiness."[15] In addition, Schechter stressed that rabbinical students and Conservative rabbis must observe *mitzvot*.[16]

Nonetheless, Schechter does not seem to have viewed practical *halakha* as an important part of the Seminary curriculum. On the one hand, the 1902 Rabbinical School curriculum included the "Codes of Moses ben Maimon, R. Jacob ben Asher, R. Joseph Caro and R. Abraham Danzig."[17] On the other hand, Schechter never mentions codes in his various references to the Rabbinical School curriculum. In 1902, he stated that a rabbi "should know everything Jewish—Bible, Talmud, Midrash, Liturgy, Jewish ethics and Jewish philosophy, Jewish history and Jewish mysticism and even Jewish folklore."[18] In 1904, he once again enumerated the subjects taught at the Seminary without mentioning codes or practical *halakha*.[19]

More important, Schechter seems to have avoided rendering practical halakhic decisions whenever possible. Bentwich, his biographer, states that Schechter received rabbinical ordination (*hatarat hora'a*),[20] "but he never exercised the rabbinical office."[21] He further states that Schechter "never assumed [the title Rabbi] and would have repudiated that title in England."[22] Furthermore, Mel Scult quotes Mathilde Schechter's memoirs to the effect that Schechter "did not care for the pulpit." He once wrote to a friend that he thanked God he was free of the "onus" of being a rabbi: "As you know, I always abhorred that profession." And Mordecai Kaplan complained that it was Schechter who "used to wither the souls of the students with his ill-timed jests about rabbis and their calling. It was he that made it fashionable for all scholars . . . in and about the Seminary to turn up their noses at the term 'rabbi.'"[23]

In light of this attitude, it is not surprising that Schechter did not view himself as a halakhic authority or express any interest in rendering halakhic decisions. In 1888 he wrote a letter to the *Jewish Chronicle* in reaction to the introduction of the triennial cycle of the Torah reading at the Berkeley Street Synagogue in London: "I am quite indifferent to the doctrinal question whether the triennial cycle ought to be considered as a most orthodox action, or fairly orthodox, or not orthodox at all. *I am only interested in the interpretation of the passage in the Talmud.*"[24] His statement clearly fits the stereotype of the Seminary professor described above: Schechter viewed himself as a scholar first and a rabbi second.

This impression is reinforced by a letter he wrote in 1901, one year before he came to the Seminary from Cambridge. He was asked at that time, along with a number of other prominent Jews, whether it was permissible to hold a funeral in the synagogue. His answer is worth reproducing because it shows his mind-set vis-à-vis practical *halakha*:

> I have, as a rule, very little to do with practical, ritual questions, falling under the heading of *She'elot* [halakhic questions addressed to rabbis], which may safely be left to the *Dayyanim* [rabbinic judges], and I feel even now reluctant to offer an opinion on such matters; but I am inclined to think that there can be no serious religious objection to carrying on a funeral service either in the synagogue or the vestry.
>
> The only disadvantage that I can see is, that it will give the synagogue a gloomy connection in the minds of the worshippers, converting it into a sort of mortuary. On the other hand, as suggested to me by a friend, this might be outweighed by the consideration that it will create a new link to bind the laity, both regular worshippers and the indifferent, with the synagogue.
>
> In olden times, they would always bring into the synagogue, the bier of a great man, such as *hakham aluf v'gaon* [a sage, a chief, a *gaon*], and there pronounce the funeral orations over his body. Who would now form the *hakham*, etc., is difficult to say, each little group claiming for its leader such a title. On the whole, it is a matter of taste, and the decision should rest upon public opinion.[25]

Finally, Schechter's assertion that he had, as a rule, very little to do with practical, ritual questions is reinforced by an incident from 13 October 1915, shortly before his death. When he was asked if a potential convert who was a priest and knew Hebrew would be exempt from circumcision, he passed the question on to Rabbi Moses Hyamson, professor of codes at the Seminary, even though the answer is obvious to any rabbi.[26]

When trying to determine the source of Schechter's attitude, it is worth noting that it apparently did not stem from his teachers at the rabbinical seminary in Vienna.[27] Both Isaac Hirsch Weiss and Meir Friedmann (Ish Shalom) published responsa in Hebrew on the burial of a non-Jew in a Jewish cemetery[28] and the latter also authored a responsum in German on the "Participation of Women in [Jewish] Worship."[29]

I believe Schechter's attitude can be traced to his devotion to, or obsession with, the scientific study of Judaism. As Neil Gillman has argued:

> From the outset, the decisive influence on the culture of the Seminary was its commitment to the *Wissenschaft* style of scholarship. For the school's founding fathers, as for their predecessors in Europe, *Wissenschaft* was more than simply a scholarly methodology, more even than an ideology. It was nothing less than their ticket of admission into the emancipation, into modernity and into the intellectual community of the West. The symbol of that integration would be the introduction of Jewish studies into the academic agenda of the modern university and its scholarly community. That could be achieved only if Judaism would be studied by the very same canons of scholarship used for the study of any other culture or body of literature. *Wissenschaft* was perceived as making Judaism worthy of belonging to the modern West, worthy of being respected.[30]

It seems that in Schechter's opinion it was more important for a rabbi to be able to write a scholarly article or produce a critical edition of a rabbinic text than to answer a question of practical *halakha*. In 1902, he stated that "the crown and climax of all learning is research."[31] He stated in that same inaugural address that

> every generation, the ancient rabbis say, which did not live to see the rebuilding of the Holy Temple must consider itself as if it had witnessed its destruction. Similarly, we must say that every age which has not made some essential contribution to the erection of the Temple of Truth and real *Wissenschaft* is bound to look upon itself as if it had been instrumental in its demolition.[32]

In this passage, Schechter compares Jewish *Wissenschaft* to the Holy Temple (*sic!*) and views it as an essential aspect of Jewish continuity.

At a later graduation, in 1908, Schechter declared:

> It would not even injure the Rabbi if he should from time to time engage in some scientific work, publishing occasionally a learned article on some historical topic, or even editing some ancient Hebrew text. . . . it *was* intended when learned institutions were created that their graduates should, by some scientific work, give confirmation of their continuing the studies in which they were initiated by their *alma mater*.[33]

Finally, in 1913, Schechter looked back on the two main reasons for reorganizing the Seminary. The first was to create a conservative tendency in the United States while the second

> was to create a school of Jewish learning . . . and give it that scientific thoroughness and finish which alone deserves the name of research as well as enable Judaism to compete with and to combat those hostile intellectual forces which are often more dangerous to us than pogroms and direct persecution.[34]

PROFESSOR SAUL LIEBERMAN (1898–1983) taught at the Seminary from 1940 until his death.[35] Author of *Tosefta Kifshutah*, *Yerushalmi Kifshuto*, *Hellenism in Jewish Palestine*, and *Greek in Jewish Palestine*, he is universally regarded as the foremost talmudist of his generation, and some regard him as one of the foremost talmudists of all times.[36] Yet he is without a doubt the model for the image of the Seminary professor described above. He published 225 books and articles, yet only four of those items are devoted to the practical halakhic problems of the 20th century.[37] This statistic becomes even more surprising when translated into quantity. Lieberman published over ninety-five hundred pages that were devoted for the most part to the explication of rabbinic texts. Yet only nineteen pages or 0.2 percent are devoted to the halakhic challenges and problems of our times.

Lieberman was the rector of the Seminary and the *posek* (decisor of Jewish law) for the Seminary synagogue from 1949 until his death. In that capacity, he dealt with whatever halakhic problems arose within that synagogue.[38] Yet there seem to have been only four occasions when he became actively involved in practical halakhic issues involving the Conservative movement or *klal yisrael* (the Jewish people).[39] The first occasion was in 1945 when Mordecai Kaplan published his controversial *Sabbath Prayer Book*. That episode will be described below in the section devoted to Louis Ginzberg.[40]

The second occasion was in 1953 when the Rabbinical Assembly tried once again to alleviate the plight of *agunot* (chained women) whose husbands had granted them a civil divorce but refused to give them a *get* (Jewish bill of divorce).[41] At that time, a Joint Law Conference was formed by the Seminary faculty and the Rabbinical Assembly, which consisted of an equal number of rabbis from each group.[42] They adopted a *takkanah* (rabbinic enactment) proposed by Lieberman that added a paragraph to the *ketubah* (marriage contract) enabling an *agunah* to force her recalcitrant husband to come to the Joint *Beit Din* (court of Jewish law), and ultimately to the civil courts, for arbitration.[43] At the time, Lieberman also tried to set up a joint *Beit Din* with Rabbi Joseph B. Soloveitchik and other prominent Orthodox rabbis, but this effort was apparently torpedoed by right-wing Orthodox opponents.[44] Nevertheless, the Lieberman *ketubah* has been widely used, though it has met with Orthodox hostility and has actually done little to alleviate the plight of the *agunah*.[45]

The third occasion was in 1958, when Prime Minister David Ben-Gurion addressed a letter to forty-three rabbis and scholars in Israel and in the Diaspora soliciting their opinion on the issue of registering children of mixed marriages whose parents—both the Jewish father and the non-Jewish mother—wish to register their children as Jews.[46] Professor Lieberman replied in no uncertain terms:

> It is perfectly clear and without a doubt that a son born to a Jew by a non-Jewish wife is not called his son and is considered a non-Jew in all respects. Any declaration . . . will not alter the situation one whit; . . . the son must meet all the

traditional legal requirements to be considered a proselyte. It is also clear that no court in Israel will in any manner agree to proselytize small children when it is known in advance that their parents will not educate them to observe the Torah and its commandments. No tragedy of the parents has the power to justify making a farce of proselytism.[47]

In the remainder of the responsum, Lieberman encourages such a mother and son to undergo conversion, and he urges the Israeli government to admit its error and return to the halakhic definition of Jewish identity.

The fourth and final occasion when Lieberman entered the halakhic fray was in the spring of 1979 when the Seminary faculty was hotly debating the ordination of women as rabbis.[48] On *Rosh Hodesh Adar* 5739 he wrote a responsum in Hebrew to H. Z. Dimitrovsky, David Weiss Halivni, Dov Zlotnick, Jose Faur, and Israel Francus.[49] He asserts on the basis of Rabbi Yehudah al-Barzeloni that "in our day" there is no real *semicha* (ordination) but only a *ketav masmich* (an ordaining document) that entitles one to be called "Rabbi" and to sit among the judges be included in the council of the *haverim* (sages). "Since a woman is not fit to judge, and she cannot become qualified for this, she cannot be ordained by this title. . . . Let us not make ourselves objects of derision and jest."[50]

Now that we have examined Lieberman's meager output of responsa, we must try to explain why such a talmudic genius refrained from writing responsa and engaging in *pesak halakha*. His own reluctance to deal with practical halakhic issues is clearly stated at the outset of his responsum on ordination:

> I would have preferred not to deal with this question at all because of hidden reasons which I do not wish to disclose. I was glad that they neither asked me nor requested me to issue a legal decision. But now I am afraid that it is forbidden me to deny kindness to others, to evade and not respond.[51]

What were his "hidden reasons"? Why did Lieberman normally avoid *pesak halakha*? I believe there are two answers to this question. He grew up in Lithuania and learned at the *mussar yeshivot* of Multch, Slobodka, and Novaredok.[52] The goal of Talmud study at Lithuanian *yeshivot* was *Torah lishma*, or Torah study for its own sake. Receiving *semicha* and deciding questions of Jewish law was not an ideal but rather a compromise forced upon the student by the need to earn a living.[53] When Lieberman moved to Jerusalem in 1928 and began to study with Y. N. Epstein, he transformed his traditional love of *Torah lishma* into the modern love of scientific/critical Talmud study that he brought with him to the Seminary in 1940.[53a] Had he remained in Europe, he would probably have become a *Rosh Yeshiva*, not a communal rabbi and *posek*. At the Seminary he became the rector, but not a halakhic authority for the community at large.

Furthermore, one gets the distinct impression that Lieberman was very ambivalent about being considered a leader of the Conservative movement. On the one hand, when he proposed his *takkanah* regarding the *ketubah* in 1953, he expressed his disdain for Orthodox rabbis opposed to all change even if it be totally halakhic.[54] In addition, we know from his surviving letters that he helped Rabbi Theodore Friedman receive permission to perform weddings in Jerusalem and defended the *gittin* (bills of divorce) executed by Rabbi Israel Silverman and other Conservative rabbis.[55]

On the other hand, he saved a number of letters from prominent Orthodox rabbis such as J. L. Maimon, Isser Yehuda Unterman, Joseph B. Soloveitchik, and Shlomo Goren but almost none from Conservative rabbis.[56] More important, in 1974 the Israeli daily *Ma'ariv* published an article claiming that Golda Meir asked Professor Lieberman to influence the Conservative movement to accept a compromise according to which there would be a yearlong moratorium on the registration of converts who make *aliya* in order to enable the *Mafdal* (National Religious Party) to join the Israeli government. Lieberman was described there as "one of the leaders of the Conservative movement and as the vice-president of the Jewish Theological Seminary in New York."[57] Lieberman wrote an indignant letter to the editor in which he denied the entire story. But, more important for our purposes, he says: "I am not one of the heads of the Conservative movement and I am not, nor have I ever been, the Vice President of the [Jewish] Theological Seminary. I teach Torah to the Jewish people and I don't understand much about politics."[58]

This statement is quite remarkable coming from a person who had been teaching at the Seminary for thirty-four years and who had been its rector since 1949! But in retrospect, Lieberman's attitude is not that surprising. He came to the Seminary at age forty-two after spending thirty years in Eastern Europe and twelve years in Jerusalem. He was very ambivalent about leaving Israel,[59] and for many years he spent half of every year in Jerusalem. He was even awarded the Israel Prize, which is only awarded to Israeli citizens. Thus, he did not come to the Seminary in 1940 out of loyalty to a specific movement but in order to engage in scientific *Torah lishma* and "to teach Torah to the Jewish people." He fulfilled both those tasks admirably. Our disappointment in his halakhic output and influence is based on the influence he *could* have had but not on any promises he ever made.

Those Who Worked Behind the Scenes: Kaplan and Finkelstein[60]

The next pair of Seminary professors we shall examine consists of Mordecai Kaplan and Louis Finkelstein. They did not write many responsa nor were they viewed as major *poskim*. Yet unlike Professors Schechter and Lieberman, they took an active interest in shaping the *halakha* of the Conservative movement. They did so by serving on the Committee on Jewish Law of the Rabbinical Assembly for quite a few years and by working behind the scenes to mold the membership and procedures of that and other committees.

Professor Mordecai Kaplan (1881–1983) taught at the Seminary from 1909 until 1963. His list of accomplishments is truly astounding: founder of the Seminary's Teachers Institute; rabbi of Kehillath Jeshurun, the Jewish Center, and the Society for the Advancement of Judaism; founder of the Young Israel movement, *The Reconstructionist* magazine, the Jewish Reconstructionist Foundation, and the Reconstructionist Rabbinical Seminary. Through his four hundred publications and his fifty-four years of teaching at the Seminary, he had a profound influence on American Jewry in general and on the Conservative movement in particular.[61]

At first glance, Kaplan would seem a very unlikely candidate to take an interest in practical *halakha*. He was ambivalent about or even hostile toward much of Jewish law. He wrote in his diary in 1905–6:

> The Talmud is tolerable considering the age they lived in and at times there really sparkles a gem of thought or morality, but the *poskim* . . . their modes of thought, their narrowness, their absolute slavery to the past. . . are below criticism, that I have to spend time upon these ridiculous laws, makes me chafe at my fate.
>
> . . . there is no doubt as to the deeply religious character which rites and ceremonies had for our fathers. But, on the other hand, there is equally no doubt as to the failure on the part of these same rites and ceremonies to call forth any authentic religious response in us.
>
> . . . Taking up the *Shulhan Arukh* [the standard code of Jewish law], let us see how much thereof we can retain.[62]

In 1933, he attended the divorce proceedings of two of his congregants at the *Beit Din* at the Seminary. He recorded in his diary that he found the proceedings "dismal and unimpressive." He felt they were quite anachronistic "in the manner of ancient formalities which are as much in place today as knee breeches and powdered wigs."[63] Furthermore, we know that he used to write on *Shabbat* and that he reluctantly allowed his four daughters to drive and smoke on *Shabbat*.[64]

Nevertheless, Kaplan wrote at least two responsa. In 1927, Rabbi Morris Silverman of Hartford, Connecticut, asked Kaplan whether it would be permissible to depict the human form in the new stained glass windows being designed for his congregation. Kaplan replied, "There is no reason at the present time for excluding the human form from being depicted in stained glass provided it does not represent the Diety or any specific personage whether hero, prophet or sage."[65]

In 1958, Kaplan was also asked by Ben-Gurion for his opinion regarding the halakhic status of a child whose Jewish father and non-Jewish mother wished to register him as Jewish. Not surprisingly, he does not discuss the halakhic aspects of the question. He rather enters into a historical disquisition in which he questions the Jewishness of the State of Israel: "It is the task of the Government to establish a modern state, not a Jewish State; an Israeli State, not a Jewish State." Nonetheless, he recommends caution in making such a drastic change in the definition of Jewishness. He suggests that the child of the non-Jewish mother be registered as a "Jewish resident."

> Should he, upon reaching maturity, chance to pledge himself formally to the observance of the religious rituals, he may be registered simply as "Jew".... In this way, the Government will fulfill its obligations without, thereby, infringing upon the accepted religious norms or touching upon questions relating to religious tradition.[66]

Yet despite his meager output of responsa, Kaplan actually played a decisive role in molding the makeup and functioning of the law committees of the Rabbinical Assembly that have persisted until today. At the United Synagogue convention in 1917, Louis Ginzberg proposed setting up a Committee on the Interpretation of Jewish Law that would reply to questions submitted by Conservative rabbis and laymen. That committee existed for ten years under the auspices of the United Synagogue, and though it had five members, Professor Ginzberg seems to have written all of the responsa himself.[67]

Kaplan and Ginzberg were lifelong combatants in their interpretation of Jewish law.[68] In 1918, Kaplan had argued against the establishment of Ginzberg's committee, arguing rather for the establishment of a genuine rabbinical court at the Seminary.[69] Their halakhic antagonism came to a head at the annual Rabbinical Assembly convention in Asbury Park, New Jersey, in July 1927. Ginzberg maintained that whatever changes were introduced by rabbis in the past were of an "unconscious nature." Those who advocated a deliberate break with the past "are undermining the very existence of Judaism." Turning to the rabbis in front of him, he thundered: "To you, I say, hands off the law!"[70] Kaplan stood up and replied that there are different types of changes. Contempt for the ancients would be bad, but deliberate change in order to deal with new and unprecedented aspects that could not have been contemplated was not really a break with the past.[71] Furthermore, at that very same convention, Rabbi Israel Goldstein took a pretty obvious stab at Ginzberg and his committee. In his address, he stated:

> In the experience of every rabbi, cases trivial as well as important come up during the year, which involve questions of Jewish Law. There ought to be provided at these conferences, a clearing house for the discussion of such cases. It is one thing to address a *She'ela* [question] and to receive a *Teshuba* [responsum] from an authority. It is quite another thing to be able to discuss both the *She'ela* and the *Teshuba*, and to discuss them in the company of peers *and not in the dumbfounding presence of a towering superior*. Even though the decision be unaltered, the discussion is itself a thing of value and certainly a valid source of stimulation and interest. To create occasions for such discussions, to keep a record of the discussions together with the decisions, would be going far

Rabbinical
Assembly conven-
tion, Asbury Park,
New Jersey, 1927.
The Seminary's
Jacob Hoschan-
der, Mordecai
Kaplan, Cyrus
Adler, and Israel
Davidson are first,
second, fourth,
and fifth from left
in the first row. In
the second row,
Louis Finkelstein
is third from left;
Max Arzt, at far
right. Morris D.
Levine stands
behind and to the
right of Finkel-
stein. *Photo by
Cole Co. Ratner
Center, JTS.*

towards making explicit whatever views and principles we hold in common, and toward helping us discover our like-mindedness as rabbis who purport to belong to the same party in Judaism.[72]

Indeed, that convention was preceded by a "round-robin" of letters from April through June 1927 between Kaplan and his followers—Rabbis Kadushin, Ruben-ovitz, Goldman, and Kohn—in which they debated whether to break away from the United Synagogue and the Rabbinical Assembly, to form "an informal committee on a question of law," or to influence the function and scope of the Committee on Jewish Law.[73] Finally, at the convention, a compromise was reached: the Law Com-mittee would be transferred from the United Synagogue to the Rabbinical Assem-bly, and the new committee would be composed of four conservative, four liberal, and two neutral rabbis. Kaplan proposed that the new body merely respond to the legal questions posed and that it possess no authority over its members.[74] The final resolution adopted at the 1927 convention reads:

> RESOLVED that a committee of ten be appointed representing the various tendencies in the Rabbinical Assembly in matters of religious and legal proce-dure. This committee shall have power to receive questions from the Rabbis, to discuss the same with them and with one another. Where a decision is unani-mous, it shall be issued as the authoritative opinion of the Rabbinical Assem-bly; otherwise the committee shall forward the majority as well as the dissent-ing opinions to the inquirer.[75]

Thus in July 1927, Kaplan and his supporters removed Ginzberg from his de facto position as chief *posek* of the Conservative movement. Ginzberg would continue to write responsa and influence the Committee on Jewish Law but not in an official capacity. More important, they set the ground rules for all subsequent Conservative law committees that remain in effect until today: under Rabbinical Assembly auspices, the committee represents all tendencies within the movement, and it disseminates simultaneous majority and minority opinions.[76] But Kaplan's influence on the Law Committee did not end in 1927. He was one of the four "liberals" appointed to the new Committee on Jewish Law. He continued to serve on this committee until 1937[77] and was appointed again in 1944–45.[78]

Finally, he played a role in the reorganization of the Committee on Jewish Law in 1948. As in 1927, the left wing of the Rabbinical Assembly wanted the Law Committee to serve as a vehicle for halakhic change, not just as a group of rabbis writing responsa. In May 1948, a vigorous debate took place at the annual convention of the Rabbinical Assembly.[79] Mordecai Kaplan was not present, but his followers emerged victorious. Boaz Cohen, a traditionalist, was replaced as chairman by Morris Adler, a liberal, and twenty-one members of the Committee on Jewish Law were not asked to serve on the new committee, which met for the first time on 16 December 1948. Mordecai Kaplan attended that meeting as a member of the "Board of Consultants of the Rabbinical Assembly Committee on Jewish Law," which seems to have been an ad hoc group created for the sole purpose of attending that one meeting. When Jacob Agus suggested that the name of the committee be changed to the "Committee on Jewish Law *and Standards*," Kaplan supported the suggestion since

> it implied that the task of the Committee would be not only to rule on questions of law, but also to deal with areas of Jewish practice [and] custom which for some members of the committee [do] not properly belong under the heading of Jewish law.[80]

The motion carried and that has been the name of the committee since 1948. Thus we see that Mordecai Kaplan, though not a *posek*, played a crucial role in molding the law committees of the Conservative movement from 1927 to 1948.

PROFESSOR LOUIS FINKELSTEIN (1895–1991) taught at the Seminary from 1920 until 1972 and was President and later Chancellor of the Seminary from 1940 until 1972.[81] At first glance, Finkelstein had all the makings of a *posek*. He was noted for his personal piety. His childhood friend Rabbi Solomon Goldman wrote to Finkelstein in honor of his fiftieth birthday: "Then there was your unswerving piety, a piety which was not burdensome but joyous."[82] His lifelong friend, Rabbi Simon Greenberg, wrote: "None of us could possibly fail to note . . . the meticulous care with which he observed not only the least of the ritual commandments of the Torah, but the ethical commandments as well."[83]

Furthermore, we know that he took the study of *halakha* very seriously. On 30 October 1916, he and his classmates Solomon Goldman and David Aronson addressed this letter "To the Faculty of the Jewish Theological Seminary":

> We, the undersigned, beg to call your attention to the fact that no provision has been made for an advanced course in codes during Seminary hours in the schedule for this year.
> Trusting that you will consider the matter, we are . . . [84]

We do not know whether the request was granted, but Finkelstein continued to study *halakha* privately with Louis Ginzberg and, in 1923, became the first Seminary graduate to receive traditional ordination (*hatarat hora'a*) from Professor Ginzberg.[85]

Later on, in 1941, Finkelstein contributed the article on "Ceremonial Law" to the *Universal Jewish Encyclopedia* in which he spelled out some of the basic laws and customs of Judaism.[86] Finally, in that same year, he published a ninety-page article entitled "The Beliefs and Practices of Judaism."[87] This monograph is a succinct and lucid introduction to Judaism that contains chapters on blessings, the synagogue and prayers, sabbath and festivals, life cycle, and the dietary laws. It was reprinted on numerous occasions[88] and was probably the best introduction to Judaism published by the Conservative movement before Isaac Klein's *Guide to Jewish Religious Practice* appeared in 1979.

Nevertheless, despite these publications and despite his service on the Committee on Jewish Law that will be described below, Finkelstein wrote few responsa and did not view himself as a *posek*. In 1942, Herbert Davis of Johnson and Johnson asked Finkelstein whether Jews would object to using hog intestines for surgical gut since there was a shortage of sheep intestines because of the war. Finkelstein immediately wrote to Professor Ginzberg and asked: "What do you think I should say to them?"[89] In 1946, a layman wrote to Finkelstein to inquire about his son's bar mitzvah portion; he promptly passed the letter on to Boaz Cohen for reply.[90] In 1956, a layman asked Finkelstein whether an Ark could be counted as the tenth man in a prayer quorum; that question was also referred to Cohen.[91]

In 1958, Finkelstein, like Lieberman and Kaplan, was asked by Ben-Gurion about registering children of mixed marriages as Jews. Finkelstein began his reply as follows:

> I must, first of all, remark that it is not my custom to offer opinions in halakhic matters. There are many scholars far more expert than I in this field; and therefore, I have no right to offer any decisions dealing with it. I will, therefore, discuss the issue you raise only from the point of view of its practical implications.[92]

What follows is, to all intents and purposes, a *teshuva*, but Finkelstein nonetheless did not view himself as a *posek*.

Even so, beginning in 1927 when the Committee on the Interpretation of Jewish Law was reorganized and transferred from the United Synagogue to the Rabbinical Assembly,[93] Finkelstein played an active role in that process as president of the Rabbinical Assembly (1928–30) and as a founding member of that law committee (1927–40).

In a series of addresses to the Rabbinical Assembly from 1927 to 1929, Finkelstein expressed his views on changing Jewish law. In 1927, he stated that permitting changes by individual rabbis and congregations is revolutionary, and revolutions can only be justified by being successful; if they bring Jews back to God and the Torah, they will take their place beside the Maccabean innovation of permitting wars of self-defense on *Shabbat* and beside the Tosafistic leniencies with regard to Gentile wine. But pending such proof of the value of these changes,

> and pending their acceptance by all Israel, some of us prefer to stand aside and watch like Eliezer at the well "steadfastly, holding our peace, to know whether the Lord hath made their way successful or not" [Genesis 24:21].
>
> As to the proposed innovations and new interpretations, there is none of us so bigoted as to refuse to cooperate with those who are attempting them, provided always that the ultimate purpose of the change is to strengthen the attachment of Israel to the whole of the Torah, and that it does not defeat its own end by striking at the fundamentals of Judaism [such as *Shabbat*].[94]

Yet in 1928, in an address entitled "Can Maimonides Still Guide Us?" Finkelstein takes a more liberal approach, advocating change through interpretation. After quoting Maimonides (*Moreh*, part 3, chapter 41) that only the *Sanhedrin* (high court of seventy-one judges) has the right to temporarily dispense with a *halakha*, Finkelstein comments:

> There is no *Bet Din Ha-Gadol* [high court of seventy-one judges] in existence . . . Yet the principle that the Law which is eternal may require modifications from time to time and place to place, is one which we may well consider, and which we may well ask our elder colleagues who are less inclined to [change] to ponder over. If Maimonides, living in Egypt in the twelfth century, could realize the need for changes in the Law . . . is it not also true that we, living in this late generation, with our many new problems, ought to make use of that power which is inherent in any rabbinic court of standing and recognition, to interpret the Law in accordance with the needs of the times?[95]

Finkelstein elaborated on this theme further in his presidential address on "Traditional Law and Modern Life" presented at the Rabbinical Assembly convention in July 1929. He stated that he was aware that our ancestors have heaped restriction upon restriction that are difficult for modern Jews to observe. Yet he rejects solving the problem by reorganizing the *Sanhedrin* both because it is unlikely to happen in our divided Jewish world and because it is unnecessary. We do not need to legislate *takkanot*, but to interpret inherited laws as our ancestors have always done.[96]

Finkelstein then states that the Jews of America really need an authoritative tribunal for the interpretation of our laws in order to limit the freedom exercised by individual rabbis. This, ideally, should be done with other groups of rabbis, but since this is not likely to occur,

> we feel justified in creating for ourselves a Committee on Jewish Law, to guide us in questions of ritual and religious adjustment. We feel we have among us men who by virtue of their learning and piety, their knowledge of general judicial science, and their experience in the world, can sit on such a committee.[97] . . . the organization of this committee on Jewish law is a matter of supreme importance. It came into being first as a compromise between opposing groups, but like many creations of the moment, it has risen far above its origin . . . it is, I think, destined to take an important place in the development of Jewish law.[98]

Louis Finkelstein himself was one of the "men" he spoke of above. He was appointed to the new committee in September 1927, as one of the four traditionalists on the committee of ten,[99] and he served until stepping down in 1940.[100]

The surviving minutes and correspondence of the Committee on Jewish Law show that Finkelstein did not attend the meetings on a regular basis, but he did participate in some of the committee's discussions, and he did write a few responsa or react to the responsa of others. He proposed inserting a clause in the *ketubah* in order to obviate the need for *halitza*.[101] He agreed to prepare a manual regarding marriage and divorce to be presented at one of the Rabbinical Assembly conventions, but it seems to have been prepared by Rabbi Ira Eisenstein.[102] He seems to have allowed a congregation to use a Protestant church for High Holy Day services under certain conditions; he corresponded with a rabbi about a certain case of *halitza*; he permitted a sanctuary to be used for secular purposes under certain circumstances; and he commented on a number of halakhic initiatives undertaken by the committee.[103]

Thus, despite his initial enthusiasm for the committee, Finkelstein made few contributions in the realm of *halakha*. And yet he made one important contribution in the realm of organization and politics. In 1930, Finkelstein stated in his presidential address to the Rabbinical Assembly that the committee needed more than ten members.[103a] On 13 November 1933, the committee decided to expand to twenty-three members. Two days later, Finkelstein wrote to Rabbi Elias Margolis, president of the Rabbinical Assembly, suggesting twenty-three names.[103b] All of those twenty-three rabbis were appointed to the committee a short time later.[103c] Thus, we see that Finkelstein excelled at working behind the scenes and in influencing the Law Committee on the political level. Indeed, this was a sign of things to come.

The third and last period of Finkelstein's involvement in Conservative *halakha* and the Law Committee began in 1949 and continued into the 1950s. As explained above, in 1948 there was an upheaval in the Committee on Jewish Law. Its name was changed and the chairman and many of its members were now left-wing disciples of Mordecai Kaplan.[104] Professor Finkelstein reacted at the next Rabbinical Assembly convention, in 1949. He announced that the Seminary faculty now

> after all these years, comes to you with the plea: We want to meet with you, as members of the Rabbinical Assembly, to think through the inter-relationships of our three institutions—the Rabbinical Assembly, the United Synagogue and the Seminary; we want to think through with you the philosophy of our movement and the fundamental principles which must guide us in our detailed decisions.[105]

Finkelstein apparently saw that the new Committee on Jewish Law and Standards was going to deal once again with the problem of the *agunah*, and he wanted to make sure that the right wing of the movement as represented by the Seminary Talmud professors would have a say. At the Rabbinical Assembly convention in 1951, Finkelstein proposed setting up a Joint Law Conference between the Rabbinical School faculty and the Rabbinical Assembly to come up with some solution to the problem of the *agunah*.[106] The Rabbinical Assembly approved this idea at its convention in 1952.[107]

In June 1952, Finkelstein went to Israel, as he explained in a letter,

> to see whether this Conference might become a World Conference . . . in the course of three years. This Conference would be attended not by people looking only to the past, but by men, who, grounded in the past like ourselves, have their main concern with the future. The establishment of such a World Conference is a basic need of our time, everywhere; and would be, in effect, the reestablishment of *Anshe Keneset Ha-Gedolah* [The Men of the Great Assembly], and just as that group built the bridge between Bible and Talmud, so our World Conference, given sufficient and effective guidance, can build the bridge between Talmudic and future Judaism.[107a]

Louis Finkelstein did not succeed in his mission; he no doubt met with the opposition of the Orthodox rabbinate in Israel. Yet this is a remarkable document for it shows that Finkelstein, who had published an entire book about the *Anshe Keneset Ha-gedolah* just two years before,[107b] actually wanted to revive that institution in order to solve the problem of the *agunah* as well as other pressing problems in Jewish law.

Yet despite his failure to establish a World Conference on Jewish Law, the initial results regarding the Joint Law Conference were swift and impressive. A Joint

Steering Committee was set up to coordinate the entire effort; a National *Beit Din*, to deal with Jewish marriage law; and a Joint Law Conference, to enact *takkanot* in order to solve the *agunah* problem.[108] Professor Finkelstein lobbied for the entire plan,[109] and it was approved by the convention along with Lieberman's above-mentioned *takkanah* for adding a paragraph to the *ketubah*.[110]

It is beyond the scope of this study to examine the subsequent history of the Joint *Beit Din* and the Joint Law Conference. Our purpose was to show Professor Finkelstein's influence on the entire enterprise; he initiated the idea in order to combat the left-wing faction in the new Committee on Jewish Law and Standards—and they knew it.[111] He got the Talmud faculty involved in a joint project with the Rabbinical Assembly for the first and only time. And he lobbied for approval of the plan at the Rabbinical Assembly convention and emerged victorious.

Thus we see that, as in the case of Mordecai Kaplan, Louis Finkelstein was not a *posek*. But he played an active role in the halakhic life of the Conservative movement in three ways—in the reorganization of the law committee in 1927 and 1933, as a member of that committee from 1927 to 1940, and as the initiator and prime mover behind the Joint Law Conference in the 1950s.

The Poskim: *Ginzberg and Cohen*[112]

PROFESSOR LOUIS GINZBERG (1873–1953) taught at the Seminary from 1902 until his death. Author of *Seridei Yerushalmi*, *Geonica*, *Legends of the Jews*, *Ginzei Schechter*, *Peirushim V'hidushim Bayerushalmi*, and more than five hundred other publications, Ginzberg is universally regarded as one of the foremost talmudists of the first half of the 20th century.[113]

However, there is one area of Ginzberg's scholarly output that has received scant attention: his responsa.[114] Although Lieberman, Finkelstein, and others have heaped praise upon his responsum regarding the use of unfermented wine for Jewish ceremonies that was published in 1922 (110–133),[115] and others made posthumous use of his final responsum regarding mixed pews in the synagogue,[116] most of Ginzberg's responsa were never published and have remained "as an unturned stone." A careful search[117] has now yielded all or part of more than a hundred of the responsa that Ginzberg wrote over a period of forty years (1913–53),[118] and they have recently been published.[119]

This cache is significant for a number of reasons. First, it disproves the common perception of Seminary professors described at the beginning of this study. Ginzberg not only felt that it was his "responsibility to provide halakhic guidance for his own day," but he was the founder and, for ten years, sole *posek* of the first Conservative law committee.

Second, all of Ginzberg's responsa except for two (on unfermented wine (110–133) and on artificial insemination (207–213)), were written in English.[120]

There are, of course, precedents for writing responsa in languages other than Hebrew. The *Geonim* wrote in Aramaic; they, along with R. Yitzhak Alfasi and Maimonides, wrote in Arabic; R. Yisrael Isserlein wrote in Yiddish;[121] and, in the 19th century, Orthodox and Reform rabbis wrote responsa in German.[122] However, Ginzberg was one of the first to write most of his responsa in English.[123] By so doing, he set the norm for all subsequent Conservative law committees in the United States, whose members wrote and continue to write most of their responsa in English.[124]

It is also worth noting the breakdown of Ginzberg's questioners. Of the ninety-three questioners, thirty-six were rabbis, twenty-four were laymen, seventeen were unidentified Jews, and sixteen were Christians. We can deduce three general conclusions from these figures: (1) They indicate active halakhic interest among both rabbis and laymen. (2) About one-sixth of Professor Ginzberg's responsa were written to non-Jews! This is undoubtedly the first time in history that a *posek* wrote formal responsa to questions posed by Christians. (3) Aside from the Orthodox community, the general public in the United States—Conservative and Reform rabbis, laymen, and Christians—saw in Ginzberg the highest halakhic authority or the most prominent halakhic figure who should be turned to in order to solve disputes between rabbis and between rabbis and congregants or to determine the authoritative "Jewish position" on the question under discussion.

Last, Ginzberg set a precedent that has been maintained until today in the Conservative movement. In a speech delivered at the United Synagogue convention in 1917, he proposed setting up a "Committee on the Interpretation of Jewish Law . . . to consist of five members learned in the law . . . to advise congregations and associates of the United Synagogue in all matters pertaining to Jewish law and custom" (43). This suggestion is surprising. Did Professor Ginzberg really need assistance? After all, he could have rendered halakhic decisions by himself, and in fact, he apparently wrote all of the responsa of that committee by himself![125] Perhaps he wanted to include other qualified rabbis in the halakhic process or he may have wanted to curb criticism that one rabbi is the *posek* for an entire movement. On the other hand, he may have been influenced by the Reform movement, which set up a similar law committee in 1907.[126] Regardless of his reasons, this practice of relying on law committees has persisted until today.

Now that we understand the general significance of this body of responsa, we should explain why Ginzberg decided to become an active *posek* and to write responsa. He explained his motives in this way:

> It is seen here in the appalling religious anarchy of the Jews where "Every man does that which is right . . . in his own eyes" [Judges 17:6]. . . . In no other country where some respect for legitimate authority still lingers among the Jews, are the religious conditions as chaotic as in ours. *Geonim* by the grace of butchers,

Rabbis by the authorization of successful wholesale dealers or manufacturers, theologians by the acclamation of still more successful bankers or lawyers and Academicians with degrees from nowhere, are only found in our country. Such a condition will exist as long as lack of authority will continue (42).[127]

Ginzberg went on to say that the true solution would be to appoint an "authoritative council . . . for the interpretation of Jewish law." But this was not feasible at the time. Since the United Synagogue allowed its members a good deal of autonomy, there would be no way for the committee to enforce its authority. He therefore recommended the formation of a Committee on the Interpretation of Jewish Law as explained above.[128]

If *pesak halakha* was so important to Louis Ginzberg, why did he not publish his numerous responsa? There is no clear-cut answer to this question, but it should be stressed that he did publish or summarize part of the responsa of the committee in articles and annual reports that appeared in the *United Synagogue Recorder* and elsewhere in the 1920s.[129] As for the majority of his responsa that were never published, he may have refrained from doing so because they were written in English. This hypothesis is supported by the fact that he did publish his lengthy responsum on unfermented wine (110–113 and Hebrew section 13–77), which was written in Hebrew. On the other hand, perhaps he did not want to take time away from his research projects and was therefore satisfied with writing the responsa and did not take the time to edit them for publication. Finally, he may have been hurt by the decision to set up an alternative law committee in 1927 and may have therefore stopped publishing his responsa.

What was Ginzberg's general approach to *halakha*? First, he was quite strict with regard to liturgical and synagogue-related issues, and here he was no doubt influenced by his pious Lithuanian upbringing.[130] This became evident on a number of occasions. In 1945, Mordecai Kaplan and three of his colleagues published the controversial *Sabbath Prayer Book*. In June of that year, the Orthodox *Agudas Harabonim* excommunicated Kaplan, and one of the young Orthodox rabbis burned a copy of the *siddur* (the prayer book) in public. In October of that year, Louis Ginzberg—along with Alexander Marx and Saul Lieberman—published a "Declaration" in a number of Hebrew and English periodicals, in which they opposed the *herem* (excommunication) and the burning of the *siddur*, but at the same time, condemned the *siddur*. They lamented the abbreviation of the *Shema*, the changes in the *Amidah*, its insipid introduction, the editing of the chapters of the Psalms and of *Lekha Dodi*, and more. They suggested a much more conservative alternative:

> We do not deny the need of the hour to attract the youth to the synagogue. But the royal road to the synagogue is the house of study and the dissemination of the Torah. However, as a temporary measure, it is proper to improve the exter-

nals of the *siddur*, to append at the conclusion of the service prayers in the vernacular, and even to repeat the *Shema* in English after the service (62).

In 1946, the Rabbinical Assembly published *The Sabbath and Festival Prayer Book*, edited by Rabbi Morris Silverman. The latter sent Professor Ginzberg a copy along with a dedication thanking him for his assistance. Ginzberg replied:

> I deeply appreciate your inscription in which you thanked me for my counsel and assistance. I wish, however, my counsel would have been more effective. Then the prayer book would have had less omissions and commissions of which I cannot approve (69).

In 1949, Ginzberg was asked to explain the phrase *mei raglayim* (urine) in the *Pittum Haketoret* prayer. At the beginning of his responsum, he remarks:

> Let me first tell you that your letter gave me a good deal of pleasure for the reason that I often have been asked by congregations whether this or that part of the Prayer Book might be left out. I am, therefore, particularly happy to see that you have in your congregation, people whose interest is in understanding the Prayer Book and not in changing it (82).

In 1947, Ginzberg reluctantly allowed one section of mixed pews in Chizuk Emunah synagogue in Baltimore in order to prevent the breakup of the synagogue. But after the fact, he wrote to the rabbi of the synagogue (in Hebrew):

> I am having second thoughts as to whether I should have interfered in the dispute in your synagogue. For you know that I am not one of those who likes "new things", and I have a special aversion to changes in the customs of the synagogue (99).[131]

Eli Ginzberg writes in *Keeper of the Law* that his father "hesitated at change," and elsewhere he speaks of his "growing conservatism."[132] These assessments bear revision in light of the entire corpus of Ginzberg's responsa. Aside from liturgy, where he was clearly a conservative, Ginzberg seems to have judged each case on its own merits and frequently arrived at a lenient decision. He permitted late Friday evening services as was customary in many congregations (109). He disproved the approach of the *Magen Avraham*, a distinguished decisor, and allowed the use of grape juice for *kiddush* in order to prevent the desecration of God's name caused by rabbis who became rich from selling wine during Prohibition (110–133). He permitted the use of a radio that had been turned on before *Shabbat* (134). He asserted that peas and green beans are not *kitniyot* (legumes) and may therefore be eaten on *Pesah* (136). He allowed the alteration of synagogue melodies, ignoring the opposition of two important authorities (138). He allowed the conversion of a Gentile woman who was already married to a Jew and permitted the woman to immerse in the *mikveh* (ritual bath) while wearing a loose-fitting bathing suit (170–171). He allowed children in mourning to attend music classes and assemblies at their public schools (202–203). He forbade performing a wedding on *Hol Hamoed* (the intermediate days of the Festivals) as decreed by the *Mishnah*, but allowed it in a case where the groom was a soldier setting sail for combat in Europe (220–222). He also helped Boaz Cohen prepare an "agency appointment" which would enable a *beit din* to write a *get* should a husband disappear in battle (226–228). Finally, he allowed women to serve on synagogue boards despite the opposition of Maimonides to women holding public office (270–271).

On the other hand, Ginzberg occasionally prohibited something not because it is technically forbidden by Jewish law but in order to preserve the "spirit of the law" or to prevent improper behavior such as *marit ayin* or *hillul hashem*.[133] He therefore prohibited Cantor Richard Tucker from working simultaneously as an opera singer because of *marit ayin*. Or as Ginzberg put it:

> There is no law prohibiting a rabbi from appearing in a cabaret, but do you think that any congregation would seriously consider having a cabaret singer as a rabbi? . . . I am . . . sure that people would find it quite strange to see their cantor one day recite the *Neilah* prayer and the following day, sing a love duet with some lady (75).[134]

Similarly, Ginzberg prohibited building a synagogue on *Shabbat* with the help of a Gentile contractor even though, technically, one can find a way around this prohibition:

> But I object to any synagogue group taking such advantage of legal loopholes . . . [We must consider] the effect of such conduct on all beholders, Jews and Gentiles alike . . . My decision, therefore, becomes not a matter of the letter, but of the spirit, and I urge the questioners not to allow this obvious desecration of our day of rest (108).

He ruled that the U. S. Army may require a Jewish soldier to cut off his beard with a scissor so that observant Jews would not use this as an excuse to avoid army service (166). Finally, and for the very same reason, he allowed a *kohen* (member of the priestly tribe) to serve in the army despite the fear of coming into contact with dead bodies (200).

Professor Ginzberg was also concerned about the unity of the Jewish people. On two occasions he expressed opposition to the use of an organ in the synagogue and on both he explained that, in addition to the halakhic problems involved, he was afraid that American Jewry would cut itself off from world Jewry and therefore this innovation should be avoided (47 and 135).

In his classic portrait of his beloved ancestor, the Vilna Gaon, Ginzberg quotes him as saying: "Do not regard the views of the *Shulhan Arukh* as binding if you think that they are not in agreement with those of the Talmud."[135] It is obvious from many places in his responsa that Louis Ginzberg took this advice to heart. In his opinion, the *halakha* is determined by the Talmud and the *rishonim* (early authorities) and not by *midrashim* (later customs) or the *aharonim* (later authorities). In his responsum on artificial insemination, Ginzberg writes at the end of the question:

> And the rabbi who asked me replied at length on the basis of the *aharonim* . . . but since it has always been my practice to base myself on the words of the Talmud and *rishonim*, I have avoided quoting his words and discussing them (Hebrew section, 85).

This approach is echoed at the end of the same responsum: "All of the above is sufficient to prove that we have not found a peg in the Talmud or in the *rishonim* on which to hang a lenient ruling in this serious matter [ibid., 126]."

Previously, in the same responsum, he rejects using the *Alpha Beta d'ven Sira* as a halakhic source:

> Yet, in any case, one cannot decide *halakha* on the basis of this legend . . . for we have learned in *Yerushalmi Peah* 2:6 [fol. 17a] . . . "One does not learn [*halakha*] . . . from *haggadot* [legends or non-legal material]." If they said this about Talmudic *haggadot*, how much moreso is it true regarding a legend from *Alpha Beta d'ven Sira* which is a late work . . . After we have seen that it is difficult to rely on a legend from *Ben Sira* in such a serious matter . . . let us see what the [Babylonian] Talmud has to say [on our subject] because "we are dependent on its word" (ibid., 99).

A similar approach lies behind his permission for a man to marry a woman whose name is identical to his mother's: "There is nothing in Jewish law prohibiting a man to marry a woman whose name is the same as the man's mother" (214). This particular custom is based on the Testament attributed to Rabbi Judah the Pious and from there it passed to *Pithei Teshuvah* and other authorities,[136] but in Professor Ginzberg's opinion these sources are clearly not "Jewish law." His lengthy responsum on the use of unfermented wine for *kiddush* is based primarily on the Talmud and the *rishonim* and opposes the opinion of the *Magen Avraham* by a careful analysis of the *rishonim* (110–133). Indeed, after refuting the *Magen Avraham* by quoting three earlier works on customs, he explicitly states: "And even though these three are worthy of being relied upon even when there is no emergency, it is not the way of the Torah to decide *halakha* according to books of customs in cases where we have strong support in the words of the *rishonim*" (Hebrew section, 62). Finally, he states in an address delivered in 1921: "The Talmud, though never promulgated as a code of law became the standard of Jewish law. . . . After the Talmud, there is no authority in the real sense of the word" (46–47).[137]

Ginzberg also appears in his responsa as a passionate defender of his people willing to engage in lengthy apologetics against anti-Semites.[138] One is impressed anew by the breadth of his knowledge and his prodigious memory[139] and is touched by his ability to write a responsum that is truly pastoral in tone.[140] Last, Ginzberg is one of the first *poskim* whose responsa are clearly influenced by Jewish *Wissenschaft* both in form and in content.[141]

Many scholars have shown that the responsa literature is a gold mine for historians and sociologists.[142] The responsa of Louis Ginzberg are no exception. They supply the historian with much important data about American Jewry between the years 1913 and 1953. Interestingly enough, "there is nothing new under the sun," and many of the questions asked then continue to be asked today.

Professor Ginzberg was asked about the sale of a synagogue,[143] synagogue construction on *Shabbat*,[144] women in the synagogue,[145] the organ,[146] art in the synagogue,[147] the direction of the synagogue,[148] dances in the synagogue basement,[149] and the dual use of a synagogue basement as a *beit midrash* (study and prayer hall) and social hall.[150] He received many enquiries about intermarriage,[151] apostates,[152] and unaffiliated Jews.[153] Then, as now, American Jews were greatly influenced by non-Jewish funeral customs, and Ginzberg attempted to combat this phenomenon.[154] Many Jews served in the U. S. Army and he therefore dealt with halakhic problems that arose in connection with World War I, World War II, and the Korean War.[155] Then, as now, there were tensions between the need for a *get* and a civil divorce.[156] Then, as now, there were ignorant rabbis or rabbis who openly transgressed Jewish law.[157] Then, as now, there were laymen who did not trust their rabbi and therefore addressed their questions to a higher authority.[158] Finally, these responsa teach us that the term "Conservative Judaism" was in use in 1924.[159]

Thus, we see that, unlike the common perception of the Seminary professor described at the beginning of this study, Louis Ginzberg did not "ignore the halakhic needs of the contemporary community." On the contrary, he founded the first Conservative law committee, chaired it for ten years, wrote most (or all) of its responsa, and continued to write responsa and provide halakhic guidance for the rest of his life.

BOAZ COHEN (1899–1968) is the last Seminary professor we shall study. Cohen taught codes at the Seminary from 1925 until his death and also served as assistant librarian from 1925 to 1950.[160] He was the author of more than 125 publications including *Kuntress Hateshuvot*, *Law and Tradition in Judaism*, and *Jewish and Roman Law*.[161] But aside from his duties at the Seminary and his scholarly publications, Cohen was *the* pivotal halakhic figure in the Conservative movement from 1932 to 1968. First of all, he was the secretary of the Central *Beit Din* of the Rabbinical Assembly, which was organized in May 1932 and continued to function at least until the 1950s.[162] He continued to perform a large number of *gittin* until his death. An idea of the number can be gleaned from the fact that in August 1966, he ordered 150 copies of a "Certificate of Divorce" from the Seminary administration.[163]

In addition, Cohen was probably the most prolific *posek* ever produced by the Conservative movement. This aspect of his career began in 1932 when he was appointed secretary of the Committee on Jewish Law of the Rabbinical Assembly, after which he served as its chairman from 1940 to 1948.[164] But the word "served" does not adequately describe his contribution to that committee because, in a sense, he *was* the committee, and without his efforts it could not have functioned. His contributions as secretary were repeatedly praised by Rabbi Julius Greenstone, who chaired the committee until 1936.[165] Rabbi Louis Epstein, his successor, expressed his appreciation "to the members of the Committee, consisting, outside of the Chairman, of the following: our Secretary, Dr. Boaz Cohen, *constituting in himself half of the Committee.*"[166] This is confirmed by Cohen's own testimony in March 1947 toward the end of his tenure as chairman:

> While the Committee on Jewish Law met only once since the beginning of the current year, *the business of the Committee is a daily preoccupation of the Chairman*, as hardly a day passes without one inquiry or another on this or that phase of Jewish law and ritual.[167]

In December 1948, the committee was reorganized and renamed, as mentioned above.[168] Rabbi David Aronson, the president of the Rabbinical Assembly, subsequently thanked "Professor Boaz Cohen for the loyal, scholarly and distinguished service he rendered to the Assembly . . . for seventeen years."[169] But Boaz Cohen did not stop writing responsa in 1948. He continued to write responsa to his colleagues and former pupils throughout the world as we shall see below. This was because he already had a reputation as *the posek* of the Conservative movement. As one Jewish woman wrote to Cohen in 1959: "Rabbi Baruch Levine referred me to you as the leading authority on Jewish law codes."[170]

When Professor Cohen died in 1968, his disciple and colleague Edward Gershfield stated that he had written "*thousands* of opinions, including many lengthy treatises, on questions of Jewish law which were brought before him."[171] This is apparently an exaggeration, but Boaz Cohen definitely wrote *hundreds* of responsa that have survived in various forms. Most of the responsa that he wrote for the Committee on Jewish Law between 1932 and 1948 are preserved in a typed volume of responsa edited by Cohen and/or Michael Higger during the 1940s. It is mentioned seven times between 1944 and 1947,[172] but its publication was probably aborted by the revolution in the Law Committee in 1948. The new, more left-wing members probably had no interest in publishing such a "conservative" volume of responsa, and Boaz Cohen himself, no longer on the committee, may have been too insulted to care. A complete copy as well as a partial copy of that volume have survived.[173] Unfortunately, Cohen or Higger removed all names, dates, and places when editing the volume! This is proven by some of the responsa that have survived in their original form with markings indicating what the secretary was supposed to type.[174] As a result, we know that Cohen's many responsa are included in that volume, but we don't know in many cases which responsa are his.[175]

Yet even without these, 274 complete or partial responsa[176] have been preserved in the Boaz Cohen archives[177] relating to a wide array of halakhic problems and topics. Sixty-one relate to *Orah Hayyim* with a heavy emphasis on kashering dishes (seven responsa) and synagogue architecture (seventeen). One hundred thirty-four relate to *Yoreh Deah* with a heavy emphasis on *kashrut* (eighteen), conversion and adoption (twenty-four), and mourning (forty-eight!). There are forty-two responsa related to *Even Haezer*—of which almost half (nineteen) are related to divorce—and an additional nine are devoted to *Hoshen Mishpat*. Finally, there are nineteen miscellaneous responsa on diverse topics such as the pillars called *Yakhin* and *Boaz*, what Daniel and his companions ate, electronic eavesdropping, and rabbinic sources on the importance of supporting orphans.[178]

Most of Cohen's responsa are in English, though at least six are in Hebrew and two in Yiddish. The questioners are mostly rabbis, but there are a number of questions from cantors, executive directors, lawyers, doctors, and women. As in the responsa of Louis Ginzberg described above, there are also questions from non-Jews, including a few professors, a monsignor from Brooklyn, a pastor from Nebraska and a lay person from New Zealand, and from non-Jewish organizations such as *Ave Maria* magazine, Standard Oil Company, and the Consumer Services Division of the City of New York.

It is worth noting that a number of the questions in Cohen's papers were addressed to the "Jewish Theological Seminary of America" and were then passed on to him for reply since he was the acknowledged halakhic expert.

The responsa are written in three basic styles. Frequently, Cohen replies with a simple answer without quoting any sources at all. Thus, a young woman asked whether she and her girlfriend could use one set of glass dishes for meat and milk. Boaz Cohen wrote: "In reply to your letter of September 20th, I wish to inform you that it is not permissible to use glass dishes for both dairy and meat."[179] He does not quote any sources nor does he explain that there are various points of view on the subject[180] nor does he try to "soften the blow." He simply rules that it is forbidden.

The second type of responsum indicates that there are various points of view and/or refers to a few basic sources. Thus, when he was asked about the proper date for a *yahrzeit* (the anniversary of a death) when the burial does not take place on the day of death, he replied:

> With regard to the observance of the *Jahrzeit*, there are several opinions recorded by the later authorities. Some authorities hold that the *Jahrzeit* is always observed on the anniversary of the day of death, others are of the opinion that if the burial was delayed a few days then the *first Jahrzeit* only is

observed on the anniversary of the day of burial, but the subsequent *Jahrzeit*s are observed on the anniversary of the day of death. For full discussion of this point, see the *Shak* and *Taz* to *Yoreh Deah* 402, 12. A summary of their views is given by the *Beer Heteb* note 11, cf. also *Pithe Teshubah* note 3.[181]

In such cases, Cohen assumes that the questioner wants to know some of the sources so that he can study the subject further on his own.

Lastly, Cohen wrote a number of full-blown, detailed responsa in which he exhibits his mastery of a wide array of sources including the Bible, Philo, Josephus, the Talmud, *Geonim*, medieval responsa and codes, and modern scholarship.[182]

Several general principles shaped Cohen's approach to Jewish law: (1) The Talmud enjoys a unique position in Jewish law and, like the Bible, its authority is indisputable.[183] (2) Jewish law has undergone a long development and must, therefore, be studied historically.[184] (3) Jewish law needs to be brought into harmony with contemporary conditions. This must be done through "interpretation, not by innovation or abrogation."[185] (4) Interpretation must be based on tradition (*matnita*) and not on pure reason (*sevara*),[186] and must be entrusted to people "versed in the *Halakhah* and sworn to the conservation of Jewish law."[187] (5) Nevertheless, "we must recognize that there are limits to genuine interpretation and that we cannot attempt to remedy all evils."[188] (6) We are anxious to solve the problem of the *agunah*, but we must not make a unilateral Conservative *takkanah* which would separate Conservative Judaism from the Jewish people.[189] (7) Finally, Cohen considered himself neither strict nor lenient: "The determining factor in our decisions is the question whether we are preserving genuine Jewish religious values or not."[190] Thus, he was lenient on autopsies but strict on reinterment of the dead; resigned to mixed seating but strongly opposed to the introduction of the organ into the synagogue.[191]

In light of Cohen's conservative approach to Jewish law, it is not surprising that his more left-wing colleagues deposed him as chairman of the Committee on Jewish Law in 1948.[192] In any case, we have demonstrated that Cohen was a prolific *posek* with a distinct writing style and legal philosophy.

Conclusion

By examining the halakhic activity of six Seminary professors, we have learned that, as usual, reality is far more complex than our stereotypes would allow. We have seen three very different attitudes toward *pesak halakha* in the period under discussion: Schechter and Lieberman did not view themselves as *poskim*. Kaplan and Finkelstein were not *poskim*, but played a crucial political role in molding and remolding the law committees of the Conservative movement. Finally, Ginzberg and Cohen were active *poskim* who dominated Conservative *halakha* for more than half a century. It now remains for future historians to investigate the subsequent influence of Seminary professors on *halakha* in the Conservative movement.[193]

1. I remember hearing this statement quite frequently at the time. For general criticism by Seminary graduates of the faculty for not teaching them how to deal with the "real world," see Marshall Sklare, *Conservative Judaism: An American Religious Movement*, 2d ed. (New York: Schocken Books, 1972), pp. 181–82, 190; Charles Liebman, *American Jewish Year Book* 69 (1968), pp. 50–53; Neil Gillman, *Proceedings of the Rabbinical Assembly* 48 (1986), pp. 41– 46; idem., *Conservative Judaism* 43, no. 2 (winter 1990–91): pp. 3–11; idem., *Conservative Judaism: The New Century* (West Orange, N.J.: Behrman House, Inc., 1993), pp. 199–201.

2. *Proceedings of the Rabbinical Assembly* 48 (1986), p. 83. I concurred in an address published in *Eit La'asot* 2 (1989): p. 38, which appeared in English translation in *Conservative Judaism* 46, no. 3 (spring 1994): pp. 37–38. Professor Schorsch and I later changed our opinion in a conversation we had in Jerusalem in the summer of 1992.

3. Gillman, *Conservative Judaism*, p. 79.

4. See Norman Bentwich, *Solomon Schechter, A Biography* (Philadelphia: Jewish Publication Society, 1938), chap. 8.

5. See below, note 160, for literature about Cohen.

6. Lastly, there were technical reasons for stopping at this date. After Boaz Cohen, the next pivotal halakhic activist on the Seminary faculty was Seymour Siegel (1927–88). Since all of his papers were donated to St. Lawrence University in upstate New York—see *Conservative Judaism* 45, no. 1 (fall 1992): p. 81—I have not yet been able to examine them and therefore decided it was preferable to end this study in 1968.

7. For Schechter, I consulted Adolph Oko, *Solomon Schechter: A Bibliography* (Cambridge: Cambridge University Press, 1938); Bentwich, *Solomon Schecter*; Abraham Karp, *Conservative Judaism: The Legacy of Solomon Schechter*, unpublished compilation, JTS Library; and Bernard Mandelbaum, *The Wisdom of Solomon Schechter* (New York: Burning Bush Press, 1963). For Lieberman, I consulted the extensive bibliography listed below in note 35 and the small collection of his correspondence that has been preserved in the Saul Lieberman Archives at the Seminary.

8. The only full-length biography remains Bentwich, *Solomon Schecter*. Also see Cyrus Adler in the *American Jewish Year Book* 5677 (1916–17) vol. 18, pp. 24–67; *Encyclopædia Judaica*, vol. 14, cols. 948–50; and Pamela Nadell, *Conservative Judaism in America: A Biographical Dictionary and Sourcebook* (Westport, Conn.: Greenwood Press, 1988), pp. 222–27. It is worth noting that Schechter himself used the phrase "Conservative Judaism" on numerous occasions. See Solomon Schechter, *Seminary Addresses and Other Papers* (New York: Burning Bush Press, 1959), p. 231, and Bentwich, *Solomon Schechter*, pp. 98, 178, 192, 340, and cf. below, note 159.

9. See Schecter, *Seminary Addresses*, pp. 6, 21–22, 85–86, 114, 128–29, 132–34, 171, 178–80, 200–01, 203, 226, 228, 231–32; Bentwich, *Solomon Schechter*, pp. 181, 184, 191–192, 207, 209, 210, 220, 237–38, 288–89, 293–97, 340; Mandelbaum, *Wisdom*, pp. 6, 112; Solomon Schechter, *Studies in Judaism*, First Series (Philadelphia: Jewish Publication Society, 1915), pp. 243 ff., and Third Series, Philadelphia, 1924, p. 74; Solomon Schechter, *Aspects of Rabbinic Theology*, 2d ed. (New York: Schocken Books, 1961), pp. 148ff; and Solomon Schechter, "An American Jewish Synod," *The American Israelite* 51, no. 42 (21 April 1905): pp. 4–5; also in *The American Hebrew* 76, no. 22 (28 April 1905): pp. 697–99.

10. Schechter, *Seminary Addresses*, p. 22.

11. For anthologies of his bon mots and important statements, see *JTS Students' Annual* 3, 1916, pp. 23–43; Abraham Karp, *Legacy*, pp. 15–23, 32–33, 37; and Mandelbaum, *Wisdom*.

12. Schechter, *Seminary Addresses*, p. 6.

13. Ibid., p. 85, and cf. Bentwich, *Solomon Schechter*, pp. 184–85.

14. Schechter, *Seminary Addresses*, p. 134.

15. Bentwich, *Solomon Schechter*, pp. 296–97.

16. Ibid., p. 181, and Schechter, *Seminary Addresses*, pp. 128–29. See, however, David Acker-man, "A Not Too Distant Mirror: The Seminary Rabbinical School Curriculum," *Conservative Judaism* 44, no. 4 (summer 1992): p. 50, who asserts that the requirement for students to observe Jewish law was absent from the 1902 curriculum and only reappeared in 1913.

17. Ibid., p. 51.

18. Schechter, *Seminary Addresses*, p. 19.

19. Ibid., pp. 57–59. And cf. below, note 84, for further proof of this *lacuna* in the Seminary curriculum.

20. For a copy of his *semicha* (ordination certificate) from Isaac Hirsch Weiss, see *JTS Students' Annual* 3 (1916), p. 13.

21. Bentwich, *Solomon Schechter*, p. 41.

22. Ibid., p. 198.

23. Mel Scult, *Judaism Faces the Twentieth Century: A Biography of Mordecai M. Kaplan* (Detroit: Wayne State University Press, 1993), p. 223.

24. *The Jewish Chronicle*, 13 January 1888, p. 6, quoted by Bentwich in *Solomon Schechter*, p. 71. Emphasis added.

25. *American Hebrew* 69, no. 4 (14 June 1901): p. 107, which was reprinted by Abraham Karp, *Legacy*, p. 62. This item is *not* listed in Oko's *Bibliography*. My thanks to Professor Karp for this reference as well as for allowing me to use him as a sounding board for some of the ideas in this study. For one more halakhic ruling by Schechter, see Jonathan Sarna, "The Debate Over Mixed Seating in the American Synagogue," in *The American Synagogue: A Sanctuary Transformed*, ed. Jack Wertheimer (Cambridge: Cambridge University Press, 1987), pp. 379–80. My thanks to David Fine for this reference.

26. The letter is located in JTS Records, Record Group 3B, faculty box 1, Moses Hyamson file. Hyamson (1862–1949) was born and raised in England where he served as a rabbi and *dayyan* until 1913 when he became "Rabbi for Life" of Congregation Orach Chaim in New York City. In 1915, he was appointed professor of codes at the Seminary, a position he held until 1940 when he was appointed professor emeritus. He is best known as the translator of Bahya's *Hovot Halevavot* and of *Sefer Hamadah* of the *Mishneh Torah* by Maimonides. He is not included in this study because he was a vice-president of the Union of Orthodox Jewish Congregations of America and clearly did not view himself as a Conservative Jew. For his biography, see *The Universal Jewish Encyclopedia* (New York: Universal Jewish Encyclopedia Co., Inc., 1941) vol. 5, p. 509, and the testimonial booklet published on 10 October 1937 in honor of his seventy-fifth birthday, which is in Record Group 3B, ibid. For his reactions to Kaplan's *Judaism as a Civilization*, see Scult, *Mordecai Kaplan*, pp. 345–46.

27. Schechter studied there from 1874 to 1879. See Bentwich, *Solomon Schechter*, pp. 35–41 and the literature cited there.

28. See *Bet Talmud*, vol. 4 (5645), pp. 65–72, 169–72, 257–65.

29. "Mitwirkung von Frauen beim Gottesdienste," *Hebrew Union College Annual* 8–9 (1931–32), pp. 518–21.

30. Neil Gillman, *Conservative Judaism* 43, p. 4, and cf. his remarks in *Proceedings of the Rabbinical Assembly* 48, pp. 41 ff.

31. Schechter, *Seminary Addresses*, p. 16 and cf. p. 214.

32. Ibid., p. 18.

33. Ibid., pp. 131–32. Also see Bentwich, *Solomon Schechter*, p. 101, where Schechter states that "what is wanting in America is a scientifically-trained Rabbi class."

34. Schechter, *Seminary Addresses*, p. 232.

35. There is, as yet, no full-length biography of Professor Lieberman. For the time being, see the following (in chronological order): Alexander Marx, *Proceedings of the Rabbinical*

Assembly 12 (1948) pp. 259–71; Eliezer Shimshon Rosenthal, *Proceedings of the American Academy for Jewish Research* 31 (1963), pp. 1–71 (Hebrew section); Tovia Preschel, *Hadoar* 42, no. 23 (11 Nissan 5723): pp. 370–71 and 381–84, also in *R. Shaul Lieberman U'foalo Hamadai*, (New York), 5723, 36 pp. (and cf. that entire issue of *Hadoar* for additional articles); *Encyclopædia Judaica*, vol. 11, cols. 218–20; Tovia Preschel, *Jewish Book Annual* 30, (5733), pp. 69–72; Gilbert Epstein, *Proceedings of the Rabbinical Assembly* 37 (1976), p. 90; Tovia Preschel, "R. Shaul Lieberman: Ishiyuto U'foalo Hamadai," *Hadoar* 56, no. 15 (Shevat 5737): pp. 229–32 also in offprint, 5738, 32 pp. (and cf. that issue of *Hadoar* for additional articles); ibid., no. 16, p. 252; ibid., no. 17, pp. 258–59; *Ma'ariv*, 24 March 1983, p. 15; *New York Times*, 24 March 1983, p. B10; Yitzhak Refael, *Sinai* 93 (5743): pp. 91–92; Paltiel Birnbaum, *Hadoar* 62, no. 20 (2 Iyar 5743): p. 318; David Weiss Halivni, ibid., vol. 62, no. 25 (15 Sivan 5743): p. 404; David Rosenthal, *Cathedra* 28 (Tammuz 5743): pp. 3–16; Dov Zlotnick, *Proceedings of the Rabbinical Assembly* 45 (1983), pp. 202–7, also in *Cornerstone* 1, no. 1 (5748): pp. 56–60; Phillip Sigal, *Judaism* 33, no. 2 (spring 1984): pp. 135–45; Shamma Friedman, *Jewish Studies* 23 (winter 5744): pp. 23–37 (in Hebrew); E. E. Urbach, Sh. Abramson, H. Z. Dimitrovsky and Shamma Friedman, *L'zikhro shel Shaul Lieberman* (Jerusalem: *The Israel Academy of Sciences and Humanities Annual*, 5744), p. 55; Seymour Siegel, *Jewish Book Annual* 41 (5744): pp. 163–67; Richard Kalmin, *Proceedings of the Rabbinical Assembly* 48 (1986), pp. 145–49; David Weiss Halivni, *Conservative Judaism* 38, no. 2 (spring 1986): pp. 5–9 (excerpted in *Cornerstone*, ibid., pp. 51–52); Norman Lamm, *Washington Jewish Week*, 27 March 1986, pp. 20–21; M. B. Lerner, *Te'udah* 4 (5746): p. 113; Yitzhak Gilat, *Bitzaron*, New Series, vol. 9 (summer-fall 5747–48): pp. 49–54; William Berkowitz, ed., *In Praise of the Master: Tributes to Professor Saul Lieberman*, (New York: American Jewish Heritage Committee, 1987), (31 unnumbered pages); Elie Wiesel, "Lessons in Devotion," in a pamphlet in possession of the author; Nadell, *Conservative Judaism*, pp. 178–80; Elijah Schochet, *Cornerstone*, ibid., pp. 53–55; Solomon Spiro, *Conservative Judaism* 46, no. 4 (summer 1994): pp. 64–84: Dov Zlotnick in Saul Lieberman, *Greek in Jewish Palestine/Hellenism in Jewish Palestine* (New York and Jerusalem: Jewish Theological Seminary of America, 1994), pp. vii–xxii. For a short autobiographical vignette, see Saul Lieberman in *Minsk Ir Va'em* (Israel: Hakibbutz Hame'uhad, 5735) vol. 1, pp. 516–19, also in Saul Lieberman, *Mekhkarim B'torat Eretz Yisrael* (Jerusalem: Magnes, 5751), pp. 608–11.

36. See E. S. Rosenthal, p. 1: "... until we can almost say about him: there was no king like him before him according to his custom and his method." Yitzhak Rafael, p. 92, writes: "I am not authorized nor do I dare assert that Prof. Rabbi Shaul Lieberman z"l was the greatest Talmud scholar in recent generations, but it seems that no one would attempt to dispute this assertion." Elijah Schochet, p. 55, states: "Rabbenu Eliyahu, the *Gaon* of Vilna, was born on the first day of Pesah, 1720. Rabbenu Sha'ul our own *Gaon*, was laid to rest on the eve of Pesah, 1983. Between them there was no other like Saul Lieberman." David Weiss Halivni, p. 8, states: "Professor Lieberman was not only a *yahid b'doro*, unique in his generation, but a *yahid b'dorotav*, unique in all generations." Jacob Neusner wrote to Lieberman on 10 December 1981: "I am enjoying *Hayerushalmi Kipshuto* so much that I wanted to tell you so ... It reminds me of why I have long ago concluded you are the greatest exegete of rabbinic texts of the 20th century and among the true greats among the ones I have studied and used—of all times." See Saul Lieberman Archives, box 6, "N-O" file.

37. See Tovia Preschel in *Sefer Hazikaron L'rabi Shaul Lieberman*, ed. Shamma Friedman, (New York and Jerusalem: Jewish Theological Seminary of America, 5753), pp. 1–28, for a complete bibliography of Lieberman's writings. The items in question are nos. 75, 114, and 220. His *ketubah* (see below) is, for some reason, not even listed in that bibliography. It is rather ironic—but telling—that Lieberman's best-known contribution to Conservative

halakha is entirely missing from the bibliography of his writings!

38. Shamma Friedman, personal communication to the author in Jerusalem, 23 December 1994.

39. There were, however, occasions when Lieberman answered individual halakhic questions. On 25 June 1941, he answered a question intended for Professor Boaz Cohen since the latter was away on vacation. See Boaz Cohen Archives, box 5, "Marriage—from R. Teller" file. Professor Elliot Dorff informed the author in February 1995 that he once sent Lieberman a halakhic question and received a written reply.

40. See below, after note 130. Jacob J. Weinstein, *Solomon Goldman: A Rabbi's Rabbi* (New York: Ktav Publishing House, Inc., 1973), p. 45, claims that Lieberman refused to get into the elevator with Kaplan after the publication of the Reconstructionist prayer book. But that report bears verification, because Weinstein has a tendency to exaggerate.

41. The Conservative movement was obsessed with this dilemma from 1930 until 1970. See David Golinkin, *An Index of Conservative Responsa and Practical Halakhic Studies: 1917-1990*, (New York: Rabbinical Assembly, 1992), pp. 38–40, and Sidney Schwarz, *Conservative Judaism* 36, no. 1 (fall 1982): pp. 37–44.

42. For Finkelstein's role in forming that body, see below, note 104 ff.

43. See *Proceedings of the Rabbinical Assembly* 17 (1953), pp. 75-79, for Lieberman's proposal and vol. 18 (1954), pp. 64–68, for the actual *takkanah*.

44. See Emanuel Rackman, *Jewish Week*, 8 May 1987, p. 28, along with Wolfe Kelman's three-page reaction which was, apparently, never printed. My thanks to Professor Jack Wertheimer for sending me a copy of Rabbi Kelman's letter.

45. For Orthodox reactions and actual court cases, see A. Leo Levin and Meyer Kramer, *New Provisions in the Ketubah* (New York: Yeshiva University, 1955); R. Eliezer Waldenberg, *Tzitz Eliezer*, vol. 5, "Petihah," paragraph 7; Norman Lamm, *Tradition* 2, no. 1 (1959): pp. 93–119; David and James Ellenson, *Conservative Judaism* 35, no. 3 (spring 1982): pp. 35–42; Irwin Haut, *Divorce in Jewish Law and Life* (New York: Sepher-Hermon Press, 1983), pp. 77–80; and Shlomo Riskin, *Women and Jewish Divorce* (Hoboken, N.J.: Ktav Publishing House, Inc., 1989), pp. 137–38.

46. This correspondence was compiled by Baruch Litvin and edited by Sidney Hoenig as *Jewish Identity: Modern Responsa and Opinions* (New York: Philipp Feldheim, Inc., 1965).

47. Ibid., p. 236.

48. For the history of the ordination debate at the Seminary, see Robert Gordis, *Judaism* 33, no. 1 (winter 1984): pp. 6–12; Arnon Bruckstein, *The Ordination of Women as Rabbis and Cantors in the Conservative Movement* (in Hebrew), (master's thesis, Hebrew University, Jerusalem, 1990); and the essay by Beth Wenger in these volumes.

49. A facsimile of his handwritten responsum appeared posthumously in *Tomeikh keHalakhah: Responsa of the Panel of Halakhic Inquiry* (Mount Vernon, N.Y.: The Union for Traditional Conservative Judaism, 1986), vol. 1, pp. 15–18, followed by an English translation by Rabbi Wayne Allen on pp. 20–22.

50. Ibid. in Hebrew, p. 18; English, p. 22. For the author's reaction to Lieberman's approach, see *Responsa of the Va'ad Halakhah of the Rabbinical Assembly of Israel* (in Hebrew), vol. 5 (5752–54), pp. 41–42, and cf. ibid., note 50 for *rishonim* (early authorities) who permit women to serve as judges.

51. *Tomeikh keHalacha*, Hebrew, p. 15; English, p. 20. Also cf. Saul Lieberman Archives, box 8, "Saul Lieberman" file where Avraham Harmon, the Israeli ambassador to Washington, asked him to make a public statement about the autopsy controversy in Israel and Lieberman begged off, saying that the Israeli government had enough problems without his adding fuel to the fire.

52. The *mussar yeshivot* were talmudic academies that emphasized the study and practice of

ethics as advocated by Rabbi Israel Salanter. Regarding Lieberman's youth and yeshiva education, see Preschel, 5723, pp. 1–4; Lieberman, *Mehkarim*, pp. 608–11; and Abramson in *L'zikhro shel Shaul Lieberman*, pp. 24–26 (all referred to in note 35 above).

53. See Gedalyahu Alon, "The Lithuanian Yeshivas," in *The Jewish Expression*, ed. Judah Goldin, (New York: Bantam Books, 1970), pp. 451–52, and Shaul Stampfer, *The Lithuanian Yeshiva* (in Hebrew) (Jerusalem: The Zalman Center for Jewish History, 1995), pp. 47, 100–2, 122, 304.

53a. For a similar assessment, see David Weiss Halivni, *The Book and the Sword* (New York: Farrar, Straus and Giroux, 1996), p. 89.

54. *Proceedings of the Rabbinical Assembly* 17 (1953), pp. 75–76.

55. Saul Lieberman Archives, box 10, "Written by Lieberman" file.

56. See ibid. as well as box 6, "M" file, "S" file, and "Lieberman archives" file.

57. *Ma'ariv* 27, no. 9177 (Thursday, 12 September 1974): p. 1.

58. See note 55 above.

59. See Louis Finkelstein in Berkowitz, *In Praise of a Master* (note 35 above; the pages are unnumbered).

60. The section on Kaplan is based primarily on Scult, *Mordecai Kaplan*, which is the most thorough biography of Kaplan to date. The section on Finkelstein is based on Burton Visotsky and Micha Oppenheim, *A Bibliography of the Writings of Louis Finkelstein* (New York: Jewish Theological Seminary of America, 1977), on the supplement by Ora Hamelsdorf in *Hadoar* 64, no. 30 (9 Tammuz 5745): pp. 488–89, and on some of his letters that were discovered in various archives.

61. Regarding Kaplan, see *Encyclopædia Judaica*, vol. 10, cols. 751–53; Nadell, *Conservative Judaism*, pp. 147–54; Emanuel Goldsmith, Mel Scult, and Robert Seltzer, eds., *The American Judaism of Mordecai Kaplan* (New York: New York University Press, 1990), which contains a complete bibliography on pp. 415–53; and Scult, *Mordecai Kaplan*.

62. Scult, *Mordecai Kaplan*, p. 92, quoting from the Kaplan diaries: 1 August 1905, 11 May 1906, and 25 May 1906.

63. Scult, *Mordecai Kaplan*, p. 299.

64. Ibid., p. 352.

65. Ibid., p. 300, quoting from a letter to Silverman dated 27 April 1927. It is worth nothing that Kaplan corresponded with some of his disciples regarding this very question in April–May 1927. See the correspondence reproduced in Herman and Mignon Rubenovitz, *The Waking Heart* (Cambridge, Mass.: Nathaniel Dame & Company, 1967), pp. 75, 76, 78.

66. Litvin and Hoenig, *Jewish Identity*, p. 235. Professor Scult told the author in November 1995 that he recalls seeing a brief responsum of Professor Kaplan regarding conscientious objection during World War II.

67. Regarding Ginzberg's role in establishing that committee and his responsa for it, see below, after note 124.

68. See Scult, *Mordecai Kaplan*, pp. 183, 209–13, etc.

69. Ibid., pp. 180–81, and the literature cited there on p. 398, note 4.

70. Ibid., p. 211.

71. Ibid., pp. 211–12.

72. *Proceedings of the Rabbinical Assembly* 1 (1927), p. 36. Emphasis added.

73. See Scult, *Mordecai Kaplan*, pp. 277–78, and note 50. For some important letters from April–June 1927 not mentioned by Scult, see Herman and Mignon Rubenovitz, *The Waking Heart*, pp. 73–84.

74. Scult, *Mordecai Kaplan*, p. 278.

75. *Proceedings of the Rabbinical Assembly* 1 (1927), p. 11. It is also quoted by Scult, *Mordecai Kaplan*, p. 278, from Kaplan's diary.

76. For the subsequent checkered history of the Committee on Jewish Law, see George Nudell, "The Clearing House: A History of the Committee on Jewish Law and Standards," fall 1979, 43 pp., unpublished. (Nudell was not aware of the existence of the Committee on the Interpretation of Jewish Law nor of the process by which the Rabbinical Assembly Committee on Jewish Law came into being in 1927.) It is worth noting that these same procedures were adopted when the *Va'ad Halakhah* (law committee) of the Rabbinical Assembly of Israel was established in 1985, although the Kaplan precedent of 1927 was not known.

77. Kaplan is mentioned as a member of the committee in *Proceedings of the Rabbinical Assembly* 3 (1929), p. 57, and in 5 (1933–38), pp. 30, 100, 169, 368.

78. *Bulletin of The Rabbinical Assembly*, 22 November 1944, p. 10.

79. *Proceedings of the Rabbinical Assembly* 12 (1948), pp. 110–92, summarized by Nudell, "The Clearing House," pp. 10–14.

80. Max Routtenberg letter to Mordecai Kaplan, 18 November 1948, in the Committee on Jewish Law and Standards Archives 1947–49 and the minutes of the Committee on Jewish Law and Standards meeting on 16 December 1948 in the Committee on Jewish Law and Standards minutes, 1930–59.

81. For thorough discussions of Finkelstein's life and career, see elsewhere in these volumes. There is, as yet, no full-length biography of Finkelstein. For the time being, see the following (in chronological order): *United Synagogue Recorder* 3, no. 3 (July 1923): p. 3; ibid. 5, no. 1 (January 1925): p. 30; *Proceedings of the Rabbinical Assembly* 9 (1945), pp. 193–223; *Time*, 15 October 1951, pp. 52–58; *Current Biography*, 1952, pp. 191–93; Herbert Parzen, *Architects of Conservative Judaism* (New York: Jonathan David Publishers, 1964), pp. 207–18; *Encyclopædia Judaica*, vol. 6, cols. 1293–95; Jacob J. Weinstein, *Solomon Goldman*, pp. 4, 11, 39–52, 72, and 259–70; Visotsky and Oppenheim, *A Bibliography*; *Hadoar* 64, no. 30 (9 Tammuz 5745): pp. 481–89 (includes six articles including the supplemental bibliography by Hamelsdorf); *New York Times*, 1 September 1985, p. 57; Nadell, *Conservative Judaism*, pp. 83–87; and Gillman, *Conservative Judaism*, pp. 69–73. Also see the following eulogies (in alphabetical order): Ezra Finkelstein, *Women's League Outlook* 62, no. 3 (spring 1992): p. 4; Judah Goldin, *Conservative Judaism* 45, no. 2 (winter 1993): pp. 19–22; Ari Goldman, *New York Times*, 30 November 1991, p. A9; Simon Greenberg, *Proceedings of the Rabbinical Assembly* 54 (1992), pp. 278–81; Abraham Karp, *American Jewish Year Book* 93 (1993), pp. 527–34; Lawrence Schiffman, *Proceedings of the American Academy for Jewish Research* 59 (1993): pp. 1–4; Menahem Schmelzer, *Jewish Studies* 32 (1992): pp. 37–45 (in Hebrew); Ismar Schorsch, *Eit La'asot: The Journal of the Alumni Association of the Seminary College*, June 1992, p. 15.

82. Weinstein, *Solomon Goldman*, p. 47.

83. Greenberg, *Proceedings of the Rabbinical Assembly* 54, p. 280, and cf. Greenberg in *Hadoar* 64, p. 483, and Gillman, *Conservative Judaism*, p. 72.

84. JTS Records, Record Group 3B, faculty box 1, Moses Hyamson files. It is ironic that many years later Finkelstein downplayed the importance of the *Shulhan Arukh* in the Seminary curriculum—see *Proceedings of the Rabbinical Assembly* 28 (1964), p. 177.

85. Nadell, *Conservative Judaism*, p. 84.

86. *Universal Jewish Encyclopedia*, vol. 3, pp. 94–103.

87. "The Beliefs and Practices of Judaism" in Louis Finkelstein, J. Elliot Ross, and William Brown, *The Religions of Democracy: Judaism, Catholicism, Protestantism in Creed and Life* (New York: Devin-Adair, 1941), pp. 1–88.

88. See Visotsky and Oppenheim, *A Bibliography*, nos. 155, 176, 195, 235, 326, 365.

89. David Golinkin, ed., *The Responsa of Professor Louis Ginzberg* (New York and Jerusalem: Jewish Theological Seminary of America, 1996), p. 315.

90. Boaz Cohen Archives, box 4, "Bar Mitzva" file.

91. Ibid., box 5, "Minyan from Lichter" file.

92. Litvin and Hoenig, *Jewish Identity*, p. 118. For another statement by Finkelstein belittling his halakhic expertise, see *Proceedings of the Rabbinical Assembly* 17 (1953), p. 63. And cf. his introduction to his father's *Seder Tefila Im Bei'ur Siah Yitzhak* (Jerusalem: Privately printed, 1968), p. 13, where he states that his father, Rabbi Simon Finkelstein, "decreed" that he should not get involved in any matters of *kashrut* and that he followed his father's advice.

93. See above, notes 70–76.

94. *Proceedings of the Rabbinical Assembly* 1 (1927), pp. 48–49.

95. Ibid., 2 (1928), p. 99.

96. Ibid., 3 (1929), pp. 27–28.

97. Ibid., p. 29.

98. Ibid., p. 30.

99. See ibid., p. 151. He was even secretary for a short time—see ibid., 4 (1930–32), p. 236.

100. For his letter of resignation, see Louis Finkelstein to Boaz Cohen, 5 November 1940, in Committee on Jewish Law and Standards archives, 1930–41. Finkelstein stated that it would not be possible for him to serve on the committee, without stating any reason. He may have no longer had the time due to his new duties as President of the Seminary which he assumed in 1940.

101. *Halitza* (Deut. 25:5-10) is a ceremony in which a childless widow indicates that her husband's brother does not wish to marry her by removing his shoe and spitting on the ground in front of him. See the Committee on Jewish Law and Standards minutes, 12 March 1934, pp. 3–4. The minutes of the next meeting are missing from the Committee on Jewish Law and Standards archives. Rabbi Louis Epstein was asked to prepare such a clause, according to the Committee on Jewish Law and Standards Minutes, 11 February 1935, p. 2, but he ruled against the idea in *Proceedings of the Rabbinical Assembly* 5 (1933–38), pp. 227-35.

102. Committee on Jewish Law and Standards minutes, 1 May 1935, p. 3; Boaz Cohen Archives, box 9, "Finkelstein, Louis" file, letter from Boaz Cohen(?) to Louis Finkelstein, 5 October 1935; and *Proceedings of the Rabbinical Assembly* 5 (1933–38), p. 168.

103. "Overflow Services in Churches" in Boaz Cohen Archives, box 5, "Miscellaneous Questions and Answers" file; loc. cit., "Halitzah from Simon" file; loc. cit., box 3, "Julius Greenstone" file; loc. cit., box 9, "Finkelstein, Louis" file.

103a. *Proceedings of the Rabbinical Assembly* 4 (1930–32), p. 10.

103b. Boaz Cohen Archives, box 3, "Elias Margolis" file.

103c. *Proceedings of the Rabbinical Assembly* 5 (1933–38), p. 100.

104. See above, notes 79–80.

105. *Proceedings of the Rabbinical Assembly* 13 (1949), p. 122, and cf. Finkelstein's entire address, pp. 117–23.

106. This proposal is not mentioned in *Proceedings of the Rabbinical Assembly* 15, 1951; it is mentioned in *Proceedings of the Rabbinical Assembly* 16 (1952), p. 53.

107. Ibid.

107a. Louis Finkelstein to Max Davidson, 17 June 1952, in JTS General Files, "Committee on Jewish Law and Standards" file. My thanks to Dr. Michael Greenbaum of the Seminary for sending me a copy of this important document. And cf. his article in *Conservative Judaism* 47, no. 4 (summer 1995): pp. 32–36 and 72 for this and other important documents.

107b. *Haperushim V'anshei Keneset Hagedolah* (New York: Jewish Theological Seminary of America, 1950), especially chaps. 4–7.

108. *Proceedings of the Rabbinical Assembly* 17 (1953), pp. 45 ff.

109. Ibid., pp. 61–65, and cf. 19 (1955), pp. 47–48.

110. Ibid., 17 (1953), p. 75 ff,. and 18 (1954), pp. 64–68.

111. See Rabbi Aaron Blumenthal in *Proceedings of the Rabbinical Assembly* 17 (1953), pp. 65–67.

112. The section on Ginzberg is based on Golinkin, *Responsa*, which contains all extant responsa of Louis Ginzberg.

113. The most important biography is Eli Ginzberg, *Keeper of the Law: Louis Ginzberg* (1966; reprint, Philadelphia: Jewish Publication Society, 1996). For an exhaustive bibliography, see Golinkin, *Responsa*, introduction, note 1. Most of what follows is taken from the author's introduction to that volume.

114. His responsa are mentioned by Louis Finkelstein, *Proceedings of the American Academy for Jewish Research* 23 (1954), p. li; David Druck, *R. Levi Ginzberg* (in Hebrew) (New York: Posy-Shoulson Press, 5694) p. 118; and especially by Eli Ginzberg in *Keeper*, chap. 10. Herbert Parzen, *Architects*, accuses Louis Ginzberg of "devoting himself completely to scientific scholarship" (p. 143), withdrawing "to his study" (ibid.), and using "his prestige through the Law Committee of the Rabbinical Assembly to maintain the status quo" (p. 145). These assertions are thoroughly disproved by Golinkin, *Responsa*. Parzen further states that Ginzberg "assumed the chairmanship of the Committee on Jewish Law of the United Synagogue" in 1916 (p. 149), but both the name of the committee and the date are inaccurate (see below, after note 124). Finally, Parzen knows of only one responsum by Ginzberg—that on grape juice written in 1922 (pp. 151–52). Thus, Parzen's account is totally inaccurate, and it is unfortunate that later scholars were misled by his article—see David Kraemer, *Proceedings of the Rabbinical Assembly* 48 (1986), pp. 153–54, 165, and Nadell, *Conservative Judaism*, pp. 100–1.

115. Saul Lieberman, *Mehkarim*, pp. 613–14 and Finkelstein, *Proceedings of the American Academy for Jewish Research*. All references in parentheses refer to the page numbers in Golinkin, *Responsa*.

116. It was published in *Conservative Judaism* 11, no. 1 (fall 1956): p. 39. It should, however, be emphasized that that letter gives only a partial picture of his views on the subject—see Golinkin, *Responsa*, pp. 90–100, for the full correspondence, as well as ibid., pp. 85–89, for his earlier responsa.

117. On the importance of publishing Conservative responsa, see Golinkin, *Index*, p. 4, and note 12.

118. A few items are obviously not responsa but were included in Golinkin, *Responsa*, because they indicate Ginzberg's active involvement in the halakhic life of American Jewry. I also included a number of his popular articles (e.g., pp. 143–50) for the same reason.

119. Golinkin, *Responsa*.

120. It should be pointed out that his English responsa were typed on a typewriter by his secretary and were therefore preserved in the form of carbon copies. On the other hand, he does not seem to have had a Hebrew secretary, so there may have been additional Hebrew responsa which he wrote by hand and of which no copy was preserved.

121. See Leket Yosher, *Yoreh Deah* (Berlin: Itzkovsky Press, 1904), pp. 19–20, for a complete responsum in Yiddish. For Yiddish words, sentences, and entire paragraphs within the responsa literature, see Zalman Shazar, *Orei Dorot* (in Hebrew) (Jerusalem: Mossad Bialik, 5731), pp. 239–319—my thanks to Dr. Elhanan Reiner for this reference—and Yosef Bar-El, *A Yiddish-Hebrew Dictionary to the Responsa of the Great Rabbis of Ashkenaz* (in Hebrew) (Ramat Gan: Bar Ilan University, 5737).

122. For Orthodox responsa, see Rabbi David Zvi Hoffman, *Melamed L'ho-il*, part 2 (Frankfurt am Main: Hermon, 1927), no. 113, and elsewhere. Also see Rabbi Salomon Abraham Trier, ed., *Rabbinische Gutachten über die Beschneidung* (Frankfurt am Main: Bach, 1844), which is an entire collection devoted to the defense of circumcision against its Reform detractors.

My thanks to Dr. Ira Robinson for the second reference. For Reform responsa, see Peter Haas in *Liberal Judaism and Halakhah*, ed. Walter Jacob (Pittsburgh: Rodef Shalom Press, 1988), pp. 39, 43–52, who describes two collections in detail.

123. For a survey of Reform responsa in English beginning in 1891, see Haas, ibid.; Walter Jacob, ed., *American Reform Responsa* (New York: Central Conference of American Rabbis, 1983), pp. xvi–xviii; and idem., in Walter Jacob and Moshe Zemer, eds., *Dynamic Jewish Law: Progressive Halakhah: Essence and Application* (Tel Aviv and Pittsburgh: Freehof Institute of Progressive Halakhah, 1991), pp. 87–105.

124. For proof of this assertion, see the responsa listed in Golinkin, *Index*.

125. The reports of that committee listed in the appendix to Golinkin, *Responsa*, point to this conclusion.

126. See the literature cited above in note 123.

127. For a similar lament regarding American Jewry penned by Rabbi Jacob David Wilowsky in Chicago in 1904, see Abraham Karp in *Perspectives on Jews and Judaism: Essays in Honor of Wolfe Kelman*, ed. Arthur Chiel (New York: Rabbinical Assembly, 1978), p. 228.

128. The latter committee was formed in September 1927. See *Proceedings of the Rabbinical Assembly* 3 (1929), pp. 57, 151. Eli Ginzberg, *My Brother's Keeper* (New Brunswick and London: Transaction Publishers, 1980), p. 25, states that Ginzberg resigned from the committee after concluding that most of the members were unqualified to participate in such deliberations. But, as we have seen above (notes 68–76), the committee was reorganized in order to exclude him.

129. See the reports of the committee listed in the appendix to Golinkin, *Responsa*.

130. See Ginzberg, *Keeper*, chap. 2, and Golinkin, *Responsa*, introduction, pp. 6–13.

131. For other strict rulings with regard to synagogue-related issues, see Golinkin, *Responsa*, pp. 78–80, 103–6, 155–63.

132. Ginzberg, *Keeper*, pp. 241–42, and Eli Ginzberg, "The Seminary Family" etc., in Chiel, *Perspectives on Jews and Judaism*, p. 125, and cf. Parzen's opinion quoted in note 114 above.

133. "Appearance of impropriety" and "the desecration of God's Name," respectively.

134. Ginzberg's reference to *Neilah* is apparently not accidental—see Finkelstein in *Proceedings of the American Academy for Jewish Research* 23 (1954), p. liii.

135. Louis Ginzberg, *Students, Scholars and Saints* (Philadelphia: Jewish Publication Society, 1928), p. 141.

136. See the literature listed in Golinkin, *Responsa*, p. 214, n. 2..

137. For a similar statement by Professor Ginzberg, see Ginzberg, *Keeper*, p. 219.

138. Golinkin, *Responsa*, pp. 143–50, 231–62.

139. Ibid., pp. 110–33, 218–19, 231–52, 269, 286–87.

140. Ibid., p. 201.

141. In form, some of his responsa read like scientific articles—see especially pp. 110–33. Regarding content, see pp. 78–83, 85–100, 155–63, 218–19, and much of chap. 6. It is interesting that Lieberman, *Mehkarim*, pp. 613–14, praises Ginzberg's responsum on grape juice (110–33): ". . . that even one of the *yeshiva* students who have nothing to do with *Hokhmat Yisrael* [the scientific study of Judaism] would see in him one of their own." Indeed, that responsum contains features that would be appreciated by a *yeshiva* student, but, in general, its questions, sources, structure, contents, and style all bear the indelible imprint of *Hokhmat Yisrael*.

142. See B. D. Weinryb in: H. J. Zimmels et al., eds., *Essays Presented to Chief Rabbi Israel Brodie*, (London: Soncino Press Limited, 1967), pp. 399–417, and the literature cited there, and Haym Soloveitchik, *The Use of Responsa as Historical Source* (in Hebrew) (Jerusalem: Zalman Shazar Center for Jewish History, 1990). There are more than fifty historical monographs based primarily on the responsa literature.

143. Golinkin, *Responsa*, pp. 105–7, 299–301.

144. Ibid., p. 108.

145. Ibid., pp. 85–100, 270–71, 300.

146. Ibid., pp. 47, 135, 305.

147. Ibid., pp. 155–63.

148. Ibid., pp. 78–80.

149. Ibid., p. 297.

150. Ibid., pp. 103–4.

151. Ibid., pp. 167–71, 311–12.

152. Ibid., pp. 164, 175, 178–184.

153. Ibid., pp. 267–68

154. Ibid., pp. 189–98, 298–99.

155. For World War I, pp. 200, 304; for World War II, pp. 84, 221–22, 226–28; for the Korean War, p. 166.

156. Ibid., pp. 224–25

157. Ibid., pp. 167–69, 199, 220–22, 302–3, 307–8.

158. Ibid., pp. 85–87, 90–100, 199, 215.

159. Ibid., for "Conservative Synagogues," p. 139 (in 1933); for "Orthodox Conservative Congregation" (*sic!*), p. 199 (undated); for "Conservative Judaism," p. 220 (in 1924); for "Conservative rabbis" p. 221 (during World War II). Regarding the term "Conservative Judaism," see Herbert Rosenblum, *Conservative Judaism: A Contemporary History* (New York: United Synagogue of America, 1983), pp. 3, 20, 22, 32, the literature cited there, and also cf. above, note 8.

160. Regarding Boaz Cohen, see the following (in chronological order): *United Synagogue Recorder* 4, no. 3 (June-July 1924): p. 14; *Who's Who in American Jewry*, vol. 3 (1938–39), p. 171; *Universal Jewish Encyclopedia*, vol. 3, p. 239; *New York Times*, 18 December 1956, p. 31 (an obituary for his second wife, Blanche Stein Cohen); a brief autobiography in Boaz Cohen Archives, box 13, "Rabinowitz, H. R." file; *New York Times*, 12 December 1968, p. 47; Edward Gershfield, *Proceedings of the Rabbinical Assembly* 33 (1969), pp. 173–75; Elias Bickerman and Edward Gershfield, *Proceedings of the American Academy for Jewish Research* 37 (1969), pp. xxix–xxxi; *Entziklopedia Ivrit*, vol. 20 (Jerusalem: Hevrah L'hotza-'ot Entziklopediyot, 5731), cols. 599–600; *Encyclopædia Judaica*, vol. 5, col. 667; Nadell, *Conservative Judaism*, pp. 53–55. This section is based on Cohen's published writings, the Boaz Cohen Archives, the Committee on Jewish Law and Standards archives, and the Committee on Jewish Law and Standards minutes.

161. See David Golinkin, "A Bibliography of the Writings of Professor Boaz Cohen," *Jewish Law Annual*, 1997 (at press).

162. See, for example, *Bulletin of the Rabbinical Assembly* 1, no. 2 (February 1938): p. 38, and ibid., 4, no. 1 (November 1940), p. 7. In the 1950s, after being removed from the Committee on Jewish Law, Boaz Cohen used to sign his responsa: "Chairman of the *Bet Din* of the Rabbinical Assembly of America." In any case, this aspect of Cohen's career bears further investigation.

163. Boaz Cohen to David Kogen in JTS Records, Record Group 15A, Rabbinical School alumni files, box 4, "Boaz Cohen" file.

164. In *Proceedings of the Rabbinical Assembly* 5 (1933–38), p. 100, Cohen is mentioned as a member of the committee, while on p. 169, he is already mentioned as secretary of the committee. In *Bulletin of the Rabbinical Assembly* 4, no. 1 (November 1940): p. 7, Cohen is first mentioned as chairman of the committee. He was removed from that position in the "revolution of 1948" described above (notes 79–80).

165. *Proceedings of the Rabbinical Assembly* 5 (1933–38), pp. 102, 169, 332.

166. Ibid., 6 (1939), p. 160. Emphasis added.

167. *Bulletin of the Rabbinical Assembly*, March 1947, p. 7. Emphasis added.

168. See above, notes 79–80.

169. *Proceedings of the Rabbinical Assembly* 13 (1949), p. 136. To the best of my knowledge, Cohen only served on the committee for *sixteen* years.

170. Boaz Cohen Archives, box 6, "Synagogue Art, Mrs. Bickelman" file.

171. *Proceedings of the Rabbinical Assembly* 33 (1969), p. 174, which he repeated in *Proceedings of the American Academy for Jewish Research* 37 (1969), p. xxxi. Emphasis added.

172. *Bulletin of the Rabbinical Assembly*, 22 November 1944, p. 1; *Conservative Judaism* 1, no. 1 (January 1945): p. 6; *Bulletin of the Rabbinical Assembly*, December 1945, p. 3; *Proceedings of the Rabbinical Assembly* 10 (1946), p. 42; memorandum from Michael Higger to Israel Goldman, 13 February 1947 in Committee on Jewish Law and Standards archives, 1947; *Bulletin of the Rabbinical Assembly*, March 1947, p. 7; *Conservative Judaism* 3, no. 3 (May 1947): p. 5; *Proceedings of the Rabbinical Assembly* 11 (1947), p. 71.

173. The complete copy has been sitting in a box in the Committee on Jewish Law and Standards archives for fifty years without anyone's being aware of its contents. I discovered it while working on Golinkin, *Responsa*. The partial copy is preserved in the Boaz Cohen Archives, box 5, "Miscellaneous Questions and Answers" file.

174. For one example among many, see Boaz Cohen Archives, box 4, "Burial, Widows from Kolatch" file. For some reason, many of the responsa related to mourning and burial have survived in both the original and truncated forms.

175. I hope to identify some of the authors of the edited responsa by comparing them with the Committee on Jewish Law and Standards minutes.

176. That is, questions alone, answers alone, or complete responsa. Of course, we have no way of knowing if all the questions were answered, but given Cohen's dedication to Jewish law and to the Committee on Jewish Law, I believe he answered almost all of them. It should be noted that the number 274 does not include letters in which Cohen answered more than one question. In other words, I counted letters, not individual questions.

177. There are a number of additional signed responsa by Cohen in the Committee on Jewish Law and Standards archives which I have not yet had a chance to sort.

178. One person even asked him for the source of a poem by Robert Browning! See Boaz Cohen Archives, box 15, "Waldman, Mark" file.

179. Boaz Cohen Archives, box 5, "Kashrut, Budgar, Sylvia" file.

180. See *Shulhan Arukh, Orah Haim*, 451:26, and Rabbi Isaac Klein, *Responsa and Halakhic Studies* (New York: Ktav, 1975), pp. 79–83.

181. Boaz Cohen Archives, box 11, "Kelman, Wolfe" file. (This is an error; the questioner was rabbi Harry Kellman.)

182. "The Repentant Apostate" in *Bulletin of the Rabbinical Assembly*, Supplement on Jewish Law 1, no. 1 (January 1941): pp. 9–11; also found in Boaz Cohen Archives, box 19, "The Repentant Apostate" file and mentioned by Higger in *Proceedings of the Rabbinical Assembly* 5 (1933–38), p. 369; "Markings on Tombstones" in *Bulletin of the Rabbinical Assembly*, ibid., pp. 12, 20, also found in Boaz Cohen Archives, box 3, "Tombstones" file, and ibid., box 6, "Tombstone from Rabbi Charry" file; "Is it Allowed to use the Organ at Religious Services?" Boaz Cohen Archives, box 3, "Organs" file which is mentioned by Higger in *Proceedings of the Rabbinical Assembly* 7 (1940), p. 28; and a responsum on the *mehitzah* in the synagogue summarized by Cohen, *Proceedings of the Rabbinical Assembly* 8 (1941–44), pp. 139–41, which he apparently wrote himself—see Boaz Cohen, *Law and Tradition in Judaism*, 2d ed. (New York: Ktav, 1969), p. 37.

183. Cohen, *Law and Tradition*, pp. 29–30, 59, and 73, and *Proceedings of the Rabbinical Assembly* 11 (1947), p. 58.

184. Cohen, *Law and Tradition*, pp. 73–74, and cf. p. 60. This approach is evident in the lengthy responsa mentioned in note 182, above.

185. Ibid., p. 71, and cf., ibid., pp. 71–73 and 58–59.

186. *Proceedings of the Rabbinical Assembly* 11 (1947), p. 55.

187. Ibid., p. 60.

188. Cohen, *Law and Tradition*, p. 60. Cf. Cohen's genuine annoyance with a rabbi who performed a wedding for a *kohen* and a divorcee and then asked Cohen for a *heter* (lenient ruling) after the fact. See Boaz Cohen Archives, box 5, "Marriage from Margolis, Morris" file.

189. Cohen, *Law and Tradition*, pp. 60, 34–35, and *Proceedings of the Rabbinical Assembly* 8 (1941–44), p. 33.

190. Cohen, *Law and Tradition*, pp. 36–37 which is repeated in a similar fashion on pp. 88–89.

191. Ibid.

192. See above, notes 79–80.

193. I suspect that research will show that the three models of halakhic involvement presented here continued after 1968 as well. Some Seminary professors were clearly not interested in *pesak halakha*. Others, such as Professors Seymour Siegel, Edward Gershfield, Joel Roth, and Mayer Rabinowitz played an active and, at times, leading role in the Committee on Jewish Law and Standards. Finally, Chancellor Gerson Cohen and others played a crucial political role in the decision to ordain women as rabbis. Regarding this last topic, see above, note 48.

BETH S. WENGER

The Politics of Women's Ordination

Jewish Law,
Institutional Power,
and the Debate over
Women in the Rabbinate

Amy Eilberg, the first woman to be ordained as a Conservative rabbi, at her ordination in 1985.
Photo by Joyce Culver. Communications Department, JTS.

BETH S. WENGER

The Politics
of Women's Ordination

Jewish Law, Institutional Power, and the
Debate over Women in the Rabbinate

ON 24 OCTOBER 1983 the faculty of the
Jewish Theological Seminary concluded one of the most protracted struggles in the
history of Conservative Judaism when it voted to ordain women as rabbis. The long
and often contentious debate over women's ordination preoccupied the Conservative Jewish community for more than a decade and precipitated a tense conflict
among the Seminary faculty, the rabbinic and lay leadership, and the emerging
feminist movement. The Conservative movement's decision to ordain women can
be written from several historical perspectives. On one level, women's entry into the
rabbinate reflected social and political developments taking place throughout the
United States, as the women's movement gained momentum and many previously
all-male institutions opened their doors to women. As a crucial moment in Jewish
feminism, the admission of women to the rabbinate signaled an important step on
the road to women's full inclusion in Jewish religious leadership. At the same time,
the debate surrounding women's ordination marked a critical phase in the history of
the Seminary and Conservative Judaism. Ordaining women as rabbis required the
Seminary to grapple with its commitment to Jewish law and with its ability to
remain relevant and responsive to the needs of the contemporary Jewish community. At stake in the decision to ordain women as rabbis was not only the granting of
equal rights to women but also the institutional fate of the Seminary, its leadership
role within the Conservative movement, and its ability to maintain a broad American Jewish constituency.

Like all pivotal institutional changes, the Seminary's decision to admit women to
the rabbinate involved a combination of social forces, political maneuvers, and
competing ideologies. The proponents of women's ordination became increasingly
vocal and insistent throughout the 1970s. A growing number of well-educated

Jewish women provided a pool of qualified female rabbinic candidates, and the organized Jewish feminist movement became a powerful lobby force. The Rabbinical Assembly (RA), the organization representing Conservative rabbis, pressured the JTS faculty to begin accepting women as rabbinical students and urged Seminary leaders to respond to the changing character of the Conservative Jewish community. Yet, at the same time, many Conservative Jews expressed strong opposition to the ordination of women. Prominent members of the JTS faculty and some leading congregational rabbis denounced women's ordination as both contrary to Jewish law and detrimental to the future of Conservative Judaism. Faced with dissension within the Seminary faculty and fears about an irreparable split in the Conservative movement, the Seminary's leadership attempted to address the issue of ordaining women in a manner both faithful to Jewish law and capable of retaining the diverse constituency within Conservative Judaism. The approximately ten-year struggle that culminated in the 1983 vote to ordain women testified to Jewish women's changing social, political, and religious roles even as it revealed the path that the Jewish Theological Seminary had chosen.

The ordination question fundamentally centered on the role of women within Conservative Judaism, but when the Seminary grappled with the issue, the key players in the debate were the established male leaders of the movement. Although the discussion revolved around a crucial redefinition of gender norms in Jewish practice, feminism and a thoughtful deliberation of gender roles were not central features in the institutional decision to accept female students at the Jewish Theological Seminary. Like so many other campaigns for women's enfranchisement, the dispute over admitting women to the rabbinate had more to do with ideological divisions, political disputes, and battles for institutional control than it did with issues of gender equality and transformation.

The Contours of the Ordination Debate: Women's Issues and Institutional Politics in the Conservative Movement

The women's ordination debate reached a feverish pitch in the 1970s, but women had been formally studying in non-rabbinic programs at JTS since the early 20th century. As early as 1903, Henrietta Szold attended rabbinic classes at the Seminary, but only after she had "assured its administration that she would not use the knowledge thus gained to seek ordination."[1] The 1909 creation of the JTS Teachers Institute attracted a regular stream of women to the Seminary student body to prepare for careers in Jewish education.[2] Female students were a constant presence at JTS, but requests for formal admission to rabbinical school remained rare before the 1960s. In 1957, Gladys Citrin, a Yeshiva-educated college student, became one of the first women to apply to the rabbinic program when she wrote to Chancellor Louis Finkelstein expressing her interest "in entering the Seminary as a rabbinical

Women students
of the Teachers
Institute at their
graduation in
1936. Simon
Greenberg is at
the podium; Sem-
inary president
Cyrus Adler
(right) and Adler's
secretary Joseph
Abrahams are
seated at the table.
*Ratner Center,
JTS.*

student."[3] Such inquiries generally received a standard reply from the Chancellor, explaining that JTS did not train women for the rabbinate and suggesting alternative Seminary programs. Long before women's ordination became a burning issue within the Conservative movement, many women were being educated alongside male rabbinical students but only a select few had expressed a desire to serve as rabbis.

By the late 1960s and 1970s, as the feminist movement became more powerful and the number of well-educated Jewish women increased, requests for admission to rabbinical school became more frequent and fervent. The presence of a significant number of college-trained women with comprehensive Jewish educations convinced many rabbis and laypeople in the Conservative movement that the time had come to consider qualified women for the rabbinate. The Reform and Reconstructionist movements had already accepted women into their rabbinical programs. By the seventies, Jewish women in the Conservative movement had benefited from equal access to secondary Jewish education and publicly celebrated their Bat Mitzvahs in the synagogue; many had also attended the movement's Ramah summer camps, and some had furthered their knowledge in college-level Jewish Studies courses. In 1976, Rabbi Al Axelrad, Hillel Director at Brandeis University, informed the JTS director of rabbinical school admissions that several talented female undergraduates at Brandeis aspired to the Conservative rabbinate. "Knowing their outstanding Jewish strengths and promise," Axelrad explained, "I simply hate to see them denied entrance into the rabbinical school of their choice."[4] Appeals to admit qualified female candidates to rabbinical school emerged from several rabbis throughout the country, most of whom had firsthand experience

Girls at Camp
Ramah in New
England, ca. 1958.
*Camp Ramah in
New England.*

working with dedicated and educated young Jewish women intent on careers in the rabbinate. Rabbi Kassel Abelson, serving a Minneapolis congregation, wrote to Chancellor Gerson Cohen about "two very fine young ladies" in his community who wanted to become rabbis. "They would prefer to go to the Seminary," Abelson insisted, "but will probably apply to the Reconstructionist Seminary or to Hebrew Union College. This represents a real loss in (WO)man power for our movement."[5] Throughout the 1970s, women candidates applied regularly to rabbinical school, among them Susannah Heschel, daughter of prominent JTS faculty member, Abraham Joshua Heschel. They were informed of the Seminary's policies, urged to pursue their educations at JTS, and encouraged to devote themselves to professional Jewish careers other than the rabbinate.[6]

Jewish women responded to the Conservative movement's policies by organizing and demanding inclusion in all arenas of Jewish life, including the rabbinate. One of the most dramatic episodes in the struggle occurred in 1972 when Ezrat Nashim, a group of committed Conservative Jewish women, interrupted the annual Rabbinical Assembly convention to present their demands. They called for women to be granted full membership and ritual rights in synagogues, insisted that all barriers to women's equality in Jewish law be removed, and asserted women's right to serve as rabbis and cantors in the Conservative movement. The members of Ezrat Nashim, who had been reared and educated as Conservative Jews, declared their personal commitment to the movement but also issued a stern reminder to its leaders:

> The educational institutions of the Conservative movement have helped women recognize their intellectual, social and spiritual potential. If the movement then denies women opportunities to demonstrate these capacities as adults, it will force them to turn from the synagogue, and to find fulfillment elsewhere.[7]

Jewish women convinced many Conservative Jewish leaders that a failure to act would result in a significant loss for the movement. The proclamations of Ezrat Nashim reflected the feminist commitment shared by a growing number of Jewish women and fueled the movement for women's ordination.

Chancellor Gerson Cohen had taken office in 1972, aware of the heightened tenor of debate over the question of women's ordination. Although he had declared a willingness to consider the issue, Cohen consistently upheld the JTS policy not to admit women, insisting that he would be guided by the Seminary's Rabbinic faculty and would search for consensus in the Conservative movement before making any changes. Despite growing support for women's ordination, Cohen understood that a significant opposition remained among Conservative rabbis and within the JTS faculty. When the Seminary faculty discussed the question of women's ordination in 1973, one faculty member reported an overwhelming sentiment "against admitting women to ordination at this time."[8] In the first years of his tenure, Cohen attempted to satisfy both sides of the controversy, steadfastly opposing ordination as detrimental to the movement but willing to offer women every other possible option. In 1974, Cohen streamlined the Seminary curriculum so that students could take classes in any department, a move that effectively opened all Rabbinical School courses to qualified women students. He wanted to convince prospective female applicants that all avenues of study were open to them; only ordination remained prohibited. The Chancellor reminded ordination proponents that "[t]he fact of the matter is that there are young ladies studying in our Rabbinical School and a full academic rabbinical program is available to them. We have as yet not admitted them to a program for ordination which is a different kettle of fish."[9] Cohen promised his critics that the Seminary was "considering this question carefully and trying to find some solution which will meet the needs of our community and satisfy the desires of the young ladies to serve as religious functionaries" albeit not as rabbis. Until the late 1970s, Chancellor Cohen maintained the Seminary's status quo, convinced that "an outright policy of ordination" would mean "tearing our Movement apart."[10]

Among the various arms of the Conservative movement, the Jewish Theological Seminary remained the most reluctant to initiate changes in women's roles, resisting reforms instituted by other branches of the movement. As early as 1955, a minority group within the Rabbinical Assembly's Committee on Jewish Law and Standards voted in favor of granting women the right to be called to the Torah. Four years later, the United Synagogue of America, the umbrella organization representing Conservative synagogues, recommended sweeping changes in women's status when it called for women to have equal voting, membership, and office-holding rights in congregational life.[11] By 1973, the RA Law Committee had approved the counting of women in a *minyan*, the prayer quorum that had traditionally required ten men.[12] Several JTS faculty members opposed the Law Committee's rulings, but they had no power to overturn them. However, the Seminary's own synagogue never instituted any of the changes proposed by other arms of the movement. At JTS, women were not counted in the *minyan* or called to the Torah and separate seating for men and women—a rare practice in most American Conservative congregations—remained the custom within the Seminary synagogue. The Seminary's gender policies stood in direct contrast to the experience of most Conservative Jews. Within the spectrum of Conservative Judaism, the Jewish Theological Seminary remained the most militant stronghold of traditional Jewish practice.

A similar pattern emerged with the question of women's ordination. The United Synagogue was the first branch of the movement to call for women to be ordained as rabbis. At its 1973 convention, the United Synagogue passed a resolution favoring "the admission of qualified women to the Rabbinical School of the Jewish Theological Seminary of America."[13] The Rabbinical Assembly also discussed similar initiatives at its annual conventions in 1975 and 1976 but tabled the motions in order to allow further study and debate. The RA had never been unanimous in its support of ordination. In fact, within the Rabbinical Assembly, a group known as the Committee for Tradition and Diversity within the Conservative Movement strenuously battled against ordination and changes in women's status.[14] At the same time, a significant faction within the RA had been pressing for women's ordination for years before bringing the matter before the annual convention in 1975.[15] The motions favoring women's admission to rabbinical school were tabled in successive years due to internal disagreements within the RA and a long-standing "gentlemen's agreement" about decision making in the Conservative movement.[16] In the words of the RA's executive vice-president, Rabbi Wolfe Kelman, "We have tried to preserve the tradition that the Rabbinical Assembly does not pass a resolution about matters which properly belongs [*sic*] to the Seminary."[17] The faculty of the Jewish Theological Seminary had always maintained the sole authority for ordaining Conservative rabbis. Even the most passionate advocates of women's ordination in the RA conceded that "It is not possible for the Rabbinical Assembly to either demand or rule for the Seminary." Proponents of women's ordination within the Rabbinical Assembly mounted increasing pressure on the Seminary by introducing motions each year. Yet, in 1976, Rabbi Fishel Pearlmutter, the most fervent leader for women's ordination within the RA, admitted to an aspiring female rabbinic candidate that despite a persistent lobbying effort, he did "not believe the Seminary [was] currently ready to respond to the call."[18]

At the heart of the Seminary's resistance to women's ordination lay a serious debate about whether Jewish law (*halakha*) permitted women to serve as rabbis. The strongest opposition emerged from senior members of the Seminary's Talmud faculty, particularly Rabbis Saul Lieberman and David Weiss Halivni, as well as several other Seminary professors and Conservative rabbis. The ordination of women involved several complex halakhic issues. The fundamental questions centered around whether women's legal exemption from performing certain obligations rendered them unfit to carry out those commandments and whether Jewish law explicitly prohibited women from fulfilling certain functions of the rabbinate. Opponents of ordination claimed that because women were not required by Jewish law to observe time-bound commandments, they could not serve as religious agents for congregations or perform basic rabbinic duties. Among the most crucial halakhic issues were women's ability to lead the congregation in prayer, serve as witnesses, and preside at wedding ceremonies. Several faculty members also questioned the legitimacy of women counting in a *minyan*, an issue that had continued to elicit controversy despite the Law Committee's endorsement of the practice. According to Rabbi Israel Francus, "A woman can never—not today, not tomorrow, not next year, and not next generation—acquire the status of a *hiyyuvit*—of one 'obligated' in relation to a *mitzvah* from whose performance she is now halakhically exempt, which would qualify her to act as agent in the performance of those *mitzvot* in behalf of men."[19] For those opposed to admitting women to the rabbinate, halakhic barriers provided insurmountable obstacles to women's ordination. In the words of Rabbi Weiss Halivni, the ordination of women in the Conservative movement defied the basic principle of "a halacha based on Revelation as interpreted by the Sages throughout the ages, a position to which the Seminary is committed from its very inception."[20]

Just as opponents of women's ordination grounded their objections in halakhic terms, so too the advocates of ordination defended their position as completely legitimate within the bounds of Jewish law. Ordination proponents insisted that barriers to women's fulfillment of commandments could be overcome through halakhic means and that Jewish law was sufficiently flexible to adapt to changing circumstances. In a lengthy responsum, Rabbi Joel Roth proposed that women be allowed to accept voluntarily the obligation to fulfill all time-bound commandments and "affirm that failure to comply with the obligation is a sin."[21] Through such mechanisms, he claimed, women's status as religious functionaries could be halakhically altered. Rabbi Robert Gordis emphasized the evolutionary capability of *halakha* and suggested the need to reconcile contemporary moral and ethical standards with Jewish law. "[F]or modern Halakhah to perpetuate [women's inferior] status in a society where women participate in all areas of life is unconscionable. . . . To bring Halakhah in this respect into conformity with our ethical standards constitutes part of the unfinished business of contemporary Judaism."[22] Ordination advocates defended the dynamic quality of the halakhic process and its ability to respond to the moral demands of women's equality. Others pointed to the need to reconsider the function of the rabbi in contemporary American society. Gordis maintained that "the rabbinate represents virtually a new calling" in modern America and that a rabbi's duties had changed dramatically since ancient times.[23] Professor Judith Hauptman, then an instructor in the Talmud Department, reiterated that claim, emphasizing that "'Rabbi' means teacher, that the person has attained a certain level of education."[24] Within the many pro-ordination opinions expressed by Seminary faculty members lay a fundamental belief that "there [were] no insurmountable halakhic objections to the granting of ordination" to women.[25] In the furor over ordaining women that raged within the Seminary, both sides of the debate fervently believed that the force of Jewish law was on their side.

For all the critical halakhic questions at the center of the debate, the women's ordination controversy was not simply a dispute over Jewish law. To be sure, the Jewish Theological Seminary wanted to retain its reputation as the guardian of *halakha* for the Conservative movement and its faculty members felt passionately about maintaining fidelity to Jewish law. Yet, social, psychological, and political attitudes proved to be equally powerful forces stirring the conflict over women's ordination. Even those who argued for the halakhic legitimacy of ordaining women often emphasized the pressing social realities compelling a change in Conservative Judaism. Committed Conservative Jews acknowledged that "the ability and willingness of women to perform rabbinic duties as well as men, the right to equal job opportunities, [and] the right to pursue a career of one's choice" provided the backdrop for any halakhic rulings on women and the rabbinate.[26] "Withholding ordination from women," argued Rabbi Simon Greenberg, "can only delay or impair the healthy integration of the Jewish woman into the Jewish society of the future."[27] Opponents of ordination often attacked the ordination movement as motivated "solely on the basis of sociological norms," but many anti-ordination opinions also drew on social and psychological rationales.[28] Dr. Mortimer Ostow, chairman of the Seminary's Department of Pastoral Psychiatry, argued his case in Freudian terms, insisting that women rabbis would threaten male self-esteem, undermine the image of rabbis as father figures, and prompt erotic fantasies from male congregants.[29] While the debate over women's ordination involved a complex discussion of women and Jewish law, its dimensions were clearly shaped by fundamental attitudes toward women and social change.

The ordination controversy also sparked a political battle within the Jewish Theological Seminary and the Conservative movement. In institutional terms, the dispute over ordaining women framed a long-standing power struggle between the Seminary and the Rabbinical Assembly. It was the RA's heightened pressure upon JTS that forced Chancellor Cohen to take action on the ordination question. Once Cohen had assumed a leading role in the debate, political turmoil swirled within the Seminary's faculty. By the late seventies, the ordination controversy threatened to undermine the leadership of Chancellor Cohen and to alienate several prominent members of the JTS faculty. The battle over admitting women to the rabbinate extended beyond issues of women's rights and responsibilities; it also exposed the ideological divisions, political tensions, and institutional battles within Conservative Judaism.

The Commission:
Deliberating the Ordination Question

The movement to admit women to the Conservative rabbinate had gained momentum throughout the 1970s, sparking discussion, debate, and controversy. However, not until 1977 did Chancellor Cohen and the Jewish Theological Seminary become the central players in what had become the most pressing and divisive issue of Conservative Judaism. Since 1975, the Rabbinical Assembly had been tabling motions that called for the Jewish Theological Seminary to admit women to its rabbinical school. When a similar resolution came before the annual convention in 1977, Rabbi Fishel Pearlmutter, who led the ordination crusade, agreed to table the resolution once again but only after securing a new course of action. Members of the RA and the JTS faculty knew that a successful RA motion endorsing the admission of women to the Seminary's Rabbinical School would exacerbate tensions between the two branches of the movement. Before the RA meeting, Chancellor Cohen had promised the Seminary faculty that he would "oppose any efforts . . . to pass a resolution concerning the admissions policy of the Rabbinical School . . . as an unacceptable intrusion into the academic affairs of the Seminary."[30] Realizing the potential damage that might occur, Chancellor Cohen negotiated a compromise solution with Fishel Pearlmutter. When he moved to table the original RA motion, Pearlmutter proposed the following substitute resolution:

> Be It Resolved that the Rabbinical Assembly respectfully petitions the Chancellor of the Jewish Theological Seminary of America to establish an interdisciplinary commission to study all aspects of the role of women as spiritual leaders in the conservative movement.
>
> Be It Further Resolved that this study commission, whose membership shall

reflect the pluralism and diversity of the Conservative movement, shall be responsible for a progress report on its findings to be presented to the Executive Council of The Rabbinical Assembly in the spring of 1978 and for a final report and recommendation at the 1979 convention of The Rabbinical Assembly.[31]

The Assembly approved the new resolution at the 1977 convention, mandating the Seminary's Chancellor to establish a commission to study the issue of women's ordination and providing a two-year deadline for a final recommendation. While some RA members perceived the move as another delay in the process, Pearlmutter explained that he "acted out of the conviction that it is better for us to work with the Seminary and accomplish the goal than for us to win a rhetorical victory, even if that would have been achieved."[32] Advocates of ordination within the RA hoped that the commission signaled the Seminary's willingness to deliberate the ordination question seriously and to bridge the widening gap between JTS and the Rabbinical Assembly.

The Commission for the Study of the Ordination of Women as Rabbis was created by the mandate of the Rabbinical Assembly but chaired by Chancellor Cohen, who selected the members and guided the deliberations. "The Seminary . . . is commonly considered to be the central institution of Conservative Judaism," explained one internal commission document, and therefore should lead any discussion about admitting women to its Rabbinical School.[33] While Cohen supervised the commission, he fully intended to heed the RA's mandate to create an interdisciplinary committee reflecting a wide range of opinion and expertise. Some rabbis and halakhic experts served on the commission, but so too did attorneys, academics, and a variety of professionals. Cohen also refused to allow the commission to become a collection of the presidents of Conservative organizations, such as the RA, Men's Club, Women's League, and United Synagogue. As Rabbi Gordon Tucker, executive director of the commission, reflected in a memo to Cohen, "the stocking of the commission with movement presidents would be disastrous . . . can't you imagine this body getting logged down in the usual nonsense that gets batted around between the arms of the movement?"[34] Therefore, Cohen decided that an honest debate of the ordination question could "best be accomplished by people who have no organizational axes to grind and thus can deal with the issue in as wide a cultural and social context as possible."[35] Cohen's criteria for choosing members of the commission was that

> the members of the commission would be people who, while they may have commitments, nevertheless have a perspective sufficiently open to allow for a change of their stand. I would therefore not appoint extreme right wingers who are intransigent about women in the rabbinate. Nor would I want people who are so committed to ordaining women as rabbis that they would automatically overrule all considerations of timing, implementation, and *halakha*.[36]

After several months of deliberation, Cohen composed a fourteen-member panel, consisting of three women and eleven men.[37] Only four members served on the JTS faculty, including Cohen and his assistant, Gordon Tucker. The others were congregational rabbis, independent scholars, attorneys, and representatives of the Jewish community. All of the members chosen declared both "open-mindedness" and an "identification with the Conservative movement," two essential qualifications for appointment.[38] The commission, Cohen claimed, reflected a diverse Jewish constituency capable of considering the ordination question from a variety of social, psychological, religious, moral, and halakhic perspectives.

The creation and composition of the commission provided an immediate source of dissension within the JTS faculty and certain quarters of the Conservative movement. Opponents of ordination believed that the commission served as a predetermined vehicle for endorsing women's admission to the rabbinate. Conservative rabbis who were convinced that ordination represented an affront to *halakha* attacked the commission's membership as insufficiently qualified to render a decision for the movement. "We believe," declared an open letter issued by the Committee for Preservation of Tradition, an anti-ordination group within the RA, "that a matter as significant and far-reaching as the ordination of women must be determined by the specialists in halachah on the Faculty of the Seminary. . . . It is they who can decide whether the ordination of women is within the spirit or contrary to halachah."[39] The commission's competency to deliberate matters of Jewish law as well as its commitment to respect halakhic principles became a constant source of conflict. The commission had been formed with the understanding that it would issue no recommendation that "would contravene or be incompatible with the requirements of halakhah."[40] In the closed deliberations of the commission, Cohen firmly declared that, "If this commission should decide that to have a woman as [a] rabbi is anti-halachic and nevertheless it votes to have women as rabbis, I will not be able to support that position."[41] Yet, despite Cohen's insistence that *halakha* would have veto power in the commission's final decision, the critics remained unconvinced.

The commission set out to deliberate the halakhic issues as well as assess the sentiments of both Conservative leaders and the laity. In their first meeting in December 1977, commission members revealed their personal attitudes toward ordination and outlined the fundamental issues at stake in the decision. The following March, the commission heard testimony from a variety of Jewish leaders, including the presidents of the Men's Club and Women's League, representatives from the Rabbinical Assembly and United Synagogue, and others. The testimony reflected a wide range of opinion regarding women's ordination. While the organizational representatives offered almost unanimous personal support for ordination, they differed about the potential consequences within the movement. Rabbi Stanley Rabinowitz declared that "from an ethical point of view," women could not be denied ordination. However, Rabbi Saul Teplitz insisted that "the Conservative Jewish community [was] . . . not prepared for this at all." Although he personally favored ordination, Simon Schwartz, president of the United Synagogue, believed that "ninety percent of the congregations would find it rather difficult to call a woman to their pulpit" and that women's ordination would "cause a great deal of dissension in almost every synagogue."[42]

Part of the commission's responsibility was to gauge the sentiments of the Conservative Jewish community. To that end, it conducted open public hearings in seven cities throughout the United States and Canada during a six-month period in 1978.[43] At the hearings, commission members welcomed "anyone who has a clearly identifiable stake in Conservative Judaism."[44] The public meetings elicited some of the most passionate and fervent testimony on both sides of the ordination debate. Local rabbis and laypeople, men and women, young and old came to express their thoughts about the ordination of women as rabbis. The majority of testimony favored admitting women to the rabbinate, but several strident opposing voices were also heard. For example, in Washington, Rabbi David Novak argued that the ordination of women would threaten the continuation of the Conservative movement "as a form of normative Judaism."[45] However, in Minneapolis, Rabbi Arnold Goodman insisted that "any delay [in ordaining women] should be regarded as an act of injustice. Indeed, in this area as in others, justice delayed is justice denied."[46] Some of the most powerful statements came not from rabbis, but from Conservative Jews who harbored strong feelings about women as rabbis. "To deny any woman the opportunity of becoming a rabbi not only cuts her off from her religion and her belief, but cuts off every woman who cares about her Judaism," declared Amy Lynn at the Washington meeting.[47] Debra Cantor, who would later be a member of the first class of women admitted to rabbinical school, traveled from Boston to testify at the New York meeting. "When I told a friend that I was going all the way to New York . . . in order to be here tonight," Cantor explained, "she said please tell them that for every one of your five minutes [to speak], there are five hundred of us who stand behind you. . . . All that we ask is the chance to study and to serve."[48] The commission recorded the opinions expressed and at the close of the hearings, concluded that "the overwhelming majority of those who chose to testify at these meetings strongly favored women's ordination."[49]

The commission's open hearings constituted an unprecedented event in the decision-making process of the Conservative movement. Never before had a crucial issue in Conservative Judaism, particularly one rooted in *halakha* and central to the future of the Seminary, been discussed in a nationwide public forum of committed Conservative Jews. Critics of the process sharply condemned the open hearings as an improper means of debating halakhic arguments. "Pressure to ordain women through public hearings and media releases is an affront to all those who take halacha seriously," declared Rabbi Weiss Halivni.[50] Yet, the commission never intended the hearings to be a democratic vote on the issue but rather to serve as a means of taking the collective pulse of the movement. As the final report of the commission explained:

> These meetings were arranged not for the purpose of counting "votes" pro or con, but rather for the purpose of gathering information on the problems which concerned the rank and file of the Movement, and the arguments which were being formulated by the laity. It was felt to be a fundamental principle of Jewish practice that any decision concerning Jewish usage, even an halakhically based decision, must take account of what will be reasonably acceptable to the community.[51]

Indeed, the commission discovered that members of the Jewish community avidly desired to express their opinions about ordination. The Chancellor and the commission received bundles of mail from Conservative Jews, both rabbis and laypeople, eager to contribute to the discussion.

In making a decision about women in the rabbinate, Chancellor Cohen and the members of the commission were particularly interested in evaluating public opinion within the movement. In addition to the hearings, they sponsored scientific surveys designed to measure attitudes toward women's ordination. The commission hoped that a scientific sampling might better portray the readiness of the movement to accept ordination. With the help of a market research firm, Yankelovich, Skelly, and White, the commission selected fourteen representative congregations and distributed questionnaires designed to determine attitudes toward women's rights in the synagogue, including the right to serve as rabbis. In a preliminary report, the firm presented the initial data which revealed that "on the whole, the prospect of a female rabbi appeals to a slight majority."[52] However, the survey also demonstrated some potentially damaging effects of ordaining women. One in ten members indicated that they would change affiliation if their congregation were to hire a female rabbi. The study also found that greater levels of observance and education correlated with a tendency to reject the idea of women's ordination.[53] Another study prepared by Charles Liebman and Saul Shapiro revealed similar data that prompted Liebman to argue that the ordination of women would be detrimental to the future of Conservative Judaism.[54] Explaining his findings before the Seminary faculty, Liebman insisted that "since observance is correlated to opinions on ordination, we would be antagonizing those upon whom we must depend for our future."[55] Yet, as many ordination advocates observed, those who claimed that women's ordination might prompt them to leave the Conservative movement represented an older segment within Conservative Jewry, while members under thirty-five years of age generally favored women's ordination. More than one-third of Conservative Jews under thirty-five reported that they might consider leaving the movement if ordination were denied to women. Therefore, it was also possible to argue that women's ordination secured rather than damaged the future of Conservative Judaism. The surveys conducted under the commission's auspices ultimately provided ample evidence to support the contentions of both sides of the ordination debate.

Within their private deliberations, commission members seriously weighed the consequences of women's ordination. At the opening commission meeting, Chancellor Cohen expressed the dilemma:

> The community may not be ready for [ordination], even if we could see our way to doing it. And therefore, if the community is not ready for it, it would be I think a theological violation for me to take what I consider a prophetic stance ... and to fight for something which would only be destructive of the community. Therefore, I am torn between my perception of women who feel that they should morally be the equal of men, and my perception that the ordination of women today would only rip the community apart.[56]

Other members of the commission shared an apprehension about the ramifications of ordination. The greatest concerns about ordaining women revolved around the possibility of permanently alienating the traditional element within Conservative Jewry, potentially provoking an irreparable split within the movement and signaling a betrayal of the movement's commitment to pluralism. A pro-ordination vote might also prompt the resignations of respected Seminary faculty members, make the Conservative movement appear less distinct from Reform and no longer faithful to Jewish law, and threaten any future relationship with the traditional religious leadership in Israel. The commission debated all these potential consequences but also considered the consequences of not ordaining women. Refusing women's ordination might spark the disaffection of Conservative Jews who felt passionately about the ethical necessity and halakhic legitimacy of ordaining women, a group that included both women and men. A negative decision on the ordination question would also make the Seminary, the leading institution of Conservative Judaism, appear antiquated and incapable of responding to contemporary needs. Such characterizations had already begun appearing in the press. One magazine article used the Seminary's architecture, its "great iron gates" and "secluded inner courtyard," to symbolize "the institution's aloofness from current changes in Judaism, even those within the Conservative movement."[57] Many commission members believed that an anti-ordination vote would send the message of a stultified religious movement and endanger the future of Conservative Judaism. As the commission debated the various angles of the ordination decision, its members came to realize that some factions of the movement would be displeased no matter what the outcome. In reaching a decision, Cohen insisted to the commission, "If the community is going to be split apart, one way or the other, let us at least take the path where our conscience leads us."[58]

For Gerson Cohen, the fourteen-month deliberation of the commission marked a turning point in his personal position on women's ordination. Cohen had assumed office at a time when the women's issue was taking center stage in the Conservative movement. In the early years of his tenure, Cohen defended the Seminary's policy not to admit women and insisted that "religious change should not be brought about by popular pressure."[59] By the time the commission had concluded its work, Cohen declared himself "passionately in favor of ordination of women."[60] According to Cohen's personal notes, his conversion came in the month before the commission's final meeting.[61] He weighed the halakhic evidence and became convinced that no serious halakhic barriers existed. While Cohen continued to express his respect for those who argued that the ordination of women contradicted Jewish law, he had not been persuaded by their arguments.[62] He also came to believe that the future of the Seminary and the Conservative movement depended upon a favorable response on women's ordination. In Cohen's estimation, "the welfare of Conservative Judaism, the supremacy of [the] Seminary, [and his] moral duty to its members" required him to advocate women's right to become rabbis.[63] At the commission's final meeting in December 1978, he told the delegation, "This year of agonizing and study has been very fruitful. It's changed me a bit, as you can see, because I really began with a prejudice against [ordination]. I am now not for it, I am passionately for it."[64]

In the most heated moments of the ordination battle, Cohen composed a personal list of the pros and cons of women's ordination. The negative consequences that he envisioned included a possible split in the faculty, the disaffection of the "right wing of the RA and [the] hard core laity," the Seminary's image in Israel, and the potential loss of students to the Orthodox movement. However, his list of the favorable reasons for ordaining women was much longer. He insisted that admitting women to the rabbinate would "prevent splinter activity in [the] RA."[65] Cohen remained profoundly concerned with retaining the Seminary's leading position within the Conservative movement. "I feel that if the Seminary is to provide leadership," he told the commission, "it has to take this role. . . . We cannot be at the tail end all the time. I would rather be at the center of this movement, controlling the ordination, regulating it . . . as an institution."[66] Cohen not only wanted the Seminary to take institutional control within the movement but was also eager to portray the Seminary as "responding to modernity." In his notes, Cohen reflected, the Seminary "can't be out of touch as we have been growing increasingly." He believed that the Seminary had committed a serious error throughout the 20th century by not placing itself at the center of Conservative Jewish life. "By holding itself aloof, it has abdicated, and it has left a vacuum." On more than one occasion, Cohen compared the Seminary's stance toward ordination with its response to Mordecai Kaplan and the nascent Reconstructionist movement that emerged from within the ranks of Conservative Judaism during the mid-20th century. Cohen believed that

Kaplan succeeded by addressing the critical issues of his day. In portraying the break of Reconstructionism from Conservative Judaism, Cohen explained, "It wasn't Kaplan's views . . . that caused the schism. . . . It was the reluctance, the unwillingness, the inability, the abdication . . . on the part of the leaders of this Seminary and the Conservative movement in terms of dealing with the realities of the changes of atmosphere and how to deal and grope with the problems halachically." Chancellor Cohen did not want to repeat the miscalculation of the Kaplan era and sharply criticized the Seminary faculty's refusal to render halakhic decisions that answered the needs of contemporary American Jews.[67] Announcing his decision to vote in favor of admitting women to the rabbinate, Cohen explained to commission members that his position reflected "not only ordination of women. It's a total upheaval of our posture towards Seminary leadership."[68]

On his list of the advantages of ordaining women, Cohen also noted, "We are losing to Orthodoxy and Reform anyway. I must lead those I have positively."[69] In the course of the commission hearings, the Chancellor became convinced that discussing the ordination question in terms of the relationship with other movements was irrelevant. He told the commission:

> I'm not concerned with Reform, nor am I concerned with Orthodoxy. I'm concerned with us. . . . I hope that no faculty will leave. But we cannot be paralyzed by that threat anymore. I hope that nobody will leave the Conservative Movement, but we cannot be threatened by that. I'd rather lose people in the Conservative Movement, and have integrity within our movement.[70]

For Cohen, the ordination of women signaled the Seminary's willingness to lead and to reinvigorate the Conservative Jewish community.

The commission held its final meeting in December 1978 when the majority of members voted in favor of women's ordination. By the time commission members convened for the last time, tensions had already begun to escalate within the movement and particularly within the JTS faculty. "I have literally not slept with calls and threats, cajoling, [and] writing" from all sides of the debate, Cohen told the commission. He also informed the members of "pressures . . . beginning to mount from the faculty."[71] JTS faculty recognized that the commission would likely vote in favor of ordination, and delegations of faculty members opposed to ordination pleaded with and threatened Cohen, insisting that "it would be disastrous for the future of Conservative Judaism if women were ordained."[72] Despite such objections, the commission issued its report recommending that "qualified women be ordained as rabbis within the Conservative Movement" and called upon the Seminary to admit women to its Rabbinical School. Eleven members signed the commission's majority report while three members dissented, writing a minority opinion that opposed admitting women to the rabbinate but advocated that "appropriate roles be created for Jewish women short of ordination."[73] In accordance with the original RA mandate, the commission reported its findings to the Rabbinical Assembly at the annual convention in Los Angeles. The commission first announced its decision in January 1979, an event so highly anticipated that the Seminary set up a recorded telephone message where interested parties could learn of the findings in the Chancellor's own words.[74] The commission then published its report and referred its recommendation to the faculty of the Jewish Theological Seminary. With the commission's work concluded, the ordination question became the province of the Seminary faculty.

Prelude to a Vote:
JTS Faculty and the Admission of Women to Rabbinical School

The commission had never been assigned the responsibility of legislating for the Conservative movement or for the Jewish Theological Seminary. Its duty was to make a recommendation on women's ordination, but the final decision about admitting women to rabbinical school rested with the JTS faculty. Even before the commission issued its report, Chancellor Cohen assured concerned faculty members that "the report, whether positive or negative will be brought to the faculty for adoption or rejection."[75] Such assurances did not, however, alleviate mounting tensions within the JTS faculty. At an emergency faculty meeting held immediately before the 1979 RA convention, faculty members began discussing the implications of the forthcoming commission report. One professor pointed out that favorable recommendations by both the RA and the commission would make it very difficult for the JTS faculty to reject women's ordination without creating an avalanche of "bad public relations." Another professor insisted that a close faculty vote, whether approving or rejecting ordination "would not give confidence" to the movement. Since most faculty members anticipated the favorable findings of the commission, ordination opponents reiterated their accusation that "halacha [had] played a subservient role" in the commission's deliberations, denouncing both the commission procedure and impending faculty vote as improper. Cohen took exception to those charges, emphasizing the commission's unwavering commitment to the primacy of *halakha* and declaring that the faculty would be given every opportunity to consider carefully all aspects of the ordination question.[76] Cohen's immediate concern was that the faculty agree to tackle the ordination issue immediately so that he could assure the RA that the Seminary would not delay the matter any longer. "The Seminary must move into the forefront by grappling with the issue," he implored faculty members, warning that if JTS failed to do so, "the institution will be discredited."[77]

Before the RA convention and release of the commission report, the Seminary faculty attempted to establish procedures for handling the ordination decision. In a heated and often angry discussion, faculty members debated whether a two-thirds or a majority vote was required on the ordination issue, ultimately deciding to maintain a majority rule. They also initiated the first of many arguments about which faculty members were entitled to vote. At the conclusion of a contentious meeting, Rabbi David Kogen presented a motion that dictated faculty procedure after the release of the commission report. Kogen proposed that the faculty

> study the following questions and submit written statements to the Chancellor for circulation to the Faculty by May 1, 1979:
>   1. Is the ordination of women in accordance with halacha?
>   2. What would be the halachic consequences of the ordination of women?
>   3. What other considerations are pertinent to the question?
> Within ten days after these papers are circulated, the faculty will meet for extended deliberation, following which it will vote its position by May 30, 1979.[78]

Despite objections from some faculty members who claimed that the May deadline "was a stratagem . . . for a 'shotgun' admission committee for September 1979," (an accusation the Chancellor called "offensive"), the motion passed and the faculty resolved to render a decision by the close of the 1979 academic year.[79]

The rancorous tenor of the faculty meeting preceding the RA convention foreshadowed the bitter struggle that gripped the JTS faculty after the publication of the commission report. The release of the commission's findings altered the nature of the ordination debate. One prospective female rabbinical student remembered that after the commission's endorsement of ordination, the mood was "overwhelmingly positive" among those hoping for women's admission to rabbinical school.[80] Even opponents of ordination generally believed that an affirmative vote on women's ordination was imminent. As one anti-ordination leader reflected, "our side is not doing well at all."[81] Although Chancellor Cohen declared that he "was resuming a neutral position as Chairman of the faculty and would no longer advocate any position" on the ordination issue, he had already become so deeply and passionately committed to women's ordination that neutrality was impossible.[82] Indeed, in his most candid moments, Cohen confided to friends and allies that he would "try to ram the commission's report down the Faculty's throats."[83] Cohen understood that a very strong minority in the faculty was "unalterably opposed" to ordination and that he could not change their views. However, he believed that he could "mitigate their sense of hurt by preparing them, briefing them."[84] Efforts to calm emotions at the Seminary during the first months of 1979 proved futile as the opposing sides of the ordination battle became increasingly strident and combative. Even before the release of the commission report, four Seminary professors warned Cohen, "You know, [the commission report] is a recommendation to the faculty, we could vote you down." Cohen replied that should that occur, "they would have to choose a different Chancellor." Although he later retracted that ultimatum, Cohen had become completely and intensely enmeshed in the furor over women's ordination.[85] In perhaps the greatest understatement of the ordination controversy, Cohen admitted to the JTS community, "It's no secret that there is considerable tension in the Seminary these days."[86]

In an attempt to ameliorate the situation and increase the potential for a peaceful resolution, Chancellor Cohen agreed to postpone the faculty vote from May to December 1979. When he acquiesced in the postponement, Cohen hoped that an acrimonious vote might be avoided if the faculty had the opportunity to discuss and reflect upon the issue. As Cohen explained to a confidant:

> Faculty opponents of the ordination of women have asked for additional time
> to formulate their statements, and I have agreed to defer the vote from May 31
> to December 1. I have hoped that by letting matters cool about ten months, I
> will be able to persuade some of the middle-of-the-roaders to assume a gradu-
> alist position whereby we will be able to give women some form of equal status,
> of course within halakhic limits.[87]

Cohen publicly defended his decision to postpone the vote as a means of allowing thorough study of all aspects of the ordination question.[88] To critics in the RA who viewed the delay as a possible betrayal, Cohen explained that, "I feel it to be my duty to try to keep the great faculty of the Seminary united even in disagreement, and this requires that I do not make anyone feel that I 'steamrolled' an issue to a vote."[89] Throughout the ordination controversy, Cohen remained a deliberate politician, balancing the need to appease his opponents with the ultimate goal of winning approval for women's ordination. As a tactical move, the delay prevented an immediate confrontation with the faculty and bolstered Cohen's image as a religious leader who encouraged intellectual dialogue and serious reflection about the ordination issue.

At the same time, the postponement also lengthened the opportunity for ideological positions to become entrenched, for emotions to build, and for the opposition to plan its strategy. By the time the new JTS academic year began in the fall of 1979, tensions at the Seminary had escalated to an unprecedented level. One professor expressed his disappointment at "the bitterness and dissent" and "the disintegration of collegiality" that characterized the Seminary faculty.[90] The entire Seminary community was preoccupied with the struggle over women's ordination. Students who favored ordination met regularly in the JTS dorms to "pore over the faculty lists and count the votes," assessing the likelihood of an affirmative vote. They believed they "had the votes" but sent delegations to any wavering faculty members who might be persuaded to vote for women's ordination.[91] In the meantime, Chancellor Cohen continued to lobby vigorously for ordination, earning increasing respect from those who wanted women admitted to the rabbinate but facing growing hostility and resentment from ordination opponents. Cohen remained resolute in the face of bitter opposition, but he certainly felt the mounting pressure. "I get moments of soul searching hesitation," he confided to a friend. "For a man in my position that's dangerous for the other side looks for the slightest show of weakness on my part."[92] By the fall of 1979, the ordination of women had become a full-fledged political battle within the Seminary, sparking heated debates and personal attacks.

One of the first areas of contention was the question of which faculty members would be allowed to cast a vote on women's ordination. Since the preceding year, faculty members had been arguing about the voting procedures of the Seminary Senate, the body that ruled on all issues affecting the institution. The senate consisted of tenured faculty members, certain administrators, and non-tenured representatives from each of the Seminary schools. At a highly charged faculty meeting, a slim majority voted to allow the full senate to decide the question of ordination. Opponents of ordination attacked that ruling, arguing that only the Rabbinical School faculty (or preferably the Talmud faculty) should determine the halakhic validity of ordination and the admissions policy of the Seminary's rabbinical school.[93] Since it appeared that a vote of the full senate would likely support ordination, the opposition grew defensive and accused Chancellor Cohen of manipulating voting procedures in order to secure a positive decision.

In November, just weeks before the scheduled vote, a group of sixteen faculty members united to challenge the ordination deliberations. In a letter to the Chancellor, they denounced the senate as an improper forum for determining Seminary policy and insisted that "the deliberate perpetuation of an admittedly inequitable structure, in an atmosphere of tension and rancor, renders the validity of all the Senate's decisions subject to serious challenge." The dissatisfied faculty members also demanded that a critical religious issue such as women's ordination "should be decided only by the most competent rabbinical authority, rather than treated as an ordinary academic or administrative question." Acting upon their objections, the group of sixteen refused to "participate in debating or voting on the question of the ordination of women unless a proper body is constituted to deal with this issue."[94] "The sixteen," which included a significant portion of the Talmud faculty, mounted a serious threat to the success of the ordination vote and to Cohen's leadership. The Chancellor recognized the challenge and spent long hours with his advisers discussing the best means to handle the increasingly militant opposition. Rabbi Yaakov Rosenberg, a trusted member of the Chancellor's Cabinet, outlined detailed scenarios of the meetings scheduled with "the sixteen" in which Cohen would offer the faculty members the option of participating in the vote, absenting themselves and abiding by the majority rule, or referring the decision to the Chancellor's discretion. Obviously, the opposition was not interested in any such arrangements, but Cohen and his advisers hoped somehow to avoid the spectacle of determining such an important issue with only half the faculty's participation. They wanted Cohen to appear firm but conciliatory, "to acknowledge the pain and anguish suffered by all" and find a suitable remedy.[95] While Cohen conducted the meetings with "the sixteen" in a calm and open manner, he confessed privately that their actions had convinced him that he could no longer "depend on the probity and honor" of the opposing faculty members. In response to the determined resistance of a strong minority, Cohen resolved to carry out the vote and "declare a complete victory for the ordination of women" with or without the participation of certain faculty members.[96]

As the furor raged among faculty members, Gerson Cohen found his leadership and future as Chancellor in serious jeopardy. The more contentious and divisive the women's issue became, the more Cohen wondered whether he "should regard the vote as a point of confidence or not." To his friends, he confided his fears that "I will not be able to function as the head of the Conservative movement if I am defeated by the vote."[97] Trusted members of the Seminary faculty managed to convince Cohen not to regard the vote as either an affirmation or an indictment of his leadership.[98] Nevertheless, Cohen wrestled with the political risks throughout the ordination controversy. The rumors that he might resign if the faculty rejected women's ordination had become so pervasive that in an open Seminary meeting with the Chancellor, one student directly inquired whether he intended to do so. Quieting the rumors, Cohen publicly declared his decision to remain Chancellor regardless of the outcome of the vote.[99] As the personal and political stakes increased, Cohen's convictions about admitting women to the rabbinate seemed to grow even stronger. "[E]very creative change in Jewish law has had consequences," he explained, but "we can no longer minister to a community of 1902 or 1952. We must legislate for a community of 1979 and, indeed, 2000, too. This is what drove me to change my position from opposition to ordination of women to support of it."[100] Having made a commitment to women's ordination, Cohen put his full political clout behind attaining that goal, alienating many faculty members in the process.

By the fall of 1979, the mood surrounding the ordination debate had shifted dramatically, from the feeling that approval of women's ordination would follow quickly on the heels of the commission report to a sense of paralysis and bitter dissension within the faculty that threatened to derail the process. Debra Cantor, a student who aspired to the rabbinate, had left the Seminary in 1977 and returned in 1979, hopeful that women would soon be admitted to rabbinical school. She recalled that the confidence about ordination that had "seemed like a sure thing" rapidly disappeared in the months preceding the scheduled December vote.[101] The minority of faculty members ardently opposed to ordination had objected loudly, refused to participate in the vote; some had even threatened to resign if women's ordination passed. Although they remained a minority, their strident opposition had become sufficiently potent to raise doubts among those that Cohen called the "middle-of-the-roaders." Some faculty members who personally favored ordination found the emotionally charged struggle over women's ordination so distasteful and painful that they began to question the wisdom of pursuing such a divisive issue. In early December, Professor Yochanan Muffs, who supported women's ordination but did not consider himself "a passionate partisan," conveyed his concerns to Gerson Cohen in a letter that reflected the sentiments of many faculty members:

> I am afraid that even if we get the votes needed for the ordination, our victory will be a pyrrhic one leaving some no recourse other than to resign and others to teach with a lack of enthusiasm. If it comes to the choice of saving the school or resolving the women's issue (which is certainly an ethical issue) I would opt for saving the school.[102]

Several faculty members who were neither virulent opponents nor enthusiastic advocates of women's ordination began to fear that the issue had become so explosive that it threatened the institutional future of the Seminary.

Professor Muffs urged Chancellor Cohen to table the vote, a proposal that many faculty members considered advisable given the stormy atmosphere that pervaded the Seminary in the winter of 1979. In a pained letter to Cohen, Professor Ismar Schorsch articulated his fears about forcing a vote on women's ordination. "In light of the acrimonious discord which is fragmenting the faculty," Schorsch argued that even a positive vote on women's ordination would prove detrimental. "Renowned members of the faculty who opposed the decision will surely seek a more hospitable climate in which to resume their scholarship, and those forced to stay will constitute a sullen and uncooperative lot, hardly an asset to the institution."[103] Cohen responded kindly to Schorsch's letter and clearly considered him an ally in the struggle. However, Cohen remained resolute, insisting, "I will not submit to or flinch from confrontation with people whose only method of argument is withdrawal from discussion with peers and of paralysing activity through threats." Chancellor Cohen refused to compromise his position. "For me to withdraw after making a promise to face the issue," he maintained, "would be to confess that the Seminary is an institution without moral fiber."[104]

Cohen's adversaries proved equally determined in battling against women's ordination. The opponents of ordination, realizing their minority status within the JTS faculty, strategically organized an independent conference outside the auspices of the Seminary. On 18 December, just before the scheduled vote, the Conference on Halakhic Process convened in Queens, New York, attracting a group of Seminary professors, Conservative rabbis, and laypeople. "The goal of this conference," explained its organizers, "is to provide a forum for as yet unheard voices of respected teachers and colleagues on questions which will determine the relationship of Halakhah and Halakhic process to the future of the Conservative Movement." At the conference, five members of the JTS Talmud faculty argued that halakhic barriers prohibited women from serving as rabbis.[105] Professor Saul Lieberman, the senior member of the Talmud Department who never wrote a formal responsum on the question of women's ordination, did not attend the gathering. However, in a note to conference participants, Lieberman declared that he "was pleased to hear that a large number of my students and friends have decided to deliberate intensely as to how to prevent the 'last spark of halakha' from being extinguished."[106] Lieberman's greetings to the conference were extremely important, for his status as the reigning Talmud scholar of the Seminary gave his opinions great influence within the Seminary community. Lieberman had conspicuously avoided any written opinions on women's ordination, and he had not joined fellow Talmud faculty members as a member of "the sixteen." Nevertheless, Lieberman was widely understood to be an opponent of women's ordination; his public endorsement of a conference explicitly organized to contest the validity of women's admission to the rabbinate simply gave greater credence to that position. The conference concluded with a resolution that its participants would "not accept as authoritative any decision on the question of the ordination of women which does not give primacy to the opinions presented by these halakhists."[107]

The halakhic positions presented at the conference were not new to the Seminary faculty, but the meeting had an enormous impact, underscoring the sharp opposition to women's ordination and further convincing some faculty members of the potential repercussions of the vote. Only two days after the conference, the Seminary Senate convened to consider a motion to table the vote on women's ordination. Ismar Schorsch, who had attended the Queens meeting "in order to see what the enemy camp looked like," proposed the tabling resolution. Schorsch had already expressed concerns that a vote might produce an irreparable split in the JTS faculty, and his visit to Queens further persuaded him of the deep divisions about the women's issue that existed within the Conservative movement.[108] Introducing the motion to table, Schorsch insisted that "there would be no winners on this issue and that the faculty had lost its civility, collegiality and much of its academic effectiveness." He supported tabling the vote as a means "to restore harmony and peace" within the Conservative movement and the JTS faculty.[109] The text of the motion read:

> For the past two years the prospect of a vote by the Seminary faculty on the question of ordaining women had preoccupied the attention of the Conservative Movement. As the time for that vote draws near, it is abundantly clear that the question has provoked unprecedented divisions at every level of the Movement. The bitter divergence of opinion threatens to inflict irreparable damage to the academic excellence of the Seminary and the pluralistic unity of the

Rabbinical Assembly. Accordingly, we move that the question be tabled until such time as a balanced committee of talmudic scholars, to be appointed by the Chancellor, has completed a systematic study of the status of women in Jewish law.[110]

The meeting, which lasted three and a half hours, included some contentious debate, with ordination advocates arguing passionately to proceed with a vote or refer the matter to the Chancellor for a final decision. However, despite the objections, the Schorsch resolution passed by a vote of 25 to 19, and the faculty adjourned without setting any definite timetable for reconsidering the issue.[111]

From Postponement to Passage: Women's Admission to the Conservative Rabbinate

Although the tabling of the vote represented a painful defeat for Chancellor Cohen, he attempted to portray the event in the best possible light. In a public address to the Seminary community, Cohen told ordination advocates "to accept this decision as a challenge and not a defeat." He pleaded for understanding and healing, praising the diversity and pluralism of the Conservative movement and its ability to withstand debate.[112] To Rabbinical Assembly members, Cohen more directly defined the vote as "tantamount to a defeat of ordination for the foreseeable future." He informed fellow Conservative rabbis that he did not intend to appoint a committee of talmudic scholars to study the women's issue, as the motion to table had suggested. Cohen felt that the commission and the papers written by Seminary faculty members constituted sufficient analysis of the problem. He rejected the notion that further study of the issue would provide any new insights, insisting that "when our Movement becomes more confident of its own identity, we will ordain women."[113]

In the meantime, the Seminary's decision to table the vote had serious repercussions throughout the Conservative movement. While opponents of ordination praised Cohen as "one of the courageous leaders, who put the welfare of the Seminary and the Conservative Movement ahead of his own interests," ordination advocates did not hesitate to express their anger and disappointment.[114] One RA member decided to withhold his contribution to the Seminary's fund-raising campaign, claiming that the faculty's failure to act was "an affront not only to the Chancellor and the commission but the body of the RA as well."[115] Fishel Pearlmutter, who had devoted years to the ordination crusade, was "deeply frustrated and personally angered" by the faculty's decision and the Chancellor's acceptance of the delay tactics. "I assumed [Cohen] meant to use every bit of his leadership," Pearlmutter wrote in a letter expressing his sense of betrayal.[116] One of the most vocal protests came from the Group for the Rabbinic Ordination of Women (GROW), an organization of rabbis, rabbinical students, and laypeople committed to realizing the goal of women's ordination. After the vote was tabled, GROW attacked the decision as "immoral" and organized rallies to denounce publicly the decision of the Seminary faculty. GROW held some of its demonstrations on the front steps of the Jewish Theological Seminary where speakers assailed the JTS faculty as a body that "feebly threw up its hands in the face of a necessary initiative."[117] The decision to table the vote may have forestalled an internal battle within the Seminary, but it did not put to rest the passionate feelings regarding women's ordination.

Chancellor Cohen reluctantly acquiesced in the faculty's decision, but he had no intention of relinquishing the long-term campaign for women's ordination. Immediately after the tabling of the vote, Cohen set out to create a new Seminary graduate program for women, designed to qualify them to serve as religious functionaries albeit not as rabbis. When opponents of ordination learned of the new program, they attacked it as "a means for achieving eventual ordination of women."[118] Accusing Cohen of preparing women for the rabbinate through subterfuge, opposing faculty members rekindled the hostility and distrust that had surrounded the ordination debate. Cohen countered by asserting his right as Chancellor to create a new academic program and emphasized that "the Conservative movement was in dire need of all the talent available to it." He informed the faculty that he "would do nothing to circumvent the faculty decision" but intended to "explore alternatives to the Rabbinate as avenues for religious ministry on the part of the women in the Jewish community."[119] By the fall of 1980, the Chancellor had created a Religious Ministry Program, entitled Shadar, under the directorship of Professor Anne Lerner. The program required a "commitment to a halakhic way of life within the parameters of the Conservative Movement" and offered graduates a Doctorate of Hebrew Letters (D.H.L.) as well as a religious title.[120]

The Shadar program represented Cohen's attempt to provide dedicated Jewish women with career alternatives and to prepare them for a time when women might be ordained. He expressed particular concern for a group of seven women who had studied in JTS graduate programs and were widely known to be prospective rabbinical students.[121] After the tabling of the vote, he wrote each of them letters and met with them several times, urging the women to remain at the Seminary and within the Conservative movement. He insisted that he would abide by the faculty's decision but firmly underscored his commitment to women's ordination.[122] The women involved understood that Cohen was their advocate. Nina Beth Cardin, who would eventually pursue a career in the rabbinate, wrote to Cohen expressing the collective confidence of the seven women who had been hoping for admission to the rabbinate. "It is very gratifying to know we, the '7,' can count on you, without any promises, to help press this case," Cardin assured the Chancellor.[123] Most of the women who aspired to the rabbinate believed that women's ordination would be approved sometime in the future, but not all were willing to wait. The Shadar program initially attracted one or two students, but most women never considered it a serious program. They wanted to become rabbis, not second-class religious functionaries. The few women who remained at the Seminary's graduate school pursued degrees in Talmud or other subjects; no one ever completed the Shadar program. Shadar was created as a means of offering some option to those women who had wanted to pursue rabbinic careers, but ultimately it served only to anger opponents of ordination who viewed it as a camouflaged rabbinic program and to disappoint women who had hoped to become Conservative rabbis.[124]

For more than three years after the creation of the Shadar program, the Seminary removed itself from any open action on the women's issue. After 1980, the ordination debate was temporarily shelved, replaced by public declarations about healing within the movement and the need to carry on with the work of Conservative Judaism. Women's ordination disappeared from the active agenda of the Seminary, but most ordination advocates believed that the issue would be revisited. "No one thought it was not going to happen," recalled Debra Cantor. "I thought it would happen in my lifetime," she remembered, "but perhaps not until I had reached my fifties."[125] Many women, including Cantor, left JTS and returned only after they could enter as rabbinical students; some women pursued rabbinic careers in other Jewish movements, while others abandoned plans for the rabbinate altogether. Within the Seminary and the Conservative movement, a range of opinion existed about when women's ordination might become a reality. After the vote was tabled in 1979, Rabbi Joel Roth, who authored an influential responsum favoring women's ordination, lamented that "the issue of the ordination of women will be a dead issue within the Seminary" and estimated that the question would be postponed "for at least fifty years, if not forever."[126] In contrast, Rabbi Fishel Pearlmutter reiterated a belief that "this set-back will be temporary. The cause of justice will proceed, and we will yet see women in the JTS Rabbinical School and ordained by the Jewish Theological Seminary."[127] In the early 1980s, the ordination debate retreated from the center stage of the Conservative movement, but the issue continued to percolate within the Seminary and the Rabbinical Assembly, and among Conservative men and women.

The Rabbinical Assembly had consistently been the force pressuring the Seminary to consider women's ordination, and it continued to advocate women's admission to rabbinical school even after the faculty tabled the issue. Although the RA membership had never unanimously supported women's ordination—and indeed a strong minority had strenuously objected to the measure—the organization had emerged as a tenacious proponent of ordination since the mid-1970s. Longtime ordination advocates within the RA, who had delayed their own ordination motion and trusted the commission and the Seminary faculty to rule on the women's issue, felt "chagrined and angered" by the decision to table the vote.[128] At the 1980 RA convention following the tabling, members adopted a mild resolution calling upon the Seminary "to discuss and vote on the motion tabled with all deliberate speed."

In a further declaration of its collective sentiment, the resolution also asserted, "The Rabbinical Assembly goes on record as favoring the ordination of women." Such motions by the RA revealed the organization's growing support of admitting women to the rabbinate but had little success in motivating the Jewish Theological Seminary to reconsider the women's issue.[129]

By the early 1980s, staunch supporters of women's ordination within the Rabbinical Assembly had grown impatient and frustrated with the inaction of JTS and moved to take matters into their own hands. For years, the RA had respected the "gentlemen's agreement" within the Conservative movement and waited for the Seminary to approve women's ordination before initiating its own measures. However, as early as 1977, Wolfe Kelman, executive vice-president of the RA, had discussed offering private ordination to qualified women if JTS proved unwilling to act.[130] After the tabling of the vote, support for women's ordination increased within the RA as did the dissatisfaction with the Seminary. "The faculty slammed the door on women who have been studying and eager to enter into full equality within the Conservative Movement," Fishel Pearlmutter told his RA colleagues. "I want to push the door back open."[131] After the Seminary postponed the decision, several RA members raised the possibility of creating a *Beit Din*, a rabbinic court, that would be empowered to ordain rabbis. In that way, the RA could act independently of JTS to admit women to the Conservative rabbinate and, in the words of one RA member, "could once again become the master of its own house."[132] Discussions about creating such a procedure remained the province of passionate ordination advocates within the RA, but the larger RA membership had become more receptive to exerting its political clout in bringing about women's ordination.

In 1983, the Rabbinical Assembly took a dramatic step toward admitting women to the Conservative rabbinate. At the annual RA convention in Dallas, Texas, the Rabbinical Assembly debated a motion to accept Beverly Magidson, a rabbi ordained by the Reform movement's Hebrew Union College, as a member of the RA. According to RA policy, rabbis ordained outside the Seminary who served in Conservative congregations or in the larger Jewish community and also met other objective criteria were eligible for RA membership. Magidson worked for the B'nai B'rith Hillel Foundation in St. Louis and earned a unanimous recommendation for admission from the RA membership committee. By accepting Magidson as a member of the RA, the Rabbinical Assembly could effectively create an avenue for allowing women to become Conservative rabbis—an avenue that completely circumvented the Jewish Theological Seminary. At the convention, rabbis on both sides of the ordination question participated in a stormy debate over whether to admit Beverly Magidson. Advocates of the move urged the RA to accept the moral and halakhic position that the Seminary had abdicated; opponents reiterated halakhic objections to women's ordination and insisted that the Conservative movement would be fractured by such a decision. In a final vote, the tally was 210 in favor of admitting Magidson and 75 opposed, a result that fell four votes short of the 75 percent required for membership.[133] Beverly Magidson was not accepted as a member of the Rabbinical Assembly, but the extremely close vote sent a clear message that the admission of female candidates to the RA would not be delayed much longer.

The Magidson episode occurred in April 1983; the following month Chancellor Cohen announced that a Seminary faculty vote on the ordination of women would take place the next fall. Cohen's declaration took the faculty and the Seminary community by surprise.[134] When the vote had been tabled three and a half years earlier, one faculty member had remarked, "No Chancellor with a modicum of sanity would wish to subject the Seminary again to the type of purgatory in which it has been suffering for these two years."[135] Indeed, Cohen had no intention of reigniting the fires of political suspicion and relentless bickering that had surrounded the previous ordination debate. From the outset, Chancellor Cohen orchestrated the 1983 vote in a manner designed to win approval for women's ordination. Professor Judith Hauptman recalled that the announcement of the impending vote arrived in faculty members' mailboxes after graduation, at the close of the 1983 academic year. Refusing to allow JTS faculty and students to become enmeshed in an acrimonious dispute, Cohen informed the community of the upcoming vote just as the institution was concluding its final exercises. Moreover, Cohen sent an early message that the decision would not be delayed or derailed. Hauptman remembered that when faculty members received Cohen's letter, "We all knew exactly what it meant. We all knew for sure it meant that women were going to be ordained." By 1983, Cohen's demeanor and strategy revealed his resolute intention to realize the goal of women's ordination.[136]

What had motivated Chancellor Cohen to act so decisively on women's ordination after the issue had been shelved for several years? The near election of Beverly Magidson clearly worried Cohen. Many of the rabbis who had opposed her election had also indicated that they favored women's ordination but preferred to see the first Conservative woman rabbi trained by the Seminary. Cohen understood that if JTS failed to act, the Rabbinical Assembly would soon begin admitting women to the Conservative rabbinate, usurping the role of the Seminary.[137] Throughout the ordination controversy, Cohen had been profoundly concerned that the Seminary remain the fountainhead of the movement. He criticized JTS for abandoning its legislative role within Conservative Jewry and was particularly fearful of relinquishing control to the Rabbinical Assembly. For Cohen, allowing the RA to become the central player in the women's issue would not only create disarray within the Conservative movement but also signal the Seminary's loss of institutional power. When Conservative Judaism moved to admit women to the rabbinate,

Chancellor Cohen wanted the Jewish Theological Seminary to be the primary force behind the decision.

In addition to the Magidson vote, many members of the Seminary community continue to mention the death of the renowned senior Talmud professor, Saul Lieberman, as a factor motivating Cohen's decision to revisit the ordination question. Lieberman died in March 1983, less than two months before Chancellor Cohen announced the upcoming vote. Lieberman had been relatively silent during the course of the ordination debate, but he was widely perceived as an ordination opponent and his Talmudic expertise carried great influence. Within the collective mythology of the Seminary, the death of Lieberman has emerged as a causal factor behind the eventual success of women's ordination. In both popular and scholarly narratives of the ordination decision, Lieberman's death is always mentioned.[138] Close advisers to the Chancellor deny that Lieberman's passing was the impetus for Cohen's tactical move, and in fact, Cohen's own writings reveal no such preoccupation with Lieberman's objections. The death of the Seminary's senior Talmud scholar may have eased Chancellor Cohen's ability to press the issue, but Cohen's primary and most vital interest throughout the long struggle for women's ordination had always been preserving the strength, integrity, and institutional power of the Seminary within the Conservative movement.[139] In that respect, it was the threat posed by the Rabbinical Assembly that emerged as the most burning issue preceding the 1983 vote.

The faculty convened for the vote on 24 October 1983 in a meeting that Cohen described as "'full of debate' but without rancor."[140] The businesslike mood of the 1983 faculty meeting stood in direct contrast to the contentious atmosphere that had characterized the previous ordination vote. The opponents of ordination, representing a significant portion of the Talmud faculty, again refused to participate in the Seminary Senate vote and denounced the voting process as an inappropriate means for determining the halakhic permissibility of women's ordination. However, this time Chancellor Cohen would not allow their absence or their objections to derail the process. In his opening remarks, Cohen declared:

> I take note that several members of this Assembly have chosen not to attend this meeting. As you all know, their decision to do so was premised on their stated conviction that this is not the proper forum for discussing and deciding the issue at hand. I believe you are all aware of my feelings about that premise . . . I shall not dwell further on it.
>
> I would like the record to show that I deeply regret the absence of some of our colleagues. It goes without saying that they are welcome at this meeting. Indeed, they belong here. With that, I ask that we turn now to a consideration of the important matter at hand, for which this meeting was called.[141]

In 1979, Cohen had been persuaded that the objections of a segment of the JTS faculty were so serious and divisive to justify tabling the vote. A few years later, how-ever, he determined that the vote would proceed despite the opposition.

The only issue of serious contention at the faculty meeting concerned the word-ing of the motion to admit women to rabbinical school and the stipulations attached to their candidacy. The original motion, introduced by Rabbi Joel Roth, proposed that women be admitted to rabbinical school "provided that they accept the obliga-tion of fulfilling the mitzvot and disavow any exemption based on distinctions between the sexes." Such a condition was not formally attached to the admission of men. Several faculty members who favored ordination objected to establishing sep-arate criteria for male and female rabbinic candidates. Professor Judith Hauptman maintained that in addition to mandating different standards for men and women, the motion would also create two classes of Jewish women, those who had assumed the obligation to fulfill all of the commandments and those who had not. Given these reservations, the faculty voted to amend Roth's original proposal and to vote on a motion that declared simply "that Jewish women be admitted to the Rabbinical School of [the] Jewish Theological Seminary as candidates for ordination as rabbis." Some faculty members spoke against the motion, arguing that halakhic barriers prohibited women's ordination altogether. Others reiterated the halakhic legitimacy of admitting women to the rabbinate and the need to respond to con-temporary demands of women's equality. The meeting proceeded relatively smoothly, with the exception of the altered wording of the original motion, and when the final votes were counted, the motion passed by a vote of 34 to 8, with one abstention.[142] The first class of women entered rabbinical school in the fall of 1984. In May 1985, Amy Eilberg, who had been pursuing advanced work in Talmud at the Seminary before matriculating as a rabbinical student, became the first woman ordained by the Conservative movement. The Rabbinical Assembly waited until Eilberg's ordination before admitting women to its membership and then permitted Beverly Magidson and other qualified non-Seminary female rabbis to become members. Ultimately, the Seminary did ordain the first woman to serve as a Con-servative rabbi.[143]

The historic vote permanently altered the character of the Jewish Theological Seminary and the Conservative rabbinate. As Chancellor Cohen declared, the Sem-inary had "achieved a major step in the equalization of women in Jewish religious life."[144] The atmosphere outside the meeting room indicated the magnitude of the decision, as aspiring female rabbinic candidates, ordination advocates, and mem-bers of the press waited anxiously at the door for news of the vote.[145] But for all its historic significance, both the faculty members involved and those who awaited the decision noted that the tension of that day paled in comparison to the tumultuous climate of 1979. Perhaps the outcome of the 1983 vote seemed more predictable, although given the stormy history of the struggle, even the most optimistic

Rabbinical
students Leslie
Gordon and
David Starr, 1986.
*Photo by Joyce
Culver. Communi-
cations Depart-
ment, JTS.*

observers refused to predict victory until the final decision was announced. Ultimately, the orderly manner in which women finally gained the right to become
rabbis presented an ironic contrast to the years of furious debate that had surrounded the question of women's ordination.

The decision to ordain women as rabbis prompted a variety of reactions within
the Seminary and throughout the Conservative movement. Not surprisingly, those
who had dedicated long years to battling for women's ordination were elated. The
night of the vote, the women of Ezrat Nashim gathered to celebrate the fulfillment
of the call they had issued over ten years earlier.[146] Jewish women who had waited
years for the opportunity to serve as Conservative rabbis began preparing to enter
the Seminary as rabbinical students. At the same time, opponents of ordination
attacked the JTS decision as a betrayal of *halakha* and a disservice to the Conservative movement. The Union for Traditional Conservative Judaism (UTCJ), an organization composed of ordination opponents, insisted that the JTS vote defied "all
norms of Jewish jurisprudence."[147] Claiming that the Seminary had repudiated the
traditional tenets of Conservative Judaism, union members created an alternative
rabbinical school, the Institute of Traditional Judaism, which admitted only men.

The UTCJ never captured a large following, but its rabbinical school attracted a prominent group of faculty and the organization remained a militant presence within the Conservative movement. The Seminary also lost its leading Talmud scholar, David Weiss Halivni, who resigned from JTS in the wake of the ordination decision, assumed a leading role in the UTCJ, and accepted a faculty appointment at neighboring Columbia University.[148] Yet, despite some significant faculty defections and the vocal opposition of a minority group, the decision to ordain women as rabbis received a generally positive response within the Seminary and among Conservative Jews. Ismar Schorsch, who proposed the 1979 tabling resolution and succeeded Gerson Cohen as Chancellor, reasoned that in the years between the tabling and the final vote a preponderant majority favoring women's ordination coalesced within the Conservative Jewish community. "What happened as a result of the delay," Schorsch explained, "was the prevention of a split down the middle; in 1983, the split occurred on the margins of the movement."[149] In the spirit of pluralism, the Conservative movement continued to respect the diversity of opinion on the women's issue. At JTS, the original synagogue that had mandated separate seating and had prohibited women's ritual participation remained in existence, complemented by a newly established egalitarian *minyan*. As a sign of the changing atmosphere at the Seminary, the new *minyan* consistently attracted a greater number of worshippers.

Although the decision to admit women to rabbinical school had been rendered, JTS had not yet begun to grapple with the profound consequences of women's entry into the rabbinate. In all the heated discussion about women's ordination, there had been little thoughtful reflection about the redefinition of gender roles and the reconceptualization of the rabbinic profession. Many observers within the JTS community noted that when women joined the rabbinic student body, "the mood of the Seminary became very different" and "there was a feeling of openness and possibility."[150] But for all its posturing about ordaining women as rabbis, the Seminary began the first year of its coed rabbinical school attempting to "carry on business as usual."[151] Presumably, the JTS Rabbinical School would continue training rabbis in the same manner but with the addition of a female constituency. Few leaders in the Seminary community anticipated the real work of including women as rabbinic leaders within the Conservative movement. Women brought a host of new challenges to the rabbinate, redefining the role of the rabbi, questioning gendered language in prayer, images of God, and creating new forms of ritual expression and spiritual leadership. The vote to admit women to rabbinical school was only a prelude to the dynamic process that would unfold once women began training and serving as rabbis in the Conservative movement.

In fact, a striking element throughout the long years of the ordination controversy was the relative absence of attention given to women's experience, gender roles, and the far-reaching implications of women serving as rabbis. To be sure, ordination advocates emphasized women's new career goals, the budding movement for equality between the sexes, and the need to overcome the sexist aspects of Jewish tradition. Critics of ordination pointed to the possible threats to masculinity, the erosion of sexual distinctions, and the supposedly temporary fad of "women's lib." However, most of the serious dialogue surrounding women's ordination involved a technical deliberation about the intricacies of Jewish law, an institutional struggle between the Rabbinical Assembly and the Seminary, and a political battle among individual leaders of the Conservative movement. In many respects, women were neither the central players nor the primary subjects within the furious dispute over whether to allow them to become rabbis. The ordination debate provided a glimpse into the ways that established male leaders viewed women and the ways that women's inclusion intersected with their larger agendas.

The discourse about ordaining women as rabbis was rooted in the political, legal, and institutional concerns of the Conservative movement not predicated upon a feminist agenda or a thoughtful deliberation about the ways that women's admission might alter the character of Conservative Judaism and its rabbinic leadership. Gerson Cohen, a man who began his tenure as Chancellor as a staunch opponent of women's ordination and concluded it as a passionate advocate, never fully grasped the feminist platform of the age. He was a foresighted institutional leader and a tactical politician interested in maintaining the strength of the Jewish Theological Seminary and the Conservative movement. For Cohen, ordaining women as rabbis became a part of realizing that larger goal. Nevertheless, without his tenacious devotion to the cause, it is doubtful that women's ordination would have succeeded in such a timely fashion.

In the most heated moments of the struggle for women's ordination, Chancellor Cohen predicted that the debate would be "a healthy phenomenon," prompting the Conservative movement "to think about substantive questions" and to awaken "from its ideological passivity."[152] Ultimately, the admission of women to the rabbinate marked only the beginning of that process. The meaningful redefinition of gender roles, the feminist reconceptualization of Conservative ideology and theology, and the practical innovations in Jewish life began to emerge only after women functioned as religious leaders within the Conservative movement. In recent years, women rabbis have gradually begun reshaping the contours of Conservative Judaism, providing fresh perspectives on Jewish tradition and new models of gendered behavior in Jewish practice. In historical terms, it is far too soon to gauge the impact of women rabbis within the Conservative Jewish community. The JTS decision to ordain women marked the conclusion of one of the most provocative chapters in the history of the Conservative movement, but it initiated a far more complex transformation that has only begun to take shape.

1. Susan Dworkin, "Henrietta Szold—Liberated Woman," in *The Jewish Woman: New Perspectives*, ed. Elizabeth Koltun (New York: Schocken Books, 1976), p. 168.

2. For more on the Teachers Institute, see the article by David Kaufman in this volume.

3. Gladys Citrin to Louis Finkelstein, 20 May 1957, Jewish Theological Seminary, Ratner Center for the Study of Conservative Judaism, Records of the Jewish Theological Seminary of America, R.G.1M–153–48 [hereafter, Ratner Center].

4. Albert Axelrad to Baruch Feldstern, 8 November 1976, Ratner Center, Commission for the Study of the Ordination of Women as Rabbis, R.G. 30, uncatalogued [hereafter, Commission Papers]. The commission papers have been catalogued since the time that I examined the collection.

5. Kassel Abelson to Gerson Cohen, 2 January 1976, Commission Papers.

6. For other examples of women applicants to the Seminary's rabbinical school, see Amy Stone, "Gentlemen's Agreement at the Seminary," *Lilith* 1, no. 3 (spring/summer 1977): pp. 13–18.

7. "Jewish Women Call For Change," document located in the Jewish Women's Resource Center, National Council of Jewish Women, New York.

8. David Kogen, cited in Stone, "Gentlemen's Agreement at the Seminary," p. 14.

9. Gerson Cohen to Kassel Abelson, 10 January 1977, Commission Papers.

10. Ibid.

11. Aaron H. Blumenthal, "An Aliyah for Women," *Proceedings of the Rabbinical Assembly* 19 (1955), pp. 168–81; Bernard Mandelbaum, "Conservative Judaism: A Direction," *Conservative Judaism* 14:1 (fall 1959); pp. 36–46.

12. See the responsum by Rabbi Phillip Sigal in Seymour Siegel, *Conservative Judaism and Jewish Law* (New York: Rabbinical Assembly, 1977), pp. 282–92; *Proceedings of the Rabbinical Assembly* 36 (1974), pp. 24–25.
    In 1954, the Law Committee had also added a new clause to the traditional ketubah designed to protect a woman from becoming an agunah in the event that her husband refused to grant her a divorce. *Proceedings of the Rabbinical Assembly* 18 (1954), pp. 55–83

13. *Proceedings of the 1973 Biennial Convention of the United Synagogue of America*, 11-15 November, 1973, pp. 108–109.

14. See, for example, letter from Usher Kirshblum to Gerson Cohen, 10 October 1975, Commission Papers.

15. The leading proponent of women's ordination in the Rabbinical Assembly, Rabbi Fishel Pearlmutter, explained his sustained effort to bring a motion before the RA in Fishel Pearlmutter to S.W. Schneider, 25 January 1980, Fishel Pearlmutter Papers, box 2, folder 4, Ratner Center, Jewish Theological Seminary of America [hereafter, Pearlmutter Papers].

16. The phrase, "Gentlemen's Agreement," was used in a *Lilith* magazine article and adequately reflects the tacit understanding between the arms of the Conservative movement. Stone, "Gentlemen's Agreement at the Seminary."

17. Wolfe Kelman to Arnold Goodman, 2 March 1977, Pearlmutter Papers, box 1, folder 2, p. 3.

18. Fishel Pearlmutter to Carol Glass, 16 March 1976, Pearlmutter Papers, box 1, folder 1, p. 2.

19. Israel Francus, "On the Ordination of Women," in *The Ordination of Women as Rabbis: Studies and Responsa* , ed. Simon Greenberg (New York: The Jewish Theological Seminary of America, 1988), p. 36.

20. David Weiss Halivni, "On Ordination of Women," in "On the Ordination of Women as Rabbis: Position Papers of the Faculty of the Jewish Theological Seminary of America," pp. 17–18. This collection of faculty papers on the question of women's ordination was circulated internally by the Seminary as a source for dialogue and study during the course of the debate. Most of the papers were later published in Greenberg, *The Ordination of Women*

as Rabbis. This volume provides an excellent discussion of the many complex halakhic issues surrounding women's ordination.

21. Joel Roth, "On the Ordination of Women as Rabbis," in Greenberg, *The Ordination of Women as Rabbis*, p. 168.

22. Robert Gordis, "The Ordination of Women," in ibid., p. 55

23. Ibid., p. 48.

24. Hauptman quoted in Reena Sigman Friedman, "Behind the Headlines: Women in the Conservative Rabbinate," *JTA Daily News Bulletin,* 17 January 1979, p. 3.

25. Joel Roth, "On the Ordination of Women as Rabbis," p. 171.

26. "Final Report of the Commission for the Study of the Ordination of Women as Rabbis," 30 January 1979, p. 9, Commission Papers. The report is also reprinted in Greenberg, *The Ordination of Women as Rabbis*, pp. 5–30.

27. Simon Greenberg, "On the Question of the Ordination of Women as Rabbis by the Jewish Theological Seminary of America," in Greenberg, *The Ordination of Women as Rabbis*, p. 86.

28. David Weiss Halivni, "On Ordination of Women," p. 17.

29. Mortimer Ostow, "Women and Change in Jewish Law, " *Conservative Judaism* 29:1 (fall 1974): pp. 5–12.

30. Minutes of the Combined Rabbinical School Faculties of the Jewish Theological Seminary of America, 3 February 1977, p. 1.

31. *Proceedings of the Rabbinical Assembly* 39 (1977), p. 139.

32. Fishel Pearlmutter, open letter to "Dear Colleague," 31 May 1977, Pearlmutter Papers, box 1, folder 2, p. 1; see also Pearlmutter's reflections on the 1977 resolution in Fishel Pearlmutter to Gerson Cohen, 18 May 1979, ibid. p. 1.

33. Gordon Tucker, "Working Paper For Members of the Commission For the Study of Women in the Rabbinate," Commission Papers, p. 4.

34. Gordon Tucker, confidential memo to Gerson Cohen, 7 September 1977, Commission Papers.

35. Press release, "Commission Named on Status of Women in Judaism, 10 November 1977, Jewish Theological Seminary of America, JTS Records, R.G. 11, Communications Department, box 8, folder 16.

36. Gerson Cohen, confidential memorandum to Wolfe Kelman, David Kogen, Stanley Schachter, and Gordon Tucker, 17 August 1977, Commission Papers.

37. The members of the Commission were: Gerson Cohen (Chancellor, JTS); Haim Dimitrovsky (Professor of Talmud, JTS); Victor Goodhill (Professor of Otologic Research, UCLA); Marion Siner Gordon (Attorney); Rivkah Harris (Assyriologist); Milton Himmelfarb (American Jewish Committee); Francine Klagsbrun (Author); Fishel Pearlmutter (Rabbi); Harry Plotkin (Attorney); Norman Redlich (Dean, NYU Law School); Elijah Schochet (Rabbi); Wilfred Shuchat (Rabbi); Seymour Siegel (Professor of Theology, JTS); Gordon Tucker (Assistant to the Chancellor, JTS; Executive Director of the Commission).

A full description of the affiliations of the Commission members can be found in "Final Report of the Commission for the Study of the Ordination of Women as Rabbis," p. 2.

38. Minutes of the Faculty Senate of the Jewish Theological Seminary of America, 8 February 1979, p. 2.

39. Usher Kirshblum, Chairman, Committee for Preservation of Tradition, "Open Letter to the Faculty, Jewish Theological Seminary," Commission Papers.

40. "Final Report of the Commission for the Study of the Ordination of Women as Rabbis," 30 January 1979, p. 4.

41. Transcript of commission meetings, 12-14 March 1978, Commission Papers, p. 442.

42. Ibid., pp. 368, 192, 117–18.

43. The hearings were held in Vancouver, Los Angeles, Minneapolis, Chicago, Washington, D.C., New York, and Toronto.

44. Gerson Cohen to Matthew Simon, 25 April 1978, Commission Papers.

45. Transcript of Washington hearing, 17 August 1978, Commission Papers, p. 48.

46. Transcript of Minneapolis hearing, 13 September, 1978, Commission Papers, p. 22.

47. Transcript of Washington hearing, Commission Papers, p. 17.

48. Transcript of New York hearing, 3 December 1978, Commission Papers.

49. "Final Report of the Commission for the Study of the Ordination of Women as Rabbis," p. 6.

50. Halivni, "On the Ordination of Women," p. 17.

51. "Final Report of the Commission for the Study of the Ordination of Women as Rabbis," pp. 5–6.

52. "Attitudes Toward Women in the Rabbinate: A Survey of Selected Conservative Congregations," Prepared for the Jewish Theological Seminary of America, January 1979, Commission Papers, p. 8.

53. Ibid., pp. 8, 13, 16.

54. Charles Liebman and Saul Shapiro, "A Survey of the Conservative Movement and Some of its Religious Attitudes," May 1979, Commission Papers.

55. Minutes of the Faculty Senate of the Jewish Theological Seminary of America, 15 May 1979, p. 4.

56. Transcript of commission meetings, 12 December 1977, Commission Papers, p. 79.

57. Stone, "Gentlemen's Agreement at the Seminary," pp. 13, 16.

58. Transcript of commission meetings, 6–7 December 1978, p. 246.

59. Gerson D. Cohen, "Statement on Women in the Rabbinate," April 1975, Commission Papers.

60. Gerson Cohen, "State of the Seminary Address to the Students," second draft, 18 November 1979, p. 11, JTS Records, Ratner Center, R.G. 11, box 60, folder 9.

61. Gerson Cohen, personal notes attached to a letter from Eli Ginzberg to Gerson Cohen, 23 March 1979, Commission Papers.

62. Gordon Tucker, interview by author, 19 November 1993. Tucker recalled that Cohen had confided to him that no members of the Commission or the faculty had been able to formulate what he considered persuasive halakhic arguments prohibiting women's ordination.

63. Gerson Cohen, personal notes attached to a letter from Eli Ginzberg to Gerson Cohen, 23 March 1979.

64. Transcript of commission meetings, 6-7 December 1978, Commission Papers, p. 251.

65. Gerson Cohen, personal notes attached to letter from Eli Ginzberg to Gerson Cohen, 23 March 1979. Ginzberg had written to Cohen, suggesting that he "put down on paper the pluses and minuses" of ordaining women. Cohen obviously took Ginzberg's advice, composing a list of pros and cons of ordination.

66. Transcript of commission meetings, 6-7 December 1978, Commission Papers, p. 246.

67. Gerson Cohen, personal notes attached to a letter from Eli Ginzberg to Gerson Cohen, 23 March 1979; transcript of commission meetings, 6–7 December 1978, Commission Papers, pp. 295, 242–43; see also Cohen, "State of the Seminary Address to the Students," second draft, 18 November, 1979, p. 9.

68. Transcript of commission meetings, 6–7 December 1978, Commission Papers, p .247.

69. Gerson Cohen, personal notes attached to a letter from Eli Ginzberg to Gerson Cohen, 23 March 1979.

70. Transcript of commission meetings, 6–7 December 1978, Commission Papers, p. 250.

71. Ibid., pp. 3, 4.

72. Gerson Cohen, memo for files and Gordon Tucker, "Summary of Meeting with Professors Dimitrovsky, Weiss-Halivni, Marcus, and Rabbi Brodie," 30 November 1978, Commission Papers.

73. "Final Report of the Commission for the Study of the Ordination of Women as Rabbis," pp. 26, 29. The three members signing the minority opinion were Haim Dimitrovsky, Elijah Schochet, and Wilfred Shuchat.

74. Gordon Tucker, interview.

75. Minutes of emergency Faculty Senate meeting, 26 December 1978, p. 1.

76. Minutes of emergency Faculty Senate meeting, 18 January 1979, pp. 1-4.

77. Ibid. , p. 6.

78. Ibid., p. 5.

79. Ibid.

80. Debra Cantor, interview by author, 21 June 1994.

81. Usher Kirshblum to Gerson Cohen, 25 May 1978, Commission Papers.

82. Minutes of the Seminary Senate meeting, 8 February 1979, p. 1.

83. Gerson Cohen to Alan M. Stroock, 7 March 1979, p. 3, Commission Papers.

84. Transcript of commission meetings, 6–7 December 1978, Commission Papers, p. 332.

85. Ibid., p. 331; Gerson Cohen, memo for files and Gordon Tucker, "Summary" 30 November 1978.

86. Gerson Cohen, "State of the Seminary Address to Students," second draft, 18 November 1979, p. 1.

87. Gerson Cohen to Alan M. Stroock, 7 March 1979, p. 3.

88. Minutes of the Seminary Senate meeting, 15 May 1979, p. 2; Gerson Cohen, "State of the Seminary Address to Students," second draft, 18 November 1979, p. 5.

89. Gerson Cohen to Fishel Pearlmutter, 30 May 1979, Pearlmutter Papers, box 2, folder 1, p. 1.

90. Yochanan Muffs to Gerson Cohen, 5 December 1979, Commission Papers.

91. Debra Cantor, interview.

92. Gerson Cohen's notes attached to letter from Eli Ginzberg to Gerson Cohen, 23 March 1979.

93. Minutes of the Seminary Senate meeting, 23 October 1979.

94. Letter from sixteen faculty members to Gerson Cohen, 6 November 1979, Commission Papers. The sixteen faculty members were: Gershon Bacon, Joseph Brodie, Haim Dimitrovsky, Jose Faur, Israel Francus, Edward Gershfield, David Weiss Halivni, Hillel Hyman, Ronald Price, Zvulun Ravid, David Resnick, Fritz Rothschild, Menahem Schmelzer, Johanna Spector, Morton Waldman, and Dov Zlotnick.

95. Yaakov G. Rosenberg, confidential memos to Gerson Cohen, 29, 30 November 1979, Commission Papers.

96. Gerson Cohen, confidential memo to Chancellor's Cabinet, 15 November 1979, Commission Papers.

97. Gerson Cohen to Eli Ginzberg, 29 May 1979, Commission Papers.

98. David Kogen to Gerson Cohen, 28 November 1978; Simon Greenberg to Gerson Cohen, 26 October 1979, Commission Papers.

99. Gerson Cohen, "State of the Seminary Address to Students," second draft, 18 November 1979, p. 29.

100. Gerson Cohen to Alan M. Stroock, 7 March 1979, p. 3.

101. Debra Cantor, interview.

102. Yochanan Muffs to Gerson Cohen, 5 December 1979, Commission Papers.

103. Ismar Schorsch to Gerson Cohen, 30 November 1979, Commission Papers.

104. Gerson Cohen to Ismar Schorsch, 10 December 1979, Commission Papers.

105. Brochure of Conference on Halakhic Process, 18 December 1979, Commission Papers.

106. Saul Lieberman, message enclosed in letter to participants in the Conference on Halakhic Process, 30 November 1979, Commission Papers.

   After Lieberman's death, some faculty members claimed that he had composed an unpublished responsum that prohibited women's ordination. However, many faculty members have questioned the validity of those claims. Gordon Tucker, interview; Judith Hauptman, interview by author, 7 March 1994.

107. "On the Ordination of Women," document enclosed in material of Conference on Halakhic Process, Commission Papers.

108. Ismar Schorsch, interview by author, 8 March 1994. Before going to the meeting, Schorsch had told Chancellor Cohen of his plans to observe the proceedings at the Queens conference.

109. Minutes of the Seminary Senate meeting, 20 December 1979, p. 3.

110. Ismar Schorsch, "Motion For Senate Consideration on December 20 1979," included in ibid.

111. Ibid., pp. 4–5.

112. "Excerpts from Remarks of Dr. Gerson D. Cohen," 15 January 1980, JTS Records, R.G. 11, box 60, folder 9.

113. Gerson Cohen, letter to "Dear Colleague", 21 December 1979, Pearlmutter Papers, box 2, folder 4.

114. Israel Francus to Gerson Cohen, 20 December 1979, Commission Papers.

115. Daniel Teplitz to Morris Friedman, 13 June 1980, Commission Papers.

116. Fishel Pearlmutter to Harold Schulweis, 11 January 1980, Pearlmutter Papers, box 2, folder 4.

117. David Wolf Silverman, draft of GROW rally speech, 18 March 1980, Jewish Women's Resource Center.

118. Gerson Cohen, and Ismar Schorsch, unsigned memorandum to members of the caucus, 14 February 1980, Commission Papers.

119. Minutes of the Seminary Senate meeting, 25 March 1980, pp. 2, 1.

120. Minutes of the Seminary Senate meeting, 20 October 1980, p. 4.

121. The seven women were: Debra S. Cantor, Nina Beth Cardin, Stephanie Dickstein, Nina Bieber Feinstein, Sharon Fliss, Carol Glass, and Beth Polebaum. See, for example, the letter written by them to the Seminary faculty, 6 December 1979, Commission Papers.

122. Gerson Cohen to Debra Cantor, 12 March 1980, Commission Papers; Debra Cantor, interview.

123. Nina Beth Cardin to Gerson Cohen, 17 February 1980, Commission Papers.

124. Debra Cantor, interview; Anne Lapidus Lerner, interview by author, 8 March 1993.

125. Ibid.

126. Minutes of the Seminary Senate meeting, 20 December 1979.

127. Fishel Pearlmutter to S.W. Schneider, 25 January 1980, p. 3.

128. Ibid.

129. *Proceedings of the Rabbinical Assembly* 42 (1980), p. 299.

130. Stone, "Gentlemen's Agreement at the Seminary," p. 17; *New York Times*, 13 January 1979, pp. 23–24.

131. Fishel Pearlmutter, letter to "Dear Colleague," 29 January 1980, Pearlmutter Papers, box 2, folder 4.

132. Morris Rubinstein to Fishel Pearlmutter, 6 February 1980, Pearlmutter Papers.

133. *Proceedings of the Rabbinical Assembly* 45 (1983), pp. 217–51.

134. Gordon Tucker, interview.

135. Minutes of the Seminary Senate meeting, 20 December 1979.

136. Judith Hauptman, interview.

137. Gordon Tucker, interview.

138. See, for example, Pamela S. Nadell, *Conservative Judaism in America: A Biographical Dictionary and Sourcebook* (Westport, CT: Greenwood Press, 1988), pp. 56, 289.

139. Gordon Tucker, Judith Hauptman, Debra Cantor, interviews.

140. *New York Times*, 25 October 1983, p. A20

141. Minutes of the meeting of the Faculty Assembly, 24 October 1983.

142. Ibid. When faculty members chose to amend Joel Roth's motion regarding women's candidacy, they also appointed a committee on implementation. That committee later accepted the conditions originally outlined in Roth's responsum that required female rabbinic candidates to assume the religious obligations once prescribed only for men. The complex decision-making process surrounding the admission of female candidates sparked some confusion and criticism within the Seminary and fueled the dispute about the procedures used to determine halakhic matters. Judith Hauptman, interview.

143. *Proceedings of the Rabbinical Assembly* 47 (1985), pp. 179–81.

144. *New York Times*, 25 October 1983, p. A20

145. Carolyn Braun, interview by author, 30 June 1994; Debra Cantor, interview.

146. Paula Hyman, telephone conversation with the author, 27 June 1994.

147. *New York Times*, 25 October 1983, p. A20

148. Edward S. Shapiro, *A Time for Healing: American Jewry Since World War II* (Baltimore: The Johns Hopkins University Press, 1992), pp. 178–79.

149. Ismar Schorsch, interview.

150. Debra Cantor, interview.

151. Carolyn Braun, interview.

152. Gerson Cohen to Alan M. Stroock, 7 March 1979.

DAVID ELLENSON & LEE BYCEL

A Seminary of Sacred Learning

The JTS Rabbinical Curriculum in Historical Perspective

SCHEDULE OF STUDIES—1902-1903.

SENIOR CLASS.

HOURS.	MONDAY.	TUESDAY.	WEDNESDAY.	THURSDAY.	FRIDAY.
9 to 10 a. m.	Pesahim, Prof. GINZBERG.	Pesahim, Prof. GINZBERG.	Pesahim, Prof. GINZBERG.	Pesahim, Prof. GINZBERG.	Pesahim, Prof. GINZBERG.
10 to 11 a. m.	History of Jewish Literature, with Specimens, Prof. SCHECHTER.	Jewish History, Prof. GINZBERG.	Philosophical and Ethical Texts, Prof. ASHER.	Judæo-Aramaic Grammar, Prof. GINZBERG.	Yerushalmi Bikkurim, Prof. SCHECHTER.
11 a. m. to 12 m.	Shulhan Aruk, Dr. DRACHMAN.	Jewish Theology, Prof. SCHECHTER.	Hebrew Grammar and Composition, Dr. DRACHMAN.	Exodus, Prof. SCHECHTER.	Biblical Archæology, Dr. ADLER.
12 m. to 1 p. m.	Midrash Bereshit Rabbah, Prof. SCHECHTER.	Berakot, Mr. JOFFE.	Psalms, Dr. DRACHMAN.	Homiletics, Prof. ASHER.	Psalms, Dr. DRACHMAN.
1 to 2 p. m.	Joshua, Dr. DRACHMAN.	Isaiah with Targum, Dr. DRACHMAN.	Berakot, Mr. JOFFE.	Isaiah with Targum, Dr. DRACHMAN.	Abot, Mr. JOFFE.

JUNIOR CLASS.

HOURS.	MONDAY.	TUESDAY.	WEDNESDAY.	THURSDAY.	FRIDAY.
3 to 4 p. m.	Hebrew Grammar and Composition, Dr. DRACHMAN.	Mishnah, R.-Ha-Shanah Yoma and Sukkah, Mr. JOFFE.	Genesis with Rashi, Dr. DRACHMAN.	Berakot, Mr. JOFFE.	
4 to 5 p. m.	Judæo-Aramaic Grammar, Prof. GINZBERG.	Baba-Meziah, Mr. JOFFE.	Jeremiah, Dr. DRACHMAN.	Baba-Meziah, Mr. JOFFE.	

Schedule of Studies, 1902–3.
Jewish Theological Seminary of America, Biennial Report, 1902–1904.

526

DAVID ELLENSON & LEE BYCEL

A Seminary of Sacred Learning

The JTS Rabbinical Curriculum
in Historical Perspective

IN A SERMON delivered at Congregation Chizzuk Emunah in Baltimore during the winter of 1886, Sabato Morais, founder of the Jewish Theological Seminary of America, made the following pledge to his audience, "A seminary of sacred learning will be set up. . . . I acknowledge that as far as it lies in *my* power, the proposed seminary shall be hallowed to one predominating purpose—to the upholding of the principles by which my ancestors lived and for which many have died. From that nursery of learning shall issue forth men whose utterances will kindle enthusiasm for the literature of Holy Writ, but whose every-day conduct will mirror forth a sincere devotion to the *tenets* of Holy Writ."[1]

For Morais and his colleagues the tasks involved in the establishment of the Seminary over the next decade were manifold. The goals these men set for themselves were surely daunting. A building had to be constructed, a faculty secured, an endowment raised, students enrolled, a library stocked, and a curriculum established. This last item—the history and evolution of the curriculum—is our subject.

In offering such a study, we are mindful that curricular specialists employ the term "curriculum" to denote "all of the experiences . . . [a student] has under the aegis of [an educational institution]." Indeed, the educational theorist Elliot Eisner divides these experiences into two categories—a written course of study which identifies the central subjects, themes, and goals that are part of an instructional program and all the other activities associated with an educational institution from which a student learns both inside and outside of the classroom. In this paper, our focus will be on the former category, what Eisner has identified as the "explicit curriculum" of an educational institution—the formal content and announced educational goals that a school, university, or seminary consciously and specifically defines.[2]

527

Our goal in this essay is therefore circumscribed. It is to present and analyze the historical context and educational aims that guided and informed the leaders of the Seminary from its inception to the present as evidenced in written records such as speeches, newspaper reports and articles, and catalogs. In so doing, we are mindful that the implicit dimensions of seminary training—the "hidden curriculum" which informs the ethos of an institution and which is not transmitted formally but through the overarching social and educational culture of a school and in the personal interactions between students and teachers that actually transpire in the classroom—may well be neglected in this study. We hope that this study, by focusing on the "explicit curriculum" of the Seminary, will nevertheless display the ongoing as well as innovative vision of the rabbinate advanced by the leadership of the Conservative movement. We also trust that this display and discussion of the constant yet evolving nature of the Seminary's curricular deliberations will shed some light on the nature and evolution of Judaism itself in 20th-century North America.

European Models

The educational and religious philosophy of the Jewish Theological Seminary of America and the initial curriculum for the training of rabbis established by the founders of JTS to reflect that philosophy did not arise in a vacuum. The leaders of the Seminary—and the Hebrew Union College, for that matter—did not have to confront the task of imagining a modern rabbinical seminary and its curriculum de novo. Instead, the outlook and curriculum that marked and defined the Seminary as a distinct institution were rooted in large part on the model of rabbinical training provided by the modern European rabbinical seminary. Zacharias Frankel and his Breslau Jewish Theological Seminary in particular were of seminal import for the men who created JTS. The name alone of the fledgling American rabbinical college testifies to the central role the Breslau Seminary played as a model for the founders of the American institution. A review of the sources and personalities associated with the creation and initial years of the Seminary makes these points abundantly clear.

Morais himself, as the first President of the Seminary and its advisory board, was a native of Italy and was in large measure informed by and possessed of Western and Central European Jewish educational models and sensibilities as he, along with his colleagues, undertook the task of forging a new American seminary. It is therefore hardly surprising that Morais, in his first report as President to the Board of Trustees of the Seminary, wrote, "What the seminaries at Breslau and Berlin, in Germany, at Buda-Pesth, in Hungary, at Rome, in Italy, are to Europe, this Jewish Theological Seminary should be to America. It [is] indeed time that New York should be in possession of such a place of Jewish learning."[3]

Morais's hopes that JTS would embody the attributes of a modern European rabbinical seminary on American soil were shared by virtually every person involved in the creation of the Seminary. Members of the original JTS faculty and its Advisory Board of Ministers such as Alexander Kohut, Frederick de Sola Mendes, and Bernard Drachman were themselves graduates of the Jewish Theological Seminary of Breslau. Others such as Aaron Wise and Marcus Jastrow were also trained in Europe and they too were shaped and informed by the ethos of the European seminary. They, like their Breslau colleagues, identified with the notion of a Positive-Historical Judaism that Zacharias Frankel as head of the Breslau Seminary had articulated, and they were particularly receptive to the educational patterns Frankel had established in his institution. The educational ideal that directed and inspired these men was not that of a traditional yeshiva on an Eastern European model. Instead, their aim was to construct a modern seminary patterned educationally after the modern European rabbinical seminary in general and the Breslau Seminary of Frankel in particular. The curriculum structured by these men in the early years of JTS will—as we shall see—bear witness to this.

In the curricula of all the European seminaries, the study of Talmud and codes occupied a central role. The yearbooks of all three of the major seminaries that served German Jewry—the Orthodox Rabbinerseminar, the Positive-Historical Jewish Theological Seminary of Breslau, and the Liberal Hochschule established by Abraham Geiger in 1872—indicate that the greatest bulk of the curriculum in these institutions was assigned to the study of rabbinical literature and codes and that the titles of subjects taught in this area were similar in each school. Particular attention was paid to Jewish laws of marriage and divorce. At the Breslau Seminary, this area was considered to be of such import that Frankel himself taught the talmudic tractates related to this theme. The laws of *Hoshen Mishpat*, the section of the *Shulhan Aruch* that deals with Jewish civil law, were totally ignored in the curricula of all three institutions. In focusing the course content of the study of rabbinical literature as they did, these schools reflected the reality of a world where Jewish civil autonomy had disappeared.[4]

Other areas of study also received considerable attention in the seven-year course of study that was prescribed for students of the Breslau Seminary. Students were expected to master the following subjects—Holy Scriptures and their exegesis, Hebrew language and grammar, historical and methodological introduction to Mishna and Talmud, history of the Jews together with a history of Jewish literature, religious philosophy and ethics according to Jewish sources, midrash, ritual practice, pedagogy, and homiletics. The modern European seminary was surely different from traditional Jewish centers of learning. It was not a yeshiva. Instead, it was an institution designed to train and educate rabbis for a contemporary western cultural setting. The expansion of the curriculum beyond the classical "four ells of

Halakha" and the modern academic categories employed to transmit Jewish knowledge to the students surely reflect this.[5]

Students at the Breslau seminary, like their counterparts at the Rabbinerseminar and the Hochschule, were required to complete their doctorate at a secular university as a prerequisite for ordination at all the German seminaries.[6] Faculty and students alike at these institutions were imbued with ideals imparted by western culture and were absolutely committed to a belief in the centrality of *Wissenschaft des Judentums,* which in turn—they believed—would lead to a proper understanding of Judaism. As Frankel himself wrote, "Without the academic study of Judaism, Judaism could not exist [in the present day]."[7]

Hebrew Union College and American Realities

The cultural ideals and models that guided the founders of the Jewish Theological Seminary of America—like their counterparts in Europe—were strongly western. Nonetheless, the founders of JTS, like Frankel and the Positive-Historical school in Europe, were quite traditional in religious orientation and observance. It was precisely this distinctive orientation and pattern of observance that led to the creation of JTS, for the religious directions that informed Morais and his colleagues were decidedly different from the sensibilities and practices that were then beginning to mark the course of American Reform. Indeed, JTS arguably arose as an "opposition Seminary" to the Hebrew Union College.[8]

Hebrew Union College, it should be remembered, initially claimed that it would not be a sectarian or denominationally distinct Reform institution. I. M. Wise himself declared in 1879 that Hebrew Union College "shall be an orthodox Jewish academy. . . . The Masoretic text of the Bible with the fundamental principle of God, revelation, Providence, immortality, righteousness, justice, truth, and freedom, is the rock of foundation, and our post biblical literature contains the material upon which and with which our structure of education is to be erected under the help of God."[9] While Wise aimed to create rabbis who were "American with heart and soul,"[10] he had, in the words of the *American Israelite*, "no ISMS or SCHISMS to impose." Instead, as his journal described it, "He will earnestly and steadily endeavour with the aid of a competent and distinguished Faculty, to open the treasures of Israel's literature to . . . reformer and orthodox, in justice to all and offence to none. . . . The Hebrew Union College . . . [intends to offer] an enlightened religious and moral training in temples grand and gorgeous as well as in the orthodox synagogue, to see Judaism in its glory and to hear it expounded intelligently."[11]

In offering this vision of the Hebrew Union College, it is clear that Wise's aim in these early years was to create a seminary that could provide rabbis for all American Israel. His true sentiments were undoubtedly not those of an Orthodox Jew. After all, in his address on the occasion of the opening of the College, Wise stated,

"Where the old Talmud appears to us contrary to the spirit of Thorah, we reject its teaching." Nevertheless, he also praised the Talmud and claimed that the rabbinical students of HUC were obligated to acquaint themselves with "the Jochanans, Gamaliels, Jehudas or Rabbina and Ashi," all great figures in rabbinical literature. Indeed, "Kenan, Welhausen, Renan, Ewald, or Smith," all modern biblical critics, were "no more reliable authorities" than these rabbinical sages. The Hebrew Union College, in its training of rabbis, would embody "historical Judaism, . . . the rock upon which the temple of Israel proudly stands and has stood these three thousand years and more. . . . There is no Judaism without Thorah and revelation. The college was established to teach the literature of Israel; to train, educate, and license rabbis for real Judaism."[12]

These words indicate that at this time Wise was greatly concerned to reassure traditionalists in the American Jewish community that his Cincinnati school would educate rabbis who had mastered the gamut of traditional Jewish literature and who could therefore serve them. He also sought to train an American Jewish clergy thoroughly conversant and comfortable with contemporary forms of academic scholarship. His outlook was informed by the model of the European rabbinical seminary no less than that of the men who would establish the Jewish Theological Seminary several years later. The curriculum he designed reflected these commitments and attitudes.

In a pamphlet entitled, "Propositions," submitted on 11 July 1878 to a "Commission appointed by the Council of the Union of American Hebrew Congregations [UAHC]," Wise defined the "Subjects, Aims, and Methods of Instruction" that were to mark the curriculum of the Hebrew Union College. Section 1 stated, "The principal subjects of the College shall be the Bible, with its Commentaries and Paraphrases, the Talmud and its Commentaries, the Jewish philosophical literature, all in their respective original tongues, the Theology, Ethics and History of the Hebrews, together with the various disciplines of Hermeneutics, Exegetics, Homiletics, Criticism, and Semitic philology." These goals were to be accomplished in two ways—through the reading of "original sources" on the basis of "scientific principles" as well as through "systematical lectures." Wise asserted that no more "than two-sevenths of the whole school time shall be devoted to the lectures." Indeed, the overwhelming bulk of instructional time—"ten out of the fourteen hours of weekly instruction"—given to the students in Judaica was "devoted to the study of original sources."[13]

Lest it appear that fourteen hours a week of instructional time in Judaica was meager, it should be noted that the first students at the College were required to do more than study Judaica. Many were teenage boys, and the College was committed to the modern seminary model of producing rabbis who were well educated in secular subjects. The College therefore granted them time during these years to devote to secular studies so that the students might thereby qualify for and earn a bachelor's degree. Only then could they stand as candidates for ordination. To this end, HUC established a Preparatory Department that had as one of its aims the grounding of the student in the linguistic, historical, philosophical, and textual foundations necessary for advanced rabbinical studies. The hours of instruction in Jewish studies were somewhat circumscribed so as to permit the student to pursue secular academic training. The student, during his years in the Preparatory Department was not only expected to earn a Bachelor of Hebrew Letters degree (*atzilei bnei yisrael*), but to earn a secular degree from a university as well. Otherwise, the student could not qualify for admission to the Collegiate Department where students were expected to engage in advanced studies so as to qualify for ordination as a rabbi. This required students to "give good evidence of their ability to pass . . . the examination for admission into such institutions as Columbia College, New York; the University of Pennsylvania (Philadelphia), or the McMicken University, Cincinnati."[14] By 1894, the College was able to state simply in its first catalog that each ordinand "must be a graduate of the University, with the degree of at least B.A. or B.L."[15]

While this first rabbinical seminary on American soil did not require an earned doctoral degree from its students to qualify for ordination as its German counterparts had, the demand that each student possess a university diploma bespeaks a comparable sensitivity to the academic ethos of the larger world. Further evidence of the Hebrew Union College's commitment to the inclusion of *Wissenschaft* in its curriculum is displayed in several other statements issued by Wise and the College. For example, in 1877 Wise contended that while the researches of Frankel, Geiger, Graetz, Luzzatto, and Zunz among others were not sufficient to qualify one as a rabbi, he left little doubt that these "excellent works" were an invaluable part of a modern rabbinical education.[16] In addition, the catalogs of the College explicitly stated that the "main object" of the "four years' course" in the Collegiate Department was "to enable the student to read and expound *scientifically* the original sources of Judaism and its History."[17] Finally, the internalization of a modern academic ethos on the part of the Hebrew Union College and its manifestation in the curriculum is evidenced in the requirement that each student write "an original thesis proving research and originality" in order to graduate as a rabbi.[18]

In his "Propositions" of 1878, Wise explicitly delineated what he expected the students of the Preparatory Department to master during their four years of study. He wrote, "Every student of the Preparatory Department shall attain competency in Jewish history; Hebrew, Chaldaic and Syriac grammar; in reading fluently the rabbinical Hebrew as used in the commentaries; and in the translation of any passage or passages from the originals of the Bible, the Mishna in *Moed* and *Nezikin*, and the Talmud from any one of the one hundred and fifty pages read in the department."[19] As the historian Michael Meyer has observed, "The curriculum devised for the Preparatory Department was remarkably, even absurdly ambitious. At the end of four years—and before beginning the Collegiate Department—a student was to have mastered Hebrew and Aramaic grammar, read in the original most of the Bible and large selections from rabbinical literature, including portions from the both the Babylonian and the Palestinian Talmuds, and familiarized himself with the entire span of Jewish history."[20]

Nevertheless, as later catalogs indicate, Wise appears to have maintained these standards. Hence, in a catalog of the 1890s, under the rubric, "Standard of Admission to Collegiate Department," it states, "Thorough knowledge of Hebrew and Aramaic grammars (Luzzatto's), and Hebrew translation from English or Aramaic; *prima vista* translation of the Biblical books and . . . readiness to read Rashi passages. In Mishna is required the knowledge of *Aboth* and at least two other *Mesachtoth* ; in Talmud, *prima vista* reading of at least fifty pages in one or more *Mesachtoth* previously prepared; also the best parts of *Sepher Hamadda* in the code of Maimonides, and history from Zerubabel to Rabbi Jochanan ben Saccai."[21]

Particularly noteworthy in view of the antinomian course upon which the Reform Movement was about to embark was the stress Wise placed on rabbinical literature and codes in the curriculum of the College during these early years. In the manner of the German rabbinical seminaries, no time was devoted to a study of Jewish civil law as contained in *Hoshen Mishpat*. However, considerable attention was given to mishnaic and talmudic tractates that were deemed to be of "ethical and historical value" such as *Aboth*, *Sanhedrin*, and *Sotah* as well as to tractates, legal codes, and responsa that dealt with matters of current concern to segments of the American rabbinate and laity such as dietary laws, personal status, and the holidays. Hence, the talmudic tractates of *Gittin*, *Kiddushin*, *Hullin*, *Yebamoth*, *Yoma*, and *Megillah* were studied as were large portions of *Berachoth*. In addition, courses were given on select chapters of *Eben Haezer* and in *Yore Deah* Hilchot *Tsedakah*, *Milah*, *Gerim*, *Bikkur Cholim*, and *Abeloth* as well as in *Orach Chayim*, Hilchot *Channuakah*, *Purim*, and *Pesach*.[22] The appearance of these texts in the curriculum of the College seems to reflect the influence of a European seminary model upon the embryonic Cincinnati institution, for such study constituted the central element in the curricula of each the major rabbinical schools of Germany and Central Europe. The significant role assigned such texts in the curriculum of the Hebrew Union College at this juncture in history indicates that the College still regarded itself as embedded in classical Jewish tradition and that it still aspired to address traditional as well as liberal segments of the American Jewish community.

The course of studies in the advanced rabbinical track at the Hebrew Union College was of course not limited to classical rabbinical texts. In the Collegiate Department, the history of Judaism from the tannaitic period through Mendelssohn and the emergence of American Judaism was covered, and readings in medieval philosophy focusing upon Albo, Saadia, and Maimonides were required. The Tanakh was studied along with classical rabbinical commentaries, *targumim*, and contemporary critical scholarship. The study of languages such as Syriac and Arabic were included in the curriculum, and homiletics as well as lectures on pastoral theology were given to the students in the realm of practical rabbinics.[23]

By 1899, Wise could look back upon his achievements as the architect of the Hebrew Union College and its curriculum with pride. In his address that year to the ordinands of the College, he stated that the College had as its object the perpetuation of "the covenant and the Thorah," the establishment of "the continuity of Judaism on this continent under the new light of a new world, a new civilization of freedom, equality, justice, and humanity, the morning dawn of the future of the human family." His curriculum was designed to facilitate that goal's attainment—to educate rabbis who could expound the "sacred lore of Israel" to an American audience.[24] Others shared his vision for the creation of an American rabbinate. However, they were certain the Hebrew Union College was not the appropriate institution for the attainment of that goal, and so they created the Jewish Theological Seminary of America.

The Jewish Theological Seminary of America: Vision and Curriculum

In the view of Morais and his colleagues, HUC had betrayed the ideal of a united American Judaism it purported to espouse by serving non-kosher food at a banquet honoring its first class of ordinands in 1883. Marcus Jastrow, the ordination speaker on that occasion, and many other persons both lay and rabbinic, were incensed by the sectarian division they felt Hebrew Union College had introduced into the life of the American Jewish community through the violation of this classical pillar of Jewish observance. Furthermore, this action contributed to the view that an alternative seminary—one more devoted to classical Jewish patterns of observance—was a necessity for American Jewry. This led Morais to assert in December 1884, "To save the religion for which Mattathias staked his existence and of which Chanukah is a glorious exponent, a seminary of learning, where *all* the ordinances of the Pentateuch, compatible with our state of dispersion, will be taught and enforced, must be set up in obedience to the demands of an enlightened 'Orthodoxy.'"[25]

Morais continued to call for the creation of a new seminary throughout 1885. The adoption of the Pittsburgh Platform by the Reform rabbinate in November of that year only reinforced his resolve. Furthermore, the theological vision articulated in the Pittsburgh Platform of Judaism as a universal religion totally in accord with the dictates of reason and absolutely hostile to the ritual and national elements traditionally associated with the Jewish religion led others to criticize HUC and caused many to rally around Morais and his proposal. A declaration in the pages of the *American Israelite* by Marcus Kohner, honorary secretary to the Trustees of

Temple Ahavath Chesed in New York, is typical of the critical sentiments shared by many others on the perceived direction of the Hebrew Union College. Kohner wrote, "At the convention of rabbis, held at Pittsburgh, several resolutions were adopted, and still others proposed, of which the Trustees of Congregation Ahavath Chesed are not in accord. I am instructed by said Trustees to state that if these articles, as adopted and proposed, are to be the instructions at the Hebrew Union College, that they, as a member of [the Union of American Hebrew Congregations], find themselves morally bound to protest against such teachings."[26]

The Pittsburgh Platform, following as it did so shortly after the infamous Cincinnati ordination banquet of 1883, caused Morais to state that his goal in the establishment of the Jewish Theological Seminary of America was to forswear the impieties of I. M. Wise's "blatant 'American Judaism'" and preserve in its stead "the pure Judaism of Moses and all the righteous in Israel."[27] Alexander Kohut gave eloquent expression to the difference in philosophy that was to distinguish the new seminary from its older sibling in Cincinnati. Kohut contended, "In the new seminary a different spirit will prevail, different impulses will pervade its teachings and animate its teachers. This spirit shall be that of *Conservative* Judaism, the *conserving* Jewish impulse which will create in the pupils of the Seminary the tendency to recognize the dual nature of Judaism and the Law; which unites theory and practice, identifies body and soul, realizes the importance of both matter and spirit, and acknowledges the necessity of observing the Law as well as studying it."[28] Only the establishment of the Jewish Theological Seminary of America could produce a class of rabbis capable of rescuing American Judaism from the compromising and destructive tendencies inherent in Cincinnati and Reform.

Morais, like Wise, had a distinct vision of Judaism, and he was determined to fashion an institution for the training of rabbis in the United States who would be able to disseminate that vision so as to give life to Jewish tradition in America. With Wise, Morais shared an enthusiasm for the United States. As Morais himself phrased it, "Heartfelt is, indeed, our devotion to the constitution of the country that has leveled inequality and clothed Israelites with all the franchises of free men." His aim was therefore to create rabbis sympathetic "with the spirit of our American institutions, . . . imbued with . . . firm and intelligent . . . patriotism."[29]

Morais was also completely committed to offering Jewish instruction in accord with a modern scientific spirit. He maintained, "The entire work of the institution must be conducted in accordance with collegiate methods now prevalent." Morais was also "gratified" by the association the Seminary had established with Columbia College during the first few years of the Seminary's existence, for it confirmed the high level of academic instruction the Seminary offered.[30] By 1896, only a decade after the Seminary had opened, he proudly claimed "We can train scholarly rabbis here in America as well as in Europe."[31]

Yet, Morais, unlike Wise, was not interested, as one admirer put it, in creating "an *American* Judaism." Rather, he was concerned about preserving "*Judaism* in America."[32] His commitment to Jewish observance as an absolute standard for ordination as a rabbi is evidenced in the Seminary's explicit statement that admission to the institution required "adherence to a mode of life consonant with Jewish laws."[33] Morais and men such as Jastrow and de Sola Mendes were committed to what they defined as historical Judaism. They were quite disturbed by what they considered to be Hebrew Union College's ever increasing drift in the direction of Reform during the latter decades of the 19th century. Their opposition to this direction not only gave birth to JTS and the Conservative movement in this country. It also caused them to assert that "fidelity and devotion to Jewish law" was a prerequisite for the rabbinical office.[34] Thus, they explicitly drew a boundary between the Seminary and the Hebrew Union College.

Morais also offered a description of the ideal course of instruction at the Seminary. He wrote, "The traditions of the fathers are therefore coeval with the written statutes of the five holy books. . . . It follows then that the Bible constitutes the primary object of our pupils' tuition; Mishnah and Talmud are studied by them as an indispensable corollary. Those branches of sacred literature with kindred ones, systematically imparted without pre-judgment by men whose characters we believe to be unassailable, must inspire the scholars with love for their religion and reverence for the ancients who honestly handed it down."[35] Or, as he observed elsewhere concerning the subject content of his nascent seminary, "The word of the Bible in its original purity shall command profound attention; its purport, when obscure, shall be sought at the hands of commentators, trustworthy by reason of their thorough acquaintance with the construction, the genius, the spirit of Holy Writ." In a tone that foreshadowed his successor Solomon Schechter's enmity towards the discipline of Higher Biblical Criticism, Morais continued, "Ewald shall not supersede our Kimchi and Nachmanides, nor shall Luzzatto be set aside to make room for Gesenius. Like the word of the Bible, so shall its history also be studied in the original, not in Kuenen, Wellhausen, or Robertson Smith; not in the works of Gentiles or Jews that deny Moses the authorship of the Pentateuch, make our patriarchs sheer myths, our priests tyrannical egotists, our Ezra a pretender, our progenitors unmitigated dupes." For Morais, as for many Jews of this era, biblical criticism was a not-so-covert form of anti-Semitism. It would have no role at the Seminary.[36]

Given the commitment Morais displayed towards Jewish observance, it is fascinating to observe that he asserted the following concerning the role to be assigned rabbinical studies in his curriculum. He stated, "It is very far from my thoughts to belittle Talmudism. . . . [However], it shall be the boast of that institute hereafter that the attendants are unsurpassing Scripturalists . . . though they may not rank foremost among skilled Talmudists. The latter have, at times, degenerated into hair-splitting disputants—*pilpulists*." It is the Bible which is "the book without which post-biblical literature lacks the foundation stone; it is simply—a castle in the air."[37]

In offering such thoughts, Morais undoubtedly reflected the influence that the bibliocentrism of occidental culture had upon him as well as his own impatience with those modes of "talmudic sophistry" that dominated certain Eastern European *yeshivot*. This latter mode of talmudic methodology would certainly find no home at JTS. On the other hand, these statements of Morais simultaneously betray the lack of influence he may have exerted over the design of the actual Seminary curriculum itself. While nothing was taught at JTS in opposition to Morais's sentiments, an investigation of the Seminary's curriculum for its rabbinical students even during these early years indicates that the study of rabbinical literature, not Bible, constituted the heart of instruction at the New York institution.

The JTS rabbinical curriculum must therefore be approached and analyzed in the fullness of a multi-layered context. The curriculum was a patrimony from the seminaries of Central Europe and Germany. At the same time, the ethos of the institution was constructed in light of the sentiments of its founders and in opposition to the specific reality of American Reform Judaism and the Hebrew Union College.

JTS offered a Preparatory Department akin to that at the Hebrew Union College and established for precisely the same reasons. Rabbinical students were required to earn a bachelor's degree and be well versed in secular subjects. The responsibility for providing an opportunity for such instruction so that candidates suitably qualified for entering the Rabbinical School of JTS could be produced thus fell upon the Seminary itself. Indeed, in many of his reports to the association, President Morais describes the valiant efforts of his young charges at the Seminary to acquire both a secular and a Jewish education that would qualify them for admission to the rabbinical program itself. In the Preparatory Department the student was instructed in Hebrew and biblical Aramaic grammar, Bible with Rashi and Targum, Mishna, and Jewish history through the tannaitic period. The curriculum of the Preparatory Department at the Seminary, though not identical with, closely paralleled the curriculum offered in the Preparatory Department of the Hebrew Union College.[38]

The most striking feature of the course of instruction offered at the Seminary and described in the various *Proceedings* of the 1890s is the seminal, though hardly surprising, role that the Breslau Seminary played in shaping the contours of its curriculum. The course of study for ordination at JTS was set for seven years in what were labeled "Junior Department" and "Senior Department." The program stressed not only Talmud and codes, but Bible, Jewish history, philosophy, midrash, homiletics and pedagogy, *hazzanut*, and lectures on Biblical archaeology. As Bernard Drachman observed, the program at the Jewish Theological Seminary of America was practically identical to that offered at the Breslau Seminary.[39] It should also be apparent that it bore strong affinities to the curriculum of the Hebrew Union College as well.

A closer look at the subjects of instruction only confirms this latter point. In Jewish philosophy, Albo, Maimonides, and Saadia were stressed, just as they were at HUC. Furthermore, approximately three-quarters of instructional time was devoted to talmudic texts and related rabbinical literature. This too was akin to the course of study at the College during this period. The tractates, codes, and laws studied also overlapped greatly with the course of instruction provided by HUC. *Gittin*, *Chulin*, *Kiddushin*, *Yore Deah*, *Eben Ha'ezer*, and *Orach Chayim* constituted the major talmudic and rabbinical legal texts and codes that were read by the students of the Seminary just as they were by the students of the College. The courses in history as well as Bible also possess titles similar to those found in the reports and catalogs of the Hebrew Union College of the 1880s and 1890s.[40]

None of this disconfirms the point that the curriculum of JTS was modeled after that of Breslau. Rather, what it does display is how deeply embedded the men who established both HUC and the Seminary were in the ethos of the German seminary and how desirous they were of patterning their institutions after the model such seminaries provided. This, more than any other factor, appears to have informed the curricula they initially established. In their minds, the route to legitimization as a serious and worthy institution of higher Jewish learning necessitated the creation of a curriculum and ethos modeled after the European seminary.

The issue here is not whether JTS or HUC, at this juncture in history, was the academic equal of the Hochschule or the Breslau Seminary. Men such as Morais or Wise—to put it mildly—were surely not the scholarly peers of Frankel or Geiger. Rather, what is crucial is that each of these men aspired to create institutions for the training of American rabbis patterned after the seminaries founded by Frankel and Geiger. One only has to read a representative statement uttered by Morais in 1890 to recognize how deeply he and his colleagues in both New York and Cincinnati had internalized the values and models of the European seminary in the creation of their own institutions. Morais noted that academic lectures on topics such as "Biblical Archaeology" and "The History of Hebrew Grammar" as well as "The Talith and the Pallium" and "The Siloam Inscription and the Moabite Stone" had been delivered at the Seminary, and he proudly observed that the *Allgemeine Zeitung des Judenthums* "devoted considerable space to an appreciative article in regard to the course of lectures delivered [at the Seminary] last summer, in which it said, 'We can with gratification observe from this that in the New World too, Jewish learning is making its way."[41] Morais and Wise, along with their colleagues, established a curriculum and institutional ethos in keeping with the ideal of the modern seminary. While the student at JTS was expected to display a level of Jewish ritual observance distinct from that of his student colleague at the Hebrew Union College, an investigation and analysis of the catalogs, reports, and articles concerning these two institutions of rabbinical training reveal no genuinely discernible differences in the curricula of the two schools during this era. With the advent of the 1900s and the appointment of Kaufmann Kohler as president of the Hebrew Union College, such differences would begin to appear, but under Wise and Morais, the legacy of Europe remained paramount in guiding the curriculum of each institution.

The Impact of Schechter

On 1 April 1902, Solomon Schechter—arguably the preeminent scholar of Judaica during his era in the English-speaking world—assumed his duties as President of the Seminary. During the thirteen years he occupied this position, Schechter succeeded in placing his stamp on the character and curriculum of the institution that he headed and through that stamp managed to influence the course of American Judaism and rabbinical training far beyond his time. Schechter was determined that the Seminary be a fertile training ground for rabbis who would be devoted to the promotion and dissemination of the Law to all Israel. Judaism, he stated to the ordination class of 1910, was principally committed to the "binding authority of law and the absolute sovereignty and grace of law. . . . Ethics are good, but laws and commandments bidden and commanded by God are better; and all such phrases as idealism, spirituality, and religiosity will avail us nothing as long as you omit to urge the great principle that the Holy One of Israel, 'in His Holiness, gave law unto His people.' . . . To urge this upon your community in all its force and all its significance seems to me the mission of the Rabbi in the present generation."[42] Furthermore, the rabbi was "not only responsible to his congregation, but to the whole of Israel for [the] preservation and perpetuation of Torah."[43] Indeed, "The Directors of this institution, by terming it the Jewish Theological Seminary of *America*," have distinctly shown their [understanding of the historical nature of Judaism and their] intention of avoiding sectarianism. . . . The Seminary to be really great will have to be catholic, and of a uniting nature."[44]

To succeed at this, the Seminary had to remain faithful to its original mandate—"the promotion of Jewish learning and the training for the Jewish ministry."[45] The legitimacy and authority of the rabbinate depended upon the ability of the Seminary to inculcate a knowledge and appreciation of the Jewish past and its literature in its graduates. It was imperative to anchor the rabbi in this way, for otherwise he could only champion a Judaism that would "turn out to be a mere caprice of the mob, or a whim of fashion, or the hobby of some willful individual, sure to disappear when viewed *sub specie æternitatis*." No "instruction suited to the needs of such an isolated and detached present [will] ever embody any features of greatness."[46]

Authentic Judaism required rabbis and teachers whose roots were firmly planted in the historical soil of traditional Jewish scholarship. A rabbi bereft of such learning was a "nude soul." For, as Schechter was to maintain in 1908, "No man in authority is greater than the source whence his authority is derived. The authority of the Rabbi is derived from the Torah; he is its servant."[47] The ongoing passion and commitment Schechter displayed to the ideal of a learned rabbinate was evident, when, in 1912, he thundered, "Judaism need not be advertised. Judaism needs to be taught."[48] Learning, Schechter maintained, was "the only safeguard against . . . sham cherubs. Piety without learning is apt . . . to degenerate into mere ranting, making religion a caricature of itself."[49]

To be sure, Schechter was not entirely impervious to the practical demands of the rabbinate. "The Rabbi," he acknowledged, "is expected to 'do things.' Upon this we are all agreed."[50] The rabbi was required to be a model for others. His home was to be "strictly Jewish," and he was obligated to "faithfully and manfully maintain [a] loyalty to Torah." Furthermore, the rabbi needed to perform "social work included under the name of *Gemilath Chasadim*," for in Judaism this formed "a part of Israel's great *Imitatio Dei*."[51] As Schechter put it, "Mercifulness and lovingkindness are, according to our sages, among the criteria distinguishing the people of Israel. You . . . know the regular Jewish expression, *Yisrael rahmanim b'nei rahmanim*, 'Israel are a compassionate people, the descendants of a compassionate people.' You have also heard of the Jewish heart. Do not fail to cultivate these sentiments and to keep them alive among your congregants."[52] At times, this meant that the rabbi was called upon to be "an organizer, a social agitator, an expert on all topics of the day."[53] Yet, all of these latter functions could be properly fulfilled only if the rabbi was a scholar. The task of the rabbi was "to think things" from a Jewish perspective. The rabbi could do this only if he was "a sound Hebrew scholar."[54]

Consequently, in his 1902 inaugural address, Schechter assigned top priority to the creation of a curriculum and the recruitment of a faculty that would enable the prospective rabbi to receive "such training as to enable him to say: '*Judæici nihil a me alienum pluto.*' 'I regard nothing Jewish as foreign to me.' He should know everything Jewish—Bible, Talmud, Midrash, Liturgy, Jewish ethics and Jewish philosophy; Jewish history and Jewish mysticism; and even Jewish folklore. None of these subjects . . . should be . . . strange to him."[55]

Such training, Schechter insisted, would be rigorous. He hoped to produce a rabbi who would be capable of engaging from "time to time . . . in some scientific work, publishing occasionally a learned article on some historical topic, or even editing some ancient Hebrew text."[56] For, as Schechter put it, "The crown and climax of all learning is research." It alone could facilitate the search for "truth."[57] It was his hope that the "spiritual destinies" of Israel "in this country" would "be presided over by men of the stamp of Dr. Kohut and Dr. Jastrow, who left us the greatest Rabbinical Dictionaries, . . . or Dr. Szold, who bequeathed to us one of the most lucid commentaries on the Book of Job."[58] To produce such men, Schechter asserted that his students obtain "a thorough and accurate knowledge of Jewish literature. . . . The duty of accuracy, even in the most minute details of a subject, cannot be shirked. . . . I know that the acquiring of details is a very tiresome and wearisome affair, and may well be described in the language of the old Rabbis: 'The part of wisdom learned under wrath.' But, unfortunately, there is no 'snapshot' process for acquiring learning. It has its methods and its laws, as ancient as time itself, and these none can evade or escape."[59] With this challenge in mind, Schechter asserted, "We—my colleagues and I—[have] tried to draw up the curriculum of studies for the classes, in such a way as to include in it almost every branch of Jewish literature. . . . [We must] attempt to bring the student on terms of acquaintance at least with all those manifestations of Jewish life and Jewish thought which may prove useful to them as future ministers, and suggestive and stimulating to them as prospective scholars."[60] For Solomon Schechter, knowledge and careful scholarship were the sine qua non that established the grounds for exercising legitimate rabbinical leadership. The education and ordination of such rabbis now became the focus of his life's work.

To aid him in the task of producing such rabbis, Schechter assembled some of the greatest scholarly luminaries of his day and appointed them to the faculty of the Seminary. Foremost among them was Louis Ginzburg, whom Schechter immediately appointed to the faculty as professor of Talmud in 1902. Over the course of the next several years he recruited Israel Friedlaender as professor of Bible and Alexander Marx to serve both as professor of history and as chief librarian. Joseph Mayor Asher, who had studied with Schechter in England, was appointed professor of homiletics. Upon his death in 1910, Mordecai Kaplan assumed that position. In addition, Israel Davidson was appointed to a faculty position as instructor in Hebrew and Rabbinics in 1905. In little more than a decade, Davidson was made a full professor.[61]

In appointing such scholarly giants to the faculty, Schechter underscored the academic seriousness of the institution he had come to head. Each of these men was a distinguished scholar, and the academic reputation of the Seminary soared with the addition of these men to the faculty. The transformation these men wrought in the atmosphere of the Seminary is attested to by Bernard Drachman in his memoirs. As Drachman observed, "A new and, from a certain point of view, more brilliant period began for [the Seminary with the ascension of Schechter to the presidency]."[62] Schechter was determined to carve out the highest academic reputation for the Seminary. There would be no room under his administration for faculty members who could not make the most significant contributions to their chosen field of scholarship. This meant men such as Drachman and Joshua Joffe—stalwarts of the Seminary during the 1890s—had to be content with comparatively minor roles as instructors under Schechter.

A brief analysis of Drachman's career at the Seminary during the first decade of the 20th century reflects the changes wrought in the atmosphere of JTS as well as the determination of Schechter to appoint only men of the greatest scholarly competence to the faculty. Drachman felt that he had been "the logical candidate for the successorship to Dr. Morais. The least to which I was logically entitled," he continued, "was a professorship in some major subject."[63] Indeed, Drachman's hopes do not appear to have been unreasonable. After all, he had served as dean of the faculty from 1889 "until the reorganization of the Seminary in 1901 under the presidency of Dr. Solomon Schechter."[64] However, Drachman was compelled to recognize that his "just claims were apparently not even considered. I was offered the position of instructor in Hebrew and acting reader of rabbinical codes." Drachman accepted this obvious demotion because he "hoped . . . that with unremitting devotion to the duties of my appointed task I would be able to win the approval of the new powers that be."[65]

Such hopes were not fulfilled. Drachman devoted himself to scholarship and in 1908 produced a work on "an abstruse Talmudic discussion or controversy between two of the greatest and most renowned Talmudic authorities of the Middle Ages, Rabbi Abraham ben David of Posquieres in France and Rabbi Zerahiah ben Isaac Ha-Levi, originally of Gerona in Spain, and afterwards a resident of Lunel in France." When Drachman presented Schechter with a copy of the book, he anticipated a warm and complimentary reception. To his dismay, "the learned head of the Seminary accepted my book most ungraciously, hardly said a word in acknowledgment thereof, and was unmistakably displeased." One year later, in 1909, Drachman "received an official letter from the board of directors of the Jewish Theological Seminary. It contained a notification that my appointment to the teaching staff was terminated and that my services would no longer be required."[66] While some have suggested that it was his commitment to Jewish Orthodoxy that found disfavor in the eyes of Schechter,[67] such an explanation seems highly implausible. If Schechter had sought to transform the Seminary into a denominationally distinct Conservative institution by purging all Orthodox persons from positions on the faculty, he would hardly have appointed—as he did—men such as Alexander Marx, a fully Orthodox Jew who was the son-in-law of the famed Orthodox savant Rabbi David Zevi Hoffmann of Berlin; or Orthodox Rabbi Moses Hyamson, formerly Dayyan of the Beth Din in London, to the Chair in Codes in 1915.[68] Instead, the whole incident with Drachman and the ultimate decision to remove him from the faculty altogether reflect Schechter's judgment that Drachman was not a first-rate scholar. Indeed, if one compares the academic attainments of Drachman with the other men Schechter appointed to the faculty, one can hardly avoid this conclusion. Schechter was absolutely committed to having only men of the highest scholarly capability and achievement instruct his students as they proceeded through their course of study.

To make sure that candidates qualified for the privilege of being taught by these men, formal standards of admission were established. Students were required to "be members of the Jewish faith [and] of good moral character." They were also "expected to observe the Jewish Sabbath and to conform to the Jewish dietary laws." Piety and character were necessary ingredients for a student's admission into rabbinical candidacy. However, they were not sufficient.[69]

Schechter further demanded that each successful candidate for admission to the Rabbinical department "should have received from a university or college in good standing the Degree of Bachelor of Arts." The Seminary was poised to become a post-baccalaureate institution. The days of devoting instructional time to the teaching of high school students had long passed. Furthermore, students were expected to pass a battery of entrance examinations on a variety of subjects prior to their admission to the rabbinical course of study. The successful candidate for admission was already to know the "elementary grammar of the Hebrew language" and was expected to display an ability to translate and interpret "the whole of the Pentateuch" at sight. The Book of Genesis, along with "Targum Onkelos and the commentary of Rashi and Rashi characters," were also to be mastered prior to admission to candidacy for the rabbinate. Familiarity with portions of the Books of Judges, Isaiah, Psalms, and Daniel was a prerequisite for admission. Beyond erudition in the Bible, the fledgling candidate was required to display his facility in rabbinical literature as well. He was required to pass an examination in the mishnaic order *Seder Moed*, and he was further expected to be familiar with the "first perek of Tractate *Berakhot*, pages 1–13." Finally, the successful candidate had to demonstrate a "general acquaintance" with Jewish liturgy and history. Schechter—in formalizing these requirements for admission—was determined that the course of instruction in the rabbinical program at JTS be conducted on an advanced level.[70]

The curriculum in the Rabbinical School, as Schechter himself phrased it, "tried . . . to include . . . almost every branch of Jewish literature."[71] At the outset of the Schechter era, the course of instruction fell into six categories—Bible, the Babylonian and Jerusalem Talmud, Jewish history and the history of Jewish literature, theology and catechism, homiletics (including elocution and pastoral work), and *hazzanut*. The course of study was to extend "over a period of four years" and involved "lectures and instruction." The student—at the completion of four years of study—was required to "pass a satisfactory examination and write a thesis approved by the Faculty" in order to "be entitled to the Degree of Rabbi."[72] These last requirements underscore and highlight the vision Schechter held of the rabbinate as a learned academic modern profession.

The actual course content of the JTS curriculum at the beginning of Schechter's administration continued to center around the study of rabbinical literature as it had under Morais. Senior students were enrolled weekly in twenty-five hours of classroom instruction. Seven hours were devoted to the study of Talmud—four hours to Tractate *Hullin,* one hour each to *Shabbath* and *Gittin,* and one hour to Tractate *Shekalim* in the Jerusalem Talmud. In addition, students engaged in the study of the *Shulhan Aruch* for four hours each week—two hours in *Yoreh Deah,* and one each in *Eben Ha-Ezar* and *Orah Haim. Hoshen Mishpat* remained totally ignored. Midrash occupied another hour of classroom instruction each week, as did Judeo-Aramaic grammar, history of Jewish literature, Jewish history, theology, and Hebrew grammar. There was a weekly one-hour lecture devoted to theology and two more hours were spent on philosophy. In the fall semester, a one-hour lecture on the Jewish calendar was delivered by Cyrus Adler, and in the spring Schechter taught the students liturgy during the same time period. Bible—in the form of Leviticus, Psalms, and Jeremiah and their traditional rabbinic commentaries—was confined to three hours a week, and one hour a week was devoted to the "practical rabbinate" under the title of homiletics.[73]

Several observations are apposite at this point. First, the content of the curriculum reveals that at this juncture in the history of the Seminary virtually no time was spent on practical training for the rabbinate. As David M. Ackerman has observed, "Homiletics included all the 'practical' training deemed necessary for the Jewish ministry. By 1912 this area filled three hours a week of class time, up from one hour in 1902, reflecting an increased awareness on the seminary's part of the need for training in such areas as education and 'ministering to the sick and dying,' all in 'preparation for the practical part of the minister's vocation.'"[74] During the course of the decade, Schechter may have been forced to concede that more than one hour each week had to be spent on issues of the practical rabbinate if his ordinands were to be prepared to fulfill their vocational tasks. Nevertheless, the small amount of time spent on such topics bespeaks his belief that a mastery of classical Jewish literature—not attention devoted to practical matters—was the prerequisite that would qualify an individual student for the title of rabbi. In this sense, the content of the curriculum was totally consonant with the sentiment Schechter had expressed years earlier when he wrote, "No man in authority is greater than the source whence his authority is derived. The authority of the Rabbi is derived from the Torah."

The heart of the JTS course of instruction during the Schechter era centered upon Talmud and related literature. The study of Talmud and codes alone comprised almost half the instructional hours. Furthermore, many of the other courses such as theology, liturgy, midrash, history of Jewish literature, and even Bible focused on classical rabbinical sources as well. Hence, the advanced Seminary student of this era—as had his student predecessor a decade earlier—devoted at least three-quarters of his week to what could be labeled classical rabbinical literature. In addition, the courses in philosophy and Jewish history were devoted to reading the works of Saadia, Halevi, and Maimonides in Hebrew. All of this testifies to the text-centered nature of the Schechter curriculum and the Schechter ideal of a rabbi as one grounded in classical Jewish sources.

The role occupied by Bible in the curriculum also merits special commentary. From its inception, the Seminary—all its pious claims to the import of critical scholarship notwithstanding—held that the Bible was off-limits to critical inquiry. Kohut had stated, "To us the Pentateuch is a *noli me tangere*! Hands off! We disclaim all honor of handling the sharp knife which cuts the Bible into a thousand pieces."[75] Schechter shared this view and, in a famous and oft-quoted phrase, equated "Higher Criticism" with "Higher Anti-semitism." In a passionate passage, he wrote, "The Bible is our sole *raison d'être*, and it is just this which the Higher anti-Semitism is seeking to destroy, denying all our claims to the past, and leaving it without hope for the future. . . . The Bible is our patent of nobility granted to us by the Almighty God, and if we disown the Bible, leaving it to the tender mercies of a Welhausen, Stade and Duhm, and other beautiful souls working away at diminishing 'the nimbus of the Chosen People,' the world will disown us."[76] Decades were to pass before the Seminary would embrace a critical approach to the teaching of Bible. During this era, and for years to follow, JTS would be content in its curriculum to avoid critical questions concerning the Bible and its authorship. Instead, as the explicit curriculum demonstrates, the hours of instruction devoted to Bible would be limited altogether, just as they had been during the Morais era. Furthermore, the instruction that was offered in Bible would be conducted—at least during these years—in accord with classical rabbinical commentary.

The Adler Years

An analysis of the catalogs published during the Adler era reveals that the curriculum during these years remained substantially unchanged. While the scope of instruction by 1917 had expanded to include midrashim, codes, and liturgy as separate subject areas,[77] this only gave formal expression to a curriculum that already was being taught.

The alterations that did emerge during the Adler years were relatively minor in terms of their impact upon the overall curriculum of the Seminary Senior Rabbinical Department. In 1919, a new subject area—Jewish Communal Studies—was developed. The inclusion of this field in the rabbinical curriculum of the Seminary "no doubt reflected," as Ackerman has put it, "Mordecai Kaplan's influence, as it indicated a shifting view of the rabbi's role. . . . While still training scholars, teachers, and preachers, the Seminary recognized a need for the performance of 'social work' and various other communal functions by American rabbis."[78] Fourteen years later (in 1933) Simon Greenberg was added to the faculty as lecturer in education.[79] However, as we shall see, such courses for the "practical ministry" never occupied more than a tiny fraction of the student's weekly schedule. Indeed, it would be a mistake to view the inclusion of these areas in the curriculum of the Seminary as reflecting any type of significant transformation in course content of the curriculum. In a representative *Register* from this period, the area of Jewish Communal Studies is described as being comprised of a single course, entitled "Problems of the Rabbinate," and one hour per week of actual class time was allotted to it. It consisted "of lectures on Jewish education, Jewish philanthropy, industrial problems, correctional work and recreational institutions."[80]

The only other significant change that occurred in the emphasis of the curriculum also took place in 1933. As Israel Davidson has observed, "On June 9, 1933, the Faculty recommended that the curriculum of the Seminary be changed, so as to concentrate on the lectures in the first two years and to enable the student to take specialized work in the Seminar courses during the third and fourth years. . . . In the third and fourth years students were [also] required to select at least one seminar chosen from among the following subjects: Bible, History and Literature, Talmud, Liturgy and Medieval Poetry, Modern Hebrew Literature, Codes, History of Religion, and Theology."[81] The thesis requirement had been abandoned as a prerequisite for ordination in 1928. As a result, Ackerman has speculated that this system of lectures and seminars "was intended to replace the old thesis requirement . . . as a means of achieving scholarly expertise in a particular field."[82] In sum, these changes in no way attenuated the commitment of the Seminary to the ideal of *Wissenschaft*. Indeed, they only reinforced the vision of the rabbi as scholar.

Otherwise, the actual hours and content of instruction throughout the 1920s remained remarkably similar to what had obtained in the curriculum during the years of the Schechter administration. Requirements for admission were by and large equivalent to what they had been during the Schechter period. Students had to observe "the Sabbath and holidays" as well as "the dietary laws." They were also required to earn the "bachelor's degree from a college or university in good standing" in order to gain admission "into the . . . upper classes" and were subjected to a battery of examinations in Bible, Hebrew grammar, and Talmud. In 1920–21, the course of study was set at seven years, and student classes were "designated as Freshman A and B, Sophomore A and B, Junior A and B, and Senior." Students who did well on their entrance examinations were allowed to be admitted to the upper classes. In this way, the Seminary took cognizance of the diverse levels of Judaica backgrounds and textual competencies that increasingly marked the members of the student body.[83]

An examination of the actual twenty-three to twenty-six hours devoted each week to formal classroom instruction throughout the 1920s and 1930s reveals that Bible continued to be studied for two to three hours per week. Again, critical study of the biblical text was eschewed in favor of rabbinical commentaries. In addition, students were required to read additional chapters of the Bible over their summer vacation and were tested upon their mastery of the text "in the Autumn soon after the beginning of the term."[84] Four to five hours were devoted to talmudic tractates such as *Yoma*, *Kiddushin*, *Sanhedrin*, *Hullin*, *Shabbat*, *Gittin*, and *Pesahim*. Texts from the *Shulhan Aruch* (with the continued exception of *Hoshen Mishpat*) were studied two hours weekly by students in the four upper classes while one to two hours weekly were spent upon Hebrew grammar and composition. Medieval Hebrew texts were studied one hour weekly, and lecture courses on the Bible and Talmud, with titles such as "Monuments and the Bible," "Biblical Archaeology," "History of the Halakhah," and "Outlines of Rabbinic Jurisprudence" comprised two hours of the weekly curriculum. One hour of medieval philosophy was required, and one hour of weekly course work was devoted in the last three years to the study of liturgy. Midrash and "Lectures on the Religious Functions of the Rabbi" received an hour each of instructional time, and three hours of lecture focused upon "Post-Biblical History" and "Literature"—each year of the latter course being devoted to texts from a different period of the Jewish past. "Courses in the Practical Ministry" were confined formally in the 1920s to two hours per week—one hour listed under the rubric, "Problems of the Rabbinate—Special Lectures," and another to *hazzanut*. In the 1930s, an additional hour under this category was devoted to "Education" and one more to "Public Speaking." Finally, all students were required to spend additional time on the study of Talmud. The more advanced students were "required to read privately . . . 30 folios" of Talmud each year while only "15 folios" were demanded of the less advanced students. In sum, the curriculum throughout the Adler administration remained overwhelmingly devoted, as it had under Schechter, to the study of texts and historical scholarship.[85]

The fidelity displayed in the curriculum to the rabbinical vision articulated by Schechter during the period of 1915 to 1940 can be explained in several ways. First, throughout these twenty-five years Adler himself was involved in a whole host of activities. In fact, throughout his incumbency as President of the Seminary, Adler did not even establish his principal residency in New York. Instead, his home remained in Philadelphia, and he divided his time between Philadelphia and New York.[86] Consequently, Adler actually had relatively little time to devote to curricular matters at the Seminary. Moreover, his admiration for Schechter was unbounded. Adler had not only been instrumental in persuading Schechter to come to the Seminary in 1902. He had also agreed to serve as chair of the Board of Directors during the Schechter administration. Adler delivered the eulogy at the funeral of his friend and coworker and said of Schechter, "Through his teachings and the inspiration of his character, he has raised up a following not only of his immediate disciples, but among the larger number that he influenced, who in their humble way will carry on his traditions of character and learning. The hope of Israel will live through him."[87]

All this reveals that Adler not only lacked the time to alter the curriculum of the Seminary in a significant manner but also had little inclination to do so. He shared the vision Schechter held of Judaism and the rabbinate and, with the exception of a few minor curricular changes, was content to allow the content and scope of the curriculum as developed by Schechter to remain undisturbed during his tenure as President.

The distinctive nature of that curriculum and the vision of the rabbinate it embodied can be highlighted when we compare it briefly to the curricula of the Rabbi Isaac Elchanan Theological Seminary of Yeshiva University and Hebrew Union College during the first decades of the 1900s. As Aaron Rothkoff has indicated, during the 1920s many members of the American Jewish community "did not understand wherein . . . Yeshiva differed from the Jewish Theological Seminary." After all, "many persons active in the administration and faculty of the Jewish Theological Seminary during this period were Orthodox or close to Orthodox in their theology and practice." Indeed, this was a period in American Jewish history when a man such as Adler could still be invited to address a convention of the Orthodox *Agudat Harabanim* on the subject of Sabbath observance. As a result, laypersons such as Louis Marshall from the board of the Seminary and Judge Otto Rosalsky of Yeshiva "felt there was no need for the community to support two major rabbinical seminaries if their religious viewpoints were so similar" and they even went so far as to advocate a merger between the two institutions during the last half of the 1920s.[88]

Rabbi Bernard Revel, president of Yeshiva, was adamantly opposed to a merger, and he took up the cudgels against such a proposal in a mimeographed article entitled "Seminary and Yeshiva" which he circulated to the entire membership of Yeshiva's Board of Directors. In the article, Revel employed the issue of curriculum as a demarcation that distinguished the two institutions from one another. Revel claimed that the students at Yeshiva—whether native or foreign born—had uniformly intensive backgrounds in the study of talmudic texts and commentaries. Consequently, study of the Talmud at Yeshiva could be conducted on a highly advanced level. Students at the Seminary generally did not possess such backgrounds in Talmud. Revel therefore asserted that the level of talmudic study at JTS could not match that of the Yeshiva. Moreover, Revel contended, students at Yeshiva also spent ten months of the year studying twenty-three hours of Talmud weekly. This was in contrast to the eight hours weekly that were devoted to Talmud and codes for eight months each year at the Seminary. "This difference in time," Revel wrote, "must show in the nature of the material presented for study, in the method pursued, and in the students' achievements." Revel conceded that the Seminary gave its students extensive training in Jewish history and literature. However, as an Orthodox rabbi, his vision of the rabbinate compelled him to assert that such study was irrelevant to qualifying an individual for rabbinical ordination. Instead, Revel held that the curriculum in a rabbinical school should focus almost exclusively on intensive talmudic study. Mastery of this literature alone could qualify the student for the title of rabbi. The level of talmudic instruction and the time allotted to it at Yeshiva reflected his vision. The content and structure of the curriculum at the Seminary reflected another.[89]

If the Seminary curriculum of this period could be perceived by the president of Yeshiva University as insufficiently devoted to the study of Talmud and overly directed towards *Wissenschaft* and academic scholarship, a different type of perception emerges if we contrast the Schechter curriculum to that of Hebrew Union College during these years. As noted earlier, there were no discernible differences in the curricula of the Seminary and HUC at the end of the era of Morais and Wise. With the selection of Kaufmann Kohler as president of the Hebrew Union College in 1903, significant distinctions in the rabbinical courses of instruction at the two institutions began to appear. This is not to say that there were not vital points of agreement between them as to the manner in which the modern rabbi should be trained and educated. After all, the two men possessed similar backgrounds. They were European born and each had an absolute command over both rabbinical literature and modern scholarship. The two worked together on a number of academic projects—notably *The Jewish Encyclopedia*—and were close personal friends. In a tone reminiscent of Schechter, Kohler, in an address he delivered at the dedication of the new building at the Jewish Theological Seminary on 26 April 1903, spoke both of the indispensable role that contemporary scholarship played in legitimating the claim of the rabbi to authority and of the obligation of the modern rabbinical school to impart such knowledge to its students. Kohler, on that occasion, asserted, "Pulpit oratory evokes tears or smiles, assent or dissent; *it is the seat of learning vested with authority which endows the man in the pulpit with the knowledge and skill to substantiate every righteous claim.*"[90] Or, as Kohler once more contended thirteen years later, "In order to be a true leader, . . . the modern rabbi must take his stand on high, keeping ever abreast of ideas, the philosophical and scientific . . . problems of the age in order to be a safe and trusted guide to the erring and struggling. . . . We need more leaders who go back to the fountains of Jewish lore and know how to strike the dry rock to make it flow with living waters of knowledge."[91]

In order to achieve this goal, Kohler, like Schechter, appointed masters of *Wissenschaft* to the faculty of HUC. During his tenure, great scholars such as Jacob Lauterbach, David Neumark, and Julian Morgenstern were added to the teaching staff. In fact, it was the aim of Kohler, as it had been of both Morais and Schechter, to create a seminary for "American Israel" that could "well boast that its work for the Jewish faith and Jewish learning" would "outdo that of European Jewry."[92] Nevertheless, the shared commitment Kohler and Schechter displayed toward the mastery of modern scholarship as a prerequisite for the rabbinical office should not mask the considerable differences in attitude that distinguished Kohler from Schechter. Nor, as alluded to above, were these differences confined to the theoretical realm. They were to find concrete expression in the content of the curriculum each man initiated.

Kohler, unlike Schechter, possessed what can charitably be described as a noticeable disdain for the Talmud. In 1904, he wrote, "There is no justification whatsoever for . . . the most precious time of the student" to be "spent upon Halakic discussions." Kohler spoke disparagingly of the "hair-splitting dialectics of the Talmud" as well as "the stagnant form of the Halakah and the inane discussions that fill so many pages of the Babylonian Gemarah." Kohler therefore contended, "A Jewish Theological School concentrating its efforts upon the Halakah resembles a medieval fortress which looks formidable to the beholder but can not hold out against the implements of modern warfare."[93] This did not mean that the Talmud and classical legal codes of the rabbinical tradition were of no import to Kohler. However, as he asserted, "The teaching of the Talmud and Codes becomes profitable for us, who are no longer bound to the Shulhan Aruk, only when such practical questions as the marriage and divorce laws, the funeral and mourning rites, or the Sabbath and Festivals are discussed, so as to be brought into relation to modern life."[94]

Kohler further distinguished himself from Schechter in his attitude toward biblical criticism and its place in the curriculum of a rabbinical school. Kohler held that it was "only in keeping with this narrow Halakistic view that Higher Criticism" could be deemed "dangerous or alien to the scope of Rabbinic theology. The entire history and literature of Judaism remains a book with seven seals to him who shuts his eyes to the disclosures of . . . modern Bible research." In what must be seen as a barb directed at Schechter, Kohler continued, "Such brilliant phraseology as is the label 'Higher Anti-Semitism' given to Higher Criticism may captivate many— baahizat enayyim—by its seeming truth, but it can not stand the test of scrutiny. . . . We cannot escape the conclusions of Higher Criticism. . . . What geology did for us in laying bare the different strata of the earth telling of the various epochs of creation, Higher Criticism does in disclosing the various stages of growth of the truth of divine revelation."[95] Furthermore, Kohler felt the Hebrew Union College, "with its outspoken Reform principle,"[96] could express its view of Judaism as one of "progress, of growth and transformation" only through the medium of "critical and historical research."[97] Biblical criticism was not to be eschewed in the curriculum of the Hebrew Union College during the Kohler administration. Instead, it was to become a handmaiden for the legitimization of Reform in what was now to be a distinctly Reform rabbinical seminary.

The curriculum taught within the walls of the Hebrew Union College during the era of Kaufmann Kohler increasingly conformed to Kohler's vision of Reform Judaism. It was a vision that conceived of Judaism in religious-spiritual categories alone and condemned Zionism as "ignorance and irreligion." Students were told by Kohler that they had two choices—to serve "a Jewish nationalism without God, or a Judaism inseparably linked to its universal God, its Torah, and its world-mission."[98] As Michael Meyer has observed, modern Hebrew literature and Zionism would find no place in the curriculum of HUC during the Kohler years. Talmud and classical rabbinical literature would recede in importance, and the Bible—particularly the books of the Prophets—would be assigned the central place in the HUC course of study.[99] An analysis of the catalogs published during these years bears out the accuracy of Meyer's observation.

By 1903, the year before Kohler was appointed as president, the ideal of a rabbinical student mastering 150 folios of Talmud prior to his entry to the five-year Collegiate Department of HUC had long since been abandoned. Nevertheless, five to six of the fifteen weekly class hours were assigned to Mishna, Talmud, and codes. Courses examined the tractates of *Gittin*, *Yebamot*, *Kiddushin*, *Ketubot*, and *Shabbat* during the five-year course of study in the Collegiate Department along with the codes relevant to these talmudic sources. Bible was confined to two to four hours a week. In addition, one- to two-credit courses in philosophy, history, grammar, modern Hebrew, and Arabic were given. Systematic theology and ethics were also taught—as they were at JTS—to students in their final year; and there was a thesis requirement. Courses in the practical rabbinate were essentially confined to homiletics in the third and fourth year and pastoral theology in the fifth.[100]

Kohler immediately sought to expand and change the curriculum. In 1904, he drew up a proposed curriculum for the College, which eliminated modern Hebrew. Furthermore, in the Preparatory Department, no Talmud at all was required. In the five-year Collegiate Department, Mishna, Talmud, and *halakha* were assigned six hours in the first two years and four credits in years three and four. In the fifth year, no Talmud was taught, though Kohler did propose that graduating students study the "History of Talmudism, Karaism, and Cabbalah" two hours weekly. A course on the "History of the Sadducees, Pharisees, and Essenes" was proposed for the fourth year. In suggesting these latter two courses, Kohler emulated the curriculum initiated by Abraham Geiger at the Berlin Hochschule, for there Geiger had included courses on the history of Jewish sectarianism as well as those groups in Jewish history that did not acknowledge the authority of the Talmud.[101] Interestingly, in light of the paramount role they were later to assume in the curriculum, Bible and commentaries were offered only three hours weekly in the first three years, and an additional hour was proposed for years four and five. Other courses in history, philosophy, grammar, midrash, haggadah, liturgy, apocalyptic and pseudepigraphic literature, Apocrypha, comparative religion, New Testament and Koran, systematic theology, and Jewish ethical literature were offered at various points during the student's matriculation in the Collegiate Department. All these academic courses were to be supplemented by practical courses on pedagogy, sabbath school work, homiletics, and elocution. These latter courses were generally restricted to two hours each week, though in the final year they were expanded to five of the twenty weekly course load hours in which each senior student was required to matriculate.[102]

The HUC 1906 catalog indicates that Kohler was not able to realize his ideal curriculum immediately. Of the 138 units prescribed for graduation over the five-year course of study in the collegiate classes, thirty units fell under the rubric of Talmud, though only ten to twelve were actually assigned to talmudic text. The other eighteen to twenty required units were taken from Mishna and codes. An equal weight of thirty credits was assigned to the study of Bible, reflecting the increasing importance attached to this subject area in the curriculum. Midrashic literature was defined as a separate subject area and was elevated to fourteen required units of study. The student took four units each year in philosophy and history, and in the third year a two-unit course in liturgy was required. Theology, homiletics, ethics, and pedagogy were assigned students during their last three years of study. Electives in all these areas, as well as Hebrew and cognate languages, music, sociology, and elocution were also provided to complete the curriculum. This curriculum is indicative of the shifts that were beginning to take place in the curriculum of HUC. Several subject areas had been added to the course of instruction extant during the Wise era. Most significantly, more weight was now assigned to Bible and midrash, while Talmud and halakhic literature—while still occupying a significant place in the HUC curriculum—started to diminish in prominence.[103] This trend, seen in nascent form in 1906, was fully manifest by 1921–22, the last year of Kohler's presidency.

Courses in a wide variety of subject areas such as philosophy, history, and midrash were still included in the 1921–22 curriculum. In addition, Kohler demanded that each student enroll in a course entitled "The History of Judaism and its Sects." Courses designed to prepare students for the practical rabbinate still constituted a relatively small part of the entire curriculum, but this area was expanded. For example, six of the fifteen class hours during the senior year were devoted to issues related to the practical rabbinate—homiletics, practical theology, ethics and pedagogy, and applied sociology. A commitment to *Wissenschaft* remained paramount, and HUC continued to stipulate a written thesis based on original research as a requirement for ordination. Most important, Kohler constructed a curriculum that centered upon the study of Bible. Classical rabbinical texts—particularly Talmud—continued to receive less and less attention. The 1921–22 catalog indicates that five to seven hours of instruction were devoted each week to Bible—particularly the prophetic books—for students during their first four years in the Collegiate Department. Talmud, in contrast, was not even taught during the first year of the advanced program. Instead, first-year students studied Mishna two hours each week. They were exposed to Talmud for three hours in the second year and two hours weekly in the third. Students in the junior and senior years were enrolled in "Topics from Hullin and Codes" for two units both semesters during the former year and in "Topics from Kiddushin, Gittin, Yebamot, and Codes" for the same amount of credit during the latter one. In sum, the student who completed his rabbinical training during the last year of Kohler's tenure as president took a minimum of twenty-seven units of Bible, but only eleven units of Mishna, Talmud, and codes by the time he completed his course of study. The curriculum of HUC at the end of the Kohler Administration displayed little fidelity to the course of instruction of the Wise era.[104]

Kohler's aim was to produce a Reform rabbi prepared to serve a denominationally distinct movement. The era of Wise, when Hebrew Union College strove to educate rabbis who could serve traditional as well as liberal Jewish American congregations, had passed. Orthodox Judaism was obviously of no concern to Kohler. Nor did this transformation in the curriculum of HUC disturb Julian Morgenstern, Kohler's successor to the presidency (in 1923). An eminent biblical scholar, Morgenstern shared the curricular vision and Jewish outlook of Kohler. This is not to say that his views and those of Kohler were identical, nor does it mean that there were no curricular changes at HUC during the Morgenstern years. The appointment of a man like Samuel S. Cohon to the faculty during the 1920s assured modern Hebrew and Zionism a voice in the life of the College that was absent during the Kohler administration. Nevertheless, Morgenstern basically perpetuated the curriculum he had inherited from Kohler during his tenure as president. The curriculum principally focused upon Bible and paid considerable attention to history and literature, philosophy, and midrash. Courses in theology and ethics persisted, and a minimum of eleven of the seventy-three total credits required for ordination were devoted to concerns of the practical rabbinate. The Talmud, in contrast, was relegated to a minor place in the curriculum. A student could complete his course of study with only eight credits in Talmud, a subject area that included Mishna and codes. The College no longer strove to imbue its graduates with a high degree of proficiency in classical rabbinical texts. Kohler's curricular vision would govern the Hebrew Union College for most of the 20th century.[105]

This analysis of the rabbinical school curricula at both Yeshiva University and Hebrew Union College during the first decades of the 20th century highlights the distinctive nature of rabbinical training offered by the Seminary. On the one hand, the Seminary clearly rejected the educational model of the yeshiva. The insularity of the traditional yeshiva curriculum perpetuated what the Seminary saw as a

553

*The JTS
Rabbinical
Curriculum
in Historical
Perspective*

limited and parochial vision of the inner life and creative dynamics of the people Israel. Conversely, the content of the HUC curriculum as it evolved under Kohler was equally unacceptable—albeit for different reasons—to men such as Schechter and his colleagues. The limited requirements of HUC in the area of talmudic literature and the elevated role assigned to Bible in the curriculum of the Reform seminary reflected what the men at JTS regarded as a truncated understanding of Judaism despite the importance Schechter and Kohler ascribed to critical study and modern scholarship.

The curriculum established in each of these three schools embodied three distinctive approaches to Judaism. The days when matters of observance alone divided the Seminary in New York from the College in Cincinnati were over. Diverse curricula now clearly differentiated these schools from one another—and by extension these differences reflected alternative visions of Judaism. They signaled the emergence of a denominationally divided Jewish community at this juncture in the American Jewish experience. An integrated mode of critical study that reflected an allegiance to rabbinic civilization as well as to modern scholarship marked the ethos of the Seminary and its curriculum. It would also serve as the distinctive hallmark of the Conservative movement.

The Finkelstein Administration: Preservation and Expansion of a Legacy

In the fall of 1940, Louis Finkelstein became the fourth President of the Jewish Theological Seminary of America. The turbulence of political events during the war years in which he assumed office as well as the practical experience he possessed as a pulpit rabbi caused Finkelstein to supplement the curriculum he inherited from Schechter and Adler in distinctive ways. Nevertheless, his own vision of the rabbinate was essentially in accord with the ideal that had been promulgated by his predecessors, and this led him to maintain the historic traditions of the Seminary as a center of both classical Jewish learning and modern scholarship. Even as he introduced curricular changes, Finkelstein's Seminary continued to display strong elements of continuity with the past.[106]

In a 1937 address at the Seminary, "Tradition in the Making: The Seminary's Interpretation of Judaism," Finkelstein outlined his own vision of Judaism as well as the approach to rabbinical training this vision entailed. In words reminiscent of Schechter, Finkelstein maintained that "the discipline of Law [w]as essential to human behavior." Through "proper conduct," one comes "to approach God." Finkelstein therefore held "that it is not enough for the establishment and strengthening of moral character to hold up a symbolically perfect personality, but that it is necessary by means of moral judgments to train a person with regard to every question of right and wrong." This perception led Finkelstein to the universalistic assertion that "Law and Discipline" were at the "core" of the "Judeo–Christian tradition." Indeed, the central legacy that Judaism had bequeathed to all humankind was the gift of law. Judaism had disseminated this ideal concerning the majesty of law and the processes attached to it throughout occidental civilization.[107]

All this caused Finkelstein to inveigh against a Reform movement that would "repudiate the discipline of Judaism on the one hand" and an Orthodox Judaism "on the other hand" that would "refuse to give" the discipline of law "the opportunity to live." These movements and their adherents "think that we have but two alternatives, to reject or to accept the law, but in either case to treat it as a dead letter. Both of these alternatives are repugnant to the whole tradition of Judaism, and it is to combat them that the Seminary was brought into being."[108] The Seminary championed a Conservative Judaism that averred that while the principles which undergirded Jewish law were eternal, the law itself was dynamic. As Finkelstein observed, "Justice, truth, mercy and love do not change—they are more real than the world in which we live. But their applications differ under varying conditions... . It is one of the great achievements of Jewish law that it provides in itself the machinery for its interpretation, its expansion, and its application to changing conditions."[109]

This understanding of Jewish law allowed Finkelstein to contend that Conservative Judaism did not embody a "break with traditional Judaism." Rather, the approach promoted by the Seminary called for a "return to it."[110] As Finkelstein asserted, "There is no quarrel between us and Isaiah, Jeremiah, Hillel, and Akiba." For the Seminary, imparting knowledge of the law and its character to the JTS students, would "do for our generation what" these great men "did for their generation."[111] To accomplish this task, the ordinand of the Seminary had to combine a mastery of classical Jewish learning and modern scholarship with a life of faith. Finkelstein wrote, "Each one of us must devote part of his day to Jewish thought and the Jewish mode of communion with God."[112] Finkelstein concluded this seminal address with the following observation, "When I was younger, I frequently wished that it might have been granted me to have lived in the first or second century and have been one of those humble students, whose names have been for the most part forgotten, but whose life and labor contributed so much happiness and goodness for all the world. Now that I am growing older, I realize that we have no need to envy our ancestors. We can do better than that—we can emulate them."[113] Finkelstein believed that the curriculum he inherited from his predecessors was designed to facilitate and foster such emulation. Consequently, he retained both the content and ethos of the traditional JTS curriculum. Simultaneously, he expanded and altered that curriculum in subtle ways.

The continuity between past and present at the Seminary that Finkelstein affirmed is evidenced in the very first catalog issued during his administration in 1940–41. The catalog called upon its candidates for admission to "be members of the Jewish faith and loyal adherents of its observances, including the Sabbath, holidays, daily prayers, and dietary laws." In addition, each prospective student was required to "hold the degree of Bachelor of Arts or Bachelor of Science" and to have a strong background in the liberal arts. Finally, each candidate was expected to "pass satisfactory examinations" in the areas of Bible, Hebrew, Talmud, and history. In Bible, this meant that each prospective student would possess "a thorough knowledge of the text" of the Pentateuch "and familiarity with the commentary of Rashi," in addition to "a thorough knowledge of the books of the Former Prophets, and the ability to translate at sight texts from the Latter Prophets and Hagiographa," while in history "a general acquaintance" was demanded. The student was further expected to demonstrate a "knowledge of Hebrew grammar" and to display an "ability to translate an English text into Hebrew." In the Talmud examination, a student was called upon "to read at sight from one of the major treatises previously studied" and was asked to indicate his "ability to read a passage of the Talmud after preparation." Finkelstein was clearly concerned that the students of the Seminary possess adequate background in Judaica and texts so that the high level of classroom instruction established by his predecessors in office could be maintained during his administration.[114]

Finkelstein, like Schechter, was also concerned that only individuals of the highest scholarly rank and achievement instruct the students of the Seminary. Men such as Louis Ginzberg, Alexander Marx, and Mordecai Kaplan continued to serve on the faculty, and others such as H. L. Ginsberg, Robert Gordis, and Boaz Cohen maintained their scholarly productivity during the early years of the Finkelstein era. Finkelstein supplemented these scholars by appointing such outstanding figures as Shalom Spiegel and Abraham Joshua Heschel to the instructional staff in 1943 and 1945 respectively, and he recognized the budding promise and talents of men such as Gerson Cohen, David Weiss Halivni, Judah Goldin, Chaim Dimitrovsky, Seymour Siegel, and Moshe Davis and gave all of them their initial appointments to the JTS faculty. However, his most significant academic appointment may well have been one that was made during his first year in office—in 1940 Saul Lieberman joined the faculty as professor of Palestinian literature and institutions.

In 1948 Lieberman became dean of the Seminary Rabbinical School. Ten years later he was named rector of the Seminary, and he continued his distinguished career as professor of Talmud until his death in 1983. His rigorous approach to learning and his absolute devotion to the study of Talmud helped to direct the Seminary rabbinical curriculum and mold the outlook of its graduates for more than four decades.[115] These characteristics and commitments—so consonant with the spirit of the Seminary since the turn of the century—are captured in the following tale which Lieberman himself related.

As Pamela Nadell has indicated, it was not uncommon for Lieberman, who

David Weiss Halivni with students in his office. *Photo by Peter J. Kaplan. Communications Department, JTS.*

"begrudged time away from his scholarship," to often be in his office at the Seminary "near midnight so that he could complete an evening's work."[116] Lieberman related that on one such occasion, "on a Saturday night," he came to his office on the fifth floor at the Seminary. "Late, at about midnight, when I stopped to ponder over a passage that I did not understand, I could hear the voice of someone studying in the dormitory. It was such a sweet voice . . . It was a real *kol Torah* —voice of Torah. . . . I must tell you that this kind of study, this voice of Torah which had the genuine longing of our ancestors for the Torah brought back to me the voice of the Yeshivoth of the old country. . . . I could not help but reflect that as long as this goes on at the Seminary, as long as these mysterious ties between the ivory tower of the fifth floor and the floors of the dormitory continue *'od lo ovdah tikvateinu* —our hope is not lost."[117] Lieberman was determined to maintain a curriculum for the rabbinical students of the Seminary that would have at its center a devotion to Talmud and classical rabbinical texts taught in accord with a modern academic spirit. Finkelstein, as well as his most influential colleagues on the faculty, shared this vision.

An analysis of the course content on the curriculum as outlined in reports from the 1950s through the 1970s bears out the accuracy of this last observation. A full description of the curriculum of the four-year Graduate Department of the Rabbinical School appears in the 1951–52 *Register*. The curriculum was a demanding one, and each student was required to enroll in a minimum of thirty-two course units in each year. Two credit courses in academic areas such as theology and American Jewish history were required in specific years. In addition, students matriculated in courses on codes, Jewish philosophy, medieval Hebrew literature, and modern Hebrew literature during four of their eight semesters of advanced rabbinical studies. The *Register* also indicates that students enrolled in two-credit courses devoted to midrash, philosophies of religion, Bible, and history during every semester that they were in attendance during their four-year course of study. One hour each week during the first three years and two hours per week during the senior year were devoted to a course in speech, and during the third and fourth years two hours weekly were spent in education. In the fourth year, one unit each semester focused on the area of practical theology, a subject described as including "public relations, adult education, and the conducting of lectures." These three last courses, combined with a two-unit course on homiletics which was taken during all eight semesters that a student was in attendance at the Rabbinical School, constituted the totality of time assigned to matters of the practical rabbinate. As in the past, Talmud and related literature were the focus of the curriculum. Each student enrolled in a five-unit class on Talmud during all eight semesters of the Graduate Rabbinical Program. The Talmud curriculum itself was described in the following terms: "A study of the Babylonian Talmud with its standard commentaries, as well as the Palestinian Talmud and the Halakhic Midrashim, pursued along philological, historical and critical lines, and supplemented by lectures on the history of rabbinic jurisprudence and literature."[118]

This curriculum conveys a clear picture of the rabbi that Finkelstein and the faculty envisioned. For, as Michael B. Greenbaum has pointed out, Finkelstein believed that "a study of the Bible, Talmud, medieval and modern Hebrew literature, will indicate the manner in which Judaism can be saved in periods of crisis [such as our own]."[119] Finkelstein therefore concurred with an attitude Salo Baron

Saul Lieberman
(right) with Louis
Finkelstein,
1960s. *Photo by
John H. Popper.
Ratner Center,
JTS.*

had expressed concerning the training of Jewish leaders. Baron had maintained that Judaism could produce farsighted leaders only if the leadership of the contemporary American Jewish community was "imbued with the accumulated wisdom of the ages of rabbis and thinkers" and "equipped with the knowledge furnished them by the methods of modern social and historical sciences."[120] Finkelstein recognized that this sentiment was totally consonant with the educational vision that had guided the Seminary rabbinical curriculum from its inception, and he was determined that it should continue to guide the education of the Conservative rabbinate. The allegiance to classical Jewish civilization and its literature and to modern scholarship that Schechter had established as the hallmark of the Seminary and its curriculum also characterized the ethos and content of the rabbinical curriculum that obtained at JTS during the Finkelstein years. In words that could have been uttered by Schechter, Finkelstein wrote that "just as [the men of the Great Assembly] built a bridge between Bible and Talmud," so men educated for the rabbinate at JTS would "build the bridge between Talmudic and future Judaism."[121]

This is not to say that the curriculum remained static during the Finkelstein administration. The most noticeable change, as David Ackerman has observed, came during the 1950s with "a new willingness on the Seminary's part to apply critical method to the study of *Humash* . . . . The advertised topic for the 1959 Prize Essay in Bible, 'The Traditions in Genesis 1:1–25:17—Resemblances to, Dependencies upon, and Contrasts with Traditions of Other People,' represented the full flowering of the new critical stance."[122] Furthermore, this trend intensified throughout the 1960s, and a course description of a class from this period entitled "Bible B—Book of Psalms," could state that the Psalms would be examined "with special attention to the findings from Ugaritic and Babylonian sources." Indeed, by the 1970s a Bible seminar could be taught that outspokenly stated it would provide an "analysis of the various sources of the Pentateuch, a comparison of the contrasting world views, and an examination of the criteria—linguistic and substantive—commonly used in dating them." Ackerman, commenting upon this development, has observed, "A far cry indeed from 'Higher Criticism Higher Anti-Semitism,' or from Kohut's description of the *Humash* as *noli me tangere*."[123] The inclusion of biblical criticism in the curriculum of the Rabbinical School surely represented a significant departure from the past. Nevertheless, catalogs of the late 1950s and early 1960s reveal few other curricular changes.[124]

During these years, the Seminary was compelled to recognize that a number of otherwise strong candidates for admission to the rabbinical program did not possess the grounding in Talmud and the familiarity with Judaica that the Seminary ideally desired for students in its four-year course. Indeed, beginning in the 1950s, fewer students came to the Seminary from Orthodox backgrounds, and their exposure to traditional Jewish texts and study was not as intense as that of their predecessors in the earlier decades of the 1900s. Though the formal course of study remained four years, the Seminary recognized that many such students lacked the requisite knowledge to complete the prescribed course of study during that time, and the 1958–59 *Register* states that those students "who require additional work to overcome deficiencies in a certain area may, upon admission, be assigned programs of five or six years."[125] While the Jewish educational training of prospective Seminary rabbinical students may have eroded over the course of the century, the Seminary was not prepared to lower its standards for these men. Instead, it would simply lengthen their tenure at the school. Consequently, as Arthur Hertzberg, writing in 1959, observed, "The Rabbinical School at the Seminary has increasingly in the last decade or so required of many of its students that they remain for five or even six years of study before being ordained, in place of the minimal four-year course."[126]

In the following year, the Seminary responded formally to its increasingly diverse student population by dividing the Rabbinical department into three divisions—the School of Judaica, the Graduate Rabbinical School, and the Department of Postgraduate Studies. The latter division provided advanced study leading to the degree of Doctor of Hebrew Literature for men who had already received rabbinical ordination. The other two divisions were devoted to a course of study that would qualify the successful student for his ordination as a rabbi. The School of Judaica involved a one- to three-year course of study. Its curriculum was "designed to permit concentration in text studies in Bible, Talmud, and Hebrew." After the satisfactory completion of all required courses, the student in the School of Judaica was required to pass written comprehensive examinations. At that juncture, the successful student received the degree of Master of Hebrew Literature. Subsequent to the completion of these studies, the student was eligible for admission to the three-year course of study in the Graduate Rabbinical School, a course of study that would lead to rabbinical ordination.[127]

Students who, "because of insufficient background in Judaica," could not pass entrance examinations in Bible, Talmud, Hebrew, and history could be admitted to the Preparatory Department of the School of Judaica for a single year. Class standing in the School of Judaica for those students who did pass the entrance examinations was determined by knowledge of Talmud. A student in the first year of the School of Judaica was expected to prepare "a minimum of 10 pages (20 sides)" in a talmudic tractate chosen from among *Ketubot, Pesahim, Shabbat, Baba Kama, Baba Mezia, Baba Batra, Kiddushin, Gittin,* or *Sanhedrin.* Second-year placement was contingent upon a mastery of "25 pages (50 sides)" in one of these tractates, while students who could demonstrate a knowledge of "50 pages (100 sides)" qualified for third-year standing.[128]

While attention was paid in the curriculum of the School of Judaica to Bible, codes, Hebrew, and midrash, the major subject studied was Talmud. In the first year, ten of sixteen class hours were spent on Talmud, though this number dropped to six hours in the second year. During the third year, Talmud was assigned nine hours each week. Thus, the curriculum of the School of Judaica focused principally on Talmud, with over half the course work demanded of the student—in keeping with the ethos and vision of the Seminary—devoted to this classical repository of Jewish wisdom and identity. The Seminary was determined to sustain its commitment to a curriculum that would produce ordinands strongly conversant in

Talmud. It is particularly noteworthy that not even a single course devoted to the practical issues and functions of the rabbinate—with the possible exception of a two-hour course on "Homiletics of Midrash" in the third year—was included in the curriculum of the School of Judaica.[129] The leadership of the Seminary in the 1960s affirmed and perpetuated the view of Schechter that the requirement for legitimate rabbinical leadership was that the rabbi possess a thorough knowledge of Torah and Talmud.

561

*The JTS
Rabbinical
Curriculum
in Historical
Perspective*

The curriculum displayed a comparable fidelity to the past in the Graduate Rabbinical School. A five-credit course in Talmud was required each semester of the first year, and four-credit Talmud courses were assigned during the final two. In addition, students in this department enrolled in two-credit courses in Bible every semester. Courses and seminars in American Jewish history, codes, history, Jewish art, Jewish philosophy, midrash, philosophies of religion, medieval Hebrew literature, and modern Hebrew literature complemented the course of study as they had in the past. Practical subjects rounded out the curriculum. These components of a Rabbinical School education continued to play a minor role in the overall curriculum—albeit, a somewhat expanded one compared to the past. Two-credit courses in education and homiletics were required each semester during both the first and second years of the program, and also a one-credit course in speech as well as a course in homiletics during the final year. In 1962, a program was initiated that required senior students to serve an internship of at least eight sessions with a rabbi in the New York area so as to better acquaint the student with the problems and challenges of the congregational rabbinate. The 1964–66 *Register* indicates that this was immediately required as part of the two-credit practical theology course for last-year students.[130] A course in pastoral psychiatry had been added to the curriculum in 1955, which, by 1964, was required of all students in the Graduate Rabbinical School during their six semesters of matriculation.[131] The first year focused on an introduction to psychiatry and psychoanalysis, while the second year centered on techniques of counseling. In the third year students were placed in social service agencies.[132] This expansion represented a clear departure from the 1960 curriculum, when this subject was limited to a single credit during both semesters of the third and final year.[133]

In response to the atmosphere of the 1960s, the curriculum began to evidence some concern with the personal issues confronting the student and the role that the individual faculty member might play in addressing these concerns. Documents from this period reflect discussions that took place concerning the role that the faculty ought to assume in advising students. The avowed aim of such advisement was to foster exchange between faculty advisers and students that would not be limited to "reviews of the subject studied." Instead, such advisement would further consider the "relevance" of the subjects that were studied as well as the "theological questions" such study might pose. In addition, "intimate personal problems" were to be addressed. The purpose of the advisement program, as one student poignantly phrased it, was to aid the student in grappling with the question, "How am I growing in knowledge, piety and wisdom in my years at school?"[134]

One can only speculate as to the success of this advisement program. Indeed, reports to the Board of Overseers during this period indicate that doubts surfaced concerning the effectiveness of the program, despite the recognition of its laudatory goals. Questions were raised concerning the competence of scholars to probe students' intimate personal problems and theological and spiritual growth. Furthermore, it was feared that such goals were dissonant with the considerable pressures put on students to master a vast amount of material.[135] After all, the commitment to academic achievement and mastery of classical rabbinic texts remained as paramount at the Seminary in this era as it had been in decades past. Students in the School of Judaica were not supposed to seek outside employment, and those in the Rabbinical department were permitted to assume part-time teaching positions or part-time rabbinic posts only with the permission of the faculty. Study remained the principal task of the student.[136]

The 1960s themselves were a time of great ferment in American society. The civil rights movement, the assassinations of John and Robert Kennedy and of Dr. Martin Luther King, Jr., as well as the horror and moral outrage expressed by many in American society concerning American involvement in Vietnam, did not leave the Academy unaffected. Student unrest was the order of the day at many universities, and student protest demonstrations were quite common on the American academic scene. JTS did not remain untouched by these developments. Indeed, the Seminary, perched as it was on the doorstep of Columbia University, was compelled to take note of these trends that were making themselves felt within the university. Students throughout the United States were demanding a greater voice in determining the course and content of their education, and this spirit found some expression at JTS. Perhaps for the first time, a committee of students and faculty was formed. And in 1967–68 a curricular review of the Graduate Rabbinical School was initiated followed by a comparable review of the School of Judaica undertaken in 1970.[137]

Two reports summarized the results of these reviews. A 1970 *Report for the Board of Overseers* states that the "new curriculum [is] centered about the classical texts of Bible and Talmud which are to be studied every year by every student in the school and . . . the rest of the academic program [structured] around a multiplicity of elective courses in a wide variety of fields."[138] The 1971 *Report for the Board of Overseers* described the changes in the School of Judaica curriculum in a similar manner and claimed that the new approach allowed for "a more flexible program" that would enable "our faculty better to meet the needs of individual students." Moreover, the School of Judaica offered electives for the first time, and the *Report* boasted that "new pedagogical approaches were attempted in Talmud courses for beginners."[139] No description of these new approaches appears in either the *Report* or the *Register* for that year. Indeed, an examination of the curricula for both the School of Judaica and the Graduate Rabbinical School as recorded for those years makes it difficult to discern what was genuinely new about these curricula.

In the last catalog issued by the Seminary under the aegis of the Finkelstein administration in 1970, entrance requirements in Bible, Hebrew, and Talmud remained essentially the same as those administered in 1940, and students in the School of Judaica were still required to devote all their efforts to study. They were not permitted to "assume the responsibilities of a student pulpit." Only students in the Graduate Rabbinical School were permitted to assume "appropriate part-time rabbinic posts" and then only at the discretion of the faculty.[140]

Most important, this 1970 catalog reveals virtually no change in course content from the curriculum that was in force at the Seminary a decade earlier. In the School of Judaica, the focus of the three-year curriculum was still on Talmud, and placement in the School remained contingent on a mastery of Talmud. There were no courses dedicated to the issues of the practical rabbinate. Indeed, the only concession to the spirit of the times was that students in the School of Judaica were permitted to take a limited number of specific courses on a pass-fail basis. In the Graduate Rabbinical School, every student remained required to enroll in at least one course in Talmud and Bible each semester. Students in the Graduate Rabbinical School were permitted a wider range of elective options than previously, and they were allowed to take all their classes on a pass-fail basis if they so desired. Other than that, the JTS rabbinical curriculum remained as it was before.[141]

During the Finkelstein era, new programs with curricular implications were also implemented. The Melton Research Center in Jewish Education opened in 1960 and, as mentioned above, the American Student Center in Jerusalem was established in 1962. The year 1965 witnessed the creation of the Morris J. and Ethel Bernstein Pastoral Psychiatry Center. Its aim was to help acquaint future rabbis with issues of human development and to provide them with the skills to recognize deviant behavior as well as the opportunity to do counseling in a supervised setting. In addition to these programs, there were several outreach activities initiated during the Finkelstein administration that informed the educational atmosphere of the Seminary. *The Eternal Light* was a well-known weekly radio program started in 1944 under the auspices of JTS. Later it became a popular Sunday morning television show. The Seminary also delved into summer camping, and Camp Ramah was created in Wisconsin in 1947. The camp was a great success, and in the years that followed, Ramah camps came to dot North America. Most of the faculty and staff who directed and served at these camps were associated with the Seminary, and many of the youth who attended these camps were destined to become the religious and lay leaders of the Conservative movement in the decades ahead. Although most of these developments did not explicitly influence the curriculum, they certainly exposed the student to a wide variety of significant experiences and influences. Any analysis of the curriculum of the Seminary would be remiss in not mentioning them.[142]

The impact of these developments upon the curriculum of the Seminary should not be exaggerated. They enriched the curriculum but hardly altered it in any meaningful way. Indeed, the bulk of programatic innovations at JTS during the Finkelstein years reflected the ongoing commitment of the Seminary to classical Jewish learning and modern scholarship.

One important new departure came about through the creation of the Lehman Institute, which was established to promote "research in the field of Talmudic Ethics, with particular emphasis upon the relevance of such study to the area of human rights." It hoped to foster publications that would "indicate the historical and philosophical background of the principles of human rights and freedom, especially as their origins may be traced to Bible and Talmud."[143] The Institute spawned a host of activities and programs aimed at rabbis and laymen alike. It also succeeded in bringing "statesmen, . . . men in positions of great responsibility," to "visit with the students, and to discuss freely their own experiences in decision-making."[144]

The primary focus of the Lehman Institute, however, was its Special Studies Program under the direction of Professor Saul Lieberman. Indeed, this program was arguably the jewel in the crown of the Seminary Rabbinical School. Seymour Siegel served as the associate dean of the program and Chaim Dimitrovsky of the Talmud department was a member of its faculty. Men such as Gerson Cohen and Finkelstein himself also taught on occasion. Rabbinical students were invited to submit applications for admission as Fellows of the Institute. The aim of the program was to allow these students to "devote their full time to the study of Rabbinics." Finkelstein and Lieberman believed that only men trained in this way would be capable of engaging in authentic Jewish scholarship. In view of the destruction of the great European centers of Torah study during World War II, it was apparent to them that graduates of this program would be crucial in perpetuating Jewish scholarship on American soil.[145]

The Special Studies Program opened with twelve students in 1957–58, and by 1970 more than fifty students had "completed its intensive course of Talmudic Studies under the direction of Professors Saul Lieberman, Chaim Zalman Dimitrovsky, and Seymour Siegel."[146] Students had to be adept at Talmud before they could qualify for admission to the program, and examinations were administered either by Lieberman or Dimitrovsky before a student was permitted to enroll. The course of study lasted three years, and students in this program were granted stipends and forbidden to engage in outside employment throughout their time at the Seminary.[147] On the other hand, these students in the Special Studies Program of the Rabbinical department were encouraged to study for their doctorates "simultaneously at other institutions of higher learning, such as Princeton and Columbia Universities," and at the Institute of Advanced Studies at the Seminary, in fields such as Talmud, Bible, medieval Jewish literature, history, and philosophy.[148]

565

The JTS
Rabbinical
Curriculum
in Historical
Perspective

As the catalogs and reports of these years indicate, students in the Special Studies Program were enrolled in thirty class hours per year for each of their three years in the program. Sixteen hours each year were devoted to Talmud. This meant that students studied Talmud with both Professors Lieberman and Dimitrovsky every semester. In addition, students enrolled in two four-credit courses in Bible as well as two seminars in Jewish ethics each year. The course in Bible often included a study of medieval Jewish Bible commentators, and the seminar on Jewish ethics often focused on a classical midrashic text such as *Pirkei d'rabbi eliezer*. Due to the academic orientation of the program, courses devoted to the tasks of the practical rabbinate were completely omitted from the curriculum of the Special Studies Program.

By 1969, the Seminary could boast of this program's success. Its graduates were not only appointed to the faculty of JTS, they were also selected to teach at a broad variety of secular institutions such as Vassar, Brown, the State University of New York, Ohio State, and Columbia.[149] Subsequent years witnessed the appointment of alumni of the Special Studies Program to the faculties of Yale, the University of Judaism, Hebrew Union College, the University of California, the University of Pennsylvania, Emory, Princeton, Brandeis, and New York University in the United States as well as universities in Canada and Israel. In addition, the Seminary itself continued to be the beneficiary of this program, and one graduate of the program, Judith Hauptman—albeit not ordained as a rabbi—became the first woman appointed to teach Talmud at JTS.[150] In short, the Special Studies Program succeeded quite well in its announced aim of educating and forming a cadre of young academics who would perpetuate and guide advanced Jewish study in the contemporary setting. It fulfilled its founders' vision of the Seminary as a fountainhead of Jewish scholarship and in this sense was emblematic of the posture JTS had adopted concerning its mission and curriculum since its inception in 1886.

In assessing the curriculum of the Seminary during the Finkelstein era, it is clear, as Neil Gillman has observed, "that Chancellor Finkelstein's primary goal was to make the Seminary into the successor of the great academies of learning that have dotted Jewish history from Palestine in the first century to Europe in the nineteenth and twentieth centuries." His goal was surely to "have the Seminary serve as the newest link in the 2000-year-old chain of great centers of Talmud Torah," and

Judith Hauptman,
1970s. *Photo by
Arnold Katz.
Communications
Department, JTS.*

without a doubt, this "goal was achieved" under his watch.[151] Finkelstein had succeeded in realizing a vision of the Seminary that Sabato Morais had articulated in the 1880s. New York now housed "a place of Jewish learning" comparable to the seminaries that had existed in Europe during the 19th century.

This is not surprising, since the Seminary had a well-established educational paradigm for the training and formation of rabbis by the time Finkelstein assumed office. The Seminary curriculum by 1940 was no longer susceptible to creation de novo. Furthermore, Finkelstein himself had been socialized into the tradition that promoted this curriculum, and he himself strove to perpetuate it. Thus, the pronounced elements of continuity in the curriculum between the Finkelstein era and that of Schechter and Adler were to be expected.

To be sure, new initiatives in the areas of curricular and educational programming were taken during the years that Finkelstein guided the Seminary. After all, the Seminary was not unaffected by events and sensibilities present in the larger world during these years, and the curriculum attempted to respond to these events. However, as our analysis has demonstrated, curricular revisions even during the 1960s were sharply bounded. In addition, the most significant curricular development during the Finkelstein administration—the Special Studies Program of the Lehman Institute—was totally consonant with an overarching vision the Seminary had promulgated since its inception. The ideal rabbi was above all expected to be learned in classical Judaica and trained in contemporary scholarhip. The Seminary's curriculum was designed to preserve and actualize that vision throughout Finkelstein's tenure.

The Seminary curriculum as it was maintained and supplemented under

Finkelstein also continued to reflect the denominational divisions that marked American Jewish life. Finkelstein and his colleagues had neither need nor desire to make reference to either Hebrew Union College or Yeshiva University in the formation of the curriculum and educational standards that would guide the Seminary. This undoubtedly reflected a genuine self-confidence the leaders of the Seminary possessed in regard to their own vision of Judaism and the rabbinate.

This is not to suggest that Finkelstein was unconcerned with or inattentive to non-Conservative varieties of Judaism. As a man schooled in the teachings of Solomon Schechter, the notion of catholic Israel, with its emphasis on the unity of the Jewish people, was an ideal to which Finkelstein was strongly committed.[152] Indeed, the curricular expression of this commitment was a program in the 1960s that brought Rabbi Eugene B. Borowitz (Reform) and Rabbi Norman Frimer (Orthodox) as well as the Orthodox theologian Michael Wyschogrod to co-teach a theology course along with Seymour Siegel to JTS rabbinical students.[153] It was surely the intent of Finkelstein and his colleagues, as it was of their predecessors, to create a nondenominational rabbinical school, one which "might reach out to all Jews" and "be a force for reconciliation and unity" among them.[154]

Yet, as already noted, the curriculum of the Seminary embodied an approach to Judaism different from that provided to Orthodox and Reform rabbinical students. Nothing in the curricula of the Finkelstein era diminished this distance. The curriculum at each major seminary—including JTS—remained consonant with the ideology of its movement.

Thus, in this period, Hebrew Union College–Jewish Institute of Religion sought "men of positive faith in the message of Judaism" as candidates for the rabbinate and demanded that these men possess "suitable qualities of character, leadership, personality and academic capacity" to serve in the rabbinical office; it did not call for these candidates to adhere to specific religious practices.[155] Furthermore, HUC-JIR allowed students with little or no background in Judaica or Hebrew to qualify for admission to the rabbinical program. Although comprehensive examinations in Hebrew, Bible, and rabbinic studies were administered to the students at the end of their second year of residence in the rabbinical program, HUC-JIR did not—unlike the Seminary—demand such examinations prior to admission. Consequently, the level of instruction in textual courses at the former could not initially be on the same plane as that of JTS. Undoubtedly, this is why the College-Institute awarded its students a baccalaureate degree—the B.H.L.—after two years of study, and not the M.H.L. as the Seminary did when its students completed the School of Judaica. Students at HUC-JIR completed an additional three years of study before receiving the M.H.L. degree.

Moreover, the curriculum at HUC-JIR did not privilege Talmud in any way. No prior knowledge of Talmud was necessary for admission to the Reform institution, and rabbinic studies was assigned no more weight in the curriculum of the first two years than was Hebrew, Bible, or speech and human relations. Nor did the focus on rabbinic studies increase during the last three years of study at HUC-JIR. Furthermore, rabbinic studies itself remained more broadly construed at HUC-JIR than at JTS. As the 1956–57 *HUC-JIR Catalogue* suggests, rabbinic studies at the College-Institute included codes, commentaries, and midrash as well as Talmud. HUC-JIR also required more courses devoted to the practical rabbinate than did the Seminary. Congregational work was required of every student. Bible retained its place as the subject of primary import. At HUC-JIR, knowledge of the Bible and its prophetic ethics were seen as essential for the prospective rabbi. The College-Institute, like the Seminary, was committed to academic scholarship. It required a rabbinic thesis prior to ordination. However, in contrast to JTS, it rejected the notion that the modern rabbi needed a thorough knowledge of rabbinical literature in general and Talmud in particular in order to qualify for ordination.

The Rabbi Isaac Elchanan Theological Seminary (RIETS) at Yeshiva University remained devoted to the study of Jewish law and committed to its application in practice. Its Orthodox student body was steeped in Talmud. Until 1958, the course of study for ordination formally lasted for two years with the entire curriculum devoted to rabbinic literature. The study of Talmud dominated: students were expected to study two tractates, and they were required—in traditional fashion—to master certain sections of *Yoreh Deah* in order to receive rabbinical ordination. Nevertheless, RIETS was not immune from the pressures the contemporary American setting exerted on the American rabbinate at mid-century. For example, demands for professionalization were heard even at this Orthodox seminary. In response, Yeshiva began in the late 1950s to require students at RIETS to obtain an advanced degree (at least an M.A.) in either an academic area or in the fields of education or communal service and social work. Furthermore, the course of study for the rabbinate was expanded in 1958 from two to three years. This added time enabled RIETS to prepare its students for the practical challenges of the rabbinate. Courses in practical rabbinics, chaplaincy, and education were therefore introduced as complements to the traditional curriculum.[156] In keeping with this ethos of higher professional standards for its rabbis, RIETS introduced written examinations at this time.[157]

Despite these developments, RIETS remained absolutely opposed to the inclusion of a critical approach derived from the Academy in its curriculum. While the motto of Yeshiva University was "*Torah u'madda*—Torah and Science," it was clear that the latter was not meant to intrude upon the former within the walls of RIETS. Rabbi Samuel Belkin, president of Yeshiva University from 1943 to 1975, was, like his predecessor Bernard Revel, a man of great erudition in the realms of both classical rabbinic literature and modern secular studies. He received his Ph.D. in

Classics from Brown University and wrote several seminal studies on Philo of Alexandria. In addition, he taught Greek at Yeshiva University. Nevertheless, he condemned the application of *Wissenschaft* to Judaism. As he phrased it, "Modern Jewish scholarship has tried to explain Judaism in terms which are alien and do not apply to it, and has attempted to force even those practices and rituals which define the relationship of man to God into the molds of current sociological and economic theories."[158] Critical academic scholarship had no place at RIETS, which viewed itself as "heir to, and modeled after, the traditional yeshivot of Europe."[159] Needless to say, such a vision did not comport with the ideology that informed Finkelstein and his colleagues at the Seminary.

The curriculum at JTS as it evolved under Finkelstein embodied the fundamental vision of rabbinical education framed by the founders of the Seminary. Its adherence to the canons of critical modern scholarship as well as its devotion to rabbinic civilization remained the distinctive trademark of a Seminary rabbinical education. Finkelstein may well have expanded upon this vision in several particulars, but he did nothing to disturb it. Indeed, our analysis of the curriculum at JTS during the Finkelstein years reveals how strongly he internalized and reinforced the Seminary's approach to the training of rabbis and the ethos and spirit of Conservative Judaism.

The Cohen and Schorsch Years: Final Developments and Directions

In 1972, Gerson Cohen succeeded Finkelstein as Chancellor of the Seminary. After succeeding Salo Baron as professor of Jewish history at Columbia University, Cohen returned to the Seminary as Jacob H. Schiff Professor of Jewish History in 1970. In selecting him as Chancellor and President, JTS once again chose a distinguished scholar from within its own ranks to head the institution.[160]

At his inauguration on 23 October 1973, which took place only a few weeks after the Yom Kippur War, Cohen proudly noted that the Seminary had been "privileged to don the mantle worn in earlier ages by the great academies of Sura and Pumbeditha, ... Volozhin and Slobodka. Like them, it has preserved the legacy of the past and translated its values into guideposts for the future." However, unlike these Jewish academies, "and in concert with the halls of learning in our free society, our Seminary has sought to examine the past critically and by the canons of dispassionate scholarship. It has done so out of the conviction that only through unflinching confrontation with the truth and only with *penetrating critical examination of its sacred tradition* can it best serve its own constituency, the Jewish people, and humanity at large in a world seething with change and challenge to the pillars of classical faith. . . . Hence, the dedication of this Seminary to Torah represents at once a commitment to knowledge of the Jewish past and present along with the provision of models by which to translate this knowledge into the idiom of the present so that it may in turn serve as beacon and inspiration for the future."[161] Cohen's vision of and for the Seminary was very much in keeping with the ideals that had long guided the institution. The beliefs expressed in his inaugural address reflect his affinity for the viewpoints of Schechter and Finkelstein, and they indicate that his administration sought continuity with the past.

As soon as Cohen assumed office new challenges appeared. The impact of the 1960s was strong and its effects lingered in American society. Writing years later, Neil Gilman identified the issues that began to be addressed at the Seminary at this time. According to Gilman, these included:

> What standing did Jewish religion have in a school dominated by the scientific, critical, and historical mind-set of a faculty committed to *Wissenschaft*? A Seminary rabbinical education did many things rather well. The one thing that it did not do in any kind of systematic way was *religious* education. Paradoxically, . . . rabbinic education at the Seminary was subversive. Not only did it neglect to train the rabbi for his main role; it actually undermined his ability to function in that role. For the better part of the century, the Seminary-trained rabbi was a prisoner of his education. Equally paradoxically, the second major shaping impulse behind the culture of the Seminary, its halakhic traditionalism, did nothing to alleviate this subversion. If anything, it exacerbated it . . . further. . . . For we all wondered: How do you combine a critical approach to Torah and halakhic traditionalism?[162]

In view of the sentiments he expressed in his inaugural address, Cohen surely would not have concurred with Gillman's assessment of the JTS curriculum. Nonetheless, Cohen began his chancellorship by doubting the efficacy of the curriculum that had been bequeathed to him. He sensed that the scholarly goals of the traditional Seminary curriculum were not necessarily those most appropriate for the training of rabbis in late 20th-century America, and he believed that they were not necessarily congruent with the religious and communal needs of the Jewish people in modern-day America. Thus, in a paper on "Jewish Identity and Jewish Collective Will" delivered at the 42nd General Assembly of the Council of Jewish Federations and Welfare Funds in 1973, Cohen made clear his commitment to the reshaping and reformulation of Jewish education—including Jewish professional education—on this continent. As he stated on that occasion, "I am consumed by the desire to draft new curricula."[163]

Cohen's address at the General Assembly should not be interpreted as a clarion call for a radical change. Such a departure would have been totally alien to his temperament and ideals. Instead, his speech indicates that he wanted rabbinical training at the Seminary to evolve with a fidelity to the past that would also address the needs of the present.

The nature and parameters of the educational vision Cohen offered can be found in an unpublished memorandum he wrote "early in his tenure as Chancellor of the Seminary." Entitled "Towards a Revision of Rabbinic Education and Training," the memorandum argued that the Seminary should produce graduates "committed to Jewish life in America." Secondly, ordinands of the Seminary should possess "a deep feeling of kinship with the Jewish national and cultural rebirth and its aspirations." This required the Conservative rabbi to be fluent "in modern Hebrew" and to be knowledgeable "of modern Jewish ideologies and movements." By the mid-1970s, JTS required that every student spend at least one year in residence at the American Student Center in Jerusalem. Finally, Cohen wrote that "JTS graduates" had to be "competent students of Torah." Unlike past expectations, this did not mean that the Seminary graduate ought to strive "for a thorough knowledge of rabbinic literature and history." Instead, the Conservative rabbi would now be trained so that he would be master "of a specific body of knowledge and its interpretations," and he would further possess the "ability to analyze them critically and mediate" them to a wider constituency. The task of the rabbi was "to make the literary and spiritual legacies of the past part of the intellectual and spiritual legacy of the modern American Jew."[164]

Ackerman, in his commentary upon this document, has noted that the memorandum reflected a shift in emphasis "from extensive cognitive knowledge to methodological knowledge. . . . Cohen's choice of the word 'mediate' was no accident. He meant for rabbis to convey and transmit 'the literary and spiritual legacies of the past' . . . to their congregants." Such training would permit Conservative rabbis, in Ackerman's view, to develop "a more collaborative, more democratic style of religious leadership. . . . Methodological knowledge would enable rabbis to help their congregants make relevant the classic body of tradition. In Neil Gillman's terminology, Conservative rabbis would now serve not as 'answerers of questions but as leaders of inquiry.'" The conclusions drawn by Ackerman from his analysis of the Cohen memorandum may be somewhat overdrawn. It is far from certain that Cohen intended rabbis to "limit their own authority to issue" Jewish legal decisions "in favor of developing a more collaborative . . . style of religious leadership."[165] Nevertheless, an investigation of the curriculum initiated by the Seminary in 1977 confirms the substance of Ackerman's observations.

The 1977–82 *Register* describes rabbinical candidates as studying the same courses that had traditionally been prescribed as prerequisites for ordination. Talmud remained at the center of the curriculum as did Bible. Midrash and codes were assigned a formal place, as were Jewish history, philosophy, and literature. In all of this there was nothing new. Neither was there anything particularly novel about the assertion, "Professional courses in homiletics, education, pastoral psychiatry, and practical theology are an integral part of the program."[166] Cohen intended no revolution in the subject content of the JTS curriculum.

Instead, the spirit of innovation Cohen promoted at the General Assembly in 1973 was put into practice via a new emphasis on skills-mastery of traditional subjects.[167] This approach was first given curricular expression in 1977 through the introduction of four progressive levels of study. Level I courses, labeled "Technical Skills," focused—in the main—on educating the student to master the vocabulary and style of the Talmud, and the methods and skills necessary for reading and understanding these classical Jewish texts. In addition, courses on this level were taught in Hebrew language, introductory homiletics, basic synagogue skills, Judaica bibliography, codes, and midrash. Level II, "Introductory Surveys," centered primarily on Bible and history. Students were required to enroll in eight Bible courses and five history courses at this level, as well as three courses on Jewish literature. Other survey courses were offered in philosophy, codes, and Mishna. Only one course in Talmud was taught in Level II. The study of Talmud at the Seminary was to retain its textual orientation. That is, students would engage in a close reading and exegesis of the texts themselves. Talmud would not be a major object of study at this level of survey. However, Talmud figured prominently in Level III courses on "Methodologies." Twelve credits per year in Talmud were required at this level, as were six credits in Bible. In addition, students were asked to enroll in three other yearlong six-credit courses. Here the student could select from among history, Jewish literature, philosophy, codes, or midrash. Finally, Level IV courses, identified as "Electives, Professional Skills and Thematic Interdisciplinary Courses," required students to enroll in courses on practical rabbinics, pastoral psychiatry, education, and homiletics. Students at this level were also called upon to matriculate in four "Synthesis" courses, two courses in Talmud, and eight other electives of their choice.[168]

In assessing the Cohen curriculum, its broad-based character—as opposed to its predecessors—is readily apparent. Bible was given additional prominence as a subject area, as was history. Students were provided with a wider range of elective options, and much more attention was devoted to professional skills. However, none of these latter changes represents a significant break with the past. Indeed, they are all consonant with earlier curricula. The Cohen curriculum was not revolutionary because Talmud and rabbinics still maintained their central place. Nevertheless, the Cohen curriculum did embody a new sensibility. As Ackerman has observed, "The shift in focus from cognitive to methodological knowledge formed the central and crucial difference between the 1977 curriculum and its predecessors."[169]

Several factors help to account for this shift in emphasis. Currents present in the larger culture itself were surely among them. The turbulence of the 1960s and its impact upon the culture and ethos of the Academy as well as its influence upon American religious life already has been alluded to. Noninstitutional expressions of religious life and renewal became common at this time, and these expressions often informed and complemented previously established patterns of institutional religiosity. In American Judaism, these patterns of religious renewal manifested themselves most prominently in the *havurah* movement in general and in works such as the first *Jewish Catalog* in 1973 which were written by individuals attached to *havurah* Judaism in particular. This movement envisioned a nonhierarchical brand of Judaism and promoted, as Riv-Ellen Prell has noted, "an expressive individualism that featured the activism of all participants."[170]

Havurah Judaism embodied the values and ethos of the American youth culture of those days. The sociologist Marshall Sklare even referred to *havurah* Judaism derisively as heralding the "greening of American Judaism."[171] Despite this, the influence of the movement was significant. As Jack Wertheimer has observed, "Originating in the American counterculture of the 1960s, Havurah Judaism and its sometime ally, the Jewish feminist movement, challenged the established institutions and movements of American Judaism to rethink their priorities and reshape their religious programs in the concluding quarter of the twentieth century. . . . Although the impact of these changes on Jewish religious life became clear only in the mid-1970s, the process of restructuring had already begun in the 1960s."[172]

The 1977 curriculum cannot be characterized as a radical departure from the course of instruction offered at the Seminary in prior decades. Nevertheless, the character of the Cohen curriculum, with its emphasis upon synthesis and mediation, did map out different directions for the students than had previous curricula. The curriculum that obtained at the Seminary at the end of the Finkelstein era "was perfectly crafted," Neil Gillman has observed, to educate those rabbis "who consciously sought an academic career."[173] The new curriculum did not abandon that vision. At the same time, the 1977 curriculum did not promote the rabbi-scholar alone as its ideal type. Rather, the Cohen curriculum was the first in the history of the Seminary to formulate a course of instruction consciously designed to prepare rabbis for their roles, in the previously quoted words of David Ackerman, "as leaders of inquiry." In so doing, this curriculum foreshadowed a more far-ranging alteration of the curriculum that was to occur a decade later during the administration of Ismar Schorsch. We will discuss that curriculum below. For now, it is sufficient to observe that the 1977 Seminary curriculum was one whose novel parameters reflected the influence of an egalitarian ethos common after the 1960s.

This worldview spawned still other developments. As Charles Liebman pointed out in his famed study, "The Training of American Rabbis," in 1968, "The textual orientation of the courses is the primary source of dissatisfaction among JTS students." Simply put, the students at the Seminary "found their courses uninspiring, and their preparation inadequate, because problems raised by Jewish philosophy, theology, or the place of Judaism in the modern world are ignored."[174] Increasing numbers of Seminary students from the 1960s on did not identify with or affirm the educational visions of Lieberman and Finkelstein. For, as Liebman phrased it, "the interrelation of textual study and social ethics was not obvious to a majority of the 1968 Seminary student body."[175] This meant, even close to two decades later, that "a certain amount of [the] coursework," was deemed "irrelevant."[176] The critique itself bespeaks the impact of an era that made such demands for relevancy commonplace. The Cohen curriculum—with it focus upon mediation—was designed in part to provide a positive response to this demand.

Undoubtedly, the most significant development affecting the curriculum was the decision by the Faculty Senate in 1983 to admit women to the Rabbinical School. The subsequent ordination of Amy Eilberg as rabbi in 1985—because it was so radical a departure from the past—signaled a climate of unprecedented openness to change at the Seminary. Indeed, the ordination of Rabbi Eilberg was preceded, as mentioned earlier, by the appointment of Judith Hauptman to the Talmud faculty. These decisions—to ordain women as rabbis and to appoint a woman as professor of Talmud—can be viewed as defining moments in the history of the Seminary. Neil Gillman explains why this is so. "The decision to ordain women will loom as a monumental turning-point in the history of the movement," Gillman has contended, because "for the first time, the school listened to the call for guidance from the movement and responded." The Seminary—in deciding to ordain women as rabbis—broke dramatically with whatever remnant remained of its Orthodox roots and "fulfilled its role as fountainhead of a *modern* religious movement."[177] In so doing, the Seminary demonstrated that it was not inured to the currents of the age. The same ethos that promoted "Havurah Judaism" was at work here, as "its sometimes ally, the Jewish feminist movement," made its presence and influence palpable at the Seminary.

Indeed, the decision by JTS to ordain women as rabbis should not be viewed in isolation from the dominant ideological and cultural currents of the time. Both the Hebrew Union College-Jewish Institute of Religion and the newly established (1968) Reconstructionist Rabbinical College—responding to the same cultural and ideological imperatives—had decided a decade earlier to grant ordination to women. Reform Rabbi Laura Geller has described the transformative power inherent in this decision as follows: "The impact of women rabbis on Judaism begins with the revolutionary idea that women's experience ought to be acknowledged and valued. . . . It means that women are subjects as well as objects, that women are fully part of the tradition. It means we must wrestle with our sacred texts to hear the voices of women just as we need to wrestle with the structure of our modern Jewish institutions to make room for women's commitment and styles. It means that we must listen to the views of others who have been silent or invisible in our tradition. It means that those texts and institutions will change as they are shaped in response to these different voices."[178]

The import of all this for the curriculum was discussed by Debra Orenstein, a 1990 ordinand of JTS. Echoing the sentiments of Geller, Orenstein, in a piece entitled, "Recovering the Forgotten Woman," charged that "the traditional curriculum" of the Seminary was "deficient because it does not fully include women. The rabbinical school curriculum represents our priorities and standards for what an educated Jew should know. It has taken the admission of women and the application of a feminist consciousness to make us aware that the education we give . . . our rabbis is distorted by its treatment of women."[179]

To be sure, the JTS curriculum was not suddenly informed by a feminist program just because of the decision to ordain women as Conservative rabbis. Rather, it opened up new possibilities.[180] As Pamela Hoffman aptly wrote in 1986, "The very presence of women [at JTS] produced a catalytic effect for it was the greatest testimony to the fact that radical, unexpected change was indeed possible."[181]

The changes evidenced in the Rabbinical School curriculum of JTS during the Cohen years were noteworthy. They were the products of all the forces and developments mentioned above. Nevertheless, the quest for synthesis and the new directions that would guide and inform that curricular quest were hardly exhausted. The novel elements Cohen introduced into the curriculum represented the first steps in the alteration of the JTS course of instruction.

Still additional changes were introduced by Ismar Schorsch, the successor of Gerson Cohen as Chancellor and President of the Seminary. An eminent scholar of German-Jewish history, Schorsch rose to the position of professor in 1976 and in 1980 became the Rabbi Herman Abramowitz Professor of Jewish History at JTS. His activities at JTS were not confined to the realm of teaching. Just as Adler had employed the administrative as well as scholarly talents of Finkelstein, so Cohen recognized the multiple skills of Schorsch. He therefore designated Schorsch as the dean of the Seminary Graduate School in 1975. In 1980 Schorsch was elevated to the office of provost. When Cohen announced his intention to resign as Chancellor, Schorsch was the natural choice to succeed him in that position.[182]

From the moment Schorsch assumed his post as Chancellor, he displayed a noticeable interest in continuing and expanding upon the innovative educational legacy Cohen had bequeathed the Seminary rabbinical program. He was well aware of the need for adjusting the old curriculum. Rabbis had to be formed in a new manner if they were to serve the Jewish people and humanity in the contemporary setting. In a 1986 speech, Schorsch declared that there was "almost no common denominator between the profession of the modern rabbi. . . and the religious leadership of the Middle Ages." He went on to assert, "If earlier the rabbi served as halakhic decisor, judge, and teacher of Talmud for advanced students, today he is a member of a profession dedicated to addressing the needs of the individual." The education of the contemporary rabbi was therefore "forced to go well beyond the

575

The JTS
Rabbinical
Curriculum
in Historical
Perspective

exclusive confines of halakhah. A mastery of secular learning has become a necessity in our day . . . The curricular narrowness which had once marked the yeshiva world" has been compelled to yield "to a deeper understanding of the complex development of a multifaceted Judaism."[183] In making these statements, Schorsch was affirming the patrimony passed on to him by his predecessors. From Morais through Cohen, all the leaders of the Seminary had advanced identical sentiments. The JTS curriculum under the Schorsch administration would continue to display its dual allegiance to classical texts and modern scholarship. Schorsch, like Cohen, would not engage in a radical revamping of the curriculum.

At the same time, Schorsch was determined to continue on the path of innovation laid out by his immediate predecessor, Gerson Cohen. Schorsch, like Cohen, was mindful that prospective rabbis needed to be trained in such a way that they could synthesize and mediate the tradition for Jews embedded in a social context dominated by "freedom and secularity."[184] For many of these Jews, precisely because of this context and the ethos engendered by it, also experienced what Schorsch identified as "religious hunger." He described the multivalent religious condition of American Jews in the following terms. Schorsch wrote:

> While the open society continues to erode inexorably the Jewish identity of many American Jews, countervailing forces are also at work returning others to the synagogue. Some come by way of the spiritual emptiness left in the wake of a life absorbed by the pursuit of wealth and pleasure. . . . Others are the noteworthy products of intensive Jewish education. . . . Ultimately, greater attention to the committed will not only enhance the case of Judaism to the uncommitted, but also make the rabbinate a more satisfying spiritual vocation.

The Seminary had to require, now as in the past, "competence" of its ordinands. However, JTS was also obligated to train its rabbis so that its graduates would possess the qualities of "compassion and courage" required of those who would "serve living Jews."[185]

The sentiments voiced by Schorsch in these writings bespeak the ongoing impact of the 1960s and the cultural currents present in that era upon the life of the Seminary. Indeed, their influence upon the Schorsch curriculum and the ethos that informed that curriculum was perhaps even more pronounced than it had been a decade earlier. The description Schorsch provided of the contemporary rabbinate as constituting a spiritual vocation indicates how ubiquitous and influential those currents were in shaping his thoughts. Schorsch had internalized many of those currents, and they would find expression in the curriculum advanced at JTS during his tenure as Chancellor.

As with Cohen, this does not mean that he abandoned or rejected the traditional content of the curriculum that had informed the Seminary since its inception. Indeed, his commitment to that content was absolute. However, Schorsch recognized the need for additional elements in order to address self-consciously the quest for meaning that now preoccupied many serious Jews in American society. A new curriculum was designed to train rabbis who, while conversant with the tradition, would, at the same time, be capable of guiding themselves and Jews in their search for meaning. Through his focus upon a skills-mastery course of study that would prepare rabbis for their roles as mediators of this process, Cohen had pointed the Seminary curriculum in this direction. The challenge confronting Schorsch was to define how this goal could be appropriately advanced.

As Pamela Hoffman, in her 1986 paper, phrased it, "the sense of imbalance in the spiritual-intellectual ecology of the Seminary" had to be overcome. There was a "need for a new 'hermeneutic'" that would help the students "make personal sense of their Jewish living and learning during their many years spent in the Seminary." This caused Hoffman to assert that the time had come to "move beyond the vision of the Finkelsteins, the Ginzbergs and the Adlers." There was, in her opinion, a pressing need "to redefine our rabbinic agenda." Hoffman was careful to point out that this call did not constitute a call for "a change in forms." Rabbinic civilization—its literature and practices—would retain its favored position in the curriculum. However, the way in which it would be taught would entail "a change in orientation and mindset."[186]

This worldview was beginning to find increasing expression in seminary education throughout North America. and its appearance at JTS was not an exclusive Conservative phenomenon. For example, the Reconstructionist Rabbinical College 1990–93 *Catalogue* asserted that its curriculum embodied "a new approach to rabbinic education. . . . This approach understands rabbinical studies as necessarily combining aspects of academic study with a personal encounter with Judaism."[187] In designing its curriculum in this way, the RRC attempted to fulfill the mandate of Mordecai Kaplan, who had stated, "A rabbinic school should furnish its students with extensive knowledge of the Jewish heritage, of human nature and social conditions, and with the ability to *synthesize* situations with which they will have to deal as rabbis." In so doing, the Reconstructionist Rabbinical College consciously rejected the model of the rabbi as authority figure. Instead, the rabbi was envisioned as a guide who would help people explore Jewish life for themselves. The rabbi, as part of the community, would work in an egalitarian spirit of cooperation with others to shape the future of Jewish life.[188]

HUC-JIR evidenced comparable curricular sensibilities at this time. In the fall of 1985, President Alfred Gottschalk of the College-Institute appointed a Task Force on Rabbinical Curriculum. In a report entitled, "Innovators of Torah: Preparing Tomorrow's Rabbis for Reform Judaism," far-ranging suggestions for an overhaul of the HUC-JIR curriculum in several areas were made. These suggestions, in large part, were aimed at better preparing students at HUC-JIR for the tasks of the rabbinate. The framers of the report hoped that the College-Institute could design a curriculum that would "foster greater appreciation of practical skills." At the same time, they were anxious not to compromise "our academic integrity." Most significantly, the authors of the report bemoaned what they saw as "a growing disparity between scholarly mastery of sources and the ability to elicit religious values and meanings from them." The same concern for mediation and synthesis that had promoted curricular adjustments at the Seminary under Cohen was also present at HUC-JIR. The report further asserted that the spiritual formation of the HUC-JIR student body ought to become a matter of paramount concern to the institution. In articulating these themes, the report reflected the educational ethos and cultural-spiritual concerns of the day.[189]

Indeed, these currents were so powerful that they even manifested themselves at Yeshiva University. In 1984–85, RIETS extended its course of study from three to four years in order to prepare its students to respond more adequately to the "new challenges" of the day and the "numerous professional responsibilities of a rabbi." A professional seminar and a practical internship were added to the curriculum. However, Jewish law and classical texts remained central in the RIETS curriculum. While *Wissenschaft* was still not allowed to intrude into the walls of Yeshiva, a new subject area labeled "Practical Halakhah" gave "additional emphasis to those areas of Jewish law where rabbinic decisions are most frequently required . . . Shabbat, kashrut, conversion, family life, and mourning." In addition, "Contemporary Halakhah" constituted "an interface between Halakhah and modern problems, seen through the prism of Responsa literature. Weekly seminars, with experts drawn from within the RIETS faculty and without, explore topics that have risen to the fore as a result of recent social, scientific, and technological developments. Topics include medicine, civil law, social and political issues, the Jewish community, and the family." All of this demonstrates that the administrators and faculty at RIETS, like their peers at the RRC and HUC-JIR, were responding out of their own sensibilities and in their own distinctive way to the cultural and social imperatives of the hour.[190]

The curricular effervescence cascading upon the Seminary during the 1980s cannot be understood apart from this larger context. The leadership and student body of the Seminary—in voicing their curricular concerns and in calling for curricular innovations—were not sealed off from the rhythms of the age. Instead, they were part of a larger movement and mood that obtained at all the other major rabbinical institutions. However, the influences were not all synchronic. They were diachronic as well. The Seminary had its own traditions. The new curriculum that JTS was poised to unveil during the 1989–90 academic year—the fruits of a curricular review process initiated at the behest of Schorsch in the mid-1980s—reflected the spirit of the age. It also bespoke the distinctive heritage of the Seminary.

Gordon Tucker, dean of the JTS Rabbinical School at that time, captured these two dimensions of the new curriculum quite well when he asserted:

> The new Rabbinical School Curriculum stands in the long seminary tradition of academic rigor and devotion to Jewish scholarship as a religious value. It differs from previous curricula in that it will overtly address the goal of transforming the bright and committed men and women who come to us into rabbis. We believe this transformation process requires great scholarly achievement but also serious attention to inner religious growth, and the development of the ability to teach, inspire and transform the lives of others.[191]

The curriculum inaugurated during the 1989–90 academic year reconfirmed and refined the shift towards the skills-mastery curriculum that had been introduced by Cohen during the previous decade. Indeed, within five years the outline and content of the new curriculum had been firmly established. As Neil Gillman has phrased it, "The entire purpose of the new Rabbinical School curriculum can be summed up in one sentence: It is designed to educate the rabbinical student to function as a religious Jew, without the slightest sacrifice of a modern mind-set, and to educate his or her congregants to do the same."[192]

The Seminary intended to achieve this end by establishing a five-year course of study for the rabbinate. As the 1994–95 *Academic Bulletin* stated, candidates for the rabbinate now as in the past:

> are expected to be living according to Jewish tradition. They should demonstrate commitment to *halakhah*. The mitzvot should guide the life of all candidates for Rabbinical School; these include, but are not limited to observance of *Shabbat* and festivals, regular daily prayer with *tallit* and *tefillin*, dietary laws, *Talmud Torah, and acts of gemilut hasadim. Women are required to accept equality of obligation for the mitzvot from which they are halakhically exempt.*"[193]

Furthermore, the Seminary still required knowledge in the areas of Hebrew language, *tanakh*, liturgy, history, and philosophy as prerequisites for admission, and the placement level of students admitted to the Rabbinical School was determined by student performance on the examinations. In addition, students entering the Rabbinical School were expected to demonstrate "the mastery of at least ten folio (*dapim*) pages of Gemara and Rashi, from no more than two chapters in the Talmud," and drawn from "*Shabbat, Pesahim, Ketubot, Gittin, Kiddushin, Bava Kamma, Bava Mezia, Bava Batra, Sanhedrin.*"[194]

While the Seminary recognized that some students entered with "advanced textual skills" that would qualify them for participation in an "Accelerated Rabbinics Program," it "assumed that most students will need to undertake preliminary work prior to embarking on the Rabbinical School Program." In stating this, the Seminary simply acknowledged what was by now a foregone conclusion concerning most potential candidates for the JTS rabbinical program—a large number of otherwise well-qualified persons who desired to receive ordination as Conservative rabbis possessed weak foundational backgrounds in Judaica. Rather than refusing such persons admission, JTS remained committed to the maintenance of a Preparatory Year Program at the Ziegler School of the University of Judaism in Los Angeles. This program was "designed to enable students to meet all of [the] standards" necessary for admission to the rabbinical course of study.[195] The actual course content of the new curriculum remained centered, as it had in the past, around the study of Talmud and rabbinic literature. During the first three years of the program, students enrolled each semester in a six-credit course devoted to a close reading of *Sanhedrin* as well as other tractates along with the major classical commentaries upon these sources. This required three-year Talmud sequence was "conducted in *shiur*[lesson]/*hevruta* [study in pairs] format. For the first hour of class, students will study in *hevrutot* in the Beit Midrash room, assisted by their course instructor. Classes will then reconvene for an hour-long *shiur*. The twice weekly *hevruta/shiur* class will be supplemented by an additional *hevruta* session." As in previous generations, approximately one-third of the time devoted to classroom instruction during these first three years was occupied by the study of Talmud text.[196]

Survey courses in ancient, medieval, and modern Jewish history, in addition to more survey courses in Bible and biblical literature and grammar were also required. Four three-credit semester courses in Hebrew, survey courses on Midrash and medieval Bible commentary, and methodology courses in Talmud in particular and Judaic studies in general rounded out the academic curriculum of the first two years of study. During the third year of the program, the student journeyed to Israel and there, in addition to Talmud, matriculated in courses devoted to Bible, Midrash text, "The Idea of Zion in Jewish History," and twelve credits in two courses entitled, "Introduction to Halakhah." The textual orientation of the curriculum remained strong. In addition, the directions Cohen had established in the 1977 curriculum remained constant. Level II courses, "Introductory Surveys," as well as Level III courses, "Methodologies," remained an integral part of the curriculum.[197]

The directions embodied in these latter courses found even stronger expression in the final two years of the five-year program. During these years, each student was required to enroll in survey courses in Jewish intellectual history and Jewish literature, as well as courses in liturgy and practical *halakha*. An additional demand was placed upon the students to "choose a field of concentration." Areas of concentration included Bible, Rabbinics, history, literature, liturgy, philosophy, or education. Students were also allowed to "propose interdisciplinary fields of concentration." The trend Cohen had initiated was thus extended and intensified under Schorsch. Cognitive knowledge remained important; however, it was no longer the primary goal of the curriculum. Instead, the Seminary curriculum was now designed to foster scholarly depth and methodological expertise in a particular discipline. In this way, the analytical skills of the students would be sharpened and they would be better prepared to fulfill their roles as mediators of the tradition for those whom they would serve.[198]

The introduction of a field of concentration into 1989–90 curriculum surely reflected the spirit of curricular experimentation that then obtained at the Seminary. However, "two wholly new curricular structures—the Rabbinical School Seminar and an intensive program of Field Work,"[199] most fully bear witness to the innovative character of what was transpiring educationally at JTS. Field work was no longer discouraged. Instead, it was designated as an integral part of the education every prospective rabbi would receive. During the final two years of enrollment, each student was

> expected to perform a significant amount of rabbinic field work . . . Specifically, in the fourth year, students will be assigned to various rabbinic settings in the field (such as congregations, hospitals, communal service agencies, schools, Hillel foundations, etc.) for several weeks at a time, in order to observe and learn about rabbinic work. During the last year of Rabbinical School, each student will be expected to work at a setting of his or her choice for up to fifteen hours a week . . . under a rabbinic mentor.

Courses in professional skills—"Senior Homiletics" and "The Rabbi, Hazzan, and the Congregation"—were also included during the senior year.[200]

The Rabbinical School Seminar, "a weekly four-hour non-academic course that covers the first three years of the rabbinical school," was the novel central feature of the new curriculum.[201] The seminar,

> in which all students must be registered every semester in each of the first three years, will not be a graded course in the usual sense. Instead, the Seminar leader will write an extensive evaluation of each student at the end of the semester. That evaluation will assess the student's progress academically, religiously, and professionally, and may serve as a basis for further advice and guidance from the Dean concerning the student's needs with respect to rabbinical training.[202]

In this setting, students were challenged to view their education as more than a collage of discrete and separate elements. Instead, they were encouraged to regard these elements as part of a greater whole. Students were called upon to identify their own thoughts and feelings concerning the nature and evolution of their own personal religious life and were presented with the opportunity to reflect upon how their academic and professional training fit into that development. In so doing, it was hoped that students themselves would articulate an ideal of Jewish life and construct an idiom that would enable them to transmit that ideal to those whom they would serve. The vision of integration and synthesis promulgated by Cohen, and affirmed by Schorsch, came to fruition in this seminar.

Neil Gillman has captured the actual workings of the Rabbinical School Seminar in the following description:

> We sit around a table, not in a traditional classroom. There are no grades, just extended narrative evaluations of each student, and these evaluations are shared with and signed by the student before they go to the Dean. And we also do a great deal of listening to *Divrei Torah*, to personal diary entries, and to position papers—not research papers, but personal statements—on topics such as: What do we mean by sin? Why do we read this particular Torah reading on Yom Kippur morning? Why is there no liturgy preceding the eating of the *Afikoman?* . . . And next year, with theology as the Seminar's agenda: How do we conceive of God? What happened at Sinai? Why mitzvah? . . . The classroom becomes an arena for a shared inquiry into issues of personal meaning, a prototype for what should happen in the synagogue itself.[203]

The new Rabbinical School curriculum surely charted significant new directions for the JTS curriculum. The notion of a skills-mastery curriculum was now firmly established. In addition, the creation of the Rabbinical School Seminar and the inclusion of supervised fieldwork as an integral part of the rabbinic course of study meant, to cite Ackerman once more, that "for the first time, practical training will consist of more than a hodge-podge of courses relegated to the curriculum's periphery."[204]

However, the impact of these changes should not be exaggerated. They ought not to be viewed as constituting a revolution in the program of instruction for Conservative rabbis. To begin with, many members of the faculty were uncomfortable with the direction these changes unleashed. As Kenneth Katz put it, "Teachers can teach only according to their own learning and temperament. If any Seminary teachers are able or disposed to give pietistic instruction, they are probably already doing so."[205] Furthermore, as Gillman has contended, "The faculty resists because the new curriculum makes demands of us that have never been made before, *that we were never trained to fulfill*, and that are not as yet fully considered when decisions about tenure and promotion are confronted."[206] Only time will determine whether the view of Katz and the charges of Gillman are well founded. In the meantime, their words should serve as a caution against those who would assert that the innovations introduced at the Seminary during the last two decades constitute a radical transformation of the curriculum.

Instead, these changes must be viewed in the context of a curriculum where the vast majority of the program remained devoted to Jewish texts. Indeed, the 1989–90 curriculum displayed prominent elements of continuity with the past. Talmud was not displaced; it was complemented. During the first three years of the program, every course, with the exception of the seminar, involved immersion in classical Jewish literature and history—even when the methods of instruction utilized to impart and organize this knowledge departed from approaches employed in the past. Furthermore, in the fourth year, fifteen units of classical Jewish learning were required each semester. Only in the fifth year did the curriculum devote as much time to professional aspects of rabbinic training as it did to its academic dimensions. As Gillman has pointed out, the new curriculum, while it reflected novel sensibilities and directions, continued to relegate professional skills courses "to the periphery" and, for the most part, confined them "to the final years of study."[207]

For Cohen and Schorsch, knowledge of rabbinics and academic scholarship—even in a skills-mastery oriented curriculum that aimed at synthesis and integration—remained the sine qua non that established the grounds for exercising legitimate rabbinical leadership. There could be no compromise on this position. These men carved out noteworthy new paths for the curriculum. Simultaneously, the curriculum they framed displayed strong elements of continuity with the past. Their faith and vision, while attuned to the needs of the present, remained anchored and rooted in the traditions and legacy of the past.

Concluding Remarks

Pamela Hoffman, writing in 1986, observed:

> Almost one hundred years ago the Jewish Theological Seminary responded to the needs of the hour by building an institution that was to become a giant in modern Jewish scholarship. Today it stands before another challenge which reflects a new day and a new era—that is, the infusion of religious passion into its own unique approach to Jewish learning as well as to its abiding commitment to Jewish law. Were it to succeed (and there is no reason why it should not), the Conservative movement would once again be making an immeasurable contribution to Jewish survival as we rapidly approach the twenty-first century.[208]

This statement allows us to measure and reflect upon the words—cited at the outset of this paper—uttered by Sabato Morais, who asserted in 1886, "A seminary of sacred learning will be set up." In making this pledge, he, along with his colleagues and cofounders, possessed a vision of rabbinic education inspired by the currents and challenges of their day. They constructed a rabbinic curriculum both informed by those currents and designed to meet those challenges. Succeeding generations of Seminary leaders have done no less. Each President and Chancellor has been subject to the exigencies and influences of his era. Each one, like his counterparts at the other major American rabbinical seminaries, has been informed by and responded to contemporaneous events and attitudes.

Students engaged
in *havruta*-style
study in the
Matthew Eisen-
feld and Sara
Duker Beit
Midrash at JTS,
1997. *Photo by
Marjorie Gersten.*

In this discussion of the JTS curriculum, we have sought to analyze the content
of the rabbinical course of study at the Seminary by illuminating how the historical
context of a particular decade or decades informed each leader as he forged a schedule of instruction that was sensitive as well as appropriate to the challenges of the
hour. By delineating those elements in the curriculum that have evolved over the
past one hundred years and by defining the trends that gave rise to those elements,
we hope that this study has yielded insight into American Judaism in general and
Conservative Judaism in particular during the past century.

At the same time, our study indicates that the leaders of JTS shared common
religious-ideological-intellectual sensibilities and judgments concerning the nature
of Judaism and the rabbinical office. These joint sensibilities and judgments allowed
them to establish a curriculum for the training of rabbis that has displayed far more
continuity than change over the course of one hundred and ten years. The vision of
the founders was a coherent one, and the trajectory they established for rabbinic
education at JTS has not veered significantly. The Seminary curriculum has always
affirmed a fidelity to rabbinic civilization. At the same time, it has consistently
championed an integrated mode of critical study. Thus, the Seminary curriculum
has embodied and been faithful to the posture of Conservative Judaism. In so doing,
it has provided a distinctive form of rabbinic education for those who have matriculated at JTS. The newest curriculum—for all the signs of innovation that mark
it—has perpetuated that posture and the ethos that animates it. The vision of the
founders has proved enduring.

1. *American Hebrew*, 19 February 1886, p. 19.
2. Elliot W. Eisner, *The Educational Imagination: On the Design and Evaluation of School Programs* (New York: Macmillan, 1994), pp. 26–27.
3. *Proceedings of the First Biennial Convention of the Jewish Theological Seminary Association,* 1888, p. 10.
4. For an English language summary of these reports, see David Ellenson, *Rabbi Esriel Hildesheimer and the Creation of a Modern Jewish Orthodoxy* (Tuscaloosa: University of Alabama Press, 1990), pp. 158 ff.
5. Ibid.
6. Ibid., p. 160.
7. Ibid.
8. The phrase, "opposition Seminary," is taken from a speech delivered by Alexander Kohut. See *American Hebrew*, 7 January 1887, p. 8.
9. *American Israelite*, 5 September 1879, p. 2.
10. *American Israelite*, 21 July 1871, p. 8.
11. *American Israelite*, 3 September 1875, p. 4.
12. David Philipson and Louis Grossman, ed., *Selected Writings of Isaac Mayer Wise,* (New York: Arno Press, reprint, 1969), pp. 395–96.
13. Isaac M. Wise, "Propositions Submitted to the Gentlemen of the Commission Appointed by the Council of the Union of American Hebrew Congregations at Milwaukee, July 11, 1878," pp. 5–6, 11. In addition, see "Report of the President of the Hebrew Union College to the President and Members of the Board of Governors of Hebrew Union College," *Proceedings of the Union of American Hebrew Congregations* 1 (1873–79), p. 336, for a confirmation of the daily time allotted to the study of texts.
14. Ibid, pp. 98, 704. By the 1890s the curriculum in the Collegiate Department had developed into a set four-year program. See the section entitled, "Course of Studies in the Collegiate Department," in *Programme of the Hebrew Union College*, 1894–95, pp. 17–19.
15. Ibid., p. 20.
16. *Proceedings of the Union of American Hebrew Congregations* 1 (July 1877): p. 342
17. *Programme of the Hebrew Union College*, 1894–95, p. 16. Emphasis ours.
18. Ibid., p. 20.
19. Wise, "Propositions," p. 15.
20. Michael Meyer, "A Centennial History of the Hebrew Union College," in *Hebrew Union College-Jewish Institute of Religion at One Hundred*, ed. Samuel Karff (Cincinnati: Hebrew Union College Press, 1975), p. 20.
21. *Programme of the Hebrew Union College*, 1894–95, p. 14.
22. Wise, "Propositions," pp. 11–13; *Proceedings of the Union of American Hebrew Congregations* 1 (July 1877, and July 1878), pp. 341 and 450; and *Proceedings of the Union of American Hebrew Congregations* 3 (July 1890), p. 2625.
23. *Catalogue of the Hebrew Union College*, 1896–97, pp. 16–20.
24. *Proceedings of the Union of American Hebrew Congregations* 5 (June 1899), pp. 4102–103.
25. *American Hebrew*, 19 December 1884, p. 84.
26. *American Israelite*, 18 December 1885, p. 6.
27. *American Hebrew* 34, no. 7, p. 100.
28. *American Hebrew*, 7 January 1887, p. 8.
29. *American Hebrew* 34, no. 7, p. 99; and *Proceedings of the Second Biennial Convention of the Jewish Theological Seminary Association* , 1890, p. 7.
30. *Proceedings of the Fourth Biennial Convention of the Jewish Theological Seminary Association,* 1894, p. 17.
31. *Proceedings of the Fifth Biennial Convention of the Jewish Theological Seminary Association,*

1896, p. 17.

32. *Proceedings of the Sixth Biennial Convention of the Jewish Theological Seminary Association,* 1898, p. 12.

33. See, for example, *Proceedings of the Third Biennial Convention of the Jewish Theological Seminary Association,* 1892, p. 39.

34. *Proceedings of the First Biennial Convention of the Jewish Theological Seminary Association,* 1888, p. 9.

35. *American Hebrew* 34, no. 7, p. 99.

36. *American Hebrew,* 19 February 1886, p. 19. Also see Morais's statement concerning the "insidious" nature of such criticism in *American Hebrew,* 7 January 1887, pp. 4–5

37. *American Hebrew,* 19 February 1986, p. 19.

38. *Proceedings of the Second Biennial Convention of the Jewish Theological Seminary Association,* 1890, pp. 52–54.

39. Bernard Drachman, *The Unfailing Light* (New York: The Rabbinical Council of America, 1948), pp. 99–109.

40. See any curriculum from the *Proceedings* of the 1890s for the course content of the instructional program offered by the Seminary during these years.

41. *Proceedings of the Second Biennial Convention of the Jewish Theological Seminary Association,* 1890, p. 10.

42. Solomon Schechter, *Seminary Addresses and Other Papers* (New York: Burning Bush Press, 1960), pp. 133–34.

43. Ibid., p. 126.

44. Ibid., pp. 48, 50.

45. Ibid., p. 14.

46. Ibid., pp. 45, 46.

47. Ibid., pp. 21, 125.

48. Ibid., p. 227.

49. Ibid., p. 131.

50. Ibid., p. 198.

51. Ibid., pp. 129, 23, 30.

52. Ibid., p. 204.

53. Ibid., p. 200.

54. Ibid., pp. 198, 200.

55. Ibid., p. 19.

56. Ibid., p. 200.

57. Ibid., p. 16.

58. Ibid., p. 199.

59. Ibid., p. 14.

60. Ibid., p. 20.

61. On these appointments, see the catalogs of the Jewish Theological Seminary—variously entitled "Register," "Announcement," or "Circular of Information"—for the years of Schechter's presidency. In addition, consult Israel Davidson, "The Academic Aspect and Growth of the Rabbinical Department—The Seminary Proper," in *The Jewish Theological Seminary of America—Semi-Centennial Volume,* ed. Cyrus Adler (New York: The Jewish Theological Seminary of America, 1939), pp. 79ff. Finally, see Drachman, *The Unfailing Light,* pp. 253–54.

62. Drachman, *The Unfailing Light,* p. 253.

63. Ibid., p. 254.

64. Ibid., p. 184.

65. Ibid., p. 254.

66. Ibid., pp. 258–60.

67. Ibid, p. 261.

68. Israel Davidson, "The Academic Aspect and Growth of the Rabbinical Department," p. 82.

69. *The Jewish Theological Seminary of America—Circular of Information*, 1903–04, pp. 5–6.

70. Ibid.

71. Schechter, *Seminary Addresses*, p. 20. In keeping with the "rationalistic outlook" of the era, texts in Jewish mysticism—Schechter's sentiments notwithstanding—were of course not included in the curriculum.

72. *The Jewish Theological Seminary of America—Circular of Information*, 1903-1904, p. 6.

73. Ibid., p. 10.

74. David M. Ackerman, "A Not Too Distant Mirror: The Seminary Rabbinical School Curriculum," *Conservative Judaism* (summer 1992): p. 51.

75. Ibid., p. 49.

76. Schechter, *Seminary Addresses*, pp. 37–38.

77. *The Jewish Theological Seminary of America—Register*, 1917–18, pp. 10–11.

78. Ackerman, "A Not Too Distant Mirror," p. 53.

79. Davidson, "The Academic Aspect and Growth of the Rabbinical Department," p. 84.

80. *The Jewish Theological Seminary of America—Register*, 1923–24, pp. 11, 15.

81. Davidson, "The Academic Aspect and Growth of the Rabbinical Department," p. 84.

82. Ackerman, "A Not Too Distant Mirror," p. 53.

83. *The Jewish Theological Seminary of America—Register*, 1923-1924, pp. 15-16. Catalogs for diverse years such as 1927–28 and 1936–37 reflect virtually the same requirements for admission. The similarity—if not identity—of these requirements bespeaks a continuity in the vision of the rabbinate held by the Seminary during the first half part of century. In fact, with allowance being made for the fact that the Seminary came to recognize that more students with little or no facility in classical Judaica desired to be admitted to the Rabbinical School at the end of the century, these requirements for admission have basically remained in force until the present day. As such, they reflect the constancy of the Seminary ideal of the rabbi as one who possesses textual competency.

84. *The Jewish Theological Seminary of America—Register* (1927–28), pp. 12–13.

85. All of these curricular details can be found in the *Jewish Theological Seminary of America—Register* for the years 1923–24, 1927–28, and 1936–37.

86. Cyrus Adler, *I Have Considered the Days* (Philadelphia: Jewish Publication Society, 1941), p. 291. This autobiographical memoir describes in great detail the myriad activities in which Adler was involved throughout his variegated and multi-faceted career.

87. Ira Robinson, ed., *Cyrus Adler: Selected Letters—Volume One* (Philadelphia: Jewish Publication Society, 1985), p. 298.

88. Aaron Rothkoff, *Bernard Revel: Builder of American Jewish Orthodoxy* (Philadelphia: Jewish Publication Society, 1972), pp. 99–103.

89. Ibid., pp. 108–10.

90. Typescript taken from the American Jewish Archives of "An Address Delivered by Kaufmann Kohler at the Dedication of the New Building of the Jewish Theological Seminary of America, April 26, 1903." Emphasis ours.

91. Kaufmann Kohler, "The Staff of Priesthood and the Staff of Leadership," in *A Living Faith: Selected Sermons and Addresses from the Literary Remains of Kaufmann Kohler*, ed. Samuel S. Cohon (Cincinnati: Hebrew Union College Press, 1948), pp. 148–49.

92. Kaufmann Kohler, "The Hebrew Union College of Yesterday and a Great Desideratum in its Curriculum Today," in *Studies, Addresses, and Personal Papers* (New York: Alumni Association of Hebrew Union College, 1931), pp. 555-57.

587

*The JTS
Rabbinical
Curriculum
in Historical
Perspective*

93. Kaufmann Kohler, "The Four Ells of the Halakah and the Requirements of a Modern Jewish Theological School," *Hebrew Union College Annual*, 1904, pp. 9–10, 17.

94. Kohler, "The Hebrew Union College of Yesterday and a Great Desideratum in its Curriculum Today," p. 558.

95. Kohler, "The Four Ells of the Halakah and the Requirements of a Modern Jewish Theological School," pp. 10, 12–13.

96. Kohler, "The College and the Seminary."

97. Kaufmann Kohler, "What the Hebrew Union College Stands For," in *Studies, Addresses, and Personal Papers*, p. 443.

98. Ibid., pp. 441–42.

99. Meyer, "A Centennial History of the Hebrew Union College," pp. 59–60.

100. *Hebrew Union College Catalog and Program*, 1903, pp. 20–24.

101. Ellenson, *Rabbi Esriel Hildesheimer and the Creation of a Modern Jewish Orthodoxy*, p. 160.

102. Kohler's proposed curriculum is found in Kohler, "The Four Ells of the Halakah and the Requirements of a Modern Jewish Theological School," pp. 21–25.

103. *Catalog of the Hebrew Union College*, 1906, pp. 59–75.

104. *Catalog of the Hebrew Union College*, 1921–22, pp. 15–23.

105. See, for example, *The Catalogue of the Hebrew Union College* (1923–24), pp. 45–51, for a representative presentation of the curriculum at HUC during the Morgenstern years. Indeed, a decade later, *The Catalogue of the Hebrew Union College*, 1932–33, pp. 61–71, displays the same emphases.

106. For interesting biographical details on Finkelstein, see Pamela S. Nadell, *Conservative Judaism in America: A Bibliographical Dictionary and Sourcebook* (Westport, Conn.: Greenwood Press, 1988), s.v., "Finkelstein, Louis."

107. Louis Finkelstein, "Tradition in the Making: The Seminary's Interpretaton of Judaism," in Adler, ed., *The Jewish Theological Seminary of America—Semi-Centennial Volume*, pp. 30 and 26–27.

108. Ibid., pp. 29–30.

109. Ibid., p. 29.

110. Ibid., p. 30.

111. Ibid.

112. Ibid., p. 32.

113. Ibid., pp. 33–34. During the period that he delivered this address, Finkelstein published two major works of scholarship that illuminate the position he advanced in this speech. The first, *Akiba: Scholar, Saint, and Martyr* (New York: Covici-Friede Publishers), appeared in 1936, while the second, his two-volume study on *The Pharisees* (Philadelphia: Jewish Publication Society), was issued in 1938. In each of these works, Finkelstein adopted an approach that has frequently been both praised and criticized as "sociological." That is, he portrayed both the Pharisees and the famed 2nd-century Tanna Rabbi Akiba as embodying an approach to Jewish law which took account of the exigencies of the day. In this way, the attitude of Rabbinic Judaism to Jewish law can be seen as akin to the description of the Jewish legal process Finkelstein delineated in this speech. Furthermore, as Finkelstein indicated, this viewpoint concerning the nature of Jewish law was promulgated at the Seminary. We do not possess sufficient expertise in Rabbinic Judaism and its antecedents to assess the scholarly claims Finkelstein put forth in either of these studies. However, it is apparent the descriptions he offered of Jewish law in both of them provided an historical warrant for the legitimacy and Jewish authenticity of a Conservative approach to Jewish law. The fruits of scholarship were clearly employed here in the service of faith. They also guided that faith and informed the ethos of the Seminary and its curriculum.

114. *The Jewish Theological Seminary of America Register*, 1940–41, p. 9.

115. Nadell, *Conservative Judaism in America*, pp. 178–79.

116. Ibid.

117. Saul Lieberman, "Response to the Introduction by Professor Alexander Marx," in *The Jewish Expression*, ed. Judah Goldin (New York: Bantam Books, 1970), p. 133.

118. *The Jewish Theological Seminary of America Register*, 1951–52, pp. 24–28.

119. Cited in Michael B. Greenbaum, "Finkelstein and His Critics," *Conservative Judaism* (summer, 1995): p. 52.

120. Ibid., p. 73.

121. Ibid., p. 72.

122. Ackerman, "A Not Too Distant Mirror," p. 55.

123. Ibid., p. 57.

124. For a representative catalog of this period which illustrates this point, see *The Jewish Theological Seminary of America Register*, 1958–59, pp. 28–31.

125. Ibid., p. 29.

126. On the educational profile of students entering the Seminary at this point in time in contrast to those who were admitted earlier, see Arthur Hertzberg, "The Conservative Rabbinate: A Sociological Study," in Joseph L. Blau, et. al., *Essays on Jewish Life and Thought Presented in Honor of Salo Wittmayer Baron* (New York: Columbia University Press, 1959), p. 309–32. For the particular quotation, see p. 330.

127. Information in this paragraph is culled from *The Jewish Theological Seminary of America Register*, 1959–60, pp. 31–35; and *The Jewish Theological Seminary of America Register*, 1964–66, pp 31–35.

128. *The Jewish Theological Seminary of America Register*, 1964–66, pp. 33–34.

129. Ibid.

130. Ibid., p. 42.

131. Ibid., p. 35.

132. *Reports for the Board of Overseers of The Jewish Theological Seminary of America*, May 1964.

133. *The Jewish Theological Seminary of America Register*, 1959–60, p. 36.

134. *Reports for the Board of Overseers of the Jewish Theological Seminary of America*, 15 November 1964, p. 9.

135. Ibid.

136. *The Jewish Theological Seminary of America Register* (1964–66), p. 37.

137. See *Report for the Board of Overseers at the Jewish Theological Seminary of America*, May 1970, p. 7; and *Report for the Board of Overseers at the Jewish Theological Seminary of America*, May 1971, p. 9. We would like to thank Rabbi Joel Rembaum of Temple Beth Am in Los Angeles—a student at JTS during this period—for drawing our attention to the matter of student representation on these committees.

138. *Report for the Board of Overseers at the Jewsh Theological Seminary of America*, May 1970, p. 7.

139. *Report for the Board of Overseers of the Jewish Theological Seminary of America*, May 1971, pp. 9–10.

140. *The Jewish Theological Seminary of America Register*, 1970–73, pp. 36ff.

141. Ibid.

142. All these programs are discussed in detail elsewhere in the volume.

143. *The Jewish Theological Seminary of America Register*, 1964–66, p. 144.

144. *Reports for the Board of Overseers of the Jewish Theological Seminary of America*, April 1962.

145. Ibid.

146. *Report for the Board of Overseers at the Jewish Theological Seminary of America*, May, 1971, p. 11.

147. This information is culled from a number of *Reports to the Board of Overseers* as well as cat-

589

*The JTS
Rabbinical
Curriculum
in Historical
Perspective*

alogs issued by the Seminary throughout the 1960s. It is also supplemented by an oral interview with Rabbi Elliot Dorff, provost of the University of Judaism, who was enrolled in the Special Studies Program during the 1960s.

148. *Report for Board of Overseers at the Jewish Theological Seminary of America*, May 1971, p. 11.

149. *Report for the Board of Overseers at the Jewish Theological Seminary of America*, May 1969, p. 12.

150. For a description of Professor Hauptman during her years as a student in the Lehman Institute, see *Report for Board of Overseers at the Jewish Theological Seminary of America*, May 1972, p. 8.

151. Neil Gillman, "The Changing Paradigm of the Conservative Rabbi," *Conservative Judaism* (winter 1991): p. 4.

152. On this point, see Michael B. Greenbaum, "Finkelstein and His Critics," pp. 55ff.

153. See *The Jewish Theological Seminary of America Register*, 1966–69, pp. 32–33; and ibid., 1970–73, pp. 32–33, 48.

154. Greenbaum, "Finkelstein and His Critics," pp. 54-58.

155. *Hebrew Union College-Jewish Institute of Religion Catalogue*, 1956–57, p. 21.

156. This information is taken from the unpaginated *Academic Bulletin—Rabbi Isaac Elchanan Theological Seminary of Yeshiva University*, 1986.

157. Rabbi Robert Hirt, vice-president for administration and professional education at RIETS, personal communication on 22 February 1996 to Lee Bycel.

158. Samuel Belkin, *In His Image: The Jewish Philosophy of Man as Expressed in Rabbinic Literature* (London and New York: Abelard-Schuman Limited, 1960), p. 16.

159. *Academic Bulletin—Rabbi Isaac Elchanan Theological Seminary of Yeshiva University*, 1986.

160. Nadell, *Conservative Judaism in America*, p. 55.

161. Gerson Cohen, "Inaugural Address," in *Inauguration of Gerson D. Cohen as Chancellor of the Jewish Theological Seminary* (New York: Jewish Theological Seminary, 1973), p. 3. Emphasis ours.

162. Neil Gillman, "The Changing Paradigm of the Conservative Rabbi," pp. 4–5.

163. Gerson Cohen, "Jewish Identity and Jewish Collective Will in America," p. 20.

164. This paragraph is taken from Ackerman, "A Not Too Distant Mirror," p. 58.

165. Ibid., p. 59.

166. *The Jewish Theological Seminary of America Register*, 1977–82, p. 35.

167. We would like to thank our colleague William Cutter, professor of education and Hebrew literature at HUC-JIR, Los Angeles, for providing us with the term, "skills-mastery," to describe the nature of such a curriculum.

168. Ackerman, "A Not Too Distant Mirror," p. 59.

169. Ibid., p. 60.

170. Riv-Ellen Prell, *Prayer and Community: The Havurah in American Judaism* (Detroit: Wayne State University Press, 1989), p. 102.

171. See Marshall Sklare, "The Greening of Judaism," *Commentary* (December, 1974): pp. 51–57, for his sharply critical remarks upon *The Jewish Catalog* and the ethos of *Havurah* Judaism.

172. Jack Wertheimer, *A People Divided: Judaism in Contemporary America* (New York: Basic Books, 1993), pp. 25–26.

173. Gillman, "The Changing Paradigm of the Conservative Rabbi," p. 6.

174. Charles Liebman, "The Training of American Rabbis," in *Aspects of the Religious Behavior of American Jews* (New York: Ktav, 1974), p. 48.

175. Ibid., p. 51.

176. Kenneth Katz, "Uninspired," *Conservative Judaism* (summer, 1986): p. 14.

177. Gillman, "The Changing Paradigm of the Conservative Rabbi," p. 10. Italics ours.

591

*The JTS
Rabbinical
Curriculum
in Historical
Perspective*

178. Laura Geller, "From Equality to Transformation: The Challenge of Women's Rabbinic Leadership," in *Woman Rabbis: Exploration and Celebration,* ed. Gary Zola (Cincinnati: HUC-JIR Rabbinic Alumni Association Press, 1996), p. 78.

179. Debra Orenstein, "Recovering the Forgotten Woman: Why We Need to Rethink the Rabbinical School Curriculum," *Direction—A Magazine of the University of Judaism* (fall 1991):p. 12.

180. See Pamela Hoffman, "A Rejoinder to Ken Katz by a Seminary Spiritualizer," *Conservative Judaism* (summer 1986).

181. Ibid., p. 25.

182. Nadell, *Conservative Judaism in America*, p. 227.

183. Ismar Schorsch, *Thoughts From 3080: Selected Addresses and Writings* (New York: Jewish Theological Seminary, 1987), pp. 21–22.

184. Ibid., p 22.

185. Ismar Schorsch, "The Modern Rabbinate—Then and Now," *Conservative Judaism* (Winter, 1991): pp. 19 and 18.

186. Hoffman, "A Rejoinder to Ken Katz by a Seminary Spiritualizer," pp. 23–24, 26.

187. *Reconstructionist Rabbinical College Catalogue*, 1990–1993, p. 7.

188. The Kaplan quotation is cited in Rebecca T. Alpert, "Reconstructionist Rabbis," *Encyclopædia Judaica Supplement* (Jerusalem: Keter, 1985), p. 101. Emphasis ours. The final point is made by Alpert herself.

189. For these quotations, as well as for a comprehensive discussion of this document, see Lee Bycel, "Tradition or Renewal: Notes on a Modern Rabbinic School Curriculum," *Religious Education* 90, no. 1 (1995): pp. 72–88.

190. This information is taken from the unpaginated *Academic Bulletin—Rabbi Isaac Elchanan Theological Seminary of Yeshiva University*, 1986.

191. 1989 Jewish Theological Seminary press release, entitled, "Jewish Theological Seminary Changes Rabbinical School Curriculum."

192. Neil Gillman, "The Changing Paradigm of the Conservative Rabbi," p. 9.

193. *The Jewish Theological Seminary Academic Bulletin*, 1994–95, p. 39. Emphasis ours.

194. Ibid., pp. 41–42.

195. Ibid., p. 42.

196. Ibid., pp. 45–46, 175–76.

197. Ibid., p. 46, and relevant sections under the rubric, "Courses of Instruction," pp. 72 ff.

198. Ibid., pp. 43-47.

199. Ackerman, "A Not Too Distant Mirror," p. 60.

200. *The Jewish Theological Seminary Academic Bulletin* , 1994–95, pp. 45, 47, 158 ff.

201. Ackerman, "A Not Too Distant Mirror," p. 60.

202. *The Jewish Theological Seminary Academic Bulletin* , 1994–95, p. 45.

203. Gillman, "The Changing Paradigm of the Conservative Rabbi," p. 10.,

204. Ackerman, "A Not Too Distant Mirror," p. 61.

205. Katz, "Uninspired," p. 17.

206. Gillman, "The Changing Paradigm of the Conservative Rabbi," p. 11. Emphasis ours.

207. Neil Gillman, "Inside or Outside? Emancipation and the Dilemmas of Conservative Judaism," *Judaism* (fall 1989): p. 415.

208. Pamela Hoffman, "A Rejoinder to Ken Katz by a Seminary Spiritualizer," p. 26.

KARLA GOLDMAN

A Respectful Rivalry

The Hebrew Union College-Jewish Institute of Religion and the Jewish Theological Seminary

On a country outing, circa 1910s, Solomon Schechter, left, and Kaufmann Kohler share a bench. Standing are Louis Ginzberg, left, and Emil G. Hirsch. *Library, JTS.*

KARLA GOLDMAN

A Respectful Rivalry

The Hebrew Union College-Jewish Institute of
Religion and the Jewish Theological Seminary

WITH THE DEATHS OF SABATO MORAIS
in 1897 and Isaac M. Wise in 1900, America's two young rabbinical seminaries
found themselves without leadership or direction. A few months after Wise's death,
the weekly Jewish newspaper, the *American Hebrew*, set forth the question as to
whether American Jews would not be better off with "one strong" institution for
teaching rabbis "instead of two weak ones."[1] In response to this inquiry, a number of
American Jewish leaders, including some of the primary financial backers of the
two seminaries, speculated about the future course of these now apparently rudder-
less institutions.

To some it seemed extraordinary that they were being asked to consider the
merger of two institutions that they believed had been founded upon the presumption of ineluctable ideological division. When Isaac M. Wise founded Cincinnati's
Hebrew Union College (HUC) in 1875, he hoped to train rabbis who would preach
a distinctive American Judaism that would become the creed of every American
Jew. It was common knowledge that those who organized in 1886 to found New
York's Jewish Theological Seminary (JTS) did so in part because of their profound
unease with both Wise's brand of Judaism and the conduct of the Hebrew Union
College.

Many exponents of traditional Judaism in the United States had initially supported Wise in his intention to create an institution that would broadly serve the
needs of American Judaism. But as became most starkly evident when shellfish was
served at the celebratory dinner after Hebrew Union College's first ordination in
1883 and when the radical planks of the 1885 Pittsburg Platform declared the negation of much of the traditional law, the Reform Judaism of Wise and his colleagues
quickly became untenable in the eyes of more traditional Jews. Growing fears of the

595

radicalism represented by Wise's school and by reformers in general created an imperative need for a traditional alternative. Offering his unsolicited response to the *American Hebrew* symposium, Sabato Morais's son, Henry, reported that "more than once" his father had "openly declared that his actual purpose had been and would always be, to offset the mischief and the destruction plain to every eye, as the result of the Cincinnati college, and those that emanated from its midst."[2]

Many participants in the 1900 symposium believed that the two institutions did indeed represent opposite ends of a radical-traditional spectrum and that their founders "were as far apart as the antipodes in their religious thought."[3] Some contributors, especially those who insisted upon the maintenance of traditional Jewish observance and doctrine, cited "irreconcilable differences of opinion" between the two schools that could admit no compromise. Curiously, however, many prominent observers and supporters of the schools who contributed to the forum were not entirely clear as to what the real differences were between the schools. A number of participants, for instance, noted that one irreconcilable difference between reformers and conservatives was the former's practice of higher biblical criticism, the scientific elucidation of the scripture's human authors.[4] During Wise's lifetime, however, this methodology and perspective had been banned on the campus of the Hebrew Union College.

Perhaps because of this sort of ambiguity over what the schools represented, a number of respondents who were not committed to the obligations of traditional Jewish observance insisted that the two institutions and their tendencies were not so far apart as they might seem. These participants argued that given the fluidity of doctrinal positions taken by American Jews, ideological distinctions should not be allowed to obscure the fact that "the fundamental objects and purposes of both [institutions] are identical."[5] This position was held by supporters of both the Reform College and the more conservative Seminary. For Jacob Schiff, for instance, issues of ideology were dwarfed by the question of geography and the foolishness of placing so important an institution in a backwater like Cincinnati, rather than in a city that could offer "large local [intellectual] resources and wealth [that] can be utilized in its favor."[6]

The appointments of Solomon Schechter as president of JTS in 1902 and of Kaufmann Kohler as president of HUC in 1903 foreclosed the possibility of merging the two schools. From the organization of the early Seminary in 1886, the leaders of both JTS and HUC have tried to set a spiritual course for American Judaism. Ideological and geographic distance often allowed each seminary to attempt to chart its own path without reference to the course being set by the other. Inevitably, however, there were times when tensions between the respective visions of the seminaries brought them into conflict with each other. In the early 20th century, under the guidance of Kaufmann Kohler and Solomon Schechter, the two schools worked from the premise that the other institution's existence called for a more explicitly ideological and positive statement of their own identity. Through this period, each defined itself in large part in opposition to whatever seemed to be represented by its rival.

In time, as each school solidified its institutional base and financial position and staked out its own distinctive religious and ideological turf, a cordial coexistence came to mark formal relations between the schools' leaders, overshadowing the more immediate rivalry that had marked the Kohler/Schechter era. Differing stances particularly towards questions of observance and the place of Jewish nationalism in American Jewish life have provided the most salient markers of division between the two schools. Yet, as ideologies have shifted, many of the specific questions at stake between the two schools have been transformed. Today, for instance, instead of contesting the wisdom of Zionism, Hebrew Union College-Jewish Institute of Religion (HUC-JIR) and JTS must consider the status of the other's year-in-Israel program and whether they should work together to challenge Orthodox control of the Israeli religious establishment.

One telling point that emerged in the 1900 symposium was that the content of the particular differences between the two institutions was not necessarily as important as the fact that there were differences. As the HUC-trained Rabbi Max Heller noted, "Tolerance is a good thing. . . . Yet in religion, earnestness, consistency, the rich glow of fervid sentiments, the clear outlining of positive convictions, are of far more primary importance." Similarly Dr. Cyrus Adler, a prime backer of the Seminary who would later become its president, worried that "amalgamation might result in the production of a body of graduates absolutely devoid of positive convictions and virility." As Heller pointed out, the coexistence of the two institutions could be vital to the self-definition of each: "Let there be a healthy and mutually respectful rivalry,—the Hebrew Union College needs it; it cannot do its best without it."[7] Levels of competition and cooperation have waxed and waned, but the energizing rivalry hoped for by Max Heller in 1900 has remained as the two seminaries continue to explore what it means to train rabbis for the contemporary world.

After the deaths of Wise and Morais, both institutions sought reorganized frameworks for their future existence. In this context, the arena for the most potential conflict between the two schools was in competition for donors. Although Hebrew Union College had depended to a large extent on the generosity of Cincinnati's Jews, its Board of Governors also hoped for continuing contributions from the liberal and affluent Jews of New York City. Jacob Schiff and Louis Marshall, two of the most prominent philanthropists in American Jewish life, both members of New York's Reform Temple Emanu El, were confronted with the legitimate expectation that they should support a liberal rabbinical school that was intended to serve Jews throughout the United States. Louis Marshall, for instance, had accepted the role of chairman of the campaign to raise $500,000 in honor of the memory of Isaac Mayer Wise. Despite the local pride that Cincinnati's prosperous Jews took in seeing their community as the fountainhead of Jewish learning in America, it seemed clear that any aspirations to continue as a national institution would depend on the school's ability to attract the interest of America's wealthiest Jews.

The views expressed by both Schiff and Marshall in the *American Hebrew*'s 1900 symposium did not augur well for those who believed that a liberal institution wherever it was located should automatically command the allegiance of liberal Jews. In their responses, Marshall and Schiff indicated their belief that a commitment to the future of American Judaism should outweigh any loyalty that they as liberal Jews owed to a particular school of progressive Judaism based in Cincinnati. In their view, matters of doctrine were merely incidental to the project of Jewish education. Thus, a range of viewpoints could easily be incorporated within the curriculum of one amalgamated school. As Schiff noted, "It is not a question of whether orthodoxy or reform should be sustained and perpetuated, the question much nearer to me is, how can Judaism be maintained as an active force in the daily life of our people."[8]

Ultimately the successful reorganization of the Seminary in 1902 depended mightily on the philanthropy of progressive Jews like Schiff and Marshall. From their point of view, a commitment to the Seminary meant investing not in Orthodoxy per se but in the enlightened and educated traditionalism represented by Solomon Schechter, whose credibility derived not from his Eastern European origins but from his scholarship and his post as a reader in rabbinics at Cambridge University. Overtures to Schechter in regard to his taking on a leadership role at the Seminary were made as early as 1892.[9] The eventual success of the effort to bring Schechter to America and the Jewish Theological Seminary rested upon commitments from a small but influential group of donors from New York and Philadelphia in the amount of $200,000.

As New York's most prominent liberal Jews pushed to secure Solomon Schechter's presence at the helm of the Seminary, HUC's leaders sought out an eminent British academician of their own. Israel Abrahams, author of *Jewish Life in the Middle Ages,* had gained scholarly renown after the publication of his book by the Jewish Publication Society in 1896.[10] In response to advances from HUC, Abrahams had intimated that he would like to make the move to America. When Schechter decided to take on the leadership of JTS, however, Abrahams accepted Schechter's vacated Cambridge University post. Abrahams apparently preferred the role of Schechter's successor to that of Schechter's rival.[11]

A few months after Schechter's actual arrival in America, the College's board chose Kaufmann Kohler, among the most respected of America's Reform rabbis, to serve as president. In some ways, Kohler was an unlikely successor to Wise. His scholarly, often rigid, approach contrasted with the energetic and compromising style pioneered by Wise. In addition, Kohler's impressive Reform pedigree derived from his father-in-law, David Einhorn, who had often been Wise's fierce antagonist. Kohler's reputation as an ultra-reformer, who had once advocated the introduction of a Sunday Sabbath for Jews, was tempered by his sincere pursuit of authentic spirituality in a rational age. Moreover, his scholarship and his respect for piety had earned him respect in more traditional circles. He was, for instance, a frequent contributor to the traditionalist-leaning *American Hebrew*. In appointing Kohler, the Cincinnati school's agents hoped to build upon his reputation to broaden the school's appeal beyond the smaller communities of the West and Midwest where Wise had found the greatest response.[12]

The establishment of the Seminary under firm financial and academic leadership evidently generated a significant response among those invested with guiding the fortunes of Hebrew Union College. Overtures to both Israel Abrahams and Kohler reflected efforts to match the anticipated strengths of Schechter in his role as institutional head. The invitation to Kohler from the chairman of HUC's Board of Governors to become the College's president noted that "in view of the recent liberal endowment of the Jewish Theological Seminary of America" with its mission to perpetuate "the old-time rigid, unyielding orthodoxy . . . the separate and independent existence of the Hebrew Union College has become an absolute necessity."[13] Kohler responded in kind, affirming "the need of an institution of Jewish learning which stands uncompromisingly and consistently for those principles of Reform and Progress, . . . which made American Judaism a power in this free country."[14]

Kohler, after twenty-four years as a rabbi at New York's Beth El, already commanded the respect of many of New York's most eminent Jews. Jacob Schiff, although he had evidently concluded that he would rather expend his resources in New York than in Cincinnati, nevertheless informed Kohler that he still wanted "to give expression of my appreciation of your election to the Presidency of the Hebrew Union College, and to mark my esteem and respect for you." Deciding to endow a scholarship in Kohler's honor, Schiff made a $2500 contribution to the College.[15] Kohler further justified the hopes of his new employers when he returned from a 1904 fund-raising trip to New York having raised $30,000 and reporting that he had "won the warm interest and goodwill of the leading Jews of the metropolis for the Cincinnati college." The potential for support from the East, Kohler indicated, rested upon the ability of donors to understand that the Seminary and the College were not simply duplicates of each other: "it being fully recognized by them that the Hebrew Union College responds to the needs of progressive American Judaism, while the Seminary stands for conservative Judaism."[16]

The appointment of both Kohler and Schechter as the leaders of their respective schools cast them into the position of leaders of the Reform and traditionalist camps in American Judaism. Given the extent to which the institutions were identified with the viewpoints and personalities of their leaders, the institutional relationship between the two schools during this period may best be understood through examination of the positions and relationship of the two presidents. The personal relationship between the two men, which was established on a basis of mutual respect even before Schechter arrived in New York, was inevitably complicated when they were cast into the leadership of two rival institutions. For the most part, the two men and their institutions maintained a formal cordiality in their public dealings with each other. Yet, the very real conflict that informed their disparate ideological positions and the extent to which they felt threatened by the advance of the other's institution created ample motivation for occasional expressions of hostility.

While Schechter was still in England, numerous correspondents alerted him to the conflicts between reformers and traditionalists that would engage him once he arrived on American soil. One writer had assured him that "there is room for two Seminaries in this great glorious country, etc. My answer was in the sense of peace, etc," Schechter reported.[17] Schechter's account suggests the bemused indifference of someone who was becoming acquainted with someone else's disputes but had not yet become engaged by them. Still, the pre-JTS Schechter had already formulated an idea of the position advocated by his future rivals and insisted that in contrast to "the Cincinnati people," those at the Seminary had to recognize that "it is time to stand by our Torah and our traditions."[18]

Both Schechter's and Kohler's public accounts of their relationship were marked by cordiality and respect. Kohler recalled that when Schechter came to New York and before he himself left for Cincinnati, they visited each other on a daily basis. In his early days as president of Hebrew Union College, Kaufmann Kohler wrote Schechter hoping for a chance to exchange notes on what he described as "our common work."[19] Kohler's installation speech celebrated the potential of "two institutions of learning" in "American Israel" to impart "new power, new light and new life" to Judaism.[20] In honoring Kohler upon his selection as HUC president, Schechter noted that some were predicting "jealousy and strife between the two colleges." Yet while Schechter acknowledged that there was much that might separate him from his colleague, he professed that "I honor and admire Dr. Kohler too much to take up the position of an antagonist."[21]

As he anticipated their future relationship, Schechter focused on their common task, noting that while there were "very many essential points about which we are still compelled to differ, the great thing is to work . . . for the glory of God and His people."[22] Once settled into his tenure at the Seminary, however, Schechter came to see the work of the Hebrew Union College and of the Reform movement in a more threatening light. In a private letter written in 1904, Schechter's disdain for advocates of Reform was reflected in his outrage that people "whose whole Judaism consists of coming in their automobiles to listen to opera singers every Friday evening" would attempt to "smuggle" their liturgies "and other hellish things" among New York's Russian Jews. Schechter characterized their missionizing techniques as "dishonest, dirty and aggressive as those of the Christian missionaries."[23]

Inevitably, Schechter's disdain for Reform took its toll on his regard for Kohler. Schechter's letters to a sympathetic graduate of HUC revealed his growing resentment at the encroachments of Reform. In 1907 he responded to an article by Kohler that he viewed as an attack on his own support of Zionism by belittling both Kohler and the HUC president's brand of Judaism. "I am not going to make him important by entering into a controversy with him," Schechter observed. Of Kohler's critique that Schechter's position seemed to support those who advocated ethical culture, Schechter noted that "it is a well-known fact here that the great majority of Felix Adler's recruits came from Temple Beth-El [Kohler's former pulpit], where they received the proper training for ultimately leaving the Synagogue."[24] On another occasion, Schechter referred facetiously to Kohler as "this great luminary" as he privately decried Kohler's apparent dismissal of the "moral and spiritual side" of traditional Judaism: "I can pardon such ignorance in a 'Goy,' but the Jew who repeats it is really wicked."[25]

When Bible scholar and HUC professor Max Margolis fell into bitter conflict with Kohler over his right to express his Zionist ideology, he turned to Schechter as a confidant, hoping for assistance in securing a new professional position. In his letters, he conveyed his most personal sentiments in Hebrew phrases. One letter, composed entirely in Hebrew and written when his position at HUC was at the crisis point, described Kohler in the most derisive of terms. In describing a Kohler Passover sermon, Margolis accused the HUC president of undermining Jewish belief and plaintively asked Schechter, "Have you ever heard such stupidity?"[26]

Schechter's own growing animosity to the tactics and position of the Reform movement and its institutions was reflected in his outrage when the Union of American Hebrew Congregations, meeting in Philadelphia in 1909, dedicated a synagogue memorial window in the image of HUC founder Isaac M. Wise. In Schechter's eyes the Wise memorial deliberately flouted traditional Jewish prohibitions against the appearance of graven human images in sacred space. "Nothing more outrageous to the Jewish conscience was ever done in this country," Schechter fumed to a sympathetic Reform colleague.[27] To a certain extent the geographical separation between the two institutions moderated the degree of direct conflict between them. Thus, when the Reform rabbis announced their intention to hold their annual meeting in New York in 1909, Schechter perceived the plan as a plot to "conquer the East," anticipating that "the Seminary and the humble writer of this letter are to be subjects of attack." When the rabbis did come to New York, he denied concern for himself noting "it is not a personal question with me," yet he railed against what he saw as attacks on traditional Judaism and its institutions and lamented the growing "abyss" "between the Reform party and the rest of Israel."[28]

Schechter's official relationship with the Hebrew Union College and the Reform movement was a subtle mixture of competition and courteous protocol. Perceived slights had to be managed delicately. In 1910, when Schechter received an inquiry from the secretary of the Central Conference of American Rabbis [CCAR], the organizational body for Reform rabbis, Schechter consulted with his lay colleagues in the leadership of JTS on how to handle the perceived affront implicit in asking the president of the Seminary to respond to the secretary of the Conference. Cyrus Adler pointed out that it would certainly have been more proper if such a request had come from "the President of their Conference," and suggested sending an acknowledgment that the letter had been received but have it "signed by some one else."[29]

Despite the basic hostility towards the Hebrew Union College that prevailed among JTS's leaders, the conservatives also understood the need for outward displays of civility. This was illustrated in 1911, when JTS leaders considered an HUC request to Schechter for the submission of a sixteen-page scholarly article. Cyrus Adler pointed out that given the responsibilities incumbent upon a busy scholar and president of a large institution, "he owes no courtesy to the head of an Institution most of whose Directors and Professors consider his Institution wrongheaded and reactionary. No act of his will alter their feelings." Yet, Adler acknowledged that while some in Cincinnati would use Schechter's refusal as an excuse to paint him as a bigot, Kohler himself "would feel profoundly injured and any personal relations that was [*sic*] established between you and him during the past years would be strained."[30]

Seminary leaders kept careful track of their own "liberality" towards representatives of HUC. Adler pointed out that the Seminary had invited Kohler to deliver lectures at the Seminary and granted honorary degrees to "outspoken opponents like Felsenthal [a Zionistic Reform rabbi from Chicago] and [Samuel] Schulman [rabbi of Temple Emanu-El]." When Schechter consulted Adler about whether he had to publish an article by HUC graduate Hyman Enelow, Adler pointed out that he had wanted "to publish something from some of that school" but that those already published from "Kohler, Rhine and Lauterbach" had "answer[ed] that purpose."[31] Institutional cordiality went only so far between the two camps. When Kohler was unable to accept an invitation to attend the dedication of Dropsie College, Cyrus Adler, its president, asked Schechter whether he thought "it necessary that I should have some other representative of the Hebrew Union College," noting that "none of the Professors there are very much to my taste." He felt he had "done my duty by them in inviting their President." Yet in the interest of "all around good will" he was willing to consider inviting a Reform rabbi to the festivities.[32]

In large part, geography cut off extensive intellectual or social exchange between members of the two schools. Yet, in an era when the faculties of the two seminaries represented the country's greatest concentration of scholars in Jewish studies, they were frequently brought together by group academic projects that drew upon the expertise of America's academic Jewish community. Representatives of the two schools encountered each other in the work of the *Jewish Encyclopedia*, the English Bible translation sponsored by the Jewish Publication Society (JPS) and the Central Conference of American Rabbis, and a series of Jewish classics sponsored by Jacob Schiff.

These projects offered a potential arena for interdenominational contact and collegiality. In 1901, before becoming president of the Hebrew Union College, Kaufmann Kohler had proclaimed that "the Jewish Encyclopedia goes forth as a peacemaker and friendly intermediary between all shades of opinion among the Jews, between Orthodoxy and Reform, Radicalism, and Conservatism, Nationalist and Cosmopolitanism."[33] At the same time, the potential of these same projects for divisiveness was readily evident. When Schechter arrived in America, he joined in the ongoing *Jewish Encyclopedia* project but privately registered his discomfort over Kohler's editorial contributions: "K[ohler] hates Rabbinic Judaism like any *goy* and has become so aggressive that the Encyclopedia will become the *rishes* [evil] of the 20th century."[34] Citing other obligations, Schechter eventually resigned from his participation in the project.

In 1908 when appointments were being considered to the JPS/CCAR Bible translation project, Mayer Sulzberger pointed out to Schechter that his presence on the committee "might, in the course of politics, result in the appointment of Kohler by [CCAR president, David] Philipson" and noted that "I should wish to spare you the unhappiness which might result from such a contingency."[35] As it turned out when the CCAR did appoint Kohler to the committee of editors, Schechter acknowledged that his own presence had also become necessary. Max Margolis who had been made executive editor of the Bible project privately observed that "the two will hardly be able to work harmoniously together." And in fact the meetings of the editors, drawn out over seven years, did not always go smoothly.[36] Nevertheless, the successful completion of this project despite moments of conflict testifies to their ability to put their differences and rivalries aside.

During Schechter's tenure, representatives of the two schools could never feel quite at ease with each other. Although they recognized their formal responsibility to cooperate in the interest of their own institutions and for the good of American Judaism, the problematic nature of interactions between the leaders of the two schools and movements could not be fully eradicated. In part, this discomfort derived simply from different personal stances towards Jewish observance. When, for instance, Reform Temple Emanu-El's rabbi Samuel Schulman invited

Final meeting of
the board of the
JPS/CCAR Bible
translation pro-
ject, held at the
Seminary, 1915.
From left: Joseph
Jacobs, Solomon
Schechter, Max
Margolis, Cyrus
Adler, David
Philipson, Kauf-
man Kohler,
Samuel Schul-
man. *Ratner
Center, JTS.*

Schechter to a dinner likely to be attended by the Kohlers and David Philipson,
Cyrus Adler reassured him that although he had felt "rather lonesome" at the event
the previous year, Schulman had advised him "in advance that the dinner was
kosher and I took his word for it."[37]

Because he believed that the coexistence of Reform and traditional strands
within American Judaism was inevitable, Kaufmann Kohler could embrace the
tension between the two seminaries as consistent with the age-old tradition of contesting schools within Judaism going back to Hillel and Shammai. Schechter's
conviction that "the reform of which Montefiore and a Kohler dream means simply
final conversion to Christianity" made him less open to a pluralistic vision for
American Judaism.[38] Even when he served as the Seminary's ceremonial representative to the older school, he remained constrained in his ability to celebrate the
benefits of coexistence. Although he accepted the invitation to attend the dedication ceremonies for HUC's new campus, Schechter refused to gloss over what he
termed his "want of sympathy with reform tendencies." Instead, he emphasized
that the Seminary and the College were "pursuing, to a certain extent, different
aims and endeavoring to realize them by largely different methods." Schechter
gracefully likened the relationship between the two schools to that prevailing
between the British government and its political foes. Like the British government
and "his majesty's opposition," JTS and HUC despite their differences were united

by a larger goal. They both pursued Jewish scholarship to educate first Jews and then all humanity in the ways of justice taught by Judaism.[39]

In the era of Kohler and Schechter each institution had pursued its own path with a competitive awareness of the other. Even protestations that they worked towards the same ends were accompanied by a vital, sometimes hostile, rivalry between the two schools. With Schechter's death in 1915 and Kohler's retirement in 1922, rivalry between the two seminaries lost its harsh ideological edge. Upon Schechter's death, the Hebrew Union College leadership sent solemn condolences to the Seminary, using the occasion to ascribe to Schechter the belief that despite any institutional differences between the Seminary and the College "in the fundamentals we are all one."[40] If this did not serve as a faithful representation of Schechter's attitude towards his Reform counterparts, it may more closely approximate the relationship that came to prevail between HUC and JTS under subsequent leaders.

Cyrus Adler became acting president of the Seminary upon Schechter's death, although he did not receive a permanent appointment as president until nine years later. As a boyhood disciple of Seminary founder Sabato Morais, Adler believed fiercely in traditional Judaism, yet he was less interested than Schechter had been in fighting for the soul of American Judaism. Intimately associated with the emergence of Conservative Judaism as a movement within American Judaism, Adler was preeminently an institution builder and administrator. Unlike Schechter, he did not consider himself a Zionist and thus held less of an animus towards the anti-Zionist position identified with HUC than did faculty members like Israel Friedlaender and other members of the JTS faculty who may also have aspired to the school's presidency. Through his close involvement with almost all the national organizations that sought to represent and serve the American Jewish community, Adler knew that he had to be able to work in coalition with those who might be ideological rivals. Serving simultaneously as the institutional head of both the Jewish Theological Seminary in New York and Dropsie College of Jewish Studies in Philadelphia, Adler was more willing than Schechter to accept the coexistence of different institutions directed towards roughly similar ends.

Toward the end of his career, Schechter had despaired of his dream of creating in America "a great centre of Jewish learning and Conservative activity." Without appropriate funding or support, he imagined his "hopes and aspirations shattered to pieces." According to Schechter, it was "the Rabbi of the 'Temple' who gets the best salary" and was awarded the best social position, while America's newer Conservative synagogues were supported only by "the lower middle class . . . still more or less in their peddling state."[41] Schechter was unable to imagine that the immigrant population which he dismissed as "the most unruly element in Jewry" could ever serve as the basis for a vital and prosperous religious movement in America.

Adler, although no less elitist in his views of community leadership than Schechter, saw that these same immigrants were the key to the future. In 1915, the year of Schechter's death, Adler explained to the United Synagogue, the federation of Conservative congregations, that he had "not the slightest doubt that in the course of ten or twenty years, at most, the ideas which lie at the basis of our movement will be the most prevalent among the Jews of America."[42] Adler was willing to trust the Seminary's future to the Americanization of the hundreds of thousands of recent immigrants who would become uncomfortable with Orthodoxy but who would be unable to find a home within Reform.

With Adler as acting president of JTS and with Julian Morgenstern succeeding Kohler as president of HUC in 1922, doctrine continued to separate the two schools, yet interactions between the Seminary and the College no longer seemed driven by institutional rivalry. In a 1923 address to the Rabbinical Assembly, Adler articulated a view of American Judaism that seemed closer to Kohler's than to Schechter's: "I cannot wholly deplore the fact that there are differences among us. When have there not been?"[43] In this speech, Adler expressed his hope that the Seminary could be broad enough to encompass this broad range of Jewry, yet he realized that there was room in American Jewry for both institutions.

In his role as president, Adler believed it was his duty to preserve positive institutional relations. In general, Adler was quite hesitant to advocate any course that might be perceived as a slight by those at Hebrew Union College. When a Conservative Cincinnati rabbi encouraged Adler to grant a special scholarship so that a Hebrew Union College student might undertake graduate study at the Seminary, Adler feared that "it would look as though I were bribing a man to leave the Hebrew Union College." According to Adler, the propriety of such a course "in view of the amicable personal relations which I try to cultivate all around, would certainly be inadvisable."[44] When informed that an issue of the *American Jewish Year Book* might focus upon the Seminary in an article on the state of graduate Jewish study in the United States, Adler noted that it would be wrong to "single out the Seminary and omit the Hebrew Union College or even the Yeshibah [*sic*]."[45] Similarly when Louis Finkelstein delivered an address on the legacy of Jacob Schiff in 1936, Adler wondered why "there [was] no mention of Mr. Schiff's great contributions to the Hebrew Union College."[46] In this era, Schechter's antagonism to Reform or a 1909 article by Israel Friedlaender that characterized an anti-Zionist biblical interpretation by then professor of Bible Julian Morgenstern as "a rehash of all that is most offensive to Jewish sentiment and Jewish dignity in 'modern scientific research,'" would have seemed quite out of place.[47]

In greetings sent in recognition of Hebrew Union College's fiftieth anniversary in 1925, Cyrus Adler, unlike his predecessor, was able to emphasize the shared goals of the two schools: "You and we have realized that we have many purposes in common." Adler did not deny differences, but he privileged commonality: "The differences in our outlook . . . have not stood in the way of hearty co-operation and friendly personal relations."[48] In his report to the Seminary faculty on his participation in the College's fifty-year jubilee celebration, Adler acknowledged that his visit to the Cincinnati campus had inspired both admiration and jealousy, admitting that "I . . . had a very strong temptation to break a Commandment." "The physical facilities of the Hebrew Union College," he told them, "are so vastly superior to our own that I can well imagine them as a superior attraction to any young student." He reported that the school's dormitory was "as comfortable as that of any college that I have ever seen," that the library was "charming," and the school's gymnasium and exercise facilities were excellent. Although Adler acknowledged that similar facilities were not a realistic possibility in New York City, he alerted his faculty to the "attention" manifested by HUC towards "the human comforts" of its students, describing them as "quite beyond anything that we have dreamed of."[49] Adler's visit to Cincinnati no doubt influenced his vision for the new JTS campus on the Upper West Side, the construction of which marked one of the chief accomplishments of his presidency.[50]

Through the 1920s, at a time when general national prosperity meant that "the demand for rabbis exceeded the supply," both seminaries were in the fortunate position of feeling that they could profitably learn from the other about how to operate an American rabbinical school.[51] Officers of the two schools frequently consulted each other in regard to matters ranging from faculty pay scales and sabbatical policy to the design of graduate programs and rabbinical diplomas.[52] In a request for information about the dormitory fees and scholarship and loan policies at HUC, Adler told Morgenstern that he hoped "to be able to take from your experience as to whether we are doing too much or what is more likely too little for our students here."[53] The possibility that the two schools might learn from each other facilitated moments of institutional if not ideological cooperation.

At the very beginning of Morgenstern's service as HUC president, the leaders of the two seminaries seemed to anticipate that they might find new ways to work together for the good of the American Jewish community. Even before Morgenstern was promoted from interim to permanent president of HUC, Cyrus Adler sought his cooperation for a proposed "organization of the Jewish educational institutions in the United States." Although Morgenstern was hesitant to commit his institution to plans that were "still only in their very preliminary stages," he and Adler did cooperate in putting together a meeting of fifteen "leaders in Jewish religious educational activities" from a number of different movements and tendencies. Despite this joint effort in the field of education, there is no evidence that the proposed plan progressed much beyond the initial meeting.[54]

Academic and personal exchange between the two faculties during this period appears to have been limited, although there were some areas in which they did come together. The American Academy for Jewish Research, founded in 1919 to encourage the production of Jewish scholarship, was the brainchild of the Seminary's Louis Ginzberg. The majority of its founding members and officers were from both the Seminary and the College.[55] In addition, Ginzberg, who had initially come to the United States expecting to be employed by Hebrew Union College, sustained close personal friendships with Zvi Diesendruck and Jacob Lauterbach of the HUC faculty.[56] The most fruitful professional relationship at this time between representatives of the two schools may have been that between the librarians. Alexander Marx of JTS and Adolph Oko of HUC sustained a collegial and productive relationship that began with Marx's input into a bibliography of Solomon Schechter's writings by Oko and extended to consultation over catalog offerings and the exchange of books and information about the policies of their respective libraries. Their relationship grew into a personal friendship with meetings in New York, Cincinnati, and most significantly, on the Jersey shore. Oko proved instrumental in helping Marx's brother Moses in securing both a job opportunity at HUC and a visa to enter the United States from Germany in 1926. Although Oko's arrogance and irascibility did not make him personally popular at HUC, his correspondence and friendship with Alexander Marx were marked by great cordiality and mutual respect.[57]

The generosity and camaraderie prevailing in this period may be best exemplified by an exchange between the two presidents on the occasion of an event that might have given rise to institutional hostility. In 1928 Julius Rosenwald had provided a vital pledge of $500,000 to the Hebrew Union College that became the cornerstone of a $4 million campaign that was completed in July 1929.[58] When Rosenwald helped funnel a generous pledge to the Jewish Theological Seminary in 1929 and appeared to be about to offer the Seminary a huge contribution in a scheme very similar to that which he had offered HUC, Cyrus Adler wrote to thank Morgenstern for "your very generous letter" written to Rosenwald expressing approbation for both the work of the Seminary and Rosenwald's gift to it. Adler assured Morgenstern that he too had disinterestedly taken occasion to speak positively of the other's school to a crucial audience of potential donors: "I had the pleasure of recommending the Hebrew Union College at a meeting some four or five months ago held at Judge Sterns's house, at which Mr. Ochs [publisher of the *New York Times* and chairman of HUC's endowment campaign] was the principal speaker." This, Adler assured his colleague was "as it should be. The things that divide us are by no means so considerable as the things that unite us."[59] Morgenstern responded in kind, celebrating the "close and cordial" relations that enabled each to "rejoice in the good fortune and progress of the other and lend what assistance we can in furthering the welfare of both institutions."[60]

There *were* limits to the celebration of mutuality. In 1926 the Hebrew Union College publicized a summer school course through which ordained rabbis could pursue the degree of "Doctor of Divinity." Cyrus Adler wrote cautiously to Morgenstern indicating the discomfort of the JTS faculty at the idea that their ordainees "should be encouraged to seek a Doctor of Divinity degree at the Hebrew Union College rather than a Doctor of Hebrew Literature degree at the Seminary." Adler indicated that friendly coexistence required the respect of certain crucial boundaries: "I think you will see my point. . . . I am sure you know that . . . I want to encourage in every way our present friendly relations and not take a step that might result in difficulties or criticism." Morgenstern responded that no one at HUC wished to "go contrary to your wishes or your judgement of what is for the best interests of your own men." He sought to assure his colleague that the College had only meant to serve those Seminary graduates who might "spontaneously desire this."[61]

The general smoothing of the Seminary's relationship with the institutions of Reform Judaism was somewhat complicated in 1922 when Stephen S. Wise founded a second rabbinical school for the training of progressive American rabbis. Although Wise assured one donor in 1924 that the Jewish Institute of Religion (JIR) was not intended "to compete with or rival the work of the Hebrew Union College or the Jewish Theological Seminary but to complement them," the Institute's Reform orientation and its New York locale inevitably brought it into potential conflict with both of the other schools.[62]

Wise, anxious to have his school acknowledged as a legitimate purveyor of rabbinical authority and training, was particularly sensitive to what he perceived as slights directed at both him and his institution. For instance, Wise believed that the Seminary, as the older New York school, owed its junior colleague every courtesy. Thus, he rather brazenly addressed Alexander Marx, the Seminary's librarian with thanks for presumably being "ready to place the facilities of the library of the Jewish Theological Seminary at the command of the members of the teaching staff and student body of the Jewish Institute of Religion." Marx responded with some haughtiness that while he may have granted library privileges to JIR's visiting European professor, Ismar Elbogen, "no statement has been authorized that the library was at the command of the teaching staff and student body of any other institution."[63]

Personal and institutional conflicts continued to muddy the relationship between the two schools for some time. Although the JIR offered honorary degrees to Professor Louis Ginzberg and to Solomon Stroock, chairman of the Seminary's Board of Directors, and invited Seminary faculty to speak at what Wise termed "important meetings of the Institute," Wise felt that these expressions of respect were not reciprocated. In Wise's view, the Seminary willfully snubbed the Institute on frequent occasions when they invited evident "second and third raters" to partici-pate in Seminary events rather than eminently qualified participants from the Insti-tute. As Wise observed privately, "It is really too insulting to be borne without com-plaint."[64] For Wise, the definitive moment in his relationship with JTS came when Louis Finkelstein, then assistant to the Seminary's president, led an effort to prevent Rabbi Wise from serving as president of the Zionist Organization of America in 1936. When Finkelstein became president of the Seminary in 1940, Wise adamantly refused to send a congratulatory message, citing the many slights of the past and "the avowed hostility of the J.T.S. to the JIR."[65] From the other side, the Seminary's view towards the Institute might be captured in Finkelstein's comment upon a Sab-bath event presided over by a JIR rabbi which included athletic games: "One never knows with these graduates of the Institute of Religion, just what they want."[66]

One intriguing connection between the different seminaries in this period was their shared interest in Mordecai Kaplan, professor of homiletics at JTS and found-ing director of its Teachers Institute. Occupying the left wing of the Seminary's ideological spectrum, Kaplan brought his students into critical engagement with the dilemmas of modern thought and of contemporary Jewish life. While this posi-tion often alienated him from other faculty members and the administration at the Seminary, it also made him attractive to those who might otherwise have been put off by Kaplan's traditional attitude towards questions of ritual observance.

In 1922, 1923, and 1927, Kaplan engaged in extended discussions with Stephen Wise about the possibility of leaving the Seminary for a post at the Institute as a potential heir to his vision of a progressive and Zionist American Judaism. Kaplan was vitally attracted by the idea that a position at JIR "might emancipate me for the larger life and the greater contribution that I might make to the cause of Judaism."[67] In 1927 he actually submitted his resignation to Adler with the intention of moving to Wise's Institute. Although Wise was willing to hire Kaplan away from the Semi-nary, he was concerned that the Institute not appear to be taking professors away from "other Jewish Theological Seminaries." Thus, the JIR leaders determined to wait until Kaplan's resignation was accepted before officially inviting him to take a post at the Institute.[68] Once confronted with the combined pleas of the teachers at the Teachers Institute, present and past Seminary students, the executive commit-tee of the Rabbinical Assembly, and the Seminary's president, however, Kaplan was unable to hold to his resolve and agreed to stay at the Seminary.[69]

Kaplan's liminal ideological status was further elaborated in 1925 when he enter-tained advances from Julian Morgenstern about a possible appointment at Hebrew Union College with the thought that the College might provide "a more congenial atmosphere" for his "views on Judaism" than the Seminary had proven to be.[70] Ultimately, Morgenstern apparently concluded that Kaplan's intense Jewish nationalism would not fit well into the HUC environment. Although one of

Kaplan's objections to the situation at the Seminary was his perception of its growing "tendency to identify itself with Orthodoxy," some of his hesitation about leaving seemed to arise from fears that he might come to feel more alienated Jewishly were he to move elsewhere.[71] Although Kaplan had hoped that HUC might prove a refuge from the "spiritually stifling environment of the Seminary," he too concluded that as isolated as he felt at the Seminary he would feel "even more alone and unhappy in the Hebrew Union College." When he rejected Wise's overtures in 1923, Kaplan reflected upon "how often I would have had many of deeply rooted Jewish habits [*sic*] jarred by the class of people with whom I would have to associate, if I were to have joined Wise's Institute."[72] Kaplan's encounters with the Reform seminaries thus highlighted the extent to which perceptions of the difference between JTS and the other schools seemed to be concentrated in distinctive approaches to Jewish observance. Many potential and active rabbinical students who felt torn between the religious and ideological positions represented by the various schools often came to Kaplan for advice.[73] In 1923 he recorded the case of one potential applicant who had told a JTS professor that although he was not currently "observant of the ceremonies," he was willing to become so. As the student related it to Kaplan, the professor then contemptuously dismissed the candidate with the observation "that he ought to have applied rather to the Hebrew Union College."[74]

The strain on resources that came with the Great Depression forced all the schools to reassess their own missions and their relationships to each other. In June 1930 representatives of the Jewish Institute of Religion, Hebrew Union College, and Jewish Theological Seminary met in New York to consider the novel situation caused by the depression, of the "over-production of Rabbis." Pressed into cooperative consultation by grim economic realities, the schools undertook no formal action but did agree that efforts should be made to limit class size.[75] In 1933, Julian Morgenstern reported that by raising standards for admission and winnowing weaker students, HUC had decreased enrollment by nearly 50 percent. He thus informed his colleagues that "the Hebrew Union College has adhered strictly to the understanding" which had been reached at the 1930 conference and sought further avenues "by which our three seminaries, either singly or in cooperation, might deal with this difficult and unhappy situation even more systematically and more constructively." Louis Finkelstein as registrar of JTS reported to Morgenstern that in accordance with the consensus of the conference, the Seminary had raised its entry requirements and thus reduced its own entering classes by two-thirds.[76]

In taking such actions, none of the schools could afford to act alone. If one school limited its size but the other schools expanded to absorb students who might have gone elsewhere, an institution might succeed only in limiting its own influence without addressing the broader problem of excess rabbis. Financial constraint forced a recognition that, despite distinctive ideological and religious stances, the

Julian Morgen-
stern (left) receiv-
ing an honorary
doctorate from
Cyrus Adler at the
Seminary, 1937.
*Ratner Center,
JTS.*

different schools were engaged in the common project of training non-Orthodox rabbis to serve a population of American and Americanizing Jews. In determining the basic framework of rabbinical education, no school could afford to move out of step with the others. Thus Finkelstein suggested the possibility that "each of the Seminaries lengthen their training in the practical work of the ministry" so that the total post-B.A. course would be increased to five years. Finkelstein reported that the Seminary faculty had already approved such a course "provided it is accepted by the other two institutions."

For the most part, the tensions of the depression and the subsequent approach of World War II pushed the different seminaries to focus upon their own internal financial and ideological concerns. They did, however, recognize that the Nazi accession to power in Germany, by threatening the careers and lives of numerous Jewish scholars, raised questions of concern to them all. Given the limited ability of these small and financially challenged schools to aid the many eminent scholars at risk, the leaders of America's institutions of Jewish learning often consulted with each other out of a sense of shared responsibility to find refuge for the various scholars who came to their attention.[77]

To Julian Morgenstern of HUC, who pushed his school to take the most prominent role among the American rabbinical seminaries in the effort to secure visas, safe passage, and jobs for as many scholars as possible, it was clear that efforts on behalf of these scholars could not be carried on unilaterally. In a tentative 1934 letter to Cyrus Adler, Morgenstern broached what he termed "a rather delicate matter." Dr. Julius Lewy was one of the many Jewish academicians who had lost his German university post when Hitler came to power in 1933. Lewy, an Assyriologist, came to the United States in 1934, filling temporary positions at Johns Hopkins University, JTS, and HUC. Morgenstern asked Adler if there was any possibility that the Seminary would employ Lewy on a more permanent basis or whether Adler was making other attempts to find a position for him. As Morgenstern pointed out, the task of aiding scholars like Lewy demanded institutional cooperation: "We must not work at cross-purposes . . . [or] in conflict with each other."[78] Much of the difficulty involved in aiding European scholars and students involved sensitive questions of scarce institutional resources. As more cases arose, the leaders of the different schools continued to consult each other, alerting each other to those in need, reporting on their own efforts, and frankly sharing their concerns about the difficulties of expending precious funds and positions on German Jews when they worried that they were not adequately serving American needs.[79]

The most successful cooperative effort of the three seminaries in relation to the refugee scholars was put forth for Ismar Elbogen, described by the interested American parties as "the foremost Jewish scholar in Germany." At the end of 1937 Elbogen was invited jointly by the "Seminary, the Hebrew Union College, the Jewish Institute of Religion, and the Dropsie College, to a research professorship in this country." Since the schools could not negotiate a fair way to divide the scholar's services, it was determined that each institution would provide Elbogen with $1000 a year while he would be left free to "carry on research."[80] Although the invitation was from all four schools, Cyrus Adler pointed out that "it would be an anomalous situation for four institutions to invite a man to come over." He suggested that "the Hebrew Union College, which is the oldest of our institutions and which took the initiative," should tender the invitation, "joined by" the other institutions.[81] The cooperative spirit of the invitation was somewhat disturbed by Stephen Wise's desire to have Elbogen give a course at JIR. Cyrus Adler pointed out that such a request might propel Elbogen into an unsatisfying career as "a peripatetic teacher in three cities of this country." Ultimately Elbogen was allowed to pursue his research with little practical obligations to his sponsors.[82]

In the midst of great events in the world beyond and involvement with their own institutional concerns, ideological rivalry between the different institutions remained on the back burner. In 1937, Julian Morgenstern was presented an honorary degree by JTS and marked the occasion with an address to the Rabbinical

Assembly. Morgenstern used the opportunity to humorously belittle the significance of differences between Reform and Conservative expressions of Judaism while he eloquently emphasized the shared purpose of the two movements.[83] Even Stephen Wise mellowed somewhat in his aversion to the Seminary. Although he maintained his criticism and wariness, he did acknowledge privately, after Finkelstein sponsored a luncheon celebration at the Seminary in honor of Wise's seventieth birthday, that Finkelstein was "acting very decently toward me."[84] Meanwhile JIR faculty members living on New York's Upper West Side developed neighborly and collegial relationships with their counterparts on the JTS faculty.[85]

In the years after the war, HUC and JTS continued to approach each other without hostility. Potential sources of conflict like the defection to JTS of Abraham Joshua Heschel, one of the scholars who came to Cincinnati to escape the long arm of the Nazis, seemed to cause little resentment. Heschel, who was committed to an observant Jewish life, had not found a comfortable environment in Cincinnati. His transfer seems to have been understood as a move that made sense for him rather than as an assault on the integrity or viability of the College. There is, for instance, no extant evidence of the kind of turmoil and vituperation that accompanied Kaplan's aborted defection to JIR.[86] Similarly Professor Shalom Spiegel's transfer from JIR to JTS in 1943 seemingly occurred without incident.[87]

In recognition of HUC's extraordinary efforts on behalf of German refugee scholars, JTS in 1946 asked Morgenstern in his capacity as president of the College to accept an expression of appreciation "for the exemplary and generous action you took in helping to save so large a number of eminent Jewish scholars from persecution and danger of death during the Nazi persecutions." Although Morgenstern professed his hesitation at accepting "any further distinction or tribute from the Jewish Theological Seminary," he accepted the citation "as the representative of the Hebrew Union College" and used the occasion to express the hope for even closer relations between the two schools "based upon the principle of complete mutuality and good will in our common endeavor."[88]

The language that Morgenstern used to describe the relationship between the two schools reflected the analysis that Will Herberg would use in *Protestant, Catholic, Jew* to capture the religious ethos of the United States during the 1950s. In this context, school and denominational loyalties could at times be subsumed in the larger goal of the strengthening of an American Judaism. For example, in 1947 Eric Werner, one of the refugee scholars brought over by HUC, turned to Morgenstern for support for his campaign to establish a school that would train cantors for American synagogues while preserving the European traditions of *hazzanut* that had been decimated by the Holocaust. Werner emphasized that the plan being pushed by the nondenominational Society for the Advancement of Jewish Liturgical Music was receiving support from cantors and musicians across the Jewish religious spec-

THE HEBREW UNION COLLEGE

CINCINNATI, OHIO

May 29, 45

Dear Professor Finkelstein:

    I wish to acknowledge the receipt of your letter of May 24 and to accept herewith the invitation to join the faculty of the Jewish Theological Seminary.

    In accepting this great task and high distinction I am fully aware of the responsibility it implies. יהי רצון שלא יארע דבר תקלה על ידי.

    I thank you from the bottom of my heart.

Cordially yours,

Abraham Heschel

Abraham Joshua
Heschel was at
Hebrew Union
College when he
wrote this letter to
Louis Finkelstein
accepting the
Seminary's invita-
tion to join its fac-
ulty. *Ratner Center,
JTS.*

Heschel lecturing
at the Seminary
soon after his
arrival in 1945.
*Photo by Virginia
F. Stern. Ratner
Center, JTS.*

trum. Although Morgenstern pointed out that America's existing rabbinical seminaries had "not reached that stage of mutual understanding and cooperation which would permit" them to cooperate in founding such an institution, he expressed an extraordinarily expansive view of the shared interests of America's religious Jewish community. He informed Werner that if, at a future date, the College was asked to take on sole sponsorship of such a school, it would not be conducted in the interests of "the so-called Reform Movement specifically, but rather . . . for . . . that positive all-embracing American Judaism towards which we seem to be trending [*sic*]."

The belief that everyone's best interests would be realized by working together towards a common goal was, of course, not always realized in practice. In planning his school, Werner, for instance, informed Morgenstern that although Yeshiva University was supportive of the plan, JTS "and its affiliated organization, the Rabbinical Assembly" were the only important groups not represented in planning sessions for the new school. Their absence was attributed by a Conservative rabbi present to "institutional jealousy." The School of Sacred Music, directed by Eric Werner, was successfully inaugurated under the auspices of HUC-JIR in 1951. Not surprisingly, perhaps, the Seminary opened a cantorial school of its own in 1952.[89]

On a practical level, HUC's librarian might do his best to "facilitate the usage of our library for graduates of the Jewish Theological Seminary," but tensions arose when the two schools attempted to work together more formally.[90] In 1945 the plans for the Seminary-sponsored Jewish Museum in New York called for the display of a valuable collection of artifacts owned by HUC that had been in storage. Given that the "Seminary has the facilities for exhibiting this collection in a most desirable way" and that "exhibition of the Hebrew Union College collection could not fail to be helpful to the interest of the college," the planners hoped for a cooperative arrangement that "would surely constitute an important service to the community as a whole." Morgenstern's response to frequent renegotiations of the terms of the joint venture was one of annoyance and concern over whether the result might "subordinat[e] the position of the Hebrew Union College in relation to the Seminary."[91]

In terms of formal recognition of each other's achievements, the exchange of honors among the different seminaries was never a fully reciprocal one. Although the schools did eventually honor each other's presidents with honorary degrees, recognition of other representatives of the various schools was offered on a much more limited basis. HUC and JIR were generous in their recognition of individuals from the Conservative seminary, particularly when compared to the Seminary's stinginess towards those from Reform institutions. In addition to the honorary degrees from Wise's Institute to Seminary faculty mentioned above, Hebrew Union College's honorary recognition of Seminary representatives included Louis Finkelstein in 1922, Louis Ginzberg in 1944, Alexander Marx in 1945, and Mordecai Kaplan in 1950.[92] These degrees presumably demonstrated the College's commitment to the sentiment that the two schools were indeed involved in a common endeavor.

In Cincinnati to receive his degree, Kaplan addressed this theme before a gathering of Reform rabbis to whom he declared that he "felt truly at home among them because of our common striving to establish a permanent future for Judaism in America." At the same time, in his diary he recorded his impression that many Reform leaders seemed to view their movement "with a sense of partisan insecurity and rivalry." On this visit and in 1948 when he served as the Seminary's representative to the inauguration of Nelson Glueck as HUC's new president, Kaplan carefully noted the ways in which the HUC environment seemed both similar to and different from his own. He was, for instance, surprised by Glueck's declaration that "I am a son of Cincinnati and I am a son of Jerusalem," observing that it took "considerable courage for a man as head of Hebrew Union College" to express himself in that fashion. He took note that picture taking preceded the Sabbath morning services and that on Saturday afternoon "here and there some one was smoking," but also that "many more would have smoked, if it weren't for the Sabbath."[93]

The relationship between HUC and JTS was redefined, geographically at least, at the beginning of Glueck's presidency when the Cincinnati school entered into a merger with Wise's Jewish Institute of Religion. Despite the desire of Glueck and the board to make the once independent New York school into a two-year preparatory school for the Cincinnati campus, resistance from Reform Jews in New York prevented the realization of the plan. Rabbi Louis Newman's defiant founding of a progressive rabbinical school of his own underscored the message that New York's expanding Reform constituency would not be left without an ordaining Reform seminary of its own. If HUC-JIR was to desert New York symbolically, critics made it clear that the field would be lost either to a new Reform-oriented school or, presumably in a reference to JTS, to "another aggressive movement in Jewish religious life."[94] The preservation of the JIR campus as a full rabbinical school within the new HUC-JIR represented a significant victory for Reform leaders in New York and brought the two oldest rabbinical seminaries in America onto the same turf.[95]

Finkelstein had welcomed Glueck as his presidential colleague with a statement of appreciation for his personal qualities and a reemphasis of the now familiar understanding of the connection between the two schools. Those at the Seminary were gratified, he wrote, "that the ties which have bound the College and the Seminary, making both institutions more effective instruments for the advancement of Jewish learning, will be continued during the future years." Early in 1950, Finkelstein expressed his dissatisfaction to Glueck about a gathering they had attended together, where they had been "placed at opposite ends of the table" and referred to as "competitors." Finkelstein suggested that the two men meet to talk about "ways we could dramatize our real cooperation so as to exorcize this particular devil." Glueck reported that he too reacted "negatively to the idea of any 'competition' between us or our institutions" and rejected competition as a viable basis of coexistence: "I said to someone recently: 'The more properly qualified institutions and people there are devoted to Judaism, the better for all of us.'"[96]

Since Glueck took little interest in the New York campus of the reorganized HUC-JIR, official relations between HUC and JTS remained grounded in Cincinnati and New York. Ironically, this geographic separation made it easier for Finkelstein to remain friends with Glueck than it had been for him to maintain a regular relationship with Stephen Wise. Finkelstein actively sought consultation and cooperation with Glueck. Thus on a number of occasions he invited his Reform counterpart to meet unofficially to explore areas of common concern. In 1959 Finkelstein noted to Glueck his feeling that it was "a pity that you and I who have been friends for so many years, meet so rarely." He suggested that the two of them get together with Samuel Belkin, president of Yeshiva University, "in a very private manner quite off the record simply to get to know one another better." Glueck heartily entered into the suggestion.[97]

Little practical cooperation emerged from such expressions of cordiality. On one occasion, they did explore the possibility of "a joint approach to one of the great foundations" to procure money to support "the secular parts" (such as the libraries) of their institutions. This initiative did not prove successful.[98] In 1960, Mordecai Kaplan convened a sort of spiritual summit of America's non-Orthodox Jewish leadership in an effort to consider the status of America's Jews. Glueck attended through Finkelstein's invitation, but Kaplan observed that Glueck "was repelled" by his idea that adult Jews go through a ritual of commitment to Judaism. Despite his success in bringing so many influential men together, Kaplan ultimately concluded that "with Jewish leaders of the kind that took part in that informal conference, there is no likelihood of their ever aiming at, to say nothing of achieving, a meeting of minds on the problem of Jewish unity and peoplehood."[99]

Although the leaders of the two seminaries may have emphasized the spirit of cooperation publicly and to each other, the expansionist tendencies of the schools and of their movements in the postwar period unavoidably created situations in which rivalry rather than cooperation dominated the formation of policy and programs. Just as rivalry between the two schools played a powerful role in the preservation of an ordaining Reform rabbinical seminary and the creation of a Conservative school for Jewish music in New York, Reform-Conservative competition for the Jewish laity was the driving force in bringing about the creation of California branches for both JTS and HUC-JIR.[100] Although local Conservative and Reform rabbis appeared willing to jointly create an institution that could offer an education in general Judaica to the Jews of Los Angeles, and although Mordecai Kaplan hoped that the University of Judaism (UJ) might offer access to Jewish civilization to all Jews, the JTS sponsors of the Los Angeles school hoped to create a bastion of Conservative Judaism in this emerging center of Jewish population on the West Coast. Simon Greenberg, provost of JTS, pushed for the creation of the University of Judaism in 1947 in an attempt to provide access to advanced Jewish education for Los Angeles's Jews and "to broaden the scope of the influence of [the Conservative] movement." As Greenberg pointed out, while the name of the school may have suggested that it "was a *Klal Yisrael* program [intended for the entire Jewish community] . . . everybody recognized that the institution was being backed by the Seminary.[101]

Although the Reform rabbis in Los Angeles felt that they needed to offset the UJ's educational outreach with a program of their own, they were initially unable to interest Glueck in their project. They turned to the Union of American Congregations, the congregational arm of the Reform movement, instead of HUC, for institutional sponsorship of their new College of Jewish Studies. Within a year, Glueck agreed to join in sponsorship and supervision of the new school, but contributed no financial support to the program until 1954.[102] Institutional rivalry soon pushed the two schools to expand their offerings beyond the glorified adult education classes that made up their initial curriculums. The progress of the Reform movement's "California School" was linked to pressure generated by the position of the UJ. In the early 1950s, Isaiah Zeldin, who was running the Reform "College of Hebrew Studies," argued that if HUC-JIR would introduce a rabbinical department at the Los Angeles school, the Reform institution could make a compelling claim on the generosity of the many members of Reform congregations who were important contributors to the University of Judaism.[103] A separate building outside of the existing synagogues became necessary in an effort to secure the benefits of academic accreditation enjoyed by the UJ. Intensive continuing rivalry between the two California branches of America's eastern religious seminaries in these years, however, was forestalled by Glueck's lack of interest. His dream of a Reform movement that would be grounded in Cincinnati and Jerusalem defused institutional competition in Los Angeles.

The appointments of Alfred Gottschalk as president of HUC-JIR and of Gerson Cohen as chancellor of the Seminary again raised the possibility that goodwill between the leaders of the two institutions would result in the realization of what Gottschalk shortly after his installation in 1972 hoped would be "a fuller and more far-reaching relationship between our two institutions." Again an HUC president articulated his belief that both institutions shared the "same orbit of concerns and interests," this time identified as "the upbuilding of Jewish life in the Diaspora and in Israel."[104]

Official relations between Gottschalk and Cohen began inauspiciously. Owing perhaps to "snafus" attendant upon the Seminary's own transition of power, no one from the Seminary was present at Gottschalk's inauguration. Thus, the usual statements of common purpose that were requisite upon changes in institutional leadership waited a few months until Gerson Cohen in a letter to Gottschalk expressed his distress at his absence from "what I think was a historic occasion and one of deep religious significance for all Jewry" and determined "to make amends somehow on behalf of myself and of our movement." Cohen hoped that the unfortunate "slight to your honor (which was, I believe, an indignity to ourselves) will serve as the catalyst and stimulus for greater cooperation than ever obtained before." Cohen earnestly stated his hope that the new presidents would "work much more closely than . . . some of our predecessors did." To attest to the sincerity of his desire "to begin a new chapter," he assured Gottschalk "that I will come to see you anywhere, any time so that we can begin to talk seriously about areas of joint interest to us" and, in an evident plea for atonement, noted "since I have never visited the Hebrew Union College in Cincinnati, I would be glad to make a trip out there."[105]

In response, Gottschalk regretted the "blatantly obvious" absence of the Seminary and its "attendant embarrassment," but assured Cohen that he did not "take this matter personally" and expressed his own openness to discussions of cooperative ventures. He specifically suggested that since both schools were working toward a compulsory year of study in Israel, they might work on "a number of joint approaches that could be developed toward our common problems in Israel."[106] Cohen did follow through with his symbolically charged offer, visiting Cincinnati for one day in May 1973, at which time he delivered a talk on "The Quest for Structure in Jewish History" and enjoyed "a very nice luncheon" that was ordered with great care. The Cincinnati dean, perhaps thinking of the divisive results of *trefa* banquets of the past, carefully instructed that "because Dr. Cohen represents Conservative Judaism, it would be most appropriate if you arrange that the luncheon be *milchik*." Suggesting a menu of cold fish, cheese, and salad, he instructed that the final menu should be cleared with him.[107]

Gottschalk and Cohen both valued the idea of cooperative pluralism. Despite carefully monitoring the directions in which the other school was choosing to expand both geographically and programmatically, the two leaders chose not to contest or challenge each other on ideological grounds. Gottschalk even suggested to Finkelstein, JTS's retired president, that if Solomon Schechter had the opportunity "to look at the College and what it represents today" he might not have felt it necessary to characterize the two schools as opponents. Abraham Joshua Heschel, according to Gottschalk, on the occasion of receiving an honorary degree from HUC-JIR, had observed that "were he at the College today he would have found no need to leave it." Gottschalk's point was not that the College-Institute had become identical to the Seminary but that the prevailing "tolerance for difference" in American Jewish life made each institution better able to appreciate the contributions of the other. Finkelstein echoed this sentiment acknowledging that "even those who do not agree with some of the [College's] views . . . have to admire its achievements."[108] In 1977, Gottschalk went so far as to observe of the way Gerson Cohen had defined Conservative Judaism to the United Synagogue: "It is exactly the way in which I have defined Reform Judaism."[109]

Gottschalk, enjoying a much more mobile presidency than his predecessors, spent time at all of the College-Institute's campuses. Although Gottschalk offered a formal academic presentation to the JTS faculty only once, his frequent visits to New York afforded him the opportunity to deepen his acquaintance with Cohen.[110] The most striking example of formal cooperation between Gottschalk and Cohen echoed the efforts promoted by Mordecai Kaplan in 1960 and by Morgenstern and Adler in 1922 to try to address the problematic state of Jewish education. In these earlier efforts seminary leaders had acted out of their perceptions that they bore some responsibility to bring order to the chaotic system of Jewish education in the United States. In 1978 Gottschalk and Cohen joined with Moshe Davis, who had previously served as a dean at the Seminary, in gathering leaders in higher Jewish education to create the International Center for University Teaching of Jewish Civilization. Meeting in New York at JTS and at the HUC-JIR campus in Cincinnati, as well as in Jerusalem, this elite group hoped to establish standards, guidelines, and resources to serve and oversee the numerous Jewish Studies programs that seemed to be proliferating throughout the world. This effort represented a recognition that the academic study of Judaism had moved beyond the bounds of the rabbinical seminary and a few university programs along with the hope that these older centers might continue to exercise oversight over less established programs. Those who attended the meetings of this group in New York and Cincinnati remarked upon their historically "unprecedented" effort in bringing together such a wide range of leaders from secular and religious institutions to address questions of "Jewish curriculum."[111]

The ability of the Reform and Conservative leaders to work together in this and other endeavors emerged from Gerson Cohen's conviction that it was time for the Conservative movement to stop deferring to the Orthodox. As Conservative Judaism focused on establishing its own institutions, it could better afford to cooperate with those representing Reform.[112] This attitude was reflected most saliently in Cohen's push towards the ordination of women at the Seminary, an important symbolic rejection of those who insisted that such a move would distance Conservative Judaism from the Jewish community as defined by the Orthodox, while accepting practices already identified with the Reform movement. In this effort, Cohen's warm relationship with Gottschalk provided him with both a consultant and confidant.[113]

While the leaders of JTS and HUC-JIR during the seventies and early eighties did not contest each other on ideological grounds and did much to advance cooperation, they could not wholly ignore the fact that they remained institutional rivals. In Israel, in California, in New York, each school had to be sensitive to the new initiatives, the programs, and the successes of the other. The decisions of the one inevitably affected the direction of the others. This was particularly the case in Israel where the schools faced the common problem of hostility from the nation's Orthodox religious establishment, but where each wanted to win turf for its own version of progressive Judaism.[114]

In 1977, Gottschalk questioned whether an adult education program that the University of Judaism in California was planning "with several reform and conservative congregations . . . overstepped the boundaries of an agreement . . . that we would not encroach institutionally on the preserves of our respective Movements." Gottschalk expressed his feeling that it would be best to avoid "this kind of competition since unquestionably the Hebrew Union College, Yeshiva University and other interested institutions would feel obliged to do likewise." Gottschalk, whose previous job had been as dean of the HUC-JIR Los Angeles campus, asked that before UJ solicited Reform congregations to support the proposed project, its leaders "consider the future effect upon the cooperation that exists between our institutions and the understanding that we so painfully arrived at so many years ago."[115]

A change of leadership at JTS and the changing emphases in trends of Jewish observance in the United States and in Israel brought many implicit understandings between HUC-JIR and JTS into question and complicated the relationship between the heirs of Schechter and Kohler. Gerson Cohen's administration ended with an exchange of presidential honorary degrees and affirmations of the "cooperation and respect which exist between our two seminaries" by Gerson Cohen. Celebration of the Seminary's centennial was marked by a declaration of "the common liberal heritage and vision of Jewish pluralism which our two institutions share" from HUC.[116] The inauguration of Ismar Schorsch as chancellor of JTS, however, reframed the relationship between the two schools with new, if familiar, tensions.

Gottschalk responded with some alarm to an account of an interview with the new JTS chancellor that appeared in *The Jerusalem Post* at the end of 1986. Gottschalk responded negatively to Schorsch's "haughty and unbecoming" dismissal of HUC-JIR's Jerusalem school as a "magnificent structure . . . yet to be filled with substance." In addition, Gottschalk took offense at Schorsch's efforts to distinguish the Conservative movement from the Reform by denigrating positions of the Reform movement on patrilineal descent and rabbinical officiation at intermarriages. Gottschalk's central concern seemed to be that instead of continuing "the period of nonpolemic confrontation in the press" that he had worked out

Gerson Cohen (right) receiving an honorary doctorate from Alfred Gottschalk (left) as Richard Scheuer, chairman of the HUC-JIR Board of Governors looks on, 1985. *Ratner Center, JTS.*

together with Gerson Cohen, Schorsch seemed to be intent upon "tear[ing] down what others have pioneered."

In response, Schorsch informed Gottschalk that as the question of the relationship between the Conservative and Reform movements "came up time and again" while he was in Israel, "the intent of my remarks throughout was to distinguish sharply between our two camps." Although Schorsch agreed that in Israel the two movements faced a "common adversary," he asserted that "there is no benefit to us to blur the distinctions." He insisted that, despite Gottschalk's hopes that the two movements "could confront in a creative and mutually cooperative way issues that affect our people," the Conservative movement in Israel could not afford to be aligned with a movement that "condones . . . officiating at mixed marriages and endorses" patrilineal descent. According to Schorsch, these positions only proved the case of those Zionists who condemned the "baneful consequences of emancipation." In the Israeli context, Schorsch argued, association with such positions could hamper efforts to convince Israelis to accept Conservatism as a legitimate expression of Judaism.

Schorsch did offer the conciliatory sentiment that "there certainly are issues of transcending importance to the Jewish community that need our joint efforts" and expressed the hope that "for all our disagreements, we will be able to identify and address them in concert, as did our predecessors." He concluded by pointing to "the relationship of Kohler and Schechter" as a hopeful model: "Conviction often forced them into open controversy, yet deep mutual respect and a common commitment to the cause of Jewish scholarship enabled them to cooperate on projects of value to the entire Jewish community."[117] Gottschalk responded that Kohler and Schechter were indeed "wonderful models," yet in the Kohler tradition, Gottschalk chose to understand their example as one of mutuality and respect for differences towards a shared goal. In the Schechter tradition, Schorsch set out to pursue a course in which Conservative Judaism in America and throughout the world would be defined, in part, by its resistance to encroachments on authentic Judaism accepted or advanced by the Reform movement.

At the end of the 20th century, the multiplicity of Jewish institutions and frameworks for the Jewish religion meant that the leaders of the Hebrew Union College-Jewish Institute of Religion and the Jewish Theological Seminary of America were not as dependent upon each other for self-definition and American Jewish identity as had been the case in the early 20th century. Yet throughout this century, at times of both conflict and cooperation, the "healthy and mutually respectful rivalry" hoped for by one contributor to the 1900 *American Hebrew* symposium has never stopped shaping the program and direction of the two schools themselves or, ultimately, the course of American Judaism of which they have been so vital a part.

1. "One Institution for Rearing Rabbis? Shall Our Theological Colleges Unite, Is it Possible, Is it Desirable? A Symposium," *American Hebrew* 67, no. 2 (25 May 1900): 36–40; 67, no. 3 (1 June 1900): pp. 69–72.

2. Henry S. Morais, letter to the editor, *American Hebrew* 67, no. 4 (8 June 1900): p. 99.

3. Bernard Drachman, "A Symposium," *American Hebrew* 67, no. 3, p. 71.

4. See, e.g., Joseph Jacobs, op. cit., p. 69; Maurice H. Harris, op. cit., p. 71.

5. Louis Marshall, "A Symposium," *American Hebrew* 67, no. 2, p. 40.

6. Jacob Schiff, op. cit., p. 38.

7. Max Heller and Cyrus Adler, "A Symposium," *American Hebrew* 67, no. 3, p. 70.

8. Jacob Schiff, "A Symposium," *American Hebrew* 67, no. 2, p. 37.

9. Alexander Kohut to Solomon Schechter, 28 April 1892, Jewish Theological Seminary Archives, New York, Collection 101, Solomon Schechter Papers, box 3.

10. Jonathan D. Sarna, *JPS, The Americanization of Jewish Culture, 1888–1988* (Philadelphia: Jewish Publication Society, 1989), p. 60.

11. Howard Allen Berman, "His Majesty's Loyal Opponents: A Comparative Study of the Presidencies of Kaufmann Kohler and Solomon Schechter," (Rabbinic thesis, Hebrew Union College—Jewish Institute of Religion, 1974), pp. 16–17.

12. Michael A. Meyer, "A Centennial History," in *Hebrew Union College-Jewish Institute of Religion at One Hundred Years,* ed. Samuel E. Karff (Cincinnati: Hebrew Union College Press, 1976), p. 53.

13. Bernhard Bettmann to Kaufmann Kohler, 10 February 1903, American Jewish Archives, Cincinnati, Manuscript Collection 29, Kohler Papers, box 1/1.

14. Kaufmann Kohler to Bernhard Bettmann, 13 February 1903, Kohler Papers, box 1/1.

15. Jacob H. Schiff to Kaufmann Kohler, 15 June 1903, Kohler Papers, box 1/4.

16. Kaufmann Kohler, quoted in Berman, "Loyal Opponents," p. 56.

17. Solomon Schechter to Cyrus Adler, 26 March 1902, Solomon Schechter Papers, box 1.

18. Solomon Schechter, quoted in Berman, "Loyal Opponents," p. 121, from Bernard Mandelbaum, *The Wisdom of Solomon Schechter.*

19. Kaufmann Kohler to Solomon Schechter, 7 October 1903, Schechter Papers, box 3.

20. Berman, "Loyal Opponents," p. 40.

21. Solomon Schechter, "Higher Criticism—Higher Anti-Semitism," in *Seminary Addresses and Other Papers* (Cincinnati: Ark Publishing Co., 1915), p. 38.

22. Solomon Schechter to Max Heller, 4 November 1904, American Jewish Archives, Manuscript Collection 33, Maximilian H. Heller Papers, box 5/5.

23. Solomon Schechter to Mayer Sulzberger, 4 October 1904, Schechter Papers, box 6.

24. Solomon Schechter to Max Heller, 1 February 1907, Heller Papers, box 5/5.

25. Solomon Schechter to Max Heller, 21 July 1907, Heller Papers, box 5/5.

26. Max Margolis to Solomon Schechter, Passover 1907, Schechter Papers, box 4.

27. Solomon Schechter to Max Heller, 4 February 1909, Schechter Papers, box 3.

28. Ibid., Solomon Schechter to Max Heller, 19 November 1909, Schechter Papers, box 3.

29. Cyrus Adler to Schechter, 17 February 1910, Schechter Papers, box 1.

30. Cyrus Adler to Solomon Schechter, 7 June 1911, JTS, Cyrus Adler Papers, box 7.

31. Cyrus Adler to Solomon Schechter, 2 August 1911, Adler Papers, box 7.

32. Cyrus Adler to Solomon Schechter, 28 January 1912, Schechter Papers, box 1.

33. *A Historic Jewish Banquet in the City of New York* [tendered to the editors and publishers of the *Jewish Encyclopedia*], (New York: P. Cowen, 1901), p. 15.

34. Meir Ben-Horin, "Solomon Schechter to Judge Mayer Sulzberger, Part II: Letters from the Seminary Period (1902-1925)," *Jewish Social Studies* 27 (April 1965): p. 79.

35. Mayer Sulzberger to Schechter, 2 August 1908, Schechter Papers, box 6.

36. Sarna, *JPS,* p. 109.

37. Adler to Schechter, 20 December 1911, Adler Papers, box 7.

38. Solomon Schechter to Mayer Sulzberger, 14 March 1905, in Ben-Horin, "Schechter to Sulzberger," p. 85.

39. Solomon Schechter, "His Majesty's Opposition," [22 January 1913] in Schechter, *Seminary Addresses*, pp. 239-44.

40. "The Board of Governors of the Hebrew Union College on the Death of Doctor Solomon Schechter," 15 December 1915, Adler Papers, box 1/2.

41. Schechter to Louis Marshall, 23 December 1913, Schechter Papers, box 4. Schechter saw JTS's deprivation in the context of HUC's abundance. Shortly before his death in 1915, frustrated by the Seminary's limited financial resources, Schechter had raged before his faculty about the school's growing inability to attract worthy students: "See what they are doing at Cincinnati. They give each man twice the amount we give. If we can't offer scholarships, we can't have any students." Mordecai Kaplan diary, 18 March 1915, JTS Archives.

42. Quoted in Herbert Parzen, *Architects of Conservative Judaism* (New York: Jonathan David Publishers, 1964), p. 104.

43. Cyrus Adler, "The Standpoint of the Seminary," 1923 address to Rabbinical Assembly, reprinted in *Tradition and Change, the Development of Conservative Judaism* , ed. Mordecai Waxman (New York: Burning Bush Press, 1958), p. 184.

44. Cyrus Adler to Louis Feinberg, 11 January 1926, Adler Papers, box 1-3.

45. Cyrus Adler to Louis Finkelstein, 12 April 1922, Adler Papers, box 1-3.

46. Cyrus Adler to Louis Finkelstein, 26 June 1936, Adler Papers, box 1-3.

47. Israel Friedlaender, "Were Our Ancestors Capable of Self-Government?" (1909) in *Past and Present, Selected Essays* (New York: Burning Bush Press, 1961), p. 48. The author thanks Baila Shargel for this citation.

48. Cyrus Adler, statement, 19 October 1925, JTS General Files, Record Group 1, folder 1A-10-95.

49. "Report of Adler," 15 November 1925, JTS General Files, folder 1A-10-95.

50. Parzen, *Architects of Conservative Judaism*, p. 95.

51. Julian Morgenstern to Cyrus Adler, 29 June 1933, JTS General Files, folder 1A-10-95.

52. Alfred M. Cohen to Cyrus Adler, 30 October 1924, Adler Papers, box 1-2. Shalom Maximon to Israel Davidson, 12 February 1931; JTS General Files; Jacob R. Marcus to registrar, JTS, 20 October 1930; Jacob R. Marcus to Israel Davidson, 25 February 1929; JTS General Files, folder 1A-10-95. Julian Morgenstern to Cyrus Adler, 9 March 1927; Morgenstern to Adler, 3 June 1927; Morgenstern to Adler, 15 February 1928; Adler to Morgenstern, 17 February 1928, American Jewish Archives, Manuscript Collection 5, Hebrew Union College Papers, box A-1/6.

53. Cyrus Adler to Julian Morgenstern, 9 November 1925, JTS General Files, folder 1A-10-95.

54. See Julian Morgenstern to Cyrus Adler: 11 April 1922, 4 May 1922, 8 August 1922, 20 November 1922; Adler to Morgenstern: 21 June 1922, 28 July 1922, 2 August 1922, 22 November 1922, 21 December 1922, 22 December 1922, 29 December 1922. HUC Papers, box A-1/6.

55. Eli Ginzberg, *Keeper of the Law: Louis Ginzberg* (Philadelphia: Jewish Publication Society, 1966), pp. 165–66.

56. Ibid., pp. 270, 274.

57. See Adolph Oko to Alexander Marx: 17 March 1916, 16 May 1923, 14 March 1924, 15 April 1926, 28 December 1926, 2 October 1928; Marx to Oko: 3 June 1918, 30 March 1925, 24 December 1926, filed under "M"[arx] and "J" [TS], American Jewish Archives, HUC Library Letterbooks.

58. Michael A. Meyer, "A Centennial History," in Karff, *Hebrew Union College*, p. 115.

59. Parzen, *Architects of Conservative Judaism*, p. 96; Julian Morgenstern to Cyrus Adler,

7 October 1929, HUC Papers, box A-1/6.

60. Julian Morgenstern to Cyrus Adler, 11 October 1929, HUC Papers, box A-1/6.

61. Cyrus Adler to Julian Morgenstern, 21 April 1926; Morgenstern to Adler, 27 April 1926; JTS Record Group, folder 1A-10-95.

62. Stephen S. Wise to Julius Rosenwald, 20 March 1924, American Jewish Archives, Manuscript Collection 19, Jewish Institute of Religion Papers, 1921-1950, box 31/5.

63. Stephen S. Wise to Alexander Marx, 11 November 1922; Alexander Marx to Stephen W. Wise, 16 November 1922; JIR Papers, box 22/3.

64. Steven S. Wise to Julian Mack, 11 May 1937, JIR Papers, box 22/3.

65. Stephen S. Wise to G[ertrude] A[delstein], 14 May 1940, JIR Papers, box 22/3.

66. Louis Finkelstein to Cyrus Adler, 12 July 1936, Adler Papers, box 1-3.

67. Kaplan diary, 1 May 1922. For Kaplan flirtations with JIR see Kaplan diary, 27 May 1921, 28 March 1922, 27 March 1922, 5 May 1922, 22 May 1922, 30 March 1923, 26 June 1923, 16 July 1923, 20 August 1923, 20 September 1923, 22 September 1923, 12 January 1927, 19 January 1927, 26 January 1927, 10 February 1927, 12 February 1927, 23 February 1927.

68. "Extract from Board of Trustees Meeting," 8 February 1927; Julian Mack to Stephen Wise, 26 January 1927; JIR Papers, box 22/1.

69. Kaplan diary, 26 January 1927, 12 February 1927, 23 February 1927.

70. Kaplan diary, 1 November 1925.

71. Mordecai Kaplan to Cyrus Adler, 31 January 1927, JIR Papers, box 22/1.

72. Kaplan diary, 22 September 1923.

73. See Kaplan diary, 18 October 1922, 7 February 1923, 27 September 1923.

74. Kaplan diary, 27 September 1923.

75. Julian Morgenstern to Cyrus Adler, 29 June 1933, JTS General Files, folder 1A-10-95.

76. Louis Finkelstein to Julian Morgenstern, 11 July 1933, JTS General Files, folder 1A-10-95.

77. For the fullest account of Hebrew Union College's efforts on behalf of German Jewish scholars, see Michael A. Meyer, "The Refugee Scholars Project of the Hebrew Union College," in *A Bicentennial Festschrift for Jacob Rader Marcus*, ed. Bertram Wallace Korn (New York: Ktav Publishing House, 1976), pp. 359-75.

78. Julian Morgenstern to Cyrus Adler, 29 January 1935, HUC Papers, box A-1/6.

79. Julian Morgenstern to Cyrus Adler 16 May 1939, JTS General Files, folder 1A-10-94; Gertrude Adelstein to Louis Finkelstein, 21 June 1938, JTS General Files, folder 1A-12-92; Morgenstern to Finkelstein, 15 June 1938, HUC papers, box A-8/9; Morgenstern to Finkelstein, 14 October 1938, HUC Papers, box A-8/9; Morgenstern to Adler, 13 December 1937, HUC papers, box A-1/6.

80. "Presented at Board Meeting," 20 December 1937, JTS Faculty Record Series B, box 1/3B-1-9.

81. Cyrus Adler to William Rosenau, 29 April 1938, JTS Record Group 1, General Files Series A, folder 1A-10-94.

82. Cyrus Adler to Stephen S. Wise, 15 May 1939. See also Stephen S. Wise to Cyrus Adler, 22 May 1939; Cyrus Adler to Stephen S. Wise, 31 May 1939; Joseph Abrahams to Stephen S. Wise, 5 July 1939, JTS faculty files, box 3B-1-9.

83. Julian Morgenstern, "Greetings," (1937) *Proceedings of the Rabbinical Assembly*, 5, 1939, pp. 355-57.

84. Harry Orlinsky to Louis Finkelstein, 1 April 1944, folder 1B-35-16 (1943-44); Stephen Wise to Henry Slonimsky, 17 May 1945, JIR papers, box 22/3.

85. Alfred Gottschalk, interview by author, 1 February 1996.

86. See, e.g., Heschel's letter of acceptance to Finkelstein, 29 May 1945: "[I] accept herewith the invitation to join the faculty of the Jewish Theological Seminary." JTS Record Group

1 General Files, file 1C-48-48. Despite some objections from the Cincinnati faculty, the New York campus of HUC-JIR presented Heschel with an honorary degree in 1972. Gottschalk, interview.

87. Pamela S. Nadell, *Conservative Judaism in America, A Biographical Dictionary and Source-book* (New York: Greenwood Press, 1988), p. 243.

88. Julian Morgenstern to Louis Finkelstein, 7 March 1946; Morgenstern to Finkelstein, 8 April 1946; Finkelstein to Morgenstern, 28 February 1946. HUC papers, box A-13/1.

89. Eric Werner to Julian Morgenstern, undated [1946]; Werner to Morgenstern, 7 January 1947; Werner to Morgenstern, 22 April 1947; Morgenstern to Werner, 21 April 1947, HUC papers, box 12/22. Elie Schleifer, interview by author, 8 January 1996.

90. Irving M. Levey to Louis Finkelstein, 28 May 1946, JTS General Files, folder 1C-48-39.

91. Alan Stroock to Julian Morgenstern, 12 January 1945; Julian Morgenstern to Alan Stroock, 16 January 1946, JTS General Files, folder 1C-48-39.

92. Seminary recognition of a member of HUC-JIR's faculty with an honorary degree did not occur until 1993 when Jacob Rader Marcus, ninety-seven-year-old elder statesman of HUC-JIR, the Reform movement, and the study of American Jewish history, was so honored.

93. Kaplan diary, 16 March 1948, 15 June 1950.

94. Temple Isaiah Israel of Chicago, "Resolution on the Unification Plan for Hebrew Union College-Jewish Institute of Religion," HUC/JIR, Gottschalk Files [uncatalogued papers], Pre-1973 Correspondence, "Merger" file drawer. Nelson Glueck to Louis I. Newman, 7 May 1948: Trying to placate Newman, Glueck assured him: "I subscribe to everything that you say with regard to the importance of our larger College of Liberal Judaism not yielding the field in New York to the J.T.S. or to any other groups," JIR papers, box 16/9.

95. See Meyer, "Centennial History," pp. 185-90.

96. Nelson Glueck to Louis Finkelstein, 31 January 1950, JTS General Files, folder 1D-59-57.

97. Louis Finkelstein to Nelson Glueck, 12 August 1959; Glueck to Finkelstein, 20 August 1959; JTS General Files, "Nelson Glueck," RG 10-175.

98. Nelson Glueck to Louis Finkelstein; 21 December 1962; Finkelstein to Glueck 27 December 1962. JTS General Files, folder 1R-204-46.

99. Kaplan diary, box 6, v. 20, pp. 112–13; 6 March 1960, 8 March 1960, 16 March 1960, 19 April 1960, pp. 114–17.

100. On the University of Judaism, see *To the Golden Cities, Pursuing the American Jewish Dream in Miami and L. A.* (New York: Free Press, 1994), pp. 129–35; on the HUC-JIR Los Angeles campus, see Meyer, "Centennial History," pp. 190-99. Moore is especially helpful on the relationship between the two schools.

101. Simon Greenberg, quoted in Moore, p. 131.

102. Meyer, "Centennial History," p. 192.

103. Moore, pp. 136–37.

104. Alfred Gottschalk to Gerson Cohen, 16 November 1971, JTS General Files, folder 1AA-278-28.

105. Gerson Cohen to Alfred Gottschalk, 6 March 1972, Gottschalk Files, file drawer: "Prior to July 1973."

106. Alfred Gottschalk to Gerson Cohen, 27 March 1972, Gottschalk Files, "Prior to July, 1973."

107. Kenneth D. Roseman to Ruth Frenkel, 6 April 1973, Gottschalk Files.

108. Alfred Gottschalk to Louis Finkelstein, 26 March 1976; Finkelstein to Gottschalk, 15 March 1976; Gottschalk Files.

109. Alfred Gottschalk to Gerson Cohen, 29 November 1977, Gottschalk Files.

110. Gerson Cohen to Alfred Gottschalk, 7 March 1979; Cohen to Gottschalk, 9 May 1973; Gottschalk to Cohen, 29 November 1977; Cohen to Gottschalk, 5 December 1977; Gottschalk Files. Gottschalk, interview.

111. See "Moshe Davis" file, "1977–78"; "International Program for University Jewish Studies" file, Gottschalk Files.

112. Nadell, *Conservative Judaism*, p. 57.

113. Gerson Cohen to Alfred Gottschalk, 10 April 1979, Gottschalk Files. Gottschalk, interview.

114. See files of both Gottschalk and Cohen for extensive clipping files as well as public relations and curricular material gathered from the other institution. See also Ezra Spicehandler to Alfred Gottschalk, 14 May 1976, "Jewish Theological Seminary" folder, in regard to JTS plan to appoint visiting annual professors at kibbutz college Oranim: "I am simply giving you this information to indicate that in this area JTS has jumped ahead of us." Gottschalk Files.

115. Alfred Gottschalk to David Lieber, 19 July 1977, "1977–78" file, Gottschalk Files.

116. Gerson Cohen to Alfred Gottschalk, 12 September 1985; "Congratulatory Resolution on the Centennial Celebrations of the Jewish Theological Seminary of America," JTS files, 1987–88, Gottschalk Files.

117. David Landau, "Seminary chancellor outlines 'ultimate goal' in Israel," *Jerusalem Post*, 12 December 1986; Alfred Gottschalk to Ismar Schorsch, 30 December 1986; Schorsch to Gottschalk, 13 January 1986[7]; Gottschalk to Schorsch, 28 January 1987; "1987–88, P-Z," Gottschalk Files.

GLENN T. MILLER

Just a Little Different

The Jewish Theological Seminary and Other Forms of American Ministerial Preparation

Union Theological Seminary seen across Broadway through the gate of
Jewish Theological Seminary, 1940s or 1950s. The tower belongs to Riverside Church.
Photo by Carée. Ratner Center, JTS.

GLENN T. MILLER

Just a Little Different

The Jewish Theological Seminary and Other
Forms of American Ministerial Preparation

Hᴏᴡ ᴅᴏᴇꜱ the Jewish Theological Seminary fit into the larger picture of American theological education? An answer to that question is not easily formulated, because American theological schools are a highly diverse group. Often the only things they seem to share are their formal structures. They are places of higher learning with libraries, teachers, and students. Usually, they are organized under the laws of a particular state and have the rights and privileges associated with a legal corporation. With few exceptions, most are small schools serving fewer than five hundred students. Almost all are seriously limited financially, and those fiscal restraints often constrict their educational mission.

Despite their small size, most seminaries are very complex institutions. While their primary mission remains the training of religious leaders, theological schools maintain a number of programs that educate people for a variety of different forms of religious service.[1] Most are conscious of having a dual character. On the one hand, they are schools of a particular religious community or tradition that deliberately seek to serve their sponsoring body. On the other hand, these same schools pride themselves on their relationship to the larger American academic community. Their faculties have the customary academic ranks; the schools provide for academic freedom, and they have the expected academic officers, such as presidents, deans, and registrars. Students often receive federal aid to help cover their educational costs. Faculty members pride themselves on their scholarship and are active in those professional associations related to their academic disciplines. The most influential faculty members are usually those who publish.

In this world of small schools, seminary officials tend to see their institutions as unique. Rarely is this claim justified; yet the Jewish Theological Seminary is truly different from most other schools that train religious leaders. This is not to say that the morphology of the school varies greatly from the seminary norm. Like most seminaries, the Jewish Theological Seminary is small and serves congregations in a particular religious tradition. The State of New York has invested a Board of Directors with the ultimate governance of the school, and the trustees, in turn, have adopted an administrative structure that has a strong President or Chancellor. Further, the school has high academic standards and a brilliant record of intellectual achievement. Despite the losses from a disastrous fire, for instance, the school boasts an excellent library, containing one of the best Judaica collections in the world. The school has high scholarly expectations for both students and members of the faculty. From the beginning, its faculty have published books and articles in their academic specialties.

Like other religious thinkers exposed to the new thought associated with science and the Enlightenment, the teachers at the Jewish Theological Seminary have had to struggle with the effects of modern thought on their community's inherited faith. The meaning of authentic Jewish life has undergone radical social and intellectual change, and JTS has struggled with the meaning of these changes for the school and its academic program.

The understanding of the rabbinate as profession dates back to the emancipation of Central and Eastern European Jews. Like their Protestant neighbors, Jews found that the governments expected their religious leaders to attend universities and to meet the secular standards required by law.[2] The mark of this European professional status was a thorough scholarly knowledge of a religious leader's own religious tradition. Although the Jewish Theological Seminary inherited this understanding of profession, the school replaced parts of this old-world approach with the more characteristically new-world definition of professionalism as "expertise" or "know-how." Especially after the election of Gerson Cohen as Chancellor in 1972, faculty, students, and administrators have shared a common professional language with others who train religious leaders. As in the case of other seminaries, periodic accreditation visits have helped the school understand better ways to perform its task.

At first glance, these points of similarity appear striking enough that one is tempted to advocate a seminary version of Will Herberg's thesis that Protestantism, Catholicism, and Judaism are becoming increasingly similar to each other.[3] The Herberg thesis provides the historian with a convenient story line: Institutions or popular movements begin with a strong, even heightened, sense of their divergence from the more common patterns of their society. Yet, despite these differences, their members yearn to be like their neighbors, and in time, they adopt characteristics of the surrounding culture. In turn, the majority ceases to see them as different. The next step is for the larger society to see them as sharing the same or similar values. Hence Herberg's claim that Americans were no longer as concerned about whether their neighbors were Protestant, Catholic, or Jewish as long as they held to a faith that provided them with moral values.[4] For seminaries, this would mean that

Catholic, Protestant, and Jewish schools had accepted a common ideal of professional training and differed primarily in terms of the specific traditions that informed differing communities.

Yet the more one tries to put the story of the Jewish Theological Seminary into this type of context, the less the school seems to fit comfortably into the larger picture.[5] One reason may be the power of belief and of ideas. Despite the pressures brought by American society on institutions to fit social and cultural norms, many institutions—perhaps more than students of American religion tend to admit—remain doggedly determined to maintain their own identity. Like other seminaries, the Jewish Theological Seminary's morphology enables it to preserve its values. Small, comparatively inexpensive institutions often can afford more cognitive distance than larger, more culturally central institutions enjoy. Curiously, the Jewish Theological Seminary's determination to remain distinctive may be the element that it shares most clearly with many other theological schools. To understand this assertion, one needs to examine briefly the general history of American theological education.

American Seminaries: Schools of Theology and Theological Schools[6]

For much of their history, theology was the stock-in-trade of American seminaries. The tendency of both Protestants and Catholics to use seminary education, ministerial preparation, and theological education as synonyms is not accidental. Since the Reformation, Protestants and Catholics have battled more over theological issues than they have over questions of morals or ritual. Further, both Catholics and Protestants used theological education to advance their cause. Protestants required a thorough course in confessional theology for ordination, and post-Trentine Catholics required residence in a seminary.[7] Of course, the identification of Christianity largely with its intellectual expression was not new. The ancient creeds stressed the importance of specific theological affirmations, and heresy or the teaching of false doctrine was the most serious sin throughout the medieval period. Nor is the theological focus any less important today. The deepest divisions among Protestant Christians are those between evangelicals who hold a strong doctrine of biblical inspiration and liberals and moderates who tend toward historical critical studies. Although Catholics are more concerned with ritual, theological differences arising from Vatican II still remain key issues. Much of the history of American theological education can be told in terms of how specific schools have treated the intellectual content of faith.

New England's Trinitarian and Unitarian Congregationalists clashed in the early 19th century over the doctrine of the Person of Christ. After the Unitarians triumphed at Harvard, the orthodox Congregationalists founded the first modern American seminary, Andover, in 1808. The school had three faculty members, a significant endowment, and a program organized around biblical studies, theology, and preaching. The instructors subscribed (signed) either the Westminster Standards or a creed specially prepared for the institution. While the school did train religious leaders, its purpose was more theological than practical. With the election of Unitarian Henry Ware to the Hollis Chair of Divinity in Harvard College, the orthodox Congregationalists of Massachusetts found themselves locked in a life-or-death battle. Putting aside their own theological differences, they established a school that they hoped would be the West Point of orthodoxy. Andover was to train the ideological leaders of the orthodox counter-offensive.

Other theological disagreements among very similar Congregational theologies led rapidly to the establishment of new schools. In Connecticut, Nathaniel Taylor, of the divinity department of Yale College, developed a theology that would support the popular revivalism of the time. While technically orthodox, Taylor's system emphasized the role of human will in religion and downplayed the doctrine of election. Taylor believed that original sin was more an inclination than something inherent in a person's physical or spiritual makeup. To Bennet Tyler, Taylor had crossed a boundary. Joining forces with Ashbel Nettleton, a more traditional Calvinist evangelist, Tyler established the Theological Institute of Connecticut (later Hartford Seminary) to defend what he believed was Christian truth.

The Congregationalists were not the only denomination to mark their theological turf with seminaries. Presbyterians wanted their school, Princeton Theological Seminary, to adhere strictly to the Westminster Confessions and Catechisms. The founders of Union Theological Seminary in New York wanted to spread a theology that would sustain the reformist impulses of New School Presbyterianism. American Lutherans bound Gettysburg Seminary to the Augsburg Confession. When that seminary's leading theologian, Samuel Schmucker, leaned toward a more ecumenical faith, other Lutherans, however, found Gettysburg too loose doctrinally. They established a more conservative seminary in Philadelphia. Even more conservative Lutherans, recent immigrants from Saxony, found Philadelphia unsound, and they established Concordia Seminary in Saint Louis to maintain the full *Book of Concord*, a collection of 16th-century Lutheran creeds.

The real stars of these early schools were the systematic theologians. The theologians set the tone for the schools and often served as the champions for the schools in the denominational battles that characterized antebellum Christianity. In many ways, this was their most important function. Andover, the largest antebellum school, rarely exceeded one hundred students, and most seminaries had twenty-five or less. While some immigrant groups were able to insist on graduate education for their pastors, this was not true for the majority of American Protestant groups. The seminary education of pastors did not become normative until after World War II.

If theology was the primary reason for the existence of antebellum schools, antebellum seminaries also began a more scholarly tradition. Leaning heavily on German models, such scholars as Moses Stuart and Edward Robinson did the spade work that established an American biblical guild.[8] The Hebrew lexicons and grammars of Wilhem Gesenius were translated as were various works by Johann Jahn, an 18th-century Catholic scholar, and a number of lesser lights. Many Americans studied in Germany, and these students forged close relationships with their teachers that formed a transatlantic network. By 1860, Americans reviewed the most significant German books within a year of their publication and often translated them within a few years. If American scholars only wrote a few original works, they were part of the larger scholarly discussion.

German universities also provided Protestant Americans another suggestion for the organization of their schools. In Germany, the ministry was interpreted as one of many civil service jobs that required particular training. German theological faculties taught courses in such areas as religious pedagogy and other practical tasks. The possibilities for this type of education intrigued American theological educators who believed that the education offered in their schools was more practical in other respects than the German model.[9]

American Catholic seminaries also began in the antebellum period. The French Revolution was the decisive event for Catholicism in the 19th century. Not only were many priests and members of religious orders executed or forced into exile, but the Church was uneasy with modern culture. The tendency in Catholic thought was to look "over the mountains" to Rome, and the tendency in Rome was to look beyond the Enlightenment to the great theologians of the 13th century, especially Thomas Aquinas. Orthodoxy and discipline were the watermarks of the pre-Vatican II church.

The first Catholic seminary was St. Mary's, established at One Mile Tavern near Baltimore in 1792. Bishop John Carroll invited the Sulpicians to establish the school. The Society of St. Sulpice was a French order that had been established in the 17th century by Jean Jacques Olier. Seminary training was the primary vocation of the Sulpician order, which developed an intense method of spiritual formation designed to form the candidate into the "image of Christ."[10] The other French order actively involved in training American priests was the Vincentian whose educational technique also stressed priestly formation. American religious orders usually made provision for the training of their own members, although some dioceses used monastic orders to train some of their candidates. Other religious orders, such as the Jesuits, were more important for their work with colleges and universities.

From Theologians to Professionals and Back Again

Symbolized by the founding of Johns Hopkins University in 1876, American higher education entered a period of rapid change after the American Civil War. Fueled by the continual expansion of the economy, the larger colleges became research universities, complete with graduate and professional schools. A few American seminaries became part of these remodeled institutions. But those schools that did not find a university home often adopted university standards or tried to do so. Particularly in Bible and church history, seminary scholarship soared. The Society of Biblical Literature and the American Society of Church History were founded in 1880 and 1888 respectively.

Whether liberal or conservative, the dominant intellectual issue for American Protestants was biblical authority. Although biblical scholars had raised penetrating questions about the date and authorship of the various biblical books, their studies did not become widely known until after 1860. At the same time, Darwin's understanding of biological evolution became widely accepted. More liberal Protestants modified their understanding of biblical authority to fit these new developments and also set about developing a theology that stressed the immanence of God in creation and history. Miracles and divine interventions were largely discarded. In contrast, conservatives held fast to traditional understandings of biblical authority and modified their position only slightly to fit the new situation.

The debate over biblical scholarship was bypassed in Catholic theological seminaries by the papal condemnation of the modernist movement in the encyclical *Pascendi* (1907). Serious Catholic use of the new methods of biblical study did not occur until World War II when the Pope allowed Catholics to use historical criticism, subject to the teaching authority of the church (*magisterium*). Despite this limited papal approval, the new scholarship was not widely used in American Catholic seminaries before Vatican II.

Biblical studies dominated the curriculum of Protestant theological schools from 1870 to 1890. By the end of this period, however, the focus of the schools began to change. Many of the changes were due to "The Third Great Awakening" that involved Protestant laypeople in a host of the church's ministries. The Sunday school movement, always significant in the United States, grew by leaps and bounds, and large Sunday school parades took place in the nation's largest cities. Missionary activists founded the Student Volunteer Movement. Its members, all college and university students, pledged themselves to go abroad to "evangelize the world in this generation." At the same time, the adoption of new fund-raising techniques helped fill church coffers.

American society was also at an exciting moment. The nation was entering into the age of the professional and the expert. Americans saw the person with specific practical knowledge as the key to the future, especially when those people could claim scientific warrants for their practices. While scholars saw the new university as a place for research, the new professionals saw it as a place for training and certification. Universities added schools in such areas as engineering, dentistry, and public health. In turn, seminaries modeled their programs on the most successful of these professional programs. The larger seminaries, such as the divinity schools of the University of Chicago and Yale University, Union Theological Seminary, and Hartford Theological Seminary Foundation began to add specialized courses in religious education. In time, these courses became sufficiently established to support professorships. At some well-endowed and progressive institutions, such as Hartford and Boston College, separate professional schools were formed for religious education and, at Hartford, missions also.

Religious education was both a program of studies and a crusade. Its advocates were convinced that the application of the new social sciences to the problems of religious leadership would regenerate the churches and, they hoped, the nation. Teachers of religious education were also deeply concerned with the development of new professional disciplines, especially in the area of psychology and human development. In many schools, the religious education professor's tentative experiments with psychology matured into independent programs in that discipline.

A key element in the development of the professional understanding of ministry was the development of field education. Protestant seminary students had often worked in local congregations to finance their studies. Field education began when such schools as Union and Hartford began to establish academic programs around this weekend work. The initial idea was that this time should have a practical use. Field education was to parallel the "practice or apprenticeship" units in other professional schools, such as practice teaching in education. Despite this theory, few schools had as strong a field education program as their rhetoric and ideals demanded. Both the schools and the students remained too dependent on the money earned by weekend employment for the schools to shape the programs completely around educational goals.

In 1925 Dr. Richard Cabot joined with Anton Boisen to offer a program of "clinical" education at Worcester State Hospital. Students worked as chaplain interns, visiting the sick in their rooms and recording their conversations for later discussion. In 1936 Cabot and Russell Dicks, chaplain at Boston State Hospital, published an influential text, *The Art of Ministering to the Sick*, that dealt with clinical theology as a means of growth.[11] Influential programs of clinical training were established in Massachusetts, New York, and Kentucky.

In time, Protestant theological educators, especially the administrators of schools, came to describe their work as professional education.[12] This understanding of theological education underlay the three studies undertaken from 1920 to 1957. The first was by Robert Kelly; the second, by William Adams Brown and Mary A. May; and the third, by H. Richard Niebuhr, James Gustafson, and Daniel Day Williams.[13] The professional ideal was very important in the work of the American Association of Theological Schools (later the Association of Theological

Schools) since it provided a way of discussing the aims and goals of seminary education without explicit attention to the theological issues that deeply divided American seminaries. The further elaboration of this model enabled the association to expand beyond the mainstream schools and encompass both evangelical and Catholic schools.

In addition to commitment to the professional understanding of ministry, 20th-century seminaries have had a deep commitment to investigating and, hopefully, influencing the church's commitment to social change. This commitment began with the development of the Social Gospel by such liberal theologians as Washington Gladden and Walter Rauschenbusch. Drawing on themes in the prophets and the teachings of Jesus, the Social Gospelers argued that Christianity had a social dimension that was as essential to its message as individual redemption. Although the Social Gospel declined, the neoorthodox theologians of the 1930s and 1940s continued to advocate Christian social involvement, and many of the most passionate debates of the depression years were about such matters as whether or not the United States should intervene in Europe.

The unrest of the 1960s increased the seminaries' interest in social issues. Theologians developed many new branches—Latin American Liberation Theology, Black Theology, Feminist Theology, and Gay and Lesbian Theology—that highlighted the need for Christianity to be involved in particular issues. At the same time, the schools themselves became more diverse, hiring black, Asian, and women instructors. Each of these contributed a different perspective on theological education that suggested the schools might view their enterprise differently. While not repudiated, the professional model no longer seemed adequate.

By the 1980s, theological education had come full circle as American theological educators asked again the question of what was theological about theological education. This round of inquiries, which began with the publication of Edward Farley's *Theologia* [14] and continued through David Kelsey's *To Understand God Truly*, suggested that the schools needed to return to a model based more on *paideia* and less on one drawn from the contemporary university. [15] What made theological education interesting and vital was not what it contributed to the professional life of any economic group, including the clergy, but the intrinsic importance of the questions that theologians asked.

Ethnic Seminaries

Ethnicity is a persistent theme in American history. The United States is largely a nation of immigrants who came to the New World with both hope for a new style of life and determination to retain some of their original culture. In *Albion's Seed,* David Hackett Fischer pointed to English regional cultural patterns in New England and the American South that have continued since colonial times. Interestingly enough, these folkways included foods and verbal particularities.[16] In a similar way every new group that has entered the United States has continued, whether deliberately or not, some of its earlier heritage and culture.

Religion and ethnicity are often linked in the American experience. The number of names with the suffix, "Mac," in most Presbyterian churches bears eloquent witness to the connection between the church and Scotch and Scotch-Irish immigration. Similarly, Lutheran congregations contain many people with German or Scandinavian names. While Catholic bishops often resisted the establishment of ethnic parishes, many parishes were in fact predominantly Irish, Italian, German, or Polish. Priests heard confession and preached in the language of the old country; sisters from the homeland staffed the school, and the congregation conversed in their familiar tongue. Following World War II, many of the children and grandchildren moved to the suburbs where they joined parishes with less discernable ethnic traditions.[17]

Ethnicity was not the reason for the existence of such congregations or denominations. The churches that served ethnic populations were very aware that they were part of the larger Christian movement, and every Sunday their members confessed that they were members of the "one holy catholic and apostolic Church." In addition, many leaders of these churches, like the first generation of American Puritans, were on an "errand into the wilderness."[18] They not only wanted their own churches to conform to their doctrinal and religious standards, they hoped that their witness might convert their homelands to their perspective. Ethnic identity only reinforced the church's religious message; it did not replace it. To be German and Lutheran seemed a more inevitable connection when one lived in a world in which many, if not most, people were neither.[19] To preserve the heritage, one preserved the faith; to preserve the faith, one preserved the heritage.

Like many other founders of seminaries that served predominantly ethnic religious movements, the founders of the Jewish Theological Seminary were self-conscious religious conservatives who wanted to preserve their ancient faith in a brave new world of democratic institutions. Like the representatives of other ethnic groups, they experienced two sides of American culture. In this new world, individuals were free to make personal choices about occupation, neighborhood, and self-identification. Although America was an almost promised land for the Jews, much painful prejudice existed in the United States. Some Jews were very conscious of the dangers concealed in the blessings of American life. As Solomon Schechter, the first President of the reorganized the Jewish Theological Seminary, said, the "first thing that the immigrant loses is his Judaism."[20] It was as if the atmosphere contained an acid that ate away at this precious *mitzvah* or that pious practice.

The pious Eastern European Jews who came toward the end of the 19th century were not comfortable with how earlier Jews, largely from Germany, had dealt with the seductiveness of the new land. Reform Judaism had drastically changed centuries-old patterns of observance and ritual. Dietary laws (*kashrut*) were more or less discarded, mixed seating was encouraged in worship, and an orderly liturgy, primarily in English, was standard. Many "temples" had organs, and some had Sunday services. To many Eastern European Jews, such an Americanized faith hardly seemed like Judaism at all. In 1883, when the organizers of the graduation dinner at Hebrew Union College served prohibited foods, the critics of Reform Judaism decided to follow a more traditional path. They wanted a Judaism that was visibly obedient to the law and, at the same time, open to the promise of the new land. A seminary was part of this program. As Cyrus Adler put it simply in 1915: "If Judaism is to be perpetuated in America, provision must be made for a learned ministry."[21]

Partly because the Jewish issues had to do with observance, the parallel between these events and the experience of other immigrant groups may be overlooked. In fact, the shock experienced by Eastern European Jews was similar to that experienced by other ethnic groups when their countrymen or members of their religious community assimilated to American norms. For instance, the new Germans who entered Pennsylvania in the 1830s and 1840s faced such a shock. Those Germans who had come to the New World in the 18th century had already laid aside many particularities of their tradition. Gettysburg Seminary symbolized these changes. Schmucker, the first president and professor of theology at Gettysburg, was deeply influenced by Reformed Christianity. In many ways, the seminary that he founded was a Lutheran copy of his alma mater, Princeton. Schmucker was also influenced by the Reformed tendency to replace formal theological statements and confessions of faith with a simple biblicism. After years of building bridges between Lutheranism and revivalism, Schmucker or his supporters published the *Definite Synodical Platform* in 1855. The *Platform* called for a revision of historic Lutheran theology to exclude such traditional doctrines as baptismal regeneration. The newer immigrants, who came from a world in which those same theological issues had created tensions and led to several schisms, were appalled at the looseness of "grape juice" Lutheranism.[22] They created their own seminary at Philadelphia, only a few miles from Gettysburg and elected Charles Porterfield Krauth as their professor of theology.[23] The Missouri Synod, founded by Saxon Lutherans, was unable to accept either of the other German Lutheran bodies as orthodox and insisted on its own style of theological education. This included two different seminaries: a practical seminary dedicated to getting ministers onto the field and an academic seminary devoted to maintaining a European style of education. Similar stories exist in the history of Dutch Calvinists, Scottish Covenanters, and other European groups.

If groups entering the United States felt a need to preserve their traditions in part through the establishment of an institution to train religious leaders, the form that this new institution would take was not as obvious. Most would have favored the establishment of universities, similar to those in their homelands, although the more pietistic distrusted such schools as secularizing agents. Ethnic leaders elected the American pattern of college followed by seminary largely because immigrant groups could not afford to establish modern universities. Late 19th-century Conservative Jews also had many options for training new rabbis. They might have used what later became university Jewish studies departments, established a rabbinical program at a major university, or participated in a university divinity school.[24] The founders of the Jewish Theological Seminary chose a "seminary" for many of the same reasons that led other ethnic leaders to a similar decision.[25] These rationales included the need to identify the institution with its constituency and the desire to retain control over the curriculum, faculty, and subject matter.

In almost all cases, the location of an ethnic seminary was, in part, a matter of economy. The Missouri Synod located Concordia Seminary in St. Louis nearby the center of Saxon Lutheran settlement,[26] and Calvin Seminary was placed conveniently in Holland, Michigan. Likewise the Jewish Theological Seminary located in New York close to the homes of large numbers of Eastern European Jewish immigrants. Location near the ethnic demographic center made the school a visible part of the community. Almost all ethnic seminaries used their schools to recruit leaders for their group and their school. A central location also enabled a school to draw on numerous community financial resources for help.

When an ethnic group sponsors a seminary, that group expects the school to be more than an educational institution. Ethnic religious groups expect their schools to assume a number of diverse roles and tasks that are not clearly related to the central mission. Most Protestant ethnic seminaries provided leadership for different areas of their church's life for a season. Once their denominations matured, however, these Protestant seminaries transferred their noneducational tasks to other agencies and confined their work to the training of religious leaders. In part, because of the small number of Jewish educational institutions, the intellectuals at the Jewish Theological Seminary have provided leadership for a number of Conservative Jewish agencies. Thus the school ran a system of Ramah camps, conducted what amounted to an ecumenical agency, served as Conservative Judaism's governance structure, worked in Israel, and produced radio and television programs. The Jewish Theological Seminary did not transfer these assignments to other bodies, leaving no clear boundary between the Seminary and the Conservative Jewish movement (denomination).

Among Protestant ethnics, language was tightly tied to generational location, even at such strongly ethnic institutions as Calvin Seminary or Concordia (Saint

Louis). The Jewish Theological Seminary shared a similar rhythm of the generations. Typically, the founders built a seminary with the second and third generation
of the ethnic group as their primary market. The first generation to attend the
seminary had to know the language in order to participate in classes and preach, and
they still retained practical knowledge of the language and cultural distinctives of
their parents. Hence, teachers made assignments in both the original language and
the newer tongue. The more able first-generation graduates could preach in both
languages. For the second and third student generations, the ability to use the
original language was desirable, but not essential. Most classes were in English, and
the churches were rapidly moving toward an English liturgy. For subsequent generations, the language was more a memory than a tool, although some retained a word
or a phrase. Library purchases followed the same pattern. During the first and second generations, the libraries acquired significant numbers of books in the original
language. By the third or fourth generation, the newer books were the standard
English texts used at other institutions.

In regard to language, the Jewish Theological Seminary was more like Catholic
than Protestant ethnic institutions. Although Hebrew began to revive among those
who immigrated to Israel or hoped to do so, most Eastern European Jews spoke the
language of their homeland or Yiddish in their daily life.[27] Hebrew, like Latin, was a
learned tongue, reserved for worship and sacred studies. In pre-Vatican II Catholic
seminaries, the church expected all students to know sufficient Latin to study theology. The Jewish Theological Seminary had a similar relationship to its holy tongue:
mastery of the language was an essential part of the sacred function.[28] As with a
priest and Latin in the Catholic church, a rabbi had to be able to use Hebrew easily
in the service and to read the most important works in that language. Those
studying to be Hebrew teachers in Jewish schools, interestingly enough, were
often more interested in Hebrew than future rabbis. The Teachers Institute used
Hebrew as its language of instruction. Inspired by the revival of spoken Hebrew
among European Zionists and in Israel and by modern Hebrew literature, the
prospective teachers had a passion for the use of Hebrew in daily life. The same was
true of those who managed the Ramah camps.

For various reasons, the Jewish Theological Seminary did not have to take the
same care with the original European languages of the immigrants, although it did
pay some attention to Yiddish. In part, this was because many East European Jews
were refugees who were fleeing pogroms or the threat of pogroms. America was a
place of safety, an oasis in a desert of hatred. One did not come to America to have
warm memories of Russia or Poland. Further, many Eastern European Jews were
not fluent in the official languages of their home governments.[29] A significant
number came from the "Pale of Settlement" where most Jewish communities were
self-contained. When Eastern Jews entered the educated elite, they tended to prefer

645

*JTS and
Other Forms
of American
Ministerial
Preparation*

Students in the
JTS cafeteria,
early 1960s.
*Ratner, Center,
JTS.*

French or German as did many members of the Russian and Polish nobility and middle classes.

After a brief period as a commuter school, the Jewish Theological Seminary adopted the residential pattern favored by the majority of American seminaries.[30] Residential schools had a common dormitory or dormitories, provisions for meals, and other "common" rooms. The residential pattern had many other advantages. If nothing else, student housing allowed a school to attract students who did not live near the institution. Without some provisions for residence, a national school would be difficult to establish or maintain. Yet, residence was more than a convenience; common life was a way of "civilizing" candidates for the ministry. Since Protestant churches often recruited their clergy from those young people who were, to use a past idiom, "poor but pious," many needed exposure to an environment that might teach them upper class manners and mores. In residential schools, young people learned how to "get along" by imitating the manners and lifestyles of their wealthier peers. The same informal training in social life that transformed a farmer's son into an urban and urbane Protestant cleric also socialized the children of immigrants into leaders of socially mobile Jewish congregations.

The Jewish Theological Seminary's concept of scholarship was also part of the school's immigrant heritage. Ethnic seminaries tend to adopt the academic standards of their homeland, insofar as they could attain them, as their own standards. Thus, Concordia Seminary in St. Louis demanded that its students arrive thoroughly prepared in the classical and biblical languages. In effect, Concordia wanted students who were products of the German *gymnasium* or an American equivalent, and many received their previous education in Missouri Synod schools. Concordia pursued theology in a thoroughly continental manner with a heavy emphasis on rigorous biblical and dogmatic study.

In its emphasis on the Breslau-Berlin model of scholarship, the Jewish Theological Seminary was doing what other immigrant seminaries did when they established their intellectual canons. They took the best European models and imported them into the new world. To sustain these standards, JTS found it useful to continue to recruit faculty members from abroad who had learned the proper scholarly arts at their source. Many faculty were graduates of the great rabbinical schools in Central Europe.

Despite the recruiting of new European faculty, irrelevance threatened most ethnic seminaries at some stage in their history. The models of scholarship that were so intellectually stimulating when a school was founded became dated when the school's students and faculty came to relate more to the intellectual questions of their American contemporaries. This apparently happened at Concordia in the 1950s when many faculty members replaced traditional German orthodoxy with American Neoorthodoxy. Likewise, American Protestant Southerners, who often behaved like an ethnic group within the United States, went through a transformation in the 1950s. Many seminaries in the "Bible belt" traded their regional orthodoxies for a system of theology more common elsewhere in the nation. At the same time, these schools adopted structures similar to those of the Northern seminaries.

In reading the accounts of the Finkelstein presidency, one senses that the Breslau-Berlin tradition was in its golden years in the 1940s and that it was a little less important to students and some faculty thereafter. By and large those changes did not occur until the late 1970s and 1980s.

The intensity of the Jewish Theological Seminary's devotion to the Breslau-Berlin intellectual style made it difficult for the Seminary to explore new models. While it maintained some of America's premier ecumenical programs in the 1940s, 1950s, and 1960s, it did not integrate these programs into the school's larger educational mission. Ironically, the Seminary separated these programs from its other tasks by calling them "Institutes." In many ways, these Institutes were similar to the various research "institutes" maintained by German universities. The Seminary's public allegiance to the older tradition, moreover, hindered needed curricular revisions. As at Concordia, the primary demand of the 1960s radical students was for a thorough curricular reform that would allow more electives and encourage educational innovation.

Almost from the beginning, the Jewish Theological Seminary wanted to be a graduate professional institution. This hope was almost universal among American Protestant theological educators from the establishment of the first seminary, Andover, in 1808. In its early history, JTS insisted that candidates undertake

bachelor's degree study at the same time as they did specialized studies for the rabbinate. When the children and grandchildren of Jewish immigrants prospered, JTS attracted a higher percentage of college graduates. However, the gradual increase in Jewish wealth alone did not change the standard. As with most Protestant seminaries, World War II was the decisive turning point.[31] When the government demobilized the troops, it provided significant scholarship aid to former military personnel through the G. I. Bill. At the same time, many people made a new commitment to religion. As a result, the Jewish Theological Seminary (and most other seminaries) had more and better qualified candidates.

An apparently unique feature of JTS—the school's tendency to see its leaders in the role of a great person—may not be as different as it first appears. At Concordia Seminary, presidents Carl F. W. Walter and Franz A. O. Pieper were seen as larger-than-life leaders within the school and the denomination. Although Abraham Kuyper—the Dutch Neo-Calvinist—never taught at Calvin, both the school and the denomination were under his spell for many years. Schechter, Adler, and Finkelstein fulfilled similar roles within the Jewish Theological Seminary's history, ethos, and mythology.

The willingness of an institution to convey high status on an individual or individuals has many sources. Joseph Campbell has identified the hero saga as a key element in human mythic consciousness, and seminaries create heroes much as other institutions do. This should not lead us to overlook other factors. The late 19th century was awash in neoromantic leadership ideologies. The idea of the hero was part of the baggage that European immigrants brought with them to America. Likewise, the American context encouraged similar ideas. Many Americans understood the Civil War as an epic battle between Lincoln and Lee. Not surprisingly then, Solomon Schechter found a hero in Abraham Lincoln.

While ethnicity alone cannot account for someone like Mordecai Kaplan, head of the Teachers Institute from 1909 to 1945,[32] Kaplan does illustrate the importance of ethnic life at the Jewish Theological Seminary. Kaplan viewed Jews primarily as an ethnic group and shaped the work at the Institute around that understanding. Israel lay at the heart of much of his "Reconstructionism." Kaplan believed in the cultural Zionism of Ahad Ha'am. Judaism was again to support a major world civilization. In contrast to the traditional piety of many in the Rabbinical School, Kaplan sloughed off the traditional Jewish belief in a transcendent God who intervenes in human history. For him, the Bible was essentially the folklore of a people. He believed that the Jews had created their own culture. This Jewish culture, he argued, had contributed to the world's culture in the past, and it was still marking humanity's path into a more ethical future. In support of his vision, Kaplan spent his life training people to use the Hebrew language and to follow Jewish practices and rituals in their daily lives. Naturally, Kaplan passionately believed in the resurrection of Hebrew as a spoken language. Kaplan had the Teachers Institute classes conducted in Hebrew, and the faculty assigned modern Hebrew literature alongside ancient and medieval texts.

Yet, for all Kaplan's deviations, his work illustrates graphically the role of the seminary in the preservation of ethnic customs and practices. While few Protestants would have proposed that their ethnic and religious identity could or should survive the "death of God," most ethnic church leaders have assumed the value of their faith to their nation's civilization. "Wherever an altar is found, there civilization exists."[33] Many immigrant Christians explicitly believed in the close relationship between religion and their national cultures. The Lutheran Church Missouri Synod and the Christian Reformed Church, for example, maintained an extensive program of cultural and religious education that went far beyond the Sunday school. In a similar fashion, the parochial school, taught by nuns from the home country, was an important mark of the Catholic ethnic parish. Teachers in these schools sought to teach students the faith's contributions to their old and new homeland.

Beyond Ethnicity

Viewing the Jewish Theological Seminary as an immigrant and later ethnic institution enables us to put the school's post–World War II development in perspective. From 1945 onward large numbers of Americans immigrated from the cities to the small towns and semirural areas that surrounded the urban areas. The young men and women who returned from World War II and Korea had unprecedented access to education and, through education, to better jobs. Federally guaranteed mortgages funded the construction of the single family homes that were increasingly popular. In his *Crabgrass Frontier: The Suburbanization of the United States*,[34] Kenneth T. Jackson noted the way in which life in the suburbs transformed the culture of former urban dwellers.[35] In particular, suburban life tended to homogenize Protestant, Catholic, and Jewish perspectives. Although many Americans became deeply involved in their churches, suburban religion tended toward faith in belief itself. Americans did not care what their neighbors believed as long as they believed something. Religion was a "private matter," something one did in one's spare time and not subject to public scrutiny.

For most European Protestant and Catholic ethnics, suburbanization marked the beginning of the end of specifically ethnic communities. Students and faculties at schools with strong ethnic backgrounds began to identify primarily with larger cultural and educational norms. By the 1950s, ethnic seminaries were beginning to seek accreditation. Most often, they first sought the approval of their regional bodies and only later of the Association of Theological Schools. The Jewish Theological Seminary sought and received Middle States Accreditation in 1954 and has passed periodically through the process for reaccreditation since then.

Accreditation was one sign of this new conformity to national standards. As in other schools, accreditation marked the movement from one reference community to another. Ethnic communities validated their seminaries informally. If a school enabled a graduate to function in a religious community, the churches or synagogues hired its graduates. This made the relationship to the community decisive for the school's survival and mission. However, accreditation created a reference community composed of similar institutions. What matters in the process is not how effectively a seminary serves its sponsors; what counts is whether a school attains the same standards as similar schools.

Student interests also moved toward conformity with the larger national norm. For instance, JTS students in the 1960s were caught up in the same ethical and cultural issues as their counterparts at Union Seminary or Columbia University. Students demonstrated against the Vietnam War, supported the "strike" at Columbia, and observed the "Day of Conscience . . . in Protest of the War" (15 October 1969). The Jewish Theological Seminary students forced their school to close temporarily in May 1970. Equally important, JTS began to demand the professional trappings that had long been part of American Protestant seminary education. In 1968 JTS students demanded a curriculum with more electives and more direct relevance to their future work as rabbis. This trend continued. According to a 1983 survey, student interests had shifted away from Zionism and Hebrew toward professional courses. Like their counterparts in other seminaries, Jewish Theological Seminary students wanted more courses in such practical areas as teaching, counseling, and spirituality. [36]

The fascination with the practical also may have been related to other serious problems facing the Jewish community. The European Jewish tradition has no analog to American religious voluntarism,[37] and some evidence exists that Judaism in America is declining demographically. For Conservative rabbis, this larger crisis is compounded by the countercultural elements in their tradition, such as the high appreciation of scholarship and of religious observance.[38] How Conservative Jews will resolve this identity crisis is not obvious. However, in pressing the Seminary to provide an educational solution to the problem, Conservative Jews are making demands similar to those made by other religious groups on their seminaries. Especially among Protestants, discussions of what is "wrong with the church" always lead, sooner or later, to the question of what is wrong with the "seminary." And Americans, who believe passionately in the ability of schools to make things better, tend to assume that the reason for their distress is that the schools have failed to respond to the people.

Although the Jewish Theological Seminary has experienced the changes that come from a weakening of ethnic identity, other trends worked against a wholesale abandonment of Jews' ethnic roots. By the mid-seventies, many Americans of various backgrounds were recovering their ethnic backgrounds.[39] In many ways, the "new ethnicity" was part of a larger search for personal selfhood. In the wake of Vietnam, the oil embargo, and massive social unrest, Americans were not sure who they were or how they related to a larger social entity. Remembered ethnicity was one way in which they forged important bonds with their past and, hence, found for themselves a different future.

For the Jewish Theological Seminary, remembered ethnicity was never easy. Unlike other Americans seeking the meaning of their past, American Jews have to struggle with two overwhelming realities. First, anti-Semitism has not disappeared, and many Jews rightly fear that it has taken new forms. Hatred tends to intensify personal identification with the larger group. Second, the national debate over American military support of Israel became acute with the 1967 and 1973 Arab-Israeli Wars. In light of the Holocaust, Conservative Jews could not deny the importance of Israel. Not only was the reestablishment of the Jewish state the most significant single event in modern Jewish history; Israel has proven an important leaven for Jews and Judaism around the world.

American Jews often assumed that other Americans shared their commitment to Israel, but the threat of war proved their assumptions false. Some Americans raised questions about American foreign policy, and there was a struggle for American support that was crucial to the military battle for Israel's survival. This made many

Jews more conscious of their relationship to Israel and more willing to join with
other Jews in supporting Israel's survival.

651

*JTS and
Other Forms
of American
Ministerial
Preparation*

While Israel was not for most Jews a remembered ethnicity, it shaped many Jews'
sense of their heritage. Thus the Jewish state provided an important secondary
source of personal identity for many American Jews, just as ethnic pride did for
many other Euro-Americans or black pride for African Americans. The Jewish Theological Seminary's educational attempts to struggle with this "created ethnicity,"
such as the year in Israel, were similar to the popular undergraduate "year abroad"
programs. Like collegiate "year abroad" programs, the JTS "year in Israel" emphasized the need to use the language in daily life and the value of a direct experience
of the culture. But, at least for some Seminary leaders and students, the year
abroad involved more than cultural knowledge. American Conservative Judaism
believes that it has a mission to the Jews of Israel and that the presence of the Seminary in Israel contributes to this mission. Globalization projects in Protestant
seminaries serve similarly as links between a school's mission and its denomination's
larger mission.

Scholarship and Community

In David Kelsey's study, *To Understand God Truly: What's Theological About a Theological School*,[40] Kelsey notes that German models of learning and instruction
deeply affected 19th-century American Protestant seminaries. From the founding
of the University of Halle near the beginning of the 18th century onward, the various German states modernized their universities to reflect Enlightenment understandings of knowledge. Similar reforms were introduced into some Slavic lands.
At the heart of the renewed German university tradition was the ideal of research or
independent, objective investigation. In theory, the task of the professor was first to
master a field of inquiry and then to make significant contributions to that field that
would, in turn, inspire the next round of research. The operative term for this
model of study was "objective." The word did not mean that the investigator's work
was necessarily free of values or that it was only descriptive. Instead, "objective"
pointed to the public character of academic discourse. What the Germans were
claiming was that any investigator who followed the best methods would reach similar or identical results.

The German term for this approach was *Wissenschaft*, a word that means knowledge, science, or scholarship. As most Germans use the word, *Wissenschaft* refers to
a disciplined attempt to understand natural and cultural phenomena. In other
words, what makes a particular study *Wissenschaft* is that the scholar self-
consciously applies a rule or a method to the subject matter. The method may be as
simple as the comparison of the texts of all existent manuscripts of a medieval
writing or as complicated as the statistical analysis of the emissions of a fusion

generator. The classical example of *Wissenschaft* in the cultural arena is the critical edition with all manuscript variations carefully noted in the margins.

Both classical Christian theology and *Wissenschaft* were concerned with the interpretation of sacred texts. Many, if not most, Protestant scholars passed easily from the older Renaissance understandings of how to study a text to the newer Enlightenment forms of analysis.[41] The ease of that transition, however, should not hide the significance of the shift. Kelsey expressed the change this way:

> In a third century AD pagan or Christian academy one might study ancient texts so as to become more deeply shaped by the virtues. On the model of a *paideia* that is what excellent schooling aims at. By contrast, the disciplines that make inquiry in the humanities in a research university genuinely critical research yielding truly public knowledge are the disciplines of the historian. In a research university one studies ancient texts to learn the truth about them, their origins, their meanings in the original settings, the history of their uses, the history of the teachings about them or the readings of them, perhaps the social or psychological dynamics that explain why such texts come to be written.[42]

Another way to make Kelsey's point might be to ask the question of who "owns" the text or has the right to interpret it. Traditionally, Christians and Jews had assumed that religious writings, whether canonical or extra canonical, belonged to the community. The new hermeneutic assigned the primary ownership of the texts to the scholars whose arts and skills were capable of determining their historical meaning. Neither the yeshiva nor the monastery had claims on a par with those of the university. If the traditional religious readings of texts were found wanting, the new scholarship discarded them, often contemptuously.

Any analysis of *Wissenschaft* must include an examination of scholars' understanding of themselves. The master of *Wissenschaft* was a professional. By 1870 the concept of professional scholar was no longer the ancient idea of the person who had mastered a body of material. It was the modern idea of a person who had mastered an approach to a subject.[43] To put this in a slogan, the scholar was no longer the person of erudition; the scholar was the master of technique. In Germany, the certification of a professional scholar was a slow process that moved from the relatively humble accomplishment of the doctor of philosophy degree to the higher achievement of the *habilitation* or second dissertation. A number of Jewish intellectuals had experienced this system in Europe. The laws of the various Central European states mandated that all candidates for religious leadership had to attend the universities. For many young rabbis, the experience of attending the university was their first real taste of Jewish emancipation and personal freedom. They loved the university, its traditions, and its practices. Likewise, Protestant Americans who studied in Germany brought the doctor of philosophy degree home with them. The opening of Johns Hopkins in 1876 was: "the most important innovation in graduate education launched during the whole period between the Civil War and the First World War. It was the first American institution to be founded as a university in the German tradition."[44] The Jewish Theological Seminary Charter of 1902 listed Jewish scholarship as the fourth of the seminary's six aims.

Once Protestant scholars secured this new type of professional status for themselves, they began to advocate a similar status and form of training for the ministry. The scholarly understanding paralleled the interest in Christian activism that accompanied the Third Great Awakening.[45] The resultant understanding of theological education as professional education is the foundation of much 20th-century Protestant thinking about ministerial education. Ironically, no similar idea of the rabbinate was common at the Jewish Theological Seminary until the presidency of Gerson Cohen and still is not as developed as among Protestants. Many have commented that JTS has exalted the role of the scholar over that of the rabbi throughout its history. This may reflect the difficulty that faculty members have had transferring their own professional status and training to their students.

The new scholarship reshaped the American seminary tradition. In order to support the newer research style, schools had to raise significant amounts of money for personnel, facilities, and libraries. John D. Rockefeller learned how much the new education cost from his personal experience. William Rainey Harper, the first president of the University of Chicago, repeatedly asked Rockefeller for just one more gift to support the school until Rockefeller's contribution had grown to more than $25 million. Other university pioneers were as needy and as determined as Harper.

Libraries and museums were the most expensive research tools, and their cost increased almost yearly. Historian Henry Preserved Smith noted:

> The method of instruction has changed from few books to many books. The student is expected to engage in research on his own account and to familiarize himself with a wide range of literature. The library must put him in possession, not of a few "standard works" but of all that has been written on his subject[46]

Americans abroad became voracious purchasers of books as schools tried to fill the lacunae on their shelves and perhaps own some significant volumes. Thus, Union (New York) had the famed Van Ness collection, and Chicago Theological Seminary, the private collection of Berlin Professor Ernst Wilhelm Hengstenberg. Mayer Sulzberger, the great collector of texts for the Jewish Theological Seminary, was not alone in his search for scholarly treasures!

The Jewish Theological Seminary has experienced the high financial costs of scholarship. The school often had to scrimp to get through a difficult period, and budgets apparently were often rearranged to grant raises to leading scholars. Like the neighboring Union Seminary, JTS required considerable financial support in order to survive. What is most remarkable, consequently, is not the occasional financial downturn; what is most notable is the number of Jews who have paid the price for the school's survival.

From the beginning, the Jewish Theological Seminary understood its work in terms of the new style of scholarly research. The roots of JTS were in the European *Wissenschaft des Judentums* movement that was actively engaged in the recovery of Jewish literary history. The school was established in the midst of a "Jewish Renaissance" [47] that included the expansion of Oriental and Judaica departments at home and abroad, the establishment of Hebrew Union College in Cincinnati, and the creation of the Jewish Publication Society. The cultural Zionism of Ahad Ha'am also generated interest in the Jewish past and its recovery.

For many faculty and perhaps some students, the Seminary's style of scholarship had its own religious romance. Solomon Schechter epitomized this aspect of the Jewish Theological Seminary tradition when he said:

> Every discovery of an ancient document giving evidence of a bygone [person] is . . . an act of resurrection in miniature. How the past suddenly rushes in upon you with all its joys and woes. And there is a spark of a human soul like yours come to light again after a disappearance of centuries, crying for sympathy and mercy. . . . You dare not neglect the appeal and slay this soul again. [48]

Through scholarly reconstruction, the past lived again. The Israel of flesh and blood lived in the Judaism of pen and paper.

Protestant seminary researchers were also deeply affected by a similar romantic historiography. German-born Philip Schaff (d. 1893), often styled the parent of American church history and the principle founder of the American Society of Church History, [49] was one of the popularizers of the romantic mode. His *The New Schaff-Herzog Encyclopedia of Religion*, [50] a multivolume summary of church history on the eve of the Great War, was a model of how German romantic theory could inspire precise study. Although not as extensive, the *New Schaff-Herzog* was similar to the later *Jewish Encyclopedia*, to which JTS scholars contributed, that capped the romantic historiographic tradition at the Seminary.

The romantic historiographic tradition provided JTS leaders with more than a framework for analysis; it provided them with an apologetic. Louis Finkelstein's concept of a Judeo-Christian heritage that united western culture was an outgrowth of this apologetic approach. In Finkelstein's *The Jews, Their History, Culture, and Religion*, the Seminary's President sought to bridge the gap between Jews and Gentiles by demonstrating their historic solidarity. [51] Although Abraham Heschel was a follower of European and Israeli existentialist Martin Buber, many elements in his philosophy and biblical studies hearkened back to a similar model. Kaplan's description of this aspect of the Jewish Theological Seminary's tradition is apt:

It was expected that such knowledge would open the eyes of non-Jews to the fact that the Jews, throughout their historical career, had been creators of significant cultural values. . . . It was assumed that non-Jews would change their attitude toward Jews as a result of this new knowledge concerning them. Thus would Jews gain the good will of their gentile neighbors, but they themselves would also arrive at a better understanding of their own people and its past.[52]

The depths that this approach to *Wissenschaft* had penetrated life at the Seminary was evident during the 1930s and 1940s. One way that JTS responded to the dark days for Judaism in Europe was by collecting what scholarly and cultural treasures they could rescue. Through these artifacts, European Judaism, if not the European Jews, would live forever in America!

Christian seminary scholars carried the *Wissenschaft* model in two directions. For American liberal scholars, science, whether literary or natural, demanded a thorough revision of Christian doctrine. On the basis of their research, liberal Protestants called for a reconsideration of traditional Christology in the light of research into the Gospels. The new theology tended to stress the immanence of God in creation. Other liberal Protestant characteristics, such as an interest in social reform, followed logically from these assumptions. A. C. McGiffert, president of Union Seminary in New York, summarized the liberal perspective on Scripture:

> Biblical criticism has had theological effects of the very greatest significance. It is not simply that our view of the Bible has changed as a result of it, but our whole view of religious authority has changed. As we have learned not to think of the Bible as a final and infallible authority, as the ultimate court of appeal in all matters of human concern, we have come to see that there is no such authority and that we need none.[53]

In contrast, Protestant conservatives were more leery of the new scholarship. Deeply suspicious of the results and conclusions reached by liberal scholars, Protestant conservatives withdrew into careful textual studies. While they pursued these studies with highly sophisticated methods, conservative methods were not designed to wrestle with the questions posed by the historical-critical approach. In many ways, Thomas Olbricht, a leading historian of American biblical studies, summarized their perspective accurately:

> They [the conservatives] too now read the Scriptures from a historic and literary prospective. Green made a clarion call for this new scholarship: "We must have an English and an American scholarship that is fitted to grapple with these questions as they arise. We need, in the ranks of the pastorate, men who can conduct Biblical researches and who can prosecute learned critical inquiries . . ." They differed only with the conclusions reached by German higher criticism. By the end of the nineteenth century, most German biblical

schools agreed that the Scriptures must be scrutinized with history at the forefront but also that skepticism in regard to historical accuracy, alleged authorship, and the unity of biblical books is healthy, if not mandatory. The [conservative] scholar, in contrast, argued that accuracy, authenticity, and integrity were all supported by history itself.[54]

Although aware of the impact of Higher Criticism on their Protestant counterparts, JTS teachers responded to historical-critical scholarship in very complex ways before 1972. Yet, no single institutional response to the issues seems to have existed. Rather, individual professors seemed to offer their own interpretation of the newer methods. Some institutional marks, however, did exist. Particularly after Adler's presidency, the Seminary featured biblical studies as one of its chief attractions. Teachers and students were apparently more open to the use of higher critical insights in the Prophets and in the Writings. Yet, taking seriously Schechter's warning against the "higher anti-Semitism," the program only touched on Torah in the entrance examinations before 1972![55] Further, the faculty appears to have studied the very important rabbinical literature primarily through the lenses of textual criticism and traditional rabbinical methods of interpretation.

I suspect that Higher Criticism did not affect the Jewish Theological Seminary as radically as it did Protestant theological schools. In part, this is because of the different place of the Bible in the two traditions. For Conservative Jews, the marks of observance are the synagogue, *kashrut*, the Sabbath, and the Land of Israel. Further, rabbinic texts remain a central feature of the tradition. These four foundations are related not only to Scripture but also to the long tradition of rabbinical interpretation. In contrast, the biblical texts constitute Protestant faith and practice. When the Scriptures are not in the Protestant foreground, the background becomes empty. The Bible is all that separates Protestantism from the chaotic void of individualism and rationalism. To touch Scripture, consequently, is to transform Protestantism in a way that is unthinkable among Jews or, for that matter, Roman Catholics.

A Slightly Different World

In attempting to put the Jewish Theological Seminary into the larger context of American theological education, ethnicity and *Wissenschaft* are useful categories. JTS shares many characteristics with Protestant and Catholic ethnic seminaries, and the problems of modern scholarship have implications for that school as well as its non-Jewish peers. Yet, after we note these points of similarity, Judaism and Christianity remain different religions. The differences between the two faiths are as important for understanding the place of the Jewish Theological Seminary among American seminaries as are the similarities between JTS and other schools. Further, although it is an associate member of the Association of Theological

Schools, the Jewish Theological Seminary did not *self-consciously* use Protestant or Catholic seminaries as models. The school's primary "reference institutions are the great research universities."[56] In addition, the Seminary has drawn insights and directions from the various institutions used to train rabbis in the long history of Judaism. The school's accreditation report in 1964 noted the institution's attempts to combine these two traditions:

657

*JTS and
Other Forms
of American
Ministerial
Preparation*

> It is fascinating to watch the development of the Seminary as it seeks to inte-
> grate two philosophies and systems of education into a dynamic and creative
> whole. Obviously, such an effort is fraught with many difficulties and perplexi-
> ties; but perhaps if it should succeed in the future even better than in the past,
> the result may be a significant contribution to the advancement of educational
> theory in this country.[57]

In this sense, the defining task of JTS is the integration of the Jewish tradition with modern, secular learning. The decision to call the Los Angeles campus the University of Judaism was in line with the deepest levels of the seminary's self-understanding.

The primary difference between JTS and the nation's Christian seminaries lies in the ethos that informs the schools' common life and their curriculum. I have found Alasdair MacIntyre's concept of practice useful in discussing these larger patterns of difference:

> By practice I am going to mean any coherent and complex form of socially
> established cooperative activity through which goods internal to that form of
> activity are realized in the course of trying to achieve those standards of excel-
> lence which are appropriate to and partially definitive of, that form of activity,
> with the result that human powers to achieve excellence, and human concep-
> tions of the ends and goods involved, are systematically extended. . . . Brick-
> laying is not a practice; architecture is. So are the enquiries of physics, chem-
> istry, and biology, and so is the work of the historian, and so are painting and
> music.[58]

While MacIntyre's definition of practice is complicated, it does highlight important aspects of practices: they convey virtue, they can improve over time, and they are attempts to find excellence. All practices are ways in which people transmit the good to others in space and time.

The root of these differences in practice goes back to the second century C.E., when the two communities laid foundations for the rabbinate and for Christian ministry. In the light of the destruction of the Temple and the reestablishment of Jerusalem as a Gentile city, the Palestinian rabbis refused to allow their tradition to die. The rabbi became the protector of the community's memory and traditions, the expert in both the written and the unwritten law, and the primary educator of the community. The rabbinical tradition, although influenced by many cultures, thus had as its central goal or purpose the preservation of a minority community that lived within the boundaries (physical, mental, or religious) set by the majority. The most important practices for this style of faith were those preserved by Conservative Judaism: synagogue, scholarship, *kashrut*, and the Sabbath. The way in which the Jewish community protected its practices was through *halakha* or decisions about the meaning of the practices delivered on a case-by-case basis. The academic life of the Rabbinical School is largely organized around studies that enable the prospective rabbi to understand and forward halakhic practices.

In contrast, Christian leadership became increasingly wed to the idea of orthodoxy or right belief. The church formulated creeds, established canons, and waged intellectual (and later physical) war on those who rejected its doctrines. To an extraordinary degree among the world's religions, Christianity became a religion of intellectual teaching or dogma. The Reformation carried this development to new heights. Each division of the church distinguished itself by a particular confession of faith and by rituals that reflected those authoritative summaries of doctrine. Other practices tended to follow the lead of theology. The churches have often excluded people from communion for theological differences, while remaining relatively tolerant about rituals and morals.

Protestant and Catholic theological education reflects the place of doctrine in Christian practice. Originally, theological education was somewhat undifferentiated. In Reformation times, European universities tended toward a fixed curriculum that often listed the specific books that students were required to read and the lectures that they were required to attend. However, Enlightenment philosophers believed that scholars should reflect on their subjects and thus discover their rational form. By the 18th century, most Protestant theologians advocated something like the fourfold curriculum of biblical studies, systematic theology, church history, and professional or practical studies. Conservative theologians believed that this curriculum had value because the Bible was the foundation of the program. In contrast, liberal theologians tended to find the unity of the curriculum in pastoral practice.[59]

Before Vatican II, Catholics favored a more scholastic or often Thomistic pattern of studies. The goal was to balance elements drawn from nature and grace. While this was reflected in a scholastic theology that blended philosophy and theology, it was also expressed through various practices of formation. Formation is the shaping of the natural form of the candidate by impressing on him the spiritual or supernatural character (form) of the priest or, in some understandings, of Christ. Traditional Catholic formation included the teaching of regular forms of prayer, frequent attendance at Holy Communion, personal spiritual direction, and the classic monastic disciplines of fasting, silence, and meditation.

Largely under the influence of the Association of Theological Schools, Catholic and Protestant practices have become more alike since the Council. Some Catholic schools have a program that resembles the Protestant fourfold curriculum, and most Protestant schools have adopted some aspects of formation. Courses on such subjects as Bible and church history tend to be similar with the greatest differences in systematic theology or dogmatics and in ethics. In some respects, the Jewish Theological Seminary has participated in the same process, at least on the formal level. Yet, the differences in the practice of Conservative Judaism compared with the two forms of western Christianity focus the same course differently. Thus a course in Torah at JTS is a quite different course than a Protestant or Catholic class on the Pentateuch, even if the instructor assigns the same readings or topics.

This style of analysis helps us avoid superficial historical comparisons. The reason that the Jewish Theological Seminary has invested few resources in the teaching of theology is that Conservative Jewish practice demands more attention to other areas. For a person to be authentically Jewish, that individual has to live out the commandments that define Jewish life. The meaning of those commandments is, consequently, of great importance. This is reflected in the considerable proportion of the curriculum devoted to Talmud and its interpretation. In contrast, doctrinal clarity is not central to authentic Jewish practice. While Jewish doctrine exists, there is no Jewish parallel to the Christian preoccupation with doctrinal details. Given the relatively small place of doctrine in Jewish practice, the type of theology taught at JTS has logically tended toward the philosophy of Judaism rather than toward the systematic exposition of Jewish teachings. Abraham Heschel's *God in Search of Man*[60] and *Man Is Not Alone: A Philosophy of Religion*[61] are good examples of this Jewish theological style.

To an outsider, the Jewish Theological Seminary appears to be a conglomerate. The school was at one time home to the United Synagogue, the Ramah camps, a radio and television empire, a Teachers Institute, a large Jewish museum, and other enterprises. Over the years, it has maintained campuses in Los Angeles and Israel. Its President and faculty have served as the spokespersons for conservative Jews in Israel. While it is a slight exaggeration, one might say that the Jewish Theological Seminary is American Conservative Judaism.[62] Earlier in this essay, the comparative shortage of intellectual leadership among Conservative Jews was suggested as one reason for this proliferation.[63] Other factors were also at work. Jewish practice does not demand the same type of organizational separations that Protestantism and Catholicism find essential to their common life. Judaism evolved in small communities, and its characteristic practices reflect the needs of such coherent communities. In contrast, both Protestantism and Catholicism traditionally were majority religions in their countries and used different institutions as internal checks and balances. For Protestants in America, voluntary societies, semi-independent denominational agencies, and colleges and seminaries provided the churches with the necessary pluralism. In Catholicism, the religious orders provided a similar diversity of voice and tasks.

Although there are many similarities between scholars at the Jewish Theological Seminary and those at Protestant and Catholic schools,[64] JTS has continued a uniquely Jewish practice of scholarship that antedates the modern world. This tradition involves a vocation to the service of texts and their interpretation. The text is expected to master the interpreter, almost to meld with its reader, and no detail is too small to influence the meaning of the whole composition. Despite the seriousness and care with which Seminary scholars study past writings, the tradition also encourages an intellectual playfulness.

From the time of the Renaissance, the goal of Protestant scholars was to strip away what time has placed between the interpreter and the past. To understand the Bible, hence, one must act as if twenty centuries of piety and scholarship did not intervene. The objects of scholarship are expected to be as fresh as the day they first appeared. In contrast, JTS has retained a tradition of study that views texts as part of a continual stream of interpretation, reinterpretation, and more reinterpretation. If the outlines are not as sharp as some contemporary scholarly theory might demand, the colors and shapes stand out more clearly. For this scholarship, a word, a vowel point, or a phrase may transform a text into a prismatic window on the Divine.

Part of the genius of any conservative movement is its ability not simply to retain the past, but to manage needed change in a way that augments the tradition. Much of historic rabbinical thought was an exercise in finding ways to modify the tradition while retaining its power to sustain the community and its practices. The Seminary's practice of scholarship and education has enabled the school and Conservative Jews to find ways of affirming cultural Zionism and later the State of Israel and the ordination of women. From an outsider's standpoint, it appears that JTS has faced a major cultural or political change every generation. Further, the institution has handled its dissenters in the main with dignity and occasionally affirmation. Few Protestant seminaries could have used the radicalism of a Mordecai Kaplan without abandoning their central mission.

At its deepest level, the most important practice at the Jewish Theological Seminary is the school's continual involvement with the religious, cultural, and—after 1948—political survival of the Jews. The art of survival has included the transmission of the stories, teaching, and habits of Judaism. Without those, Judaism vanishes as does Jewish ethnic identity. But JTS has done more than continue a cultural tradition. The school has experimented with a radical ecumenism that dared to bring together scholars and leaders from the Christian and the Jewish communities. While these meetings did not always work miracles, they had an impact on events.

661

*JTS and
Other Forms
of American
Ministerial
Preparation*

Louis Finkelstein (left) with Reinhold Niebuhr of neighboring Union Theological Seminary during a meeting of the Institute for Religious and Social Studies at JTS, 1946. *Photo by Virginia F. Stern. Ratner Center, JTS.*

They contributed to the post-Vatican II Catholic awareness of the historic and continuing place of Judaism in God's work of human redemption, and some liberal Protestants had their first personal encounter with a non-Protestant world there. While the story has not ended, I believe that the Seminary's work in Israel will make a significant contribution to the Jewish state. Like the ancient prophets, the Jewish Theological Seminary intellectuals have reminded secular Israelis that God, not the power of their arms, is the source of their power.

The Jewish Theological Seminary's configuration of practices is an important part of the ecology of American theological education, in part because it differs from both Protestantism and Catholicism. If at one level, one wishes to celebrate the school's similarities with other institutions that train religious leaders, one also wants to rejoice in the continuation of a Jewish pattern of education and excellence. Without the Jewish Theological Seminary, American theological education would be significantly poorer.

1. The tendency is for the schools to educate fewer people for ordained service and more people for a variety of religious occupations.

2. Catholic leaders occasionally resisted the new professionalism. The *Kulturkampf,* a battle between Bismarck's Germany and the Catholic Church was partially over whether Prussia and other German states had the right to mandate university education for priests.

3. Will Herberg, *Protestant, Catholic, Jew: An Essay in American Religious Sociology* (1960; reprint, Chicago: University of Chicago Press, 1983).

4. There is considerable material critiquing the thesis of vanishing ethnicity. The classic is Nathan Glazer and Daniel Moynihan, *Beyond the Melting Pot: The Negroes, Puerto Ricans, Jews, Italians, and Irish of New York City* (Cambridge: Harvard University Press, 1963); see also Richard Polenberg, *One Nation Indivisible: Class, Race, and Ethnicity in the United States Since 1938* (New York: Viking Press, 1980), and Reed Ueda, *Postwar Immigrant America: A Social History* (Boston: St. Martin's Press, 1994).

5. I began this study with a strong belief that the Jewish Theological Seminary fit larger American religious patterns. While I did find similarities, such as the secularizing impact of accreditation, I came to the end of my own study convinced that the similarities were more on the surface than substantial. Every time that I have returned to the essay with my faith in the power of those elements that unite the Jewish Theological Seminary with other similar institutions, the less I am able to convince myself of my own rhetoric.

6. For a more extensive discussion, see Glenn Miller and Robert Lynn, "Christian Theological Education," in *Encyclopedia of the American Religious Experience,* ed. Charles Lippy and Peter Williams (New York: Charles Scribner's Sons, 1988), vol. 3, pp. 1627–52. Also see Glenn T. Miller, *Piety and Intellect* (Atlanta: Scholar's Press, 1990).

7. The 16th-century Council of Trent set the content of much Catholic doctrine and practice before Vatican II. One of its decrees required dioceses to establish seminaries for the training of priests.

8. Jerry Wayne Brown, *The Rise of Biblical Criticism in America.* (Middletown: Wesleyan University Press, 1969).

9. Edward Robinson "Theological Education in Germany" *The Biblical Repository* 1, no. 1 (1831): p. 207.

10. Christopher J. Kauffman, *Tradition and Transformation in Catholic Culture: The Priests of Saint Sulpice in the United States from 1791 to the Present.* (New York: Macmillan; London: Collier Macmillan, 1987). William Stephen Morris, *The Seminary Movement in the United States: Projects, Foundations, and Early Development, 1833–1866.* (Washington D.C.: Catholic University of America, 1932).

11. Russell Dicks and Richard Cabot, *The Art of Ministering to the Sick* (New York: The Macmillan Company, 1936). Although its critics claimed that clinical training was atheological, the movement advocated an inductive approach to theological issues; that is, learning who God was through the encounter with other people.

12. In contrast, many faculty members saw their work as more similar to teachers in colleges and universities and spoke about "their disciplines" and "their work."

13. Robert Kelly, *Theological Education in America: A Study of One Hundred-Sixty-One Theological Schools in the United States and Canada* (New York: George Doran and Company, 1924). William Adams Brown and Mark May, *The Institutions That Train Ministers, vol. 3, The Education of American Ministers* (New York: The Institute for Religious and Social Research, 1934); and H. Richard Niebuhr, Daniel Day Williams, and James M. Gustafson, *The Advancement of Theological Education* (New York: Harper & Brothers, 1957).

14. Edward Farley, *Theologia, the Fragmentation and Unity of Theological Education* (Philadelphia: Fortress Press, c. 1983). David Kelsey, *To Understand God Truly: What's Theological About a Theological School* (Louisville, Ky.: Westminster/John Knox Press, 1992).

15. The Greek word, *paideia*, originally referred to the combination of literary and moral education received by the upper classes in ancient Greece and Rome. The purpose of *paideia* was to teach students leadership skills that would enable them to function effectively in the ancient empires. The word does not always have this clear a meaning, however, in many discussions of contemporary theological education where it tends to point to an educational style that deemphasizes scientific and critical study in favor of studies that deal more with religious experience, internal attitudes, and personal orientation.

16. David Hackett Fischer, *Albion's Seed: Four British Folkways in America* (New York: Oxford University Press, 1989).

17. Stephen J. Shaw, " An Oak Among Churches: St. Boniface Parish, Chicago, 1864–1990" in *American Congregations*, ed. James P. Wind and James W. Lewis (Chicago: University of Chicago Press, 1991), vol. 1, pp. 349–93.

18. Perry Miller, *Errand into the Wilderness* (Cambridge: Belknap Press of Harvard University Press, 1956). Miller argued that the earliest Puritans came to America in order to demonstrate to their old-world counterparts that a fully reformed church was possible and desirable. The hope was that England would learn its true nature from its apparent dissenters. In a similar way, many ethnic churches believe that the purity of their faith will attract people in the old country to their cause. The Missouri Synod Lutherans have sent "missionaries" to Germany to gather churches similar to their own.

19. White American Christians are more likely to be active in local congregations than their European counterparts. While ethnicity is not the only reason for this difference, church membership offers one way to distinguish oneself and one's group from the larger mass of the American population. In other words, ethnicity is a form of secondary identity.

20. Cited in Mel Scult, "Schechter's Seminary," in these volumes.

21. Ira Robinson, "Cyrus Adler, President of the Jewish Theological Seminary, 1915–1940," in these volumes. From the 1915 commencement service.

22. Schmucker's adherents followed the example of the Methodists and Presbyterians in substituting non-alcoholic drinks for the wine in communion.

23. The story of the founding of Philadelphia Seminary and of the confessional and ritual issues involved can be found in Adolph Spaeth, *Charles Porterfield Krauth*, 2 vols. (New York: Christian Literature Co., 1898–1909); Abdel Wentz, *History of the Gettysburg Theological Seminary of the General Synod of the Evangelical Lutheran Church in the United States and of the United Lutheran Church in America, Gettysburg, Pennsylvania, 1826–1926* (Philadelphia: Printed for the Seminary by the United Lutheran Publication House, 1927); Abdel Ross Wentz, *Pioneer in Christian Unity: Samuel Simon Schmucker* (Philadelphia: Fortress Press, 1967).

24. Harold Wechsler notes that all of these options were investigated. See his essay, "The Jewish Theological Seminary of America in American Higher Education," in these volumes.

25. The term "seminary" lacked specific meaning in the 19th century, and the founders of new schools rarely used the word with any care or precision. In talking about the decision to found a "seminary," I mean only that they elected a freestanding institution that specialized in training ministers to accomplish their aims. I suspect that the founders of the Jewish Theological Seminary probably had the European seminar or research department as much in mind as they did American Protestant and Catholic institutions for the training of ministers. The Latin *seminarium* means a seedbed where young plants are nurtured. However, I suspect that once the school was called a "seminary," students and constituents began to measure it by other institutions bearing the same name.

26. Carl Stamm Meyer, *From Log Cabin to Luther Tower: Concordia Seminary During One Hundred and Twenty-Five Years a More Excellent Ministry, 1839–1964* (St. Louis: Concordia Publishing House, 1965), chaps. 1 and 2.

27. See the following paragraph for more details on the Eastern European Jews and language.

28. The revival of modern spoken Hebrew in Israel and both cultural and political Zionism gave instruction in Hebrew many meanings for American Jews and, hence, deeply influenced language study at JTS. While this essay could deal with many reasons for the revival of interest in the ancient language, I decided to restrict the discussion in the text to two parts of what appears to have been a larger discussion.

29. Eastern Europe was not linguistically unified. Almost every Eastern Europe empire had substantial minorities that did not speak or write the languages of the ruling classes.

30. The residential pattern began to weaken in the 1980s as theological students became older and elected to commute to nearby schools rather than move to a more central seminary.

31. Only a handful of schools met the pre-World War II standard of the American Association of Theological Schools that all candidates for advanced degrees hold the bachelor of arts degree. By the 1950s, however, compliance with this standard was almost uniform across the Association.

32. The Teachers Institute was a division of the Jewish Theological Seminary that educated people to teach in Jewish schools—especially to teach Hebrew and other aspects of Judaism.

33. Joseph de Maistre (1753–1821) cited in *The Columbia Dictionary of Quotations* (New York: Columbia University Press, 1993).

34. Kenneth T. Jackson, *The Crabgrass Frontier: The Suburbanization of the United States* (New York: Cambridge University Press, 1985).

35. Unlike the cities, where various ethnic groups had maintained their own enclaves, the suburbs tended to place people of different background and faiths next to one another. One had neighbors who came from another ethnic background, and this made it harder for people to turn others into a "they."

36. N. W. Cohen, "Diaspora Plus Palestine, Religion Plus Nationalism: The Seminary and Zionism, 1902–1948," in these volumes.

37. To an outsider, one of the most fascinating links in Jewish history is the close relationship between the world of the rabbi and a socially identifiable community that are often contiguous to one another. In Europe (including the Ottoman Empire), this link was maintained by granting the rabbi and other Jewish leaders a quasi-legal status as the authority with whom the state could deal in the event of ethnic tensions. It was also maintained by religious laws that commanded Jews to live within walking distance of the synagogue and thus to maintain community, even when not compelled by legal pressure. For a season, these communities were maintained in the United States by Jews who settled near their synagogues. But as the synagogue became less the center of a parish and more a gathered community, rabbinic authority (always weak in America) receded.

38. Cohen, "Diaspora Plus Palestine."

39. David A Hollinger, *Post-Ethnic America* (New York: Basic Books, 1995) has a good account of the ways in which Americans have handled issues of ethnicity in the recent past. See also Harold Stein, *The Ethnic Imperative: Examining the New White Ethnic Movement* (University Park: Pennsylvania State University Press, 1977).

40. David Kelsey, *To Understand God Truly*, chap. 4, pp. 78–98.

41. Philology was an important point of transition. As one studied how words and grammatical forms changed over centuries, one came to have a better understanding of how text changed in that same period.

42. Kelsey, *To Understand God Truly*, p. 85. Kelsey's understanding of ancient *paideia* needs some social enrichment. One purpose of ancient *paideia* was to train the ruling classes in a certain rhetoric that enabled them to cooperate with each other. See Peter Brown, *Power and Persuasion in Late Antiquity: Towards a Christian Empire* (Madison: University of Wisconsin Press, 1992), especially chap. 1, "Power and Elites."

665

*JTS and
Other Forms
of American
Ministerial
Preparation*

43. Barton J. Bledstein, *The Culture of Professionalism: The Middle Class and the Development of Higher Education* (New York: W. W. Norton, 1976).

44. John Brubacker, *Higher Education in Transition: An American History: 1636–1956* (New York: Harper and Row, 1958), p. 176.

45. Ibid., p. 10.

46. Henry Preserved Smith, *The Heretic's Defense; A Footnote to History* (New York: Scribner's 1926), p. 121–22. Smith, who was librarian at Union Theological Seminary in New York, exaggerated the overall change. Every survey of Protestant theological education has noted that few students do sufficient work in the library.

47. Jonathan A. Sarna, "Two Traditions of Seminary Scholarship," in these volumes. The term "Jewish Renaissance" is from a quote by Cyrus Adler.

48. Scult, "Schechter's Seminary."

49. Schaff was extremely influential in American historical scholarship. Some of the recent literature on his work includes: George H. Shriver, *Philip Schaff: Christian Scholar and Ecumenical Prophet: Centennial Biography for the American Society of Church History* (Macon, Ga.: Mercer University Press, 1987); James Hastings Nichols *Romanticism in American Theology: Nevin and Schaff at Mercersburg* (Chicago: University of Chicago Press, 1961); Klaus Penzel, *Philip Schaff, Historian and Ambassador of the Universal Church: Selected Writings Edited and With Introductions* (Macon, Ga.: Mercer University Press, 1991).

50. Johann Jakob Herzog, Philip Schaff, Samuel Macauley Jackson, and Albert Hauck, *The New Schaff-Herzog Encyclopedia of Religious Knowledge* (New York: Funk & Wagnalls [1908–1914]).

51. Louis Finkelstein, *The Jews: Their History, Culture, and Religion* (New York: Harper, 1949).

52. Sarna, "Two Traditions of Seminary Scholarship."

53. A. C. McGiffert, "The Progress of Theological Thought in the Past Fifty Years," *American Journal of Theology* 19 (July 1916).

54. Thomas Olbricht, "Intellectual Ferment and Instruction in the Scriptures: The Bible in Higher Education," in *The Bible In American Education*, ed. David Barr and Nicholas Piediscalzi (Philadelphia: Fortress Press, 1982), p. 98.

55. Baila R. Shargel, "The Texture of Seminary Life during the Finkelstein Era," in these volumes.

56. Harold S. Wechsler, "The Jewish Theological Seminary of America in American Higher Education."

57. Ibid.

58. Alasdair MacIntyre, *After Virtue: A Study in Moral Theory*, 2d ed. (Notre Dame, Ind.: University of Notre Dame Press, 1984), p. 187.

59. Edward Farley, *Theologia, the Fragmentation and Unity of Theological Education* (Philadelphia: Fortress Press, 1983).

60. Abraham Joshua Heschel, *God in Search of Man; A Philosophy of Judaism* (New York: Farrar, Straus and Giroux, 1955).

61. Abraham Joshua Heschel, *Man Is Not Alone: A Philosophy of Religion.* (New York: Farrar, Straus and Giroux, 1951).

62. The word "denomination" is not as useful as it might seem. The divisions in Judaism are only superficially similar to Protestant divisions. For one thing, the issues that divide Jews tend to be questions of ritual and not questions of belief.

63. See above, note 2.

64. See above, note 6.

FRED BEUTTLER

For the World at Large

*Intergroup Activities at the
Jewish Theological Seminary*

Leaders of the Conference on Science, Philosophy and Religion, Columbia University, 1949. From left: Lyman Bryson, Louis Finkelstein, F. Ernest Johnson, Edgar S. Brightman, Richard P. McKeon. *Ratner Center, JTS.*

FRED BEUTTLER

For the World at Large

Intergroup Activities at the
Jewish Theological Seminary

Unfortunately we cannot expect to produce a super-Maimonides or a super-
Aquinas to deal with modern science. . . . We need not a book, but a School
which shall continually present to the religious world the facts of Science and
interpret them at once in terms of religious and ethical values. . . . Whether the
Seminary is prepared to undertake such a task, I do not know. I do know that in
the long run nothing it can do either for Judaism or religion can be more important. Until now we have been essentially a school for Jewish history: it is time
that we become also a school of religion and ethics, not only for ourselves, but,
taking the example of Maimonides, for the world at large. . . . It is our coming
of age.   —Louis Finkelstein to Cyrus Adler, 26 July 1939

ONE OF THE MORE important,
innovative, and indeed unique programs in the history of religion and education
was the Jewish Theological Seminary's office of intergroup activities.[1] Comprising
over the course of its history a series of lectureships, an annual interdisciplinary
academic conference on democratic ethics, an ecumenical theological students
program, a continuing education program for clergy, faculty seminars, and an early
"think-tank" on ethics, intergroup activities at the Seminary are essentially alternative forms for the embodiment of a single idea.

This idea was Louis Finkelstein's central vision, the fulfillment of which was one
of his "highest aspirations" and, arguably, one of the more important works of his
academic life. Finkelstein's vision was of a "spiritual federalism," a modern synthesis of the various fields of knowledge at the service of a faith that would be certain of
its convictions yet civil and public in its expression. This modern synthesis would
be ongoing, a continual process of "corporate thinking" that would apply the model
of scientific research to the discovery and furtherance of consensual moral values.
At the center would be an educational and scholarly institution that would both
develop new knowledge and integrate it with traditional truth, creating a progres-

669

sive orthodoxy, faithful to the tradition yet open to new truths. Not exclusively nor even primarily Jewish, this school would provide a philosophical center for study and reflection, interpreting the tradition in light of the present, but more important, the present in light of tradition. In many ways, Finkelstein hoped that the intergroup activities would provide for world intellectual life what the Jewish Theological Seminary was to the larger Jewish community: a moral center. For the Jewish community to provide this would truly be its "coming of age" and, indeed, a partial fulfillment of its messianic mission.

Given the centrality of this idea, it is artificial to tell the story of the intergroup activities through its institutional forms: the Institute for Religious and Social Studies; the Conference on Science, Philosophy and Religion; and the Institute on Ethics. Each organization was part of a continuing experiment to implement this central vision. Institutional development was to culminate in an international university centered on the study of ethics, to be called the World Academy of Ethics. This academy was to be truly collaborative, providing a continuous dialogue on moral problems between committed scholars who would reflect and interpret their respective religious and philosophical traditions in light of modern knowledge. In many ways the Enlightenment dream of a true "republic of letters," the vision harkens back to the scholarly ideal of Medieval Spain, where Jew, Christian, and Muslim studied and thought in humble civility and where the scholar provided leadership for his community.

From its beginnings in the late 1930s, through its maturation in the 1940s and 1950s, to its partial abandonment in the 1960s, this vision underwent numerous modifications and developments. It is difficult to tell the story of an idea embodied in several institutional forms, that produced more than ten thousand pages of original research and as many of verbatim transcripts of various discussions, dialogues, and debates. Yet it is clear that in the Conference and the Institute there took place some of the most inclusive discussions on ethics and democracy that America has ever had. They were ultimately unable to develop the comprehensive moral framework for democratic values that was their final goal, but they did develop techniques and models for realizing a truly inclusive universal ethics that would incorporate the best of the various religious and philosophical traditions. While they were unsuccessful in reaching Louis Finkelstein's lofty goals, the story of intergroup activities at the Jewish Theological Seminary does provide the most promising prototype for healing our fragmented moral order, for it established the contours of an inclusive community dedicated to continuous dialogue on moral values.

Beginnings

The various structures designed to implement intergroup activities at the Seminary cannot be understood without careful attention to their immediate historical contexts. As the European crisis loomed in the late 1930s, Louis Finkelstein was convinced that this was a symptom of a more fundamental crisis in Western civilization. Germany was widely considered the most civilized nation in the West, with its great universities, science, and intellectual culture. Since the Enlightenment, Jewish and German culture had evolved together. The Seminary itself combined German-style research with traditional Judaism, seeing itself in continuity with the *Wissenschaft des Judentums* school of German Jewish university scholars. The rise of Nazism and militant anti-Semitism therefore came as a profound shock. If the most highly educated nation on earth could lapse so completely and so rapidly into barbarism, what did that mean for the whole heritage of the West? Hitler's election and rise to power represented a profound threat to democracy and freedom everywhere. It is against this context that the beginning of the Seminary's intergroup activities needs to be interpreted. For this was not just another scholarly venture; rather, it was seen by Finkelstein and others as a desperate attempt to mobilize a generally isolationist American intellectual community to defend democracy and religious liberty.

In order to gain acceptance of his minority faith in an increasingly anti-Semitic America, Louis Finkelstein and the Jewish Theological Seminary decided to launch two related ventures in the late 1930s, the Institute for Religious and Social Studies (IRSS) and the Conference on Science, Philosophy and Religion (CSPR). The Institute was originally designed to broaden the training of the JTS rabbinical students by introducing them to prominent scholars in other fields, including other religious traditions. The Conference, on the other hand, was designed to provide a venue for an ongoing dialogue on ethics between scholars in the various academic disciplines and religious traditions, a kind of ecumenical Talmud.

In addition to their stated purpose, these projects had two further goals in common, aims specific to Conservative Judaism—to strengthen Judaism by broadening its vision and to introduce a respectable, intelligent, and faithful Judaism to mainstream American culture. Louis Finkelstein, in a shrewd yet subtle strategy, sought to counteract secularism and anti-Semitism with an indirect approach. Strengthening the place of religion in intellectual life would gain respect for Judaism, and mediating between Protestants and Catholics, believers and unbelievers, would also help secure the place of minority faiths. This was a subtle strategy and was soon subject to serious criticism within the Seminary and larger Jewish communities. Many thought that these intergroup activities were merely a "goodwill" movement, diluting the Seminary from its essential function of rabbinical training.[2]

Yet in the end one needs to consider the strategy an overwhelming success. Whatever the specific difficulties with the intergroup activities—over format, theme, technique, and subject matter—it did serve to expand the Seminary's influence into the mainstream of American intellectual life. No longer a comparative backwater, the Seminary, through the IRSS and the CSPR, became an internationally known address, with scholars from around the country and the world traveling to what was still predominantly a school to train rabbis. And perhaps most important, it helped open up American intellectual life to Jewish scholars, irreversibly expanding the old Protestant and ex-Protestant academy.[3]

The Institute for Religious and Social Studies was designed to be a forum for the continuing education of area pastors, priests, and rabbis and for the broader training of seminary students at the JTS and neighboring seminaries, such as Union Theological Seminary across the street. Ecumenical in scope, the Institute sought to introduce religious leaders and students to other traditions, as well as to the latest in scientific and social scientific research. It was founded in 1938 as a lecture series under the name of the "Institute for Interdenominational Studies," and from these early beginnings the IRSS grew to a weekly session of three lectures and the Tuesday luncheon at the Seminary, as well as two satellite centers and several faculty seminars. After a significant cutback in 1969–70, the Institute operated a reduced program in the 1970s and 1980s, but in 1995 a major grant from Louis Stein established a sizable endowment and allowed for an expanded program. Renamed the Louis Finkelstein Institute for Religious and Social Studies, the Institute plans on extending Finkelstein's vision while retaining its function of aiding pastoral and seminary student education through ecumenical dialogue on contemporary ethical issues.

The Institute provided a major forum for the expansion of ecumenism and inter-religious dialogue[4] in the post–World War II period, as well as serving as a means for the introduction of mainstream learning into religious discourse. As the end of the war approached, the Institute expanded to other regional seminary centers. In 1944 a series was started at the University of Chicago under the leadership of political scientist and Catholic layman Jerome G. Kerwin, and the following year a series began in Boston with the cooperation of the American Academy of Arts and Sciences. Both of these experiments proved reasonably successful, but financial considerations at the JTS led to their demise in 1953. Another program under Institute sponsorship was a series of faculty seminars composed of scholars from a variety of disciplines and institutions, mostly from the New York area. Several of these seminars lasted for a number of years, including the seminar on religion and art in the late 1940s led by Paul Tillich and John LaFarge, S. J., and the seminars on responsibility in society under the direction of Lyman Bryson, Thomas K. Finletter, and Leo Rosten.

Within its first year the Institute commenced a publishing program, distributing some of the lectures as pamphlets. Soon the Institute decided to publish the lectures in book form, a series that grew to almost thirty volumes, such as *Religion and the World Order* (1944), *Labor's Relation to Church and Community* (1947), *American Spiritual Autobiographies* (1948), *American Education and Religion: The Problem of*

Religion in the Schools (1952), *Patterns of Ethics in America Today* (1957), and *The*
Assault on Poverty and Individual Responsibility (1965). Arranged as they are around
a lecture series and study course, the Institute volumes hold together rather well
conceptually, providing an excellent overview of contemporary thought on the various topics under discussion.

In contrast to the Institute for Religious and Social Studies, the mission of the
Conference on Science, Philosophy and Religion was not the further education of
clergy, but rather the transformation of American intellectual life. It sought to
counter the fragmentation of the academy, to "federalize" intellectual life under a
common goal of democratic values. To do this it did not sponsor guest speakers but
instead commissioned prominent academics to draft papers on a given topic from
their disciplinary perspective and then assembled a wide range of scholars from
numerous other disciplines to comment upon these essays. The main point was not
the papers themselves but rather the dialogue generated by opposing interpretations of the problem at hand. As such, the Conference was oriented not toward
professional clergy or young scholars beginning their careers, like the IRSS, but
rather toward a high level dialogue among the best talents in the American university system. Its aim was not the dissemination of knowledge but rather moral
progress through the *integration* of knowledge.

In the mid-1950s the Seminary added another organization with a slightly
different aim to its program in intergroup activities, the Institute on Ethics. Administered within the IRSS, the Institute on Ethics sought to further the scholarly
emphasis of the Conference on a more continual basis. Instead of the limited
dialogue allowed by annual meetings, the Institute on Ethics sought to focus the dialogue by meeting in a smaller group over a more sustained length of time. It was
hoped that this concentration of energies would produce more concrete results.
This somewhat short-lived group was basically made up of the same inner circle
involved in the CSPR and the IRSS and, as will become evident later on in this
study, with much the same results.

To any outsider, it is evident that the Seminary's intergroup activities were part
of the same general strategy—to create what one member of the inner circle, political scientist Harold Lasswell, described as an "organized American conscience."
Many both inside and outside the Seminary were unclear as to the exact differences
between the CSPR, the IRSS, and the Institute on Ethics. They met at different
times and in different formats but often considered similar problems with similar
scholarly resources. Yet because of their different aims, moral progress versus the
dissemination of knowledge, they had different histories. It is significant as well that
the Institute for Religious and Social Studies, with its focus on "applied" knowledge, still exists, while the Conference, oriented towards "basic" research and
dialogue, was seen by 1970 as outside the necessary purpose of the Seminary.

Through the various intergroup activities, the Seminary reached thousands of people as active participants, audience members, and students. Attendance for the first four decades of the various programs reached over seventy-five thousand;[5] each year the IRSS enrolled between one and two hundred clergy for each lecture series. In the Conference, more than six hundred prominent scholars published a paper or comment in the Conference volumes; thousands attended Conference meetings over the years.[6] There were about a hundred who considered this one of their intellectual homes, serving either on its board of directors or consistently attending, submitting papers, and actively participating in its sessions.

An inner circle of scholars developed rather slowly as the need arose for more central direction and consensual leadership of the intergroup activities, but they provided the continuity necessary to sustain the intergroup activities over the decades. While several drifted in and out, the inner circle was rather stable, centered of course around Louis Finkelstein. Other members of this somewhat informal group included Teachers College educator Lyman Bryson; Columbia political sociologist Robert M. MacIver; educator and Protestant ecumenist F. Ernest Johnson; political scientist Harold Lasswell; John LaFarge, S. J., the editor of the Jesuit journal, *America;* Harvard astronomer Harlow Shapley; and philosopher of science Philipp Frank. By the late 1940s others became closely involved, including University of Chicago philosopher Richard McKeon, Clarence Faust of the Ford Foundation, Nobel laureate physicist I. I. Rabi, John Courtney Murray, S. J., biologist Hudson Hoagland, and Rabbi Simon Greenberg of the JTS. Administering the intergroup activities and soon an active member of the inner circle was Jessica Feingold, later to become the director of the Seminary's office of intergroup activities. After Louis Finkelstein, the most important member was Lyman Bryson, a professor of education at Teachers College and pioneer in adult education for CBS radio. A secularist and close follower of John Dewey, Bryson formed his life around a belief in democratic individualism based on secular scientific knowledge made accessible to all. Finkelstein and Bryson barely knew each other in 1940 but soon developed a close working friendship, perhaps made stronger because of their basic philosophical and religious differences and which only ended at Bryson's death in 1959. This relationship is indicative of the range of religious and philosophical traditions represented, and it is here, among the inner circle, that Louis Finkelstein's goal of "team thinking" came closest to realization.

Funding Intergroup Activities

Much of the early opposition at the JTS surrounding the intergroup activities was overcome in part because of Louis Finkelstein's great success as a fund-raiser. In 1937 Finkelstein became the first provost of the Seminary, where he concentrated on improving contact with the new Conservative congregations and increasing the

Seminary's funding base. When he assumed the position, contributions were under $25,000 per year, from about two thousand donors. By 1939-40, contributions had risen to $70,000; almost $100,000 was raised the following year; and by the 1944-45 school year, contributions reached $517,000 from more than forty thousand donors.[7] It was this massive infusion of funds that allowed Finkelstein to expand the Seminary's intergroup activities.

He knew, though, that intergroup activities needed to be separately funded in order to insulate them from interference. While still provost, Louis Finkelstein turned to Lucius Littauer (1859–1944), a philanthropist and former Congressman. The connection between Littauer and Finkelstein illustrates an interesting problem in the relationship between Jewish philanthropy and the intergroup activities. Were Jewish interests best served by concentrating resources on improving religious adherence among the laity or by raising the intellectual status of religion through interaction with other traditions and disciplines? Littauer, and many within the Jewish community, would only grudgingly accept even the importance of the latter, but Littauer did provide the seed money out of which Finkelstein was able to begin the Institute for Religious and Social Studies and the Seminary's larger intergroup activities program.

Littauer was from the same generation of German Jewish businessmen that initially funded the reorganized Seminary, but he had never been particularly close to the Jewish community. A five-term Republican Congressman, Littauer endowed at Harvard, his alma mater, one of the first professorships in Jewish literature and philosophy in America and provided more than $2 million for the establishment of Harvard's Graduate School of Public Administration in 1935–37.[8] One of Littauer's main concerns was the rise in anti-Semitism.[9] For two years, from 1937 to 1939, Finkelstein courted the philanthropist, making him an honorary JTS alumnus and presenting him ambitious proposals for a Bible institute and endowed professorships. Littauer was open to such an institute, but he was more concerned with having the Seminary train lay Bible leaders and organize reading groups, for he was suspicious of research programs.[10] In late 1938 Littauer gave his first gift, of $5000, to establish the "Institute of Interdenominational Studies" at the Seminary, "to give breadth to the better knowledge of Judaism and the Jewish interpretation of the Bible."[11]

That November the first Institute address was given by Nobel laureate Arthur H. Compton, a physicist from the University of Chicago. In "The Religion of a Scientist," Compton put forth the design argument for the existence of God and suggested a form of theistic evolution as the mechanism for creation. He explained how science could give a moral and ethical outlook that paralleled religious belief and how "the laws of nature are the method in which our intelligent God works."

While Finkelstein was pleased with the lecture series and the formal establishment of the Institute of Interdenominational Studies (soon changed to the Institute for Religious and Social Studies, the IRSS), he had much larger ambitions for the Seminary. Merely sponsoring lectures would not further religious development and belief, for Finkelstein thought that only in these ways could Judaism be strengthened, anti-Semitism reduced, and democratic values preserved. His experience in ecumenical affairs was mixed, for such organizations as the National Conference of Christians and Jews were rather superficial. He turned to the religious leaders in the immediate neighborhood—at Riverside Church, at the headquarters of the Federal Council of Churches, and at Union Theological Seminary—as a base for his ecumenical projects. Throughout 1939 he worked towards achieving his larger vision of a truly interdenominational and interdisciplinary institution centered at the Jewish Theological Seminary. In early November 1939, Finkelstein met with several major religious leaders and scientists to begin planning for a major conference in the fall of 1940, what was to become the first meeting of the Conference on Science, Philosophy and Religion.

Finkelstein wrote Littauer about the meeting, describing the proposed conference as an "immense step forward in the development of religion. . . . None of us could recall another meeting of this type," when Catholics, Protestants, and Jews had gathered to discuss common religious aims. "We hope to impress the statesmen and lay leaders of the world," Finkelstein explained, "with the basic unity of ideals of Science and Religion; and through them and the educators, to make this school and its ramifications, an effective bulwark against the insidious spread of Nazi and Communist doctrines in this country." Finkelstein hoped to establish a "Lucius Littauer School of Religion, Science and Democracy," centered around an ecumenical graduate school based on a new curriculum, on "the scientific basis for religion," "the place of religion in the history of civilization," and "the study of the historical relationship of Western religions." This new school would counter the "lack of influence of religious teachers among intellectual groups" not by emphasizing denominational distinctions but rather by focusing on "general religious teaching," in addition to training ministers and rabbis. Finkelstein was convinced that only a Jewish institution could sponsor it and that it was essential for the position of Judaism within America as a whole.

Littauer angrily rejected Finkelstein's proposal, especially the ecumenical graduate school and interdisciplinary scholarly conferences, and was particularly embittered over Finkelstein's refusal to go to Christian organizations to raise money. Littauer saw little point in a "goodwill" effort and resented the shift away from layleadership training and study programs. Finkelstein was deeply disappointed but explained the need to emphasize their shared belief in immortality, "the cornerstone for faith in human dignity and equality and therefore the ultimate bulwark of democracy."[12]

Littauer was right in challenging Finkelstein to approach Christian organizations as well to raise funds for the new project but not for the right reasons. The dilemma that Finkelstein faced in the late 1930s was that Christians would not have given more than a token place to Jews in any "Judeo-Christian" organization. If Jews were to have any influence in an organization such as this, they would need to sponsor it. Yet to survive, it needed broader financial support. Unfortunately, this was not forthcoming. Littauer refused to fund the Conference on Science, Philosophy and Religion but still remained the patron of the Institute for Religious and Social Studies. Finkelstein convinced him of the importance of the Institute, which at that point was evolving into an ecumenical organization sponsoring weekly lectures and publications for students from the local seminaries, rabbis, and ministers. Littauer continued to support the IRSS for $5000 annually, but after his death in 1944 his foundation abruptly cut off funds.

The relationship between Littauer and the intergroup activities at the Seminary is illustrative of the larger problems with funding that continued to plague the intergroup activities. Finkelstein's success in creating a secure fiscal base for the Seminary enabled him to fund the Conference through the Seminary's own budget, providing a subsidy by sharing staff, physical plant, and other resources. He also shifted funds from the IRSS budget, using this method to circumvent Littauer's opposition to interdisciplinary and ecumenical activities. The initial freedom this gave Finkelstein came at a price, however. By relying so closely on Seminary subsidy, the Conference and the Institute came to be seen as too closely identified with the JTS, rather than being a point where various religious traditions and intellectual disciplines met on more equal footing. When the Seminary's resources became more limited in the mid-1960s, there was no long tradition of shared financial responsibility for the Conference or the Institute. They had become too linked with the Seminary, and when the JTS lost interest, there was no other institution willing to take over. Finkelstein was somewhat successful in raising minor grant money, and there were attempts to interest large individual donors like Littauer, but these could not replace strong institutional commitments.

The Conference on Science, Philosophy and Religion

While the Institute for Religious and Social Studies antedated the Conference on Science, Philosophy and Religion, in the early years it was evident that the Conference was the most important part of the Seminary's intergroup activities. This was the necessary first step in the realization of Finkelstein's vision. The Institute made the Seminary known throughout the greater New York area, but the Conference made the Seminary known throughout the world.

Formally incorporated as "The Conference on Science, Philosophy and Religion, in Their Relation to a Democratic Way of Life, Inc.," the Conference was

A meeting of the CSPR fellows, Columbia University, 1955. From left: Louis Finkelstein, Clarence H. Faust, Lyman Bryson, Robert M. MacIver. *Photo by Maurey Garber. Ratner Center, JTS.*

created to mobilize American academics for the defense of democracy, yet the war was merely an occasion for an experiment in truly inclusive reflection on the democratic moral order. The early history demonstrates Louis Finkelstein's desires to make it truly inclusive: the Conference was the first time in American history that representatives of Protestantism, Catholicism, Judaism, *and* secular humanism met for continuous discussion on ethics. Finkelstein was also careful to invite representatives of most university disciplines: natural and physical scientists; philosophers, including Thomists, pragmatists, logical positivists, and Platonists; social scientists, from anthropologists to sociologists; and most major brands of theologians. Within its first year it also included prominent African American and women scholars.

The stormy first Conference established the major lines of disagreement, between liberal forms of religion and positivistic conceptions of science. Two controversies the first year, between philosophers Mortimer Adler and Sidney Hook and over Albert Einstein's criticism of theistic religion, fixed an image on the mind of the learned public that was difficult to shake. The Adler-Hook controversy painted the Conference as a reactionary counterattack by religious traditionalists against progressive democracy, for the partisans of Hook, including John Dewey and the influential journal *Partisan Review*, targeted the Conference as the leading element in a "New Medievalism." The problem with Einstein's address was almost the opposite one—the popular press lambasted his rejection of an "anthropomorphic God." As this latter controversy was more directed at Einstein himself, the Conference was unscathed, although Finkelstein could not get the chastened physicist to submit anything else. The Adler-Hook controversy was more significant, for it still colors historiographic perceptions of the Conference. The irony, however, is that neither figure had anything to do with the Conference after that first year. Hook attacked it as a hotbed of Adler's medieval scholasticism and antidemocratic elitism, and Adler saw it as doomed from the start, but both were wrong.

The initial planning session for the Conference was in November 1939, two months after the Nazi invasion of Poland. Finkelstein assembled ten representatives, seven from theological seminaries—along with political scientist Harold Lasswell, Nobel laureate Arthur Compton, and astronomer Harlow Shapley—for a meeting to plan a continuing conference to "integrate" science, philosophy, and religion for the "advancement of democracy." After gaining broad support, Finkelstein, assisted by Jessica Feingold, began work preparing for the upcoming conference. A draft statement, signed by seventy-nine "founding members" and reprinted on page 1 of the *New York Times*, proclaimed that the fundamental weakness of democracy in face of totalitarian threats was the lack of "an adequately formulated philosophy." Democracy had become increasingly secular: "Divorced from God, and deprived of its religious foundations, Democracy [was] a mere convenience with little power to move or inspire." To support the democratic way of life, it was essential to create a framework of ideas and beliefs, based on the religious faith in the Fatherhood of God, human dignity, equality, and individual immortality. The *New York Times* saw this as an "intellectual declaration of independence" and hoped that the Conference would create a formula for democratic ideas, relevant in terms of social issues like housing, food, clothing, health, and science: "We need a new Social Contract, a new Declaration of the Rights of Man. If the conference can help to give us that it will become a worthy successor of the Encyclopedists."[13]

That summer Finkelstein and the rest of the Conference planners struggled to fulfill those inflated expectations. The strongest challenge came from Mortimer Adler, then allied with University of Chicago president Robert M. Hutchins in an attempt to reorganize the curriculum around "great books." Invited because of his role in the Chicago fight, Adler sent a long memo to the Conference insisting upon its unanimous repudiation of positivism, by which he meant the equating of science with knowledge and the reduction of religion and philosophy to mere opinion. This repudiation was the "basic function" of the Conference, the only thing that could "justify its existence," in Adler's words. Without it, it should "disband, for there is no point in considering the place of philosophy and religion in our culture if they are merely opinion."[14]

A month prior to the first Conference, the founding members wrestled with the Conference format and agenda, especially Adler's criticisms. The discussion about

Adler's proposals demonstrated the broad diversity of opinion within the Conference and the difficulty in finding ways to deal democratically with questions of ultimate truth. Most agreed that the Conference was awash in a "tremendous amount of vagueness," but Adler's dogmatism was repulsive to most present. Biblical archeologist William F. Albright declared that it was "absolutely impossible" for the group to accept Adler's scholastic premises. The Conference needed to be "democratic," and that required experimentation. It also had to start with common ground, however tenuous. Albright did not deny the legitimacy of Adler's Aristotelianism but insisted that it was only a minority position. Sociologist Robert MacIver thought that Adler's scheme "would in one way ruin our Conference." Rather than a formula to relate science, philosophy, and religion, the main question was "how we can sustain, develop, promulgate certain values." Different people approached democratic values through different means.

At the meeting Adler defended himself, insisting that he did not intend to limit free speech within the Conference but explaining that "the aim of free speech is not to go on being free." The goal of free speech was agreement, for dialogue must have as its aim to "so change both our minds together that we ultimately approach real common ground, I mean an actual sharing of the same ideas and truth." If this was not the point, the Conference in Adler's view was meaningless.

Finkelstein disagreed. "It might be worthwhile for two people to understand each other even if they can't possibly agree," he countered. "I haven't the slightest intention of ever becoming a Catholic, and I haven't the slightest desire to ask Professor [Jacques] Maritain to become a Jew." Maritain, a prominent French Catholic philosopher, had given an address at the Seminary and participated in the early years of the Conference. Though they had some irreconcilable premises, Finkelstein admitted, "If we can't work together, then I will say not only this Conference is hopeless but Christian civilization [*sic*] is hopeless."[15]

Seeking common ground, Lyman Bryson suggested that they could agree in principle that religion and philosophy were knowledge equal to science. This would be the intellectual foundation of the Conference, that philosophers and theologians did have access to certain truths. Adler adamantly rejected this: "Either philosophy is superior to science, as knowledge, both theoretically and practically, or it doesn't exist." Finkelstein proposed another means of accommodation. Scientific truths were tentative, and because of this, they were "universally wrong, because they are expected to be superseded or incorporated into bigger construction." The astronomer Harlow Shapley agreed. Religious truths, Finkelstein went on, were "not expected to be tentative, but expected to be permanent." In that sense, scientific truths were "inferior" to religious truths, dynamic rather than eternal. For example, it was not possible to predict the state of astronomy or archeology a century in the future, but Finkelstein could tell "what the teachings of Judaism are going to be in the year 10,000 if there be any Judaism left." Regardless of Adler's predictable objections, the Conference planners accepted these accommodations, placing the Conference on an inductive, experimental, and democratic path towards consensus on democratic values.

The First Conference

The first Conference on Science, Philosophy and Religion opened on Monday, 9 September 1940, with more than five hundred prominent intellectuals, scholars, and members of the press under tents in the Seminary's courtyard. It was less than three months after the fall of France. In the opening address, Louis Finkelstein declared that the "collapse of Western Civilization" was "a result of its intellectual disunity." "We believe the military struggle in Europe to be but one phase, perhaps a minor phase, of a far greater conflict, namely that between ideas which make for the development, and those which make for the destruction of human culture." Finkelstein argued that the increased specialization of knowledge had contributed to a moral and spiritual vacuum within Europe, fatally separating scientific research from ethical reflection, "facts" from "values." The major aim of this first Conference meeting was to create a consensus on certain key moral and intellectual values through collaborative "corporate thinking," applying the model of scientific research to the discovery of common moral values. Finkelstein argued that the organization must be based on two fundamental principles: the belief in "the dignity, worth, and moral responsibility of the individual, as a child and creature of God," and the conviction that "there is nothing in the world above universal truth." Within the context of these two values, academic disciplines and religious traditions would "become a pluralistic but well regulated universe of thought." Only on this foundation could democratic values be sustained.[16]

Many of the speakers that first day echoed Finkelstein, attempting to develop the newly evolving ideology of "the Judeo-Christian tradition."[17] They were careful, though, to argue that democracy was not based exclusively upon Protestant Christianity, an all too common sentiment of the American people at the time. Within this context, democracy was not an end in itself but rather "the best means for realizing" the supreme end of a fellowship of all humanity, in the words of University of Chicago theologian Edwin Aubrey. Others were careful to warn that democracy was more like a family than a political party, as emphasized by Columbia sociologist Robert M. MacIver, and thus did not need a common creed but rather organic unity.[18]

One common theme was that the current war was merely a symptom of a deeper crisis of the spirit, indeed of the whole Western tradition itself. Pitirim Sorokin, a former member of the Kerensky government in revolutionary Russia and the first head of Harvard's sociology department, argued that the war was a stage in the dissolution of a culture that had overemphasized the material world and had denigrated the realm of the ideal and spiritual. Sorokin called for a new synthetic culture that would include scientific advances but would see humans as bearers of absolute value, true spiritual ends. Columbia College dean Harry Carman agreed: "We have perhaps unconsciously allowed materialistic forces to make our lives shallow and empty and to neglect those 'life-sustaining, life-preserving, life-forwarding areas'—the family, the land and the self."[19]

Not everyone agreed with this foundation, nor that this was the best way to defend democracy. One large part of the audience agreed with Yale religious historian Erwin R. Goodenough, who insisted that he did not come to commit himself "to a definite program of life and philosophy of civilization." Modern scholars were fighting for "the right to keep one's mind open without forming preconceived statements of philosophy, civilization, or anything else."[20] Critics from more pragmatic and scientific viewpoints, such as Philipp Frank and Lyman Bryson, agreed that there was a deep crisis, although they argued that it was precisely the more absolutist and spiritual values that had caused it.

On the opposite side was Mortimer Adler, who agreed that the crisis was caused by a failure to establish a definite philosophy but who considered the Conference to be fundamentally flawed. Adler had offered to withdraw from the Conference, but Finkelstein, Lyman Bryson, and Jacques Maritain urged him to remain. As Finkelstein explained: "I cannot believe that it is going to serve the Conference ill. It is always good to have a good deal of self-examination."[21] Finkelstein was concerned with keeping the Conference as inclusive as possible, and to eliminate Adler would silence one coherent position. If the Conference were to work towards a consensus on moral values, it could not exclude any viable philosophical alternative, however unpopular. This is perhaps the most significant aspect of the Adler controversy— Finkelstein wanted the severest criticisms *within* the group, for only through this form of inclusive dialogue could true progress be made.[22]

The major conflict of the first Conference, and indeed of the American intellectual community for a decade, was that between neo-Thomistic realism and scientific pragmatism. French neo-Thomist philosopher Jacques Maritain spoke first, arguing for a hierarchy of values that could sustain democracy: "There is no unity of the multiple without order in diversity, and therefore, without a hierarchy of degrees. In the world of politics, one of the ills of modern democracies was the false ideology which led many to believe that a democratic society must be a *non-hierarchical whole*." Democratic principles put "political justice and legal relations in first place," creating "hierarchies founded upon liberty."[23]

Mortimer Adler's speech, "God and the Professors," was a more vitriolic assertion of the same position. It had two major parts, one an attack on the Conference itself and the other a program for reforming American intellectual life based on a rejection of "positivism" in favor of Thomistic realism. Adler was skeptical of any collection of professors, for academics came to speak their minds not change them, and thus all the Conference could do was register opposing viewpoints without reaching any conclusions. At the root of this was contemporary "positivism," by which he meant that only science had a claim to knowledge, with philosophy reduced to opinion and religion mere superstition. Adler declared:

> I say that the most serious threat to Democracy is the positivism of the professors, which dominates every aspect of modern education and is the central corruption of modern culture. Democracy has much more to fear from the mentality of its teachers than from the nihilism of Hitler. It is the same nihilism in both cases, but Hitler's is more honest and consistent, less blurred by subtleties and queasy qualifications, and hence less dangerous.[24]

Adler proposed a series of propositions "to serve like intellectual litmus paper to bring out the acid of positivism." He asserted that philosophy was "public knowledge, not private opinion," just like science, and indeed, that philosophy was superior to science, in that science concerned means, not ends, and could not make "a single judgment about good and bad, right and wrong, in terms of the ends of human life."

Adler agreed with Finkelstein that the crisis of the West was due to a failure to integrate modern science with religious truth and that the solution was a grand cultural synthesis, like that of Aquinas and Maimonides, but he accused the Conference of not seeking this with any coherent method. The Conference had to affirm his principles in order to succeed; otherwise its failure would be even more tragic. Positivists could not claim, as Adler did, that democracy was "the *best* political order," for in their minds this was only opinion. "Without the truths of philosophy and religion, Democracy has no rational foundation," and thus to most pragmatists, American democracy was merely "a cult, a local prejudice, a traditional persuasion." It was for these reasons that Adler concluded: "We have more to fear from our professors than from Hitler. . . . Whether Hitler wins or not, the culture which is formed by such education cannot support what democracy we have against interior decay."[25]

New York University philosopher Sidney Hook was the scheduled respondent, reading a measured reply against almost every one of Adler's assertions. To proclaim America was in danger more from professors than Hitler was "not merely false, but irresponsible," for the professors' only crime was disagreeing with Adler. Hook denied that the cause of totalitarianism was positivism, dismissing Adler's philosophical propositions, for "the progress of scientific knowledge flies full in the face of every one of his assumptions about the nature of knowledge." Hook thought it ironic that there was "more universal *agreement*" about scientific ideas, "which make no pretense of being self-evidently true, than about any axioms or self-evident truths which have ever been advanced." To Hook, the moral of this was simple: "Our hope lies in building the values and attitudes of scientific method more firmly into the living tissues of the democratic way of life." The assembled intellectuals and academics roared their approval.[26]

Albert Einstein's paper was equally controversial. The physicist's main point, as the *New York Times* headlined it, was that a "Religion of Good" was "more worthy than 'concept of a personal God.'"[27] Einstein distinguished between science, which he saw as limited to facts, and religion, as concerned with value judgments. The realms of science and religion were inherently dependent upon each other: "Science without religion is lame, religion without science is blind." But this did not include a personal God: "The more a man is imbued with the ordered regularity of all events, the firmer becomes his conviction that there is not room left by the side of this ordered regularity for causes of a different nature," such as from human or Divine will. Religious people should "give up the doctrine of a personal God . . . to avail themselves of those forces which are capable of cultivating the Good, the True, and the Beautiful in humanity itself." Science could purify religion "of the dross of anthropomorphism," contributing to "a religious spiritualization of our understanding of life," for the path of "genuine religiosity" lay in "striving after rational knowledge."[28]

While much of this was as old as Newton, the arguments excited the popular press. Many of the other scientific papers pushed Einstein's arguments further, especially making the connection with democracy explicit. Philosopher of science Philipp Frank argued that democracy was best preserved by inculcating the "scientific spirit," although with religious values doing "what science is unable to do, that is, set up certain goals for both private and social human life and influence the disposition of human beings in favor of these goals."[29] Political scientist Harold Lasswell argued for a "science of democracy" which would use social instruments to transmit "a unified view of the goals of our society," to realize "democracy in life."[30]

By its end, the first Conference established fundamental agreement over the necessity of defending democracy philosophically, but there emerged two broad positions over how that was best accomplished. At the extreme opposite ends were philosophers Adler and Hook, neither of whom was committed to an inclusive dialogue and neither of whom accepted invitations to return to the Conference. Both Adler's dogmatic Thomism and Hook's dogmatic pragmatism had their adherents in the Conference, but with this difference: those in the Conference committed themselves to working out a synthesis of these positions, a democratic philosophy that would include both metaphysical truths and pragmatic scientific method. It never would resolve this systematically, although it did somewhat on a personal level. The conclusion to that first Conference was perhaps best provided by William

F. Albright: "I have a strong suspicion that one of the principal reasons why our Conference is succeeding so well as it promises to succeed is that our Chairman is neither Protestant or Catholic, nor liberal Jew, nor liberal Protestant, nor scientist. He is a conservative Jew. He knows from the outset that we cannot achieve unity and that this is not a parliament of religions, it is not a liberal congress of any sort. . . ; it is a congress where we all aim at one kind of unity, and that unity is a unity of goal."[31]

The Public Face of the Conference

In the first few years of its existence, the Conference on Science, Philosophy and Religion established some very clear patterns and methods of dialogue that would persist throughout its history. The dominant debate would remain between adherents of a moderate Judeo-Christian tradition and scientistic pragmatism. This divide was not between theologian and scientist, but rather the lines of philosophical division cut across disciplinary boundaries. Scientists were often the strongest defenders of the Judeo-Christian tradition, while some theologians pushed pragmatism as a method into faith itself.

After some experimentation with group papers and other forms of collaboration, the Conference settled down to its mature method. Already by the second Conference, papers were not read publicly; instead, copies were distributed a week or so beforehand with only brief summaries allowed at the Conference sessions, a technique that left maximum time for discussion. Over the years they would adopt other methods for dealing with the problem of too much material, with sometimes the moderator having responsibility for summarizing papers or for finding some coherent themes. One persistent problem was that there were almost always too many monographs, sometimes upwards of eight or ten per session, with fifty or sixty over three or four days.

By the third Conference the group had excluded the public from the working sessions, later adding public lectures in the evenings. This narrowed the range of participants and limited the more irrelevant comments from the crowd. One essential technique that distinguished the Conference was the practice of almost always having plenary sessions. To build a modern synthesis on ethics required broad collaboration, so it was vital for theologians to hear technical papers in science and for scientists to wrestle with philosophical issues. Often the most perceptive comments came from those outside a given discipline; the necessity of explaining positions to outsiders forced scholars to broaden their own work, leading to a true "republic of letters."

In these early years there emerged one of the most fundamental problems of the Conference, one that would really limit its larger influence. The decision was made to publish the collected papers in a single annual volume. Thus there were in reality two separate Conferences each year—the published material, which eventually grew to eighteen volumes of dense academic prose, and the actual meetings themselves. As Lyman Bryson once admitted: "The curious thing is that our symposium as published bears a very slight relation to our meeting. They are two different things. The papers are discussed, they are not read."[32] The published material is a mass of academic papers, sometimes sixty to a volume, with little or no coherence between them. At most there was only a cursory introduction, often not even that. Published along with the papers were comments, printed variously as footnotes or appendixes, which gave the appearance of scholarly criticism, but these comments were usually submitted before the Conference itself. In many respects, the Conference volumes could have been published *before* the actual meetings. Unfortunately, the published writings had little to do with the scholarly dialogue that was the true work of the Conference.

If one were to focus on the most fundamental failure of the Conference, it would be here—in the separation of its publications from the integrated dialogue within the actual meetings. Both the published papers and the meetings themselves have real value, of course, but there was no *public* attempt at integration. There were only halfhearted efforts to discuss conclusions within the Conference itself, so as a result many of the conclusions reached were often lost from year to year, leading to much repetition of the same arguments, with little progress. There were one or two attempts at writing a synthetic book that would incorporate the cumulative insights of the Conference, but none was completed. The obvious alternative, a quarterly journal, was never really discussed until the mid-1960s, far too late. A journal would have become the common focus for their vision of an international intellectual community, providing the possibility not only of building up a constituency but also creating the continuing dialogue necessary for a modern synthesis.

Another problem, although one generally outside the Conference's control, was its inability to develop on philosophical issues "the kind of team thinking which has been introduced into science and other fields." Louis Finkelstein put the problem in its simplest terms: the "best men" in a specific field could not or would not put in the year or two necessary, and younger scholars did not have the breadth of experience necessary for truly productive "co-thinking."[33] In many ways also the departmentalization and professionalization of American academic life militated against the success of the Conference—the reward structures of academic disciplines did not really allow for this kind of research or collaboration to count for tenure or promotion.

"Spiritual Democracy" and Moral Order

The true significance of the Conference is therefore not what is in the published volumes but rather what went on in the meetings themselves. What was a Conference actually like? What were the topics of debate, and what was the level of the discussions? Were any broad conclusions reached? Perhaps the best way to answer these questions would be to examine a series of Conferences on a typical issue.

One of the most important periods in the history of the Conference was between 1944 and 1948. That was probably its high point. Victory over the Nazis was in sight, and the Cold War had not begun. By 1947 relations between the West and the Soviet Union were chilling, and they froze solid over the next two years. In 1944 most scholars were concerned with issues of postwar reconstruction, the bases of a just and durable peace. The Conference had been founded initially to mobilize American scholars to defend democracy against Nazism; it easily made the transition in the postwar period to working toward the creation of a new internationalism, but many within it were profoundly alienated from American politics as the Cold War developed. The Conference was not a place for hard-line anticommunists nor advocates of an American Century. Rather, the Conference worked out a vision of a true world community and world culture, which would be neither Western nor Oriental. As the possibilities of an inclusive world community narrowed in the late 1940s, the Conference participants seemed almost visibly to lose their sense of intellectual excitement.

Perhaps only after the end of the Cold War is it possible to see the significance of the Conference debates in this period. There was a real window of opportunity in these years, of alternatives to renewed ideological conflict, and this may provide the most important long-term impact of the Conference. The idea of an inclusive world culture involved concepts of national sovereignty, cultural relativism, and the pos-

Robert MacIver addresses a meeting of the eighth CSPR, American Philosophical Society, Philadelphia, 1947. Swami Akhilananda and Simon Greenberg are the second and fourth from the left in the first row facing him. Also present are F. Ernest Johnson, Richard P. McKeon, Ben Zion Bokser, Alain Locke, and, at far right, Jessica Feingold. *Photo by Press Syndicate, Chicago. Ratner Center, JTS.*

sibility of ethical integration among different absolute values, and the Conference in this period continually discussed these issues. Throughout these years, there was a broad consensus among the participants that peace was best maintained by concentrating on the "fundamental attitudes" of peoples rather than the specific machinery of international organizations. As Louis Finkelstein put it, if there were the same "incompetent statesmen" and the same "moral breakdown" of the interwar period, "it would lead straight to a war no matter what [kind of institutional framework] we had."[34]

A focus on values provided for the development of a "common universal discourse" among the Conference participants, allowing the fundamental chasm between ethical positions to become clear. The Conference was generally divided between those who believed there were universal, ethical norms, binding on all people, versus those who believed that ideas are "ultimately and incorrigibly diverse; that cultural relativism is not a doctrine or a creed, but a discovery," and that all that was possible were small pragmatic agreements. At root this was a clash between an inclusive ethical universalism versus an ethical pluralism, one that is ultimately unreconcilable, but in spite of this disagreement, as Lyman Bryson put it, "All of the people at both extremes recognize . . . that whether the Jewish-Christian tradition is adequate or not, you have to find out about the Hindu, the Chinese, and the other great groups and cultures in the world."[35]

Certain figures within the Conference, such as anthropologist Margaret Mead and African American philosopher Alain Locke, were clear advocates of a philosophy of "cultural relativism," but over the course of the debates within the CSPR they modified this to a broad inclusivist ethic. Cultural relativism they interpreted in a weak sense; to be sensitive to "cultural correlatives, that is to say, different ways to express really the same unitary values."[36] Rather than expressions of ethical pluralism, this form of cultural relativism assumed some universal human essence that was not limited to Western or American values. This was a true ethical universalism. Various members of the Conference tried to reconcile cultural relativism with absolute moral principles, such as Locke's suggestion that absolutists should base their universals on "the common experience of humanity on a comparative and objective basis," rather than deductive assertions. Others insisted upon more pragmatic tests, with ethics and indeed religions regarded as "parts of technology."[37] Yet a rough consensus developed within the Conference on the question of cultural relativism and absolute moral principles, which insisted that "rights" needed to be considered absolute, especially the protection of individual personality, while equally insisting that the question of the good was relative to cultures and cultural groups.

There was a broad consensus on the uniqueness of religious traditions and an equally suspicious fear of a universal world culture based upon material power. As

689

*For the World
at Large:
Intergroup
Activities
at JTS*

Anthropologist
Margaret Mead
speaks at the
Institute for Reli-
gious and Social
Studies, JTS,
1946. Lyman
Bryson is at left.
*Photo by Virginia
F. Stern. Ratner
Center, JTS.*

the Buddhist scholar Taraknath Das insisted, there was a fundamental difference between Western and Oriental cultures. Western culture was leading towards a world culture, but it was a "culture for power and the culture for materialism, the foundation of the present curse which is afflicting the world today." The "founda-tions of Oriental culture takes man as a whole, man's inner being," an insight the West had in Judaism and Christianity two millennia ago, but now the West had neglected the whole of humanity by "giving up the most fundamental things of a human being, the human relation, and taking humanity at large." "You can build all your machines, . . . your League of Nations, you can build all your universities, but they will be of no consequence if that foundation is lacking."[38]

Yet the role of religion and ethics in postwar reconstruction, in establishing a new world order, was always a contested one. Missionary Christianity came under frequent assault. As anthropologist Clyde Kluckhohn put it, while Christianity would create "a world order of unquestionably high ethical principles," it shared with Nazism and Communism the demand that the order be on its own terms. "It seems to me that we ought to face the proposition that Christianity in some respects is perhaps the greatest stumbling block to the only kind of world order which seems . . . a possible one." World religions, while necessary, needed to admit "the tenet that there is no single way of life, from a religious point of view, which is adequate to the needs of all human beings."[39]

Not everyone agreed with this optimistic liberalism, however. "Why should religion . . . that part of the human adventure which appeals to the most sacred, the innermost spiritual feelings of a man, be asked to abdicate and to admit all other groups, religious groups on equality?" countered archaeologist William F. Albright. Religion required "zeal and a conviction that one's own cause is right."[40] Others attacked this as intolerant. The Hindu Krishnalal Shridharani thought that Albright's was "the most irreligious attitude in the world," for it assumed "you are holier than the other person." Hinduism did not care what creed was preached but rather looked at one's conduct. Any world organization needed to be based on world community, and this could only be "on the basis of principles that are acceptable to the whole world and not to a particular community alone, however dominant that community may be."[41]

Yet all religious traditions were not "absolutely equal," insisted sociologist Talcott Parsons. What was needed was a "discriminating selection among elements in other religious traditions." American religion was not strictly exclusive, but evidenced a larger unity in diversity. "There is a most intimate relationship between religion and social solidarity," explained Parsons, "the deeper sentiments which do bind the members of a society together in such a way that harmonious social life is possible." In some respects, the United States did have "a common religion," yet it allowed for great religious diversity.[42]

Many thought that there was a world civilization evolving, in some way following the American model. One common element was a "tendency to reject all absolutisms" based on science and democratic politics. "The essence of democratic politics," insisted international political scientist Quincy Wright, "was completely relativistic," for right was based on fluctuating majorities. Perhaps, he concluded, "tolerance could be the religion of . . . a world civilization."[43] But others thought tolerance too thin a foundation for a world culture. Pitirim Sorokin argued that mere tolerance eliminated divisions between right and wrong, between ignorance and knowledge. All existing religions had "two sets of values": the belief in some absolute value, called God or whatever, outside empirical reality, and a common ethical code. "Here you have foundations which already exist." It was impossible to build one world from a mere "negative tolerance," but on this religious ethic it could be done.

One possible foundation for a world moral order was based on John Dewey's vision of the common school, where group prejudice was reduced through democracy in action. This could include learning the classics of all spiritual traditions, allowing students to see the spiritual and ethical unity of all faiths, and providing for the shared belief in "the right of the other person to live out his own conscientious convictions and see himself as experimenting to discover fuller truth."[44]

Dewey's method provided an essential basis for common action, but in the view of many, it confused democracy and religion. Gerald Walsh, S. J., insisted on distinguishing democracy as "a way of life . . . a perfectly human thing," from religion, which was "a way of salvation . . . a very divine thing." Mixing the two led to dangerous confusion. "We can be quite united on the way of life, but why pry into our way of salvation?" Natural law could provide the basis for the way of life, provided it was not to formulate a universal way of salvation. That should be the focus of the Conference, on creating "a world democracy, as a way of life in terms of the natural law, shared by all men, and can leave to the conscience or to revelation the notion of a way of salvation."[45]

The relationship between the vision of a world community and the reality of the postwar world forced the question of power on the Conference, but many there were suspicious of the emerging Cold War realism. Many thought the United Nations flawed, because it went too far in protecting national sovereignty and assumed the continuation of Western political imperialism. The sixth Conference met merely two weeks after the explosion of the atomic bombs, and this raised fundamental questions involving the moral uses of power. What the Conference represented in these debates is best illustrated by their reactions to several papers given by political scientist Hans Morgenthau in the immediate postwar years. Morgenthau contrasted political action and moral action, warning that any possible reconciliation, any politics based on morality, would be "uneasy, precarious, even paradoxical, and ever liable to turn into renewed conflict" because of the inherent political sinfulness of humans.[46] Morgenthau received a lot of the grounding for his tragic realism from Reinhold Niebuhr. Niebuhr never participated in the Conference, although he occasionally presented papers for the IRSS, and it seems plausible that one reason why is that he considered the Conference too idealistic.[47] Certainly that was the case with Morgenthau.

Some thought Morgenthau's cautions correct, but others found that he had left humanity in an "insufferable" moral dilemma. As F. Ernest Johnson confessed, "I believe that there is a difference between right and good, and if one finds it necessary to make a choice between the two evils, if he chooses the lesser, he is not choosing unmixed good, but he is choosing the right." Lyman Bryson thought Morgenthau's revival of the concept of sin a useful corrective to liberal optimism, but that any notion of inherent sinfulness in politics was a rather common-sensical point. Morgenthau missed Johnson's dilemma, of the necessity of choosing "acts which will accomplish as much good in the face of necessary evil as is possible."

Morgenthau did not want to leave anyone "in a moral no-man's land" but insisted "that there is no clear-cut solution to the problem of political ethics." The atomic bomb posed an "insoluble ethical problem" in that it achieved a good end through bad means. He hoped that his realist position "would eliminate certain self-delusive references to the justice of one's own political position," making "political action more scientific," as people realized that it was not justice, but rather power, that they were aiming at.[48]

The consensus of the Conference was that Morgenthau's cautions had a clear practical effect in the short term, but what was really needed was a picture of the developing future with a full achievement of a moral order. Morgenthau's ideas seemed rather obvious to most of the group; they wanted to move beyond to something more constructive. Political ethics were only relative, and in that sense, it was much like the progress of science, as Finkelstein thought, "in any particular point we are choosing between an inadequate construction and a more inadequate construction. . . . If you choose out of two evil actions the one that is less evil, you have done what is good in the eyes of God."[49]

The problem of ethical uses of political power was one in which the Conference continually struggled. Cold War realism was only beginning its takeover of political thought in America and had not taken over the Conference. Hans Morgenthau's realism was met with deep skepticism, yet the alternative was not a simpleminded idealism as is often portrayed. If most of the Conference planners fell into Reinhold Niebuhr's category of "naive children of light," it was not for want of reflection.

One chief objection to political realism was that it necessarily led to a "steady succession of wars" that could only be ended by a single world community. Law followed community, Massachusetts Institute of Technology historian Karl Deutsch maintained, for the habit of cooperation preceded government. It was this emphasis upon ethical community "from below" that Louis Finkelstein stressed, hoping that peace would be built from within, "on how strong we are morally." American policy abroad should be oriented around a sense of world "moral and spiritual leadership," a responsibility that required the United States to solve its internal problems of racial segregation and intergroup conflict. Only if America was seen to stand for both power and true democracy would it have anything "concrete" to give the world.[50]

The Conference viewed the national and international arenas as intrinsically linked. Just as America had developed a larger community based on a federal model, so could world community develop. The participants saw America as a laboratory for the problems of cultural integration. The black sociologist Charles S. Johnson, soon to become president of Fisk University, declared: "We have in America in microcosm . . . the problems that we envision in the discussions of the integration of human cultures over the world." It was true, Johnson argued, that the world was moving towards a single culture, and just as social controls needed to be directed against "free competition in the economic sphere in the interests of free competition itself," so it was equally desirable to control human relations in a democratic framework "in the interests of human relations themselves." Johnson applied this to the state of the American Negro, enumerating the many barriers to full black integration. The ability to solve this problem on equitable terms, Johnson implied, foretold the ability to create the desired equitable world community.[51]

Perhaps the discussion that most illustrates the orientation of the Conference participants towards internationalism was at the eighth Conference. Held in 1947, only a few months after the Truman Doctrine and the Marshall Plan enshrined the theory of containment into U.S. foreign policy, the Conference explored a relationship with UNESCO, the United Nations Educational, Scientific and Cultural Organization. Through discussions on UNESCO, the Conference added two additional men to its inner circle, University of Chicago philosopher Richard McKeon and John Courtney Murray, S. J. Many of the CSPR participants were members of the U.S. National Commission of UNESCO, including Lyman Bryson, who was on the executive committee. McKeon was one of the primary authors of UNESCO's declaration of human rights. The image of the Conference struggling to advance the vision of UNESCO at the same time the Cold War was hardening points to how out of step many in the Conference felt throughout the late Truman and Eisenhower eras.

Even while becoming increasingly estranged from the dominant Cold War realism of American foreign policy, the Conference sought common philosophical ground, in Philipp Frank's words, the "great possibility of agreement which is independent of the opinion about ultimate values."[52] This was the essence of what Bryson called "spiritual democracy." Quoting Jacques Maritain's speech before UNESCO in 1947, Bryson urged this as the explanation of what the Conference itself represented. Maritain had said:

> I am quite certain that my way of justifying belief in the rights of men and the ideal of liberty, equality and fraternity, is the only way with a firm foundation in truth. This does not prevent me from being in agreement on those practical convictions with people who are certain that their ways of justifying them, entirely different from mine or opposed to mine in its theoretical dynamism, is equally the only way to truth. If both believed in a democratic charter, a Christian and a rationalist would still give mutually incompatible justifications for their belief. If their hearts and minds and blood were involved, then they would fight each other for them. And God forbid that I should say it doesn't matter which of the two is right! It matters essentially. The fact remains that on the practical expression of this charter, they are in agreement and can formulate common principles of action.[53]

If human experience were like a building, as Maritain had suggested at an earlier CSPR, with logical empirical knowledge as the "basement," the main purpose of the Conference should be to gain agreement on the "second story," on "intermediate generalities," where ultimates meet in practical action. The Conference itself had reached the "first floor" of common experience and because of that it had great value regardless of any larger purpose, but Bryson did not think it was possible to reach agreement on the "upper stories" unless the CSPR members made the Conference "the main event of our intellectual lives." They were still "amateurs."[54] But this common experience was immensely valuable, thought Quincy Wright, for it was the only place he knew where inhabitants of different third floors could meet. He wanted to make the Conference even more complete by adding Confucians, Buddhists, and Communists to see if they could reach agreement on the first floor of scientific humanism and natural law while avoiding metaphysical issues as the fundamental cause of conflict.[55]

Was then the ultimate purpose of the group to come to an agreement, or to be as representative as possible? Cultural anthropologist Ruth Benedict felt that "the object of a conference such as this is to get unity, or agreement. . . . We don't want the people who disagree with us to be converted. We want them to use their strengths."[56] It was not to reach agreement, but as Bryson put it, to discover the limits of the universe of discourse, to see where the common first level ended and the third floor of conflicting convictions began.

By 1948, then, the participants began to articulate what the Conference had become. It had evolved over the previous decade, from a search for common values into a great conversation, without the goal of final agreement. While it could be argued that this was implicit all along, even going back to Finkelstein's comments on the Conference's purpose against Mortimer Adler's ideas, here it seemed that the experiment and the method had succeeded.

In some ways this was a distinctively Jewish contribution to the vision of a common ethical community. In spite of several strong advocates for creating a Christian world through conversions, or the advocates of some grand cultural synthesis, there was another alternative. Rabbi Ben Zion Bokser of the Forest Hills Jewish Center suggested that they should follow the model of the Jewish missionaries described by Josephus, whose goal was to create "god-fearers," to lead people to accept the universal moral values inherent in Judaism without requiring the acceptance of the particular religious symbols. The problem with conversion, insisted Rabbi Bokser, was that it denied "the authenticity of the elements of faith and life which other peoples represent" and thus negated "the principle of universality." This was one of the fundamental insights of Judaism: "Every expression of life, to the extent that within itself it manifests creative activity of God, must have authentic elements." No expression of life was wholly true or wholly false, for the world was too complex for that. Rabbi Bokser used the oft-cited image of the Tower of Babel, but rather than being punishment, it was how God introduced "the element of change and diversity, so that men might become differentiated into distinct universes, going off into their own directions," resulting in "a richer culture for all." Each culture, as well as each individual, had a divine purpose to fulfill; without it, the world would be diminished. "Every religion, like every culture," he explained, "surely has an obvious duty to testify to its own truth, but that comes about in a simple process of expounding its views . . . but not in the sense of seeking to make formal converts." This, he urged, was the model of tolerance and community that the Conference itself represented.[57]

The conversation the Conference had become did not fulfill Louis Finkelstein's larger vision, however. Affirming the uniqueness and authenticity of the various disciplines and religious traditions was essential, but the conversation needed to reach some form of agreement. He was not satisfied to rest in something that Bryson considered "magnificently inconclusive."[58] As Finkelstein admitted, one major contribution of the Conference was that scholars saw that their disciplines were not ends in themselves: "Maybe it is a good thing for us, to come here and have to justify our existence in our pursuits in the eyes of one another." Finkelstein hoped that one day they could spend enough time together "to do a little more than just catch those glimpses which we catch here of one another, where the glimpses will become, instead of mere strokes of lightning, a continuous ray of light." Yet even lightning strikes "light up the world a bit, and show us how broad and large it is, even if they also show us how dark it is."[59]

An Organized Conscience and the Spirit of Mohonk

The desire to create this "continuous ray of light" constantly pushed Louis Finkel-stein toward other ways to fulfill his vision. In July 1944 he invited a small group, including Lyman Bryson, Robert MacIver, Harlow Shapley, and Harold Lasswell, to go to Amherst to discuss the future of the Conference and the larger vision of the Seminary's intergroup activities. This group later established a sort of base at Mohonk Mountain House in the Hudson valley near Poughkeepsie, New York. It was at these Mohonk weekends that the inner circle planned the upcoming year's meetings of both the IRSS and the CSPR. While it later added a few members, including Richard McKeon, F. Ernest Johnson, John LaFarge, S. J., Clarence Faust, Simon Greenberg, Hudson Hoagland, John Courtney Murray, S. J., and Jessica Feingold, it remained relatively stable, becoming the core inner circle and planning body of the Conference and the Institute, the real moral center of the JTS intergroup activities. What they later called "the spirit of Mohonk" developed out of these close, intensive discussions leading to the future successes and failures of the Conference and the Institute.[60]

The discussions at Amherst centered around the future mandate of the Conference. Most agreed with Lyman Bryson's desire to further the method of collaborative thinking, seeking to combine the practical attitudes of "men of affairs" with the deliberative reflection of "men of thought," a combination Bryson thought "a necessity for maintaining democracy." Finkelstein, however, wanted the group to concentrate on using this method as a means of resolving moral conflict. "Western civilization has a dynamic quality which is responsible for technological power," he pointed out, but which was "in conflict with the moral traditions of the Jewish-Christian cultures. The great problem of progress is to retain dynamism for technological achievement while substituting charity for aggression."

Harold Lasswell saw the future for the Conference as "an organized conscience for American civilization," that would formulate "a basic moral platform . . . indicating at proper occasions how the general principles applied." Most agreed with Lasswell that the essential task of the Conference was to be a "national conscience." The Conference had succeeded as a gathering of scholars, but most at Amherst thought it a failure, because, as one put it, "we have been haunted by the desire to achieve a practical effect in changing American public opinion and influencing policy." The way to strengthen the moral order was to clarify the cultural norms of American society. The Conference should not be a public information agency but rather issue "statements of its basic principles as a kind of continual platform, experimenting with the concurrent application of those principles to specific problems in order to make explicit the design of the hoped for moral order," with "a statement of choice as to which values should be sacrificed for other possible values."

Sometime after midnight one night while at Amherst, Harold Lasswell and Harlow Shapley were talking about how to work beyond the frustrations of the Conferences through setting up a sort of school or institute. Finkelstein had a vague form of this idea in the back of his mind since 1939 but kept it rather to himself, preferring to have others develop the idea. Around 2 A.M. Shapley remembered some lines from Emily Dickinson: "It might be easier to fail with Land in sight / Than gain my Blue Peninsula to perish of Delight," and this school had a name, the "Blue Peninsula Academy." This would be a working organization of about "one-hundred flexibly minded American men and women who are sensitive to the problems of the 'Moral Order' and competent to contribute knowledge, experience and inspiration in a positive intellectual adventure." The first step would be "the construction of a social-cultural 'platform' for Western civilization, with a collection of clearly described and generally acceptable 'planks.'" The next step would be to survey the implementation of these principles, with a final step "a systematic and prolonged assault on the Tyranny of the Unknown, through a detailed list of unsolved problems." The group at Amherst unanimously endorsed the idea, and it was to remain a topic at subsequent meetings of the inner circle at Mohonk. A fulfillment of Louis Finkelstein's vision for intergroup activities back in 1939, Amherst demonstrated how widely the vision was shared, even among individuals who differed drastically on philosophical grounds. An organized American conscience, on truly inclusive grounds, was to become the Conference ideal.

While the Conference and the Institute continued throughout the decade after World War II, working on areas of world peace, international organization, intergroup conflict, and goals for American education, the Blue Peninsula Academy was to constantly be in the background, returning again in the mid-1950s when Louis Finkelstein and the inner circle began serious planning for the realization of their dream.

The Institute for Religious and Social Studies

When Louis Finkelstein was provost of the Seminary, he presented to Cyrus Adler a plan for an "Institute of Interdenominational Studies." At the Seminary's Semi-Centennial Celebration, several of the speakers—including New York Governor Herbert Lehmann, Columbia President Nicholas Murray Butler, and Dr. Henry Sloane Coffin of Union Theological Seminary—urged the necessity of recognizing the common elements of the Jewish and Christian traditions, and Finkelstein wanted to expand this recognition throughout American society. "America's achievements in industry, commerce and science," he wrote to Cyrus Adler, "will be eclipsed for the future historian by her singular contribution to man's spiritual life," the recognition that democracy was "a way of life and thought, based on the religious faith in human dignity and immortality." Finkelstein wanted to create a spiritual federalism, to have American spiritual life reflect "the same genius for disciplined cooperation which has made possible its federal system of government."[61] The IRSS was to help develop this by working towards practical and personal cooperation.

On Monday evening, 24 October 1938, the first Institute classes began. There were four courses that first term: "The History of the Second Jewish Commonwealth," taught by Alexander Marx; "Jewish Life Under the Law," taught by Louis Finkelstein; "Introduction to Philo," taught by Yale religions professor Erwin R. Goodenough; and the "Septuagint in its Relation to the New Testament," taught by Alexander Sperber of the JTS.

In his report to the Seminary's board two years later, Louis Finkelstein explained the significance of the Institute. He was excited at the emergence of a new vocabulary, of the phrase "Hebrew-Christian tradition," or "Judaeo-Christian tradition," for it demonstrated the "recognition of Judaism as a religion in the same basis as Christianity." More fundamental was its significance as a symbol:

> In a sense, nothing which has occurred in centuries of Jewish and Christian thought, is more important for the future of religion than the fact that men of different faiths are coming together to study religious problems. None of the men attending these courses has any thought of submerging the distinctive teachings of his own denomination in a new universal religion. Each means to preserve his separate tradition. But each has come to recognize not only that

F. Ernest Johnson
leads an Institute
for Religious and
Social Studies
class, 1945. *Photo
by Virginia F.
Stern. Ratner Cen-
ter, JTS.*

the preservation of these separate traditions need not involve antagonism, but
that cooperation between religions will strengthen individual denominations.[62]

Finkelstein considered the Institute "unique both historically and in the modern
world." It offered "a ray of hope," and its "existence is at once a tribute to American
democracy and a bulwark for its preservation. Where friendship and a conscious
common purpose exist between devotees of different faiths, absolutist pseudo-
religions will find it difficult to obtain a foothold."[63]

By the 1940–41 academic year, its name had been changed to the Institute for
Religious Studies, and it was advertised as "A Graduate School Conducted by
Catholic, Jewish and Protestant Scholars." That year it sponsored courses on "The
Religious Background of American Constitutional Democracy," with a month each
of lectures by a Protestant, Catholic, and Jewish scholar; "Current Trends in Christian and Jewish Theology"; another course, "Two Ancient Philosophers and the
Problems of the Present Day," on Augustine and Rabbi Akiba; and the beginning of
the Tuesday luncheon series, with various lecturers. One hope throughout these
years was granting academic credit for the courses, but the "complications involved
seemed insurmountable."

Over the years, the IRSS grew to include several other activities, including a
working group on art and religion, monthly faculty seminars, and even a manuscript prize on "problems of group adjustment." The core of its program, however,
remained the lecture series. What did it accomplish? Its most concrete legacy was

699

*For the World
at Large:
Intergroup
Activities
at JTS*

Institute for Reli-
gious and Social
Studies luncheon
meeting, JTS
1947. From left:
Louis Finkelstein
(back to camera),
Ben Zion Bokser,
Luther A. Weigle,
Swami Nikhi-
lananda. *Photo by
Virginia F. Stern.
Ratner Center,
JTS.*

almost thirty volumes of addresses on a wide variety of topics, published over three
decades. These published addresses are generally more coherent than the Conference volumes, for they are based on a single topic with clearly identified positions.
For example, *Patterns of Ethics in America Today* includes chapters on the ethics of
Judaism, Roman Catholicism, Protestantism, Ethical Culture, "Rational Ethics,"
and "Ethical Frontiers," each a concise treatment from a distinctive ethical tradition. The IRSS volumes were also more accessible, for the lectures emphasized
more the dissemination of knowledge than its advance. Often the addresses would
be too general, even platitudinous, but overall they provide a good introduction to
the various topics addressed.

The method of publication of the IRSS volumes was also rather different from
the CSPR published material. The CSPR program committee commissioned
papers that were distributed beforehand and published with minimal editing. With
the IRSS lecture series, topics were set by the program committee and lecturers
assigned, but often the lectures were published from stenograph records, and occasionally with some of the audience questions, giving the IRSS volumes a more
immediate feel. Oftentimes, the IRSS lectures were a synopsis from a writer's
previous work on the subject, condensed into an hour's lecture. As one confessed at
the beginning of his talk, "Much of what I am about to say has been plagiarized
from my previous writings on the subject."[64]

The purpose of the IRSS was dissemination of knowledge, rather than creation
or integration, so often the IRSS volumes were more general in scope. Many of the

topics would be similar to the themes of an upcoming Conference. Occasionally, papers commissioned for a CSPR would serve as the basis for an IRSS lecture series. The IRSS publications were always more readable and were more easily adapted for classroom use. Perhaps the best way to understand the Institute is to examine its discussions on three common topics—democracy and world order, ethics and American social policy, and the various series of "spiritual autobiographies."

Democracy and the World Order

One consistent theme of the IRSS lecture series, especially in the 1940s, was the foundation of a stable democratic political order. While some of the addresses only treated issues of world order implicitly, the assumption behind the series was "that whatever makes for perfecting the democratic process in all its phases, for the promotion of justice and equity, and for the enrichment of personality has a bearing on the organization of the world for peace and cooperation."[65]

Louis Finkelstein's 1943 address on "collaboration for world order" provided the conceptual underpinnings of the series. It was clear to Finkelstein, in that year before D-Day, that a decisive victory of the "United Nations" was essential to world peace, as was a form of international governmental machinery. The main contribution scholarship could make, insisted Finkelstein, was to clarify cultural standards, for ethical confusion was one of the spiritual causes of war: "Through a series of confusions and misunderstandings, a large part of mankind has lost the ability to reach decisions regarding private and public affairs in terms of unequivocal and definite standards of conduct and thought." Without accepted principles of behavior, people feel "an impelling necessity to surrender to a leader. The need to reach decisions without premises to base them induces a profound psychological misery," a "gnawing doubt" that was "insufferable." Western culture had clearly defined goals in certain fields, such as in medicine and the military, but once outside those limited areas, "we lose guidance, for lack of clearly defined objectives. In the rest of our life, we must face the necessity of determining the wisdom of a proposed course, without knowing the goal."

Improved techniques in science and increases in knowledge of other cultural traditions had all contributed to moral confusion. Much of modern culture was "self-contradictory," leading to mental illness in individuals and irrational politics in nations. Finkelstein recognized the plural nature of Western culture but also urged the removal of its contradictions: "It is not possible to maintain a culture which teaches at the same time the importance of service, and also the value of domination, which inculcates the duty of charity, and also maintains that charity begins at home; which pays lip service to God, but at the same time rejects the practices implicit in recognition of His being." Failure to do so will make "our children . . . regard as the foremost achievement of our civilization its multiplication of personal comforts and its intensification of physical pleasures." Finkelstein concluded with his vision for the immediate agenda of the IRSS in regard to democracy and world order: "The integration in our culture of a system of values which can be summarized for the individual as a guide for his approach to the detailed problems of his life, to give him a viewpoint from which he can evaluate the flux of events, is the vital necessity of our time."[66]

Other expressions of world order were more theoretical, such as Boston personalist philosopher Edgar S. Brightman's call for a "philosophy of world community." Brightman, a mentor of Martin Luther King, Jr., argued that humanity's common humanness, natural environment, common stock of knowledge, and interdependence were the "facts of necessary community," and he hoped for the eventual formation of a "world community organized on the principles of organic pluralism, providing economic and governmental regimentation within the bounds of cultural freedom." This "Faith in World Community" was "an inevitable corollary of faith in God."[67]

In addition to calling for a Jewish homeland, Mordecai Kaplan proposed specifically Jewish contributions to a reconstructed world order by focusing on the relationship of Jewish life to democracy. Mordecai Kaplan argued that the "general trend of Jewish life and teaching has so closely paralleled the trend of democracy that it is no exaggeration to say that the faith and fate of Jewry are bound up with the faith and fate of democracy," for "the prophetic element" within Judaism "illumines the *meaning* of democracy," and "the Torah element points the way to what is necessary to make democracy *work*."[68]

The broad interdisciplinary and ecumenical range of the treatment of these issues is illustrated by the series, "Foundations of Democracy," presented during the academic year of 1944-45 and published a couple of years later. This series opened with an introductory lecture on the contemporary crisis in modern democracy, delivered by F. Ernest Johnson, where he argued that the crisis was much deeper than the war itself. Western democracies had been unable to create loyalty and "an all-consuming devotion to common ends." To Johnson, one of the major problems in democracy was the gulf between major systems of thought, such as laissez-faire economics and the New Deal, but it was essential "to think out the function in a democracy of that sustained tension between opposites which keeps them in precarious balance but in vital interrelationship."[69]

In a pattern typical of the IRSS volumes, there is a surprising amount of controversy and even contradiction within the lecture series itself. This was a conscious attempt to work out in practice what Johnson argued for in theory, of the sustained tension between opposites. After Louis Finkelstein surveyed the "Hebrew Sources" of democracy, George N. Shuster, president of Hunter College, argued for the very real contribution of the Middle Ages to the advance of democracy, from the establishment of universal law and representative institutions, to the separation of church from the state, to the creation of organized societies of free citizens in towns and guilds.

Yet a couple of weeks later, Horace Kallen, then a dean at the New School for Social Research, contradicted most of Finkelstein's and Shuster's ideas in his talk on the "Humanistic Sources of Democracy." Combining a discussion of the American founders with Renaissance humanists, Kallen insisted that the former "did not look to any hidden metaphysical equality" in setting up their experiment in democracy; rather, they based it on a respect for difference, on "the equal rights of different people to life, liberty and the pursuit of happiness." The "dogma" of divine election, either in a Jewish sense of chosen people or in a Christian sense of elected individuals, was merely "a means of making and supporting invidious distinctions between man and man." "Although holders of this dogma have recently discoursed eloquently and at length about 'the infinite value of the human personality,' they have not really meant any and every personality, with all its differences on its head. They have really meant personality that agrees with them." Democracy negates this, insisted Kallen, and his version of democracy, based upon ideas of Thomas Jefferson and John Dewey, was the only version that allows for this difference. "It alone affirms, without any fear of challenge or contradiction, the 'infinite value of human personality.'" This was against any vision of a god, for as Kallen retranslated Job 13:15, he had Job say: "Behold, He will slay me; I shall not survive; nevertheless will I maintain my ways before Him." For Kallen, the humanist tradition meant democracy but a democracy based upon absolute method. "The ends are the Many. The means become the One, generated by the Many."[70]

Characteristic of the IRSS approach to questions of internationalism and democracy was the lecture series on "Great Expressions of Human Rights," delivered in the 1948–49 academic year. The fourteen addresses included traditional topics, such as the *Magna Carta*, Milton's *Areopagitica*, and the American Bill of Rights, but also more inclusive expressions, such as that found in the Confucian tradition as interpreted by Harvard professor Wing-Tsit Chan, the prophetic tradition of Micah by Robert Gordis of the JTS, and the *Ethics of the Fathers* by Rabbi Ben Zion Bokser of the Forest Hills Jewish Center. Of special note was one of the earliest comments on the Universal Declaration of Human Rights, by Roger N. Baldwin of the American Civil Liberties Union, who hoped "that in the tortured development of an international morality through the United Nations, the years 1948 and 1949 [would] mark the laying of cornerstones of universality in human rights," although he was cautious about their success in the midst of "the not-so-cold war."[71] Robert MacIver, the editor, included about a hundred pages of historical documents, making this volume ideal for classroom use.

These topics, on issues of democracy and world order, are indicative of how the IRSS contributed a distinctively Jewish approach to the topic of democracy and world order. There was seldom any "preaching" on the particularly Jewish role in human rights, for example. There were examples from Jewish history and literature, including a long talk in the 1944–45 series by Mordecai Kaplan on "Palestine, An Experiment in Democracy" that was later published as "Democracy and Zionism." The Jewish contribution was never the dominant note of any of the lecture series. This is significant, for by sponsoring the lectures, it made the Jewish tradition accessible to those outside it in a much more subtle and effective way than if its role was more explicit or even triumphal.

Ethics and American Social Policy

The IRSS was perhaps more widely known for its work in applying religious and ethical perspectives to American society. In this realm of practical ethics, the IRSS worked out an early version of multigroup relations, developing a distinctive idiom through the use of the term "group," as in "intergroup" or "multigroup." The IRSS preferred these comparatively neutral terms, rather than using terms like race, religion, ethnicity or class, suggesting a clear understanding that democracy is made up of legitimate subdivisions that could work together but were not to be formed into a unitary whole. A later generation would call this "multiculturalism," yet the IRSS affirmed both diversity and unity. The IRSS constantly expressed "its deep interest in the challenge to unity and brotherhood raised by the prejudice and discrimination that separate group from group," insisting that "the greatest peril of modern society is the exclusiveness of group against group."[72] For more than fifty years, the IRSS has tried to make American social policy reflect this vision of intergroup brotherhood.

The first published lecture series of the IRSS was *Group Relations and Group Antagonisms*, which featured representatives of various minority groups considering their problems from the perspective of national welfare and from the viewpoint of the effects on their own group. Lectures included a discussion of Italian Americans by Max Ascoli; "The Negro Group" by Alain Locke; a chapter on the Chinese, the Roman Catholics, and various Eastern European groups; an essay on the Jewish minority by Louis Finkelstein; a chapter on "The Soviet Solution of the Minorities Problem" by Jacob Robinson; and "Minorities and the Autonomy of India" by Krishnalal Shridharani. "This small volume," one reviewer wrote, "has the distinction, in spite of its dry and flat title, of being the most recent and able introduction to the majority-minorities relationship in the United States and abroad."[73]

It was not the Institute's desire to create a single American culture. In "The Ordering of a Multigroup Society," Robert MacIver formulated the working philosophy of the IRSS. The major task was to make America a "multigroup society" where differences between groups would not be eliminated, but only disabilities removed. He called for "the thesis of the common": "There is a great fundamental premise . . . that what we have in common is more fundamental than what we have separately, that that which unites us is deeper, more profound, more important, more real, than that which separates us." MacIver called for going beyond "the narrow group ethics that tend to dominate us," which, without a "great binding faith," simply separates group from group. "Each group has its own purposes, and it struggles for these purposes. So we have the ethics of the group but we haven't the ethics of the whole. We have to get beyond the fragmentation ethics of a divided society." MacIver and the IRSS did not envision a unitary ethic, but rather a broad universal ethic as a sort of umbrella with group ethics underneath. "Our age needs a new . . . charter that will think not of the relations of individuals, but of the relations of group, so that groups may be unified freely without loss, without prejudice, within the whole."[74]

This thesis of the common was one of the constant themes of the IRSS in the mid-1940s. The lecture series "Unity and Difference" focused on this topic, looking at divisions based on race, ethnicity, economics, and religion. Louis Finkelstein provided "Three Paths to the Common Good" by urging groups to emphasize common interests, long-range views, and "the spiritual aspects of life as against its material ones." Finkelstein constantly stressed the long view of things, realizing that alternatives narrow "the nearer we approach a crisis." He also pushed for the spiritual: "If we can persuade ourselves not only intellectually, but also emotionally, that the human spirit and spiritual values are the truly important aspects of life, we will find others to follow that concept. . . . interest in material things divides mankind, while interest in spiritual things unites them. This is natural, for of material things there is a limited supply to meet an unlimited need, while to spiritual things there can be no limit, for we create them ourselves." The solution to problems of the spirit will lead to the solution of physical problems, but "if man concentrates on material problems, he will endanger his material existence and lose his spiritual life."[75]

Many of the IRSS lecture series concentrated on the dissemination of applied social science, for example, when Robert MacIver analyzed crime statistics in Chicago.[76] Arguably the most influential course the IRSS sponsored applied social science to race relations, analyzing "The Costs of Discrimination to the United States," from November 1947 through February 1948. The series was introduced by MacIver who declared: "If we have any spiritual strength as a people it must lie in something we have in common, not in the creeds that divide us. . . . It means that beyond our differences there must be the fiber of solidarity." To abandon differences would lead to sterility, but to mandate uniformity would mean "spiritual death." MacIver considered the "vision of belonging together" as "the first and most eternal problem of social man—to take these differences of ours and harmonize them into a people's unity."[77] Racial discrimination was a betrayal of this national faith.

Most of the lectures concentrated on the specifics of racial discrimination against the Negro, including restrictive covenants in housing contracts, discrimination in trade unions, churches, and the law. The most influential address of the course was by New York University professor of education Theodore Brameld on educational costs. After providing depressing figures on disparities of educational spending in the South and segregated schools, Brameld focused on "the more qualitative and immaterial side," such as costs "in conflict and confusion of values," of the "sacrifice of integrity" of universities with quota systems, and especially costs "in the denial of self-realization, of the maximum fulfillment of personality and group associations by boys and girls, men and women, who are refused completely equal educational opportunity because of skin color or religious faith." Brameld proposed several actions, including support for the President's Commission on Civil Rights, tests on the constitutionality of segregated schools and quotas, struggles for equal pay and tenure for minorities, qualitative experiments to test the psychological effects of prejudice, and intercultural education at all levels. It was Brameld's essay that the U.S. Supreme Court cited as a corroborating authority in the school desegregation case, *Brown v. Board of Education*.[78] The most disastrous cost of discrimination was not economic but spiritual. As MacIver concluded: "Intergroup discrimination has been destroying the spiritual heritage of America and if we lose that heritage we dissolve into scrambling, hustling, power seeking, profit seeking groups denuded of worth, without dignity among ourselves, and without respect from the rest of the world."

In the middle of the 1950s the IRSS sponsored lectures on less political topics, such as on "spiritual problems in literature," religious symbolism, and "patterns of faith," but towards the end of the decade the IRSS returned to practical issues. In the year 1959–60 the IRSS sponsored the series on "Dilemmas of Youth in America Today," looking at questions of the postponement of adulthood, the "tragic use of leisure time," pressures towards conformity, urbanization, and "the ambiguities of public morality." Some lamented the "hangover" from the McCarthy era, in the political timidity and passivity of students, while another perceptively noted the distinctively modern problem of "the understood child," who "has his own pathology stemming from the lack of the opportunity for rebellion against parents who understand him rather than direct him."[79]

The final IRSS series that reached published form took place in 1963–64, on issues of poverty. Like many of the IRSS studies, this dealt with an issue of immediate national debate and included most of the major perspectives. Directed to keep statistics to a minimum, the lecturers pushed for the abolition of abject poverty, urging world and especially national planning to eliminate destitution. The winter of 1963–64 was a time when it was possible to say that "United States resources provide no significant limit for altering existing policies to do away with poverty."[80] That January President Johnson declared war on poverty, and soon thereafter Daniel Patrick Moynihan, then with the Department of Labor, presented his strategies for implementing this before the IRSS. The series anticipated most of the major issues at that time, including medical insurance for the elderly and indigent, divergences in race and problems in migration of rural peoples to cities, poverty in Puerto Rico, and American responsibilities abroad. Reviews of *The Assault on Poverty* were quite favorable, although the issue developed so rapidly that by the time the lectures were published it appeared rather conservative. The first riots had taken place after the series had ended, causing one reviewer to complain: "None of these commentators suggests a role for protest organizations, militant local movements, or outbreaks of violence in achieving needed social change. Nor do they hint at any 'latent functions' of poverty for the affluent majority."[81] In spite of the radicalness of the times, the IRSS demonstrated that it was in the center of the more reflective liberal opinion on this critical issue.

Spiritual Autobiographies, Insights, and Discoveries

In the decade after World War II, the IRSS also sponsored five different lecture series on "spiritual autobiographies," anticipating the 1950s religious revival by several years.[82] These lectures compose one of the most fascinating series of autobiographical reflections in the culture at that time. The IRSS planners encouraged the lecturers to interpret the genre broadly, and many revealed a profound spirituality in everyday life.

The first series was from labor leaders. A director of social insurance for the A. F. L. described his transformation from Methodist minister to union activist. He had personally given up his religious faith, finding in labor conflicts "a peace that I have not known anywhere else." "Maybe it is a curious twist of nature," he reflected, "but only when engaged in a good hard fight to accomplish something to improve life for the workers in our unions, do I find an inner peace and satisfaction that I think is comparable to religious experience."[83] Another, an organizer for the Transport Workers Union, was deeply religious, and indeed, his Christianity motivated him for his work with the CIO. Others organized their spiritual lives around secular moral values, such as a dean of the New School for Social Research who admitted that "My fundamental beliefs are the products of three converging influences . . . history, America, and Jefferson." Another testified that "my autobiography of the spirit is intertwined with the effort to bring practical and humane meanings to these words—'administration,' 'science,' 'love,' 'democracy,' 'education,' and 'high religion.'"[84]

Louis Finkelstein edited two of these volumes, the first of which included a fascinating spiritual autobiography of his father, but he never narrated his own story. Fortunately, others associated with the intergroup activities did. Lyman Bryson, Hudson Hoagland, Ordway Tead, and Karl Deutsch all contributed, with philosopher Richard McKeon writing two, one where he organized his life around the history of philosophy, the reorganization of the University of Chicago, and the founding of UNESCO, and the other where he discovered a profound insight while reading Plato. Simon Greenberg, vice-chancellor of the JTS, wrote on "The Revelation of Human Love," describing his inner life molded around three factors: prayer, "love of the Hebrew language," and "joy in the traditional observance of the Sabbath, Festival and dietary laws." He learned a sense of accountability for all actions from the legend of the little finger, which recorded in heaven the deeds of each day, and he became conscious of "the reality of human love" when his father bought him a sled he had not asked for. His father's love "laid the foundations for my unwavering faith and conviction that human beings can be and are moved to act from motives of love, and that our greatest need as human beings is to be both the objects of the love of other human beings and the bestowers of love upon them."[85] Other significant figures whom the IRSS encouraged to narrate their lives were Julian Morgenstern, then president of Hebrew Union College, and Judith Berlin Lieberman, the daughter of Rabbi Meir Berlin and wife of JTS professor Saul Lieberman. All of these autobiographies point to what one reviewer said was the real value of this work, "how men who reject each other's most fundamental beliefs can work so well together when they have deep respect for human dignity."[86]

The story of the IRSS was not of course limited to its publications. It has sponsored numerous other activities throughout its history. There were several long-running faculty seminars, one started by Lyman Bryson in 1953, which met monthly into the 1960s and included such scholars as Daniel Bell, John C. Bennett, Charles Frankel, Simon Greenberg, Thomas K. Finletter, Gerson Cohen, and Bernard Mandelbaum. In 1960 another faculty seminar formed, composed of younger academics from the Morningside Heights area, including Donald R. Campion, S. J., Lawrence A. Cremin, Daniel Greenberg, Robert S. Johann, S. J., Robert W. Lynn, Roger Shinn, and Seymour Siegel, among others. In June 1958 the IRSS welcomed three Islamic scholars, the dean of theology at the University of Tehran and two professors of religious jurisprudence, who explored Jewish history during the Persian/Babylonian period, and in 1959 the Maharaja of Mysore, India, presented a paper on "The Concept of Power in Indian Philosophic Thought" before the IRSS. In the late 1960s the IRSS sponsored the "Transcultural Seminar on Tradition and Change" and for several years focused on the "Enhancement of Civilization in New York City," even commissioning a study of squatter families displaced by building projects on Morningside Heights.

After the 1969–70 budget cutbacks, the IRSS was reduced in scope, but it still provided an essential part of the Seminary's program. In spite of its topical nature, there was strong continuity in its purpose, as seen for example through a typical lecture series, "Pluralism and Politics: Puzzles for Religious Committees" in the 1984–85 academic year. Lectures that year included "Reflections on the Political Season," delivered right after the election by a Baptist minister and a Reform Rabbi, two lectures on "Black-Jewish Relations," a lecture by a U.S. congressman, and analyses of urban problems by a director of a settlement house, a Catholic bishop, and the director of social action for the Union of American Hebrew Congregations. As Baptist minister Carl E. Flemister, then chairman of the IRSS, said in advertising the series, "The agenda for the future is being shaped by the reality of how little we have in our world. Today we are being confronted by the homeless, the hungry, the captive, . . . in our nation and throughout the world. Our ability to meet this confrontation will be measured by our sense of justice and our continuing faith in the God of the Exodus who leads people and nations from slavery to freedom." Throughout its history the IRSS continued to demonstrate that mutual understanding and cooperation among religious groups could strengthen American democracy.[87]

The Grand Vision: The Institute on Ethics and the World Academy

For all the successes of the CSPR and the IRSS, these organizations embodied only part of Louis Finkelstein's plan for a transformed Judaism and American intellectual life. The Conference was too limited in scope, for the meetings were only of short duration and often rather unfocused. The Institute, on the other hand, was oriented more toward the dissemination of knowledge and was directed toward clergy and theological students—worthy goals, but still less than an ethical university on the cutting edges of scholarly reflection.

The dream of a new school, a Blue Peninsula Academy, was in the background throughout the 1940s and early 1950s. After a year or so of study the Conference was reorganized on a permanent basis in 1950, with an inner circle represented on its board plus a larger group of "Fellows" who were supposed to act like consultants, but this reform did not really change the nature of the Conference itself. Between 1952 and 1954 the Conference concentrated on the relationship between symbolism and values, meeting less frequently but with more of a focus. During this time Finkelstein began to draft possible plans to realize his grand vision. In 1953 he urged the Seminary to develop a "Philosophy Center," for, as he saw it, "the most urgent need of America and civilization today is the formulation of a philosophy system which would explain them to themselves." This would not be a system imposed from above but rather the philosophy "inherent in the basic institutions and decisions of America and the free world," clarified and made explicit. Comparing the process of democracy with the way a judge made his decisions, there was an inner coherence and symmetry, though often unconscious; the task of the philosophy center would be to discover this "inner harmony." This process of clarifying American democracy would make explicit its goals, and he believed that these goals "would have the support of the vast majority of mankind." Because of this, he insisted that "few institutions could contribute more greatly to the security of the Republic and the free world than the proposed 'Philosophy Center.'"[88]

The 1950s were a decade when this type of thinking was common in American circles. The emphasis upon consensus permeates historical writing and cultural commentary, yet there seems to be something qualitatively different about Finkelstein's vision. His call for a "philosophy center" is somewhat ambiguous. Clearly in the memo he meant a physical place, but it would also become the center of American philosophy, not a place but rather an ideal. Should America have a center? Walter Lippmann thought it needed a "public philosophy," but his brand of neo-stoicism would not appeal to the majority. Many scholars thought more like historian Daniel Boorstin, who held that it was the "genius" of the American people that they did not have a common philosophy. Finkelstein, however, was convinced of the necessity of developing a moral consensus, one that could be explained and even exported to others.

By the mid-1950s Finkelstein thought that the intergroup activities had matured enough to begin implementing this philosophy center idea. The 1955 Conference, on "Aspects of Human Equality," returned the CSPR to a closer focus on contemporary ethical issues, and the following spring he decided it was time to create the first Institute on Ethics as the next step in the proposed World Academy of Ethics.

Finkelstein folded this enlargement of the intergroup activities into a larger campaign to expand the entire Seminary's program. In September 1955, Finkelstein, speaking for the Seminary's board, the Rabbinical Assembly, and the United Synagogue, announced a ten-year, $32 million campaign that would expand the programs of the Seminary and its branches in Los Angeles and Jerusalem, including buildings, endowed professorships, $1 million for a conference center, and $1.5 million for the IRSS. While incorporating traditional areas of Seminary interest, such as religious education, along with new programs in mental health, the expansion plan concentrated on areas of ethics.

The Institute on Ethics

The Conference itself was too limited a format to accommodate sustained ethical reflection on a given topic. Whatever its successes, it could not do what it was initially envisioned as accomplishing. For all its efforts at formulating a "universe of discourse," it had not become an organized American conscience. It was simply too

Jessica Feingold
and Lyman
Bryson at a
meeting of the
Institute on
Ethics at Mohonk
Mountain House,
1958. *Photo by
Virginia F. Stern.
Ratner Center,
JTS.*

large and met too infrequently to have much impact. The semiannual retreat and planning weekends at the Mohonk Mountain House did provide a more focused time, but these also were too limited. What was needed was a monthlong Mohonk, a sustained conversation with a select group of participants on a given ethical topic, with the goal of producing a moral "platform."

This sustained Mohonk was to be the next experiment designed to implement Finkelstein's initial vision. Called the Institute on Ethics and housed administratively in the Institute for Religious and Social Studies, it was envisioned as being a cross between the Conference and the Institute, combining the frequency and topicality of the Institute with the basic research and advanced scholarly level of the Conference. Much of the intergroup work in 1955 and 1956 went to implementing this new and exciting experiment. Clarence Faust was selected to direct the Institute on Ethics, an optimistic move on the part of Finkelstein and the other members of the inner circle, for Faust had recently been appointed president of the Ford Foundation's Fund for the Advancement of Education.

In April 1956, the inner circle met at Mohonk to set the agenda for the Institute on Ethics.[89] Narrowing the focus of the 1955 CSPR, Faust and the group decided to concentrate on "Equality of Opportunity." One problem with the fifteenth CSPR, on "Aspects of Human Equality," was that attempts to formulate ethical middle ground too often gained universality by becoming too abstract. Faust suggested the group develop a series of "equivalent statements" of "corresponding ethical axioms or premises" from the diverse ethical positions, which would be "a collective ethical preface to the concrete and specific concerns of the Institute." Practical proposals to further equality of opportunity were also needed, so participants divided into specific problem areas, such as barriers to equality of opportunity among peoples, in higher education, in the development of education, in "social and civic judgment," and in the development of "individual excellence." Finkelstein hoped that the group could also could "mine" a "common core of ethical teaching" from all great religious and philosophical traditions to serve as a foundation for this program.[90]

That June the Institute on Ethics met for the first time, after several months of preparation by six drafting committees, each focused on specific barriers to equality of opportunity. While the study ranged from equality among nations and peoples to

On the grounds of Mohonk Mountain House, 1958. From left: N. A. Nikam, Sterling McMurrin, Louis Finkelstein, I. I. Rabi, John P. Plamenatz (seated), Seymour Siegel. *Photo by Virginia F. Stern. Ratner Center, JTS.*

equalizing access to higher education, the most immediate concerned barriers among various racial, national, gender, and religious groups. One preparatory committee, led by John P. Plamenatz and Liston Pope, compared the practice of apartheid in South Africa with the condition of the Negro in the American South, seeking to find areas for hope in the latter while lamenting barriers in both. Another committee, with Philipp Frank and John Courtney Murray, S. J., looked at "barriers in the cultivation of individual excellence," specifically problems within higher education. Much of this work concerned common complaints over the failure of the university to reach its ideal—as Philipp Frank said, that "the role of scientist as a leader in human conduct has been disparaged," or as Murray put it, that increased specialization had led to a loss of intellectual order, "the greatest need of the university," and that the current disorder was the greatest barrier to intellectual opportunity.

At Mohonk, the group worked through each of the drafts. The report on racial, ethnic, and religious group discrimination was criticized for omitting social class and gender issues. In addition, the working group raised the problem of the minority group's self-conception as related to the dominant society's view. Could the negative reaction to barriers be transformed into positive, constructive reactions? And what would happen to insulated communities when larger societal barriers came down? The group struggled to discover ethical principles "that would aid in the formulation of polities that minimize[d] barriers to equality of opportunity among all groups, while still attempting to preserve the rights of *every* individual to maximal self-fulfillment in the process of group self-determination." The group succeeded in developing questions for further ethical reflection, but it fell short of developing clear ethical guidelines to reconcile individual and group self-determination.[91]

Several outsiders were perplexed at the direction taken by some of the working groups. Regarding individual excellence, much of the report focused on the legitimacy of inequality within a democratic society. This focus, combined with criticism of the intellectual disorder of the modern university, left several confused at how this related to removing barriers. Physicist Richard Feynman, a future Nobel prize winner, thought that "fragmentation of knowledge has very little to do with ethical issues of equality of opportunity"; he thought the meeting would be concerned with more mundane issues like race segregation in the South, quotas in medical schools, and the access of the poor to higher education. More specifically, he wondered why the group did not address such questions as inequality of talents, for it seemed that advanced education enhanced latent inequalities, rather than reduced them: "How are we to state the principles of equality so that this magnification of inequality is not an unethical procedure, but rather, is justified?" Without answers to questions like these, Feynman did not see the purpose of Mohonk and wondered whether his contribution was worth anything.[92] In many ways, though, Feynman's criticisms overlooked the hidden agenda of the Institute, which was to be a preliminary experiment towards the World Academy of Ethics. As such, the focus on intellectual barriers within the university, rather than more external and mundane barriers, was warranted. The latter were rather easy to solve intellectually; no one present would have defended racial quotas or opposed student loans. It was the more intellectual barriers that needed to be resolved before the World Academy could begin.

That summer the group struggled with the shape of future expansion. Harold Lasswell argued for a social scientific approach, with a team of staff researchers headed up by seniors scholars like himself and Finkelstein, while Richard McKeon urged a more free-ranging dialogue on a humanistic model, a further development along the lines of the June Mohonk. In late August 1956, the inner circle again got together for a series of meetings to plan the next stage. Even given the polar distance between Lasswell and McKeon, they agreed that they were dissatisfied with the current state of American universities. The black sociologist Charles S. Johnson hoped to move towards something like the French Academy, while Quincy Wright urged universities to become more independent of other institutions of society, like the church, the state, and the business corporation.

In many ways the June Institute on Ethics was rather disappointing. In late July Finkelstein spoke with Harold Lasswell about their progress, complaining that the quality of the papers was generally poor, and in spite of all the courtesy, "there is a feeling that as a group accomplishment it doesn't amount to much, if anything at all."[93] While useful, the results were not publishable. In many ways this was the perennial dilemma of the Conference itself. It was not possible to publish the results on equality of opportunity in that collaborative form, but to give the material to a single author would make it his project rather than the results of the group as a whole. Assigning six authors to the book would help reflect the collaborative nature of the Institute on Ethics, but it would not be as good as a single work. The critical problem was finding this single author, who could represent the diversity within the group yet communicate its findings. The question was never resolved.[94]

Toward the World Academy

By the late fall of 1956 Finkelstein felt confident enough to draft a confidential memo for the Seminary community, arguing that the World Academy was "the next major step in the development of the Seminary and of Judaism." It was "imperative for the Seminary to undertake broader social responsibilities" by becoming a "world center of ethics." Finkelstein was careful to place this proposed expansion in the history of the Seminary, showing the continuities with the work of Solomon Schechter. Schechter's strategy was to overcome the perceived inferiority of Judaism through scholarship addressed to the larger English-speaking world, rather than primarily to the Jewish community. This strategy was instrumental in changing the attitude of British and American theologians towards Judaism, moving them away from their former anti-Semitism. The Institute for Religious and Social Studies built upon this framework, along with the Conference, the Institute on Ethics and, in a more popular direction, *The Eternal Light* radio series.

As Finkelstein related in the memo, one of the immediate causes for the concentrated effort on the World Academy was a request from the Rockefeller Brothers Fund for "help in formulating the ethical principles" of a major study then in progress. In addition to the more outward looking efforts, it was critical in Finkelstein's mind to strengthen the ethical understanding of the Jewish community, and with that he concentrated Seminary resources on the study of the Talmud. Judaism had "probably the longest continuous tradition of ethical discussion extant," but this "immense treasure-house" was unknown to all but a few Talmud scholars. Finkelstein sought to create an Institute of Biblical and Talmudic Ethics, "unique in the world and unique in history," to concentrate on contemporary ethical problems and propose solutions.[95]

All these were preliminary to the major proposal, the World Academy of Ethics. This academy was "a further development of the Institute on Ethics, and would seek to formulate answers to the daily problems of modern men, in terms of the great religious and philosophical traditions covering human relations, problems of modern social science, and those of the man of action." At this stage, Finkelstein envisaged this as operated by the Seminary, with about fifty senior scholars of all fields, faiths, and parts of the world. "Here they would live together and think through together, as a team," various pressing ethical problems, such as interreligious relations. The academy would be "a unique center for ethical counseling," such as that requested by the Rockefeller Brothers Fund and would have a scholarship program, like the Rhodes scholarships in England, to disseminate this approach.

Finkelstein realized that only an institution like the JTS could sponsor this academy. Universities were too locked into specialized disciplines to work effectively, but most important, it could not be sponsored by any other religious group than the Jews, "for all other religions seek converts to themselves," but "Judaism does not seek converts." It was natural then for Jews "to promote a federalism among faiths and philosophies, instead of conquest of all by itself."[96]

This idea of "spiritual federalism" was a powerful one, and over the following year Finkelstein and his staff worked hard on developing a "blueprint" for the World Academy. This blueprint was to be the major planning document, working towards the realization of the World Academy in four or so years. Finkelstein was concerned that the "moral confusion" caused by competing ethical standards had led to "material paralysis," where people of no common values could find no common grounds for action. "Men who have inconsistent values cannot lead consistent lives. Men who cannot communicate morally cannot cooperate practically." Yet the goal was not conformity, but rather "clarification." This would be provided by the World Academy, "an international, interdenominational, interdisciplinary body which will conduct a coordinated assault on the obscurity and confusion which shrouds the ethical issues of our age." It was to be "a university of the finest religious, philosophic, humanistic, and scientific thought," having a "permanent nucleus of renowned scholars" along with a staff of visiting students, "to experience on a continuing basis the intimate communication, the mutual enlightenment, the indispensable cross-fertilization which is the only manner in which men can arrive at a true community of moral ideas."

Not to codify, but to clarify: this was the minimal goal of the World Academy. But behind this was a larger vision: to be "the center of a vital radiation of ethical faith to a tossing world." Finkelstein saw it as a collection of "firsts": "The first great effort to create a universe of ethical discourse among the intellectuals leaders of the world, the first global effort to analyze the content of five millennia of ethical thought, the first systematic application of science and philosophy to the inspirations of religious thought—these are goals to set men's minds afire." Clearly Finkelstein's mind was set afire by this vision. But could he convince enough people of the need to raise the requisite funding for the bricks and mortar? His first move was to gain what he called a "spiritual subscription to the program itself"; then the needed money would come.[97]

By the fall of 1957 the blueprint had taken shape.[98] The World Academy of Ethics was to form the "fourth leg" of the world's table, in RCA chairman David Sarnoff's metaphor, for while the scientific, economic, and political legs had all grown stronger, the ethical leg had atrophied and "almost withered away." Central to the World Academy was the interdisciplinary and interdenominational university, where scholars and men of affairs could be in residence for weeks or years, free from immediate responsibilities. "The fundamental principle . . . [was] the absolute freedom of participants to determine the methods and procedures of their work." The World Academy would also include other departments, such as an "Institute for Practical Ethics for Everyday Living," where the scholar and layman could come together; "Ethics Workshops" and "Ethics Clinics," targeted at younger leaders, where "men of affairs . . . might retreat to take stock of themselves and their world." It would become a "World Center for Advanced Ethical Study" for younger scholars, along with sponsoring an "Ethics Library for the World" on microform and numerous regional conferences at various international centers, such as Paris, Istanbul, New Delhi, and Rio de Janeiro.

The blueprint even contained budget and site information. The World Academy was to be housed in either a rural retreat setting about thirty miles from New York

City, with several multipurpose buildings, a "cafetorium," a library, staff and faculty houses, and an endowed "Meditation House," built from "identical gifts from distinguished followers of the Buddhist, Catholic, Hindu, Islamic, Jewish and Protestant Faiths"; or on Jumel Terrace, between 160th and 162nd streets in New York City. The urban site was preferable: "With $1,500,000 in funds, the World Academy, complete with housing facility, library, and auditorium, could rise on historic Jumel Terrace site in from two to three years." Another site investigated included the old World's Fair grounds in Flushing Meadows, Long Island, but that was dismissed as impractical.

Closely related to the World Academy plans was the proposed "Ethics Village" of the Seminary, which was to tie the various programs on ethics together as a unified whole through the creation of a new campus site, complete with housing, conference rooms, and endowed professorships. This was to be directed primarily at the Jewish community first, to strengthen its ethical sense in order to "spur a moral revolution" in America so that the nation could undertake moral, rather than merely material leadership in the world. America's current moral failure was especially painful to American Jews: "For Jews bring to their adopted lands everywhere an ethical heritage that involves weighty responsibility. Just as the Quaker is identified with peace, the Jew is identified with ethical living, and this heritage is one he cannot easily abandon." The visit of Chief Justice Earl Warren to study talmudic ethics had "brought an understandable gleam of satisfaction" to the Seminary community, but this included "bitter regret" over the neglect of the Talmud by all but specialists. The Ethics Village was to be the capstone of a three-point program to reinvigorate the ethical heritage of Judaism, which would also include an English translation of the Talmud, a multi-volume history of Jewish ethical reflection, and a manual of the ethics of the Talmud. The ultimate hope of the Ethics Village was to become a "'cathedral center' of Judaism, a gathering place for the best in Jewish life," to embrace first the Conservative community, then the rest of American Jews, then Americans, "and ultimately the whole world." To do anything less, was to "fail our glorious past, our endangered today, and the generations unborn. Above all, [to] fail God Himself." While written for a public relations document designed to raise upwards of $3 million for site and endowment, these words do express Finkelstein's central vision of a Judaism both outward looking and faithful to its heritage.[99]

The move towards the Ethics Village was part of a larger plan to reshape the Conservative movement as "an ethical force." To do that he planned to start with a summer camp in July and August 1958, with around forty rabbis and their families, to be the first "Fellows" of the Lehman Institute on Talmudic Ethics. "It seems to me," Finkelstein wrote to the Seminary officers, "that we will not only have to carry on these studies, but actually carry on a crusade, so to speak, for higher moral standards and higher moral sensitivity in all parts of the Conservative movement. I think too, that the time has come for a redefinition of Conservative Judaism as more than a midway between Reform and Orthodoxy, but rather as an ethical force."[100]

The Rockefeller-Kissinger Special Studies Project

It was during the planning stages for the World Academy that the Institute on Ethics came closest to fulfilling its policy advising function, but it was here also that the future plans were to be frustrated. Louis Finkelstein had been approached by Henry Kissinger and Nelson Rockefeller in late 1956 to have the Institute on Ethics become an advisory panel on ethics. In retrospect, this relationship with Kissinger and the Rockefeller Brothers Fund was the best chance to implement Finkelstein's vision for the World Academy, but the poor showing of the Institute on Ethics doomed its further expansion.

In 1956 Nelson Rockefeller appointed the young Kissinger as the director of a policy planning group that was to prepare his run for U.S. president. The Special Studies Project was to define the major problems and opportunities open for the United States over the next decade or so, to serve as a basis for national policy. Kissinger assembled a bipartisan panel composed of some of the major policy advisors in the country, including former Assistant Secretary of State Adolf A. Berle, former ambassador Chester Bowles, economist Arthur F. Burns, General Lucius Clay, Carnegie Corporation president John W. Gardner, Rockefeller Foundation president Dean Rusk and RCA chairman David Sarnoff. In addition, Kissinger assembled six teams of policy experts, three focused on domestic issues, (the economy, education, and democratic processes) and three on foreign policy questions (international objectives, military policy, and economic issues).[101] In its initial formation Kissinger and Rockefeller conceived that the whole project would provide a "moral framework of national purpose," but they soon realized that they would need expert advice in this specific area as well.

Early in the project, the planners realized that it would flounder "in a sea of expediency," in Kissinger's words, unless the six panels were given moral and philosophical guidance on "the most fundamental questions." Kissinger approached Finkelstein to have the Institute on Ethics provide this ethical guidance. In the fall of 1956, the Seminary's Institute on Ethics had become an unofficial panel of the Special Studies Project, and by the next spring Institute members Louis Finkelstein, Lyman Bryson, Clarence Faust, Richard McKeon, Robert MacIver, John LaFarge, S. J., John Courtney Murray, S. J., and Robert Calhoun had become Panel VII, on "The Moral Framework of National Purpose." Because of its long experience in interdisciplinary and interreligious dialogue, and because it was the most inclusive body of moral philosophers then in existence, it seemed a logical choice to provide moral guidance.

Kissinger proposed several questions to the group: Was the Judeo-Christian tradition "sufficiently universal to afford a basis of community with other cultures"? Could the moral philosophers explain and apply the concept of "human dignity" in secular terms? Specifically, Kissinger wanted to know whether the concept of human dignity could provide guidelines for political, social, economic, and national security objectives. Kissinger had just published a book that was climbing the best-seller lists, where he argued that the United States should move its strategic doctrine from the Eisenhower-Dulles doctrine of massive retaliation towards a conception of limited nuclear war, but he knew that this was a technical problem; he had avoided the crucial question of when this type of war would be justified. That was probably his most important question for Panel VII: What are we "willing to die for in terms of values"?[102]

The moral confusion that Finkelstein had diagnosed was demonstrated in the project's other panels. Even in the age of consensus, the policy makers had little conception of the "overriding purposes" of America, and thus could not adequately address issues such as cold war strategy or resources allocation. Panel VII struggled in its early meetings to provide this sort of ethical criteria. Richard McKeon accepted the chairmanship of the panel, suggesting that it had two tasks: to improve moral thinking and to increase its influence in policy making. McKeon sought to use his earlier ethic of responsibility, which he had sketched out at Mohonk in June 1956, expanded to the scope of the nation. As a basis of discussion, McKeon's ethic of responsibility was too systematic, but it seemed promising to the group.

Attempts to tackle the other panels' questions, for example over the moral implications of economic abundance, quickly became bogged down in abstractions and anecdotalism. A. A. Berle, observing the stalled discussions, pleaded with the philosophers for guidance in establishing international objectives, especially as the end of European empires forced the issue of a new world order outside of bipolarity. What should America stand for abroad? "I am not a philosopher," he explained, "and at my best all I can do is to describe a vast, empty and aching void which has to be filled."[103] Kissinger agreed with Berle, that the moral framework panel had bogged down in abstractions rather than addressing the deep moral dilemmas of the other panels, especially "the formulation of some ultimate end." While professional philosophers found this question "naive," Kissinger emphasized that policy makers had to face this question:

> This morning I spoke to a chairman of one of the subpanels and he said: 'Can we really talk about international objectives until we are willing to decide what principles we are willing to die for?' Now, again I'm sure a trained philosopher can prove that this is a meaningless question. It seems, however, to him and to the people on that panel a very meaningful one, and I am not sure they would be very reassured by being told it is not a meaningful question. *They have to answer it.*[104]

Kissinger implored Panel VII not be too "fastidious" in definitions but rather to give clear moral guidance. The other panels "have all dealt with technical problems but they want to know why they should do what they have been doing." They agreed that they wanted a world with "justice," but they could not define it. "This is what they would ask."[105]

But the Institute on Ethics circle shied away from that responsibility. F. Ernest Johnson was dismayed at the awesome burden implicit in their role as "Lords Spiritual," admitting he was "scared" of that responsibility. They were resisting their duty of providing moral guidance. Kissinger wanted the panel to focus on the deep questions, not definitions or abstractions: "To me the striking thing in this project has been the concern of the very practical people for what may strike individuals like yourselves . . . as elementary questions." The policy makers were confused over the meaning and purpose of "both the policy and the technical choices which constantly come before them." The other panels were constantly asking "what our philosophy is and what it is that we should project abroad." While it may be a philosophically unanswerable question, they "have to give an answer to that in the terms of their own life."[106]

It seemed what Rockefeller and Kissinger were looking for was something like an updated Declaration of Independence. The moral philosophers had to bridge the gap between "philosophical refinement and individual purpose," however difficult, for this is what the other subpanels required.[107] The Institute on Ethics group tried to find this consensus by focusing on narrow issues raised in the other reports, especially America's "spiritual preparedness for war." Kissinger pushed the group to consider ultimate questions. He could understand a strategic threat but not a threat to fundamental American values. Here personally he was on shaky ground; he needed moral guidance, and he knew it. But the assembled moral philosophers refused to provide it. "We should know what we are willing to resist and what we are willing to fight for." The panel had to come up with at least a framework for answering these questions, Kissinger emphasized. "There is no way of dodging this specific issue."[108]

The group tried their best to dodge it, however. Robert MacIver was deeply critical of Kissinger's whole line of argument: "I think any attempt to think of a morally limited war is quite unrealistic," especially given nuclear weapons. John Courtney Murray suggested that the biggest problem was the unpreparedness of the American people for a limited war. Could Americans admit defeat with unused nuclear weapons in their arsenal? McKeon argued that our "fundamental beliefs" were more valuable than mere survival. What was needed was the "democratic equivalent of an ideology," a universalist "mode of life" that would undergird U.S. foreign relations. Finkelstein proposed that the ultimate American national purpose should be the development of "a human climate in which such a great evil as war itself at any level would not happen."[109] But these were questions, not programs for action.

Kissinger and Nelson Rockefeller were frustrated at the moral philosophers' lack of progress, but in spite of the lack of consensus, the organizers still considered Panel VII essential. Kissinger wanted them to provide an overarching framework for national purpose, unifying all the policy proposals under an umbrella of moral concern, for this was to be the introduction to the final report.[110] This was to be the "program of action" to reach the ultimate ends of American society. Harvard political scientist William Yandell Elliott pushed the panel to see that any moral framework required "assumptions about an ultimate order of the universe," which the Judeo-Christian tradition provided. This superseded questions of religious pluralism, for only on this foundation was America bonded in community, which transcends this country and offers "the only ultimate way toward dealing with other religions and other peoples."[111]

The panel was resistant to this universalism and instead focused on the moral implications of limited nuclear war, perhaps the key policy recommendation of the Special Studies Project. It was clear that the possibility of nuclear extinction radically changed the moral situation. Several on the panel argued the immorality of any type of nuclear war, but McKeon countered that national extinction could result from a decadent individualism. Several refused to put it so starkly. The maintenance of national security was not primarily the problem of what individuals would die for but rather "the problem of determining under what conditions the claims of national security would be approbated in favor of a higher value."[112] Yet the philosophers refused to define any value hierarchy.

The questions of individual life and resource allocation raised by other panels forced the consideration of numerous problems, such as juvenile delinquency and criteria to choose between competing social objectives. Kissinger recounted that one panel "didn't know how to choose" between social goods. "They had a list they had spent several months working out," but after accepting certain national security expenditures, they could not decide on social welfare issues. "They literally didn't know on what basis to make the choice."[113]

Finkelstein suggested that the major reason for this impasse was a reliance upon individualism, for to make that the foundation of national purpose would always leave one without a criterion to choose between social goods, but the panel did not suggest any clear alternatives. The moral philosophers saw their role as merely clarifying the right questions, rather than being responsible for giving the right answers. They refused to sketch out the moral framework.

The lack of a clear consensus or, indeed, any conclusions to the moral framework panel's discussions made the issue of a report rather problematic. In late April 1957 Robert Heilbroner tried to articulate the sense of the panel thus far. "A condition of disorder grips the world," he wrote, "a condition manifested by a worldwide mood of inward uncertainty." An underlying "moral vacuity" expressed itself in a "haziness of purpose" and a "feebleness of spirit." A fair description of the world, it described the moral framework panel even better.[114] Heilbroner proposed a framework combining the Judeo-Christian ethic and the U.S. political tradition, arguing that Americans valued the dignity of the individual, the subordination to transcendent order, and the belief that moral individuals in cooperation will reach moral conclusions. Kissinger was impressed with the draft, but the panel and especially McKeon thought it weak and erroneous. Kissinger pushed Heilbroner to include more of religion's role, especially its insistence upon a "natural law" above the state and the existence of institutions above and beyond state control.[115] McKeon, on the other hand, thought the draft an exercise in self-justification, especially the idea that world society was moving in an American direction.

721

*For the World
at Large:
Intergroup
Activities
at JTS*

In June 1957, John Courtney Murray presented his framework for a moral foreign policy. American international conduct must be based on the sacredness of man and the secular concept of reason, law, science, and progress.[116] "If America lost this sense of its identity, it would in the deepest sense fail to survive." This consensus judged American policies on the basis of its common social goals: civic order, justice, freedom, public welfare, and common defense—"universally valid" categories implemented in a constitutional system. The American political culture, Father Murray contended, while pragmatic, was not pragmatism, for it presupposed that "some perennially and universally valid answers have been given to the three great human questions: What can a man know? What ought a man do? What may a man hope? And it insists that they have been answered in politically relevant ways." The one absolute value is the sacredness of the individual, derived from the Judeo-Christian tradition and from which the secular naturalist dissents. "What I'm trying to say," he insisted, "is that the American consensus admits dissent but recognizes that dissent is still dissent." On the basis of these propositions, moral principles were subject to analysis and could decide conflicts of values based upon the moral order, "the hierarchy of ends inherent in the nature of man."[117] Americans had defined an international common good as "prosperity for all, and peace amid pluralism." Self-interest must then be subsumed under this more universal moral claim. He stressed the urgency of the international realm, especially in the context of the emerging new nations.

Yet even on this clear statement of values from one of their own, Finkelstein and the others still could not agree. Did American democracy have a central moral core that would clearly recognize dissent? Or was democratic procedure sufficient? Kissinger knew the latter was inadequate, but the moral philosophers could not agree upon the content of this central moral core.

Much of the summer and fall of 1957 went into drafting the other six panel reports. Early in 1958 the Rockefeller Brothers Fund published Kissinger's report on military issues, with its recommendations for massive increases in defense spending. Other reports followed, with printing runs in the hundreds of thousands. Their major objectives accomplished, Rockefeller and Kissinger left the project in late May. But the report on the "Moral Framework of National Purpose" remained unpublished. The group was to continue working on the report over the next two years, but their findings were finally subsumed under the report on "The Power of the Democratic Idea," philosopher Charles Frankel's tribute to procedural democracy released in 1960. Rather than address the idea of a moral framework of national purpose, the report left these broader questions to individuals to resolve.

While this is not the place to analyze fully the reasons for the failure of the Institute on Ethics group to provide this "moral framework of national purpose," it is clear that there was not a moral consensus within the group that it could use as a basis for an "American conscience." The Special Studies Project was the closest they came to realizing this goal, but many within the group balked at the responsibility. The increasing calls for ethical values in public policy in the late 1950s obscures the major issue of the inability of moral philosophers to establish a consensual scale for ethical values, a hierarchy that would help policy planners by suggesting clear criteria for political judgments. The Special Studies Project assumed that a broad bipartisan consensus could be reached on matters of national and international policy, and to a large extent it was, with many of their recommendations adopted by the Kennedy administration. This consensus makes the failure of the "moral framework" panel even more problematic. The main problem, it seemed, was the refusal to establish a clear hierarchy of normative values. The group was caught in a transition between the model of the moral philosopher speaking to a coherent community and the emerging bureaucratic model of the "ethics expert" on call and at the bidding of a specific contractor or employer.

At the November 1957 Mohonk, much of the discussion centered on the ethical issues involved in Hudson Hoagland's research in oral contraceptives, but lingering in the background was the Rockefeller study. Clarence Faust, in his review of the Rockefeller meetings, pointed out that they liked the idea of a project on "love," even going so far as to ask Father LaFarge to prepare a paper on it, but he had submitted one on urbanization. Faust said that the Rockefellers were "looking for neither formulations nor solutions; they were searching for illumination, for an ethical base. They said that they knew the 'hows' of decision-making, but wanted to know the 'whys'." Finkelstein complained that "the Rockefellers felt that they had been doing things right, but wanted to know *why* they were right."[118]

Whatever his suspicions of the motives of the Rockefeller-Kissinger group, and they were probably accurate, it seems that the direction Finkelstein took was the wrong way to reach the fulfillment of his grand vision. He saw one of the functions of the World Academy to be an ethical consultant, accepting queries from groups like the Rockefeller-Kissinger project, much like a denominational body would from associated congregations. Yet the authority of the World Academy had not been established, let alone any acceptance of its legitimacy in a radically pluralist America. The road to this authority was *through* groups like the Rockefeller-Kissinger project, not around it. Finkelstein's dismissal of this was fatal to the further realization of his grand vision.

It was not a question of selling one's ethical soul, for it was not a requirement to support Kissinger's program of larger defense spending and limited nuclear war. That the Institute on Ethics failed to reach any broad agreement demonstrated that the group had little to offer of utility to policy makers. The group failed its test case. When the time came to function as an organized conscience, the group floundered. Finkelstein did not see the importance of this for the larger fulfillment of his vision; during this period he concentrated on planning for the World Academy, convinced that this was the more immediate concern. Yet part of the tragic element to this story is that when the vision was closest to being realized, of becoming an organized conscience to American culture, the opportunity was missed.

Several months after the Rockefellers initially approached the Institute on Ethics, Finkelstein requested $200,000 as start-up money for the World Academy of Ethics from the Rockefeller Brothers Fund. A representative of the fund had participated in the Institute on Ethics in 1956 and found it "an interesting and stimulating group," but others at the fund found it rather confused. Throughout 1957 Finkelstein met with its officers in an attempt to sell the foundation on the World Academy and a major project on the ethics of the Talmud. Predictably, the fund was cold to the latter project but thought the World Academy, while wildly ambitious, had possibilities. According to the fund's officers, however, there was "still no clear picture of what the Academy will do, who will be involved in it, and how it will maintain itself in the future." Finkelstein had secured $45,000 from the Food Fair Foundation, set up by the grocery store chain, and a couple of smaller grants, but he needed the Rockefeller grant to make the World Academy a reality. Discussions continued through all of 1957 and into early 1958, but the Brothers Fund decided against such a large grant. As a consolation, they gave a one-time grant of $15,000 to the IRSS. The fund considered Finkelstein's dream "completely lacking in reality," but as his group represented "a consequential core of leading philosophers and theologians" who had "stimulating discussions across religious and philosophical boundaries," the fund saw value in encouraging it to continue.[119] Fundamental to its decision was the experience of foundation administrators in working with the Institute on Ethics during the Special Studies Project.

Finkelstein used their small grant to fund the June 1958 Institute on Ethics at Mohonk, along with several smaller discussions throughout the following year. The Institute concentrated on issues of population control, drug abuse, and atomic energy, with the most interesting discussions centering on Institute executive committee member Hudson Hoagland's research on a birth control pill. In 1959 Finkelstein embarked on a long trip to Europe and Israel, with one of his main tasks to drum up intellectual support for his World Academy. That August there was a reduced Conference meeting on "One World—One Ethics?" but the papers were not publishable.

Planning for the 1960 Conference on Science, Philosophy and Religion presented one possible direction for the realization of the World Academy, although it also revealed significant differences of opinion in the direction of the Seminary's intergroup activities. Political scientists Harold Lasswell and Harlan Cleveland were chosen to organize the Conference, under the theme of "Challenges to Traditional Ethics: Government, Politics and Administration." Held at the JTS from 29 August to 1 September, this Conference moved towards a more explicit public policy focus, rather than the more religious and ethical concerns of Louis Finkelstein. While quite successful, this Conference represented the last big effort to use this format for wide-ranging ethical dialogue. It was to be six years before the Conference met again, this time with a more narrow focus, "Approaches to Education for Character: Strategies for Change in Higher Education."

A Diminished Vision: Intergroup Activities in the 1960s

After the 1960 Conference and given the difficulty in raising funds, Louis Finkelstein decided against the rather ambitious building program and the World Academy and instead sought to expand the Institute on Ethics internationally, to create a World Institute on Ethics. Fund-raising was still a problem, and equally pressing was the aging of the inner circle. Finkelstein was sixty-five, and other members, such as F. Ernest Johnson and Robert MacIver, were even older. Lyman Bryson had died in the spring of 1959, a couple of weeks after Richard McKeon was seriously injured in an automobile accident. After 1960 there was a more active attempt to recruit younger scholars, a new generation to implement the vision. Many first became involved through the Institute for Religious and Social Studies, especially a new IRSS Faculty Seminar that started in 1960. Four of the most important in this second generation were Robert Johann, S. J., Teachers College professor Lawrence Cremin, sociologist C. Eric Lincoln, and religious historian Robert Wood Lynn.

Throughout the early 1960s the group concerned itself with ways to implement the international aspects of the World Institute. A group of Latin American scholars, along with some Asians, had come to the Seminary in August 1961 to plan a conference on "The Ethics of Mutual Involvement." Discussions and plans centered on holding a conference in Indonesia or perhaps India. Harold Lasswell pushed to have a series of meetings of forty to fifty people each sometime in 1962. At Mohonk that October, Finkelstein explained what he saw as the purpose of the group: "The state of the world in 1961 is the worst that it has been in all of history," yet the imminent threat of nuclear war was not something on which to build plans. No one "plans his life on the supposition that he will die tomorrow." Finkelstein assumed that the world would "muddle through" the immediate crisis, but what was necessary was to raise the moral tone of Americans to forestall other crises. "We all agree that the only way the free world can survive is not by boasting of a high standard of living. . . . The things we need to emphasize in the life of our nation are: justice, morals, spiritual integrity, love between humans, peace, and moral values." Science had dramatically increased, but ethics had stagnated. "It has been a long time since America has produced a great ethicist, if ever. The person we are seeking to fill this role is not a man at all—he is a procedure, and institution. Can we bring this about here?"[120]

By late October 1961, Alan M. Stroock, chairman of the Board of Directors of the JTS, had been sold on the idea, as he praised the intergroup activities program:

> For over twenty years, we have experimented with the possibility of mutual cross-fertilization between different disciplines. We have brought together, in common discourse, minister and rabbi, priest and scientist, scholar and statesman. Our success in achieving some kind of consensus here has encouraged us to believe that we have developed important techniques for continuing efforts in this direction—which risky though they may be, are also the only risks that today are really worth taking.[121]

In January 1962 at Mohonk the group concentrated on planning for the Southeast Asian conference. Aside from the persistent need for funding, the most important need was for a director, someone who could go "to people's offices" and make "them miserable reminding them about Mohonk," someone who could "help spawn little Mohonks." Two additional members were businessmen Ben Dillingham III and Oliver Iselin, Jr. Dillingham had some rather strong ideas about what the World Institute should be, even so far as pushing the new East-West Center then being built with State Department money in Hawaii as a possible base for the World Institute.

The additions of new members diluted the focus of the group, however. Finkelstein was rather irritated by the lack of progress in planning for the new Institute. "I don't believe this group is ready to go to India or to project a World Academy of Ethics. First we need to learn to have a Mohonk meeting." Too few had come prepared or done their homework. "We are not clear in our own minds what we want to do."[122]

The international conference postponed, work progressed over the following year on clarifying what they wanted to do. The task of drafting a program for a World Institute on Ethics was given to Robert Johann, S. J., who in October 1962, presented his "Blueprint for Action" centered around the idea of justice. The criterion for justice in a condition of radical pluralism implied, to Johann and the others, "a willingness on the part of the politically and culturally divided peoples of the world to institute a joint inquiry into what may be considered just in the concrete situations of interaction in which they find themselves." The point of the inquiry was not confrontation "but an adjustment of practical intentions, . . . on the level of action." The goal of the World Institute was "not a comprehensive philosophy on which all can agree that the world needs today, but a genuine, working accord in areas of common concern." Without this effort, "justice in the world is impossible." The World Institute's agenda was to be on questions of common, practical concern, those "arising precisely as byproducts of the active interrelationship of different peoples and cultures," especially "a close scrutiny of the *means* actually being used" to achieve mutual goals. Areas for discussion included questions of overpopulation and economic development, free access to information, the possible "opposition between the real welfare of the people and the principle of self-determination" in newly independent areas, and questions of neutralism and intervention in the Cold War. The World Institute on Ethics was not to be a world forum, a world parliament, nor a world court but rather a "practical effort of qualified spokesmen from the different peoples and cultures in today's world to determine jointly the ingredients of justice in the various actual and specific conflicts of intention that divide them."[123] While promising, it was almost like starting over, back where they were almost eight years before.

By late February 1963, Louis Finkelstein was rather discouraged. He was seriously thinking about refunding some of the initial contributions that had come in to fund the World Institute, including money from Oliver Iselin, Jr., the General Electric Foundation, and Alan M. Stroock. In preparation for the June Mohonk, Finkelstein admitted: "It is clear we are not now in a position to implement the resolutions to organize the World Institute on Ethics." No one had stepped forward to direct the organization or undertake its fund-raising efforts. He had hoped to concentrate on an initial international conference, but he concluded that now, "on the whole the whole project probably is not ready for such action," or even to hire a full-time director. Finkelstein realized he had to place the formal organization, "on ice" but he hoped, "not in the deep freeze."[124]

While the grand plans for an ongoing institutionalized international dialogue on ethics never materialized, the other elements of the Seminary's intergroup activities continued throughout the 1960s. Two Conferences were held, including one in 1966 in Chicago on "Education for Character," and the IRSS continued its full schedule of Tuesday luncheons and lecture programs. For two years, 1966–67 and 1967–68, there was an experimental "Transcultural Seminar on Tradition and Change" for graduate students under the direction of Jessica Feingold, but it did not continue—in many ways a victim of similar loss of direction and commitment that doomed the Conference and the Institute on Ethics. The IRSS had hired an outside evaluator to assess its results, and while she thought that overall the program should continue, it suffered from a "lack of focus" and "a clear purpose." More damaging was the attitude of the faculty members, for none of them assumed continued responsibility for the program, leaving it to the administrators to provide continuity.[125]

This loss of direction and commitment was the main cause of the decline in the intergroup activities in the late 1960s. As Robert Wood Lynn, an active member of the second generation later reflected, the Conference and the Institute for Religious and Social Studies shifted in the 1960s, a result of "a growing sense that none of us cared deeply enough about the Conference to commit ourselves to the task of providing new energy and a promising agenda." There were several reasons for this, including the increasing pull of academic careers during a period of a massive expansion of higher education, pushing people more deeply into their specialties rather than toward "such vaguely defined intellectual ventures." Social movements of the 1960s also had a profound impact, yet it is unclear why the existing organizations were not used as channels for reflecting on contemporary social events, especially after the relative commercial success of an IRSS book like *The Assault on Poverty* (1965). Lynn considers that the increased fragmentation of theology throughout the 1960s was a prime cause, but as the early history shows, there never was even a moderate consensus in the Conference along theological lines. A more likely explanation was the absence of an ideological opponent to focus scholarly attention, like Nazism and Communism in the 1940s and 1950s. Yet fatal to the vision was the older generation's inability to pass on the vision to another generation. As Lynn admits, "The fundamental problem was the failure of my generation to give new life to this organization."[126]

In one final effort to recreate enthusiasm for the idea of an international dialogue on ethics, Finkelstein sent Jessica Feingold on a world tour from October 1969 through April 1970. She traveled first to Hawaii, where she met with Harlan Cleveland, then president of the University of Hawaii and former CSPR executive committee member, about the prospect of a future Conference in Hawaii. She also met with numerous professors and government officials, before traveling to Japan; Taiwan; Indonesia; Thailand; India, where she was welcomed by the Maharaja of Mysore; to Iran; and finally to Switzerland and Portugal before returning to New York. She had had close consultations with more than one hundred and fifty scholars, government officials, and religious leaders. The Conference itself was well known through its publications, and the contacts were useful, but on her return it was clear that there was no way to rebuild enthusiasm for the Conference. The Seminary was in the midst of a serious financial crisis, and funds from other sources were also in short supply. By May 1970 Louis Finkelstein was approaching retirement, and with that, the vision of the Department of Intergroup Activities as "the Seminary's window to the world" was losing its guiding spirit.

Intergroup activities continued at the Seminary after Finkelstein's retirement, although at a reduced level. The main agency was the Institute for Religious and Social Studies, which continued its lecture series and luncheons under the direction of Jessica Feingold and Carlotta Damanda. The story does not end there, however. With support from the 1995 Louis Stein endowment and its new name, the Louis Finkelstein Institute for Religious and Social Studies, the Institute has moved to reassert its place as a major center of ecumenical activity. Now under the direction of Dr. Burton L. Visotzky, a graduate of the Seminary, the Institute promises in part to fulfill Louis Finkelstein's initial vision of a continuing conversation on issues of ethical concern to the religious community.

Conclusions and Outcomes

If the Jewish Theological Seminary's program of intergroup activities was one of the more significant intellectual events in 20th-century America, what did it accomplish? Any form of assessment raises a number of questions, such as the outcomes of their collaborative effort, the models and techniques that remain valid, the causes of decline, and the place of interdisciplinary groups in a modern university-dominated intellectual environment. At the heart of these organizations—the Institute for Religious and Social Studies, the Conference on Science, Philosophy and Religion, and the Institute on Ethics—lies Louis Finkelstein's animating vision of an ongoing modern synthesis of traditional religious truth with modern scientific knowledge. This collaborative effort was to develop a truly inclusive universal ethics, not a lowest common denominator of duties but a high level synthesis of practical action and moral guidance. This vision of conviction combined with civility was to become an "organized conscience," with all major voices and responsible positions represented. It was to culminate in the World Academy of Ethics, a permanent scholarly center dedicated to continuous moral reflection.

In assessing the results of the intergroup activities, it would be a mistake to dismiss the World Academy as a fantasy. Finkelstein was too great a scholar and too far-seeing an administrator to be dismissed that easily. This was to be the capstone to a remarkable career, which his more scholarly work sought to embody in large-scale collaborative projects like *The Jews: Their History, Culture, and Religion* (1949). While the other intergroup activities differed in function and immediate purpose, they were different institutional embodiments of the same idea, experiments that could be learned from in order to fulfill the grander vision. After the collapse of the World Academy, however, much of the energy went out of the other programs. They did have important immediate impact, especially in the lives of their participants, and the continued success of the Institute demonstrated the critical nature of intergroup education. It seems that the history of these institutions demonstrates a paradox, that lower expectations lead to greater success, for the Institute was quite successful, the Conference less so.

As the inner circle aged, it grew more detached from the cutting edges of American intellectual life. It never did develop an adequate method of recruitment and renewal, a failure that was one of the most damaging to the vision. The "spirit of Mohonk" that was to sustain the intergroup activities and really create the possibilities of a truly inclusive ethical universalism was not all that transferable. Philosophers may consider ideas eternal, yet ideas, even grand visions like Finkelstein's, exist in a historical context. It may be that seemingly accidental factors like personality conflicts, car wrecks, and the sudden death of a principal participant may drastically affect the success of an organization. An idea may never reach maturity due to problems with its implementation rather than difficulties intrinsic to the idea itself.

It took time to develop a "universe of discourse" around ethical issues and to communicate within this universe, especially as the American university community was designed to further specialization rather than synthesis. The Seminary's intergroup activities were clearly counter-cyclical, for the direction of American intellectual life was toward specialization, not integration. While it was true that the 1950s were a golden age for religious ecumenism, religion was not a major participant in intellectual discourse. The IRSS and its mission could be seen within the broader bounds of ecumenical discussion, and indeed, it flourished then, but the Conference and the Institute on Ethics attempted to cross more problematic boundaries, boundaries rigidly defended and with structural rewards almost exclusively in the opposite direction. The GI Bill and the 1960s expansion of higher education encouraged these trends against the integration of knowledge and in favor of the "multiversity."

While many outside factors militated against the success of Finkelstein's vision, there were some serious difficulties in its conception. One does not want to eliminate the hope of a universal ethics or a world community, but the creation of a World Academy of Ethics may not have been the most strategic use of resources. Under Finkelstein's direction, the inner circle of participants never developed a rigorous method for ethical discussion, and as such, there were few cumulative results. As can be seen in the Rockefeller study, the lack of a sound method left the group with rather vague abstractions. Finkelstein's focus on the "clarification" of values was also quite weak; for "an American conscience" to be effective, it needed to proclaim principles, not shrink from taking a position. More troubling, it seems that Finkelstein's desire for inclusion was premature. An initial focus on the ethics of the "Judeo-Christian tradition" could have provided a solid foundation from which to reach out to interested secularists and other religious traditions. His instincts were right; leadership had to come from a Jewish institution, but as the intergroup activities developed, the distinctively Jewish perspective was rather quickly diluted and the group was left with vague abstractions. Rather than serving as a means of illumination, the institutions designed to implement Finkelstein's vision left the American moral order almost as confused as before.

In spite of its inability to reach its highest goals, it seems that, on balance, the intergroup activities were successful. The IRSS and the CSPR were unique programs; never before in America was there as inclusive and sustained a dialogue on religion and ethics as at the Conference. It established a model of discussion that provided for mutual understanding across widely divergent philosophical and religious traditions. Much of its success lay in the impact it had on its participants. While it failed to create a consensual moral framework, it did provide one model as to how it could be done in the future. The Institute was a profound success, affecting thousands of lives through its theological student and clergy programs. A more subtle but equally important impact was the assistance the intergroup activities gave to the establishment of Jewish studies within American universities after World War II. Finally, the wide acceptance of the idea of a "Judeo-Christian tradition" was in large part due directly to the IRSS and the CSPR. Never again would Judaism be seen as outside the American democratic tradition.

Was Louis Finkelstein wrong when he said that intergroup activities were the Seminary's "coming of age"? After the end of the Finkelstein era, the Seminary turned inward, repudiating his vision, but with the revival of the Institute for Religious and Social Studies, it seems that the Seminary is returning to ecumenical leadership. He always held up the model of Medieval Spain, when Jew, Christian, and Muslim worked, studied, and conversed together, each certain in his own conviction yet treating the other with humble civility. Finkelstein's plans would have pushed the Seminary too far, though, for an emphasis on civil dialogue often serves to diminish convictions in a later generation, requiring an inward turn to reinforce and strengthen belief in the truthfulness of the faith. What seems evident now, as the 20th century nears its end, is that the moral confusion and sense of crisis Louis Finkelstein saw has returned. Perhaps in the future, the Seminary can revive his original vision, learn from the many mistakes of its history and find new ways to implement it, so that the Seminary can again become a center of religion and ethics, a model of progressive orthodoxy, not only for itself, but "for the world at large."

731

Notes to:
For the World
at Large:
Intergroup
Activities
at JTS

1. The author expresses special thanks to Jessica Feingold and Carlotta Damanda, both past directors of the Seminary's Intergroup Activities, whose unceasingly labor did so much to make Louis Finkelstein's vision a reality, and without whose help, encouragement, and friendship, this study could not have been accomplished.

2. Indeed, the criticism of the IRSS and the CSPR grew so heated by 1945 that Finkelstein seriously considered resigning. He stayed only after winning a vote of confidence from the Seminary board in April 1945. See the discussion in Michael Greenbaum's dissertation, "Mission Conflict in Religiously Affiliated Institutions of Higher Education: The Jewish Theological Seminary of America During The Presidency of Louis Finkelstein, 1940–1955," (Ph.D. diss., Teachers College, Columbia University, 1994), esp. chap. 5, "The Seminary's Critics," pp. 91–109.

3. The creation of Jewish studies programs in universities after World War II, one of Finkelstein's goals behind the intergroup activities, was seen by Simon Greenberg as one of the most important developments of Judaism in this century, almost equal to the establishment of the State of Israel. Interview by author, August 1992.

4 The Seminary developed a distinctive idiom for referring to these efforts, preferring "intergroup" to such terms as "interreligious" or "interfaith." Louis Finkelstein used only "intergroup." There was only one faith, he often insisted, and that was faith in God.

5. See Jessica Feingold, "Up From Isolation—Intergroup Activities at the Seminary," in *Judaism* 27, no. 3 (summer 1978): p. 289.

6. For a complete bibliography of all the Conference articles, see the author's doctoral dissertation, "Organizing an American Conscience: The Conference on Science, Philosophy and Religion, 1940–1968," (Ph.D. diss., University of Chicago Department of History, March 1995).

7. Pamela Nadell, *Conservative Judaism in America: A Biographical Dictionary and Sourcebook* (Westport, Conn.: Greenwood Press, 1988), pp. 278–79.

8. See the article on Littauer in the *Dictionary of American Biography*.

9. Finkelstein handwritten notes, 23 March 1937, JTS General Files, box 16, file 87.

10. Finkelstein to Lewis Strauss, 5 May 1937, JTS General Files, box 16, file 85.

11. Littauer to Finkelstein, 19 September 1938; 16 December 1938, JTS General Files, box 16, file 85.

12. Finkelstein to Littauer, 3, 7, 8 November 1939, JTS General Files, box 16, file 86.

13. The *New York Times*, 1 June 1940; See also the editorial on 9 June 1940.

14. "Statement by Mortimer Adler on the Fundamental Position of the Conference on Science, Philosophy and Religion," n.d., University of Chicago Special Collections, Robert M. Hutchins Papers, Addenda, box 42, folder 3.

15. Founders meeting, 9 August 1940, pp. 33-40, JTS Record Group 5 CSPR, Series F, *Proceedings*, box 36, folder 2.

16. Louis Finkelstein, "The Aims of the Conference," in *Science, Philosophy and Religion* (New York: The Conference on Science, Philosophy and Religion, 1941), pp. 19, 11. Citations to the published Conference volumes will subsequently use the acronym followed by the first number referring to the volume and the second to the page, as: CSPR 1: 19, 11. Citations to the unpublished verbatim transcripts of Conference sessions, which are in R.G. 5 CSPR, Series f, will include a 'T': CSPR 1 T: 12.

17. Some historians consider the Conference to be one of the main centers for the development of this ideology. See the discussion on the Judeo-Christian tradition in Mark Silk, *Spiritual Politics: Religion and America Since World War II* (New York: Simon and Schuster, 1989), pp. 41–43. Transcripts are also available on microfilm.

18. CSPR 1:87–88.

19. CSPR 1:43–48.

20. CSPR 1T, founders meeting: p. 28.

21. CSPR 1T, founders meeting: p. 70.

22. Compare Sidney Hook's account in *Out of Step: An Unquiet Life in the 20th Century* (New York: Harper and Row, 1987), pp. 335f. Hook was surprised that Adler's "strongest apparent supporter" was Finkelstein, suggesting that Finkelstein's motive was dislike for Hook, since many bright rabbinical candidates had decided to study with Hook. Based on the archives and Finkelstein's larger purpose, it is evident that rather than supporting Adler, Finkelstein's goal was to include all possible opinions, something that Hook could not understand. See also Adler's *Philosopher at Large: An Intellectual Autobiography* (New York: Macmillan, 1977), esp. pp. 185-89, and his *A Second Look in the Review Mirror* (New York: Macmillan, 1992).

23. CSPR 1:177-82.

24. CSPR 1:128.

25. CSPR 1:136-37.

26. Sidney Hook's address was reprinted as "The New Medievalism," in *The New Republic*, 28 October 1940, pp. 605-6. Hook carried his attack further in *Partisan Review* and later helped form a rival organization, the Conference on the Scientific Spirit and the Democratic Faith.

27. The *New York Times*, 11 September 1940. Einstein's paper became notorious in the popular religious press, which interpreted Einstein's meaning as atheistic. The physicist was surprised and deeply upset by the public criticism, claiming he had been mistranslated; he was opposed to the concept of an "anthropomorphic God." In the original German manuscript, Einstein does use this term. In many ways, though, Einstein's complaint was specious, for a denial of an anthropomorphic God would not have made headlines, but the theologians were equally opposed to this deistic conception of the Divine. Louis Finkelstein was especially disturbed at Einstein's exclusion of prayer. See the correspondence between Finkelstein and Einstein in JTS General Files, Series A, Box 7.

28. CSPR 1:213-14.

29. CSPR 1:223-28.

30. CSPR 1:240-47.

31. CSPR 1T founders meeting: p. 47.

32. CSPR 5T: 605.

33. CSPR 8T: 5-11.

34. CSPR 4T:158.

35. CSPR 4T:356-59.

36. CSPR 4T: 395.

37. CSPR 4T:383-88.

38. CSPR 5T: 143-46.

39. CSPR 5T:301-2.

40. CSPR 5T:306.

41. CSPR 5T: 309-10.

42. CSPR 5T:311-12.

43. CSPR 5T:314-17.

44. CSPR 5T:336.

45. CSPR 5T:338-39.

46. CSPR 6T:143.

47. See Reinhold Niebuhr, *Children of Light and Children of Darkness* (New York: Scribner's, 1944).

48. CSPR 6T:157, 167, 171.

49. CSPR 6T: 191-92.

733

Notes to:
For the World
at Large:
Intergroup
Activities
at JTS

50. CSPR 7T:360-70.

51. CSPR 7:250, 275.

52. CSPR 9T: 412.

53. Jacques Maritain, introduction to *Human Rights: Comments and Interpretations*, ed. UNESCO (New York: Columbia University Press, 1949), pp. 10-11.

54. CSPR 9T: 382ff.

55. CSPR 9T: 440.

56. CSPR 9T:457.

57. CSPR 6T: 485-86.

58. CSPR 7T:180.

59. CSPR 10T Phil.: 59.

60. The minutes of the Amherst meeting are in the JTS archives, CSPR Records, box 2, Amherst meeting minutes, 24–26 July 1944. All quotations are from the typed minutes compiled after the meeting.

61. "Confidential Memoranda I," JTS R.G. 16, box 1, folder 22.

62. "Report on Institute of Interdenominational Studies," 20 February 1940, p. 8, JTS R.G. 16, box 1.

63. Ibid, p. 10.

64. Norman Cousins, "World Citizenship," in *World Order: Its Intellectual and Cultural Foundations*, ed. F. Ernest Johnson (New York: Institute for Religious Studies, 1945), p. 210.

65. Introduction to *World Order*, p. vii.

66. Louis Finkelstein, "Collaboration for World Order," in *World Order*, pp. 8–12.

67. Edgar S. Brightman, "The Philosophy of World Community," in *World Order*, p. 30.

68. Mordecai Kaplan, "The Jewish Contribution to a World Order," in *World Order*, p. 138.

69. F. Ernest Johnson, "The Crisis of Modern Democracy," in *The Foundations of Democracy* (New York: Institute for Religious and Social Studies, 1947), pp. 7, 13.

70. Horace Kallen, "Humanistic Sources," in *Foundations of Democracy*, pp. 69, 73, 83, 86.

71. Roger N. Baldwin, "The International Bill of Rights," in *Great Expressions of Human Rights*, ed. R. M. MacIver, (New York: Institute for Religious and Social Studies, 1950), p. 210.

72. See R. M. MacIver, preface to *Civilization and Group Relationships* (New York: Institute for Religious Studies, 1945), pp. ix, x.

73. J. S. Roucek, *The Annual of the American Academy of Arts and Sciences*, 233:256, May 1944.

74. R. M. MacIver, "The Ordering of a Multigroup Society," in *Civilization and Group Relationships*, pp. 166–69.

75. Louis Finkelstein, "Three Paths to the Common Good," in *Unity and Difference in American Life*, ed. R. M. MacIver (New York: Institute for Religious and Social Studies, 1947), p. 12.

76. They appeared to demonstrate high crime rates for Negroes, but when controlled for literacy, poverty, and education, the crime rates for blacks and whites were basically identical. See MacIver, "The Need for a Change of Attitude," in *Civilization and Group Relationships*, pp. 7–10.

77. R. M. MacIver, "Our Strength and Our Weakness," in *Discrimination and National Welfare* (New York: Institute for Religious and Social Studies, 1949), p. 2.

78. *Brown v. Board of Education*, 347 US 483, 494 fn. 10.

79. Harold Taylor, "The Ambiguities of Public Morality: A Problem for World Youth," in *Dilemmas of Youth in America Today*, ed. R. M. MacIver (New York: Harper, 1961), p. 122.

80. R. M. MacIver, ed., *The Assault on Poverty: And Individual Responsibility* (New York: Institute for Religious and Social Studies, 1965), p. 32.

81. Warner Bloomberg, in *American Sociological Review* 31 (June 1966): p. 420.

82. See *Labor's Relation to Church and Community* (1947), *American Spiritual Autobiographies* (1948), *Moments of Personal Discovery* (1952), *Thirteen Americans: Their Spiritual Autobiographies* (1953) and *The Hour of Insight* (1953).

83. Nelson H. Cruikshank, "I Have Found in Conflicts a Peace," in *Labor's Relation to Church and Community,* ed. Liston Pope (New York: Institute for Religious and Social Studies, 1947), p. 167.

84. Ordway Tead, in *Thirteen Americans: Their Spiritual Autobiographies,* ed. Louis Finkelstein, (New York: Harper, 1953), p. 29.

85. Simon Greenberg, "The Revelation of Human Love," in *The Hour of Insight,* ed. R. M. MacIver (New York: Institute for Religious and Social Studies, 1954), pp. 100–1.

86. A. L. Sachar, review of *American Spiritual Autobiographies,* ed. Louis Finkelstein, *New York Herald Tribune Weekly Book Review,* 1 May 1949, p. 21.

87. "Program of Lectures and Discussions, 1984–85," IRSS, IRSS files.

88. "1953 Memo," JTS R.G. 16, box 71, file 35.

89. At Mohonk that weekend were Louis Finkelstein, Clarence Faust, F. Ernest Johnson, Robert MacIver, Richard McKeon, I. I. Rabi, Hudson Hoagland, Simon Greenberg, Harry J. Carman, Jessica Feingold, Charles S. Johnson, and several others.

90. Report by A. Durwood Foster, Lake Mohonk meeting 6–8 April 1956, JTS R.G. 16, IRSS, box 67.

91. Discussion of Committee V, 27 June 1956. pp. 3, 8, JTS R.G. 16, IRSS, box 68.

92. Discussion of Committee I, 27 June 1956, pp., 5, 10-12, JTS R.G. 16, IRSS, box 68. See also the account in Richard P. Feynman, *"Surely You're Joking, Mr. Feynman!": Adventures of a Curious Character* (New York: Bantam, 1985), pp. 253–59.

93. Transcript of meeting between Finkelstein and Lasswell, 26 July 1956, JTS R.G. 16, box 71, file 28.

94. Business meeting at the Columbia Men's Faculty Club, 29 August 1956, JTS R.G. 5 CSPR, box 39, file 29.

95. This was later to become the Herbert H. Lehman Institute of Talmudic Ethics, 1958–66, established with much fanfare after U.S. Supreme Court Chief Justice Earl Warren spent a weekend in September 1957 studying talmudic ethics at the Seminary.

96. Louis Finkelstein, "Confidential Memo," November 1956, JTS R.G. 16, box 98, file 13.

97. Toward a World Academy of Ethics, "n. d.", draft document, JTS R.G. 16, box 99, file 4.

98. "Blueprint: World Academy of Ethics" (finished volume), JTS R.G. 16, box 98.

99. "The Ethics Village," JTS R.G. 16, box 98, file 17.

100. Finkelstein to Seminary officers, 25 October 1957, JTS R.G. 16, box 98, file 17.

101. For a complete listing of the participants, as well as the final reports, see Rockefeller Brothers Fund, *Prospect for America* (Garden City, N.Y.: Doubleday, 1958–1961), pp. xiv–xxvi.

102. Rockefeller Archive Center (RAC), Rockefeller Brothers Fund (RBF), Special Studies Project (SSP) V4G, box 49, file 558: "The Framework of National Purpose," preliminary draft, February 1957. The Rockefeller Archive Center is housed in North Tarrytown, New York.

103. "Transcript of Meeting," 8 April 1957, at 21–22, RAC RBF SSP V4G, box 48, file 553.

104. Idem, pp. 66–67.

105. Ibid.

106. Idem, pp. 32.

107. Idem, pp. 33–34.

108. Idem, pp. 85–86, 84.

109. Idem, pp. 76, 91.

110. "Transcript of Meeting No. 4," 20 May 1957, RAC RBF SSP V4G box 48, file 557. Cf. McKeon's memo, in file 556.

111. Idem, pp. 26, 30.

112. Idem, pp. 76–81.

113. Idem, pp. 100.

114. "Heilbroner Drafts," "Draft 1," 26 April 1957, RAC RBF SSP V4G box 49, file 559.

115. "Robert Heilbroner," Kissinger to Heilbroner, 13 June 1957, RAC RBF SSP V4G, box 48, file 540.

116. For further insight into Murray's conception of international politics in this period, see his *We Hold These Truths: Catholic Reflections on the American Proposition* (New York: Sheed and Ward, 1960).

117. J. C. Murray, "Remarks at Overall Panel Meeting," 19 June 1957, RAC RBF SSP V4G box 48, file 545, pp. 7, 10, 20–21.

118. Report of Planning Meeting of Institute of Ethics Mohonk, 1–3 November 1957, JTS R.G. 16, box 72, file 11.

119. "Jewish Theological Seminary," 1956–1958, RAC RBF file.

120. Institute on Ethics, Mohonk, 6–8 October 1961, pp. 22, plus Sunday session, separately paginated, p .4, JTS R.G. 16, box 75, file 21.

121. Institute on Ethics, Mohonk, 6–8 October 1961, JTS R.G. 16, box 75, file 20.

122. Institute on Ethics, Mohonk, 26–28 January 1962, Proceedings, p. 19, JTS R.G. 16, box 75, file 23.

123. Robert Johann, S. J., "The World Institute on Ethics: A Blueprint for Action," JTS R.G. 16, box 98, file 3, pp. 9, 12, 19.

124. Louis Finkelstein, "Draft for Mohonk Discussants," 17 May 1963, JTS R.G. 16, box 98, file 13a.

125. See Susan N. Kranz, *Evaluation of the Transcultural Seminar on Tradition and Change, on Values in the Twentieth Century* (New York: Center for Urban Education, 1969), pp. 60–65.

126. Robert Wood Lynn to the author, 25 April 1991.

VIRGINIA LIESON BRERETON

Religious Educators at The Jewish Theological Seminary and the Wider Educational World

Pupils at the Teachers Institute's model school at the Inwood Hebrew Congregation, late 1940s. *Photo by Virginia Stern. Ratner Center, JTS.*

VIRGINIA LIESON BRERETON

Religious Educators at The Jewish Theological Seminary and the Wider Educational World

I N a 1993 interfaith symposium on religious education, Joseph Lukinsky, professor of Jewish education at Jewish Theological Seminary, asked to comment from a Jewish perspective, observed:

> I doubt if there are many *important* interactions between Jewish education and the field of general "religious education" despite the fact that Jewish educators have participated in the Religious Education Association since its founding, gaining from and contributing to the relationship. Many apparent similarities are probably parallels related to the *zeitgeist*.[1]

Lukinsky's comment helps capture the mixture of strangeness and familiarity felt by Jewish and Christian educators when they have regarded each other across the divide of their separate and quite distinct traditions. One goal of this essay is to examine both the sense of strangeness and that of familiarity.

There have been plenty of sources for both, the reasons for the separation of Christian and Jewish educators being perhaps most self-evident. Many themes are important to American Jews that matter less to most Christians: Israel and Zionism, the Jewish educator's emphasis on the rigorous learning of Hebrew and on a set of complex texts (other than the Pentateuch) virtually unknown to Christians; and centuries of Jewish political, cultural, and social history that are seldom taught outside Jewish settings or Jewish studies departments. Then there is the bane of most Jews—Christians' penchant for proselytizing them or at least thinking of them as

739

incomplete Christians. Finally, there is (often) physical separation, the fact that Jews and Christians have often lived in different sections of the nation or different parts of the same metropolis, and sometimes spoken different languages and practiced different politics. Indeed, much of the separation has been intentional; for the sake of religious identity and community, Jewish and Christian leaders—particularly Jews—have needed to be mindful of and emphasize their distinctions.

On the other hand, considerable common ground between Jewish and Christian educators can be traced to the connections linking both to the wider educational world (part of Lukinsky's *zeitgeist*)—especially to the educational progressivism of John Dewey and his colleagues at Columbia University Teachers College. The closeness was particularly marked in the case of Jewish and Christian educators in New York City, many of whom actually studied with Dewey and his associates as well as read their books. Furthermore, the 20th-century ecumenical movement, gathering strength as the century has gone on, has encouraged Jewish and Christian educators to explore commonalities. And religious educators, both Jewish and Christian, have been thrown together by adversity; they have increasingly had to cope with the competition from other "educators" that were unknown in the 19th century: radio, television and MTV, movies, tapes and CDs, and video games. Not only have these "educators" absorbed time that might otherwise be devoted to religious learning; they have often taught very contrary lessons.

One clarification: my essay focuses particularly upon the specific religious educators associated with Jewish Theological Seminary and Union Theological Seminary, New York. Occasionally, however, it ranges more broadly to the Conservative movement within American Judaism, for which JTS has been the academic and religious center, and occasionally to Judaism as a whole; similarly, it sometimes moves beyond UTS to comment on liberal Protestantism more generally. Roman Catholic educators are largely missing from this story until the early sixties, when they started forging more connections with Jewish and Protestant educators. JTS and Conservative Judaism's connections with evangelical Protestants have been minimal; thus, the latter enter our comparative story hardly at all.

To some degree I have finessed the issue of periodization, for I am of necessity dealing simultaneously with several different periodization schemes: JTS and the Conservative movement, liberal Protestantism, progressive education, and American Catholicism—none of which coincide. While Eastern European immigration, the Holocaust, and the establishment of the State of Israel stand out in a history of Conservative Jewish education at JTS, World War I and the advent of neoorthodoxy are probably the defining events for liberal Protestantism—although in the nature of things there are arguments within each group of religious historians about which markers are most important. I attempt to tell a several-layered story, an attempt that carries some risks to clarity.

Early Links

741

*Religious
Educators
at Jewish
Theological
Seminary*

In the first decades of the 20th century JTS educators had relatively little contact with Christian religious educators, at least little that has left any public record. A few Jewish educators joined the Religious Education Association when it was formed in 1903, but they were not associated with JTS. Moreover, Jewish involvement in the early REA seems to have been minimal, and certainly the ethos of the early REA was overwhelmingly liberal Protestant.[2] Up through the twenties, Jewish educators contributed occasional essays to the REA publication, *Religious Education*, but their purpose seems to have been mainly to inform the Protestant educational world what Jewish education was all about. (Authors felt they had to explain terms like "bar mitzvah," for instance.) The articles celebrate the accomplishments of Jewish education rather than rehearse its problems (which, as we know from other contexts, the Jewish educators themselves felt keenly).[3]

Here and there, however, we glimpse exceptions to the general lack of contacts between JTS and Christian educators. We see evidence of links between JTS and UTS educators. Emanuel Gamoran, a preeminent Jewish educator, had studied and taught at the Teachers Institute at JTS, was a student of Samson Benderly of the New York City Bureau of Jewish Education, and was considered close enough to the Protestant religious educator at Union, George A. Coe, to write one of the tributes to him in the 1952 memorial issue of *Religious Education*. Gamoran had not studied under Coe, but

> my contacts with him through the Religious Education Association [in the teens and early twenties particularly] and the religious activities at Teachers College and on the Columbia campus in general gave me a most clear indication of his personality. As president of the Jewish Forum at Teachers College it was my privilege to represent the Jewish group either in religious activities at Teachers College itself or on various occasions on the Columbia campus. No one was second to Dr. Coe in willingness to render service to religious groups and causes.[4]

Gamoran took this memorial occasion to praise Coe's understanding and appreciation of cultural pluralism, a concept important to the Jewish graduate students at Teachers College and the Teachers Institute, but his highest encomium was reserved for Coe's grasp of a core truth of Judaism:

> The concept of religion as separate from life is, . . . foreign to Jewish classical thinking on the subject. Judaism is a way of life. . . . His [the Jew's] religion . . . is not of the year-end or even week-end variety. Hence we have a Hebrew term for the words "faith," "law," "custom," but we have no term for the word "religion." It has always appeared to me that among the non-Jews, three men came closest to appreciating our concept. These are John Dewey, William Heard Kilpatrick, and George Albert Coe. The last, because he was at work in the field of

religious education, read many of the Jewish writings on the subject and therefore came close to the Jewish group at Teachers College.[5]

We get another glimpse of connections in another memorial issue of *Religious Education*. In 1951, upon the death of Harrison Elliott, Israel S. Chipkin, a student of
Benderly and of Mordecai Kaplan, the director of the Teachers Institute at JTS,
and later a close associate of Kaplan on the faculty of JTS, penned a testimonial to
the longtime professor of religious education at Union Seminary:

> I want to acknowledge with reverence and appreciation the friendship which I
> experienced over the years he and I worked together. I learned much from him.
> . . . I am indebted to him for his kindness and encouragement to me. He was
> always ready to accept my invitations to attend Jewish educational conferences.
> He participated and contributed much to them in speech and in writing. He
> familiarized himself with the most important writing in the field of Jewish
> education.[6]

Israel S. Chipkin,
ca. 1930s. *Ratner
Center, JTS.*

Indeed, Elliott's 1941 essay, "Relationship of
Religious Education to Public Education," is
apparently the first essay by a Christian educator
to appear in the journal *Jewish Education*.[7]

Testimonials such as Chipkin's and Gamoran's
inevitably contain a degree of the honorific, of
course, and may be as much a tribute to fifties-
style Jewish-Christian ecumenism as evidence of
friendships among actual persons. But still, at the
very least, they testify to periodic interactions
between JTS and UTS religious education faculty and personnel, the existence of mutual
respect, and perhaps they bespeak deeper meet-
ings of the mind than we are aware of. No doubt, too, these men were linked by the
experience of living and working as scholars in cosmopolitan New York City—and
eventually (after 1930) as academic neighbors on Morningside Heights.

The Deweyan Connection

If it is hard to trace the exact nature of the traffic between JTS and Union Seminary's Department of Religious Education, it is clear that there was all manner of
travel between JTS and Teachers College on the one hand and UTS and Teachers
College on the other hand. As early as 1900 or 1901 in Baltimore, Samson Benderly,
who would later direct the Bureau of Religious Education in the New York Kehillah
and play a major role in shaping the education of prospective teachers at the Teachers Institute of JTS, was avidly following the writing of Teachers College teachers

such as Dewey and E. L. Thorndike. Rebecca Brickner, Benderly's student and associate, recalled that around 1900

> the scientific work in general education done by the Columbia University Teachers College group, was coming to the fore. No sooner were the works of Thorndike and Dewey published, than Benderly had them on his desk. He was filling himself with the newly acquired "Chochmah" [wisdom] of these educators. In the mornings he would read, and in the afternoons he would test out these newly acquired theories.[8]

Mordecai Kaplan also testified to the influence of Teachers College on Jewish educators at the Teachers Institute:

> From the very beginning the Teachers Institute sensed the importance of relating the Jewish training to general pedagogic training. In order that the Jewish teacher might be respected it was necessary that in addition to a thorough Jewish training he should receive advanced scientific pedagogic training. For this reason those specializing in Jewish education were given the opportunity to do advanced work at Teachers College, Columbia University.[9]

And most Teachers Institute students did indeed take advantage of the opportunity. Arthur Goren in his history of the New York Kehillah puts the matter more strongly than Kaplan: "In one sense, the young professionals of the Bureau replaced scriptural authority with Dewey's educational philosophy."[10] "The young professionals" at the Bureau of Jewish Education were, in addition to being Benderly's students—"Benderly's Boys," as they were called—almost without exception alumni/ae of the JTS Teachers Institute. In 1937 *Jewish Education* published a letter by the Teachers Institute's Israel S. Chipkin, "Greetings to Professor William Heard Kilpatrick" (of Teachers College) from his "pupils, disciples and admirers in the field of Jewish education, in Jewish center work and in Jewish social work."[11] Kilpatrick's teaching was particularly valued because, building on the pedagogical principles of Dewey, he had been able to lend them more practical application.

Teachers College returned the compliment; by 1930 it was providing a course in "Principles and Problems of Jewish Education." The first classes were taught by Leo Honor, who also taught at JTS; Israel Chipkin, instructor and registrar at JTS, offered the course after 1932. The course lasted until the late thirties.

Not everyone at JTS was comfortable about the powerful influence exerted upon Jewish students by Teachers College faculty. Mordecai Kaplan and Solomon Schechter, President of JTS between 1902 and 1915, would have preferred to have the teachers-in-training follow the full rabbinic course at the seminary, with the result that they would be connected more thoroughly and securely to Jewish tradition. But Benderly, afraid that these future teachers might be lured into the more prestigious rabbinate, demurred and prevailed.[12] Teachers Institute students

Teachers College, 1936. *Special Collections, Milbank Memorial Library, Teachers College, Columia University.*

divided their time between their campus and Teachers College and usually ended up with Teachers College/Columbia doctorates.

Well-known religious educators at Union Seminary too went to school at Teachers College. George Albert Coe (at UTS 1909–22) and Harrison Elliott (1924–50), immersed themselves in the scientific and progressive pedagogy of Dewey, Thorndike, and Kilpatrick. By the time Coe accepted the appointment at Union, Brian Tippen writes, he "had been working in relation to Dewey's thought for a decade. . . . Thorndike's research on educational psychology at Teachers College and Dewey's arrival at Columbia echoed academic trends that Coe represented and with which he could cooperate."[13] Elliott, who succeeded his teacher Coe at Union, was also a follower of Dewey, Kilpatrick, and other Teachers College faculty; he earned an M.A. at Teachers College in the early twenties and was especially powerfully influenced by Dewey's *How We Think* (1910).[14]

It was at once daring and safe for Jewish and Protestant religious scholars to study with Dewey at Teachers College. His religious naturalism was well known to them and sometimes regretted. He had stopped going to church when he started teaching at the University of Chicago in 1894 and was quite obviously uninterested in the details of theological thought. For all of this, Jewish students must have found him too "Protestant" at times; not surprisingly, Dewey had never entirely shed the language he had learned from his devout Protestant mother. As a matter of fact, he

745

*Religious
Educators
at Jewish
Theological
Seminary*

Teachers Institute
student Tziporah
Heckelman at the
Institute's model
school at the
Inwood Hebrew
Congregation,
late 1940s. *Photo
by Virginia F.
Stern. Ratner
Center, JTS.*

could sound quite Christian and quite Protestant even when he wasn't specifically
addressing the subject of religion. And it may be that his Protestant students were
more comfortable celebrating his ideas of lifelong "growth" and "change" and of
instrumentalism in all areas of human activity including religion than his Jewish
students, who also felt strongly attached to "tradition."

Yet even his Jewish followers could see Dewey as reassuringly "religious." If he
had sloughed off the particularities of Protestant belief, he still saw the universe as
generally shaped by benevolent purpose and remained far from antireligious. As
Alan Ryan, Dewey's most recent biographer, argues,

> For those who doubted that "science" could tell us all we needed about politics,
> and who held that religion or ethics must fill the gap, Dewey had a consistent
> answer. The contrast between science and art, science and ethics, science and
> religion was illusory. Properly understood, the scientific attitude was continu-
> ous with the religious attitude; properly understood, what scientists do when
> they try to understand the world is not very different from what any of us do
> when we try to decide what to think and what to do; properly understood, the
> scientist's search for order is not so different from the artist's search for order.[15]

Thus, it was possible for Jewish and Protestant admirers of Dewey to think of themselves as both scientific educators and serious persons of faith. For those at JTS who
insisted upon the legitimacy of the scientific study of Judaism (as did Protestants at

UTS in regard to theology and scripture), Dewey's persuasive confidence in the harmony of faith and science must have acted as a powerful draw.

As a consequence of their connections with Teachers College and Dewey, then, Jewish and Protestant educators ended up sharing much in common. Both groups learned to consider the needs, interests, and psychology of the child as the starting point in designing curriculum and teaching methods. For them the reform of teaching usually meant rejecting recitation and lecture, especially for young children, and incorporating a pedagogy that stressed children's active engagement with objects and materials. Music, art, film, and drama became important in religious education classrooms. Jewish educators reacted against the *hederim*, the elementary-level schools for Jewish children imported from Eastern Europe, which have been immortalized in immigrant literature as noisy, chaotic dens of mechanical recitation and indifferent instructors. For their part, Christian educational reformers such as Coe at Union Seminary criticized the Sunday school's dull content and teaching methods that grasped at fragments of Bible, failed to foster moral character, and made no attempt to learn from the social sciences.[16] For both groups of educators, reform meant a teaching practice that was thoroughly scientific, ethical, and religious.

As attentive students of Dewey, both Jewish and Protestant educators came to see education as fundamentally *social*. They viewed interactions in the classroom as important preparation for children's participation in a democracy (and for Jews, in the Jewish community) and emphasized the continuities between the school and the rest of the child's environment. Education, whether public or religious, should school children in democracy, they believed. Religious education should also be democratic in the sense of being inclusive and extended to children (and adults for that matter) who had not been reached before. During the teens Jewish educators began designing large, once-a-week classes for Jewish children not in Jewish schools[17] and extended their purview to girls, whose religious education had been largely ignored in Europe. Protestants had long sent girls to Sunday school, but they concentrated on expanding their efforts to urban populations who they claimed had thus far been neglected.

These reformist educators, Christian and Jewish, endorsed graded lessons, efficiency, and the practice of coordinating among different levels and kinds of education. (In the rather heterogeneous world of Jewish education order and efficiency were strong desiderata.) They stressed the training of teachers in the "science of pedagogy," employing actual observation in laboratory schools and supervised practice as teachers. (Teachers College had a demonstration Sunday school that was transferred to UTS in 1910; during the teens JTS took advantage of selected model schools run by the Kehillah's Bureau of Education.) In these ways, Jewish and Protestant educators influenced by the Teachers College faculty came to think of religious education as an area for serious scientific research, necessitating the deployment of the social sciences—especially psychology—as well as the theological and biblical disciplines.

Perhaps as important as anything else for Jewish educators, Dewey and others embraced cultural pluralism, the recognition and appreciation of cultural differences in America. The result was that Jews concluded with some relief that it was possible to educate children to be both truly Jewish and truly American; for their part Protestants such as those at Union learned that Jews could be good Americans without becoming Christians, that, in fact, a diverse religious culture was to be celebrated rather than lamented. These were important commonalities and furnished the basis for dialogue between JTS and UTS educators. Yet naturally substantial differences persisted as well. Above all, there was the very real (and sometimes justified) suspicion among Jews that Protestants' chief objective in approaching them was to convert them, no matter how subtly they seemed to go about it. And there was the lingering ambivalence, even among liberal Protestants, about whether the very essence of evangelical faith did not in fact demand the proselytization of Jews.

But even when evangelizing goals were clearly renounced and the renunciations were believed, substantial differences remained between Jewish and Protestant educators. Above all, Jews in the movement represented by JTS had come to associate Jewish religious education with the very important task of learning Hebrew. Since the acquisition of any foreign language consumes immense amounts of time, it was clear early on that Jewish religious education had to demand much more of a student's time and energy than the Protestant Sunday school's one hour a week.

The issue of Hebrew separated Christian and Jewish educators in other ways. Much discussion of reform in Jewish education focused on better, more efficient, and more interesting ways to teach Hebrew. Early in the 20th century, stimulated by Zionism, Jewish reformers had introduced *Ivrit bi-Ivrit*, a way to teach modern Hebrew through actual conversation rather than through grammar, vocabulary, and rote word-by-word translation of a biblical text. Enlightened and humane as this approach was in many respects, the modern Hebrew that was learned by ear was quite different from written biblical Hebrew, leaving vexed questions that Jewish educators are to this day still trying to settle: Is mastery of Hebrew meant to connect American Jews closer to modern-day Israel, or is it intended primarily to aid in the study and discussion of Jewish sacred texts? Since lay Christians had seldom read the Bible in any other language than the vernacular, this was a discussion that went over their heads.

Furthermore, for most Jews, Jewish education meant acquiring familiarity with the long history of Judaism and with the multiple dimensions of contemporary Jewish culture (e.g., Hebrew folksongs, Zionism, Yiddish theater, modern Hebrew literature)—dimensions that Protestants might have considered "secular" but that Jews often did not. (Certainly Mordecai Kaplan, with his conviction that Judaism is a "civilization," did not.) In contrast, Protestant Sunday school students were so immersed in a basically Protestant milieu that they did not need explicit Sunday school teaching about Protestant cultural traditions.

In fact, if Jewish and Christian educators had attempted to engage in dialogue between 1900 and 1940, they would quickly have come to wonder whether in fact they meant anything comparable when they used the phrase "religious education." Protestants weren't always sure what they meant, of course, and debated the issue frequently. Their nomenclature also shifted, from "religious" to "Christian" education and later sometimes to "church school," reflecting their uncertainties and disagreements. But Protestants usually had in mind a relatively limited collection of topics: the Bible (in English), ethics or morality, and a little bit of doctrine or theology. Jews were even less certain where the boundaries of "religious education" lay; usually they were assumed to take in Hebrew, Torah and the prayers, synagogue practices, and Jewish history and traditions. But, much as those studies involved, they might not end there. The confusion is reflected in Alexander Dushkin's description of the establishment of the Jewish Education Committee in New York in 1939: "There was discussion whether Jewish nationalism, Zionism, and Yiddish are or are not Jewish 'religious' education."[18] And the debate was joined again in the early forties when the seminary considered changing the degrees of Bachelor, Master, and Doctor of Jewish Pedagogy to Bachelor, Master, and Doctor of Religious Education:

> When a proposal was made to change the degrees to Bachelor and Master of Religious Education—in line with the degrees offered by non-Jewish institutions, some of the Faculty demurred. They wanted to know how a degree in *religious* education could be offered for secular and 'pagan' ideas reflected in some of the Hebrew literature taught in the Hebrew literature classes, such as Tchernichovsky's "Ode to Apollo." But when Dr. Kaplan defined his ideas of religion, and showed how it encompassed even the literary creations of Shneur and Tchernichovsky and Berichevsky as well as Bialik and Ahad Haam, they were reconciled to the idea of a degree in religious education.[19]

A Dialogue Begun in Earnest

Gradually Protestant and Conservative Jewish educators, reflecting a national trend, entered more and more into dialogue with each other. (For both groups the dialogue with Roman Catholics developed more slowly.) Generally speaking, the growing ecumenical movement and also the increasing assimilation of the Eastern European immigrants account for the growing conversation, but we can trace educators' efforts to some particular factors. First, in the late twenties and early thirties, the "goodwill" movement began to encourage conversation between Jews and Christians. One of the earliest efforts took place under the auspices of the Federal Council of Churches, in the Committee for Goodwill Between Jews and Protestants. In 1927 this committee was eclipsed by the National Conference of Christians and Jews, which in 1929 organized the first of a number of seminars on relations among religious groups (interestingly, the initial one was in JTS territory, at Columbia University). Through its characteristic symposiums, roundtables, and panels, each with Protestant, Catholic, and Jewish representation, the NCCJ promoted better religious understanding. Its practice of always including Protestant, Catholic, and Jewish spokespersons established the precedent, which would be confirmed in the fifties in Will Herberg's *Catholic-Protestant-Jew* (1955), for conceiving the American religious landscape as a parity of the "three major faiths."[20]

Probably even more important than the goodwill movement in bringing Jewish, Protestant, and Catholic *educators* together for dialogue, however, was the discussion concerning religion and the public schools. This discussion had two focal points: the role (if any) of the teaching of/about religion in the public schools; and the merits of released time (also sometimes referred to as "dismissed time," or "weekday classes"). These issues, especially released time, began to be aired occasionally as early as the teens; weekday religious education upon the model of the "Gary Plan," which had been implemented in 1916, was in fact the subject of several essays published in a 1916 issue of *Religious Education*. Three of the discussants there were Jews, all with JTS ties: Samson Benderly, Isaac Berkson, and Judah Magnes.[21] Despite this early encounter, though, the subject of released time remained a peripheral concern for most Jews until the forties, when New York City, where the majority of American Jews lived, adopted released time (in 1941), making it a more pressing issue among Jewish educators. Also propelling Jewish interest was a particularly animated discussion in the larger society about the teaching of religion in the public schools: whether it was necessary, desirable, and whether it could be done constitutionally. (Probably the high point of this discussion occurred in 1947, with the publication of the American Council on Education's *The Relation of Religion to Public Education*. The report was reproduced in *Religious Education* the same year, along with "evaluations" of the report, among which were three by Jewish educational leaders.)

The religion and public education debate typically occurred in symposia or roundtable formats, either before a live audience or in journals like *Religious Education*. In theory, Catholic spokespersons were generally well disposed toward the idea of religion in the public schools, though, committed as they were to parochial schools, it was not really their fight. The Jewish pronouncements tended to take the negative or at least skeptical position on mixing religion and public education; as traditional advocates of strict separation between church and state, Jewish leaders warned against introducing religion as a subject into public schools; unlike some Protestants they did not believe it was possible to train a classroom teacher to offer objective or neutral instruction on the subject of religion.[22] (Liberal Protestants were nervous on this score but more eager than Jews to try it out.) Nor on the whole were Jews enthusiastic about released or dismissed time, again partly on the grounds of the necessity for keeping church and state separate. But even when Jewish educators satisfied themselves that released time was being handled with complete neutrality by the schools, they still found released time to be of dubious value: one paltry hour a week (the usual amount allowed for released time) would hardly make much difference to Jewish instruction. They were also worried—as it turned out needlessly—that Jewish parents, if given the choice between released time classes and the more intense classes of the usual religious educational curriculum, would elect the released classes as cheaper and less time consuming.

Interestingly, some Jewish educators had the sense of being pressured into the above debates. Alexander Dushkin recalled that "our Protestant and Catholic colleagues made our cooperation in this [released time] a test of interfaith goodwill." He went on, "Personally I was ambivalent; I considered it neither harmful nor valuable and went along with the board in the attitude of *kabdehu ve-hashdehu*— respect it and suspect it'."[23] Yet, despite skepticism like Dushkin's, it appears that Jewish educators got into the habit of dialogue with their counterparts in other faiths on matters of educational importance.

AT JTS BY ABOUT MIDCENTURY there were two categories of influence—those that encouraged educators to turn to the outside educational world for ideas and inspiration and those that made them turn inward to cultivate and consolidate Jewish (and specifically Conservative Jewish) identity. After World War II American Jews—and of course world Jewry—were preoccupied by two sets of circumstances—the Holocaust and the 1948 establishment of the State of Israel. The old guard was also changing at JTS and on Morningside Heights. Mordecai Kaplan retired in 1945 after nearly half a century on the faculty; Dewey, Kilpatrick, and Thorndike had passed from the scene at Teachers College (in 1930, 1938, and 1940 respectively). Though the influence of Dewey and his cohorts certainly persisted at JTS and UTS—as a quick look at the literature produced by faculty in the past few decades will verify—new educators (many of them influenced by Dewey, it must be said) provided educational models and questions, and Judaism's own imperatives dictated other educational directions JTS people would choose.

One of the most important departures taken by JTS educators after World War II was their very successful experiment with religious camping. In fact, many of the educators connected to JTS, if asked about the seminary's single most significant contribution to religious education, would point to the 1947 establishment of the

Ramah camps. Ismar Schorsch, the current Seminary Chancellor, writes, "I am firmly convinced that in terms of social import, in terms of lives affected, Ramah is the most important venture ever undertaken by the Seminary."[24] Ironically, given the importance of this development for JTS, neither the birth nor the growth of the Ramah movement has received much notice from Christian educators.

This lack of notice was not because Christian educators themselves were uninterested in summer camping. By the time Ramah entered the scene it joined a well-established religious camping enterprise; the initial church-sponsored camp had appeared in 1880, and the first of a series of successful YMCA camps dated from 1885 (on Lake Champlain). Despite a number of Christian (and secular) precedents, however, Ramah was modeled not upon these so much as upon earlier Jewish experiments in camping. (See Michael Brown's essay elsewhere in these volumes.)

Clearly Camp Ramah created an intense environment (a "total educational environment," according to Seymour Fox).[25] The camps ran for eight-week sessions; Hebrew was the official language; Zionism was a guiding spirit (eventually many counselors came from Israel); dietary and other laws were taken seriously; and part of the day was devoted to classes in Hebrew and Judaic studies (in addition to more typical camp classes such as music and crafts). A "professor-in-residence" (usually from JTS) was on hand for the summer. The counselors were a dedicated group, often former Ramahniks themselves.

Gerson Cohen described Ramah as addressing "the basic problem of Jewish education... the gap that lay between what the Jewish school was teaching and what the Jewish child experienced in his home." He went on,

> The young founders sought to bridge the gap by providing a new milieu and a framework which could act as a surrogate home. To recapture the spirit and substance of the Jewish home as it had been in Eastern Europe and the Zionist reality as it developed in Israel, they devised a very special medium, a camp in which rituals were made integral to the cultural context as a whole and where Jewishness became part of the natural environment.[26]

Joseph Reimer recalled Ramah "in its first generation" as "an ideologically-driven utopian experiment."[27] Ramah was obviously more intense and more intentional than most Christian camps; perhaps this helps explain why it received scant attention from Christians. Compared to Ramah's substantial summerlong commitment, Christian camps usually lasted one or at most two weeks. As befit an institution so closely (and uniquely) tied to a seminary, Ramah was heavily "academic," whereas Christian camps normally carefully distinguished between the goals of camp and those of church or Sunday school. Christian camp manuals typically cautioned that camp should never feel like school to campers; Ramah leaders had no such compunctions. And of course Christian camps did less to initiate campers into a whole way of life; insofar as they were concerned about induction into a way of life at all,

Counselors
engaged in one of
Camp Ramah's
most important
activities—study.
Camp Ramah in
the Poconos,
1950s. *Photo by
Virginia F. Stern.
Ratner Center,
JTS.*

they were interested in forming good Americans—honest, cooperative, gregarious, able to make decisions and assume leadership. Worship and prayer came into the Christian camp purview, but they were assumed to arise almost naturally out of sustained contact with the beauty of the natural environment. Ramah leaders were less willing to just let prayer "happen" but systematically cultivated its practice.

In recent years, Ramah and Christian camps have probably come to resemble each other more than earlier, though more in response to common cultural factors than to any actual consultation. As families have seemed more and more fragile, camp leaders on all sides have dropped the rhetoric that sometimes treated the family as delinquent in its religious duties and as interfering in the program of the camp. Instead, the camping experience has often come to include the family, for all or part of the session. And as is common with movements that start out with such élan, some of the earlier dedication and energy has yielded to routine.[28]

Important as Ramah has been to the postwar seminary in developing new generations of Conservative leadership and in providing a laboratory for JTS religious educators,[29] much has gone on inside the seminary as well. Religious educators at JTS, especially since about 1960, have devoted a good deal of attention to the issue of how to "translate" (the word often used) the scholarship concerning Jewish texts and Jewish tradition into curriculum, both for children and adults. This "translation" is not easy: like Protestant and Catholic scholarship that has followed the

753

*Religious
Educators
at Jewish
Theological
Seminary*

Melton Center
publications,
1980s. *Melton
Center, JTS.*

canons of modern academic disciplines, Jewish scholarship in the Conservative
movement too has tended to be relativizing. And of course that scholarship is complex and does not easily lend itself to lay people's (or children's) understanding. Nor
does the privileging of ancient texts (sometimes in Hebrew) and ancient ideas
always rest easily with the progressive education principle of making the interest of
child (or older student) central to the educational enterprise.

Much of the JTS religious educational endeavor in recent decades has taken
place under the institutional umbrella of the Melton Research Center established at
the Seminary in 1960 and funded by Samuel Melton of Columbus, Ohio. In the
early days of the Melton Center, a "Melton Faculty Seminar" was convened—and

was ongoing for several years—for the purpose of examining the question of how Jewish scholarship could be conveyed in actual Jewish school curriculum (the seminar has become legendary in Seminary annals; many who recall it remember it as an intellectual Golden Era). The plan devised by the seminar, outlined in a 1963 "blueprint" entitled "The Melton Research Center: a Plan for Jewish Education," called for a group of Jewish scholars to write up their areas of specialty in a way that could then be translated, through a process of classroom testing and teacher training, to the religious school curriculum. The first volume of scholarship completed in this projected collection, by Nahum Sarna, a JTS biblical scholar, was on Genesis. Sarna's study, which took a comparative religions approach, was turned into manuals for teachers and students by Leonard Gardner and Louis Newman. Classroom experience, however, revealed that the "translation" was still difficult for teachers to use. Eventually an accessible and successful volume was produced by a seasoned classroom teacher, Ruth Zielenziger (*Genesis: A New Teachers Guide*, 1979; *Genesis: A New Student Workbook*, 1980). Zielenziger, joined by colleagues, set to work training teachers to use the new curriculum.[30]

For a number of years the Melton Center concentrated on its Bible curriculum and the training of teachers to use it (some of the projected scholarly volumes originally planned in the faculty seminar never got written). A manual on Exodus was produced in 1984 by Zielenziger (*Exodus: A Teachers Guide*). Melton Center personnel, committed to the study of Torah in Hebrew, also put a great deal of thought into producing a Hebrew language curriculum. In recent years the Center has branched out beyond Bible and language curriculum to materials on prayer, holidays, Jewish history, Israel, and the family. Melton Center curricular materials—even those meant for young children—have tended to carry a good deal of scholarly weight; indeed, it seems quite audacious (if not downright foolhardy) for a curriculum on Genesis to *start* with a scholarly volume on the subject and proceed to "translate" it into terms children and lay people can understand—and then turn around and repeat the same basic pattern in other subjects. The Melton biblical materials have been highly enough regarded to be used in secular public school classes. Somewhat surprisingly, I am not aware of any study by Christian educators of the Melton materials. One would think, given the frequent criticisms of Sunday school materials as intellectually vacuous (and of religious education as marginal to theological seminaries), that the JTS curricula and the process by which they were developed would attract attention from Christian educators.

Another component of the Melton Center activity—also worthy of examination by Christian educators—has been for JTS educators to train teachers in the use of Melton materials, either on the Morningside Heights campus, in special settings in the summer, or in the synagogue schools where the materials have been tried.

In seeking to establish camps and create Bible teaching materials and educate teachers (the Seminary also created a supplementary high school, Prozdor, in 1951), the educators at JTS have tended to follow some of the same paths set out by their predecessors early in the century: they have reached out to secular educational thinkers. They no longer looked with the same intensity to Teachers College; indeed, the gurus of education were no longer nearly so concentrated in one place as they once were. Between 1960 and 1975 JTS educators turned most often to secular educators at the University of Chicago, to Ralph Tyler[31] and above all to Joseph Schwab, longtime teacher of biology and of education at the University of Chicago (1930–74) and creator of a well-known curriculum for teaching biology. By all accounts, Schwab's charismatic personality supplied much of the stimulus that made the Melton Faculty Seminars so exciting. He had been at the center of experiments in undergraduate education during Robert Hutchins's administration at Chicago, using discussion of the "great books" as a basis. When these experiments ended in the late fifties, Schwab had sought new arenas for his interest in the philosophy of teaching. One such arena turned out to be Jewish education. Though Schwab was a secular Jew, his interest in great books and in the role of education in the preservation of tradition and the shaping of ethical values apparently found a nice fit with the teaching of Jewish religion and culture. His main contributions to JTS efforts in religious education were a dedication to critical and free "inquiry" (à la Dewey) in the classroom—no less in matters of religion, at least once children were old enough; an interest in the structure of disciplines that would have encouraged the expectations of the Melton seminar that children could grasp all the essentials of a complex subject (Genesis, e.g., or Jewish history) if only it was presented to them properly; an attention to the child's emotional and psychological as well as intellectual life; and a concern for the development of "character."[32] Seymour Fox, a close associate of Schwab's at Chicago, a professor of education at JTS (1956–66) and dean of the Teachers Institute (1959–66) until he left for Hebrew University, was an ally in propagating Schwab's ideas in the seminary's educational endeavors, and himself quite a compelling personality.

The Dialogues Deepened

By the sixties the scope of possible topics for interfaith dialogue had expanded. In the forties and early fifties, it had been increasingly common for Jews and Christians to discuss topics of mutual concern such as released time and religion in the public schools. Certainly the essays of educators with ties to JTS appear in the pages of *Religious Education*; in the forties, for instance, we see articles by Samuel Dinin, Alexander Dushkin (two), and Robert Gordis. As the sense of shared concerns grew in the sixties, the dialogue did also. In the face of what they perceived as a growing "secularism," many Protestants had come to feel as beleaguered as Jews had in the face of a dominant Christian culture (in fact, the movements for released time and religion in the public schools had been earlier symptoms of growing Protestant anxiety about their ebbing influence in the culture). It had become clear to Protestant leaders that their children no longer automatically imbibed a Christian ethos in the public school or the neighborhood, and certainly not in the mall or the media. Nor did it seem as if the public schools would be judged a feasible place for the teaching of religion any time soon; indeed, if they taught about religion in a balanced, inclusive, and constitutionally permissible manner—about the best that could be expected—the goals of Protestant nurture in particular would hardly be served. If the younger generation was going to grow up Christian at all, religious education would have to assume a heavier burden than before. But released time—a mere hour a week—had proven to be less than a panacea, and the impetus behind it began to fade in the sixties. Likewise, the celebrated *Presbyterian Faith and Life Curriculum* (1947)—widely copied by other Protestant denominations—had fallen short of its promises. One of its major aims, to shift more of the responsibility for religious education from the school to the family, failed in the end to attract the desired involvement from the parents of Sunday school pupils. The agonized question remained: How could Sunday schools of one hour a week—the chief form of Protestant education—accomplish what was needed? All this at a time when the very notion of schooling itself was being called into question by thinkers like Ivan Illich (*Deschooling Society*, 1970). By turns schooling was regarded as all too effective and efficient—at oppressing children—or as downright irrelevant, because the other cultural "educators" were so much more powerful.

Beginning in the sixties, American Roman Catholic educators, who had long relied upon their system of parochial schools shored up by the existence of the old Catholic ethnic communities, started to question their educational assumptions. First, they came to the recognition that, given the decline in religious vocations and the unlikelihood of substantial public aid to their schools, they were going to have difficulties maintaining their parochial system at its present level, let alone expanding it. Accordingly, they came to acknowledge that the substantial portion of Catholic children in public schools (never less than 50 percent of the total of Catholic children) was never likely to diminish very much. If such children were to receive a religious education at all, they would have to be included in a system of supplementary education that, thus far, the church had failed to take very seriously. Catholic educators, who had passed through the heyday of progressive education impervious or hostile to its appeal, now discovered the attractions of a child-centered, experience-oriented pedagogical approach. And partly as a result of Vatican II in the early sixties, the American Catholic church began to welcome contacts with other faiths. All of these factors—the sense of beleaguered parochial schools, their new commitment to supplemental religious education, the increasing ecumenism, and their openness to progressive pedagogy—gave them much more in common with Jewish and Protestant educators than heretofore and prepared them to engage in dialogue.

The signs of greatly increased interchange among religious educators of diverse faiths were legion. More than ever before, educators wrote articles for each others' journals. On occasion they taught in each others' seminaries and in other venues where religious educators were being trained. For example, Michael A. Signer, professor of Jewish history at Hebrew Union College-Jewish Institute of Religion, served also as an instructor in the Advanced Catechetical Ministries Course for the Catholic Archdiocese of Los Angeles; the Catholic religious educator Mary Boys moved in 1995 from Boston College to the faculty of Union Seminary. *Religious Education* lost much of its former liberal Protestant identity. In 1987 Jack Spiro, a rabbi, succeeded the Presbyterian John Westerhoff as editor. The conventions of the REA began to attract more Catholics than Protestants[33] (the proportion of Jewish educators at REA conventions remained small). Among educators ardent and sometimes desperate for a more effective pedagogy, promising new ideas and approaches to religious education tended to cause concurrent ripples across the groups. For instance, in recent years Protestant and Jewish educators have begun to ponder the traditionally Catholic concept of religious education as "formation." Accordingly, in 1987 *Religious Education* organized its fall issue around that theme. There were contributions by Protestant religious educators, of course, and Rabbi Jack Spiro wrote on "Formative Process in Jewish Education," while Catholic Berard Marthaler addressed the subject from a Catholic perspective. And Jewish and Christian educators have begun to converge on issues that once sharply separated them. As Catholics were growing more critical of parochial schooling, Jewish groups became less enchanted with public education and began to embrace day schools in remarkable numbers (some of the initiatives, including the Solomon Schechter Day Schools, involved JTS faculty or alumni/ae). Thus, on the matter of religious day schooling, Jews and Catholics sometimes met in the middle—something that could hardly have been predicted in 1925 or even 1945. Religious educators from all three traditions agonized over their teenagers; the teens were obviously critical years for religious development, yet it also appeared that youth fled more determinedly than ever from formal religious instruction. Accordingly, Jewish and Christian educators continued to experiment with youth groups, summer camping, and, in the case of Jews, trips to Israel.

As religious educators have critiqued their own educational traditions in recent years, they have increasingly looked quite explicitly to other faiths for instruction. Thus, in a 1981 essay Mary Boys was ready to assert that unless Christians achieve a sympathetic understanding of Judaism, they will lack a true understanding of their own faith. She wrote that "entrance into the questions" of Jewish-Christian relations "permits deeper penetration into the labyrinthine mystery of faith; confrontation with Judaism offers Christians fertile, new insights into faith, as well as some sobering perspectives on a faith too glibly expressed."[34] At the same time, Jeffrey Schein, an instructor at the Temin Center for Jewish Education at the Reconstructionist Rabbinical College (an educational outgrowth of Mordecai Kaplan's ideas), struggling to bridge the dichotomy between moral thought (or study) and moral action, advised his fellow religionists to break out of "a certain Jewish parochialism implicit in treating the relationship between study and moral action as a uniquely Jewish phenomenon." How about seeking insights, he asked, from Robert Bellah's *Habits of the Heart* and Alasdair MacIntyre's *After Virtue*? He added, "We share the difficulties of the impeded dialectic with other educators. We have much to learn from conversations with Christian educators and secular educators who are concerned with moral education."[35] Michael Signer sought to bridge the divide that has opened up as a result of the common Jewish conviction that theology is a Christian and "not a Jewish thing": "I am aware that many scholars claim that systematic theology is 'alien' to Judaism as a mode of discourse for explanation." But Jews, through their long contact with Christian culture, have become more attuned to systematic presentation: "It is clear that a new hermeneutic is developing with respect to classical Jewish sources and their presentation to a Western-educated Jewish lay audience."[36] Another Conservative Jewish educator, Elliott Dorff of the University of Judaism faculty in Los Angeles, argued that Jews need to be able to speak more comfortably about God than they have been accustomed to do, and appealed to the Christian example:

> Belief in God is not only intellectually possible, but experientially important, and Jews need to be much more open about how and why. Here we can learn from our Christian brothers and sisters who talk about God much more openly than Jews are used to doing. . . . we must confront the issues and develop theologically and educationally sophisticated ways of reintroducing God into Jewish education.[37]

Jewish education must be different from Christian, he cautioned, "But we must also be aware of the fact that we can learn from others, as others learn from us."[38] Michael Signer summarizes the mounting reasons for Jews and Christian educators to come together more than they have in the past: "The world grows larger around us. We recognize that the ways of the West are no longer the ways of the world. The human family reflected from our satellites is neither Jewish nor Christian. From this perspective we have more in common than we perhaps ever thought possible before."[39]

As Dorff's caution above suggests, there are limits to dialogue, of course—or at least limits to how much each group, given its own particular interests, can or will learn from the others. Liberal Protestantism, one of the groups traditionally most amenable to dialogue with Jews, has become more theologically oriented in recent decades, due in part to the proddings of neoorthodoxy; this theological preoccupation may at times have made Protestants' conversations with their Jewish counterparts more rather than less difficult. At the same time, Jewish educators (not excluding Reform Judaism) have become more serious about the meaning of *halakha* (the law) and its implications for religious practice—ruminations not particularly accessible to faith-righteous Protestants (or to Catholics either). Jewish educators have other concerns of their own. Sara S. Lee, director of education at the School of Education of Hebrew Union College in Los Angeles, reminds us: "While God and Torah have parallels in other religious traditions, the centrality of the People of Israel and the Land of Israel are idiosyncratic to Judaism."[40] The issue of Messianism, she adds, remains a vexed issue between Jews and Christians. Jews must worry about their survival as a people in America in a way Protestants and Catholics do not, at least not to date. Yet she too argues that religious leaders in the 20th century, as they tackle similar tasks of religious nurture in the face of powerful influences like secularity, the homogenization of American culture, and the impact of the electronic media on youth, must pool their intellectual and imaginative resources; they can each of them use all the help they can get.

As for JTS in particular, in the past two and a half decades it has widened its search of the educational world both secular and religious for educational ideas. The Chicago influence (as represented by Tyler, Schwab, and Fox) has waned, though it continues in the person of Lee Schulman of Stanford University, who studied at the University of Chicago School of Education under Schwab and who consults at JTS. But there are more diverse sources. Neil Gillman, professor of Jewish philosophy at JTS, in discussing how to teach Jewish children to pray—beyond going through the motions—recommended seeking inspiration from the "stages of faith" ideas of the Protestant educator, James Fowler.[41] In "Education for Change: Toward a Model of Jewish Teacher Education" (1988), Barry Holtz and Eduardo Rauch, the codirectors of the Melton Center between 1981 and 1994, demonstrated an engagement with many of the most celebrated educators of our time. In discussing the education of younger children they cited Jean Piaget, and they turned to Lawrence Kohlberg for older youngsters; they quoted B. F. Skinner (mostly as an example of what *not* to do). They borrowed from writing process teachers like Donald Graves and from well-known writing process techniques like journals and autobiography. They invoked the use of metaphorical forms of thinking, based, e.g., on William J. J. Gordon (*Synectics*), and looked to British teacher-educators like Peter Abbs. In company with other educators of our time, they tried to go beyond the notion of education as appealing primarily to the reason or intellect; rather it must use emotion, intuition, and even forms of meditation. (Holtz and Rauch quote Arthur Green approvingly in opposition to Jewish educators who "condemn silent meditation as *goyish*.") Holtz and Rauch were even more catholic than their predecessors in their resort to the social sciences; in addition to psychology they also employ anthropology, for instance ethnographers who describe the training of a traditional healer among the Kung of the Kalahari Desert. And they quoted Christian theologians freely.[42]

One place Morningside Heights religious educators from different traditions have come together over the past ten years is in a seminar on religious education, rotated among the campuses and team-taught by Joseph Lukinsky of JTS, Douglas Sloan of Teachers College, and, until his recent retirement, William Kennedy of Union Seminary. Much of the seminar discussion has revolved around the use of secular educational strategies in religious education: storytelling, synectics, mimesis, and journal writing.[43] Despite the enthusiastic participation of Lukinsky, though, the enrollment of Jewish education students in the seminar has remained relatively low.[44]

Perhaps these low figures are reasons for caution about ecumenical claims; though in many ways it seems as if Jewish educators and their Catholic and Protestant counterparts have moved closer both personally and intellectually, the gaps have persisted. In 1981 Ruth Zielenziger, the staff member of the Melton Center who wrote *Teaching Genesis* and *Teaching Exodus*, attended a convention of the Religious Education Association in East Lansing, Michigan, and reported on her experience for the Melton Center Journal (her piece was later reprinted in *Religious Education*). A native of Israel, she tells us she had lived in suburban America for some time, where Christians and Jews mingled regularly—the Christians attending bar/bat mitzvahs and the Jews attending Catholic wakes. But that casual ecumenism had not prepared her for the more searching ecumenism of the convention. On the way from the airport to the convention site she encountered a Catholic sister who in the course of the conversation confided in her, "You're the first Jew I ever met."[45]

Zielenziger was one of only five Jews among the two hundred attendants; she had requested kosher food, but the food service had interpreted that to mean only that she wouldn't eat pork or drink wine. But misunderstandings and miscommunications went well beyond dietary matters. She examined a beautiful set of Methodist Sunday school materials, wondering whether she could get ideas from them, and saw that "a notation in a lovely picture book indicates that Jerusalem is located in ancient Palestine. I am sure that this is not intended to be a political statement, and yet. . . ." She attended an ecumenical worship service, but couldn't understand the statement, "We celebrate your love, oh Yahwe," and wondered how it would even translate into Hebrew. Nor could she bring herself to utter "Yahwe." When the assembly repeated the Lord's Prayer, she thought,

> I find myself the only one to whom the words "give us our daily bread" mean
> what they mean in "Birkat Hamazon," namely an expression of thanks to God

and a supplication for His continued love and protection. To others these words evoke echoes of "the partaking of the messianic banquet." I have no idea of what this means.[46]

Christians she encountered evinced a genuine curiosity about Judaism, but they confounded her by assuming that there was one Jewish position on all issues. In the end Zielenziger was glad she had attended the convention—she learned a lot—but her report leaves us with an overwhelming impression of how much unknowing separates Christians and Jewish educators when they really start to talk theologically or liturgically.

In 1925 it would have been unlikely for anyone at JTS to have attended an REA convention, or even considered it. That Zielenziger went is a sign of ecumenism and the willingness of JTS people to learn from and to teach Christian educators. Yet the learning and teaching seems to have gone on at a fairly basic level, and Zielenziger, as is clear from her words quoted above, often felt she and the others were talking different languages. Jews and Christians are still sometimes strangers, and Jews still feel the need to practice Dushkin's behest to "respect" and "suspect."

And yet—that *zeitgeist* that Lukinsky talked about earlier is no small thing. And by the recent decades we *are* indeed talking about a powerful *zeitgeist*: a majority of religious educators—at least at the leadership level—Jewish, Protestant, and Catholic, share a commitment to what, broadly speaking, can be called progressive education. They may have derived it from diverse sources, but derive it they did. Underneath their thinking still lurk John Dewey, Johan Pestalozzi, Maria Montessori, and other progressive educators—and, sometimes more overtly, the successors and disciples of Dewey. Thus, at least in theory, the student remains central in all "enlightened" religious pedagogy. However compelling and demanding the content of the Jewish school curriculum, for instance, the needs and interests of the child must be taken seriously. And it is no longer possible for religious educators to ponder schools without thinking of the relationship of schools to other educators, formal and informal: families, youth groups, Israel, summer camps, and the churches and synagogues themselves. Nor can educators discuss education for very long without also talking, like good Deweyans, about "community" and "society." (The sense that all communities, particularly religious, seem to be at risk currently has reinforced this Deweyan influence.) And there is much more to that *zeitgeist*: the pervasive professionalization of the educator (at least at the director of religious education level) that ensures certain common "professional" interests (salary, similar academic credentials, concerns about status); the nervousness about a secular world not notably friendly to religious interests; lately, the increased interest in all traditions in the cultivation of "spirituality"; and the recognition of the importance of the family as educator (or, to put it the other way, the futility of most religious education without the cooperation of the family). In the end, then, Christians and

Jews are religiously speaking both strangers and intimates, as Joseph Lukinsky suggested. One thing seems clear, however: that whatever their real differences, Jewish and Christian educators have enough in common and enough to learn from each other that they can benefit from many more years of dialogue on this vexed subject of religious education.

1. Joseph S. Lukinsky, "A Response to Brian Tippen," *Religious Education* 88 (fall 1993): p. 624.

2. Stephen A. Schmidt, *A History of the Religious Education Association* (Birmingham, Ala.: Religious Education Association, 1983), pp. 34–35.

3. See, e.g., Rabbi Louis Grossman, "Jewish Religious Education. The Training of Jewish Teachers of Religion," *Religious Education* 6 (1911–12): pp. 276–81.

4. Emanuel Gamoran, "An Appreciation" [of George Coe] *Religious Education* 47 (1952): pp. 108–9.

5. Ibid., p. 109.

6. Israel S. Chipkin, "[Harrison S. Elliott] As an Interfaith Worker," *Religious Education* 46 (1951): p. 261.

7. Harrison S. Elliott, "Relationship of Religious Education to Public Education," *Jewish Education* 13 (September 1941): pp. 92–98.

8. Rebecca Brickner, "As I Remember Dr. Benderly," *Jewish Education* 20 (summer 1949): p. 56.

9. Mordecai Kaplan, "The Teachers Institute," in *The Jewish Theological Seminary of America: Semi-Centennial Volume,* ed. Cyrus Adler (New York: Jewish Theological Seminary of America, 1939), p. 140.

10. Arthur Goren, *New York Jews and the Quest for Community: The Kehillah Experiment, 1908–1922* (New York: Columbia University Press, 1970), p. 119.

11. Israel S. Chipkin, "Greetings to Professor William Heard Kilpatrick," *Jewish Education* 9, no. 2 (April-June 1937): p. 51.

12. Mel Scult, *Judaism Faces the Twentieth Century: a Biography of Mordecai Kaplan* (Detroit: Wayne State University, 1993), p. 123.

13. Brian A. Tippen, "A Historical Look at the Succession of Major Professors of Religious Education at Union Theological Seminary in New York," *Religious Education* 88, no. 4 (fall 1993): p. 508.

14. Ibid., p. 508.

15. Alan Ryan, *John Dewey and the High Tide of American Liberalism* (New York: Norton, 1995), p. 21. Ryan in general is interested in the ways that Dewey continued to be "religious" and "Protestant," albeit with a difference.

16. E.g., see George A. Coe, *What Is Christian Education?* (New York: Scribner's, 1929), pp. 13 ff.

17. Goren, *New York Jews*, p. 111.

18. Alexander Dushkin, *Living Bridge: Memoirs of an Educator* (Jerusalem: Keter, 1975), p. 146.

19. Samuel Dinin, "Professor Mordecai Kaplan," *The Bulletin of the Alumni Association* (JTS), (May 1981): p. 7.

20. For the history of Jewish-Christian relations see Benny Kraut, "A Wary Collaboration: Jews, Catholics and the Protestant Good Will Movement," in *Between the Times: The Travail of the Protestant Establishment in America, 1900–1960,* ed. William R. Hutchison (Cambridge: Cambridge University Press, 1989); James E. Pitt, *Adventures in Brotherhood* (New York: Farrar, Straus and Co., 1955); Lance J. Sussman, "'Toward a Better Understanding': The Rise of the Interfaith Movement in America and the Role of Rabbi Isaac Landman," *American Jewish Archives* 34 (1982): pp. 35–51.

21. See Samson Benderly, "Standard Curriculum for Jewish Week-Day Religious School"; [Isaac Berkson], "Jewish Week-Day Religious Education and the Gary Schedule"; J.L. Magnes, "Attitude of the Jews Toward Week-Day Religious Education," *Religious Education* 11 (1916): pp. 526–31, 345–49, 226–30.

22. Ben M. Edidin, "Released Time in the Jewish Community," *Religious Education* 41 (1946): pp. 16–19; Rabbi Leon Fram, "Evaluations of the Relation of Religion to Public Education—the Basic Principles," *Religious Education* 42 (1947): pp. 173–175; Solomon B.

Freehof, "Evaluations of the Relation of Religion to Public Education—the Basic Principles," *Religious Education* 42 (1947): pp. 163–65.

23. Dushkin, *Living Bridge*, p. 161.

24. Sylvia C. Ettenberg and Geraldine Rosenfield, *The Ramah Experience: Community and Commitment* (New York: The Jewish Theological Seminary of America, 1989), p. 185.

25. Ibid., p. 20.

26. Ibid., p. 40.

27. Ibid., p. 57.

28. Many of the essays in the Ettenberg volume convey this sense of routinization.

29. E.g., Joseph S. Lukinsky derived his data for his doctoral dissertation from his observations at Ramah. "Teaching Responsibility: A Case Study in Curriculum Development" (Ph.D. diss., Harvard Graduate School of Education, 1968).

30. Ruth Zielenziger, "A History of the Bible Program of the Melton Research Center With Special Reference to the Curricular Principles on Which It Is Based" (Ph.D. diss., Jewish Theological Seminary, 1989).

31. Tyler's best-known book is *Basic Principles of Curriculum and Instruction* (Chicago: University of Chicago Press, 1949).

32. Schwab's ideas on the structure of discipline were similar to those of Jerome Bruner; Schwab was convinced he had arrived at them before Bruner, but obviously Bruner has received most of the credit. Schwab spent a year at Teachers College on a fellowship during the thirties and probably imbibed Deweyan influence then; he also read a great deal of Dewey later on when he was pondering issues of the undergraduate curriculum at Chicago. Schwab was also influenced—like many of the great books advocates—by his reading of Aristotle. One prime locus for Schwab's concern with the emotions is his essay "Eros and Education." Schwab's essays are difficult to read; even his admirers attest to this difficulty. Apparently the essays were most effective when one had had classroom contact with Schwab and therefore had more context for his written work. In regard to free inquiry, Schwab felt secular subjects should always be taught in this manner, whether younger or older students were involved; in regard to the teaching of matters connected with religious tradition, the younger students should not be taught inquiry. "These matters will be participated in by the child as a privileged sharing of the adult world, not queried, or 'whyed.'" (Schwab, "The Religiously Oriented School in the United States: A Memorandum on Policy," *Conservative Judaism* 18, no. 3 [spring 1964]: p. 11.) But by the time children were about twelve they were ready for an inquiry approach to religion.

    For a useful collection of Schwab's most important essays (including "Eros and Education") see *Joseph J. Schwab: Science, Curriculum and Liberal Education: Selected Essays*, ed. Ian Westbury and Neil J. Wilkof (Chicago: University of Chicago, 1978). See also the introduction to this collection. For analysis of Schwab's educational thought, see Elliot Eisner, "No Easy Answers: Joseph Schwab's Contributions to Curriculum," *Curriculum Inquiry* 14, no. 2 (1984): pp. 201–10; Henrietta Schwartz, "Dialogue: Schwab's 'Practical 4' and its Corroboration in Recent History," *Curriculum Inquiry* 14, no. 4 (1984): pp. 437–63; Lee S. Shulman, "The Practical and the Eclectic: A Deliberation on Teaching and Educational Research," *Curriculum Inquiry* 14, no. 2 (1984): pp. 183–200; Seymour Fox, "Dialogue: The Vitality of Theory in Schwab's Conception of the Practical," *Curriculum Inquiry* 15, no. 1 (1985): pp. 63–89; Ralph W. Tyler, "Dialogue II. Personal Reflections on The Practical 4," *Curriculum Inquiry* 14, no. 1 (1984): pp. 97–102. For Schwab on religious education in particular, see "The Religiously Oriented School."

33. Schmidt, *A History*, p. 164

34. Mary Boys, "Questions 'Which Touch on the Heart of Our Faith,'" *Religious Education* 76 (November-December 1981): p. 656.

35. Jeffrey Schein, "Moral Thought and Moral Action: Toward an Agenda for Future Research in Jewish Education," *Jewish Education* 86, no. 2 (spring 1991): p. 247.

36. Michael A. Signer, "*Communitas et Universitas*: From Theory to Practice in Judaeo-Christian Studies," in *When Jews and Christians Meet*, ed. Jakob J. Petuchowski (Albany: State University of New York, 1988), p. 82.

37. Elliot N. Dorff, "A Renewed Understanding of Mission and Method in Jewish Education," *Religious Education* 79, no. 1 (winter 1984): p. 84.

38. Ibid., p. 85.

39. Signer, "*Communitas*," p. 78.

40. Sara S. Lee, "An Educational Perspective on Interreligious Dialogue: a Jewish View," *Religious Education* 86, no. 2 (1991): p.187.

41. Ettenberg, *The Ramah Experience*, p. 89.

42. Barry W. Holtz and Eduardo Rauch, "Education for Change: Toward a Model of Jewish Teacher Education." *Studies in Jewish Education*, vol. 3 (Jerusalem: The Magnes Press, The Hebrew University, 1988).

43. Joseph S. Lukinsky, "Narratives and the Program in Religion and Education," *Union Seminary Quarterly Review* 47 (1993): p. 73–88.

44. Joseph S. Lukinsky, interview by author, 7 June 1995.

45. Ruth Zielenziger, "Meeting the Others," *Melton Center Journal* (spring 1982): p. 28.

46. Ibid.

HAROLD S. WECHSLER

The Jewish Theological Seminary of America in American Higher Education

The Jewish Theological Seminary and its neighbors on Morningside Heights, 1931.
(1) Jewish Theological Seminary; (2) Juilliard School of Music, now Manhattan School of
Music; (3) Union Theological Seminary; (4) Teachers College; (5) Columbia University;
(6) Barnard College. Riverside Church is in the foreground. *Photo by Fairchild Aerial Surveys.
Ratner Center, JTS.*

HAROLD S. WECHSLER

The Jewish Theological Seminary of America in American Higher Education

By ALL ACCOUNTS, the March 1937 dinner commemorating the fiftieth anniversary of the founding of the Jewish Theological Seminary was a grand occasion. A stellar lineup of after-dinner speakers addressed a roomful of dignitaries and an international radio audience.[1] First, philanthropist Lucius Littauer introduced the Reverend Harry E. Fosdick of neighboring Riverside Church. Then JTS president Cyrus Adler introduced the main speaker, Harvard president James B. Conant.

The printed version of Conant's address was entitled "Learning's Necessity for an Able Minister," an allusion to Joseph Sedgwick's 17th-century pamphlet defending the English universities against the attacks of Cromwellian "levellers." But the address neither dealt with the education of the clergy, nor rehearsed "Jewish contributions" to western civilization. A "contributions speech" made to this audience at this time would have appeared condescending—Conant's very presence was ample recognition of the Seminary's place in the academic world.[2] During its tricentennial celebration, held the previous year, Harvard included Jewish learning in its academic pantheon and recognized the leadership of the Seminary—by then known as the "Jewish Harvard"[3]—by awarding JTS scholar Louis Ginzberg the sole honorary degree granted in this field.[4]

Instead, Conant drew a parallel between the anti-intellectuals of the 17th century and of modern times and then discussed the role of scholars of all disciplines in educating the American *laity*, especially the place of values in a world of facts and the role of historical knowledge in that education.[5] The reciprocal invitations and the content of Conant's talk foreshadowed strengthened relations between the Seminary and secular universities, relations that had languished for a generation. Conant (and Fosdick) suggested an intellectual direction for these relations. The

769

response of a new generation of Seminary officials helped to bring a semi-isolated institution into the higher education mainstream.[6]

This essay traces the Seminary's relationships with American colleges and universities from its founding in 1886 through the end of the administration of Louis Finkelstein (1972). Early interactions between the Seminary and other academic institutions often involved arrangements for the simultaneous secular education of its students at Columbia College (later, Columbia University), the University of the City of New York (later New York University), and the College of the City of New York (later the City College of New York). The need to "articulate" with these colleges raised a number of questions: What was the proper age of admission? What academic preparation should be required? Should undergraduate liberal education precede or accompany Seminary work? Should the Seminary charge tuition? How could the Seminary maximize the educational advantages attendant upon its location on Morningside Heights after its move from midtown Manhattan in 1902? Articulation issues proved nettlesome during the presidency of Sabato Morais (1886–97), who established working relationships with several local colleges. But Solomon Schechter (1902–15) and Cyrus Adler—first as chair of the Seminary board (1902–15), then as JTS Acting President and President (1915–40)—drew upon their extensive exposure to secular institutions to resolve them. Administrative relationships between the Seminary and other institutions waned during the first decades of the 20th century as an intensification of academic anti-Semitism led many university administrators to seek greater distance from Jewish constituents after 1910. The movement culminated in a public controversy over restrictions on admission of Jewish students to Harvard in 1922.[7]

But the interaction between JTS and other institutions also involved other less tangible factors. The Seminary oriented itself towards a few "reference" universities, including Columbia, Johns Hopkins, Harvard, and Pennsylvania, that provided the norms governing much of American graduate education. These norms included a "scientific" or "research" ethos for the study of Judaism, academic freedom, a full-time faculty, an emphasis on scholarship, professional instruction on the graduate level, and standardized entrance requirements.

The Seminary, under Solomon Schechter and Cyrus Adler, did not seek "recognition" from the reference universities. American universities, both leaders noted, devoted little attention to Jewish learning, a condition unlikely to change during their tenures. But Schechter and Adler, desiring to promote the Seminary's leadership in this field, adopted norms generated by these universities, independent of the quantity or quality of direct encounters.

By the time Louis Finkelstein assumed the presidency in 1940, relationships with other universities began to improve as academic anti-Semitism went on the defensive. Finkelstein responded to Conant's invitation to define a broader role for

JTS and for Jewish learning in American higher education by opting initially for interinstitutional projects involving faculty participation. These projects attempted to strengthen intergroup relations and academic freedom, unify the key branches of knowledge (including religion), and promote the study of American Jewish history.[8] They alerted the academic world to potential contributions of the Seminary and Seminary officials to the role they could play in a more hospitable academic climate. The Seminary's participation in "mainstream" endeavors may have helped pave the way for the appearance of Jewish learning on college and university campuses. In any case, many colleges and universities that introduced Jewish learning later appointed Seminary graduates to their faculties. Some formal arrangements involving students also emerged from these interinstitutional contacts. A 1953 agreement between JTS and Columbia's School of General Studies foreshadowed more than a half dozen agreements negotiated over the next generation.

James Bryant Conant, president of Harvard University, ca. 1937. *Photo by Underwood and Underwood. Ratner Center, JTS.*

But increased frequency and intensity of institutional interaction called into question the Seminary's future ability to adopt American academic norms *selectively*. Adler and Schechter sought to retain a *gemeinschaft*—a community balancing university practices with inspiration from the yeshiva and from the old-time American college. Infrequent contacts with colleges and universities, combined with the opening of a one-acre campus containing contiguous classrooms, dormitories, a kosher "commons," and a synagogue, facilitated the cultivation of "community." But pressure—some perceived, some real—to conform to the academic mainstream accompanied heightened institutional contacts. The question remained where to draw the line. Adopting "more" norms did not mean "all." The Seminary's decision in the early 1950s to seek accreditation from the Middle States Association, the regional accrediting association, was implicit recognition of the need for further accommodation. But the tension endured. Looking forward from the 1953 agreement with Columbia and the 1954 accreditation visit, Seminary leaders were forced to ask whether the JTS of the last third of the 20th century would more closely resemble a college or a university or would be sui generis.

The Old Seminary: Great Expectations

The late 19th century was a time of major institution building, both in the American Jewish and the American academic communities. The establishment of seminaries by what became the three major movements in 20th-century Jewish life—Hebrew Union College 1875, JTS in 1886, and Rabbi Isaac Elchanan Seminary (RIETS, forerunner of Yeshiva College) in 1896—occurred while reformers of American higher education nurtured a new university format. The simultaneous evolution of seminary and university affected the relationships and norms that governed JTS, the seminary with the strongest university connections. But first: what was the "proper" relationship between secular and Judaic studies in the preparation of American rabbis?

Most Jews saw little of relevance in the typical 19th century American college. The more traditional Jews argued against any connection. The yeshiva, they argued, was not limited to the education of rabbis—study of the Torah was the requisite education for Jews, regardless of professional goals. Secular education, at least past the elementary level, detracted from time devoted to Torah, thereby threatening the strength of the student's reverence for Judaism. RIETS, located on the Lower East Side of New York City, omitted secular studies for several decades—a decision leading to a 1908 rebellion among students who desired curricular inclusion of secular subjects. The controversy remained unresolved until 1928 when President Bernard Revel created an undergraduate division under the institution's aegis. Late 19th-century advocates of a secular component in the education of rabbis considered the anticollegiate argument ahistorical. "For the first time," wrote Cyrus Adler,

> Jews in America had to face an attitude brought over from Eastern Europe that secular learning, or indeed any learning which was not acquired from the Talmud and the Codes, or had anything to do with the Gentile world, could not be permitted as part of the training of a rabbi; in fact, unfitted him for the purpose, and that the English language itself was not to be employed.[9]

To the contrary, requiring members of the European rabbinate to possess a secular education had a lengthy history. "The plan that we have applied," he noted in 1923 while serving as JTS president, "is not a novelty but a steady development of several thousand years."[10] JTS founders, he added, had both a traditional Jewish and a secular education obtained in many different Western European nations. Most, he wrote, had resided in the United States for at least a generation—long enough to understand prevailing practices.[11] "It was natural," Adler continued, "that this group of men should look to the education of a Jewish Rabbinate which combined Jewish learning and adherence to tradition with secular knowledge." His conclusion permitted him to refute allegations that the Seminary defended "downtown or ultra-Russian orthodoxy where learning is limited to Talmud."[12] The Seminary, he pointed out:

> on the other hand, following the methods existing in Western Europe and deriving something from the methods of the American colleges, had developed

along lines similar to those of the Jews' College in London, the Seminaries in Berlin, Breslau, Paris, Budapest and even Constantinople, in which the real question was not so much that of a greater or lesser orthodoxy, as the combination of Jewish studies with secular knowledge. It was realized, of course, that since the secular education required time, and that all the attention of the student could not be given to Jewish studies, as it was in the *yeshivas*, improved scientific methods of imparting Jewish knowledge must be found."[13]

Seminary officials, though committed to a secular education obtained at the nascent universities, considered and rejected several alternative configurations. Some Reform rabbis saw university-based interdenominational divinity schools as attractive vehicles for rabbinical education, once these schools appointed the appropriate faculty members. Bernhard Felsenthal, a prominent Chicago rabbi, showed his faith in a "scientific" approach to religion and theology. With an appointment in talmudic and midrashic literature, he suggested, the newly opened University of Chicago (1892) "might render service even as a Jewish-theological Seminary."[14] Emil G. Hirsch of Chicago's Temple Sinai already taught at the divinity school of this nominally Baptist university. "Seminaries," wrote Hirsch, who was not well disposed towards Isaac Mayer Wise, the leader of Hebrew Union College, "are survivals of the unfittest."[15] Both rabbis counted on the support of President William Rainey Harper, himself a Hebraist, for a Judaic presence at the Chicago divinity school.

But most American Jews, including the founders of the Seminary, were more skeptical of the environment offered by universities.[16] Incorporation of Protestant seminaries into universities, observers noted, had proceeded more slowly than absorption of schools for physicians or lawyers, the other two classical professions. University-based divinity schools and theology departments were expected to teach from the broadest and most objective perspective, but leaders of seminaries, usually founded to advance specific doctrines, often could not agree to this norm. Conversely, leaders of universities frequently reassured students, alumni, and benefactors that their institutions would remain "Christian" despite growing acceptance of a norm of *Wissenschaft*.

A university sponsored by the Jewish community would, of course, meet these objections, and the Seminary's founders contemplated this option when discussing the disposition of a bequest by Hyman Gratz for "the establishment and support of a college for the education of Jews residing in the city and county of Philadelphia." In 1894, Adler, Morais, Sulzberger, et al., who played key roles in determining the use of the bequest, asked sympathetic presidents of emerging universities, including Seth Low of Columbia and Charles W. Eliot of Harvard, about the feasibility of establishing a Jewish university in America. These presidents had expanded their own institutions vertically by creating universities out of colleges, or horizontally by adding new departments to existing institutions. But they advised against either course in this case, noting potential problems in acquiring legitimacy and in attaining a sound financial status, if the university was funded at the proposed level. Cyrus Adler retained this vision but found few sympathizers during his lifetime.[17]

The Seminary's founders also gave brief consideration to a university-based Hebrew department. A query to Seth Low as to whether the Gratz funds might be used for this purpose brought a negative reply. Semitics departments, Low noted, offered coursework in comparative Semitic studies, not Judaica, which was not at the scholarly forefront.[18] He therefore advised a one-course maximum. Neither a Jewish university nor a Hebrew department, added JTS President Sabato Morais, would produce needed rabbis nor Hebrew teachers.[19]

Finally, some Jews proposed expansion of a current practice: sending young Americans to Europe for a combined education at universities and seminaries. The Breslau Seminary, often considered the model for JTS, facilitated simultaneous study at neighboring universities. But the results of European university study gave pause to the founders of the New York seminary. Several candidates for the rabbinate from prominent American Jewish families made this journey, and some, on their return, assumed the rabbinical posts reserved for them. But others opted for academic positions. Richard Gottheil, for example, son of Rabbi Gustave Gottheil of Temple Emanu-El, a prominent Reform temple in New York City, became a professor of Semitics and Rabbinics at Columbia. Still others, including Felix Adler, son of Rabbi Samuel Adler, also of Temple Emanu-El, strayed from Judaism entirely after secular studies in Europe.

The distressing results of exposure to European universities were not confined to the liberal wing of American Judaism. Morris Jastrow resigned from a junior post at Philadelphia's Rodeph Shalom in 1886, the year of the Seminary's founding, shortly after returning to the United States following four years of studies in Europe. Morris, son of Marcus Jastrow, rabbi of Rodeph Shalom Congregation and a founder of JTS, would have succeeded to that pulpit upon his father's retirement. The culprit, many JTS founders concluded, was the Higher Criticism taught at the European universities, which made religion an "object of analysis."

A domestic theological seminary, in partnership with an American university less enamored with the Higher Criticism, the majority of concerned Jewish leaders concluded, might assure that Judaism became a sympathetic "subject of study" for rabbinical candidates.[20] The dominant factions among what became the Reform and Conservative movements, therefore opted for freestanding seminaries confining themselves to religious education, while requiring students to register for secular studies at contiguous universities—the University of Cincinnati in the case of HUC and several New York City colleges in the case of JTS.

This solution resembled the practice of Christian seminaries that accepted the invitations of universities such as Columbia, Chicago, and Berkeley to proximate locations and to working relationships; invitations arising from a desire to demonstrate that "non-denominational" did not mean "Godless."[21] The Jewish seminaries that opted for contiguity gained several advantages. A secular education became a sine qua non; the liberal arts college could acculturate and educate Jewish students, while the seminaries restricted themselves to Judaic subjects. And if the neighboring university had a Semitics department—as did Columbia and the University of the City of New York—the seminary might forego cognate linguistic instruction, thereby conserving resources.

One contemporary summarized the presumed advantages of a contiguous, free-standing seminary:

> Their students were to be trained deeply and truly in the Hebrew language, literature and history, but yet they were to receive at the same time, a university education. They were to imbibe the waters from the fountains of Hebrew inspiration and assimilate them with the progress of the Nineteenth and Twentieth centuries.[22]

Seminary founders drew upon a generation of experience in Philadelphia in contemplating relations with their secular neighbors in New York. Several founders had associations with Philadelphia's short-lived Maimonides College (1865–73). That small college cultivated close relations with the University of Pennsylvania by preparing their secondary school level students for the university's entrance examinations. Some founders of Maimonides College furthered these ties by sending their own children or close relatives to that university, including Morris Jastrow, whose father taught at Maimonides, and Cyrus Adler, a nephew of Mayer Sulzberger.[23] These connections permitted leaders of the Jewish community to observe the university firsthand. Morais was the first Jew to receive an honorary doctor of laws from Pennsylvania (1887) and to interact with its officials.[24]

The strength of the relationship between contiguous colleges and the New York seminary, the founders concluded, depended on the support of the college or university president. Sympathetic presidents, such as Pennsylvania's William Pepper, Chicago's William Rainey Harper, and Harvard's Charles Eliot, assured Jewish representation in the work of their Semitics departments. The founders therefore successfully cultivated and received significant support from Seth Low, president of Columbia from 1889 to 1901. Low came off Columbia's board of trustees to serve as president between his tenures as mayor of Brooklyn (1881–85) and mayor of Greater New York (1901–3).

"Columbia University, under the presidency of Seth Low," wrote Cyrus Adler, "placed the Seminary in the same relationship to the University as was held by the Union Theological Seminary and the General Theological Seminary."[25] Writing about arrangements for the registration and tuition of seminary students, Adler was incorrect; Columbia had different agreements with UTS and JTS.[26] But technicalities aside, Low desired a close working relationship with the Seminary.[27] The opening of the JTS building on Lexington Avenue in May 1892 made Columbia the college closest physically to the Seminary. Speaking on that occasion, Low declared that Columbia would not open its own divinity school—the Divinity School of the University of Chicago had opened only days earlier—but would rely for theological instruction on existing seminaries, including JTS. The relationship between Low and the Seminary's directors remained cordial throughout the tenure of the Columbia president.[28] Columbia officials, for example, did not discourage the Seminary's 1902 move to Morningside Heights in upper Manhattan—six years after the university's own northward migration.

But official Columbia maintained this attitude despite the opposition of Richard Gottheil, whose half-century tenure at Columbia began shortly before the opening of the Seminary. In 1886, Gustave Gottheil and a group of Temple Emanu-El congregants funded a position in Semitics and Rabbinics at Columbia for five years, and Columbia, in turn, appointed Richard Gottheil to the post. Gottheil, in a vulnerable position as a professor dependent on external subsides, may have seen the founding of the Seminary as providing religious and professional competition. In any case, during the summer of 1887, Gottheil and Rabbi Solomon Solis-Cohen, a member of the JTS board, engaged in a intense written exchange over the need for a seminary in New York. Solis-Cohen, arguing for the primacy of the Seminary's life-or-death $100,000 endowment campaign, denounced HUC's rival drive, which would enable the Cincinnati institution "to continue its work of destruction; to enable it to train ministers to throw ridicule upon the laws of Moses; to overturn the labor of the prophets, to trample underfoot the hedges of the Sages." He concluded: "Let those who are tired of Judaism, and wish to see the religion of their fathers destroyed, respond liberally to the appeal."[29]

Gottheil, who just completed the first year of his Columbia professorship, countered that all support should go to HUC's campaign, since Reform Jewry took the lead in creating most Jewish eleemosynary institutions. JTS would "turn out Jesuitical, narrow-minded, fanatical teachers of religion." He added, "I declare it to be a crying wrong that one cent of money should be given to this hotbed of exclusiveness and of down-right bigotry."[30]

Neither HUC nor JTS folded as a result of this "War of the Doctors." But Robert Fierstien's history of the Seminary's early years notes one effect: "a residue of hard feelings that could only serve to hurt the Seminary's hopes of raising support from moderate Reform elements of American Jewry."[31] Gottheil may have seen the new Seminary as competition for the scarce resources that Reform Jews had to invest in higher Jewish education—a genuine concern since Reform Jews provided funding critical to the Seminary's reorganization several years later. Gottheil's

opposition did not halt the opening of the Seminary, though it may have influenced his advice to Low, who consulted Gottheil on the future of the Gratz bequest.

During the 1890s, Low personally determined Columbia's relationship with JTS. But Columbia had a new president by the time the Seminary moved to Morningside Heights. And Nicholas Murray Butler, who led Columbia for almost a half century (1902–45), evinced less interest in sustaining this cooperation than his predecessor. As a result, Richard Gottheil (a college classmate of Butler) became Columbia's main arbiter of relations with JTS until his death in 1937.

777

*The Jewish
Theological
Seminary in
American
Higher
Education*

Nicholas Murray
Butler, president
of Columbia Uni-
versity, speaks at
the Seminary's
Semi-Centennial
celebration, 1937.
*Ratner Center,
JTS.*

The Reorganized Seminary: Self-Containment

SELECTIVE NORM ADAPTATION. Beginning with Solomon Schechter, the 20th-century presidents of JTS knew the university world from the inside. Membership on the faculties of Cambridge University and of Johns Hopkins University, respectively, gave Schechter and Cyrus Adler an understanding of the norms and mores of academic life. Daniel Coit Gilman, the first president of Johns Hopkins (1876-1901), which styled itself as America's first "true" university, also taught Adler about academic governance and administration. The two men agreed on most academic matters, and their administrations *selectively* borrowed norms and practices evolving at contemporary universities consistent with the Seminary's goals.

Adoption of a scientific ethos for teaching and research was of primary importance. "We must insist that the teaching in the Seminary be conducted along scientific lines," Schechter argued. "We must have 'Wissenschaft.'" he insisted. "This is the only way to save Judaism in this country or elsewhere. We cannot and will not perpetrate 'Sluzch' or 'Bialistock' here."[32] "The development of Jewish science," he continued, ". . . would enable us to compete with other institutions of higher learning."

Schechter deliberately used the word "compete"; he viewed most European universities as rivals where faculty members used "'shock-tactics' of Higher Bible Criticism" that thoroughly corrupted Semitic studies.[33] "You know what I think of this school and their apostle Paul [Haupt—Adler's teacher at Johns Hopkins]," he wrote. But, he added, these tactics were an *abuse* of valid methods that the Seminary could enlist to the defense of traditional Judaism. Schechter would consider a division of labor between university-based studies of Semitic languages and literatures and Seminary-based post-biblical studies (he assumed that no American university would seriously venture into the Seminary's intellectual turf) but only on his terms. Acceptance of scholarly norms, combined with wariness of universities, set the Seminary's direction for decades.

JTS officials adopted other practices developed at neighboring universities, including a full-time faculty that devoted its time to teaching and scholarship.[34] Many reformers of professional education, noting the success of Johns Hopkins, advocated the exclusive use of full-time faculty. The 1910 Carnegie Foundation report on medical education in America, written by Abraham Flexner, another admirer of Gilman, argued for appointment of full-time clinicians to medical school faculties. Free of the demands of private practice, these clinicians would be "teachers of teachers" whose students would in turn assure widespread reliance on scientific knowledge and a scientific spirit of inquiry.[35]

Similarly, part-time rabbis would not dominate the reorganized Seminary faculty. The often overwhelming demands of the moment, Schechter and Adler believed, deterred capable scholars from devoting time to Jewish learning.[36] "Those equipped for scholarly work were busy men—rabbis, lawyers, teachers in colleges, physicians, or men occupied 'in engrossing administrative work,'" wrote historian Moshe Davis of Adler's views. Adler exempted only two scholar-rabbis, Bernhard Felsenthal and Marcus Jastrow. "For the rest, scientific work is done by stealth, or when they should be sleeping or taking a walk."[37] Sabato Morais himself, Adler well knew, was a part-timer who retained the Mikvah Israel pulpit in Philadelphia while leading the New York Seminary. A full-time faculty in Jewish learning, argued Schechter and Adler, would assure the dominance of Jewish science within the movement for traditional Judaism in America by allowing ample time for its production and dissemination.[38]

Schechter and Adler demonstrated caution when appointing new faculty members. "No person," wrote Adler, "has an inherent right to be a professor in a particular institution and the governing body, whatever it may be, whether Trustees or Faculty, indicates their trend of opinion by the selection of professors."[39] At the Seminary, noted historian Herbert Parzen, Schechter, and Adler kept positions vacant rather than appoint scholars who might not represent the traditional viewpoint. Adler did battle with his faculty over appointments—he, for example, appointed the ideologically "safe" Jacob Hoschander to a chair in Bible without faculty consultation.[40]

Schechter and Adler, some historians note, not only adopted academic norms that nurtured the growth of the Seminary, they also lived up to norms that universities sometimes found convenient to ignore. Perhaps in response to the Hoschander incident, the Seminary administration defended the academic freedom of faculty members, once aboard, from communal attacks. Adler, for example, resisted demands from influential members of the Conservative movement to remove Mordecai Kaplan from the faculty. "Academic freedom," Adler wrote,

> means that once a professor is in a given institution he may teach the subject for which he is selected according to his lights—in other words, according to what he believes to be the truth. It further means that a professor is free to express his opinions on any subject just as any other man is, but when he expresses his opinions outside of the field for which he is elected, it is his duty to make it clear that he is speaking in his own name and not in behalf of his institution."[41]

Even Herbert Parzen, often critical of Adler, gave him high marks for his defense of academic freedom. Adler's actions may have affected Kaplan's decision to reject several offers to move to the rival Jewish Institute of Religion during the 1920s—a move that would have strengthened Stephen Wise's institute.[42]

At neighboring Columbia, in contrast, controversies surrounding academic freedom during World War I contributed to the dismissals and resignations of several prominent faculty members.[43] JTS also took a stronger stance than HUC, which in 1907 suffered the forced resignations of three faculty members, in part because of their adherence to Zionism.[44]

The 1902 reorganization of the Seminary sought to bring its mode of governance into greater conformance with American academic tradition. The new charter replaced the Seminary's governing board of congregational representatives with a self-perpetuating board of directors, the standard practice at American colleges and universities since the 18th century.[45] "I myself have never been very enthusiastic about the idea of securing large popular support for institutions of higher learning," Adler later wrote. "The whole history of higher learning has shown that it is in the main dependent upon the support of the few, or, where this is in accordance with public provision, by the State."[46] Self-perpetuating boards, Adler believed, helped to assure consistent academic policies, as well as financial support. These boards, Adler added approvingly, also prevented domination of universities by the faculty, the typical pattern of medieval European universities.[47]

But neither Schechter nor Adler imported the entirety of American academic norms and practices. American universities, Adler believed, were neither designed nor suited to teach "subjective" humanistic subjects "in which opinion plays a large part from the Jewish point of view."[48] He listed philosophy, history, ethics, and sociology but singled out the social sciences as popularizing the viewpoint that traditional religion (read Judaism) was "dysfunctional."[49] Thus, when several JTS students asked Adler to add a course on religion from a social scientific standpoint, he replied, "You mean the thing called social psychology. . . . I don't believe in the whole business. There is no such thing as a psychology of the Jewish people. Anyone that would undertake to teach such a subject is a charlatan."[50] Having rejected the Higher Criticism, neither Schechter nor Adler countenanced other "challenges" to traditional Judaism. A student might enroll in undergraduate social science courses prior to admission to the Seminary, but these subjects would not appear in the JTS curriculum. Louis Finkelstein, Adler's successor, displayed a more charitable attitude.[51]

Schechter and Adler had additional concerns about the direction of American higher education. The two presidents recruited scholars who grew to preeminence, but Adler wrote that he "never became an entire convert to the Hopkins idea of a University which, while it called for students and required teaching, made that secondary to research."[52] Members of the Seminary faculty should emphasize the direct instruction of rabbis and teachers. "I am sure you know that I agree with you on the power of ideas, but these ideas have to be promulgated," Adler told Louis Finkelstein. "One way of promulgating ideas is to write books and pamphlets, but I think in the long run the best way is to train people to teach other people and when I say other people I mean finally those who teach the hundreds of thousands."[53]

Perhaps most important, universities did not retain the salutary aspects of an academic *gemeinschaft*. "Dr. Schechter," recalled Cyrus Adler, "was not much of an organizing man and as he very tersely put it, always believed in organisms rather than organizations." But this emphasis, Adler added, had a positive component. "The President of the Seminary," he insisted, "whoever he may be, ought give a great deal of time to the Professors and the students of the Seminary. There are many human and scholastic problems which in a small institution have to come to the head and cannot be delegated to another."[54] Later generations of academic observers noted many shortcomings in the administration of the Seminary, but remedying these deficiencies, JTS officials would argue, should not require the sacrifice of community.

Adler's acceptance of many academic norms, his distaste for university administrators who invoked these norms only when convenient—such as when universities suspended academic freedom protections or meritocratic admissions criteria—and his rejection of other norms led to his renewed advocacy for a Jewish university in America. Adler made the suggestion at the time of the founding of Dropsie (1906), during World War I, and again prior to the founding of Hebrew University (1925). The proposed university would build upon existing Jewish institutions of higher learning, including JTS, Gratz, Dropsie, and the JTS Teachers Institute. Fear of the social sciences would not be a problem at a university under Jewish auspices. "Research and instruction in Jewish Pedagogics and Philanthropic and Communal work could be instituted," he added. "Jewish journalism, still largely in the amateur stage, could be taught as a profession; the scope of the teaching of Jewish literature could be greatly extended[;] American Jewish History should become a regular subject of instruction."[55]

Gratz and the Teachers Institute would serve as preparatory institutions for

Dropsie and the Seminary. Adler's plan envisioned identical curricula at the teachers colleges, "with uniform entrance examinations and conditions for the bestowal of the certificate." These curricula would then become the requirements for admission to JTS and Dropsie. A closer relationship between Dropsie and the Seminary would include "an exchange of residence and of credits, a uniform and coordinated system of publications, in cases of exceptional specialties even the interchange of professors or lecturers or for the sake of economy the use of a single man in both institutions."[56] These concepts reflected contemporary initiatives among secular universities: committees on standardized secondary school curricula and uniform entrance requirements flourished between 1890 and 1910; the College Entrance Examination Board was founded in 1901 to assure uniformity in entrance examinations; and universities, notably including the University of Chicago, envisioned feeder colleges that would free them up to offer advanced work exclusively.

Adler, living at a time when existing Jewish institutions suffered recurrent financial reverses, found little support for a project of this scope. He remained content to require a secular education for JTS students and to adopt the desirable features of universities, while keeping at arm's length from them.

INTERINSTITUTIONAL RELATIONS: THE SECULAR EDUCATION REQUIREMENT. The directors of the Seminary never wavered in their belief in the need for the liberal education of rabbis.[57] The board initially called for a *simultaneous* liberal education, which implied contiguity and frequent contacts with secular colleges. An early bulletin, for example, stated:

> Secular Education—The Trustees and Faculty of the Seminary will exercise supervision over the secular studies of the students and will secure for the pupils every advantage possible at Columbia College or at the University of the City of New York. *All graduates will be required to have a secular collegiate education.*[58]

The Seminary's lay supporters concurred with Cyrus Adler's repeated call for "general culture," certified by a bachelor's degree "preferably in the humanities, in a recognized College or University."[59] Louis Marshall, a Reform Jew and a key backer of the 1902 reorganization, believed that "secular higher education was an important element in the acculturation of Jews in America." Even "to have a 'secular' college in a yeshiva setting," he argued, "would constitute a large step backward."[60]

JTS thus joined HUC in insisting that a secondary school secular education was not sufficient for candidates for a rabbinical degree. "It was customary," recalled Cyrus Adler, "to admit to the Seminary young students who had completed their High School course, make arrangements for their College education and graduate them about the time they would receive their degree of Bachelor of Arts."[61] Local colleges facilitated these arrangements, though some accounts suggest that even at the outset, JTS officials saw the simultaneous registration of students as a less than ideal method of reconciling the desirable and the possible. "The Seminary had to grow from the bottom up," wrote one historian. "First it had to be a preparatory school before it could attempt to be a college, much less offer graduate work of the quality required to train the modern Rabbi envisioned by Morais."[62] In any case, during the Morais years, the average age of the student body rose due to increased enrollment of college level students.

Simultaneous study at a secular and sectarian institution implied conflicts. JTS officials had to refute charges made by Orthodox Jews that "by insisting upon a college education, [the Seminary] curtailed the amount of time which could be devoted to Jewish studies."[63] The Seminary began its classes in the late afternoon, after its students completed secular studies at the College of the City of New York on 23rd Street or at the University of the City of New York in Greenwich Village—neither site far from the Seminary's first downtown homes. Columbia, located at 49th Street and Madison Avenue until its move in 1896 to Morningside Heights, was ten blocks from the mansion at 736 Lexington Avenue at 59th Street that became the Seminary's home in 1892. Students who opted for the thirty-six-block walk between the Seminary and CCNY after Columbia's move uptown had little time and energy for Seminary work.[64] JTS students, Cyrus Adler later noted:

> went to college in the morning and early hours of the afternoon, and then came to their Bible and rabbinic studies in the late afternoon and evening, when they were tired out with their regular college work. This was not the most happy arrangement. It is reported that students sometimes fell asleep over their great folios of the Talmud. The plan had its advantages in that the students were under the influence of the Seminary for eight years and sometimes more. But the scholastic disadvantages were very great.[65]

Seminary officials announced the creation of a secular department in 1894 to remedy these disadvantages.[66] "Various circumstances operated to hinder the progress of several pupils in the College of the City of New York," Seminary Association president Joseph Blumenthal noted,

> where the demands of the curriculum, particularly in the mathematical branches, were of an inordinately burdensome character. We have, therefore, been compelled to establish an academic department, with two competent instructors, and six students are now pursuing their secular studies in this department, which includes instruction in Latin, Greek, German, history, English Literature, algebra, geometry, physics, and advanced English.[67]

According to historian Robert Fierstien, Seminary publications made no subsequent mention of this department. In fact, two years later Blumenthal complained that the Seminary still lacked a way "to accommodate the severe demands upon the time of our students made by the pursuit of secular studies in college, with the necessity of doing full justice to the requirements of our curriculum and schedule of studies here in the Seminary."[68] The Seminary Association added to the difficulty in 1896 by requiring a bachelor's degree before ordination, but JTS soon began to admit older students and to distinguish between a preparatory and a senior class. Those palliatives lasted until the Schechter administration insisted on a new requirement of secular, collegiate-level education *prior* to admission to the Rabbinical School.

"The gradual turning of the Seminary into a post-graduate school," wrote Cyrus Adler, "was, next to the choosing of the new Faculty, the most important achievement of Schechter's administration.[69] Requiring completion of college, Adler noted in 1905, permitted JTS officials "to carefully sift the students and to ensure the fact that they were men of cultivation, old enough to know their own minds, and to properly appreciate the seriousness of the calling which they were to pursue."[70]

Adler did not link the secular education requirement, per se, to American academic norms, but he knew that American professional schools, including Protestant seminaries, were gradually requiring applicants for admission to have completed a college education. Graduate level admission, contemporary reformers insisted, provided professional schools with liberally educated, well-socialized students who could then devote time exclusively to professional study.[71] Secular professional schools also elevated the age of entrance, added specific academic entrance requirements, and lengthened their curricula—toward the same assurance of adequate preparation and maturity.[72] Woodrow Wilson, then a professor at Princeton, approved these trends:

> The community, if it be wise, . . . will wish the physician to be something more than an empiric, capable himself of sure-footed search for the origins and determining conditions of disease; will desire to find in the preacher something larger and more generous in temper and endowment than dogmatism—even the liberal spirit of a serious and withal practical philosophy; will look for dignified parts of learning in the lawyer, something better than practical shrewdness and successful chicane, a capacity to rise at need to the point of view of the jurist, as if aware of the great and permanent principles of large-eyed justice. The average individual, on the other hand, will be eager to make his way as rapidly as possible to business; and when once business engagements begin to press upon him, his thought will adjust itself to them. If the habit of carrying special cases up into the region of general principles—where alone the real light of discovery burns—be not formed during the period of preparation, it will hardly come afterward, when the special cases crowd fast and the general principles remain remote.[73]

In moving to university status at the end of the 19th century, Columbia committed itself to raising the admission requirement to most of its professional schools to the graduate level. This measure required enticements, since obtaining a license to practice from the state did not yet require graduate level professional studies, and since some competing professional schools continued to admit students with high school diplomas or less. The Columbia answer was a "combined course of study"—an undergraduate liberal education and a graduate level professional education, with the senior collegiate year serving a dual liberal and professional purpose. JTS and Columbia never created a combined course, but the Seminary exercised flexibility in admission of seniors after the shift to graduate status.

Cyrus Adler and his fellow JTS directors took advantage of the Seminary's reorganization and Schechter's arrival to opt for graduate level admission. Requiring a bachelor's degree, they concluded, would assure an older, presumably more mature, student body for the Seminary, permit recruitment of students from noncontiguous institutions, and reduce the need for graduate level interinstitutional cooperation, a course Schechter considered prudent.[74] Most important, Seminary students could realistically be expected to devote their entire time to Jewish learning—no more divided loyalties.[75] A Seminary-ordained rabbi, Adler argued:

> should be a man of sound general education when he enters, and that whilst here, he should devote himself to building upon this foundation a structure of Jewish scholarship, which, in the end, will be translated into Jewish work in the pulpit, in the schoolroom, the general community, and occasionally, let us hope, in the enrichment of Jewish learning.

During the student's residence at the Seminary, Adler added, "We want not only the best of him, but the whole of him."[76]

The simultaneous diversification of the undergraduate curriculum provided an added incentive. Many educators at late 19th-century professional schools favored replacing the traditional, prescribed undergraduate curriculum that emphasized Greek, Latin, and mathematics with an elective curriculum that included the sciences, the social sciences, literature, and history. Just as medical school officials could then require undergraduate studies in biology, chemistry, and physics prior to admission, JTS, throughout the Schechter years, asked that prospective students study English literature, rhetoric, and composition; ancient and medieval history; philosophy, psychology, and logic; and German, Greek, and Latin.

But a shift to graduate level education came at a price. Dependence for a student's undergraduate education and socialization on a secular or secularizing college, or perhaps even on a college that retained denominational ties meant a loss of direct academic and social influence on potential students—some of whom might even decide on another career—during these years. The shift would also result in a large age spread within the JTS student body during the years of transition.

The undergraduate elective system also had a downside. Students admitted on the graduate level, Seminary authorities recognized, might lack basic Judaic education. The Seminary, during the early Schechter years, required entrance examinations in elementary Hebrew and Biblical Aramaic grammar, Bible, and *Mishna* and *Gemara* and announced that Harvard "has established a group of studies leading to the Bachelor's Degree which includes the foregoing subjects required for admission." Several prominent universities, including Columbia, Johns Hopkins, Pennsylvania, and Chicago, the Seminary catalogue added, "agreed to provide instruction necessary for admission to the Seminary."[77] But the elective system made the needed instruction escapable, and most other colleges did not offer the required coursework. Early 20th-century efforts to include Hebrew among elective courses sputtered at best, except at other seminaries; other aspects of Jewish learning went entirely unrepresented.[78] The Seminary faculty could therefore expect admittees to possess a liberal education and a degree of acculturation, but until Jewish studies courses became popular on campus after World War II, the faculty had to rely on informal, secondary-level, or ancillary Judaic preparation.[79] Even so, for some time it was the exceptional candidate for rabbinical study who did not know at least some biblical Hebrew and have some mastery of the Pentateuch.[80]

The problem had its parallels in secular institutions since not all American colleges could prepare students in all subjects required or recommended for admission to a given graduate or professional school. Few academic institutions, then or now, could avoid the need to reconcile the desirable with the possible. But the problem grew in magnitude since, as time passed, the Seminary could not assume that informal and religious school preparation would provide adequate preparation. By 1929, the list of entrance requirements had so fallen into disuse that Mordecai Kaplan recommended that "the Seminary draw up a list of subjects which candidates for admission into the Seminary should pursue during their college career."[81] The Hebrew deficiency proved especially vexing. In 1930, the Seminary faculty voted to advise candidates for admission that the catalogue regulation stating "Seniors at college are *also* admitted into the Seminary" applied "only in cases where students are exceptionally equipped in Hebrew. As a rule, applications will not be looked upon favorably unless the candidates have already completed their college course."[82] The issue became more pronounced with each decade, and by 1965 Judaic entrance requirements became minimal—in part reflecting the belief that access to the Seminary's rabbinical program should not be denied to students who developed a strong sense of mission during the college years.[83] These concerns also led JTS to reenter the undergraduate field, first by adding a teacher education component, then by creating the Seminary College and finally by negotiating cooperative agreements with liberal arts colleges, beginning in 1954.[84]

INTERINSTITUTIONAL RELATIONS: TIES WITH SEMITICS DEPARTMENTS. As he disembarked from the ship that brought him to the Seminary's helm, Solomon Schechter differentiated between the province of universities and Jewish seminaries.[85] "He spoke of the courses in Semitic studies offered in English universities," noted the correspondent for the *American Hebrew*. "The purpose was to increase the knowledge of students in Old Testament studies, but the purpose of a Jewish institution for higher education necessarily includes more essential matter, the study of post-Biblical literature."[86] Semitics departments in universities, Adler concurred, should not exclude Rabbinics, but both leaders insisted that the subject was best studied at the Seminary, which accorded it primacy and a supportive environment.[87]

Insistence on a Jewish environment for Jewish learning reflected Schechter's concern that Semitics departments and other units of contiguous universities might lure away Seminary students. Several rabbis, such as Stephen Wise and Louis Newman, both in the Reform camp, obtained their Ph.D.'s from Columbia's Semitics department. So did some faculty members who taught at seminaries, including Max Margolis, another Gottheil student.[88] Teachers College, the school of education affiliated with Columbia, also offered competition. "What really angered him [Schechter]," wrote historian Baila Round Shargel,

> was the knowledge that these students [Isaac Berkson and Alexander Dushkin] would not matriculate into the Seminary's rabbinical school; instead they would enroll in Columbia University's Graduate School of Education. There they would sit at the feet of [John] Dewey and [William S.] Kilpatrick rather than [Louis] Ginzberg and [Alexander] Marx. At the termination of their studies, they would not receive rabbinical degrees but the more prestigious Ph.D. There loomed the distinct possibility that these young men, rather than the rabbis he trained, would assume the leadership of the American Jewish community, that the Kehillah, rather than the Jewish Theological Seminary, would become the dominant Jewish institution in New York.[89]

Schechter even saw potential competition from Dropsie College and from Adler's proposed Jewish university, even though the plan envisioned a central role for the Seminary in the education of lay leaders as well as rabbis.[90]

Adler, though less concerned about competition, also minimized the potential contributions of Semitics departments to Jewish scholarship, much less Jewish leadership. "The amount of work done was comparatively insignificant," said the holder of the first American Ph.D. in Semitics (Johns Hopkins, 1887). "The number of men taking their Ph.D. in Semitics had been so small as to give no great encouragement for the development of Hebrew scholarship." Adler knew that several rabbis, including William Rosenau, who became a prominent member of the Reform movement and a governor of HUC, followed him to study Semitics at Johns

787

*The Jewish
Theological
Seminary in
American
Higher
Education*

Low Library
overlooks West
116th Street (now
College Walk) in
this view of
Columbia Univer-
sity, ca. 1902.
*Columbiana Col-
lection, Columbia
University.*

Hopkins.[91] But these departments waned in strength during the early 20th century, and Adler provided potential supporters of Jewish scholarship with a strong incentive to think of the Seminary: "The coming of Dr. Schechter," he said in 1902, "would no doubt arouse an enthusiasm for Hebrew scholarship which would have fruitful results."[92]

Relations with the Columbia Semitics department and with Richard Gottheil, the department's mainstay for a half century, improved after Schechter assumed the presidency in 1902. The two men sustained a personal and scholarly relationship that began during Gottheil's graduate studies in Europe in the 1880s. At the time, Schechter, the master, agreed to disagree with Gottheil about his student's intellectual future. Gottheil gave primacy to Semitics, though the field took a non-Judaic direction, and Schechter would have had him keep a Judaic orientation.[93] Reuniting master and student permitted a salutary division of labor:

> Professor Richard Gottheil claimed the distinction of being one of Dr. Schechter's first pupils. He spoke [at a welcome banquet for Schechter] of the connection of the Seminary and Columbia University whose Semitics department was under his direction. It was another story of the dog and his tail. Whether Columbia University's Semitics department would wag the Seminary or vice versa. But whether the Seminary should prove the tail or the dog, he was sure they would work together in perfect harmony.[94]

This view was consistent with the ambivalence of a man who opposed the Seminary's creation and who saw donations from Temple Emanu-El congregants go to the Seminary rather than to his department. It also reflects Gottheil's commitment to Semitic studies as the field had evolved in American universities.[95] Disciplinary recognition, university-based Semitists believed, resulted from discovering and decoding new languages, not from incremental advances in knowledge about a language whose structure was already well known, or from exegetical commentaries. They therefore offered Hebrew only as a propaedeutic study and specialized in another Semitic language or in comparative linguistic analysis.[96] The Seminary, from Gottheil's perspective, should educate scholars in Judaica, thereby freeing his department to respond to disciplinary developments.

During the Schechter administration, the Columbia Semitics department and the Seminary—neither threatened with extinction—recognized the virtues of a contiguous location, at least nominally, and viewed their academic provinces as complementary. Gottheil lectured at Schechter's Seminary, and they and their wives visited each other's homes.[97] Columbia under Nicholas Murray Butler initially continued Seth Low's policy of granting registration, tuition waivers, library privileges, and credit for seminary coursework to students from local seminaries, including JTS. The policy paid off. "The number of newly admitted students to the Seminary," Schechter wrote Gottheil in 1909, "was considerable, and a large number attend your Columbia classes."[98]

The working relationship did not resolve all ambiguities.[99] Columbia solved a revenue flow problem by limiting tuition exemptions to graduate students in 1905–6, when JTS had not yet completed the transition to graduate level instruction. But Gottheil remained concerned that some JTS students viewed the Seminary as a "back door" to a Columbia education.[100] "I do think it is true," he told Butler in 1911, "that the privileges of the Seminary have, in some cases, been misused and that students have matriculated their [*sic*] in order to avail themselves of the free tuition at the University. This is an abuse which ought not to be permitted."

Butler was undisturbed—cordial interinstitutional relations were still worth the risk of abuse. "I have no doubt," he wrote, "that in all of the Seminaries interested with us, applications are received from students who merely wish to use those Seminaries as a way of getting free admission to the University."[101] But the Seminary faculty shared Gottheil's concern. In 1911, Israel Friedlaender wrote to Schechter, who was on leave:

> The Faculty has passed several resolutions insuring a more regular attendance of the students. . . . It seems clear to me that the latitude, which the students are given in attending Columbia University, is largely responsible for their irregularity at the Seminary. I have noticed it particularly during the mid-winter examinations at Columbia, which make it impossible for a number of students to attend regularly during that period. Several students have applied to me during the winter for permission to take up Post-graduate courses at Columbia, as this permission is required by the University authorities, but I told them that in your absence I did not feel justified in granting them this privilege.[102]

Gottheil, hearing rumors of broader Seminary dissatisfaction, assured himself "that there was absolutely no feeling against Columbia, and least of all against our department." JTS officials, he added are "most thankful for the privileges it enjoys at the University. The only cause for complaint that the Seminary Faculty has is that some of the students neglect altogether their Seminary work for the lectures at Columbia. This is a matter for adjustment by the Seminary Faculty and does not concern us at all."[103]

Resolutions on attendance passed by the Seminary faculty and raising Seminary admission to the graduate level reduced the problem, and here the situation rested for more than a decade. Gottheil and Schechter arrived at a modus vivendi involving the division of intellectual labor that took advantage of institutional contiguity—and personal relations tempered potential conflicts until after Schechter's death in 1915.

Relations with Columbia deteriorated markedly during the years of Cyrus Adler's leadership. Experience with university life made Adler wary about the price that Jews and Jewish learning might pay for academic "recognition."[104] He also chided universities for failing to adhere to their stated norms.[105] The quota on admission of Jewish undergraduates to Harvard, proposed by President Lowell in 1922, showed how academic anti-Semitism undermined the meritocratic norms of elite institutions. "If a university is a seat of learning," Adler contended,

> then it should become, as President [Ernest Martin] Hopkins of Dartmouth said a few days ago, an aristocracy of brains and nothing else should count. If this theory is to be applied only to the post-graduate department and professional schools whilst the colleges are to be held as a sort of country club in which good manners and sports are tests for entrance, let us know.[106]

Adler knew of Columbia's attempts to limit its Jewish student population, beginning about 1910, and academic anti-Semitism partly accounts for deteriorating relations between the two institutions.[107]

Adler also watched the atrophy of Semitics departments in the first decades of the 20th century. Columbia, for example, did not replace John D. Prince when he left the Columbia Semitics department, and Richard Gottheil remained the only professor in that department until his death in 1936. Morris Jastrow, still teaching at the University of Pennsylvania in 1919, questioned the future of the subject in American universities:

> The preponderance of the natural sciences in this country at the present time, is such that even among educated persons those who devote their careers to the old "Humanities" are looked upon as "back numbers," left over from a passing generation, while those who choose such outlandish subjects as Assyrian or Arabic or Sanskrit or Persian are regarded in the light of intellectual freaks.[108]

This trend, Adler knew, reduced potential competition. But he also knew that universities had not turned off the spigot to help the Seminary.

Finally, JTS, for Adler, was not simply an academic institution specializing in an otherwise neglected subject; it produced the religious and, perhaps, the lay communal leaders needed to preserve the Jewish tradition in America. Adler, unlike Reform rabbis Emil Hirsch and Bernhard Felsenthal, would not entertain delegating the preparation of rabbis to universities. The study of Judaism required a protected environment to assure that it remain a "subject of study," rather than an "object of analysis."

Adler, America's greatest entrepreneur for Jewish learning before World War II, rarely attempted projects involving university participation, and the intrusion of international politics after World War I gave him a specific reason to remain aloof from Columbia.[109] Richard Gottheil and Israel Friedlaender were both politically active Zionists. But in 1918, Gottheil, a strong supporter of the Triple Alliance, denounced Friedlaender for alleged pro-German sympathies at the outset of the war, and Friedlaender was compelled to resign membership on an American Red Cross commission to Palestine and Syria. Instead he became a member-at-large of the Joint Distribution Committee and in 1920 went to the Ukraine as its representative, where he was murdered during a pogrom. Many observers—the Seminary faculty included—blamed Gottheil and Stephen Wise for creating the circumstances leading to Friedlaender's death.[110] The tragedy, added to Gottheil's adherence to Reform Judaism and to Zionism, ended any chance of serious cooperation between the Columbia Semitics department and JTS, the fountainhead of Conservatism, led by the non-Zionist Adler.[111]

In 1925, Columbia limited tuition waivers and registration reciprocity to "institutions which by definite administrative arrangement have joined with the University in common educational enterprises." Columbia's affiliation agreement with Union Theological Seminary included "a definite administrative arrangement"; the JTS agreement did not.[112] Whereas in 1905 Schechter and the JTS board extensively discussed a similar possibility, in 1925 the Seminary paid scant attention to the decision.[113] Adler and Butler exchanged letters; Adler informed the Seminary faculty and students, but only after asking his secretary to determine "exactly what the present arrangement was with Columbia University."[114] The arrangement ended at the end of the academic year.

Three years later, when Linda Miller, a Temple Emanu-El congregant and recent widow of businessman Nathan L. Miller, endowed a professorship of Jewish History, Literature, and Institutions at Columbia, the university's search committee included representation from Union Theological Seminary, but not from JTS, or from any other Jewish institution of higher learning. Such a search by a major American university for a full-time faculty member in any field of Jewish learning

Barnard College (with columns), Riverside Church (tall tower), and Union Theological Seminary (lower tower) line Broadway in this view looking north from West 116th Street, 1938. *Columbiana Collection, Columbia University.*

was virtually unprecedented, and the Seminary faculty members kept themselves informed of developments. But, despite close connections with Linda Miller, Seminary staff played at most an informal, consultative role.[115] Committee members met with Adler as they fashioned a short list of candidates that included the eventual appointee, Salo W. Baron, a faculty member at the rival Jewish Institute of Religion.[116] Prompt consultation with Adler in 1936 might have spared Columbia the embarrassment of offering Richard Gottheil's chair to George Antonius, a partisan in contemporary Middle Eastern politics with no scholarly credentials, only to rescind the offer when members of the Jewish community protested the error.[117]

Relationships with Columbia, and indeed with most colleges and universities, remained minimal and correct during the remainder of the Adler administration.[118] The few ongoing contacts centered on the extracurriculum and the library.[119] Ad hoc contacts centered on admissions-related questions, such as evaluating an unknown credential presented by a student.[120] From this state—a far cry from the vision of the Seminary founders and reorganizers—a turnaround soon began.[121]

The Finkelstein Administration: Into the Mainstream

"Learning's Necessity," James Conant's semicentennial speech, marked a significant turn in the Seminary's place in American higher education, coming less than a year after the death of Richard Gottheil, two years before the outbreak of World War II, and three years before the death of Cyrus Adler. Henry S. Hendricks, a member of the Semi-Centennial Committee, responded enthusiastically to

Conant's invitation to contemplate a role in the education of the laity: "We conceive of the function of this institution," Hendricks noted, "as something broader than a school for the education of Rabbis and preachers and teachers in Israel, and thereby indirectly teaching and upholding Judaism." He added: "Even as Harvard stands as a lighthouse illuminating the world with the wisdom of knowledge, so we see the Seminary standing as a lighthouse directly illuminating its sphere of influence with the wisdom of Judaism and blending that wisdom with the general wisdom of mankind."[122]

Necessities of time and scarcity of resources complemented Cyrus Adler's predisposition toward looking inward. But Conant had invited Seminary officials to contemplate its relationship to a larger, perhaps increasingly congenial academic world. How could the Seminary educate the Jewish laity, many of whom attended American colleges and universities? And, as Conant suggested, did the Seminary have a role in educating non-Jews to "relive the rich experiences of the human race by the cultivation of those 'precious parts of antiquity which give necessarie light to the present in matters of State, Law and History and the understanding of good authors'?" Could one do so without taking the Jewish contribution into account? How did one, reprising an issue raised by Cyrus Adler, deal with the subjective? And how would the Seminary deal with other educators who shared these concerns?

Adler, who remained President for three years after the semicentennial, remained skeptical about an expanded role for JTS. He approved, for example, an interdenominational course—envisioning comparisons of Jewish and Christian fundamentals, once "anybody can agree as to what are the fundamentals of Judaism and Christianity." But could the Seminary substantially improve relations between Christians and Jews? "As I have told you a number of times," he wrote Finkelstein:

> I think this Seminary ought to play its part, but I do not think it can play the major role. Its people will not be selected from that point of view and there are other and larger forces both for it and against it. You must remember that there are a great many people who are anti-Jewish who are not Christians, but simply heathens, and how on earth the Seminary is going to be the agency to cope with that I cannot say.[123]

Louis Finkelstein, who assumed the Seminary presidency in 1940, set the Seminary on the path of growth and interinstitutional involvement implied in Conant's address.[124] Finkelstein was more comfortable with interdenominational dialogue on religion and with the relationship of Jewish learning to the humanities. He also believed that the social sciences, which Adler had eschewed, could reinforce Jewish tradition. "Together with these advances in Biblical study and natural science," he wrote, "has come a deeper understanding of psychology and sociology, those infant sciences which give so much promise for the future of mankind." He continued:

793

*The Jewish
Theological
Seminary in
American
Higher
Education*

From left: Robert
M. MacIver,
Louis Finkelstein,
John Courtney
Murray, S.J.,
Swami Akhila-
nanda, and Alain
Locke at the
eighth Confer-
ence of Science,
Philosophy and
Religion, Ameri-
can Philosophical
Society, Philadel-
phia, 1947. *Photo
by Press Syndicate,
Chicago. Ratner
Center, JTS.*

Only a few blocks away from us, at Teachers College, experiments were performed in character training which definitely establish the fact that moral
habits must be inculcated one by one, and cannot be given *en bloc* to the child or
an adult. Properly interpreted these experiments bear very nearly on the essential controversy between Paul, who rejected the Law, and the Rabbis who
defended it. It is becoming increasingly obvious that it is not enough for the
establishment and strengthening of moral character to hold up a symbolically
perfect personality, but that it is necessary, by means of moral judgments, to
train a person with regard to every question of right and wrong."[125]

Other chapters in these volumes address the Seminary's postwar intellectual history. Here, we examine the institutional implications of a move to the mainstream.
During its third quarter century, the Seminary routinized consultation with representatives of a spectrum of higher education institutions—usually through their
associational representatives. This routinization led to pressures to accept the
entirety of academic norms, but Finkelstein did not abandon the Seminary's policy
of selective adaptation. JTS reiterated its distinctiveness when mainstream practice
appeared threatening or irrelevant.

Finkelstein first nurtured informal contacts between Seminary faculty and staff
members and their colleagues in colleges and universities. These contacts laid the

groundwork for more formality—first projects, then programs, and finally agreements.[126] Fred Beuttler's essay in this volume describes one important early contact: Finkelstein's involvement with the Seminary-sponsored Conference on Science, Philosophy and Religion. The Conference, organized at JTS, but held at Columbia and at other sites, placed Seminary faculty and staff in close contact with many university-based intellectuals. College and university faculty members led other Seminary-sponsored projects, including the Institute for Religious and Social Studies.

Finkelstein's interest in intergroup relations became another point of entry. Some colleges and universities, made aware of the consequences of their prior discriminatory actions, attempted to reduce barriers to access and to reduce prejudice against enrolled minority students. Finkelstein participated in discussions on admissions discrimination and campus anti-Semitism sponsored by the American Council on Education, the "umbrella" group representing American higher education and its Committee on Religion and Education. He also worked with the National Conference of Christians and Jews and with several Jewish defense organizations that sponsored the intergroup activities of Columbia sociologist Robert MacIver.[127] Finkelstein also served on the advisory panel for the American Academic Freedom Project, which published historical and contemporary surveys of academic freedom at the height of the McCarthy era and strengthened ties between the Seminary and several Columbia departments. Philanthropist Louis Rabinowitz, a strong supporter of Jewish learning, financed the project; his close ties to Columbia's School of General Studies and to JTS facilitated agreement on a joint program of undergraduate education announced by the two institutions in 1953.[128]

JTS helped nurture Judaic aspects of some university-based disciplines, including religion and history. Seminary officials, for example, built on their relationship with Salo Baron to establish closer ties to the Columbia history department. Allan Nevins, Baron's Columbia colleague, was recruited to codirect the Seminary's American Jewish History Center (established 1953) with Moshe Davis. This center published studies of local Jewish history, written by university-based history professors.[129] The pattern of nurture established for American Jewish history would be repeated as other aspects of Jewish learning entered the academic mainstream.[130]

Contacts, projects, programs, and disciplinary interactions led to a series of formal agreements with divisions of Columbia. In 1930, the Seminary had established a joint program with neighboring Teachers College permitting students, usually women, to receive a bachelor of science in education from Teachers College and a bachelor of Jewish pedagogy from the Seminary's Teachers Institute.[131] The joint program suffered when the Teachers Institute fell on hard times during the depression, but the precedent remained on the books and provided guidance and encouragement to later generations of officials.

795

*The Jewish
Theological
Seminary in
American
Higher
Education*

Louis Finkelstein
(left) with Colum-
bia president
Grayson Kirk
after signing the
agreement that
established the
joint program
between the two
schools, 1953.
*Photo by Arnold
Katz. Ratner
Center, JTS.*

In 1953, officials representing the Seminary and Columbia's School of General Studies agreed that students at the Teachers Institute and the Seminary College of Jewish Studies could apply sixty-four credits toward language and elective course requirements for the B.S. degree at General Studies. The Seminary, in turn, agreed to accept sixty hours completed at General Studies towards the liberal arts require- ments for its bachelor of Hebrew literature degree. A later generation saw the joint program in grandiloquent terms: a step towards including Jewish learning in the undergraduate curriculum. This inclusion, some observers noted, marked a philo- sophical change from a "melting pot" theory ("the notion that a standardized higher education was the only key to the American mainstream and that ethnic heritage or religious tradition had no place in the liberal arts curriculum") to a philosophy based on cultural pluralism ("The Joint Program continues to help American Jews understand their heritage") and to place Judaic scholarship in the main stream of academic life.[132] But in 1953 Seminary officials saw the agreement as a practical way of solving the long-standing problem of integrating general and Judaic education of potential rabbinical students and of fulfilling Conant's call to educate the laity— joint program graduates were expected to enter Jewish communal and educational posts, as well as the secular professions. This program signaled the Seminary's will- ingness to work with Columbia divisions that repudiated anti-Semitism; programs with Barnard and the School of Social Work followed in the 1970s.

Taken together, these arrangements permitted the Seminary to define a place in the higher education mainstream and to free up scarce resources for investment in other directions. Nowhere is the commitment to this path more visible than in the Seminary's participation in the accreditation process devised by higher education institutions earlier in the century.

Extant records do not identify a single event or factor leading to the Seminary's decision to seek accreditation from the Middle States Association of Colleges and Secondary Schools.[133] The decision may have been related to the Seminary's improving interinstitutional relations or to a desire for the recognition that accreditation brought. It also may have arisen from implications that Columbia students who participated in the joint program with General Studies[134] might worry that the unaccredited status of JTS would affect their applications for admission to professional or graduate school, or for a job. The joint program had also forced the Seminary to contemplate the technicalities of student credits and transcripts, acceptability of coursework done elsewhere for its degrees, and, conversely, the acceptability of its coursework by other colleges and universities. Accreditors, Seminary officials may have thought, might help with the requisite bureaucratization or professionalization of some functions and in the adoption of standard academic terminologies.

But accreditation, Seminary officials understood, encompassed more than validation of coursework. The process began with a self-study of the entire Seminary and ended with a wide-ranging report submitted by a team of visitors representing institutions of higher education accredited by the Middle States Association. Would and should the Seminary "measure up" to the expectations of American academic life? The self-studies and the reports issued by the accrediting teams produced during the first two reviews, conducted in 1954 and 1964, ratified and reinforced JTS's move towards the academic "mainstream." The processes also forced members of the Seminary community to ask "how far?"

The self-study that began the 1954 accreditation permitted the Seminary to contemplate the implications of an expanded role, but neither the self-study, the visit by the accrediting committee, nor its final report *forced* changes in goals or practices.[135] Middle States accreditors conducted the first evaluation with a light touch; they used the occasion to learn how to evaluate a seminary—a relatively new experience for the Middle States Association—and, in addition, a seminary with a second new campus in Los Angeles that fell under the jurisdiction of another accrediting association.[136]

The accrediting committee report identified few academic problems. It praised the statement of aims and purposes found in the Seminary's charter as "more than a mere paper objective"; instead, it was "a guide to the day by day operation of the institution far more than is ordinarily the case in American institutions of higher education."[137] The committee asked Seminary officials to address three issues. First, adherence to the stated mission translated into a need to cover many biblical and rabbinical texts. This need led to an "almost unbelievable" student workload and to inattention to contemporary issues. Second, expanding the Seminary's functions resulted in a proliferation in the types of degrees awarded by the Seminary. Third, some students who desired academic careers in Jewish learning felt forced into the rabbinical program to gain access to members of the faculty of the Rabbinical department. This complaint echoed the concerns of doctoral candidates in some business and law schools, who had to complete the professional program before turning to doctoral work. Seminary officials acknowledged these problems, but lacking resources, they took up to two decades to resolve them.[138]

The accrediting committee, noting the Seminary's growth into miniversity status and its increased interactions with other institutions, also suggested changes in the organizational structure created by Adler. Too many divisions reported directly to Finkelstein, despite an administrative shuffle in 1951; yet a vice-chancellor reported directly to the overseers, not to the Chancellor. Growth, the committee warned, "will add to the administrative duties, which are already consuming a great deal of the time and energy of the officers. It therefore becomes highly important that the Seminary restudy its organization and that officers of great scholarly ability be relieved of those administrative duties which can be fulfilled by less scholarly persons."[139]

Similarly, the Seminary's Board of Directors and its committees handled too many administrative details; yet the institution had a separate board of directors for the library.[140] By this time, most American colleges and universities more or less adhered to the dictum, "Boards set policy; administrations implement policy," but subsequent accrediting teams revisited this issue.

These recommendations for administrative reform were offered with some hesitation. "The Seminary thinks of itself as the relatively small and compact institution," the committee concluded, "which it has been until recently, a brotherhood were [*sic*] the responsibilities could be shared on a personal basis. It has reason to be proud of its accomplishments and of its harmonious relations." Admiring "the spirit of the Seminary and the success of the methods which have been followed," accrediting team members acknowledged the value of informality:

> This lack of clear-cut authority and responsibility seems not to have interfered with successful and harmonious operation. The organization is a relatively small one; more important, the incumbents of these positions have known each other a long time either as fellow students or as teacher and student, and each has dedicated his life to the work of the Seminary.

The Seminary should relieve its academic officers of administrative detail, but it should also maintain "its insistence that all of its officers of educational administration shall continue to be scholars." As in the case of the Seminary's adherence to its "mission statement," by this insistence, the committee concluded, the Seminary "will have solved a problem which has proved too difficult for most American institutions of higher education," namely, living up to stated norms.[141]

The problem, noted the committee, was that the Seminary was no longer a *gemeinschaft*: "The responsibilities of the institution have grown and are bound to grow," stated the accreditation report. "A clearer realization of this changed outlook, would lead to improvements in organization."[142]

The reluctance of the accrediting committee to criticize faculty "inbreeding" reflects its ambivalence about recommending that the Seminary adopt academic norms on a wholesale basis. Hiring one's own graduates, the committee decided, may be appropriate in the Seminary environment, even if it was an undesirable practice at universities that wished to display intellectual diversity:

> The Committee is at a loss what to say about inbreeding of the faculty. The Jewish Theological Seminary of America is the only institution in the United States preparing rabbis for Conservative Judaism. In the past it obtained teachers from the rabbinical institutions of the old world. With the possible exception of Israel these sources are no longer available. The Chancellor and faculty are keenly aware of the value of bringing in scholars from other institutions but apparently the Seminary must recruit its faculty entirely or almost entirely from its own graduates. Progress has been made in developing a plan to have all its rabbinical students spend one year of their course studying in Jerusalem."[143]

The committee felt on stronger ground in asking Seminary officials to reconsider their policy of granting full tuition to nearly all students in the Rabbinical School. At the turn of the century, only the divinity schools at Harvard and Chicago charged their students full tuition. Both schools were not only affiliated with universities, they also advocated "scientific" theological studies. Other divinity schools attempted to maintain low or free tuition policies, but a desire for equity among university divisions, combined with rising costs, often led to the imposition of tuition charges during the ensuing decades. Many seminaries, including Union Theological Seminary, followed suit. The committee, noting this trend, as well as the ability of most JTS students to pay at least a nominal charge, recommended this course for the Seminary.[144] But Seminary officials, despite considerable financial duress, resisted this step for another fifteen years.

The committee felt most comfortable in recommending the Seminary's adherence to mainstream norms in its ventures into formal relations with other academic institutions. The report noted two key advantages accruing to the Seminary from the joint program with Columbia: "For one thing, it makes available to the students of the Seminary the very considerable offerings of one of the largest universities in the world. Even more important, the joint curriculum constitutes a norm by which students of the Seminary who are doing or have done their general collegiate work at other institutions may be judged."[145]

The committee recognized the difficulties in moving from isolation to mainstream but suggested that the move could not be effected entirely on its own terms. The joint program, for example, was partly aimed at providing public high school teacher certification in Hebrew language and literature, a language that met the New York State Education Department's secondary school language requirements. But the program, the committee suggested, may have maintained its steep requirements in Hebrew studies at the expense of teacher preparation.[146] Clarification of purpose—a necessity in times of growth—was as important in planning teacher preparation programs as in contemplating non-rabbinical graduate education.[147] Within the pedagogical portion of the joint program, the committee added, the Seminary might profit from experience elsewhere: "It would seem that as the joint program is further developed, the situation experienced by student teachers in other subject fields should be explored with public school authorities."[148]

The Seminary "worked," concluded the accrediting team, despite the ambiguities that marked periods of change:

> The Seminary is ever alert to carry out its very broad purposes in its own special field of interest by whatever means commend themselves as most likely to be effective with the particular group to whom they are addressed. It is remarkable that so broad and diverse a program can be carried out, while at the same time there exists almost in the very air within the Seminary buildings an unremitting emphasis upon the importance of and the necessity for the highest standards of scholarship and research. . . .
>
> The Committee has not the slightest doubt of the effectiveness of the program and believes that the Seminary is to be commended on its academic standards, on the competence of its faculty members, on the correlation between its objectives and curricula, and on the service it is rendering to its constituency.[149]

The problems associated with the growth in the Seminary's internal functions and external relations did not impede accreditation by the Middle States Association. But would Seminary address these issues in the decade between visits? Would it come to resemble other institutions of higher education? Or could it continue to blur the distinction between *gemeinschaft* and *gesellschaft*, between community and society? The future of doctoral work became the key vehicle for dealing with this issue in the 1964 accreditation site visit.

Between accreditation team visits, JTS amended its charter to include many goals defined by Louis Finkelstein during his first two decades of Seminary leadership. These goals included "the integration of Jewish and general philosophy of learning . . . the promotion of better understanding among people of different religious and ethnic backgrounds, [and] the fostering of deeper insights into the philosophy of religion."[150] The level of interinstitutional interaction, if anything, increased after the charter revision. So did the normative pulls exerted by the academic mainstream.

Seminary officials confronted the implications of these increases as they contemplated future offerings in graduate education. A "boom in religious studies," that is, increased undergraduate interest in religion during the 1950s and 1960s, resulted in the growth of religion departments at public and independent colleges. Columbia, stimulated by the Reverend James A. Pike, the university chaplain and head of the religion department, offered more than thirty courses by the early 1960s, the largest undergraduate offering in America.[151] This boom reinforced the Seminary's prominence in an important academic conversation, but should the Seminary take the next step by expanding its nonrabbinical graduate programs to help fill the demand for religion and Judaica professors?[152]

By 1964, the Seminary had awarded ninety-eight doctorates through its Doctor of Hebrew Literature program, open to graduates of the rabbinical department, and thirty-eight Seminary graduates taught at JTS or at other institutions of higher learning. But the D.H.L. program, noted the Middle States accrediting team, was offered on a part-time basis, mainly in the summers, and was staffed by visiting faculty members. The team questioned the quality of advisement and instruction.[153] Ordained rabbis without the Ph.D., some less sympathetic critics charged, might serve as "jacks-of-all-trades," thereby raising questions about quality while denying positions to Ph.D.'s from the growing number of Jewish studies programs at secular institutions.[154]

The Seminary faculty placed its hopes for future innovation in graduate study in its Herbert H. Lehman Institute of Talmudic Ethics, which offered an intensive full-time residential Ph.D. program, including a more demanding thesis than required for the D.H.L. Initially, the Seminary granted the Ph.D. only to the best graduates of the Rabbinical department, but students in history became eligible for this degree in 1970 with the appointment of Gerson D. Cohen to the faculty.[155] The Seminary defended the program as a place where students might absorb the best of Jerusalem and Athens, thereby developing a commitment to JTS and to Conservative Judaism:

> The emphasis is placed on the relevance of insights found in the Talmud to the problems of our own time, especially to character training and ethical decision-making. The course of study thus follows the established pattern of the ancient Jewish academies, demonstrating the relevance of study and wisdom to the good life. The Institute is also part of the university tradition of the western world, in that it makes full use of the techniques of modern critical scholarship. Without the high promise shown by the graduates of this program, the future of this Seminary, deprived of its best source of faculty replacements, would be extremely uncertain.[156]

The 1964 accreditation team identified several weaknesses in the Institute's program: it lacked a critical mass of students; its degree requirements were vague; and some of its faculty appeared indifferent. The team asked the Seminary to consider a more substantial step—a doctoral track for potential college and university instructors that did not require completing the rabbinical course.[157]

The faculty could not dismiss this suggestion out of hand. A "nontheological" doctoral course had a better chance of attracting a viable student cohort, since colleges and universities were more likely to hire students with a doctorate, a degree with wide acceptance. Faculty members knew they would soon have to replenish their own ranks and continued to defend "inbreeding," but they also knew that most universities frowned on inbreeding, and that the Middle States Association looked for a high proportion of doctorates among faculty members at accredited institutions.

Implementing a doctoral program, Seminary faculty members and administrators understood, required careful consideration. Would the program divert talented students from the rabbinate into university-based Judaica programs, and would the Seminary admit women and non-Jews to graduate work? Conversely, should the Seminary hire professors who received their doctorates in graduate Judaica programs at universities? Such professors might not be rabbis, nor even committed to Conservative Judaism.

This discussion, initiated by the Middle States team, went unresolved until several years into the administration of Gerson Cohen. Universities in the 1960s, the height of the "academic revolution," had high standards and precise expectations for graduate education.[158] The accreditors did not *force* JTS to engage in non-rabbinical graduate education, but external scrutiny became inevitable once the Seminary's *voluntary* involvement with secular institutions grew to include the preparation of Judaica professors.

The 1964 accrediting team found little change in key issues related to finance, governance, and administration. Rabbinical students still did not pay tuition; some directors did not adequately support the Seminary; reliance on an annual fund drive would no longer do.[159] Faculty members still performed functions left elsewhere to administrators, and administrators still did not always perform the functions suggested by their titles.[160] The Seminary's tradition of informality still resulted in vague degree requirements, inconsistent academic policies, inadequate record-keeping, lax protection of student records, and insufficient precautions against fire and theft.

The committee contrasted the Seminary's informality with the bureaucratized practices of partner institutions. Miniversity status implied consistency and specificity; informality had already become a liability in some instances and could degenerate into amateurishness. "If the amateur methods used by the present staff [of the library of the University of Judaism] are not abandoned," the team warned, "the growth of the collection will quickly intensify the unsatisfactory aspects of this makeshift cataloguing and classification."[161]

Nor had the Seminary solved the most vexing problems associated with its relations with other colleges and universities. The committee, though unaware of the fate of undergraduates at JTS six decades earlier, noted that joint program students wrestled with an "unbelievable" double workload. These students either devoted enormous energy to their work or opted out. The 1958 charter amendments provided for a liberal arts college, a reinvention of the never-implemented 1894 solution. But the Seminary faculty would not lighten the load, and enrollments in the joint program remained chronically low.

The report of the 1964 accrediting team, like its predecessor, ended with an upbeat conclusion. JTS graduates, all agreed, "tend to be firmly grounded in two cultures." The team's report echoed the words of Cyrus Adler and Louis Marshall: "The general academic requirements for entrance into the various graduate departments insure an excellent college background, while the Seminary's own standards of scholarship assure its graduates of unusual competence in Jewish studies."[162]

The main problems still resided in administration and student support, and JTS officials promised to address these concerns. But these officials reiterated their policy of selective adaptation of academic norms. "The whole structure of the Seminary," they responded, "is thus a curious amalgam of modern American academic organization and educational goals and traditions stemming from earlier Rabbinic academies, going back to the beginnings of the Christian Era, perhaps even earlier." Their report continued:

> It is fascinating to watch the development of the Seminary as it seeks to integrate two philosophies and systems of education into a dynamic and creative whole. Obviously such an effort is fraught with many difficulties and perplexities; but perhaps if it should succeed in the future even better than in the past, the result may be a significant contribution to the advancement of educational theory in this country.[163]

The Seminary's administrators and faculty respected and responded to the representatives of secular American higher education. But even as these officials signaled a commitment to integrating two philosophies and to learning from secular academic practice, a part of the Seminary psyche retained the conviction of Cyrus Adler that the "mainstream" could learn some important lessons from this mini-city on a hill.

Conclusion

The Seminary, in its relations with American colleges and universities, was an exporter and importer. It exported knowledge after World War II—first through projects and programs, later though its graduates as faculty members in secular colleges and universities. Its willingness to import academic norms and to subject itself to the scrutiny of representatives of these norms made it easier for its faculty and graduates to traverse the road between Athens and Jerusalem.

Interinstitutional relations grew slowly; other decisions had priority. The joint program with Columbia's School of General Studies began half a century after the Seminary's move to Morningside Heights; similar agreements with Barnard and the School of Social Work awaited the 1970s. Each agreement permitted limitations on what the Seminary had to do by itself. The agreements with General Studies and Barnard substituted for the liberal arts college contemplated in the 1958 charter amendments. The agreement with Columbia's School of Social Work gave the Seminary access to social work instruction without opening its own school; in contrast, Yeshiva University opened its Wurzweiler School of Social Work in 1957.

JTS students, agreed accreditors and insiders, imbibed the knowledge of two worlds. But could the Seminary continue to balance Athens and Jerusalem? Historian Douglas Sloan identifies four key tensions between the American collegiate and university models: instruction versus research, the humanities versus science, values instruction versus moral neutrality, and developing the "whole" person versus educating experts. Many colleges, he adds, resolved these tensions in favor of the "university" position, the second position in each dyad. American seminaries, he suggests, preserved some aspects of the liberal arts college: the humanities held sway, and values were ever present. But seminaries vacillated on the teaching-research and whole person-expert axes.

JTS officials wished to bridge these dualisms. "The purpose of the Seminary," they noted, "is, of course, the preservation in America of authentic Judaism, a religious tradition which we believe has an important contribution to make to civilization, in addition to its vital spiritual significance to the Jews themselves." Judaism's emphasis on study as a mode of worship, these officials added, meant that "rabbis must also have an unusual commitment to study, and an appreciation of the scholarly enterprise."[164]

The 1964 accreditors noted the Seminary's success in attaining this goal: "The lifelong devotion to study," the committee noted, "is a marked characteristic of all Seminary graduates." The publications of graduates and the teaching posts filled by alumni reflected this devotion; so did "the contributions to Jewish scholarship made by graduates who have followed professional careers in science, law, medicine, government, and business." Perhaps most important, the alumni, especially graduates of the Rabbinical department, imparted this orientation to their congregants. Conservative synagogues, noted the 1964 self-study, often offered significant adult education programs: "Although American Jews have shown a growing willingness to devote some of their leisure to study of their heritage, it is safe to say that they would not be enrolling in serious courses in large numbers were their spiritual leaders not setting them an example of regular study."[165]

Research at the Seminary was not an end unto itself—a charge often leveled against university departments in the 1960s. It was, and ought to be, said Seminary administrators, integrated with instruction. "One of the strengths which we bring to this task [of imbuing an ethic of study], is our senior faculty, which numbers among its members some of the foremost research scholars in Judaism in the world," noted these officials. "As Solomon Schechter, former president of the Seminary, once said, the strength of an institution like this lies in the opportunity offered its students to associate with great men." Rabbinical School students, they added, "associate with the giants of their time, and they learn from them by example, as well as in the classroom." There was a reciprocal effect: "The emphasis which our tradition places upon study and education helps these great scholars to function effectively as classroom teachers." "Like rabbinic scholars through the ages," they concluded, "our professors are also gifted teachers, and, devoted as they are to their individual scholarly projects, none of them would willingly give up his teaching assignments."[166]

Through cultivating teaching *and* research, the Seminary guarded against losing the sense of community it had nurtured for three quarters of a century and against becoming indistinguishable from a secular research institute. Seminary officials preferred to retain their own middle ground for as long as possible and to live with ambiguities, if necessary, rather than adopt university norms wholesale.

Members of the Seminary faculty must have felt this sense strongly in the 1960s, as they watched many university students seek community in institutions not designed for that purpose and as they grappled with the need to recruit their successors. Preserving a sense of community was vital, not only to infuse the Conservative movement with the desirability of "study as a mode of worship" but also to retain faculty members. If secular colleges and universities were becoming more hospitable to Jewish learning and if the Seminary simultaneously lost its distinctiveness, what would prevent a potential teaching "giant" from accepting a lucrative offer from a secular institution? Would faculty members base career decisions on economic and status considerations, rather than on the need to preserve and advance traditional Judaism?

"The faculty of the Rabbinical Department is more than just a teaching faculty," wrote an optimistic Seminary publicist in the 1960s, "It is a fraternity of scholars in their fields—Bible, Talmud, Rabbinics, etc." An exclusive fraternity, too, with admission requirements including a lifetime of Judaic studies, a strong secular education, and a commitment to traditional Judaism. "We think, and so far experience has proven," the publicist added, "that we will be able to hold on to our best people so long as we maintain this special scholarly fellowship which makes it possible for a young man who stays here as a reader or instructor to be associated with the leading experts in his field. Only time will tell whether we will be able to continue this attraction."[167]

Coda: The Cohen Administration

In 1972, Gerson Cohen succeeded Louis Finkelstein as Seminary Chancellor. One Middle States Association official compared the two men: "Louis Finkelstein lived in the world of ideas; Gerson Cohen must face the real world in terms of limited resources."[168] The comparison was not entirely fair. Finkelstein was quite familiar with limited resources; Cohen, with the world of ideas. But soon after he entered office, Cohen, found that confronting the "real world" had become more difficult. Coming from the history department at Columbia—the first Seminary leader to have previously held a regular faculty appointment in a secular American university since Cyrus Adler's tenure at Johns Hopkins in the 1880s and 1890s—Cohen observed the complex relationship between the success of Jewish learning in these institutions and the intensified competition for students, faculty, and benefactors. He also noted the onset of "the new depression in higher education," a round of budgetary cutbacks that followed sustained growth.[169]

Cohen's response, a commitment to continued distinctiveness combined with the need to address financial realities, did not result in institutional isolation.[170] Instead, he expanded nondenominational graduate programs through collaboration with neighboring seminaries and graduate departments.[171] He established new cooperative undergraduate and professional programs with Columbia, Teachers College, and Hofstra University[172] and imposed tuition on rabbinical students, a major departure from prior practice.[173] Finally, he continued to adopt academic, administrative, and financial procedures routinely used by colleges and universities, including, notably, a probationary period for junior faculty members.[174]

The creation of a separate graduate school in the mid-1970s was perhaps the most significant response.[175] The self-study preceding the 1974 visit of the Middle States accrediting team raised questions about the growing centrality of graduate education, the lack of curricular coordination between programs, and the lack of support services for graduate students.[176] Seminary officials noted the growth of masters level enrollments, which they attributed to the proliferation of undergraduate Judaica programs on secular campuses. These officials had also become dissatisfied with the structure of the Institute for Advanced Studies in the Humanities, the new name for the Lehman Institute. The program still attracted few students, even fewer philanthropic donations, and virtually no public support. Last, they perceived a need for a completely remodeled D.H.L. that would move from being "an appendage of the general rabbinical school program" to a solid preparation for rabbis who wished to teach Jewish studies courses in colleges located near their

Gerson Cohen
(seated, left) and
Columbia presi-
dent William J.
McGill renew the
joint agreement
between the Sem-
inary and Colum-
bia, 1978. Stand-
ing, from left:
Ward Dennis,
dean, and Leslie
Shanken, director
of admissions for
Columbia's
School of General
Studies, and Ivan
Marcus, dean of
the Seminary
College of Jewish
Studies. *Photo by
Arnold Katz. Rat-
ner Center, JTS.*

synagogues. The solution appeared to be a unified graduate school, led by a dean
with responsibility for all nonprofessional graduate work.

Within the next five years, New York State authorized the Seminary to offer the
Ph.D. in Judaic studies, as well as in Rabbinics and Jewish history, the M.A. in
Judaic studies, and the D.H.L. in theology. The Seminary thus addressed Solomon
Schechter's fear of losing influence over students to other Morningside Heights
institutions by expanding its own doctoral level work. The price paid was that the
Seminary could no longer be assured of having "the whole" of any student. The
graduate school initiative permitted, and often required, students to take courses at
the Graduate Center of the City University of New York, Columbia, and even
UTS. The 1974 accreditation team saw this step as a salutary combination of academic expansion and fiscal restraint; neither Schechter nor Adler would have agreed.

Other challenges to "community" accompanied the expansion of graduate education, including the growth of off-campus residence and part-time study. By 1978,
the "academic and non-theological" divisions, which were "open to qualified men
and women, regardless of religion, race, or national origin," enrolled three-fourths
of all JTS students. Staffed by a larger faculty that included more part-timers who
also taught at secular colleges and universities, these divisions awarded the same
degrees as secular universities, prepared their students to teach in those institu-

tions, and required considerable administrative rationalization and interinstitutional coordination. Could a Seminary with a growing nontheological component retain the "special scholarly fellowship" manifested in the "paradoxical combination of critical scholarly inquiry and passionate commitment to Torah and its value as a guide to contemporary living" that its leaders still claimed as its motive force?[177] The Seminary wrestled with that question during the next two decades.

Cohen, like Finkelstein, acknowledged the inevitability and importance of interaction between the Seminary and secular colleges and universities and of incorporating the norms of higher education. But, also like Finkelstein, he found that every move towards these ends posed its own challenge to the Seminary's ability to continue the encounter *on its own terms*.

1. W1-XAL, supported by the World Wide Broadcasting Foundation, broadcast the talk. The same nonprofit educational network had broadcast the Harvard Tercentenary celebration the previous year. WEAF and the NBC network also broadcast the speech.

2. "I should like the Jewish people of the country to realize the full significance of what is involved in this visit by the President of the oldest university in America to our own great institution. His coming here forms a fitting climax to the tribute which was paid to the Seminary at Harvard's Tercentenary when the Degree of Doctor of Theology was awarded to our Professor of Talmud, Louis Ginzberg." Draft of letter to be sent to out of town rabbis, 21 January 1937. Records of the Jewish Theological Seminary of America, Jewish Theological Seminary of America (hereinafter RJTSA), Record Group (R.G.) 11, Communications Department, 1930s-1980s, 11c-18-22: "James Bryant Conant Meeting, 1937" file.

3. Conant decided to accept the invitation "because of the distinction of JTS and because the invitation comes through Mr. Felix Warburg, who has been not only a generous benefactor to Harvard, but also a wise leader of public opinion in New York City." Conant to Henry James, 17 November 1936, RJTSA, R.G. 11, Communications Department, 1930s-1980s, 11c-18-21: "James Bryant Conant Dinners, 1937" file.

4. Ginzberg's essay, "Jewish Folklore: East and West," was included in Harvard Tercentenary Conference of Arts and Sciences, *Independence, Convergence, and Borrowing in Institutions, Thought and Art* (Cambridge: Harvard University Press, 1937), a Harvard Tercentenary Publication, and Ginzberg spoke at a summer 1936 Harvard Tercentenary symposium.

5. James B. Conant et al., *Learning's Necessity [for an Able Minister]* (New York: The Jewish Theological Seminary of America, 1937). The Seminary assigned the title, but Conant remarked, "The education of religious leaders is not my theme tonight. It would be indeed most presumptuous of me to attempt to discuss such matters here. My concern is with the education of laymen" (pp. 19-20). The speech argued for appreciation of the history of the basic fields of knowledge and for transcending the immediate for an understanding of the origins and evolution of institutions, law, and the humanities. In addressing the education of the laity instead of an educated ministry, Conant launched a lengthy debate over the Seminary's role in educating lay intellectual and social leadership in the history and traditions of Judaism.

6. JTS director Alan Stroock subsequently told Fosdick that some younger supporters were attempting to assure that JTS would "remain in the future a means of integrating religion in terms of a liberal outlook on life." Stroock to Fosdick, 17 March 1937, RJTSA, R. G. 11, Communications Department, 1930s-1980s, 11c-18-21: "James Bryant Conant Dinners, 1937" file.

7. See Marcia G. Synnott, *The Half-Opened Door: Discrimination and Admissions at Harvard, Yale, and Princeton, 1900-1970* (Westport, Conn.: Greenwood Press, 1979), and Harold S. Wechsler, *The Qualified Student: A History of Selective College Admission in America* (New York: Wiley-Interscience, 1977), chap. 7.

8. Fred W. Beuttler discusses the Seminary's intergroup activities in "For the World at Large: Intergroup Activities at the Jewish Theological Seminary," another essay in this history.

9. Cyrus Adler, "The Standpoint of the Seminary," in *Tradition and Change: The Development of Conservative Judaism*, ed. Mordecai Waxman (New York: The Burning Bush Press, 1958), p. 180.

10. Ibid., p. 181.

11. "Morais came from Leghorn, Italy; Kohut from Hungary; Jastrow was born in Warsaw; Szold in Hungary; and Mendes had his training in England. Both Jastrow and Kohut were graduates of German universities, and Morais drew his inspiration from Samuel David Luzzatto." George A. Kohut was the relative newcomer to America. Ibid.

12. *American Hebrew* 58, no. 19 (13 March 1896): p. 532, as quoted in Yehezkel Wyszkowski, "The American Hebrew Views the Jewish Community in the United States, 1879-1884, 1894-1898, and 1903-1908" (Ph.D. diss., Yeshiva University, 1979), p. 428.

13. Adler, "The Standpoint of the Seminary," p. 181.

14. "Hebrew Grammar, Reading of the O.T. and philological comments upon it, Introduction in the books of the O.T., and c., also Semitic languages and literatures in a wider sense, these and other branches the Jewish students might study under you and other non-Jewish Professors." Felsenthal to Harper, 25 February 1892, University Presidents' Papers, University of Chicago Special Collections, box 65, file 5. Felsenthal added a disclaimer that "this is only a thought hastily thrown out," but he may have the name of Max L. Margolis in mind. Margolis had just completed his doctoral studies under Columbia Semitics professor Richard Gottheil. Gottheil had recently communicated to Felsenthal on his behalf.

15. See Moshe Davis, *The Emergence of Conservative Judaism: The Historical School in 19th Century America* (Philadelphia, Pa.: The Jewish Publication Society of America, 1963), pp. 179–80, and Emil G. Hirsch, "Ministerial Training," *The Reform Advocate* 7 (9 June 1894): p. 293.

16. Jewish students did occasionally enroll in the divinity school. Neither Columbia nor Pennsylvania, the two logical eastern sites for such an arrangement, opened a divinity school, but a similar proposal would have drawn even less support from the more conservative Jews in the East.

17. See Louis I. Newman, *A Jewish University in America?* (New York: Bloch Publishing Co., 1923).

18. Before replying, Low consulted Richard Gottheil, a member of the university's Semitics department with decided views about the Seminary. See below.

19. Marshall Sklare, *Conservative Judaism: An American Religious Movement* (Glencoe, Ill.: Free Press, 1955), pp. 249–51. The existence of JTS precluded the revival of Maimonides College in Philadelphia, so the funds could be used most advantageously by educating Jewish teachers and preparing students for JTS. Gratz College, founded in 1895, would perform these functions, and JTS listed Gratz among the colleges that prepared students to meet the Seminary's entrance requirements. The retention of Seminary graduate Henry Speaker (1895) as the founding principal of Gratz, a position he held for about thirty years, facilitated articulation between the curricula of the two institutions.

20. Adler made this distinction in 1925, when discussing the mission of the proposed Institute of Jewish Studies at Hebrew University. "How could it be supposed . . . ," he wrote, "that any subject concerned with Jewish learning can be studied from a purely objective point of view. Things that affect the lives or have affected the lives of millions of people over the course of many centuries, whether it be the Bible or the Talmud or the Jewish Law, can be approached from two definite points of view. The one is the acceptance of the ancient document until it is proved to be wrong. This in effect is the traditional view. The other point of view is the sceptical which doubts the ancient document . . . unless there are other ancient documents to corroborate it. And this latter is definitely not the Jewish point of view. The moment that the latter attitude is assumed, Jewish learning becomes the object of analysis and not the subject of study." As for the need for sympathy, Adler added, "The person who believes that the Bible is largely made up of fictitious documents or the Talmud is a collection of rubbish might be able to read and explain and discuss every point in both of these great collections of literature perfectly and yet would never advance the knowledge of either." Adler's defense of traditional Judaism was even more adamant when applied to the Seminary. Adler to Sol Rosenbloom, 20 March 1925, in *Cyrus Adler: Selected Letters* 2 vols., ed. Ira Robinson (Philadelphia and New York: Jewish Publication Society of America and Jewish Theological Seminary of America, 1985),vol. 2, p. 112.

21. See Natalie A. Naylor, "The Theological Seminary in the Configuration of American Higher Education," *History of Education Quarterly* 17 (spring 1977): pp. 17–30.

22. Daniel P. Hayes, "The New Jewish Theological Seminary," *American Hebrew*, 22 April 1902, p. 685.

23. The university subsequently awarded an honorary degree to Morais. The Pennsylvania Semitics department, despite the presence of Morris Jastrow, did not have a distinctly Jewish bent either in personnel, intellectual agenda, or community support, and neither Gratz College (1895) nor Dropsie (1906) maintained close ties to the university.

24. Davis, *The Emergence of Conservative Judaism*, p. 355.

25. Cyrus Adler, "Semi-Centennial Address," in *The Jewish Theological Seminary of America Semicentennial Volume*, ed. Cyrus Adler, (New York: Jewish Theological Seminary of America, 1939), p. 8. Practically, this meant granting free tuition to qualified students.

26. Prior to 1891, the students of JTS, along with UTS and the General Theological Seminary, could register for courses in Columbia's undergraduate division. In 1891, Columbia and Union Theological Seminary negotiated a complex agreement that not only admitted recommended students into Columbia graduate level courses without charge, but also applied course work completed at UTS towards completion of minor requirements for Columbia degrees and granted a UTS faculty member nonvoting membership on the Columbia University Council. "The Union Theological Seminary," in *Charters, Acts of the Legislature, Official Documents, and Records*, 3 vols., ed. John B. Pine (New York: Printed for Columbia University, 1920), 1: 290–29. The near-simultaneous agreement between JTS and Columbia extended registration privileges for recommended JTS students to the philosophy and political science faculties but did not extend to the other areas. Ibid., vol. 1, pp. 262–63. In 1925, Columbia distinguished between UTS and the Seminary when terminating its free tuition privileges. Adler wrote in 1939, well after relations between Columbia and JTS took a decided turn for the worse.

27. "The further prosecution of Mr. [Joseph] Hertz's secular studies rendered necessary an application on the part of the Trustees of the Seminary to the Trustees of Columbia College to secure for him the advantages of that institution gratuitously. It is extremely gratifying to express here the appreciation of the Trustees, for the generous and courteous spirit manifested by President Low and the Board of Trustees of Columbia College, in placing the Seminary in the same relation to the College which is borne by the Union Theological Seminary and the General Theological Seminary, by admitting our students to its School of Arts and School of Philosophy. Considering the standing of Columbia as one of the few great Universities in this country, and the splendid professional staff constituting its faculty, it is not easy to overestimate the importance and value of this act of generosity on the part of the President and Trustees of Columbia College." *Proceedings of the Third Biennial Convention of the Jewish Theological Seminary Association Held in the City of New York, Sunday, Adar, 28th, 5652, March 27, 1892* (New York: Press of Philip Cowen, 1892), p. 16.

28. Schiff and Low were especially friendly; Low resigned from the Columbia trustees in 1914 when the board restricted automatic access to campus facilities to Christian groups. See Wechsler, *The Qualified Student*, chap. 7, and idem. "Low, Seth," *Encyclopedia of New York City* (New Haven and London: Yale University Press, 1995), p. 691.

29. Solomon Solis-Cohen, "Under Which Flag?" *American Hebrew* 22 July 1887, p. 163.

30. Richard Gottheil, "Under Which Flag?" *American Hebrew* 29 July 1887, pp. 180, 179.

31. Robert E. Fierstien, *A Different Spirit: The Jewish Theological Seminary of America, 1886–1902* (New York: The Jewish Theological Seminary of America, 1990), pp. 75–76. Fierstien lists Henry Pereira Mendes as a Solis-Cohen defender, while Kaufmann Kohler, later president of HUC, supported Gottheil. "Perhaps the most sensible words uttered in the entire

811

*The Jewish
Theological
Seminary in
American
Higher
Education*

episode," Fierstien concluded, "came from an anonymous letter-writer from Washington D.C.—probably Cyrus Adler—who asserted that there was room for both colleges in the American Jewish community: 'Yer pays yer money, ye takes yer choice. . . . It is our boast that we are charitable in *deed*. Why then should we not be charitable in *thought*?'" See *American Hebrew*, 19 August 1887, p. 21.

32. Quoted in Bernard Mandelbaum, *The Wisdom of Solomon Schechter* (New York: The Burning Bush Press, 1963), p. 119.

33. Solomon Schechter, *Seminary Addresses and Other Papers* (Cincinnati: Ark Publishing, 1915), p. viii.

34. The newly recruited faculty members were to be young, as well as full time. "In those days I was President of the Board of Directors and was in very close contact with Doctor Schechter. I had with me the tradition of Johns Hopkins University and treasured in my memory a statement of President Daniel C. Gilman, that with the exception of his first three choices for the Faculty, he was going to pick out young men, his dictum being, 'I would rather have men with their future before them than with their future behind them.' At all events, Schechter's choices were wise, and there has developed here a combination of learning, research, careful training for the ministry, and devotion and piety." Adler, "Semi-Centennial Address," p. 11.

35. See Abraham Flexner, *Medical Education in the United States and Canada* (New York: Carnegie Foundation for the Advancement of Teaching, 1910), and Steven C. Wheatley, "Abraham Flexner and the Politics of Educational Reform," *History of Higher Education Annual* 8 (1988): pp. 45–58.

36. Neither Abraham Flexner nor Adler would have academics withdraw to their laboratories or studies. See Adler's comments on the primacy of teaching, below. The careers of the two midwestern Jewish educators merit sustained comparison. Both used Johns Hopkins as a reference point; both were deeply involved in academic life, but as builders, facilitators, and reformers—not as scholars. Both believed in *Wissenschaft* and in grand plans. Democracy is deficient, wrote Flexner, "in the ability to conceive and to execute comprehensive designs." But neither reformer was enamored with the need for extensive educational bureaucracies. See Wheatley, "Abraham Flexner and the Politics of Educational Reform," p. 51.

37. Davis, *The Emergence of Conservative Judaism*, pp. 257–58.

38. See Jonathan Sarna, "Cyrus Adler and the Development of American Jewish Culture: The 'Scholar-Doer' as a Jewish Communal Leader," *American Jewish History* 78, no. 3 (March 1989): pp. 382–94. But note that Adler was for many years a part-time President of the Seminary.

39. Adler to Sol Rosenbloom, in *Cyrus Adler: Selected Letters*, vol. 2, pp. 110–11.

40. Parzen, *Architects of Conservative Judaism*, p. 96.

41. Adler to Sol Rosenbloom, in *Cyrus Adler: Selected Letters*, vol. 2, pp. 110–13. Similarly, Israel Friedlaender's work for the Bureau of Jewish Education may have earned him a reprimand and may have damaged his chances of succeeding Schechter as Seminary President, but the work did not get him fired. Baila Round Shargel, *Practical Dreamer: Israel Friedlaender and the Shaping of American Judaism* (New York: The Jewish Theological Seminary of America, 1985).

42. "We differ in our views upon aspects of Judaism as I believe you differ from most of your colleagues in the Seminary Faculty. You have shown great ability as a teacher and organizer and have made great personal sacrifices for the Seminary. We are all modern men, we do not engage in inquisitions or excommunications or heresy hunting and we are bound up in the general doctrine of academic freedom. How far this applies in a theological seminary which teaches subjects that are bound to be taught subjectively, in which faith, tradition,

even inherited prejudice if you please, must have a part is a subject we have never discussed but which probably ought to be discussed either between us or with the entire Faculty." Adler to Kaplan, 21 September 1923, in *Cyrus Adler: Selected Letters*, vol. 2, p. 80.

43. See Walter P. Metzger *Academic Freedom in the Age of the University* (New York: Columbia University Press, 1961), and William Summerscales, *Affirmation and Dissent: Columbia's Response to the Crisis of World War One* (New York: Teachers College Press, 1970).

44. The "non-Zionist" Adler capitalized on this event by hiring two HUC protagonists, Max Margolis and Henry Malter, for the Dropsie College faculty. Adler took seriously the norms he did adopt. He protested, for example, the unthinking manner in which the founders of a new university in Palestine seemed to be going about their work: "What I have in mind is that having entered upon the whole question of Palestine without real fore-thought does not involve establishing a University in the same haphazard way with the expectation that we shall muddle through. Sometimes it is possible to bluff in Politics, but you cannot bluff through a University." Adler to Joseph Hertz, 13 December 1922, in *Cyrus Adler: Selected Letters*, vol.2, p. 61.

45. Adler to Adolphus Simeon Solomons, 15 May 1901, in *Cyrus Adler: Selected Letters*, vol. 1, p. 88.

46. Adler to Schiff, 13 August 1919, in *Cyrus Adler: Selected Letters*, vol. 1, p. 383. Popular financial support, Adler continued, was sporadic: "It is difficult to convince the man in the street that higher institutions of learning are a real need and while he may give under pres-sure or in the enthusiasm of a campaign, I am not sanguine that continued support can be secured in this way. One year subscriptions may be paid up and the second year will show a falling off and by the third year there will be the need for another campaign. Of course if there is no other way, as there probably is not, the popular appeal must be made and I for one should go very heartily into it."

47. Adler often reiterated his faith in the conservatism of a self-perpetuating board of direc-tors. During the early 1920s, philanthropist Sol Rosenbloom expressed willingness to fund a Jewish or Semitic department at a contemplated Jewish university in Palestine so long as instruction "would be carried on along traditional lines and not fall into the hands of a group of radicals which might well be possible." Adler noted that Otto Warburg, a propo-nent of, and eventual teacher at, this university "seemed to think that a group of men might associate themselves together and become a Faculty, as it were, by natural selection, and that some unknown persons might provide the funds and look after the details of manage-ment." Admitting that medieval universities "did arise in this way by a sort of voluntary association of masters and pupils," Adler added, "I very much doubt whether this method can be followed with safety at the present time." "The only way to assure a fairly consistent policy for such a Department would be to place it in the hands of a Board of Governors or Directors representing institutions whose policy was reasonably fixed, as far as anything is fixed in this world of ours," he concluded. Adler to Joseph Hertz, 13 December 1922, in *Cyrus Adler: Selected Letters*, vol. 2, p. 60. Closer to home, Adler would later see the direc-tors as a counteractant to the popularity of faculty member Mordecai Kaplan.

48. Adler to Schiff, 26 September 1916, in *Cyrus Adler: Selected Letters*, vol. 1, p. 321.

49. The teachings of Mordecai Kaplan, who studied sociology with Columbia's Franklin Gid-dings, reinforced his belief. "Only in the light of what these newer sciences of human life have taught us," Kaplan wrote, "can we comprehend what is amiss with this spiritual con-dition today and lay plans for making religion function again." See Mel Scult, *Judaism Faces the Twentieth Century: A Biography of Mordecai M. Kaplan* (Detroit: Wayne State University Press, 1993), p. 217.

50. Ibid., p. 218. By the 1930s, Adler pulled back a bit. He agreed with Louis Finkelstein that the proposed Institute for Interdenominational Studies should include a discussion of sci-

ence and religion, "and I also agree that psychology and religion is something that has to be considered." Adler to Finkelstein, 31 July 1939, in *Cyrus Adler: Selected Letters*, vol. 2, p. 367. In any case, the Seminary did not retreat from its insistence on an undergraduate education prior to admission—an education that probably included these subjects.

51. In 1930, the faculty twice debated the conditions under which the students might issue invitations to non-Jews to lecture at the Seminary. The faculty agreed to sanction an invitation issued "to a well-known scholar, but not to men who are merely known for their eloquence." Faculty minutes, 15 January 1930. The faculty, under this policy, subsequently approved an invitation issued to A. V. Williams Jackson, a Sanskritist who taught at Columbia. Ibid., 17 March 1930. Adler had earlier opposed a suggestion to include professors of Semitics at a forthcoming JTS dinner. "It seems to me," he wrote, "that little is gained by this sort of 'liberalism' and that the whole character of the evening might be changed. Please give me your advice. I should want [Ignar] Goldziher to feel perfectly free to speak of Jewish affairs in Europe, if he will, and this he could not do if the Goyim were present." Adler to Schechter, 22 September 1904, in *Cyrus Adler: Selected Letters*, vol. 1, pp. 105–06.

52. Cyrus Adler, *I Have Considered the Days* (Philadelphia: The Jewish Publication Society of America, 1945), p. 181.

53. Adler to Finkelstein, 31 July 1939, in *Cyrus Adler: Selected Letters*, vol. 2, p. 368.

54. Adler to Jacob H. Schiff, 11 November 1919, in ibid., vol. 1, pp. 398, 399. Several years later, Adler told Felix Warburg that Judah Magnes, as head of the Hebrew University, "overburdened himself with details—at least he does things which the Registrar or Secretary should do—he has not yet acquired that highest skill of administration, never to do anything that he can get someone else to do. I know you think I have the same fault but at least I can recognize it in another." Adler to Warburg, 12 August 1926, ibid., vol. 2, p. 134.

55. Adler to Schiff, 26 September 1916, in ibid., vol. 1, p. 321. See also Adler to Schiff, 17 January 1918, ibid., pp. 345–46. See also Louis Finkelstein, "The Jewish Theological Seminary as a University of Judaism," *Jewish Exponent*, 14 September 1945, in which Finkelstein called for the study of contemporary Judaism at the Seminary.

56. Adler to Schiff, 26 September 1916, in *Cyrus Adler: Selected Letters*, vol. 1, p. 321. He envisioned administrative centralization, mentioning a common employment bureau—also a common move at contemporary universities. Adler advocated many of these positions when consulted about creation of a Jewish university in Palestine after World War I.

57. "In 1896, the trustees formally agreed with the recommendation of Dr. Morais that no student should be ordained unless he had first received a college or university degree." *JTSA Proceedings*, 1896, p. 36, as quoted in Fierstien, *A Different Spirit*, p. 78.

58. Davis, *The Emergence of Conservative Judaism*, p. 241. Since many of the students were born in Europe, they often applied with a more extensive Jewish knowledge; and students with advanced standing were admitted to higher classes. In 1890, the trustees decided that "no student over twenty-one years of age shall be admitted unless qualified to enter college, nor anyone over twenty-five years of age, unless possessed of secular education equivalent to the requirement for the degree of Bachelor of Arts." *JTSA Proceedings*, 1890, p. 50, as quoted in Fierstien, *A Different Spirit*, p. 78.

59. "Adler's address at the second commencement of the Jewish Theological Seminary of America, 18 June 1905," in *Cyrus Adler: Selected Letters*, vol. 1, p. 114.

60. Marshall to Adler, 29 December 1925, as quoted in Scult, *Judaism Faces the Twentieth Century*, p. 214. "The point has been made many times," wrote Scult, "that laymen never see the theological niceties observed by rabbis and scholars. Marshall, a Reform Jew, saw no reason why there shouldn't be one strong traditional Seminary instead of two weak ones. He believed that a merger might help put an end to the yeshiva's plans to establish a college. Marshall denounced the college plan publicly as an attempt to establish a

'Ghetto Institution'." Ibid.

61. Adler, "Semi-Centennial Address," p. 8. Practically, this meant granting free tuition to qualified students.

62. Simon Greenberg, *Men of Vision*, p. 6. Unpublished paper, JTS library.

63. Aaron Rothkoff, *Bernard Revel: Builder of American Orthodoxy* (Philadelphia: Jewish Publication Society of America, 1972), p. 16.

64. Fierstien, *A Different Spirit*, p. 79.

65. Adler, "Semi-Centennial Address," p. 13.

66. The Seminary also contracted with Robert Houston, a CCNY professor, to teach elocution. Fierstien, *A Different Spirit*, p. 91.

67. President Joseph Blumenthal, 1894 report to the Seminary Association Convention, *JTSA Proceedings*, 1894, p. 16.

68. *JTSA Proceedings*, 1896, p. 17. Fierstien could not find any mention of the department in the *American Hebrew*, his source for much of the Seminary's early history. See Fierstien, *A Different Spirit*, p. 87.

69. Adler, "Semi-Centennial Address," p. 13.

70. "Adler's address at the second commencement of the Jewish Theological Seminary of America, 18 June 1905," in *Cyrus Adler: Selected Letters*, vol. 1, p. 114.

71. See Naylor, "The Theological Seminary," passim.

72. John S. Brubacher and Willis Rudy, in their history of American higher education, state that by the turn of the century over 10 percent of all clergy, college teachers, lawyers, and doctors had college and professional or graduate instruction. John S. Brubacher and Willis Rudy, *Higher Education in Transition: A History of American Colleges and Universities* (New York: Harper and Row, 1976), p. 203. See also Hugh Hawkins, "American Universities and the Inclusion of Professional Schools," *History of Higher Education Annual* 13 (1993): pp. 53-68. The Seminary continued to accept college seniors whose home institution permitted joint enrollments. See *JTSA Register*, 1909–10, p. 9.

73. Woodrow Wilson, "Should an Antecedent Liberal Education Be Required of Students in Law, Medicine, and Theology?" in *The Public Papers of Woodrow Wilson*, vol. 1: *College and State: Educational, Literary, and Political Papers (1875–1913)*, ed. Ray Stannard Baker and William E. Dodd (New York and London: Harper and Brothers, 1925–27), pp. 223–24.

74. See the next section. Semitist Paul Haupt of Johns Hopkins, who accepted the Higher Criticism, argued that a theological education might best *precede* a graduate education in a Semitics department. See Gilman to Haupt, 27 October 1884, Daniel C. Gilman Papers, Johns Hopkins University Archives, "Paul Haupt" file.

75. Schechter even opposed close cooperation with newly founded Dropsie College (1906) in Philadelphia, over which Adler, still head of the Seminary board, presided. This opposition did not stem from fear of the Higher Criticism but from a challenge to the Seminary's primacy in Jewish learning. Adler, on the other hand, urged close cooperation—even a university confederation among Jewish colleges and seminaries, a plan that came to naught.

76. "Adler's address at the second commencement of the Jewish Theological Seminary of America, 18 June 1905," in *Cyrus Adler: Selected Letters*, vol. 1, p. 114. As for extending the course of study, Adler concluded, "If the needs of the community and his own private inclinations render it possible for him to stay with us a fifth year and earn the Degree of Doctor of Hebrew Literature, the community, the man, and the Institution will all be the gainers."

77. *JTSA Register*, 1909–10, p. 10. "The President reported that he had communicated with the authorities of various colleges in regard to the adoption of a curriculum in Hebrew which would conform to the preliminary requirements of the Seminary, and that satisfactory arrangements had been made with the following institutions: Harvard University,

Columbia University, Johns Hopkins University and the University of Pennsylvania." Directors meeting, 29 March 1903, *JTSA Biennial Report, 1902–1904* (New York: Jewish Theological Seminary of America, 1906), p. 39. The *Register* for 1909–10 added that Gratz College provided appropriate preparation.

78. Israel Friedlaender, according to Baila Shargel, proposed to Lee Kohns, a businessman and City College trustee, that CCNY "initiate a program of instruction in Semitic languages, especially Hebrew and Arabic. Among his arguments was one calculated to appeal to a practical-minded, socially conscious 'uptown Jew': the inclusion of Hebrew in the curriculum of a public institution would somehow encourage good behavior on the part of the children of the Russian immigrants, thereby preventing the emergence of 'an army of Lefty Louies and Gyp the Bloods.'" The proposal, which as a by-product would have provided another source of rabbinical students better-versed in Hebrew, went nowhere. Shargel, *Practical Dreamer*, pp. 134–35. JTS faculty, including Louis Ginzberg, occasionally participated in Menorah activities through the 1920s. But Menorah's leaders preferred that Jewish learning grow in universities, not in seminaries. See Paul Ritterband and Harold S. Wechsler, *Jewish Learning in American Universities: The First Century* (Bloomington and Indianapolis: Indiana University Press, 1994), chap. 6.

79. "At JTS, 74 percent of the students had at least nine years of Jewish studies before college entrance, but only 41 percent received most of their education in all-day schools; 47 percent in supplementary afternoon schools, and 9 percent in Sunday schools. Thirty percent of the students at JTS had no formal program of Jewish studies while at college. In other words, a substantial number of students entered JTS with a good deal less than the best Jewish educational background." Charles S. Liebman, "The Training of American Rabbis," *American Jewish Yearbook* 69 (1968): p. 15.

"A comparison of the Jewish educational backgrounds of first- and last-year students at YU showed no differences. At JTS, however, first-year students had less Jewish education: among first-year students, fewer had nine years or more of Jewish education before college (57 percent, compared with 74 percent of last-year students); more had attended Sunday school (12 percent compared with 5 percent); and fewer attended all-day schools (16 percent, compared with 42 percent); slightly fewer (67 percent, compared with 74 percent), were enrolled in a formal Jewish-studies program while at college." Ibid., p. 16.

80. Gottheil and Schechter arranged for the simultaneous enrollment of one student who lacked any Hebrew preparation but was studying the language with Gottheil at Columbia. See Schechter to Gottheil, 2 November 1903, Solomon Schechter Papers, JTS, "Professor Richard Gottheil" file.

81. JTS faculty minutes, 23 October 1929.

82. JTS faculty minutes, 12 May 1930. Examination of the faculty minutes for these years suggests that most admissions conditions imposed by the faculty were for deficiencies in Hebrew.

83. A 1965 faculty discussion about the "weaker" students in the School of Judaica was typical. Professor Dimitrovsky noted that "many of them were lacking in basic Jewish knowledge, and particularly in the knowledge of the prayer book." The faculty asked Rabbi [Neil] Gillman to consider remedies, including summer session work. JTS faculty minutes, 19 May 1965, p. 58.

84. Seminary faculty member Israel Friedlaender placed this viewpoint in a broad context: "Until contemporary times," summarized Baila Shargel, Friedlaender's biographer, "educated people invariably determined the direction of Jewish life. As committed Jews pursuing a higher education, you are therefore the rightful leaders of tomorrow. Join organizations established to perpetuate traditional Judaism, support Jewish culture, be faithful to Zion. Above all, pursue Jewish learning, leaving philanthropy to those untutored in the

more exalted callings of Jewish life." Shargel, *Practical Dreamer*, p. 134.

85. See Ritterband and Wechsler, *Jewish Learning in American Universities*, chap. 4.

86. "Dr. Schechter Arrives," *American Hebrew*, 18 April 1902, p. 657.

87. Adler expressed this sentiment when replying to Daniel Coit Gilman's request for advice to a candidate for admission to the Semitics Seminary at Johns Hopkins: "With regard to Rabbinical studies he might be informed that instruction is now given in Mishnaic Hebrew and that one course in this branch will probably be given each year, that it would hardly come within the scope of the Semitic Department, which makes comparative philology its end, to dwell especially on Rabbinical studies." Adler to Gilman, 31 May 1889, in *Cyrus Adler: Selected Letters*, vol. 1, p. 16.

88. Margolis may have been a particular cause for concern since Gottheil helped him obtain a teaching position at HUC. But Adler retained Margolis for the Dropsie faculty after HUC forced his resignation.

89. Shargel, *Practical Dreamer*, pp. 129–30.

90. Adler to Schiff, 25 November 1906, in *Cyrus Adler: Selected Letters*, vol. 1, pp. 128–30.

91. Adler's characterization of the intellectual odyssey of Max Margolis may best sum up his mature view on the potential for university-based doctoral work in Semitics to advance Jewish learning. Studies at Berlin and Columbia, he wrote, gave Margolis, "a broader field of knowledge, but so impressed was he with the primary importance of the Bible and Jewish studies that he absorbed all the new knowledge, brought it back and utilized it for that which was nearest to the Jewish soul." Cyrus Adler, "Max Leopold Margolis," *American Jewish Yearbook* 35 (1933–34): p. 144. Margolis agreed. While contemplating a second tenure in Cincinnati, he wrote, "I feel that I belong there rather than in a secular institution where my Jewish knowledge lies idle." See Margolis to Joseph Stolz, 2 January 1905, Max Margolis Collection, American Jewish Archives, Cincinnati, Ohio. Margolis taught at HUC twice and then at Adler's Dropsie from 1909 until his death in 1922. On his career, see also Richard Gottheil, A. V. Williams Jackson, and Ludlow S. Bill, "The Life and Work of Max Leopold Margolis," *Journal of the American Oriental Society* 52 (1932): pp. 106-9; Robert Gordis, "The Life of Professor Max Leopold Margolis: An Appreciation," in Dropsie College for Hebrew and Cognate Learning Alumni Association, *Max Leopold Margolis: Scholar and Teacher* (Philadelphia, Pa.: Dropsie College, 1952), chap. 1; and Leonard J. Greenspoon, *Max Leopold Margolis: A Scholar's Scholar* (Atlanta, Ga.: Scholars Press, 1987).

92. "Judean Banquet to Professor Schechter," *American Hebrew*, 6 June 1902, p. 75.

93. See Ritterband and Wechsler, *Jewish Learning in American Universities*, chaps. 3 and 4.

94. *American Hebrew*, 6 June 1902, p. 75.

95. Shortly after Gustave Gottheil's death the following year, some Emanu-El congregants did create a Gustave Gottheil lectureship at Columbia as a memorial.

96. "As a language Hebrew is not of central and primary interest," wrote Union Theological Seminary president Francis Brown, one of the first men to teach Assyriology in America. "Its vocabulary is not the most ample. Its structure has suffered from the wear and tear of use. Truth requires that we find its place among others of its group by comparing its qualities with theirs, and without the glamour of its association. When we have disposed of it philologically, as the facts require, we shall be all the freer to respect its contents and interpret its messages." Francis Brown, "Semitic Studies in America," *Johns Hopkins University Circular* 214 (1909): pp. 242–43.

97. See Schechter to Gottheil, 28 May 1903, Solomon Schechter Papers, JTS, "Prof. Richard Gottheil" file.

98. Schechter to Gottheil, 18 November 1909, Ibid.

99. "The number of students of your institution taking advantage of the opportunities offered

to them for study at Columbia is steadily increasing," wrote the Columbia registrar in 1903. Rudolph Tombo to Schechter, 27 February 1903, RJTSA, R. G. 1, General Files, 1902– 72, 1A-5-47. NYU, in 1913-1914, similarly agreed to admit Seminary students to graduate courses and to waive tuition charges. Tuition at the Seminary was free.

100. There were actually two problems: the tuition waivers and the frequent petitions for Columbia degree credit brought by students from local seminaries for work completed at those seminaries. Limiting tuition waivers to graduate students would be problematic as long as the Seminary retained a "Preparatory Class" of undergraduate students. During the weaning process, Seminary officials attempted to assure parity of treatment with other seminaries. See Tombo to Schechter, 10 October 1905; Jacob Schiff to Louis Marshall, 23 October 1905, and Marshall to Schechter, 24 October 1905 in RJTSA, R. G. 1, General Files, 1902–72, 1A-5-47, "Columbia University" file. As for degree credit, Gottheil felt the need for a uniform policy:

> If we have done right in accepting such courses, it is imperative that some standard should be adopted in order that we may know what courses in these seminaries are to be counted as leading to a degree, and in order to preserve the standard of our own degrees. The Hebrew instruction in some of the seminaries is good; in others, I'm afraid, it is very bad. I feel that it is not wise to leave this matter to the discretion of the individual professor, as at times he is quite unable to form a just estimate of the character of the work done. It is also manifestly unjust to demand the same amount of work in Hebrew from a student in the Drew Theological Seminary as we ought to demand from one in the Jewish Theological Seminary. In former years I have tried to arrange such matters in conference with the Dean of the School of Philosophy. But as other seminaries are gaining the privilege of sending their students to us, the question becomes more complicated. Some definite line of policy, ought, I venture to think, to be laid down.

Gottheil added a long-term policy consideration, "If we proceed upon these lines, are we not running the danger of becoming in a number of cases, merely an examining body, similar to the University of London? This appears to me to be an undesirable development." A 1905 committee that included Gottheil concluded that work completed at UTS and GTS could be counted in lieu of work done at Columbia for higher degrees. Other seminaries could send their students to Columbia to study and receive a tuition waiver, as long as those institutions accepted Columbia students under the same terms. See Gottheil to Robert W. Rogers, 2 November 1906, Letter-Book of Richard J.H. Gottheil, 1906–8, Rare Book Room, Columbia University Libraries.

101. Butler to Gottheil, 28 April 1911, Columbia University Files, 408 Low Memorial Library, "RJH Gottheil" file, 1910–18.

102. Friedlaender to Schechter, 16 February 1911, Solomon Schechter Papers, JTS, 101-2, box 2, "Israel Friedlaender" file.

103. Gottheil to Butler 27 April 1911, Columbia University Files, "RJH Gottheil" file, 1910–18.

104. Adler's admiration for Daniel Coit Gilman, for example, did not translate into admiration for his successors at Johns Hopkins. When the Hopkins trustees asked Adler to request $2 million of Jacob Schiff for the university's endowment fund, Adler demurred. "I do not see why the Johns Hopkins University turns so naturally to Jewish millionaires," he wrote in 1910. "They [the Johns Hopkins trustees] would have been in a better position to do so if they had elected a Jew to one of the numerous vacancies which have occurred during the past ten or fifteen years." Adler to Herbert Friedenwald, 21 October 1910, in *Cyrus Adler: Selected Letters*, vol. 1, pp. 187–88. Adler suggested several possible donors, including James Speyer who eventually gave money to Johns Hopkins for a professorship, and noted

that he recently solicited several other gifts from Schiff. To Friedenwald's suggestion that Baltimore, through Johns Hopkins, strongly affected the American Jewish intellectual life, Adler replied: "The influence that you speak of on the Jewish intellectual life of Baltimore as compared with New York and Philadelphia would not be a strong argument to hand out to a New Yorker nor would I be able to hand it out even if I thought it wise, because I have never noticed it." Schiff, in turn, criticized Columbia for similarly excluding Jews from trustee ranks. See Wechsler, *The Qualified Student*, chap. 4.

105. This knowledge arose in part from personal experience. He withdrew his daughter's application for admission to Bryn Mawr when an indifferent college administration would not permit her to make up an entrance examination, scheduled for *shabbat*. "Bryn Mawr College, I believe, was founded by a distinguished member of the Society of Friends and its Trustees belong to that Society," he wrote. "I remember being present either at the opening of Bryn Mawr or at the dedication of one of its most important halls and James Russell Lowell delivered the dedicatory address. I thought—at the time maybe a young hopeful man—that here would be an institution founded by a man belonging to a sect which had itself been bitterly persecuted, which would always recognize and accord the student religious tolerance. I have myself passed through the University of Pennsylvania, through Johns Hopkins University, where I was also a teacher, and spent sixteen years on the staff of the Smithsonian Institution, and was never required or even expected to disregard any of my religious observances." Adler to Marion Park, 19 September 1923, in *Cyrus Adler: Selected Letters*, vol. 2, pp. 78–79.

106. Adler to Marshall, 22 September 1922, in *Cyrus Adler: Selected Letters*, vol. 2, p. 54. Adler added: "My opinion is that if Harvard cannot be convinced that by making discriminations it is doing an illiberal and uncivilized thing, she will not be won over by an enumeration of our eminent people or our sufferings in the past."

107. See Wechsler, *The Qualified Student*, chap. 7. Adler was not impressed with Nicholas Murray Butler's leadership ability. In 1920, a year in which Butler sought the U.S. presidency, Adler unsuccessfully attempted to enlist Herbert Hoover into the presidential campaign. See Adler to Hoover, 24 February 1920, in *Cyrus Adler: Selected Letters*, vol. 2, pp. 3–4.

108. Morris Jastrow, Jr., "Supplementary Account of Thirty Years' Progress in Semitic Studies, and Discussion of Dr. Peters' Paper," in *Thirty Years of Oriental Studies Issued in Commemoration of Thirty Years of Activity of the Oriental Club of Philadelphia*, ed. Roland Kent (Philadelphia: Intelligencer Printing Co., 1918), pp. 64–72, quotations from pp. 67, 69.

109. The American Jewish Historical Society remained a small enterprise located at, and associated with, the Seminary. The Jewish Publication Society only occasionally published a book by a university-based author. The *Jewish Encyclopedia* included both university and seminary-based scholars, but it was an early project (1901–05)—and one of great magnitude. The Bible published by the Jewish Publication Society (1917), under Adler's nurture, was a product of a unified Jewish scholarly community, not of university and seminary-based academics as originally envisaged.

110. Parzen, *Architects of Conservative Judaism*, chap. 7, and Shargel, *Practical Dreamer*, passim.

111. During the 1920s, Gottheil, acknowledging the need for a Jewish seminary in New York, accepted the chair of the governing board of the new Jewish Institute of Religion—directed by Stephen S. Wise, for whom Adler had little love. While contemplating membership on the Board of Governors of the newly established Hebrew University, Adler wrote, "The insistence of yourself and others of the presence of Dr. Stephen S. Wise on this board is not likely to make for my continued cooperation, at least, if I have to sit in the room with that gentleman very often." Adler to Magnes, 21 July 1926, in *Cyrus Adler: Selected Letters*, vol. 2, p. 130. The feeling was mutual. In 1928, Wise, then JIR president, complained to Max Margolis about the omission of any mention of the Institute in the lat-

ter's one-volume history of the Jews. Wise deemed Margolis's reply unsatisfactory and wrote but did not send: "I exonerate you in the matter of the omission of the name of the Jewish Institute of Religion in your volume of the so-called 'History of the Jewish People.' I have reason to know, for a number of years, that they who serve the Chairman of the Jewish Publication Society or the President of Dropsie College must do his bidding, whether voiced or unvoiced." See Wise to Margolis, undated, unsent, Jewish Institute of Religion Papers, American Jewish Archives, box 19 26/6, "Max Margolis" file. Gottheil supported Wise's failed bids to lure Mordecai Kaplan from JTS to JIR, as well as Wise's nomination of Kaplan to the Nathan Miller Chair at Columbia in 1928. See Ritterband and Wechsler, *Jewish Learning in American Universities*, chap. 7.

112. The list included General, Drew, Jewish, Reformed Dutch, St. Joseph's, and Bloomfield Theological Seminaries. Columbia officials noted that the policy led to inequities in educational policy and to requests from other institutions for similar privileges. UTS, which retained credit and tuition privileges, had instituted tuition charges several years earlier, leading to further complications.

113. See note 100.

114. Nicholas Murray Butler to Adler, 9 December 1924; Adler to Butler, 23 December 1924; Frank Fackenthal to Adler, 6 January 1925, 14 January 1925; and Adler to Joseph B. Abrahams, 10 February 1925 (source of quotation), RJTSA, R. G. 1, General Files, 1902-1972, 1A-5, "Columbia University" file. Adler and the JTS faculty agreed to express "the hope that notwithstanding the fact that their official relations have been severed, the two Institutions will remain on friendly footing." See "Extract from the minutes of the meeting of the Faculty, February 3, 1925," Adler to Butler, 9 February 1925, ibid. We have no indication of Gottheil's response, but a simultaneous controversy gave Gottheil little opportunity to change the decision even if he wanted to. Gottheil relied upon Ginzberg's evaluation of a thesis based on the Talmud. Ginzberg approved the dissertation, which was later published despite its many admitted weaknesses. Gottheil protested that the incident would damage his attempts to secure greater cooperation between Columbia and JTS. See Ritterband and Wechsler, *Jewish Learning in American Universities*, pp. 145-47.

115. See Ritterband and Wechsler, *Jewish Learning in American Universities*, chap. 7, especially note 36.

116. Herbert Schneider to Cyrus Adler, 31 October 1929, Adler to Schneider, 6 November 1929, RJTSA, R. G. 1, General Files, 1902-1972, 1A-5-27.

117. See Ritterband and Wechsler, *Jewish Learning in American Universities*, chap. 4, and Adler to Julian Morgenstern, 23 October 1936 in *Cyrus Adler: Selected Letters*, vol. 2, pp. 320-21.

118. In 1935, Adler may have injected a touch of sarcasm in declining an invitation issued by Columbia to celebrate the 800th anniversary of Maimonides, when he wrote: "I desire however to express my sincere gratification at the fact that Columbia University is celebrating the anniversary of this most distinguished philosopher, physician, priest, and Jewish leader of the Middle Ages." Adler to "The Secretary," Columbia University, 31 March 1935, RJTSA, R. G. 1, General Files, 1902-72, 1A-5-27, "Columbia University" file. Adler had wished to facilitate the editing of a definitive text of the writings of Maimonides, but the project came to naught. Adler to Louis Ginzberg, 17 July 1928, and Adler to Moses Schorr, 9 January 1929, in *Cyrus Adler: Selected Letters*, vol. 2, pp. 155-56, 164.

119. During the second decade of the century, a Students' House began to provide kosher meals to JTS and Columbia students—eighty in the late teens. Adler to Warburg, 10 November 1919, in *Cyrus Adler: Selected Letters*, vol. 1, p. 396. Later the Seminary dedicated some space to a meeting area for Columbia students. Finkelstein to Jacob Weinstein, 30 September 1932; Weinstein to Finkelstein, 3 October 1932; Finkelstein to Adler, 2 November 1932; and Finkelstein to Weinstein, 21 November 1932, RJTSA, R. G. 1, General Files, 1902-72,

1A-5-27 "Columbia University".

120. JTS followed the same admissions requirements as the Columbia Graduate Faculties. Smaller or specialized academic institutions, instead of "accrediting" on their own, often relied on lists maintained by universities or accrediting associations. Finkelstein to "Dean, Graduate School, Columbia University," 7 February, 1934; Adam L. Jones to Finkelstein, 12 February 1934, RJTSA, R. G. 1, General Files, 1902–72, 1A-5-27. The relationships between admissions officers were virtually nonexistent, and it sometimes took a while for Seminary officials to obtain a response to their inquiries. See, for example, Louis Finkelstein to the Registrar, Harvard University, 25 September 1933; Hazel F. Stanley to Finkelstein, 26 September 1933; David Fleisher to Finkelstein, 4 October 1933; and Finkelstein to Fleisher, 9 October, 1933, RJTSA, R. G. 1, General Files, 1902–72, 1A-10-71, "Harvard University" file.

121. Other Jewish seminaries also displayed aloofness. Neither HUC nor Yeshiva maintained strong ties with universities during the interwar years. There were two exceptions: Harvard and JIR briefly shared the services of Harry Wolfson prior to the endowment of the Nathan Littauer Chair in Jewish Literature and Philosophy in 1925, and Salo Baron continued to teach at JIR for several years after his appointment to the Columbia faculty in 1929.

122. "Address of Henry S. Hendricks," in Conant et al., *"Learning's Necessity [for an Able Minister],"* p. 32.

123. Adler to Finkelstein, 21 July 1939, in *Cyrus Adler: Selected Letters*, vol. 2, p. 364.

124. See Michael B. Greenbaum, "Mission Conflict in Religiously Affiliated Institutions of Higher Education: The Jewish Theological Seminary of America During the Presidency of Louis Finkelstein, 1940–1955" (Ph.D. diss., Teachers College, Columbia University, 1994).

125. Louis Finkelstein, "Tradition in the Making," in *Tradition and Change*, pp. 190, 191.

126. See Jessica Feingold, "Up From Isolation—Intergroup Activities at the Seminary," *Judaism* 27, no. 3 (summer 1978): pp. 283–91. Commentators often used the term "isolation" to characterize the Adler years.

127. See Robert Morrison MacIver, *As a Tale That is Told: The Autobiography of R. M. MacIver* (Chicago: University of Chicago Press, 1968).

128. Philanthropist Louis Rabinowitz supported the project. Rabinowitz also funded projects that promoted Jewish learning at universities and seminaries, notably the Yale Judaica series.

129. Historian Jeffrey Gurock, in his recent history of American Jewish Historical Society publications, called Nevins "a constant and influential consultant to the center." Jeffrey S. Gurock, "From *Publications* to *American Jewish History*: The Journal of the American Jewish Historical Society and the Writing of American Jewish History," *American Jewish History* 81, no. 2 (winter 1993–94): p. 224. JTS also housed the American Jewish Historical Society throughout its New York years. The AJHS was under the strong influence of Baron and his students during the 1950s, and the Seminary benefited from Baron's advocacy for the study of American Jewish history within mainline historical associations and among university-based colleagues. Ibid., pp. 221–22, 226. By the mid-1970s, more than twenty-five colleges offered coursework in American Jewish history. Ibid., pp. 246–47.

130. "The intellectual as well as geographical proximity to Baron at Columbia gave JTS an avenue of discourse with a major American university." Michael Panitz, "The Jewish Theological Seminary and the Academic Study of Judaism," in *The Seminary at 100: Reflections on the Jewish Theological Seminary and the Conservative Movement*, ed. Nina Beth Cardin and David Wolf Silverman (New York: The Rabbinical Assembly and the Jewish Theological Seminary of America, 1987), p. 166.

131. Cyrus Adler, "Semi-Centennial Address," pp. 16–17.

132. "Seminary College Celebrates Anniversary of Joint Program with Columbia," in Jewish Theological Seminary of America, *Bulletin: News for Congregational Editors* 22, no. 7 (Nissan, 5738): p. 1.

133. The Middle States Association opened the process to seminaries in 1951. The North Central Association, arguing that it wished to accredit only institutions that offered general education programs, did not follow suit. See Louis G. Geiger, *Voluntary Accreditation: A History of the North Central Association, 1945–1970* (Menasha, Wis.: North Central Association, 1970), p. 92.

134. The move may also have been related to a need to accredit the University of Judaism, which emphasized general and adult education, not rabbinical studies.

135. "The Jewish Theological Seminary is more than a theological seminary. . . . It is more nearly a university. . . . Moreover the Seminary is more than a university since it has almost an organic connection with the United Synagogue of America and the Rabbinical Assembly of America. . . . The Seminary constitutes the capstone of the educational and research program of the Conservative Jewish movement of America, as well as its intellectual, and to a large extent its spiritual undergirding." "Report on the Evaluation of The Jewish Theological Seminary of America, New York, New York and Los Angeles, California By A Committee of the Middle States Association of Colleges and Secondary Schools Assisted, for the California Branch, By a Committee of the Western College Association, February 24, 1954, March 7–10, 1954," RJTSA, R. G. 1, General Files, 1902–1972, 1J-129, p. 2.

136. The jurisdictional issues preoccupied Middle States officials prior to their visit to the Seminary and were subject to considerable discussion and modification thereafter. See correspondence in files on the Jewish Theological Seminary of America in the Middle States Association Archives, Philadelphia, Pa. (hereinafter MSAA).

137. "Report on the Evaluation of The Jewish Theological Seminary of America," p. 3. The clear relation between goals, curriculum, and instructional method, the committee added, suggested that the statement of purpose derived from the Seminary's activities, not vice versa. Ibid.

138. "At least one member of this committee sensed some resentment of this [unavailability of Rabbinical School faculty members] by students who wish to continue in scholarship and find it necessary to accept the rabbinate in order to get the best training the Seminary has to offer." But the committee immediately reassured the association, "The faculty is aware of this difficulty and steps are now being taken to prepare programs for A.M. and Ph.D. degrees to be awarded in course for graduate work by non-rabbinical students or by rabbinical students who might prefer these degrees to the D.H.L." "Report on the Evaluation of The Jewish Theological Seminary of America," p. 5.

139. "Report on the Evaluation of The Jewish Theological Seminary of America," pp. 16-20, quotation from p. 19.

140. Especially its executive committee, and its administrative committee, a recently created subcommittee created when the executive committee was enlarged. Executive committee report, 7 June 1953, Board of Directors minutes, JTS.

141. "Report on the Evaluation of The Jewish Theological Seminary of America," p. 20. The committee did not comment on the doctrinal tensions existing between Kaplan, his colleagues, and Seminary benefactors, the most obvious case of the Seminary's adherence to a norm that secular colleges and universities sometimes compromised.

142. "Report on the Evaluation of The Jewish Theological Seminary of America," pp. 16-20, quotation from p. 19.

143. Ibid., p. 18. "Almost all the senior members of the faculty are men of great renown and are acknowledged to be among the foremost authorities in the world in their respective subjects," the committee reported. "They have chosen the younger men. Their choice has

allegedly been based primarily on considerations of scholarly ability, and by this standard it seems to have been completely justified." Ibid., p. 4.

144. Ibid., p. 22.

145. Ibid., p. 7.

146. "The effectiveness of academic preparation in the combination program will depend upon (a) how realistically it meets the subject matter needs of the teaching situations in which students find themselves, (b) how clearly it is related to the previous preparation of the students, (c) how well the teaching demonstrates effective methodology, and (d) how extensively instruction results in thorough understanding as opposed to mere memorization." Ibid., p. 8.

147. "The question arises as to whether the five year program for the preparation of teachers of Hebrew is intended to produce master teachers, or to lead on to doctoral studies, or to do both. Careful consideration should be given to this matter." Ibid.

148. "The effectiveness of the professional preparation, which is to be developed, in the joint program will depend upon (a) how well the professional offerings provide for individual needs, (b) how extensively instruction is based upon research findings which are reported in theses and professional journals, (c) how well learning experiences are provided for, and (d) how well the instructors developed for student use up-to-date annotated bibliographies designed to encourage wide reading." "Report on the Evaluation of The Jewish Theological Seminary of America," p. 8. The 1974 accreditation report commended the teacher-training program, save for insufficient exposure to the classroom. "Report to the Faculty, Administration, Trustees of the Jewish Theological Seminary of America by An Evaluation Team Representing the Commission on Higher Education of the Middle States Association. Prepared after study of the institution's self-evaluation report and a visit to the campus on October 27–30, 1974," MSAA, p. 5.

149. "Report on the Evaluation of The Jewish Theological Seminary of America," pp. 12–13.

150. Amendments adopted 28 March 1958 quotation from "Evaluation Report, March 8–11, 1964," JTS Records, 1T-225-24, "Middle States Association" file, p. 9.

151. "Religion on the Campus," *Columbia College Today* (spring-summer 1963): p. 16.

152. This number would increase to over 150 within a decade: "In its 1974 Self-Study, JTS listed over 150 graduates of its various schools who were serving in college and university teaching positions. While this list included graduates serving on the JTS and University of Judaism faculties there remained nearly 100 JTS alumni staffing Judaica programs in North America as well as Israel." Michael Panitz, "The Jewish Theological Seminary and the Academic Study of Judaism," pp. 167–68.

153. "Evaluation Report, March 8–11, 1964," pp. 23–24. Many professional fields were then reassessing the appropriateness of the first professional degree as a prerequisite for doctoral work—the MBA for a business doctorate, for example. See Robert Aaron Gordon and James E. Howell, *Higher Education for Business* (New York: Columbia University Press, 1959). The committee similarly took to task the MSM and DSM programs of the Cantors Institute and Seminary, College of Jewish Music, which were staffed by part-time faculty members, and were heavily reliant on the resources of other institutions (pp. 27–28).

154. Increased supply of university-educated Judaica scholars did not force out the rabbinical contingent; the field, as the Seminary's statistics suggest, continued to display a disproportionate number of rabbis and part-time instructors. See Arnold J. Band, "AJS Survey of the Field of Jewish Studies," *Association for Jewish Studies Newsletter* 24 (March 1979).

155. "Evaluation Report, March 8-11, 1964," pp. 23, 25.

156. "Progress report presented by: The Jewish Theological Seminary of America," 1 April 1966, MSAA, p. 4.

157. A 1986 essay, written by Michael Panitz, minimized the distinction: "After the 1964 visit of

the Middle States accreditation team, and at that body's urging, JTS implemented a Ph.D. training program. . . . True, graduates with the degree of Doctor of Hebrew Literature had successfully entered academic teaching, but the Ph.D. was the recognized coin of the university realm." Panitz, "The Jewish Theological Seminary and the Academic Study of Judaism," pp. 167–68. The distinction, in the eyes of the accreditors, Band, and others, was substantive, and was not simply over nomenclature. See Arnold J. Band, "Jewish Studies in American Liberal-Arts Colleges and Universities," *American Jewish Yearbook* 67 (1966): pp. 3–30.

158. Christopher Jencks and David Riesman, *The Academic Revolution* (Garden City, N.Y.: Doubleday, 1967).

159. "One cannot meet with the Executive Committee of the Board of Directors without being aware of the financial and professional strength of the board. Leadership by the Chancellor can only result in the means to provide the buildings, the annual support and the endowment for the future of this educational institution dedicated to the conservative movement of Jewry in the United States." "Evaluation Report, 8–11 March 1964," p. 51.

160. Ibid., p. 14. The registrar of the Teachers Institute, the report stated, was actually the student adviser; the dean of students had little to do with students.

161. Ibid., p. 75.

162. Ibid., p. 49. "At the undergraduate level," the report continued, "such curriculum planning as that involved in the Combined Program with the School of General Studies at Columbia University gives students a thorough background in both areas."

163. "Progress report, 1966," p. 8.

164. Ibid., p. 2.

165. "Evaluation Report, March 8–11, 1964," p. 50.

166. "Progress report, 1966," p. 2.

167. Marjorie Wyler to Ed Wakin, 12 April 1967, RJTSA, R. G. 11, Communications Department Records, 1930s–1980s, 11c-65-17, "Campus Boom in Religion" file.

168. Martha E. Church to K. Roald Bergethon, 25 January 1973, MSAA, "Jewish Theological Seminary of America" file.

169. Earl F. Cheit, *The New Depression in Higher Education: A Study of Financial Conditions at 41 Colleges and Universities* (New York: McGraw-Hill, 1971).

170. "In an age of limited resources," wrote one dean, "we should try to avoid duplication and schools must learn to work with each other to supplement each others strengths." Neil Gillman to Gerson Cohen, 11 September 1975, RJTSA, R. G. 11, Communications Department, 1930s–1980s, 11c-33-37, "Hofstra University, 1970s" file.

171. The graduate program in ancient Judaism involved cooperation with UTS and Columbia, for example. Recall that Columbia terminated similar arrangements during the Adler administration. Informal and semi-formal relationships nurtured by several Columbia departments, notably history through Baron, Cohen, and Nevins, paved the way.

172. One dean, for example, justified a proposed joint program between the Seminary College and Barnard as an alternative for students who might otherwise attend Brandeis. Ivan G. Marcus, "A Proposal for Interinstitutional Cooperation between Barnard College and the Seminary College of Jewish Studies," 10 April 1978, RJTSA, R. G. 11, Communications Department, 1930s–1980s, 11c-10-3, "Barnard College/Seminary Agreement, 1979" file.

173. The Middle States evaluating team called for further significant increases, but Seminary officials responded that tuition increases in the undergraduate division might prompt students to enroll in other institutions with Judaica programs, that already overworked students would have to accept more part-time employment, that students in the rabbinical program had paid no tuition at all until recently, and that agreements made with its students restricted the size of any forthcoming increases. "The imposition of even the current

tuition by the seminary's Rabbinical School," argued Seminary officials, "was a daring move in a community of Jewish seminaries, many of which offer full tuition scholarships to their students as a matter of course." The Seminary's reference group thus remained the Jewish seminaries that continued heavy student subsidies, not universities that charged amounts closer to "true costs." "Response by the Faculty, Administration, Trustees of The Jewish Theological Seminary of America to the report by the Evaluating Team Representing the Commission on Higher Education of the Middle States Association," 15 January 1975, MSAA, "Jewish Theological Seminary of America" file, pp. 3–4.

174. The Seminary had finally compiled a faculty handbook that included a tenure code with a probationary period. Faculty members were henceforth subject to uniform procedures, and knew about the benefits and obligations of their positions. But the probationary period ended any expectation that the initial appointment came with a presumption of tenure. "As for junior faculty, the decision to put into effect a policy of termination of appointment was a wise one," the accrediting team wrote. "No institution can operate with full academic effectiveness if appointment to its faculty carries with it automatic life tenure. It must be free to reconsider earlier appointment decisions and to adjust its instructional program to changing needs and challenges." "Report to the Faculty, Administration, Trustees of the Jewish Theological Seminary of America by An Evaluation Team Representing the Commission on Higher Education of the Middle States Association. Prepared after study of the institution's self-evaluation report and a visit to the campus on October 27-30, 1974," p. 6. The Seminary hired a full-time registrar in 1975. See David C. Kogen to Harry Porter, 19 June 1975, MSAA, "Jewish Theological Seminary of America" file.

175. Introduction to Graduate Studies at the Seminary," and "The Graduate School," RJTSA, R. G. 11, Communications Department, 1930s-1980s, 11c-33-19, "Graduate School: 1970s–1980s" file, 1979.

176. Much of the visit had focused on familiar administrative and financial matters—the structure and function of the board of trustees, the use of funds for endowment and for operating expenses, the blurred administrative lines, and the duplication and coordination of courses—urging further conformance to "best practices" in higher education, concepts that had been refined, revised, and even challenged during the previous twenty years. The team's comment on course duplication shows the halting manner in which the Seminary accepted the opportunities and responsibilities associated with interinstitutional cooperation. The team, noting the "importance of coordinating both curriculum and even the scheduling of courses with the other institutions on Morningside Heights," challenged JTS officials to fulfill their obligations: "Either needless duplication of courses in any given term or blocking the availability of courses to students of one institution by thoughtless scheduling is to be avoided in this era of academic austerity. The fact that some of the part-time faculty at JTS teach at other neighboring institutions provides both the opportunity and the obligation to involve them in departmental planning at the very specific level of what will be taught, where and when." "Report to the Faculty, Administration, Trustees of the Jewish Theological Seminary of America by An Evaluation Team Representing the Commission on Higher Education of the Middle States Association. Prepared after study of the institution's self-evaluation report and a visit to the campus on October 27-30, 1974," p. 6.

177. The estimate of the proportion of students enrolled in the nontheological divisions appears in Marcus, "A Proposal for Interinstitutional Cooperation between Barnard College and the Seminary College of Jewish Studies," 10 April 1978. The phrase "paradoxical combination" appears in Gillman to Cohen, 11 September 1975, RJTSA, R.G. 11, Communications Department, 1930s-1980s, 11c-33-37, "Hofstra University, 1970s" file. A decade earlier, Louis Finkelstein contemplated the implications of an enlarged component

of part-time, teaching-oriented faculty when he and Middle States officials discussed methods of expanding academic governance to include these categories. Finkelstein to F. Taylor Jones, 23 March 1965 and 30 March 1965; Jones to Finkelstein, 26 March 1965, RJTSA, R. G. 1, General Files, 1902-1972, 1U-234-7, "Middle States Association" file.

Index

of, I:432n135; reponsa of,
II:468-470, II:481n176
Cohen, Burton, I:617, I:830,
I:832, I:836, I:847, I:848
Cohen, Gerson D., *I:234,*
I:234-268, *I:238, I:242,
I:358, I:368, I:393, I:407,*
II:103, *II:221, II:428,
II:623, II:806;* adminis-
trative team of, I:239;
appointment of to JTS
faculty, II:556; and Beit
Midrash, II:245; and Can-
tors Institute, I:773; as
Chancellor, I:236-237,
I:502-503, I:554; and
Commission for the Study
of the Ordination of
Women in the Rabbinate,
II:494-495, II:519n37; and
curriculum, II:569-573;
faculty hiring practices of,
I:245; on faculty of Teach-
ers Institute, I:596; and
Gottschalk, II:619-621; on
graduate program, I:241;
historical analogies on
Judaism, I:260; and Insti-
tute for Religious and
Social Studies, II:707; on
interfaith programs,
II:267n133; and Israel,
I:250-256, II:202, II:219-
221, II:221-222, II:235-
240; leadership of, I:236-
237; as librarian, I:539,
I:705, *I:706;* and library,
I:697-698; meeting with
Peres, *II:233;* and Melton
Faculty Seminar, I:617; on
nature of JTS, I:261; office
location of, I:433n156;
priorities of, I:239; with
Rabbinical School faculty
and students, *I:246;* and
Ramah, I:844, I:853n84,
II:751; resignation of,
I:262; and Teachers Insti-

tute, I:616, I:618-619;
views of mission of JTS,
I:237; with visitors, *I:252;*
and *Wissenschaft des Juden-
tums,* I:317-318; on women
in Ramah camps,
II:441n78; and women's
ordination, I:255-258,
II:498-500, II:502-504; on
women's ordination,
II:430-431, II:489,
II:520nn62,65; writings
of, II:74, II:571; and Zion-
ist movement, II:269n155;
on Zucker, I:409
Cohen, Harry K., I:707
Cohen, Jack, II:103
Cohen, Jeremy, I:828
Cohen, Mark, I:563n115
Cohen, Max, I:19, I:26, I:28
Cohen, Naomi W., I:389,
I:559n49, II:267n133,
II:269n155
Cohen, Rose, I:605
Cohen, Samuel M., I:486,
I:507-508n45, II:135,
II:410, II:424
Cohen, Shaye J. D., I:389,
I:513n95
Cohen, Steven M., I:466n37
Cohon, Samuel S., II:553
College Entrance Examina-
tion Board, II:781. *See also*
Entrance examinations
College of Jewish Music,
I:775
College of Jewish Studies
(HUC), II:619
College of Jewish Studies
(Spertus), II:96
Collegiate Department,
II:585n14
Collegio Rabbinico Italiano,
I:658
Columbia University, I:25,
I:273, I:397, I:552, II:192-
194, II:260n32. *See also*
Joint Programs; and cross-

registration with JTS,
I:243; joint program with
Teachers Institute, I:608,
I:616; and JTS students,
II:810n26, II:817nn99,100;
relationship with JTS,
II:775-776; and Semitics
department, II:787-789
Combined Program of
Studies, I:616
Commentary (magazine),
II:347
*The Commentary of David
Kimhi on the Book of Isaiah*
(Finkelstein), I:164
Commission for the Study of
the Ordination of Women
in the Rabbinate, I:257,
II:493-501, II:519n37
Commission on the Ideology
of Conservative Judaism,
II:433
Committee for Goodwill
Between Jews and Protes-
tants, II:749
Committee for Preservation
of Tradition, II:495
Committee on Jewish Law
and Standards, II:456,
II:490
Committee on Refugee
Jewish Ministers, II:277
Committee on the Interpre-
tation of Jewish Law,
II:454, II:458
Communications Depart-
ment, I:424n7, II:112n28
Compton, Arthur H., II:675-
676, II:679
Conant, James Bryant, I:303,
I:808nn3,5, II:366, *II:771,*
II:791-792
Concordia Seminary, II:636,
II:643, II:645-646, II:647
Conference on Halakhic
Process, II:506-507
Conference on Science,
Philosophy and Religion,

TRADITION RENEWED was designed and produced by Scott-Martin Kosofsky at the Philidor Company in Boston. Betsy Sarles was his primary design assistant and Steve Dyer helped in the early stages of text formatting. Some of the photographs, especially the oldest ones, were badly damaged or survived only in copies, and required extensive restoration. This work was carried out electronically and was done by Betsy Sarles, Sophie Kosofsky, and Scott-Martin Kosofsky. Suzanne Kaufman printed many of the photographs from negatives made much earlier, mostly by Virginia F. Stern.

Mr. Kosofsky made a new typeface for these volumes called Philidor Erhardt, based on the "real Dutch types" offered by the Erhardt foundry in Leipzig in the mid-18th century. Though Daniel Berkeley Updike conjectured that these types were of 17th-century origin, Mr. Kosofsky believes they may be the early work of Johann Michael Fleischman, a very popular type cutter who worked for the Enschedé foundry in Haarlem during much of the 18th century. The great contrast between their thick and thin lines and the angularity of their serifs suggest Fleischman's hand. While the types retain most of the characteristics of Dutch and English "oldstyles" of the early 18th century, their weight and presence seem to look forward to later in the century. In that spirit, several "modern" types were chosen for the titles, subtitles, and initials: Didot roman, Berthold Bodoni italic, and Bauer Bodoni Titling—an interesting combination, if not exactly an orthodox one.

The images were scanned mostly by Aurora Graphics in Portsmouth, New Hampshire, who also made the final page films. The more fragile ones were scanned at the Philidor Company. The book was printed by Universal-Nimrod in Westwood, Massachusetts, on acid-free paper made by Glatfelter in Pennsylvania. The binding was done by Acme Bookbinding in Charlestown, Massachusetts, using a linen cloth made in North Carolina by Holliston.